Giving You the Knowledge, Skills, and Confidence to Succeed

Learn from real-life examples

Model documents, including a number of "ineffective/effective" pairs, are annotated with constructive criticism to show why specific writing tactics are either successful or unsuccessful. (See examples on pp.136, 224, 249, 448, 569, and 588.)

Benefits: By clearly seeing what works—and why—in a variety of professional documents, you quickly gain the insights you need to improve your own writing.

Develop essential new-media skills

You are probably an active user of electronic media already, but the way these tools are used in the workplace is often quite different from the way you use them. *Business Communication Today* shows you how to meet professional expectations when using instant messaging, blogs, wikis, social networking, podcasts, and other technologies. (See examples on pp. 50, 82, 153, 157, 220, and 262.)

Benefits: Successfully adapt what you already know about new media and the social communication model to the practices and quality standards you'll encounter in the workplace.

Practice writing skills by solving real-life business challenges

More than 140 communication cases let students practice writing real business documents as they explore a wide range of tactical and strategic communication challenges in every major business medium. (See examples on pp. 236-241, 339-345, 498-504, 556, and 615-617.)

Benefits: Cases give you the opportunity to develop skills you can apply on the job—and to show future employers you're ready to make the leap from student to professional communicator.

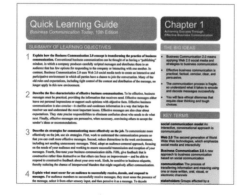

Review chapter concepts and key terms

Hit all the high points of every chapter in just two pages with downloadable Quick Learning Guides prepared by the authors.

Benefits: Spend less time studying and preparing for exams—while ensuring you can understand and recall the essential concepts from every chapter.

Get the latest information and advice with Real-Time Updates

A unique integration of print and electronic media, the Real-Time Updates service provides fresh content throughout the course to reinforce learning and to keep the class relevant.

Benefits: You can stay up to date with the trends and techniques of professional business communication and be ready to hit the ground running the day you graduate.

Discover a proven process for writing better messages in less time

The time-tested three-step writing process helps you craft a variety of messages for print and electronic media quickly and easily. (See examples on pp. 247, 510, and 568.)

Benefits: Reduce the time and energy it takes to create effective business messages, both during college and throughout your entire career.

Find answers quickly with the Handbook of Grammar, Mechanics, and Usage

The integrated Handbook of Grammar, Mechanics, and Usage offers summaries of essential points of grammar, mechanics, and usage plus helpful lists of frequently confused, misused, and misspelled words. (See p. H-1.)

Benefits: The handbook helps take the work and worry out of grammar, mechanics, and usage.

Simplify and accelerate learning with mybcommlab

This unique online study tool helps you identify and improve weak areas through focused practice. Test your understanding of the concepts presented in the text and explore additional materials that will bring the ideas to life in video, activities, and an online multimedia ebook.

Benefits: Make the best use of your time by identifying the areas where you need to improve, reviewing the appropriate concepts and skills, and practicing the specific techniques that will help you communicate more effectively.

PEARSON
mybcommlab™

In mybcommlab there are activities for every facet of the course to help you achieve the key learning objectives in writing, grammar, and presentation skills.

Customized Study Plans

Customized Study Plans keep you on track throughout the semester.

You complete a pre-test, and the results generate a customized study plan, complete with remediation activities. Study plans tag incorrect questions from the pre-test to the appropriate textbook learning objective, enabling you to concentrate on only the topics that you need help with. Tools to help you study include flash cards, eBook reading assignments, document makeovers, and grammar and writing tutorials.

After you complete the remediation activities, you may take a post-test to validate that you have mastered the learning objectives.

Robust Self-Study and Practice Tools

Peer Review capabilities so that you can focus on the writing process as they critique each other's work.

Model Documents help you understand the "why" and the "how" of polished communication.

Sample Presentations reinforce the presentations heard in class.

Video Applications reinforce the concepts covered in lecture.

BUSINESS COMMUNICATION TODAY

GLOBAL EDITION

BUSINESS COMMUNICATION TODAY

GLOBAL EDITION

Tenth Edition

COURTLAND L. BOVÉE

Professor of Business Communication
C. Allen Paul Distinguished Chair
Grossmont College

JOHN V. THILL

Chairman and Chief Executive Officer
Global Communication Strategies

Boston   Columbus   Indianapolis   New York   San Francisco   Upper Saddle River
Amsterdam   Cape Town   Dubai   London   Madrid   Milan   Munich   Paris   Montreal   Toronto
Delhi   Mexico City   Sao Paulo   Sydney   Hong Kong   Seoul   Singapore   Taipei   Tokyo

Editorial Director: Sally Yagan
Editor in Chief: Eric Svendsen
Acquisitions Editor: James Heine
Acquisitions Editor, Global Edition: Steven Jackson
Editorial Assistant: Karin Williams
Director of Marketing: Patrice Lumumba Jones
Director of International Marketing: Ann Oravetz
Senior Marketing Manager: Anne Fahlgren
Marketing Assistant: Susan Osterlitz
Senior Managing Editor: Judy Leale
Project Manager: Karalyn Holland
Senior Operations Supervisor: Arnold Vila
Senior Operations Specialist: Arnold Vila
Senior Art Director: Janet Slowik
Text and Cover Designer: Kris Carney

Manager, Visual Research: Beth Brenzel
Photo Researcher: Sheila Norman
Manager, Rights and Permissions: Zina Arabia
Image Permission Coordinator: Nancy Seise
Manager, Cover Visual Research & Permissions: Karen Sanatar
Cover Art: © Tom Grill/Corbis
Full-Service Project Management: GGS Higher Education Resources, a Division of PreMedia Global, Inc.
Composition: GGS Higher Education Resources, a Division of PreMedia Global, Inc.
Printer/Binder: Quebecor World Color/Versailles
Cover Printer: Lehigh-Phoenix Color/Hagerstown
Text Font: 10.5/12 Minion

Credits and acknowledgments borrowed from other sources and reproduced, with permission, in this textbook appear on appropriate page within text (or on page AC-1).

Microsoft® and Windows® are registered trademarks of the Microsoft Corporation in the U.S.A. and other countries. Screen shots and icons reprinted with permission from the Microsoft Corporation. This book is not sponsored or endorsed by or affiliated with the Microsoft Corporation.

If you purchased this book within the United States or Canada you should be aware that it has been imported without the approval of the Publisher or the Author.

Prentice Hall
is an imprint of

10 9 8 7 6 5 4 3 2
ISBN 10: 0-13-246458-6
ISBN 13: 978-0-13-246458-1

Contents in Brief

Contents

8 Contents

Preface

Looking for a Competitive Advantage That Will Help You at Every Stage of Your Career?

Communication is one the most fundamental elements of business, whether it's a research team gathering clues about market trends or an inspirational leader guiding a company in pursuit of shared goals. Effective communication is essential to success for both organizations and individuals, and ineffective communication is often the cause of minor mistakes, major strategic blunders, and catastrophic failures. No matter what profession you want to pursue, the ability to communicate will be an essential skill—and a skill that employers expect you to have when you enter the workforce.

This course introduces you to the fundamental principles of business communication and gives you an opportunity to develop your communication skills. You'll discover how business communication differs from personal and social communication, and you'll see how today's companies are using blogging, podcasting, video, wikis, and other innovative technologies. You'll learn a simple three-step writing process that works for all types of writing and speaking projects, both in college and on the job. Along the way, you'll gain valuable insights into ethics, etiquette, listening, teamwork, and nonverbal communication. Plus, you'll learn effective strategies for the many different types of communication challenges you'll face on the job, from routine messages about transactions to complex reports and websites.

Colleges and universities vary in the prerequisites established for a business communication course, but we advise taking at least one course in English composition before taking this class. Having completed some coursework in business studies will also give you a better perspective on communication challenges in the workplace. However, we have taken special care not to assume any in-depth business experience, so you can use *Business Communication Today*, Tenth Edition, successfully even if you have limited on-the-job experience or business coursework.

HOW THIS COURSE WILL HELP YOU

Few courses can offer the three-for-the-price-of-one value you get from a business communication class. Check out these benefits:

- **In your other classes.** The communication skills you learn in this class can help you in virtually every other course you will take in college. From simple homework assignments to complicated team projects to oral presentations, you'll be able to communicate more effectively with less time and effort.
- **During your job search.** You can reduce the stress of searching for a job and stand out from the competition. As you'll see in Chapters 18 and 19, every activity in the job search process relies on communication. The better you can communicate, the more successful you'll be in landing interesting and rewarding work.
- **On the job.** After you get a great job, the time and energy you have invested in this course will continue to yield benefits year after year. As you tackle each project and every new challenge, influential company leaders—the people who largely determine how quickly you'll get promoted and how much you'll earn—will be paying close attention to how well you communicate. They will observe your interactions with colleagues, customers,

and business partners. They'll take note of how well you can collect data, find the essential ideas buried under mountains of information, and convey those points to other people. They'll observe your ability to adapt to different audiences and circumstances. They'll be watching when you encounter tough situations that require careful attention to ethics and etiquette. All this may sound daunting, but every insight you gain and every skill you develop in this course will help you shine in your future career.

HOW TO SUCCEED IN THIS COURSE

Although this course explores a wide range of message types and covers quite a lot of territory, the underlying structure of the course is actually rather simple. You'll learn a few basic concepts, identify some key skills to use and procedures to follow, and then practice, practice, practice. Whether you're writing a blog posting in response to one of the real-company cases or drafting a copy of your own résumé, you'll be practicing the same skills again and again. With feedback and reinforcement from your instructor and your classmates, your confidence will grow, and the work will become easier and more enjoyable.

The following sections offer advice on approaching each assignment, using your textbook, and taking advantage of some other helpful resources.

Approaching Each Assignment

In the spirit of practice and improvement, you will have a number of writing (and possibly speaking) assignments throughout this course. These suggestions will help you produce better results with less effort:

- **Don't panic!** If the thought of writing a report or giving a speech sends a chill up your spine, you're not alone. Everybody feels that way when they are first learning business communication skills, and even experienced professionals can feel nervous about major projects. Keeping three points in mind will help. First, every project can be broken down into a series of small, manageable tasks. Don't let a big project overwhelm you; it's nothing more than a bunch of smaller tasks. Second, remind yourself that you have the skills you need to accomplish each task. As you move through the course, the assignments are carefully designed to match the skills you've developed up to that point. Third, if you feel panic creeping up on you, take a break and regain your perspective.
- **Focus on one task at a time.** A common mistake is trying to organize and express your ideas while simultaneously worrying about audience reactions, grammar, spelling, formatting, page design, print quality, and a dozen other factors. You must fight the temptation to do everything at once; otherwise, your frustration will soar, and your productivity will plummet. In particular, don't worry about grammar, spelling, and word choices during your first draft. Concentrate on the organization of your ideas first, then on the way you express those ideas, and then on the presentation and production of your messages. Following the three-step writing process is an ideal way to focus on one task at a time in a logical sequence.
- **Give yourself plenty of time.** With any school project, putting things off to the last minute creates unnecessary stress. Writing and speaking projects in particular are much easier if you tackle them in small stages, with breaks in between, rather than try to get everything done in one frantic blast. Moreover, there will be instances when you simply get stuck on a project; the best thing to do in such a situation is walk away and give your mind a break. If you allow room for this in your schedule, you'll minimize the frustration and spend less time overall on your homework, too.
- **Step back and assess each project before you start.** The writing and speaking projects you'll have in this course cover a wide range of communication scenarios, and it's essential that you adapt your approach to each new challenge. Resist the urge to dive in and start writing without a plan. Ponder an assignment for a while, consider the various approaches you might take, and think carefully about your objectives before you start writing. It is frustrating to get stuck halfway through because you're not sure what you're trying to say or you've wandered off track. Spend a little time planning, and you'll spend a lot less time writing.

- **Use the three-step writing process.** The essential planning tasks are the first step in the three-step writing process, which you'll learn about in Chapter 4 and use throughout the course. This process has been developed and refined by professional writers with decades of experience and thousands of projects, ranging from simple e-mail messages to 600-page textbooks. It works; take advantage of it.
- **Learn from the examples and model documents.** This textbook offers dozens of realistic examples of business messages, many with notes along the sides that explain strong and weak points. Study these and any other examples that your instructor provides. Learn what works and what doesn't work, and apply these lessons to your own writing.
- **Learn from experience.** Learn from the feedback you get from your instructor and from other students. Don't take the criticism personally; your instructor and your classmates are commenting about the work, not about you. View every piece of feedback as an opportunity to improve.

Using This Textbook Package

This book and its accompanying online resources introduce you to the key concepts in business communication while helping you develop essential skills. As you read each chapter, start by studying the learning objectives. These help you identify the most important concepts in the chapter and give you a feel for what you'll be learning. Following the learning objectives, the "Communication Close-up" tells a brief story of how a particular business professional met a real-life communication challenge by using the same concepts and skills you'll be learning in the chapter.

As you work your way through the chapter, compare the advice given with the various examples, both the brief in-text examples and the stand-alone model documents. Also, keep an eye out for the Real-Time Updates Learn More elements in each chapter. These videos, podcasts, presentations, and other online media provide informative and entertaining enhancements to the text material.

At the end of each chapter, read the "Summary of Learning Objectives" carefully to confirm that you've met each objective. You can also download the two-page Quick Learning Guide to review the essential points from the chapter.

Each chapter includes a variety of questions and activities that help you gauge how well you've learned the material and are able to apply it to realistic business scenarios. Several chapters have activities with downloadable media such as podcasts; if your instructor assigns these, follow the instructions in the text to locate the correct files.

In addition to the 19 chapters of the text, here are some special features that will help you succeed in the course and on the job:

- **Prologue: Building a Career with Your Communication Skills.** This brief section (immediately following this Preface) helps you understand today's dynamic workplace, the steps you can take to adapt to the job market, and the importance of creating an employment portfolio.
- **Handbook.** The Handbook of Grammar, Mechanics, and Usage (see page H-1) serves as a convenient reference of essential business English.
- **mybcommlab.com.** Use mybcommlab.com to test your understanding of the concepts presented in each chapter and explore additional materials that will bring the ideas to life in videos, activities, and an online multimedia e-book.
- **Real-Time Updates.** You can use this unique newsfeed service to make sure you're always up to date on important topics. Plus, at strategic points in every chapter, you are directed to the Real-Time Updates website to get the latest information about specific subjects. To sign up via RSS, visit http://realtimeupdates.com/bct. You can also access Real-Time Updates through mybcommlab.com.

- **Quick Learning Guides.** These downloadable, two-page study guides were specially prepared by the authors to help you study for exams or review important concepts whenever you need a quick refresher.
- **Business Communication Web Search.** We developed this revolutionary approach to searching so that you can quickly access more than 325 search engines. The tool uses a simple and intuitive interface engineered to help you find precisely what you want, whether it's PowerPoint files, Adobe Acrobat PDFs, Microsoft Word documents, Excel files, videos, or podcasts.
- **Companion Website.** This text's Companion Website, at www.pearsonglobal editions.com/bovee, offers free access to document makeovers, a student version of the PowerPoint package, an updated list of featured websites, the English–Spanish Audio Glossary of Business Terms, an online version of the Handbook of Grammar, Mechanics, and Usage, and the Business Communication Study Hall, which helps you brush up on several aspects of business communication— grammar, writing skills, critical thinking, report writing, résumés, and PowerPoint development.
- **Study Guide.** This text offers a study guide, which includes a variety of review questions and study quizzes. Page references to the review questions and quizzes are included. You can purchase the study guide by visiting: www.pearsonglobal editions.com/bovee

ABOUT THE AUTHORS

Courtland L. Bovée and John V. Thill have been leading textbook authors for more than two decades, introducing millions of students to the fields of business and business communication. Their award-winning texts are distinguished by proven pedagogical features, extensive selections of contemporary case studies, hundreds of real-life examples, engaging writing, thorough research, and a unique integration of print and electronic resources. Each new edition reflects the authors' commitment to continuous refinement and improvement, particularly in terms of modeling the latest practices in business and the use of technology.

Professor Bovée has 22 years of teaching experience at Grossmont College in San Diego, where he has received teaching honors and was accorded that institution's C. Allen Paul Distinguished Chair. Mr. Thill is a prominent communications consultant who has worked with organizations ranging from Fortune 500 multinationals to entrepreneurial start-ups. He formerly held positions with Pacific Bell and Texaco.

ACKNOWLEDGMENTS

This tenth edition of *Business Communication Today* reflects the professional experience of a large team of contributors and advisors. We express our thanks to the many individuals whose valuable suggestions and constructive comments influenced the success of this book:

Michelle Boucher, Southwestern College
Nicole A. Buzzetto-More, University of Maryland, Eastern Shore
Lana W. Carnes, Eastern Kentucky University
Rebecca Cline, Middle Georgia College
Steven Deeley, Santiago Canyon College
Cynthia Evans, University of Northern Colorado
Duane Franceschi, Canyon College
Jeffrey Goddin, Indiana University
Roxanne B. Hamilton, Landmark College

Hal P. Kingsley, Trocaire College
Lisa B. Martin, Piedmont Technical College
Mabry M. O'Donnell, Marietta College
Brenda Rhodes, Northeastern Junior College
Sarah K. Rodgers, Owens Community College
Karen J. Roush, Independence Community College
Jessica Stoudenmire, El Camino College
Tracy K. Tunwall, Mount Mercy College
Joyce W. Twing, Vermont Technical College
Kathi Vosevich, Shorter College
Mark C. Zorn, Butler County Community College

Pearson wish to thank the following people for their work on the Global Edition:

Dr Bashir, King Abdulaziz University, Saudi Arabia
Susanna Chui, Hong Kong Baptist University, Hong Kong
Dr Radhika Jaidev, SIM University, Singapore
Dr Janie H M Liew, University Malaysia Sabah (UMS), Malaysia
Kitty Szeto, The Chinese University of Hong Kong, Hong Kong
Dr Muhammad E Ulhaque, King Abdulaziz University, Saudi Arabia

Reviewers of Previous Editions

We especially want to thank these reviewers, whose detailed and perceptive comments resulted in excellent refinements:

Timothy Alder, Pennsylvania State University—University Park
Heather Allman, University of West Florida
Janice Cooke, University of New Orleans
Terry Engebrertsen, Idaho State University
Joyce Hicks, Valparaiso University
Lynda Hodge, Guilford Technical Community College
Mary Humphrys, University of Toledo
Iris Johnson, Virginia Commonwealth University
Marsha Kruger, University of Nebraska—Omaha
Marianna Larsen, Utah State University
Anita Leffel, University of Texas—San Antonio
Richard Malamud, California State University—Dominguez Hills
Thomas Marshall, Robert Morris University
Leanne Maunu, Palomar College
Michael Mclane, University of Texas—San Antonio
Bronna McNeely, Midwestern State University
Holly Payne, University of Southern Indiana
Kathy Peacock, Utah State University
Folke Person, Idaho State University
Diza Sauers, University of Arizona
Lucinda Sinclair, Longwood University
Rodney Smith, University of Dubuque
Bruce Strom, University of Indianapolis
Dana Swesen, Utah State University
Dennielle True, Florida Gulf Coast University
Robyn Walker, University of Arizona
Judy Walton, Howard University

Reviewers of Document Makeovers

We sincerely thank the following reviewers for their assistance with the Document Makeovers:

Lisa Barley, Eastern Michigan University
Marcia Bordman, Gallaudet University
Jean Bush-Bacelis, Eastern Michigan University
Bobbye Davis, Southern Louisiana University
Cynthia Drexel, Western State College
Kenneth Gibbs, Worcester State College
Ellen Leathers, Bradley University
Diana McKowen, Indiana University
Bobbie Nicholson, Mars Hill College
Andrew Smith, Holyoke Community College
Jay Stubblefield, North Carolina Wesleyan College
Dawn Wallace, South Eastern Louisiana University

Reviewers of Model Documents

The many model documents in the text and their accompanying annotations received invaluable review from

Diane Todd Bucci, Robert Morris University
Dacia Charlesworth, Indiana University–Purdue University Fort Wayne
Avon Crismore, Indiana University
Nancy Goehring, Monterey Peninsula College
James Hatfield, Florida Community College at Jacksonville
Estelle Kochis, Suffolk County Community College
Sherry Robertson, Arizona State University

Personal Acknowledgments

We wish to extend a heartfelt thanks to our many friends, acquaintances, and business associates who provided materials or agreed to be interviewed so that we could bring the real world into the classroom.

A very special acknowledgment goes to George Dovel, whose superb writing and editorial skills, distinguished background, and wealth of business experience assured clarity and completeness in this project. Also, recognition and thanks to Jackie Estrada for her outstanding skills and excellent attention to details. Her creation of the Peak Performance Grammar and Mechanics material is especially noteworthy. Paul Straley's professionalism and keen eye for quality were invaluable.

We also feel it is important to acknowledge and thank the Association for Business Communication, an organization whose meetings and publications provide a valuable forum for the exchange of ideas and for professional growth.

In addition, we would like to thank the supplement authors who prepared material for this new edition. They include Dacia Charlesworth, Indiana University–Purdue University Fort Wayne; Myles Hassell, University of New Orleans; William Peirce, University of Maryland University College; and Jay Stubblefield, North Carolina Wesleyan College.

We want to extend our warmest appreciation to the devoted professionals at Prentice Hall. They include Jerome Grant, president; Sally Yagan, editorial director; James Heine, acquisitions editor; Nikki Jones, marketing manager; Ashley Santora, product development manager, Karin Williams, editorial assistant; all of Prentice Hall Business Publishing;

and the outstanding Prentice Hall sales representatives. Finally, we thank Judy Leale, senior managing editor of production, and Karalyn Holland, production project manager, for their dedication; and we are grateful to Heidi Allgair, senior production editor at GGS Higher Education Resources, a division of Premedia Global, Inc.; Janet Slowik, senior art director; and Ilze Lemisis, interior designer, for their superb work.

Courtland L. Bovée
John V. Thill

Dedication

This book is dedicated to you and the more than two million students who have used this book in years past. We appreciate the opportunity to play a role in your education, and we wish you success and satisfaction in your studies and in your career.

Courtland L. Bovée
John V. Thill

Take advantage of this FREE online service that extends the value of your textbook with fresh multimedia content every weekday

You can access Real-Time Updates through mybcommlab or by visiting

www.real-timeupdates.com/bct

Business Communication Today's **Real-Time Updates** makes it easy to learn from the pros, get great ideas for class projects, and stay up to date with the world of business communication. This unique service provides weekly content updates that keep your textbook current and reinforce the concepts you learn in class. Simply visit the website to find podcasts, PowerPoint presentations, online videos, PDFs, and articles—or get new items delivered to your desktop automatically via RSS newsreader.

Prologue

Building a Career with Your Communication Skills

USING THIS COURSE TO HELP LAUNCH YOUR CAREER

This course will help you develop vital communication skills that you'll use throughout your career—and those skills can help you launch an interesting and rewarding career, too. This brief prologue sets the stage by helping you understand today's dynamic workplace, the steps you can take to adapt to the job market, and the importance of creating an employment portfolio. Take a few minutes to read these sections while you think about the career you hope to create for yourself.

UNDERSTANDING TODAY'S DYNAMIC WORKPLACE

Social, political, and financial events continue to change workplace conditions from year to year, so the job market you read about this year might not be the same market you try to enter a year or two from now. However, you can count on a few forces that are likely to affect your entry into the job market and your career success in years to come:[1]

- **Instability and opportunity.** In addition to broad economic cycles, your career will likely be affected by globalization, mergers and acquisitions, short-term mentality driven by the demands of stockholders, ethical upheavals, and the relentless quest for lower costs. On the plus side, new opportunities, new companies, and even entire industries can appear almost overnight. In fact, trying to make a long-term career plan might not be a wise use of your time anyway. As retired Lockheed Martin CEO Norman Augustine puts it, "There are just too many changes ahead, too many things that are going to happen that you can't anticipate."[2]

- **Responsibility for your own career.** The idea of lifetime employment, in which employees spend their entire working lives with a single firm that takes care of them throughout their careers, is all but gone in many industries. Boeing, the Chicago-based aerospace giant, speaks of lifetime *employability*, rather than lifetime employment, putting the responsibility on employees to track market needs and keep their skills up to date—even changing careers, if necessary. In fact, most U.S. employees will not only change employers multiple times but will even change careers anywhere from three to five times over their working lives.

- **Growth of small business.** Small businesses employ about half of the private-sector workforce in this country and create somewhere between two-thirds and three-quarters of new jobs, so chances are good that you'll work for a small firm at some point. One expert predicts that before long, 80 percent of the U.S. labor force will be working for firms employing fewer than 200 people.

- **Increase in independent contractors.** The nature of employment itself is changing for many people. As companies try to become more flexible, more employees are going solo and setting up shop as independent contractors, sometimes selling their services back to the very companies they just left.

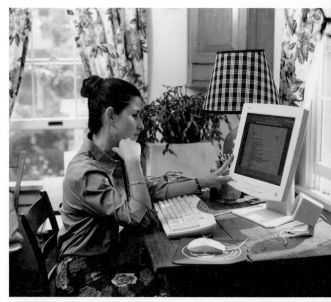

Would you like to pursue a career in business but have the flexibility to work from home? Many professionals now do so, as either independent contractors or corporate employees who telecommute.

- **Changing view of job-hopping.** Given all these changes, job-hopping doesn't have quite the negative connotation it once had. Even so, you still need to be careful about "jumping ship" at every new opportunity. Recruiting and integrating new employees takes time and costs money, and most employers are reluctant to invest in someone who has a history of switching jobs numerous times without good reason.

What do all these forces mean to you? First, take charge of your career—and stay in charge of it. Understand your options, have a plan, and don't count on others to watch out for your future. Second, as you will learn throughout this course, understanding your audience is key to successful communication, starting with understanding how employers view today's job market.

How Employers View Today's Job Market

From the employer's perspective, the employment process is a question of balance. Maintaining a stable workforce can improve practically every aspect of business performance, yet many employers want the flexibility to shrink and expand payrolls as business conditions change. Employers obviously want to attract the best talent, but the best talent is more expensive and more vulnerable to offers from competitors, so there are always financial trade-offs to consider.

Employers also struggle with the ups and downs of the economy. When unemployment is low, the balance of power shifts to employees, and employers have to compete in order to attract and keep top talent. When unemployment is high, the power shifts back to employers, who can afford to be more selective and less accommodating. In other words, pay attention to the economy; at times you can be more aggressive in your demands, but at other times you should be more accommodating.

Many employers now fill some labor needs by hiring temporary workers or engaging contractors on a project-by-project basis. Many U.S. employers are now also more willing to move jobs to cheaper labor markets outside the country and to recruit globally to fill positions in the United States. Both trends have stirred controversy, especially in the technology sector, as U.S. firms recruit top engineers and scientists from other countries while shifting mid- and low-range jobs to India, China, Russia, the Philippines, and other countries with lower wage structures.[3]

What Employers Look for in Job Applicants

Given the forces in the contemporary workplace, employers are looking for people who can adapt to the new dynamics of the business world, can survive and thrive in fluid and uncertain situations, and continue to learn throughout their careers. Companies want team players with strong work records, leaders who are versatile, and employees with diversified skills and varied job experience.[4] In addition, most employers expect college graduates to be sensitive to cultural differences and to have a sound understanding of international affairs.[5] In some cases, your chances of being hired are better if you've studied abroad, learned another language, or can otherwise demonstrate an appreciation of other cultures.

ADAPTING TO TODAY'S JOB MARKET

Adapting to the workplace is a lifelong process of seeking the best fit between what you want to do and what employers are willing to pay you to do. For instance, if money is more important to you than anything else, you can certainly pursue jobs that promise high pay; just be aware that most of these jobs require years of experience, and many produce a lot of stress, require frequent travel, or have other potential drawbacks you'll want to consider. In contrast, if location, lifestyle, intriguing work, or other factors are more important to you, you may well have to sacrifice some level of pay to achieve them. The important question is to know what you want to do, what you have to offer, and how to make yourself more attractive to employers.

What Do You Want to Do?

Economic necessities and the vagaries of the marketplace will influence much of what happens in your career, of course; nevertheless, it's wise to start your employment search by examining your own values and interests. Identify what you want to do first and then see whether you can find a position that satisfies you at a personal level while also meeting your financial needs:

- **What would you like to do every day?** Research occupations that interest you. Find out what people really do every day. Ask friends, relatives, or alumni from your school. Read interviews with people in various professions to get a sense for what their careers are like.
- **How would you like to work?** Consider how much independence you want on the job, how much variety you like, and whether you prefer to work with products, machines, people, ideas, figures, or some combination thereof. Do you prefer constant change or a predictable role?
- **What specific compensation do you expect?** What do you hope to earn in your first year? What's your ultimate earnings goal? Are you willing to settle for less money in order to do something you really love?
- **Can you establish some general career goals?** Consider where you'd like to start, where you'd like to go from there, and the ultimate position you'd like to attain.
- **What size company would you prefer?** Do you like the idea of working for a small, entrepreneurial operation or a large corporation?
- **What sort of corporate culture are you most comfortable with?** Would you be happy in a formal hierarchy with clear reporting relationships? Or do you prefer less structure? Teamwork or individualism? Do you like a competitive environment?
- **What location would you like?** Would you like to work in a city, a suburb, a small town, an industrial area, or an uptown setting? Do you favor a particular part of the country? Another country?

Filling out the assessment in Table 1 might help you get a clearer picture of the nature of work you would like to pursue in your career.

What Do You Have to Offer?

Knowing what you *want* to do is one thing. Knowing what you *can* do is another. You may already have a good idea of what you can offer employers. If not, some brainstorming can help you identify your skills, interests, and characteristics. Start by jotting down 10 achievements you're proud of, such as learning to ski, taking a prize-winning photo, tutoring a child, or editing your school paper. Think carefully about what specific skills these achievements demanded of you. For example, leadership skills, speaking ability, and artistic talent may have helped you coordinate a winning presentation to your school's administration. As you analyze your achievements, you'll begin to recognize a pattern of skills. Which of them might be valuable to potential employers?

Next, look at your educational preparation, work experience, and extracurricular activities. What do your knowledge and experience qualify you to do? What have you learned from volunteer work or class projects that could benefit you on the job? Have you held any offices, won any awards or scholarships, mastered a second language?

Take stock of your personal characteristics. Are you aggressive, a born leader? Or would you rather follow? Are you outgoing, articulate, great with people? Or do you prefer working alone? Make a list of what you believe are your four or five most important qualities. Ask a relative or friend to rate your traits as well.

If you're having difficulty figuring out your interests, characteristics, or capabilities, consult your college placement office. Many campuses administer a variety of tests to help you identify interests, aptitudes, and personality traits. These tests won't reveal your "perfect" job, but they'll help you focus on the types of work best suited to your personality.

TABLE 1.1 Career Self-Assessment

What work-related activities and situations do you prefer? Evaluate your preferences in each of the areas in this table and use the results to help guide your job search.

ACTIVITY OR SITUATION	STRONGLY AGREE	AGREE	DISAGREE	NO PREFERENCE
1. I want to work independently.				
2. I want variety in my work.				
3. I want to work with people.				
4. I want to work with technology.				
5. I want physical work.				
6. I want mental work.				
7. I want to work for a large organization.				
8. I want to work for a nonprofit organization.				
9. I want to work for a small family business.				
10. I want to work for a service business.				
11. I want to start or buy a business someday.				
12. I want regular, predictable work hours.				
13. I want to work in a city location.				
14. I want to work in a small town or suburb.				
15. I want to work in another country.				
16. I want to work outdoors.				
17. I want to work in a structured environment.				
18. I want to avoid risk as much as possible.				
19. I want to enjoy my work, even if that means making less money.				
20. I want to become a high-level corporate manager.				

How Can You Make Yourself More Valuable?

While you're figuring out what you want from a job and what you can offer an employer, you can take positive steps toward building your career. First, look for volunteer projects, temporary jobs, freelance work, or internships that will help expand your experience base and skill set. These temporary assignments not only help you gain valuable experience and relevant contacts but also provide you with important references and with items for your employment portfolio (see the following section).[6]

Second, considering applying your talents to *crowdsourcing* projects, in which companies and nonprofit organizations invite the public to contribute solutions to various challenges. For example, Fellowforce (www.fellowforce.com) posts projects involving advertising, business writing, photography, graphic design, programming, strategy development, and other skills.[7] Even if your contributions aren't chosen, you still have solutions to real business problems that you can show to potential employers as examples of your work.

Third, learn more about the industry or industries in which you want to work and stay on top of new developments. Join networks of professional colleagues and friends who can help you keep up with trends and events. Many professional societies have student chapters or offer students discounted memberships. Take courses and pursue other educational or life experiences that would be hard to get while working full time.

Even after an employer hires you, it's a good idea to continue improving your skills in order to distinguish yourself from your peers and to make yourself more valuable to current and potential employers. Acquire as much technical knowledge as you can, build broad-based life experience, and develop your social skills. Learn to respond to change in positive, constructive ways; doing so will help you adapt if your "perfect" career path eludes your grasp. Learn to see each job, even so-called entry-level jobs, as an opportunity to learn more and to expand your knowledge, experience, and social skills. Share what you know with others instead of hoarding knowledge in the hope of becoming indispensable; helping others excel is a valuable skill.[8]

BUILDING AN EMPLOYMENT PORTFOLIO

Employers want proof that you have the skills to succeed on the job, but even if you don't have much relevant work experience, you can use your college classes to assemble that proof. Simply create and maintain an **employment portfolio**, which is a collection of projects that demonstrate your skills and knowledge. You can create both a *print portfolio* and an *e-portfolio*; both can help with your career effort. A print portfolio gives you something tangible to bring to interviews, and it lets you collect project results that might not be easy to show online, such as a handsomely bound report.

An e-portfolio is a multimedia presentation of your skills and experiences.[9] Think of it as a website that contains your résumé, work samples, letters of recommendation, articles you have written, and other information about you and your skills. Be creative. For example, a student who was pursuing a degree in meteorology added to his e-portfolio a video clip of himself delivering a weather forecast.[10] Your e-portfolio can be burned on a CD-ROM for physical distribution or, more commonly, posted online—whether it's a personal website, your college's site (if student pages are available), or a networking site such as www.collegegrad.com or www.creativeshake.com. To see a selection of student e-portfolios from colleges around the United States, go to http://real-timeupdates.com/bct, click on "Student Assignments," and then locate the link to student e-portfolios.

Throughout the course, pay close attention to the activities and cases marked "Portfolio Builder" (they start in Chapter 7). These items will make particularly good samples of not only your communication skills but your ability to understand and solve business-related challenges. By combining these projects with samples from your other courses, you can create a compelling portfolio by the time you're ready to start interviewing. Your portfolio is also a great resource for writing your résumé because it reminds you of all the great work you've done over the years. Moreover, you can continue to refine and expand your portfolio throughout your career; many professionals use e-portfolios to advertise their services, for instance (see Figure 1).

As you assemble your portfolio, collect anything that shows your ability to perform, whether in school, on the job, or in other venues. However, you *must* check with an employer before including any items that you created while you were an employee. Many business documents contain confidential information that companies don't want distributed to outside audiences.

For each item you add to your portfolio, write a brief description that helps people understand the meaning and significance of the project. Include such items as these:

- **Background.** Why did you undertake this project? Was it a school project, an article you wrote on your own initiative, and so on?
- **Project objectives.** Explain the project's goals, if relevant.
- **Collaborators.** If you worked with others, be sure to mention that and discuss team dynamics, if appropriate. For instance, if you led the team or worked with others long distance as a *virtual team*, point that out.
- **Constraints.** Sometimes the most impressive thing about a project is the time or budget constraints under which it was created. If these apply to a project, consider mentioning them in a way that doesn't sound like an excuse for poor quality. If you had only one week to create a website, for example, you might say that "One of the intriguing challenges of this project was the deadline; I had only one week to design, compose, test, and publish this material."

FIGURE 1 **Professional Portfolio**

Erik Jonsson, a digital media designer, uses e-portfolio services such as Behance.net (**www .behance.net/erikj**) to display samples of his work. Potential clients or business partners can click on the images shown here to learn more about each project. No matter what your intended profession or level of experience, you can use an e-portfolio to help potential employers learn more about your skills and qualifications.

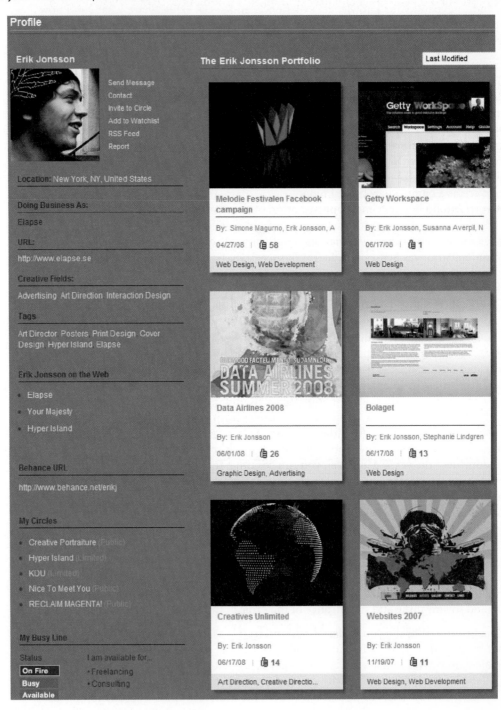

- **Outcomes.** If the project's goals were measurable, what was the result? For example, if you wrote a letter, soliciting donations for a charitable cause, how much money did you raise?
- **Learning experience.** If appropriate, describe what you learned during the course of the project.

Keep in mind that the portfolio itself is a communication project, too, so be sure to apply everything you'll learn in this course about effective communication and good design. Assume that every potential employer will find your e-portfolio site (even if you don't tell them about it) and don't include anything that could come back to haunt you. Also, if you have anything on Facebook, MySpace, or any other social networking site that could be embarrassing, remove it immediately.

To get started, first check with the career center at your college; many schools now offer e-portfolio systems for their students. (Some schools now require e-portfolios, so you may already be building one.) You can also find plenty of advice online; search for "e-portfolio" or "student portfolio." Finally, consider reading a book such as *Portfolios for Technical and Professional Communicators*, by Herb J. Smith and Kim Haimes-Korn. This book is intended for communication specialists, but it offers great advice for anyone who wants to create a compelling employment portfolio.

Best wishes for success in this course and in your career!

BUSINESS COMMUNICATION TODAY

GLOBAL EDITION

Part 1

Understanding the Foundations of Business Communication

No other skill will help your career in as many different ways as communication will. Discover what business communication is all about and learn how to adapt your communication experiences in life and college to the business world. Improve your skills in such vital areas as team interaction, etiquette, listening, and nonverbal communication. Explore the advantages and the challenges of a diverse workforce and develop the skills that every communicator needs to succeed in today's multicultural business environment.

Achieving Success Through Effective Business Communication

Learning Objectives
After studying this chapter, you will be able to

1 Explain how the Business Communication 2.0 concept is transforming the practice of business communication

2 Describe the five characteristics of effective business communication

3 Describe six strategies for communicating more effectively on the job

4 Explain what must occur for an audience to successfully receive, decode, and respond to messages

5 Explain four strategies for successfully using communication technology

6 Discuss the importance of ethics in business communication and differentiate between ethical dilemmas and ethical lapses

Communication Close-up at Six Apart

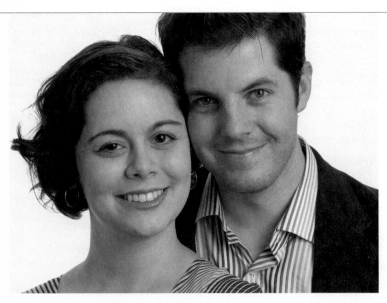

Through the company she co-founded with her husband, Ben, Six Apart's Mena Trott is an influential figure in the world of blogging.

www.sixapart.com

Many people transform personal interests into successful business enterprises. Mena Trott used her hobby to help start a revolution. She was among the first wave of web users to keep a *web log*, or *blog*, an online journal that can cover any topic from politics to pets. As the popularity of Trott's blog grew, the rudimentary blogging tools available at the time couldn't keep up. Trott and her husband, Ben, decided to create their own software that would handle high-volume blogging—and make it easy for anyone to blog.

The Trotts' first product, Movable Type, caught on quickly as web users around the world welcomed the opportunity to become instant online publishers. Before long, Ben and Mena become first-name celebrities in the "blogosphere," and an effort that had started as an extension of a hobby soon grew into a multinational firm that now lays claim to being the world's leading provider of blogging tools and services. (The Trotts named their new company Six Apart in honor of the fact that the two of them were born just six days apart.)

With help from companies such as Six Apart, bloggers began to influence virtually every aspect of contemporary life, from politics to journalism to business. The best of these business blogs tear down the barriers that can make companies seem impersonal or unresponsive. Companies ranging from Boeing to General Motors to Microsoft now use blogs to put a human face on commercial organizations, and millions of people read these blogs to keep up on the latest news about the products and companies that interest them.

Six Apart continues to offer consumers and businesspeople new ways to communicate, such as making its TypePad blogging system available on Apple's popular iPhone. Blogging is changing so rapidly that it's hard to predict what the future holds for Six Apart, but Trott summed up the impact of blogging when she said, "I can't imagine where we'll be in a year, let alone five years, but I'm certain web logging is here to stay."[1]

GETTING READY FOR BUSINESS COMMUNICATION 2.0

Back in the old days—you know, two or three years ago—business communication was largely defined by a *publishing* or *broadcasting* mindset. Externally, a company released carefully scripted messages to a mass audience that often had few, if any, ways to respond. Likewise, customers and other interested parties had few ways to connect with one another to ask questions, share information, or offer support. Internally, communication tended to follow the same "we talk, you listen" model, with upper managers issuing directives to lower-level supervisors and employees.

However, thanks to the efforts of innovators such as Mena Trott (profiled in the chapter-opening Communication Close-up), a variety of technologies have enabled and inspired a new approach to business communication. In contrast to the publishing mindset, this new **social communication model** is *interactive* and *conversational*. As corporate communication specialist Caroline Kealey puts it, traditional practices of "issuing messages through static, hierarchical and largely one-way channels are fading into obsolescence."[2] The audience is no longer a passive recipient of messages but an active participant in the conversation. Just as **Web 2.0** signifies the second generation of World Wide Web technologies (blogs, wikis, podcasts, and other *social media* tools that you'll read about in Chapter 7), **Business Communication 2.0** is a convenient label for this new approach to business communication.

On the surface, this approach might look like it's just added a few new media tools, such as blogs, podcasts, and wikis. However, as Figure 1.1 shows, the changes are much deeper and more profound. In a typical "1.0" approach, messages are scripted by designated communicators, approved by someone in authority, distributed through selected channels, and delivered without modification to a passive audience that is not invited or even expected to respond. In the 2.0 approach, the rules change dramatically; none of these assumptions can be taken for granted.

Of course, no company, no matter how enthusiastically it embraces the 2.0 mindset, is going to be run as a social club in which everyone has a say and a vote. Instead, a hybrid approach is emerging in which some communications (such as strategic plans and policy documents) follow the traditional approach and others (such as project management updates and customer support messages) follow the 2.0 approach.

Throughout this book, you'll find many discussions of how the nature of business communication is changing. Here are some of the major Business Communication 2.0 topics you'll read about:

- Social networking technologies (Chapter 2)
- Social media (including blogs and podcasts) for short messages (Chapter 7)
- The challenge of negative information spread through social media (Chapter 9)
- Social commerce and new approaches to persuasive messages (Chapter 10)
- Social bookmarking and tagging as research tools (Chapter 11)
- Social media (wikis) for longer messages (Chapter 14)
- Social media tools used in recruiting and job searches (Chapter 18)

1 LEARNING OBJECTIVE

Explain how the Business Communication 2.0 concept is transforming the practice of business communication

The conversational and interactive social communication model is revolutionizing business communication.

Practically every assumption about business communication needs to be reconsidered under the Business Communication 2.0 approach.

REAL-TIME UPDATES
Learn More

See how businesses are using Facebook, YouTube, and other social media

Social media expert Ben Wills discusses the growing role of social media in business. Go to **http://real-timeupdates.com/bct** and click on "Learn More." If you are using mybcommlab, you can access Real-Time Updates within each chapter or under Student Study Tools.

FIGURE 1.1 Business Communication: 1.0 Versus 2.0
Business Communication 2.0 differs from conventional communication strategies
and practices in a number of significant ways.

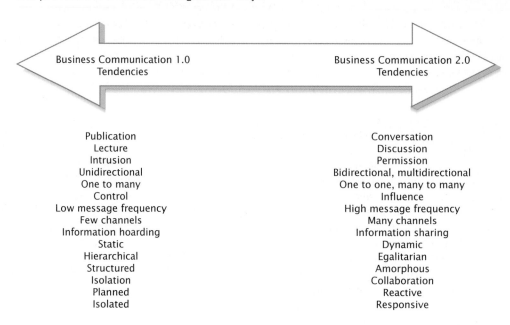

Business Communication 1.0 Tendencies	Business Communication 2.0 Tendencies
Publication	Conversation
Lecture	Discussion
Intrusion	Permission
Unidirectional	Bidirectional, multidirectional
One to many	One to one, many to many
Control	Influence
Low message frequency	High message frequency
Few channels	Many channels
Information hoarding	Information sharing
Static	Dynamic
Hierarchical	Egalitarian
Structured	Amorphous
Isolation	Collaboration
Planned	Reactive
Isolated	Responsive

If you're an active user of Web 2.0 technologies, you'll fit right in with this new communication environment—and possibly even have a head start on more experienced professionals who are still adapting to the new tools and techniques (see "Business Communication 2.0: Putting Their Communication Skills to Work"). For the latest information on communicating in a Web 2.0 environment, visit http://real-timeupdates.com/bct and select Chapter 1.

ACHIEVING SUCCESS IN TODAY'S COMPETITIVE ENVIRONMENT

Communication skills are essential to your career success.

Whether you want to follow in the footsteps of Mena Trott and start your own company or find your place in an existing firm, communication skills will be essential to your success. In fact, if you're looking for a surefire way to stand out from your competition, improving your communication skills may be the single most important step you can take. Employers often express frustration at the poor communication skills of many employees—particularly recent college graduates who haven't yet learned how to adapt their communication styles to a professional business environment. If you learn to write well, speak well, listen well, and recognize the appropriate way to communicate in various business situations, you'll gain a major advantage that will serve you throughout your career.[3]

Communication is the process of transferring information and meaning between *senders* and *receivers*, using one or more written, oral, visual, or electronic channels. The essence of communication is sharing—providing data, information, and insights in an exchange that benefits both you and the people with whom you are communicating.[4] Effective communication helps businesses in numerous ways. These benefits include[5]

Effective communication yields numerous business benefits.

- Stronger decision making based on timely, reliable information
- Faster problem solving, in which less time is spent on understanding problems and more is spent on creating solutions
- Earlier warning of potential problems, from rising business costs to critical safety issues
- Increased productivity and lower costs (In the words of business writing expert Jack Appleman, "bad writing wastes time, and time is money."[6])
- Stronger business relationships
- Clearer and more persuasive marketing messages
- Enhanced professional images for both employers and companies

Business Communication 2.0

Putting Their Communication Skills to Work

The authors have recently met a number of young professionals who use the latest media tools to improve communication in their work. Here are a few of their stories:

- Meg Stivison (University of Massachusetts–Amherst) writes a blog and maintains a Flickr photo-sharing collection for the Stickley Museum at Craftsman Farms in Cary, North Carolina.
- Aga Westfall (Northern Arizona University) of The Santy Agency, an advertising firm in Phoenix, Arizona, uses the Twitter microblogging tool for research and networking.
- Melissa Popp (Millersville University), who is employed by Best Buy in Dover, Delaware, uses YouTube to educate her customers about electronic products.
- Matthew Nederlanden (Palm Beach Atlantic University) of Pompano Beach, Florida, just launched a new *crowdsourcing* advertising agency that allows anyone to create a concept for a commercial, post it on YouTube, and get paid based on how many people view it.
- Jerrold Thompson (Evergreen State College) of Clinton, Washington, just launched In My Life Video, a service that produces personal autobiographies. The skills he honed in class helped him write content for his website and a script for a promotional video he posted on YouTube.
- Philip Beech (Brooks Institute of Photography) of Portland, Oregon, uses Facebook to communicate with other Home Video Studio franchise owners and to promote his business to prospective clients.

- Chris Millichap (University of Wisconsin–Madison) of Chicago, Illinois, uses Facebook to promote Boosh Magazine, an online college entertainment publication.
- Matthew Meyer (Indiana University) of Oakland, California, is an e-learning developer for Adecco who has written and produced a series of training podcasts for a major pharmaceutical client.
- Liz Wise (Art Institute of Colorado) and her colleagues at Drillspot.com, a tools and hardware website based in Boulder, Colorado, use a wiki to minimize the number of meetings held and to store and share instructions for tasks and procedures.
- Ted Rubin (SUNY Purchase) of Atlanta, Georgia, is a remote server support analyst for Career Connection who uses Really Simple Syndication (RSS) newsfeeds to receive updates from vendors and to track the continuous results from his searches on Google News.

CAREER APPLICATIONS

1. If you are currently working, how could you use electronic media to improve the way you communicate with customers or colleagues? (If you're not currently working, think about a job you had in the past or think about a friend's or classmate's job for this exercise.)
2. In what ways have you used electronic media in your college classes? Can you identify any disadvantages of using these media to communicate with instructors and classmates?

- Greater employee engagement with their work, leading to higher employee satisfaction and lower employee turnover
- Better financial results and higher return for investors

Effective communication strengthens the connection between a company and all its **stakeholders**, those groups affected in some way by the company's actions: customers, employees, shareholders, suppliers, neighbors, the community, and the nation.[7] Conversely, when communication breaks down, the results can be anything from time wasting to tragic. At every stage of your career, communication will help you succeed, and the higher you rise in your organization, the more important communication becomes. Top managers spend as much as 85 percent of their time communicating with others.[8]

Communicating in Organizational Settings

Messages flow into, through, and out of business organizations in a variety of ways. **Internal communication** takes place between people inside a company, whereas **external communication** takes place between a company and outside parties.

Every organization has a **formal communication network**, in which ideas and information flow along the lines of command (the hierarchical levels) in the company's organization structure (see Figure 1.2). Although these communication efforts might use social media, they tend to follow the conventional Business Communication 1.0 mindset.

Throughout the internal formal network, information flows in three directions. *Downward communication* flows from executives to employees, conveying executive

A formal communication network mirrors the company's organizational structure.

FIGURE 1.2   Formal Communication Network

A formal communication network, defined by the relationships between the various job positions in an organization, generally follows Business Communication 1.0 conventions. Messages can flow *upward* (from a lower-level employee to a higher-level employee), *downward* (from a higher-level employee to a lower-level employee), and *horizontally* (across the organization, between employees at the same or similar levels).

decisions and providing information that helps employees do their jobs. *Upward communication* flows from employees to executives, providing insight into problems, trends, opportunities, grievances, and performance—thus allowing executives to solve problems and make intelligent decisions. *Horizontal communication* flows between departments to help employees share information, coordinate tasks, and solve complex problems.[9]

Every organization also has an **informal communication network**, often referred to as the *grapevine* or the *rumor mill*, that encompasses all communication that takes place outside the formal network. Some of this informal communication takes place naturally as a result of employee interaction both on the job and in social settings, and some of it takes place when the formal network doesn't provide information that employees want. In fact, the inherent limitations of formal communication networks helped spur the growth of social media and the Business Communication 2.0 concept.

Social media play an increasingly important role in the informal communication network.

Recognizing Effective Communication

You can have the greatest ideas in the world, but they're no good to your company or your career if you can't express them clearly and persuasively. To make your messages effective, you need to make them practical, factual, concise, clear, and persuasive:[10]

2 **LEARNING OBJECTIVE**

Describe the five characteristics of effective business communication

- **Provide practical information.** Give recipients useful information, whether it's to help them perform a desired action or understand a new company policy. For instance, if you review the various product blogs on Six Apart's website (www.sixapart.com/about/ourblogs), you'll see that every posting provides information that advances the cause of blogging in some way. As blogging continues to grow, so do the business opportunities for Six Apart.
- **Give facts rather than vague impressions.** Use concrete language, specific detail, and information that is clear, convincing, accurate, and ethical. When an opinion is called for, present compelling evidence to support your conclusion. If you're using an internal company blog to alert people to a potential problem, don't just complain about the

FIGURE 1.3 Ineffective Business Communication
At first glance, this e-mail message looks like a reasonable attempt at communicating with the members of a project team. However, review the blue annotations to see just how many problems the message really has.

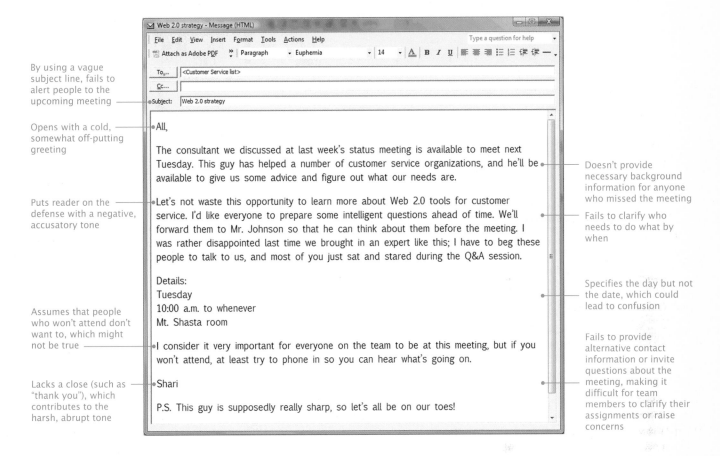

By using a vague subject line, fails to alert people to the upcoming meeting

Opens with a cold, somewhat off-putting greeting

Puts reader on the defense with a negative, accusatory tone

Assumes that people who won't attend don't want to, which might not be true

Lacks a close (such as "thank you"), which contributes to the harsh, abrupt tone

Doesn't provide necessary background information for anyone who missed the meeting

Fails to clarify who needs to do what by when

Specifies the day but not the date, which could lead to confusion

Fails to provide alternative contact information or invite questions about the meeting, making it difficult for team members to clarify their assignments or raise concerns

situation. Describe the circumstances, explain why it is in fact a problem, and, if appropriate, suggest potential solutions.

- **Present information in a concise, efficient manner.** Audiences appreciate—and respond more positively to—messages that highlight and summarize essential points rather than messages buried under mountains of disorganized facts and figures.
- **Clarify expectations and responsibilities.** Write messages to generate a specific response from a specific audience. Clearly state what you expect from audience members or what you can do for them.
- **Offer compelling, persuasive arguments and recommendations.** Show your readers precisely how they will benefit from responding to your message the way you want them to.

Keep these five important characteristics in mind as you review Figure 1.3 and Figure 1.4. At first glance, both e-mails appear to be well constructed, but Figure 1.4 is far more effective, as the comments in blue explain.

Understanding What Employers Expect from You

In any business-related career, employers expect you to be competent at a wide range of communication tasks. Fortunately, the skills that employers expect from you are the same skills that will help you advance in your career:[11]

- Organizing ideas and information logically and completely
- Expressing ideas and information coherently and persuasively—in oral, written, visual, and electronic media

Employers expect you to possess a wide range of communication skills.

FIGURE 1.4   Effective Business Communication
This improved version of the e-mail message from Figure 1.3 does a much better job of communicating the essential information the team members need in order to effectively prepare for the meeting.

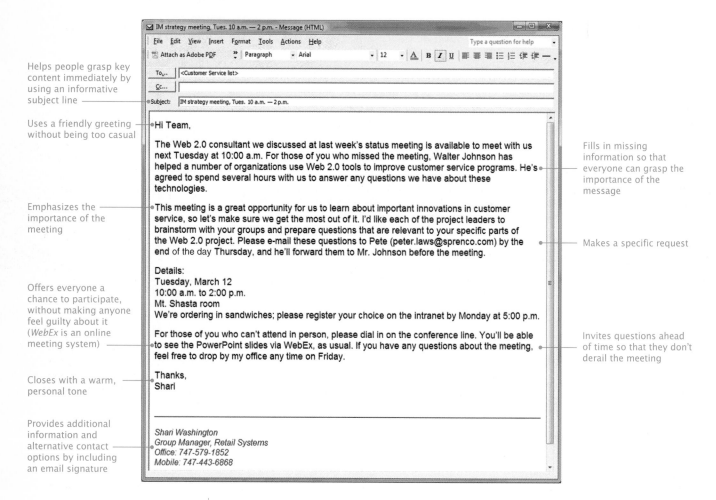

Helps people grasp key content immediately by using an informative subject line

Uses a friendly greeting without being too casual

Emphasizes the importance of the meeting

Offers everyone a chance to participate, without making anyone feel guilty about it (*WebEx* is an online meeting system)

Closes with a warm, personal tone

Provides additional information and alternative contact options by including an email signature

Fills in missing information so that everyone can grasp the importance of the message

Makes a specific request

Invites questions ahead of time so that they don't derail the meeting

- Actively listening to others
- Communicating effectively with people from diverse backgrounds and experiences
- Using communication technologies effectively and efficiently
- Following accepted standards of grammar, spelling, and other aspects of high-quality writing and speaking
- Adapting your messages and communication styles to specific audiences and situations
- Communicating in a civilized manner that reflects contemporary expectations of business etiquette, even when dealing with indifferent or hostile audiences
- Communicating ethically, even when choices aren't crystal clear
- Managing your time wisely and using resources efficiently

You'll have the opportunity to practice these skills throughout this course—but don't stop there. Successful professionals continue to hone communication skills throughout their careers.

Understanding the Unique Challenges of Business Communication

Although you have been communicating with some success your entire life, business communication is often more complicated and demanding than the social communication you typically engage in with family, friends, and school associates. Five issues help illustrate why business communication requires a high level of skill and attention: the globalization of business and the increase in workforce diversity, the increasing value of business information, the pervasiveness of technology, the evolution of organizational structures, and the growing reliance on teamwork.

The Globalization of Business and the Increase in Workforce Diversity

Today's businesses increasingly reach across international borders to market their products, partner with other businesses, and employ workers and executives—an effort known as **globalization**. Many U.S. companies rely on exports for a significant portion of their sales, sometimes up to 50 percent or more, and managers and employees in these firms need to communicate with many other cultures. Moreover, thousands of companies from all around the world vie for a share of the massive U.S. market, so chances are you'll do business with or even work for a company based in another country at some point in your career.

As people and products cross borders, businesses are paying more attention to **workforce diversity**—all the differences among the people who work together, including differences in age, gender, sexual orientation, education, cultural background, religion, ability, and life experience. As Chapter 3 discusses, successful companies realize two important facts: (1) A diverse workforce can yield a significant competitive advantage by bringing new ideas and new communication skills, and (2) the more diverse their workforce, the more attention must be paid to communication.

The Increasing Value of Business Information

As global competition for talent, customers, and resources continues to grow, the importance of information continues to escalate as well. Even companies not usually associated with the so-called Information Age often rely on **knowledge workers**, employees at all levels of an organization who specialize in acquiring, processing, and communicating information. Three examples help to illustrate the value of information in today's economy:

Successful companies know that diverse workforces can create powerful competitive advantages, but they require close attention to communication in order to eliminate barriers between groups with different communication styles.

- **Competitive insights.** The more a company knows about its competitors and their plans, the better able it will be to adjust its own business plans.
- **Customer needs.** Most companies invest significant time and money in the effort to understand the needs of their customers, and this information needs to be analyzed and summarized in order to develop goods and services that better satisfy customer needs.
- **Regulations and guidelines.** Today's businesses must understand and follow a wide range of government regulations and guidelines covering such areas as employment, environment, taxes, and accounting.

Information has become one of the most important resources in business today.

No matter what the specific type of information, the better you are able to understand it, use it, and communicate it to others, the more competitive you and your company will be.

The Pervasiveness of Technology

The innovations that enable the Business Communication 2.0 approach highlight an important fact of business communication today: Technology influences virtually every aspect of the field. To benefit from this technology, however, you need to have at least a basic level of skills. If your level of technical expertise doesn't keep up with that of your colleagues and co-workers, the imbalance can put you at a disadvantage and complicate the communication process. Throughout this course, you'll learn how to use numerous technological tools and systems more effectively.

Business communication today is heavily dependent on a growing array of technologies.

The Evolution of Organizational Structures

Every firm has a particular structure that defines the relationships between various units in the company, and these relationships influence the nature and quality of communication throughout the organization. *Tall structures* have many layers of management between the lowest and highest positions, so they can suffer communication breakdowns and delays as messages are passed up and down through multiple layers.[12]

To overcome such problems, many businesses are adopting *flat structures* that reduce the number of layers. With fewer layers, communication generally flows faster and with

Organizations with tall structures may unintentionally restrict the flow of information; flatter structures can make it easier to communicate effectively.

fewer disruptions and distortions. On the other hand, with fewer formal lines of control and communication in these organizations, individual employees are expected to assume more responsibility for communication—particularly in the horizontal direction, from department to department across the company.

Specific types of organization structures present unique communication challenges. In a *matrix structure*, for example, employees report to two managers at the same time, such as a project manager and a department manager. The need to coordinate workloads, schedules, and other matters increases the communication burden on everyone involved. In a *network structure*, sometimes known as a *virtual organization*, a company supplements the talents of its employees with services from one or more external partners. For instance, a company might focus on the research and development of new products while relying on partners to manufacture, sell, and service those products. Communicating across these multiple boundaries requires extra planning and diligence—particularly because each company in the network might be a partner in several other networks.

Newer types of organization structures such as matrixes and networks present new communication challenges.

Regardless of the particular structure a company uses, your communication efforts will also be influenced by the organization's **corporate culture**, the mixture of values, traditions, and habits that give a company its atmosphere and personality. Successful companies encourage employee contributions by ensuring that communication flows freely down, up, and across the organization chart. Open climates encourage candor and honesty, helping employees feel free enough to admit their mistakes, disagree with the boss, and share negative or unwelcome information.

Open corporate cultures benefit from free-flowing information and employee input.

The Growing Reliance on Teamwork

Both traditional and innovative company structures can rely heavily on teamwork, and you will probably find yourself on dozens of teams throughout your career. Teams are commonly used in business today, but they're not always successful—and a key reason that teams fail to meet their objectives is poor communication. Chapter 2 offers insights into the complex dynamics of team communication and identifies skills you need in order to be an effective communicator in group settings.

Working in a team makes you especially responsible for communicating effectively.

3 LEARNING OBJECTIVE

Describe six strategies for communicating more effectively on the job

COMMUNICATING MORE EFFECTIVELY ON THE JOB

Communication in today's business environment is clearly a challenge, but you can meet that challenge by learning to connect with your audiences, minimizing distractions, adopting an audience-centered approach, improving your basic communication skills, using constructive feedback, and being sensitive to business etiquette.

Connecting with Your Audience

You have no doubt had experiences in which a single word or even just a glance successfully communicated what you wanted to say—as well as experiences in which you talked for hours or sent what seemed like a million messages but just couldn't get your audience to understand your point. Why do some efforts succeed and others fail?

Human communication is a complex process with many opportunities for messages to get lost, ignored, or misinterpreted. Fortunately, by understanding this process, you can improve the odds that your messages will reach their intended audiences and produce the intended effects.

The Communication Process

Viewing communication as a process helps you identify steps you can take to improve your success as a communicator.

By viewing communication as a process (Figure 1.5), you can identify and improve the skills you need to be more successful. Many variations on this process model exist, but these eight steps provide a practical overview:

1. **The sender has an idea.** Whether a communication effort will ultimately be effective starts right here. For example, if you have a clear idea about a procedure change that will save your company time and money, the communication process is off to a strong start. On the other hand, if all you want to do is complain about how the company is wasting

FIGURE 1.5 The Communication Process
These eight steps illustrate how ideas travel from sender to receiver. After you explore the process in more detail in the following pages, Figure 1.8 on page 52 offers advice on improving your skills at each step.

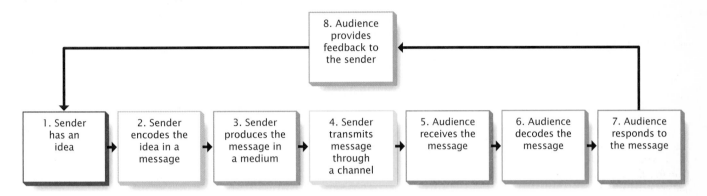

time and money, but you don't know how to fix the situation, you might be able to get your point across, but you probably won't communicate anything of value to your audience.

2. **The sender encodes the idea as a message.** When you put your idea into a message (words, images, or a combination of both), you are **encoding** it. Much of the focus of this course is on developing the skills needed to successfully encode your ideas into effective messages.

3. **The sender produces the message in a transmittable medium.** With the appropriate message to express your idea, you now need some way to present that message to your intended audience. As you'll read in Chapter 4, media for transmitting messages can be divided into *oral, written, visual,* and *electronic* forms. Selecting the best medium for each message is an important communication skill, particularly as electronic media options continue to multiply.

4. **The sender transmits the message through a channel.** Just as technology continues to increase the number of media options at your disposal, it continues to provide new **communication channels** you can use to transmit your messages. The distinction between medium and channel can get a bit murky, but think of the medium as the *form* a message takes and the channel as the system used to *deliver* the message. The channel can be a face-to-face conversation, the Internet, another company—any method or system capable of delivering messages.

5. **The audience receives the message.** If all goes well, your message survives the trip through the channel and arrives at your intended audience. However, mere arrival at the destination is not a guarantee that the message will be noticed or understood correctly. As "How Audiences Receive Messages" (page 46) explains, many messages are either ignored or misinterpreted as noise.

6. **The audience decodes the message.** If the message is actually received, the audience then needs to extract your idea from the message, a step known as **decoding**. "How Audiences Decode Messages" (page 47) takes a closer look at this complex and subtle step in the process.

7. **The audience responds to the message.** By crafting your messages in ways that show the benefits of responding, you can increase the chances that your audiences will respond as you'd like them to. However, as "How Audiences Respond to Messages" (page 48) points out, audience members need to remember your message long enough to act on it, they need to be able to act on it as you want them to, and they need to be motivated to respond.

8. The audience provides feedback to sender. In addition to responding (or not responding) to the message, audience members may give **feedback** that helps you evaluate the effectiveness of your communication effort. Sometimes feedback can be subtle and difficult to interpret. For example, a listener looking away while you're talking might be trying to conceal confusion or might be angry and trying to control his or her emotions. Other times, feedback is direct and easy to interpret, as when someone says he or she doesn't understand you, thinks your idea is brilliant, or can't hear you.

Bear in mind that this process description represents just one instance of communicating a single message between a sender and a receiver. Particularly in situations that use social media to invite contributions from all interested parties, an ongoing discussion could involve dozens or hundreds of exchanges like the one just described.

The following sections take a closer look at two important aspects of the process: environmental barriers that can block or distort messages and the steps audiences take to receive, decode, and respond to messages.

Barriers in the Communication Environment

Within any communication environment, messages can be disrupted by a variety of **communication barriers**. These include noise and distractions, competing messages, filters, and channel breakdowns:

A number of barriers can block or distort messages before they reach the intended audience.

- **Noise and distractions.** External distractions range from uncomfortable meeting rooms to crowded computer screens with instant messages and reminders popping up all over the place. The common habit of *multitasking*, attempting more than one task at a time, is practically guaranteed to create communication distractions. Internal distractions are thoughts and emotions that prevent audiences from focusing on incoming messages. For instance, a person worried about losing his job might ignore any message that doesn't apply to his immediate concerns.
- **Competing messages.** Having your audience's undivided attention is a rare luxury. In most cases, you must compete with other messages that are trying to reach your audience at the same time. Any message that is more compelling than yours can pull the audience's attention away; this is one of the reasons it is so essential to craft messages that your audience will care about.
- **Filters.** Messages can be blocked or distorted by *filters*, any human or technological interventions between the sender and the receiver. Filtering can be both intentional (such as automatically filing e-mail messages based on sender or content) or unintentional (such as an overly aggressive *spam* filter that deletes legitimate e-mail). As you read earlier, the structure and culture of an organization can also inhibit the flow of vital messages. And, in some cases, the people or companies you rely on to deliver your message can distort it or filter it to meet their own needs.
- **Channel breakdowns.** Sometimes the channel simply breaks down and fails to deliver your message at all. A colleague you were counting on to deliver a message to your boss might have forgotten to do so, or a computer server might have crashed and prevented your blog from updating.

As a communicator, try to be aware of any barriers that could prevent your messages from reaching their intended audiences. As a manager, keep an eye out for any organizational barriers that could be inhibiting the flow of information.

Inside the Mind of Your Audience

After a message works its way through the communication channel and reaches the intended audience, it encounters a whole new set of challenges. Understanding how audiences receive, decode, and respond to messages will help you create more effective messages.

How Audiences Receive Messages   For an audience member to receive a message, three events need to occur: The receiver has to *sense* the presence of a message, *select* it from all the other messages clamoring for attention, and *perceive* it as an actual message (as opposed to random, pointless noise).[13] You can appreciate the magnitude of this challenge by driving down any busy street in a commercial section of town. You'll encounter literally hundreds of messages—billboards, posters, store window displays, other people's thumping car stereos, pedestrians waving or talking on mobile phones, car horns, street signs, traffic lights, and so on. However, you sense, select, and perceive only a small fraction of these messages.

Today's business audiences are much like drivers on busy streets. They are inundated with so many messages and so much noise that they can miss or ignore many of the messages intended for them. Through this course, you will learn a variety of techniques to craft messages that get noticed. In general, follow these five principles to increase your chances of success:

Message overload is a constant challenge in contemporary life; your messages must compete with many others clamoring for the audience's attention.

- **Consider audience expectations.** Deliver messages using the media and channels that the audience expects. If colleagues expect meeting notices to be delivered by e-mail, don't suddenly switch gears and start delivering the notices via blog postings without telling anyone. Of course, sometimes going *against* expectations can stimulate audience attention, which is why advertisers sometimes do wacky and creative things to get your attention. However, for most business communication efforts, following the expectations of your audience is the most efficient way to get your message across.
- **Ensure ease of use.** Even if audiences are actively looking for your messages, they probably won't see the messages if you make them hard to find, hard to access, or hard to read. Poorly designed websites with confusing navigation are common culprits in this respect.
- **Emphasize familiarity.** Use words, images, and designs that are familiar to your audience. For example, most visitors to company websites now expect to see information about the company on a page called "About Us."
- **Practice empathy.** Make sure your messages speak to the audience by clearly addressing *their* wants and needs—not yours. People are inclined to notice messages that relate to their individual concerns.[14]
- **Design for compatibility.** For the many messages delivered electronically these days, be sure to verify technological compatibility with your audience. For instance, if your website requires visitors to have the Adobe Flash capability on their computers, you won't reach those audience members who don't have that software installed.

How Audiences Decode Messages   A received message doesn't "mean" anything until the recipient decodes it and assigns meaning to it, and there is no guarantee that your audience will assign the same meaning that you intended. Even well-crafted, well-intentioned communication efforts can fail at this stage because assigning meaning through decoding is a highly personal process that is influenced by culture, individual experience, learning and thinking styles, hopes, fears, and even temporary moods. Moreover, audiences tend to extract the meaning they expect to get from a message, even if it's the opposite of what the sender intended.[15] In fact, rather than extract your meaning, it's more accurate to say that audience members re-create their own meaning—or meanings—from the message.

Decoding a message to assign meaning to it is a complicated and often highly personal process.

As you'll discover in Chapter 3, culture shapes people's views of the world in profound ways, from determinations of right and wrong to details such as the symbolic meanings attached to specific colors. For instance, because U.S. culture celebrates youth and individual accomplishment, it is "natural" for people raised in this country to admire young, independent-minded leaders who rebel against older, established ways of doing business. A culture such as Japan's, however, generally places a higher value on respect for older colleagues, consensus decision making, and group accomplishment. Given these differences, a younger colleague's bold proposal to radically reshape business strategy could be interpreted more positively in one culture than in the other—quite independent of the proposal's merits alone.

At an individual level, beliefs and biases influence the meaning that audiences extract from messages. For instance, the human brain organizes incoming sensations into a mental "map" that represents each person's individual **perception** of reality. If a detail doesn't quite fit for any reason, people are inclined to distort the information rather than rearrange their mental map—a process known as **selective perception**.[16] For example, an executive who

Selective perception occurs when people ignore or distort incoming information to fit their preconceived notions of reality.

has staked her reputation on a particular business strategy might distort or ignore evidence that suggests the strategy is failing.

Differences in language and usage also influence received meaning. If you ask an employee to send you a report on sales figures "as soon as possible," does that mean within 10 seconds, 10 minutes, or 10 days? By clarifying expectations and resolving potential ambiguities in your messages, you can minimize such uncertainties. In general, the more experiences you share with another person, the more likely you are to share perception and thus share meaning (see Figure 1.6).

Individual thinking styles are another important factor in message decoding. For example, someone who places a high value on objective analysis and clear logic might interpret a message differently from someone who values emotion or intuition (reaching conclusions without using rational processes).

How Audiences Respond to Messages   You are almost there. Your message has been delivered, received, and correctly decoded. Now what? Will audience members respond in the way you'd like them to? Only if three events occur.

First, the recipient has to *remember* the message long enough to act on it. Simplifying greatly, memory works in several stages: *Sensory memory* momentarily captures incoming data from the senses; then, whatever the recipient pays attention to is transferred to *short-term memory*. Information in short-term memory will quickly disappear if it isn't transferred to *long-term memory*, which can be done either actively (such as when a person memorizes a list of items) or passively (such as when a new piece of information connects with something else the recipient already has stored in long-term memory). Finally, the information needs to be *retrieved* when the recipient wants to act on it.[17] In general, people find it easier to remember and retrieve information that is important to them personally or professionally. Consequently, by communicating in ways that are sensitive to your audience's wants and needs, you greatly increase the chance that your messages will be remembered and retrieved.

Second, the recipient has to be *able* to respond as you wish. Obviously, if recipients simply cannot do what you want them to do, they will not respond according to your plan. By understanding your audience (you'll learn more about audience analysis in Chapter 4), you can work to minimize these scenarios.

Third, the recipient has to be *motivated* to respond. You'll encounter many situations in which your audience has the option of responding but isn't required to. For instance, a record company may or may not offer your band a contract, or your boss may or may not respond to your request for a raise. Throughout this course, you'll learn techniques for crafting messages that can help motivate readers to respond.

Audiences will likely respond to a message if they remember it, if they're able to respond, and if they're properly motivated to respond.

By explaining how audiences will benefit by responding to your messages, you'll increase their motivation to respond.

FIGURE 1.6   **How Shared Experience Affects Understanding**
The more that two people or two groups of people share experiences—personal, professional, and cultural—the more likely it is that receivers will extract the intended meanings that senders encode into the messages.

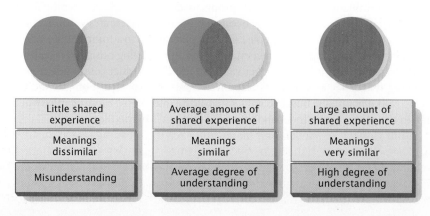

Minimizing Distractions

Although distractions are a major problem in business communication, everyone in an organization can help minimize them. A small dose of common sense and courtesy goes a long way. Turn off that mobile phone before you step into a meeting. Don't talk across the tops of other people's cubicles. Be sensitive to personal differences, too; for instance, some people enjoy working with music on, but music is an enormous distraction for others.[18]

Take steps to insulate yourself from distractions, too. Don't let e-mail, IM, telephone calls, or Twitter updates interrupt you every minute of the day. Set aside time to attend to messages all at once so that you can focus the rest of the time.

Finally, recognize that emotions—yours and your audience's—can create distractions. Try to overcome these distractions by being aware of your own feelings and by anticipating emotional reactions from others.[19] For example, when communicating about an emotionally charged situation, choose your words carefully to minimize overreactions that could keep your message from getting through.

Overcome distractions by
- *Using common sense and courtesy*
- *Not sending unnecessary messages*
- *Not isolating yourself*
- *Informing receivers of message priority*

Communicating in emotionally charged situations requires extra care.

Adopting an Audience-Centered Approach

An **audience-centered approach** involves understanding and respecting the members of your audience and making every effort to get your message across in a way that is meaningful to them (see Figure 1.7). This approach is also known as adopting the **"you" attitude**, in contrast to messages that are about "me." Learn as much as possible about the biases, education, age, status, style, and personal and professional concerns of your receivers. If you're addressing people you don't know and you're unable to find out more about them, try to project yourself into their position by using common sense and imagination. This ability to relate to the needs of others is a key part of *emotional intelligence*, which is widely considered to be a vital characteristic of successful managers and leaders.[20] The more you know about the people you're communicating with, the easier it will be to concentrate on their needs—which, in turn, will make it easier for them to hear your message, understand it, and respond positively.

Recognizing and adapting to the diverse styles of all the audiences you will encounter on the job will improve not only the effectiveness of your communication but also the quality of your working relationships.[21] The audience-centered approach is emphasized throughout this book, so you'll have plenty of opportunity to practice this approach.

Keeping your audience's needs in mind helps you ensure successful messages.

Fine-Tuning Your Business Communication Skills

Your skills as a communicator will be as much a factor in your business success as anything else you'll do in your career. No matter what your skill level at any given time, opportunities to improve are numerous and usually easy to find. Many employers provide communication training in both general skills and specific scenarios, but don't wait. Begin mastering your skills now, using this course and the opportunity to practice in an environment that provides honest and constructive feedback. You'll have ample opportunity to plan and produce documents, collaborate in teams, listen effectively, improve nonverbal communication, use a variety of technologies, and communicate across cultures—all skills that will serve your career well.

Work on your communication skills now, before you start (or restart) your business career.

Giving—and Responding to—Constructive Feedback

You will encounter numerous situations in which you are expected to give and receive feedback regarding communication efforts. Whether giving or receiving criticism, be sure to do so in a constructive way. **Constructive feedback**, sometimes called *constructive criticism*, focuses on the process and outcomes of communication, not on the people involved (see Table 1.1). In contrast, **destructive feedback** simply criticizes with no effort to stimulate improvement.[22] For example, "This proposal is a confusing mess, and you failed to convince me of anything" is destructive feedback. Your goal is to be more constructive: "Your proposal could be more effective, with a clearer description of the manufacturing process

Constructive feedback focuses on improvement, not personal criticism.

FIGURE 1.7 Audience-Centered Communication
This blog post from the developers of the popular TypePad blogging system demonstrates concern for the audience in several ways, including content that addresses audience interests, a design that makes the content easy to absorb, and the opportunity for readers to participate in the conversation.

January 16, 2008

Shiny new icon for the iPhone and iPod Touch

Have an iPhone or iPod Touch? If you add the TypePad for iPhone web app as a webclip to your iPhone's home screen, you'll now get a bright icon that will look great alongside your other favorite iPhone apps and websites.

Offers links to additional information

Adding it is easy. After you've updated your iPhone to version 1.1.3, visit i.typepad.com in Safari and click on the "+" button in the toolbar at the bottom of the screen. Now you'll have a quick and easy way to sign in to TypePad from your iPhone, and a great-looking TypePad icon on your home screen!

Update: And here's a tip on how you can add your own custom icon for your blog, in case any of your readers add your blog to their iPhone's home screen as a webclip.

1. Create your own custom 57x57 icon, and save it in PNG format.
2. Name that file "apple-touch-icon.png"
3. Upload it to the main folder of your account by signing into TypePad and visiting Control Panel > Files.

Provides technical instructions in an easy-to-follow numbered list

It's that easy! The next time someone saves your blog as a webclip on their iPhone, they'll get your pretty icon instead of an automatically generated screenshot.

Supports quick reading with an open, uncluttered design

Posted by Michael Sippey on January 16, 2008 at 04:41 PM in Mobile | Permalink

TrackBack

TrackBack URL for this entry:
http://www.typepad.com/t/trackback/174921/25201430
Listed below are links to weblogs that reference Shiny new icon for the iPhone and iPod Touch:

Comments

Great. Now back to work on better stats:-)

Posted by: Petur Jonsson | January 16, 2008 at 05:50 PM

Offers a commenting feature so that readers can join the conversation (notice the friendly but firm tone of this reader's comments as he asks for a product improvement)

Try to react unemotionally when you receive constructive feedback.

you advocate and a well-organized explanation of why the positives outweigh the negatives." When giving feedback, avoid personal attacks and give the person clear guidelines for improvement.

When you receive constructive feedback, resist the urge to defend your work or deny the validity of the feedback. Remaining open to criticism isn't easy when you've poured your heart and soul into a project, but feedback is a valuable opportunity to learn and improve. Try to disconnect your emotions from the work and view it simply as something—a thing apart from yourself—that you can make better. Many writers find it helpful to step back, think about the feedback for a while, and let their emotions settle down before diving in to make corrections. Of course, don't automatically assume that even well-intentioned feedback is necessarily correct. You have the responsibility for the final content and quality of every message you produce, so make sure that any suggested changes are valid.

TABLE 1.1 Giving Constructive Feedback

HOW TO BE CONSTRUCTIVE	EXPLANATION
Think through your suggested changes carefully.	Because many business documents must illustrate complex relationships between ideas and other information, isolated and superficial edits can do more harm than good.
Discuss improvements rather than flaws.	Instead of saying "this is confusing," explain how the writing can be improved to make it clearer.
Focus on controllable behavior.	Because the writer may not have control over every variable that affected the quality of the message, focus on the aspects the writer can control.
Be specific.	Comments such as "I don't get this" or "Make this clearer" don't identify what the writer needs to fix.
Keep feedback impersonal.	Focus comments on the message, not the person who created it.
Verify understanding.	Ask for confirmation from the recipient to make sure that the person understands your feedback.
Provide your feedback in a timely fashion.	Make sure the writer will have sufficient time to implement the changes you suggest.
Highlight any limitations your feedback may have.	If you didn't have time to give the document a thorough edit, or if you're not an expert in some aspect of the content, let the writer know so that he or she can handle your comments appropriately.

Being Sensitive to Business Etiquette

A vital element of audience-centered communication is **etiquette**, the expected norms of behavior in any particular situation. In today's hectic, competitive world, etiquette might seem a quaint and outdated notion. However, the way you conduct yourself and interact with others can have a profound influence on your company's success and your career. When executives hire and promote you, they expect your behavior to protect the company's reputation. The more you understand such expectations, the better chance you have of avoiding career-damaging mistakes.

Understanding communication etiquette can help you avoid needless blunders.

Throughout this book, you'll encounter etiquette advice for a variety of business situations, but even if you don't know the specific expectations in a given situation, some general guidelines will get you through any rough spots. Start by being sensitive to the fact that etiquette is culturally based, and people from different cultures can have different expectations about the same situation. Something you find appalling or embarrassing might be business as usual for a colleague and vice versa.

Long lists of etiquette "rules" can be overwhelming, and you'll never be able to memorize all of them. Fortunately, you can count on three principles to get you through any situation: respect, courtesy, and common sense. Moreover, following these principles will encourage forgiveness if you do happen to make a mistake. As you prepare to encounter new situations, take some time to learn the expectations of the other people involved. Travel guidebooks are a great source of information about norms and customs in other countries. Check to see if your library has online access to the CultureGrams database, or review the country profiles at www.kwintessential.co.uk or www.culturecrossing.com. Don't be afraid to ask questions, either. People will respect your concern and curiosity. You will gradually accumulate considerable knowledge, which will help you feel comfortable and be effective in a wide range of business situations.

Respect, courtesy, and common sense will get you through most etiquette challenges on the job.

FIGURE 1.8 Becoming an Effective Business Communicator

The communication process presents many opportunities for messages to get lost, distorted, or misinterpreted as they travel from sender to receiver. Fortunately, you can take action at every step in the process to increase your chances of success.

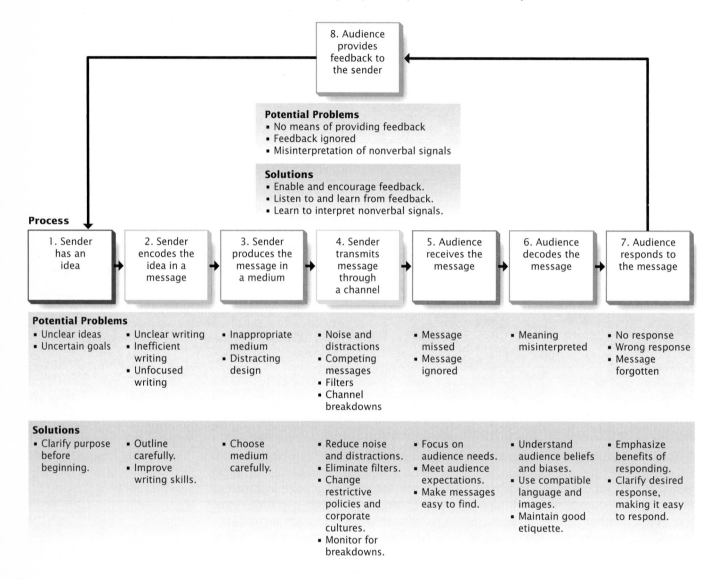

Applying What You've Learned to the Communication Process

Now that you have some additional insights into what makes communication succeed, take another look at the communication process model. Figure 1.8 identifies the key challenges in the process and summarizes the steps you can take along the way to become a more effective communicator.

5 LEARNING OBJECTIVE

Explain four strategies for successfully using communication technology

USING TECHNOLOGY TO IMPROVE BUSINESS COMMUNICATION

Today's businesses rely heavily on technology to facilitate the communication process. In fact, many of the technologies you might use in your personal life, from microblogs to video games to virtual worlds, are also used in business. You will find technology discussed extensively throughout this book, with specific advice on using both common and emerging tools. The four-page photo essay "Powerful Tools for Communicating Efficiently" (see pages 54–57) provides an overview of the technologies that connect people in offices, factories, and other business settings.

Anyone who has used a computer, a smartphone, or other advanced gadget knows that the benefits of technology are not automatic. Poorly designed or inappropriately used technology can hinder communication more than it helps. To communicate effectively, learn to keep technology in perspective, guard against information overload and information addiction, use technological tools productively, and disengage from the computer frequently to communicate in person.

Communicating in today's business environment requires at least a basic level of technological competence.

Keeping Technology in Perspective

Perhaps the single most important point to remember about technology is that it is simply a tool, a means by which you can accomplish certain tasks. Technology is an aid to interpersonal communication, not a replacement for it. Technology can't think for you or communicate for you, and if you lack some essential skills, technology can't fill in the gaps. Your spell checker is happy to run all your words through a dictionary, but it doesn't know whether you're using the correct words or crafting powerful sentences.

Don't rely too much on technology or let it overwhelm the communication process.

While this advice might sound obvious, it is easy to get caught up in the "gee whiz" factor, particularly when new and different technologies first appear. No matter how exotic or cutting edge it may be, technology has value only if it helps deliver the right information to the right people at the right time.

Guarding Against Information Overload and Information Addiction

The overuse or misuse of communication technology can lead to **information overload**, in which people receive more information than they can effectively process. Information overload makes it difficult to discriminate between useful and useless information, lowers productivity, and amplifies employee stress both on the job and at home—even to the point of causing health and relationship problems.[23] Information overload has become such a serious productivity concern that research organizations such as the Information Overload Research Group have been founded to search for solutions.[24]

Information overload results when people receive more information than they can effectively process.

As a recipient, you often have some level of control over the number and types of messages you choose to receive. For example, corporate e-mail systems usually have powerful filtering and tagging capabilities that can automatically sort incoming messages based on criteria you set. Use this feature to isolate high-priority messages that deserve your attention. Also, be wary of subscribing to too many blog feeds, Twitter groups, and other sources of recurring messages. Separate your *need-to-know* information from *nice-to-know* information and make sure the latter doesn't drown out the former.

As a sender, you can help reduce information overload by making sure you don't send unnecessary messages. You don't want to undercommunicate, but sending unnecessary messages or sending the right message to the wrong people is almost as bad. In addition, if

An important step in reducing information overload is to avoid sending unnecessary messages.

you must send a message that isn't urgent or crucial, let people know so they can prioritize. If a report requires no action from recipients, tell them up front so they don't have to search through it, looking for action items that apply to them. Also, most communication systems let you mark messages as urgent; however, use this feature only when it is truly needed. Sending too many so-called urgent messages that aren't really urgent will lead to annoyance and anxiety, not action.

Beyond simple overload, some workers are beginning to show signs of *information technology addiction*—to the point of craving the stimulation of being connected practically around the clock, even while on vacation. While employees who refuse to disconnect from their work might sound like a manager's dream, being constantly "plugged in" often does more harm than good. Too much work, like too much information, can

 REAL-TIME UPDATES
Learn More

Steps you can take to help reduce information overload

Everyone needs to play a part in reducing the burden of too much data and information in the work environment; this document has plenty of helpful tips. Go to **http://real-timeupdates .com/bct** and click on "Learn More." If you are using mybcommlab, you can access Real-Time Updates within each chapter or under Student Study Tools.

(*Text continues on page 58*)

Powerful Tools for Communicating Effectively

The tools of business communication evolve with every new generation of digital technology. Selecting the right tool for each situation can enhance your business communication in many ways. In today's flexible office settings, communication technology helps people keep in touch and stay productive. When co-workers in different cities need to collaborate, they can meet and share ideas without costly travel. Manufacturers use communication technology to keep track of parts, orders, and shipments—and to keep customers well-informed. Those same customers can also communicate with companies in many ways at any time of day or night.

Electronic Presentations

Combining a color projector with a laptop or personal digital assistant (PDA) running the right software lets people give business presentations that are enhanced with sound, animation, and website hyperlinks.

Wireless Networks

Wireless access lets workers with laptop PCs and other devices stay connected from just about anywhere—around the corporate campus and from coffee shops, airports, hotels, and other remote locations.

REDEFINING THE OFFICE

Technology makes it easier for people to stay connected with co-workers and retrieve needed information. Some maintain that connection without having a permanent office, a desktop PC, or even a big filing cabinet. For example, Sun Microsystems lets staff members choose to work either at the main office or at remote offices called "drop-in centers." Many Sun facilities have specially equipped "iWork" areas where phone and computer connections can be quickly reconfigured to meet individual requirements.

Virtual Meeting Spaces

A number of companies (such as Cranial Tap, whose virtual headquarters is shown here) are experimenting with meeting spaces in virtual worlds such as Second Life. Advantages include being able to explore three-dimensional product models and data visualization displays.

Electronic Whiteboards

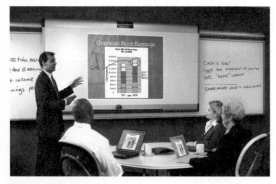

Electronic whiteboards can capture, store, and e-mail the results of brainstorming sessions and other meetings. The newest versions work with electronic presentations, too, letting users write and draw directly on displayed slides.

Unified Communications

Many workers can now access all their voice and e-mail communication through a single portal. *Follow-me phone service* automatically forwards incoming calls to remote sites, home offices, or mobile phones. Integrated systems can retrieve voice-mail messages via computer or read e-mail messages over the phone.

Wikis

Wikis promote collaboration by simplifying the process of creating and editing online content. Anyone with access (some wikis are private, while some are public) can add and modify pages as new information becomes available.

Web-Based Meetings

Web-based meetings allow team members from all over the world to collaborate online. Various systems support instant messaging, live video, real-time editing tools, and more.

COLLABORATING

Working in teams is essential in almost every business. Teamwork can become complicated, however, when team members work in different parts of the company, in different time zones, or even for different companies. Technology helps bridge the distance by making it possible to brainstorm, attend virtual meetings, and share files from widely separated locations. Communication technology also helps companies save money on costly business travel without losing most of the benefits of face-to-face collaboration.

Shared Workspaces

Online workspaces such as eRoom and Groove make it easy for far-flung team members to access shared files anywhere, anytime. Accessible through a browser, the workspace contains a collection of folders and has built-in intelligence to control which team members can read, edit, and save specific files.

Videoconferencing and Telepresence

Videoconferencing provides many of the same benefits as in-person meetings at a fraction of the cost. Advanced systems feature *telepresence*, in which the video images are life sized and extremely realistic.

Voice Technologies

The human voice is being supplemented by a variety of technologies. *Voice synthesis* regenerates a human speaking voice from computer files. *Voice recognition* converts human speech to computer-compatible data.

RSS Newsfeeds and Aggregators

Aggregators, sometimes called *newsreaders*, automatically collect information about new blog postings and podcasts via Really Simple Syndication (RSS) newsfeeds. They give audiences more control over the content they receive from businesses. Businesses are now sending some messages to internal and external audiences via RSS newsfeeds instead of e-mail.

Extranets

Extranets are secure, private websites and networks that share information with suppliers, business partners, and customers. Think of an extranet as an extension of a company intranet that is available to people outside the organization by invitation only.

SHARING THE LATEST INFORMATION

Companies use a variety of communication technologies to create products and services and deliver them to customers. The ability to easily access and share the latest information improves the flow and timing of supplies, lowers operating costs, and boosts financial performance. Easy information access also helps companies respond to customer needs by providing them timely, accurate information and service and by delivering the right products to them at the right time.

Supply Chain Management Software

Manufacturers, distributors, and retailers now automatically share information that used to require labor-intensive manual reporting. Improved information flow increases report accuracy and helps each company in the *supply chain* manage stock levels.

Social Tagging and Bookmarking

Audiences become part of the communication channel when they find and recommend online content through tagging and bookmarking sites such as Delicious.com.

Location and Tracking Technologies

Location and tracking technologies can replace manual reporting. Radio-frequency identification (RFID) tags enable automated tracking of goods and containers. Geographic data from the Global Positioning System (GPS) enables new forms of communication, such as location-based advertising (getting an ad on your mobile phone from a store you're walking past, for instance) and remote monitoring of medical patients and trucking fleets.

Online Customer Support

For online shoppers who need instant help, many retail websites make it easy to connect with a live sales rep via phone or instant messaging. In addition, software tools known as *virtual agents* or *bots* can perform a variety of communication tasks, such as answering simple questions and responding to requests for electronic documents.

Podcasts

With the portability and convenience of downloadable audio and video recordings, podcasts have quickly become a popular means of delivering everything from college lectures to marketing messages. Podcasts are also used for internal communication, replacing conference calls, newsletters, and other media.

INTERACTING WITH CUSTOMERS

Maintaining an open dialog with customers is a great way to gain a better understanding of their likes and dislikes. Today's communication technologies make it easier for customers to interact with a company whenever, wherever, and however they wish. A well-coordinated approach to phone, web, and in-store communication helps a company build stronger relationships with its existing customers, which increases the chances of doing more business with each one.

Help Lines

Some people prefer the personal touch of contact by phone. Moreover, some companies assign preferred customers special ID numbers that let them jump to the front of the calling queue. Many companies offer multilingual support as well.

In-Store Kiosks

Staples is among the retailers that let shoppers buy from the web while they're still in the store. Web-connected kiosks give customers quick access to thousands of in-store items and many more that are available online.

Blogs

Blogs let companies connect with customers and other audiences in a fast and informal way. Commenting features let audiences participate in the conversation, too.

raise stress, increase exhaustion, and interfere with personal relationships. As Rutgers University professor Gayle Porter puts it, "Employers rightfully provide programs to help workers with chemical or substance addictions. Addiction to technology can be equally damaging to the mental health of the worker."[25]

Using Technological Tools Productively

E-mail, IM, the World Wide Web, and other technologies are key parts of what has been called the "information technology paradox," in which information tools can waste as much time as they save. In fact, many employers are so concerned about productivity losses from personal use of the Internet and e-mail at work that they are placing restrictions on how employees can use them, such as installing software that limits Internet access to business-related sites during working hours.[26]

Managers need to help ensure that employee can productively use the communication tools at their disposal.

Managers need to guide their employees in productive use of information tools because the speed and simplicity of these tools is also one of their greatest weaknesses: It's too easy to send too many messages and to subscribe to too many blog feeds, Twitter groups, and other information sources. The flood of messages from an expanding array of electronic sources can significantly affect employees' ability to focus on their work. In one study, workers exposed to a constant barrage of e-mail, IM, and phone calls experienced an average 10-point drop in their functioning IQ.[27]

Simply knowing how to use your tools can make a big difference in your productivity. You don't have to become an expert in most cases, but you need to be familiar with the basic features and functions of the tools you are expected to use on the job. As a manager, you also need to ensure that your employees have sufficient training to productively use the tools you expect them to use.

Another major productivity consideration is personal use of music players, IM, blogging, and other technological tools (and toys) on the job. Few companies go to the extreme of banning all personal use of such technologies at work or of trying to restrict employees' personal blogs, but every company needs to address this issue—and address it again every time a new technology shows up. For instance, inappropriate web surfing not only distracts employees from work responsibilities but can also leave employers open to lawsuits for sexual harassment if inappropriate images are displayed in or transmitted around the company.[28] Blogging has created another set of managerial challenges, given the risk that employee blogs can expose confidential information or damage a firm's reputation in the marketplace. With all these technologies, the best solution lies in developing clear policies that are enforced evenly for all employees.[29]

Reconnecting with People

No matter how much technology is involved, communication is about people connecting with people.

Let's say you IM a colleague asking how she did with her sales presentation to an important client, and her answer comes back simply as "Fine." What does *fine* mean? Is an order expected soon? Or did she lose the sale and doesn't want to talk about it? If you visit with her in person, or at least talk over the phone, she might provide additional information, or you might be able to offer advice or support during a difficult time.

Moreover, even the best technologies cannot truly match the rich experience of person-to-person contact. For example, *telepresence* videoconferencing systems (discussed in Chapter 2) can create a convincing illusion of everyone being in the same room, even if they are thousands of kilometers apart. However, even enthusiastic users know that this technology has limits. Jill Smart, an executive with the consulting firm Accenture, often takes advantage of the company's advanced telepresence facilities but still travels frequently to meet with clients—particularly clients in other countries and cultures. "You get things from being there, over breakfast and dinner, building relationships face to face."[30]

6 LEARNING OBJECTIVE

Discuss the importance of ethics in business communication and differentiate between ethical dilemmas and ethical lapses

MAKING ETHICAL COMMUNICATION CHOICES

Ethics are the accepted principles of conduct that govern behavior within a society. Put another way, ethical principles define the boundary between right and wrong. Former Supreme Court Justice Potter Stewart defined ethics as "knowing the difference between what you have a right to do and what is the right thing to do."[31] To make the right choices as a business communicator, you have a responsibility to think through not only what you say but also the consequences of saying it.

Ethical behavior is a companywide concern, but because communication efforts are the public face of a company, they are subjected to particularly rigorous scrutiny from regulators, legislators, investors, consumer groups, environmental groups, labor organizations, and anyone else affected by business activities. **Ethical communication** includes all relevant information, is true in every sense, and is not deceptive in any way. In contrast, unethical communication can distort the truth or manipulate audiences in a variety of ways:[32]

- **Plagiarism.** Plagiarism is presenting someone else's words or other creative product as your own. Note that plagiarism can be illegal if it violates a **copyright**, which is a form of legal protection for the expression of creative ideas.[33]
- **Omitting essential information.** Information is essential if your audience needs it to make an intelligent, objective decision. For example, homebuyers in an Orlando, Florida, housing development were sold houses without being told that the area was once a U.S. Army firing range and that live bombs and ammunition are still buried in multiple locations around the neighborhood.[34]
- **Selective misquoting.** Distorting or hiding the true intent of someone else's words is unethical.
- **Misrepresenting numbers.** Statistics and other data can be unethically manipulated by increasing or decreasing numbers, exaggerating, altering statistics, or omitting numeric data.
- **Distorting visuals.** Images can be manipulated in unethical ways, such as making a product seem bigger than it really is or changing the scale of graphs and charts to exaggerate or conceal differences.
- **Failing to respect privacy or information security needs.** Ethical concerns involve more than just the content of messages. Failing to respect the privacy of others or failing to adequately protect information entrusted to your care can also be considered unethical (and is sometimes illegal).

Any time you try to mislead an audience, the result is unethical communication.

In some situations, ethical choices are clear, but in others, the right path is not always easy to identify. Deciding what is ethical can be a considerable challenge in complex business situations.

Distinguishing Ethical Dilemmas from Ethical Lapses

Every company has responsibilities to its multiple stakeholders, and those various groups often have competing interests. An **ethical dilemma** involves making a choice when the alternatives aren't completely wrong or completely right. Perhaps two conflicting alternatives are both ethical and valid, or perhaps the alternatives lie somewhere in the gray area between clearly right and clearly wrong. Suppose you are the chief executive of a company whose sales are declining, and you might be forced to reduce costs by laying off 100 employees. You've decided to monitor sales for two more months before making this tough decision. Here's your dilemma: Do you tell the workforce now that 100 jobs could disappear in the near future? Telling them now would give people more time to look for new jobs and adjust their finances—clearly a good thing. However, if you tell them now, essential employees might leave immediately to find new jobs, which could drive down sales even more—and possibly force you to eventually lay off even more than 100 employees. And what if you tell them now, and many people leave but then sales improve enough in the next two months that you can avoid the layoffs? You will have unnecessarily disrupted many careers and families. Situations such as these often have no clear answer.

In contrast, an **ethical lapse** is a clearly unethical choice. If you tell employees their jobs are "absolutely safe" even though you know there is a strong likelihood that some of them

An ethical dilemma is a choice between alternatives that may all be ethical and valid.

An ethical lapse is making a choice that you know to be unethical.

FIGURE 1.9 **Unethical Communication**

The writers of this memo clearly want the company to continue funding their pet project, even though the marketing research doesn't support such a decision. By comparing this memo with the version shown in Figure 1.10, you can see how the writers twisted the truth and omitted evidence in order to put a positive "spin" on the research.

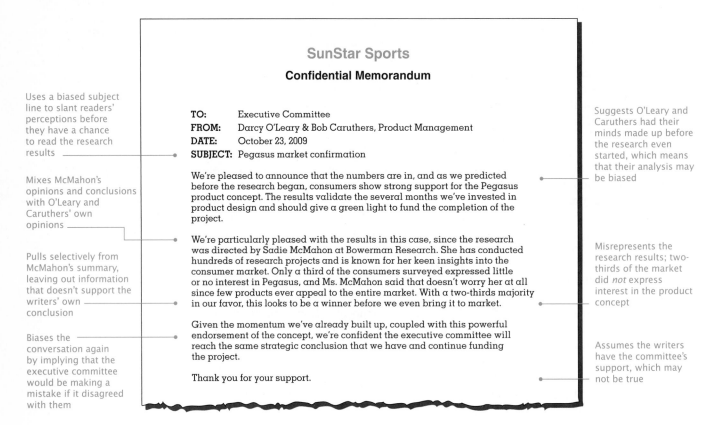

Uses a biased subject line to slant readers' perceptions before they have a chance to read the research results

Mixes McMahon's opinions and conclusions with O'Leary and Caruthers' own opinions

Pulls selectively from McMahon's summary, leaving out information that doesn't support the writers' own conclusion

Biases the conversation again by implying that the executive committee would be making a mistake if it disagreed with them

Suggests O'Leary and Caruthers had their minds made up before the research even started, which means that their analysis may be biased

Misrepresents the research results; two-thirds of the market did *not* express interest in the product concept

Assumes the writers have the committee's support, which may not be true

SunStar Sports

Confidential Memorandum

TO: Executive Committee
FROM: Darcy O'Leary & Bob Caruthers, Product Management
DATE: October 23, 2009
SUBJECT: Pegasus market confirmation

We're pleased to announce that the numbers are in, and as we predicted before the research began, consumers show strong support for the Pegasus product concept. The results validate the several months we've invested in product design and should give a green light to fund the completion of the project.

We're particularly pleased with the results in this case, since the research was directed by Sadie McMahon at Bowerman Research. She has conducted hundreds of research projects and is known for her keen insights into the consumer market. Only a third of the consumers surveyed expressed little or no interest in Pegasus, and Ms. McMahon said that doesn't worry her at all since few products ever appeal to the entire market. With a two-thirds majority in our favor, this looks to be a winner before we even bring it to market.

Given the momentum we've already built up, coupled with this powerful endorsement of the concept, we're confident the executive committee will reach the same strategic conclusion that we have and continue funding the project.

Thank you for your support.

will be laid off, you have committed an ethical lapse. With both internal and external communication efforts, the pressure to produce results or justify decisions can make unethical communication a tempting choice. (Compare the messages in Figure 1.9 and Figure 1.10.)

Ensuring Ethical Communication

Ensuring ethical business communication requires three elements: ethical individuals, ethical company leadership, and the appropriate policies and structures to support employees' efforts to make ethical choices.[35] Moreover, these three elements need to work in harmony. If employees see company executives making unethical decisions and flouting company guidelines, they might conclude that the guidelines are meaningless and emulate their bosses' unethical behavior.

Responsible employers establish clear ethical guidelines for their employees to follow.

Employers have a responsibility to establish clear guidelines for ethical behavior, including ethical business communication. In a global survey by the International Association of Business Communicators, 70 percent of communication professionals said their companies clearly define what is considered ethical and unethical behavior.[36] On a less encouraging note, in a 2007 survey, 56 percent of U.S. employees said they have observed unethical behavior by people in their organizations—and more than 40 percent of those who witnessed unethical behavior did not report it.[37]

Many companies establish an explicit ethics policy by using a written **code of ethics** to help employees determine what is acceptable. For example, Gap Inc. (the owner of the Gap, Banana Republic, and Old Navy retail chains), publishes a detailed Code of Business Conduct for its employees, addressing such areas as conflicts of interest, product integrity, health and safety, protection of company assets and information, and political activities by employees.[38] A code

FIGURE 1.10   Ethical Communication
This version of the memo shown in Figure 1.9 presents the evidence in a more honest and ethical manner.

Tries not to "sell" the conclusion ahead of time, using an even-handed subject line

Offers full disclosure of all the background information

Provides the complete text of the researcher's summary

Separates the researcher's observations and opinions from the writers' own

Invites further discussion of the situation

Emphasizes the skills of the researcher without biasing the readers regarding her conclusions

Explains that more in-depth information will be available soon but emphasizes the importance of reviewing this summary right now

Illustrates clearly that the market expert is concerned about the project

States clearly and honestly that the project will not live up to original hopes

SunStar Sports
Confidential Memorandum

TO: Executive Committee
FROM: Darcy O'Leary & Bob Caruthers, Product Management
DATE: October 23, 2009
SUBJECT: Market research summary for Pegasus project

The market research for the Pegasus Project concluded last week with phone interviews of 236 sporting goods buyers in 18 states. As in the past, we used Bowerman Research to conduct the interviews, under the guidance of Bowerman's survey supervisor, Sadie McMahon. Ms. McMahon has directed surveys on more than 200 consumer products, and we've learned to place a great deal of confidence in her market insights.

A complete report, including all raw data and verbatim quotes, will be available for downloading on the Engineering Department intranet by the end of next week. However, in light of the project-funding discussions going on this week, we believe the conclusions from the research warrant your immediate attention.

Sadie McMahon's research summary

Consumer interest in the new product code-named Pegasus is decidedly mixed, with 34% expressing little or no interest in the product but 37% expressing moderate to strong interest. The remaining 29% expressed confusion about the basic product concept and were therefore unable to specify their level of interest. The segment expressing little or no interest is not a cause for concern in most cases; few products appeal to the entire consumer market.

However, the portion of the market expressing confusion about the fundamental design of the product is definitely cause for concern. We rarely see more than 10 or 15% confusion at this stage of the design process. A 29% confusion figure suggests that the product design does not fit many consumers' expectations and that it might be difficult to sell if SunStar goes ahead with production.

Our recommendations

At $7.6 million, the development costs for Pegasus are too high to proceed with this much uncertainty. The business case we prepared at the beginning of the project indicated that at least 50% consumer acceptance would be needed in order to generate enough sales to produce an acceptable return on the engineering investment. We would need to convince nearly half of the "confused" segment in order to reach that threshold. We recommend that further development be put on hold until the design can be clarified and validated with another round of consumer testing.

Please contact Darcy at ext. 2354 or Bob at ext. 2360 if you have any questions or concerns.

is often part of a larger program of employee training and communication channels that allow employees to ask questions and report instances of questionable ethics. To ensure ongoing compliance with their codes of ethics, many companies also conduct **ethics audits** to monitor ethical progress and to point out any weaknesses that need to be addressed.

However, whether or not formal guidelines are in place, every employee has a responsibility to communicate in an ethical manner. In the absence of clear guidelines, ask yourself the following questions about your business communications:[39]

- Have you defined the situation fairly and accurately?
- What is your intention in communicating this message?
- What impact will this message have on the people who receive it, or who might be affected by it?

Business Communication 2.0

Who's Responsible Here?

When companies engage in *comparative advertising*, making explicit comparisons between their products and those of their competitors, complaints of false statements and defamation are fairly common. In that sense, a lawsuit that Subway recently filed against Quiznos is not in itself unusual. Subway claims that Quiznos made unfair and untrue comparisons about the size and meat content of one of its sandwiches and failed to disclose the fact that the larger Quiznos sandwich cost nearly twice as much as the Subway sandwich.

What makes this case unusual—and gives it potentially far-reaching impact for business communication—is the Web 2.0 angle of *user-generated content* (UGC). As part of its efforts to promote this particular sandwich, Quiznos sponsored a contest in which members of the public were invited to create their own commercials. The contest encouraged people to highlight the "meat, no meat" theme, suggesting that the Quiznos sandwich had copious amounts of beef, while the Subway had far less. More than 100 people submitted videos, which were posted to a Quiznos website and to iFilm, a now-defunct video clip website owned by the media giant Viacom.

Subway's lawsuit claims that some of the videos contain false and disparaging content for which Quiznos and iFilm should be held liable. Subway asserts that Quiznos specifically encouraged contestants to promote one product at the expense of the other, so it should not be immune from responsibility. Quiznos's lawyers responded by claiming that the company did not create these videos and is therefore not liable. "We're just facilitating consumers who go out and create their own expression in the form of a commercial." The company tried to have the UGC part of the lawsuit dismissed by claiming the same immunity that YouTube and other services have regarding the content on their websites, but a judge refused, saying the law that protects YouTube (the Communications Decency Act) doesn't necessarily protect Quiznos in this case.

Contests involving consumer-generated ads and other forms of UGC have become popular in recent years, but if Quiznos is found liable (legal action is ongoing), the trend of inviting UGC could shrink dramatically because other companies won't want to expose themselves to similar lawsuits.

CAREER APPLICATIONS

1. Legal issues aside, in your opinion, is Quiznos ethically responsible for any false or misleading information that may be found in the user-generated videos? Why or why not?
2. Most consumers lack the skills and equipment needed to produce professional-quality video commercials. Why would companies such as Quiznos invite them to create commercials?

If you can't decide whether a choice is ethical, picture yourself explaining it to someone whose opinion you value.

- Will the message achieve the greatest possible good while doing the least possible harm?
- Will the assumptions you've made change over time? That is, will a decision that seems ethical now seem unethical in the future?
- Are you comfortable with your decision? Would you be embarrassed if it were printed in tomorrow's newspaper or spread across the Internet? Think about a person whom you admire and ask yourself what he or she would think of your decision.

Ensuring Legal Communication

Business communication is governed by a wide variety of laws designed to ensure accurate, complete messages.

In addition to ethical guidelines, business communication is also bound by a wide variety of laws and regulations, including the following areas:

- **Promotional communication.** Marketing specialists need to be aware of the many laws that govern truth and accuracy in advertising. These laws address such issues as false and deceptive advertising, misleading or inaccurate labels on product packages, and "bait and switch" tactics in which a store advertises a lower-priced product to lure consumers into a store but then tries to sell them a more expensive item.[40] Chapter 10 explores this area in more detail.
- **Contracts.** A **contract** is a legally binding promise between two parties, in which one party makes a specified offer and the other party accepts. Contracts are fundamental to virtually every aspect of business, from product sales to property rental to credit cards and loans to professional service agreements.[41]
- **Employment communication.** A variety of local, state/provincial, and national laws govern communication between employers and both potential and current employees. For example, in some countries job descriptions must be written in a way that doesn't intentionally or unintentionally discriminate against women, minorities, or people with disabilities.[42]

- **Intellectual property.** In an age when instant global connectivity makes copying and retransmitting electronic files effortless, the protection of intellectual property (IP) has become a widespread concern. **Intellectual property** includes patents, copyrighted materials, trade secrets, and even Internet domain names.[43] Bloggers need to be particularly careful about IP protection, given the carefree way that some post the work of others without offering proper credit. For guidelines on this hot topic, get the free *Legal Guide for Bloggers* at www.eff.org/bloggers/lg.

- **Financial reporting.** Finance and accounting professionals who work for publicly traded companies (those that sell stock to the public) must adhere to stringent reporting laws. For instance, a number of corporations have recently been targets of both government investigations and shareholder lawsuits for offering misleading descriptions of financial results and revenue forecasts.

- **Defamation.** Negative comments about another party raise the possibility of **defamation**, the intentional communication of false statements that damage character or reputation.[44] (Written defamation is called *libel*; spoken defamation is called *slander*.) Someone suing for defamation must prove (1) that the statement is false, (2) that the language is injurious to the person's reputation, and (3) that the statement has been published.

If you have any doubts about the legality of a message you intend to distribute, ask for advice from your company's legal department. A small dose of caution can prevent huge legal headaches and protect your company's reputation in the marketplace.

For the latest information on ethical and legal issues in business communication, visit http://real-timeupdates.com/bct and click on Chapter 1.

Document Makeover

Improve This Memo

To practice correcting drafts of actual documents, visit the "Document Makeovers" section in either mybcommlab or the Companion Website for this text (visit www.pearsonglobaleditions.com/bovee, select *Business Communication Today*, Tenth Edition, and click its Companion Website link).

If mybcommlab is being used in your class, see your User Guide for specific instructions on how to access the content for this chapter. If you are accessing this feature through the Companion Website, click on "Document Makeovers" and then select Chapter 1. You will find a memo that contains problems and errors related to what you've learned in this chapter about improving business communication. Use the Final Draft decision tool to create an improved version of this memo. Check the message for ethical communication and an audience-centered approach.

Communication Challenges at Six Apart

In 2007, Ben and Mena Trott promoted Chris Alden to president and CEO of Six Apart. Alden plays a vital role in keeping communication flowing within the company and between the company and external audiences. To help him with a growing workload of communication tasks, he has recently hired you as an assistant with special responsibilities for communication. Use your knowledge of communication to choose the best response for each of the following situations. Be prepared to explain why your choice is best.

Individual Challenge: One of the reasons for Six Apart's success is its friendly, open style of communication with its customers, even the occasional customers who make unrealistic demands or expect special treatment. Unfortunately, you've learned that some of the customer service representatives have been letting their emotions get in the way when dealing with these difficult people. Several customers have complained about rude treatment. You're sensitive to the situation because you know that customer service can be a difficult job. However, a reputation for hostile customer service could spell doom for the company, so you need to communicate your concerns immediately. Draft the first sentence of an internal blog posting that you will write for the customer service staff to initiate a discussion on this subject.

Team Challenge: Six Apart has developed a corporate culture that reflects both the engaging personalities of Ben and Mena Trott and the informal vibe of the blogosphere. However, as the company continues to grow, new employees bring a variety of communication styles and expectations. In particular, the new accounting manager tends to communicate in a formal, distant style that some company old-timers find off-putting and impersonal. Several of these people have expressed concern that the new manager "doesn't fit in," even though she's doing a great job otherwise. Draft a short e-mail message to Alden, advising him on handling this situation.

SUMMARY OF LEARNING OBJECTIVES

1 **Explain how the Business Communication 2.0 concept is transforming the practice of business communication.** Conventional business communication can be thought of as having a "publishing" mindset, in which a company produces carefully scripted messages and distributes them to an audience that has few options for responding to the company or interacting with one another. In contrast, Business Communication 2.0 uses Web 2.0 social media tools to create an interactive and participative environment in which all parties have a chance to join the conversation. Many of the old rules and expectations, including tight control of the content and distribution of the message, no longer apply in this new environment.

2 **Describe the five characteristics of effective business communication.** To be effective, business messages must be practical, providing the information that receivers need. Effective messages either leave out personal impressions or support such opinions with objective facts. Effective business communication is also concise—it clarifies and condenses information in a way that helps the receiver see and understand the most important issues. Effective messages are also clear about expectations. They state precise responsibilities to eliminate confusion about who needs to do what next. Finally, effective messages are persuasive, when necessary, convincing others to accept the sender's ideas or recommendations.

3 **Describe six strategies for communicating more effectively on the job.** To communicate more effectively on the job, use six strategies. First, work to understand the communication process so that you can craft more effective messages. Second, reduce distractions in the work environment, including not sending unnecessary messages. Third, adopt an audience-centered approach, focusing on the needs of your audience and working to ensure successful transmission and reception of your messages. Fourth, fine-tune your business communication skills. Fifth, give feedback that is constructive rather than destructive so that others can focus on improvement— and be able to respond to constructive feedback about your own work. Sixth, be sensitive to business etiquette, thereby reducing the chance of interpersonal blunders that might negatively affect communication.

4 **Explain what must occur for an audience to successfully receive, decode, and respond to messages.** For audience members to successfully receive messages, they must sense the presence of the message, select it from other sensory input, and then perceive it as a message. To decode messages successfully, they need to extract the same meaning that the sender encoded into the message. And to respond in a manner that the sender would consider successful, audience members need to remember the message, have the ability to respond to it, and have the motivation to respond.

5 **Explain four strategies for successfully using communication technology.** First, be sure to keep technology in perspective. Make sure that it supports the communication effort rather than overwhelming or disrupting it. Second, guard against information overload and information technology addiction. Third, learn how to use technological tools productively. Doing so allows you to focus on communicating rather than on the tool being used. Fourth, by reconnecting in person from time to time, you ensure that communication is successful and that technology doesn't come between you and the people you need to reach.

6 **Discuss the importance of ethics in business communication and differentiate between ethical dilemmas and ethical lapses.** Ethical communication is particularly important in business because communication is the public face of a company, which is why communication efforts are intensely scrutinized by company stakeholders. The difference between an ethical dilemma and an ethical lapse is a question of clarity. An ethical dilemma occurs when the choice is unclear because two or more alternatives seem equally right or equally wrong. In contrast, an ethical lapse occurs when a person makes a conscious choice that is clearly unethical.

PEARSON
mybcommlab™

Log on to www.mybcommlab.com to access the following study and assessment aids associated with this chapter:

- Video applications
- Real-Time Updates
- Peer review activity
- Quick Learning Guides

- Pre/post test
- Personalized study plan
- Model documents
- Sample presentations

If you are not using mybcommlab, you can access the Real-Time Updates and Quick Learning Guides through http://real-timeupdates.com/bct. The Quick Learning Guide (located under "Learn More" on the website) hits all the high points of this chapter in just two pages. This guide, especially prepared by the authors, will help you study for exams or review important concepts whenever you need a quick refresher.

Test Your Knowledge

1. How will your communication skills contribute to your company's success?
2. What three principles will help you minimize missteps in business etiquette?
3. How does formal communication differ from informal communication?
4. In what directions can information travel within an organization's formal hierarchy?
5. How does the social communication model differ from traditional business communication practices?
6. What steps have to occur before an audience member perceives the presence of an incoming message?
7. Why should communicators take an audience-centered approach to communication?
8. How is communication affected by information overload?
9. How can you make sure your feedback is constructive?
10. Why is ethical communication important?

Apply Your Knowledge

1. How are blogs, wikis, and other Web 2.0 technologies changing the practice of business communication?
2. Is it possible for companies to be too dependent on communication technology? Explain briefly.
3. How can a lack of shared experience between sender and receiver result in communication failures?
4. How does the presence of a reader comments feature on a corporate blog reflect audience-centered communication?
5. **Ethical Choices** Because of your excellent communication skills, your boss always asks you to write his reports for him. When you overhear the CEO complimenting him on his logical organization and clear writing style, your boss responds as if he'd written all those reports himself. What kind of ethical choice does your boss's response represent? What can you do in this situation? Briefly explain your solution and your reasoning.

Practice Your Knowledge

Message for Analysis

Read the following blog posting and then (1) analyze whether the message is effective or ineffective communication (be sure to explain why) and (2) revise the message so that it follows this chapter's guidelines.

It has come to my attention that many of you are lying on your time cards. If you come in late, you should not put 8:00 on your card. If you take a long lunch, you should not put 1:00 on your time card. I will not stand for this type of cheating. I simply have no choice but to institute an employee monitoring system. Beginning next Monday, video cameras will be installed at all entrances to the building, and your entry and exit times will be logged each time you use electronic key cards to enter or leave.

Anyone who is late for work or late coming back from lunch more than three times will have to answer to me. I don't care if you had to take a nap or if you girls had to shop. This is a place of business, and we do not want to be taken advantage of by slackers who are cheaters to boot.

It is too bad that a few bad apples always have to spoil things for everyone.

Exercises

Active links for all websites in this chapter can be found online. If mybcommlab is being used in your class, see your User Guide for instructions on accessing the content for this chapter. Otherwise, visit www.pearsonglobaleditions.com/bovee, locate *Business Communication Today*, Tenth Edition, click the Companion Website link, select Chapter 1, and then click on "Featured Websites." Please note that links to sites that become inactive after publication of the book will be removed from the Featured Websites section.

1.1 **Business Communication 2.0: Convincing Your Colleagues to Open the Door** You are the customer service manager for a company that sells a software package used by not-for-profit organizations to plan and manage fundraising campaigns. The powerful software is complicated enough to require a fairly extensive user's manual, and the company has always provided a printed manual to customers. Customers frequently e-mail your department with questions about using the software and suggestions for using the software to maximize fundraising efforts. You know that many customers could benefit from the answers to those questions and the suggestions from fellow customers, but with a printed manual issued once every couple years, you don't have any way to collect and distribute this information in a timely fashion.

You've been researching wikis and believe this would be a great way to let customers participate in an ongoing conversation about using the software. In fact, you'd like to convert the printed manual to a wiki on which any registered customer could add or edit pages. Rather than spend thousands of dollars printing a manual that is difficult to expand or update, the wiki would be a "living" document that continually evolves as people ask and answer questions and offer suggestions. The rest of the management team is extremely nervous, however. "We're the experts—not the customer," one says. Another asks, "How can we ensure the quality of the information if any customer can change it?" They don't deny that customers have valuable information to add; they just don't want customers to have control of an important company document. Making up any information you need, write a brief e-mail to your colleagues, explaining the benefits of letting customers contribute to a wiki-based user manual. (You can refer to pages 71–72 to learn more about wikis.)

1.2 **Effective Business Communication: Understanding the Difference** Bring to class a sales message that you received in the mail or via e-mail. Comment on how well the communication
  a. provides practical information
  b. gives facts rather than impressions
  c. clarifies and condenses information
  d. states precise responsibilities
  e. persuades others and offers recommendations

1.3 **Internal Communication: Planning the Flow** For the following tasks, identify the necessary direction of communication (downward, upward, horizontal), suggest an appropriate type (or types) of communication (casual conversation, formal interview, meeting, workshop, web conference, instant message, memo, blog, bulletin board notice, and so on), and briefly explain your suggestions.
  a. As human resources manager, you want to announce details about this year's company picnic.
  b. As director of internal communication, you want to convince top management of the need for an internal executive blog.

  c. As production manager, you want to make sure that both the sales manager and the finance manager receive your scheduling estimates.
  d. As marketing manager, you want to help employees throughout the company understand the marketplace and customer needs.

1.4 **Ethical Choices** In less than a page, explain why you think each of the following is or is not ethical.
  a. Keeping quiet about a possible environmental hazard you've just discovered in your company's processing plant
  b. Overselling the benefits of instant messaging to your company's managers; they never seem to understand the benefits of technology, so you believe it's the only way to convince them to make the right choice
  c. Telling an associate and close friend that she needs to pay more attention to her work responsibilities, or management will fire her
  d. Recommending the purchase of excess equipment to use up your allocated funds before the end of the fiscal year so that your budget won't be cut next year

1.5 **The Changing Workplace: Personal Expression at Work** Blogging has become a popular way for employees to communicate with customers and other parties outside the company. In some cases, employee blogs have been quite beneficial for both companies and their customers by providing helpful information and "putting a human face" on other formal and imposing corporations. However, in some other cases, employees have been fired for posting information that their employers said was inappropriate. One particular area of concern is criticism of the company or individual managers. Should employees be allowed to criticize their employers in a public forum such as a blog? In a brief e-mail message, argue for or against company policies that prohibit critical information in employee blogs.

1.6 **Internet** Cisco, a leading manufacturer of equipment for the Internet and corporate networks, has developed a code of ethics that it expects employees to abide by. Visit the company's website, at www.cisco.com, and find the code of conduct. In a brief paragraph, describe three specific examples of things you could do that would violate these provisions; then list at least three opportunities that Cisco provides its employees to report ethics violations or ask questions regarding ethical dilemmas.

1.7 **Communication Etiquette** Potential customers frequently visit your production facility before making purchase decisions. You and the people who report to you in the sales department have received extensive training in etiquette issues because you deal with high-profile clients so often. However, the rest of the workforce has not received such training, and you worry that someone might inadvertently say or do something that would offend one of these potential customers. In a two-paragraph e-mail, explain to the general manager why you think anyone who might come in contact with customers should receive basic etiquette training.

1.8 Ethical Choices Knowing that you have numerous friends throughout the company, your boss relies on you for feedback concerning employee morale and other issues affecting the staff. She recently asked you to start reporting any behavior that might violate company policies, from taking home office supplies to making personal long-distance calls. List the issues you'd like to discuss with her before you respond to her request.

1.9 Formal Communication: Self-Introduction Write an e-mail message or prepare an oral presentation introducing yourself to your instructor and your class. Include such things as your background, interests, achievements, and goals. If you write an e-mail message, keep it under one normal screen in length, and use Figure 1.4 as a model for the format. If you prepare an oral presentation, plan to speak for no more than two minutes.

1.10 Teamwork Your boss has asked your work group to research and report on corporate child-care facilities. Of course, you'll want to know who (besides your boss) will be reading your report. Working with two team members, list four or five other things you'll want to know about the situation and about your audience before starting your research. Briefly explain why each of the items on your list is important.

1.11 Communication Process: Analyzing Miscommunication Use the eight phases of the communication process to analyze a miscommunication you've recently had with a co-worker, supervisor, classmate, teacher, friend, or family member. What idea were you trying to share? How did you encode and transmit it? Did the receiver get the message? Did the receiver correctly decode the message? How do you know? Based on your analysis, identify and explain the barriers that prevented your successful communication in this instance.

1.12 Ethical Choices You've been given the critical assignment of selecting the site for your company's new plant. After months of negotiations with landowners, numerous cost calculations, and investments in ecological, social, and community impact studies, you are about to recommend building the new plant on the Lansing River site. Now, just 15 minutes before your big presentation to top management, you discover a possible mistake in your calculations: Site-purchase costs appear to be $500,000 more than you calculated, nearly 10 percent over budget. You don't have time to recheck all your figures, so you're tempted to just go ahead with your recommendation and ignore any discrepancies. You're worried that management won't approve this purchase if you can't present a clean,

unqualified solution. You also know that many projects run over their original estimates, so you can probably work the extra cost into the budget later. On your way to the meeting room, you make your final decision. In a few paragraphs, explain the decision you make.

1.13 Communication Etiquette In group meetings, some of your colleagues have a habit of interrupting and arguing with the speaker, taking credit for ideas that aren't theirs, and shooting down ideas they don't agree with. You're the newest person in the group and not sure if this is accepted behavior in this company, but it concerns you both personally and professionally. Should you go with the flow and adopt their behavior or stick with your own communication style, even though you might get lost in the noise? In two paragraphs, explain the pros and cons of both approaches.

Expand Your Knowledge

Exploring the Best of the Web

Check Out These Resources at the Business Writer's Free Library

www.managementhelp.org/commskls/cmm_writ.htm
The Business Writer's Free Library is an excellence resource for business communication material. Categories of information include basic composition skills, basic writing skills, correspondence, reference material, and general resources and advice. Log on and read about the most common errors in English, become a word detective, ask Miss Grammar, review samples of common forms of correspondence, fine-tune your interpersonal skills, join a newsgroup, and more. Follow the links and improve your effectiveness as a business communicator.

1. What are some common causes of problems in internal communication?
2. What is the value of diversity in the workplace?
3. Why is bad etiquette bad for business?

Sharpening Your Career Skills Online

Bovée and Thill's Business Communication Web Search, at http://businesscommunicationblog.com/websearch, is a unique research tool designed specifically for business communication research. Use the Web Search function to find an online video, a podcast, or a PowerPoint presentation that explains at least one essential business communication skill. Write a brief e-mail message to your instructor, describing the item that you found and summarizing the career skills information you learned from it.

Mastering Team and Interpersonal Communication

Learning Objectives
After studying this chapter, you will be able to

1 Highlight the advantages and disadvantages of working in teams

2 Identify eight guidelines for successful collaborative writing

3 Explain how meeting technologies can help participants communicate more successfully and describe the emerging role of social networking technologies in business communication

4 Describe the listening process and explain how good listeners overcome barriers at each stage of the process

5 Clarify the importance of nonverbal communication and briefly describe six categories of nonverbal expression

6 Discuss the importance of business etiquette

Communication Close-up at Rosen Law Firm

Lee Rosen's law firm uses a wiki to manage thousands of documents while boosting teamwork and collaboration.

www.rosen.com

When communication tools function at their best, they can go beyond mere facilitation to transformation. Such was the case at Rosen Law Firm, based in Raleigh, North Carolina. Lee Rosen, the firm's owner and chief executive, wanted to replace an expensive, complicated, and inflexible computer system that employees relied on for everything from contact lists to appointment calendars to document storage. The solution he chose for his small law firm was a wiki, the same technology that enables nearly 100,000 people around the world to contribute to Wikipedia.

The wiki certainly helped cut costs, and it also did much more. In addition to handling much of the firm's document storage and formal communication, the wiki introduced an informal social element that is helping employees bond as a community. Many employees have added personal pages with information about themselves, helping employees get to know their colleagues on a more intimate level.

In implementing the wiki, Rosen faced a common challenge with new communication tools: getting people to give up familiar ways of doing things and embrace change. Knowing that the value of a company wiki depends on the level of employee contribution—and that having some of the staff switch while others cling to old ways would seriously disrupt communication—he encouraged use of the new wiki with a friendly competition. For each page an employee created during the three-month competition, he or she was given one possible combination to the company safe, which contained a $1,000 cash prize. From time to time, Rosen also forced use of the wiki by publishing important information only on the wiki.

As often happens when companies face significant changes, the move to the wiki did cause some turmoil. Two camps of employees argued over the best way to organize information and got caught up in an "edit war" on the wiki, repeatedly undoing each other's decisions. They eventually reached a compromise that resolved the disagreement and had lasting benefits for teamwork and interpersonal communication across the firm. According to Rosen, "It forced everybody to learn about each other's job."[1]

COMMUNICATING EFFECTIVELY IN TEAMS

The teamwork interactions among the employees at Rosen Law Firm (profiled in the chapter-opening Communication Close-up) represent one of the essential elements of interpersonal communication. A **team** is a unit of two or more people who share a mission and the responsibility for working to achieve a common goal.[2] **Problem-solving teams** and **task forces** assemble to resolve specific issues and then disband when their goals have been accomplished. Such teams are often *cross-functional*, pulling together people from a variety of departments who have different areas of expertise and responsibility. The diversity of opinions and experiences can lead to better decisions, but competing interests can lead to tensions that highlight the need for effective communication.

Team members have a shared mission and are collectively responsible for their work.

Committees are formal teams that usually have a long life span and can become a permanent part of the organizational structure. Committees typically deal with regularly recurring tasks, such as an executive committee that meets monthly to plan strategies and review results.

Whatever the purpose and function of a team, you and your fellow team members must be able to communicate effectively with each other and with people outside your team. As Chapter 1 points out, this ability often requires taking on additional responsibility for communication: sharing information with team members, listening carefully to their inputs, and crafting messages that reflect the team's collective ideas and opinions.

Effective communication is essential to every aspect of team performance.

Advantages and Disadvantages of Teams

When teams are successful, they can improve productivity, creativity, employee involvement, and even job security.[3] Teams are often at the core of **participative management**, the effort to involve employees in the company's decision making. Teams can play a vital role in helping an organization reach its goals, but they are not appropriate for every situation—and even when they are appropriate, companies need to weigh both the advantages and disadvantages of a team-based approach. A successful team can provide a number of advantages:[4]

1 LEARNING OBJECTIVE

Highlight the advantages and disadvantages of working in teams

- **Increased information and knowledge.** By pooling the experience of several individuals, a team has access to more information in the decision-making process.
- **Increased diversity of views.** Team members can bring a variety of perspectives to the decision-making process. Keep in mind, however, that unless these diverse viewpoints are guided by a shared goal, the multiple perspectives can hamper a team's efforts.[5]
- **Increased acceptance of a solution.** Those who participate in making a decision are more likely to support it and encourage others to accept it.
- **Higher performance levels.** Working in teams can unleash new levels of creativity and energy in workers who share a sense of purpose and mutual accountability. Effective teams can be better than top-performing individuals at solving complex problems.[6] Furthermore, teams fill an individual worker's need to belong to a group, reduce employee boredom, increase feelings of dignity and self-worth, and reduce stress and tension between workers.

Effective teams can pool knowledge, take advantage of diverse viewpoints, and increase acceptance of solutions the team proposes.

Teams need to avoid the negative impact of groupthink, hidden agendas, and excessive costs.

Although teamwork has many advantages, it also has a number of potential disadvantages. At the worst, working in teams can be a frustrating waste of time. Teams need to be aware of and work to counter the following potential disadvantages:

- **Groupthink.** Like other social structures, business teams can generate tremendous pressures to conform with accepted norms of behavior. **Groupthink** occurs when peer pressures cause individual team members to withhold contrary or unpopular opinions. The result can be decisions that are worse than the choices the team members might have made individually.
- **Hidden agendas.** Some team members may have a **hidden agenda**—private, counterproductive motives, such as a desire to take control of the group, to undermine someone else on the team, or to pursue a business goal that runs counter to the team's mission.
- **Cost.** Aligning schedules, arranging meetings, and coordinating individual parts of a project can eat up a lot of time and money.

Characteristics of Effective Teams

To be effective collaborators in a team setting, you and your colleagues must recognize that each individual brings valuable assets, knowledge, and skills to the team. Strong collaborators are willing to exchange information, examine issues, and work through conflicts that arise. They trust each other and work toward the greater good of the team and organization rather than focus on personal agendas.[7]

Effective teams have a clear sense of purpose, open and honest communication, consensus-based decision making, creativity, and effective conflict resolution.

The most effective teams have a clear objective and a shared sense of purpose, communicate openly and honestly, reach decisions by consensus, think creatively, and know how to resolve conflict.[8] Learning these team skills takes time and practice, so U.S. companies now teach teamwork more frequently than any other aspect of business.[9]

In contrast, unsuccessful teamwork can waste time and money, generate lower-quality work, and frustrate both managers and employees. A lack of trust is cited as the most common reason for the failure of teams. A lack of trust can result from team members being suspicious of one another's motives or ability to contribute.[10] Another common reason for failure is poor communication, particularly when teams operate across cultures, countries, and time zones.[11] Poor communication can also result from basic differences in conversational styles. Some people expect conversation to follow an orderly pattern in which team members wait their turn to speak. Others view conversation as more spontaneous and are comfortable with an overlapping, interactive style.[12]

Collaborative Communication

When a team collaborates on reports, websites, presentations, and other communication projects, the collective energy and expertise of the various members can lead to results that transcend what each individual could do otherwise.[13] However, collaborating on team messages requires special effort; the following section offers a number of helpful guidelines.

2 LEARNING OBJECTIVE

Identify eight guidelines for successful collaborative writing

Guidelines for Collaborative Writing

In any collaborative effort, it's important to recognize that team members coming from different backgrounds may have different work habits or priorities: A technical expert may focus on accuracy and scientific standards; an editor may be more concerned about organization and coherence; and a manager may focus on schedules, cost, and corporate goals. In addition, team members differ in writing styles and personality traits—two factors that can complicate the creative nature of communication.

To collaborate effectively, everyone involved must be flexible and open to other opinions, focusing on team objectives rather than on individual priorities.[14] Successful writers know that most ideas can be expressed in many ways, so they avoid the "my way is best" attitude. The following guidelines will help you collaborate more successfully:[15]

Successful collaboration requires a number of steps, from selecting the right partners and agreeing on project goals to establishing clear processes and avoiding writing as a group.

- **Select collaborators carefully.** Choose a combination of people who have the experience, information, and talent needed for each project.
- **Agree on project goals before you start.** Starting without a clear idea of what the team hopes to accomplish inevitably leads to frustration and wasted time.

- **Give your team time to bond before diving in.** If people haven't had the opportunity to work together before, make sure they can get to know each other before being asked to collaborate.
- **Clarify individual responsibilities.** Because members will be depending on each other, make sure individual responsibilities are clear, including who is supposed to do what and by when.
- **Establish clear processes.** Make sure everyone knows how the work will be done, including checkpoints and decisions to be made along the way.
- **Avoid writing as a group.** The actual composition is the only part of developing team messages that does not usually benefit from group participation. Group writing is often a slow, painful process that delivers bland results. In most cases, the best approach is to plan, research, and outline together but assign the task of writing to one person or divide larger projects among multiple writers. If you divide the writing, try to have one person do a final revision pass to ensure a consistent style. (See Chapter 14 for specific advice regarding wiki writing.)
- **Make sure tools and techniques are ready and compatible across the team.** Even minor details such as different versions of software can delay projects. If you plan to use technology for sharing or presenting materials, test the system before work begins. (See the following section for more on collaboration technologies.)
- **Check to see how things are going along the way.** Don't assume that everything is working just because you don't hear anything negative.

Technologies for Collaborative Writing

A variety of collaboration tools exist to help teams write together, including group review and editing features in both word processors and the Adobe Acrobat electronic document system, multiauthor blogs, and **content management systems** that organize and control the content for websites. Each of these tools addresses specific needs, but none offers quite the level of direct collaboration as a wiki. A **wiki**, from the Hawaiian word for *quick*, is a website that allows anyone with access to add new material and edit existing material (see Figure 2.1). Public wikis allow any registered user to edit pages; private wikis such as the one in use at Rosen Law Firm (featured at the beginning of the chapter) are accessible only with permission. Private wikis can be quite large when needed. For instance, Yahoo! uses private wikis to facilitate communication among hundreds of team members around the world involved in creating and documenting new services.[16] Chapter 14 offers guidelines for effective wiki collaboration.

Collaboration tools include multiauthor blogs, content management systems, and wikis.

Key benefits of wikis include simple operation—writers don't need to know any of the techniques normally required to create web content—and the freedom to post new or revised material without prior approval. This approach is quite different from a content management system, in which both the organization of the website and the *workflow* (the rules for creating, editing, reviewing, and approving content) are tightly controlled.[17] With a wiki, if you see a way to improve a particular page or want to add a new page, you simply edit or write, using your web browser, and it's done. A content management system is a great tool for maintaining consistent presentation on a company's primary public website, whereas a wiki allows a team to collaborate with speed and flexibility.

Benefits of wikis include simple operation and the ability to post new or revised material instantly, without a formal review process.

Enterprise wiki systems extend the wiki concept with additional features for business use that ensure information quality and confidentiality and also provide the speed and flexibility of a wiki. For instance, *access control* lets a team leader identify who is allowed to read and modify a wiki. *Change monitoring* alerts team members when significant changes or additions are made. And *rollback* allows a team to "travel back in time" to see all previous versions of pages.[18]

In addition to webpages, many teams work on a wide variety of other file types, including word processing files, spreadsheets, and presentations. To facilitate collaboration on a broad scale, using a variety of resources, many teams now take advantage of **groupware**, computer-based systems that let people communicate, share files, present materials, and work on documents simultaneously. **Shared workspaces** are online "virtual offices" that give everyone on a team access to the same set of resources and information: databases,

FIGURE 2.1   Using a Wiki for Collaborative Communication

This page from the Public Relations Wiki (http://pr.wikia.com) shows the features typically used to create and edit wiki pages.

Shows the title of the page being edited ("Crisis management")

Offers a variety of tips on adding text styles, inserting images, and performing other tasks

Provides a variety of quick formatting tools

Displays the text being edited

Provides a variety of links and instructions for completing pages

Lists common markup codes for page formatting; these can be inserted into the page text just by clicking the mouse

calendars, project plans, pertinent instant messaging and e-mail exchanges, shared reference materials, and team-created documents (see Figure 2.2). To maintain security, shared work-spaces and other team resources are hosted on *intranets* (restricted-access websites that are open to employees only) or *extranets* (restricted sites that are available to employees and to outside parties by invitation only).

Most groupware systems have built-in intelligence to control which team members can read, edit, and save specific files. *Revision control* goes one step further: It allows only one person at a time to check out a given file or document and records all the changes that person makes. This feature prevents two people from independently editing the same report at the same time and thereby creating two different versions of the same document.[19]

Group Dynamics

Group dynamics are the interactions and processes that take place in a team.

The interactions and processes that take place among the members of a team are called **group dynamics**. Productive teams tend to develop rules of interaction that are conducive to business. Often unstated, these rules become group **norms**—informal standards of conduct that members share and that guide member behavior. For example, some teams develop a casual approach to schedules, with members routinely showing up 10 or 15 minutes late for meetings, while other teams expect strict adherence to time commitments. Group dynamics are influenced by several factors: the roles that team members assume, the current phase of team development, the team's success in resolving conflict, and the team's success in overcoming resistance.

FIGURE 2.2 Shared Workspaces

Shared workspaces, such as this example from Microsoft's Office Live Workspace system, give virtual teams instant access to the documents, calendars, and other files and information needed for successful collaboration. Carefully designed intranet tools such as this can boost team productivity and help prevent communication breakdowns.

Assuming Team Roles

Members of a team can play various roles, which fall into three categories (see Table 2.1). Members who assume **self-oriented roles** are motivated mainly to fulfill personal needs, so they tend to be less productive than other members. "Dream teams" composed of multiple superstars often don't perform as well as one might expect because high-performing individuals can have trouble putting the team's needs ahead of their own.[20] In addition, highly skilled and experienced people with difficult personalities might not contribute for the simple reason that other team members may avoid interacting with them.[21] Far more likely to contribute to team goals are members who assume **team-maintenance roles** to help everyone work well together and those who assume **task-oriented roles** to help the team reach its goals.[22]

Each member of a group plays a role that affects the outcome of the group's activities.

Roles can change over time. For instance, in a self-directed team with no formal leader, someone may assume a task-oriented leadership role early in the team's evolution. If this person doesn't prove to be a capable leader, someone else may emerge as a leader as the group searches for more effective direction.[23]

Allowing for Team Evolution

Teams typically evolve through a number of phases on their way to becoming productive (see Figure 2.3). A variety of models have been proposed to describe the evolution toward becoming a productive team. Here is how one commonly used model identifies the phases a problem-solving team goes through as it evolves:[24]

Teams typically evolve through a variety of phases, such as orientation, conflict, brainstorming, emergence, and reinforcement.

1. **Orientation.** Team members socialize, establish their roles, and begin to define their task or purpose. Many companies use a variety of team-building exercises and activities

TABLE 2.1 Team Roles—Functional and Dysfunctional

DYSFUNCTIONAL: SELF-ORIENTED ROLES	FUNCTIONAL: TEAM-MAINTENANCE ROLES	FUNCTIONAL: TASK-FACILITATING ROLES
Controlling: Dominating others by exhibiting superiority or authority	**Encouraging:** Drawing out other members by showing verbal and nonverbal support, praise, or agreement	**Initiating:** Getting the team started on a line of inquiry
Withdrawing: Retiring from the team either by becoming silent or by refusing to deal with a particular aspect of the team's work	**Harmonizing:** Reconciling differences among team members through mediation or by using humor to relieve tension	**Information giving or seeking:** Offering (or seeking) information relevant to questions facing the team
Attention seeking: Calling attention to oneself and demanding recognition from others	**Compromising:** Offering to yield on a point in the interest of reaching a mutually acceptable decision	**Coordinating:** Showing relationships among ideas, clarifying issues, summarizing what the team has done
Diverting: Focusing the team's discussion on topics of interest to the individual rather than on those relevant to the task		**Procedure setting:** Suggesting decision-making procedures that will move the team toward a goal

to help teams break down barriers and develop a sense of shared purpose.[25] Note that team building can be a particular challenge with geographically dispersed virtual teams (see page 79) because the members may never meet in person. Sharing a "team operating agreement" that sets expectations for online meetings, communication processes, and decision making can help teams overcome the disadvantages of distance.[26]

2. **Conflict.** Team members begin to discuss their positions and become more assertive in establishing their roles. Disagreements and uncertainties are natural in this phase.

3. **Brainstorming.** Team members air all the options and fully discuss the pros and cons. At the end of this phase, members begin to settle on a single solution to the problem. Note that while group brainstorming remains a highly popular activity in today's companies, it may not always be the most productive way to generate new ideas. Some research indicates that having people brainstorm individually and then bring their ideas to a group meeting is more successful.[27]

4. **Emergence.** Consensus is reached when the team finds a solution that all members are willing to support (even if they have reservations).

5. **Reinforcement.** The team clarifies and summarizes the agreed-upon solution. Members receive their assignments for carrying out the group's decision, and they make arrangements for following up on those assignments.

You may also hear the process defined as *forming, storming, norming, performing,* and *adjourning,* the phases identified by researcher Bruce Tuckman when he proposed one of the earliest models of group development.[28] Regardless of the model you consider, these stages

FIGURE 2.3 Phases of Group Development
Groups generally progress through several stages on their way to becoming productive and reaching their objectives.

1. Orientation	2. Conflict	3. Brainstorming	4. Emergence	5. Reinforcement
Team members get to know each other and establish roles.	Different opinions and perspectives begin to emerge.	Team members explore their options and evaluate alternatives.	The team reaches a consensus on the chosen decision.	Team harmony is reestablished, and plans are made to put the decision into action.

are a general framework for team development. Some teams may move forward and backward through several stages before they become productive, and other teams may be productive right away, even while some or all members are in a state of conflict.[29]

Resolving Conflict

Conflict in team activities can arise for a number of reasons: competition for resources; disagreement over goals or responsibilities; poor communication; power struggles; or fundamental differences in values, attitudes, and personalities.[30] Although the term *conflict* sounds negative, conflict isn't necessarily bad. Conflict can be *constructive* if it forces important issues into the open, increases the involvement of team members, and generates creative ideas for solving a problem. Teamwork isn't necessarily about happiness and harmony; even teams that have some interpersonal friction can excel with effective leadership and team players committed to strong results. As teamwork experts Andy Boynton and Bill Fischer put it, "Virtuoso teams are not about getting polite results."[31]

Conflict in teams can be either constructive or destructive.

In contrast, conflict is *destructive* if it diverts energy from more important issues, destroys the morale of teams or individual team members, or polarizes or divides the team.[32] Destructive conflict can lead to *win–lose* or *lose–lose* outcomes, in which one or both sides lose, to the detriment of the entire team. If you approach conflict with the idea that both sides can satisfy their goals to at least some extent (a *win–win strategy*), you can minimize losses for everyone. For a win–win strategy to work, everybody must believe that (1) it's possible to find a solution that both parties can accept, (2) cooperation is better for the organization than competition, (3) the other party can be trusted, and (4) greater power or status doesn't entitle one party to impose a solution.

The following seven measures can help team members successfully resolve conflict:

- **Proaction.** Deal with minor conflict before it becomes major conflict.
- **Communication.** Get those directly involved in a conflict to participate in resolving it.
- **Openness.** Get feelings out in the open before dealing with the main issues.
- **Research.** Seek factual reasons for a problem before seeking solutions.
- **Flexibility.** Don't let anyone lock into a position before considering other solutions.
- **Fair play.** Insist on fair outcomes and don't let anyone avoid a fair solution by hiding behind the rules.
- **Alliance.** Get opponents to fight together against an "outside force" instead of against each other.

Overcoming Resistance

One particular type of conflict that can affect team progress is resistance to change. Sometimes this resistance is clearly irrational, such as when people resist any kind of change, whether it makes sense or not. Sometimes, however, resistance is perfectly logical. A change may require someone to relinquish authority or give up comfortable ways of doing things. If someone is resisting change, you can be persuasive with calm, reasonable communication:

When you encounter resistance or hostility, try to maintain your composure and address the other person's emotional needs.

- **Express understanding.** You might say, "I understand that this change might be difficult, and if I were in your position, I might be reluctant myself." Help the other person relax and talk about his or her anxiety so that you have a chance to offer reassurance.[33]
- **Bring resistance out into the open.** When people are noncommittal and silent, they may be tuning you out without even knowing why. Continuing with your argument is futile. Deal directly with the resistance, without accusing. You might say, "You seem cool to this idea. Have I made some faulty assumptions?" Such questions force people to face and define their resistance.[34]
- **Evaluate others' objections fairly.** Use active listening to focus on what the other person is expressing, both the words and the feelings. Get the person to open up so that you can

REAL-TIME UPDATES
Learn More

Use negotiation skills to resolve conflicts

Learn how to resolve conflicts through the win–win strategies of empathetic negotiation. Go to **http://real-timeupdates.com/bct** and click on "Learn More." If you are using mybcommlab, you can access Real-Time Updates within each chapter or under Student Study Tools.

understand the basis for the resistance. Others' objections may raise legitimate points that you'll need to discuss, or they may reveal problems that you'll need to minimize.[35]

Sometimes you need to address the other party's emotional needs before attempting to resolve underlying conflict.

- **Hold your arguments until the other person is ready for them.** Getting your point across depends as much on the other person's frame of mind as it does on your arguments. You can't assume that a strong argument will speak for itself. By becoming more audience centered, you will learn to address the other person's emotional needs first.

Social Networks and Virtual Communities

Chapter 1 explains how social media and the Web 2.0 approach are redefining business communication. Within that context, **social networking technologies** are redefining teamwork and team communication by helping erase the constraints of geographic and organization boundaries. In addition to enabling and enhancing teamwork, social networks have numerous other business applications and benefits (see Table 2.2).

Social networking technologies are becoming vital communication linkages in many companies.

The two fundamental elements of social networking technology are *profiles* (the information stored about each member of the network) and *connections* (mechanisms for finding and communicating with other members.)[36] If you're familiar with MySpace or Facebook, you have a basic idea of how social networks function. Business-oriented networks such as LinkedIn (www.linkedin.com), Ryze (www.ryze.com), and Xing (www.xing.com) function in much the same way, and they also have the potential to become vital elements of an organization's structure and communication channels. For example, some companies use social networking technologies to form *virtual communities* or *communities of practice* that link employees with similar professional interests throughout the company and sometimes with

TABLE 2.2   Business Uses of Social Networking Technology

BUSINESS CHALLENGE	EXAMPLE OF SOCIAL NETWORKING IN ACTION
Supporting customers	Allowing customers to develop close relationships with product experts within the company
Integrating new employees	Helping new employees navigate their way through the organization, finding experts, mentors, and other important contacts
Easing the transition after reorganizations and mergers	Helping employees connect and bond after internal staff reorganizations or mergers with other organizations
Overcoming structural barriers in communication channels	Bypassing the formal communication system in order to deliver information where it is needed in a timely fashion
Assembling teams	Identifying the best people, both inside the company and in other companies, to collaborate on projects
Fostering the growth of communities	Helping people with similar—or complementary—interests and skills find each other in order to provide mutual assistance and development
Solving problems	Finding "pockets of knowledge" within the organization—the expertise and experience of individual employees
Preparing for major meetings and events	Giving participants a way to meet before an event takes place, helping to ensure that the meeting or event becomes more productive more quickly
Accelerating the evolution of teams	Accelerating the sometimes slow process of getting to know one another and identifying individual areas of expertise
Maintaining business relationships	Giving people an easy way to stay in contact after meetings and conferences
Sharing and distributing information	Making it easy for employees to share information with people who may need it—and for people who need information to find employees who might have it
Finding potential customers, business partners, and employees	Identifying strong candidates by matching user profiles with current business needs and linking existing member profiles

customers and suppliers as well. Given its ability to connect people across organizational boundaries, networking technology is an essential element of the network organizational structure discussed on page 44 in Chapter 1.

The heavy-equipment manufacturer Caterpillar has more than 2,700 virtual teams or communities that discuss problems and share insights into improving quality and productivity. In some companies, these teams or communities are informal and "organic," springing up and growing as employees connect with one another. In other companies, including Caterpillar, they are planned and managed in a more formal fashion.[37] The huge advantage that social networking brings to these team efforts is in identifying the best people to collaborate on each problem or project, no matter where they are located around the world or what their official roles are in the organization.

REAL-TIME UPDATES
Learn More

Social media for professionals

See several intriguing new examples of social networks designed exclusively for members of certain professions or industries. Go to **http://real-timeupdates.com/bct** and click on "Learn More." If you are using mybcommlab, you can access Real-Time Updates within each chapter or under Student Study Tools.

MAKING YOUR MEETINGS MORE PRODUCTIVE

Well-run meetings can help you solve problems, develop ideas, and identify opportunities. Much of your workplace communication is likely to occur in small-group meetings; therefore, your ability to contribute to the company and to be recognized for those contributions will depend on your meeting skills.

Much of the communication you participate in will take place in meetings.

Unfortunately, many meetings are unproductive. In one study, senior and middle managers reported that only 56 percent of their meetings were actually productive and that 25 percent of them could have been replaced by a phone call or a memo.[38] The three most frequently reported problems with meetings are getting off the subject, not having an agenda, and running too long.[39] You can help ensure productive meetings by preparing carefully, conducting meetings efficiently, and using meeting technologies wisely.

A single poorly run meeting can waste thousands of dollars.

Preparing for Meetings

Careful preparation helps you avoid the two biggest meeting mistakes: (1) holding a meeting when a blog posting or some other message would do the job and (2) holding a meeting without a specific goal in mind. Before you even begin preparing for a meeting, make sure holding a meeting is truly necessary. Once you're sure, proceed with four preparation tasks:

- **Identify your purpose.** *Informational meetings* involve sharing information and answering audience questions. *Decision-making meetings* involve persuasion, analysis, problem solving, and planning. Whatever your purpose, identify what the best possible result of the meeting would be (such as "we carefully evaluated all three product ideas and decided which one to invest in"). Use this hoped-for result to shape the direction and content of the meeting.[40]
- **Select participants for the meeting.** Be sure to invite everyone who needs to participate—but don't invite anyone who doesn't need to be there. The more people you have, the longer it will take to reach consensus. Meetings with more than 10 or 12 people can become unmanageable if everyone is expected to participate in the discussion and decision making.
- **Choose the time and prepare the facility.** Morning meetings can be more productive than afternoon sessions because people are fresher and not yet involved in the various problems and concerns of their working days. After selecting the time, plan the facility and layout carefully. For instance, if you want to encourage interaction, arranging chairs in a circle or U shape is more effective than seating in rows. Plus, give some attention to details such as room temperature, lighting, ventilation, acoustics, and refreshments; any of these details can make or break a meeting. If the meeting will take place online, you need to consider a variety of other factors (see page 79).
- **Set the agenda.** The success of a meeting depends on the preparation of the participants. Distribute a carefully written agenda to participants, giving them enough time to

To ensure a successful meeting, decide on your purpose ahead of time, select the right participants, choose the time and facility carefully, and set a clear agenda.

FIGURE 2.4   Typical Meeting Agenda

Agenda formats vary widely, depending on the complexity of the meeting and the presentation technologies that will be used. For an online meeting, for instance, a good approach is to first send a detailed planning agenda in advance of the meeting so that presenters know what they need to prepare. You can then create a simpler display agenda similar to this one to guide the progress of the meeting.

prepare as needed (see Figure 2.4). A productive agenda answers three key questions: (1) What do we need to do in this meeting to accomplish our goals? (2) What issues will be of greatest importance to all participants? (3) What information must be available in order to discuss these issues?[41]

Conducting and Contributing to Efficient Meetings

Everyone shares the responsibility for successful meetings.

Everyone in a meeting shares the responsibility for making the meeting productive. If you're the designated leader of a meeting, however, you have an extra degree of responsibility and accountability. To ensure productive meetings, be sure to do the following:

- **Keep the discussion on track.** A good meeting leader draws out the best ideas the group has to offer and resolves differences of opinion while maintaining progress toward achieving the meeting's purpose and staying on schedule.
- **Follow agreed-upon rules.** The larger the meeting, the more formal you need to be to maintain order. Formal meetings use **parliamentary procedure**, a time-tested method for planning and running effective meetings. The best-known guide to this procedure is *Robert's Rules of Order*.
- **Encourage participation.** On occasion, some participants will be too quiet and others too talkative. The quiet participants may be shy, they may be expressing disagreement or resistance, or they may be working on unrelated tasks. Draw them out by asking for their input on issues that pertain to them.

REAL-TIME UPDATES
Learn More

Keep those meetings on track with simple parliamentary procedures

These condensed guidelines to parliamentary procedures can help a group transform meetings from chaos to controlled efficiency. Go to **http://real-timeupdates.com/bct** and click on "Learn More." If you are using mybcommlab, you can access Real-Time Updates within each chapter or under Student Study Tools.

✓ **CHECKLIST: Improving Meeting Productivity**

A. Prepare carefully.
- Make sure the meeting is necessary.
- Decide on your purpose.
- Select participants carefully.
- Choose the time and prepare the facility.
- Establish and distribute a clear agenda.

B. Lead effectively and participate fully.
- Keep the meeting on track.
- Follow agreed-upon rules.
- Encourage participation.
- Participate actively.
- Close effectively.

- **Participate actively.** If you're a meeting participant, try to contribute to both the subject of the meeting and the smooth interaction of the group. Speak up if you have something useful to say but don't monopolize the discussion or talk simply to bring attention to yourself.
- **Close effectively.** At the conclusion of the meeting, verify that the objectives have been met or arrange for follow-up work, if needed. Either summarize the general conclusion of the discussion or the actions to be taken. Make sure all participants have a chance to clear up any misunderstandings.

To review the tasks that contribute to productive meetings, refer to "Checklist: Improving Meeting Productivity."

For formal meetings, it's good practice to appoint one person to record the **minutes**, a summary of the important information presented and the decisions made during a meeting. In smaller or informal meetings, attendees often make their own notes on their copies of the agenda. In either case, a clear record of the decisions made and the people responsible for follow-up action is essential. If your company doesn't have a specific format for minutes, follow the generic format shown in Figure 2.5.

Using Meeting Technologies

You can expect to use a variety of meeting-related technologies throughout your career. In some instances, technology is used to promote interaction among participates in the same location, such as *electronic whiteboards* that can print or e-mail information recorded on them during a meeting and a variety of *electronic presentation tools* (see Chapter 17).

The focus of most meeting technologies is to enable participation among people in two or more locations. These technologies have spurred the emergence of **virtual teams**, whose members work in different locations and interact electronically in **virtual meetings**.

The simplest of the long-distance meeting tools provide communication through a single medium, such as audio **teleconferencing**, in which three or more people are connected by phone simultaneously. When you are invited to participate in a teleconference, you are typically given a special phone number and a meeting access code to ensure the privacy of the session. Instant messaging chat sessions can also serve as virtual meetings, with people participating by typing instead of talking.

Videoconferencing combines audio communication with live video, letting team members

3 LEARNING OBJECTIVE

Explain how meeting technologies can help participants communicate more successfully and describe the emerging role of social networking technologies in business communication

How many people are in this conference room in Chicago? Only the two people in the foreground; the other six are in Atlanta and London. Virtual meeting technologies such as this *telepresence* system connect people spread across the country or around the world.

FIGURE 2.5 Typical Minutes of a Meeting

Intranets and blogs are commonly used to distribute meeting minutes. The specific format of minutes is less important than making sure you record all the key information, particularly regarding responsibilities assigned during the meeting. No matter what medium is used, key elements of meeting minutes include a list of those present and a list of those who were invited but didn't attend, followed by the times the meeting started and ended, all major decisions reached at the meeting, all assignments of tasks to meeting participants, and all subjects that were deferred to a later meeting. Minutes objectively summarize important discussions, noting the names of those who contributed major points. Outlines, subheadings, and lists help organize the minutes; additional documentation is noted in the minutes and attached.

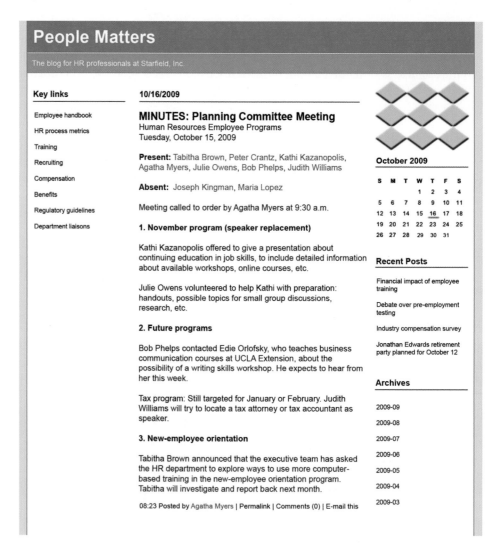

see each other, demonstrate products, and transmit other visual information. Videoconferencing can take place using PC-based systems over the World Wide Web or through dedicated networks with specially built rooms. The most advanced systems feature *telepresence*, in which the interaction feels so lifelike that participants can forget that the person "sitting" on the other side of the table is actually in another city.[42]

Web-based meeting systems combine the best of instant messaging, shared workspaces, and videoconferencing with other tools such as *virtual whiteboards* that let teams

FIGURE 2.6 Web-Based Meetings

You can expect to participate in many online meetings during your career. Web-based meeting systems offer powerful tools for communication, and you need to be proficient at using these tools to be effective during online meetings.

collaborate in real time (see Figure 2.6). Using such systems, attendees can log on from a desktop or laptop PC, a PDA, or even a web-enabled mobile phone from almost anywhere in the world.

Technology continues to create intriguing opportunities for online interaction. For instance, one of the newest virtual tools is *online brainstorming*, in which companies conduct "idea campaigns" to generate new ideas from people across the organization. These range from small team meetings to huge events such as IBM's giant InnovationJam, in which 100,000 IBM employees, family members, and customers from 160 countries were invited to brainstorm online for three days. In fact, online brainstorming has proven so successful that IBM now offers its Jam services to other companies.[43]

Companies are also beginning to experiment with virtual meetings and other communication activities in *virtual worlds*, most notably Second Life (www.secondlife.com). In much the same way that gamers can create and control characters (often known as *avatars*) in a multiplayer video game, professionals can create online versions of themselves to participate in meetings, training sessions, sales presentations, and other activities (see Figure 2.7). To learn more about business communication in Second Life, you can read the Business Communicators of Second Life blog at http://freshtakes.typepad.com/sl_communicators.

For the latest information on meeting technologies, visit http://real-timeupdates .com/bct and click on Chapter 2.

FIGURE 2.7 Virtual Meetings in a Virtual World
Cranial Tap, whose online headquarters is shown here, is one of a growing number of firms that use Second Life as a virtual meeting place.

IMPROVING YOUR LISTENING SKILLS

Listening is one of the most important skills in the workplace.

Effective listening strengthens organizational relationships, enhances product delivery, alerts an organization to opportunities for innovation, and allows an organization to manage diversity both in the workforce and in the customers it serves.[44] Companies whose employees and managers listen effectively stay in touch, up to date, and out of trouble. Some 80 percent of top executives say that listening is the most important skill needed to get things done in the workplace.[45] In fact, many of the leading business schools in the United States, for example, have begun retooling their curricula in recent years to put more emphasis on "soft skills" such as listening.[46]

Poor listening skills can cost companies millions of dollars a year as a result of lost opportunities, legal mistakes, and other errors. Effective listening is vital to the process of building trust not only between organizations but also between individuals.[47] Throughout your career, effective listening will give you a competitive edge, enhancing your performance and thus the influence you have within your company and your industry.

Recognizing Various Types of Listening

To be a good listener, adapt the way you listen to suit the situation.

Effective listeners recognize several types of listening and choose the best approach for each situation. The primary goal of **content listening** is to understand and retain the speaker's message. Because you're not evaluating the information at this point, it doesn't matter whether you agree or disagree, approve or disapprove—only that you understand. Try to overlook the speaker's style and any limitations in the presentation; just focus on the information.[48]

The goal of **critical listening** is to understand and evaluate the meaning of the speaker's message on several levels: the logic of the argument, the strength of the evidence, the validity of the conclusions, the implications of the message, the speaker's intentions and motives, and the omission of any important or relevant points. If you're skeptical, ask questions to explore the speaker's point of view and credibility. Be on the lookout for bias that could color the way the information is presented and be careful to separate opinions from facts.[49]

The goal of **empathic listening** is to understand the speaker's feelings, needs, and wants so that you can appreciate his or her point of view, regardless of whether you share that perspective. By listening with empathy, you help the individual vent the emotions that prevent a calm, clear-headed approach to the subject. Avoid the temptation to jump in with advice unless the person specifically asks for it. Also, don't judge the speaker's feelings and don't try to tell people they shouldn't feel this or that emotion. Instead, let the speaker know that you appreciate his or her feelings and understand the situation. After you establish that connection, you can help the speaker move on to search for a solution.[50]

No matter what mode they are using at any given time, effective listeners try to engage in **active listening**, making a conscious effort to turn off their own filters and biases to truly hear and understand what the other party is saying. They ask questions to verify key points and encourage the speaker through positive body language.[51]

Understanding the Listening Process

Listening is a far more complex process than most people think—and most of us aren't very good at it. People typically listen at no better than a 25 percent efficiency rate, remember only about half of what's said during a 10-minute conversation, and forget half of that within 48 hours.[52] Furthermore, when questioned about material they've just heard, they are likely to get the facts mixed up.[53]

Listening follows the same sequence as the general communication process model described in Chapter 1 (page 52), with the added challenge that it happens in real time. To listen effectively, you need to successfully complete five separate steps:[54]

1. **Receiving.** You start by physically hearing the message and acknowledging it. Physical reception can be blocked by noise, impaired hearing, or inattention. Some experts also include nonverbal messages as part of this stage because these factors influence the listening process as well.

2. **Decoding.** Your next step is to assign meaning to sounds, which you do according to your own values, beliefs, ideas, expectations, roles, needs, and personal history.

3. **Remembering.** Before you can act on the information, you need to store it for future processing. As you learned in Chapter 1, incoming messages must first be captured in short-term memory before being transferred to long-term memory for more permanent storage.

4. **Evaluating.** Your next step is to evaluate the message by applying critical thinking skills to separate fact from opinion and evaluate the quality of the evidence.

5. **Responding.** After you've evaluated the speaker's message, you react. If you're communicating one-on-one or in a small group, the initial response generally takes the form of verbal feedback. If you're one of many in an audience, your initial response may take the form of applause, laughter, or silence. Later on, you may act on what you have heard.

If any one of these steps breaks down, the listening process becomes less effective or even fails entirely. As both a sender and a receiver, you can reduce the failure rate by recognizing and overcoming a variety of physical and mental barriers to effective listening.

Overcoming Barriers to Effective Listening

Good listeners look for ways to overcome potential barriers throughout the listening process (see Table 2.3). For instance, simply avoiding interrupting the speaker removes many potential barriers. If you have questions, wait until the speaker has finished speaking. Rustling papers, tapping on a PDA, and checking the time are just a few of the nonverbal behaviors that can interrupt a speaker and hamper listening for everyone.

Listening involves five steps: receiving, decoding, remembering, evaluating, and responding.

Good listeners actively try to overcome the barriers to successful listening.

TABLE 2.3   What Makes an Effective Listener?

EFFECTIVE LISTENERS	INEFFECTIVE LISTENERS
• Listen actively.	• Listen passively.
• Take careful and complete notes.	• Take no notes or ineffective notes.
• Make frequent eye contact with the speaker (depending on the culture).	• Make little or no eye contact.
• Stay focused on the speaker and the content.	• Allow their minds to wander; are easily distracted.
• Mentally paraphrase key points to maintain attention level and ensure comprehension.	• Fail to paraphrase.
• Adjust listening style to the situation.	• Listen with the same style, regardless of the situation.
• Give the speaker nonverbal cues (such as nodding to show agreement or raising eyebrows to show surprise or skepticism).	• Fail to give the speaker nonverbal feedback.
• Save questions or points of disagreement until an appropriate time.	• Interrupt whenever they disagree or don't understand.
• Overlook stylistic differences and focus on the speaker's message.	• Are distracted by or unduly influenced by stylistic differences; are judgmental.
• Make distinctions between main points and supporting details.	• Are unable to distinguish main points from details.
• Look for opportunities to learn.	• Assume that they already know everything that's important to know.

Selective listening is one of the most common barriers to effective listening. If your mind wanders, you may stay tuned out until you hear a word or phrase that gets your attention again. But by that time, you're unable to recall what the speaker *actually* said; instead, you remember what you *think* the speaker probably said.[55]

One reason listeners' minds tend to wander is that people think faster than they speak. Most people speak at about 120 to 150 words per minute, but listeners can process audio information at up to 500 words per minute.[56] In other words, your brain has a lot of free time whenever you're listening, and if you don't focus, it will find a thousand other things to think about.

Your mind can process information much faster than most speakers talk, so you need to focus to listen effectively.

Overcoming interpretation barriers can be difficult because you may not even be aware of them. As Chapter 1 notes, selective perception leads listeners to mold messages to fit their own conceptual frameworks. Listeners sometimes make up their minds before fully hearing the speaker's message, or they engage in defensive listening—protecting their self-esteem by tuning out anything that doesn't confirm their view of themselves.

Even when your intentions are good, remember that you can still misinterpret incoming messages if you and the speaker don't share enough language or experience. When listening to a speaker whose native language or life experience is different from yours, try to paraphrase that person's ideas. Give the speaker a chance to confirm what you think you heard or to correct any misinterpretation.

Overcoming memory barriers is a comparatively easy problem to solve, but it takes some work. One simple rule: Don't count on your memory. If the information is crucial, record it. You can hold information in short-term memory by repeating it silently or organizing a long list of items into several shorter lists. To store information in long-term memory—particularly information that you might not be immediately interested in—four techniques can help: (1) Associate new information with something closely related (such as the

REAL-TIME UPDATES
Learn More

Are you a good listener?

Most of us believe we are good listeners, but the constant communication breakdowns in business and personal settings is evidence that we could all improve. Go to **http://real-timeupdates.com/bct** and click on "Learn More." If you are using mybcommlab, you can access Real-Time Updates within each chapter or under Student Study Tools.

✓ CHECKLIST: Overcoming Barriers to Effective Listening

- Control whatever barriers to physical reception you can (such as avoiding interrupting speakers by asking questions or by exhibiting disruptive nonverbal behaviors).
- Avoid selective listening by focusing on the speaker and carefully analyzing what you hear.
- Keep an open mind by avoiding any prejudgment and by not listening defensively.

- Try to paraphrase the speaker's ideas, giving that person a chance to confirm or correct your interpretation.
- Don't count on your memory; write down or record important information.
- Improve your short-term memory by repeating information or breaking it into shorter lists.
- Improve your long-term memory by using association, categorization, visualization, and mnemonics.

restaurant in which you met a new client), (2) categorize the new information into logical groups (such as alphabetizing the names of products you're trying to remember), (3) visualize words and ideas as pictures, and (4) create mnemonics such as acronyms or rhymes. Note that all four techniques have an important factor in common: You have to *do* something to make the information stick.

For a reminder of the steps you can take to overcome listening barriers, see "Checklist: Overcoming Barriers to Effective Listening."

IMPROVING YOUR NONVERBAL COMMUNICATION SKILLS

Nonverbal communication is the interpersonal process of sending and receiving information, both intentionally and unintentionally, without using written or spoken language. Nonverbal signals play a vital role in communication because they can strengthen a verbal message (when the nonverbal signals match the spoken words), weaken a verbal message (when nonverbal signals don't match the words), or replace words entirely. For example, you might tell a client that a project is coming along nicely, but your forced smile and nervous glances send an entirely different message. In fact, nonverbal communication often conveys more to listeners than the words you speak—particularly when they're trying to decide how you really feel about a situation or when they're trying to judge your credibility and aptitude for leadership.[57]

Recognizing Nonverbal Communication

Paying special attention to nonverbal signals in the workplace will enhance your ability to communicate successfully. Moreover, as you interact with business associates from other backgrounds, you'll discover that some nonverbal signals don't necessarily translate across cultures. You'll learn more about cultural influences on nonverbal communication in Chapter 3. The range and variety of nonverbal signals are almost endless, but you can grasp the basics by studying six general categories:

- **Facial expression.** Your face is the primary vehicle for expressing your emotions; it reveals both the type and the intensity of your feelings.[58] Your eyes are especially effective for indicating attention and interest, influencing others, regulating interaction, and establishing dominance.[59]
- **Gesture and posture.** The way you position and move your body expresses both specific and general messages, some voluntary and some involuntary. Many gestures—a wave of the hand, for example—have specific and intentional meanings. Other types of body movement are unintentional and express more general messages. Slouching, leaning forward, fidgeting, and walking briskly are all unconscious signals that reveal whether you feel confident or nervous, friendly or hostile, assertive or passive, powerful or powerless.

5 LEARNING OBJECTIVE

Clarify the importance of nonverbal communication and briefly describe six categories of nonverbal expression

Nonverbal communication supplements spoken language.

Nonverbal signals include facial expression, gestures and posture, vocal characteristics, personal appearance, touch, and use of time and space.

COMMUNICATING ACROSS CULTURES

Actions Speak Louder Than Words All Around the World

The weeklong meeting with your new business partner in Hong Kong went well. Over the long dinners during which you hashed out various details of the contract, you also sensed a friendship beginning to form. Your business partner was even kind enough to drive you to the airport when you left on Friday afternoon. As you said good-bye, you impulsively reached out to give him a quick hug around the shoulder, with one arm only, to express that new sense of friendship. You were quite surprised when he stood as stiff as a statue and didn't return the gesture. What happened to the friendship? Had you misread the signals all week?

No, you probably just missed a key point of nonverbal behavior in Hong Kong culture, where businesspeople are unaccustomed to colleagues making any kind of physical contact. Nonverbal cues vary widely between cultures, as you can see by comparing a couple of fairly subtle differences:

- Canadian listeners nod to signal agreement.
- Japanese listeners nod to indicate only that they have understood.
- British listeners stare at the speaker, blinking their eyes to indicate understanding.
- People in the United States are taught that it's impolite to stare.

To adjust your nonverbal communication to other cultures, learn as much as you can. Consult books, seminars, and motion pictures on cultural differences. Try renting movies and television shows from other countries. Examine illustrations in news and business magazines to get an idea of expected business dress and personal space. Above all, remain flexible as you interact with people from other cultures.

CAREER APPLICATIONS

1. Explain how watching a movie from another country could help you prepare to interpret nonverbal behavior from that culture correctly—or incorrectly.
2. One of your co-workers is originally from Saudi Arabia. You like him, and the two of you work well together. However, he stands so close when you speak with him that it makes you uncomfortable. Do you tell him of your discomfort or try to cover it up?

- **Vocal characteristics.** Voice carries both intentional and unintentional messages. A speaker can intentionally control pitch, pace, and stress to convey a specific message. For instance, consider the question "What are you doing?" with the emphasis on *what* versus the emphasis on *you*. Unintentional vocal characteristics can convey happiness, surprise, fear, and other emotions (for example, fear often increases the pitch and the pace of your speaking voice).
- **Personal appearance.** People respond to others on the basis of their physical appearance, sometimes fairly and other times unfairly. Although an individual's body type and facial features impose limitations, people can control grooming, clothing, accessories, and overall personal style. If your goal is to make a good impression, adopt the style of the people you want to impress.
- **Touch.** Touch is an important way to convey warmth, comfort, and reassurance—as well as control. Touch is so powerful, in fact, that it is governed by cultural customs that establish who can touch whom and how in various circumstances. In the United States and Great Britain, for instance, people usually touch less frequently than people in France or Costa Rica. Even within each culture's norms, however, individual attitudes toward touch vary widely. A manager might be comfortable using hugs to express support or congratulations, but his or her subordinates could interpret those hugs as either a show of dominance or sexual interest.[60] Touch is a complex subject. The best advice: When in doubt, don't touch.
- **Time and space.** Like touch, time and space can be used to assert authority, imply intimacy, and send other nonverbal messages. For instance, some people try to demonstrate their own importance or disregard for others by making other people wait; others show respect by being on time. The manipulation of space works in a similar way. For example, the decision to respect or violate someone's "private space" sends a powerful nonverbal signal.

✓ **CHECKLIST:** | **Improving Nonverbal Communication Skills**

- Understand the roles that nonverbal signals play in communication, complementing verbal language by strengthening, weakening, or replacing words.
- Nonverbal signals often reveal the truth, sometimes conveying more to listeners than spoken words.
- Note that facial expressions (especially eye contact) reveal the type and intensity of a speaker's feelings.
- Watch for cues from gestures and posture.
- Listen for vocal characteristics that signal who the speaker is, the speaker's relationship with the audience, and the emotions underlying the speaker's words.
- Recognize that listeners are influenced by physical appearance.
- Be careful with physical contact; touch can convey positive attributes but can also be interpreted as dominance or sexual interest.
- Pay attention to the use of time and space.

Using Nonverbal Communication Effectively

Paying attention to nonverbal cues will make you both a better speaker and a better listener. When you're talking, be more conscious of the nonverbal cues you could be sending. Are they effective without being manipulative? Consider a situation in which an employee has come to you to talk about a raise. This situation is a stressful one for the employee, so don't say you're interested in what she has to tell you and then spend your time glancing at your computer or checking your watch. Conversely, if you already know you won't be able to give her the raise, be honest in your expression of emotions. Don't overcompensate for your own stress by smiling too broadly or shaking her hand too vigorously. Both nonverbal signals would raise her hopes without justification. In either case, match your nonverbal cues to the tone of the situation.

Work to make sure your nonverbal signals match the tone and content of your spoken communication.

Also consider the nonverbal signals you send when you're not talking—the clothes you wear, the way you sit, the way you walk. Are you talking like a serious business professional but dressing like you belong in a dance club or a frat house? (Appropriate clothing for work situations is discussed in the next section, on business etiquette.)

What signals does your personal appearance send?

When you listen, be sure to pay attention to the speaker's nonverbal cues. Do they amplify the spoken words or contradict them? Is the speaker intentionally using nonverbal signals to send you a message that he or she can't put into words? Be observant but don't assume that you can "read someone like a book." Nonverbal signals are powerful, but they aren't infallible. Contrary to popular belief, for instance, just because someone doesn't look you squarely in the eye doesn't mean he or she is lying.[61] If something doesn't feel right, ask the speaker an honest and respectful question; doing so may clear everything up, or it may uncover issues you need to explore further. See "Checklist: Improving Nonverbal Communication Skills" for a summary of key ideas regarding nonverbal skills.

DEVELOPING YOUR BUSINESS ETIQUETTE

You may have noticed a common thread running through the topics of successful teamwork, productive meetings, effective listening, and nonverbal communication: All these activities depend on mutual respect and consideration among all participants. As Chapter 1 notes, etiquette is now considered an essential business skill. Nobody wants to work with someone who is rude to colleagues or an embarrassment to the company. Moreover, shabby treatment of others in the workplace can be a huge drain on morale and productivity.[62] Poor etiquette can drive away customers, investors, and other critical audiences—and it can limit your career potential. This section addresses some key etiquette points to remember when you're in the workplace, out in public, and online.

6 **LEARNING OBJECTIVE**

Discuss the importance of business etiquette

Etiquette is an essential element of every aspect of business communication.

Etiquette in the Workplace

Workplace etiquette includes a variety of behaviors, habits, and aspects of nonverbal communication. Although it isn't always thought of an as element of etiquette, your personal appearance in the workplace sends a strong signal to managers, colleagues, and customers.

Personal appearance can have considerable impact on your success in business.

TABLE 2.4   Assembling a Business Wardrobe

1 SMOOTH AND FINISHED (START WITH THIS)	2 ELEGANT AND REFINED (TO COLUMN 1, ADD THIS)	3 CRISP AND STARCHY (TO COLUMN 2, ADD THIS)	4 UP-TO-THE-MINUTE TRENDY (TO COLUMN 3, ADD THIS)
1. Choose well-tailored clothing that fits well; it doesn't have to be expensive, but it does have to fit and be appropriate for business.	1. Choose form-fitting (but not skin-tight) clothing—not swinging or flowing fabrics, frills, or fussy trimmings.	1. Wear blouses or shirts that are or appear starched.	1. Supplement your foundation with pieces that reflect the latest styles.
2. Keep buttons, zippers, and hemlines in good repair.	2. Choose muted tones and soft colors or classics, such as a dark blue suit or a basic black dress.	2. Choose closed top-button shirts or button-down shirt collars, higher-neckline blouses, or long sleeves with French cuffs and cuff links.	2. Add a few pieces in bold colors but wear them sparingly to avoid a garish appearance.
3. Select shoes that are comfortable enough for long days but neither too casual nor too dressy for the office; keep shoes clean and in good condition.	3. If possible, select a few classic pieces of jewelry (such as a string of pearls or diamond cuff links) for formal occasions.	3. Wear creased trousers or a longer skirt hemline.	3. Embellish your look with the latest jewelry and hairstyles but keep the overall effect looking professional.
4. Make sure the fabrics you wear are clean, are carefully pressed, and do not wrinkle easily.	4. Wear jackets that complement an outfit and lend an air of formality to your appearance. Avoid jackets with more than two tones; one color should dominate.		
5. Choose colors that flatter your height, weight, skin tone, and style; sales advisors in good clothing stores can help you choose.			

Pay attention to the style of dress where you work and adjust your style to match. Expectations for specific jobs, companies, and industries can vary widely. The financial industries tend to be more formal than high technology, for instance, and sales and executive positions usually involve more formal expectations than positions in engineering or manufacturing. Observe others and don't be afraid to ask for advice. If you're not sure, dress modestly and simply—earn a reputation for what you can *do*, not for what you can wear. Table 2.4 offers some general guidelines on assembling a business wardrobe that's cost-effective and flexible.

Grooming is as important as attire. Pay close attention to cleanliness and avoid using products with powerful scents, such as perfumed soaps, colognes, shampoos, and aftershave lotions (many people are bothered by these products, and some are allergic to them). Shampoo frequently, keep hands and nails neatly manicured, use mouthwash and deodorant, and make regular trips to a barber or hair stylist.[63] Some companies have specific policies regarding hairstyles, which you may be expected to follow.[64]

If you work in a conventional office setting, you'll spend as much time with your office-mates as you spend with family and friends. Personal demeanor is therefore a vital element of workplace harmony. No one expects (or wants) you to be artificially upbeat and bubbly every second of the day, but a single negative personality can make an entire office miserable and unproductive. Every person in the company has a responsibility to contribute to a positive, energetic work environment.

Plan important phone calls as carefully as you plan meetings.

Given the telephone's central role in business communication, phone skills are essential in most professions. Because phone calls lack the visual richness of face-to-face conversations, you have to rely on your attitude and tone of voice to convey confidence and professionalism. Table 2.5 on page 90 summarizes helpful tips for placing and receiving phone calls in a confident, professional manner.

If you're accustomed to using your mobile phone anywhere and everywhere, get ready to change your habits. Mobile phones are causing so much disruption in the workplace that some senior executives now ban their use in meetings.[65] Other companies prohibit their use throughout the entire workday. Even if mobile phones aren't banned in your office, don't let yours become a source of annoyance to your colleagues.

Etiquette in Social Settings

From business lunches to industry conferences, you may represent your company when you're out in public. Make sure your appearance and actions are appropriate to the situation. Get to know the customs of the culture when you meet new people. For example, in North America, a firm handshake is expected when two people meet, whereas a respectful bow of the head is more appropriate in Japan. If you are expected to shake hands, be aware that the passive "dead fish" handshake creates an extremely negative impression. If you are physically able, always stand when shaking someone's hand.

You represent your company when you're in public, so etiquette continues to be important outside the organization's walls.

When introducing yourself, include a brief description of your role in the company. When introducing two other people, speak their first and last names clearly and then try to offer some information (perhaps a shared professional interest) to help the two people ease into a conversation.[66] Generally speaking, the lower-ranking person is introduced to the senior-ranking person, without regard to gender.[67]

Business is often conducted over meals, and knowing the basics of dining etiquette will make you more effective in these situations.[68] Start by choosing foods that are easy to eat. Avoid alcoholic beverages in most instances, but if one is appropriate, save it for the end of the meal. Leave business documents under your chair until entrée plates have been removed; the business aspect of the meal doesn't usually begin until then.

Inappropriate use of mobile phones and other devices is a sign of disrespect.

Ethics Detective

How Did "We" Turn into "I"?

You are employed in the marketing department of a multinational company with its regional office at Oman (Jordan). The head of the department called you and told you that from today on you two will work as a team. After that he gave you certain guidelines and asked you to prepare a marketing plan. You spent almost two weeks and made a very comprehensive plan to market the products. Although your boss did not participate in the development phase, he appreciated your effort toward the plan and asked you to give him a printed copy as well as the electronic copy of the plan. While you were preparing the final copy you included the name of your boss along with your name as plan initiators. You gave him the hard copy, as well as the electronic copy, of the plan. Three weeks later, your boss was out of the office when you received a phone call from the CEO's secretary who asked you, as the number-two person in the department, to change some things in the plan. The secretary sent you the electronic copy of the marketing plan through e-mail. Once you saw the plan, you were shocked to see that your boss removed your name from the document, so that only his name was included as the plan initiator. You also noticed that the author name on the soft copy was also changed. You were furious. You spoke to one of your friends about this matter, but she could not give you any advice.

ANALYSIS

Is it fair to remove a person's name from a document when that person has worked hard to produce that document? Is your boss's action correct? What will your reaction be in this situation? Will you ask your boss about this? Or will you bring the matter to the notice of the CEO's secretary while discussing the requested changes. What consequences will you face if you discuss this matter with the CEO's secretary?

TABLE 2.5   Quick Tips for Improving Your Phone Skills

GENERAL TIPS	PLACING CALLS	RECEIVING CALLS	USING VOICE MAIL
Use frequent verbal responses that show you're listening ("Oh yes," "I see," "That's right").	Be ready before you call so that you don't waste the other person's time.	Answer promptly and with a smile so that you sound friendly and positive.	When recording your outgoing message, make it brief and professional.
Increase your volume just slightly to convey your confidence.	Minimize distractions and avoid making noise that could annoy the other party.	Identify yourself and your company. (Some companies have specific guidelines on what to say when you answer.)	If you can, record temporary greetings on days when you are unavailable all day so that callers will know you're gone for the day.
Don't speak in a monotone; vary your pitch and inflections so people know you're interested.	Identify yourself and your organization, briefly describe why you're calling, and verify that you've called at a good time.	Establish the needs of your caller by asking, "How may I help you?" If you know the caller's name, use it.	Check your voice-mail messages regularly and return all necessary calls within 24 hours.
Slow down when conversing with people whose native language isn't the same as yours.	Don't take up too much time. Speak quickly and clearly and get right to the point of the call.	If you can, answer questions promptly and efficiently; if you can't help, tell the caller what you can do for him or her.	Leave simple, clear messages, with your name, number, purpose for calling, and times when you can be reached.
Stay focused on the call throughout; others can easily tell when you're not paying attention.	Close in a friendly, positive manner and double-check all vital information, such as meeting times and dates.	If you must forward a call or put someone on hold, explain what you are doing before you do it.	State your name and telephone number slowly so that the other person can easily write them down; repeat both if the other person doesn't know you.
		If you forward a call to someone else, try to speak with that person first to verify that he or she is available and to introduce the caller.	Be careful what you say; most voice-mail systems allow users to forward messages to anyone else in the system.
		If you take a message for someone else, be complete and accurate, including the caller's name, number, and organization.	Replay your message before leaving the system to make sure it is clear and complete.

Just as in the office, when you use your mobile phone in public, you send the message that people around you aren't as important as your call and that you don't respect your caller's privacy.[69] If it's not a matter of life and death, or at least an urgent request from your boss or a customer, wait until you're back in the office.

Finally, always remember that business meals are a forum for business, period. Don't get on your soapbox about politics, religion, or any other topic that's likely to stir up emotions. Don't complain about work, don't ask deeply personal questions, avoid profanity, and be careful with humor—a joke that entertains some people could easily offend others.

REAL-TIME UPDATES
Learn More

Don't let etiquette blunders derail your career

Get great advice on developing professional telephone skills, making a positive impression while dining, and dressing for success in any career environment (including great tips on buying business suits). Go to **http://real-timeupdates .com/bct** and click on "Learn More." If you are using mybcommlab, you can access Real-Time Updates within each chapter or under Student Study Tools.

Etiquette Online

Electronic media seem to be a breeding ground for poor etiquette. Learn the basics of professional online behavior to avoid mistakes that could hurt your company or your career. Here are some guidelines to follow whenever you are representing your company while using electronic media:[70]

- **Avoid personal attacks.** The anonymous and instantaneous nature of online communication can cause even level-headed people to strike out in blog postings and on message threads.
- **Stay focused on the original topic.** If you want to change the subject of an e-mail exchange, a forum discussion, or a blog comment thread, start a new message.

- **Don't present opinions as facts; supports facts with evidence.** This guideline applies to all communication, of course, but online venues in particular seem to tempt people into presenting their beliefs and opinions as unassailable truths.
- **Follow basic expectations of spelling, punctuation, and capitalization.** Sending acronym-filled messages that look like you're texting your high school buddies makes you look like an amateur.
- **Use virus protection and keep it up to date.** Sending or posting a file that contains a computer virus is rude.
- **Ask if this is a good time for an IM chat.** Don't assume that just because a person is showing as "available" on your IM system that he or she wants to chat with you right this instant.
- **Watch your language and keep your emotions under control.** A moment of indiscretion could haunt you forever.
- **Avoid multitasking while using IM.** You might think you're saving time by doing a dozen things at once, but you're probably making the other person wait while you bounce back and forth between IM and your other tasks.
- **Never assume privacy.** Assume that anything you type will be stored forever, could be forwarded to other people, and might be read by your boss or the company's security staff.
- **Don't use "reply all" in e-mail unless everyone can benefit from your reply.** If one or more recipients of an e-mail message don't need the information in your reply, remove their addresses before you send.
- **Don't waste others' time with sloppy, confusing, or incomplete messages.** Doing so is disrespectful.

When you represent your company online, you must adhere to a high standard of etiquette and respect for others.

Communication Challenges at Rosen Law Firm

You recently joined Rosen Law Firm and quickly became an enthusiastic user of the company's internal wiki. In your brief time being involved with the wiki, you have observed some behavior that runs counter to the spirit of collaborative writing. Study these two scenarios and decide how to respond.

Individual Challenge: One particular employee keeps editing your pages on the wiki, often making changes that appear to add no value, as far as you can see. She doesn't seem to be editing other employees' pages nearly so often, so you are beginning to wonder if she has a personal grudge against you. You want to address this uncomfortable situation without dragging your boss into it. First, decide how to approach your contentious colleague. Should you drop by her office unannounced, call her on the phone, send her an e-mail message, or perhaps insert a sarcastic comment about excessive editing on one of her wiki pages? Second, whichever mode of communication you've chosen, outline the message you think you should share with her.

Team Challenge: A common dilemma in every form of collaborative writing is deciding how soon to share early drafts with your colleagues in order to get their feedback and contributions. Should you send out an unpolished rough draft for the team's input before investing a lot of time in polishing and formatting, or should you do a second or third draft to enhance readability—knowing that the team might delete entire sections that you've worked hard to polish? On the Rosen wiki, some contributors seem to go into "grammar attack mode" whenever a rough draft appears. They seem to ignore the message and content altogether and instead focus on punctuation, grammar, and formatting concerns. With a small team of fellow students, draft some brief guidelines for wiki contributors, conveying these three points: (1) Punctuation, grammar, and formatting are definitely important, but worrying about them too early in the writing process can hamper the free exploration of ideas and information; (2) when reviewing early drafts, wiki users need to make a conscious effort to look past the presentation and focus on the information; and (3) contributors who post rough drafts seeking input should make the pages at least minimally readable so that reviewers can focus on the content and ideas. (To learn more about editing and working with wikis, you can peek ahead to page 190 in Chapter 6 and page 453 in Chapter 14.)

SUMMARY OF LEARNING OBJECTIVES

1 **Highlight the advantages and disadvantages of working in teams.** Teams can achieve a higher level of performance than individuals because of the combined intelligence and energy of the group. Motivation and creativity can flourish in team settings. Moreover, individuals tend to perform better because they achieve a sense of purpose by belonging to a group. Teams also bring more input and a greater diversity of views, which tends to result in better decisions. And because team members participate in the decision process, they are more committed to seeing the results succeed. Teams are not without disadvantages, however. Poorly managed teams can be a waste of everyone's time. For example, if members are pressured to conform, they may develop groupthink, which can lead to poor-quality decisions and ill-advised actions. Some members may let their private motives get in the way.

2 **Identify eight guidelines for successful collaborative writing.** Collaborative communication is a great opportunity for teams to pool their diverse talents and knowledge to produce messages that are of higher quality than any single team member could produce on his or her own. However, collaborative writing requires close attention. Select team members carefully to balance talents and viewpoints and be sure to agree on project goals at the outset to avoid confusion and wasted time. If a team hasn't worked together before, make sure team members have time to get to know one another. Next, make sure that everyone clearly understands individual responsibilities, processes, and tools. Also, resist the temptation to write as a group; research and plan as a group but assign the task of writing to one person or assign separate sections to individual writers and have one person edit them all. Finally, make sure tools and techniques are compatible across the team.

3 **Explain how meeting technologies can help participants communicate more successfully and describe the emerging role of social networking technologies in business communication.** Tools such as whiteboards and electronic presentations promote interaction among people in a single physical location, but most meeting-related technologies focus on enabling participation among people in two or more locations. These tools range from simple audio teleconferencing and IM chat sessions to videoconferences, telepresence systems, and web-based meetings. Shared workspaces give teams instant access to a common set of project resources, including documents, databases, schedules, and other materials. Social networking technologies are redefining teamwork and business communication by helping to erase the constraints of geographic and organization boundaries. By making it easy for members of a network to locate and communicate with other members who possess specific knowledge and skills, these technologies help in numerous aspects of running a business, including supporting customers; integrating new employees and assisting with reorganizations; overcoming communication barriers in the organization structure; assembling and fostering the growth of teams and virtual communities; maintaining business relationships; and finding potential customers, employees, and business partners.

4 **Describe the listening process and explain how good listeners overcome barriers at each stage of the process.** The listening process involves five activities: (1) receiving (physically hearing the message), (2) decoding (assigning meaning to what you hear), (3) remembering (storing the message for future reference), (4) evaluating (thinking about the message), and (5) responding (reacting to the message, taking action, or giving feedback). Several barriers can interfere with the listening process. To improve reception, minimize distractions by holding questions until the speaker finishes and avoiding distracting nonverbal behaviors. To improve decoding and interpretation, avoid prejudgment and defensive listening by taking a patient, open-minded approach. To improve remembering, store information for the short term by repeating it to yourself or breaking a long list into several shorter lists. Also, transfer information from short-term to long-term memory through association, categorization, visualization, and mnemonics. To improve evaluating, overcome selective listening by focusing on the speaker, taking careful notes, mentally paraphrasing what's being said, and analyzing the speaker's argument. To improve responding, react naturally when appropriate and plan out any response to a more complex message.

5 **Clarify the importance of nonverbal communication and briefly describe six categories of nonverbal expression.** Nonverbal communication is important because actions speak louder than words. Body language is more difficult to control than words and may reveal a person's true feelings, motivation, or character. Therefore, people believe nonverbal signals over words. In addition, nonverbal communication is more efficient; with a wave of your hand or a wink, you can streamline your thoughts—without much thought. Types of nonverbal expression include facial expression, gestures and posture, vocal characteristics, personal appearance, touching behavior, and use of time and space.

6 **Discuss the importance of business etiquette.**   Attention to etiquette is essential to success in every form of business communication—so much so that etiquette is considered an important business skill. Poor etiquette can hinder team efforts, drain morale and productivity, drive away customers and investors, and limit your career potential.

PEARSON
mybcommlab

Log on to www.mybcommlab.com to access the following study and assessment aids associated with this chapter:

- Video applications
- Real-Time Updates
- Peer review activity
- Quick Learning Guides
- Pre/post test
- Personalized study plan
- Model documents
- Sample presentations

If you are not using mybcommlab, you can access the Real-Time Updates and Quick Learning Guides through http://real-timeupdates.com/bct. The Quick Learning Guide (located under "Learn More" on the website) hits all the high points of this chapter in just two pages. This guide, especially prepared by the authors, will help you study for exams or review important concepts whenever you need a quick refresher.

Test Your Knowledge

1. How can organizations and employees benefit from successful teamwork?
2. As a team or department leader, what steps can you take to ensure that your meetings are successful and efficient?
3. How can employees and companies take advantage of social networking technologies?
4. What is groupthink, and how can it affect an organization?
5. How can organizations help team members successfully resolve conflict?
6. Why is etiquette an important business skill?
7. Why would a company use a wiki to support team collaboration rather than a content management system?
8. What are the main activities that make up the listening process?
9. How does content listening differ from critical listening and empathic listening?
10. In what six ways can an individual communicate nonverbally?

Apply Your Knowledge

1. How can nonverbal communication help you run a meeting? How can it help you call a meeting to order, emphasize important topics, show approval, express reservations, regulate the flow of conversation, and invite a colleague to continue with a comment?
2. Whenever your boss asks for feedback during department meetings, she blasts anyone who offers criticism, which causes people to agree with everything she says. You want to talk to her about it, but what should you say? List some of the points you want to make when you discuss this issue with your boss.
3. Is conflict in a team good or bad? Explain your answer.
4. You and another manager in your company disagree about whether employees should be encouraged to create online profiles on LinkedIn and other business-oriented social networking websites. You say these connections can be valuable to employees by helping them meet their peers throughout the industry and valuable to the company by identifying potential sales leads and business partners. The other manager says that encouraging employees to become better known in the industry will only make it easier for competitors to lure them away with enticing job offers. Write a brief e-mail message that outlines your argument. (Make up any information you need about the company and its industry.)
5. **Ethical Choices** Strange instant messages occasionally pop up on your computer screen during your team's virtual meetings, followed quickly by embarrassed apologies from one of your colleagues in another city. You eventually figure out that this person is working from home, even though he says he's in the office; moreover, the messages suggest that he's running a sideline business from his home. You're concerned about the frequent disruptions, not to mention your colleague's potential ethical violations. What should you do? Explain your choice.

Practice Your Knowledge

You are the president of a student unit and have made the following notes for your meeting. Prepare a formal agenda by putting the following items in the logical order and rewriting, where necessary, to make the phrases more consistent:

Student unit meeting, 3:00 P.M., Monday, October 19, 2009.
Future meetings: The student unit will assemble after every four weeks.
Student unit will guide the freshmen joining the university.
I will call the meeting to order.
Student unit secretary will be nominated from the elected members.
Meeting will take place in Conference Room 1.
Meeting will be telecasted on the university television network.
Duties of the members will be approved.

Agenda points:

  How to guide the junior and senior students in taking
   courses

  Accommodation problems

  Nomination of secretary

  How to advise the freshmen

Distribution of student unit bylaws to members.

Exercises

Active links for all websites in this chapter can be found online. If mybcommlab is being used in your class, see your User Guide for instructions on accessing the content for this chapter. Otherwise, visit **www.pearsonglobaleditions.com/bovee**, locate *Business Communication Today*, Tenth Edition, click the Companion Website link, select Chapter 2, and then click on "Featured Websites." Please note that links to sites that become inactive after publication of the book will be removed from the Featured Websites section.

2.1   **Teamwork**   Form a team with one of your classmates, and attend any university, college, or community society/group meeting. During the meeting, be an observer and take the notes individually. Do not compare your notes with your teammate until you write a paper highlighting the following:

 a.   What kind of meeting it was, when it was convened, who participated, and what the agenda was

 b.   How you judge the leader's ability at the following:
  Articulating the meeting's goals
  Engaging the members in meaningful discussion

 c.   How you judge the group as a whole for the following:
  Group's dynamics
  Group's listening skills

 d.   How you judge the members for the following:
  Listening skills
  Making decisions
  Voting

 e.   Whether the members reach decisions by consensus, whether members with dissenting opinions get a chance to voice their objections, and whether there are any communication barriers

 Now compare your notes with your teammate. Justify how you can account for any differences.

2.2   **Team Communication: Overcoming Barriers**   Every month, each employee in your department is expected to give a brief oral presentation on the status of his or her project. However, your department has recently hired an employee who has a severe speech impediment that prevents people from understanding most of what he has to say. As department manager, how will you resolve this dilemma? Please explain.

2.3   **Team Development: Resolving Conflict**   Describe a recent conflict you had with a team member at work or at school and explain how you resolved it. Did you find a solution that was acceptable to both of you and to the team?

2.4   **Ethical Choices**   During team meetings, one member constantly calls for votes or decisions before all the members have voiced their views. As the leader, you asked this member privately about his behavior. He replied that he was trying to move the team toward its goals, but you are concerned that he is really trying to take control. How can you deal with this situation without removing the member from the group?

2.5   **Online Communication: Staying on Track with Blog Replies**   As the leader of a product development team, you write a daily blog to inform team members of questions, concerns, and other developments related to your project. Team members are always encouraged to reply to your online posts, but lately a number of people have been wandering off track with their replies, raising new issues in the middle of a discussion thread or posting on matters unrelated to the item to which they're replying. The blog is becoming less useful for everyone because individual message threads no longer stick to a single topic. Write a brief blog posting, three or four sentences at most, courteously reminding readers why it's important to stick to the subject at hand when replying to blog items.

2.6   **Internet**   Visit the PolyVision website, at **www.websterboards.com**, and read about electronic whiteboards. What advantages do you see in using this kind of whiteboard during a meeting? Draft a short e-mail message to your boss, outlining the product's advantages.

2.7   **Telephones and Voice Mail**   Late on a Friday afternoon, you learn that the facilities department is going to move you—and your computer, your desk, and all your files—to another office first thing Monday morning. However, you have an important client meeting scheduled in your office for Monday afternoon, and you need to finalize some contract details on Monday morning. You simply can't lose access to your office at this point, and you're more than a little annoyed that your boss didn't ask you before approving the move. He has already left for the day, but you know he usually checks his voice mail over the weekend, so you decide to leave a message, asking him to cancel the move or at least call you at home as soon as possible. Using the voice mail guidelines listed in Table 2.5, plan your message (use an imaginary phone number as your contact number and make up any other details you need for the call). As directed by your instructor, submit either a written script of the message or a podcast recording of the actual message.

2.8   **Nonverbal Communication: Analyzing Written Messages**   Select a business letter and envelope that you have received at work or home. Analyze their appearance. What nonverbal messages do they send? Are these messages consistent with the content of the letter? If not, what could the sender have done to make the nonverbal communication consistent with the verbal communication?

2.9   **Nonverbal Communication: Analyzing Body Language**   Describe what the following body movements suggest when someone exhibits them during a conversation. How do such movements influence your interpretation of spoken words?

a. Shifting one's body continuously while seated
b. Twirling and playing with one's hair
c. Sitting in a sprawled position
d. Rolling one's eyes
e. Extending a weak handshake

2.10 Etiquette: Coaching New Hires As the local manager of an international accounting firm, you place high priority on professional etiquette. Not only does it communicate respect to your clients, it also instills confidence in your firm by showing that you and your staff are aware of and able to meet the expectations of almost any audience. Earlier today, you took four recently hired college graduates to lunch with an important client. You've done this for years, and it's usually an upbeat experience for everyone, but today's lunch was a disaster. One of the new employees made not one, not two, but *three* calls on his mobile phone during lunch. Another interrupted the client several times and even got into a mild argument. The third employee kept making sarcastic jokes about politics, making everyone at the table uncomfortable. And the fourth showed up dressed like she was expecting to bale hay or work in coal mine, not have a business lunch in a posh restaurant. You've already called the client to apologize, but now you need to coach these employees on proper business etiquette. Draft a brief memo to these employees, explaining why etiquette is so important to the company's success—and to their individual careers.

2.11 Listening Skills: Self-Assessment How good are your listening skills? Use the following chart to rate yourself on each element of listening. Then examine your ratings to identify where you are strongest and where you can improve, using the tips in this chapter.

ELEMENT OF LISTENING	ALWAYS	FREQUENTLY	OCCASIONALLY	NEVER
1. I look for areas of interest when people speak.	_____	_____	_____	_____
2. I focus on content rather than delivery.	_____	_____	_____	_____
3. I wait to respond until I understand the content.	_____	_____	_____	_____
4. I listen for ideas and themes, not isolated facts.	_____	_____	_____	_____
5. I take careful notes to make sure I understand and analyze the message correctly.	_____	_____	_____	_____
6. I really concentrate on what speakers are saying.	_____	_____	_____	_____
7. I stay focused even when the ideas are complex.	_____	_____	_____	_____
8. I keep an open mind despite emotionally charged language.	_____	_____	_____	_____

| Expand Your Knowledge

Exploring the Best of the Web
Make Your Meetings More Productive

www.effectivemeetings.com

From preparing effective agendas to dealing with "meeting addicts," the Effective Meetings website offers advice to make business meetings more productive. Peruse the list of articles and answer the following questions.

1. What are four questions to ask to determine whether a meeting is necessary? (Look under Meeting Basics.)
2. What steps can you take to make sure meetings start and end on schedule? (Look under Meeting Planning.)
3. How can a "scrum meeting" help a team stay on target toward meeting its goals? (Look under Teams.)

Sharpening Your Career Skills Online

Bovée and Thill's Business Communication Web Search, at http://businesscommunicationblog.com/websearch, is a unique research tool designed specifically for business communication research. Use the Web Search function to find an online video, a podcast, or a PowerPoint presentation that offers advice on improving your active listening skills in business situations. Write a brief e-mail message to your instructor, describing the item that you found and summarizing the career skills information you learned from it.

Communicating in a World of Diversity

Learning Objectives

After studying this chapter, you will be able to

1 Discuss the opportunities and challenges of intercultural communication

2 Define *culture* and explain how culture is learned

3 Define *ethnocentrism* and *stereotyping* and give three suggestions for overcoming these limiting mindsets

4 Explain the importance of recognizing cultural variations and list eight categories of cultural differences

5 Identify steps you can take to improve your intercultural communication skills

6 List seven recommendations for writing clearly in multilanguage business environments

Communication Close-up at IBM

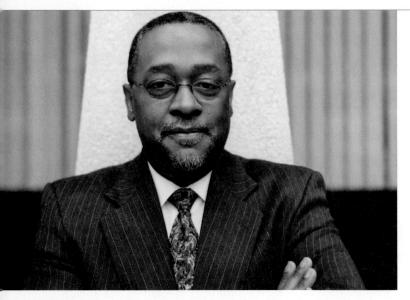

Ron Glover oversees IBM's efforts to build competitive advantage by capitalizing on the benefits of a diverse workforce.

www.ibm.com

The *I* in IBM stands for *International*, but it could just as easily stand for *Intercultural*, as a testament to the computer giant's long-standing commitment to embracing diversity. Ron Glover, IBM's vice president of global workforce diversity, knows from years of experience that communicating successfully across cultures is no simple task, however—particularly in a company that employs more than 350,000 people and sells to customers in roughly 175 countries around the world.

Language presents a formidable barrier to communication when you consider that IBM's employees speak more than 165 languages. But language is just one of many elements that play a role in communication between cultures. Differences in age, ethnic background, gender, sexual orientation, physical ability, and economic status can all affect the communication process. Glover emphasizes that "to operate successfully, we must be especially mindful of how we respect and value differences among people in countries and regions." He recognizes that these differences represent both a challenge and an opportunity, and a key part of his job is helping IBM executives and employees work together in a way that transforms their cultural differences into a critical business strength. Diversity, he explains, is "an essential aspect of IBM's broader business strategy."

Throughout its long history of employing and working with people from a variety of cultures, IBM has learned some powerful lessons. Perhaps the most significant is its conclusion that successfully managing a diverse workforce and competing in a diverse marketplace starts with embracing those differences, not trying to ignore them or pretending they don't affect interpersonal communication. Take Ron Glover's advice when he says that even if your company never does business outside the United States, "you will need to effectively engage differences to remain viable in the economy of the future."[1]

UNDERSTANDING THE OPPORTUNITIES AND CHALLENGES OF COMMUNICATION IN A DIVERSE WORLD

IBM's experience (profiled in the chapter-opening Communication Close-up) illustrates both the challenges and the opportunities for business professionals who know how to communicate with diverse audiences. Although the concept is often framed in terms of ethnic background, a broader and more useful definition of **diversity** "includes all the characteristics and experiences that define each of us as individuals."[2] As you'll learn in this chapter, these characteristics and experiences can have a profound effect on the way businesspeople communicate.

Diversity includes all the characteristics that define people as individuals.

Intercultural communication is the process of sending and receiving messages between people whose cultural backgrounds could lead them to interpret verbal and nonverbal signs differently. Every attempt to send and receive messages is influenced by culture, so to communicate successfully, you need a basic grasp of the cultural differences you may encounter and how you should handle them. Your efforts to recognize and bridge cultural differences will open up business opportunities throughout the world and maximize the contributions of all the employees in a diverse workforce.

The Opportunities in a Global Marketplace

You might be a business manager looking for new customers or fresh talent. You might be an employee looking for new work opportunities. Either way, chances are good that you'll be looking across international borders sometime in your career.

Thanks to communication and transportation technologies, natural boundaries and national borders are no longer the impassable barriers they once were. Local markets are opening to worldwide competition as businesses of all sizes look for new growth opportunities outside their own countries. Thousands of U.S. businesses depend on exports for significant portions of their revenues. Every year, these companies export hundreds of billions of dollars worth of materials and merchandise, along with billions more in personal and professional services. If you work in one of these companies, you may well be called on to visit or at least communicate with a wide variety of people who speak languages other than English and who live in cultures quite different from what you're used to (see Figure 3.1). Of the top 10 export markets for U.S. products, only two, Canada and Great Britain, speak English as an official language—and Canada also has French as an official language.[3]

1 LEARNING OBJECTIVE

Discuss the opportunities and challenges of intercultural communication

You will communicate with people from other cultures throughout your career.

The Advantages of a Diverse Workforce

Even if you never visit another country or transact business on a global scale, you will interact with colleagues from a variety of cultures, with a wide range of characteristics and life experiences. Over the past few decades, many innovative companies have changed the way they approach diversity, from seeing it as a legal requirement (providing equal opportunities for all) to seeing it as a strategic opportunity to connect with customers and take advantage of the broadest possible pool of talent.[4] Smart business leaders such as IBM's Ron Glover recognize the competitive advantages of a diverse workforce that offers a broader spectrum of viewpoints and ideas, helps companies understand and identify with diverse markets, and enables companies to benefit from a wider range of employee talents. According to Glover, more diverse teams tend to be more innovative over the long term than more homogeneous teams.[5]

The diversity of today's workforce brings distinct advantages to businesses:
- *A broader range of views and ideas*
- *A better understanding of diverse, fragmented markets*
- *A broader pool of talent from which to recruit*

FIGURE 3.1 Languages of the World

This map illustrates the incredible array of languages used around the world. Each dot represents the geographic center of one of the more than 6,900 languages tracked by the linguistic research firm SIL International. Even if all your business communication takes place in English, you will interact with audience members who speak a variety of other native languages.

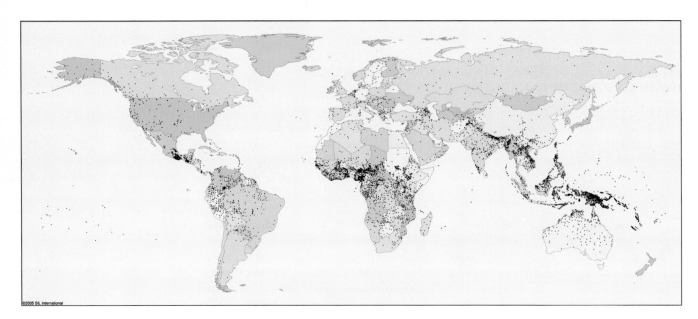

Diversity is simply a fact of life for all companies. The United States has been a nation of immigrants from the beginning, and that trend continues today. The western and northern Europeans who made up the bulk of immigrants during the United States' early years now share space with people from across Asia, Africa, eastern Europe, and other parts of the world. Even the term *minority*, as it applies to nonwhite residents, makes less and less sense every year: In two states (California and New Mexico), in several dozen large cities, and in several hundred counties across the United States, Caucasian Americans make up less than half the population.[6] This pattern of immigration isn't unique to the United States. For example, workers from Africa, Asia, and the Middle East are moving to Europe in search of new opportunities, while workers from India, the Philippines, and Southeast Asia contribute to the employment base of the Middle East.[7]

However, you and your colleagues don't need to be recent immigrants to constitute a diverse workforce. Differences in everything from age and gender to religion and ethnic heritage to geography and military experience enrich the workplace. Both immigration and workforce diversity create advantages—and challenges—for business communicators throughout the world.

The Challenges of Intercultural Communication

A company's cultural diversity affects how its business messages are conceived, composed, delivered, received, and interpreted.

Today's increasingly diverse workforce encompasses a wide range of skills, traditions, backgrounds, experiences, outlooks, and attitudes toward work—all of which can affect communication in the workplace. Supervisors face the challenge of connecting with these diverse employees, motivating them, and fostering cooperation and harmony among them. Teams face the challenge of working together closely, and companies are challenged to coexist peacefully with business partners and with the community as a whole.

Culture influences everything about communication, including
* *Language*
* *Nonverbal signals*
* *Word meaning*
* *Time and space issues*
* *Rules of human relationships*

The interaction of culture and communication is so pervasive that separating the two is virtually impossible. The way you communicate—from the language you speak and the nonverbal signals you send to the way you perceive other people—is influenced by the culture in which you were raised. The meaning of words, the significance of gestures, the importance of time and space, the rules of human relationships—these and many other aspects of communication are defined by culture. To a large degree, your culture influences the way you think, which naturally affects the way you communicate as both a sender and a receiver.[8] So you can see that intercultural communication is much more complicated than simply matching language between sender and receiver. It goes beyond mere words to beliefs, values, and emotions.

Think back to the communication process model you studied in Chapter 1 (page 44). Elements of human diversity can affect communication at every stage of the communication process, from the ideas a person deems important enough to share to the habits and expectations of giving feedback. In particular, your instinct is to encode your message using the assumptions of *your* culture. However, members of your audience decode your message according to the assumptions of *their* culture. The greater the difference between cultures, the greater the chance for misunderstanding.[9] For example, the American-made movie *Hollywood Buddha* was advertised with posters showing the star of the movie sitting on the head of a statue of Buddha. Such a depiction may have few spiritual implications for non-Buddhists, but it was a serious insult to many Buddhists—so much

Communication among people of diverse cultural backgrounds and life experiences is not always easy, but doing it successfully can create tremendous strategic advantages.

so that Buddhists in a number of countries took to the streets in protest, and the government of Thailand (where Buddhism is the predominant religion) was prompted to create a guidebook to help foreigners understand and respect Thai culture.[10]

Throughout this chapter, you'll see numerous examples of how communication styles and habits vary from one culture to another. These examples are intended to illustrate the major themes of intercultural communication, not to give an exhaustive list of styles and habits of any particular culture. With an understanding of these major themes, you'll be prepared to explore the specifics of any culture.

ENHANCING YOUR SENSITIVITY TO CULTURE AND DIVERSITY

The good news is that you're already an expert in culture, at least in the culture in which you grew up. You understand how your society works, how people are expected to communicate, what common gestures and facial expressions mean, and so on. The bad news is that because you're such an expert in your own culture, your communication is largely automatic; that is, you rarely stop to think about the communication rules you're following. An important step toward successful intercultural communication is becoming more aware of these rules and of the way they influence your communication.

Understanding the Concept of Culture

Culture is a shared system of symbols, beliefs, attitudes, values, expectations, and norms for behavior. Your cultural background influences the way you prioritize what is important in life, helps define your attitude toward what is appropriate in a situation, and establishes rules of behavior.[11]

Actually, you belong to several cultures. In addition to the culture you share with all the people who live in your own country, you belong to other cultural groups, including an ethnic group, possibly a religious group, and perhaps a profession that has its own special language and customs. With its large population and long history of immigration, the United States is home to a vast array of cultures. As one indication of this diversity, the inhabitants of this country now speak more than 160 languages.[12] In contrast, Japan is much more homogeneous, having only a few distinct cultural groups.[13]

Members of a given culture tend to have similar assumptions about how people should think, behave, and communicate, and they all tend to act on those assumptions in much the

2 LEARNING OBJECTIVE

Define *culture* and explain how culture is learned

Culture is a shared system of symbols, beliefs, attitudes, values, expectations, and behavior norms.

You belong to several cultures, each of which affects the way you communicate.

same way. Cultures can differ widely and vary in their rate of change, their degree of complexity, and their tolerance toward outsiders. These differences affect the level of trust and openness that you can achieve when communicating with people of other cultures.

You learn culture both directly (by being instructed) and indirectly (by observing others).

People learn culture directly and indirectly from other members of their group. As you grow up in a culture, you are taught by the group's members who you are and how best to function in that culture. Sometimes you are explicitly told which behaviors are acceptable; at other times you learn by observing which values work best in a particular group. In these ways, culture is passed on from person to person and from generation to generation.[14]

Cultures tend to offer views of life that are both coherent (internally logical) and complete (answer all of life's big questions).

In addition to being automatic, culture tends to be *coherent*; that is, a culture appears to be fairly logical and consistent when viewed from the inside. Certain norms within a culture may not make sense to someone outside the culture, but they probably make sense to those inside. Such coherence generally helps a culture function more smoothly internally, but it can create disharmony between cultures that don't view the world in the same way.

Finally, cultures tend to be *complete*; that is, they provide most of their members with most of the answers to life's big questions. This idea of completeness dulls or even suppresses curiosity about life in other cultures. Not surprisingly, such completeness can complicate communication with other cultures.[15]

3 LEARNING OBJECTIVE

Define *ethnocentrism* and *stereotyping* and give three suggestions for overcoming these limiting mindsets

Ethnocentrism is the tendency to judge other groups according to the standards, behaviors, and customs of one's own group.

Stereotyping is assigning generalized attributes to an individual on the basis of membership in a particular group.

Cultural pluralism is the acceptance of multiple cultures on their own terms.

You can avoid ethnocentrism and stereotyping by avoiding assumptions and judgments and by accepting differences.

Overcoming Ethnocentrism and Stereotyping

Ethnocentrism is the tendency to judge other groups according to the standards, behaviors, and customs of one's own group. Given the automatic influence of one's own culture, when people compare their culture to others, they often conclude that their own group is superior.[16] An even more extreme reaction is **xenophobia**, a fear of strangers and foreigners. Clearly, businesspeople who take these views are not likely to communicate successfully across cultures.

Distorted views of other cultures or groups also result from **stereotyping**, assigning a wide range of generalized attributes to an individual on the basis of membership in a particular culture or social group. For instance, assuming that an older colleague will be out of touch with the youth market or that a younger colleague can't be an inspiring leader are examples of stereotyping age groups.

Those who want to show respect for other people and to communicate effectively in business need to adopt a more positive viewpoint, in the form of **cultural pluralism**—the practice of accepting multiple cultures on their own terms. When crossing cultural boundaries, you'll be even more effective if you move beyond simple acceptance and adapt your communication style to that of the new cultures you encounter—even integrating aspects of those cultures into your own.[17] A few simple habits can help:

- **Avoiding assumptions.** Don't assume that others will act the same way you do, use language and symbols the same way you do, or even operate from the same values and beliefs. For instance, in a comparison of the 10 most important values in three cultures, people from the United States had *no* values in common with people from Japanese or Arab cultures.[18]
- **Avoiding judgments.** When people act differently, don't conclude that they are in error or that their way is invalid or inferior.
- **Acknowledging distinctions.** Don't ignore the differences between another person's culture and your own.

Unfortunately, overcoming ethnocentrism and stereotyping is not a simple task, even for people who are highly motivated to do so. Moreover, research suggests that people often have beliefs and biases that they're not even aware of—and that may even conflict with the beliefs they *think* they have. (To see if you have some of these *implicit beliefs*, visit the Project Implicit website, at https://implicit.harvard.edu/implicit, and take some of the simple online tests.)[19]

4 LEARNING OBJECTIVE

Explain the importance of recognizing cultural variations and list eight categories of cultural differences

Recognizing Variations in a Diverse World

You can begin to learn how people in other cultures want to be treated by recognizing and accommodating eight main types of cultural differences: contextual, legal and ethical, social, nonverbal, age, gender, religious, and ability.

COMMUNICATING ACROSS CULTURES

Test Your Intercultural Knowledge

Even well-intentioned businesspeople can make mistakes if they aren't aware of simple but important cultural differences. Can you spot the erroneous assumptions in these scenarios?

1. You're tired of the discussion, and you want to move on to a new topic. You ask your Australian business associate, "Can we table this for a while?" To your dismay, your colleague ignores the request and keeps right on discussing the topic.

2. You finally made the long trip overseas to meet the new director of your German division. Despite slow traffic, you arrive only four minutes late. His door is shut, so you knock on it and walk in. The chair is too far away from the desk, so you pick it up and move it closer. Then you lean over the desk, stick out your hand and say, "Good morning, Hans. It's nice to meet you." Why is his reaction so chilly?

3. Your meeting went better than you'd ever expected. In fact, you found the Japanese representative for your new advertising agency to be very agreeable; she said yes to just about everything. When you share your enthusiasm with your boss, he doesn't appear very excited. Why?

Here's what went wrong in each situation:

1. To "table" something in Australia means to bring it forward for discussion, the opposite of the usual U.S. meaning.

2. You've just broken four rules of German polite behavior: punctuality, privacy, personal space, and proper greetings. In time-conscious Germany, guests should never arrive even a few minutes late. Also, Germans like their privacy and space, and many adhere to formal greetings of "Frau" and "Herr," even if the business association has lasted for years.

3. The word *yes* may not always mean "yes" in the Western sense. Japanese people may say *yes* to confirm that they have heard or understood something but not necessarily to indicate that they agree with it. You'll seldom get a direct no. Some of the ways that Japanese people say no indirectly include "It will be difficult," "I will ask my supervisor," "I'm not sure," "We will think about it," and "I see."

CAREER APPLICATIONS

1. Have you ever been on the receiving end of an intercultural communication error, such as when someone inadvertently used an inappropriate gesture or figure of speech? How did you respond?

2. After arriving late at the office of the German colleague, what would have been a better way to handle the situation?

Contextual Differences

Every attempt at communication occurs within a **cultural context**, the pattern of physical cues, environmental stimuli, and implicit understanding that convey meaning between two members of the same culture. However, cultures around the world vary widely in the role that context plays in communication (see Figure 3.2).

In a **high-context culture**, people rely less on verbal communication and more on the context of nonverbal actions and environmental setting to convey meaning. For instance, a Chinese speaker expects the receiver to discover the essence of a message and uses indirectness and metaphor to provide a web of meaning.[20] In high-context cultures, the rules of everyday life are rarely explicit; instead, as individuals grow up, they learn how to recognize situational cues (such as gestures and tone of voice) and how to respond as expected.[21] The primary role of communication is building relationships, not exchanging information.[22]

In a **low-context culture**, people rely more on verbal communication and less on circumstances and cues to convey meaning. In such cultures, rules and expectations are usually spelled out through explicit statements such as "Please wait until I'm finished" or "You're welcome to browse."[23] The primary task of communication in low-context cultures is exchanging information.[24]

Contextual differences are apparent in the way people approach situations such as decision making, problem solving, and negotiating. For instance, in low-context cultures, businesspeople tend to focus on the results of the decisions they face, a reflection of the cultural emphasis on logic and progress (for example, "Will this be good for our company? For my career?"). In comparison, higher-context cultures emphasize the means or the method by which a decision will be made. Building or protecting relationships can be as important as the facts and information used in making the decisions.[25] Consequently, negotiators working on business deals in such cultures may spend most of their time together building relationships rather than hammering out contractual details.

Cultural context is a pattern of physical cues, environmental stimuli, and implicit understanding that conveys meaning between members of the same culture.

High-context cultures rely heavily on nonverbal actions and environmental setting to convey meaning; low-context cultures rely more on explicit verbal communication.

Low-context cultures tend to value written agreements and interpret laws strictly, whereas high-context cultures view adherence to laws as being more flexible.

FIGURE 3.2 How Cultural Context Affects Business
Cultural context influences the nature of business communication in many ways. Note that these are generalized assessments of each culture; contextual variations can be found within each culture and from one individual to another.

IN LOW-CONTEXT CULTURES	IN HIGH-CONTEXT CULTURES
Executive offices are separate with controlled access.	Executive offices are shared and open to all.
Workers rely on detailed background information.	Workers do not expect or want detailed information.
Information is highly centralized and controlled.	Information is shared with everyone.
Objective data are valued over subjective relationships.	Subjective relationships are valued over objective data.
Business and social relationships are discrete.	Business and social relationships overlap.
Competence is valued as much as position and status.	Position and status are valued much more than competence.
Meetings have fixed agendas and plenty of advance notice.	Meetings are often called on short notice, and key people always accept.

Swiss German · German · Scandinavian · American · French · British · Italian · Spanish · Greek · Arab · Chinese · Japanese

Low-context cultures ←——————————————————————→ High-context cultures

The distinctions between high and low context are generalizations, of course, but they are important to keep in mind as guidelines. Communication tactics that work well in a high-context culture may backfire in a low-context culture and vice versa.

Legal and Ethical Differences

Cultural context influences legal and ethical behavior, which in turn can affect communication. For example, because low-context cultures value the written word, they consider written agreements binding. But high-context cultures put less emphasis on the written word and consider personal pledges more important than contracts. They also tend to take a more flexible approach regarding adherence to the law, whereas low-context cultures adhere to the law strictly.[26]

Honesty and respect are cornerstones of ethical communication, regardless of culture.

As you conduct business around the world, you'll find that both legal systems and ethical standards differ from culture to culture. Making ethical choices across cultures can seem complicated, but you can keep your messages ethical by applying four basic principles:[27]

- **Actively seek mutual ground.** To allow the clearest possible exchange of information, both parties must be flexible and avoid insisting that an interaction take place strictly in terms of one culture or another.
- **Send and receive messages without judgment.** To allow information to flow freely, both parties must recognize that values vary from culture to culture, and they must trust each other.
- **Send messages that are honest.** To ensure that information is true, both parties must see things as they are—not as they would like them to be. Both parties must be fully aware of their personal and cultural biases.
- **Show respect for cultural differences.** To protect the basic human rights of both parties, each must understand and acknowledge the other's needs and preserve each other's dignity by communicating without deception.

REAL-TIME UPDATES
Learn More

Video guide puts culture in context

Enjoy a pictorial tour of cultures around the world as you learn more about communication across the spectrum of cultural context. Go to **http://real-timeupdates.com/bct** and click on "Learn More." If you are using mybcommlab, you can access Real-Time Updates within each chapter or under Student Study Tools.

Social Differences

The nature of social behavior varies among cultures, sometimes dramatically. Wal-Mart learned this lesson the hard way when the giant retailer tried to expand into Germany. Store clerks resisted the company requirement of always smiling at customers—a cornerstone of customer relationship strategies in the United States—because customers sometimes misinterpreted smiling as flirting. Wal-Mart dropped the requirement but, after a number of other cultural and strategic missteps, eventually left the German market.[28]

Some behavioral rules are formal and specifically articulated (table manners are a good example), and others are informal and learned over time (such as the comfortable distance to stand from a colleague during a discussion). The combination of formal and informal rules influences the overall behavior of most people in a society most of the time. In addition to the factors already discussed, social norms can vary from culture to culture in the following areas:

Formal rules of etiquette are explicit and well defined, but informal rules are learned through observation and imitation.

- **Attitudes toward work and success.** Many U.S. citizens hold the view that material comfort earned by individual effort is a sign of superiority and that people who work hard are better than those who don't. This view is reflected in the number of hours that U.S. employees work every year.
- **Roles and status.** Culture dictates, or at least tries to dictate, the roles that people play, including who communicates with whom, what they communicate, and in what way. For example, in some countries women still don't play a prominent role in business, so women executives who visit these countries may find that they're not taken seriously as businesspeople.[29] Culture also dictates how people show respect and signify rank. For example, people in the United States show respect by addressing top managers as "Mr. Roberts" or "Ms. Gutierrez." However, people in China are addressed according to their official titles, such as "President" or "Manager."[30]

Respect and rank are reflected differently from culture to culture in the way people are addressed and in their working environment.

- **Use of manners.** What is polite in one culture may be considered rude in another. For instance, asking a colleague "How was your weekend?" is a common way of making small talk in the United States, but the question sounds intrusive to people in cultures in which business and private lives are seen as totally separate. Research a country's expectations before you visit and watch carefully and learn after you arrive.

The rules of polite behavior vary from country to country.

- **Concepts of time.** People in high-context cultures see time as a way to plan the business day efficiently, often focusing on only one task during each scheduled period and viewing time as a limited resource. However, executives from low-context cultures often see time as more flexible. Meeting a deadline is less important than building a business relationship.[31] Trying to coax a team into staying on a strict schedule would be an attractive attribute in U.S. companies but could be viewed as pushy and overbearing in other cultures.

Attitudes toward time, such as strict adherence to meeting schedules, vary throughout the world.

- **Future orientation.** Successful companies tend to have a strong *future orientation*, planning for and investing in the future, but national cultures around the world vary widely in this viewpoint (see Figure 3.3). Some societies encourage a long-term outlook that emphasizes planning and investing—making sacrifices in the short term for the promise of better outcomes in the future. Others are oriented more toward the present, even to the point of viewing the future as hopelessly remote and not worth planning for.[32]
- **Openness and inclusiveness.** At both the national level and within smaller groups, cultures vary on how open they are to accepting people from other cultures and people who don't necessarily fit the prevailing norms within the culture. An unwillingness to accommodate others can range from outright exclusion to subtle pressures to conform to majority expectations. IBM has long been a leader in the effort to create an inclusive environment that ensures fair opportunities for both employees and external business partners. Executive-led task forces at the company represent women; Asian American, African American, Hispanic American, and Native American people; people with disabilities; and gay, lesbian, bisexual, and transgender employees. Diversity is embraced at the employee level through more than 100 networking groups that unite people who have a variety of talents and interests.[33]

Cultures around the world exhibit varying degrees of openness toward outsiders and people whose personal identities don't align with prevailing social norms.

FIGURE 3.3 Future Orientation and National Competitiveness
Countries vary widely in the degree to which they are willing to embrace and invest in the future. As this graph shows, there appears to be a strong correlation between a country's future orientation and its ability to compete in global markets. A culture's attitude about the future is one of several social elements that influence the communication process.

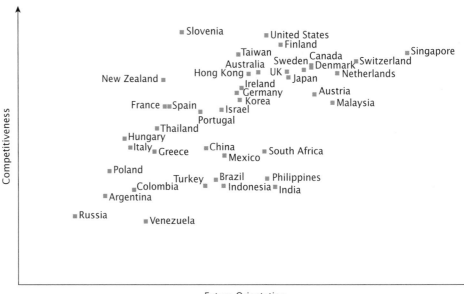

Future Orientation
(cultural support for delayed gratification, planning, and investment)

Nonverbal Differences

The meanings of nonverbal signals vary widely from culture to culture, so you can't rely on assumptions.

As discussed in Chapter 2, nonverbal communication can be a reliable guide to determining the meaning of a message—but this holds true only if the sender and receiver assign the same meaning to nonverbal signals. For instance, the simplest hand gestures have different meanings in different cultures. A gesture that communicates good luck in Brazil is the equivalent of giving someone "the finger" in Colombia.[34] Don't assume that the gestures you grew up with will translate to another culture; doing so could lead to embarrassing mistakes (see Figure 3.4).

When you have the opportunity to interact with people in another culture, the best advice is to study the culture in advance and then observe the way people behave in the following areas:

- **Greetings.** Do people shake hands, bow, or kiss lightly (on one side of the face or both)? Do people shake hands only when first introduced and every time they say hello or good-bye?
- **Personal space.** When people are conversing, do they stand closer together or farther away than you are accustomed to?
- **Touching.** Do people touch each other on the arm to emphasize a point or slap each other on the back to show congratulations? Or do they refrain from touching altogether?
- **Facial expressions.** Do people shake their heads to indicate "no" and nod them to indicate "yes"? This is what people are accustomed to in the United States, but it is not universal.
- **Eye contact.** Do people make frequent eye contact or avoid it? Frequent eye contact is often taken as a sign of honesty and openness in the United States, but in other cultures it can be a sign of aggressiveness or lack of respect.
- **Posture.** Do people slouch and relax in the office and in public, or do they sit up and stand up straight?
- **Formality.** In general, does the culture seem more or less formal than yours?

FIGURE 3.4   Avoiding Nonverbal Mishaps

The smile is about the only nonverbal gesture that has the same meaning in all cultures. But even a simple smile isn't all that simple. People in many cultures do not smile at strangers as much as people in the United States do, so travelers from the United States are sometimes put off by what they consider unfriendly responses from strangers. Conversely, people from other cultures can be put off by the U.S. habit of frequent smiling, which some view as insincere.

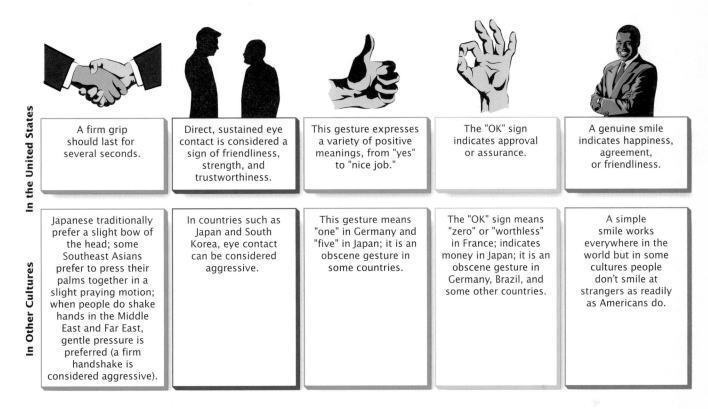

	In the United States	In Other Cultures
	A firm grip should last for several seconds.	Japanese traditionally prefer a slight bow of the head; some Southeast Asians prefer to press their palms together in a slight praying motion; when people do shake hands in the Middle East and Far East, gentle pressure is preferred (a firm handshake is considered aggressive).
	Direct, sustained eye contact is considered a sign of friendliness, strength, and trustworthiness.	In countries such as Japan and South Korea, eye contact can be considered aggressive.
	This gesture expresses a variety of positive meanings, from "yes" to "nice job."	This gesture means "one" in Germany and "five" in Japan; it is an obscene gesture in some countries.
	The "OK" sign indicates approval or assurance.	The "OK" sign means "zero" or "worthless" in France; indicates money in Japan; it is an obscene gesture in Germany, Brazil, and some other countries.
	A genuine smile indicates happiness, agreement, or friendliness.	A simple smile works everywhere in the world but in some cultures people don't smile at strangers as readily as Americans do.

Following the lead of people who grew up in the culture is not only a great way to learn but a good way to show respect as well.

Age Differences

In U.S. culture, youth is associated with strength, energy, possibilities, and freedom. In contrast, age is often associated with declining powers and a loss of respect and authority. However, older workers can offer broader experience, the benefits of important business relationships nurtured over many years, and high degrees of "practical intelligence"—the ability to solve complex, poorly defined problems.[35]

In contrast, in cultures that value age and seniority, longevity earns respect and increasing power and freedom. For instance, in many Asian societies, the oldest employees hold the most powerful jobs, the most impressive titles, and the greatest degrees of freedom and decision-making authority. If a younger employee disagrees with one of these senior executives, the discussion is never conducted in public. The notion of "saving face," of avoiding public embarrassment, is too strong. Instead, if a senior person seems to be in error about something, other employees will find a quiet, private way to communicate whatever information they feel is necessary.[36]

In addition to cultural values associated with various life stages, the multiple generations within a culture present another dimension of diversity. Today's workplaces can have as many as four distinct generations working side by side, generally defined as *traditionalists* (those born before 1946), *baby boomers* (born between 1946 and 1964), *generation X* (born between 1965 and 1980), and *generation Y* (born after 1980).[37] Each of these generations has been shaped by dramatically different world events and social trends, so it is not surprising

A culture's views on youth and aging affect how people communicate with one another.

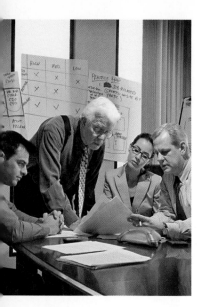

Communication styles and expectations can vary widely among age groups, putting extra demands on teams that include workers of varying ages.

Broadly speaking, men tend to emphasize content in their messages, and woman tend to emphasize relationship maintenance.

that they often have different values, expectations, and communication habits. As with all other cultural matters, success in building bridges starts with understanding the gaps between the two sides.

Gender Differences

The perception of men and women in business varies from culture to culture, and these differences can affect communication efforts. In some cultures, men hold most or all positions of authority, and women are expected to play a more subservient role. Female executives who visit these cultures may not be taken seriously until they successfully handle challenges to their knowledge, capabilities, and patience.[38]

As more women enter the workforce and take on positions of increasing responsibility, enlightened company leaders are making a point to examine past assumptions and practices.[39] For instance, company cultures that have been dominated by men for years may have adopted communication habits that some women have difficulty relating to—such as the frequent use of sports metaphors or the acceptance of coarse language.

Whatever the culture, evidence suggests that men and women tend to have slightly different communication styles. Broadly speaking, men tend to emphasize content in their communication efforts, whereas women place a higher premium on relationship maintenance.[40] This difference can create friction when two parties in a conversation have different needs and expectations from the interchange. Again, these are broad generalizations that do not apply to every person in every situation, but keeping them in mind can help men and women overcome communication hurdles in the workplace.

Religious Differences

Religion is a dominant force in many cultures and the source of many differences between cultures.[41] The effort to accommodate employees' life interests on a broader scale has led a number of companies to address the issue of religion in the workplace. As one of the most personal and influential aspects of life, religion brings potential for controversy in a work setting. On the one hand, some employees feel they should be able to express their beliefs in the workplace and not be forced to "check their faith at the door" when they come to work. On the other hand, companies want to avoid situations in which openly expressed religious differences cause friction between employees or distract employees from their responsibilities. To help address such concerns, firms such as Ford, Intel, Texas Instruments, and American Airlines allow employees to form faith-based employee support groups as part of their diversity strategies. In contrast, Procter & Gamble is among the companies that don't allow organized religious activities at their facilities.[42]

U.S. law requires employers to accommodate employees' religious beliefs to a reasonable degree.

Religion in the workplace is a complex and contentious issue—and it's getting more so every year, at least as measured by a significant rise in the number of religious discrimination lawsuits.[43] Beyond accommodating individual beliefs to a reasonable degree, as required by U.S. law, companies occasionally need to resolve situations that pit one group of employees against another or against the company's policies.[44] As more companies work to establish inclusive workplaces, and as more employees seek to integrate religious convictions into their daily work, you can expect to see this issue being discussed at many companies in the coming years.

Ability Differences

Assistive technologies help employers create more inclusive workplaces and benefit from the contributions of people with physical or cognitive impairments.

Colleagues and customers with disabilities that affect communication represent an important aspect of the diversity picture. People whose hearing, vision, cognitive ability, or physical ability to operate computers is impaired can be at a significant disadvantage in today's workplace. As with other elements of diversity, success starts with respect for individuals and sensitivity to differences. Employers can also invest in a variety of *assistive technologies* that help people with disabilities perform activities that might otherwise be difficult or impossible. These technologies include devices and systems that help people communicate orally and visually, interact with computers and other equipment, and enjoy greater mobility in the workplace. For example, designers can emphasize *web accessibility*, taking steps to make websites more accessible to people whose vision is limited. Assistive technologies create a vital link for thousands of employees with disabilities, giving them opportunities to pursue a greater range of career paths and giving employers access to a broader base of talent. With the United States heading for a potentially serious shortage of workers in a few years, the economy will need all the workers who can make a contribution, and assistive technologies will be an important part of the solution.[45]

Adapting to Other Business Cultures

Culture is obviously a complex topic that requires a lifetime commitment to learning and growth. You'll find a variety of specific tips in "Improving Intercultural Communication Skills," starting on page 108, but here are four general guidelines that can help all business communicators improve their cultural competency:

- **Become aware of your own biases.** Successful intercultural communication requires more than just an understanding of the other party's culture; you need to understand your own culture and the way it shapes your communication habits.[46] For instance, knowing that you value independence and individual accomplishment will help you communicate more successfully in a culture that values consensus and group harmony.
- **Ignore the "Golden Rule."** You probably heard this growing up: "Treat people the way you want to be treated." The problem with the Golden Rule is that people *don't* always want to be treated the same way you want to be treated, particularly across cultural boundaries. The best approach: Treat people the way *they* want to be treated.
- **Exercise tolerance, flexibility, and respect.** As IBM's Ron Glover puts it, "To the greatest extent possible, we try to manage our people and our practices in ways that are respectful of the core principles of any given country or organization or culture."[47]
- **Practice patience and maintain a sense of humor.** Even the most committed and attuned business professionals can make mistakes in intercultural communication, so it is vital for all parties to be patient with one another. As business becomes ever more global, even the most tradition-bound cultures are learning to deal with outsiders more patiently and overlook occasional cultural blunders.[48] A sense of humor is a helpful asset as well, allowing people to move past awkward and embarrassing moments. When you make a mistake, simply apologize, if appropriate, ask the other person to explain the accepted way, and then move on.

An important step in understanding and adapting to other cultures is to recognize the influences that your own culture has on your communication habits.

Adapting to U.S. Business Culture

If you grew up or live in a culture outside the U.S., you can apply all the concepts and skills in this chapter to help work with companies that have a U.S. business culture. Here are some key points to remember to facilitate business communication with U.S. companies.[49]

The values espoused by U.S. culture include individualism, equality, and privacy.

- **Individualism.** In contrast to cultures that value group harmony and group success, U.S. culture generally expects individuals to succeed by their own efforts, and it rewards individual success. Even though teamwork is emphasized in many companies, competition between individuals is expected and even encouraged in many cases.
- **Equality.** Although the country's historical record on equality has not always been positive, and inequalities still exist, equality is considered a core American value. This applies to race, gender, social background, and even age. To a greater degree than people in many other cultures, Americans believe that every person should be given the opportunity to pursue whatever dreams and goals he or she has in life.
- **Privacy and personal space.** People in the Unites States are accustomed to a fair amount of privacy, and this

REAL-TIME UPDATES
Learn More

Overcoming culture shock

This entertaining five-part video series shares the experience of an Israeli journalist undergoing culture shock when coming to graduate school in New York City, and it offers help and encouragement to anyone living in a new culture for the first time. Go to **http://real-timeupdates.com/bct** and click on "Learn More." If you are using mybcommlab, you can access Real-Time Updates within each chapter or under Student Study Tools.

includes their "personal space" at work. For example, they expect you to knock before entering a closed office and to avoid asking questions about personal beliefs or activities until they get to know you well.

- **Time and schedules.** U.S. businesses value punctuality and the efficient use of time. For instance, meetings are expected to start and end at designated times.
- **Religion.** The United States does not have an official state religion. Many religions are practiced throughout the country, and people are expected to respect each other's beliefs.
- **Communication style.** Communication tends to be direct and focused on content and transactions, not relationships or group harmony.

These are generalizations, of course. Any nation of more than 300 million people will exhibit a wide variety of behaviors. However, following these guidelines will help you succeed in most business communication situations.

5 LEARNING OBJECTIVE

Identify steps you can take to improve your intercultural communication skills

IMPROVING INTERCULTURAL COMMUNICATION SKILLS

Communicating successfully between cultures requires a variety of skills (see Figure 3.5). You can improve your intercultural skills throughout your career by studying other cultures and languages, respecting preferences for communication styles, learning to write and speak

FIGURE 3.5 Components of Successful Intercultural Communication
Communicating in a diverse business environment is not always an easy task, but you can continue to improve your sensitivity and build your skills as you progress in your career.

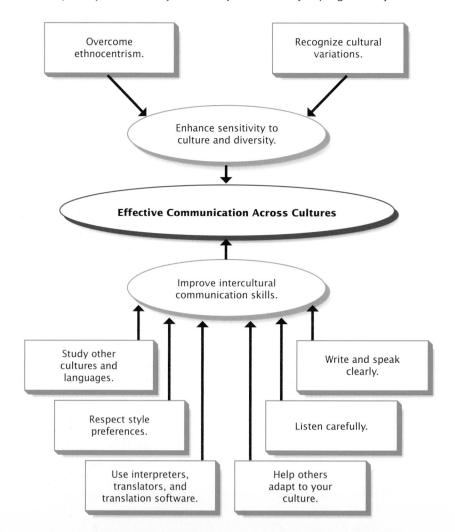

clearly, listening carefully, knowing when to use interpreters and translators, and helping others adapt to your culture.

Studying Other Cultures

Effectively adapting your communication efforts to another culture requires not only knowledge about the culture but also both the ability and the motivation to change your personal habits as needed.[50] Fortunately, you don't need to learn about the whole world all at once. Many companies appoint specialists for specific countries or regions, giving employees a chance to focus on just one culture at a time. Some firms also provide resources to help employees prepare for interaction with other cultures. On IBM's Global Workforce Diversity intranet site, for instance, employees can click on the "GoingGlobal" link to learn about customs in specific cultures.[51]

Even a small amount of research and practice will help you get through many business situations. In addition, most people respond positively to honest effort and good intentions, and many business associates will help you along if you show an interest in learning more about their cultures.

Numerous websites (such as www.culturecrossing.com) and books offer advice on traveling to and working in specific cultures. Also try to sample newspapers, magazines, and even the music and movies of another country. For instance, a movie can demonstrate nonverbal customs even if you don't grasp the language. (However, be careful not to rely solely on entertainment products. If people in other countries based their opinions of U.S. culture only on the silly teen flicks and violent action movies that the United States exports around the globe, what sort of impression do you imagine they'd get?) For some of the key issues to research before doing business in another country, refer to Table 3.1.

Studying Other Languages

Consider what it must be like to work at IBM, where the global workforce speaks more than 165 languages. Without the ability to communicate in more than one language, how could this diverse group of people ever conduct business? As commerce continues to become more globalized, the demand for multilingual communicators continues to grow as well. For instance, with so many U.S. and British companies outsourcing business functions to facilities in India, many Indians now view English skills as an important career asset. Conversely, China's continued growth as a manufacturing powerhouse is prompting many professionals in the United Sates and other countries to learn Mandarin, the official language in China.[52]

A number of U.S. companies are teaching their English-speaking employees a second language to facilitate communication with customers and co-workers. The Target retail chain is among those sponsoring basic Spanish classes for English-speaking supervisors of immigrant employees. Elsewhere around the United States, enrollment is growing in specialized classes such as health-care Spanish and Spanish for professionals.[53] Informal coaching is helpful, too, such as having English- and Spanish-speaking employees teach each other a few business or technical terms every day.[54]

Even if your colleagues or customers in another country speak your language, it's worth the time and energy to learn common phrases in theirs. Learning the basics not only helps you get through everyday business and social situations but also demonstrates your commitment to the business relationship. After all, the other person probably spent years learning your language.

Finally, don't assume that people from two countries who speak the same language speak it the same way. The French spoken in Quebec and other parts of Canada is often noticeably different from the French spoken in France. Similarly, it's often said that the United States and the United Kingdom are two countries divided by a common language. For instance, *period* (punctuation), *elevator*, and *gasoline* in the United States are *full stop*, *lift*, and *petrol* in the United Kingdom.

Successful intercultural communication can require the modification of personal communication habits.

Making an effort to learn about another person's culture is a sign of respect.

English is the most prevalent language in international business, but don't assume that everyone understands it or speaks it the same way.

TABLE 3.1   Doing Business in Other Cultures

ACTION	DETAILS TO CONSIDER
Understand social customs	• How do people react to strangers? Are they friendly? Hostile? Reserved? • How do people greet each other? Should you bow? Nod? Shake hands? • How do you express appreciation for an invitation to lunch, dinner, or someone's home? Should you bring a gift? Send flowers? Write a thank-you note? • Are any phrases, facial expressions, or hand gestures considered rude? • How do you attract the attention of a waiter? Do you tip the waiter? • When is it rude to refuse an invitation? How do you refuse politely? • What topics may or may not be discussed in a social setting? In a business setting? • How do social customs dictate interaction between men and women? Between younger people and older people?
Learn about clothing and food preferences	• What occasions require special clothing? • What colors are associated with mourning? Love? Joy? • Are some types of clothing considered taboo for one gender or the other? • How many times a day do people eat? • How are hands or utensils used when eating? • Where is the seat of honor at a table?
Assess political patterns	• How stable is the political situation? • Does the political situation affect businesses in and out of the country? • Is it appropriate to talk politics in social or business situations?
Understand religious and social beliefs	• To which religious groups do people belong? • Which places, objects, actions, and events are sacred? • Do religious beliefs affect communication between men and women or between any other groups? • Is there a tolerance for minority religions? • How do religious holidays affect business and government activities? • Does religion require or prohibit eating specific foods? At specific times?
Learn about economic and business institutions	• Is the society homogeneous or heterogeneous? • What languages are spoken? • What are the primary resources and principal products? • Are businesses generally large? Family controlled? Government controlled? • What are the generally accepted working hours? • How do people view scheduled appointments? • Are people expected to socialize before conducting business?
Appraise the nature of ethics, values, and laws	• Is money or a gift expected in exchange for arranging business transactions? • Do people value competitiveness or cooperation? • What are the attitudes toward work? Toward money? • Is politeness more important than factual honesty?

Respecting Preferences for Communication Style

Communication style—including the level of directness, the degree of formality, preferences for written versus spoken communication, and other factors—varies widely from culture to culture. Knowing what your communication partners expect can help you adapt to their particular style. Once again, watching and learning are the best ways to improve your skills. However, you can infer some generalities by learning more about the culture. For instance, U.S. workers typically prefer an open and direct communication style; they find other styles frustrating or suspect. Directness is also valued in Sweden as a sign of efficiency; but, unlike with discussions in the United States, heated debates and confrontations are unusual. Italian, German, and French executives don't soften up colleagues with praise before they criticize—doing so seems manipulative to them. However, professionals from high-context cultures, such as Japan or China, tend to be less direct.[55] Finally, in general,

Business Communication 2.0

The Web 2.0 Way to Learn a New Language

Taking classes with a skilled teacher and getting real-life practice while living in another country are proven ways to learn a new language, but what if neither of these options is available to you? Thanks to the growth of social networking technology and other Web 2.0 communication tools, independent language learners now have a multitude of online learning options.

Palabea (www.palabea.net) is a great example of the possibilities of the Web 2.0 approach to learning. By adapting social networking concepts for the unique demands of language learning, this service offers numerous helpful features:

- **Online chat with other language learners.** No matter what language you're trying to learn, someone somewhere in the world speaks it—and is trying to learn your language. Palabea lets you connect and help each other with text, audio, or video chat.
- **Connections to native speakers in your local area.** Palabea can connect you with nearby native speakers of the language you're trying to learn.

- **User-generated content.** Palabea offers a growing collection of podcasts, video lectures, documents, and other learning tools, all contributed by members.
- **Virtual classrooms.** Just as online meeting systems let business colleagues collaborate in real time on reports and other documents, Palabea's virtual classrooms let members meet online to review and correct translations and other projects.

Palabea is just one of many online resources that can help language learners. The Free Language website (http://freelanguage.org) offers links to free resources for several dozen languages.

CAREER APPLICATIONS

1. How could a multinational company such as IBM benefit from the capabilities offered by Palabea and similar websites?
2. As a manager, would you be comfortable having employees use a free service such as Palabea before sending them on important overseas assignments? Why or why not?

---

business correspondence in other countries is often more formal than the style used by U.S. businesspeople (see Figure 3.6).

Writing Clearly

When sending written communication to businesspeople from another culture, familiarize yourself with their written communication preferences and adapt your approach, style, and tone to meet their expectations. Follow these recommendations:[56]

- **Use simple, clear language.** Use precise words that don't have the potential to confuse with multiple meanings. For instance, the word *right* has several dozen different meanings and usages, so look for a synonym that conveys the precise meaning you intend, such as *correct, appropriate, desirable, moral, authentic,* or *privilege*.[57]
- **Be brief.** Use simple sentences and short paragraphs, breaking information into smaller chunks that are easier for your reader to capture and translate. Remember that your messages need to be translated one word at a time.[58]
- **Use transitional elements.** Help readers follow your train of thought by using plenty of transitional words and phrases. Precede related points with expressions such as *in addition* and *first, second,* and *third.*
- **Address international correspondence properly.** Refer to Table A.1 through Table A.5 in Appendix A for an explanation of different address elements and salutations commonly used in certain foreign countries.
- **Cite numbers and dates carefully.** In the United States, 12-05-09 means December 5, 2009, but in many other countries, it means May 12, 2009. Dates in Japan and China are usually expressed with the year first, followed by the month and then the day; therefore, to write December 5, 2009, in Japan, write it as 2009-12-05. Similarly, 1.000 means one with three decimal places in the United States and Great Britain, but it means one thousand in many European countries.

6 LEARNING OBJECTIVE

List seven recommendations for writing clearly in multilanguage business environments

Clarity and simplicity are essential when writing to or speaking with people who don't share your native language.

FIGURE 3.6 Effective German Business Letter (Translated)
In Germany, business letters usually open with a reference to the business relationship and close with a compliment to the recipient. In this letter written by a supplier to a nearby retailer, you can see that the tone is more formal than would typically be used in the United States.

- **Avoid slang, idiomatic phrases, and business jargon.** Everyday speech and writing are full of slang and **idiomatic phrases**, phrases that mean more than the sum of their literal parts. Many of these informal usages are so deeply ingrained, in fact, that you may not even be aware that you're using them. Examples from U.S. English include phrases such as "Off the top of my head" and "More bang for the buck." Your audience may have no idea what you're talking about when you use such phrases.

- **Avoid humor and other references to popular culture.** Jokes and references to popular entertainment usually rely on subtle cultural issues that might be completely unknown to your audience.

Humor does not "travel well" because it usually relies on intimate knowledge of a particular culture.

Although some of these differences may seem trivial, meeting the expectations of an international audience illustrates both knowledge of and respect for the other cultures (see Figure 3.7 and Figure 3.8).

FIGURE 3.7 Ineffective Intercultural Letter
This letter from a U.S. sales representative to a manager in France exhibits several intercultural mistakes, including the informal tone and use of U.S. slang. Compare this with the improved version in Figure 3.8.

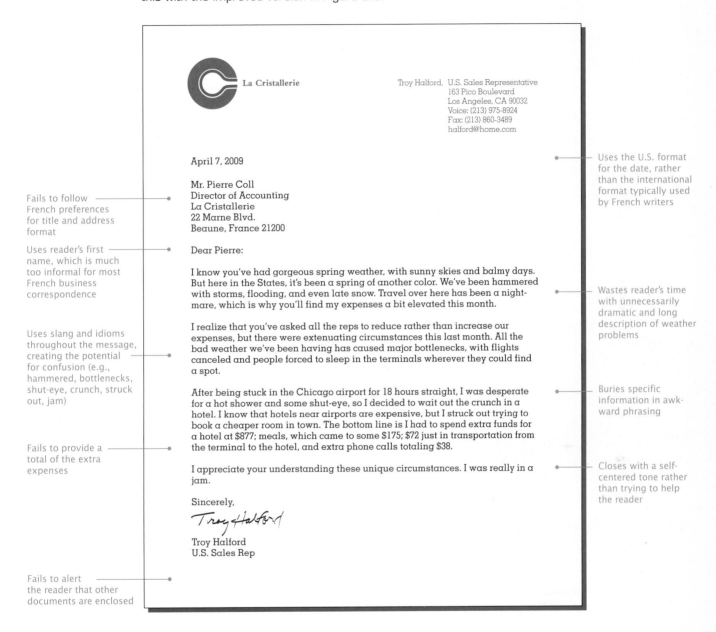

Speaking and Listening Carefully

Languages vary considerably in the significance of tone, pitch, speed, and volume. The English word *progress* can be a noun or a verb, depending on which syllable you accent. In Chinese, the meaning of the word *mà* changes, depending on the speaker's tone; it can mean *mother, pileup, horse,* or *scold.* Routine Arabic speech can sound excited or angry to an English-speaking U.S. listener.[59]

When talking with people whose native language is different from yours, remember that the processing of even everyday conversations can be difficult. For instance, speakers from the United States are notorious for stringing together multiple words into a single, mystifying pseudoword, such as turning "Did you eat yet?" into "Jeetyet?" The French language uses a concept known as *liaison,* in which one word is intentionally joined with the next. Without a lot

FIGURE 3.8 Effective Intercultural Letter

This version of the letter in Figure 3.7 follows French standards for correspondence and is also easier to read and to scan.

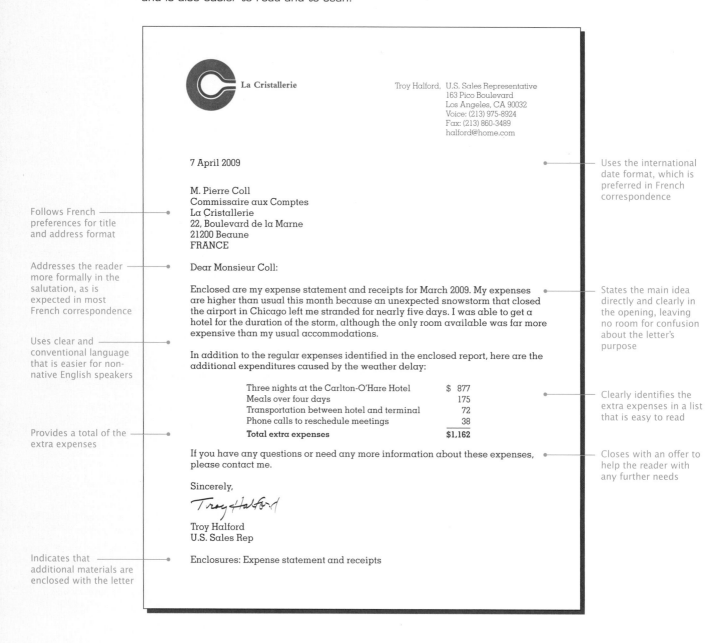

Follows French preferences for title and address format

Addresses the reader more formally in the salutation, as is expected in most French correspondence

Uses clear and conventional language that is easier for non-native English speakers

Provides a total of the extra expenses

Indicates that additional materials are enclosed with the letter

Uses the international date format, which is preferred in French correspondence

States the main idea directly and clearly in the opening, leaving no room for confusion about the letter's purpose

Clearly identifies the extra expenses in a list that is easy to read

Closes with an offer to help the reader with any further needs

---

Speaking clearly and getting plenty of feedback are two of the keys to successful intercultural conversations.

To listen more effectively in intercultural situations, accept what you hear without judgment and let people finish what they have to say.

of practice, new French speakers have a hard time telling when one word ends and the next one begins.

To be more effective in intercultural conversations, remember these tips: (1) Speak slowly and clearly; (2) don't rephrase until it's obviously necessary (immediately rephrasing something you've just said doubles the translation workload for the listener); (3) look for and ask for feedback to make sure your message is getting through; (4) don't talk down to the other person by overenunciating words or oversimplifying sentences; and (5) at the end of the conversation, double-check to make sure you and the listener agree on what has been said and decided.

As a listener, you'll need some practice to get a sense of vocal patterns. The key is simply to accept what you hear first, without jumping to conclusions about meaning or motivation. Let other people finish what they have to say. If you interrupt, you may miss something important. You'll also show a lack of respect. If you do not understand a comment, ask the person to repeat it. Any momentary awkwardness you might feel in asking for extra help is less important than the risk of unsuccessful communication.

Using Interpreters, Translators, and Translation Software

You may encounter business situations that require using an *interpreter* (for spoken communication) or a *translator* (for written communication). Interpreters and translators can be expensive, but skilled professionals provide invaluable assistance for communicating in other cultural contexts.[60] Keeping up with current language usage in a given country or culture is also critical in order to avoid embarrassing blunders. Landor Associates, a leading marketing agency, usually engages three native-language speakers to review translated materials to make sure the sense of the message is compatible with current usage and slang in a given country.[61] Some companies use *back-translation* to ensure accuracy. Once a translator encodes a message into another language, a different translator retranslates the same message into the original language. This back-translation is then compared with the original message to discover any errors or discrepancies.

Experienced international speakers, such as Dr. Eric Schmidt, Google's chairman and CEO, are careful to incorporate culture and language variations into their communication efforts.

The time and cost required for professional translation has encouraged the development of **machine translation**, any form of computerized intelligence used to translate one language to another. Dedicated software tools and online services such as WorldLingo (www.worldlingo.com) offer various forms of automated translation. Major search engines let you request translated versions of the websites you find. Although none of these tools can translate as well as human translators, they can be quite useful with individual words and short phrases, and they can often give you the overall gist of a message.[62]

For important business communication, use a professional interpreter (for oral communication) or translator (for written communication).

Helping Others Adapt to Your Culture

Whether a younger person is unaccustomed to the formalities of a large corporation or a colleague from another country is working on a team with you, look for opportunities to help people fit in and adapt their communication style. For example, if a non-native English speaker is making mistakes that could hurt his or her credibility, you can offer advice on the appropriate words and phrases to use. Most language learners truly appreciate this sort of assistance, as long as it is offered in a respectful manner. Moreover, chances are that while you're helping, you'll learn something about the other person's culture and language, too.

Help others adapt to your culture; doing so will create a more productive workplace and teach you about their cultures as well.

✓ **CHECKLIST** **Improving Intercultural Communication Skills**

- Understand your own culture so that you can recognize its influences on your communication habits.
- Study other cultures so that you can appreciate cultural variations.
- Study the languages of people with whom you communicate, even if you can learn only a few basic words and phrases.
- Help nonnative speakers learn your language.
- Respect cultural preferences for communication style.

- Write clearly, using brief messages, simple language, generous transitions, and appropriate international conventions.
- Avoid slang, humor, and references to popular culture.
- Speak clearly and slowly, giving listeners time to translate your words.
- Ask for feedback to ensure successful communication.
- Listen carefully and ask speakers to repeat anything you don't understand.
- Use interpreters and translators for important messages.

Document Makeover

Improve This Letter

To practice correcting drafts of actual documents, visit the "Document Makeovers" section in either mybcommlab or the Companion Website for this text.

If mybcommlab is being used in your class, see your User Guide for specific instructions on how to access the content for this chapter. If you are accessing this feature through the Companion Website, click on "Document Makeovers" and then select Chapter 3. You will find a letter that contains problems and errors related to what you've learned in this chapter about developing effective intercultural communication skills. Use the Final Draft decision tool to create an improved version of this letter. Check the message for a communication style that keeps the message brief; does not become too familiar or informal; uses transitional elements appropriately; and avoids slang, idioms, jargon, and technical language.

You can also take steps to simplify the communication process. For example, oral communication in a second language is usually more difficult than written forms of communication, so instead of asking a foreign colleague to provide information in a conference call, you could set up an intranet site where the person can file a written report. Similarly, using instant messaging, e-mail, or blogging is often easier for colleagues with different native languages than participating in live conversations.

Whatever assistance you can provide will be greatly appreciated because smart businesspeople recognize the value of intercultural communication skills. Moreover, chances are that while you're helping others, you'll learn something about other cultures, too.

For a brief summary of ideas to improve intercultural communication in the workplace, see "Checklist: Improving Intercultural Communication Skills." For additional information on communicating in a world of diversity, visit http://real-timeupdates.com/bct and click on Chapter 3.

Communication Challenges at IBM

Ron Glover is responsible for overall diversity planning and strategy at IBM, but every manager throughout the company is expected to foster a climate of inclusion and support for employees of every cultural background. As a team leader in one of IBM's software development labs, you're learning to exercise sound business judgment and use good listening skills to help resolve situations that arise within your diverse group of employees. How would you address these challenges?

Individual Challenge: Vasily Pevsner, a Russian immigrant, has worked in the department for five years. He works well alone, but he resists working with other employees, even in team settings where collaboration is expected. Given the importance that you place on teamwork, how should you handle the situation? List several alternatives for addressing this dilemma, identify which one you would choose, and explain why you would choose this one.

Team Challenge: Your employees are breaking into ethnically based cliques. Members of ethnic groups eat together, socialize together, and often chat in their native languages while they work. You appreciate how these groups give their members a sense of community, but you worry that these informal communication channels are alienating nonmembers and fragmenting the flow of information. How can you encourage a stronger sense of community and teamwork across your department? Brainstorm at least three steps you can take to encourage better cross-cultural communication in your group.

SUMMARY OF LEARNING OBJECTIVES

1 **Discuss the opportunities and challenges of intercultural communication.** The global marketplace spans natural boundaries and national borders, allowing worldwide competition between businesses of all sizes. Therefore, today's businesspeople are likely to communicate across international borders with people who live in different cultures. Moreover, even domestic workforces are becoming more and more diverse, with employees having different national, religious, and ethnic backgrounds. In this environment, companies can benefit from a broad range of viewpoints and ideas, get a good understanding of diverse markets, and recruit workers from the broadest possible pool of talent. However, intercultural communication presents challenges as well, including motivating diverse employees to cooperate and to work together in teams as well as understanding enough about how culture affects language to prevent miscommunication.

2 **Define *culture*, and explain how culture is learned.** Culture is a shared system of symbols, beliefs, attitudes, values, expectations, and norms for behavior. Culture is

learned by listening to advice from other members of a society and by observing their behaviors. This double-edged method uses direct and indirect learning to ensure that culture is passed from person to person and from generation to generation.

3 **Define *ethnocentrism* and *stereotyping*, and give three suggestions for overcoming these limiting mindsets.**   Ethnocentrism is the tendency to judge other groups according to the standards, behaviors, and customs of one's own group. Stereotyping is assigning a wide range of generalized attributes to individuals on the basis of their membership in a particular culture or social group, without considering an individual's unique characteristics. To overcome ethnocentrism and stereotyping, follow three suggestions: (1) Avoid assumptions, (2) avoid judgments, and (3) acknowledge distinctions.

4 **Explain the importance of recognizing cultural variations, and list eight categories of cultural differences.**   People from different cultures encode and decode messages differently, increasing the chances of misunderstanding. By recognizing and accommodating cultural differences, we avoid automatically assuming that everyone's thoughts and actions are just like ours. Begin by focusing on eight categories of differences: contextual differences (the degree to which a culture relies on verbal or nonverbal actions to convey meaning), legal and ethical differences (the degree to which laws and ethics are regarded and obeyed), social differences (how members value work and success, recognize status, define manners, and think about time), nonverbal differences (differing attitudes toward greetings, personal space, touching, facial expression, eye contact, posture, and formality), age differences (how members think about youth, seniority, and longevity), gender differences (how men and women communicate), religious differences (how beliefs affect workplace relationships), and ability differences (inclusive strategies that enable people with disabilities to more fully communicate with the rest of the workforce).

5 **Identify the steps you can take to improve your intercultural communication skills.**   Communicating successfully between cultures requires a variety of skills, all of which you can continue to improve throughout your career. Make your intercultural communication effective by studying other cultures; studying other languages; respecting your audience's preferences for communication style; writing as clearly as possible; speaking as clearly as you can; listening carefully; using interpreters, translators, and translation software when necessary; and helping others adapt to your own culture.

6 **List seven recommendations for writing clearly in multilanguage business environments.**   It's important to take extra care with your writing, adapting your approach, style, and tone to meet audience expectations. To write effectively to multilingual audiences, follow these recommendations: (1) Use simple, clear language; (2) be brief; (3) use transitional elements; (4) address international correspondence properly; (5) cite numbers and dates carefully; (6) avoid slang, idiomatic phrases, and unfamiliar jargon; and (7) minimize or avoid humor and references to popular culture.

PEARSON mybcommlab

Log on to **www.mybcommlab.com** to access the following study and assessment aids associated with this chapter:

- Video applications
- Real-Time Updates
- Peer review activity
- Quick Learning Guides

- Pre/post test
- Personalized study plan
- Model documents
- Sample presentations

If you are not using mybcommlab, you can access the Real-Time Updates and Quick Learning Guides through http://real-timeupdates.com/bct. The Quick Learning Guide (located under "Learn More" on the website) hits all the high points of this chapter in just two pages. This guide, especially prepared by the authors, will help you study for exams or review important concepts whenever you need a quick refresher.

Test Your Knowledge

1. How have market globalization and cultural diversity contributed to the increased importance of intercultural communication?
2. What are the potential advantages of a diverse workforce?
3. How do high-context cultures differ from low-context cultures?
4. In addition to contextual differences, what other categories of cultural differences exist?
5. What is ethnocentrism, and how can it be overcome in communication?

6. What four principles apply to ethical intercultural communication?

7. Why is it important to understand your own culture when attempting to communicate with people from other cultures?

8. What are some ways to improve speaking and listening skills when communicating with people of other cultures?

9. What are the risks of using computerized translation when you need to read a document written in another language?

10. What steps can you take to help someone from another culture adapt to your culture?

Apply Your Knowledge

1. What are some of the intercultural differences that managers of a U.S.-based firm might encounter during a series of business meetings with a China-based company whose managers speak English fairly well?

2. What are some of the intercultural communication issues to consider when deciding whether to accept a job in an overseas branch of a U.S. company? How about a job in the United States with a local branch of a foreign-owned firm? Explain.

3. How do you think company managers from a country that has a relatively homogeneous culture might react when they do business with the culturally diverse staff of a company based in a less homogeneous country? Explain your answer.

4. Make a list of the top five priorities in your life (for example, fame, wealth, family, spirituality, peace of mind, individuality, artistic expression). Compare your list with the priorities that appear to be valued in the culture in which you are currently living. (You can be as broad or as narrow as you like in defining *culture* for this exercise, such as overall U.S. culture or culture in your college or university.) Do your personal priorities align with the culture's priorities? If not, how might this disparity affect your communication with other members of the culture?

5. **Ethical Choices** Your office in Turkey desperately needs the supplies that have been sitting in Turkish customs for a month. Should you bribe a customs official to speed up delivery? Explain your decision.

Practice Your Knowledge

Message for Analysis

You are working in a culturally diverse organization in Dubai. Recently, you received new, transferred employees from Jordan, Egypt, and Lebanon. Your boss wants to send an e-mail to all recently transferred employees in your department. The employees understand English, but your boss asks you to review his message for clarity. What changes would you suggest to your boss and why? Would you consider this message to be audience centered? Why or why not? The e-mail is as follows:

> I wanted to welcome you ASAP to our little family here in Dubai. It's high time we shook hands in person and not just across the countries. I'm pleased about getting to know you all, and I will do my level best to see you well in Dubai.

Exercises

Active links for all websites in this chapter can be found online. If mybcommlab is being used in your class, see your User Guide for instructions on accessing the content for this chapter. Otherwise, visit www.pearsonglobaleditions.com/bovee, locate *Business Communication Today*, Tenth Edition, click the Companion Website link, select Chapter 3, and then click on "Featured Websites." Please note that links to sites that become inactive after publication of the book will be removed from the Featured Websites section.

3.1 **Intercultural Sensitivity: Recognizing Variations** You represent a Canadian toy company that's negotiating to buy miniature truck wheels from a manufacturer in Osaka, Japan. In your first meeting, you explain that your company expects to control the design of the wheels as well as the materials that are used to make them. The manufacturer's representative looks down and says softly, "Perhaps that will be difficult." You press for agreement, and to emphasize your willingness to buy, you show the prepared contract you've brought with you. However, the manufacturer seems increasingly vague and uninterested. What cultural differences may be interfering with effective communication in this situation? Explain.

3.2 **Ethical Choices** A U.S. manager wants to ship machine parts to a West African country, but a government official there expects a special payment before allowing the shipment into the country. How can the two sides resolve their different approaches without violating U.S. rules against bribing foreign officials? On the basis of the information presented in Chapter 1, would you consider this situation an ethical dilemma or an ethical lapse? Please explain.

3.3 **Teamwork** Working with two other students, prepare a list of 10 examples of slang (in your own language) that might be misinterpreted or misunderstood during a business conversation with someone from another culture. Next to each example, suggest other words you might use to convey the same message. Do the alternatives mean *exactly* the same as the original slang or idiom?

3.4 **Intercultural Communication: Studying Cultures** Choose a specific country, such as India, Portugal, Bolivia, Thailand, or Nigeria, with which you are not familiar. Research the culture and write a brief summary of what a U.S. manager would need to know about concepts of personal space and rules of social behavior in order to conduct business successfully in that country.

3.5 **Multicultural Workforce: Bridging Differences** Differences in gender, age, and physical abilities contribute to the diversity of today's workforce. Working with a classmate, role-play a conversation in which
a. a woman is being interviewed for a job by a male personnel manager.
b. an older person is being interviewed for a job by a younger personnel manager.

c. an employee who is a native speaker of English is being interviewed for a job by a hiring manager who is a recent immigrant with relatively poor English skills.

How did differences between the applicant and the interviewer shape the communication? What can you do to improve communication in such situations?

3.6   Intercultural Sensitivity: Understanding Attitudes   As the director of marketing for a telecommunications firm based in Germany, you're negotiating with an official in Guangzhou, China, who's in charge of selecting a new telephone system for the city. You insist that the specifications be spelled out in the contract. However, your Chinese counterpart seems to have little interest in technical and financial details. What can you do or say to break this intercultural deadlock and obtain the contract so that both parties are comfortable?

3.7   Cultural Variations: Ability Differences   You are a new manager at K & J Brick, a masonry products company that is now run by the two sons of the man who founded it 50 years ago. For years, the co-owners have invited the management team to a wilderness lodge for a combination of outdoor sports and annual business planning meetings. You don't want to miss the event, but you know that the outdoor activities weren't designed for someone with your physical impairments. Draft a short memo to the rest of the management team, suggesting changes to the annual event that will allow all managers to participate.

3.8   Culture and Time: Dealing with Variations   When a company knows that a scheduled delivery time given by an overseas firm is likely to be flexible, managers may buy in larger quantities or may order more often to avoid running out of product before the next delivery. Identify three other management decisions that may be influenced by differing cultural concepts of time and make notes for a short (two-minute) presentation to your class.

3.9   Intercultural Communication: Using Interpreters   Imagine that you're the lead negotiator for a company that's trying to buy a factory in Prague, the capital of the Czech Republic. Although you haven't spent much time in the country in the past decade, your parents grew up near Prague, so you understand and speak the language fairly well. However, you wonder about the advantages and disadvantages of using an interpreter anyway. For example, you may have more time to think if you wait for an intermediary to translate the other side's position. Decide whether to hire an interpreter and write a brief e-mail message (two or three paragraphs) explaining your decision.

3.10   Internet: Translation Software   Explore the powers and limitations of computer translation at Babel Fish, http://babelfish.yahoo.com. Click on "Translate" and enter a sentence such as "We are enclosing a purchase order for four dozen computer monitors." Select "English to Spanish" and click to complete the translation. Once

you've read the Spanish version, cut and paste it into the "text for translation" box, select "Spanish to English," and click to translate. Try translating the same English sentence into German, French, or Italian and then back into English. How do the results of each translation differ? What are the implications for the use of automated translation services and back-translation? How could you use this website to sharpen your intercultural communication skills? Summarize your findings in a brief report.

3.11   Intercultural Communication: Improving Skills   You've been assigned to host a group of Swedish college students who are visiting your college for the next two weeks. They've all studied English, but this is their first trip to your area. Make a list of at least eight slang terms and idioms they are likely to hear on campus. How will you explain each phrase? When speaking with the Swedish students, what word or words might you substitute for each slang term or idiom?

3.12   Intercultural Communication: Podcasting   Your company was one of the first to use podcasting (see page 225 for more information) as a business communication tool. Executives frequently record messages (such as monthly sales summaries) and post them on the company's intranet site; employees from the 14 offices in Europe, Asia, and North America then download the files to their music players and listen to the messages while riding the train to work, eating lunch at their desks, and so on. Your boss asks you to draft the opening statement for a podcast that will announce a revenue drop caused by intensive competitive pressure. She reviews your script and hands it back with a gentle explanation that it needs to be revised for international listeners. Improve the following statement in as many ways as you can:

> Howdy, comrades. Shouldn't surprise anyone that we took a beating this year, given the insane pricing moves our knucklehead competitors have been making. I mean, how those clowns can keep turning a profit is beyond me, what with steel costs still going through the roof and labor costs heating up—even in countries where everybody goes to find cheap labor—and hazardous waste disposal regs adding to operating costs, too.

Expand Your Knowledge

Exploring the Best of the Web

Cultural Savvy for Competitive Advantage

www.executiveplanet.com

Want to be more competitive when doing business across borders? Executive Planet offers quick introductions to expected business practices in a number of countries, from setting up appointments to giving gifts to negotiating deals. Visit www.executiveplanet.com and browse the country reports to answer the following questions.

1. What sort of clothes should you pack for a business trip to Mexico that will include both meetings and social events?
2. You've been trying to sell your products to a Saudi Arabian company whose executives treat you to an extravagant evening of dining and entertainment. Can you take this as a positive sign that they're likely to buy from you?
3. You collect antique clocks as a hobby, and you plan to give one of your favorites to the president of a Chinese company you plan to visit. Would such a gift likely help or hurt your relationship with this person?

Sharpening Your Career Skills Online

Bovée and Thill's Business Communication Web Search, at http://businesscommunicationblog.com/websearch, is a unique research tool designed specifically for business communication research. Use the Web Search function to find a website, video, podcast, or PowerPoint presentation that offers advice on communicating with business contacts in another country or culture. Write a brief e-mail message to your instructor, describing the item that you found and summarizing the career skills information you learned from it.

Part 2

Applying the Three-Step Writing Process

Every professional can learn to write more effectively while spending less time and energy creating effective messages. Discover a proven writing process that divides the challenge of communicating into three simple steps: planning, writing, and completing messages. The process works for everything from blog posts to formal reports to your résumé. With a bit of practice, you'll be using the process to write more effectively without even thinking about it.

Planning Business Messages

Learning Objectives

After studying this chapter, you will be able to

1. Describe the three-step writing process

2. Explain why it's important to analyze the situation and define your purpose carefully before writing a message

3. Discuss information-gathering options for simple messages and identify three attributes of quality information

4. List the factors to consider when choosing the most appropriate medium for a message

5. Explain why good organization is important to both you and your audience

6. Explain the differences between the direct and indirect approaches to organizing a message

Communication Close-up at H&R Block

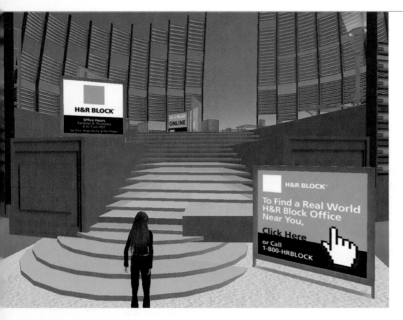

H&R Block Island in the virtual world Second Life is just one of many social media efforts that Paula Drum and her team at H&R Block use to communicate with customers about tax preparation services.

www.hrblock.com

Many U.S. taxpayers don't think about their taxes until they absolutely have to, and then they want to think about taxes as little as possible. In this context of extreme apathy, Paula Drum, H&R Block's vice president of marketing for digital tax solutions, certainly has a challenge on her hands when she wants to communicate with taxpayers about her company's tax preparation products and services.

H&R Block is the leading tax-preparation firm in the United States, with a range of options for virtually every class of taxpayer. Those who want to avoid the laborious chore of doing their own taxes can hand the job over to a tax professional in one of the company's 13,000 offices nationwide. In contrast, those taxpayers who are willing to do most or all of the work themselves can chose from a variety of digital alternatives, including both PC software and web-based solutions.

Although tax preparation is one of the least exciting consumer experiences, Drum and her staff have developed a reputation for creative communication efforts that make use of the latest innovations in social media. For example, in a recent product launch that noted media expert Shel Israel characterized as "among the most extensive business-to-consumer social media campaigns in history," Drum and her crew used a variety of techniques to connect with potential customers: video on YouTube (including a contest for user-created videos), profiles on MySpace and Facebook, Twitter microblogging, and "H&R Block Island" in the virtual world Second Life.

Drum's innovations aren't simply about technology, however. In the spirit of Business Communication 2.0 (see Chapter 1), she emphasizes a conversational, two-way approach in which the company listens as carefully as it speaks. For example, her staffers follow a large number of Twitter users who have asked tax questions in the past, with the goal of maintaining an open channel of communication. Sometimes H&R Block personnel answer specific tax questions, and sometimes they just "offer moral support," according to Drum.

Particularly coming from a company that has a stodgy, old-school image in the minds of many people, this cutting-edge communication has surprised more than a few social media observers. Perhaps even more amazing is that Drum has actually generated some interest in the field of tax preparation.[1]

UNDERSTANDING THE THREE-STEP WRITING PROCESS

The emphasis that H&R Block's Paula Drum (profiled in the chapter-opening Communication Close-up) puts on connecting with customers is a lesson that applies to every business message. Even if you're not dealing with customers, your messages need to make a connection with their intended recipients. By following a proven process, you can learn to create successful messages that meet audience needs and highlight your skills as a perceptive business professional.

The three-step writing process (see Figure 4.1) helps ensure that your messages are both *effective* (meeting your audience's needs and getting your points across) and *efficient* (making the best use of your time and your audience's time):

- **Step 1: Planning business messages.** To plan any message, first *analyze the situation* by defining your purpose and developing a profile of your audience. When you're sure what you need to accomplish with your message, *gather information* that will meet your audience's needs. Next, *select the right medium* (oral, written, visual, or electronic) to deliver your message. Then *organize the information* by defining your main idea, limiting your scope, selecting the direct or indirect approach, and outlining your content. Planning messages is the focus of this chapter.

1 LEARNING OBJECTIVE

Describe the three-step writing process

The three-step writing process consists of planning, writing, and completing your message.

FIGURE 4.1 The Three-Step Writing Process
This three-step process will help you create more effective messages in any medium. As you get more practice with the process, it will become easier and more automatic.

1 Plan →	**2 Write** →	**3 Complete**
Analyze the Situation Define your purpose and develop an audience profile.	**Adapt to Your Audience** Be sensitive to audience needs by using a "you" attitude, politeness, positive emphasis, and unbiased language. Build a strong relationship with your audience by establishing your credibility and projecting your company's preferred image. Control your style with a conversational tone, plain English, and appropriate voice.	**Revise the Message** Evaluate content and review readability, edit and rewrite for conciseness and clarity.
Gather Information Determine audience needs and obtain the information necessary to satisfy those needs.		**Produce the Message** Use effective design elements and suitable layout for a clean, professional appearance.
Select the Right Medium Select the best medium for delivering your message.		**Proofread the Message** Review for errors in layout, spelling, and mechanics.
Organize the Information Define your main idea, limit your scope, select a direct or an indirect approach, and outline your content.	**Compose the Message** Choose strong words that will help you create effective sentences and coherent paragraphs.	**Distribute the Message** Deliver your message using the chosen medium; make sure all documents and all relevant files are distributed successfully.

- **Step 2: Writing business messages.** After you've planned your message, *adapt to your audience* with sensitivity, relationship skills, and an appropriate writing style. Then you're ready to *compose your message* by choosing strong words, creating effective sentences, and developing coherent paragraphs. Writing business messages is discussed in Chapter 5.
- **Step 3: Completing business messages.** After writing your first draft, *revise your message* by evaluating the content, reviewing readability, and editing and rewriting until your message comes across concisely and clearly, with correct grammar, proper punctuation, and effective format. Next, *produce your message.* Put it into the form that your audience will receive and review all design and layout decisions for an attractive, professional appearance. *Proofread* the final product to ensure high quality and then *distribute your message.* Completing business messages is discussed in Chapter 6.

Throughout this book, you'll learn how to apply these steps to a wide variety of business messages: short messages such as e-mails and blog postings (Chapters 7 through 10), longer messages such as reports and wikis (Chapters 13 through 15), oral presentations (Chapters 16 and 17), and the employment messages you can use to build a great career (Chapters 18 and 19).

Optimizing Your Writing Time

As a starting point, allot half your available time for planning, one-quarter for writing, and one-quarter for completing your messages—but adjust these percentages for each project.

The more you use the three-step writing process, the more intuitive and automatic it will become. You'll also get better at allotting your time for each task during a writing project. Start by adding up how much time you have to spend on a given project. (In business, as in school, you'll never have as much time as you'd like!) Then, as a general rule, set aside roughly 50 percent of that time for planning, 25 percent for writing, and 25 percent for completing.

Devoting only a quarter of your time to writing might sound odd, but it makes sense for two reasons. First, doing a thorough job of planning is necessary to make sure you provide the right information in the right format to the right people. Planning can take a lot of work for a complicated project, but here's the good news: With careful planning, the actual writing is faster, easier, and a lot less stressful.

Second, it is always wise to set aside plenty of time for the completing step, particularly for long or complex messages. If you rush through or skip any of these tasks, you run the risk of spoiling all your hard work by delivering poor-quality messages.

Of course, the 50–25–25 time allotment can vary significantly from project to project. Simpler and shorter messages require less planning than long reports, websites, and other complex projects. Also, the time required to produce and distribute messages can vary widely, depending on the media, the size of the audience, and other factors. Start with the 50–25–25 split as a guideline and use your best judgment for each project.

Planning Effectively

Trying to save time by skimping on planning usually costs you more time in the long run.

As soon as the need to create a message appears, inexperienced communicators are often tempted to dive directly into writing. However, even a few minutes of planning can save hours of rework and frustration later on. Analyzing your audience helps you find and assemble the facts they're looking for and deliver that information in a concise and compelling way. Planning your message reduces indecision as you write, and it reduces rework during the completing step. Careful planning can also save you from embarrassing blunders that could hurt your company or your career. With a solid plan in place, you're ready to move forward with analyzing your situation.

2 LEARNING OBJECTIVE

Explain why it's important to analyze the situation and define your purpose carefully before writing a message

ANALYZING YOUR SITUATION

A successful message starts with a clear purpose that connects the sender's needs with the audience's needs. Identifying your purpose and your audience is usually a straightforward task for simple, routine messages. However, this task can be more demanding in more intricate

FIGURE 4.2 The Relationship Between General Purpose and Communicator Control
Your control over a message is inversely related to the degree of audience participation.
The more participation from the audience, the less control you'll have, and vice versa.

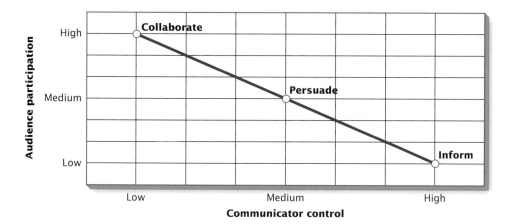

situations. For instance, if you need to communicate about a shipping problem between your Beijing and Los Angeles factories, your purpose might simply be to alert upper management to the situation, or it might involve asking the two factory managers to explore and solve the problem. These two scenarios have different purposes and different audiences, so they require distinctly different messages. If you launch directly into writing without clarifying both your purpose and your audience, you'll waste time and energy, and you'll probably generate a less-effective message.

Defining Your Purpose

All business messages have a **general purpose**: to inform, to persuade, or to collaborate with the audience. In addition to defining the overall direction of your message, the general purpose also determines both the appropriate degree of audience participation and the amount of control you have over your message (see Figure 4.2). Informing your audience typically requires little interaction. Audience members absorb the information and accept or reject it, but they don't contribute to message content. You control the message. In contrast, persuading an audience often involves some degree of participation, such as giving people the chance to ask questions so that you can address any concerns. Nevertheless, you need to retain a moderate amount of message control. At the other extreme, to collaborate with people, you want and need maximum participation. Your control of the message is reduced because you must adjust to new input as the collaboration progresses.

Your general purpose may be to inform, to persuade, or to collaborate.

Within the scope of its general purpose, each message also has a **specific purpose**, which identifies what you hope to accomplish with your message and what your audience should do or think after receiving your message. For instance, is your goal simply to update your audience about some upcoming event, or do you want people to take immediate action? State your specific purpose as precisely as possible, even to the point of identifying which audience members should respond, how they should respond, and when.

To determine the specific purpose, think of how the audience's ideas or behavior should be affected by the message.

After you have defined your specific purpose, take a moment for a reality check. Decide whether that purpose merits the time and effort required for you to prepare and send the message—and for your audience to spend the time required to read it, view it, or listen to it. Test your purpose by asking these four questions:

- **Will anything change as a result of your message?** Don't contribute to information overload by sending messages that won't change anything. For instance, if you don't like your company's latest advertising campaign but you're not in a position to influence it, sending a critical message to your colleagues won't change anything and won't benefit anyone.

Defer sending a message, or do not send it at all, if
- *Nothing will change as a result of sending it*
- *The purpose is not realistic*
- *The timing is not right*
- *The purpose is not acceptable to your organization*

- **Is your purpose realistic?** Recognizing whether a goal is realistic is an important part of having good business sense. For example, if you request a raise while the company is struggling, you night send the message that you're not tuned into the situation around you.
- **Is the time right?** People who are busy or distracted when they receive your message are less likely to pay attention to it. For example, many professions and departments have recurring cycles in their workloads, and messages sent during peak times may be ignored.
- **Is your purpose acceptable to your organization?** Your company's business objectives and policies, and even laws that apply to your particular industry, may dictate whether a particular purpose is acceptable.

When you are satisfied that you have a clear and meaningful purpose and that this is a smart time to proceed, your next step is to understand the members of your audience and their needs.

Developing an Audience Profile

Before audience members will take the time to read or listen to your messages, they need to be interested in what you're saying. They need to see what's in it for them: How will listening to your advice or doing what you ask help them, personally or professionally? The more you know about your audience members, their needs, and their expectations, the more effectively you'll be able to communicate with them. For an example of the kind of information that is helpful to compile in an audience analysis, see Figure 4.3. Follow these steps to conduct a thorough audience analysis:

FIGURE 4.3 Audience Analysis Helps You Plan Your Message
For simple, routine messages, you usually don't need to analyze your audience in depth. However, for complex messages or messages for indifferent or hostile audiences, take the time to study their information needs and potential reactions to your message.

Audience analysis notes

Project: A report recommending that we close down the on-site exercise facility and subsidize private memberships at local health clubs.

- **Primary audience:** Nicole Perazzo, vice president of operations, and her supervisory team.

- **Size and geographic distribution:** Nine managers total; Nicole and five of her staff are here on site; three other supervisors are based in Hong Kong.

- **Composition:** All have experience in operations management, but several are new to the company.

- **Level of understanding:** All will no doubt understand the financial considerations, but the newer managers may not understand the importance of the on-site exercise facility to many of our employees.

- **Expectations and preferences.** They're expecting a firm recommendation, backed up with well-thought-out financial rationale and suggestions for communicating the bad news to employees. For a decision of this magnitude, a formal report is appropriate; e-mail distribution is expected.

- **Probable reaction.** From one-on-one discussions, I know that several of the managers receiving this report are active users of the on-site facility and won't welcome the suggestion that we should shut it down. However, some nonexercisers generally think it's a luxury the company can't afford. Audience reactions will range from highly positive to highly negative; the report should focus on overcoming the highly negative reactions since they're the ones I need to convince.

- **Identify your primary audience.** For some messages, certain audience members may be more important than others. Don't ignore the needs of less influential members but make sure you address the concerns of the key decision makers.
- **Determine audience size and geographic distribution.** A message aimed at 10,000 people spread around the globe will probably require a different approach than one aimed at a dozen people down the hall.
- **Determine audience composition.** Look for both similarities and differences in culture, language, age, education, organizational rank and status, attitudes, experience, motivations, and any other factors that could affect the successful reception and decoding of your message.
- **Gauge audience members' level of understanding.** If audience members share your general background, they'll probably understand your material without difficulty. If not, your message will need an element of education, and deciding how much information to include can be a challenge. Include only enough information to accomplish the specific purpose of your message. For example, to promote tax-preparation software, Paula Drum and her colleagues at H&R Block focus on simpler, high-level audience concerns such as ease of use and the ability to avoid overpaying one's taxes—not on the gory details of tax laws.
- **Understand audience expectations and preferences.** Will members of your audience expect complete details or just a summary of the main points? In general, for internal communication, the higher up the organization your message goes, the fewer details people want to see.
- **Forecast probable audience reaction.** As you'll read later in the chapter, potential audience reaction affects message organization. If you expect a favorable response, you can state conclusions and recommendations up front and offer minimal supporting evidence. If you expect skepticism, you can introduce conclusions gradually and with more proof.

Ask yourself some key questions about your audience:
- *Who are the most important people in the audience?*
- *How many people do you need to reach?*
- *How much do they already know about the subject?*
- *What is their probable reaction to your message?*

If audience members have different levels of understanding of the topic, aim your message at the most influential decision makers.

To win over a skeptical audience, use a gradual approach and plenty of evidence.

GATHERING INFORMATION

When you have a clear picture of your audience, your next step is to assemble the information that you will include in your message. For simple messages, you may already have all the information at hand, but for more complex messages, you may need to do considerable research and analysis before you're ready to begin writing. Chapter 11 explores formal techniques for finding, evaluating, and processing information. Meanwhile, you can often use a variety of informal techniques to gather insights and guide your research efforts:

- **Consider the audience's perspective.** Put yourself in the audience's position; what are these people thinking, feeling, or planning? What information do they need to move forward?
- **Read reports and other company documents.** Annual reports, financial statements, news releases, blogs by industry experts, marketing reports, and customer surveys are just a few of the many potential sources. Find out whether your company has a *knowledge-management system*, a centralized database that collects the experiences and insights of employees throughout the organization.
- **Talk with supervisors, colleagues, or customers.** Fellow workers and customers may have information you need, or they may know what your audience will be interested in.
- **Ask your audience for input.** If you're unsure what audience members need from your message, ask them. Admitting you don't know but want to meet their needs will impress an audience more than guessing and getting it wrong.

3 **LEARNING OBJECTIVE**

Discuss information-gathering options for simple messages and identify three attributes of quality information

Uncovering Audience Needs

In many situations, your audience's information needs are readily apparent; in others, your audience may be unable to articulate exactly what is needed. If someone makes a vague or broad request, ask questions to narrow the focus. If your boss says, "Find out everything you can about Interscope Records," narrow the investigation by asking which aspect of the company and its business is most important. Asking a question or two often forces the person to think through the request and define more precisely what is required.

If you're given a vague request, ask questions to clarify it before you plan a response.

If appropriate, include additional information that might be helpful, even though the requester didn't specifically ask for it.

In addition, try to think of information needs that your audience may not have expressed. Suppose you've been asked to compare two health insurance plans for your firm's employees, but your research has uncovered a third alternative that might be even better. You could then expand your report to include a brief explanation of why the third plan should be considered and compare it to the two original plans. Use judgment, however; in some situations you need to provide only what the audience expects and nothing more.

Finding Your Focus

You may encounter situations in which the assignment or objective is so vague that you have no idea how to get started in determining what the audience needs to know. In such cases, you can use some *discovery techniques* to help generate ideas and uncover possible avenues to research. One popular technique is **free writing**, in which you write whatever comes to mind, without stopping to make any corrections, for a set period of time. The big advantage of free writing is that you silence your "inner critic" and just express ideas as they come to you. You might end up with a rambling mess by any conventional measure, but that's not important. Within that tangle of expressions, you might also find some useful ideas and angles that hadn't occurred to you yet—perhaps the crucial idea that will jumpstart the entire project.

The best discovery option in some cases might not be writing at all, but rather *sketching*. If you're unable to come up with any words, grab a sketchpad and starting drawing. While you're thinking visually, your brain might release some great ideas that were trapped behind words.

The techniques listed under "Defining Your Main Idea" on page 138 can also be helpful if you don't know where to start.

Providing Required Information

Test the completeness of your document by making sure it answers all six journalistic questions: who, what, when, where, why, and how.

After you've defined your audience's information needs, be sure you satisfy those needs completely. One good way to test the thoroughness of your message is to use the **journalistic approach**: Check to see whether your message answers *who, what, when, where, why,* and *how.* Using this method, you can quickly tell whether a message fails to deliver. For example, consider this message requesting information from employees:

> We are exploring ways to reduce our office space leasing costs and would like your input on a proposed plan in which employees who telecommute on alternate days could share offices. Please let me know what you think of this proposal.

The message fails to tell employees everything they need to know in order to provide meaningful responses. The *what* could be improved by identifying the specific information points the writer needs from employees (such as whether individual telecommuting patterns are predictable enough to allow scheduling of shared offices). The writer also doesn't specify *when* the responses are needed or *how* the employees should respond. By failing to address such points, the request is likely to generate a variety of responses, some possibly helpful but some probably not.

To gauge the quality of the information you provide in your messages, check to ensure that the information is accurate, ethical, and pertinent.

Be Sure the Information Is Accurate

Be certain that the information you provide is accurate and that the commitments you make can be kept.

Inaccurate information in business messages can cause a host of problems, from embarrassment and lost productivity to serious safety and legal issues. You may commit the organization to promises it isn't able to keep—and the error could harm your reputation as a reliable businessperson. Thanks to the Internet, inaccurate information may persist for years after you distribute it.

You can minimize mistakes by double-checking every piece of information you collect. If you are consulting sources outside the organization, ask yourself whether they are current and reliable. You must be particularly careful when using sources you find online. As you'll see in Chapter 11, the simplicity of online publishing and the frequent lack of editorial oversight call for extra care in using online information. Be sure to review any mathematical or financial calculations. Check all dates and schedules and examine your own assumptions and conclusions to be certain they are valid.

Ethics Detective

Am I Getting the Whole Story?

Recently you read a report that states, "Obesity has reached epidemic proportions globally, with more than 1 billion adults overweight—at least 300 million of them clinically obese—and is a major contributor to the global burden of chronic disease and disability. Often coexisting in developing countries with under-nutrition, obesity is a complex condition, with serious social and psychological dimensions, affecting virtually all ages and socioeconomic groups."

You are overweight but not obese; although you tried various diets, you could not lose weight. One of your friends told you that there is a paid program on one of the TV channels about a medication that can reduce weight up to 18 pounds per month. You also found an advertisement for the medication in one of the magazines. You watched the TV show, and you noticed that the spokesperson and his visitors were emphasizing only one point—that with this medication you can lose weight without cutting any food from your diet or without doing any exercise. Second, the spokesperson guaranteed that if the medication does not work, you will get your money back.

You decided to telephone the company, and you asked them about the advertisement and the claim that exercising or changing your diet is not required. The company representative confirmed this claim and assured you that if you do not lose weight within the prescribed period they will return your money. You paid the fee with your credit card, and the next day you received the medication. When you opened the package, you found a brochure stating that to lose weight you have to follow the instructions; otherwise, the medication will not be effective and you will not be able to get your money back. The instructions were as follows:

You have to take the medicine according to the Medicine Chart.

You have to cut out all food except the one described in the Nutrition Chart.

You have to do certain exercises on a regular basis as prescribed in the Exercise Chart.

ANALYSIS

Were the TV spokesperson and the company representative guilty of an ethical lapse in this case? If you think so, explain what you think the lapse is and why you believe it is unethical. If you don't think so, explain why you think the statements given by the spokesperson or company representative qualify as ethical business practices.

Be Sure the Information Is Ethical

By working hard to ensure the accuracy of the information you gather, you'll also avoid many ethical problems in your messages. If you do make an honest mistake, such as delivering information you initially thought to be true but later found to be false, contact the recipients of the message immediately and correct the error. No one can reasonably fault you in such circumstances, and people will respect your honesty.

Messages can also be unethical if important information is omitted or glossed over. (see "Ethics Detective: Am I Getting the Whole Story?"). Of course, as a business professional, you may have legal or other sound business reasons for not including every detail about every matter. Just how much detail should you include? Make sure you include enough detail to avoid misleading your audience. If you're unsure how much information your audience needs, offer as much as you believe best fits your definition of complete and then offer to provide more upon request.

A clear sense of ethics should guide your decisions when determining how much detail to include in your message.

Be Sure the Information Is Pertinent

When gathering information for your message, remember that some points will be more important to your audience than others. Audience members will appreciate your efforts to prioritize the information they need and filter out the information they don't. Moreover, by focusing on the information that concerns your audience the most, you increase your chances of accomplishing your own communication goals.

Audiences respond best to information that has been filtered and prioritized to meet their needs.

If you don't know your audience or if you're communicating with a large group of people who have diverse interests, use common sense to identify points of interest. Audience factors such as age, job, location, income, and education can give you a clue. If you're trying to sell memberships in a health club, you might adjust your message for athletes, busy professionals, families, and people in different locations or in different income brackets. The comprehensive facilities and professional trainers would appeal to athletes, whereas the low monthly rates would appeal to college students on tight budgets.

Rely on common sense if you don't know enough about your audience to know exactly what will interest them.

Some messages necessarily reach audiences with a diverse mix of educational levels, subject awareness, and other variables. In these cases, your only choice is to try to accommodate the likely range of audience members (see Figure 4.4).

FIGURE 4.4 An Audience-Focused Report (Selected Pages)
These two pages from a local water district's annual water quality report do a good job of presenting a technical subject to the general public (all the households in this particular city). Notice how the report presents scientific information accurately and supplements it with clear explanations of what the information means and how it pertains to water users.

Helps readers understand the scientific terms used to describe water quality

Provides helpful contact information

Shows test results in appropriate scientific format but helps nontechnical readers by explaining what the various substances are and whether the water complies with government standards

Answers a question that many concerned customers are likely to have

Helps readers grasp significance of very small numbers by providing a selection of analogous measurements

SELECTING THE RIGHT MEDIUM

Selecting the best medium for your message can make the difference between effective and ineffective communication.[2] A **medium** is the form through which you choose to communicate a message. You may choose to talk with someone face to face, post to a blog, send an e-mail message, or create a webcast; the range of media possibilities is wide and growing wider all the time. Although media categories have become increasingly blurred in recent years, for the sake of discussion, you can think of media as being *oral, written, visual,* or *electronic* (which often combines several media types).

Oral Media

Oral media include face-to-face conversations, interviews, speeches, and in-person presentations and meetings. By giving communicators the ability to see, hear, and react to each other, oral media are useful for encouraging people to ask questions, make comments, and work together to reach a consensus or decision. For example, experts recommend that managers engage in frequent "walk-arounds," chatting with employees to get input, answer their questions, and interpret important business events and trends.[3]

Oral communication is best when you need to encourage interaction, express emotions, or monitor emotional responses.

Of course, if you don't want a lot of questions or interaction, using oral media can be an unwise choice. However, consider your audience carefully before deciding to limit interaction by choosing a different medium. As a manager, you will encounter unpleasant situations (declining an employee's request for a raise, for example) in which sending an e-mail message or otherwise avoiding personal contact will seem appealing to you. However, in many such cases, you owe the other party the opportunity to ask questions or express concerns. Moreover, facing the tough situations in person will earn you a reputation as an honest, caring manager.

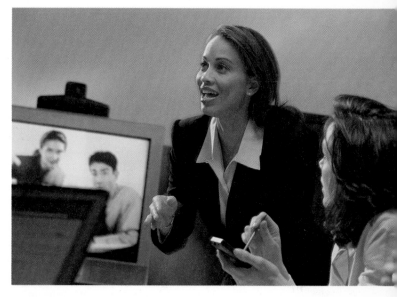

The higher you rise in an organization, the more time you'll spending talking and listening. Your ability to communicate with people from virtually any background will be key to your success.

Written Media

Written messages take many forms, from traditional memos to glossy reports that rival magazines in production quality. **Memos** are brief printed documents traditionally used for the routine, day-to-day exchange of information within an organization. In many organizations, IM, e-mail, blogs, and other electronic media have largely replaced paper memos.

Printed messages have been replaced in many instances by electronic media, although the print medium still has a place in business today.

Letters are brief written messages generally sent to recipients outside the organization. In addition to conveying a particular message, they perform an important public relations function in fostering good working relationships with customers, suppliers, and others. Many organizations rely on *form letters* to save time and money on routine communication. Form letters are particularly handy for such one-time mass mailings as sales messages about products, information about organizational activities, and goodwill messages such as seasonal greetings.

Reports and proposals are usually longer than memos and letters, although both can be created in memo or letter format. These documents come in a variety of lengths, ranging from a few pages to several hundred, and are usually fairly formal in tone. Chapters 13 through 15 discuss reports and proposals in detail.

Visual Media

Traditional business messages rely primarily on text, with occasional support from graphical elements such as charts, graphs, or diagrams to help illustrate points discussed in the text. However, many business communicators are discovering the power of messages in which the visual element is dominant and supported by small amounts of text. For the

In some situations, a message that is predominantly visual, with text used to support the illustration, can be more effective than a message that relies primarily on text.

FIGURE 4.5 Visual Media

In traditional business messages, visual elements usually support the text. However, in some instances, the message can be presented more effectively by reversing that relationship—basing the message on a dominant visual and using text to support that image.

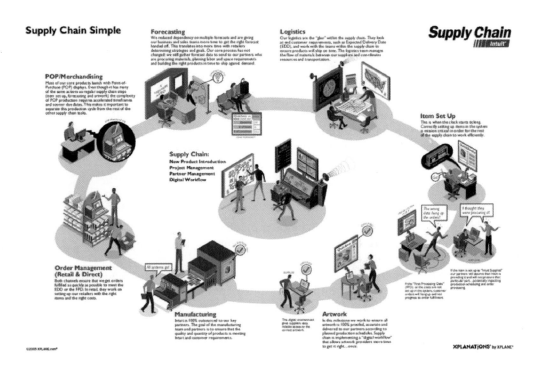

purposes of this discussion, you can think of *visual media* as any format in which one or more visual elements play a central role in conveying the message content (see Figure 4.5).

Messages that combine powerful visuals with supporting text can be effective for a number of reasons. Today's audiences are pressed for time and bombarded with messages, so anything that communicates quickly is welcome. Visuals are also effective at describing complex ideas and processes because they can reduce the work required for an audience to identify the parts and relationships that make up the whole. Also, in a multilingual business world, diagrams, symbols, and other images can lower communication barriers by requiring less language processing. Finally, visual depictions can be easier to remember than purely textual descriptions or explanations.

Electronic Media

In general, use electronic media to deliver messages quickly, to reach widely dispersed audiences, and to take advantage of rich multimedia formats.

The range of electronic media is broad and continues to grow even broader, from phone calls and podcasts to blogs and wikis to e-mail and text messaging. When you want to make a powerful impression, using electronic media can increase the excitement and visual appeal with interactivity, animation, audio, and video.

The growth of electronic communication options is both a blessing and a curse for business communicators. On the one hand, you have more tools than ever before to choose from, with more ways to deliver rational and emotional content. On the other hand, the sheer range of choices can complicate your job because you often need to choose among multiple media, and you need to know how to use each medium successfully.

Today's audiences can get frustrated with the sheer number of electronic media in the workplace.

From the audience's perspective, a common frustration with electronic media is lack of integration, with people being forced to use to an ever-growing arsenal of separate but overlapping media options in order to stay informed.[4] As the options multiply, with information appearing in e-mail messages, IM, intranets, blogs, shared online workspaces, social networks, Twitter updates, wikis, and whatever else is invented next, the struggle to monitor multiple sources of information can consume considerable time and energy. To minimize

FIGURE 4.6 Electronic Oral Media

Many websites now feature talking animated figures, sometimes called *avatars*, offering website visitors a more engaging experience.

frustration and maximize productivity, company managers should establish clear expectations for the use of electronic media and carefully integrate—or officially choose *not* to use—each new media innovation.

You'll learn more about using electronic media throughout this book (in Chapter 7, in particular), but for now, here is a quick overview of the major electronic media being used in business:

- **Electronic versions of oral media.** These media include telephone calls, teleconferencing, voice-mail messages, audio recordings such as compact discs and podcasts, voice synthesis (creating audio signals from computer data), voice recognition (converting audio signals to computer data), and even animated online characters (see Figure 4.6). The simple telephone call is still a vital communication link for many organizations, but even it has joined the Internet age, thanks to *Internet telephony*, also known by the technical term VoIP (which stands for *Voice over IP*, the Internet Protocol). Although telephone calls can't convey all the nonverbal signals of an in-person conversation, they can convey quite a few, including tone of voice, pace, laughter, pauses, and so on. Using voice mail is a handy way to send brief messages when an immediate response isn't crucial, but it's a poor choice for lengthy messages because the information is difficult to retrieve. You'll learn about podcasts in particular in Chapter 7.
- **Electronic versions of written media.** These options range from e-mail and IM to blogs, websites, social networks, and wikis. These media are in a state of constant change, in terms of both what is available and who tends to use which media. For example, e-mail has been a primary business medium for the past decade or two, but it is being replaced in many cases by IM, blogs, text messaging, and communication via social networks.[5] Chapter 7 takes a closer look at e-mail, IM, blogs, and social networks; Chapter 14 discusses wikis in more detail.
- **Electronic versions of visual media.** These choices can include electronic presentations (using Microsoft PowerPoint and other software), computer animation (using software such as Adobe Flash to create many of the animated sequences you see on websites, for example), and video. Businesses have made extensive use of video (particularly for training, new product promotions, and executive announcements) for years—first on tape, then on DVD, and now online. Video is also incorporated in podcasting, creating *vidcasts*, and in blogging, creating *video blogs* (*vlogs*) and *mobile blogs* (*moblogs*).[6] **Multimedia** refers to use of two or more media to craft a single message, typically some combination of audio, video, text, and visual graphics.

For more on the latest innovations in electronic media, visit **http://real-timeupdates .com/bct** and click on Chapter 4.

4 LEARNING OBJECTIVE

List the factors to consider when choosing the most appropriate medium for a message

Complicated messages often benefit from richer media.

Factors to Consider When Choosing Media

In some situations, you have little or no choice of which medium to use. For instance, your department might use IM for all short internal messages and a wiki for longer status reports, and you'll be expected to use those media as well. In other situations, you'll have the opportunity to choose the medium (or media) for a particular message. Table 4.1 lists the general advantages and disadvantages of each medium. In addition, be sure to consider how your message is affected by these important factors:

- **Media richness.** Richness is a medium's ability to (1) convey a message through more than one *informational cue* (visual, verbal, and vocal), (2) facilitate feedback, and (3) establish personal focus. The richest medium is face-to-face communication; it's personal, it provides immediate feedback (verbal and nonverbal), and it conveys the emotion behind a message.[7] Multimedia presentations and multimedia webpages are also quite rich, with the ability to present images, animation, text, music, sound effects, and other elements. Many electronic media are also *interactive*, in that they enable audiences to participate in the communication process. For example, a website can allow visitors to select the types of information they want to see, to provide feedback, or to use a variety of online calculators or other tools. At the other end of the continuum are the leanest media—those that communicate in the simplest ways, provide no opportunity

TABLE 4.1 Media Advantages and Disadvantages

MEDIA TYPE	ADVANTAGES	DISADVANTAGES
Oral	• Provide opportunity for immediate feedback • Promote interaction • Involve rich nonverbal cues (both physical gesture and vocal inflection) • Allow the expression of the emotions behind the message	• Restrict participation to those physically present • Unless recorded, provide no permanent, verifiable record of the communication • In most cases, reduce communicator's control over the message • Other than for messages that are prewritten and rehearsed, offer no opportunity to revise or edit spoken words
Written	• Allow you to plan and control your message • Reach geographically dispersed audiences • Offer a permanent, verifiable record • Minimize the distortion that can result with oral and some forms of electronic messages • Can be used to avoid immediate interactions • Can help you control the emotional aspects of an interchange by eliminating interpersonal communication	• Usually not conducive to speedy feedback • Lack the rich nonverbal cues provided by oral media • Often take more time and more resources to create and distribute • For elaborate documents, can require special skills in preparation and production
Visual	• Can convey complex ideas and relationships quickly • Often less intimidating than long blocks of text, particularly for nonnative readers • Can reduce the burden on the audience to figure out how the pieces fit	• Can require artistic skills to design • Require some technical skills to create • Can require more time to create than an equivalent amount of text • More difficult to transmit and store than simple textual messages
Electronic	• Deliver messages quickly • Reach geographically dispersed audiences • Offer the persuasive power of multimedia formats • Can increase accessibility and openness in an organization	• Are easy to overuse (sending too many messages to too many recipients) • Present privacy risks and concerns (exposing confidential data; employer monitoring of e-mail, IM, and blogs; accidental forwarding) • Present security risks (viruses and spyware) • Create productivity concerns (frequent interruptions, lack of integration among multiple electronic media in use at the same time, and time wasted on nonbusiness uses)

FIGURE 4.7 Media Richness

Business media vary widely in terms of *richness*, which is the number of informational cues available, the medium's ability to incorporate feedback, and the degree to which the medium can be personalized.

Leaner:
fewer cues,
no interactivity,
no personal focus

Standard reports
Static webpages
Mass media
Posters & signs

Custom reports
Letters & memos
E-mail & IM
Wikis
Blogs
Podcasts

Telephone calls
Teleconferencing
Video (including
vodcasts,
vlogs,
video IM)

Face-to-face
conversations
Multimedia
presentations
Multimedia
webpages
Virtual reality

Richer:
multiple cues,
interactive,
personalized

for audience feedback, and aren't personalized (see Figure 4.7). In general, use richer media to send nonroutine or complex messages, to humanize your presence throughout the organization, to communicate caring to employees, and to gain employee commitment to company goals. Use leaner media to send routine messages or to transfer information that doesn't require significant explanation.[8]

- **Message formality.** Your media choice is a nonverbal signal that affects the style and tone of your message. For example, a printed memo letter is likely to be perceived as a more formal gesture than an e-mail message.

- **Media limitations.** Every medium has limitations. While face-to-face communication is one of the richest media, it's also one of the most restrictive because you and your audience must be in the same place at the same time.[9] Similarly, IM is perfect for communicating simple, straightforward messages, but it is ineffective for sending complex messages.

- **Urgency.** Some media establish a connection with the audience faster than others, so choose wisely if your message is urgent. For example, talking to someone over the phone is faster than using e-mail, particularly if the recipient doesn't check his or her messages frequently. However, be sure to respect audience members' time and workloads. If a message isn't urgent and doesn't require immediate feedback, choose a medium such as e-mail that allows people to respond at their convenience.

- **Cost.** Cost is both a real financial factor and a perceived nonverbal signal. For instance, creating an interactive multimedia version of a report or proposal and distributing it via DVD is considerably more expensive than creating a basic word processor file and distributing it as an e-mail attachment. And the nonverbal signal that the DVD sends could be positive or negative, depending on the circumstances. If that expensive DVD contains a sales presentation intended for potential buyers of luxury condominiums, it will send a positive signal of sophistication and professionalism. In contrast, if the DVD contains a routine report for your boss, the nonverbal signal could well be that you can't be trusted to spend your time or the company's money wisely.

- **Audience preferences.** Be sure to consider which medium or media your audience expects or prefers.[10] What would you think if your college tried to deliver your diploma as an e-mail attachment? You'd expect the college to hand the diploma to you at graduation or mail it to you. In addition, some cultures tend to favor one channel over another. For example, the United States, Canada, and Germany emphasize written messages, whereas Japan emphasizes oral messages—perhaps because its high-context culture carries so much of the message in nonverbal cues and "between-the-lines" interpretation.[11]

Some media deliver messages faster than others; avoid using instantaneous delivery to create a false sense of urgency.

When choosing the appropriate medium, don't forget to consider your audience's preferences and expectations.

After you select the best medium for your purpose, situation, and audience, you are ready to start thinking about the organization of your message.

FIGURE 4.8 Improving the Organization of a Message

The improved version of this e-mail message is clear and efficient, presenting only the necessary information in a logical sequence.

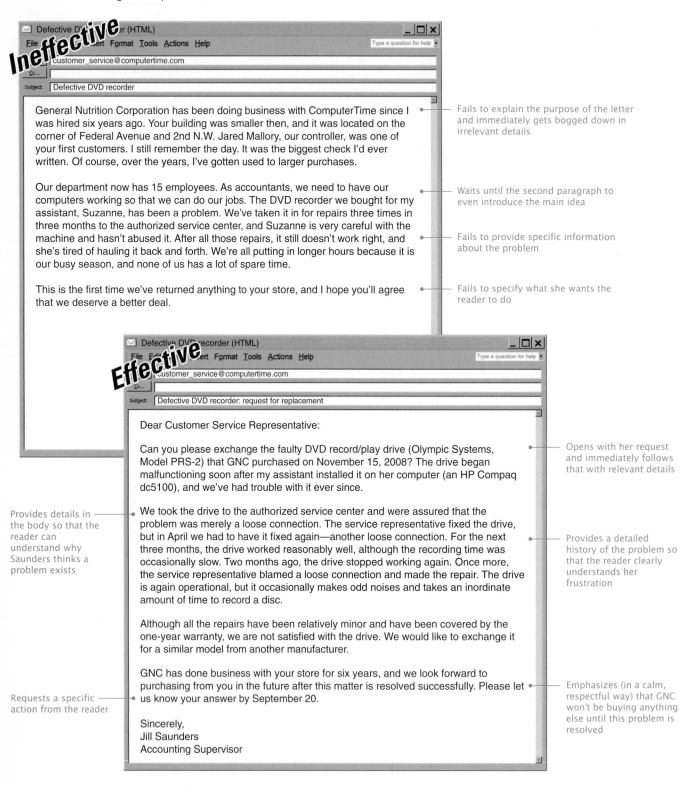

ORGANIZING YOUR INFORMATION

Organization can make the difference between success and failure. Compare the two versions of the message in Figure 4.8. The ineffective version exhibits several common organization mistakes: taking too long to get to the point, including irrelevant material, getting ideas mixed up, and leaving out necessary information.

The ability to present information in an organized fashion is an essential business skill.

Recognizing the Importance of Good Organization

Good organization helps your readers or listeners in three key ways. First, it helps them understand your message. In a well-organized message, you make the main point clear at the outset, present additional points to support that main idea, and satisfy all the information needs of the audience. But if your message is poorly organized, your meaning can be obscured, and your audiences may form inaccurate conclusions about what you've written or said.

Second, good organization helps receivers accept your message. If your writing appears confused and disorganized, people will likely conclude that the *thinking* behind the writing is also confused and disorganized. Moreover, effective messages often require a bit more than simple, clear logic. A diplomatic approach helps receivers accept your message, even if it's not exactly what they want to hear (see Figure 4.9). In contrast, a poorly organized message on an emotionally charged topic can alienate the audience before you have the chance to get your point across.

5 **LEARNING OBJECTIVE**

Explain why good organization is important to both you and your audience

Good organization helps audience members understand your message, accept your message, and save time.

FIGURE 4.9 Message Demonstrating a Diplomatic Organization Plan
In the case of ComputerTime's response to Jill Saunders's request for a replacement product from a different manufacturer, ComputerTime isn't able to do exactly what Saunders requested. (It has arranged a replacement from the same manufacturer instead.) Consequently, the response letter from Linda Davis has a negative aspect to it, but the style of the letter is tactful and positive.

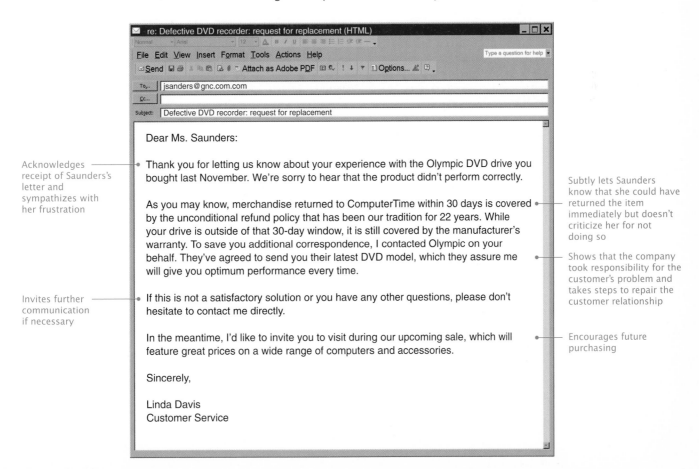

Third, good organization saves your audience time. Well-organized messages are efficient. They contain only relevant ideas, and they are brief. Moreover, each piece of information is located in a logical place in the overall flow; each section builds on the one before to create a coherent whole, without forcing people to look for missing pieces.

Good organization saves you time and energy in the writing and completing phases.

In addition to saving time and energy for your readers, good organization saves you time and consumes less of your creative energy. Writing proceeds more quickly because you don't waste time putting ideas in the wrong places or composing material that you don't need. You spend far less time rewriting, trying to extract sensible meaning from disorganized rambling.

Good organizational skills are also good for your career because they help you develop a reputation as a clear thinker who cares about your readers. If you get a reputation as a disorganized communicator, people will begin to ignore your messages and question your thinking skills. In other words, poorly organized messages are bad for business and bad for your career.

Defining Your Main Idea

The topic is the overall subject; the main idea is a specific statement about the topic.

The **topic** of your message is the overall subject, and your **main idea** is a specific statement about that topic (see Table 4.2). For example, if you believe that the current system of using paper forms for filing employee insurance claims is expensive and slow, you might craft a message in which the topic is employee insurance claims and the main idea is that a new web-based claim-filing system would reduce costs for the company and reduce reimbursement delays for employees.

In longer documents and presentations, you often need to unify a mass of material with a main idea that encompasses all the individual points you want to make. Finding a common thread through all these points can be a challenge. Sometimes you won't even be sure what your main idea is until you sort through the information. For tough assignments like these, consider a variety of techniques to generate creative ideas:

- **Brainstorming.** Working alone or with others, generate as many ideas and questions as you can, without stopping to criticize or organize. After you capture all these pieces, look for patterns and connections to help identify the main idea and the groups of supporting ideas. For example, if your main idea concerns whether to open a new restaurant in Denver, you'll probably find a group of ideas related to financial return, another related to competition, and so on. Identifying such groups helps you see the major issues that will lead you to a conclusion you can feel confident about.
- **Journalistic approach.** Introduced earlier in the chapter, the journalistic approach asks *who, what, when, where, why,* and *how* questions to distill major ideas from unorganized information.
- **Question-and-answer chain.** Start with a key question, from the audience's perspective, and work back toward your message. In most cases, you'll find that each answer

TABLE 4.2 Defining Topic and Main Idea

GENERAL PURPOSE	SPECIFIC PURPOSE	TOPIC	MAIN IDEA
To inform	Teach customer service representatives how to edit and expand the technical support wiki	Technical support wiki	Careful, thorough edits and additions to the wiki help the entire department provide better customer support.
To persuade	Convince top managers to increase spending on research and development	Funding for research and development	Competitors spend more than we do on research and development, enabling them to create more innovative products.
To collaborate	Solicit ideas for a companywide incentive system that ties wages to profits	Incentive pay	Tying wages to profits motivates employees and reduces compensation costs in tough years.

FIGURE 4.10 Using the Mind-Mapping Technique to Plan a Writing Project

Mind mapping is a helpful technique for identifying and organizing the many ideas and pieces of information that a complex writing task usually entails. Software (MindJet's MindManager in this case) makes it easy to create graphical output—such as this diagram, which shows the writer's own concerns about a report, her insights into the audience's concerns, and several issues related to writing and distributing the report.

generates new questions until you identify the information that needs to be in your message.

- **Storyteller's tour.** Some writers find it best to talk through a communication challenge before they try to write. Record yourself as you describe what you intend to write. Then listen to the playback, identify ways to tighten and clarify the message, and repeat the process until you distill the main idea down to a single concise message.
- **Mind mapping.** You can generate and organize ideas using a graphic method called *mind mapping*. Start with a main idea and then branch out to connect every other related idea that comes to mind (see Figure 4.10). You can learn more about mind mapping from the Mind Mapping Software Weblog, at http://mindmapping.typepad.com, and try a free online tool at http://bubbl.us.[12]

> **REAL-TIME UPDATES**
> **Learn More**
>
> **Wrap your mind around mind mapping**
>
> See mind mapping in action in this colorfully illustrated presentation. Go to **http://real-timeupdates.com/bct** and click on "Learn More." If you are using mybcommlab, you can access Real-Time Updates within each chapter or under Student Study Tools.

Limiting Your Scope

The **scope** of a message is the range of information presented, the overall length of the message, and the level of detail—all of which need to correspond to the main idea. Some business messages have a preset length limit, whether from a boss's instructions, the technology you're using, or a time frame, such as individual speaker slots during a seminar. Even if you don't have a preset length, it's vital to limit yourself to the scope needed to convey your message—and no more.

If your audience expects you to deliver a message of a certain length (such as a 10-page report or a 10-minute presentation), be sure to consider your main idea statement in the context of this length limitation. You may find that you have a compelling main idea but that there's no way you can cover it adequately in the space or time allowed. In this case, you'll need to narrow your main idea or, if appropriate, use this first message to provide a high-level overview of your material and then deliver additional supporting information by some other means.

Whatever the length of your message, keep the number of major supporting points to half a dozen or so. If you can get your idea across with fewer than that, all the better. Listing 20 or 30 supporting points might feel as though you're being thorough, but your audience

Limit the number of support points; having fewer, stronger points is a better approach than using many, weaker points.

is likely to view such detail as rambling and mind numbing. Instead, look for ways to group supporting points under major headings, such as finance, customers, competitors, employees, or whatever is appropriate for your subject. You may need to refine your major supporting points so that you have a smaller number with greater impact.

If your message needs to be brief, your main idea will have to be easy to understand and easy to accept. However, if your message can be somewhat longer, you can develop the major points in more detail. How much space you need to communicate and support your main idea depends on your subject, your audience members' familiarity with the material and their receptivity to your conclusions, and your credibility with them. You'll need fewer words to present routine information to a knowledgeable audience that already knows and respects you. You'll need more words to build a consensus about a complex and controversial subject, especially if the members of your audience are skeptical or hostile strangers.

Choosing Between Direct and Indirect Approaches

6 LEARNING OBJECTIVE

Explain the differences between the direct and indirect approaches to organizing a message

Use the direct approach if the audience's reaction is likely to be positive and the indirect approach if it is likely to be negative.

After you've defined your main idea and supporting points, you're ready to decide on the sequence you will use to present your information. You have two basic options:

● **The direct approach.** When you know your audience will be receptive to your message, use the **direct approach**: Start with the main idea (such as a recommendation, a conclusion, or a request) and follow that with your supporting evidence.

● **The indirect approach.** When your audience will be skeptical about or even resistant to your message, use the **indirect approach**: Start with the evidence first and build your case before presenting the main idea.

To choose between these two alternatives, analyze your audience's likely reaction to your purpose and message (see Figure 4.11). Bear in mind, however, that Figure 4.11 presents only general guidelines; always consider the unique circumstances of each message and audience situation. The following sections offer more insight on choosing the best approach for routine and positive messages, negative messages, and persuasive messages.

FIGURE 4.11 Choosing Between the Direct and Indirect Approaches
Think about the way your audience is likely to respond before choosing your approach.

	Direct Approach	**Indirect Approach**	
Audience Reaction	Eager/interested/ pleased/neutral	Displeased	Uninterested/unwilling
Message Opening	Start with the main idea, the request, or the good news.	Start with a neutral statement that acts as a transition to the reasons for the bad news.	Start with a statement or question that captures attention.
Message Body	Provide necessary details.	Give reasons to justify a negative answer. State or imply the bad news, and make a positive suggestion.	Arouse the audience's interest in the subject. Build the audience's desire to comply.
Message Close	Close with a cordial comment, a reference to the good news, or a statement about the specific action desired.	Close cordially.	Request action.

Routine and Positive Messages

The most straightforward business messages are *routine* and *positive* messages. Routine messages involve the daily matters of operating a business, from placing orders to updating employees about process changes. When you're providing routine information as part of your regular business, your audience will probably be neutral—neither pleased nor displeased. Positive messages convey some sort of good news, whether you're announcing a price cut, accepting an invitation, or congratulating a colleague. In most instances, your audience will be pleased to hear from you.

Aside from being easy to understand, such messages are easy to prepare. In most cases, you can use the direct approach. In the opening, state your main idea directly. If you have good news to share, conveying that right away puts your audience members in a positive frame of mind and encourages them to be receptive to whatever else you have to say. The body of your message can then provide all necessary details. The close is cordial and emphasizes your good news or makes a statement about the specific action desired. Routine and positive messages are discussed in greater detail in Chapter 8.

Routine and positive messages nearly always use the direct approach.

Negative Messages

In any profession, you will face situations in which you need to deliver bad news. Because your audience will be disappointed, these messages usually benefit from the indirect approach—putting the evidence first and building up to the main idea. This approach strengthens your case as you go along, making the receiver more receptive to the eventual conclusion. It also treats the receiver in a more sensitive manner, which helps you retain as much goodwill as possible. Astute businesspeople know that every person they encounter could be a potential customer, supplier, or contributor or could influence someone who is a customer, supplier, or contributor.

Successful communicators take extra care with negative messages. They often open with a neutral statement that acts as a transition to the reasons for the bad news. In the body, they give the reasons that justify the negative answer, announcement, or information before they state or imply the bad news. And they are always careful to close cordially. Negative messages are discussed further in Chapter 9.

In many situations, you can cushion the blow of negative news by introducing it with other, more positive information.

Persuasive Messages

Persuasive messages present a special communication challenge because you're asking your audience to give, do, or change something, whether it's buying a product or agreeing to fund a new project. Before you try to persuade people to do something, you need to capture their attention and get them to consider your message with an open mind. In other words, the indirect approach is usually ideal for persuasive messages. Open with an interesting point and provide supporting facts that encourage your audience to continue paying attention. Then use the body of the message to build interest in the subject and arouse audience members' desire to respond. Once you have them thinking, you can introduce your main idea and request the desired action. Persuasive messages are discussed at greater length in Chapter 10.

Persuasive messages can be a challenge because you're asking your audience to give up something, such as time, money, beliefs, or habits.

Outlining Your Content

After you have chosen the right approach, it's time to figure out the most logical and effective way to present your major points and supporting details. Even if you've resisted creating outlines in your school assignments over the years, try to get into the habit of creating outlines when you're preparing business messages. You'll save time, get better results, and do a better job of navigating through complicated business situations. Even if you're just jotting down three or four points on a notepad, making a plan and sticking to it will help you cover the important details.

When you're preparing a longer, more complex message, an outline is indispensable because it helps you visualize the relationships among the various parts. Without an outline,

REAL-TIME UPDATES
Learn More

Get helpful tips on creating an outline for any project

Learn these proven steps for creating robust, practical outlines. Go to **http:// real-timeupdates.com/bct** and click on "Learn More." If you are using mybcommlab, you can access Real-Time Updates within each chapter or under Student Study Tools.

FIGURE 4.12 Two Common Outline Forms

Your company may have a tradition of using a particular outline form for formal reports and other documents. If not, either of these two approaches will work for almost any writing project.

Alphanumeric Outline

I. First major point
  A. First subpoint
  B. Second subpoint
    1. Evidence
    2. Evidence
      a. Detail
      b. Detail
    3. Evidence
  C. Third subpoint
II. Second major point
  A. First subpoint
    1. Evidence
    2. Evidence
  B. Second subpoint

Decimal Outline

I.0 First major point
  1.1 First subpoint
  1.2 Second subpoint
    1.2.1 Evidence
    1.2.2 Evidence
      1.2.2.1 Detail
      1.2.2.2 Detail
    1.2.3 Evidence
  1.3 Third subpoint
2.0 Second major point
  2.1 First subpoint
    2.1.1 Evidence
    2.1.2 Evidence
  2.2 Second subpoint

Particularly with longer messages, using an outline is an indispensable way to visualize how all the points will fit together.

you may be inclined to ramble. As you're describing one point, another point may occur to you, so you describe it as well. One detour leads to another, and before you know it, you've forgotten the original point and wasted precious time and energy.

You're no doubt familiar with the basic outline formats that identify each point with a number or letter and that indent certain points to show which ones are of equal status. A good outline divides a topic into at least two parts, restricts each subdivision to one category, and ensures that each subdivision is separate and distinct (see Figure 4.12).

You may want to experiment with other organizational schemes in addition to traditional outlines.

Another way to visualize the outline of your message is to create an organization chart similar to the charts used to show a company's management structure (see Figure 4.13). Show the main idea, like the top executive in a company, in the highest-level box to establish the big picture. The lower-level ideas, like lower-level employees, provide the details. All the ideas are logically organized into divisions of thought, just as a company is organized into divisions and departments.[13] Using a visual chart instead of a traditional outline has

FIGURE 4.13 Organization Chart Method for Outlining

The organization chart approach is helpful when you're faced with a large variety of facts, figures, and other bits of information and aren't quite sure how they all might relate to one another. When you gather pieces of evidence together under major points, a clearer picture of the main idea will emerge.

✓ **CHECKLIST** | **Planning Business Messages**

A. Analyze the situation.
- Determine whether the purpose of your message is to inform, persuade, or collaborate.
- Identify what you want your audience to think or do after receiving the message.
- Make sure your purpose is worthwhile and realistic.
- Make sure the time is right for your message.
- Make sure your purpose is acceptable to your organization.
- Identify the primary audience.
- Determine the size and composition of your audience.
- Estimate your audience's level of understanding and probable reaction to your message.

B. Gather information.
- Decide whether to use formal or informal techniques for gathering information.
- Find out what your audience needs to know.
- Provide all required information and make sure it's accurate, ethical, and pertinent.

C. Select the best medium for your message.
- Understand the advantages and disadvantages of oral, written, visual, and electronic media.
- Consider media richness, formality, media limitations, urgency, cost, and audience preference.

D. Organize your information.
- Define your main idea.
- Limit your scope.
- Choose the direct or indirect approach.
- Outline content by starting with the main idea, adding major points, and illustrating with evidence.

many benefits. Charts help you (1) see the various levels of ideas and how the parts fit together, (2) develop new ideas, and (3) restructure your information flow. The mind-mapping technique used to generate ideas works in a similar way.

Whichever outlining or organizing scheme you use, start your message with the main idea, follow that with major supporting points, and then illustrate these points with evidence.

Start with the Main Idea

The main idea helps you establish the goals and general strategy of the message, and it summarizes two vital considerations: (1) *what* you want your audience members to do or think and (2) *why* they should do so. Everything in your message should either support the main idea or explain its implications. As discussed earlier, the direct approach states the main idea quickly and directly, whereas the indirect approach delays the main idea until after the evidence is presented.

State the Major Points

You need to support your main idea with major points that clarify and explain your ideas in more concrete terms. If your purpose is to inform and the material is factual, your major points may be based on something physical or financial—something you can visualize or measure, such as activities to be performed, functional units, spatial or chronological relationships, or parts of a whole. When you're describing a process, the major points are almost inevitably steps in the process. When you're describing an object, the major points often correspond to the parts of the object. When you're giving a historical account, major points represent events in the chronological chain of events. If your purpose is to persuade or to collaborate, select major points that develop a line of reasoning or a logical argument that proves your central message and motivates your audience to act.

Major supporting points clarify and explain your main idea.

Illustrate with Evidence

After you've defined the main idea and identified major supporting points, you're ready to illustrate each of those points with specific evidence that helps audience members understand, accept, and remember your message. For example, if you're advocating that your company increase its advertising budget, you can support your major point by providing evidence that your most successful competitors spend more on advertising than you do. You can also describe a case in which a particular competitor increased its advertising budget and achieved

Each major point must be supported with enough specific evidence to be convincing, but don't pile on so much evidence that your message becomes overly long or boring.

TABLE 4.3 Six Types of Detail

TYPE OF DETAIL	EXAMPLE	COMMENT
Facts and figures	Sales are strong this month. We have two new contracts worth $5 million and a good chance of winning another worth $2.5 million.	Adds more credibility than any other type. Can become boring if used excessively. Most common type used in business.
Example or illustration	We've spent four months trying to hire recent accounting graduates, but so far, only one person has joined our firm. One candidate told me that she would love to work for us, but she can get $10,000 more a year elsewhere.	Adds life to a message, but one example does not prove a point. Idea must be supported by other evidence as well.
Description	Upscale hamburger restaurants target burger lovers who want more than the convenience and low prices of a McDonald's. These places feature wine and beer, half-pound burgers, and generous side dishes (nachos, potato skins). Atmosphere is key.	Helps audience visualize the subject by creating a sensory impression. Does not prove a point but clarifies it and makes it memorable. Begins with an overview of the function; defines its purpose, lists major parts, and explains how it operates.
Narration	Under former management, executives worked in blue jeans, meetings rarely started on time, and lunches ran long. When Jim Wilson became CEO, he completely overhauled the operation. A Harvard MBA who favors Brooks Brothers suits, Wilson has cut the product line in half and chopped $12 million off expenses.	Works well for attracting attention and explaining ideas but lacks statistical validity.
Reference to authority	I discussed this idea with Jackie Loman in the Chicago plant, and she was very supportive. As you know, Jackie has been in charge of that plant for the past six years. She is confident that we can speed up the number 2 line by 150 units an hour if we add another worker.	Bolsters a case while adding variety and credibility. Works only if authority is recognized and respected by audience.
Visual aids	Graphs, charts, and tables.	Helps audience grasp specific data. Used more in memos and reports than in letters.

an impressive sales gain as a result. Perhaps you can show that over the past five years, your firm's sales have gone up and down in response to the amount spent on advertising.

The appropriate number of levels in an outline is determined by the depth and breadth of information you plan to include. Long and complex reports and other documents obviously require more extensive outlines. Just remember that every level needs to fit in a logical hierarchy from high-level concepts and ideas down to finer and finer levels of detail.

To a certain extent, the more evidence you provide, the more conclusive your case will be. If your subject is complex and unfamiliar or if your audience is skeptical, you may need a lot of facts and figures to demonstrate your points. On the other hand, if your subject is routine and your audience is positively inclined, you can be more sparing with the evidence. You want to provide enough support to be convincing but not so much that your message becomes boring or inefficient.

Another way to keep your audience interested is to vary the type of detail you include. As you draft your message, try to incorporate the methods described in Table 4.3. Switch from facts and figures to narration, add a dash of description, and throw in some examples or a reference to authority. If doing so makes sense, you can reinforce all these details with visual aids.

Document Makeover

Improve This Letter

To practice correcting drafts of actual documents, visit the "Document Makeovers" section in either mybcommlab or the Companion Website for this text.

If mybcommlab is being used in your class, see your User Guide for specific instructions on how to access the content for this chapter. If you are accessing this feature through the Companion Website, click on "Document Makeovers" and then select Chapter 4. You will find a letter that contains problems and errors related to what you've learned in this chapter about planning and organizing business messages. Use the Final Draft decision tool to create an improved version of this letter. Check the document for audience focus, the right choice of medium, and the proper choice of direct or indirect approach.

If your schedule permits, put your outline aside for a day or two before you begin composing your first draft. Then review it with a fresh eye, looking for opportunities to improve the flow of ideas. For a reminder of the planning tasks involved in preparing your messages, see "Checklist: Planning Business Messages on page 143."

Communication Challenges at H&R Block

Paula Drum was impressed enough with your communication skills and social media experience to add you to the team that markets H&R Block's digital tax-preparation solutions. Using the insights you gained in this chapter, address these two communication challenges.

Individual Challenge: The first assignment Drum gives you is to write a 50-word introduction to the TaxCut software product line that can be used whenever the company needs a concise summary. For example, your text will be loaded into the IM chat system so that whenever anyone asks about TaxCut, customer service representatives can send your text with just one mouse click. Visit **www.hrblock.com** and click on "Software" to read about the various versions of TaxCut. Use this information to write your 50-word summary and then e-mail it to your instructor.

Team Challenge: An ongoing dilemma for marketers in many industries is trying to offer targeted products and services that meet the needs of specific market segments without creating so many versions that the range of choices overwhelms the consumer. For example, H&R Block is in the business of simplifying tax preparation, but it currently offers ten separate digital product and service options—five versions of the TaxCut software and five online alternatives. Simply helping consumers understand the choices available can become a considerable communication challenge in its own respect. Visit **www.hrblock.com** and click on "Online" to review the web-based options the company currently offers. With a team of classmates, analyze the design and content of this webpage in terms of its ability to help any taxpayer understand the various options and choose the one that meets his or her unique needs. For example, are the services clearly distinguished from one another, and can the average taxpayer understand the distinctions being made? What improvements might you suggest? Write a one-page summary of your analysis and recommendations.

SUMMARY OF LEARNING OBJECTIVES

1 **Describe the three-step writing process.** (1) Planning consists of four tasks: analyzing the situation (defining your purpose and profiling your audience), gathering the information to meet your audience's needs, selecting the best medium for the message and the situation, and organizing the information (defining your main idea, limiting your scope, selecting an approach, and outlining your content). (2) The writing step consists of two tasks: adapting to your audience and composing the message. Adapt your message to your audience by being sensitive to audience needs, building a strong relationship with your audience, and controlling your style. Compose your message by drafting your thoughts with strong words, effective sentences, and coherent paragraphs. (3) Completing your message consists of four tasks: revising your message by evaluating content and then rewriting and editing for clarity and conciseness, producing your message by using effective design elements and suitable delivery methods, proofreading your message for mistakes in spelling and mechanics, and distributing it in a way that meets both your needs and your audience's needs.

2 **Explain why it's important to analyze the situation and define your purpose carefully before writing a message.** You must know enough about your purpose to shape your message in a way that will achieve your goal. Moreover, without a clear purpose to guide you, you are bound to waste time and energy. To decide whether you should proceed with your message, answer four questions: (1) Will anything change as a result of this message? (2) Is my purpose realistic? (3) Is this the right time for this message? (4) Is the purpose acceptable to my organization?

3 **Discuss information-gathering options for simple messages and identify three attributes of quality information.** Gathering the information that will fulfill your audience's needs is a vital step before you attempt to organize your content. For more complex documents, you may need to plan a research project to acquire all the necessary information. However, for simple messages, if you don't already have all the information you need, you can gather it by using other methods, such as considering the audience's perspective, reading

existing reports and other company documents, talking with supervisors and others who have information and insight, and asking your audience members directly for their input. To determine whether the information you've gathered is good enough, verify that it is accurate, ethical, and pertinent to the audience's needs.

4 **List the factors to consider when choosing the most appropriate medium for a message.** The first factor to consider is media richness. Richness is determined by the medium's ability to (1) convey a message using more than one informational cue, such as sound, motion, nonverbal cues, and so on; (2) facilitate feedback; and (3) establish personal focus. Other factors to consider when selecting media include the level of formality, the specific limitations of each medium, the level of urgency, the cost of various media options, and your audience's preferences.

5 **Explain why good organization is important to both you and your audience.** When you organize messages carefully, you save time and conserve creative energy because the writing process is quicker and you spend less time rewriting. Good organization also helps your audience members understand your message, it helps them accept your message, and it saves them time as well.

6 **Explain the differences between the direct and indirect approaches to organizing a message.** The fundamental difference between the direct and indirect approaches is the order in which information is presented in the message. With the direct approach, you start with the main idea and follow that with your supporting evidence that will help people understand and accept the main idea. In contrast, with the indirect approach, you lay out your evidence first, building your case one key point at a time, and then introduce your main idea.

PEARSON
mybcommlab™

Log on to **www.mybcommlab.com** to access the following study and assessment aids associated with this chapter:

- Video applications
- Real-Time Updates
- Peer review activity
- Quick learning guides

- Pre/post test
- Personalized study plan
- Model documents
- Sample presentations

If you are not using mybcommlab, you can access the Real-Time Updates and Quick Learning Guides through **http://real-timeupdates.com/bct**. The Quick Learning Guide (located under "Learn More" on the website) hits all the high points of this chapter in just two pages. This guide, especially prepared by the authors, will help you study for exams or review important concepts whenever you need a quick refresher.

Test Your Knowledge

1. What are the three major steps in the writing process?
2. What two types of purposes do all business messages have?
3. What do you need to know in order to develop an audience profile?
4. What is the value of free writing and other discovery techniques?
5. What three factors determine media richness?
6. What are the main advantages of oral media? Of written media? Of visual media? Of electronic media?
7. How does the topic of a message differ from its main idea?
8. What is the process for organizing messages?
9. Why is it important to limit the scope of a message?
10. What three elements do you need to consider when choosing between the direct and indirect approaches?

Apply Your Knowledge

1. Some writers argue that planning messages wastes time because they inevitably change their plans as they go along. How would you respond to this argument? Briefly explain.

2. As a member of the public relations department, which medium (or media) would you recommend using to inform the local community that your toxic-waste cleanup program has been successful? Why?
3. Would you use the direct or indirect approach to ask employees to work overtime to meet an important deadline? Please explain.
4. You have been invited to speak at an annual industry conference. After preparing the outline for your presentation, you see that you've identified 14 different points to support your main idea. Should you move ahead with creating the slides for your presentation or move back and rethink your outline? Why?
5. **Ethical Choices** A day after sending an e-mail to all 1,800 employees in your company regarding income tax implications of the company's retirement plan, you discover that one of the sources you relied on for your information plagiarized from other sources. Your quickly double-check all the information in your message and confirm that it is accurate. However, you are concerned about using plagiarized information, even though you did nothing wrong. Write a brief e-mail message to your instructor, explaining how you would handle the situation.

Practice Your Knowledge

Message for Analysis

A writer is working on an insurance information brochure and is having trouble grouping the ideas logically into an outline. Using the following information, prepare the outline, paying attention to the appropriate hierarchy of ideas. If necessary, rewrite phrases to make them all consistent.

Accident Protection Insurance Plan

- Coverage is only pennies a day
- Benefit is $100,000 for accidental death on common carrier
- Benefit is $100 a day for hospitalization as result of motor vehicle or common carrier accident
- Benefit is $20,000 for accidental death in motor vehicle accident
- Individual coverage is only $17.85 per quarter; family coverage is just $26.85 per quarter
- No physical exam or health questions
- Convenient payment—billed quarterly
- Guaranteed acceptance for all applicants
- No individual rate increases
- Free, no-obligation examination period
- Cash paid in addition to any other insurance carried
- Covers accidental death when riding as fare-paying passenger on public transportation, including buses, trains, jets, ships, trolleys, subways, or any other common carrier
- Covers accidental death in motor vehicle accidents occurring while driving or riding in or on automobile, truck, camper, motor home, or nonmotorized bicycle

Exercises

Active links for all websites in this chapter can be found online. If mybcommlab is being used in your class, see your User Guide for instructions on accessing the content for this chapter. Otherwise, visit www.pearsonglobaleditions.com/bovee, locate *Business Communication Today*, Tenth Edition, click the Companion Website link, select Chapter 4, and then click on "Featured Websites." Please note that links to sites that become inactive after publication of the book will be removed from the Featured Websites section.

4.1 Message Planning Skills: Self-Assessment How good are you at planning business messages? Use the chart below to rate yourself on each element of planning an audience-centered business message. Then examine your ratings to identify where you are strongest and where you can improve, using the tips in this chapter.

4.2 Planning Messages: General and Specific Purposes Make a list of communication tasks you'll need to accomplish in the next week or so (for example, a homework assignment, an e-mail message to an instructor, a job application, or a speech to a class). For each, determine a general and a specific purpose.

4.3 Planning Messages: Specific Purpose For each of the following communication tasks, state a specific purpose (if you have trouble, try beginning with "I want to . . .").
- **a.** A report to your boss, the store manager, about the outdated items in the warehouse
- **b.** A memo to clients about your booth at the upcoming trade show
- **c.** A letter to a customer who hasn't made a payment for three months
- **d.** A memo to employees about the department's high phone bills
- **e.** A phone call to a supplier, checking on an overdue parts shipment
- **f.** A report to future users of the computer program you have chosen to handle the company's mailing list

4.4 Planning Messages: Audience Profile For each communication task that follows, write brief answers to three questions: Who is the audience? What is the audience's general attitude toward my subject? What does the audience need to know?
- **a.** A final-notice collection letter from an appliance manufacturer to an appliance dealer that is 3 months behind on payments, sent 10 days before initiating legal collection procedures
- **b.** An advertisement for digital cameras
- **c.** A proposal to top management, suggesting that the four sales regions in the United States be combined into just two regions
- **d.** Fliers to be attached to doorknobs in the neighborhood, announcing reduced rates for chimney cleaning or repairs
- **e.** A cover letter sent along with your résumé to a potential employer
- **f.** A website that describes the services offered by a consulting firm that helps accounting managers comply with government regulations

ELEMENT OF PLANNING	ALWAYS	FREQUENTLY	OCCASIONALLY	NEVER
1. I start by defining my purpose.	___	___	___	___
2. I analyze my audience before writing a message.	___	___	___	___
3. I investigate what my audience wants to know.	___	___	___	___
4. I check that my information is accurate, ethical, and pertinent.	___	___	___	___
5. I consider my audience and purpose when selecting media.	___	___	___	___

4.5 **Meeting Audience Needs: Necessary Information** Choose a fairly simple electronic device (such as a digital music player or digital camera) that you know how to operate well. Write two sets of instructions for operating the device: one set for a reader who has never used that type of device and one set for someone who is generally familiar with that type of machine but has never operated the specific model. Briefly explain how your two audiences affect your instructions.

4.6 **Selecting Media: Defining the Purpose** List five messages you have received lately, such as direct-mail promotions, letters, e-mail messages, phone solicitations, and lectures. For each, determine the general purpose and the specific purpose; then answer the following questions: (1) Was the message well timed? (2) Did the sender choose an appropriate medium for the message? (3) Was the sender's purpose realistic?

4.7 **Selecting Media: Identifying an Audience** Barbara Marquardt is in charge of public relations for a cruise line that operates out of Miami. She is shocked to read a letter in a local newspaper from a disgruntled passenger, complaining about the service and entertainment on a recent cruise. Marquardt will have to respond to these publicized criticisms in some way. What audiences will she need to consider in her response? What medium should she choose? If the letter had been published in a travel publication widely read by travel agents and cruise travelers, how might her course of action have differed? Summarize your recommendations in an e-mail message.

4.8 **Teamwork: Audience Analysis** Your team has been studying a new method for testing the durability of your company's power tools. Now the team needs to prepare three separate reports on the findings: first, a report for the administrator who will decide whether to purchase the equipment needed for this new testing method; second, a report for the company's engineers who design and develop the hand tools; and third, a report for the trainers who will be showing workers how to use the new equipment. To determine the audience's needs for each of these reports, the team has listed the following questions: (1) Who are the readers? (2) Why will they read my report? (3) Do they need introductory or background material? (4) Do they need definitions of terms? (5) What level or type of language is needed? (6) What level of detail is needed? (7) What result does my report aim for? Working with two other students, answer the questions for each of these audiences and summarize your analysis in a brief report:
a. The administrator
b. The engineers
c. The trainers

4.9 **Internet: Planning Your Message** Go to the PepsiCo website, at **www.pepsico.com**, and locate the latest annual report under the Investors tab. Read the annual report's letter to shareholders. Who is the audience for this message? What is the general purpose of the message? What do you think this audience wants to know from the chairman of PepsiCo? Summarize your answers in a brief (one-page) memo or oral presentation.

4.10 **Message Organization: Outlining Your Content** Using the improved version of the GNC e-mail message in Figure 4.8, draw an organizational chart similar to the one shown in Figure 4.13. Fill in the main idea, the major points, and the evidence provided in this letter. (*Note:* Your diagram may be smaller than the one shown in Figure 4.13.)

4.11 **Message Organization: Limiting Scope** Suppose you are preparing to recommend that top management install a new heating system that uses the cogeneration process. The following information is in your files. Eliminate topics that aren't essential and then arrange the other topics so that your report will give top managers a clear understanding of the heating system and a balanced, concise justification for installing it.
- History of the development of the cogeneration heating process
- Scientific credentials of the developers of the process
- Risks assumed in using this process
- Your plan for installing the equipment in the headquarters building
- Stories about the successful use of cogeneration technology in comparable facilities
- Specifications of the equipment that would be installed
- Plans for disposing of the old heating equipment
- Costs of installing and running the new equipment
- Advantages and disadvantages of using the new process
- Detailed 10-year cost projections
- Estimates of the time needed to phase in the new system
- Alternative systems that management might want to consider

4.12 **Message Organization: Choosing an Approach** Indicate whether the direct or indirect approach would be best in each of the following situations and briefly explain why. Would any of these messages be inappropriate for e-mail? Explain.
a. A message to the owner of an automobile dealership, complaining about poor service work
b. A message from a recent college graduate, requesting a letter of recommendation from a former instructor
c. A message turning down a job applicant
d. A message announcing that because of high air-conditioning costs, the plant temperature will be held at 78°F during the summer
e. A message from an advertising agency to a troublesome long-term client, explaining that the agency will no longer be able to work on the client's account.

4.13 **Message Organization: Audience Focus** If you were trying to persuade people to take the following actions, how would you organize your argument?

   a. You want your boss to approve your plan for hiring two new people.

   b. You want to be hired for a job.

   c. You want to be granted a business loan.

   d. You want to collect a small amount of money from a regular customer whose account is slightly past due.

   e. You want to collect a large amount of money from a customer whose account is seriously past due.

4.14 **Ethical Choices: Providing Information** Your supervisor, whom you respect, has asked you to withhold important information that you think should be included in a report you are preparing. Disobeying him could be disastrous for your relationship and your career. Obeying him could violate your personal code of ethics. What should you do? On the basis of the discussion in Chapter 1, would you consider this situation to be an ethical dilemma or an ethical lapse? Please explain.

4.15 **Three-Step Process: Other Applications** How can the material discussed in this chapter also apply to meetings, as discussed in Chapter 2? (*Hint:* Review the section headings in this chapter and think about making your meetings more productive.)

| Expand Your Knowledge

Exploring the Best of the Web

Ready to Make a Buck on Blogging?

www.problogger.net

Millions of people now blog for fun or free, but a few are figuring out how to earn part or all of their income from their blogging efforts. ProBlogger (www.problogger.net) can help you get started with advice on setting up a blog, using Google's popular AdSense program, and identifying multiple ways to generate income with a blog. Explore ProBlogger's advice and answer these questions:

   1. What are the various ways bloggers can make money from their work?

   2. How can you go about choosing a topic for a blog?

   3. How can the Google AdSense program help bloggers cover their costs and perhaps even turn a profit?

Sharpening Your Career Skills Online

Bovée and Thill's Business Communication Web Search, at http://businesscommunicationblog.com/websearch, is a unique research tool designed specifically for business communication research. Use the Web Search function to find a website, video, podcast, or PowerPoint presentation that offers advice on planning a report, speech, or other business message. Write a brief e-mail message to your instructor, describing the item that you found and summarizing the career skills information you learned from it.

Writing Business Messages

Learning Objectives

After studying this chapter, you will be able to

1 Explain the importance of adapting to your audiences and list three techniques for doing so

2 Explain why establishing credibility is vital to the success of your communication efforts

3 Discuss four ways of achieving a businesslike tone with a style that is clear and concise

4 Briefly describe how to select words that are not only correct but also effective

5 Explain how sentence style affects emphasis in a message

6 List five ways to develop unified, coherent paragraphs

Communication Close-up at Creative Commons

Joi Ito, CEO of Creative Commons, uses a variety of communication vehicles to convince copyright owners to explore new ways of sharing and protecting their creative works.

http://creativecommons.org

Have you ever noticed that tiny © symbol on books, DVDs, music CDs, and other media products? It means that the person or organization that created the item is granted *copyright* protection, the exclusive legal right to produce, distribute, and sell that creation. Anyone who wants to resell, redistribute, or adapt such works usually needs to secure permission from the current copyright holder.

However, what if you *want* people to remix the song you just recorded or use your graphical designs in whatever artistic compositions they might want to create? Or if you want to give away some of your creative works to get your name out there, without giving up all your legal rights to them? Alternatively, suppose you need a few photos or a video clip for a website? Other than for limited personal and educational use, a conventional copyright requires every person to negotiate a contract for every application or adaptation of every piece of work he or she wants to use.

The search for some middle ground between "all rights reserved" and simply giving your work away led Stanford University law professor Lawrence Lessig to co-found Creative Commons. This nonprofit organization's goal is to provide a simple, free, and legal way for musicians, artists, writers, teachers, scientists, and others to collaborate and benefit through the sharing of art and ideas. Instead of the everything-or-nothing approach of traditional copyright, Creative Commons offers a more flexible range of "some rights reserved" options.

In 2008, Japanese venture capitalist Joichi ("Joi") Ito took over as CEO, bringing an entrepreneur's perspective to the Creative Commons business model. Through a variety of media, Ito continues to promote the benefits of simplifying the legal constraints on sharing and reusing intellectual property, whether for creative expression or scientific research. Millions of Creative Commons licenses have been initiated for musical works, images, short films, educational materials, novels, and more. This approach can't solve the entire dilemma of copyrights in the digital age, and not everyone agrees with the Creative Commons model, but it has created an easier way for creative people to communicate and collaborate.[1]

BRINGING YOUR IDEAS TO LIFE

As they work to persuade their audiences to consider new forms of copyright protection, Joi Ito and his colleagues at Creative Commons (profiled in the chapter-opening Communication Close-up) realize it takes more than just a great idea to change the way people think. Expressing ideas clearly and persuasively starts with adapting to one's audience.

1 **LEARNING OBJECTIVE**

Explain the importance of adapting to your audiences and list three techniques for doing so

ADAPTING TO YOUR AUDIENCE

Whether consciously or not, audiences greet most incoming messages with a selfish question: "What's in this for me?" If your intended audience members think a message does not apply to them or doesn't meet their needs, they won't be inclined to pay attention to it. Follow the example set by the Creative Commons website, which addresses a diverse audience of artists, lawyers, and business professionals but fine-tunes specific messages for each group of people.

Readers and listeners want to know how your messages will benefit them.

Providing the right information in the right format is essential, but it's not the only important aspect of adapting to your audience. You may also need to adjust your writing or speaking style for specific situations, and doing so requires a concerted effort for most communicators. For example, you might have a terse, "just the facts" style of writing that works well in most situations but can be off-putting when some diplomacy or sensitivity is required. Conversely, if you have a warm, conversational style in which your personality tends to shine through, you may need to adjust to a more direct, objective style for communicating about the most serious matters.

Adapting to your audience can mean altering your natural communication style to match specific situations.

To adapt to your audiences in a way that provides a compelling answer to the "What's in this for me?" question, be sensitive to your audience members' needs, build strong relationships, and control your style to maintain a professional tone.

Being Sensitive to Your Audience's Needs

If your readers or listeners don't think you understand or care about their needs, they won't pay attention, plain and simple. You can improve your audience sensitivity by adopting the "you" attitude, maintaining good standards of etiquette, emphasizing the positive, and using bias-free language.

Using the "You" Attitude

Chapter 1 introduced the notion of audience-centered communication and the "you" attitude—speaking and writing in terms of your audience's wishes, interests, hopes, and preferences. On the simplest level, you can adopt the "you" attitude by replacing terms such as *I, me, mine, we, us,* and *ours* with *you* and *yours*:

The "you" attitude is best implemented by expressing your message in terms of the audience's interests and needs.

INSTEAD OF THIS

Tuesday is the only day that we can promise quick response to purchase order requests; we are swamped the rest of the week.

We offer MP3 players with 50, 75, or 100 gigabytes of storage capacity.

WRITE THIS

If you need a quick response, please submit your purchase order requests on Tuesday.

You can choose an MP3 player with 50, 75, or 100 gigabytes of storage

Messages that emphasize "I" and "we" risk sounding selfish and uninterested in the audience. Such messages feel like they are all about the sender, not the receiver.

However, the "you" attitude is more than simply using particular pronouns; it's a matter of genuine interest and concern. You can use *you* 25 times in a single page and still ignore your audience's true concerns. If you're talking to a retailer, try to think like a retailer; if you're dealing with a production supervisor, put yourself in that position; if you're writing to a dissatisfied customer, imagine how you would feel at the other end of the transaction.

Be aware that on some occasions, it's better to avoid using *you*, particularly if doing so will sound overly authoritative or accusing:

Avoid using you *and* yours *when doing so*
* *Makes you sound dictatorial*
* *Could make someone else feel unnecessarily guilty*
* *Goes against your organization's style*
* *Is inappropriate for the culture*

INSTEAD OF THIS	WRITE THIS
You failed to deliver the customer's order on time.	The customer didn't receive the order on time.
	or
	Let's figure out a system that will ensure on-time deliveries.
You must correct all five copies by noon.	All five copies must be corrected by noon.

As you practice using the "you" attitude, be sure to consider the attitudes of other cultures and the policies of your organization. In some cultures, it is improper to single out one person's achievements because the whole team is responsible for the outcome; in that case, using the pronoun *we* or *our* (when you and your audience are part of the same team) would be more appropriate. Similarly, some companies have a tradition of avoiding references to *you* and *I* in most messages and reports.

Maintaining Standards of Etiquette

You know how it feels to be treated inconsiderately; when that happens, you probably react emotionally and then pay less attention to the offending message. By being courteous to members of your audience, you show consideration for them and foster a more successful environment for communication.

Although you may be tempted now and then to be brutally frank, try to express the facts in a kind and thoughtful manner.

On occasions when you experience frustration with co-workers, customers, or others, you may be tempted to say what you think in blunt terms. But venting your emotions rarely improves the situation and can jeopardize your audience's goodwill. Demonstrate your diplomatic skills by controlling your emotions and communicating calmly and politely:

INSTEAD OF THIS	WRITE THIS
Once again, you've managed to bring down the entire website through your incompetent programming.	Let's review the last website update to explore ways to improve the process.
You've been sitting on our order for two weeks, and we need it now!	Our production schedules depend on timely delivery of parts and supplies, but we have not yet received the order you promised to deliver two weeks ago. Please respond today with a firm delivery commitment.

Use extra tact when communicating with people higher up the organization chart or outside the company.

Of course, some situations require more diplomacy than others. If you know your audience well, a less formal approach may be more appropriate. However, when you are communicating with people who outrank you or with people outside your organization, an added measure of courtesy is usually needed.

Written communication and most forms of electronic media generally require more tact than oral communication (Figure 5.1). When you're speaking, your words are softened by your tone of voice and facial expression. Plus, you can adjust your approach according to the feedback you get. If you inadvertently offend someone in writing or in a podcast, for example, you usually don't get the immediate feedback you would need to resolve the situation. In fact, you may never know that you offended your audience.

FIGURE 5.1 Fostering a Positive Relationship with an Audience
In the "ineffective" example, notice how the customer service agent's unfortunate word choices immediately derail this IM exchange. In the "effective" example, a more sensitive approach allows both people to focus on solving the problem.

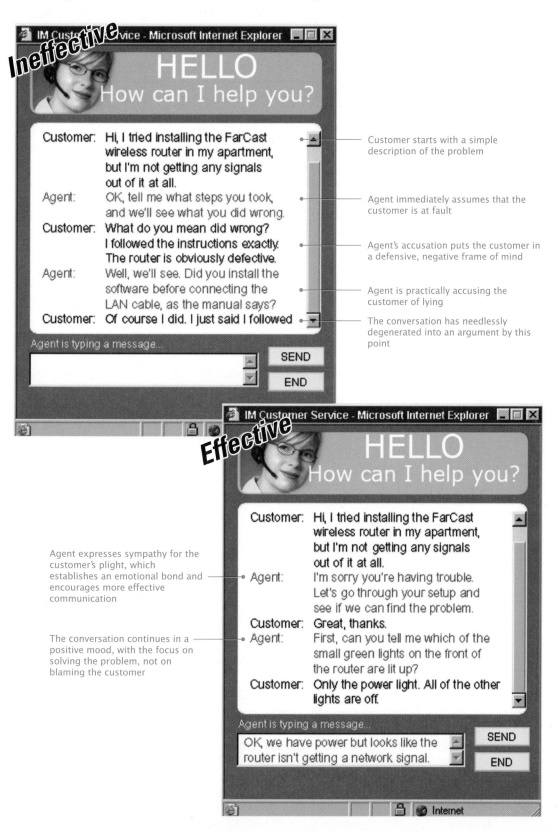

Emphasizing the Positive

You can communicate negative news without being negative.

During your career, you will have many occasions in which you need to communicate bad news. As you rise through the ranks of management, you will encounter situations in which unpleasant news can significantly affect the personal and financial well-being of employees, customers, and investors. However, there is a big difference between delivering negative news and being negative. When the tone of your message is negative, you put unnecessary strain on business relationships, which can cause people to distance themselves from you and your ideas.

Never try to hide negative news, but always be on the lookout for positive points that will foster a good relationship with your audience:[2]

INSTEAD OF THIS	WRITE THIS
It is impossible to repair your laptop today.	Your computer can be ready by Tuesday. Would you like a loaner until then?
We apologize for inconveniencing you during our remodeling.	The renovations now under way will help us serve you better.
We wasted $300,000 advertising in that magazine.	Our $300,000 advertising investment did not pay off; let's analyze the experience and apply the insights to future campaigns.

When you are offering criticism or advice, focus on what the person can do to improve.

When you find it necessary to criticize or correct, don't dwell on the other person's mistakes. Avoid referring to failures, problems, or shortcomings. Focus instead on what the audience members can do to improve:

INSTEAD OF THIS	WRITE THIS
The problem with this department is a failure to control costs.	The performance of this department can be improved by tightening cost controls.
You failed to provide all the necessary information on the previous screen.	Please review the items marked in red on the previous screen so that we can process your order as quickly as possible.

Show your audience members how they will benefit from complying with your message.

If you're trying to persuade audience members to buy a product, pay a bill, or perform a service for you, emphasize what's in it for them. Don't focus on why *you* want them to do something. An individual who sees the possibility for personal benefit is more likely to respond positively to your appeal:

INSTEAD OF THIS	WRITE THIS
We will notify all three credit reporting agencies if you do not pay your overdue bill within 10 days.	Paying your overdue bill within 10 days will prevent a negative entry on your credit record.
I am tired of seeing so many errors in the customer service blog.	Proofreading your blog postings will help you avoid embarrassing mistakes that generate more customer service complaints.

Try to avoid words with unnecessarily negative connotations; use meaningful euphemisms instead.

In general, try to state your message without using words that may hurt or offend your audience. Substitute *euphemisms* (milder equivalents) for words or phrases that have unpleasant associations. You can be honest without being harsh. Gentle language won't change the facts, but it will make them more acceptable:

INSTEAD OF THIS	WRITE THIS
Cheap merchandise	Economy merchandise
Failing	Underperforming
Fake	Imitation or faux

On the other hand, don't carry euphemisms to extremes, or your audience will view your efforts as insincere. And if you're too subtle, people won't know what you're talking about. If employees need to become 10 percent more productive to save the company from bankruptcy, don't tell them they need to "make positive performance adjustments"—tell them they need to become 10 percent more productive.

Also, when using euphemisms, you walk a fine line between softening the blow and hiding the facts. It would be unethical to speak to your local community about the disposal of "manufacturing by-products" when you're really talking about toxic waste. Such an attempt to hide the facts would likely backfire as well, damaging your business image and reputation. Even if it is unpleasant, people respond better to an honest message delivered with integrity than they do to a sugar-coated message that obscures the truth.

Using Bias-Free Language

Chapter 3 points out that you are often unaware of the influence of your own culture on your behavior, and this circumstance extends to the language you use. Any bias present in your culture is likely to show up in your language, often in subtle ways that you may not even recognize. However, chances are that your audience will.

Biases present in your culture are likely to show up in your language, making it important to understand these cultural forces.

Bias-free language avoids words and phrases that unfairly and even unethically categorize or stigmatize people in ways related to gender, race, ethnicity, age, or disability. Contrary to what some may think, biased language is not simply about "labels." To a significant degree, language reflects the way we think and what we believe, and biased language may well perpetuate the underlying stereotypes and prejudices that it represents.[3] Moreover, because communication is all about perception, simply *being* fair and objective isn't enough. To establish a good relationship with your audience, you must also *appear* to be fair.[4] Good communicators make every effort to change biased language (see Table 5.1). Bias can come in a variety of forms:

- **Gender bias.** Avoid sexist language by using the same label for everyone (don't call a woman *chairperson* and then call a man *chairman;* use *chair, chairperson,* or *chairman* consistently). Rather than refer to all individuals as *he,* reword sentences to use the plural *they* or avoid using a pronoun altogether. Note that the preferred title for women in business is *Ms.,* unless the individual asks to be addressed as *Miss* or *Mrs.* or has some other title, such as *Dr.*
- **Racial and ethnic bias.** Avoid language suggesting that members of a racial or ethnic group have stereotypical characteristics. The best solution is to avoid identifying people by race or ethnic origin unless such a label is relevant to the matter at hand—and it rarely is.
- **Age bias.** As with gender, race, and ethnic background, mention the age of a person only when it is relevant. Moreover, be careful of the context in which you use words that refer to age. Such words carry a variety of positive and negative connotations—and not only when referring to people beyond a certain age. For example, *young* can imply youthfulness, inexperience, or even immaturity, depending on how it's used.
- **Disability bias.** As with other labels, physical, mental, sensory, or emotional impairments should never be mentioned in business messages unless those conditions are directly relevant to the subject. If you must refer to someone's disability, put the person first and the disability second.[5] For example, by saying "employees with physical handicaps," not "handicapped employees," you focus on the whole person, not the disability. Finally, never use outdated terminology such as *crippled* or *retarded.*

REAL-TIME UPDATES

Learn More

Get detailed advice on using bias-free language

This in-depth guide offers practical tips for avoiding many types of cultural bias in your writing and speaking. Go to **http://real-timeupdates .com/bct** and click on "Learn More." If you are using mybcommlab, you can access Real-Time Updates within each chapter or under Student Study Tools.

Building Strong Relationships with Your Audience

Whether a one-time interaction or a series of exchanges over the course of many months or years, successful communication relies on a positive relationship existing between sender

TABLE 5.1   Overcoming Bias in Language

EXAMPLES	UNACCEPTABLE	PREFERABLE
Gender Bias		
Using words containing *man*	Man-made	Artificial, synthetic, manufactured, constructed, human-made
	Mankind	Humanity, human beings, human race, people
	Manpower	Workers, workforce
	Businessman	Executive, manager, businessperson, professional
	Salesman	Sales representative, salesperson
	Foreman	Supervisor
Using female-gender words	Actress, stewardess	Actor, flight attendant
Using special designations	Woman doctor, male nurse	Doctor, nurse
Using *he* to refer to "everyone"	The average worker . . . he	The average worker . . . he or she
		OR
		Average workers . . . they
Identifying roles with gender	The typical executive spends four hours of his day in meetings.	Most executives spend four hours a day in meetings.
	the consumer . . . she	consumers . . . they
	the nurse/teacher . . . she	nurses/teachers . . . they
Identifying women by marital status	Mrs. Norm Lindstrom	Maria Lindstrom
		OR
		Ms. Maria Lindstrom
	Norm Lindstrom and Ms. Drake	Norm Lindstrom and Maria Drake
		OR
		Mr. Lindstrom and Ms. Drake
Racial and Ethnic Bias		
Assigning stereotypes	Not surprisingly, Shing-Tung Yau excels in mathematics.	Shing-Tung Yau excels in mathematics.
Identifying people by race or ethnicity	Mario M. Cuomo, Italian-American politician and ex-governor of New York	Mario M. Cuomo, politician and ex-governor of New York
Age Bias		
Including age when irrelevant	Mary Kirazy, 58, has just joined our trust department.	Mary Kirazy has just joined our trust department.
Disability Bias		
Putting the disability before the person	Disabled workers face many barriers on the job.	Workers with physical disabilities face many barriers on the job.
	An epileptic, Tracy has no trouble doing her job.	Tracy's epilepsy has no effect on her job performance.

2 LEARNING OBJECTIVE

Explain why establishing credibility is vital to the success of your communication efforts

and receiver. Establishing your credibility and projecting your company's image are two vital steps in building and fostering positive business relationships.

Establishing Your Credibility

Audience responses to your messages depend heavily on your **credibility**, a measure of your believability, based on how reliable you are and how much trust you evoke in others. With audiences who already know you, you've already established some degree of credibility, based on past communication efforts. As long as you haven't let people down in the past,

FIGURE 5.2 Building Credibility
Lisa Ford is a highly regarded expert in the field of customer service, but she still takes care to communicate her qualifications as a presenter so that potential audience members who aren't familiar with her work can appreciate the expertise she has to offer.

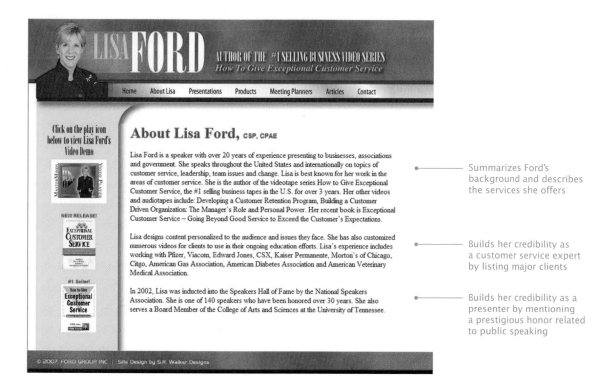

Summarizes Ford's background and describes the services she offers

Builds her credibility as a customer service expert by listing major clients

Builds her credibility as a presenter by mentioning a prestigious honor related to public speaking

they are inclined to accept each new message from you. However, with audiences that don't know you, you need to establish credibility before they'll accept—or perhaps even pay attention to—your messages (see Figure 5.2). To build, maintain, or repair your credibility, emphasize the following characteristics:

People are more likely to react positively to your message when they have confidence in you.

- **Honesty.** Demonstrating honesty and integrity will earn you the respect of your audiences, even if they don't always agree with or welcome your messages.
- **Objectivity.** Show that you can distance yourself from emotional situations and look at all sides of an issue.
- **Awareness of audience needs.** Let your audiences know that you understand what's important to them.
- **Credentials, knowledge, and expertise.** Audiences need to know that you have whatever it takes to back up your message, whether it's education, professional certification, special training, past successes, or simply the fact that you've done your research.
- **Endorsements.** An *endorsement* is a statement on your behalf by someone who is accepted by your audience as an expert. If your audiences don't know anything about you, try to get assistance from someone they do know and trust.
- **Performance.** Demonstrating impressive communication skills is not enough; people need to know they can count on you to get the job done.
- **Confidence.** Audiences need to know that you believe in yourself and your message. If you are convinced that your message is sound, you can state your case confidently, without sounding boastful or arrogant.
- **Communication style.** Support your points with evidence, not empty terms such as *amazing, incredible,* or *extraordinary.*

To enhance your credibility, emphasize such factors as honesty, objectivity, and awareness of audience needs.

- **Sincerity.** When you offer praise, don't use *hyperbole*, such as "you are the most fantastic employee I could ever imagine." Instead, point out specific qualities that warrant praise.

In addition, audiences need to know that you believe in yourself and your message. If you lack faith in yourself, you're likely to communicate an uncertain attitude that undermines your credibility. In contrast, if you are convinced that your message is sound, you can state your case with authority so that your audience has no doubts. Try to avoid phrases containing words such as *if*, *hope*, and *trust*, which can drain the audience's confidence in your message:

INSTEAD OF THIS	WRITE THIS
We hope this recommendation will be helpful.	We're glad to make this recommendation.
If you'd like to order, please visit our website	To order, please visit our website.
We trust that you'll want to extend your service contract.	By extending your service contract, you can continue to enjoy top-notch performance from your equipment.

Finally, keep in mind that credibility can take a long time to establish—and it can be wiped out in an instant. An occasional mistake or letdown is usually forgiven, but major lapses in honesty or integrity can destroy your reputation. On the other hand, when you do establish credibility, communication becomes much easier because you no longer have to spend time and energy convincing people that you are a trustworthy source of information and ideas.

Projecting Your Company's Image

Your company's interests and reputation take precedence over your personal communication style.

When you communicate with anyone outside your organization, it is more than a conversation between two individuals. You represent your company and therefore play a vital role in helping the company build and maintain positive relationships with all its stakeholders. Most successful companies work hard to foster a specific public image, and your external communication efforts need to project that image. As part of this responsibility, the interests and preferred communication style of your company must take precedence over your own views and personal communication style.

Many organizations have specific communication guidelines that show everything from the correct use of the company name to preferred abbreviations and other grammatical details. Specifying a desired style of communication is more difficult, however. Observe more experienced colleagues to see how they communicate and never hesitate to ask for editorial help to make sure you're conveying the appropriate tone. For instance, with clients entrusting thousands or millions of dollars to it, an investment firm communicates in a style quite different from that of a clothing retailer. And a clothing retailer specializing in high-quality business attire communicates in a different style than a store catering to the latest trends in casual wear.

Controlling Your Style and Tone

3 LEARNING OBJECTIVE

Discuss four ways of achieving a businesslike tone with a style that is clear and concise

Your communication **style** involves the choices you make to express yourself: the words you select, the manner in which you use those words in sentences, and the way you build paragraphs from individual sentences. Your style creates a certain **tone**, or overall impression, in your messages. You can vary your style to sound forceful or objective, personal or formal, colorful or dry. The right choice depends on the nature of your message and your relationship with the reader. Although style can be refined during the revision phase (see Chapter 6), you'll save time and a lot of rewriting if you use a style that allows you to achieve the desired tone from the start.

Using a Conversational Tone

The tone of your business messages can range from informal to conversational to formal. If you're in a large organization and you're communicating with your superiors or with customers, your tone may tend to be more formal and respectful.[6] However, that formal tone might sound distant and cold if used with close colleagues.

Most business messages aim for a conversational style that is warm but businesslike.

Compare the three versions of the message in Table 5.2. The first is too formal and stuffy for today's audiences, whereas the third is inappropriately casual for business. The second message demonstrates the conversational tone used in most business communication—plain language that sounds businesslike without being stuffy, full of jargon, or sounding like texting between two friends who are out clubbing. You can achieve a tone that is conversational but still businesslike by following these guidelines:

- **Understand the difference between texting and writing.** The casual, acronym-laden language used in text messaging and IM between friends is not considered professional business writing. Yes, texting style is an efficient way for friends to communicate—particularly taking into account the limitations of a phone keypad—but if you want to be taken seriously in business, you simply cannot write like this on the job.
- **Avoid stale and pompous language.** To achieve a businesslike tone, you might be tempted to adopt such phrases as "attached please find" and "please be advised that."

TABLE 5.2 Finding the Right Tone

TONE	EXAMPLE
Stuffy: too formal for today's audiences	Dear Ms. Navarro: Enclosed please find the information that was requested during our telephone communication of May 14. As was mentioned at that time, Midville Hospital has significantly more doctors of exceptional quality than any other health facility in the region. As you were also informed, our organization has quite an impressive network of doctors and other health-care professionals with offices located throughout the province. In the event that you should need a specialist, our professionals will be able to make an appropriate recommendation. In the event that you have questions or would like additional information, you may certainly contact me during regular business hours. Most sincerely yours, Samuel G. Berenz
Conversational: just right for most business communication	Dear Ms. Navarro: Here's the information you requested during our phone conversation on Friday. As I mentioned, Midville Hospital has the highest-rated doctors and more of them than any other hospital in the region. In addition, we have a vast network of doctors and other health professionals with offices throughout the province. If you need a specialist, they can refer you to the right one. If you would like more information, please call any time between 9:00 and 5:00, Monday through Friday. Sincerely, Samuel G. Berenz
Unprofessional: too casual for business communication	Here's the 411 you requested. IMHO, we have more and better doctors than any other hospital in the region. FYI, we also have a large group of doctors and other health professionals w/offices close to U at work/home. If U need a specialist, they'll refer U to the right one. Any ? just ring or msg. L8R, S

TABLE 5.3 Weeding Out Obsolete Phrases

OBSOLETE PHRASE	UP-TO-DATE REPLACEMENT
we are in receipt of	we received
kindly advise	please let me/us know
attached please find	enclosed is or I/we have enclosed
it has come to my attention	I have just learned or [someone] has just informed me
the undersigned	I/we
in due course	(specify a time or date)
permit me to say that	(omit; just say whatever you need to say)
pursuant to	(omit; just say whatever you need to say)
in closing, I'd like to say	(omit; just say whatever you need to say)
we wish to inform you that	(omit; just say whatever you need to say)
please be advised that	(omit; just say whatever you need to say)

While these phrases were once common in business, they sound stale and pompous to contemporary audiences (see Table 5.3).

- **Avoid preaching and bragging.** Few things are more irritating than know-it-alls who like to preach or brag. However, if you need to remind your audience of something that should be obvious, try to work in the information casually, perhaps in the middle of a paragraph, where it will sound like a secondary comment rather than a major revelation. Also, avoid bragging about your accomplishments or those of your organization (unless your audience is a part of your organization and you are celebrating a group achievement).

- **Be careful with intimacy.** Business messages should generally avoid intimacy, such as sharing personal details or adopting a casual, unprofessional tone. However, when you have a close relationship with audience members, such as among the members of a close-knit team, a more intimate tone is sometimes appropriate and even expected.

- **Be careful with humor.** In most situations, you have little to gain from humor and potentially much to lose. Never use humor in formal messages or when you're communicating across cultural boundaries. Humor can easily backfire and divert attention from your message. If you don't know your audience well or you're not skilled at using humor in a business setting, don't use it at all.

Using Plain Language

What do you think this sentence is trying to say?

> We continually exist to synergistically supply value-added deliverables such that we may continue to proactively maintain enterprise-wide data to stay competitive in tomorrow's world.[7]

Audiences can understand and act on plain English without reading it over and over.

If you don't have any idea what it means, you're not alone. However, this is a real sentence from a real company, written in an attempt to explain what the company does and why. This sort of incomprehensible, buzzword-filled writing is driving a widespread call to use *plain language* (or *plain English* specifically when English is involved).

Using plain language is a way of presenting information in a simple, unadorned style so that your audience can easily grasp your meaning, without struggling through specialized, technical, or convoluted language. The Plain English Campaign (a nonprofit group in England that's campaigning for clear language) defines *plain English* as language "that the intended audience can read, understand and act upon the first time they read it."[8] You can see how this definition supports using the "you" attitude and shows respect for your audience. In addition, plain language can make companies more productive and more profitable

COMMUNICATING ACROSS CULTURES

Communicating with a Global Audience on the Web

Reaching an international audience on the web involves more than simply offering translations of the English language. Successful global sites address the needs of international customers in five ways:

1. **Consider the reader's perspective.** Many communication elements that you may take for granted may be interpreted differently by audiences in different countries. Should you use the metric system, different notations for times or dates, or even different names for countries? For example, German citizens don't refer to their country by the English word *Germany*; it's *Deutschland* to them. Review the entire online experience and look for ways to improve communication, including such helpful tools as interactive currency converters and translation dictionaries.
2. **Take cultural differences into account.** For instance, because humor is rooted in cultural norms, U.S. humor may not be so funny to readers from other countries. Avoid idioms and references that aren't universally recognized, such as "putting all your eggs in one basket" or "jumping out of the frying pan into the fire."
3. **Keep the message clear.** Choose simple, unambiguous words; construct short, clear, sentences; and write in the active voice whenever possible. Define abbreviations, acronyms, and words an international audience may not be familiar with.
4. **Complement language with visuals.** Use drawings, photos, videos, and other visual elements to support written messages.
5. **Consult local experts.** Seek the advice of local experts about phrases and references that may be expected. Even terms as simple as *homepage* differ from country to country. Spanish readers refer to the "first page," or *pagina inicial,* whereas the French term is "welcome page," or *page d'accueil.*

CAREER APPLICATIONS

1. Visit Sony's Global Headquarters website, at www.sony.net, and find Sony's music websites for Australia (www.sonymusic.com.au), France (www.sonymusic.fr), and Germany (www.sonybmg.de). How does Sony localize each country's site?
2. Compare Sony's international sites to IBM's global webpages, at www.ibm.com/us/, www.ibm.com/au/, www.ibm.com/fr/, and www.ibm.com/de/. How does Sony's approach differ from IBM's? Do both corporations successfully address the needs of a global audience? Write a two-paragraph summary that compares the international sites of the two companies.

---

simply because people spend less time trying to figure out messages that are confusing or aren't written to meet their needs.[9]

On the Creative Commons website, for instance, licensing terms are available in two versions: a complete "legal code" document that spells out contractual details in specific legal terms that meet the needs of legal professionals and a second version labeled "license deed," which explains the licensing terms in nontechnical language that anyone can understand.[10]

Bear in mind that plain language doesn't have to be simplistic, dull, or imprecise. The point is to be clear, not lifeless. Also, be sure to consider the needs and expectations of your audience. For instance, scientific, technical, legal, and other specialized messages often require specialized terminology. Use these specific terms whenever you need to; just be sure to use them in clearly constructed sentences and well-organized paragraphs.

Even though readers overwhelmingly appreciate plain language and its merits have been demonstrated in a variety of audience tests,[11] murky, pompous, and unnecessarily complex writing is still more common than it should be. One reason is that writers are sometimes unsure about their own writing skills and about the impact their messages will have. They mistakenly believe that packaging simple ideas in complex writing makes their messages seem more impressive. Another reason is inadequate planning, which results in documents that meander in search of a message. A third reason is that some writers intentionally try to create distance between themselves and their audiences. Whatever the cause, the result of unnecessarily complex writing is always the same: ineffective communication that wastes time, wastes money, and annoys those who come in contact with it.

Selecting the Active or Passive Voice

Your choice of the active or passive voice affects the tone of your message. You are using the **active voice** when the subject performs the action and the object receives the action: "John rented the office." You're using the **passive voice** when the subject receives the action: "The

TABLE 5.4 Choosing the Active or Passive Voice

In general, avoid the passive voice in order to make your writing lively and direct.

DULL AND INDIRECT IN THE PASSIVE VOICE	LIVELY AND DIRECT IN THE ACTIVE VOICE
The new procedure was developed by the operations team.	The operations team developed the new procedure.
Legal problems are created by this contract.	This contract creates legal problems.
Reception preparations have been undertaken by our PR people for the new CEO's arrival.	Our PR people have begun planning a reception for the new CEO.

However, the passive voice is helpful when you need to be diplomatic or want to focus attention on problems or solutions rather than on people.

ACCUSATORY OR SELF-CONGRATULATORY IN THE ACTIVE VOICE	MORE DIPLOMATIC IN THE PASSIVE VOICE
You lost the shipment.	The shipment was lost.
I recruited seven engineers last month.	Seven engineers were recruited last month.
We are investigating the high rate of failures on the final assembly line.	The high rate of failures on the final assembly line is being investigated.

office was rented by John." As you can see, the passive voice combines the helping verb *to be* with a form of the verb that is usually similar to the past tense. When you use active sentences, your messages generally sound less formal and make it easier for readers to figure out who performed the action (see Table 5.4). In contrast, using the passive voice deemphasizes the subject and implies that the action was done by something or someone.

Active sentences are usually stronger than passive ones.

Using the active voice helps make your writing more direct, livelier, and easier to read. In contrast, the passive voice is not wrong grammatically, but it is often cumbersome, can be unnecessarily vague, and can make sentences overly long. In most cases, the active voice is your best choice.[12] Nevertheless, using the passive voice can help you demonstrate the "you" attitude in some situations:

Use passive sentences to soften bad news, to put yourself in the background, or to create an impersonal tone.

- When you want to be diplomatic about pointing out a problem or an error of some kind (the passive version seems less like an accusation)
- When you want to point out what's being done without taking or attributing either the credit or the blame (the passive version shifts the spotlight away from the person or persons involved)
- When you want to avoid personal pronouns in order to create an objective tone (the passive version may be used in a formal report, for example)

For example, to explain its 90-day limit on product returns, Gap says the following on its website: "Merchandise returned more than 90 days after the purchase date will not be eligible for a refund,"[13] instead of saying something like "You cannot return products more than 90 days after the purchase date." The second half of Table 5.4 illustrates several other situations in which the passive voice helps you focus your message on your audience.

COMPOSING YOUR MESSAGE

After you have decided how to adapt to your audience, you're ready to begin composing your message. As you write your first draft, let your creativity flow. Don't try to draft and edit at the same time or worry about getting everything perfect. Make up words if you can't think of the right word, draw pictures, talk out loud—do whatever it takes to get the ideas out of your head and onto your computer screen or a piece of paper. If you've planned well, you'll have time to revise and refine the material later, before showing it to anyone. In fact, many writers find it helpful to establish a personal rule of *never* showing a first draft to anyone. By working in this "safe zone," away from the critical eyes of others, your mind will stay free to think clearly and creatively.

If you get stuck and feel unable to write, try to overcome writer's block by jogging your brain in creative ways. The introduction is often the hardest part to write, so put it aside and work on whichever parts of the document you're most comfortable with at any given moment. In most cases, you don't need to write the sections in any particular order.[14] Work on nontext elements such as graphics or your cover page. Revisit your purpose and confirm your intent in writing the message. Give yourself a mental break by switching to a different project. Sometimes all you need to do is start writing without worrying about the words you're using or how they will sound to the audience. Words will start flowing, your mind will engage, and the writing will come easier.

As you create and refine your messages, learn to view your writing at three levels: strong words, effective sentences, and coherent paragraphs.

Choosing Strong Words

Successful writers pay close attention to the correct use of words.[15] If you make grammatical or usage errors, you lose credibility with your audience—even if your message is otherwise correct. Poor grammar implies that you're uninformed, and audiences may choose not to trust an uninformed source. Moreover, poor grammar can imply that you don't respect your audience enough to get things right.

Correctness is the first consideration when choosing words.

The "rules" of grammar and usage can be a source of worry for writers because some of these rules are complex and some evolve over time. Even professional editors and grammarians occasionally have questions about correct usage, and they sometimes disagree about the answers. For example, the word *data* is the plural form of *datum*, yet some experts now prefer to treat *data* as a singular noun when it's used in nonscientific material to refer to a body of information.

With practice, you'll become more skilled in making correct choices over time. If you have doubts about what is correct, you have many ways to find the answer. Check the "Handbook of Grammar, Mechanics, and Usage" at the end of this book or consult the many special reference books and resources available in libraries, in bookstores, and on the Internet.

If you're not sure of correct grammar or usage, look it up; you'll avoid embarrassing mistakes and learn at the same time.

Effectiveness is the second consideration when choosing words.

In addition to using words correctly, successful writers and speakers take care to find the most effective words and phrases to use. English is a rich language that has assimilated thousands of words from many other languages, so you often have a variety of options when choosing words. Selecting and using words effectively is often more challenging than using words correctly because it's a matter of judgment and experience. Careful writers continue to work at their craft to find words that communicate well and to avoid those that are worn out or meaningless (see Figure 5.3). Reading widely is the best way to expand your vocabulary and thereby give yourself more options when it's time to choose words in your own writing. As you expand your vocabulary, you'll make better choices because you'll understand the difference between denotative and connotative meaning and you'll know how to balance abstract and concrete terms.

Understanding Denotation and Connotation

A word may have both a denotative and a connotative meaning. The **denotative meaning** is the literal, or dictionary, meaning. The **connotative meaning** includes all the associations and feelings evoked by the word.

The denotative meaning of *desk* is "a piece of furniture with a flat work surface and various drawers for storage." The connotative meaning of *desk* may include thoughts associated with work or study, but the word *desk* has fairly neutral connotations—neither strong nor emotional. However, some words have much stronger connotations than others and should be used with care. For example, the connotations of the word *fail* are negative and can carry strong emotional meaning. If you say that the sales department *failed* to meet its annual quota, the connotative meaning suggests that the group is inferior, incompetent, or below some standard of performance. However, the reason for not achieving 100 percent might be an inferior product, incorrect pricing, or some other factor outside the control of

Many words have both a denotative (explicit, specific) meaning and a connotative (implicit, associative) meaning.

REAL-TIME UPDATES
Learn More

Grammar questions? Click here for help

This comprehensive online guide can help you out of just about any grammar dilemma. Go to **http://real-timeupdates.com/bct** and click on "Learn More." If you are using mybcommlab, you can access Real-Time Updates within each chapter or under Student Study Tools.

FIGURE 5.3   Choosing Strong Words

Through the use of such words and phrases as *premiere showcase*, *latest news*, *innovators*, and *industry leaders*, this email message promotes the many benefits of the annual VTCE trade show.

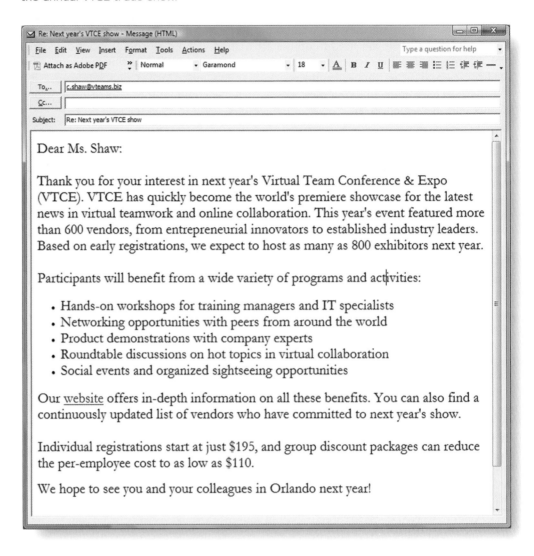

the sales department. In contrast, by saying that the sales department achieved 85 percent of its quota, you clearly communicate that the results were less than expected—without triggering all the negative emotions associated with *failure*.

Balancing Abstraction and Concreteness

The more abstract a word is, the more it is removed from the tangible, objective world that can be perceived with the senses.

Words vary dramatically in the degree of abstraction or concreteness they convey. An **abstract word** expresses a concept, quality, or characteristic. Abstractions are usually broad, encompassing a category of ideas, and they are often intellectual, academic, or philosophical. *Love, honor, progress, tradition,* and *beauty* are abstractions, as are such important business concepts as *productivity, profits, quality,* and *motivation*. In contrast, a **concrete word** stands for something you can touch, see, or visualize. Most concrete terms are anchored in the tangible, material world. *Chair, table, horse, rose, kick, kiss, red, green,* and *two* are concrete words; they are direct, clear, and exact. Incidentally, technology continues to generate new words and new meanings that describe things that don't have a physical presence but are nonetheless concrete: *software, website, signal,* and *code* are all concrete terms as well.

Concrete words are often more effective than abstract words because they are more precise, but that isn't always the case. For example, try to rewrite this sentence without using the underlined abstract words:

> We hold these <u>truths</u> to be <u>self-evident</u>, that all men are <u>created equal</u>, that they are <u>endowed</u> by their <u>Creator</u> with certain <u>unalienable Rights</u>, that among these are <u>Life</u>, <u>Liberty</u>, and the <u>Pursuit of Happiness</u>.

In business communication, use concrete, specific terms whenever possible; use abstractions only when necessary.

As you can see, the Declaration of Independence needs abstractions, and so do most business messages. (You'll also note that *men* would be replaced with *people* or another gender-neutral term, had this sentence been written in the 21st century rather than the 18th century.) Abstractions let you rise above the common and tangible.

Even though they're indispensable, abstractions can be troublesome. They tend to be fuzzy and subject to multiple interpretations. Moreover, because they seem less "real," getting readers excited about ideas can be challenging, especially if the ideas are unrelated to concrete experience. The best way to minimize such problems is to blend abstract terms with concrete ones, the general with the specific. State the concept and then pin it down with details expressed in more concrete terms. Save the abstractions for ideas that cannot be expressed any other way.

Because words such as *small, numerous, sizable, near, soon, good,* and *fine* are imprecise, try to replace them with terms that are more specific. For example, instead of referring to a *sizable loss,* talk about a *loss of $32 million.*

Finding Words That Communicate Well

By practicing your writing, learning from experienced writers and editors, and reading extensively, you'll find it easier to choose words that communicate exactly what you want to say. When you compose your business messages, think carefully to find the most powerful words for each situation and to avoid obscure words, clichés, and buzzwords that are turning into clichés (see Table 5.5):

Try to use words that are powerful and familiar.

- **Choose powerful words.** Choose words that express your thoughts clearly, specifically, and dynamically. Nouns and verbs are the most concrete words and should do most of the work in your messages. Verbs are especially powerful because they tell what's happening in the sentence, so make them dynamic and specific. For instance, you could replace *fall* with *plummet, drop,* or *decline* to suggest the magnitude of a decrease. Here's another helpful clue: If you find yourself using a lot of adjectives and adverbs, you're probably trying to compensate for weak nouns and verbs. Saying that *sales plummeted* is stronger and more efficient than saying *sales dropped dramatically* or *sales experienced a dramatic drop.*
- **Choose familiar words.** You'll communicate best with words that are familiar to both you and your readers. Efforts to improve a situation certainly can be *ameliorative,* but saying they are *helpful* is a lot more effective. Moreover, trying to use an unfamiliar word for the first time in an important document can lead to embarrassing mistakes.
- **Avoid clichés and be careful with buzzwords.** Although familiar words are generally the best choice, avoid *clichés*—terms and phrases so common that they have lost some of their power to communicate. *Buzzwords,* newly coined terms often associated with technology, business, or cultural changes, are slightly more difficult to handle than clichés because in small doses and in the right situation, they can be useful. The careful use of a buzzword can signal that you're an insider, someone in the know.[16] However, buzzwords quickly become clichés, and using them too late in their "life cycle" can mark you as an outsider desperately trying to look like an insider. When people use clichés and overuse buzzwords, they often sound as though they don't know how to express themselves otherwise and don't invest the energy required for original writing.[17]
- **Use jargon carefully.** *Jargon,* the specialized language of a particular profession or industry, has a bad reputation, but it's not always bad. Using jargon is usually an efficient way to communicate within the specific groups that understand these terms. After all, that's how jargon develops in the first place, as people with similar interests develop ways to communicate complex ideas quickly. For instance, when a recording engineer wants to communicate that a particular piece of music is devoid of reverberation and other sound effects, it's a lot easier to simply describe the track as "dry." Of course, to people who

Avoid clichés, be extremely careful with trendy buzzwords, and use jargon only when your audience is completely familiar with it.

aren't familiar with such insider terms, jargon is meaningless and intimidating—one more reason it's important to understand your audience before you start writing.

As you read for business or pleasure, take note of words that strike you as effective and then try to use those words in your own writing. If you need help finding the right words, try some of the visual dictionaries and thesauruses available online. For example, Visuwords (www.visuwords.com) shows words that are similar to or different from a given word and helps you see subtle differences to find the perfect word.[18]

TABLE 5.5 Selected Examples of Finding Powerful Words

WEAK WORDS AND PHRASES	STRONGER ALTERNATIVES (EFFECTIVE USAGE DEPENDS ON THE SITUATION)
Increase (as a verb)	Accelerate, amplify, augment, enlarge, escalate, expand, extend, magnify, multiply, soar, swell
Decrease (as a verb)	Curb, cut back, depreciate, dwindle, shrink, slacken
Large, small	(use a specific number, such as $100 million)
Good	Admirable, beneficial, desirable, flawless, pleasant, sound, superior, worthy
Bad	Abysmal, corrupt, deficient, flawed, inadequate, inferior, poor, substandard, worthless
We are committed to providing . . .	We provide . . .
It is in our best interest to . . .	We should . . .

UNFAMILIAR WORDS	FAMILIAR WORDS
Ascertain	Find out, learn
Consummate	Close, bring about
Peruse	Read, study
Circumvent	Avoid
Unequivocal	Certain

CLICHÉS AND BUZZWORDS	PLAIN LANGUAGE
An uphill battle	A challenge
Writing on the wall	Prediction
Call the shots	Lead
Take by storm	Attack
Costs an arm and a leg	Expensive
A new ballgame	Fresh start
Fall through the cracks	Be overlooked
Think outside the box	Be creative
Run it up the flagpole	Find out what people think about it
Eat our own dog food	Use our own products
Mission-critical	Vital
Disintermediate	Get rid of
Green light (as a verb)	Approve
Architect (as a verb)	Design
Space (as in, "we compete in the XYZ space")	Market or industry
Blocking and tackling	Basic skills
Trying to boil the ocean	Working frantically but without focus
Human capital	People, employees, workforce
Low-hanging fruit	Tasks that are easy to complete or sales that are easy to close
Pushback	Resistance

Creating Effective Sentences

Arranging your carefully chosen words in effective sentences is the next step in creating powerful messages. Start by selecting the optimum type of sentence to communicate each point you want to make.

Choosing from the Four Types of Sentences

Sentences come in four basic varieties: simple, compound, complex, and compound–complex. A **simple sentence** has one main *clause* (a single subject and a single predicate), although it may be expanded by nouns and pronouns that serve as objects of the action and by modifying phrases. Here's an example with the subject noun underlined once and the predicate verb underlined twice:

A simple sentence has one main clause.

> Profits increased in the past year.

A **compound sentence** has two main clauses that express two or more independent but related thoughts of equal importance, usually joined by *and*, *but*, or *or*. In effect, a compound sentence is a merger of two or more simple sentences (independent clauses) that are related. For example:

A compound sentence has two main clauses.

> Wage rates have declined by 5 percent, and employee turnover has been high.

The independent clauses in a compound sentence are always separated by a comma or by a semicolon (in which case the conjunction—*and*, *but*, *or*—is dropped).

A **complex sentence** expresses one main thought (the independent clause) and one or more subordinate, related thoughts (dependent clauses that cannot stand alone as valid sentences). Independent and dependent clauses are usually separated by a comma. In this example, "Although you may question Gerald's conclusions" is a subordinate thought expressed in a dependent clause:

A complex sentence has one main clause and one subordinate clause.

> Although you may question Gerald's conclusions, you must admit that his research is thorough.

A **compound-complex sentence** has two main clauses, at least one of which contains a subordinate clause:

A compound-complex sentence has two main clauses and at least one dependent clause.

> Profits have increased in the past year, and although you may question Gerald's conclusions, you must admit that his research is thorough.

When constructing sentences, choose the form that matches the relationship of the ideas you want to express. If you have two ideas of equal importance, express them as two simple sentences or as one compound sentence. However, if one of the ideas is less important than the other, place it in a dependent clause to form a complex sentence. For example, although the following compound sentence uses a conjunction to join two ideas, they aren't truly equal:

> The chemical products division is the strongest in the company, and its management techniques should be adopted by the other divisions.

By making the first thought subordinate to the second, you establish a cause-and-effect relationship. The following complex sentence is much more effective:

> Because the chemical products division is the strongest in the company, its management techniques should be adopted by the other divisions.

Writing is usually more effective if it balances all four sentence types.

To make your writing as effective as possible, strive for variety and balance, using all four sentence types. If you use too many simple sentences, you won't be able to properly express the relationships among your ideas, and your writing will sound choppy and abrupt. At the other extreme, a long series of compound, complex, or compound–complex sentences can be tiring to read.

5 LEARNING
OBJECTIVE

Explain how sentence
style affects emphasis
in a message

You can emphasize ideas in a sentence by
- *Devoting more words to them*
- *Putting them at the beginning or at the end of the sentence*
- *Making them the subject of the sentence*

Using Sentence Style to Emphasize Key Thoughts

In every message, some ideas are more important than others. You can emphasize these key ideas through your sentence style. One obvious technique is to give important points the most space. When you want to call attention to a thought, use extra words to describe it. Consider this sentence:

> The chairperson called for a vote of the shareholders.

To emphasize the importance of the chairperson, you might describe her more fully:

> Having considerable experience in corporate takeover battles, the chairperson called for a vote of the shareholders.

You can increase the emphasis even more by adding a separate, short sentence to augment the first:

> The chairperson called for a vote of the shareholders. She has considerable experience in corporate takeover battles.

You can also call attention to a thought by making it the subject of the sentence. In the following example, the emphasis is on the person:

> I can write letters much more quickly by using a computer.

However, by changing the subject, the computer takes center stage:

> The computer enables me to write letters much more quickly.

Another way to emphasize an idea is to place it either at the beginning or at the end of a sentence:

> **Less emphatic:**   We are cutting the price to stimulate demand.
> **More emphatic:**   To stimulate demand, we are cutting the price.

Dependent clauses can determine emphasis.

In complex sentences, the placement of the dependent clause hinges on the relationship between the ideas expressed. If you want to emphasize the subordinate idea, put the dependent clause at the end of the sentence (the most emphatic position) or at the beginning (the second most emphatic position). If you want to downplay the idea, put the dependent clause within the sentence:

> **Most emphatic:**   The electronic parts are manufactured in Mexico, *which has lower wage rates than the United States.*
> **Emphatic:**   *Because wage rates are lower in Mexico than in the United States,* the electronic parts are manufactured there.
> **Least emphatic:**   Mexico, *which has lower wage rates than the United States,* was selected as the production site for the electronic parts.

FIGURE 5.4 Unified Paragraphs
In two brief paragraphs, Whirlpool assured its trade partners (retailers and commercial laundries) that business would continue as usual after its acquisition of Magtag.

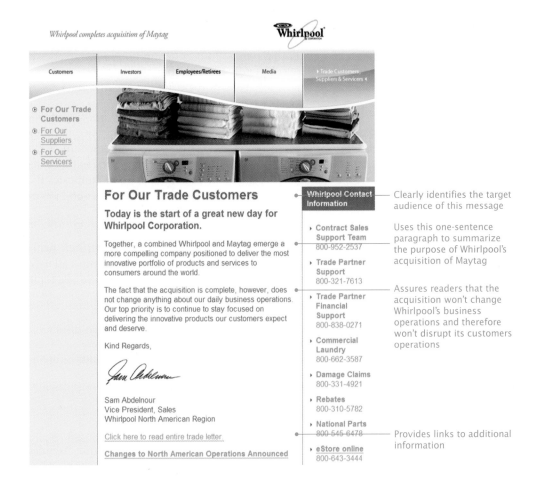

Techniques such as these give you a great deal of control over the way your audience interprets what you have to say.

Crafting Unified, Coherent Paragraphs

Paragraphs organize sentences related to the same general topic. Readers expect every paragraph to be *unified*—focusing on a single topic—and *coherent*—presenting ideas in a logically connected way. By carefully arranging the elements of each paragraph, you help your readers grasp the main idea of your document and understand how the specific pieces of support material back up that idea (see Figure 5.4).

Elements of a Paragraph

Paragraphs vary widely in length and form, but a typical paragraph contains three basic elements: a topic sentence, support sentences that develop the topic, and transitional words and phrases.

Topic Sentence   An effective paragraph deals with a single topic, and the sentence that introduces that topic is called the **topic sentence.** In informal and creative writing, the topic sentence may be implied rather than stated. In business writing, the topic sentence is generally explicit and is often the first sentence in the paragraph. The topic sentence gives

Most paragraphs consist of
- *A topic sentence that reveals the subject of the paragraph*
- *Related sentences that support and expand the topic*
- *Transitions that help readers move between sentences and between paragraphs*

readers a summary of the general idea that will be covered in the rest of the paragraph. The following examples show how a topic sentence can introduce the subject and suggest the way the subject will be developed:

> The medical products division has been troubled for many years by public relations problems. [In the rest of the paragraph, readers will learn the details of the problems.]
>
> To get a refund, please supply us with the following information. [The details of the necessary information will be described in the rest of the paragraph.]

In addition to helping your readers, topic sentences help you as a writer because they remind you of the purpose of each paragraph and thereby help you stay focused. In fact, a good way to test the effectiveness of your writing is to prepare a summary version that consists of only the first sentences of all your paragraphs. If this summary communicates the essence of your message in a sensible, compelling way, you've probably done a good job of presenting your information.[19]

Support Sentences   In most paragraphs, the topic sentence needs to be explained, justified, or extended with one or more support sentences. These related sentences must all have a bearing on the general subject and must provide enough specific details to make the topic clear:

> The medical products division has been troubled for many years by public relations problems. Since 2002 the local newspaper has published 15 articles that portray the division in a negative light. We have been accused of everything from mistreating laboratory animals to polluting the local groundwater. Our facility has been described as a health hazard. Our scientists are referred to as "Frankensteins," and our profits are considered "obscene."

The support sentences are all more specific than the topic sentence. Each one provides another piece of evidence to demonstrate the general truth of the main thought. Also, each sentence is clearly related to the general idea being developed, which gives the paragraph unity. A paragraph is well developed when it contains enough information to make the topic sentence convincing and interesting and doesn't contain any extraneous, unrelated sentences.

Transitions   **Transitions** are words or phrases that tie together ideas by showing how one thought is related to another. They also alert the reader to what lies ahead so that shifts and changes don't cause confusion. In addition to helping readers understand the connections you're trying to make, transitions give your writing a smooth, even flow.

Transitional elements include
- *Connecting words (conjunctions)*
- *Repeated words or phrases*
- *Pronouns*
- *Words that are frequently paired*

Ideally, you begin planning transitions while you're outlining, as you decide how the various ideas and blocks of information will be arranged and connected.[20] You can establish transitions in a variety of ways:

- **Use connecting words.** Use words such as *and, but, or, nevertheless, however, in addition,* and so on.
- **Echo a word or phrase from a previous paragraph or sentence.** "A system should be established for monitoring inventory levels. *This system* will provide . . . ."
- **Use a pronoun that refers to a noun used previously.** "Ms. Arthur is the leading candidate for the president's position. *She* has excellent qualifications."
- **Use words that are frequently paired.** "The machine has a *minimum* output of . . . . Its *maximum* output is . . . ."

Some transitions serve as mood changers, alerting the reader to a change in mood from the previous material. Some announce a total contrast with what's gone on before, some announce a causal relationship, and some signal a change in time. Here is a list of transitions frequently used to move readers smoothly between sentences and paragraphs:

> **Additional detail:**   moreover, furthermore, in addition, besides, first, second, third, finally
>
> **Causal relationship:**   therefore, because, accordingly, thus, consequently, hence, as a result, so
>
> **Comparison:**   similarly, here again, likewise, in comparison, still
>
> **Contrast:**   yet, conversely, whereas, nevertheless, on the other hand, however, but, nonetheless
>
> **Condition:**   although, if
>
> **Illustration:**   for example, in particular, in this case, for instance
>
> **Time sequence:**   formerly, after, when, meanwhile, sometimes
>
> **Intensification:**   indeed, in fact, in any event
>
> **Summary:**   in brief, in short, to sum up
>
> **Repetition:**   that is, in other words, as mentioned earlier

Consider using a transition whenever it could help the reader understand your ideas and follow you from point to point. You can use transitions inside paragraphs to tie related points together and between paragraphs to ease the shift from one distinct thought to another. In longer reports, a transition that links major sections or chapters may be a complete paragraph that serves as a mini-introduction to the next section or as a summary of the ideas presented in the section just ending. Here's an example:

> Given the nature of this product, our alternatives are limited. As the previous section indicates, we can stop making it altogether, improve it, or continue with the current model. Each of these alternatives has advantages and disadvantages, which are discussed in the following section.

This paragraph makes it clear to the reader that the analysis of the problem (offered in the previous section) is now over and that the document is making a transition to an analysis of the possible solutions (to be offered in the next section).

Five Ways to Develop a Paragraph

You have a variety of options for developing paragraphs. Five of the most common approaches are illustration, comparison or contrast, cause and effect, classification, and problem and solution (see Table 5.6).

In practice, you'll occasionally combine two or more methods of development in a single paragraph. For instance, you could begin by using illustration, shift to comparison or contrast, and then shift to problem and solution. However, when combining approaches, do so carefully so that you don't lose readers partway through the paragraph. In addition, before settling for the first approach that comes to mind, consider the alternatives. Think through various methods before committing yourself, or even write several test paragraphs to see which method works best. By avoiding the easy habit of repeating the same old paragraph pattern time after time, you can keep your writing fresh and interesting.

USING TECHNOLOGY TO COMPOSE AND SHAPE YOUR MESSAGES

Take advantage of the tools in your word processor or online publishing systems to write more efficiently and effectively. The names and details vary from system to system, but you'll probably find most of these capabilities:

- **Style sheets and templates.** *Style sheets* are master lists of predefined styles (typeface, type size, and so on) for headlines, paragraph text, and so on. (Here, the word *style* should not be confused with *writing style*, discussed earlier in the chapter.) Many

6 **LEARNING OBJECTIVE**

List five ways to develop unified, coherent paragraphs

Five ways to develop paragraphs:
- *Illustration*
- *Comparison or contrast*
- *Cause and effect*
- *Classification*
- *Problem and solution*

Take full advantage of your software's formatting capabilities to help produce effective, professional messages in less time.

TABLE 5.6   Five Techniques for Developing Paragraphs

TECHNIQUE	DESCRIPTION	EXAMPLE
Illustration	Giving examples that demonstrate the general idea	Some of our most popular products are available through local distributors. For example, Everett & Lemmings carries our frozen soups and entrees. The J. B. Green Company carries our complete line of seasonings, as well as the frozen soups. Wilmont Foods, also a major distributor, now carries our new line of frozen desserts.
Comparison or contrast	Using similarities or differences to develop the topic	When the company was small, the recruiting function could be handled informally. The need for new employees was limited, and each manager could comfortably screen and hire her or his own staff. However, our successful bid on the Owens contract means that we will be doubling our labor force over the next six months. To hire that many people without disrupting our ongoing activities, we will create a separate recruiting group within the human resources department.
Cause and effect	Focusing on the reasons for something	The heavy-duty fabric of your Wanderer tent probably broke down for one of two reasons: (1) a sharp object punctured the fabric, and without reinforcement, the hole was enlarged by the stress of pitching the tent daily for a week or (2) the fibers gradually rotted because the tent was folded and stored while still wet.
Classification	Showing how a general idea is broken into specific categories	Successful candidates for our supervisor trainee program generally come from one of several groups. The largest group by far consists of recent graduates of accredited business management programs. The next largest group comes from within our own company, as we try to promote promising staff workers to positions of greater responsibility. Finally, we occasionally accept candidates with outstanding supervisory experience in related industries.
Problem and solution	Presenting a problem and then discussing the solution	Selling handmade toys online is a challenge because consumers are accustomed to buying heavily advertised toys from major chain stores or well-known websites such as Amazon.com. However, if we develop an appealing website, we can compete on the basis of product novelty and quality. In addition, we can provide unusual crafts at a competitive price: a rocking horse of birch, with a hand-knit tail and mane; a music box with the child's name painted on the top; and a real teepee, made by Native American artisans.

organizations provide employees with approved style sheets to ensure a consistent look for all company documents. Moreover, style sheets can eliminate hours of design time by making many of your choices for you. *Templates* can go beyond style sheets by defining such factors as page design, available fonts, and other features. A template can also include *boilerplate*, a section of text that is reused from document to document.

- **Smart documents.** *Smart documents* are word processor files based on special templates that can retrieve information from databases and other information sources. For example, a smart document can pull data directly from the sales department's reporting system and insert these figures into ready-made tables in a monthly sales report.
- **Master documents.** Long reports with multiple sections are sometimes easier to handle as multiple *subdocuments*, particularly if different authors are in charge of the different sections. Using a *master document*, you can then organize and integrate all the subdocuments when you're ready to print and distribute the report.
- **Autocompletion.** *Autocompletion* inserts a ready-made block of text when you type the first few characters, which saves time and reduces errors. For example, instead of typing your company's name, address, phone number, fax number, e-mail address, and website URL, you can set the software to enter all this information as soon as you type the first three letters of the company name.

PEARSON
mybcommlab™

Log on to **www.mybcommlab.com** to access the following study and assessment aids associated with this chapter:

- Video applications
- Real-Time Updates
- Peer review activity
- Quick Learning Guides

- Pre/post test
- Personalized study plan
- Model documents
- Sample presentations

If you are not using mybcommlab, you can access the Real-Time Updates and Quick Learning Guides through **http://real-timeupdates.com/bct**. The Quick Learning Guide (located under "Learn More" on the website) hits all the high points of this chapter in just two pages. This guide, especially prepared by the authors, will help you study for exams or review important concepts whenever you need a quick refresher.

Test Your Knowledge

1. Do you have to use the word *you* in order to demonstrate the "you" attitude? Why or why not?
2. Why is it important to establish your credibility when communicating with an audience of strangers?
3. How does using bias-free language help communicators establish a good relationship with their audiences?
4. How does the denotative meaning of a word differ from its connotative meaning?
5. How can you use sentence style to emphasize key thoughts?
6. How does an abstract word differ from a concrete word?
7. In what three situations is the passive voice appropriate?
8. How can topic sentences help readers?
9. How can topic sentences help writers?
10. What functions do transitions serve?

Apply Your Knowledge

1. How can you apply the "you" attitude when you don't know your audience personally?
2. How can a lack of planning or a lack of confidence lead to messages that are murky or pompous?
3. What steps can you take to make abstract concepts such as *opportunity* feel more concrete in your messages?
4. Should you bother using transitional elements if the logical sequence of your message is obvious? Why or why not?
5. **Ethical Choices** Eleven million people in the United States are allergic to one or more food ingredients. Each year, 30,000 of these people end up in the emergency room after suffering allergic reactions, and hundreds of them die. Many of these tragic events are tied to poorly written food labels that either fail to identify dangerous allergens or use scientific terms that most consumers don't recognize.[21] Do food manufacturers have a responsibility to ensure that consumers read, understand, and follow warnings on food products? Explain your answer.

Practice Your Knowledge

Messages for Analysis

Read the following e-mail draft and then (1) analyze the strengths and weaknesses of each sentence and (2) revise the document so that it follows this chapter's guidelines. The message was written by the marketing manager of an online retailer of baby-related products in the hope of becoming a retail outlet for Inglesina strollers and high chairs. As a manufacturer of stylish, top-quality products, Inglesina (based in Italy) is extremely selective about the retail outlets through which it allows its products to be sold.

> Our e-tailing site, **www.BestBabyGear.com**, specializes in only the very best products for parents of newborns, infants, and toddlers. We constantly scour the world looking for products that are good enough and well-built enough and classy enough—good enough that is to take their place alongside the hundreds of other carefully selected products that adorn the pages of our award-winning website, **www.bestbabygear.com**. We aim for the fences every time we select a product to join this portfolio; we don't want to waste our time with onesey-twosey products that might sell a half dozen units per annum—no, we want every product to be a top-drawer success, selling at least one hundred units per specific model per year in order to justify our expense and hassle factor in adding it to the abovementioned portfolio. After careful consideration, we thusly concluded that your Inglesina lines meet our needs and would therefore like to add it.

Exercises

Active links for all websites in this chapter can be found online. If mybcommlab is being used in your class, see your User Guide for instructions on accessing the content for this chapter. Otherwise, visit **www.pearsonglobaleditions.com/bovee**, locate *Business Communication Today*, Tenth Edition, click the Companion Website link, select Chapter 5, and then click on "Featured Websites." Please note that links to sites that become inactive after publication of the book will be removed from the Featured Websites section.

5.1 **Audience Relationship: Courteous Communication** Substitute a better phrase for each of the following:
   a. You claim that
   b. It is not our policy to
   c. You neglected to
   d. In which you assert
   e. We are sorry you are dissatisfied
   f. You failed to enclose
   g. We request that you send us
   h. Apparently you overlooked our terms

i. We have been very patient

j. We are at a loss to understand

5.2 **Audience Relationship: The "You" Attitude** Rewrite these sentences to reflect your audience's viewpoint.

a. Your e-mail order cannot be processed; we request that you use the order form on our website instead.

b. We insist that you always bring your credit card to the store.

c. We want to get rid of all our 15-inch LCD screens to make room in our warehouse for the new 19-, 23-, and 35-inch monitors. Thus, we are offering a 25 percent discount on all sales of 15-inch models this week.

d. I am applying for the position of bookkeeper in your office. I feel my grades prove that I am bright and capable, and I think I can do a good job for you.

e. As requested, we are sending the refund for $25.

f. If you cared about doing a good job, you would've made the extra effort required to learn how to use the machinery properly.

g. Your strategy presentation this morning absolutely blew me away; there's no way we can fail with all the brilliant ideas you've pulled together—I'm so glad you're running the company now!

h. Regarding your e-mail message from September 28 regarding the slow payment of your invoice, it's important for you to realize that we've just undergone a massive upgrade of our accounts payable system and payments have been delayed for everybody, not just you.

i. I know I'm late with the asset valuation report, but I haven't been feeling well and I just haven't had the energy needed to work through the numbers yet.

j. With all the online news sources available today, I can't believe you didn't know that MyTravel and Thomas Cook were in merger talks—I mean, you don't even have to get up from your computer to learn this!

5.3 **Audience Relationship: Emphasize the Positive** Revise these sentences to be positive rather than negative.

a. To avoid damage to your credit rating, please remit payment within 10 days.

b. We don't offer refunds on returned merchandise that is soiled.

c. Because we are temporarily out of Baby Cry dolls, we won't be able to ship your order for 10 days.

d. You failed to specify the color of the blouse that you ordered.

e. You should have realized that waterbeds will freeze in unheated houses during winter. Therefore, our guarantee does not cover the valve damage, and you must pay the $9.50 valve-replacement fee (plus postage).

5.4 **Audience Relationship: Euphemisms** Provide euphemisms for the following words and phrases:

a. Stubborn

b. Wrong

c. Stupid

d. Incompetent

e. Loudmouth

5.5 **Audience Relationship: Bias-Free Language** Rewrite each of the following to eliminate bias:

a. For an Indian, Maggie certainly is outgoing.

b. He needs a wheelchair, but he doesn't let his handicap affect his job performance.

c. A pilot must have the ability to stay calm under pressure, and then he must be trained to cope with any problem that arises.

d. Candidate Renata Parsons, married and the mother of a teenager, will attend the debate.

e. Senior citizen Sam Nugent is still an active salesman.

5.6 **Ethical Choices** Your company has been a major employer in the local community for years, but shifts in the global marketplace have forced some changes in the company's long-term direction. In fact, the company plans to reduce local staffing by as much as 50 percent over the next 5 to 10 years, starting with a small layoff next month. The size and timing of future layoffs have not been decided, although there is little doubt that more layoffs will happen at some point. In the first draft of a letter aimed at community leaders, you write that "this first layoff is part of a continuing series of staff reductions anticipated over the next several years." However, your boss is concerned about the vagueness and negative tone of the language and asks you to rewrite that sentence to read "this layoff is part of the company's ongoing efforts to continually align its resources with global market conditions." Do you think this suggested wording is ethical, given the company's economic influence in the community? Explain your answer in an e-mail message to your instructor.

5.7 **Message Composition: Controlling Style** Rewrite the following e-mail to customer Betty Crandall so that it conveys a helpful, personal, and interested tone:

We received your order complaint via our website response system. Owing to the fact that you neglected to include the size of the dress you ordered, please be advised that no shipment of your order was made, but the aforementioned shipment will occur at such time as we are in receipt of the aforementioned information.

5.8 **Message Composition: Selecting Words** Write a concrete phrase for each of these vague phrases:

a. Sometime this spring

b. A substantial savings

c. A large number attended

d. Increased efficiency

e. Expanded the work area

f. Flatten the website structure

5.9 **Message Composition: Selecting Words** List terms that are stronger than the following:

a. Ran after

b. Seasonal ups and downs

c. Bright

d. Suddenly rises

e. Moves forward

5.10 Message Composition: Selecting Words As you rewrite these sentences, replace the clichés and buzzwords with plain language (if you don't recognize any of these terms, you can find definitions online):

a. Being a jack-of-all-trades, Dave worked well in his new general manager job.

b. Moving Leslie into the accounting department, where she was literally a fish out of water, was like putting a square peg into a round hole, if you get my drift.

c. My only takeaway from the offsite was that Laird threw his entire department under the bus for missing the deadline.

d. I've love to help with that project, but I'm bandwidth-constrained.

e. The board green-lighted our initiative to repurpose our consumer products for the commercial space.

5.11 Message Composition: Selecting Words Suggest short, simple words to replace each of the following:

a. Inaugurate

b. Terminate

c. Utilize

d. Anticipate

e. Assistance

f. Endeavor

g. Ascertain

h. Procure

i. Consummate

j. Advise

k. Alteration

l. Forwarded

m. Fabricate

n. Nevertheless

o. Substantial

5.12 Message Composition: Selecting Words Write up-to-date, less-stuffy versions of these phrases; write *none* if you think there is no appropriate substitute or "delete" if the phrase should simply be deleted:

a. As per your instructions

b. Attached herewith

c. In lieu of

d. In reply I wish to state

e. Please be advised that

5.13 Message Composition: Creating Sentences Suppose that end-of-term frustrations have produced this e-mail message to Professor Anne Brewer from a student who believes he should have received a B in his accounting class. If this message were recast into three or four clear sentences, the teacher might be more receptive to the student's argument. Rewrite the message to show how you would improve it:

I think that I was unfairly awarded a C in your accounting class this term, and I am asking you to change the grade to a B. It was a difficult term. I don't get any money from home, and I have to work mornings at the Pancake House (as a cook), so I had to rush to make your class, and those two times that I missed class were because they wouldn't let me off work because of special events at the Pancake House (unlike some other students who just take off when they choose). On the midterm examination, I originally got a 75 percent, but you said in class that there were two different ways to answer the third question and that you would change the grades of students who used the "optimal cost" method and had been counted off 6 points for doing this. I don't think that you took this into account, because I got 80 percent on the final, which is clearly a B. Anyway, whatever you decide, I just want to tell you that I really enjoyed this class, and I thank you for making accounting so interesting.

5.14 Message Composition: Creating Sentences Rewrite each sentence so that it is active rather than passive:

a. The raw data are entered into the customer relationship management system by the sales representative each Friday.

b. High profits are publicized by management.

c. The policies announced in the directive were implemented by the staff.

d. Our computers are serviced by the Santee Company.

e. The employees were represented by Janet Hogan.

5.15 Message Composition: Writing Paragraphs In the following paragraph, identify the topic sentence and the related sentences (those that support the idea of the topic sentence):

Sync is a snap with Auto-Sync. By default, iTunes automatically copies your entire music library to iPod and deletes songs on iPod that are not listed in iTunes. Or you can use Playlist Sync and select the playlists you want to sync with your iPod. If you have more songs in your iTunes library than you can fit on your iPod, let iTunes create a playlist to fill your iPod, or just update your iPod by dragging over individual songs.[22]

Now add a topic sentence to this paragraph:

Our analysis of the customer experience should start before golfers even drive through the front gate here at Glencoe Meadows; it should start when they phone in or log onto our website to reserve tee times. When they do arrive, the first few stages in the process are also vital: the condition of the grounds leading up to the club house, the reception they receive when they drop off their clubs, and the ease of parking. From that point, how well are we doing with check-in at the pro shop, openings at the driving range, and timely scheduling at the first tee? Then there's everything associated with playing the course itself and returning to the club house at the end of the round.

5.16 Teamwork Working with four other students, divide the following five topics among yourselves and each write one paragraph on your selected topic. Be sure each student uses a different technique when writing his or her paragraph: One student should use the illustration technique, one the comparison or contrast technique, one a discussion of cause and effect, one the classification technique, and one a discussion of problem and solution. Then exchange paragraphs within the team and pick out the main idea and general purpose of the paragraph one of your teammates wrote. Was everyone able to correctly identify the main idea and purpose? If not, suggest how the paragraph could be rewritten for clarity.

  a. Types of digital cameras (or dogs or automobiles) available for sale
  b. Advantages and disadvantages of eating at fast-food restaurants
  c. Finding that first full-time job
  d. Good qualities of my car (or house, or apartment, or neighborhood)
  e. How to make a dessert (or barbecue a steak or make coffee)

5.17 Internet Download the Security and Exchange Commission's (SEC's) *A Plain English Handbook*, from www.sec.gov/pdf/handbook.pdf. In one or two sentences, summarize what the SEC means by the phrase *plain English*. Now scan the SEC's introduction to mutual funds at www.sec.gov/investor/pubs/inwsmf.htm. Does this information follow the SEC's plain English guidelines? Cite several examples that support your assessment.

5.18 Message Organization: Transitional Elements Add transitional elements to the following sentences to improve the flow of ideas. (*Note:* You may need to eliminate or add some words to smooth out your sentences.)

  a. Robin Li realized numerous opportunities in search engine business in the China market. Robin Li was determined to make a buzz in the reality market. Li utilized his knowledge after working in different companies. He worked in Infoseek for two years. He worked in IDD Information Services for three years. Robin Li and Eric Yu set up Baidu in 2000. After nine years, Baidu is the largest Chinese search engine. Baidu has over 70% market share. Baidu is the third largest independent search engine in the world. In 2005, Baidu completed its successful IPO on NASDAQ. In 2007, Baidu was the first Chinese company to be included in the NASDAQ-100 index.
  b. To compete with dominant players in the airline industry, Oasis Airlines used a low-cost strategy. The low-price air tickets provided an alternative for budget travelers. Travelers switched to Oasis Airlines from traditional dominant players. For two years, the business was doing great. Surging oil prices began to hit the company. The company tried to look for partners to put cash into the company. The company tried to seek bail-out from other companies. In the end, Oasis Airlines could not find any help and went out of business.
  c. In every part of Hong Kong, you will always see the sign of Café de Coral. Café de Coral is a fast-food restaurant chain that serves both Chinese and Western

food at a budget price. It was established in 1968. Café de Coral has over 100 outlets all over Hong Kong and over 20 in mainland China. Café de Coral group expanded rapidly. It acquired other restaurants. It acquired The Spaghetti House in 1991. It acquired Oliver's Super Sandwiches in 2003. Such moves allowed Café de Coral group to strengthen its business in Hong Kong. Café de Coral group is the largest Chinese fast-food restaurant group in Hong Kong and in the world.

5.19 Ethical Choices Under what circumstances would you consider the use of terms that are high in connotative meaning to be ethical? When would you consider it to be unethical? Explain your reasoning.

Expand Your Knowledge

Exploring the Best of the Web
Compose a Better Business Message
http://owl.english.purdue.edu
At Purdue University's Online Writing Lab (OWL), http://owl.english.purdue.edu, you'll find tools to help you improve your business messages. For advice on composing written messages, for help with grammar, and for referrals to other information sources, you'd be wise to visit this site. Purdue's OWL offers online services and an introduction to Internet search tools. You can also download a variety of handouts on writing skills. Check out the resources at the OWL homepage and then answer the following questions. (Note that some of the advice you read on OWL may differ from the advice in your textbook in some respects.)

  1. Explain why positive wording in a message is more effective than negative wording. Why should you be concerned about the position of good news or bad news in your written message?
  2. What six factors of tone should you consider when conveying your message to your audience?
  3. What points should you include in the close of your business message? Why?

Sharpening Your Career Skills Online
Bovée and Thill's Business Communication Web Search, at http://businesscommunicationblog.com/websearch, is a unique research tool designed specifically for business communication research. Use the Web Search function to find a website, video, PDF document, or PowerPoint presentation that offers advice on writing effective sentences. Write a brief e-mail message to your instructor, describing the item that you found and summarizing the career skills information you learned from it.

Completing Business Messages

6

Learning Objectives

After studying this chapter, you will be able to

1. Discuss the value of careful revision and list the main tasks involved in completing a business message

2. List four writing techniques you can use to improve the readability of your messages

3. Describe the steps you can take to improve the clarity of your writing and to make your writing more concise

4. Explain how design elements help determine the effectiveness of your documents

5. List eight tips for improving message quality through careful proofreading

6. Discuss the most important issues to consider when distributing your messages

Communication Close-up at Mercedes-AMG

Elegant design and attention to every detail are hallmarks of Mercedes-AMG automobiles, and that same concern for quality design is reflected in the company's communication efforts.

www.mercedes-amg.com

Every business message tries to create a particular impression in the minds of the audience. What if the impression you want to create is how it feels to drive one of the world's most luxurious cars that has been customized with one of the world's most powerful engines? Merely saying the words *power* and *luxury* isn't likely to be too convincing in today's advertising-saturated world.

The German firm AMG is revered among automotive connoisseurs for its high-performance engines, which are available in special Mercedes-Benz models. To promote the newest models, the marketing communication specialists at the Mercedes-AMG partnership knew they needed to go beyond mere words and photos and use every media option and design technique possible to reach their target audience. "Our goal was to create immersive experiences that build an emotional connection between the Mercedes-AMG brand and automotive enthusiasts," said Scott Preacher, vice president of Mercedes-AMG's interactive advertising agency, Avenue A I Razorfish. The result was an innovative multimedia website that won the Webby award from the International Academy of Digital Arts and Sciences, considered by many to be the online media equivalent of an Oscar or Emmy.

When visitors "start" the virtual engine to begin a virtual tour of the AMG factory in Affalterbach, Germany, their web browsers even shake slightly to suggest the physical sensation of firing up the mighty AMG engine they can hear growling through their computer speakers. Visitors "drive" to the factory via online video and then enter various buildings to learn more about Mercedes-AMG products.

The message of powerful luxury is delivered in ways that business communicators could only dream about even a few years ago, and it does so with ageless attention to quality. In every respect—word choices, color palette, photography, audio, video, and interactive features—the website reflects the renowned "fit and finish" of the cars it represents.[1]

MOVING BEYOND YOUR FIRST DRAFT

First drafts are rarely as effective as they could be, so take the time to improve them through revision.

Your business messages may not require the sophisticated design or technology of the Mercedes-AMG website (profiled in the chapter-opening Communication Close-up), but they can benefit from the same rigorous attention to detail in the third step of the three-step writing process: completing your messages.

After you've completed a first draft, you may be tempted to breathe a sigh of relief, send the message on its way, and move on to the next project. Resist the temptation. Successful communicators recognize that the first draft is rarely as tight, clear, and compelling as it needs to be. Careful revision can mean the difference between a rambling, unfocused message and a lively, direct message that gets results. The third step of the three-step writing process involves four key tasks: revising your message to achieve optimum quality and then producing, proofreading, and distributing it.

1 LEARNING OBJECTIVE

Discuss the value of careful revision and list the main tasks involved in completing a business message

In any medium, readers tend to equate the quality of your writing with the quality of your thinking.

If you have time, put aside your draft for a day or two before you begin the revision process.

REVISING YOUR MESSAGE

The revision task can vary somewhat, depending on the medium and the nature of your message. For informal messages to internal audiences, particularly when using instant messaging, text messaging, e-mail, or blogging, the revision process is often as simple as quickly looking over your message to correct any mistakes before sending or posting it. However, don't fall into the common trap of thinking that you don't need to worry about grammar, spelling, clarity, and other fundamentals of good writing when you use these media. These qualities can be *especially* important in electronic media, particularly if these messages are the only contact your audience has with you. Audiences are likely to equate the quality of your writing with the quality of your thinking. Poor-quality messages create an impression of poor-quality thinking. Moreover, even minor errors can cause confusion, frustration, and costly delays.

With more complex messages, try to put your draft aside for a day or two before you begin the revision process so that you can approach the material with a fresh eye. Then start with the "big picture," making sure that the document accomplishes your overall goals before moving to finer points, such as readability, clarity, and conciseness. Compare the letters in Figures 6.1 and 6.2 for an example of how careful revision improves a customer letter.

Evaluating Your Content, Organization, Style, and Tone

When you begin the revision process, focus your attention on content, organization, style, and tone. To evaluate the content of your message, answer these questions:

- Is the information accurate?
- Is the information relevant to the audience?
- Is there enough information to satisfy the readers' needs?
- Is there a good balance between general information (giving readers enough background information to appreciate the message) and specific information (giving readers the details they need to understand the message)?

When you are satisfied with the content of your message, you can review its organization. Answer another set of questions:

- Are all the points covered in the most logical order?
- Do the most important ideas receive the most space, and are they placed in the most prominent positions?

FIGURE 6.1 Improving a Customer Letter Through Careful Revision
Careful revision makes this draft shorter, clearer, and more focused. These *proofreading symbols* (see Appendix C) are still widely used when printed documents are edited and revised. However, in many instances you'll use the electronic markup features in your word processor or other software, as shown later in this chapter, on page 191.

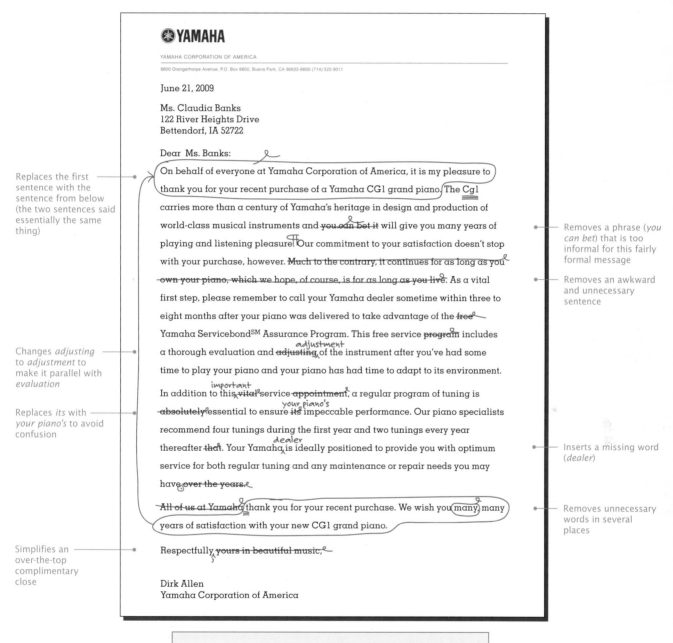

FIGURE 6.2   Revised Customer Letter

This revised letter provides the requested information more clearly, in a more organized fashion, with a friendlier style, and with precise mechanics.

YAMAHA

YAMAHA CORPORATION OF AMERICA

6600 Orangethorpe Avenue, P.O. Box 6600, Buena Park, CA 90622-6600 (714) 522-9011

June 21, 2009

Ms. Claudia Banks
122 River Heights Drive
Bettendorf, IA 52722

Dear Ms. Banks:

Thank you for your recent purchase. We wish you many years of satisfaction with your new CG1 grand piano. The CG1 carries more than a century of Yamaha's heritage in design and production of world-class musical instruments and will give you many years of playing and listening pleasure.

Our commitment to your satisfaction doesn't stop with your purchase, however. As a vital first step, please remember to call your Yamaha dealer sometime within three to eight months after your piano was delivered to take advantage of the Yamaha Servicebond℠ Assurance Program. This free service includes a thorough evaluation and adjustment of the instrument after you've had some time to play your piano and your piano has had time to adapt to its environment.

In addition to this important service, a regular program of tuning is essential to ensure your piano's impeccable performance. Our piano specialists recommend four tunings during the first year and two tunings every year thereafter. Your Yamaha dealer is ideally positioned to provide you with optimum service for both regular tuning and any maintenance or repair needs you may have.

Respectfully,

Dirk Allen
Yamaha Corporation of America

- Would the message be more convincing if it were arranged in another sequence?
- Are any points repeated unnecessarily?
- Are details grouped together logically, or are some still scattered through the document?

With the content in place and effectively organized, next consider whether you have achieved the right style and tone for your audience. Is your writing formal enough to meet the audience's expectations, without being too formal or academic? Is it too casual for a serious subject? Does your message emphasize the audience's needs over your own?

Spend a few extra moments on the beginning and end of your message; these sections usually have the greatest impact on the audience. Be sure that the opening is relevant, interesting, and geared to the reader's probable reaction. In longer messages, ensure that the first few paragraphs establish the subject, purpose, and organization of the material. Review the conclusion to be sure that it summarizes the main idea and leaves the audience with a positive impression.

The beginning and end of a message usually have the greatest impact on your readers, so make sure they are clear, concise, and compelling.

Reviewing for Readability

After confirming the content, organization, style, and tone of your message, make a second pass to improve *readability*. Most professionals are inundated with more reading material than they can ever hope to consume, and they'll appreciate your efforts to make your documents easier to read. You'll benefit from this effort, too: If you earn a reputation for creating well-crafted documents that respect the audience's time, people will pay more attention to your work.

You may be familiar with one of the many indexes that have been developed over the years in an attempt to measure readability. For example, the Flesch-Kincaid Grade Level score computes reading difficulty relative to grade-level achievement, with, for instance, a score of 10 suggesting that a document can be read and understood by the average 10th grader. Most business documents score in the 8–11 range. Technical documents often score in the 12–14 range. A similar scoring system, the Flesch Reading Ease score, ranks documents on a 100-point scale; the higher the score, the easier the document is to read. If these measurements aren't built into your word processing software, you can find a number of calculators for various indexes at websites such as www.editcentral.com.

Readability indexes offer a useful reference point, but they are limited by what they are able to measure: word length, number of syllables, sentence length, and paragraph length. They can't measure any of the other factors that affect readability, such as document design, the "you" attitude, clear sentence structure, smooth transitions, and proper word usage. Compare these two paragraphs:

> Readability indexes offer a useful reference point, but they are all limited by what they are able to measure: word length, number of syllables, sentence length, and paragraph length. They can't measure any of the other factors that affect readability, from "you" orientation to writing clarity to document design.
>
> Readability indexes can help. But they don't measure everything. They don't measure whether your writing clarity is good. They don't measure whether your document design is good or not. Reading indexes are based on word length, syllables, sentences, and paragraphs.

The first paragraph scores 12.0 on grade level and 27.4 on reading ease. The second paragraph scores much better on both grade level (8.9) and reading ease (45.8). However, the second example is choppy, unsophisticated, and poorly organized. As a general rule, then, don't assume that a piece of text is readable if it scores well on a readability index—or that it is difficult to read if it doesn't score well.

Beyond using shorter words and simpler sentences, you can improve the readability of a message by making the document interesting and easy to skim. Most business audiences— particularly influential senior managers—tend to skim documents, looking for key ideas, conclusions, and recommendations. If they determine that a document contains valuable information or requires a response, they will read it more carefully when time permits. Four techniques will make your message easier to read and easier to skim varying sentence length, using shorter paragraphs, using lists and bullets instead of narrative, and adding effective headings and subheadings.

Varying Your Sentence Length

Varying the length of your sentences is a creative way to make your messages interesting and readable. By choosing words and sentence structure with care, you can create a rhythm that emphasizes important points, enlivens your writing style, and makes information more appealing to your reader. For example, a short sentence that highlights a conclusion at the end of a substantial paragraph of evidence makes your key message stand out. Try for a mixture of sentences that are short (up to 15 words or so), medium (15–25 words), and long (more than 25 words).

Each sentence length has its advantages. Short sentences can be processed quickly and are easier for nonnative speakers and translators to interpret. Medium-length sentences are

Readability formulas can give you a helpful indication, but they can't measure everything that affects readability.

2 **LEARNING OBJECTIVE**

List four writing techniques you can use to improve the readability of your messages

The effort to make your documents more readable will pay for itself in greater career success.

To keep readers' interest, use a variety of long, medium, and short sentences.

Communication Miscues

Inaccurate Food Labels Cost Consumers' Confidence

Many consumers rely on food labels when they shop in supermarkets. When they are uncertain about their purchases, consumers refer to the information on the food labels regarding the ingredients, the nutrition, and date of expiration on the labels. Accurate food labels are especially important for people who have medical conditions.

In early 2007, the Center for Food Safety in Hong Kong received complaints from members of the public of oily diarrhea after eating fish products labeled as "codfish." Believing that the fish product was cod, as labeled on the package, 14 customers suffered from oily diarrhea after eating what was in fact oilfish, which they bought from ParknShop, one of the largest supermarket chains in Hong Kong. The confusion was caused by the store's use of the name *cod*. In the market, *cod* was used as the common name of a range of fish species, including some that do not fall into the scientific classification of cod. Instead of using *oilfish* on the labels, ParknShop used *cod* on the labels. Oilfish is edible but is generally not good for human consumption as it contains wax esters, which cannot be digested like traditional fats in the human body.

This incident has raised much public concern over the accuracy of food labels and the edibility of fish products related to cod and oilfish. The public demands the manufacturers or the retailers to be responsible for accurate food labels on the products they sell. After the incident, ParknShop recalled all oilfish products from all outlets, and its parent company, A.S. Watson Group (HK), was fined HK$45,000 (US$5,800) for selling oilfish labeled as cod. In response to the public concern, the Center for Food Safety later issued a set of guidelines on identification and labeling of oilfish and cod. The guidelines serve to advise the fish trade in the appropriate labeling of "oilfish" and "cod" so as to prevent further confusion of these two types of fish products in the market.[2]

CAREER APPLICATIONS

1. Why are food and nutrition labels so important for consumers in general?
2. Aside from food and nutrition labels, what other situations have you encountered in your life in which confusing labels, signs, instructions, or other messages created a health or safety hazard? Choose one of these situations and write a brief description of the poor communication and your advice on how it could have been improved.

useful for showing the relationships among ideas. Long sentences are often the best for conveying complex ideas, listing multiple related points, or summarizing or previewing information.

Of course, each sentence length also has disadvantages. Too many short sentences in a row can make your writing choppy. Medium sentences lack the punch of short sentences and the informative power of longer sentences. Long sentences can be difficult to understand because they contain more information and usually have a more complicated structure. Because readers can absorb only a few words per glance, longer sentences are also more difficult to skim. By choosing the best sentence length for each communication need and remembering to mix sentence lengths for variety, you'll get your points across while keeping your messages lively and interesting.

Keeping Your Paragraphs Short

Long paragraphs are visually intimidating and can be difficult to read.

Large blocks of text can be visually daunting, so the optimum paragraph length is short to medium in most cases. Unless you break up your thoughts somehow, you'll end up with lengthy paragraphs that are guaranteed to intimidate even the most dedicated reader. Short paragraphs, generally 100 words or fewer (this paragraph has 81 words), are easier to read than long ones, and they make your writing look inviting. You can also emphasize ideas by isolating them in short, forceful paragraphs.

However, don't go overboard with short paragraphs. In particular, be careful to use one-sentence paragraphs only occasionally and only for emphasis. Also, if you need to divide a subject into several pieces in order to keep paragraphs short, be sure to help your readers keep the ideas connected by guiding them with plenty of transitional elements.

Using Lists and Bullets to Clarify and Emphasize

An effective alternative to using conventional sentences is to set off important ideas in a list—a series of words, names, or other items. Lists can show the sequence of your ideas, heighten their impact visually, and increase the likelihood that a reader will find key points. In addition, lists help simplify complex subjects, highlight main points, break up a page or screen visually, ease the skimming process for busy readers, and give readers a breather. Consider the difference between the following two presentations of the same information:

Lists are effective tools for highlighting and simplifying material.

NARRATIVE	LIST
Owning your own business has many potential advantages. One is the opportunity to pursue your own personal passion. Another advantage is the satisfaction of working for yourself. As a sole proprietor, you also have the advantage of privacy because you do not have to reveal your financial information or plans to anyone.	Owning your own business has three advantages: • Opportunity to pursue personal passion • Satisfaction of working for yourself • Financial privacy

You can separate list items with numbers, letters, or bullets (a general term for any kind of graphical element that precedes each item). Bullets are generally preferred over numbers, unless the list is in some logical sequence or ranking or you need to refer to specific list items elsewhere in the document. For example, the following three steps need to be performed in the order indicated, and the numbers make that clear:

1. Find out how many employees would like on-site day-care facilities.
2. Determine how much space the day-care center would require.
3. Estimate the cost of converting a conference room for the on-site facility.

Lists are easier to locate and read if the entire numbered or bulleted section is set off by a blank line before and after, as the preceding examples demonstrate. Furthermore, make sure to introduce lists clearly so that people know what they're about to read. One way to introduce lists is to make them a part of the introductory sentence:

The board of directors met to discuss the revised annual budget. To keep expenses in line with declining sales, the directors voted to

- Cut everyone's salary by 10 percent
- Close the employee cafeteria
- Reduce travel expenses

Another way to introduce a list is to precede it with a complete introductory sentence, followed by a colon:

The decline in company profit is attributable to four factors:

- Slower holiday sales
- Increased transportation and fuel costs
- Higher employee wages
- Slower inventory turnover

Regardless of the format you choose, the items in a list should be parallel; that is, they should all use the same grammatical pattern. For example, if one list item begins with a verb, every item should begin with a verb. If one item is a noun phrase, every one should be a noun phrase:

NONPARALLEL LIST ITEMS (A MIX OF VERB AND NOUN PHRASES)	PARALLEL LIST ITEMS (ALL VERB PHRASES)
• Improve our bottom line	• Improving our bottom line
• Identification of new foreign markets for our products	• Identifying new foreign markets for our products
• Global market strategies	• Developing our global market strategies
• Issues regarding pricing and packaging size	• Resolving pricing and packaging issues

TABLE 6.1 Achieving Parallelism

METHOD	EXAMPLE
Parallel words	The letter was approved by Clausen, Whittaker, Merlin, and Carlucci.
Parallel phrases	We are gaining market share in supermarkets, in department stores, and in specialty stores.
Parallel clauses	I'd like to discuss the issue after Vicki gives her presentation but before Marvin shows his slides.
Parallel sentences	In 2007 we exported 30 percent of our production. In 2008 we exported 50 percent.

Parallel forms are easier to read and skim. You can create parallelism by repeating the pattern in words, phrases, clauses, or entire sentences (see Table 6.1).

Adding Headings and Subheadings

Use headings and subheadings to show the organization of your material, draw the reader's attention to key points, and show connections between ideas.

A **heading** is a brief title that tells readers about the content of the section that follows. **Subheadings** are subordinate to headings, indicating subsections with a major section. Headings and subheadings serve these important functions:

- **Organization.** Headings show your reader at a glance how the document is organized. They act as labels to group related paragraphs together and organize lengthy material into shorter sections.
- **Attention.** Informative, inviting, and in some cases intriguing headings grab the reader's attention, make the text easier to read, and help the reader find the parts he or she needs to read—or skip.
- **Connection.** Using headings and subheadings together helps readers see the relationship between main ideas and subordinate ones so that they can understand your message more easily. Moreover, headings and subheadings visually indicate shifts from one idea to the next.

Informative headings are generally more helpful than descriptive ones.

Headings fall into two categories. **Descriptive headings**, such as "Cost Considerations," identify a topic but do little more. **Informative headings**, such as "A New Way to Cut Costs," guide readers to think in a certain way about the topic. They are also helpful in guiding your work as a writer, especially if written in terms of questions you plan to address in your document. Well-written informative headings are self-contained, which means readers can read just the headings and subheadings and understand them without reading the rest of the document. For example, "Introduction" conveys little information, whereas the heading "Staffing Shortages Cost the Company $150,000 Last Year" provides a key piece of information and captures the reader's attention. Whatever types of headings you choose, keep them brief and use parallel construction throughout the entire document.

3 **LEARNING OBJECTIVE**

Describe the steps you can take to improve the clarity of your writing and to make your writing more concise

Editing for Clarity and Conciseness

After you've reviewed and revised your message for readability, your next step is to make sure your message is as clear and as concise as possible. To ensure clarity, look closely at your paragraph organization, sentence structure, and word choices. Perhaps a sentence is so complicated that readers can't unravel it. You might have chosen a word that is so vague that readers can interpret it in several ways. Sentence B may not be a logical sequel to sentence A, or an important word may be used incorrectly.[3]

See Table 6.2 for examples of the following tips:

Clarity is essential to getting your message across accurately and efficiently.

- **Break up overly long sentences.** If you find yourself stuck in a long sentence, you're probably trying to make the sentence do more than it can reasonably do, such as expressing two dissimilar thoughts or peppering the reader with too many pieces of supporting evidence at once. (Did you notice how difficult this long sentence was to read?)

TABLE 6.2 Revising for Clarity

ISSUES TO REVIEW	INEFFECTIVE	EFFECTIVE
Overly Long Sentences Taking compound sentences too far	The magazine will be published January 1, and I'd better meet the deadline if I want my article included because we want the article to appear before the trade show.	The magazine will be published January 1. I'd better meet the deadline because we want the article to appear before the trade show.
Hedging Sentences Overqualifying sentences	I believe that Mr. Johnson's employment record seems to show that he may be capable of handling the position.	Mr. Johnson's employment record shows that he is capable of handling the position.
Unparallel Sentences Using dissimilar construction for similar ideas	Mr. Simms had been drenched with rain, bombarded with telephone calls, and his boss shouted at him. To waste time and missing deadlines are bad habits.	Mr. Sims had been drenched with rain, bombarded with telephone calls, and shouted at by his boss. Wasting time and missing deadlines are bad habits.
Dangling Modifiers Placing modifiers close to the wrong nouns and verbs	Walking to the office, a red sports car passed her. Reduced by 25 percent, Europe had its lowest semiconductor output in a decade.	A red sports car passed her while she was walking to the office. Europe reduced semiconductor output by 25 percent, its lowest output in a decade.
Long Noun Sequences Stringing too many nouns together	The window sash installation company will give us an estimate on Friday.	The company that installs window sashes will give us an estimate on Friday.
Camouflaged Verbs Changing verbs and nouns into adjectives Changing verbs into nouns	The manager undertook implementation of the rules. Verification of the shipments occurs weekly. reach a conclusion about give consideration to	The manager implemented the rules. We verify shipments weekly. conclude consider
Sentence Structure Separating subject and predicate Separating adjectives, adverbs, or prepositional phrases from the words they modify	A 10% decline in market share, which resulted from quality problems and an aggressive sales campaign by Armitage, the market leader in the Northeast, was the major problem in 2008. Our antique desk lends an air of strength and substance with thick legs and large drawers.	The major problem in 2008 was a 10% loss of market share, which resulted from quality problems and an aggressive sales campaign by Armitage, the market leader in the Northeast. With its thick legs and large drawers, our antique desk lends an air of strength and substance.
Awkward References	The Law Office and the Accounting Office distribute computer supplies for legal secretaries and beginning accountants, respectively.	The Law Office distributes computer supplies for legal secretaries; the Accounting Office distributes those for beginning accountants.

- **Rewrite hedging sentences.** *Hedging* means pulling back from making an absolutely certain, definitive statement about a topic. Granted, sometimes you have to write *may* or *seems* to avoid stating a judgment as a fact. However, when you hedge too often or without good reason, you come across as being unsure of what you're saying.
- **Impose parallelism.** When you have two or more similar ideas to express, make them parallel by using the same grammatical construction. Parallelism shows that the ideas are related, of similar importance, and on the same level of generality.

If you qualify or hedge too often, you undermine your credibility.

- **Correct dangling modifiers.** Sometimes a modifier is not just an adjective or an adverb but an entire phrase modifying a noun or a verb. Be careful not to leave this type of modifier *dangling*, with no connection to the subject of the sentence. The first ineffective example under "Dangling Modifiers" in Table 6.2 implies that the red sports car has both an office and the legs to walk there. The second example shows one frequent cause of dangling modifiers: passive construction.
- **Reword long noun sequences.** When multiple nouns are strung together as modifiers, the resulting sentence can be hard to read. See if a single well-chosen word will do the job. If the nouns are all necessary, consider moving one or more to a modifying phrase, as shown in Table 6.2.
- **Replace camouflaged verbs.** Watch for words that end in *-ion, -tion, -ing, -ment, -ant, -ent, -ence, -ance,* and *-ency.* These endings often change verbs into nouns and adjectives, requiring you to add a verb in order to get your point across.
- **Clarify sentence structure.** Keep the subject and predicate of a sentence as close together as possible. When the subject and predicate are far apart, readers may need to read the sentence twice to figure out who did what. Similarly, adjectives, adverbs, and prepositional phrases usually make the most sense when they're placed as close as possible to the words they modify.
- **Clarify awkward references.** If you want readers to refer to a specific point in a document, avoid vague references such as *the above-mentioned, as mentioned above, the aforementioned, the former, the latter,* and *respectively.* Use a specific pointer such as "as described in the second paragraph on page 56."

Camouflaged verbs are verbs that have been changed into nouns; they often increase the length of a sentence without adding any value.

Subject and predicate should be placed as close together as possible, as should modifiers and the words they modify.

These efforts to improve clarity often reduce overall word count, so at this point you've probably eliminated most of the excess. The next step is to examine the text with the specific goal of reducing the number of words you use. Readers appreciate conciseness and are more likely to read your documents if you have a reputation for efficient writing. The good news is that many first drafts can be cut by as much as 50 percent.[4] See Table 6.3 for examples of the following tips:

Improving clarity often makes messages shorter, but you can make them shorter still by using some specific revision techniques.

- **Delete unnecessary words and phrases.** To test whether a word or phrase is essential, try the sentence without it. If the meaning doesn't change, leave it out. For instance, *very* is often simply clutter. There's no need to call someone "very methodical." The person is either methodical or not. In addition, avoid the clutter of too many or poorly placed relative pronouns (*who, that, which*). Even articles can be excessive (such as repeating *the* in a list of items). However, well-placed relative pronouns and articles prevent confusion, so make sure you don't obscure the meaning of the sentence by removing them.
- **Shorten long words and phrases.** Short words and phrases are generally more vivid and easier to read than long ones. Also, by using infinitives (the "to" form of a verb) in place of some phrases, you can often shorten sentences while making them clearer.
- **Eliminate redundancies.** In some word combinations, the words say the same thing. For instance, "visible to the eye" is redundant because *visible* is enough without further clarification; "to the eye" adds nothing.
- **Recast "It is/There are" starters.** If you start a sentence with an indefinite pronoun such as *it* or *there*, odds are the sentence could be shorter and more active. For instance, "We believe..." is a stronger opening than "It is believed that..."

Early drafts often have words and phrases that don't add anything and can easily be cut out.

As you rewrite, concentrate on how each word contributes to an effective sentence and on how each sentence helps build a coherent paragraph. For a reminder of the tasks involved in revision, see "Checklist: Revising Business Messages."

Sometimes you'll find that the most difficult problem in a sentence can be solved by simply removing the problem itself. When you come upon a troublesome element, ask yourself, "Do I need it at all?" Possibly not. In fact, you may find that it was giving you so much grief precisely because it was trying to do an unnecessary job.[5] Once you remove the troublesome element, the afflicted sentence will spring to life and breathe normally. Take advantage of the "undo" and "redo" functions in your software to experiment with adding and removing various elements.

If you're struggling to fix a particular problem, you might be able to solve it simply by deleting the troublesome phrase or sentence.

TABLE 6.3 Revising for Conciseness

ISSUES TO REVIEW	INEFFECTIVE	EFFECTIVE
Unnecessary Words and Phrases		
Using wordy phrases	for the sum of	for
	in the event that	if
	prior to the start of	before
	in the near future	soon
	at this point in time	now
	due to the fact that	because
	in view of the fact that	because
	until such time as	when
	with reference to	about
Using too many relative pronouns	Cars that are sold after January will not have a six-month warranty.	Cars sold after January will not have a six-month warranty.
	Employees who are driving to work should park in the underground garage.	Employees driving to work should park in the underground garage.
		OR
		Employees should park in the underground garage.
Using too few relative pronouns	The project manager told the engineers last week the specifications were changed.	The project manager told the engineers last week that the specifications were changed.
		OR
		The project manager told the engineers that last week the specifications were changed.
Long Words and Phrases		
Using overly long words	During the preceding year, the company accelerated productive operations.	Last year the company sped up operations.
	The action was predicated on the assumption that the company was operating at a financial deficit.	The action was based on the belief that the company was losing money.
Using wordy phrases rather than infinitives	If you want success as a writer, you must work hard.	To succeed as a writer, you must work hard.
	He went to the library for the purpose of studying.	He went to the library to study.
	The employer increased salaries so that she could improve morale.	The employer increased salaries to improve morale.
Redundancies		
Repeating meanings	absolutely complete	complete
	basic fundamentals	fundamentals
	follows after	follows
	free and clear	free
	refer back	refer
	repeat again	repeat
	collect together	collect
	future plans	plans
	return back	return
	important essentials	essentials
	end result	result
	actual truth	truth
	final outcome	outcome

(continued)

TABLE 6.3 Revising for Conciseness *(continued)*

ISSUES TO REVIEW	INEFFECTIVE	EFFECTIVE
Redundancies *(continued)*	uniquely unusual	unique
	surrounded on all sides	surrounded
Using double modifiers	modern, up-to-date equipment	modern equipment
It Is/There Are Starters	It would be appreciated if you would sign the lease today.	Please sign the lease today.
Starting sentences with *It* or *There*	There are five employees in this division who were late to work today.	Five employees in this division were late to work today.

Evaluating, Editing, and Revising the Work of Others

Evaluating and revising the work of others is an important responsibility.

At many points in your career, you will be asked to evaluate, edit, or revise the work of others. Whether you're suggesting improvements or actually making the improvements yourself (as you might on a wiki site, for example), you can make a contribution by using all the skills you've learned in this chapter as well as in Chapters 4 and 5.

Before you dive into someone else's work, recognize the dual responsibility that doing so entails. First, unless you've been specifically asked to rewrite something in your own style or change the emphasis of the message, remember that your job is to help the other writer succeed at his or her task, not to impose your writing style or pursue your own agenda. In other words, make sure your input focuses on making the piece more effective, not on making it more like something you would've written. Second, make sure you understand the writer's intent before you begin suggesting or making changes. If you try to edit or revise without knowing what the writer hoped to accomplish, you run the risk of making the piece less effective, not more. With those thoughts in mind, answer the following questions as you evaluate someone else's writing:

- What is the purpose of this document or message?
- Who is the target audience?
- What information does the audience need?
- Does the document provide this information in a well-organized way?
- Does the writing demonstrate the "you" attitude toward the audience?
- Is the tone of the writing appropriate for the audience?
- Can the readability be improved?

✓ **CHECKLIST** **Revising Business Messages**

A. Evaluate content, organization, style, and tone.
- Make sure the information is accurate, relevant, and sufficient.
- Check that all necessary points appear in logical order.
- Verify that you present enough support to make the main idea convincing and interesting.
- Be sure the beginning and end are effective.
- Make sure you've achieved the right tone.

B. Review for readability.
- Consider using a readability index but be sure to interpret the answer carefully.
- Use a mix of short and long sentences.
- Keep paragraphs short.
- Use bulleted and numbered lists to emphasize key points.
- Make the document easy to scan with headings and subheadings.

C. Edit for clarity.
- Break up overly long sentences and rewrite hedging sentences.
- Impose parallelism to simplify reading.
- Correct dangling modifiers.
- Reword long noun sequences and replace camouflaged verbs.
- Clarify sentence structure and awkward references.

D. Edit for conciseness.
- Delete unnecessary words and phrases.
- Shorten long words and phrases.
- Eliminate redundancies.
- Rewrite sentences that start with "It is" or "There are."

- Is the writing clear? If not, how can it be improved?
- Is the writing as concise as it could be?
- Does the design support the intended message?

You can read more about using these skills in the context of wiki writing in Chapter 14.

Using Technology to Revise Your Message

When it's time to revise and polish your message, software features can help you add, delete, and move text, using functions such as *cut and paste* (taking a block of text out of one section of a document and pasting it in somewhere else) and *search and replace* (finding words or phrases and changing them if you need to). Be careful using the "replace all" option; it can result in unintended errors. For example, finding *power* and replacing all occurrences with *strength* will also change the word *powerful* to *strengthful*, which isn't a word.

Software tools such as *revision marks* (look for the *track changes* feature) and *commenting* keep track of proposed editing changes electronically and provide a history of a document's revisions. In Microsoft Word, for example, revisions appear in a different text color than the original text (see Figure 6.3), giving you a chance to review changes before accepting or rejecting them. Adobe Acrobat lets you attach comments to PDF files (see Figure 6.4). (Note that Adobe Acrobat is not the same product as the free Adobe Reader.) Using revision marks and commenting features is also a great way to keep track of editing changes made by team members. Both Word and Acrobat let you use different colors for each reviewer, so you can keep everyone's comments separate.

Revision marks and commenting features are great ways to track the revision process when multiple reviewers are involved.

FIGURE 6.3   Revision Marks in Microsoft Word
Microsoft Word, the most commonly used word processor in business offices, offers handy tools for reviewing draft documents. In this example, text to be added is shown in blue, and text to be deleted is shown in red. The writer can then choose to accept or reject each suggested change.

FIGURE 6.4 Comments Attached to a PDF File
Adobe Acrobat lets reviewers attach comments to any document in PDF format, even if it was originally created using software that the reviewers don't have.

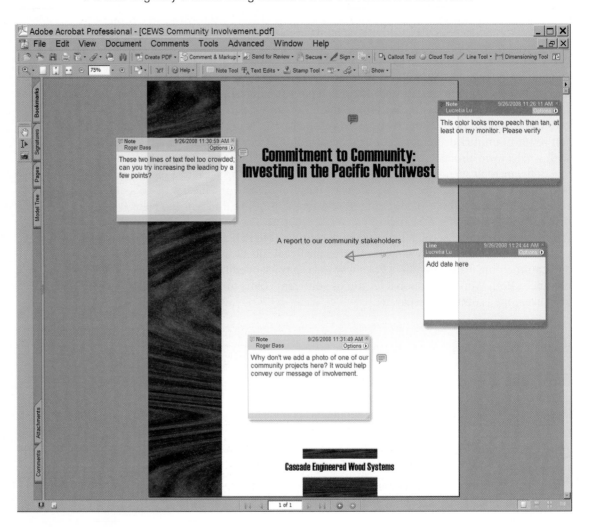

Spell checkers, grammar checkers, style checker, and computerized thesauruses can all help with the revision process, but they can't take the place of good writing and editing skills.

In addition to the many revision tools, four software functions can help bring out the best in your documents. First, a *spell checker* compares your document with an electronic dictionary, highlights unrecognized words, and suggests correct spellings. Spell checkers are wonderful for finding typos, but they are no substitute for good spelling skills. For example, if you use *their* when you mean to use *there*, your spell checker won't notice because *their* is spelled correctly. Plus, some of the "errors" that the spell checker indicates may actually be proper names, technical words, words that you misspelled on purpose, web addresses, or simply words the spell checker doesn't know. It's up to you to decide whether each flagged word should be corrected or left alone, to find the errors that your spell checker has overlooked, and to catch problems that the spell checker itself might introduce (such as inserting unwanted hyphens or suggesting incorrect word replacements).

Second, a computer *thesaurus* gives you alternative words, just as a printed thesaurus does. A computer thesaurus is much faster and lets you try multiple alternatives in just a few seconds to see which works best. The best uses of any thesaurus, printed or computerized, are to find fresh, interesting words when you've been using the same word too many times and to find words that most accurately convey your intended meaning. Don't use a thesaurus simply to find impressive words, however.

Third, a *grammar checker* tries to do for your grammar what a spell checker does for your spelling. Because the program doesn't have a clue about what you're trying to say, it can't tell whether you've said it clearly or completely. However, grammar checkers can highlight items you should consider changing, such as passive voice, long sentences, and words that tend to be misused.

Fourth, a *style checker* can monitor your word and sentence choices and suggest alternatives that might produce more effective writing. For instance, the style-checking options in Microsoft Word range from basic issues, such as spelling out numbers and using contractions, to more subjective matters, such as sentence structure and the use of technical terminology.

By all means, use any software tools that you find helpful when revising your documents. Just remember that it's unwise to rely on them to do all your revision work, and you're responsible for the final product.

PRODUCING YOUR MESSAGE

Now it's time to put your hard work on display. The *production quality* of your message—the total effect of page or screen design, graphical elements, typography, and so on—plays an important role in the effectiveness of your message. A polished, inviting design not only makes your material easier to read but also conveys a sense of professionalism and importance.[6]

Production quality affects readability and audience perceptions of you and your message.

Designing for Readability

Design affects readability in two important ways. First, if used carefully, design elements can improve the effectiveness of your message. If used poorly, design elements can act as barriers, blocking your communication. For example, people age 65 and over are the fastest-growing segment of online consumers in the United States, but many websites don't take into account the natural changes that occur in eyesight as people age. Older people often find it difficult to read the small type that is common on websites—and many websites make the mistake of preventing viewers from enlarging type size in their browsers.[7]

Second, the visual design sends a nonverbal message to your readers, influencing their perceptions of the communication before they read a single word (see Figure 6.5). For example, the elegant style of the Mercedes-AMG website conveys a message that matches the nature of the products themselves. The black, silver, gray, and white color palette sends a distinctly different message than a website with vibrant or clashing colors would send.

Document design sends strong nonverbal signals. Make sure they are positive and appropriate signals.

Effective design helps you establish the tone of your document and helps guide your readers through your message. To achieve an effective design, pay careful attention to the following design elements:

- **Consistency.** Throughout each message, be consistent in your use of margins, typeface, type size, and space. Also be consistent when using recurring design elements, such as vertical lines, columns, and borders. In many cases, you'll want to be consistent from message to message as well; that way, audiences who receive multiple messages from you recognize your documents and know what to expect.

Aim for consistent design within each message and from message to message.

- **Balance.** Balance is a subjective issue. One document may have a formal, rigid design in which the various elements are placed in a grid pattern, while another may have a less formal design in which elements flow more freely across the page—and both could be in balance. Like the tone of your language, visual balance can be too formal, just right, or too informal for a given message.

- **Restraint.** Strive for simplicity in design. Elegant simplicity, using only enough text, graphics, audio, and video to get each point across, is one of the reasons the Mercedes-AMG website is so effective. Don't clutter your message with too many design elements, too much highlighting, too many colors, or too many decorative touches. Let "simpler" and "fewer" be your guiding concepts.

Simple designs are usually more effective than more complex designs.

- **Detail.** Pay attention to details that affect your design and thus your message. For instance, extremely wide columns of text can be difficult to read; in many cases a better solution is to split the text into two narrower columns.

You can make both printed and electronic messages more effective by understanding the use of white space, margins and line justification, typefaces, and type styles.

4 **LEARNING OBJECTIVE**

Explain how design elements help determine the effectiveness of your documents

FIGURE 6.5 **Ineffective and Effective Document Design**

Compare these two e-mail screens. They contain virtually the same information but send dramatically different messages to the reader. The unprofessional appearance of the "ineffective" version makes it uninviting and difficult to read. The amateurish use of color is distracting. In contrast, the "effective" version is clear, inviting, and easy to either read entirely or scan quickly.

Ineffective callouts:
- Disrupts the flow with horizontal lines that add no information value
- Uses font styles inconsistently and unnecessarily
- Obscures ranked list within the paragraph, making it difficult to distinguish from the rest of the text
- Complicates reading with an unnecessary background color

Effective callouts:
- Uses fonts and colors consistently throughout
- Uses white space and paragraph headings effectively to make the document easy to skim
- Draws attention to important points with an easy-to-understand graphic
- Balances graphics, text, and color to create a polished appearance and to lend credibility

White Space

Any space that doesn't contain text or artwork, both in print and online, is considered **white space**. (Note that "white space" isn't necessarily white; it is simply blank.) These unused areas provide visual contrast and important resting points for your readers. White space includes the open area surrounding headings, margins, paragraph indents, space around images, vertical space between columns, and horizontal space between paragraphs or lines of text. To increase the chance that readers will read your messages, be generous with white space; it makes pages and screens feel less intimidating and easier to read.[8]

White space separates elements in a document and helps guide the reader's eye.

Margins and Justification

Margins define the space around text and between text columns. In addition to their width, the look and feel of margins is influenced by the way you arrange lines of text, which can be set (1) *justified* (which means they are *flush,* or aligned vertically, on the left and also flush on the right), (2) flush left with a *ragged-right* margin, (3) flush right with a *ragged-left* margin, or (4) centered. This paragraph is justified, whereas the paragraphs in Figure 6.2 on page 182 are flush left with a ragged-right margin.

Magazines, newspapers, and books often use justified type because it can accommodate more text in a given space. However, justified type needs to be used with care. First, it creates a denser look because the uniform line lengths decrease the amount of the white space along the right margin. Second, it produces a more formal and less personalized look. Third, unless it is used with some skill and attention, justified type can be more difficult to read because it can produce large gaps between words and excessive hyphenation at the ends of lines. The publishing specialists who create magazines, newspapers, and books have the time and skill needed to carefully adjust character and word spacing to eliminate these problems. (In extreme cases, sentences are even rewritten in order to improve the appearance of the printed page.) Because most business communicators don't have that time or skill, it's best to avoid justified type in most business documents.

Most business documents use a flush-left margin and a ragged-right margin.

In contrast to justified type, flush-left, ragged-right type creates a more open appearance on the page, producing a less formal and more contemporary look. Spacing between words is consistent, and only long words that fall at the ends of lines are hyphenated.

Centered type is rarely used for text paragraphs but is commonly used for headings and subheadings. Flush-right, ragged-left type is rarely used in business documents.

Typefaces

Typeface or **font** refers to the physical design of letters, numbers, and other text characters. The choice of typefaces influences the tone of your message, making it look authoritative or friendly, businesslike or casual, classic or modern, and so on. In other words, typefaces send nonverbal signals independent of what the words themselves say, so be sure to choose fonts that are appropriate for your message (see Table 6.4). Computers offer dozens of font choices, but most of these are inappropriate for general business usage.

TABLE 6.4 Typeface Purposes and Personalities

SERIF TYPEFACES (BEST FOR TEXT)	SANS SERIF TYPEFACES (BEST FOR HEADLINES; SOME WORK WELL FOR TEXT)	SPECIALITY TYPEFACES (FOR DECORATIVE PURPOSES ONLY)
Bookman Old Style	Arial	ANNA
Century Schoolbook	**Eras Bold**	Bauhaus
Courier	Franklin Gothic Book	EDWARDIAN
Garamond	Frutiger	Lucida Handwriting
Rockwell	Gill Sans	Old English
Times Roman	Verdana	STENCIL

Serif typefaces are commonly used for regular paragraph text; sans serif typefaces are commonly used for headings and subheadings.

Serif typefaces have small crosslines (called serifs) at the ends of each letter stroke. Serif typefaces such as Times Roman are commonly used for regular paragraph text (as in this book), but they can look busy and cluttered when set in large sizes for headings.

Sans serif typefaces have no serifs (*sans* is French for "without"). The visual simplicity of sans serif typefaces such as Helvetica and Arial makes them ideal for the larger sizes used in headlines. However, these typefaces can be difficult to read in long blocks of text. They look best when surrounded by plenty of white space—as in headings or in widely spaced lines of text.

For most documents, generally avoid using more than two typefaces, although if you want to make captions or another special text element stand out, you can use a third font for that.[9] You can't go too far wrong with a sans serif typeface (such as Arial) for heads and subheads and a serif typeface (such as Times New Roman) for text and captions. Using too many typefaces clutters a document and can produce an amateurish look (as seen in Figure 6.5).

Type Styles

Type style refers to any modification that lends contrast or emphasis to type, including boldface, italic, underlining, color, and other highlighting and decorative styles. Using boldface type for subheads breaks up long expanses of text. You can also boldface individual words or phrases to draw more attention to them. For example, the key terms in each chapter in this book are set in bold. Italic type also creates emphasis, although not as pronounced as boldface. Italic type has specific uses as well, such as highlighting quotations and indicating foreign words, irony, humor, book and movie titles, and unconventional usage.

Avoid using any type style in ways that might interfere with reading.

As a general rule, avoid using any style in a way that slows your audience's progress through the message. For instance, underlining or using all-uppercase letters can interfere with a reader's ability to recognize the shapes of words, and shadowed or outlined type can seriously hinder legibility. Also, avoid overusing any type style. For example, putting too many words in boldface dilutes the impact of the special treatment by creating too many focal points in the paragraph.

Type size is an important consideration as well. For most printed business messages, use a size of 10 to 12 points for regular text and 12 to 18 points for headings and subheadings (1 point is approximately 1/72 inch). Resist the temptation to reduce type size too much in order to squeeze in extra text or to enlarge it to fill up space. Type that is too small is hard to read, whereas extra-large type looks unprofessional. Be particularly careful with small type online. Small type that looks fine on a medium-resolution screen can be hard to read on both low-resolution screens (because these displays can make letters look jagged or fuzzy) and high-resolution screens (because these monitors reduce the apparent size of the type even further).

Designing Multimedia Documents

A **multimedia document** contains a combination of text, graphics, photographs, audio, animation, video, and interactivity (such as hyperlinks that access webpages or software programs). Most electronic media now support multiple media formats, so you have a variety of options for creating multimedia documents. For example, you can add photos to a word processor file, audio commentary to a PDF, video clips to a blog posting, and animation to webpages.

As rich media, multimedia documents can convey large amounts of information quickly, engage people in multiple ways, express emotions, and allow recipients to personalize the communication process to their own needs. However, these documents are more difficult to create than documents that contain only text and static images. To design and create multimedia documents, you need to consider the following factors:

Multimedia documents can be powerful communication vehicles, but they require more time, tools, and skills to create.

- **Creative and technical skills.** Depending on what you need to accomplish, creating and integrating multimedia elements can require some creative and technical skills. Fortunately, many basic tasks, such as adding photographs or video clips to a webpage, have gotten much easier in recent years. And even if you don't have the advantage of formal training in design, by studying successful examples such as the Mercedes-AMG website, you can start to get a feel for what works and what doesn't.

FIGURE 6.6 Multimedia Tools

Software such as Adobe Photoshop Elements makes it easy for anyone with basic computer skills to create and modify content for multimedia documents. A simple *cropping* operation on a photo is shown here.

- **Tools.** The hardware and software tools needed to create and integrate media elements are now widely available and generally affordable. For example, with simpler and less expensive consumer versions of professional photo and video editing software, you can often perform all the tasks you need for business multimedia (see Figure 6.6).
- **Time and cost.** The time and cost of creating multimedia documents has dropped dramatically in recent years. However, you still need to consider time and cost—and exercise good judgment when deciding whether to include multimedia and how much to include. Make sure the time and money you plan to spend will be paid back in communication effectiveness.
- **Content.** To include various media elements in a document, you obviously need to create or acquire them. If you have the skills, time, and tools, you might be able to create graphics or other media elements. If not, you'll need to find these items and secure the right to use them. Millions of graphics, photos, video clips, and other elements are available online, but you need to make sure you can legally use each item. One good option is to search Creative Commons (**www.creativecommons.org**) for multimedia elements available for use at no charge but with various restrictions (such as giving the creator credit).
- **Message structure.** Multimedia documents often lack a rigid linear structure from beginning to end, which means you need to plan for readers to take multiple, individualized paths through the material. In other words, a conventional outline is often inadequate. Chapter 13 discusses the challenge of *information architecture*, the structure and navigational flow of websites and other multimedia documents.
- **Compatibility.** Some multimedia elements require specific software to be installed on the recipient's viewing device. Another challenge is the variety of screen sizes and resolutions, from large, high-resolution computer monitors to tiny, low-resolution mobile phone displays. Make sure you understand the demands your message will place on the audience.

Make sure you have the legal right to use any media elements that you include in your documents.

Using Technology to Produce Your Message

Production tools vary widely, depending on the software and systems you're using. Some IM and e-mail systems offer limited formatting and production capabilities, whereas most word processors now offer some capabilities that rival those of professional publishing software for many day-to-day business needs. *Desktop publishing* software such as QuarkXPress and Adobe InDesign goes beyond word processing, offering more advanced and precise layout capabilities that meet the technical demands of publication-quality printing. (These programs are used mainly by design professionals.)

For online content, web publishing systems make it easy to produce great-looking webpages quickly. Similarly, most blogging systems now simplify the production of blog content, letting you rapidly post new material without worrying too much about design or production. Multimedia production tools such as Microsoft Producer let you combine slides, audio commentary, video clips, and other features into computer-based presentations that once cost thousands of dollars to create.

Learning to use the basic features of your communication tools will help you produce better messages in less time.

No matter what system you're using, become familiar with the basic formatting capabilities. A few hours of exploration on your own or an introductory training course can help you dramatically improve the production quality of your documents. Depending on the types of messages you're creating, you'll benefit from being proficient with the following features:

- **Templates and stylesheets.** As Chapter 5 notes, you can save a tremendous amount of time by using templates and stylesheets. Many companies provide these to their employees to ensure a consistent look and feel for all print and online documents.
- **Page setup.** Use page setup to control margins, orientation (*portrait* is vertical; *landscape* is horizontal), and the location of *headers* (text and graphics that repeat at the top of every page) and *footers* (similar to headers but at the bottom of the page).
- **Column formatting.** Most business documents use a single column of text per page, but multiple columns can be an attractive format for documents such as newsletters. Columns are also handy for formatting long lists.
- **Paragraph formatting.** Take advantage of paragraph formatting controls to enhance the look of your documents. For instance, you can offset quotations by increasing margin width around a single paragraph, subtly compress line spacing to fit a document on a single page, or use hanging indents to offset the first line of a paragraph.
- **Numbered and bulleted lists.** Let your word processor or online publishing system do the busywork of formatting numbered and bulleted lists. It can also automatically renumber lists when you add or remove items, saving you the embarrassment of misnumbered lists.
- **Tables.** Tables are great for displaying any information that lends itself to rows and columns, including calendars, numeric data, comparisons, and multicolumn bullet lists. Use paragraph and font formatting thoughtfully within tables for the best look.
- **Pictures, text boxes, and objects.** Word processors let you insert a wide variety of *pictures* (using industry-standard formats such as JPEG and GIF). *Text boxes* are small blocks of text that stand apart from the main text and can be placed anywhere on the page; they are great for captions, callouts, margin notes, and so on. *Objects* can be anything from a spreadsheet to a sound clip to an engineering drawing. Similarly, blogging systems, wikis, and other web development tools let you insert a variety of pictures, audio and video clips, and other multimedia elements.

By improving the appearance of your documents with these tools, you'll improve your readers' impressions of you and your messages, too.

Letters typically have the following elements:
- *Preprinted letterhead stationery*
- *Date*
- *Inside address*
- *Salutation*
- *Complimentary close*
- *Signature block*

Formatting Formal Letters and Memos

Formal business letters usually follow certain design conventions, as the letter in Figure 6.2 (see page 182) illustrates. Most business letters are printed on *letterhead stationery*, which includes the company's name, address, and other contact information. The first element to appear after the letterhead is the date, followed by the inside address, which identifies the person receiving the letter. Next is the salutation, usually in the form of *Dear Mr.* or

FIGURE 6.7 A Typical Business Memo

This document shows the elements usually included in a formal business memo. Note that in many instances today, this information would be transmitted via e-mail instead of a printed memo.

Uses standard company memo stationery with title indicating that this is a memo

Uses four standard headings for memos

Does not begin with a salutation

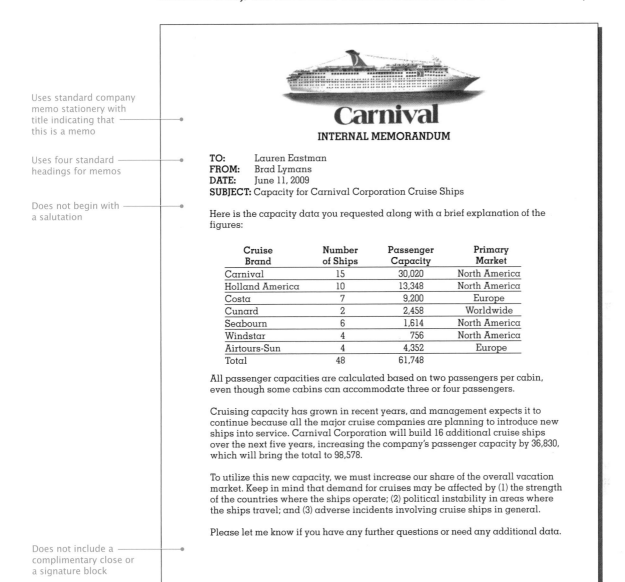

Carnival
INTERNAL MEMORANDUM

TO: Lauren Eastman
FROM: Brad Lymans
DATE: June 11, 2009
SUBJECT: Capacity for Carnival Corporation Cruise Ships

Here is the capacity data you requested along with a brief explanation of the figures:

Cruise Brand	Number of Ships	Passenger Capacity	Primary Market
Carnival	15	30,020	North America
Holland America	10	13,348	North America
Costa	7	9,200	Europe
Cunard	2	2,458	Worldwide
Seabourn	6	1,614	North America
Windstar	4	756	North America
Airtours-Sun	4	4,352	Europe
Total	48	61,748	

All passenger capacities are calculated based on two passengers per cabin, even though some cabins can accommodate three or four passengers.

Cruising capacity has grown in recent years, and management expects it to continue because all the major cruise companies are planning to introduce new ships into service. Carnival Corporation will build 16 additional cruise ships over the next five years, increasing the company's passenger capacity by 36,830, which will bring the total to 98,578.

To utilize this new capacity, we must increase our share of the overall vacation market. Keep in mind that demand for cruises may be affected by (1) the strength of the countries where the ships operate; (2) political instability in areas where the ships travel; and (3) adverse incidents involving cruise ships in general.

Please let me know if you have any further questions or need any additional data.

Does not include a complimentary close or a signature block

Ms. Last Name. The message comes next, followed by the complimentary close, usually *Sincerely* or *Cordially.* And last comes the signature block: space for the signature, followed by the sender's printed name and title. Your company will probably have a standard format to follow for letters, possibly along with a template in Microsoft Word or whatever word processor is standard in the organization. For in-depth information on letter formats, see Appendix A, "Format and Layout of Business Documents."

Like letters, business memos usually follow a preset design (see Figure 6.7). Memos have largely been replaced by e-mail, IM, and other electronic media in many companies, but if they are still in use at the firm you join, the company may have a standard format or template for you to use. Most memos begin with a title such as *Memo, Memorandum,* or *Interoffice Correspondence.* Following that are usually four headings: *Date, To, From,* and *Subject.* (*Re:*, short for *Regarding,* is sometimes used instead of *Subject.*) Memos usually don't use a salutation, complimentary close, or signature, although signing your initials next to your name on the *From* line is standard practice in most companies. Bear in mind that memos are often distributed without sealed envelopes, so they are less private than most other message formats.

Memos are usually identified by a title such as Memo or Memorandum.

5 LEARNING OBJECTIVE

List eight tips for improving message quality through careful proofreading

A methodical approach to proofreading will help you find the problems that need to be fixed.

Your brain can fool you into overlooking errors when proofreading.

PROOFREADING YOUR MESSAGE

Proofreading is the quality inspection stage for your documents, your last chance to make sure that your document is ready to carry your message—and your reputation—to the intended audience. Even a small mistake can doom your efforts, so take proofreading seriously.

Look for two types of problems: (1) undetected mistakes from the writing, design, and layout stages and (2) mistakes that crept in during production. For the first category, you can review format and layout guidelines in Appendix A on page A-1 and brush up on writing basics with Handbook of Grammar, Mechanics, and Usage on page H-1. The second category can include anything from computer glitches such as missing fonts to broken web links to problems with the ink used in printing. Be particularly vigilant with complex documents and complex production processes that involve teams of people and multiple computers. Strange things can happen as files move from computer to computer, especially when lots of fonts and multimedia elements are involved.

Far from being a casual scan up and down the page or screen, proofreading should be a methodical procedure in which you look for specific problems that may occur. Use these techniques from professional proofreaders to help ensure high-quality output:

- **Make multiple passes.** Go through the document several times, focusing on a different aspect each time. For instance, look for content errors the first time and layout errors the second time.
- **Use perceptual tricks.** You've probably experienced the frustration of reading over something a dozen times and still missing an obvious error that was staring you right in the face. This happens because your brain has developed a wonderful skill of subconsciously supplying missing pieces and correcting mistakes when it "knows" what is supposed to be on the page. To keep your brain from tricking you, you need to trick it by changing the way you process the visual information. Try (1) reading each page backward, from the bottom to the top, (2) placing your finger under each word and reading it silently, (3) making a slit in a sheet of paper that reveals only one line of type at a time, and (4) reading the document aloud and pronouncing each word carefully.
- **Double-check high-priority items.** Double-check the spelling of names and the accuracy of dates, addresses, and any number that could cause grief if incorrect (such as telling a potential employer that you'd be happy to work for $5,000 a year when you meant to say $50,000).
- **Give yourself some distance.** If possible, don't proofread immediately after finishing a document; let your brain wander off to new topics and then come back fresh later on.
- **Be vigilant.** Avoid reading large amounts of material in one sitting and try not to proofread when you're tired.
- **Stay focused.** Concentrate on what you're doing. Try to block out distractions and focus as completely as possible on your proofreading task.
- **Review complex electronic documents on paper.** Some people have trouble proofreading webpages, online reports, and other electronic documents on-screen. If you have trouble, try to print the materials so you can review them on paper.
- **Take your time.** Quick proofreading is not careful proofreading.

The amount of time you need to spend on proofing depends on the length and complexity of the document and the situation. A typo in an e-mail message to your team may not be a big deal; but a typo in a financial report, a contract, or a medical file certainly could be serious. As with every

✓ CHECKLIST   Proofing Business Messages

A. Look for writing errors.
- Typographical mistakes
- Misspelled words
- Grammatical errors
- Punctuation mistakes

B. Look for missing elements.
- Missing text sections
- Missing exhibits (drawings, tables, photographs, charts, graphs, online images, and so on)
- Missing source notes, copyright notices, or other reference items

C. Look for design, formatting, and programming mistakes.
- Incorrect or inconsistent font selections
- Problems with column sizing, spacing, and alignment
- Incorrect margins
- Incorrect special characters
- Clumsy line and page breaks
- Problems with page numbers
- Problems with page headers and footers
- Lack of adherence to company standards
- Inactive or incorrect links
- Downloadable files not stored in the appropriate folder

other task in the writing process, with proofreading, practice helps—you become not only more familiar with what errors to look for but also more skilled in identifying those errors. See "Checklist: Proofing Business Messages" for a handy list of items to review during proofing.

DISTRIBUTING YOUR MESSAGE

With the production finished, you're ready to distribute your message. As with every other aspect of business communication, your options for distribution multiply with every advance in technology. In some cases, the choice is obvious: Just click the Send button in your e-mail program, and your message is on its way. In other cases, such as when you have a 100-page report with full-color graphics or a multimedia presentation that is too big to e-mail, you need to plan the distribution carefully so that your message is received by everyone who needs it. When choosing a means to distribute messages, consider the following factors:

- **Cost.** Cost isn't a concern for most messages, but for lengthy reports or multimedia productions, it may well be. Printing, binding, and delivering reports can be expensive, so weigh the cost versus the benefits before you decide. If you're trying to land a million-dollar client, spending $1,000 on presentation materials could be a wise investment.
- **Convenience.** How much work is involved for you and your audience? Although it's easy to attach a document to an IM or e-mail message, things might not be so simple for the people on the other end. They may not have access to a printer, might be accessing your message from slow wireless connections or on handheld devices with tiny screens, or might not have the software needed to open your file. If you're sending large files as IM or e-mail attachments, consider using a file-compression utility to shrink the file first (but make sure your recipients have the means to expand the files upon arrival). For extremely large files, see whether your audience would prefer a CD-ROM or DVD instead.
- **Time.** How soon does the message need to reach the audience? Don't waste money on overnight delivery if the recipient won't read the report for a week.
- **Security and privacy.** The convenience offered by IM, e-mail, blogs, and other technologies needs to be weighed against security and privacy concerns. For the most sensitive documents, your company will probably restrict

6 LEARNING OBJECTIVE

Discuss the most important issues to consider when distributing your messages

Make sure your delivery method is convenient for your audience members.

Document Makeover

Improve This Letter

To practice correcting drafts of actual documents, visit the "Document Makeovers" section in either mybcommlab or the Companion Website for this text.

If mybcommlab is being used in your class, see your User Guide for specific instructions on how to access the content for this chapter. If you are accessing this feature through the Companion Website, click on "Document Makeovers" and then select Chapter 6. You will find a letter that contains problems and errors related to what you've learned in this chapter about revising messages. Use the Final Draft decision tool to create an improved version of this letter. Check the message for organization, readability, clarity, and conciseness.

both the people who can receive the documents and the means you can use to distribute them. In addition, most computer users are wary of opening attachments these days. Instead of sending word processor files (which are vulnerable to macro viruses and other risks), you can convert your documents to PDF files using Adobe Acrobat or an equivalent product.

Chapter 7 offers more advice on distributing podcasts, blogs, and other messages in electronic formats. For news on the latest advances in message distribution technologies, visit http://real-timeupdates.com/bct and click on Chapter 6.

Communication Challenges at Mercedes-AMG

You've just joined the Mercedes-AMG marketing team as a communication specialist. Your duties include creating new material for the Mercedes-AMG website and, occasionally, reviewing materials created by your colleagues. Using what you've learned in this chapter about revising for readability, clarity, and conciseness, address these challenges.[10]

Individual Challenge: You've been asked to review the following statement that concerns the protection of personal data collected from website visitors (Daimler is the parent company of Mercedes-Benz, so its name appears in all legal documentation):

Daimler appreciates your interest in its products and your visit to this web site. Your privacy is important to us and we want you to feel comfortable visiting our site. The protection of your privacy in the processing of your personal data is an important concern to which we pay special attention during our business processes. Personal data collected during visits to

our web site are processed by us according to the legal provisions valid for the countries in which the web sites are maintained. In addition, our data protection policy complies with the Data Protection Code of Conduct applicable companywide for Daimler. The Daimler web site may include, however, links to other web sites which are not covered by this privacy statement.

Without losing any essential information, reduce the number of words in this statement by at least 20 percent (it is currently 123 words long).

Team Challenge: In a section that discusses the history of AMG from its founding as a manufacturer of race car engines, the Mercedes-AMG website includes the following sentence: "The technology transfer from the race circuit to the road is still an integral part of the company's philosophy, which is to the benefit of every Mercedes-AMG customer." In a team with two or three other students, first study this sentence to decide what it means. Then, individually, rewrite the sentence without using the term *technology transfer*. Reconvene as a team, share your individual rewrites, and decide which revision is most effective.

SUMMARY OF LEARNING OBJECTIVES

1 Discuss the value of careful revision, and list the main tasks involved in completing a business message. Revision is a vital step in producing effective business messages; even if the first draft conveys the necessary information, chances are it can be made tighter, clearer, and more compelling—making it more successful for you. Revision occurs throughout the writing process, after you complete the first draft of your business message, and again after you produce the final version. Revision consists of three main tasks: (1) evaluating content, organization, style, and tone; (2) reviewing for

readability; and (3) editing for clarity and conciseness. After you revise your message, you complete it by using design elements to give your message a professional look, proofreading the final version after it has been produced, and distributing it to your audience.

2 List four writing techniques you can use to improve the readability of your messages. The four techniques that improve readability are varying sentence length, keeping paragraphs short, using lists and bullets, and adding headings and subheadings. Varying sentence length helps keep your writing fresh and dynamic while giving you a chance to emphasize the most important points. Paragraphs, on the other hand, are usually best kept short to make it easier for readers to consume your information in manageable chunks. Lists and bullets are effective devices for delineating sets of items, steps in a procedure, or other collections of related information. Headings and subheadings organize your message, call attention to important information, and help readers make connections between related pieces of information.

3 Describe the steps you can take to improve the clarity of your writing and to make your writing more concise. To clarify your message, (1) break up overly long sentences, (2) rewrite hedging sentences, (3) impose parallelism, (4) correct dangling modifiers, (5) reword long noun sequences, (6) replace camouflaged verbs, (7) clarify sentence structure, and (8) clarify awkward references. To make messages more concise, (1) delete unnecessary words and phrases, (2) shorten overly long words and phrases, (3) eliminate redundancies, and (4) recast sentences that begin with "It is" and "There are."

4 Explain how design elements help determine the effectiveness of your documents. White space provides contrast and gives readers a resting point. Margins define the space around the text and contribute to the amount of white space. Margins can affect both readability and the overall visual appeal of your messages. Typefaces influence the tone of the message and should be chosen carefully for each use to ensure maximum readability. Type styles such as boldface, italics, and underlining provide contrast or emphasis.

5 List eight tips for improving message quality through careful proofreading. Proofreading should be more than just a quick glance through the document. Use the techniques the pros use to make sure your documents are top quality: (1) Make multiple passes, looking for specific types of problems each time; (2) use perceptual tricks such as reading aloud or reading backward to prevent your brain from fooling you by filling in pieces or correcting errors; (3) double-check high-priority items such as names, dates, addresses, and financial data; (4) give yourself some distance by putting the document aside for a few hours or even a few days if possible; (5) stay vigilant by proofing only small sections at a time and not proofing when you are tired; (6) stay focused on your work; (7) review complex electronic documents on paper if possible; and (8) take your time.

6 Discuss the most important issues to consider when distributing your messages. Consider cost, convenience, time, security, and privacy when choosing the method to distribute your messages. Cost isn't a major issue for most messages, although production, printing, and distribution of lengthy or complex reports can be a concern. In general, balance the cost with the importance and urgency of the message. Make sure the distribution method is convenient for your audience; it might be easy for you to simply attach a document to an e-mail message, but that might not be the best approach for a given audience. As with cost, balance the time factor with your needs and the needs of your audience. Finally, consider security and privacy issues before distributing documents that contain sensitive or confidential information.

PEARSON mybcommlab™

Log on to **www.mybcommlab.com** to access the following study and assessment aids associated with this chapter:

- Video applications
- Real-Time Updates
- Peer review activity
- Quick Learning Guides

- Pre/post test
- Personalized study plan
- Model documents
- Sample presentations

If you are not using mybcommlab, you can access the Real-Time Updates and Quick Learning Guides through **http://real-timeupdates.com/bct**. The Quick Learning Guide (located under "Learn More" on the website) hits all the high points of this chapter in just two pages. This guide, especially prepared by the authors, will help you study for exams or review important concepts whenever you need a quick refresher.

❙ Test Your Knowledge

1. What are the three main tasks involved in revising a business message?
2. How can you increase the readability of your paragraphs?
3. What functions do headings serve?
4. What are some ways you can make a document more concise?
5. What computer tools can you use when revising messages?
6. What is parallel construction, and why is it important?
7. Why is it a good idea to use verbs instead of noun phrases?
8. How do readers benefit from white space?

9. Why is proofreading an important part of the writing process?
10. What factors should you consider when choosing a distribution method for your messages?

Apply Your Knowledge

1. Why is it helpful to put your first draft aside for a while before you begin the editing process?
2. How do careful revision and quality document production reflect the "you" attitude?
3. Why is it important to spend extra time reviewing and polishing the beginning and end of a message?
4. How can you demonstrate good business judgment when it comes to multimedia documents?
5. **Ethical Choices** What are the ethical implications of murky, complex writing in a document that is supposed to explain how customers can appeal the result of a decision made in the company's favor during a dispute?

Practice Your Knowledge

Messages for Analysis

Message 6.A: Improving Readability

Analyze the strengths and weaknesses of this message and then revise it so that it follows the guidelines in Chapters 4 through 6:

> As an organization, the North American Personal Motorsports Marketing Association has committed ourselves to helping our members—a diverse group comprising of dealers of motorcycles, all-terrain vehicles, Snowmobiles, and personal watercraft—achieve their business objectives. Consequently, our organization, which usually goes under the initials NAPMMA, has the following aims, goals, and objectives. Firstly, we endeavor to aid or assist our members in reaching their business objectives. Second, NAPMMA communicates ("lobbying" in slang terms) with local, state, and national governmental agencies and leaders on issues of importance to our members. And lastly, we educate the motorsports public, that being current motorsports vehicle owners, and prospective owners of said vehicles, on the safe and enjoyable operation of they're vehicles.

Message 6.B: Improving the Layout of a Word Document

To access this message, visit http://real-timeupdates.com/bct, click on "Student Assignments," select Chapter 6, and then select Page 204, Message 6.B. Download and open the Microsoft Word document. Using the various page, paragraph, and font formatting options available in your word processor, modify the formatting of the document so that its visual tone matches the tone of the message.

Message 6.C: Helping Another Writer Improve Readability

To access this message, visit http://real-timeupdates.com/bct, click on "Student Assignments," select Chapter 6, and then select Page 204, Message 6.C. Download and open the Microsoft Word document. Using your knowledge of effective writing and the tips

on page 190 for evaluating the work of other writers, evaluate this message. After you set Microsoft Word to track changes, make any necessary corrections. Insert comments, as needed, to explain your changes to the author.

Exercises

Active links for all websites in this chapter can be found online. If mybcommlab is being used in your class, see your User Guide for instructions on accessing the content for this chapter. Otherwise, visit www.pearsonglobaleditions.com/bovee, locate *Business Communication Today*, Tenth Edition, click the Companion Website link, select Chapter 6, and then click on "Featured Websites." Please note that links to sites that become inactive after publication of the book will be removed from the Featured Websites section.

6.1 **Message Readability: Writing Paragraphs** Rewrite the following paragraph to vary the length of the sentences and to shorten the paragraph so it looks more inviting to readers:

> Although major league baseball remains popular, more people are attending minor league baseball games because they can spend less on admission, snacks, and parking and still enjoy the excitement of America's pastime. Connecticut, for example, has three AA minor league teams, including the New Haven Ravens, who are affiliated with the St. Louis Cardinals; the Norwich Navigators, who are affiliated with the New York Yankees; and the New Britain Rock Cats, who are affiliated with the Minnesota Twins. These teams play in relatively small stadiums, so fans are close enough to see and hear everything, from the swing of the bat connecting with the ball to the thud of the ball landing in the outfielder's glove. Best of all, the cost of a family outing to see rising stars play in a local minor league game is just a fraction of what the family would spend to attend a major league game in a much larger, more crowded stadium.

6.2 **Message Readability: Using Bullets** Rewrite the following paragraph using a parallel bulleted list and one introductory sentence:

> Our forensic accounting services provide the insights needed to resolve disputes, recover losses, and manage risk intelligently. One of our areas of practice is insurance claims accounting and preparation services, designed to help you maximize recovery of insured value. Another practice area is dispute advisory, in which we can assist with discovery, expert witness testimony, and economic analysis. A third practice: construction consulting. This service helps our clients understand why large-scale construction projects fail to meet schedule or budget requirements. Fourth, we offer general investigative and forensic accounting services, including fraud detection and proof of loss analysis.[11]

6.3 **Revising Messages: Clarity** Break the following sentences into shorter ones by adding more periods and revise as needed for smooth flow:
  a. The next time you write something, check your average sentence length in a 100-word passage, and if your sentences average more than 16 to 20 words, see whether you can break up some of the sentences.

b. Don't do what the village blacksmith did when he instructed his apprentice as follows: "When I take the shoe out of the fire, I'll lay it on the anvil, and when I nod my head, you hit it with the hammer." The apprentice did just as he was told, and now he's the village blacksmith.

c. Unfortunately, no gadget will produce excellent writing, but using a yardstick like the Fog Index gives us some guideposts to follow for making writing easier to read because its two factors remind us to use short sentences and simple words.

d. Know the flexibility of the written word and its power to convey an idea, and know how to make your words behave so that your readers will understand.

e. Words mean different things to different people, and a word such as *block* may mean city block, butcher block, engine block, auction block, or several other things.

6.4 **Revising Messages: Conciseness** Cross out unnecessary words in the following phrases:

  a. Consensus of opinion

  b. New innovations

  c. Long period of time

  d. At a price of $50

  e. Still remains

6.5 **Revising Messages: Conciseness** Revise the following sentences, using shorter, simpler words:

  a. The antiquated calculator is ineffectual for solving sophisticated problems.

  b. It is imperative that the pay increments be terminated before an inordinate deficit is accumulated.

  c. There was unanimity among the executives that Ms. Jackson's idiosyncrasies were cause for a mandatory meeting with the company's personnel director.

  d. The impending liquidation of the company's assets was cause for jubilation among the company's competitors.

  e. The expectations of the president for a stock dividend were accentuated by the preponderance of evidence that the company was in good financial condition.

6.6 **Revising Messages: Conciseness** Use infinitives as substitutes for the overly long phrases in these sentences:

  a. For living, I require money.

  b. They did not find sufficient evidence for believing in the future.

  c. Bringing about the destruction of a dream is tragic.

6.7 **Revising Messages: Conciseness** Rephrase the following in fewer words:

  a. In the near future

  b. In the event that

  c. In order that

  d. For the purpose of

  e. With regard to

  f. It may be that

  g. In very few cases

  h. With reference to

  i. At the present time

  j. There is no doubt that

6.8 **Revising Messages: Conciseness** Revise to condense these sentences to as few words as possible:

  a. We are of the conviction that writing is important.

  b. In all probability, we're likely to have a price increase.

  c. Our goals include making a determination about that in the near future.

  d. When all is said and done at the conclusion of this experiment, I'd like to summarize the final windup.

  e. After a trial period of three weeks, during which time she worked for a total of 15 full working days, we found her work was sufficiently satisfactory so that we offered her full-time work.

6.9 **Revising Messages: Modifiers** Remove all the unnecessary modifiers from these sentences:

  a. Tremendously high pay increases were given to the extraordinarily skilled and extremely conscientious employees.

  b. The union's proposals were highly inflationary, extremely demanding, and exceptionally bold.

6.10 **Revising Messages: Hedging** Rewrite these sentences so that they no longer contain any hedging:

  a. It would appear that someone apparently entered illegally.

  b. It may be possible that sometime in the near future the situation is likely to improve.

  c. Your report seems to suggest that we might be losing money.

  d. I believe Nancy apparently has somewhat greater influence over employees in the e-marketing department.

  e. It seems as if this letter of resignation means you might be leaving us.

6.11 **Revising Messages: Indefinite Starters** Rewrite these sentences to eliminate the indefinite starters:

  a. There are several examples here to show that Elaine can't hold a position very long.

  b. It would be greatly appreciated if every employee would make a generous contribution to Mildred Cook's retirement party.

  c. It has been learned in Washington today from generally reliable sources that an important announcement will be made shortly by the White House.

  d. There is a rule that states that we cannot work overtime without permission.

  e. It would be great if you could work late for the next three Saturdays.

6.12 **Revising Messages: Parallelism** Revise these sentences in order to present the ideas in parallel form:

  a. Mr. Hill is expected to lecture three days a week, to counsel two days a week, and must write for publication in his spare time.

  b. She knows not only accounting, but she also reads Latin.

c. Both applicants had families, college degrees, and were in their thirties, with considerable accounting experience but few social connections.

d. This book was exciting, well written, and held my interest.

e. Don is both a hard worker and he knows bookkeeping.

6.13   Revising Messages: Awkward References   Revise the following sentences to delete the awkward references:

a. The vice president in charge of sales and the production manager are responsible for the keys to 34A and 35A, respectively.

b. The keys to 34A and 35A are in executive hands, with the former belonging to the vice president in charge of sales and the latter belonging to the production manager.

c. The keys to 34A and 35A have been given to the production manager, with the aforementioned keys being gold embossed.

d. A laser printer and an inkjet printer were delivered to John and Megan, respectively.

e. The walnut desk is more expensive than the oak desk, the former costing $300 more than the latter.

6.14   Revising Messages: Dangling Modifiers   Rewrite these sentences to clarify the dangling modifiers:

a. Full of trash and ripped-up newspapers, we left Dallas on a plane that apparently hadn't been cleaned in days.

b. Lying on the shelf, Ruby found the operations manual.

c. With leaking plumbing and outdated wiring, I don't think we should buy that property.

d. Being cluttered and filthy, Sandy took the whole afternoon to clean up her desk.

e. After proofreading every word, the letter was ready to be signed.

6.15   Revising Messages: Noun Sequences   Rewrite the following sentences to eliminate the long strings of nouns:

a. The focus of the meeting was a discussion of the bank interest rate deregulation issue.

b. Following the government task force report recommendations, we are revising our job applicant evaluation procedures.

c. The production department quality assurance program components include employee training, supplier cooperation, and computerized detection equipment.

d. The supermarket warehouse inventory reduction plan will be implemented next month.

e. The State University business school graduate placement program is one of the best in the country.

6.16   Revising Messages: Sentence Structure   Rearrange the following sentences to bring the subjects closer to their verbs:

a. Trudy, when she first saw the bull pawing the ground, ran.

b. It was Terri who, according to Ted, who is probably the worst gossip in the office (Tom excepted), mailed the wrong order.

c. William Oberstreet, in his book *Investment Capital Reconsidered*, writes of the mistakes that bankers through the decades have made.

d. Judy Schimmel, after passing up several sensible investment opportunities, despite the warnings of her friends and family, invested her inheritance in a jojoba plantation.

e. The president of U-Stor-It, which was on the brink of bankruptcy after the warehouse fire, the worst tragedy in the history of the company, prepared a press announcement.

6.17   Revising Messages: Camouflaged Verbs   Rewrite each sentence so that the verbs are no longer camouflaged:

a. Adaptation to the new rules was performed easily by the employees.

b. The assessor will make a determination of the tax due.

c. Verification of the identity of the employees must be made daily.

d. The board of directors made a recommendation that Mr. Ronson be assigned to a new division.

e. The auditing procedure on the books was performed by the vice president.

6.18   Producing Messages: Design Elements   Review a copy of the syllabus your instructor provided for this course. Which design elements were used to improve readability? Can you identify ways to make the document easier to read or more user friendly in general? Create your own version, experimenting with different design elements and design choices. How do your changes affect readability? Exchange documents with another student and critique each other's work.

6.19   Web Design   Visit the stock market page of Bloomberg's website at **www.bloomberg.com** and evaluate the use of design in presenting the latest news. What design improvements can you suggest to enhance readability of the information posted on this page? Summarize your recommendations in an e-mail message to your instructor.

6.20   Teamwork   Team up with another student and exchange your revised versions of Message 6.A (in the exercises under "Messages for Analysis"). Evaluate each other's work to see if it could be improved. After you have critiqued each other's work, take a moment to examine the way you expressed your comments and the way you felt listening to the other student's comments. Can you identify ways to improve the critiquing process in situations such as this? For example, did your comments focus on the writing and not the writer?

6.21   Proofreading Messages: E-Mail   Proofread the following e-mail message and revise it to correct any problems you find:

Our final company orrientation of the year will be held on Dec. 20. In preparation for this sesssion, please order 20 copies of the Policy handbook, the confidentiality agreenemt, the employee benefits Manual, please let me know if you anticipate any delays in obtaining these materials.

6.22   Ethical Choices   The time and energy required for careful revision can often benefit you or your company directly, such as by increasing the probability that website visitors will buy your products. But what about situations in which the quality of your writing and revision work really doesn't stand to benefit you directly? For instance, assume that you are putting a notice on your website, informing the local community about some upcoming construction to your manufacturing plant. The work will disrupt traffic for nearly a year and generate a significant amount of noise and air pollution, but knowing the specific dates and times of various construction activities will allow people to adjust their commutes and other activities to minimize the negative impact on their daily lives. However, your company does not sell products in the local area, so the people affected by all this are not potential customers. Moreover, providing accurate information to the surrounding community and updating it as the project progresses will take time away from your other job responsibilities. Do you have an ethical obligation to keep the local community informed with accurate, up-to-date information? Why or why not?

Expand Your Knowledge

Exploring the Best of the Web

Write It Right: Tips to Help You Rethink and Revise

www.powa.org

Are you sure that readers perceive your written message as you intended? If you want help revising a message that you're completing, use the Paradigm Online Writing Assistant (POWA; www.powa.org). With this interactive writer's guide, you can select topics to get tips on how to edit your work, reshape your thoughts, and rewrite for clarity. Read discussions about perfecting your writing skills, complete one of the many online activities provided to reinforce what you've learned, or join a special-interest group to talk about writing. At POWA's website, you'll learn how to improve the final draft of your message. (Note that you may find advice that differs in some respects from the information in this textbook.) Explore POWA's advice and then answer the following questions:

1. Why is it better to write out ideas in a rough format and later reread your message to revise its content? When revising your message, what questions can you ask about your writing?
2. Name the four elements of the "writing context." Imagine that you're the reader of your message. What questions might you ask?
3. When you revise a written message, what is the purpose of "tightening"? What is one way to tighten your writing as you complete a message?

Sharpening Your Career Skills Online

Bovée and Thill's Business Communication Web Search, at http://businesscommunicationblog.com/websearch, is a unique research tool designed specifically for business communication research. Use the Web Search function to find a website, video, PDF document, or PowerPoint presentation that offers advice on effective proofreading. Write a brief e-mail message to your instructor, describing the item that you found and summarizing the career skills information you learned from it.

Part 3

Crafting Brief Messages

Most of your communication on the job will be through brief messages, from Twitter updates and text messages to formal letters that might run to several pages. Learning how to write these messages effectively is key to maintaining productive working relationships with colleagues and customers. Start by adapting what you probably already know about electronic media to the professional challenges of business communication. Then learn specific techniques for crafting routine, positive, negative, and persuasive messages—techniques that will help you in everything from getting a raise to calming an angry customer to promoting your next great idea.

Crafting Messages for Electronic Media

Learning Objectives

After studying this chapter, you will be able to

1 Compare the strengths and weaknesses of the electronic media available for short messages

2 Outline six guidelines for creating successful social media content

3 Explain the need to treat e-mail as a professional medium and identify the qualities of an effective e-mail subject line

4 Identify guidelines for successful instant messaging (IM) in the workplace

5 Describe the role of blogging in business communication today and explain how to adapt the three-step writing process to blogging

6 Explain how to adapt the three-step writing process to podcasting

Communication Close-up at Southwest Airlines

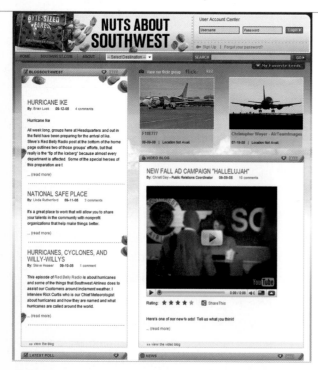

Southwest Airlines's multiauthor blog, Nuts About Southwest, features a variety of entertaining writers from around the company.

www.blogsouthwest.com

Southwest Airlines's blog is usually a love fest—or a "luv" fest, to use one of the company's favorite words. In fact, the blog's official name is Nuts About Southwest. A typical post might highlight the community service efforts of a group of employees or congratulate a team of Southwest mechanics for winning gold at the Aviation Maintenance Olympics. Devoted customers post enthusiastic comments on nearly every article, and many seem to have bonded in virtual friendship with dozens of employees on the Emerging Media Team who take turns writing the blog.

Bill Owens probably didn't expect a bubbly reception to a rather workaday post titled "Why can't I make reservations further in advance?" in which he calmly explained why the company usually didn't let customers make reservations as far into the future as other airlines do.

But he probably wasn't expecting the response he *did* get, either. In his words, "Talk about sticking your head in a hornet's nest!" Instead of the usual dozen or so happy responses to a typical post, he received several hundred responses—many of which expressed disappointment, unhappiness, and downright anger. Customers described one scenario after another in which they had a real need to book travel farther in advance than Southwest allowed, and many complained that the policy was forcing them to fly other airlines. Some Southwest employees chimed in, too, expressing their frustration with not being able to meet customer needs at times.

After bravely and patiently addressing specific customer responses over a period of several months, Owens responded with a new post titled "I blogged. You flamed. We changed." In this message, he explained that the company had listened and was changing its scheduling policies to better accommodate customer needs.

In fact, feedback from blog readers is so important that Southwest CEO Colleen Barrett considers the blog a "customer service laboratory" that helps the company learn how to better serve its customers.[1]

CHOOSING ELECTRONIC MEDIA FOR BRIEF MESSAGES

Southwest's experience with customer feedback (profiled in the chapter-opening Communication Close-up) is just one of many cases in which electronic media and Web 2.0 media in particular are changing business communication. In fact, with so many media options for brief messages, a key challenge these days is often figuring out which is the best medium for each message:

- **Social networks and user-generated content sites.** Social networking sites such as Facebook and user-generated content sites such as Flickr and YouTube provide a variety of communication tools, including user comments and personal profiles, that support brief messages. In addition, a number of companies now host their own social networking sites, where product enthusiasts interact by sharing personal stories, offering advice, and commenting on products and company news—all brief-message functions that replace more traditional media options. For example, Specialized, a major bicycle manufacturer based in Morgan Hill, California, hosts the Specialized Riders Club (www.specializedriders.com), where customers can interact with each other and the professional riders the company sponsors.[2]

- **E-mail.** Thanks to its high speed and low cost, e-mail is now a primary medium for most companies. However, as technologies continue to evolve and users tire of fighting the flood of spam, viruses, and other problems related to e-mail, this medium is being replaced in many instances by instant messaging, blogging, wikis, and other tools that provide better support for instant communication and real-time collaboration.

- **Instant messaging (IM).** After consumers around the world began to adopt IM as a faster and simpler alternative to e-mail, businesses weren't far behind; computer-based IM usage now rivals e-mail in many companies. IM offers even greater speed than e-mail, as well as simple operation and—so far at least—fewer problems with unwanted messages or security and privacy problems.

- **Text messaging.** Small screen sizes and the lack of a regular keyboard on many phone devices make text messaging somewhat less convenient than computer-based IM. However, text messaging is beginning to make inroads into business communication in such areas as marketing, customer service (airline flight updates and credit reporting alerts, for example), and online banking.[3]

- **Blogs.** The ability to update content quickly and easily makes blogs a natural medium when communicators need to get messages out in a hurry; bloggers can also publish information to vast audiences with relatively little effort.

- **Podcasts.** You may be familiar with podcasts as the online equivalent of recorded radio or video broadcasts (video podcasts are often called

LEARNING OBJECTIVE

1

Compare the strengths and weaknesses of the electronic media available for short messages

REAL-TIME UPDATES
Learn More

Explore the business value of social networking

See how businesses can improve internal and external communication with social networking tools. Go to **http://real-timeupdates.com/bct** and click on "Learn More." If you are using mybcommlab, you can access Real-Time Updates within each chapter or under Student Study Tools.

Carleton University in Ottawa, Ontario, Canada, reaches students all over the world with its lecture vodcasts.

vidcasts or *vodcasts*). Businesses are now using podcasts to replace or supplement conference calls, training courses, and other communication activities.

- **Online video.** Creating high-quality videos (such as for formal training and marketing activities) requires some time and expertise, but even the simple video functions now widely available in cameras and mobile phones can be useful for research interviews, location surveys, product demonstrations, and other communication tasks.

Most of your business communication is likely to be via electronic means, but don't dismiss the benefits of printed messages. While e-mail and other electronic media have largely replaced traditional printed memos for internal communication, letters are still used frequently for external communication. (For more on formatting printed letters and memos, see Chapter 6 and Appendix A.) Here are several situations in which you should consider using a printed message rather than electronic alternatives:

- **When you want to make a formal impression.** For special messages, such as sending congratulations or condolences, the formality of printed documents usually makes them a much better choice than electronic messages.
- **When you are legally required to provide information in printed form.** Business contracts and government regulations sometimes require that information be provided on paper.
- **When you want to stand out from the flood of electronic messages.** If your audience's computers are overflowing with e-mail, IM, and newsfeeds, a printed message could stand out enough to get noticed.
- **When you need a permanent, unchangeable, or secure record.** Letters and memos are reliable. Once printed, they can't be erased with a single keystroke or secretly modified by a recipient the way e-mail messages can be. They also can't be forwarded nearly as easily as most electronic media, and there's no danger of accidentally clicking Reply All and embarrassing yourself in the eyes of the entire company when responding on paper. Letters also offer greater security than regular e-mail because they can be sealed in envelopes to be kept away from prying eyes.

Again, most of your on-the-job communication is going to be through electronic media, which is the focus of this chapter. The following sections offer advice on creating content for social media and using e-mail, IM, blogging, and podcasting for business communication. Another vital Web 2.0 medium, wikis, is covered in Chapter 14.

Consider using printed messages
- *To create a more formal impression*
- *When you are legally or contractually required to do so*
- *To stand out from electronic messages*
- *When you need a permanent or secure record.*

CREATING CONTENT FOR SOCIAL MEDIA

Writing for social media requires a different approach than that used for traditional business media.

As Chapter 1 points out in the discussion of Business Communication 2.0, social media change the relationship between sender and receiver. Because the relationship has changed, the nature of the messages between them needs to change as well. Whether you're writing a blog or posting a product demonstration video to YouTube, consider these tips for creating successful content for social media:[4]

2 LEARNING OBJECTIVE

Outline six guidelines for creating successful social media content

- **Remember that it's a conversation, not a lecture or a sales pitch.** One of the great appeals of social media is the feeling of conversation, of people talking *with* one another instead of one person talking *at* everyone else. Companies that try to maintain the old "we talk, you listen" mindset are likely to be ignored in the social media landscape.
- **Write informally but not carelessly.** Write as a human being, not as a cog in a faceless corporate machine. At the same time, don't get sloppy; no one wants to slog through misspelled words and half-baked sentences, looking for a message.
- **Create concise, specific, and informative headlines.** Avoid the temptation to engage in clever wordplay with headlines. This advice applies to all forms of business communication, of course, but it is essential for social media. Readers, especially

those who might potentially spread your name and your ideas around the web, don't want to spend the time and energy required to figure out what your witty headlines mean. Search engines won't know what they mean, either, so fewer people will find your content.

- **Get involved and stay involved.** Social media understandably make some business-people nervous because they don't permit a high level of control over messages. Companies and individual executives can and do get criticized all the time in social media. However, don't hide from criticism. Take the opportunity to correct misinformation or explain how mistakes will be fixed.
- **If you need to promote something, do so indirectly.** Just as you wouldn't hit people with a company sales pitch during an informal social gathering, refrain from blatant promotional efforts in social media. For example, instead of listing selling features of a product, tell a story about how the product changed someone's life.
- **Be transparent and honest.** Honesty is always essential, of course, but a particular issue that has tripped up a few companies in recent years is hiding behind an online blogging persona—either a fictitious character whose writing is actually done by a corporate marketing specialist or a real person who fails to disclose an affiliation with a corporate sponsor.

CREATING EFFECTIVE E-MAIL MESSAGES

E-mail in the workplace is a more formal medium than you are probably accustomed to for personal communication (see Figure 7.1). It's important to approach e-mail as a professional communication medium and an important company resource, as explained in the following section.

Treating E-Mail as a Professional Communication Medium

The most important single point to recognize about e-mail in the workplace is that business e-mail is dramatically different from personal e-mail. The expectations of writing quality are higher, and the consequences of bad writing or poor judgment can be much more serious. For example, e-mail and other electronic message forms have been used as evidence in numerous lawsuits and criminal investigations involving everything from sexual harassment to financial fraud.[5] Other e-mail concerns include the possibility of disclosing confidential information and exposing company networks to security problems.

To minimize the potential for trouble, many companies now have formal e-mail policies that specify how employees can use e-mail, including restrictions against using company e-mail service for personal messages and sending material that might be deemed objectionable. More than one-quarter of U.S. employers have terminated employees for misuse of company e-mail systems, according to one survey.[6] In addition, roughly the same percentage of employers now monitor internal e-mail, and half of them monitor external e-mail. This monitoring can involve both automated scans using software programmed to look for sensitive content and manual scans in which security staff actually read selected e-mail messages.[7]

E-mail hygiene refers to all the efforts that companies are making to keep e-mail clean and safe—from spam blocking and virus protection to content filtering.[8] Regardless of formal policies, every e-mail user has a responsibility to avoid actions that could cause trouble, from downloading virus-infected software to sending objectionable photographs.

3 LEARNING OBJECTIVE

Explain the need to treat e-mail as a professional medium and identify the qualities of an effective e-mail subject line

Because e-mail presents considerable technical and legal hazards, many companies have formal e-mail policies.

REAL-TIME UPDATES
Learn More
Take a crash course in e-mail etiquette

Learn career-enhancing tips on using e-mail in professional settings. Go to **http://real-timeupdates.com/bct** and click on "Learn More." If you are using mybcommlab, you can access Real-Time Updates within each chapter or under Student Study Tools.

FIGURE 7.1 E-Mail for Business Communication

In this response to an e-mail query from a colleague, Elaine Burgman takes advantage of her e-mail system's features to create an efficient and effective message.

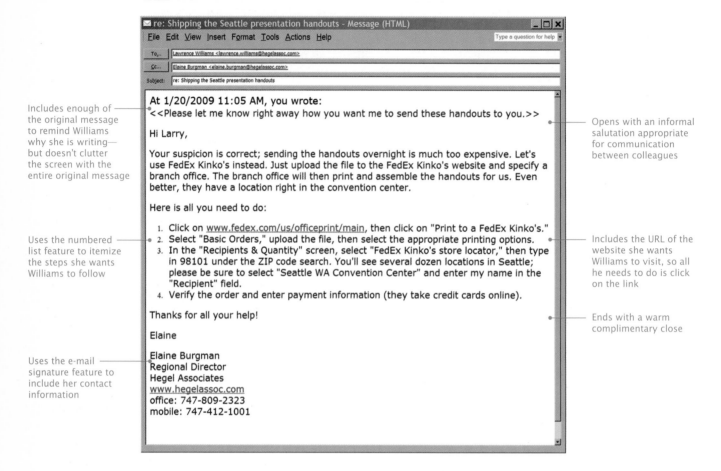

Includes enough of the original message to remind Williams why she is writing—but doesn't clutter the screen with the entire original message

Uses the numbered list feature to itemize the steps she wants Williams to follow

Uses the e-mail signature feature to include her contact information

Opens with an informal salutation appropriate for communication between colleagues

Includes the URL of the website she wants Williams to visit, so all he needs to do is click on the link

Ends with a warm complimentary close

> **re: Shipping the Seattle presentation handouts - Message (HTML)**
>
> File Edit View Insert Format Tools Actions Help   Type a question for help ▾
>
> To..: Lawrence Williams <lawrence.williams@hegelassoc.com>
> Cc...: Elaine Burgman <elaine.burgman@hegelassoc.com>
> Subject: re: Shipping the Seattle presentation handouts
>
> At 1/20/2009 11:05 AM, you wrote:
> <<Please let me know right away how you want me to send these handouts to you.>>
>
> Hi Larry,
>
> Your suspicion is correct; sending the handouts overnight is much too expensive. Let's use FedEx Kinko's instead. Just upload the file to the FedEx Kinko's website and specify a branch office. The branch office will then print and assemble the handouts for us. Even better, they have a location right in the convention center.
>
> Here is all you need to do:
>
> 1. Click on www.fedex.com/us/officeprint/main, then click on "Print to a FedEx Kinko's."
> 2. Select "Basic Orders," upload the file, then select the appropriate printing options.
> 3. In the "Recipients & Quantity" screen, select "FedEx Kinko's store locator," then type in 98101 under the ZIP code search. You'll see several dozen locations in Seattle; please be sure to select "Seattle WA Convention Center" and enter my name in the "Recipient" field.
> 4. Verify the order and enter payment information (they take credit cards online).
>
> Thanks for all your help!
>
> Elaine
>
> Elaine Burgman
> Regional Director
> Hegel Associates
> www.hegelassoc.com
> office: 747-809-2323
> mobile: 747-412-1001

Adapting the Three-Step Process for Successful E-Mail

E-mail messages can range from simple one-paragraph memos to multipage reports, and the three-step writing process can help you in every instance. With practice, you'll be able to complete the various planning, writing, and completing tasks in a manner of minutes for most messages. In addition to the skills you've practiced in Chapters 4 through 6, apply the guidelines in the following sections.

Planning E-Mail Messages

Attention to etiquette is vital with e-mail communication.

The ease of e-mail communication is its greatest strength—and its greatest weakness. Because sending e-mail is so easy, e-mail is often misused and overused, thereby undermining its effectiveness. Many busy professionals struggle to keep up with the flow of e-mail messages—some report receiving as many as 50 messages an hour from colleagues and clients.[9] The flood of messages from an expanding array of electronic sources can significantly affect employees' ability to focus on their work. In fact, one recent study found that workers exposed to a constant barrage of e-mail, IM, and phone calls experienced an average 10-point drop in their functioning IQ.[10] In addition to making sure every e-mail you send is necessary so that you don't contribute to the deluge of messages of dubious importance, you can help keep electronic messages from causing problems in your organization by following the tips in Table 7.1.

Do your part to stem the flood of e-mail by making sure you don't send unnecessary messages or cc people who don't really need to see particular messages.

When analyzing your audience, think twice before using the *cc* (courtesy copy) function to send copies to multiple recipients. Let's say you send a message to your boss and cc five colleagues simply because you want them to see that you're giving the boss some good information. Those five people now not only have to read your message but might also feel

TABLE 7.1 Tips for Effective E-Mail Messages

TIP	WHY IT'S IMPORTANT
When you request information or action, make it clear what you're asking for, why it's important, and how soon you need it; don't make your reader write back for details.	People will be tempted to ignore your messages if they're not clear what you want or how soon you want it.
When responding to a request, either paraphrase the request or include enough of the original message to remind the reader what you're replying to.	Some businesspeople get several hundred or more e-mail messages every day and may need to be reminded what your specific response is about.
If possible, avoid sending long, complex messages via e-mail.	Long messages are easier to read as printed reports or web content.
Adjust the level of formality to the message and the audience.	Overly formal messages to colleagues are perceived as stuffy and distant; overly informal messages to customers or top executives are perceived as disrespectful.
Activate a signature file, which automatically pastes your contact information into every message you create.	You save the trouble of retyping vital information and ensure that recipients know how to reach you through other means.
Don't let unread messages pile up in your in-box.	You'll miss important information and create the impression that you're ignoring other people.
Never type in all caps.	ALL CAPS ARE INTERPRETED AS SCREAMING.
Don't over-format your messages with background colors, colored type, complicated fonts, and so on.	Such messages can be difficult and annoying to read on-screen.
Remember that messages can be forwarded anywhere and saved forever.	A moment of anger or poor judgment could haunt you for the rest of your career.
Use the "return receipt requested" feature only for the most critical messages.	This feature triggers a message back to you whenever someone receives or opens your message; many consider this an invasion of privacy.
Make sure your computer has up-to-date virus protection.	One of the worst breaches of "netiquette" is unknowingly infecting other computers because you haven't protected your own system.
Pay attention to grammar, spelling, and capitalization.	Some people don't think e-mail needs formal rules, but careless messages make you look unprofessional and can annoy readers.
Use acronyms sparingly.	Acronyms such as *IMHO* ("in my humble opinion") and *LOL* ("laughing out loud") can be useful in informal correspondence between close colleagues, but don't use them in important messages.

compelled to reply so that the boss doesn't think they're being negligent. Then everyone will start replying to *those* replies, and on and on. What should have been a single message exchange between you and your boss quickly turns into a flurry of messages that wastes a lot of time.

Finally, be sure to respect the chain of command. In many companies, any employee can e-mail anyone else, including the president and CEO. However, take care that you don't abuse this freedom. For instance, don't send an e-mail complaint straight to the top just because it's easy to do so. Your e-mail will usually be more effective if you follow the organizational hierarchy and give each person a chance to address the situation in turn.

Writing E-Mail Messages

Many people, particularly young professionals accustomed to using electronic media for personal communication, assume that the standards and expectations of business communication don't apply to e-mail. Granted, you don't need to compose perfect works of literature to inform people that lunch will be served in the conference room, but even in routine matters, well-crafted messages demonstrate professionalism and respect for your audience. The time you might save with careless e-mail writing isn't worth the damage it can do to your career.[11]

Careless writing might save you time, but it costs your readers time.

First, haphazard planning and sloppy writing may require less time for writers, but they usually demand *more* time from readers forced to dig the meaning out of misspelled words, confusing sentences, and disjointed paragraphs. Making readers do work you should have done is the very antithesis of the "you" attitude. Second, people who care about effective communication—a group that includes most senior executives, the people who often decide whether you'll get promoted and how much you'll get paid—often judge the quality of your *work* by the quality of your *writing*. Third, at the click of somebody else's mouse, e-mail messages can travel to places you never imagined, including the CEO's computer screen, a lawyer's office, or off into the blogosphere. Always assume that whatever you write in an e-mail message will be stored forever and could become public knowledge inside or outside the firm.

A poorly written subject line could lead to a message being deleted or ignored.

Writing Effective Subject Lines The subject line might seem like a minor detail, but it's actually one of the most important parts of every e-mail message because it helps recipients decide which messages to read and when to read them. Missing or poorly written subject lines often result in messages being deleted without even being opened. To capture your audience's attention, make sure your subject line is informative and compelling. Go beyond simply describing or classifying your message; use the opportunity to build interest with keywords, quotations, directions, or questions:[12]

INEFFECTIVE SUBJECT LINE	EFFECTIVE SUBJECT LINE
July sales results	July sales results: good news and bad news
Friday meeting	Be ready for some tough questions at Friday's meeting
Marketing reports	Marketing reports are due Monday morning
Employee parking	Revised resurfacing schedule for parking lot
Status report	Website redesign is falling behind schedule

Consider the first of these examples. "July sales results" accurately describes the content of the message, but "July sales results: good news and bad news" is more intriguing. Readers will want to know why some news is good and some is bad. "Status report" doesn't even specify which project the report is about, but "Website redesign is falling behind schedule" identifies the project and alerts people to a problem.

Also, if you and someone else are replying back and forth based on the same original message, periodically modify the subject line of your message to reflect the revised message content. When numerous messages have identical subject lines, trying to find a particular one can be confusing and frustrating.

Keep your emotions in check when you compose e-mail messages; flaming can damage relationships and reputations.

Keeping Your Emotions Under Control Given the spontaneous nature of e-mail (and other electronic media), you may sometimes need to work hard to keep your emotions under control. A message that contains insensitive, insulting, or critical comments is called a *flame*. If you're angry, calm down before composing an e-mail message. If you do write an emotionally charged message, let it sit for at least a day and then revise it or even delete it. Ask yourself two questions: First, "Would I say this to my audience face to face?" And second, "Am I comfortable with this message becoming a permanent part of the company's communication history?" Remember that a living, breathing human being is on the receiving end of your communication—and that your message can be forwarded easily and stored forever.

Completing E-Mail Messages

Don't let the speed and simplicity of e-mail lull you into thinking that careless presentation is acceptable. Particularly for important messages, a few moments of revising and proofing might save you hours of headaches and damage control. Also, lean in favor of simplicity

✓ CHECKLIST: Creating Effective E-Mail Messages

A. Treat e-mail as a professional communication medium.
- Remember that business e-mail is more formal than personal e-mail.
- Recognize that e-mail messages carry the same legal weight as other business documents.
- Follow company e-mail policy; understand the restrictions your company places on e-mail usage.
- Practice good e-mail hygiene by not opening suspicious messages, keeping virus protection up to date, and following other company guidelines.

B. Adapt the three-step process for effective e-mail.
- Make sure every e-mail message you send is necessary.

- Don't cc or bcc anyone who doesn't really need to see the message.
- Follow the chain of command.
- Pay attention to the quality of your writing and use correct grammar, spelling, and punctuation.
- Make your subject lines informative by clearly identifying the purpose of your message.
- Make your subject lines compelling by wording them in a way that intrigues your audiences.
- Update the subject line if you reply to the same message back and forth multiple times.
- Keep your emotions under control.
- Don't mark messages as "urgent" unless they truly are urgent.

when it comes to producing your e-mail messages. A clean, easily readable font, in black on a white background, is sufficient for nearly all e-mail messages.

Take advantage of your e-mail system's ability to include a *signature* (most corporate systems support this). This is a small text file that is automatically appended to your outgoing messages. Use it to include your full name, job title, company, and contact information. A signature gives your messages a more professional appearance and makes it easy for others to communicate with you through multiple channels.

When you're ready to distribute your message, pause to verify what you're doing before you click Send. Double-check your addressees to make sure you've included everyone necessary—and no one else. Don't click Reply All when you mean to click Reply. The difference could be embarrassing or even career threatening. Don't include people in the cc (courtesy copy) or bcc (blind courtesy copy) fields unless you know how these features work. (Everyone who receives the message can see who is on the cc line but not who is on the bcc line.) Also, don't set the message priority to "high" or "urgent" unless your message is truly urgent.

To review the tips and techniques for successful e-mail, see "Checklist: Creating Effective E-Mail Messages" or click on Chapter 7 at http://real-timeupdates.com/bct.

CREATING EFFECTIVE INSTANT MESSAGES AND TEXT MESSAGES

While e-mail is here to stay as a business medium, its disadvantages—including viruses, spam, and rampant overuse—are driving many people to explore alternatives.[13] One of the most popular of those alternatives is instant messaging (IM). For both routine communication and exchanges during online meetings, IM is now widely used throughout the business world and is beginning to overtake and even replace e-mail for internal communication in many companies.[14] IM capabilities are also being embedded into other communication media, including e-mail and social networks, further extending the reach of this convenient technology.[15] Business-grade IM systems offer a range of capabilities, including basic chat, *presence awareness* (the ability to quickly see which people are at their desks and available to IM), remote display of documents, video capabilities, remote control of other computers, automated newsfeeds from blogs and websites, and automated *bot* (derived from the word *robot*) capabilities in which a computer can carry on simple conversations.[16]

IM is taking the place of e-mail for much of the routine communication in many companies.

Phone-based **text messaging** has long been popular in other parts of the world, where it is often referred to as *short messaging service* (*SMS*) and was widely available for years before it caught on in North America. Text messaging applications in business include marketing (alerting customers about new sale prices, for example), customer service (such as airline flight status, package tracking, and appointment reminders), security (for example,

Phone-based text messaging is fast and portable but not yet as versatile as computer-based IM.

authenticating mobile banking transactions), crisis management (such as updating all employees working at a disaster scene), and process monitoring (alerting computer technicians to system failures, for example).[17]

Because IM is currently more versatile and more widely used in business than text messaging, the following sections focus on IM. However, as text messaging evolves along with wireless devices and networking, you can expect that many of the benefits, risks, and guidelines that pertain to IM will eventually pertain to text messaging as well.

Understanding the Benefits and Risks of IM

IM offers many benefits:
- *Rapid response*
- *Low cost*
- *Ability to mimic conversation*
- *Wide availability*

The benefits of IM include the possibility of rapid response to urgent messages, lower cost than phone calls, ability to mimic conversation more closely than e-mail, and availability on a wide range of devices, from PCs to mobile phones to personal digital assistants (PDAs).[18] In addition, because it more closely resembles one-on-one conversation, IM doesn't get misused as a one-to-many broadcast method as often as e-mail does.[19]

Of course, wherever technology goes, trouble seems to follow. The potential drawbacks of IM include security problems (computer viruses, network infiltration, and the possibility that sensitive messages might be intercepted by outsiders), the need for *user authentication* (making sure that online correspondents are really who they appear to be), the challenge of logging messages for later review and archiving, incompatibility between competing IM systems, and *spim* (unsolicited commercial messages, similar to e-mail spam). Fortunately, with the growth of *enterprise instant messaging* (*EIM*), or IM systems designed for large-scale corporate use, many of these problems are being overcome. However, security remains a significant concern for corporate IM systems.[20]

Adapting the Three-Step Process for Successful IM

Although instant messages are often conceived, written, and sent within a matter of seconds, the principles of the three-step process still apply:

- **Planning instant messages.** View every IM exchange as a conversation; while you may not deliberately plan every individual statement you make or question you pose, take a moment to plan the overall exchange. If you're requesting something, think through exactly what you need and the most effective way to ask for it. If someone is asking you for something, consider his or her needs and your ability to meet them before you respond. And although you rarely organize instant messages in the sense of creating an outline, try to deliver information in a coherent, complete way that minimizes the number of individual messages required.
- **Writing instant messages.** As with e-mail, the appropriate writing style for business IM is more formal than the style you may be accustomed to with personal IM or text messaging. You should generally avoid IM acronyms (such as *FWIW* for "for what it's worth" or *HTH* for "hope that helps") except when communicating with close colleagues. In the IM exchange in Figure 7.2, notice how the participants communicate quickly and rather informally but still maintain good etiquette and a professional tone. This style is even more important if you or your staff use IM to communicate with customers and other outside audiences.
- **Completing instant messages.** One of the biggest attractions of IM is that the completing step is so easy. You don't have to produce the message in the usual sense, and distribution is as simple as clicking the Send button. However, don't skip over the revising and proofreading tasks. Quickly scan each message before you send to make sure you don't have any missing or misspelled words and that your message is clear and complete.

When using IM, be aware of the potential for constant interruptions and wasted time.

To use IM effectively, keep in mind some important behavioral issues: the potential for constant interruptions, the ease of accidentally mixing personal and business messages, the risk of being out of the loop (if a hot discussion or an impromptu meeting flares up when you're away from your PC or other IM device), and the "vast potential for wasted time" (in the words of MIT labor economist David Autor). On top of all that, users are at the mercy of other people's typing abilities, which can make IM agonizingly slow.[21]

FIGURE 7.2 Instant Messaging for Business Communication

Instant messaging is widely used in business, but you should not use the same informal style of communication you probably use for IM with your friends and family.

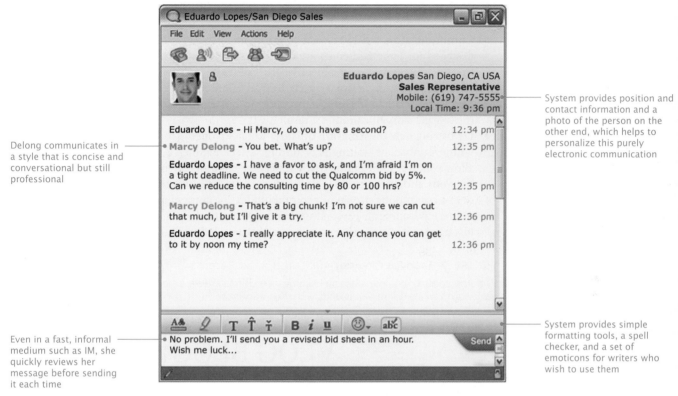

Delong communicates in a style that is concise and conversational but still professional

System provides position and contact information and a photo of the person on the other end, which helps to personalize this purely electronic communication

Even in a fast, informal medium such as IM, she quickly reviews her message before sending it each time

System provides simple formatting tools, a spell checker, and a set of emoticons for writers who wish to use them

Regardless of the system you're using, you can make IM more efficient and effective by following these tips:[22]

- Unless a meeting is scheduled, make yourself unavailable when you need to focus on other work.
- If you're not on a secure system, don't send confidential information.
- Be extremely careful about sending personal messages—they have a tendency to pop up on other people's computers at embarrassing moments.
- Don't use IM for important but impromptu meetings if you can't verify that everyone concerned will be available.
- Unless your system is set up for it, don't use IM for lengthy, complex messages; e-mail is better for those.
- Try to avoid carrying on multiple IM conversations at once, to minimize the chance of sending messages to the wrong people or making one person wait while you tend to another conversation.
- Follow all security guidelines designed to keep your company's information and systems safe from attack.

To review the advice for effective IM in the workplace, see "Checklist: Using IM Productively" or click on Chapter 7 at **http://real-timeupdates.com/bct**.

4 **LEARNING OBJECTIVE**

Identify guidelines for successful instant messaging (IM) in the workplace

Understand the guidelines for successful business IM before you begin to use it.

✓ **CHECKLIST:** **Using IM Productively**

- Pay attention to security and privacy issues and be sure to follow all company guidelines.
- Treat IM as a professional communication medium, not an informal, personal tool; avoid using IM slang with all but close colleagues.

- Maintain good etiquette, even during simple exchanges.
- Protect your own productivity by making yourself unavailable when you need to focus.
- In most instances, don't use IM for confidential messages, complex messages, or personal messages.

CREATING EFFECTIVE BUSINESS BLOGS

Blogs encourage interaction with a large, geographically dispersed audience.

To an extent perhaps unmatched by any other medium, blogs can engage large, widely distributed audiences. In a sense, a blog combines the global reach and reference value of a conventional website with the conversational exchanges of e-mail or IM. Good business blogs pay close attention to several important elements:

- **Communicating with personal style and an authentic voice.** Most business messages designed for large audiences are carefully scripted and written in a "corporate voice" that is impersonal and objective. In contrast, successful business blogs such as Southwest Airlines's are written by individuals and exhibit their personal style. Audiences relate to this fresh approach and often build closer emotional bonds with the blogger's organization as a result.
- **Delivering new information quickly.** Today's blogging tools let you post new material within minutes of writing it or filming it (see Figure 7.3). Not only does this feature allow you to respond quickly when needed—such as during a corporate crisis—it also lets your audiences know that an active conversation is taking place. Blogs that don't offer a continuous stream of new and interesting content are quickly ignored in today's online environment. Topics don't need to be earth shaking or cutting edge, either. They just need to be things that people care about and are willing to spend time reading. For

FIGURE 7.3 Video Blogging

With the addition of video, blogging becomes a true multimedia experience that gives bloggers an easy way to share sights and sounds with their audiences.

instance, Harold Baker, a researcher at Clorox, blogs for the company under the name "Dr. Laundry," dispensing helpful advice on removing stains and tackling other household chores.[23]

- **Choosing topics of peak interest to audiences.** Successful blogs cover topics that readers care about. General Motors's popular FastLane blog (http://fastlane. gmblogs.com) features top executives writing about GM automobiles and responding to questions and criticisms from car enthusiasts. The people who read the blog and write comments obviously care about cars and want the latest information from GM.[24]

- **Encouraging audiences to join the conversation.** Not all blogs invite comments, although most do. These comments can be a valuable source of news, information, and insights. In addition, the relatively informal nature of blogging seems to make it easier for company representatives to let their guards down and converse with their audiences. Of course, not all comments are helpful or appropriate, which is why many bloggers review all comments and select the most helpful or interesting ones to post.

Given the unique ability of blogs to convey topical information quickly and in a conversational format, their rapid adoption by businesses in virtually every industry should come as no surprise. The following sections offer an overview of the business applications of blogging, and Table 7.2 offers a number of suggestions for successful blogging.

Most business blogs invite readers to leave comments, although many review comments before displaying them.

Understanding the Business Applications of Blogging

Blogs are a potential solution whenever you have a continuing stream of information to share with an online audience—and particularly when you want the audience to have the opportunity to respond. Here are some of the many ways businesses are using blogs:[25]

- **Project management and team communication.** Using blogs is a good way to keep project teams up to date, particularly when team members are geographically dispersed. For instance, the trip reports that employees file after visiting customers or other external parties can be enhanced vividly with *mobile blogs*, or *moblogs*. Thanks to the convenience of camera phones and other multimedia wireless devices, employees on the go can send text, audio, images, and video to their colleagues. Conversely, mobile employees can also stay in touch with their team blogs by using handheld devices.

- **Company news.** Companies can use blogs to keep employees informed about general business matters, from facility news to benefit updates. Blogs also serve as online community forums, giving everyone in the company a chance to raise questions and voice concerns by using the commenting feature.

- **Customer support.** Building on the tradition of online customer support forums that have been around since the earliest days of the Internet, customer support blogs answer questions, offers tips and advice, and inform customers about new products.

- **Public relations and media relations.** Many company employees and even high-ranking executives now share company news with both the general public and journalists via their blogs. The Nuts About Southwest blog featured at the beginning of the chapter is a great example.

- **Recruiting.** Using a blog is a great way to let potential employees know more about your company, the people who work there, and the nature of the company culture.

- **Policy and issue discussions.** Executive blogs in particular provide a public forum for discussing legislation, regulations, and other broad issues of interest to an organization.

- **Crisis communication.** Using blogs is an efficient way to provide up-to-the-minute information during emergencies, correct misinformation, or respond to rumors.

5 **LEARNING OBJECTIVE**

Describe the role of blogging in business communication today and explain how to adapt the three-step writing process to blogging

The business applications of blogs include a wide range of internal and external communication tasks.

Moblogs are blogs adapted for display on mobile devices such as phones.

TABLE 7.2 Tips for Effective Business Blogging

TIP	WHY IT'S IMPORTANT
Don't blog without a clear plan.	Without a clear plan, your blog is likely to wander from topic to topic and fail to build a sense of community with your audience.
Post frequently; the whole point of a blog is fresh material.	If you won't have a constant supply of new information or new links, create a traditional website instead.
Make it about your audience and the issues that are important to them.	Readers want to know how your blog will help them, entertain them, or give them a chance to communicate with others who have similar interests.
Write in an authentic voice; never create an artificial character who supposedly writes a blog.	*Flogs*, or fake blogs, violate the spirit of blogging, show disrespect for your audience, and may turn audiences against you as soon as they uncover the truth.
Link generously—but carefully.	Providing interesting links to other blogs and websites is a fundamental aspect of blogging, but make sure the links will be of value to your readers and don't point to inappropriate material.
Keep it brief.	Most online readers don't have the patience to read lengthy reports.
Don't post anything you wouldn't want the entire world to see.	Future employers, government regulators, competitors, journalists, and community critics are just a few of the people who might eventually see what you've written.
Don't engage in blatant product promotion.	Readers who think they're being advertised to will stop reading.
Take time to write compelling, specific headlines for your posts.	Readers usually decide within a few seconds whether to read your posts; boring or vague headlines will turn them away instantly.
Pay attention to spelling, grammar, and mechanics.	No matter how smart or experienced you are, poor-quality writing undermines your credibility with intelligent audiences.
Respond to criticism openly and honestly.	Hiding sends the message that you don't have a valid response to the criticism. If your critics are wrong, patiently explain why you think they're wrong. If they are right, explain how you'll fix the situation.
Listen and learn.	If you don't take the time to analyze the comments people leave on your blog or the comments other bloggers make about you, you're missing out on one of the most valuable aspects of blogging.
Respect intellectual property.	You not only have an ethical obligation to not use material you don't own, doing so can also violate copyright laws.
Be scrupulously honest and careful with facts.	Honesty is an absolute requirement for every ethical business communicator, of course, but you need to be extra careful online because inaccuracies (both intentional and unintentional) are likely to be discovered quickly and shared widely.

- **Market research.** Blogs can be a clever mechanism for soliciting feedback from customers and experts in the marketplace. In addition to using their own blogs for research, today's companies need to monitor blogs that are likely to discuss them, their executives, and their products. Negative product reviews, rumors, and other information can spread across the globe in a matter of hours, and managers need to know what the online community is saying—whether it's positive or negative. *Reputation analysts* such as Evolve24 (**www.evolve24.com**) have developed ways to automatically monitor blogs and other online sources to see what people are saying about their corporate clients and evaluate risks and opportunities in the global online conversation.[26]
- **Brainstorming.** Online brainstorming via blogs offers a way for people to toss around ideas and build on each others' contributions.
- **Viral marketing.** The interconnected nature of the blogosphere makes it a natural vehicle for spreading the word about your company and your products. Bloggers often make a point to provide links to other blogs and websites that interest them, giving

Blogs are an ideal medium for viral marketing, the organic spread of messages from one audience member to another.

marketers a great opportunity to spread their messages. *Viral marketing* refers to the transmission of messages in much the same way that biological viruses are transmitted from person to person.

- **E-mail replacement.** As spam filters and message overload make it increasingly difficult to reach people via e-mail, many companies have turned to using blogs as a way to distribute information to customers and other audiences.

- **News syndication.** Blogging allows both individuals and companies to become publishers of news and other information. Syndication is explained on page 228.

- **Community building.** Blogging is a great way to connect people with similar interests. **Microblogging**, of which Twitter (http://twitter.com) is the best-known example, is blogging on a small scale, using computers, IM, or mobile phones. Starbucks, Whole Foods Markets, The Home Depot, and Comcast are among the growing number of firms using Twitter to build communities of enthusiasts who participate in research studies or other conversations or who simply want to follow along with news and events that involve their favorite products or companies.[27]

REAL-TIME UPDATES
Learn More

Convincing corporate holdouts of the value of business blogs

If you need to convince anyone that a blog can be good for business—including why blogs outperform static webpages in search engine results—check out this compelling presentation. Go to **http://real-timeupdates.com/bct** and click on "Learn More." If you are using mybcommlab, you can access Real-Time Updates within each chapter or under Student Study Tools.

The possibilities of blogs are almost unlimited, so be on the lookout for new ways to use them to foster positive relationships with colleagues, customers, and other important audiences (see Figure 7.4).

Adapting the Three-Step Process for Successful Blogging

The three-step writing process is easy to adapt to blogging tasks. The planning step is particularly important if you're considering starting a blog because you're planning an entire communication channel, not just a single message. Pay close attention to your audience, your purpose, and your scope:

- **Audience.** Except for team project blogs and other efforts with an obvious and well-defined audience, defining your target audience can be challenging. You want an audience large enough to justify the time you'll be investing but narrow enough that you can provide a clear focus for the blog. For instance, if you work for a firm that develops computer games, would you focus your blog on "hardcore" players, the type who spend thousands of dollars on super-fast PCs optimized for video games, or would you broaden the reach to include all video gamers? The decision often comes down to business strategy.

- **Purpose.** Unlike a personal blog, in which you typically write about whatever interests you, a business blog needs to have a business-related purpose that is important to your company and to your chosen audience. Moreover, the *general purpose* of your blog must "have legs"—that is, it needs to be something that can drive the blog's content for months or years and provide a cohesive framework for the *specific purpose* of each blog post. And like many websites, business blogs often need to address more than one purpose. For instance, Adam C. Haver writes the blog for SendOutCards, a Salt Lake City, Utah, greeting card company. Haver explains that the blog has two purposes: keeping the company's distribution partners up to date and giving outsiders "an inside look at our company."[28]

- **Scope.** Defining the scope of your blog can be a bit tricky. You want to cover a subject area that is broad enough to offer discussion possibilities for months or years but narrow enough to have an identifiable focus. For instance, GM's FastLane blog is about GM automobiles only—not GM's stock price, labor negotiations, and so on. Moreover, the scope of your blog needs to remain fairly stable so that you can build an audience over time. If you start out discussing product support but then shift to talking about your company's advertising programs, you'll probably lose readers along the way.

Before you launch a blog, make sure you have a clear understanding of your target audience, the purpose of your blog, and the scope of subjects you plan to cover.

FIGURE 7.4 Elements of an Effective Business Blog

Blogs exist in many forms and formats, but visitors expect a few basic elements, such as access to archives, links to related information, and a convenient way to subscribe to an automatic newsfeed. Note the style and tone of the writing in this blog; it is far more engaging and conversational than the traditional "corporate voice." Moreover, it is about the *customers*, not the *company*.

The headline and tagline combine to clearly indicate the source and the nature of this blog

Postings can be either complete articles or introductions that have links to the complete pieces

Postings are accompanied by a line that indicates who posted the material and when; most blogs also allow visitors to comment on posts

A calendar with hotlinks is one way to provide quick access to postings from previous days

Related and interesting links, to both regular websites and other blogs, are a feature of nearly every blog

Many blogs offer a search box to let visitors find past articles

Most blogs provide one or more ways for readers to subscribe via a newsfeed

Careful planning needs to continue with each message. Unless you're posting to a restricted-access blog, such as an internal blog on a company intranet, you can never be sure who might see your posts. Other bloggers might link to them months or years later. Also, if you are not writing an official company blog but rather blogging as an individual employee, make sure you understand your employer's blogging guidelines. More and more companies are putting policies in place to prevent employee missteps with blogging.[29]

Write blog posts in a comfortable—but not careless—style.

Write in a comfortable, personal style. Blog audiences don't want to hear from your company; they want to hear from *you*. Bear in mind, though, that *comfortable* does not mean *careless*. Sloppy writing damages your credibility. In addition, while audiences expect you to be knowledgeable in the subject area your blog covers, you don't need to know everything about a topic. If you don't have all the information yourself, provide links to other blogs and websites that supply relevant information. In fact, many blog audiences consider carefully screened links to be an essential part of blogging.

✓ **CHECKLIST:**   **Blogging for Business**

- Consider creating a blog whenever you have a continuing stream of information to share with an online audience.
- Identify an audience that is broad enough to justify the effort but narrow enough to have common interests.
- Identify a purpose that is comprehensive enough to provide ideas for a continuing stream of posts.
- Consider the scope of your blog carefully; make it broad enough to attract an audience but narrow enough to keep you focused.

- Communicate with a personal style and an authentic voice but don't write carelessly.
- Deliver new information quickly.
- Choose topics of peak interest to your audience.
- Encourage audiences to join the conversation.
- Offer a newsfeed option so that subscribers can get automatic updates.

Completing messages for your blog is usually quite easy. Evaluate the content and readability of your message, proofread to correct any errors, and post using your blogging system's tools for doing so. If your blog doesn't already have one, be sure to include one or more *newsfeed* options so that your audience can automatically receive updates of new blog posts (see "Distributing Blog and Podcast Content" on page 228).

"Checklist: Blogging for Business" summarizes some of the key points to remember when creating and writing a business blog. You can also visit **http://real-timeupdates.com/ bct** and click on Chapter 7 for the latest advice on blogging.

CREATING EFFECTIVE PODCASTS

Podcasting offers a number of interesting possibilities for business communication. Its most obvious use is to replace existing audio and video messages, such as one-way teleconferences in which a speaker provides information without expecting to engage in conversation with the listeners. Training is another good use of podcasting. One of the first podcasts recorded by technical experts at IBM gave other employees advice on setting up blogs, for example.[30] Sales representatives who travel to meet with potential customers can listen to audio podcasts or view video podcasts to get the latest information on their companies' products. Podcasts are also an increasingly common feature on blogs, letting audiences listen to or watch recordings of their favorite bloggers. New services can even transcribe blogs into podcasts and vice versa.[31]

As more businesspeople become comfortable with podcasting, it should find applications in a variety of new areas, wherever audio or video content can convey business messages effectively. For instance, real estate agents can record audio podcasts that potential homebuyers can listen to while walking through houses. Marketing departments can replace expensive printed brochures with video podcasts that demonstrate new products in action. Human resources departments can offer video tours of their companies to entice new recruits.

Podcasting can be used to deliver a wide range of audio and video messages.

Adapting the Three-Step Process for Successful Podcasting

Although it might not seem obvious at first, the three-step writing process adapts quite nicely to podcasting. You've already chosen the medium, so focus the planning step on analyzing the situation, gathering the information you'll need, and organizing your material. One vital planning step depends on whether you intend to create podcasts for limited use and distribution (such as a weekly audio update to your virtual team) or to create a *podcasting channel* with regular recordings on a consistent theme, designed for a wider public audience.

As with planning a blog, if you intend to create a podcasting channel, be sure to think through the range of topics you want to address over time to verify that you have

6 LEARNING OBJECTIVE

Explain how to adapt the three-step writing process to podcasting

If you plan to create a podcast channel, make sure your subject has "legs"—enough interesting topics to sustain an ongoing effort.

Business Communication 2.0

Help! I'm Drowning in Social Media!

Anyone who has sampled today's social media offerings has probably experienced this situation: You find a few fascinating blogs, a few interesting people to follow on Twitter, a couple of podcast channels with helpful business tips, and then wham—within a few hours of signing up, your computer is overflowing with updates. Even if every new item is useful (which is rather unlikely), you receive so many that you can't stay ahead of the incoming flood. Between Twitter updates, RSS newsfeeds, e-mail, instant messaging, and social networks—not to mention a desk phone and a mobile phone—today's business professionals could easily spend their entire days just trying to keep up with incoming messages and never get any work done.

To keep social media from turning into a source of stress and information anxiety, consider these tips:

- **Understand what information you really need in order to excel in your current projects and along your intended career path.** Unfortunately, taking this advice is even trickier than it sounds because you can't always know what you need to know, so you can't always predict which sources will be helpful. However, don't gather information simply because it is interesting or entertaining; collect information that is useful or at least potentially useful.

- **Face the fact that you cannot possibly handle every update from every potentially interesting and helpful source.** You have to set priorities and make tough choices to protect yourself from information overload.
- **Add new information sources slowly.** Give yourself a chance to adjust to the flow and judge the usefulness of each new source.
- **Prune your sources vigorously and frequently.** Bloggers run out of things to say; your needs and interests change; higher-priority sources appear.
- **Remember that information is an enabler, a means to an end.** Collecting vast amounts of information won't get you a sweet promotion with a big, juicy raise. *Using* information creatively and intelligently will.

CAREER APPLICATIONS

1. How can you determine whether a social media source is worth paying attention to?
2. Should you allow any information source to interrupt your work flow during the day (even just to signal that a new message is available)? Why or why not?

---

a sustainable purpose. If you plan to comment on the stock market or breaking news in your industry, for instance, you'll have a recurring source of topics to discuss. In contrast, if you plan to share marketing ideas for small business owners, make sure you have or can find plenty of ideas over time so that your podcasting efforts don't run out of steam. If you bounce from one theme to another over time, you risk losing your audience.[32]

Generous use of previews, transitions, and reviews helps podcast audiences follow the thread of your recording.

As you organize and begin to think about the words or images you'll use as content, pay close attention to previews, transitions, and reviews. These steering devices are especially vital in audio and video recordings because these formats lack the "street signs" (such as headings) that audiences rely on in print media. Moreover, scanning back and forth to find specific parts of an audio or video message is much more difficult than with textual messages, so you need to do everything possible to make sure your audience successfully receives and interprets your message on the first try. Another way to help listeners and viewers is to provide detailed written descriptions of your podcasts (on your blog, for example) so that they understand what each recording offers.

One of the attractions of podcasting is the conversational, person-to-person feel of the recordings, so unless you need to capture exact wording, speaking from an outline and notes rather than a prepared script is often the best choice. However, no one wants to listen to rambling podcasts that struggle to make a point, so don't try to make up your content on the fly. An effective podcast, like an effective story, has a clear beginning, middle, and end.

Plan your podcast content carefully; edits are much more difficult to make than in textual messages.

In the completing step, keep in mind that making edits is much more difficult with audio or video than with textual media. Take extra care to revise your script or think through your speaking notes before you begin to record. You don't want to get halfway through the recording process and realize that you should have said something else in the introduction.

Finally, consider integrating your podcasting efforts with a related blog. Not only can you provide additional information, you can use the commenting feature of the blog to encourage feedback from your audience.[33]

Assembling a Podcasting System

The equipment needed to record podcasts depends on the degree of production quality you want to achieve. For the most basic podcasts, such as those you might record for internal audiences, most contemporary personal computers probably have the equipment you need: a low-cost microphone (most laptop computers now have built-in microphones), a sound card to convert the microphone signal to digital format (most computers have them now), and some recording software (free versions are available online). Many handheld digital recorders can also record audio files that you can upload to a PC for editing and distribution.

However, a basic system might not deliver the audio quality or production flexibility you need for a public podcast. For instance, the microphone built into your laptop can't reproduce sound nearly as well as a professional-quality microphone can, and because it's physically located on the computer, the built-in microphone will pick up the noise from the computer's fan. Similarly, the low-cost sound cards built into many computers can add a significant amount of noise to your signal.[34]

If you require higher production quality or greater flexibility, you'll need additional pieces of hardware and software, such as an audio processor (to filter out extraneous noise and otherwise improve the audio signal), a mixer (to combine multiple audio or video signals), a better microphone, and more sophisticated recording and editing software (see Figure 7.5). You may also need to improve the acoustics of the room in which you are recording in order to minimize echoes, noise, and other problems. To learn more about the technical requirements of podcasting, pick up one of the many books on the subject. Some of them even come with free recording software.[35]

For a quick review of the key points of business podcasting, see "Checklist: Planning and Producing Business Podcasts." For news on the latest developments in podcasting, visit http://real-timeupdates.com/bct and click on Chapter 7.

For basic podcasts, your computer probably has most of the hardware you already need, and you can download recording software.

REAL-TIME UPDATES
Learn More
Step-by-step advice for recording your first podcast
You'll be podcasting in no time which includes step-by-step instructions for using the free Audacity audio recording software. Go to **http://real-timeupdates.com/bct** and click on "Learn More." If you are using mybcommlab, you can access Real-Time Updates within each chapter or under Student Study Tools.

With a few upgrades beyond a basic computer, you can assemble a studio capable of producing professional-quality podcasts.

For higher-quality podcasts, you'll probably need additional hardware and software.

FIGURE 7.5 The Podcasting Process
Creating a podcast requires just a few easy steps, and basic podcasts can be created using free or low-cost hardware and software.

1. Install recording software → 2. Connect and verify microphone → 3. Click the record button and start talking → 4. Review your file and edit if needed → 5. Convert file to MP3 format and save → 6. Create and validate your feed → 7. Upload your file and let RSS alert your subscribers

✓ CHECKLIST: **Planning and Producing Business Podcasts**

- Consider podcasting whenever you have the opportunity to replace existing audio or video messages.
- If you plan a podcast channel with a regular stream of new content, make sure you've identified a theme or purpose that is rich enough to sustain your effort.
- Pay close attention to previews, transitions, and reviews to help prevent your audience from getting lost.
- Decide whether you want to improvise your podcast or speak or film from a written script.

- If you improvise, do enough planning and organization to avoid floundering and rambling in search of a point.
- Remember that editing is much more difficult to do with audio or video than with textual media and plan your content and recording carefully.
- Consider linking your podcast to a blog in order to provide additional information and a forum for audience feedback.
- Syndicate your podcast, if appropriate, via RSS enclosures.

DISTRIBUTING BLOG AND PODCAST CONTENT

With today's blog and podcast technologies, you can easily reach a vast audience—an audience that can continue to grow as your readers or listeners help spread the word for you.

Syndicating Your Content

Syndication is the process of distributing blog and podcast content via feeds.

The distribution process for blogs and podcasts is called **syndication** (see Figure 7.6).[36] As a content creator, you initiate syndication by creating a **feed**, or *newsfeed*, a file that contains information about the items you have written or recorded. In the case of podcasts, the audio or video file is enclosed within the feed file as well. Several formats now exist for these feeds; the most common is known as **RSS**, which is short for *really simple syndication*. (Although this process sounds fairly technical, popular blogging and podcasting systems take care of most of the details for you.) The benefit of syndication via an RSS feed is that you have the potential to build up a vast audience over time, provided that you offer compelling content and make that content easy to find.

Aggregators automatically collect information about new blog posts and podcasts.

On the receiving end, audiences subscribe to your content either through their web browser or using a piece of software called an **aggregator** or a *newsreader*. (*Aggregating* is simply another word for *collecting*.) Basic aggregators can collect messages with both text and static images, and some aggregators specialize in certain types of media. Aggregators specifically for podcasts are usually called **podcatchers**. Whenever you create a feed for a new blog post or podcast, your subscribers are automatically alerted via the feed. In the case of blogs, aggregators usually display a headline and brief summary of your post. Anyone

FIGURE 7.6 The Syndication Process for Blogs

The publish/subscribe model lets bloggers reach a potentially vast audience and lets audiences automatically acquire fresh content from an unlimited number of sources.

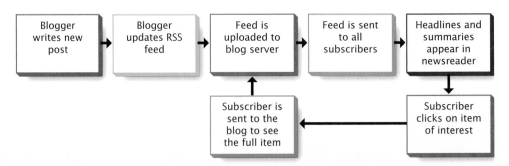

FIGURE 7.7 Viewing Blog Updates in Web Browsers

With newsfeed capability now built into web browsers, collecting updates from your favorite bloggers and news sources is effortless.

who wants to read the full item can click on the headline to be directed back to your blog to see the entire post (see Figure 7.7). In the case of podcasts, subscribers can choose to have new podcasts downloaded to their computer or other device automatically, or they can download them manually. For audiences, the key benefit of syndication is automatically collecting interesting content from many sources in a variety of formats. In a sense, it's like creating personal versions of the Internet.

Connecting with Audiences

Of course, content creators and audiences need ways to find each other for blogging and podcasting to have any value. This connection can happen in a variety of ways. The most fundamental step for bloggers is to add the feed capability to their blogs so that interested audiences can easily subscribe through their aggregators. Bloggers and podcasters can also take advantage of services such as Google's FeedBurner (www.feedburner.com), which make sure files are properly formatted and help publicize content.[37]

Adding feed capability is the most important step in staying connected with your blog or podcast audiences.

Beyond that, bloggers and podcasters can get themselves listed in a variety of directories, some of which specialize in blogs (such as Technorati, www.technorati.com), others in podcasts (such as Juice, http://juicereceiver.sourceforge.net), and others in two or more media types (such as Mefeedia, http://mefeedia.com, which covers podcasts and vodcasts).

Document Makeover

Improve This Blog

To practice correcting drafts of actual documents, visit the "Document Makeovers" section in either mybcommlab or the Companion Website for this text.

If mybcommlab is being used in your class, see your User Guide for specific instructions on how to access the content for this chapter. If you are accessing this feature through the Companion Website, click on "Document Makeovers" and then select Chapter 7. You will find a blog post that contains problems and errors related to what you've learned in this chapter about writing for electronic media. Use the Final Draft decision tool to create an improved version of this post.

Bloggers can help each other find audiences by listing favorite blogs in their blogrolls.

Content creators can also make their material easier to find through **tagging**, which involves assigning descriptive words to each post or podcast. For instance, for a blog post on clever techniques for attracting new employees, you might tag the post with the word *recruiting*. Visitors to your blog who want to read everything you've written about recruiting just click on that word to see all your posts on that subject. Tagging can also help audiences locate your posts on blog trackers such as Technorati or on *social bookmarking* or *social news* sites such as Delicious (http://delicious.com) and Digg (www.digg.com). You can read more about social bookmarking as a research tool in Chapter 11.

Bloggers can help each other by identifying blogs they themselves read. This list, called a *blogroll*, can be found on many blogs. In addition, when bloggers comment on individual posts on other blogs, they can use a feature called *trackback* to let readers of the original post know that other bloggers have commented on it. Both blogrolls and trackbacks help "spread the word" for bloggers by showing audiences other blogs they might like.

Communication Challenges at Southwest Airlines

You recently joined the corporate communications group at Southwest Airlines, and one of your responsibilities is overseeing the Nuts About Southwest blog. Study the scenarios that follow and apply what you learned about blogging in this chapter to choose the best course of action.

Individual Challenge: Pressure is building to stop the practice of moderating the blog by reviewing reader comments and selecting which ones will appear on the blog. You've received a number of adamant messages saying that Nuts About Southwest won't be a "real" blog until anyone is allowed to write any sort of comment without being "censored" by the company. However, you know that every blog is vulnerable to rude, inappropriate, and irrelevant comments, and you don't want Nuts About Southwest to turn into a free-for-all shouting match. You also want to avoid the all-too-common problem of a comment thread wandering way off topic and thereby aggravating everyone who is trying to follow the original discussion. Write a brief statement to be included in the blog's User's Guide, explaining the company's reasons for continuing to moderate comments.

Team Challenge: One member of the Emerging Media Team is about to retire, so you need to recruit another employee to take her place on the blog. You earlier sent out a companywide e-mail message asking interested candidates to submit a sample blog entry. Each entry should start with a brief paragraph introducing the writer. With a team of fellow students, discuss the style of these four entries. Which of the following seems like the most

compatible style for Nuts About Southwest? Summarize your recommendation in an e-mail message to your instructor.

From Candidate A: Hi everyone! I'm Janice McNathan, and I couldn't be more excited to be joining the Nuts About Southwest blog cuz—hey, I'm nuts! I've worked at some goofball companies before, but nobody has as much fun as the loonies here at Southwest, so I know I'm going to have a great time writing for this blog!

From Candidate B: Howdy folks, Charlie Parker here. No, not the famous jazz musician! I'm just a lowly fuel inventory auditor here in Dallas. Pretty much, I keep tabs on the fuel that goes into our planes and I make sure we get the best deals possible and all the paperwork stays in order. I can't promise any exciting stories of adventure like the pilots and other people write here, but I'll keep my eyes peeled around the airport here, and maybe something interesting will come up.

From Candidate C: I'm Rick Munoz, and I've always wanted to be a professional writer. My career sort of took a detour, though, and I wound up as a programmer who works behind the scenes at the Southwest website. I really appreciate this opportunity to hone my craft, and who knows—maybe this will be the break I need to make it as a "real" writer. You'll be able to say "I knew that guy before he became famous!"

From Candidate D: Excuse me while I wipe the grease off my hands; I don't want to mess up this shiny new keyboard! Hi, I'm Kristal Yan, an airframe and powerplant mechanic at Southwest's facility in Oakland, California. I've been an avid reader of Nuts About Southwest since it started, and I really look forward to participating in this wonderful worldwide conversation. I hope to provide some interesting observations from a mechanic's perspective, and I hope you'll feel free to ask any questions you may have about how we keep Southwest's planes running smoothly and safely.

SUMMARY OF LEARNING OBJECTIVES

1 Compare the strengths and weaknesses of the electronic media available for short messages. Web 2.0 technologies such as social networks and user-generated content sites provide commenting features, personal profiles, and other tools that facilitate short-message communication. E-mail offers high speed, low cost, and widespread availability, but it suffers from overuse and a variety of spam, security, and privacy problems. Instant messaging is even faster than e-mail, is simple to use, and hasn't yet accumulated problems with spam, security, and privacy to the same degree that e-mail has. Text messaging offers high speed as well, with the added benefit of portability. Its primary disadvantage relates to convenience and flexibility; it can't yet perform the wide array of functions now available in business-grade IM. Blogging offers a fast, simple way to publish information online and to reach wide audiences. Blogging's biggest downside is competition from the millions of other blogs on the Internet. Podcasts offer a simple way for anyone to broadcast audio or video messages. They do require more work to create than blogs, and high-quality podcasts require both a modest set of specialized equipment and plenty of network bandwidth. Finally, don't dismiss the value of printed memos and letters, even if most of your communication is electronic. Although they lack the speed, richness, and convenience of electronic media, they offer a degree of formality that is sometimes hard to achieve with electronic media. Printed letters also offer more stability and security than many electronic media.

2 Outline six guidelines for creating successful social media content. Because Web 2.0 technologies and expectations change the relationship between sender and receiver, the nature of the messages between them needs to change as well. Six guidelines for effective social media content are (1) remember that it's a conversation, not a lecture; (2) write informally but not carelessly; (3) create concise, specific, and informative headlines that aren't "cute" or clever; (4) get involved and stay involved with online conversation about your products and your company; (5) if you need to promote something, do so indirectly; and (6) be transparent and honest.

3 Explain the need to treat e-mail as a professional medium, and identify the qualities of an effective e-mail subject line. In the business use of e-mail, the expectations of writing quality are higher than for informal e-mail, and the consequences of bad writing or poor judgment can be serious. Users therefore need to treat it as a professional medium and a vital company resource. The wording of an e-mail message's subject line often determines whether and when recipients open and read the message. Effective subjects lines are both informative (concisely identifying what the message is about) and compelling (giving readers a reason to read the message).

4 Identify guidelines for successful instant messaging (IM) in the workplace. Use IM productively and effectively by making yourself unavailable when you need to focus on other work, refraining from sending confidential information if you're not on a secure system, refraining from sending personal messages at work, not using IM for impromptu meetings if you can't verify that everyone concerned will be available, not using IM for lengthy and complex messages, avoiding carrying on multiple IM conversations at once, avoiding IM slang with anyone other than close colleagues, and keeping spim filters and other security and privacy measures current.

5 Describe the role of blogging in business communication today, and explain how to adapt the three-step writing process to blogging. Blogs are used in numerous ways in business today, including for project management and team communication, company news, customer support, public relations and media relations, employee recruiting, policy and issue discussions, crisis communication, market research, brainstorming, viral marketing, e-mail replacement, news syndication, and community building. In adapting the three-step process to blogging, planning is particularly important when you start a blog because you're planning an entire communication channel, not just a single message. First, identifying your target audience is a vital step because you want an audience large enough to justify the time you'll be investing but narrow enough that you can provide an identifiable focus for the blog. Second, identifying your purpose is important because you want a purpose that will last beyond your initial posts. You don't want to start a blog and then run out of things to write about within a few weeks or months. Third, identifying your scope is important so that audiences can identify what your blog is about. A scope that is too narrow will limit both your available topic possibilities and your target audience. A scope that is too broad will make your blog seem vague and hard to pin down. When you begin writing, write in a comfortable, personal style while still taking care to write professionally and clearly.

6 Explain how to adapt the three-step writing process to podcasting. Although you'll be recording audio or video when creating podcasts, rather than writing messages, using the three-step process is an effective way to develop podcasts. Focus the planning step on analyzing the situation, gathering the information you'll need, and organizing your material. If you plan to create a series of podcasts on a given theme (the equivalent of starting a radio or TV show), make sure you've identified a range of topics extensive enough to keep your podcasts going over time. As you organize and begin to think about the words or images you'll use as content, pay close attention to previews, transitions, and reviews so that audiences don't get lost while listening or watching. Before you record, think through what you plan to say or shoot so that you don't ramble while trying to make your key points. Finally, consider the necessary level of production quality; good-quality podcasts usually require some specialized hardware and software.

PEARSON mybcommlab

Log on to www.mybcommlab.com to access the following study and assessment aids associated with this chapter:

- Video applications
- Real-Time Updates
- Peer review activity
- Quick learning guides
- Pre/post test
- Personalized study plan
- Model documents
- Sample presentations

If you are not using mybcommlab, you can access the Real-Time Updates and Quick Learning Guides through http://real-timeupdates.com/bct. The Quick Learning Guide (located under "Learn More" on the website) hits all the high points of this chapter in just two pages. This guide, especially prepared by the authors, will help you study for exams or review important concepts whenever you need a quick refresher.

Test Your Knowledge

1. How can websites such as Facebook and YouTube function as media for short messages?
2. Why are subject lines important in e-mail messages?
3. How does the overuse of e-mail (sending too many messages to too many people) lower productivity?
4. What are the benefits of using IM in business communication?
5. Should you use common IM abbreviations such as *IMHO* (in my humble opinion) or *TY* (thank you) in business IM? Why or why not?
6. Why does a personal style of writing help blogs build stronger relationships with audiences?
7. Why is it important to have a long-term, sustainable purpose in mind before you begin creating and syndicating a blog or podcasts?
8. How can blogs help with viral marketing efforts?
9. Could a podcast replace an employee newsletter that is currently printed and mailed to employees' homes? Why or why not?
10. How does syndication help blog and podcast creators reach a wider audience?

Apply Your Knowledge

1. Is instant messaging replacing many instances of e-mail for the same reasons that e-mail replaced many instances of printed memos and letters? Explain your answer.
2. If one of the benefits of blogging is the personal, intimate style of writing, is it a good idea to limit your creativity by adhering to conventional rules of grammar, spelling, and mechanics? Why or why not?
3. In your work as a video game designer, you know that eager players search the web for any scrap of information they can find about upcoming releases. In fact, to build interest, your company's public relations department carefully doles out small bits of information in the months before a new title hits the market. However, you and others in the company are also concerned about competitors getting their hands on all this "prerelease" information. If they learn too much too soon, they can use the information to improve their own products more quickly. You and several other designers and programmers maintain blogs that give players insights into game design techniques and that occasionally share tips and tricks. You have thousands of readers, and you know your blog helps build customer loyalty. The company president wants to

ban blogging entirely so that bloggers don't accidentally share too much prerelease information about upcoming games. Would this be a wise move? Why or why not?

4. In what ways does carefully planning a podcast reflect the "you" attitude?

5. **Ethical Choices** You work for a midsize freight delivery company that has been using text messaging as the primary communication channel between drivers and the central dispatch office. Drivers send a text message to confirm the time and location whenever they've made a delivery or a pickup, and whenever dispatchers get an urgent request from a customer, they send messages to the trucks to find out who is nearby and available. This manual system is clumsy and prone to errors, and the company's owners want to replace it with a fully computerized mapping system that uses the global positioning system (GPS) to automatically monitor the location of every truck in the fleet. Some drivers are in an uproar over the plan, saying it invades their privacy by tracking their every move all day long. Should the company proceed with the plan even though some drivers object? Summarize your opinion in a brief e-mail message to your instructor (or blog post, if your course uses a blog).

Practice Your Knowledge

Messages for Analysis

Message 7.A: Improving IM Skills

Review this IM exchange and explain how the salesperson could have responded more effectively to the customer.

Customer: My name is Sara and I bought a vacuum cleaner from you after you did a demonstration at my house last week.

Salesperson: Yes—how can I help you?

Customer: The machine keeps shutting off after I have used it for just a few minutes.

Salesperson: Oh that's normal.

Customer: Really? But what do I do about that?

Salesperson: Nothing—that's the way the machine is built to prevent the motor from heating up.

Customer: You mean I have to live with this problem?

Salesperson: Yes.

Customer: But I have a big house and very little time to do my cleaning. I can't be waiting for the machine to cool down every few minutes before I start vacuuming again.

Salesperson: Sorry, I can't so anything about it.

Customer: But why didn't you tell me about this during the demonstration?

Salesperson: It's in the manual.

Message 7.B: Drafting Effective Blog Posts

Revise this blog post based on what you've learned in this chapter.

[headline]

Exasperated

[post]

Yesterday was a bad day, indeed, for our institution. One of our potential students had written to the national newspaper complaining that our staff at the Student Admissions desk had been totally inefficient and unhelpful to her when she called to make some enquiries. You would all agree with me that such bad publicity in a national daily can seriously affect our image. We are after all a private educational organization and we need all the student enrollment we can muster to keep afloat! And such service or, pardon me, the lack of it, is unforgivable! If our Student Admission staff don't buck up and do something about the quality of their service, we're totally sunk baby! So whoever you are that attended to that call, buck up will you or we'll all be paying for your sins. Get what I mean??

As for all of you others in this institution who speak to the public in one way or another, it's time you took some classes too. Hey there's nothing wrong with brushing up every now and then on our service skills. And for those of you who have no clue about what I'm saying, there's a "Brush up your service!" course offered right here in our own institution—maybe you should check it out. You may learn something, you know.

Message 7.C: Plan a Better Podcast

To access this message, visit http://real-timeupdates.com/bct, click on "Student Assignments," select Chapter 7, and then select page 233, Message 7.C. Download and listen to this podcast. Identify at least three ways in which the podcast could be improved and draft a brief e-mail message that you could send to the podcaster, giving your suggestions for improvement.

Exercises

Active links for all websites in this chapter can be found online. If mybcommlab is being used in your class, see your User Guide for instructions on accessing the content for this chapter. Otherwise, visit www.pearsonglobaleditions.com/bovee, locate *Business Communication Today*, Tenth Edition, click the Companion Website link, select Chapter 7, and then click on "Featured Websites." Please note that links to sites that become inactive after publication of the book will be removed from the Featured Websites section.

7.1 **Choose Your Medium: Selecting the Best Technology for a Message** For each of these message needs, choose a medium that you think would work effectively and explain your choice. (More than one medium could work in some cases; just be able to support your particular choice.)

a. A technical support service for people trying to use their digital music players

b. A message of condolence to the family of an employee who passed away recently

c. A message from the CEO of a small company, explaining that she is leaving the company to join a competitor

d. A series of observations on the state of the industry

e. A series of messages, questions, and answers surrounding the work of a project team

7.2 **E-Mail: Making Subject Lines Informative** Using your imagination to make up whatever details you need, revise the following e-mail subject lines to make them more informative:

a. New budget figures

b. Marketing brochure—your opinion

c. Production schedule

7.3   E-Mail: Message Outlining a New Employee Procedure
The following e-mail message contains numerous information errors related to what you've learned about planning and writing business messages. Using the information it contains, write a more effective version.

To: Wilson Wu <wwu@gmail.com>

Subject: The new rule is for all of you to obey

I know that some of you may not like the new rule about fixed lunch time arrangement. However, we management have been displeased with seeing clerical staff eating your lunch or heating your lunch boxes when you are supposed to be working at your desk. We can't afford being embarrassed in front of visitors by your behavior. You make us look bad to our visitors. We therefore have decided that all of you MUST follow fixed lunch time from 1 to 2 pm. from Monday to Friday. This is a mandatory rule for all clerical staff. Let me remind you that those who do not obey the rule will be penalized at the regular monthly staff meetings.

Starting from Monday, February 23, you can start to eat, heat your lunch box, or leave for lunch ONLY when the clock strikes 1pm and you should be back at your desk at 2pm. Do not try to leave for lunch earlier than 1pm or come back later than 2pm. There will be no exceptions to this new rule! Everybody needs to obey it!

I am not asking for your opinion about the new rule. I know that there are already complaints over the grapevine and I hope this e-mail will clarify all misunderstandings and end all rumors.

Wilson Wu

Manager

Personnel department

7.4   Instant Messaging: Let's Get Professional   Your firm, which makes professional paint sprayers, uses IM extensively for internal communication and frequently for external communication with customers and suppliers. Several customers have recently forwarded copies of messages they've received from your staff, asking if you know how casually some employees are treating this important medium. You decide to revise parts of several messages to show your staff a more appropriate writing style. Rewrite these sentences, making up any information you need, to convey a more businesslike style and tone. (Look up the acronyms online if you need to.)

a. IMHO, our quad turbo sprayer is best model 4U.

b. No prob; happy2help!

c. FWIW, I use the L400 myself & it rocks

d. Most cust see 20–30% reduct in fumes w/this sprayer—of course, YMMV.

7.5   Blogging: Keeping Emotions Under Control   The members of the project team, of which you are the leader, have enthusiastically embraced blogging as a communication medium. Unfortunately, as emotions heat up during the project, some of the blog postings are getting too casual, too personal, and even sloppy. Because your boss and other managers around the company also read this project blog, you don't want the team to look unprofessional in anyone's eyes. Revise the following blog posting so that it communicates in a more businesslike manner while retaining the informal, conversational tone of a blog. (Be sure to correct any spelling and punctuation mistakes you find as well.)

Well, folks, as you're all aware, we lost the bid of revamping the Bank of Commerce's official website to Techmen Networking last week. Yesterday I got wind of the winning bid from my buddy in Techmen that we lost by only 5,000!! We lost by only 5,000! How shameful! We look like fools for not getting the project even though we sent our best men to do the presentation. And the time that we spent in preparing the 3 different groovy templates! We worked so hard as we all wanted the project so bad. Certainly, we all thought it was sure win. By only 5,000, all our efforts went straight down into the ditch. I've been saying to the accounting guys all the time in the last 2 months that we gotta cut our bid quick to gain the upper hand in this project. Those guys would only jeer at my idea and insisted on a fixed 20% markup. If only they had listened to me before finalizing the bid! Yes, of course we can't bend backwards by more lowering of our company's profit margins but now see the results. After losing this project, we won't even have enough tasks to keep everyone in our department busy in this quarter. Let's pray that no one of us will get axed because of this.

7.6   Blogging: Blog Post Informing Employees About an Office Relocation   From what you've learned about effective blogging as well as planning and writing business messages in general, you should be able to identify numerous errors made by the writer of the following blog post. After identifying the flaws, draft a version that fixes them.

Get Ready!

We are hoping to be back at work soon, with everything running smoothly, same production schedule and no late projects or missed deadlines. So you need to clean out your desk, put your stuff in boxes, and clean off the walls. You can put the items you had up on your walls in boxes, also.

We have provided boxes. The move will happen this weekend. We'll be in our new offices when you arrive on Monday.

We will not be responsible for personal belongings during the move.

Posted by David Burke at 10:42 AM 09-27-09

7.7   Podcasting: Where Are We Going with This, Boss?   You begin recording a weekly podcast to share information with your large and far-flung staff. After a month, you ask for feedback from several of your subordinates, and you're disappointed to learn that some people stopped listening to the podcast after the first couple weeks. Someone eventually admits that many staffers feel the recordings are too long and rambling, and the information they contain isn't valuable enough to justify the time it takes to listen. You aren't pleased, but you want to improve. An assistant transcribes the introduction to last week's podcast so you can review it. You immediately see two problems. Revise the introduction based on what you've learned in this chapter.

So there I am, having lunch with Selma Gill, who just joined and took over the Northeast sales region from Jackson Stroud. In walks our beloved CEO with Selma's old boss at Uni-Plex; turns out they were finalizing a deal to co-brand our products and theirs and to set up a joint distribution program in all four domestic regions. Pretty funny, huh? Selma left Uni-Plex because she wanted to sell our products instead, and now she's back selling her old stuff, too. Anyway, try to chat with her when you can; she knows the biz inside and out and probably can offer insight into just about any sales challenge you might be running up against. We'll post more info on the co-brand deal next week; should be a boost for all of us. Other than those two news items, the other big news this week is the change in commission reporting. I'll go into the details in minute, but when you log onto the intranet, you'll now see your sales results split out by product line and industry sector. Hope this helps you see where you're doing well and where you might beef things up a bit. Oh yeah, I almost forgot the most important bit. Speaking of our beloved CEO, Thomas is going to be our guest of honor, so to speak, at quarterly sales meeting next week and wants an update on how petroleum prices are affecting customer behavior. Each district manager should be ready with a brief reports. After I go through the commission reporting scheme, I'll outline what you need to prepare.

Expand Your Knowledge

Exploring the Best of the Web

Ready to Start Blogging?

www.website101.com/RSS-Blogs-Blogging

Blogging is easy to do if you have the right information. Start with these helpful tutorials. More than 30 brief articles cover everything from creating a blog to attracting more readers to setting up RSS newsfeeds. Learn techniques for adding audio and photo files to your blog. Review how search engines treat blogs and how you can use search engines to help more people find your blog. Then answer the following questions:

1. What are five ways to attract more readers to your blog?
2. Why are blogs good for marketing?
3. What is a newsfeed, and why is it a vital part of blogging?

Sharpening Your Career Skills Online

Bovée and Thill's Business Communication Web Search, at http://businesscommunicationblog.com/websearch, is a unique research tool designed specifically for business communication research. Use the Web Search function to find a website, video, PDF document, podcast, or PowerPoint presentation that offers advice on using social media in business. Write a brief e-mail message to your instructor, describing the item that you found and summarizing the career skills information you learned from it.

CASES
Applying the Three-Step Writing Process to Cases
Apply each step to the following cases, as assigned by your instructor.

1 Plan → 2 Write → 3 Complete

Analyze the Situation
Identify both your general purpose and your specific purpose. Clarify exactly what you want your audience to think, feel, or believe after receiving your message. Profile your primary audience, including their backgrounds, differences, similarities, and likely reactions to your message.

Gather Information
Identify the information your audience will need to receive, as well as other information you may need in order to craft an effective message. Select the right medium. The medium is identified for each case here, but when on the job, make sure your medium is both acceptable to the audience and appropriate for the message.

Organize the Information
Define your main idea, limit your scope, choose a direct or indirect approach, and outline necessary support points and other evidence.

Adapt to Your Audience
Show sensitivity to audience needs with a "you"attitude, politeness, positive emphasis, and bias-free language. Understand how much credibility you already have— and how much you may need to establish. Project your company's image by maintaining an appropriate style and tone. Consider cultural variations and the differing needs of internal and external audiences.

Compose the Message
For written messages, draft your message using clear but sensitive words, effective sentences, and coherent paragraphs. For podcasts, outline your message and draft speaking notes to ensure smooth recording; use plenty of previews, transitions, and review to help audiences follow along.

Revise the Message
Evaluate content and review readability, then edit and rewrite for conciseness and clarity.

Produce the Message
For written messages, use effective design elements and suitable layout for a clean, professional appearance. For podcasts, record your messages using whatever equipment you have available (professional podcasts may require upgraded equipment).

Proofread the Message
Review for errors in layout, spelling, and mechanics. Listen to podcasts to check for recording problems.

Distribute the Message
Deliver your message using the chosen medium; make sure all documents and all relevant files are distributed successfully.

BLOGGING SKILLS

1. Selling without selling: Blog posting about a GPS rescue. Promoting products through customer success stories can be a great marketing tactic, as long as you keep the customer as the "star" of the story and don't promote the product too blatantly. You've recently joined Garmin, a leading manufacturer of electronic navigation equipment, including a popular line of handheld global positioning system (GPS) devices used by hikers, kayakers, and others who venture off the beaten path.

Your task: As a communication specialist, your responsibilities include writing blog posts that highlight dramatic stories in which people used Garmin GPS units to rescue themselves or others from potentially dangerous situations. Visit Garmin's website, at www.garmin.com/whatsNew/adventures.html. Select a customer story that involves a wilderness rescue in which a Garmin product played an important role. Using the information provided by the customer, rewrite the story in the third person (changing "I" or "we" references to "he," "she," or "they") for an audience that isn't familiar with the product in question. Subtly work in references to the product and the benefits it provided in this scenario but keep the focus on the customer. Limit yourself to 400 words.

BLOGGING SKILLS

2. Come on to Comic-Con: Explaining the benefits of attending. Comic-Con International is an annual convention that highlights a wide variety of pop culture and entertainment media, from comic books and collectibles to video games and movies. From its early start as a comic book convention that attracted several hundred fans and publishing industry insiders, Comic-Con has become a major international event with more than 100,000 attendees.

Your task: Several readers of your pop culture blog have been asking for your recommendation about visiting Comic-Con in

San Diego next summer. Write a two- or three-paragraph post for your blog that explains what Comic-Con is and what visitors can expect to experience at the convention. Be sure to address your post to fans, not industry insiders. You can learn more at www .comic-con.org.[38]

E-MAIL SKILLS

3. Keeping the fans happy: Analyzing advertising on ESPN.com. ESPN leads the pack both online and off. Its well-known cable television sports channels are staple fare for sports enthusiasts, and ESPN.com (http://espn.go.com) is the leader in sports websites, too. Advertisers flock to ESPN.com because it delivers millions of visitors in the prime 18- to 34-year-old demographic group. With a continually refreshed offering of sporting news, columnists, video replays, and fantasy leagues (online competitions in which participants choose players for their teams, and the outcome is based on how well the real players do in actual live competition), ESPN.com has become one of the major advertising venues on the web.

As an up-and-coming web producer for ESPN.com, you're concerned about the rumblings of discontent you've heard from friends and read in various blogs and other sources. ESPN.com remains popular with millions of sports fans, but some say they are getting tired of all the ads—both ads on the site itself and pop-up ads. A few say they are switching to other websites that have fewer advertising intrusions. Your site traffic numbers are holding fairly steady for now, but you're worried that the few visitors leaving ESPN.com might be the start of a significant exodus in the future.

Your task: Write an e-mail message to your manager, expressing your concern about the amount of advertising content on ESPN.com. Acknowledge that advertising is a vital source of revenue, but share what you've learned about site visitors who claim to be migrating to other sites. Offer to lead a comprehensive review effort to compare the advertising presence on ESPN.com with that of other sports websites and explore ways to maintain strong advertising sales without alienating readers.[39]

E-MAIL SKILLS

4. Clothes for real women: Changing the look at La Maison Simons. The physical difference between the women who model clothes and women who buy them has long been a point of contention for shoppers—and a point of concern for health advocates who say that top fashion models have become too thin in recent years. Not only is the super-thin look unhealthy for the models, but critics says it encourages eating disorders among girls and women who aspire to look like them.

Some industry insiders admit that the images portrayed in fashion advertising are often unrealistic. Designer and television host Tim Gunn says the problem starts with an unrealistic assumption in the illustration stage, when designers are sketching new clothes. "The way in which we illustrate [a model's body] is seven heads high, which isn't normal. We're always striving to have the same look of the illustration on the runway, and it's impossible. You have a few—forgive me—freaky people who can approximate that size and shape, but this look is not part of the real world."

Models weren't always much thinner than the general population, and the pendulum seems to be swinging back toward more normal body types—at least slightly. In the summer of 2008, La Maison Simons, a Canadian retailer, pulled its back-to-school catalog following complaints that its models were too thin; the company replaced the catalog and issued an apology. Ken Downing, fashion director at the upscale American retailer Neiman-Marcus, explains, "Any retailer has to consider [its] customer and who [it's] trying to appeal to. There are models of all shapes and sizes, and the people who do the advertising and marketing really have to be conscious that they're portraying healthy, beautiful women of many ages and many colors from many backgrounds."[40]

Your task: Imagine that you're the director of catalog operations at La Maison Simons, and you want to make sure that the embarrassing episode with the summer 2008 catalog isn't repeated. Write a brief e-mail to the catalog staff, outlining the company's new policy of using only models with healthy body mass indexes. (Make up any information you need to draft the message.) You can visit the company's website, at www.simons.ca, to learn more about its products, and you can research body mass index at a variety of health-related websites.

E-MAIL SKILLS

5. There must be an opportunity in here somewhere: The Number of Visitors to Singapore Has Declined This Year Compared to Last Year. In February 2009, the number of visitor arrivals dipped by 15.2% compared to February 2008, (http://www.singstat.gov.sg). A number of factors have contributed to this problem, the main one being the global recession that has made potential tourists more cautious about spending on vacations abroad. The Singapore Tourism Board (STB) is concerned about this declining trend and would like to organize a series of cultural programs to ameliorate if not reverse this downward trend. In your job as head researcher for the STB, you have to suggest activities that the board could plan and organize to attract tourists for the rest of the year. You will then propose these to the board for consideration so that a decision can be made and the promotional material can be designed for the STB website as well as for distribution to travel agencies, embassies, hotels, and other places of interest in Singapore.

Your task: With your team of researchers at STB, brainstorm possible cultural events that showcase the various ethnic groups in Singapore, their customs, traditions, food, traditional attire, language, music, dance, festivals, and so forth. In an e-mail to all the cultural societies in Singapore, suggest the events you have in mind and the possible dates for these events. Seek their feedback on your suggestions and invite alternative suggestions on the events as well as the dates. Further, request their assistance and the involvement of their members in these events. Finally, state clearly that you will be proposing these ideas to the management and a decision will be made, which you will communicate to them by a specific date in the future.

E-MAIL SKILLS   PORTFOLIO BUILDER

6. A Bright Future Is Near: Lately, the petrochemical manufacturing companies in the Middle East region, especially in the Gulf Cooperation Council (GCC) countries, have been bearing the brunt of the global financial downturn. International prices of commodity chemicals have been decreasing and export volumes have dwindled substantially.

Your task: Write an e-mail to be addressed to major stockholders of petrochemical businesses in the GCC countries extolling the prospects for a bright future. You can use the argument that petrochemical-based commodity chemicals are used by people everywhere and that demand is bound to increase with time. The petrochemical manufacturing business in the GCC countries enjoys clear advantages over that of other developed countries due to low cost, proximity, and abundance of raw material sources of hydrocarbons.

BLOGGING SKILLS

7. Blog Posting Seeking Views of Employees on Developments in the New Age Paper. Currently, the *New Age Paper*, a tabloid-size newspaper in Singapore, comes out only on weekdays and targets young readers between the ages of 13 and 25. Its most popular sections are the sports, fashion, and movie sections. The paper also carries a weekly column called "Heart-to-Heart" to which young readers contribute their views on a range of local and international current issues. Since the introduction of this column, the circulation has increased. While the daily circulation is about 100,000, on Wednesdays when "Heart-to-Heart" appears, the readership increases by 2,000 during the school term and 5,000 during school vacations.

As the director of personnel for this paper, you want to get your employees' views on the launch of a weekend edition of the *New Age Paper*, with special features that cater to the slightly older, working reader. Along with these new sections the management would like to introduce a special readers' section similar to "Heart-to-Heart" but targeted at the adult working reader. This section, "Your Turn," will provide adult working readers with a platform for airing their views on issues that specifically concern them.

Currently, you manage an internal blog to encourage active participation from your employees and to strengthen the organizational culture of consensus and cooperation.

Your task: Write a short posting about the weekend edition and the new readers' section. Include the following in your posting:

   Information to your employees about the weekend edition that management would like to launch

   That the weekend edition will cater to the interests of the working adult segment of the population between the ages of 26 and 35

   That you would like to invite employees' comments and suggestions in connection with this idea

IM SKILLS

8. The very definition of confusion: Helping consumers sort out high-definition television. High-definition television can be a joy to watch—but, oh, what a pain to buy. The field is littered with competing technologies and arcane terminology that is meaningless to most consumers. Moreover, it's nearly impossible to define one technical term without invoking two or three others, leaving consumers swimming in an alphanumeric soup of confusion. The manufacturers themselves can't even agree on which of the *18* different digital TV formats truly qualify as "high definition." As a sales support manager for Crutchfield www.crutchfield.com, a leading online retailer of audio and video systems, you understand the frustration buyers feel; your staff is deluged daily by their questions.

Your task: To help your staff respond quickly to consumers who ask questions via Crutchfield's online IM chat service, you are developing a set of "canned" responses to common questions. When a consumer asks one of these questions, a sales advisor can simply click on the ready-made answer. Start by writing concise, consumer-friendly definitions of the following terms: resolution, HDTV, 1080p, and HDMI. Explore the Crutchfield Learning Center (visit www.crutchfield.com, click on "Learn" and then "Home Theater & Audio") to learn more about these terms. Answers.com and CNET.com are two other handy sources.[41]

PODCASTING SKILLS   PORTFOLIO BUILDER

9. Based on my experience: Recommending your college or university. With any purchase decision, from a restaurant meal to a college education, recommendations from satisfied customers are often the strongest promotional messages.

Your task: Write a script for a one- to two-minute podcast (roughly 150 to 250 words), explaining why your college or university is a good place to get an education. Your audience is high school juniors and seniors. You can choose to craft a general message, something that would be useful to all prospective students, or you can focus on a specific academic discipline, the athletic program, or some other important aspect of your college experience. Either way, make sure your introductory comments make it clear whether you are offering a general recommendation or a specific recommendation. If your instructor asks you to do so, record the podcast and submit the file electronically.

PODCASTING SKILLS

10. Based on my experience: Suggestions for improving your college or university. Every organization, no matter how successfully it operates, can find ways to improve its customer service.

Your task: Write a script for a one- to two-minute podcast (roughly 150 to 250 words), identifying at least one way in which your college experience could have been or still could be improved through specific changes in policies, programs, facilities, or other elements. Your audience is the school's administration. Offer constructive criticism and specific arguments about why your suggestions would help you—and possibly other students as well. Be sure to focus on meaningful and practical opportunities for improvement. If your instructor asks you to do so, record the podcast and submit the file electronically.

BLOGGING SKILLS

11. Look sharp: Travel safety tips for new employees. As the travel director for a global management consulting firm, your responsibilities range from finding the best travel deals to helping new employees learn the ins and outs of low-risk, low-stress travels. One of the ways in which you dispense helpful advice is through an internal blog.

Your task: Research advice for safe travel and identify at least six tips that every employee in your company should know. Write a brief blog post that introduces and identifies the six tips.

E-MAIL SKILLS

12. Your work does matter: Encouraging an unhappy colleague. You certainly appreciate your company's "virtual team" policy of letting employees live wherever they want and using technology to communicate and collaborate. The company is headquartered in a large urban area, but you get to live in the mountains, only a step or two away from some of the best fly fishing in the world. Most of the time, this approach to work couldn't get any better.

However, the lack of face-to-face contact with your colleagues definitely has disadvantages. For example, when a teammate seems to be upset about something, you wish you could go for a walk with the person and talk it out rather than rely on phone calls, e-mail, or IM. In the past couple weeks, Chris Grogan, the graphic designer working with you on a new e-commerce website project, seems to be complaining about everything. His negative attitude is starting to wear down the team's enthusiasm at a critical point in the project. In particular, he has complained several times that no one on the team seems to care about his design work. It is rarely mentioned in team teleconferences, and no one asks him about it. That part is true, actually, but the reason is that there is nothing wrong with his work—some critical technical issues unrelated to the graphic design are consuming everyone's attention.

Your task: After a couple unsuccessful attempts at encouraging Grogan over the phone, you decide to write a brief e-mail message to assure him of the importance of his work on this project and the quality of his efforts. Let him know that graphic design is a critical part of the project's success and that as soon as those technical issues are resolved and the project is completed, everyone will have a chance to appreciate his contribution to the project. Make up whatever details you need to craft your message.

E-MAIL SKILLS

13. She's one of us: Promoting a new lifestyle magazine. Consumers looking for beauty, health, and lifestyle magazines have an almost endless array of choices, but even in this crowded field, Logan Olson found her own niche. Olson, who was born with congenital heart disease, suffered a heart attack at age 16 that left her in a coma and caused serious brain damage. The active and outgoing teen had to relearn everything from sitting up to feeding herself. As she recovered, she looked for help and advice in conquering such daily challenges as finding fashionable clothes that were easier to put on and makeup that was easier to apply. Mainstream beauty magazines didn't seem to offer any information for young women with disabilities, so she started her own magazine. Oprah Winfrey has *Oprah*, and now Logan Olson has *Logan*. The magazine not only gives young women tips on buying and using a variety of products but lets women with disabilities know there are others like them, facing and meeting the same challenges.

Your task: Write a promotional e-mail message to be sent to young women with disabilities as well as families and friends who might like to give gift subscriptions, promoting the benefits of subscribing to *Logan*. You can learn more about *Logan* at www.loganmagazine.com.[42]

E-MAIL SKILLS   PORTFOLIO BUILDER

14. We're the one: Explaining why a company should hire your firm. You work for Brainbench (www.brainbench.com), one of many companies that offer employee screening services. Brainbench's offerings include a variety of online products and consulting services, all designed to help employers find and develop the best possible employees. For example, Brainbench's Pre-Hire Testing products help employers test for job skills, communication skills, personality, and employment history red flags (such as chronic absenteeism or performance problems). Employers use these test results to either screen out candidates entirely or ask focused interview questions about areas of concern.

Sonja Williamson, the human resources director of a large retail company, has just e-mailed your sales team. She would like an overview of the Pre-Hire Testing products and some background on your company.

Your task: Write an e-mail response to Williamson's query. Be sure to thank her for her interest, briefly describe the Pre-Hire Testing products, and summarize Brainbench's qualifications. Include at least one hyperlink to the Brainbench website and consider attaching one or more PDF files from the website as well.

E-MAIL SKILLS

15. Firing the customer: When a particular customer is always wrong. Many companies operate on the principle that the customer is always right, even when the customer *isn't* right. They take any steps necessary to ensure happy customers, lots of repeat sales, and a positive reputation among potential buyers. Overall, this is a smart and successful approach to business. However, most companies eventually encounter a nightmare customer who drains so much time, energy, and profits that the only sensible option is to refuse the customer's business. For example, the nightmare customer might be someone who constantly berates you and your employees, repeatedly makes outlandish demands for refunds and discounts, or simply requires so much help that you not only lose money on this person but also no longer have enough time to help your other customers. "Firing" a customer is an unpleasant step that should be taken only in the most extreme cases and only after other remedies have been attempted (such as talking with the customer about the problem), but it is sometimes necessary for the well-being of your employees and your company.

Your task: If you are currently working or have held a job in the recent past, imagine that you've encountered just such a customer. If you don't have job experience to call on, imagine that you work in a retail location somewhere around campus or in your neighborhood. Identify the type of behavior this imaginary customer exhibits and the reasons the behavior can no longer be accepted. Write a brief e-mail message to the customer to explain that you will no longer be able to accommodate him or her as a customer. Calmly explain why you have had to reach this difficult decision. Maintain a professional tone and keep your emotions in check.

PODCASTING SKILLS

16. Podcasting pitch: Training people to sell your favorite product. What product do you own (or use regularly) that you can't live without? It could be something as seemingly minor as a favorite pen or something as significant as a medical device that you literally can't live without. Now imagine you're a salesperson for this product; think about how you would sell it to potential buyers. How would you describe it and how would you explain the benefits of owning it? After you've thought about how you would present the product to others, imagine that you've been promoted to sales manager, and it is your job to train other people to sell the product.

Your task: Write the script for a brief podcast (200 to 300 words) that summarizes for your sales staff the most important points to convey about the product. Imagine that they'll listen to your podcast while driving to a customer's location or preparing for the day's activity in a retail store (depending on the nature of the product). Be sure to give your staffers a concise overview message about the product and several key support points.

E-MAIL SKILLS

17. Time to think: E-mail message requesting a change in your workload. The description of your job as a global marketing manager for New Balance is full of responsibilities that require creative thinking, from predicting consumer and retailing trends to establishing seasonal priorities for the global merchandising effort. You love these challenges—in fact, they're the main reason you took the job with this respected maker of athletic shoes and apparel. Unfortunately, between department meetings, status reports, budgets, and an endless array of other required chores, you hardly have time to think at all, much less engage in the sort of unstructured, "blue sky" thinking that is crucial to creative strategizing. You have virtually no time at work for such thinking, and after 50 or 60 hours a week at the office or on the road, you're too exhausted to brainstorm on your own time.

Your task: Write an e-mail to your boss, Paul Heffernan, the executive vice president of global marketing, persuading him that you need to reshuffle your assignments to free up more time to think. This is a tricky request because you know that Heffernan faces the same challenge. However, you're convinced that by spending less time on tasks that could be done by someone else (or perhaps shouldn't be done at all), you'll be able to do a better job of creating marketing strategies—and maybe even set a good example for other New Balance executives. You have a preliminary list of changes you'd like to make, but you know you need to discuss the entire scope of your job with Heffernan before finalizing the list. Your purpose: Invite him to lunch to begin a discussion of reshaping your responsibilities.[43]

BLOGGING SKILLS

18. Everybody's doing it, and maybe it's not so bad: Dispelling some misconceptions about teenagers and video games. The fact that 97 percent of American youth ages 12 to 17 play video games is not much of a surprise, but more than a few nongaming adults might be surprised to learn that game playing might not be quite the social and civic catastrophe it is sometimes made out to be. A recent study by the Pew Internet & American Life Project puts a least a few cracks in the stereotyped image of gamers being loners who live out violent fantasies while learning few if any skills that could make them positive members of society.[44]

Your task: Imagine that you're on the public relations staff at the Entertainment Software Association (ESA), an industry group that represents the interests of video game companies. You'd like to share the results of the Pew survey with parents to help ease their concerns. Visit http://real-timeupdates.com/bct, click on "Student Assignments," Chapter 7, and then Case 18. Download this PDF file, which is a summary of the Pew results. Find at least three positive aspects of video game playing and write a brief message that could be posted on an ESA public affairs blog.

E-MAIL SKILLS   PORTFOLIO BUILDER

19. Safe at any angle: Explaining the benefits of side-impact safety features. One-quarter of all motor vehicle accidents that involve children under age 12 are side-impact crashes—and these crashes result in higher rates of injuries and fatalities than those with front or rear impacts.[45]

Your task: You work in the consumer information department at Britax, a leading manufacturer of car seats. Your manager has asked you to prepare an e-mail message that can be sent out whenever parents request information about side-impact crashes and the safety features of Britax seats. Start by researching side-impact crashes at www.britaxusa.com (click on "Safety Center" and then "Side Impact Protection Revealed"). Write a three-paragraph message that explains the seriousness of side-impact crashes, describes how injuries and fatalities can be minimized in these crashes, and describes how Britax's car seats are designed to help protect children in side-impact crashes.

BLOGGING SKILLS

20. Airfare auction: Alerting JetBlue's Twitter fans about fare auctions on eBay. JetBlue is known for its innovations in customer service and customer communication, including its pioneering use of the Twitter microblogging system. Thousands of JetBlue fans and customers follow the company on Twitter to get updates on flight status during weather disruptions, facility upgrades, and other news.[46]

Your task: Write a Twitter update that announces the limited-time availability of flights and travel packages (flights plus hotel rooms, for example) at JetBlue's store on eBay. The key selling point is that travelers may be able to purchase flights they want at steep discounts. Include the URL http://jetblue.com/ebay/. The URL takes up 24 characters, so you have a maximum of 116 characters for the rest of your message, including spaces. (The limit for Twitter updates is 140 characters.)

E-MAIL SKILLS

21. No exaggeration: Short e-mail describing internship duties. You've been laboring all summer at an internship, learning how business is conducted. You've done work nobody else wanted to do, but that's okay. Even the smallest tasks can make a good impression on your future résumé.

This morning, your supervisor asks you to write a description of the job you've been doing. "Include everything, even the filing," she suggests, "and address it to me in an e-mail message." She says a future boss might assign such a task prior to a performance review. "You can practice describing your work without exaggeration—or too much modesty," she says, smiling.

Your task: Using good techniques for short messages and relying on your real-life work experience, write an e-mail that will impress your supervisor. Make up any details you need.

BLOGGING SKILLS

22. Meet the parents: Blog post announcing the acquisition of Golden West. As the human resources director for Golden West Financial, you know how proud your fellow employees are to work for one of the most admired banking companies in the United States. Golden West, which serves retail customers through its World Savings Bank branches across the West, was founded in Oakland, California, in the 1960s by the husband-and-wife team Herbert and Marion Sandler. For decades, Golden West flourished as an independent company, but in 2006, the Sandlers decided to sell Golden West to Wachovia, a financial giant based in Charlotte, North Carolina.

Over the coming weeks, you'll provide Golden West employees with more information about the impact of the huge deal, but for now, you want them to be aware of four key points:

- The deal allows Golden West to expand beyond its core offering of home mortgages to provide other financial services that its customers have requested for some time.
- The Sandlers carefully selected Wachovia because of its compatible values of integrity, customer-first business practices, and teamwork.
- World Savings Bank operations will continue from existing locations under the existing World Savings Bank brand name. New financial services from Wachovia will be added over time.
- The company's commitment to providing excellent career opportunities for women and minorities will not change.[47]

Your task: Write a short post for Golden West's internal blog, announcing the deal and communicating the four aforementioned key points listed (in your own words). Close by telling your colleagues how excited you are about the deal and that you'll be providing more information in the days and weeks ahead.

E-MAIL SKILLS

23. Environmental planning: E-mail announcing a committee meeting. You've probably worked as a volunteer on a committee or with team members for class assignments. You know how hard it is to get a diverse group of individuals together for a productive meeting. Maybe you've tried different locations—one member's home or a table at the library. This time you're going to suggest a local restaurant.

The committee you're leading is a volunteer group planning a trash-clearing project at an area park. Your meeting goal is to brainstorm ways to encourage public participation in this environmental event, to be held next Earth Day.

Your task: Develop a short e-mail message, telling committee members about the meeting. Include time, date, duration, and location (choose a place you know). Mention the meeting goal to encourage attendance.

PODCASTING SKILLS

24. Why me? Introducing yourself to a potential employer. While writing the many letters and e-mail messages that are part of the job search process, you find yourself wishing that you could just talk to some of these companies so your personality could shine through. Well, you've just gotten that opportunity. One of the companies that you've applied to has e-mailed you back, asking you to submit a two-minute podcast, introducing yourself and explaining why you would be a good person to hire.

Your task: Identify a company that you'd like to work for after graduation and select a job that would be a good match for your skills and interests. Write a script for a two-minute podcast (roughly 250 words). Introduce yourself and the position you're applying for, describe your background, and explain why you think you're a good candidate for the job. Make up any details you need. If your instructor asks you to do so, record the podcast and submit the file.

SOCIAL NETWORKING SKILLS

25. "Hi, my name is . . .": Introducing yourself on a business network. Business networking websites such as www.linkedin.com, www.ryze.com, and www.spoke.com have become popular places for professionals to make connections that would be difficult or impossible to make without the Internet. You might be familiar with MySpace.com or Friendster.com, sites that help individuals meet through networks of people they already know and trust. These business-oriented sites follow the same principle, but instead of using them to find new friends or dates, you use them to find new customers, new suppliers, or other important business connections. For instance, you might find that the ideal contact person in a company you'd like to do business with is the aunt of your boss's tennis partner.

An important aspect of business networking is being able to provide a clear description of your professional background and interests. For example, a manufacturing consultant can list the industries in which she has experience, the types of projects she has worked on, and the nature of work she'd like to pursue in the future (such as a full-time position for a company or additional independent projects).

Your task: Write a brief statement, introducing yourself, including your educational background, your job history, and the types of connections you'd like to make. Feel free to "fast forward" to your graduation and list your degree, the business specialty you plan to pursue, and any relevant experience. If you have business experience already, feel free to use that information instead. Make sure your statement is clear, concise (no more than two sentences), and compelling so that anyone looking for someone like you would want to get in touch with you after reading your introduction.

Writing Routine and Positive Messages

Learning Objectives

After studying this chapter, you will be able to

1 Apply the three-step writing process to routine and positive messages

2 Outline an effective strategy for writing routine requests

3 Explain how to ask for specific action in a courteous manner

4 Describe a strategy for writing routine replies and positive messages

5 Discuss the importance of knowing who is responsible when granting claims and requests for adjustment

6 Describe the importance of goodwill messages and explain how to make them effective

Communication Close-up at Get Satisfaction

Under the direction of co-founder and CEO Thor Muller, Get Satisfaction is creating a new way for companies and their customers to exchange routine messages.

http://getsatisfaction.com

For about as long as online communication has been possible, frustrated customers have been going online to complain about faulty products, confusing instructions, and poor service. When Web 2.0 tools hit the scene a few years ago, giving even nontechnical consumers a ready voice, the stream of "I need help!" messages turned into a full-time flood. On product review and shopping websites, enthusiast blogs, and various "complaint sites," consumers can vent their frustrations and ask for help when they feel they aren't getting satisfaction from the companies with which they do business.

These various websites can occasionally provide answers, but they suffer from four fundamental drawbacks. First, they are randomly scattered all over the Web, so many consumers are never quite sure where to look for help. Second, the right experts from the right companies often aren't involved, meaning that customers often have to rely on each other—which sometimes works but sometimes doesn't. Third, even companies that make a valiant effort to keep their customers satisfied know that everyone can benefit if customers can share ideas, learn from one another, and participate in ongoing conversation. Fourth, companies often find that multiple customers have the same routine questions, but communicating with every customer individually can be time-consuming and expensive.

The San Francisco–based startup Get Satisfaction is working to address all these issues. CEO Thor Muller explains that the company is "creating a kind of social network designed for companies and customers to communicate with each other." Consumers can post questions or complaints and request e-mail notification whenever a response is posted. If someone else has already posted the same complaint, all a visitor needs do is ask to be notified when the issue is resolved, saving time for the people asking and answering questions. Consumers can also suggest ideas for new products and services or improvements to existing offerings.

On the other side of the relationship, employees from companies that sell products and services can register as official representatives to answer questions, solve problems, and solicit feedback. As both knowledgeable consumers and company representatives provide answers and solutions, the responses voted most useful rise to the top, ensuring that visitors always get the most helpful information available. Companies can also put a *widget* on their websites to direct customer service inquiries to the Get Satisfaction site or replicate the Get Satisfaction capabilities right on their own websites. Plus, the "Overhead" feature lets companies monitor Twitter conversations about their products, so they can stay tuned in to complaints, questions, and compliments. As Muller explains, "When customers start to converge and talk, for many companies this is gold—real engagement with current or future customers."[1]

USING THE THREE-STEP WRITING PROCESS FOR ROUTINE AND POSITIVE MESSAGES

1 LEARNING OBJECTIVE

Apply the three-step writing process to routine and positive messages

Get Satisfaction's Thor Muller (profiled in the chapter-opening Communication Close-up) knows that much of the vital communication between a company and its customers is about routine matters, from product operation hints and technical support to refunds and ordering glitches. Whether you're writing these messages in a Web 2.0 environment such as Get Satisfaction's website or using more conventional tools, the three-step writing process gives you a great way to produce these messages effectively and efficiently.

Step 1: Planning a Routine or Positive Message

Even though planning routine and positive messages may take only a few minutes, the four tasks of planning still apply. First, analyze the situation, making sure that your purpose is clear and that you know enough about your audience to craft a successful message. Second, gather the information your audience needs to know. Third, select the right medium for the message, the audience, and the particular situation at hand. Fourth, organize your information effectively. Throughout this chapter, you'll learn more about performing all four of these tasks for a variety of routine and positive message types.

Even simple, routine messages can benefit from thoughtful planning.

Step 2: Writing a Routine or Positive Message

With all messages, you need to adapt to your audience by being sensitive to their needs: Maintain the "you" attitude, be polite, emphasize the positive, and use bias-free language. To strengthen your relationship with your audience, establish your credibility and project your company's image. And keep in mind that even if you normally use a conversational tone, some messages need to be more formal than others. Finally, use plain English and try to use the active voice as much as possible.

With some practice, you'll be able to compose most routine messages quickly. Your main idea is probably well defined already; just be sure you stick to it by limiting the scope of your message (see Figure 8.1).

In most cases, your readers will be interested or at least neutral, so you can usually adopt the direct approach for routine and positive messages: Open with a clear statement of the main idea, include all necessary details in the body, and then close cordially. Keep in mind that even though these messages are the least complicated to write, communicating across cultural boundaries can be challenging, especially if you're not familiar with the cultural differences involved.

For routine requests and positive messages
- *Open by stating the request or main idea*
- *Give necessary details in the body*
- *Close with a cordial request for specific action*

Step 3: Completing a Routine or Positive Message

No matter how brief or straightforward your message, maximize its impact by giving yourself plenty of time to revise, produce, proofread, and distribute it. First, revise your message by evaluating content and organization to make sure you've said what you want to in the order you want to say it. Review your message's readability. Edit and rewrite to

FIGURE 8.1 Routine Messages

Routine and positive messages are best conveyed using the direct approach. Google uses this blog to keep users of its AdWords search engine advertising system up to date on maintenance interruptions and other important news.

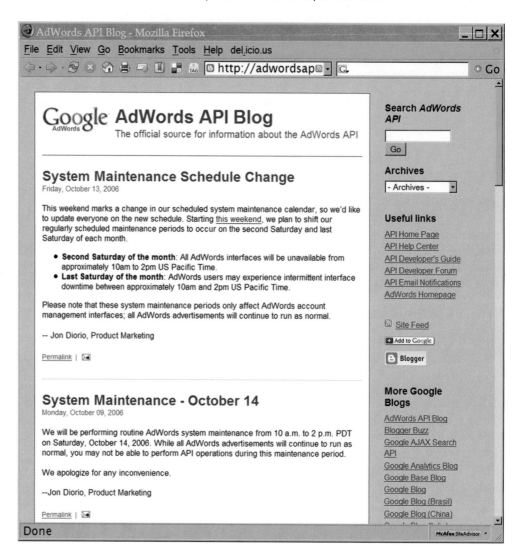

make it concise and clear. Second, design your document to suit your purpose and your audience. Even simple messages can benefit from careful font selection, the wise use of white space, and other design choices. Next, proofread the final version of your message, looking for typos, errors in spelling and mechanics, alignment problems, poor print quality, and so on. Finally, choose a distribution method that balances cost, convenience, time, security, and privacy. Refer to Chapter 7 for the most common media formats for brief messages.

MAKING ROUTINE REQUESTS

Making requests—for information, action, products, adjustments, or other matters—is a routine part of business. In most cases, your audience will be prepared to comply, as long as you're not being unreasonable or asking people to do something they would expect you to do yourself. By applying a clear strategy and tailoring your approach to each situation, you'll be able to generate effective requests quickly.

Strategy for Routine Requests

Like all other business messages, a routine request has three parts: an opening, a body, and a close. Using the direct approach, open with your main idea, which is a clear statement of your request. Use the body to give details and justify your request. Finally, close by requesting specific action.

2 **LEARNING OBJECTIVE**

Outline an effective strategy for writing routine requests

Stating Your Request Up Front

Begin routine requests by placing your initial request first; up front is where it stands out and gets the most attention. Of course, getting right to the point should not be interpreted as license to be abrupt or tactless:

Take care that your direct approach doesn't come across as abrupt or tactless.

- **Pay attention to tone.** Even though you expect a favorable response, the tone of your initial request is important. Instead of demanding action ("Send me the latest personnel cost data"), soften your request with words such as *please* and *I would appreciate.*
- **Assume that your audience will comply.** An impatient demand for rapid service isn't necessary. You can generally assume that your readers will comply with your request when they clearly understand the reason for it.
- **Be specific.** State precisely what you want. For example, if you request the latest market data from your research department, be sure to say whether you want a 1-page summary or 100 pages of raw data.

Explaining and Justifying Your Request

Use the body of your message to explain your request. Make the explanation a smooth and logical outgrowth of your opening remarks. If possible, point out how complying with the request could benefit the reader. For instance, if you would like some assistance interpreting complex quality-control data, you might point out how a better understanding of quality-control issues would improve customer satisfaction and ultimately lead to higher profits for the entire company.

Whether you're writing a formal letter or a simple instant message, you can use the body of your request to list a series of questions. This list of questions helps organize your message and helps your audience identify the information you need. Just keep in mind a few basics:

Using a list format helps readers sort through multiple questions or requests.

- **Ask the most important questions first.** If cost is your main concern, you might begin with a question such as "What is the cost for shipping the merchandise by air versus truck?" Then you might want to ask more specific but related questions about, say, discounts for paying early.
- **Ask only relevant questions.** To help expedite the response to your request, ask only questions that are central to your main request. Doing so will generate an answer sooner and make better use of the other person's time.
- **Deal with only one topic per question.** If you have an unusual or complex request, break it down into specific, individual questions so that the reader can address each one separately. Don't put the burden of untangling a complicated request on your reader. This consideration not only shows respect for your audience's time but also gets you a more accurate answer in less time.

Requesting Specific Action in a Courteous Close

Close your message with three important elements: (1) a specific request, (2) information about how you can be reached (if it isn't obvious), and (3) an expression of appreciation or goodwill. When you ask readers to perform a specific action, ask that they respond by a specific time, if appropriate (for example, "Please send the figures by May 5 so that I can return first-quarter results to you before the May 20 conference"). Plus, by including your phone number, e-mail address, office hours, and other contact information, you help your readers respond easily.

Conclude your message by sincerely expressing your goodwill and appreciation. However, don't thank the reader "in advance" for cooperating. If the reader's reply warrants a

3 **LEARNING OBJECTIVE**

Explain how to ask for specific action in a courteous manner

Close request messages with
- *A request for some specific action*
- *Information about how you can be reached*
- *An expression of appreciation*

✔ **CHECKLIST:**   **Writing Routine Requests**

A. State your request up front.
- Write in a polite, undemanding, personal tone.
- Use the direct approach because your audience will probably respond favorably to your request.
- Be specific and precise in your request.

B. Explain and justify your request.
- Justify the request or explain its importance.
- Explain any potential benefits of responding.

- Ask the most important questions first.
- Break complex requests into individual questions that are limited to only one topic each.

C. Request specific action in a courteous close.
- Make it easy to comply by including appropriate contact information.
- Express your gratitude.
- Clearly state any important deadlines for the request.

word of thanks, send it after you've received the reply. To review, see "Checklist: Writing Routine Requests."

Common Examples of Routine Requests

Many of the routine messages you'll be writing will likely fall into a few main categories: asking for information and action, asking for recommendations, and making claims and requesting adjustments.

Asking for Information and Action

When you need to know about something, elicit an opinion from someone, or request a simple action, you usually need only ask. In essence, simple requests say

- What you want to know or what you want readers to do
- Why you're making the request
- Why it may be in your readers' interest to help you

For simple, straightforward requests for information or action, use the direct approach.

If your reader is able to do what you want, such a straightforward request gets the job done quickly. Use the direct approach by opening with a clear statement of your reason for writing. In the body, provide whatever explanation is needed to justify your request. Then close with a specific description of what you expect and include a deadline, if appropriate (see Figure 8.2). In some situations, readers might be unwilling to respond unless they understand how the request benefits them, so be sure to include this information in your explanation. You can assume some shared background when communicating about a routine matter to someone in the same company.

In contrast to requests sent internally, those sent to people outside the organization usually adopt a more formal tone, as in the following example:

Dear Bioverse:

Makes overall request in polite form (no question mark) ———•

Please provide additional information on distribution opportunities for your Healthy Ponds product line, as mentioned on your website. Enviro Domestic is a 20-year-old firm with a well-established design, retail, and service presence in the Oklahoma City area, and we believe your bioremediation products would make a compelling addition to our offerings.

Identifies the writer's affiliation and reason for writing ———•

Specifies exactly what the writer wants to know to assist the recipient in responding ———•

In particular, we would appreciate answers to the following questions:

1. Do you offer exclusive regional distribution contracts?
2. Do you offer factory training for sales and service specialists?
3. Do you plan to expand beyond water bioremediation solutions into other landscaping products?

Closes with a polite request and specific answer deadline ———•

Please let us hear from you by February 15.

FIGURE 8.2 Effective Message Requesting Action

In this e-mail request to district managers across the country, Helene Clausen asks them to fill out an attached information collection form. Although the request is not unusual and responding to it is part of the managers' responsibility, Clausen asks for their help in a courteous manner and points out the benefits of responding.

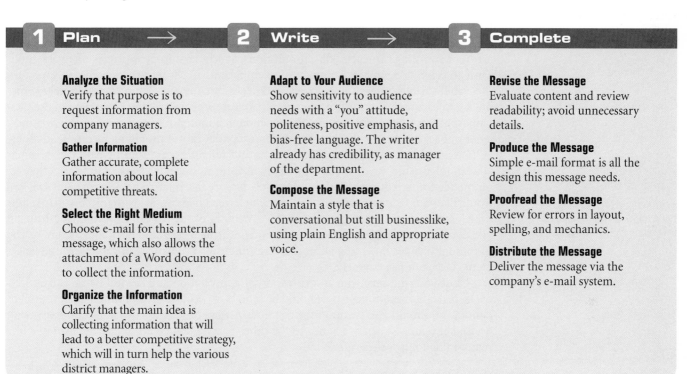

1 Plan →

Analyze the Situation
Verify that purpose is to request information from company managers.

Gather Information
Gather accurate, complete information about local competitive threats.

Select the Right Medium
Choose e-mail for this internal message, which also allows the attachment of a Word document to collect the information.

Organize the Information
Clarify that the main idea is collecting information that will lead to a better competitive strategy, which will in turn help the various district managers.

2 Write →

Adapt to Your Audience
Show sensitivity to audience needs with a "you" attitude, politeness, positive emphasis, and bias-free language. The writer already has credibility, as manager of the department.

Compose the Message
Maintain a style that is conversational but still businesslike, using plain English and appropriate voice.

3 Complete

Revise the Message
Evaluate content and review readability; avoid unnecessary details.

Produce the Message
Simple e-mail format is all the design this message needs.

Proofread the Message
Review for errors in layout, spelling, and mechanics.

Distribute the Message
Deliver the message via the company's e-mail system.

Identifies the subject of the e-mail

Acknowledges that responding to the request will require some work, but the result will benefit everyone

Gets right to the point of the message

Explains the benefit of responding to the request

Provides a clear and meaningful deadline, then closes in a courteous manner

Eudora - [All District Mgrs, Competitive Threat Analysis]

File   Edit   Mailbox   Message   Transfer   Special   Tools   Window   Help

To: <All District Mgrs>
From: hh_clausen@early-ed.com
Subject: Competitive Threat Analysis
Cc:
Bcc:
Attached: C:\Strategic planning\Competitive Analysis template.doc;

Hello everyone,

At last week's off-site meeting, Charles asked me to coordinate our companywide competitive threat analysis project. In order to devise a comprehensive strategic response that is sensitive to local market variations, we need your individual insights and advice.

To minimize the effort for you and to ensure consistent data collection across all regions, I've attached a template that identifies all the key questions we'd like to have answered. I realize this will require several hours of work on your part, but the result will be a truly nationwide look at our competitive situation. From this information, we can create a plan for next fiscal year that makes the best use of finite resources while adapting to your local district needs.

To allow sufficient time to compile your inputs before the November 13 board meeting, please e-mail your responses to me by November 8. Thanks for your help and timely attention to this important project.

Helene

Helene H. Clausen
Director, Strategic Initiatives
Early Education Solutions, Inc.
14445 Lawson Blvd, Suite 455
Denver, CO 80201
tel: 303-555-1200
fax: 303-555-1210
www.early-ed.com

A more complex request might require not only greater detail but also information on how responding will benefit the reader.

Asking for Recommendations

Always ask for permission before using someone as a reference.

The need to inquire about people arises often in business. For example, before extending credit or awarding contracts, jobs, promotions, or scholarships, companies often ask applicants to supply references. Companies ask applicants to list references who can vouch for their ability, skills, integrity, character, and fitness for the job. Before you volunteer someone's name as a reference, ask permission to do so. Some people don't want you to use their names, perhaps because they don't know enough about you to feel comfortable writing a letter or because they or their employers have a policy of not providing recommendations.

Refresh the memory of any potential reference you haven't been in touch with for a while.

Because requests for recommendations and references are routine, you can organize your inquiry using the direct approach. Open your message by clearly stating why the recommendation is required (if it's not for a job, be sure to explain what it is for) and that you would like your reader to write the letter. If you haven't had contact with the person for some time, use the opening to trigger the reader's memory of the relationship you had, the dates of association, and any special events that might bring a clear and favorable picture of you to mind. Consider including an updated résumé if you've had significant career advancement since your last contact.

Close your message with an expression of appreciation and the full name and address of the person to whom the letter should be sent. When asking for an immediate recommendation, you should also mention the deadline. Always be sure to enclose a stamped, preaddressed envelope as a convenience to the other party. Figure 8.3 provides an example of a request that follows these guidelines.

Making Claims and Requesting Adjustments

In claim letters
- *Explain the problem and give details*
- *Provide backup information*
- *Request specific action*

Be prepared to document your claim. Send copies and keep the original documents.

If you're dissatisfied with a company's product or service, you can opt to make a **claim** (a formal complaint) or request an **adjustment** (a settlement of a claim). In either case, it's important to maintain a professional tone in all your communication, no matter how angry or frustrated you are. Keeping your cool will help you get the situation resolved sooner.

In most cases, and especially in your first message, assume that a fair adjustment will be made and use a direct request. Open with a straightforward statement of the problem. In the body, give a complete, specific explanation of the details; provide any information an adjuster would need to verify your complaint. In your close, politely request specific action or convey a sincere desire to find a solution. And, if appropriate, suggest that the business relationship will continue if the problem is solved satisfactorily. Be prepared to back up your claim with invoices, sales receipts, canceled checks, dated correspondence, and any other relevant documents. Send copies and keep the originals for your files.

If the remedy is obvious, tell your reader exactly what you expect from the company, such as exchanging incorrectly shipped merchandise for the right item or issuing a refund if the item is out of stock. In some cases, you might ask the reader to resolve a problem. However, if you're uncertain about the precise nature of the trouble, you could ask the company to make an assessment and then advise you on how the situation could be fixed. Supply your contact information so that the company can discuss the situation with you,

✓ **CHECKLIST:** **Making Claims and Requesting Adjustments**

- Maintain a professional tone, even if you're extremely frustrated.
- Open with a straightforward statement of the problem.
- Provide specific details in the body.
- Present facts honestly and clearly.

- Politely summarize the desired action in the closing.
- Clearly state what you expect as a fair settlement or ask the reader to propose a fair adjustment.
- Explain the benefits of complying with the request, such as your continued patronage.

FIGURE 8.3 Effective Letter Requesting a Recommendation
This writer uses the direct approach when asking for a recommendation from a former professor. Note how she takes care to refresh the professor's memory because she took the class a year and a half ago. She also indicates the date by which the letter is needed and points to the enclosure of a stamped, preaddressed envelope.

1 Plan →

Analyze the Situation
Verify that the purpose is to request a recommendation letter from a college professor.

Gather Information
Gather information on classes and dates to help the reader recall you and to clarify the position you seek.

Select the Right Medium
The letter format gives this message an appropriate level of formality, although many professors prefer to be contacted by e-mail.

Organize the Information
Messages like this are common and expected, so a direct approach is fine.

2 Write →

Adapt to Your Audience
Show sensitivity to audience needs with a "you" attitude, politeness, positive emphasis, and bias-free language.

Compose the Message
Style is respectful and businesslike, while still using plain English and appropriate voice.

3 Complete

Revise the Message
Evaluate content and review readability; avoid unnecessary details.

Produce the Message
Simple letter format is all the design this message needs.

Proofread the Message
Review for errors in layout, spelling, and mechanics.

Distribute the Message
Deliver the message via postal mail or e-mail if you have the professor's e-mail address.

1181 Ashport Drive
Tate Springs, TN 38101
March 14, 2009

Professor Lyndon Kenton
School of Business
University of Tennessee, Knoxville
Knoxville, TN 37916

Dear Professor Kenton:

I recently interviewed with Strategic Investments and have been called for a second interview for their Analyst Training Program (ATP). They have requested at least one recommendation from a professor, and I immediately thought of you. May I have a letter of recommendation from you?

As you may recall, I took BUS 485, Financial Analysis, from you in the fall of 2007. I enjoyed the class and finished the term with an "A." Professor Kenton, your comments on assertiveness and cold-calling impressed me beyond the scope of the actual course material. In fact, taking your course helped me decide on a future as a financial analyst.

My enclosed résumé includes all my relevant work experience and volunteer activities. I would also like to add that I've handled the financial planning for our family since my father passed away several years ago. Although I initially learned by trial and error, I have increasingly applied my business training in deciding what stocks or bonds to trade. This, I believe, has given me a practical edge over others who may be applying for the same job.

If possible, Ms. Blackmon in Human Resources needs to receive your letter by March 30. For your convenience, I've enclosed a preaddressed, stamped envelope.

I appreciate your time and effort in writing this letter of recommendation for me. It will be great to put my education to work, and I'll keep you informed of my progress. Thank you for your consideration in this matter.

Sincerely,

Joanne Tucker

Joanne Tucker

Enclosure

Includes information near the opening to refresh the reader's memory about this former student

Gives a deadline for response and includes information about the person expecting the recommendation

Opens by stating the purpose of the letter and making the request, assuming the reader will want to comply with the request

Refers to résumé in the body and mentions experience that could set applicant apart from other candidates

Mentions the pre-addressed, stamped envelope to encourage a timely response if necessary. Compare the ineffective and effective versions in Figure 8.4 for an example of making a claim.

A rational, clear, and courteous approach is best for any routine request. To review the tasks involved in making claims and requesting adjustments, see "Checklist: Making Claims and Requesting Adjustments."

FIGURE 8.4 Ineffective and Effective Versions of a Claim
Note the difference in tone and information content in these two versions. The ineffective version is emotional and unprofessional, whereas the effective version communicates calmly and clearly.

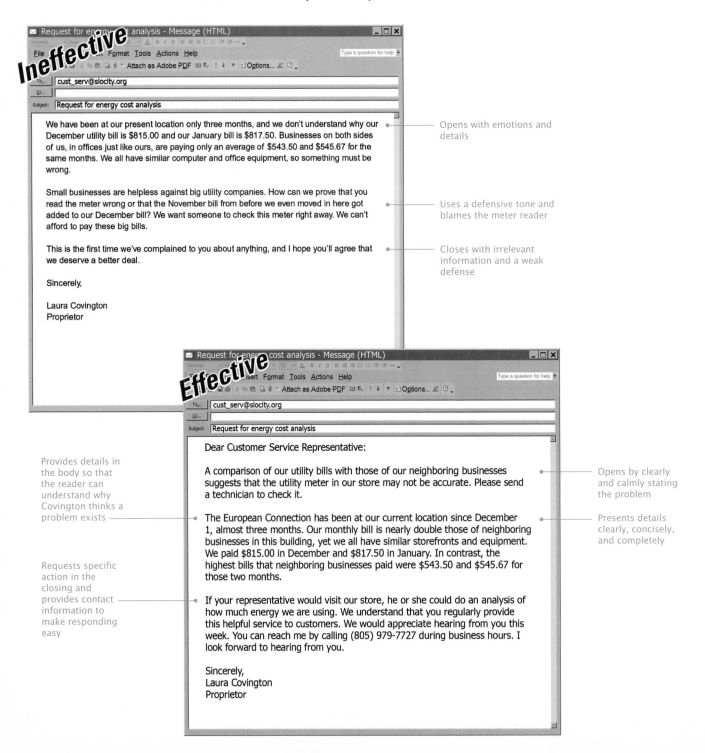

SENDING ROUTINE REPLIES AND POSITIVE MESSAGES

Just as you'll make numerous requests for information and action throughout your career, you'll also respond to requests and send a variety of positive messages. You have several goals for such messages: to communicate the information or the good news, to answer all questions, to provide all required details, and to leave your reader with a good impression of you and your firm.

Strategy for Routine Replies and Positive Messages

Like a request, a routine reply or positive message has an opening, a body, and a close. Because readers receiving these messages will generally be interested in what you have to say, you can usually use the direct approach. Place your main idea (the positive reply or the good news) in the opening, use the body to explain all the relevant details, and close cordially—perhaps highlighting a benefit to your reader.

Starting with the Main Idea

By opening routine and positive messages with the main idea or good news, you're preparing your audience for the detail that follows. Make your opening clear and concise. Although the following introductory statements make the same point, one is cluttered with unnecessary information that buries the purpose, whereas the other is brief and to the point:

INSTEAD OF THIS	WRITE THIS
I am pleased to inform you that after careful consideration of a diverse and talented pool of applicants, each of whom did a thorough job of analyzing Trask Horton Pharmaceuticals's training needs, we have selected your bid.	Trask Horton Pharmaceuticals has accepted your bid to provide public speaking and presentation training to the sales staff.

The best way to write a clear opening is to have a clear idea of what you want to say. Before you put one word on paper, ask yourself, "What is the single most important message I have for the audience?"

Providing Necessary Details and Explanation

Use the body to explain your point completely so that your audience won't be confused or doubtful about your meaning. As you provide the details, maintain the supportive tone established in the opening. This tone is easy to continue when your message is entirely positive, as in this example:

> Your educational background and internship have impressed us, and we believe you would be a valuable addition to Green Valley Properties. As discussed during your interview, your salary will be $4,300 per month, plus benefits. Please plan to meet with our benefits manager, Paula Sanchez, at 8 a.m. on Monday, March 21. She will assist you with all the paperwork necessary to tailor our benefit package to your family situation. She will also arrange various orientation activities to help you acclimate to our company.

However, if your routine message is mixed and must convey mildly disappointing information, put the negative portion of your message into as favorable a context as possible:

INSTEAD OF THIS	WRITE THIS
No, we no longer carry the Sportsgirl line of sweaters.	The new Olympic line has replaced the Sportsgirl sweaters that you asked about. Olympic features a wider range of colors and sizes and more contemporary styling.

---

4 LEARNING OBJECTIVE

Describe a strategy for writing routine replies and positive messages

Use the direct approach for positive messages.

Prepare your audience for the detail that follows by beginning your positive message with the main idea or good news.

Look for ways to present negative information in a positive context.

✓ CHECKLIST: Writing Routine Replies and Positive Messages

A. Start with the main idea.
- Be clear and concise.
- Identify the single most important message before you start writing.

B. Provide necessary details and explanation.
- Explain your point completely to eliminate any confusion or lingering doubts.
- Maintain a supportive tone throughout.

- Embed negative statements in positive contexts or balance them with positive alternatives.
- Talk favorably about the choices the customer has made.

C. End with a courteous close.
- Let your readers know that you have their personal well-being in mind.
- If further action is required, tell readers how to proceed and encourage them to act promptly.

In this example, the more complete description is less negative and emphasizes how the recipient can benefit from the change. Be careful, though: You can use negative information in this type of message *only* if you're reasonably sure the audience will respond positively. Otherwise, use the indirect approach (discussed in Chapter 9).

If you are communicating with a customer, you might also want to use the body of your message to assure the customer of the wisdom of his or her purchase selection (without being condescending or self-congratulatory). Using such favorable comments, often known as *resale*, is a good way to build customer relationships. These comments are commonly included in acknowledgments of orders and other routine announcements to customers, and they are most effective when they are relatively short and specific:

> The zipper on the laptop carrying case you purchased is double-stitched and guaranteed for the life of the product.
>
> The KitchenAid mixer you ordered is our best-selling model. It should meet your cooking needs for many years.

Ending with a Courteous Close

Make sure audience members understand what to do next and how that action will benefit them.

Your message is most likely to succeed if your readers are left feeling that you have their best interests in mind. You can accomplish this task either by highlighting a benefit to the audience or by expressing appreciation or goodwill. If follow-up action is required, clearly state who will do what next. See "Checklist: Writing Routine Replies and Positive Messages" to review the primary tasks involved in this type of business message.

Common Examples of Routine Replies and Positive Messages

Most routine and positive messages fall into six main categories: answers to requests for information and action, grants of claims and requests for adjustment, recommendations, informative messages, good-news announcements, and goodwill messages.

Answering Requests for Information and Action

Every professional answers requests for information and action from time to time. If the response to a request is a simple "yes" or some other straightforward information, the direct approach is appropriate. A prompt, gracious, and thorough response will positively influence how people think about you and the organization you represent (see Figure 8.5).

To handle repetitive queries quickly and consistently, companies usually develop form responses that can be customized as needed (see Figure 8.6). These ready-made message templates can be printed forms, word-processor documents, e-mail templates, or blocks of instant messaging text that can be dropped into a messaging window with the click of a mouse.

When you're answering requests and a potential sale is involved, you have three main goals: (1) to respond to the inquiry and answer all questions, (2) to leave your reader with

FIGURE 8.5   Effective IM Response to an Information Request

This quick and courteous exchange is typical of IM communication in such areas as customer service and technical support. The agent (Janice) solves the problem quickly and leaves the customer with a positive impression of the company.

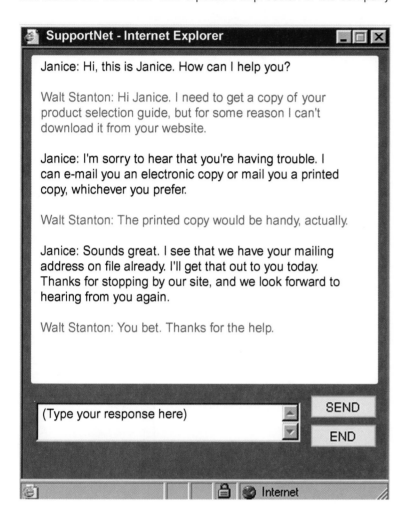

a good impression of you and your firm, and (3) to encourage the future sale. The following message meets all three objectives:

Here is the brochure "Entertainment Unlimited" that you requested. This booklet describes the vast array of entertainment options available to you with an Ocean Satellite Device (OSD).

On page 46 you'll find a list of the 338 channels that the OSD brings into your home. You'll have access to movie, sports, and music channels; 24-hour news channels; local channels; and all the major television networks. OSD gives you a clearer picture and more precise sound than those old-fashioned dishes that took up most of your yard—and OSD uses only a small dish that mounts easily on your roof.

More music, more cartoons, more experts, more news, and more sports are available to you with OSD than with any other cable or satellite connection in this region. It's all there, right at your fingertips.

Just call us at 1-800-786-4331, and an OSD representative will come to your home to answer your questions. You'll love the programming and the low monthly cost. Call us today!

Starts with a clear statement of the main point, which is responding to a consumer inquiry

Creates a positive impression of the product offered

Encourages readers to move towards a purchase by continuing to highlight product benefits

Points toward the sale confidently

FIGURE 8.6 Personalized Reply to a Request for Information
This e-mail message personalizes a standardized response by including the recipient's name in the greeting.

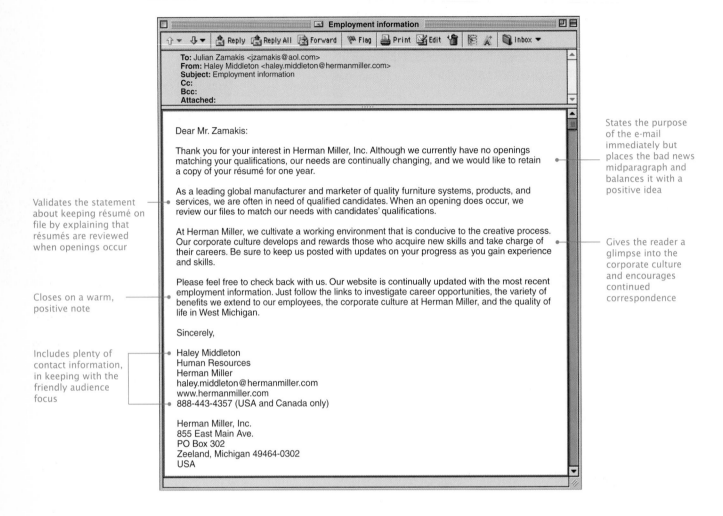

States the purpose of the e-mail immediately but places the bad news midparagraph and balances it with a positive idea

Validates the statement about keeping résumé on file by explaining that résumés are reviewed when openings occur

Gives the reader a glimpse into the corporate culture and encourages continued correspondence

Closes on a warm, positive note

Includes plenty of contact information, in keeping with the friendly audience focus

---

Granting Claims and Requests for Adjustment

Even the best-run companies make mistakes, from shipping the wrong order to billing a customer's credit card inaccurately. In other cases, a customer or a third party might be responsible for a mistake, such as misusing a product or damaging a product in shipment. Each of these events represents a turning point in your relationship with your customer. If you handle the situation well, your customer is likely to be even more loyal than before because you've proven that you're serious about customer satisfaction. However, if a customer believes that you mishandled a complaint, you'll make the situation even worse. Dissatisfied customers often take their business elsewhere without notice and tell numerous friends and colleagues about the negative experience. A transaction that might be worth only a few dollars by itself could cost you many times that amount in lost business. In other words, every mistake is an opportunity to improve a relationship.

Your response to a customer complaint depends on your company's policies for resolving such issues and your assessment of whether the company, the customer, or some third party is at fault.

Responding to a Claim When Your Company Is at Fault Before you respond after your company has made a mistake, make sure you know your company's policies, which might dictate specific legal and financial steps to be taken. For serious problems that go beyond routine errors, your company should have a *crisis management plan* that outlines communication steps both inside and outside the organization (see Chapter 9).

5 **LEARNING OBJECTIVE**

Discuss the importance of knowing who is responsible when granting claims and requests for adjustment

Most routine responses should take your company's specific policies into account and do the following:

- **Acknowledge receipt of the customer's claim or complaint.** Even if you can't solve the problem immediately, at least let the other party know that somebody is listening.
- **Take (or assign) personal responsibility for setting matters straight.** Customers want to know that someone is listening and responding.
- **Sympathize with the customer's inconvenience or frustration.** Letting the customer see that you're on his or her side helps defuse the emotional element of the situation.
- **Explain precisely how you have resolved or plan to resolve the situation.** If you can respond exactly as the customer requested, be sure to communicate that. If you can't, explain why.
- **Take steps to repair the relationship.** Keeping your existing customers is almost always less expensive than acquiring new customers, so look for ways to mend the relationship and encourage future business.
- **Follow up to verify that your response was correct.** Follow-up not only helps improve customer service but also gives you another opportunity to show how much you care about your customer.

In addition to taking these positive steps, maintain a professional demeanor. Don't blame anyone in your organization by name; don't make exaggerated, insincere apologies; don't imply that the customer is at fault; and don't promise more than you can deliver.

As with requests for information or action, companies often create customizable templates for granting claims and requests for adjustment. In the following example, a large online clothing company created an e-mail form to respond to customers who complain that they haven't received exactly what was ordered:

Handling routine communication in a friendly, audience-focused way is one of the many reasons that the Alexandria, Virginia, bank Burke & Hebert enjoys almost fanatical customer loyalty. President Hunt Burke helps ensure that customer inquires are handled promptly and that his staff communicate in a friendly, audience-focused way.

Your e-mail message concerning your recent Klondike order has been forwarded to our director of order fulfillment. Your complete satisfaction is our goal, and a customer service representative will contact you within 48 hours to assist with the issues raised in your letter.

In the meantime, please accept the enclosed $5 gift certificate as a token of our appreciation for your business. Whether you're skiing or driving a snowmobile, Klondike Gear offers you the best protection from wind, snow, and cold—and Klondike has been taking care of customers' outdoor needs for over 27 years.

Thank you for taking the time to write to us. Your input helps us better serve you and all our customers.

Acknowledges receipt of the customer's message

Explains what will happen next and when, without making promises the writer can't keep

Takes steps to repair the relationship and ensure continued business

Closes with a statement of the company's concern for all its customers

---

Responding to a Claim When the Customer Is at Fault Communication about a claim is a delicate matter when the customer is clearly at fault. If you refuse the claim, you may lose your customer—as well as many of the customer's friends and colleagues, who will hear only one side of the dispute. You must weigh the cost of making the adjustment against the cost of losing future business from one or more customers. Some companies have strict guidelines on responding to such claims, whereas others give individual employees and managers some leeway in making case-by-case decisions.

If you choose to grant a claim, you can simply open with the good news, being sure to specify exactly what you're agreeing to do. The body of the message is tricky because you want to discourage such claims in the future by steering the customer in the right direction. For example, customers sometimes misuse products or fail to follow the terms of service agreements, such as forgetting to cancel hotel reservations at least 24 hours in advance and thereby incurring the cost of one night's stay. Even if you do grant a particular claim, you don't want to imply that you will grant similar claims in the future. The challenge is to diplomatically remind the customer of proper usage or procedures without being condescending ("Perhaps you failed to read the instructions carefully") or preachy ("You should know that wool shrinks in hot water"). Close in a courteous manner that expresses your appreciation for the customer's business (see Figure 8.7).

If you grant a claim when the customer is at fault, look for diplomatic ways to discourage the errant behavior in the future.

FIGURE 8.7 Responding to a Claim When the Buyer Is at Fault
In the interest of positive customer relationships, this company agreed to provide replacement parts for a customer's in-line skates, even though the product is outside its warranty period. (For the sake of clarity, the content of the customer's original e-mail message is not reproduced here.)

1 Plan →

Analyze the Situation
The purpose is to grant the customer's claim, tactfully educate him, and encourage further business.

Gather Information
Gather information on product care, warranties, and resale information.

Select the Right Medium
An e-mail message is appropriate in this case because the customer contacted the company via e-mail.

Organize the Information
You're responding with a positive answer, so a direct approach is fine.

2 Write →

Adapt to Your Audience
Show sensitivity to audience needs with a "you" attitude, politeness, positive emphasis, and bias-free language.

Compose the Message
Style is respectful while still managing to educate the customer on product usage and maintenance.

3 Complete

Revise the Message
Evaluate content and review readability; avoid unnecessary details.

Produce the Message
Emphasize a clean, professional appearance.

Proofread the Message
Review for errors in layout, spelling, and mechanics.

Distribute the Message
E-mail the reply.

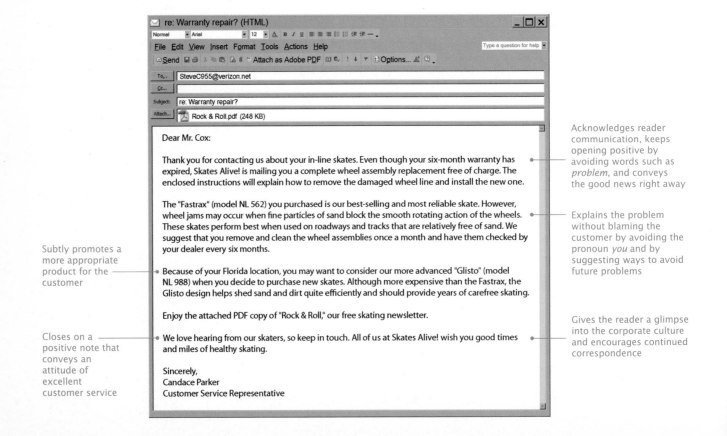

Subtly promotes a more appropriate product for the customer

Closes on a positive note that conveys an attitude of excellent customer service

Acknowledges reader communication, keeps opening positive by avoiding words such as *problem*, and conveys the good news right away

Explains the problem without blaming the customer by avoiding the pronoun *you* and by suggesting ways to avoid future problems

Gives the reader a glimpse into the corporate culture and encourages continued correspondence

---

re: Warranty repair? (HTML)

To...: SteveC955@verizon.net
Cc...:
Subject: re: Warranty repair?
Attach...: Rock & Roll.pdf (248 KB)

Dear Mr. Cox:

Thank you for contacting us about your in-line skates. Even though your six-month warranty has expired, Skates Alive! is mailing you a complete wheel assembly replacement free of charge. The enclosed instructions will explain how to remove the damaged wheel line and install the new one.

The "Fastrax" (model NL 562) you purchased is our best-selling and most reliable skate. However, wheel jams may occur when fine particles of sand block the smooth rotating action of the wheels. These skates perform best when used on roadways and tracks that are relatively free of sand. We suggest that you remove and clean the wheel assemblies once a month and have them checked by your dealer every six months.

Because of your Florida location, you may want to consider our more advanced "Glisto" (model NL 988) when you decide to purchase new skates. Although more expensive than the Fastrax, the Glisto design helps shed sand and dirt quite efficiently and should provide years of carefree skating.

Enjoy the attached PDF copy of "Rock & Roll," our free skating newsletter.

We love hearing from our skaters, so keep in touch. All of us at Skates Alive! wish you good times and miles of healthy skating.

Sincerely,
Candace Parker
Customer Service Representative

✓ CHECKLIST: Granting Claims and Adjustment Requests

A. Responding when your company is at fault
- Be aware of your company's policies in such cases before you respond.
- For serious situations, refer to the company's crisis management plan.
- Start by acknowledging receipt of the claim or complaint.
- Take or assign personal responsibility for resolving the situation.
- Sympathize with the customer's frustration.
- Explain how you have resolved the situation (or plan to).
- Take steps to repair the customer relationship.
- Verify your response with the customer and keep the lines of communication open.

B. Responding when the customer is at fault
- Weigh the cost of complying with or refusing the request.
- If you choose to comply, open with the good news.
- Use the body of the message to respectfully educate the customer about steps needed to avoid a similar outcome in the future.
- Close with an appreciation for the customer's business.

C. Responding when a third party is at fault
- Evaluate the situation and review your company's policies before responding.
- Avoid placing blame; focus on the solution.
- Regardless of who is responsible for resolving the situation, let the customer know what will happen to resolve the problem.

Responding to a Claim When a Third Party Is at Fault   Sometimes neither your company nor your customer is at fault. For example, ordering a book from Amazon.com involves not only Amazon.com but also a delivery service such as FedEx or the U.S. Postal Service, the publisher and possibly a distributor of the book, a credit card issuer, and a company that processes credit card transactions. Any one of these other partners might be at fault in the event of a problem, but the customer is likely to blame Amazon.com because that is the entity primarily responsible for the transaction.

No general scheme applies to every case involving a third party, so evaluate the situation carefully and know your company's policies before responding. For instance, an online retailer and the companies that manufacture its merchandise might have an agreement which specifies that the manufacturers automatically handle all complaints about product quality. However, regardless of who eventually resolves the problem, if customers contact you, you need to respond with messages that explain how the problem will be solved. Pointing fingers is unproductive and unprofessional; resolving the situation is the only issue customers care about. See "Checklist: Granting Claims and Adjustment Requests" to review the tasks involved in these kinds of business messages.

When a third party is at fault, your response depends on your company's agreements with that organization.

Providing Recommendations

When writing a letter of recommendation, your goal is to convince readers that the person being recommended has the characteristics necessary for the job, project assignment, scholarship, or other objective the person is seeking. A successful recommendation letter contains a number of relevant details:

- The candidate's full name
- The position or other objective the candidate is seeking
- The nature of your relationship with the candidate
- An indication of whether you're answering a request from the person or taking the initiative to write
- Facts and evidence relevant to the candidate and the opportunity
- A comparison of this candidate's potential with that of peers, if available (for example, "Ms. Jonasson consistently ranked in the top 10 percent of her class")
- Your overall evaluation of the candidate's suitability for the opportunity

As surprising as this might sound, the most difficult recommendation letters to write are often those for truly outstanding candidates. Your audience will have trouble believing uninterrupted praise for someone's talents and accomplishments. To enhance

Communication Miscues

When Recommendation Letters Lead to Lawsuits

Recommendation letters are classified as routine messages, but with all the legal troubles they can get employers into these days, they've become anything but routine. Over the years, employees have won thousands of lawsuits that charged former employers with defamation related to job recommendations. In addition to charges of defamation—which can be successfully defended if the "defamatory" statements are proven to be true—employers have been sued for retaliation by ex-employees who believed that negative letters were written expressly for purposes of revenge. And as if that weren't enough, employers have even sued each other over recommendation letters when the recipient of a letter believed the writer failed to disclose important negative information.

No wonder many companies now refuse to divulge anything more than job titles and dates of employment. But even that doesn't always solve the problem: Ex-employees have been known to sue for retaliation when their employers refused to write on their behalf. (This refusal to write recommendations also causes problems for hiring companies. If they can't get any real background information on job candidates, they risk hiring employees who lack the necessary skills or who are disruptive or even dangerous in the workplace.)

For companies that let managers write recommendations, what sort of information should or should not be included? Even though the majority of states now have laws protecting companies against recommendation-related lawsuits when the employer acts in good faith, individual cases vary so much that no specific guidelines can ever apply to all cases. However, answering the following questions before drafting a recommendation letter will help you avoid trouble:

- Does the party receiving this personal information have a legitimate right to it?
- Does all the information I've presented relate directly to the job or benefit being sought?
- Have I put the candidate's case as strongly and as honestly as I can?
- Have I avoided overstating the candidate's abilities or otherwise misleading the reader?
- Have I based all my statements on firsthand knowledge and provable facts?

No matter what the circumstances, experts also advise that you always consult your human resources or legal department for advice.

CAREER APPLICATIONS

1. A former employee was often late for work but was an excellent and fast worker who got along well with everyone. Do you think it's important to mention the tardiness to potential employers? If so, how would you handle it?
2. Step outside yourself for a moment and write a letter of recommendation about you from a former employer's perspective. Make sure your letter embodies honesty, integrity, and prudence.

REAL-TIME UPDATES
Learn More

Get expert tips on writing (or requesting) a letter of recommendation

Find helpful advice on employment recommendations, academic recommendations, and character references. Go to http://real-timeupdates.com/bct and click on "Learn More." If you are using mybcommlab, you can access Real-Time Updates within each chapter or under Student Study Tools.

A serious shortcoming cannot be ignored in letters of recommendation, but beware of being libelous:
- *Include only relevant, factual information*
- *Avoid value judgments*
- *Balance criticisms with favorable points*

your credibility—and the candidate's—illustrate your general points with specific examples that point out the candidate's abilities and fitness for the job opening.

Most candidates aren't perfect, however, and you'll need to decide how to handle each situation that comes your way. Omitting a reference to someone's shortcomings may be tempting, especially if the shortcomings are irrelevant to the demands of the job in question. Even so, you have an obligation to refer to any serious shortcoming that could be related to job performance. You owe it to your audience, to your own conscience, and even to better-qualified candidates. You don't have to present the shortcomings as simple criticisms, however. A good option is to list them as areas for improvement or as areas the person might be working on now.

The danger in writing a critical letter is that you might inadvertently engage in *libel*, publishing a false and malicious written statement that injures the candidate's reputation. On the other hand, if that negative information is truthful and relevant, it may be unethical and even illegal to omit it from your recommendation.

If you must refer to a shortcoming, you can best protect yourself by sticking to the facts, avoiding value judgments, and placing your criticism in the context of a generally favorable recommendation, as in Figure 8.8. In this letter, the writer supports all statements and judgments with evidence.

FIGURE 8.8   Effective Recommendation Letter
This letter clearly states the nature of the writer's relationship to the candidate and provides specific examples to support the writer's endorsements.

 AIRBUS

November 15, 2009

Ms. Clarice Gailey
Director of Operations
McNally and Associates, Inc.
8688 Southgate Ave.
Augusta, GA 30906

Dear Ms. Gailey:

I am pleased to recommend Talvin Biswas for the marketing position at McNally and Associates. Mr. Biswas has worked with Airbus Americas as an intern for the past two summers while pursuing his degree in marketing and advertising. His duties included customer correspondence, web content updates, and direct-mail campaign planning.

As his supervisor, in addition to knowing his work here, I also know that Mr. Biswas has served as secretary for the International Business Association at the University of Michigan. He tutored other international students in the university's writing center. His fluency in three languages (English, French, and Hindi) and sensitivity to other cultures will make him an immediate contributor to your international operations.

Mr. Biswas is a thoughtful and careful professional who will not hesitate to contribute ideas when invited to do so. In addition, because Mr. Biswas learns and adapts quickly, he will learn your company's methods with ease.

Mr. Biswas will make an excellent addition to your staff at McNally and Associates. If I can provide any additional information, please call me at the number below. If you prefer to communicate by e-mail, please contact me at angela_leclerc@airbus.com.

Sincerely,

Angela LeClerc

Angela LeClerc
Vice President, Marketing

AIRBUS INDUSTRIE OF NORTH AMERICA, INC.
198 Van Buren Street • Suite 300 • Herndon, VA 20170
Telephone (703) 834-3400 • Facsimile (703) 834-3440 • Website: www.airbus.com

---

Before you dash off any recommendation letter, even for someone you know closely and respect without reservation, keep in mind that every time you write a recommendation, you're putting your own reputation on the line. If the person's shortcomings are so pronounced that you don't think he or she is a good fit for the job, the only choice is to not write the letter at all. Unless your relationship with the person warrants an explanation, simply suggest that someone else might be in a better position to provide a recommendation.

Creating Informative Messages

Companies send a variety of routine informative messages, from updated policies to reminder notices. Use the opening of informative messages to state the purpose and briefly mention the nature of the information you are providing. Unlike the replies discussed earlier, informative messages are not solicited by your reader, so make it clear up front why the reader is receiving this particular message. Provide the necessary details in the body and end your message with a courteous close.

When writing informative messages
- *State the purpose in the opening and briefly mention the nature of the information you are providing*
- *Provide necessary details in the body*
- *End with a courteous close*

Most informative communications are neutral. That is, they stimulate neither a positive nor a negative response from readers. For example, when you send departmental meeting announcements and reminder notices, you'll generally receive a neutral response from your readers (unless the purpose of the meeting is unwelcome). Simply present the factual information in the body of the message and don't worry too much about the reader's attitude toward the information.

Some informative messages may require additional care. For instance, policy statements or procedural changes may be good news for a company, perhaps by saving money. However, it may not be obvious to employees that such savings may make available additional employee resources or even pay raises. In instances in which the reader may not initially view the information positively, use the body of the message to highlight the potential benefits from the reader's perspective.

Announcing Good News

To develop and maintain good relationships, smart companies recognize that it's good business to spread the word about positive developments. These can include opening new facilities, hiring a new executive, introducing new products or services, or sponsoring community events. Because good news is always welcome, use the direct approach.

Writing to a successful job applicant is one of the most pleasant good-news messages you might have the opportunity to write. The following example uses the direct approach and provides information that the recipient needs:

Welcome to Lake Valley Rehabilitation Center. A number of excellent candidates were interviewed, but your educational background and recent experience at Memorial Hospital make you the best person for the position of medical records supervisor.

Announces news in friendly, welcoming tone

As we discussed, your salary is $39,200 a year. We would like you to begin on Monday, February 1. Please come to my office at 9 a.m. I will give you an in-depth orientation to Lake Valley and discuss the various company benefits available to you. You can also sign all the necessary employment documents.

Confirms important details

After lunch, Vanessa Jackson will take you to the medical records department and introduce you to your staff. I look forward to seeing you on February 1.

Explains first day's of routine to ease the new employee's uncertainty

Job-offer letters should be reviewed by legal experts familiar with employment law because they can be legally binding contracts.

Although messages like these are pleasant to write, they require careful planning and evaluation in order to avoid legal troubles. For instance, messages that imply lifetime employment or otherwise make promises about the length or conditions of employment can be interpreted as legally binding contracts, even if you never intended to make such promises. Similarly, downplaying potentially negative news (such as rumors of a takeover) that turns out to affect the hired person in a negative way can be judged as fraud. Consequently, experts advise that a company's legal staff either scrutinize each offer letter or create standardized content to use in such letters.[2]

Good-news announcements are usually communicated via a letter or a **news release**, also known as a *press release*, a specialized document used to share relevant information with the local or national news media. (News releases are also used to announce negative news, such as plant closings.) In most companies, news releases are usually prepared or at least supervised by specially trained writers in the public relations department. The content follows the customary pattern for a positive message: good news followed by details and a positive close. However, traditional news releases have a critical difference: You're not writing directly to the ultimate audience (such as the readers of a newspaper); you're trying to interest an editor or a reporter in a story, and that person will then write the material that is eventually read by the larger audience. To write a successful news release, keep the following points in mind:[3]

- Above all else, make sure your information is newsworthy and relevant to the specific publications or websites to which you are sending it. Editors are overwhelmed with news releases, and those without real news content are disposed of quickly—and can damage the writer's credibility, too.

- Focus on one subject; don't try to pack a single news release with multiple, unrelated news items.
- Put your most important idea first. Don't force editors to hunt for the news.
- Be brief: Break up long sentences and keep paragraphs short.
- Eliminate clutter, such as redundancy and extraneous facts.
- Be as specific as possible.
- Minimize self-congratulatory adjectives and adverbs; if the content of your message is newsworthy, the media professionals will be interested in the news on its own merits.
- Follow established industry conventions for style, punctuation, and format.

As with many other aspects of business communication, the process of creating and distributing news releases and other media materials is continually improved by technological advances. Online distribution systems such as PR Newswire and BusinessWire make it easy for even the smallest companies to reach editors and reporters at the most prominent publications around the world. Many companies also create special media pages on their websites that contain their latest news releases, company background information, and archives of past news releases.

Until recently, news releases were intended only for members of the news media and were crafted in a way to provide information to reporters who would then write their own articles if the subject matter was interesting to their readers. Thanks to the Internet, however, the nature of the news release is changing. Many companies now view it as general-purpose tool for communicating directly with customers and other audiences, creating *direct-to-consumer news releases* (see Figure 8.9). As new-media expert David Meerman Scott puts it, "Millions of people read press releases directly, unfiltered by the media. You need to be speaking directly to them."[4]

Fostering Goodwill

6 LEARNING OBJECTIVE

Describe the importance of goodwill messages and explain how to make them effective

All business messages should be written with an eye toward fostering goodwill among business contacts, but some messages are written primarily and specifically to build goodwill. You can use these messages to enhance your relationships with customers, colleagues, and other businesspeople by sending friendly—even unexpected—notes with no direct business purpose.

Effective goodwill messages must be sincere and honest. Otherwise, you'll appear to be interested in personal gain rather than in benefiting customers, fellow workers, or your organization. To come across as sincere, avoid exaggerating and back up any compliments with specific points. In addition, readers often regard more restrained praise as being more sincere. Consider the following example:

Goodwill is the positive feeling that encourages people to maintain a business relationship.

Make sure compliments are sincere and honest.

INSTEAD OF THIS

Words cannot express my appreciation for the great job you did. Thanks. No one could have done it better. You're terrific! You've made the whole firm sit up and take notice, and we are ecstatic to have you working here.

WRITE THIS

Thanks again for taking charge of the meeting in my absence and doing such an excellent job. With just an hour's notice, you managed to pull the legal and public relations departments together so that we could present a united front in the negotiations. Your dedication and communication abilities have been noted and are truly appreciated.

Sending Congratulations   One prime opportunity for sending goodwill messages is to congratulate individuals or companies for significant business achievements—perhaps for being promoted or for attaining product sales milestones (see Figure 8.10). Other reasons for sending congratulations include the highlights in people's personal lives, such as weddings, births, graduations, and success in nonbusiness competitions. You may congratulate business acquaintances on their own achievements or on the accomplishments of a family member. You may also take note of personal events, even if you don't know the reader well. If you're already friendly with the reader, a more personal tone is appropriate.

Taking note of significant events in someone's personal life helps cement a business relationship.

FIGURE 8.9 Announcing Positive News
Blogs have become a popular mechanism for announcing positive company news. Some companies even forgo the traditional news release in favor of controlling and distributing such messages themselves.

Congratulations can also be incorporated into promotional campaigns, such as when companies send messages to new parents or to recent homebuyers. Some companies even develop a mailing list of potential customers by assigning an employee to clip newspaper announcements of births, engagements, weddings, and graduations or to obtain information on real estate transactions in the local community. Then they introduce themselves by sending out a form letter that might read like this:

> Congratulations on your new home! All of us at Klemper Security Solutions hope it brings you and your family many years of security and happiness.
>
> Please accept the enclosed *Homeowner's Guide to Home Security* with our compliments. It lists a number of simple steps you can take to keep your home, your family, and your possessions safe.

This simple message has a natural, friendly tone, even though the sender has never met the recipient.

An effective message of appreciation documents a person's contributions.

Sending Messages of Appreciation   An important managerial quality is the ability to recognize the contributions of employees, colleagues, suppliers, and other associates. Your praise does more than just make the person feel good; it encourages further excellence. Moreover, a message of appreciation may become an important part of someone's personnel file. So when you write a message of appreciation, try to specifically mention the person

FIGURE 8.10   Congratulating Business Partners
Goodwill messages serve a variety of business functions. In this announcement, Business Objects congratulates several of its customers on achieving a level of excellence in *business intelligence* (the acquisition and application of information to business decisions).

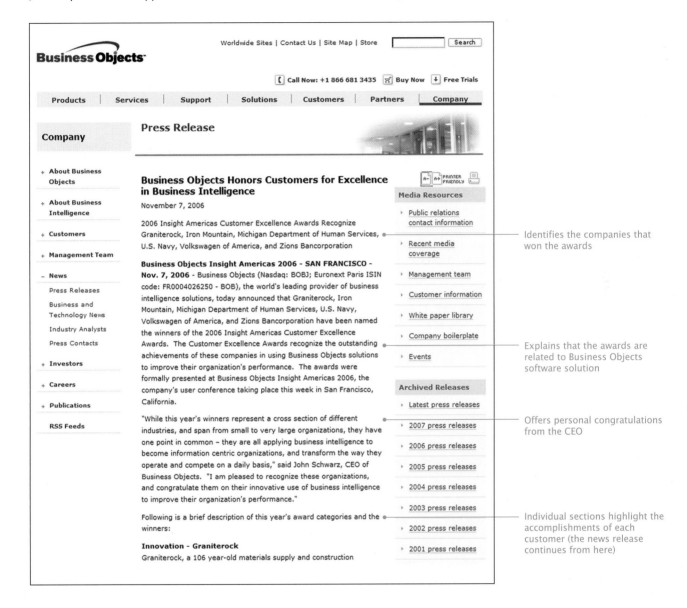

or people you want to praise. The brief message that follows expresses gratitude and reveals the happy result:

> Thank you and everyone on your team for the heroic efforts you took to bring our servers back up after last Friday's flood. We were able to restore business right on schedule first thing Monday morning. You went far beyond the level of contractual service in restoring our data center within 16 hours. I would especially like to highlight the contribution of networking specialist Julienne Marks, who worked for 12 straight hours to reconnect our Internet service. If I can serve as a reference in your future sales activities, please do not hesitate to ask.

Offering Condolences   In times of serious trouble and deep sadness, well-written condolences and expressions of sympathy can mean a great deal to people who've experienced loss. This type of message is difficult to write, but don't let the difficulty of the task keep you from responding promptly.

The primary purpose of condolence messages is to let the reader know that you and the organization you represent care about the person's loss.

CHECKLIST: Sending Goodwill Messages

- Be sincere and honest.
- Don't exaggerate or use vague, grandiose language; support positive statements with specific evidence.
- Use congratulatory messages to build goodwill with clients and colleagues.
- Send messages of appreciation to emphasize how much you value the work of others.
- When sending condolence messages, open with a brief statement of sympathy followed by an expression of how much the deceased person meant to you or your firm (as appropriate); close by offering your best wishes for the future.

REAL-TIME UPDATES
Learn More

Simple rules for writing effective thank-you notes

These tips are easy to adapt to any business or social occasions in which you need to express appreciation. Go to **http://real-timeupdates .com/bct** and click on "Learn More." If you are using mybcommlab, you can access Real-Time Updates within each chapter or under Student Study Tools.

Document Makeover

Improve This E-Mail Message

To practice correcting drafts of actual documents, visit the "Document Makeovers" section in either mybcommlab or the Companion Website for this text.

If mybcommlab is being used in your class, see your User Guide for specific instructions on how to access the content for this chapter. If you are accessing this feature through the Companion Website, click on "Document Makeovers" and then select Chapter 8. You will find an e-mail message that contains problems and errors related to what you've learned in this chapter about routine, good news, and goodwill messages. Use the Final Draft decision tool to create an improved version of this routine e-mail. Check the message for skilled presentation of the main idea, clarity of detail, appropriate use of resale, and the inclusion of a courteous close.

Open a condolence message with a brief statement of sympathy, such as "I am deeply sorry to hear of your loss" in the event of a death, for example. In the body, mention the good qualities or the positive contributions made by the deceased. State what the person meant to you or your colleagues. In closing, you can offer your condolences and your best wishes. Here are a few general suggestions for writing condolence messages:

- **Keep reminiscences brief.** Recount a memory or an anecdote (even a humorous one), but don't dwell on the details of the loss, lest you add to the reader's anguish.
- **Write in your own words.** Write as if you were speaking privately to the person. Don't quote "poetic" passages or use stilted or formal phrases. If the loss is a death, refer to it as such rather than as "passing away" or "departing."
- **Be tactful.** Mention your shock and dismay but remember that bereaved and distressed loved ones take little comfort in lines such as "Richard was too young to die" or "Starting all over again will be so difficult." Try to strike a balance between superficial expressions of sympathy and painful references to a happier past or the likelihood of a bleak future.
- **Take special care.** Be sure to spell names correctly and be accurate in your review of facts. Try to be prompt.
- **Write about special qualities of the deceased.** You may have to rely on reputation to do this, but let the grieving person know you valued his or her loved one.
- **Write about special qualities of the bereaved person.** A pat on the back helps a bereaved family member feel more confident about handling things during such a traumatic time.[5]

Supervisor George Bigalow sent the following condolence letter to his administrative assistant, Janice Case, after learning of the death of Janice's husband:

> My sympathy to you and your children. All your friends at Carter Electric were so very sorry to learn of John's death. Although I never had the opportunity to meet him, I do know how very special he was to you. Your tales of your family's camping trips and his rafting expeditions were always memorable.

To review the tasks involved in writing goodwill messages, see "Checklist: Sending Goodwill Messages." For the latest information on writing routine and positive messages, visit http://real-timeupdates.com/bct.

Communication Challenges at Get Satisfaction

After reading the many helpful responses you, as a representative of your company, posted on the Get Satisfaction website, Thor Muller invited you to join the Get Satisfaction team as a customer service specialist; your job is to communicate with the companies that use Get Satisfaction's online services. Take what you've learned in this chapter and put it to good use as you address the following challenges. (View some of the postings for various companies on **http://getsatisfaction.com** to get a feel for how the system works.)

Individual Challenge: When people are frustrated with a problem and are trying to discuss it via a lean medium such as online postings, emotions can sometimes boil over. You've been monitoring a conversation between a representative for one of the companies that uses Get Satisfaction and one of its customers. Over the past couple days, their online conversation has turned into an ugly argument, with accusations of incompetence and even dishonesty flying back and forth. Although the situation doesn't involve Get Satisfaction directly, you think it reflects poorly on your company—and it certainly isn't doing anybody any good to let this "flame war" keep raging. Write a brief post (which you can e-mail to your instructor) that acknowledges the frustration both sides are obviously feeling and offer to act as an intermediary to help get the problem resolved. Make up any information you need in order to complete the message.

Team Challenge: Get Satisfaction has just made available an upgrade to its website software in *beta release* form (a free version of software that companies encourage people to use as a way to see if anything needs to be changed or fixed before the official product is released). However, the company hasn't yet announced how much the new upgrade is going to cost when it is officially released, so not surprisingly, more than a few interested customers have written questions about the anticipated price. Small business owners in particular want to know if a less-expensive version (perhaps with

fewer features) will be available to small companies. When you asked your boss for help in answering this question, he suggested that you send the following response:

> To be as open and transparent about our pricing thinking as possible, I have to be up front: We can't speak to exact pricing yet, because we're still working on those details. We didn't want that to hold up release/use/testing of these new features, which is why we're releasing them on a "try first" beta basis right now, with the caveat that pricing will be a factor in the future for those companies who choose to continue using them.
>
> What we can say is that we are *very* committed to two things:
>
> 1) Making sure that it's a pricing structure that does in fact work both for small companies and large ones, and that if there is a tiered structure, that it scales according to a reliable set of figures/metrics that reflect those size differences.
>
> 2) Always offering a free version that has a minimum level of utility for those companies that can't for whatever reason pay.
>
> We're pretty excited about the new tools and the new functionality and want to see them spread as far and as wide as possible, so that's a significant consideration as we look to our pricing plan as well. But, you know, we've got to pay the bills somehow. :)
>
> Further updates as events warrant.[6]

This answer provides as much information as the company can release right now, but you think it can be more concise. (It is currently about 200 words.) In teams, as designated by your instructor, have each team member independently revise this message to make it no longer than 100 words. After everyone on the team has written a new draft, have each person share his or her version with the rest of the team. As a team, decide which version is best and then e-mail it to your instructor.

SUMMARY OF LEARNING OBJECTIVES

1 **Apply the three-step writing process to routine and positive messages.** Even though routine messages are usually short and simple, they benefit from the three-step writing process. Planning routine messages may take only a few moments to (1) analyze your purpose and audience, (2) investigate your readers' needs and make sure that you have all the facts to satisfy them, and (3) adapt your message to your audience through your choice of medium and your use of the "you" attitude. When writing routine messages, use the direct approach if your readers will be positive (or neutral) and have minimal cultural differences. Completing routine messages means making them as professional as possible by (1) revising for clarity and conciseness, (2) selecting appropriate design elements and delivery methods, and (3) carefully proofreading.

2 Outline an effective strategy for writing routine requests. When writing a routine request, open by stating your specific request. Avoid being abrupt or tactless: Pay attention to tone, assume that your audience will comply, avoid personal introductions, end polite requests with a period, and be specific. Use the middle of a routine request to justify your request and explain its importance. Close a routine request by asking for specific action (including a deadline, if possible) and expressing goodwill. Be sure to include all contact information so that your reader can respond easily.

3 Explain how to ask for specific action in a courteous manner. A courteous close contains three important elements: (1) a specific request, (2) information about how you can be reached (if it isn't obvious), and (3) an expression of appreciation or goodwill.

4 Describe a strategy for writing routine replies and positive messages. First, open your message with a clear and concise statement of the main idea or your good news. Second, in the body of your message, provide the details and explanations necessary to meet the audience's information needs. If your message has a mix of positive and negative information, try to put the negative news in a positive context. If you are communicating with customers, you can also use the body of the message to share marketing and customer relationship information. Third, end your message with a courteous close that indicates to your audience members that you have their best interests at heart.

5 Discuss the importance of knowing who is responsible when granting claims and requests for adjustment. Your response to a claim or a request for an adjustment can vary significantly, depending on which party you determine to be at fault. If your company is at fault, your message should acknowledge receipt of the customer's claim or complaint, take responsibility, sympathize with the customer, explain how you will resolve the situation, take steps to repair the relationship, and keep the lines of communication open. If the customer is at fault, you have to decide whether to grant the claim in the interest of keeping the customer's business. If a third party is at fault, your response will be determined by whatever arrangements are in place between your company and the third party.

6 Describe the importance of goodwill messages, and explain how to make them effective. Goodwill messages are important for building relationships with customers, colleagues, and other businesspeople. These friendly, unexpected notes have no direct business purpose, but they make people feel good about doing business with the sender. To make goodwill messages effective, make them honest and sincere. Avoid exaggerating, back up compliments with specific points, and give restrained praise.

PEARSON mybcommlab™

Log on to **www.mybcommlab.com** to access the following study and assessment aids associated with this chapter:

- Video applications
- Real-Time Updates
- Peer review activity
- Quick Learning Guides

- Pre/post test
- Personalized study plan
- Model documents
- Sample presentations

If you are not using mybcommlab, you can access the Real-Time Updates and Quick Learning Guides through **http://real-timeupdates.com/bct**. The Quick Learning Guide (located under "Learn More" on the website) hits all the high points of this chapter in just two pages. This guide, especially prepared by the authors, will help you study for exams or review important concepts whenever you need a quick refresher.

| Test Your Knowledge

1. When is a request routine?
2. What are three guidelines for asking a series of questions in a routine request?
3. What information should be included in a routine request?
4. Should you use the direct or indirect approach for most routine messages? Why?
5. Where in a routine message should you state your actual request?

6. How does a claim differ from an adjustment?
7. How does the question of fault affect what you say in a message granting a claim?
8. What is the appropriate strategy for responding to a request for a recommendation about a job candidate whose performance was poor?
9. How can you avoid sounding insincere when writing a goodwill message?
10. What are some of the guidelines for writing condolence messages?

Apply Your Knowledge

1. Why is it good practice to explain why replying to a request could benefit the reader?
2. The latest issue of a local business newspaper names 10 area executives who have exhibited excellent leadership skills in the past year. You are currently searching for a job, and a friend suggests that you write each executive a congratulatory letter and mention in passing that you are looking for new career opportunities and would appreciate the opportunity for an interview. Is this a smart strategy? Why or why not?
3. You've been asked to write a letter of recommendation for an employee who worked for you some years ago. You recall that the employee did an admirable job, but you can't remember any specific information at this point. Should you write the letter anyway? Explain.
4. Every time you send a direct-request e-mail message to Ted Jackson, who works in another department in your company, he delays or refuses to comply. You're beginning to get impatient. Should you send Jackson a memo to ask what's wrong? Complain to your supervisor about Jackson's uncooperative attitude? Arrange a face-to-face meeting with Jackson? Bring up the problem at the next staff meeting? Explain your answer.
5. **Ethical Choices** You have a complaint against one of your suppliers, but you have no documentation to back it up. Should you request an adjustment anyway? Why or why not?

Practice Your Knowledge

Messages for Analysis

Read the following messages and then (1) analyze the strengths and weaknesses of each sentence and (2) revise each document so that it follows this chapter's guidelines.

Message 8.A: Requesting Routine Information from a Business

I have recently arrived in Singapore to take up a job and would like to own a car but I keep hearing all kinds of acronyms related to car ownership and use which are absolutely confusing and frustrating. What on earth are COE and PARF? And what about CBD and ERP? It's all a complete mystery to me and I was hoping that if I wrote to you, the Land Transport Authority of Singapore, I would be able to get the information from the horse's mouth.

Message 8.B: Making Claims and Requests for Adjustment

I bought my Paulsons home theater system which includes an LCD flat screen, 42 inch television set, DVD player, and two speakers just last month at Kun Wah Electricals in Singapore. However, the second time I used the DVD player, the eject button jammed and my DVD got stuck inside the player. I took it back to Kun Wah but they said I should take it to the manufacturer. So I took my DVD player to your Paulsons factory for repairs thinking that since the set was still under warranty, I would not have to pay for anything. However, I was told that I had to pay for the replaced parts as the warranty did not cover parts replacement. This is ridiculous and indeed, shoddy

treatment of your customers. I'm writing to you now because I refuse to pay for any parts and I want my DVD set to be repaired and returned to me as soon as possible at no cost or I shall not be buying any more Paulsons stuff.

You can reply to me via e-mail at this same address. In the event that you cannot satisfy my request, I demand a full refund for the faulty set.

Message 8.C: Responding to Claims and Adjustment Requests When the Customer Is at Fault

I received your e-mail requesting free replacement of faulty parts for your Paulsons DVD player or a full refund. Actually I can't understand why the DVD got jammed so soon after you started using it. It could have happened because you pushed the "Stop" and "Eject" buttons at the same time but it could also be because you pushed one button after the other too quickly. Anyway I totally understand your frustration at being told that you had to pay for the replaced parts while your set was still under warranty. However, if you had read the fine print on the warranty card you would have noticed that it is indeed our policy to charge for replacement of faulty parts even when the set is under warranty.

Maybe the communication between you and our repairs people could have been handled better. Clearly, you're upset by what transpired between the two of you. But you must understand that we have no control over that because maintenance and repairs for Paulsons has long been outsourced to another company. You'll be happy to note nonetheless that just for this time around, we've decided to absorb the cost of the repairs even though faulty parts were replaced. You can collect your set when the repairs are done—they will call you.

Next time you operate the DVD set do remember the little tips I've given you about the "Stop" and "Eject" buttons just so you don't make the same mistake again.

Message 8.D: Letter of Recommendation

We received your e-mail requesting information about Chan Joo Khim. In case you're wondering why I'm replying to you instead of my boss, it's because I'm the Personnel Director for Zen Electronics and I have access to confidential information about all our staff. You will understand why I'm most equipped to answer your questions about Chan Joo Khim.

Generally I would say that Joo Khim was an above average employee in most areas of performance. He was in our employ from January 21, 2004, until early this year. During that period he was appraised for his performance at least four times and he generally received either an A or a B on all those occasions with A being a top score as you might have guessed. However, Joo Khim did take a fair bit of medical leave on occasion which was a bit odd for someone so young. He was also not very punctual to work in the mornings although he usually worked late in the evenings and delivered his work on schedule.

By and large, however, Chan Joo Khim was a good employee who could be entrusted with work.

Exercises

Active links for all websites in this chapter can be found online. If mybcommlab is being used in your class, see your User Guide for instructions on accessing the content for this chapter. Otherwise, visit **www.pearsonglobaleditions.com/bovee**, locate *Business Communication Today*, Tenth Edition, click the Companion Website link, select Chapter 8, and then click on "Featured Websites." Please note that links to sites that become inactive after publication of the book will be removed from the Featured Websites section.

8.1   **Revising Messages: Directness and Conciseness**   Revise the following short e-mail messages so that they are more direct and concise; develop a subject line for each revised message.

   a. I'm writing to you in response to your request last week via e-mail for a laptop computer and portable projector to be placed in the chosen venue in preparation for your seminar on cultural festivals in Singapore and Malaysia. We have noted your request and will be happy to provide the necessary equipment for your seminar. You also mentioned in your e-mail that you needed to have Internet access for this seminar. We have checked the cable points in the classroom and found that they are faulty. As such you will not be able to access the Internet during your seminar. For this reason, you may want to consider requesting a change of venue for your seminar. You can write in to the Estates Management Department of the university for this. After that, you may write another e-mail to us requesting the same equipment to be placed in the new venue.

   b. We appreciate your feedback regarding the inconvenience you experienced as a result of the mix-up in dates of your flight reservations from Singapore to Penang. We apologize for the error which happened due to a technical glitch in our online ticketing system. As you know, sometimes such errors are unavoidable. We understand that you missed your intended flight as a result of this and are upset with us. However, we have made a new reservation for you and we hope that you can still travel with Air Archipelago. To compensate you for the inconvenience caused we are giving you a 20% discount on your return ticket to Ho Chih Min city. Please e-mail us to say if you are agreeable to this arrangement.

   c. We're sorry for the delay in replying to you regarding the appointment you have sought with our Managing Director. Currently, we are rather busy with moving our office from Shenton Way in the heart of Singapore to our new premises in Sembawang in the northern part of the island. However, you will be happy to note that the Managing Director has been able to squeeze a few minutes in between moving to see you. How are you for a quick coffee at 10.30am on Friday this week? As it's Tuesday today, do get back to me by tomorrow so that we can fix the appointment.

   d. This is to inform all of you that starting next Monday coffee, tea, and biscuits will not be provided to staff at the mid-morning and mid-afternoon break times. We have been observing that a lot of times the coffee, tea, and biscuits served are wasted as staff prefer to bring or buy their own to suit their individual tastes. Instead we will be placing two large flasks of hot water in the pantry for anyone who might want to make his or her own tea or coffee.

8.2   **Revising Messages: Directness and Conciseness**   Rewrite the following sentences so that they are direct and concise. If necessary, break your answer into two sentences.

   a. We wanted to invite you to our special 40% off by-invitation-only sale; the sale is taking place on November 9.

   b. We wanted to let you know that we are giving a tote bag and a voucher for five iTunes downloads with every $50 donation you make to our radio station.

   c. The director planned to go to the meeting that will be held on Monday at a little before 11 a.m.

   d. In today's meeting, we were happy to have the opportunity to welcome Paul Eccelson, who reviewed the shopping cart function on our website and offered some great advice; if you have any questions about these new forms, feel free to call him at his office.

8.3   **Internet**   Visit the Workplace eCards section of the Blue Mountain site, at **www.bluemountain.com**, and analyze one of the electronic greeting cards bearing a goodwill message of appreciation for good performance. Under what circumstances would you send this electronic message? How could you personalize it for the recipient and the occasion? What would be an appropriate close for this message?

8.4   **Teamwork**   With another student, identify the purpose and select the most appropriate medium for communicating the following written messages. Next, consider how the audience is likely to respond to each message. Based on this audience analysis, determine whether the direct or indirect approach would be effective for each message and explain your reasoning.

   a. A notice to all employees about the placement of recycling bins by the elevator doors

   b. The first late-payment notice to a good customer who usually pays his bills on time

8.5   **Revising Messages: Conciseness, Courteousness, and Specificity**   Critique the following closing paragraphs. How would you rewrite each to be concise, courteous, and specific?

   a. I need your response sometime soon so I can order the parts in time for your service appointment. Otherwise, your air-conditioning system may not be in tip-top condition for the start of the summer season.

   b. Thank you in advance for sending me as much information as you can about your products. I look forward to receiving your package in the very near future.

   c. To schedule an appointment with one of our knowledgeable mortgage specialists in your area, you can always call our hotline at 1-800-555-8765. This is also the number to call if you have more questions about mortgage rates, closing procedures, or any other aspect of the mortgage process. Remember, we're here to make the home-buying experience as painless as possible.

8.6 **Ethical Choices** Your company markets a line of automotive accessories for people who like to "tune" their cars for maximum performance. A customer has just written a furious e-mail, claiming that a supercharger he purchased from your website didn't deliver the extra engine power he expected. Your company has a standard refund process to handle situations such as this, and you have the information you need to inform the customer about that. You also have information that could help the customer find a more compatible supercharger from one of your competitors, but the customer's e-mail message is so abusive that you don't feel obligated to help. Is this an appropriate response? Why or why not?

Expand Your Knowledge

Exploring the Best of the Web

Recommended Advice for Recommendation Letters

http://businessmajors.about.com
Whether you're continuing on to graduate school or entering the workforce with your undergraduate degree, recommendation letters could play an important role in the next few steps of your career. From selecting the people to ask for recommendation letters to knowing what makes an effective letter, About.com extends the advice offered in this chapter with real-life examples and suggestions. Visit About.com's Business Majors website and click on "Recommendation Letters." Read the advice you find and answer the following questions:

1. What is a good process for identifying the best people to ask for recommendation letters?
2. What information should you provide to letter writers to help them produce credible and compelling letters on your behalf?
3. What are the most common mistakes you need to avoid with recommendation letters?

Sharpening Your Career Skills Online

Bovée and Thill's Business Communication Web Search, at http://businesscommunicationblog.com/websearch, is a unique research tool designed specifically for business communication research. Use the Web Search function to find a website, video, PDF document, podcast, or PowerPoint presentation that offers advice on writing goodwill messages such as thank-you notes or congratulatory letters. Write a brief e-mail message to your instructor, describing the item that you found and summarizing the career skills information you learned from it.

CASES

Applying the Three-Step Writing Process to Cases

Apply each step to the following cases, as assigned by your instructor.

ROUTINE REQUESTS

E-MAIL SKILLS

1. Breathing life back into your biotech career: E-mail requesting a recommendation. After five years of work in the human resources department at Cell Genesys (a company that is developing cancer treatment drugs), you were laid off in a round of cost-cutting moves that rippled through the biotech industry in recent years. The good news is that you found stable employment in the grocery distribution industry. The bad news is that in the three years since you left Cell Genesys, you have truly missed working in the exciting biotechnology field and having the opportunity to be a part of something as important as helping people recover from life-threatening diseases. You know that careers in biotech are uncertain, but you have a few dollars in the bank now, and you're willing to ride that rollercoaster again.

Your task: Draft an e-mail to Calvin Morris, your old boss at Cell Genesys, reminding him of the time you worked together and asking him to write a letter of recommendation for you.[7]

IM SKILLS

2. Trans-global exchange: Instant message request for information from Chinese manufacturer. Thank goodness your company, Diagonal Imports, chose the Sametime enterprise instant messaging software produced by IBM Lotus. Other products also allow you to carry on real-time exchanges with colleagues on the other side of the planet, but Sametime supports bidirectional machine translation, and you're going to need it.

The problem is that production on a popular line of decorative lighting appliances produced at your Chinese manufacturing plant inexplicably came to a halt last month. As the product manager in the United States, you have many resources you could call on to help, such as new sources for faulty parts. But you can't do anything if you don't know the details. You've tried telephoning top managers in China, but they're evasive, telling you only what they think you want to hear.

Finally, your friend Kuei-chen Tsao has returned from a business trip. You met her during your trip to China last year. She doesn't speak English, but she's the line engineer responsible for this particular product: a fiber-optic lighting display that features a plastic base with a rotating color wheel. As the wheel turns, light emitted from the spray of fiber-optic threads changes color in soothing patterns. Product #3347XM is one of Diagonal's most popular items, and you have orders from novelty stores around the United States waiting to be filled. Kuei-chen should be able to explain the problem, determine whether you can help, and tell you how long before regular shipping resumes.

Your task: Write the first of what you hope will be a productive instant message exchange with Kuei-chen. Remember that your words will be machine translated.[8]

TEXT MESSAGING SKILLS

3. Tracking the new product buzz: Text message to colleagues at a trade show. The vast Consumer Electronics Show (CES) is the premier promotional event in the industry. More than 130,000 industry insiders from all over the world come to see the exciting new products on display from nearly 1,500 companies—everything from video game gadgets to Internet-enabled refrigerators with built-in computer screens. You've just stumbled on a video game controller that has a built-in webcam to allow networked gamers to see and hear each other while they play. Your company also makes game controllers, and you're worried that your customers will flock to this new controller-cam. You need to know how much buzz is circulating around the show: Have people seen it? What are they saying about it? Are they excited about it?

Your task: Compose a text message to your colleagues at the show, alerting them to the new controller-cam and asking them to listen for any buzz it might be generating among the attendees at the Las Vegas Convention Center and the several surrounding hotels where the show takes place. Here's the catch: Your text-messaging service limits messages to 160 characters, including spaces and punctuation, so your message can't be any longer than this.[9]

4. Step on it: Letter to Floorgraphics requesting information about underfoot advertising. You work for Alberta Greenwood, owner of Better Bike and Ski Shop. Yesterday, Alberta met with the Schwinn sales representative, Tom Beeker, who urged her to sign a contract with Floorgraphics. That company leases floor space from retail stores and creates and sells floor ads to manufacturers such as Schwinn. Floorgraphics will pay Alberta a fee for leasing the floor space, as well as a percentage for every ad it sells. Alberta was definitely interested and turned to you after Beeker left.

"Tom says that advertising decals on the floor in front of the product reach consumers right where they're standing when making a decision," explained Alberta. "He says the ads increase sales from 25 to 75 percent."

You both look down at the dusty floor, and Alberta laughs. "It seems funny that manufacturers will pay hard cash to put their names where customers are going to track dirt all over them! But if Tom's telling the truth, we could profit three ways: from the leasing fee, the increased sales of products being advertised, and the share in ad revenues. That's not so funny."

Your task: Alberta Greenwood asks you to write a letter for her signature to CEO Richard Rebh at Floorgraphics, Inc. (5 Vaughn Dr., Princeton, NJ 08540) asking for financial details and practical information about the ads. For example, how will you clean your floors? Who installs and removes the ads? Can you terminate the lease if you don't like the ads?[10]

E-MAIL SKILLS

5. Sour note: Requesting a refund for repeated service outages. Love at first listen is the only way to describe the way you felt when you discovered SongThrong.com. You enjoy dozens of styles of music, from Afrobeat and Tropicalia to mainstream pop and the occasional blast of industrial metal, and SongThrong.com has them all for only $9.99 a month. You can explore every genre imaginable, listening to as many tracks as you like for a fixed monthly fee. The service sounded too good to be true—and sadly, it was. The service was so unreliable that you began keeping note of when it was unavailable. Last month, it was down for all or part of 12 days—well over a third of the month. As much as you like it, you've had enough.

Your task: Write an e-mail to support@songthrong.com, requesting a full refund. To get the $9.99 monthly rate, you prepaid for an entire year ($119.88), and you've been a subscriber for two months now. You know the service has been out for at least part of time on 12 separate days last month, and while you didn't track outages during the first month, you believe it was about the same number of days.

6. Unhappy customer: Claim letter requesting an adjustment. As a consumer, you've probably bought something that didn't work right or paid for a service that did not turn out the way you expected. Maybe it was a pair of jeans with a rip in a seam that you didn't find until you got home or a watch that broke a week after you bought it. Or maybe your family hired a lawn service to do some yard work—and no one from the company showed up on the day promised; and when the gardeners finally appeared, they did not do what they'd been hired for but did other things that wound up damaging valuable plants.

Your task: Choose an incident from your own experience and write a claim letter, asking for a refund, repair, replacement, or other adjustment. You'll need to include all the details of the transaction, plus your contact address and phone number. If you can't think of such an experience, make up details for an imaginary situation. If your experience is real, you might want to mail the letter. The reply you receive will provide a good test of your claim-writing skills.

E-MAIL SKILLS

7. A juicy position: E-mail requesting information about careers at Jamba Juice. You did not expect to find a job while working out at 24-Hour Fitness, but you're willing to explore an opportunity when it appears. As you were buying a smoothie at the Jamba Juice bar inside the gym, you overheard the manager talking about the company's incentives for employees, especially those interested in becoming managers. You ask her about it, and she suggests you log on to the company's website (www.jambajuice.com) for more information.

You're still in business school, and you need a part-time job. Finding one at a company that offers a good future after graduation would be even better than simply earning some money to keep you going now. You check the Jamba Juice website. You discover that the juice-bar chain has created a good reputation in the health, fitness, and nutrition industry. Also, you can submit your résumé online for an entry-level job. That sounds promising. If you could start now while finishing your degree, you'd be in a prime spot for promotion once you graduate. You start to wonder if Jamba Juice could be a long-term career opportunity.

Your task: Write an e-mail message requesting additional information about careers and advancement at Jamba Juice. First, visit www.jambajuice.com to learn all that you can about the company; then compose your message. Specifically, ask for information about career long-term advancement beyond the store level, to corporate management. You might want to mention that you're still in school, studying business (make up any details you need).[11]

E-MAIL SKILLS

8. Streamlining Arabian Fun Fair (AFF) Company Business. Arabian Fun Fair (AFF) Co. has been a well-established name in the movie and game rental business in Egypt, Jordan, Lebanon, and some of the Gulf Cooperation Council (GCC) countries, with its headquarter at Beirut. Over the last 10 years the company has established more than 800 retail outlets in the region. Two years back, Hamdi Affendi took over as the area manager of Oman (Jordan), having more than 100 retail outlets. To improve the cash inflows of the outlets, on his own initiative, he started a paradigm shift in the business strategy of the company. In each retail outlet he introduced new display counters for computer peripherals, tie-in toys, and children's dry and edible attractions like candy, potato chips, comic magazines, and so forth. His intention was to diversify the core business of movie and game rentals. To implement the expansive business strategy, he diverted company funds to increase the warehousing and inventory capacity of the company. Consequently, the actual business of the company was adversely affected, which prompted the company higher-ups to move in to rectify the situation. Ammar Barakati, the marketing general manager, flew in to Oman from Beirut. In view of the seriousness of the situation, Mr. Barakati immediately suspended Mr. Affendi.

Because you are the deputy manager of the Oman office, Mr. Barakati called you and asked you to take charge of the business, and instructed you to concentrate on the core business of the company. He also instructed you to write an e-mail message to all the retail managers in your area to get feedback on whether major cash inflow sources are from movies and game rentals, movies and game sales, or peripherals like candy bars and so forth. Mr. Barakati has given you 10 days to prepare a comprehensive report based on the feedback of all the retail outlets to improve the company business in your region.

Your task: Draft a comprehensive e-mail addressed to all retail managers informing them about the change in the administrative setup and incorporating the instructions given by Mr. Barakati. The e-mail should have a comprehensive questionnaire so that the feedback is consistent and useful.

ROUTINE MESSAGES

BLOGGING SKILLS

9. Here's how it will work: Explaining the brainstorming process. Austin, Texas, advertising agency GSD&M Advertising brainstorms new advertising ideas using a process it calls *dynamic collaboration*. A hand-picked team of insiders and outsiders is briefed on the project and given a key question or two to answer. The team members then sit down at computers and anonymously submit as many responses as they can within five minutes. The project moderators then pore over these responses, looking for any sparks that can ignite new ways of understanding and reaching out to consumers.

Your task: For these brainstorming sessions, GSD&M recruits an eclectic mix of participants from inside and outside the agency—figures as diverse as economists and professional video gamers. To make sure everyone understands the brainstorming guidelines, prepare a message to be posted on the project blog. In your own words, convey the following four points as clearly and succinctly as you can:

- **Be yourself.** We want input from as many perspectives as possible, which is why we recruit such a diverse array of participants. Don't try to get into what you believe is the mind-set of an advertising specialist; we want you to approach the given challenge using whatever analytical and creative skills you normally employ in your daily work.
- **Create, don't edit.** Don't edit, refine, or self-censor while you're typing during the initial five-minute session. We don't care if your ideas are formatted beautifully, phrased poetically, or even spelled correctly. Just crank 'em out as quickly as you can.
- **It's about the ideas, not the participants.** Just so you know up front, all ideas are collected anonymously. We can't tell who submitted the brilliant ideas, the boring ideas, or the already-tried-that ideas. So while you won't get personal credit, you can also be crazy and fearless. Go for it!
- **The winning ideas will be subjected to the toughest of tests.** Just in case you're worried about submitting ideas that could be risky, expensive, or difficult to implement—don't fret. As we narrow down the possibilities, the few that remain will be judged, poked, prodded, and assessed from every angle. In other words, let us worry about containing the fire; you come up with the sparks.[12]

PODCASTING SKILLS   PORTFOLIO BUILDER

10. Listening to business: Using the iPod to train employees. As a training specialist in Winnebago Industry's human resources department, you're always on the lookout for new ways to help employees learn vital job skills. While watching a production worker page through a training manual while learning how to assemble a new recreational vehicle, you get what seems to be a great idea: Record the assembly instructions as audio files that workers can listen to while performing the necessary steps. With audio instructions, they wouldn't need to keep shifting their eyes between the product and the manual—and constantly losing their place. They could focus on the product and listen for each instruction. Plus, the new system wouldn't cost much at all; any computer can record the audio files, and you'd simply make them available on an intranet site for download into iPods or other digital music players.

Your task: You immediately run your new idea past your boss, who has heard about podcasting but doesn't think it has any place in business. He asks you to prove the viability of the idea by recording a demonstration. Choose a process that you engage in yourself—anything from replacing the strings on a guitar to sewing a quilt to changing the oil in a car—and write a brief (one page or less) description of the process that could be recorded as an audio file. Think carefully about the limitations of the audio format as a replacement for printed text (for instance, do you need to tell people to pause the audio while they perform a time-consuming task?). If directed by your instructor, record your instructions as a podcast.

PORTFOLIO BUILDER

11. Got it covered? Letter from American Express about SUV rentals. You can always tell when fall arrives at American Express—you are deluged with complaints from customers who have just received their summer vacation bills. Often these angry calls are about a shock-inducing damage repair bill from a car rental agency. Vacation car rentals can be a lot more complicated than most people think. Here's what happens.

Your credit card customers are standing at the Hertz or Avis counter, ready to drive away, when the agent suggests an upgrade to, say, a Ford Expedition or another large SUV. Feeling happy-go-lucky on vacation, your customers say, "Why not?" and hand over their American Express card.

As they drive off in large vehicles that many are unaccustomed to handling, 9 out of 10 are unaware that the most common accidents among rental cars take place at low speeds in parking lots. Plus, the upgraded vehicle they're driving is no longer fully covered either by their regular auto insurance or by the secondary car rental insurance they expect from American Express. If they've agreed to pay the additional $10 to $25 a day for the car rental agency's "collision and liability damage waiver fee," they will be able to walk away from any accident with no liability. Otherwise, they're running a costly risk.

Soon they pull into a shopping mall with the kids to pick up the forgotten sunscreen and sodas, where they discover that luxury road-warrior mobile is not so easy to park in stalls designed in the 1970s and 1980s, when compact cars were all the rage. *Thwack*—there goes the door panel. *Crunch*—a rear bumper into a light post. *Wham!* There goes the family bank account, but they don't realize it yet—not until they receive the bill from the rental agency, the one that comes *after* their auto insurance and credit card companies have already paid as much as they're going to pay for damages.

Auto insurers typically provide the same coverage for rentals as you carry on your own car. When customers use their credit card to pay for car rentals, American Express offers secondary protection that generally covers any remaining, unpaid damages. But there are important exceptions. Neither insurance nor credit card companies will pay the "loss of vehicle use fees" that car rental agencies always tack on. These fees can run into thousands of dollars, based on the agency's revenue losses while the car is in the repair shop. When your customers are billed for this fee, they invariably call you, angrily demanding to know why American Express won't pay it. And if they've rented an SUV, they're even angrier.

American Express Green and Gold cards provide secondary coverage up to $55,000, and the Platinum card extends that to $75,000. But large SUVs such as the Ford Expedition, the GMC Yukon, and the Chevrolet Suburban are not covered at all. Such exclusions are common. For instance, Diners Club specifically excludes "high-value, special interest or exotic cars"—such as the Ferraris, Maseratis, and even Rolls Royces that are urged on customers by rental agencies.

Your task: As assistant vice president of customer service, you'd like to keep the phone lines cooler this summer and fall. It's April, so there's still time. Write a form letter to be sent to all American Express customers, urging them to check their rental car coverages, advising them against renting vehicles that are larger than they really require, and encouraging them to consider paying the rental agency's daily loss waiver fees.[13]

BLOGGING SKILLS   PORTFOLIO BUILDER

12. Now hear this: Not-so-subtle request from the boss for better listening skills. You are normally an easygoing manager who gives your employees a lot of leeway in using their own personal communication styles. However, the weekly staff meeting this morning pushed you over the edge. People were interrupting one another, asking questions that had already been answered, sending text messages during presentations, and exhibiting just about every other poor listening habit imaginable.

Your task: Review the advice in Chapter 2 on good listening skills and then write a post for the internal company blog. Emphasize the importance of effective listening and list at least five steps your employees can take to become better listeners.

E-MAIL SKILLS   PORTFOLIO BUILDER

13. Temper, temper: E-mail to Metro Power employees about technology failures. This is the third time in two months that your company, Metro Power, has had to escort an employee from the building after a violent episode. Frankly, everyone is a little frightened by this development. As a human resources administrator, you have the unhappy task of trying to quell the storm.

Metro Power rarely fires employees, preferring to transfer them to new responsibilities, which may either draw out their finer points (and prove better for everyone in the long run) or help them decide to seek greener pastures. But in three cases, you had no choice. In one incident, a man punched out his computer screen after the system failed. In another, a man threw his keyboard across the room when he couldn't get access to the company's intranet. And in a third incident, a woman kicked a printer while screaming obscenities.

In all three cases, co-workers were terrified by these sudden outbursts. Too many disgruntled workers have committed too many violent acts against others in recent years; and whenever workers lose their temper on the job these days, it causes great fear—not to mention financial losses from the destruction of property and the disruption of workflow.

People are on edge at Metro Power right now. Rising energy costs, public and government scrutiny, and cries of price gouging are causing additional work and stress for all your employees. Plus, too much overtime, unrealistic expectations for overworked departments, and high demands on sensitive equipment are contributing to the problem. Tempers are frayed, and nerves strained. You're concerned that these three incidents are just the tip of the iceberg.

Your department head suggests that you write a reminder to all employees about controlling tempers in the workplace. "Tell them that technology glitches are commonplace and not some unholy disaster. And remind them to report routine computer failures to Bart Stone. He'll get to them in due course."

You say nothing to contradict her idea, but you wonder how to do what she asks without sounding trite or condescending. You don't want to sound like some nagging parent; if you do, no one will pay attention to your message. You sigh deeply as your boss strolls calmly back to her office. You're fairly certain that every employee already knows about reporting computer failures to Bart Stone, assistant director of information services.

Even so, you can think of a few suggestions that might be helpful, such as taking a walk to cool down and recognizing that machines, like humans, are not infallible. You want cooler heads to prevail, but that's just the sort of cliché you'd like to avoid in your message.

Your task: Write the e-mail message to all employees. Instead of uttering platitudes or wagging your finger, include preventive maintenance tips for office equipment, such as turning off systems at night, keeping food and liquids away from keyboards, making use of dusting sprays and special cloths, and so on. Your boss also asked you to make it clear that abusive behavior will be reprimanded, so include that point in a tactful way.[14]

ROUTINE REPLIES

E-MAIL SKILLS   PORTFOLIO BUILDER

14. Window shopping at Wal-Mart: Offering advice to the webmaster. Wal-Mart has grown to international success because it rarely fails to capitalize on a marketing scheme, and its website is no exception. To make sure the website remains effective and relevant, the webmaster asks various people to check out the site and give their feedback. As administrative assistant to Wal-Mart's director of marketing, you have just received a request from the webmaster to visit Wal-Mart's website and give your feedback.

Your task: Visit www.walmart.com and do some online "window shopping." As you browse through the site, consider the language, layout, graphics, and overall ease of use. In particular, look for aspects of the site that might be confusing or frustrating—annoyances that could prompt shoppers to abandon their quests and head to a competitor such as Target. Summarize your findings and recommendations in an e-mail message to the webmaster.

15. The special courier: Letter of recommendation for an old friend. In today's mail, you get a letter from Non-Stop Messenger Service, 899 Sparks St., Ottawa, Ontario K1A 0G9, Canada. It concerns a friend of yours who has applied for a job. Here is the letter:

Kathryn Norquist has applied for the position of special courier with our firm, and she has given us your name as a reference. Our special couriers convey materials of considerable value or confidentiality to their recipients. It is not an easy job. Special couriers must sometimes remain alert for periods of up to 20 hours, and they cannot expect to follow the usual "three square meals and a full night's sleep" routine because they often travel long distances on short notice. On occasion, a special courier must react quickly and decisively to threatening situations.

For this type of work, we hire only people of unquestioned integrity, as demonstrated both by their public records and by references from people, like you, who have known them personally or professionally.

We would appreciate a letter from you, supplying detailed answers to the following questions: (1) How long and in what circumstances have you known the applicant? (2) What qualities does she possess that would qualify her for the position of special courier? (3) What qualities might need to be improved before she is put on permanent assignment in this job?

As vice president of human resources at UPS, you know how much weight a strong personal reference can carry, and you don't really mind that Kathryn never contacted you for permission to list your name—that's Kathryn. You met her during your sophomore year at San Diego State University—that would have been 1994—and you two were roommates for several years after. Her undergraduate degree was in journalism, and her investigative reporting was relentless. You have never known anyone who could match Kathryn's stamina when she was on a story. Of course, when she was between stories, she could sleep longer and do less than anyone else you have ever known.

After a few years of reporting, Kathryn went back to school and earned her MBA from the University of San Diego. After that, you lost track of her for a while. Somebody said that she had joined the FBI—or was it the CIA?—you never really knew. You received a couple of postcards from Paris and one from Madrid.

Two years ago, you met Kathryn for dinner. Only in town for the evening, she was on her way to Borneo to "do the text" for a photographer friend of hers who worked for *National Geographic*. You read the article last year on the shrinking habitat for orangutans. It was powerful.

Although you're in no position to say much about Kathryn's career accomplishments, you can certainly recommend her energy and enthusiasm, her ability to focus on a task or an assignment, her devotion to ethics, and her style. She always seems unshakable—organized, thorough, and honorable—whether digging into political corruption or trudging the jungles of Borneo. You're not sure that her free spirit would flourish in a courier's position, and you wonder if she is a bit overqualified for the job. But knowing Kathryn, you're confident she wouldn't apply for a position unless she truly wanted it.

Your task: Supplying any details you can think of, write as supportive a letter as possible about your friend Kathryn to Roscoe de la Penda, Human Resources Specialist, Non-Stop Messenger.

E-MAIL SKILLS

16. Red dirt to go: Positive e-mail reply from Paradise Sportswear. As the owner of Paradise Sportswear in Hawaii, Robert Hedin was nearly done in by Hurricane Iniki in 1992, which wiped out his first silk-screened and airbrushed T-shirt business. He tried again, but then Hawaii's red dirt started seeping into his warehouse and ruining his inventory. Finally, a friend suggested that he stop trying to fight Mother Nature. Hedin took the hint: He mortgaged his condo and began producing Red Dirt Shirts, all made with dye created from the troublesome local dirt.

Bingo. Hedin's Red Dirt Sportswear designs are so popular, they're being snapped up by locals and tourists in Hedin's eight Paradise Sportswear retail outlets and in every Kmart on the islands. Hedin even added a new line, Lava Blues, made with real Hawaiian lava rock.

"You can make 500 shirts with a bucket of dirt," grins Hedin as he shows you around the operation on your first day. He's just a few years away from the usual retirement age, but he looks like a kid who's finally found the right playground.

Recently, Hedin decided to capitulate to all the requests he's received from retail outlets on the mainland. Buyers kept coming to the islands on vacation, discovering Hedin's "natural" sportswear, and begging him to set up a deal. For a long time, his answer was no; he simply couldn't handle the extra work. But now he's hired you.

As special sales representative, you'll help Hedin expand slowly into this new territory, starting with one store. Wholesaling to the local Kmarts is easy enough, but handling all the arrangements for shipping to the mainland would be too much for the current staff. So you'll start with the company Hedin has chosen to become the first mainland retailer to sell Red Dirt and Lava Blues sportswear: Surf's Up in Chicago, Illinois—of all places. The boss figures that with less competition than he'd find on either coast, his island-influenced sportswear will be a big hit in Chicago, especially in the dead of winter.

Your task: Write a positive response to the e-mail received from Surf's Up buyer Ronald Draeger, who says he fell in love with the Paradise clothing concept while on a surfing trip to Maui. Let him know he'll have a temporary exclusive and that you'll be sending a credit application and other materials by snail mail. His e-mail address is surfsup@insnet.com.[15]

E-MAIL SKILLS

17. Auto-talk: E-mail messages for Highway Bytes computers to send automatically. You are director of customer services at Highway Bytes, which markets a series of small, handlebar-mounted computers for bicyclists. These Cycle Computers do everything, from computing speed and distance traveled to displaying street maps. Serious cyclists love them, but your company is growing so fast that you can't keep up with all the customer service requests you receive every day. Your boss wants not only to speed up response time but also to reduce staffing costs and allow your technical experts the time they need to focus on the most difficult and important questions.

You've just been reading about automated response systems, and you quickly review a few articles before discussing the options with your boss. Artificial intelligence researchers have been working for decades to design systems that can actually converse with customers, ask questions, and respond to requests. Some of today's systems have vocabularies of thousands of words and the ability to understand simple sentences. For example, *chatterbots* are automated bots that can actually mimic human conversation. (You can see what it's like to carry on a conversation with some of these bots by visiting www.botspot.com, clicking on Artificial Life Bots, and then selecting Chatterbots.)

Unfortunately, even though chatterbots hold a lot of promise, human communication is so complex that a truly automated customer service agent could take years to perfect (and may even prove to be impossible). However, the simplest automated systems are called *autoresponders*, or *on-demand e-mail*. They are fast and extremely inexpensive. They have no built-in intelligence, so they do nothing more than send back the same reply to every message they receive.

You explain to your boss that although some of the messages you receive require the attention of your product specialists, many are simply requests for straightforward information. In fact, the customer service staff already answers some 70 percent of e-mail queries with three ready-made attachments:

- **Installing Your Cycle Computer.** This attachment gives customers advice on installing the cycle computer the first time or reinstalling it on a new bike. In most cases, the computer and wheel sensor bolt directly to the bike without modification, but certain bikes do require extra work.
- **Troubleshooting Your Cycle Computer.** This attachment provides a step-by-step guide to figuring out what might be wrong with a malfunctioning cycle computer. Most problems are simple, such as dead batteries or loose wires, but others are beyond the capabilities of your typical customer.
- **Upgrading the Software in Your Cycle Computer.** This attachment tells customers how to attach the cycle computer to their home or office PC and download new software from Highway Bytes.

Your boss is enthusiastic when you explain that you can program your current e-mail system to look for specific words in incoming messages and then respond, based on what it finds. For example, if a customer message contains the word *installation*, you can program the system to reply with the *Installing Your Cycle Computer* attachment. This reconfigured system should be able to handle a sizable portion of the hundreds of e-mails your customer service group gets every week.

Your task: First, draft a list of keywords that you want your e-mail system to look for. You need to be creative and spend some time with a thesaurus. Identify all the words and word combinations that could identify a message as pertaining to one of the three subject areas. For instance, the word *attach* would probably indicate a need for the installation material, whereas *new software* would most likely suggest a need for the upgrade attachment.

Second, draft three short e-mail messages, one to accompany each of the ready-made attachments, explaining that the attached document answers the most common questions on a particular subject (installation, troubleshooting, or upgrading). Your messages should invite recipients to write back if the attached document doesn't solve the problem—and don't forget to provide the e-mail address: support2@highwaybytes.com.

Third, draft a fourth message to be sent out whenever your new system is unable to figure out what the customer is asking for. Simply thank the customer for writing and explain that the query will be passed on to a customer service specialist who will respond shortly.

E-MAIL SKILLS

18. Lighten up: E-mail reply to a website designer at Organizers Unlimited. When Kendra Williams, owner of Organizers Unlimited, wanted to create a website to sell her Superclean Organizer, she asked you, her assistant, to find a designer. After some research, you found three promising individuals. Williams chose Pete Womack, whose résumé impressed both of you. Now he's e-mailed his first design proposal, and Williams is not happy.

"I detest cluttered websites!" she explodes. "This homepage has too many graphics and animations, too much 'dancing baloney.' He must have included at least a megabyte of bouncing cotton balls and jogging soap bars! Clever, maybe, but we don't want it! If the homepage takes too long to load, our customers won't wait for it, and we'll lose sales."

Williams's dislike of clutter is what inspired her to invent the Superclean Organizer in the first place, a neat device for organizing bathroom items.

Your task: "You found him," says Williams. "Now you can answer and tell him what's wrong with this design." Before you write the e-mail reply to Womack explaining the need for a simpler homepage, read some of the articles offering tips at www.sitepoint.com. On the homepage, under "Before You Code," select "Site Planning." Under "Design and Layout," select "Design Principles." Use the ideas you find to support your message.[16]

E-MAIL SKILLS

19. Recommending a Talented Person. Altavista is a famous tourist travel company with its headquarters in Islamabad, Pakistan. Its regional office in Cairo, Egypt, is headed by you. You strongly believe in public relations for business promotion. Today, you had a happy surprise when you received an e-mail from one of your prominent female customers, Mrs. Salma Sallami, to whom you recently provided business services. Salma runs a boutique business in Alexandria, Egypt, for bridal and party dresses. Salma is opening a new branch in the posh area of Cairo. She has asked if you could recommend a talented woman to be manager of her new outlet in Cairo.

Through your business contacts, you happen to know Miss Arouba personally, whom you consider the right person for the job. In reply to Salma's e-mail, you are happy to recommend Miss Arouba after getting her consent. As an introduction, you could mention in the e-mail how she has been successfully managing an international boutique for the last two years. She is a well-educated and well-groomed person and fluent in French, English, and Arabic. In visits to her boutique you found that she is quick, friendly, and good at sizing up a customer's preferences.

Your task: Write an e-mail reply to Salma, recommending Miss Arouba to her for the manager position for the new branch in Cairo. Also mention her personality, drive, and business acumen, which could be further explored in an interview with her.

20. Impressive trainee: Letter of recommendation for a top-notch intern. As a project manager at Orbitz, one of the largest online travel services in the world, you've seen plenty of college interns in action. However, few have impressed you as much as Maxine "Max" Chenault. For one thing, she learned how to navigate the company's content management system virtually overnight and always used it properly, whereas other interns sometimes left things in a hopeless mess. She asked lots of intelligent questions about the business. You've been teaching her blogging and website design principles, and she's picked them up rapidly. Moreover, she is always on time, professional, and eager to assist. Also, she didn't mind doing mundane tasks.

On the downside, Chenault is a popular student. Early on, you often found her busy on the phone planning her many social activities when you needed her help. However, after you had a brief talk with her, this problem vanished.

You'll be sorry to see Chenault leave when she returns to school in the fall, but you're pleased to respond when she asks you for a letter of recommendation. She's not sure where she'll apply for work after graduation or what career path she'll choose, so she asks you to keep the letter fairly general.

Your task: Working with a team of your classmates, discuss what should and should not be in the letter. Prepare an outline based on your discussion and then draft the letter.

IM SKILLS

21. Encouraging the Modern Way of Farming: Writing a Letter Granting Credit to Alzarra'a Alhaditha Co. (Modern Agricultural Company). Food security has topped the policy agenda in the Persian Gulf region following rampant inflation in 2008. As a joint venture, a mega-farming project between Middle Eastern and Egyptian investors has been launched by Modern Agricultural Company. The company has already started the project near the Aswan Dam on 50,000 acres of land. The company envisages that its crops of rice, wheat, and barley will be mainly exported to the Persian Gulf region staring in 2009. The company has decided to employ the most modern techniques of farming, including the GPS satellite technology to let the farmers know their exact location as well as that of their equipment in the vast farmland.

Modern Agricultural Company has sought a loan of $1.5 million from your bank, headquartered in Cairo, Egypt. You have been forwarded the loan application for you to evaluate and inform the management of the Modern Agricultural Company of your decision. After receiving the experts' report you have decided to extend the loan on terms and conditions mutually acceptable to the parties, in view of ample solvency of the project.

Your task: Write a letter addressed to the CEO of Modern Agricultural Company at their headquarters in Cairo informing him of the good news.

POSITIVE MESSAGES

BLOGGING SKILLS   PORTFOLIO BUILDER

22. Leveraging the good news: Blog announcement of a prestigious professional award. You and your staff in the public relations (PR) department at Epson of America were delighted when the communication campaign you created for the new Picture-Mate Personal Photo Lab (www.epson.com/picturemate) was awarded the prestigious Silver Anvil award by the Public Relations Society of America. Now you'd like to give your team a pat on the back by sharing the news with the rest of the company.

Your task: Write a one-paragraph message for the PR department blog (which is read by people throughout the company but is not accessible outside the company) announcing the award. Take care not to "toot your own horn" as the manager of the PR department. Use the opportunity to compliment the rest of the company for designing and producing such an innovative product.[17]

23. Intercultural condolences: Letter conveying sympathy at IBM. You've been working for two years as administrative assistant to Ron Glover, vice president of global workforce diversity at IBM in Armonk, New York. Chana Panichpapiboon has been with Glover even longer than you have, and, sadly, her husband was

killed (along with 19 others) in a bus accident yesterday. The bus skidded on icy pavement into a deep ravine, tipping over and crushing the occupants before rescue workers could get to them.

You met Surin last year at a company banquet. You can still picture his warm smile and the easy way he joked with you and others over chicken Florentine, even though you were complete strangers to him. He was only 32 years old, and he left Chana two children, a 12-year-old boy, Arsa, and a 10-year-old girl, Veera. His death is a terrible tragedy.

Normally, you'd write a condolence letter immediately. But Chana is a native of Thailand, and so was Surin. You know you better do a little research first. Is Chana Buddhist or Catholic? Is there anything about the typical Western practice of expressing sympathy that might be inappropriate? Offensive?

After making some discreet inquiries among Chana's closest friends at work, you've learned that she is Theravada Buddhist, as are most people in Thailand. From a reference work in the company library about doing business around the world, you've gleaned only that, in the beliefs of many people in Thailand, "the person takes precedence over rule or law" and "people gain their social position as a result of karma, not personal achievement," which means Chana may believe in reincarnation. But the book also says that Theravada Buddhists are free to choose which precepts of their religion, if any, they will follow. So Chana's beliefs are still a mystery.

You do know that her husband was very important to her and much loved by all their family. That, at least, is universal. And you're toying with a phrase you once read, "The hand of time lightly lays, softly soothing sorrow's wound." Is it appropriate?

Your task: You've decided to handwrite the condolence note on a blank greeting card you've found that bears a peaceful, "Eastern-flavor" image. You know you're risking a cultural gaffe, but at least you won't commit the greater offense of not writing at all. Choose the most sincere wording you can, which should resonate through any differences in custom or tradition.[18]

BLOGGING SKILLS   PORTFOLIO BUILDER

24. Green is the new green: Blog update on energy savings. Adobe Systems is well known as the maker of Acrobat, Photoshop, Flash, and other programs that are fundamental tools in the Internet Age. It is also becoming well known as one of the "greenest" companies in the United States, adopting a variety of techniques and technologies that have not only reduced its energy usage considerably but also cut nearly $1 million a year from its utility bills. In 2006, Adobe became the first company ever to receive the Platinum Certification from the U.S. Green Building Council.

Your task: Write a one- or two-paragraph post for an internal blog at Adobe, letting employees know how well the company is doing in its efforts to reduce energy usage and thanking employees for the energy-saving ideas they've submitted and the individual efforts they've made to reduce, reuse, and recycle. Learn more about the company's accomplishments by searching for the news release "Adobe Headquarters Awarded Highest Honors from U.S. Green Building Council," available on the Adobe website, at www.adobe.com/aboutadobe/pressroom. Select a few key details from this news release to include in your message.[19]

25. Congrats on that: Complimenting a former business acquaintance for national recognition. You pull the new issue of *Fortune* magazine out of the stack of mail and are quite pleased to see Indra Nooyi on the cover. Not only was Nooyi recently appointed CEO of PepsiCo, but *Fortune* has just named her the most powerful woman in American business. You got to know her briefly when PepsiCo acquired your previous employer, Quaker Oats, in 2001. You haven't spoken to her since then, but you have followed her accomplishments in the business media.

Your task: Write a brief letter (no more than one page), congratulating Nooyi on her promotion to CEO and on being recognized by *Fortune*. Make up any details you need to create a credible message. You can learn more about Nooyi's career and accomplishments in the news release "PepsiCo's Board of Directors Appoints Indra K. Nooyi as Chief Executive Officer Effective October 1, 2006," on the PepsiCo website, www.pepsico.com (look under "News," "PepsiCo Releases," "2006"). Address the letter to Indra Nooyi, CEO, PepsiCo, Inc., 700 Anderson Hill Road, Purchase, NY 10577.

26. Expressing Sympathy: Condolence Letter Addressed to the Safety Officer of the Construction Project. As a project manager of a leading construction company engaged in large projects on the western coast of Saudi Arabia, you have been informed about a tragic road accident involving the family of Mr. Ali Allawi, your safety officer on the project, on which 200 people of different nationalities are working. Mr. Allawi's wife and daughter were returning from two months vacation in Oman, Jordan, when, in route from the Jeddah, Saudi Arabia, airport, on the company transport, they were involved in the tragic and fatal accident. Mr. Allawi is totally shattered by the accident. He has been a competent safety officer, caring about the safety of all workers on the site. You have known Mr. Allawi for about 10 years. Your family has met his family on different social and religious occasions. All your subordinates have expressed their earnest desire to formally send a condolence message to Mr. Allawi, sharing his grief and praying for the fortitude to bear this tragic loss. You can comfort him by assuring that, although right now he is devastated by the tragedy, through strength of conviction and faith he can overcome this grief in time. In the letter, also express the feelings of all ranks and files of the company, mentioning the point that how Mr. Allawi, by his sense of duty and sympathetic attitude toward his subordinates, has earned the respect of his colleagues in the company. On a personal note, remember the good nature of his wife and his daughter, expressing heartfelt condolences on behalf of your family.

Your task: Write a formal condolence letter addressed to Mr. Allawi on behalf of the company. Give it a personal touch as befitting a family friend, as well.

Writing Negative Messages

Learning Objectives

After studying this chapter, you will be able to

1 Apply the three-step writing process to negative messages

2 Explain the differences between the direct and the indirect approaches to negative messages, including when it's appropriate to use each one

3 Identify the risks of using the indirect approach and explain how to avoid such problems

4 Explain the importance of maintaining high standards of ethics and etiquette when delivering negative messages

5 Explain the role of communication in crisis management

6 List three guidelines for delivering negative news to job applicants and give a brief explanation of each one

Communication Close-up at KPMG

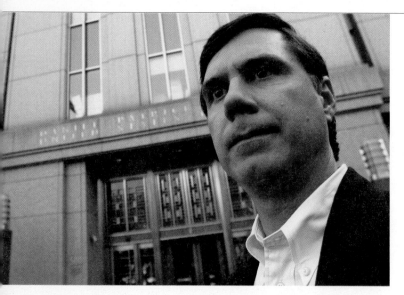

When the accounting firm KPMG publicly apologized for the illegal actions of some of its partners (one of whom, Jeffrey Eischeid, is shown here leaving the courthouse), the admission of guilt helped save the firm from potentially devastating criminal charges but might well have worked against it in numerous client lawsuits.

www.us.kpmg.com

When businesses make mistakes, should they apologize? Traditional thinking says they can't afford to because doing so would be an admission of guilt that could be used against them in lawsuits. However, an emerging school of thought says that apologizing isn't as risky as previously believed and that courts tend to show leniency toward companies that express remorse after making mistakes.

The large accounting firm KPMG faced this situation when the Internal Revenue Service ruled that certain *tax shelters* (investments created primarily to reduce tax burdens) the company had been recommending for some of its wealthy clients were illegal. Soon after, KPMG faced a criminal investigation and multiple lawsuits from individual clients who accused the company of encouraging them to break the law. Just a few years earlier, KPMG competitor Arthur Andersen had been convicted in criminal matters of a different type and had collapsed as a result, putting 85,000 people out of work.

KPMG faced a classic dilemma. If it apologized in an effort to avoid criminal prosecution, that might be seen as an admission of guilt that could be used against it in all those civil suits.

Apparently deciding that the risk of a possible criminal charge was greater than the risk of apologizing, the company issued the following statement: "KPMG takes full responsibility for the unlawful conduct by former KPMG partners . . . and we deeply regret that it occurred." The apology seemed to help the company, as the firm avoided a criminal indictment by agreeing to pay a fine of nearly a half-billion dollars and agreeing to get out of the tax shelter business. More than a dozen employees also face

criminal charges that remain unresolved; initial convictions were later dismissed, but the U.S. government is trying to reopen the case.

The admission of guilt was certainly welcomed by lawyers representing KPMG clients. "It's stunning. Obviously, it's very helpful," said one. That optimism seemed warranted, as the firm was later forced to pay most of its tax shelter clients a total of more than $150 million, and lawsuits from the remaining clients are likely to drag on for years.[1]

USING THE THREE-STEP WRITING PROCESS FOR NEGATIVES MESSAGES

1 LEARNING OBJECTIVE

Apply the three-step writing process to negative messages

Chances are slim that you'll ever need to issue a message like KPMG's (profiled in the chapter-opening Communication Close-up), but communicating other kinds of negative news is a fact of life for all business professionals, from rejecting job applicants to telling customers that shipments will be late to turning down speaking invitations.

When you need to send a negative message, you have five goals: (1) to convey the bad news, (2) to gain acceptance for the bad news, (3) to maintain as much goodwill as possible with your audience, (4) to maintain a good image for your organization, and (5) if appropriate, to reduce or eliminate the need for future correspondence on the matter (however, in a few cases, you may want to encourage discussion). Five goals are clearly a lot to accomplish in one message. However, by learning some simple techniques and following the three-step process, you can develop negative messages that reduce the stress for everyone involved and improve the effectiveness of your communication efforts.

Five goals of negative messages:
- *Give the bad news*
- *Ensure acceptance of the bad news*
- *Maintain reader's goodwill*
- *Maintain organization's good image*
- *Minimize or eliminate future correspondence on the matter, as appropriate*

Step 1: Planning a Negative Message

When planning negative messages, you can't avoid the fact that your audience does not want to hear what you have to say. To minimize the damage to business relationships and to encourage the acceptance of your message, analyze the situation carefully to better understand the context in which the recipient will process your message.

Analysis, investigation, and adaptation help you avoid alienating your readers.

Be sure to consider your purpose thoroughly—whether it's straightforward (such as rejecting a job applicant) or more complicated (such as drafting a negative performance review, in which you not only give the employee feedback on past performance but also help the person develop a plan to improve future performance). Similarly, your audience profile can be simple and obvious in some situations (such as rejecting a credit request) and far more complex in others (such as telling a business partner that you've decided to terminate the partnership).

With a clear purpose and your audience's needs in mind, identify and gather the information your audience requires in order to understand and accept your message. Negative messages can be intensely personal to the recipient, and in many cases, recipients have a right to expect a thorough explanation of your answer.

Selecting the right medium is critical. Experts advise that bad news for employees be delivered in person whenever possible, both to show respect for the employees and to give them an opportunity to ask questions. Of course, delivering bad news is never easy, and an increasing number of managers appear to be using e-mail and other electronic media to convey negative messages to employees.[2]

When preparing negative messages, choose the medium with care.

Defining your main idea in a negative message is often more complicated than simply saying no. For instance, if you need to respond to a hardworking employee who requested a raise, your message might go beyond saying no to explaining how she can improve her performance by working smarter, not just harder.

Appropriate organization helps readers accept your negative news.

Step 2: Writing a Negative Message

When you are adapting a negative message to your audience, pay close attention to effectiveness and diplomacy. After all, your audience does not want to hear bad news or might disagree strongly with you, so messages perceived as being unclear or unkind will amplify the audience's stress.

TABLE 9.1 Choosing Positive Words

EXAMPLES OF NEGATIVE PHRASINGS	POSITIVE ALTERNATIVES
Your request *doesn't make any sense.*	Please clarify your request.
The *damage won't be fixed* for a week.	The item will be repaired next week.
Although it wasn't *our fault,* there will be an *unavoidable delay* in your order.	We will process your order as soon as we receive an aluminum shipment from our supplier, which we expect to happen within 10 days.
You are clearly *dissatisfied.*	I recognize that the product did not live up to your expectations.
I was *shocked* to learn that you're *unhappy.*	Thank you for sharing your concerns about your shopping experience.
Unfortunately, we haven't received it.	The item hasn't arrived yet.
The enclosed statement is *wrong.*	Please verify the enclosed statement and provide a correct copy.

If your credibility hasn't already been established with the audience, lay out your qualifications for making the decision in question. Recipients of negative messages who don't think you are credible are more likely to challenge your decision or reject your message. And, as always, projecting and protecting your company's image are prime concerns; if you're not careful, a negative answer could spin out of control into negative feelings about your company.

When you use language that conveys respect and avoids an accusing tone, you protect your audience's pride. This kind of communication etiquette is always important, but it demands special care with negative messages. Moreover, you can ease the sense of disappointment by using positive words rather than negative, counterproductive ones (see Table 9.1).

Step 3: Completing a Negative Message

Your need for careful attention to detail continues as you complete your message. Revise your content to make sure everything is clear, complete, and concise—bearing in mind that even small flaws are magnified as readers react to your negative news. Produce clean, professional documents and proofread carefully to eliminate mistakes. Finally, be especially sure that your negative messages are delivered promptly and successfully; waiting for bad news is difficult, and wondering whether a message was lost makes it worse.

DEVELOPING NEGATIVE MESSAGES

As you apply the three-step writing process to negative messages, keep three important aspects in mind. First, before you organize the main points of a message, determine whether it will be better to use the direct or indirect approach (see Figure 9.1). Second, before composing your message, be sensitive to variations across cultures or between internal and external audiences. Third, to fulfill the spirit of audience focus, be sure you maintain high ethical standards.

2 LEARNING OBJECTIVE

Explain the differences between the direct and the indirect approaches to negative messages, including when it's appropriate to use each one

Choosing the Better Approach

To choose an approach for negative business messages—direct or indirect—answer the following questions:

- **Will the bad news come as a shock?** The direct approach is fine for business situations in which people understand the possibility of receiving bad news. However, if the bad news might come as a shock to readers, use the indirect approach to help them prepare for it.
- **Does the audience prefer short messages that get right to the point?** For example, if you know that your boss always wants brief messages that get right to the point, use the direct approach.

FIGURE 9.1 Choosing the Indirect or Direct Approach for Negative Messages
Analyze the situation carefully before choosing your approach to organizing negative messages.

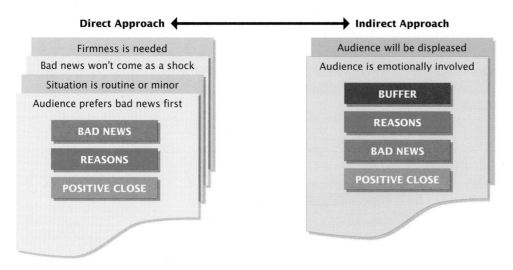

- **How important is this news to the audience?** For minor or routine scenarios, the direct approach is nearly always better. However, if the audience has an emotional investment in the situation or the consequences are considerable, the indirect approach is less jarring.
- **Do you need to maintain a close working relationship with the audience?** The indirect approach makes it easier to soften the blow of bad news and can therefore be the better choice when you need to preserve a good relationship.
- **Do you need to get the audience's attention?** If someone hasn't responded to repeated indirect messages, the direct approach can help you get his or her attention. In some situations, you have no choice but to confront an employee or other party with a forceful message, and the direct approach is better in these uncomfortable cases. Conversely, if readers have grown accustomed to routine, nonemergency messages from you but then you have a real crisis on your hands that demands their immediate attention, the direct approach is better. For example, like most other lenders, the home mortgage giant Countrywide (now part of Bank of America) sends customers a variety of routine and promotional messages—many of which are no doubt tossed aside without being read. However, after an employee illegally sold highly sensitive personal information that exposed customers to potential identify theft, the company used the direct approach in a letter to affected customers. The letter announced the theft in the first sentence, and then it went on to outline exactly what types of information were stolen.[3] Anyone taking even a cursory glance at the letter would recognize that this was not a routine message.
- **What is your organization's preferred style?** Companies often have a distinct communication style, ranging from blunt and direct to gentle and indirect. However, going against expectations can be an effective way to get people's attention in a dramatic way.

You need to consider a variety of factors when choosing between the direct and indirect approaches for negative messages.

No matter which approach you choose for a given message, don't lose sight of your purpose and your audience. A sensitive, personal tone can be more important to your readers than your choice of message organization.[4]

Using the Direct Approach Effectively

A negative message using the direct approach opens with the bad news, proceeds to the reasons for the situation or the decision, and ends with a positive statement aimed at maintaining a good relationship with the audience (see Figure 9.2). Depending on the circumstances, the message may also offer alternatives or a plan of action to fix the situation under discussion. Stating the bad news at the beginning can have two advantages: (1) It makes a shorter message possible, and (2) it allows the audience to reach the main idea of the message in less time.

Use the direct approach when your negative answer or information will have minimal personal impact.

FIGURE 9.2   Negative Message Using the Direct Approach
Spherion Corporation, a recruiting and staffing firm based in Fort Lauderdale, Florida, conducts monthly surveys of the U.S. workforce. The company used the direct approach to announce a decline in employee confidence.

Opening with a Clear Statement of the Bad News   No matter what the news is, come right out and say it. However, even if the news is likely to be devastating, maintain a calm, professional tone that keeps the focus on the news and not on individual failures or other personal factors. Also, if necessary, remind the reader why you're writing.

The amount of detail you should provide depends on your relationship with the audience.

Providing Reasons and Additional Information   In most cases, you follow the direct opening with an explanation of why the news is negative. The extent of your explanation depends on the nature of the news and your relationship with the reader. For example, if you want to preserve a long-standing relationship with an important customer, a detailed explanation could well be worth the extra effort such a message would require.

However, you will encounter some situations in which explaining negative news is neither appropriate nor helpful, such as when the reasons are confidential, excessively complicated, or irrelevant to the reader. To maintain a cordial working relationship with the reader, you might want to explain why you can't provide the information.

Should you apologize when delivering bad news? As the KPMG vignette at the beginning of the chapter illustrates, the answer isn't quite as simple as one might think. The notion of *apology* is hard to pin down. To some people, it simply means an expression of sympathy that something negative has happened to another person. At the other extreme, it means admitting fault and taking responsibility for specific compensations or corrections to atone for the mistake.

Some experts have advised that a company should never apologize, even when it knows it has made a mistake, as the apology might be taken as a confession of guilt that could be used against the company in a lawsuit. This is the dilemma KPMG faced when deciding how to respond to illegal actions taken by a few of its employees. However, several states have laws that specifically prevent expressions of sympathy from being used as evidence of legal liability. In fact, judges, juries, and plaintiffs tend to be more forgiving of companies that express sympathy for wronged parties; moreover, an apology can help repair a company's reputation. Recently, some prosecutors have begun pressing executives to publicly admit guilt and apologize as part of the settlement of criminal cases—unlike the common tactic of paying fines but refusing to admit any wrongdoing.[5]

Although corporate apologies have been more common in recent years, the worldwide crises in the business and consumer credit markets that began in 2008 might signal a new phase in apology strategies. After the failure of risky investment strategies led to billions of dollars in corporate losses, massive layoffs, the collapse of some of the United States' biggest banking companies, and widespread damage to the U.S. economy, the lack of public apologies angered both U.S. consumers and executives in other companies. As the crisis continues to unfold and inevitable lawsuits appear, it remains to be seen whether any top managers in the firms at the center of the calamity will step forward with apologies.[6]

The best general advice in the event of a serious mistake or accident is to immediately and sincerely express sympathy and offer help if appropriate, without admitting guilt; then seek the advice of your company's lawyers before elaborating. As one survey concluded, "The risks of making an apology are low, and the potential reward is high."[7]

No matter how trivial or serious the situation, if you do apologize, make it a real apology. Don't say you're sorry "if anyone was offended" by what you did—this statement implies that you're not sorry at all and that it's the other party's fault for being offended.[8] Moreover, if appropriate, explain what steps you are taking to avoid similar mistakes in the future.

Closing on a Positive Note After you've explained the negative news, close the message in a positive but still honest and respectful manner. Consider offering your readers an alternative solution if you can. Depending on the situation, you might also explain how you or your organization plan to respond to the negative news.

Using the Indirect Approach Effectively

The indirect approach helps readers prepare for the bad news by presenting the reasons for it first. However, the indirect approach is *not* meant to obscure bad news, delay it, or limit your responsibility. Rather, the purpose of this approach is to ease the blow and help readers accept the situation. When done poorly, the indirect approach can be disrespectful and even unethical. But when done well, it is a good example of audience-oriented communication crafted with attention to ethics and etiquette. Showing consideration for the feelings of others is never dishonest.

Opening with a Buffer Messages using the indirect approach open with a **buffer**: a neutral, noncontroversial statement that establishes common ground with the reader (refer to Figure 9.1). A good buffer can express your appreciation for being considered (if you're responding to a request), assure your reader of your attention to the request, or indicate your understanding of the reader's needs. A good buffer also needs to be relevant and sincere. In contrast, a poorly written buffer might trivialize the reader's concerns, divert attention from

After an explosion that killed one employee and worried local residents about the potential release of toxic chemicals, Bayer CropScience plant manager Nick Crosby said that "We are truly sorry for the serious issues caused by the incident at our facility. . . . We understand the anxiety in the community resulting from the incident." He also apologized to people living near the Institute, West Virginia, plant for failing to clarify that there was no danger of toxic emissions: "We could have communicated, and we should have communicated, much better with the community that night."

3 LEARNING OBJECTIVE

Identify the risks of using the indirect approach and explain how to avoid such problems

Use the indirect approach when some preparation will help your audience accept your bad news.

A well-written buffer establishes common ground with the reader.

the problem with insincere flattery or irrelevant material, or mislead the reader into thinking your message actually contains good news.

Consider these possible responses to a manager of the order-fulfillment department who requested some temporary staffing help from your department (a request you won't be able to fulfill):

Establishes common ground with the reader and validates the concerns that prompted the original request—without promising a positive answer

• Our department shares your goal of processing orders quickly and efficiently.

Establishes common ground, but in a negative way that downplays the recipient's concerns

• As result of the last downsizing, every department in the company is running shorthanded.

Potentially misleads the reader into concluding that you will comply with the request

• You folks are doing a great job over there, and I'd love to be able to help out.

Trivializes the reader's concerns by opening with an irrelevant issue

• Those new state labor regulations are driving me crazy over here; how about in your department?

Only the first of these buffers can be considered effective; the other three are likely to damage your relationship with the other manager—and lower his or her opinion of you. Table 9.2 shows several types of effective buffers you could use to tactfully open a negative message.

A poorly written buffer may mislead or insult the reader.

Given the damage that a poorly composed buffer can do, consider every buffer carefully before you send it. Is it respectful? Is it relevant? Is it neutral, implying neither yes nor no? Does it provide a smooth transition to the reasons that follow? If you can answer yes to every question, you can proceed confidently to the next section of your message. However, if a little voice inside your head tells you that your buffer sounds insincere or misleading, it probably is, in which case you'll need to rewrite it.

Phrase your reasons to signal the negative news ahead.

Providing Reasons and Additional Information   An effective buffer serves as a stepping-stone to the next part of your message, in which you build up the explanations and information that will culminate in your negative news. An ideal explanation section leads readers

TABLE 9.2   Types of Buffers

BUFFER TYPE	STRATEGY	EXAMPLE
Agreement	Find a point on which you and the reader share similar views.	We both know how hard it is to make a profit in this industry.
Appreciation	Express sincere thanks for receiving something.	Your check for $127.17 arrived yesterday. Thank you.
Cooperation	Convey your willingness to help in any way you realistically can.	Employee Services is here to assist all associates with their health insurance, retirement planning, and continuing education needs.
Fairness	Assure the reader that you've closely examined and carefully considered the problem, or mention an appropriate action that has already been taken.	For the past week, we have had our bandwidth monitoring tools running around the clock to track your actual upload and download speeds.
Good news	Start with the part of your message that is favorable.	We have credited your account in the amount of $14.95 to cover the cost of return shipping.
Praise	Find an attribute or an achievement to compliment.	The Stratford Group clearly has an impressive record of accomplishment in helping clients resolve financial reporting problems.
Resale	Favorably discuss the product or company related to the subject of the letter.	With their heavy-duty, full-suspension hardware and fine veneers, the desks and file cabinets in our Montclair line have long been popular with value-conscious professionals.
Understanding	Demonstrate that you understand the reader's goals and needs.	So that you can more easily find the printer with the features you need, we are enclosing a brochure that describes all the Epson printers currently available.

to your conclusion before you come right out and say it. In other words, before you actually say no, the reader has followed your line of reasoning and is ready for the answer. By giving your reasons effectively, you help maintain focus on the issues at hand and defuse the emotions that always accompany significantly bad news.

As you lay out your reasons, guide your reader's response by starting with the most positive points first and moving forward to increasingly negative ones. Be concise but provide enough detail for the audience to understand your reasons. You need to convince your audience that your decision is justified, fair, and logical. If appropriate, you can use the explanation section to suggest how the negative news might in fact benefit your reader in some way—but only if this is true and only if you can do so without offending your audience.

Avoid hiding behind company policy to cushion your bad news. If you say, "Company policy forbids our hiring anyone who does not have two years' supervisory experience," you imply that you won't consider anyone on his or her individual merits. Skilled and sympathetic communicators explain company policy (without referring to it as "policy") so that the audience can try to meet the requirements at a later time. Consider this response to an employee:

> *Don't hide behind "company policy" when you deliver bad news; present logical answers instead.*

Because these management positions are quite challenging, the human relations department has researched the qualifications needed to succeed in them. The findings show that the two most important qualifications are a bachelor's degree in business administration and two years' supervisory experience.

 Shows the reader that the decision is based on a methodical analysis of the company's needs and not on some arbitrary guideline

Establishes the criteria behind the decision and lets the reader know what to expect

This paragraph does a good job of stating reasons for the refusal:

- It provides enough detail to logically support the refusal.
- It implies that the applicant is better off avoiding a program in which he or she might fail.
- It shows that the company's policy is based on experience and careful analysis.
- It doesn't offer an apology for the decision because no one is at fault.
- It avoids negative personal expressions (such as "You do not meet our requirements").

> *Well-written reasons are*
> - *Detailed*
> - *Tactful*
> - *Individualized*
> - *Unapologetic if no one is at fault*
> - *Positive*

Even valid, well-thought-out reasons won't convince every reader in every situation. However, if you've done a good job of laying out your reasoning, you've done everything you can to prepare the reader for the main idea, which is the negative news itself.

Continuing with a Clear Statement of the Bad News
After you've prepared the audience to receive the bad news, the next task is to present the news as clearly and as kindly as possible. Three techniques are especially useful for saying no. First, de-emphasize the bad news:

> *To handle bad news carefully*
> - *De-emphasize the bad news visually and grammatically*
> - *Use a conditional statement, if appropriate*
> - *Tell what you did do, not what you didn't do*

- Minimize the space or time devoted to the bad news—without trivializing it or withholding any important information.
- Subordinate bad news in a complex or compound sentence ("My department is already shorthanded, so I'll need all my staff for at least the next two months"). This construction presents the bad news in the middle of the sentence, the point of least emphasis.
- Embed bad news in the middle of a paragraph or use parenthetical expressions ("Our profits, which are down, are only part of the picture").

However, keep in mind that it's possible to abuse de-emphasis. For instance, if the primary point of your message is that profits are down, it would be inappropriate to marginalize that news by burying it in the middle of a sentence. State the negative news clearly and then make a smooth transition to any positive news that might balance the story.

Second, use a conditional (*if* or *when*) statement to imply that the audience could have received, or might someday receive, a favorable answer ("When you have more managerial experience, you are welcome to reapply"). Such a statement could motivate applicants to improve their qualifications.

Third, emphasize what you can do or have done rather than what you cannot do. Say "We sell exclusively through retailers, and the one nearest you that carries our merchandise is . . ." rather than "We are unable to serve you, so please call your nearest dealer." Also, by implying the bad news, you may not need to actually state it ("The five positions currently open have been filled with people whose qualifications match those uncovered in our research"). By focusing on the facts and implying the bad news, you make the impact less personal.

When implying bad news, however, be sure your audience will be able to grasp the entire message—including the bad news. Withholding negative information or overemphasizing positive information is unethical and unfair to your reader. If an implied message might lead to uncertainty, state your decision in direct terms. Just be sure to avoid overly blunt statements that are likely to cause pain and anger:

INSTEAD OF THIS	WRITE THIS
I *must refuse* your request.	I will be out of town on the day you need me.
We *must deny* your application.	The position has been filled.
I *am unable* to grant your request.	Contact us again when you have established . . .
We *cannot afford to* continue the program.	The program will conclude on May 1.
Much as I would like to attend . . .	Our budget meeting ends too late for me to attend.
We *must turn down* your extension request.	Please send in your payment by June 14.

A positive close
- *Builds goodwill*
- *Offers a suggestion for action*
- *Provides a look toward the future*

Closing on a Positive Note   As in the direct approach, the close in the indirect approach offers an opportunity to emphasize your respect for your audience, even though you've just delivered unpleasant news. Express best wishes without ending on a falsely upbeat note. If you can find a positive angle that's meaningful to your audience, by all means consider adding it to your conclusion. However, don't try to pretend that the negative news didn't happen or that it won't affect the reader. Suggest alternative solutions if such information is available. If you've asked readers to decide between alternatives or to take some action, make sure that they know what to do, when to do it, and how to do it. Whatever type of conclusion you use, follow these guidelines:

- **Avoid a negative or uncertain conclusion.** Don't refer to, repeat, or apologize for the bad news. Refrain from expressing any doubt that your reasons will be accepted. (Avoid statements such as "I trust our decision is satisfactory.")
- **Limit future correspondence.** Encourage additional communication *only* if you're willing to discuss your decision further. (If you're not, avoid wording such as "If you have further questions, please write.")
- **Be optimistic about the future.** Don't anticipate problems that haven't occurred yet. (Avoid statements such as "Should you have further problems, please let us know.")
- **Be sincere.** Steer clear of clichés that are insincere in view of the bad news. (If you can't help, don't say, "If we can be of any help, please contact us.")

Keep in mind that the close is the last thing audience members have to remember you by. Even though they're disappointed, leave them with the impression that they were treated with respect.

Adapting to Your Audience

The disappointing nature of negative messages requires that you maintain your audience focus and be as sensitive as possible to audience needs. As part of this effort, you may need to adapt your message to cultural differences or to the differences between internal and external audiences.

Cultural Variations

Bad news is unwelcome in any language, but the conventions for conveying it can vary considerably from culture to culture. For instance, French business letters are traditionally quite formal and writer oriented, often without reference to audience needs or benefits. Moreover, when the news is bad, French writers take the direct approach. They open with a reference to the problem or previous correspondence and then state the bad news clearly. While they don't refer to the audience's needs, they often do apologize and express regret for the problem.[9]

In contrast, Japanese letters traditionally open with remarks about the season, business prosperity, or health. When the news is bad, these opening formalities serve as the buffer. Explanations and apologies follow, and then comes the bad news or refusal. Japanese writers protect their readers' feelings by wording the bad news ambiguously. Western readers may even misinterpret this vague language as a condition of acceptance rather than as the refusal it actually is.[10]

Whenever you are communicating across cultures, use the tone, organization, and other cultural conventions that your audience expects. Only then can you avoid the inappropriate or even offensive approaches that could jeopardize your business relationship.[11]

Expectations for the handling of bad news vary from culture to culture.

Internal Versus External Audiences

Internal audiences often have expectations for negative messages that differ from those of external audiences. In some cases, the two groups can interpret the news in different or even opposite ways. For example, employees will react negatively to news of an impending layoff, but company shareholders might welcome the news as evidence that management is trying to control costs. In addition, if a negative message such as news of a layoff is being sent to internal and external audiences, employees will expect not only more detail but also to be informed before the public is told.

Negative messages to outside audiences require attention to the diverse nature of the audience and the concern for confidentiality of internal information. A single message might have a half-dozen audiences, all with differing opinions and agendas. You may not be able to explain things to the level of detail that some of these people want if doing so would release proprietary information such as future product plans.

Compared to external audiences, internal audiences often expect more detail in negative messages.

You may need to adjust the content of negative messages for various external audiences.

Maintaining High Standards of Ethics and Etiquette

All business messages demand attention to ethics and etiquette, of course, but these considerations take on special importance when you are delivering bad news—for several reasons. First, a variety of laws and regulations dictate the content and delivery of many business messages with potentially negative content, such as the release of financial information by a public company. Second, negative messages can have a significant negative impact on the lives of those receiving them. Even if the news is conveyed legally and conscientiously, good ethical practice demands that these situations be approached with care and sensitivity. Third, emotions often run high when negative messages are involved, for both the sender and the receiver. Senders need to not only manage their own emotions but also consider the emotional state of their audiences.

The challenge of sending—and receiving—negative messages fosters a tendency to delay, downplay, or distort the bad news (see "Ethics Detective: Solving the Case of the Deceptive Soft Sell").[12] However, doing so may be unethical, if not illegal. In recent years, numerous companies have been sued by shareholders, consumers, employees, and government regulators for allegedly withholding or delaying negative information in such areas as company finances, environmental hazards, and product safety. In many of these cases, the problem was slow, incomplete, or inaccurate communication between the company and external stakeholders. In others, problems stemmed from a reluctance to send or receive negative news within the organization.

Effectively sharing bad news within an organization requires commitment from everyone involved. Employees must commit to sending negative messages when necessary and to doing so in a timely fashion, even when that is unpleasant or difficult. Conversely, managers must commit to maintaining open communication channels, truly listening when employees have negative information to share, and not punishing employees who deliver bad news.

4 LEARNING OBJECTIVE

Explain the importance of maintaining high standards of ethics and etiquette when delivering negative messages

Sharing bad news effectively requires commitment from everyone in the organization.

Ethics Detective

Solving the Case of the Deceptive Soft Sell

You and your colleagues are nervous. Sales have been declining for months, and you see evidence of budget tightening all over the place—the fruit and pastries have disappeared from the coffee stations, accountants are going over expense reports with magnifying glasses, and managers are slow to replace people who leave the company. Instant messages fly around the office; everyone wants to know if anyone has heard anything about layoffs.

The job market in your area is weak, and you know you might have to sell your house—in one of the weakest housing markets in memory—and move your family out of state to find another position in your field. If your job is eliminated, you're ready to cope with the loss, but you need as much time as possible. You breathe a sigh of relief when the following item from the CEO appears on the company's internal blog:

> With news of workforce adjustments elsewhere in our industry, we realize many of you are concerned about the possibility here. I'd like to reassure all of you that

we remain confident in the company's fundamental business strategy, and the executive team is examining all facets of company operations to ensure our continued financial strength.

The message calms your fears. Should it?

ANALYSIS

A month later, the CEO announces a layoff of 20 percent of the company's workforce—nearly 700 people. You're shocked by the news because you felt reassured by the blog posting from last month. In light of what happened, you retrieve a copy of the newsletter and reread the CEO's message. Does it seem ethical now? Why or why not? If you had been in charge of writing this newsletter item and your hands were tied because you couldn't come out and announce the layoffs yet, how would you have rewritten the message?

Negative situations can put your sense of self-control and business etiquette to the test.

Employees who observe unethical or illegal behavior within their companies and are unable to resolve the problems through normal channels may have no choice but to resort to **whistleblowing**—expressing their concerns through company ethics hot lines or even going to the news media if they perceive no other options. The decision to "blow the whistle" on one's own employer is rarely easy or without consequences; more than 80 percent of whistleblowers in a recent survey said they were punished in some way for coming forward with their concerns.[13] Although whistleblowing is sometimes characterized as "ratting on" colleagues or managers, it has an essential function. According to international business expert Alex MacBeath, "Whistleblowing can be an invaluable way to alert management to poor business practice within the workplace. Often whistleblowing can be the only way that information about issues such as rule breaking, criminal activity, cover-ups, and fraud can be brought to management's attention before serious damage is suffered."[14] Recognizing the value of this feedback, many companies have formal reporting mechanisms that give employees a way to voice ethical and legal concerns to management.

Finally, recognize that some negative news scenarios will test your self-control and tempt you to respond with a personal attack. However, keep in mind that negative messages can have a lasting impact on the people who receive them and the people who send them. As a communicator, you have a responsibility to minimize the negative impact of your negative messages through careful planning and sensitive, objective writing. As much as possible, focus on the actions or conditions that led to the negative news, not on personal shortcomings or character issues. Develop a reputation as a professional who can handle the toughest situations with dignity.

For a reminder of successful strategies for creating negative messages, see "Checklist: Creating Negative Messages."

EXPLORING COMMON EXAMPLES OF NEGATIVE MESSAGES

The following sections offer examples of the most common negative messages, dealing with topics such as routine business matters, organizational news, and employment messages.

✓ **CHECKLIST:** **Creating Negative Messages**

A. Choose the better approach.
- Consider using the direct approach when the audience is aware of the possibility of negative news, when the reader is not emotionally involved in the message, when you know that the reader would prefer the bad news first, when you know that firmness is necessary, and when you want to discourage a response.
- Consider using the indirect approach when the news is likely to come as a shock or surprise, when your audience has a high emotional investment in the outcome, and when you want to maintain a good relationship with the audience.

B. For the indirect approach, open with an effective buffer.
- Establish common ground with the audience.
- Validate the request, if you are responding to a request.
- Don't trivialize the reader's concerns.
- Don't mislead the reader into thinking the coming news might be positive.

C. Provide reasons and additional information.
- Explain why the news is negative.
- Adjust the amount of detail to fit the situation and the audience.

- Avoid explanations when the reasons are confidential, excessively complicated, or irrelevant to the reader.
- If appropriate, state how you plan to correct or respond to the negative news.
- Seek the advice of company lawyers if you're unsure what to say.

D. Clearly state the bad news.
- State the bad news as positively as possible, using tactful wording.
- To help protect readers' feelings, de-emphasize the bad news by minimizing the space devoted to it, subordinating it, or embedding it.
- If your response might change in the future if circumstances change, explain the conditions to the reader.
- Emphasize what you can or have done rather than what you can't or won't do.

E. Close on a positive note.
- Express best wishes without being falsely positive.
- Suggest actions readers might take, if appropriate, and provide them with necessary information.
- Encourage further communication only if you're willing to discuss the situation further.
- Keep a positive outlook on the future.

Sending Negative Messages on Routine Business Matters

As you progress in your career and become more visible in your industry and community, you will receive a variety of invitations to speak at private or public functions or to volunteer your time for a variety of organizations. In addition, routine business matters such as credit applications and requests for adjustment will often require you to make negative responses. Neither you nor your company will be able to say yes to every request, so crafting negative responses quickly and graciously is an important skill for many professionals.

Refusing Routine Requests

When you are unable to meet a request, your primary communication challenge is to give a clear negative response without generating negative feelings or damaging either your personal reputation or the company's. As simple as these messages may appear to be, they can test your skills as a communicator because you often need to deliver negative information while maintaining a positive relationship with the other party.

When turning down an invitation or a request for a favor, consider your relationship with the reader.

The direct approach works best for most routine negative responses. It not only helps your audience get your answer quickly and move on to other possibilities but also helps you save time because the direct approach is often easier to write than the indirect approach.

The indirect approach works best when the stakes are high for you or for the receiver, when you or your company has an established relationship with the person making the request, or when you're forced to decline a request that you might have said yes to in the past (see Figure 9.3).

Consider the following points as you develop your routine negative messages:

- **Manage your time carefully.** Focus your time on the most important relationships and requests and get in the habit of crafting quick standard responses for less important situations.

FIGURE 9.3 Effective Letter Declining a Routine Request

May Yee Kwan's company has a long-standing relationship with the college Sandra Wofford represents and wants to maintain that positive relationship, but she can't meet this particular request. To communicate negative news, she therefore uses the indirect approach. If Kwan and Wofford shared a closer relationship (if they worked together in a volunteer organization, for instance), the direct approach might be more appropriate.

1 Plan →

Analyze the Situation

Verify that the purpose is to decline a request and offer alternatives; audience is likely to be surprised by the refusal.

Gather Information

Determine audience needs and obtain the necessary information.

Select the Right Medium

For formal messages, printed letters on company letterhead are best.

Organize the Information

The main idea is to refuse the request so limit your scope to that; select the indirect approach based on the audience and the situation.

2 Write →

Adapt to Your Audience

Adjust the level of formality based on your degree of familiarity with the audience; maintain a positive relationship by using the "you" attitude, politeness, positive emphasis, and bias-free language.

Compose the Message

Use a conversational but professional style and keep the message brief, clear, and as helpful as possible.

3 Complete

Revise the Message

Evaluate content and review readability to make sure the negative information won't be misinterpreted; make sure your tone stays positive without being artificial.

Produce the Message

Maintain a clean, professional appearance on company letterhead.

Proofread the Message

Review for errors in layout, spelling, and mechanics.

Distribute the Message

Deliver your message using the chosen medium.

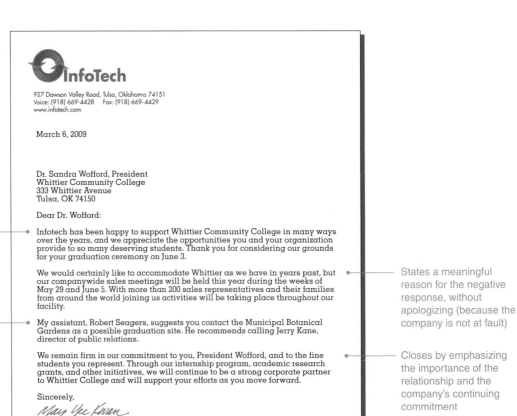

Buffers negative response by demonstrating respect and recapping the request

Suggests an alternative, showing that Kwan cares about the college and has given the matter some thought

States a meaningful reason for the negative response, without apologizing (because the company is not at fault)

Closes by emphasizing the importance of the relationship and the company's continuing commitment

- **If the matter is closed, don't imply that it's still open.** If your answer is truly no, don't use phrases such as "Let me think about it and get back to you" as a way to delay saying no.
- **Offer alternative ideas if you can.** If you can help, great. However, remember to use your time wisely in such matters. Unless the relationship is vital to your company, you probably shouldn't spend time researching alternatives for the other person.
- **Don't imply that other assistance or information might be available if it isn't.** Don't close your negative message with a cheery but insincere "Please contact us if we can offer any additional assistance." An empty attempt to mollify hostile feelings could simply lead to another request you'll have to refuse.

If you aren't in a position to offer additional information or assistance, don't imply that you are.

Handling Bad News About Transactions

Bad news about transactions, the sale and delivery of products and services, is always unwelcome and usually unexpected. Such messages have three goals: (1) to modify the customer's expectations, (2) to explain how you plan to resolve the situation, and (3) to repair whatever damage might have been done to the business relationship.

The specific content and tone of each message can vary widely, depending on the nature of the transaction and your relationship with the customer. Telling an individual consumer that his new sweater will be arriving a week later than you promised is a much simpler task than telling Toyota that 30,000 transmission parts will be a week late, especially when you know the company will be forced to idle a multimillion-dollar production facility as a result.

Some negative messages regarding transactions carry significant financial and legal ramifications.

If you haven't done anything specific to set the customer's expectations—such as promising delivery within 24 hours—the message simply needs to inform the customer of the situation, with little or no emphasis on apologies (see Figure 9.4). Bear in mind, though, in this age of online ordering and overnight delivery, that customers have become conditioned to expect instantaneous fulfillment of nearly every transaction, even if you haven't promised anything.

Your approach to bad news about business transactions depends on the customer's expectations.

If you did set the customer's expectations and now find that you can't meet them, your task is more complicated. In addition to resetting those expectations and explaining how you'll resolve the problem, you may need to include an element of apology. The scope of the apology depends on the magnitude of the mistake. For the customer who ordered the sweater, a simple apology followed by a clear statement of when the sweater will arrive would probably be sufficient. For larger business-to-business transactions, the customer may want an explanation of what went wrong to determine whether you'll be able to perform as you promise in the future.

If you've failed to meet expectations that you set for the customer, you should consider including an element of apology.

To help repair the damage to the relationship and encourage repeat business, many companies offer discounts on future purchases, free merchandise, or other considerations. Even modest efforts can go a long way to rebuilding a customer's confidence in your company. However, you don't always have a choice. Business-to-business purchasing contracts often include performance clauses that legally entitle the customer to discounts or other restitution in the event of late delivery. To review the concepts covered in this section, see "Checklist: Handling Bad News About Transactions."

Refusing Claims and Requests for Adjustment

Almost every customer who makes a claim or requests an adjustment is emotionally involved; therefore, the indirect method is usually the best approach for a refusal. To avoid accepting responsibility for the unfortunate situation and avoid blaming or accusing the

Use the indirect approach in most cases of refusing claims.

✓ **CHECKLIST:** **Handling Bad News About Transactions**

- Reset the customer's expectations regarding the transaction.
- Explain what happened and why, if appropriate.
- Explain how you'll resolve the situation.

- Repair any damage done to the business relationship, perhaps offering future discounts, free merchandise, or other considerations.
- Offer a professional, businesslike expression of apology if your organization made a mistake.

FIGURE 9.4 Effective E-Mail Advising of a Back Order

This message, which is a combination of good and bad news, uses the indirect approach—with the good news serving as a buffer for the bad news. In this case, the customer wasn't promised delivery by a certain date, so the writer simply informs the customer when to expect the rest of the order. The writer also takes steps to repair the relationship and encourage future business with her firm.

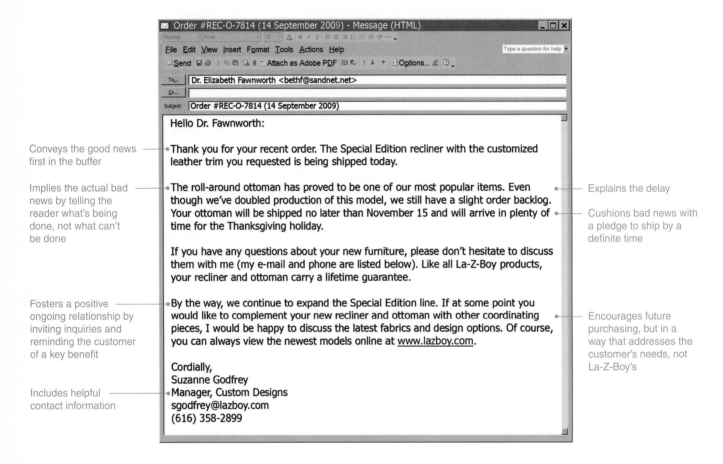

Conveys the good news first in the buffer

Implies the actual bad news by telling the reader what's being done, not what can't be done

Fosters a positive ongoing relationship by inviting inquiries and reminding the customer of a key benefit

Includes helpful contact information

Explains the delay

Cushions bad news with a pledge to ship by a definite time

Encourages future purchasing, but in a way that addresses the customer's needs, not La-Z-Boy's

customer, pay special attention to the tone of your letter. A tactful and courteous message can build goodwill even while denying the claim (see Figure 9.5).

When refusing a claim
- *Demonstrate your understanding of the complaint*
- *Explain your refusal*
- *Suggest alternative action*

When refusing a claim, avoid language that might have a negative impact on the reader. Instead, demonstrate that you understand and have considered the complaint carefully. Then, even if the claim is unreasonable, rationally explain why you are refusing the request, without hiding behind "company policy." End the message on a respectful and action-oriented note.

If you deal with enough customers over a long enough period, chances are you'll get a request that is particularly outrageous. You might even be positive that the person is being dishonest. However, you need to control your emotions and approach the situation as calmly as possible to avoid saying or writing anything that the recipient might interpret as defamation (see page 63 in Chapter 1). To avoid being accused of defamation, follow these guidelines:

You can help avoid committing defamation by not responding emotionally or abusively.

- Refrain from using any kind of abusive language or terms that could be considered defamatory.
- Provide accurate information and stick to the facts.
- Never let anger or malice motivate your messages.
- Consult your company's legal advisers whenever you think a message might have legal consequences.
- Communicate honestly and make sure that you believe what you're saying is true.
- Emphasize a desire for a good relationship in the future.

FIGURE 9.5   Effective Letter Refusing a Claim

Daniel Lindmeier, who purchased a digital video camera from Village Electronics a year ago, wrote to say that the unit doesn't work properly and to inquire about the warranty. He incorrectly believed that the warranty covers one year, when it actually covers only three months. In this response, Walter Brodie uses the indirect approach to convey the bad news and to offer additional helpful information.

1 Plan →

Analyze the Situation

Verify that the purpose is to refuse a warranty claim and offer repairs; audience's likely reaction will be disappointment and surprise.

Gather Information

Gather information on warranty policies and procedures, repair services, and resale information.

Select the Right Medium

Choose the best medium for delivering your message; for formal messages, printed letters on company letterhead are best.

Organize the Information

Your main idea is to refuse the claim and promote an alternative solution; select an indirect approach based on the audience and the situation.

2 Write →

Adapt to Your Audience

Adjust the level of formality based on degree of familiarity with the audience; maintain a positive relationship by using the "you" attitude, politeness, positive emphasis, and bias-free language.

Compose the Message

Use a conversational but professional style and keep the message brief, clear, and as helpful as possible.

3 Complete

Revise the Message

Evaluate content and review readability to make sure the negative information won't be misinterpreted; make sure your tone stays positive without being artificial.

Produce the Message

Emphasize a clean, professional appearance appropriate for a letter on company stationery.

Proofread the Message

Review for errors in layout, spelling, and mechanics.

Distribute the Message

Deliver your message using the chosen medium; make sure the reader receives any necessary support documents as well.

293

- Use the indirect approach because the reader is expecting or hoping for a positive response.
- Indicate your full understanding of the nature of the complaint.
- Explain why you are refusing the request, without hiding behind company policy.
- Provide an accurate, factual account of the transaction.

- Emphasize ways things should have been handled rather than dwell on the reader's negligence.
- Avoid any appearance of defamation.
- Avoid expressing personal opinions.
- End with a positive, friendly, helpful close.
- Make any suggested action easy for readers to comply with.

Remember that nothing positive can come out of antagonizing a customer, even one who has verbally abused you or your colleagues. Reject the claim or request for adjustment in a professional manner and move on to the next challenge. For a brief review of the tasks involved when refusing claims, see "Checklist: Refusing Claims."

Sending Negative Organizational News

As a manager, you may need to issue negative announcements regarding some aspect of your products, services, or operations. Most of these scenarios have unique challenges that must be addressed on a case-by-case basis, but the general advice offered here applies to all of them. One key difference among all these messages is whether you have time to plan the announcement. The following section addresses negative messages that you do have time to plan for, and "Communicating in a Crisis" offers advice on communication during emergencies.

Communicating Under Normal Circumstances

Negative organizational messages to external audiences can require extensive planning.

Businesses must convey a range of negative messages regarding their ongoing operations. As you plan such messages, take extra care to consider all your audiences and their unique needs. Keep in mind that a significant negative event such as a plant closing can affect hundreds or thousands of people in many organizations. Employees need to find new jobs, get training in new skills, or perhaps get emergency financial help. School districts may have to adjust budgets and staffing levels if many of your employees plan to move in search of new jobs. Your customers need to find new suppliers. Your suppliers may need to find other customers of their own. Government agencies may need to react to everything from a decrease in tax revenues to an influx of people seeking unemployment benefits.

When making negative announcements, follow these guidelines:

Give people as much time as possible to react to negative organizational news.

- **Match your approach to the situation.** A modest price increase won't shock most customers, so the direct approach is fine. However, canceling a product that people count on is another matter, so building up to the news via the indirect approach might be better.
- **Consider the unique needs of each group.** As the plant closing example illustrates, various people have different information needs.
- **Give each audience enough time to react as needed.** For instance, employees, particularly high-level professionals and managers, may need up to six months or more to find new jobs.
- **Give yourself enough time to plan and manage a response.** Chances are you're going to be hit with complaints, questions, or product returns after you make your announcement, so make sure you're ready with answers and additional follow-up information.
- **Look for positive angles but don't exude false optimism.** If eliminating a seldom-used employee benefit means employees will save money, by all means promote that positive angle. On the other hand, laying off 10,000 people does not give them "an opportunity to explore new horizons." It's a traumatic event that can affect employees, their families, and their communities for years. The best you may be able to do is to thank people for their past support and wish them well in the future.

- **Minimize the element of surprise whenever possible.** This step can require considerable judgment on your part, as well as awareness of any applicable laws. In general, if you recognize that current trends are pointing toward negative results sometime in the near future, it's often best to let your audience know ahead of time.
- **Seek expert advice if you're not sure.** Many significant negative announcements have important technical, financial, or legal elements that require the expertise of lawyers, accountants, or other specialists.

Ask for legal help and other assistance if you're not sure how to handle a significant negative announcement.

Negative situations will test your skills as a communicator and leader. People may turn to you and say, "Okay, so things are bad; now what do we do?" Inspirational leaders try to seize such opportunities as a chance to reshape or reinvigorate the organization, and they offer encouragement to those around them (see Figure 9.6).

Communicating in a Crisis

5 LEARNING OBJECTIVE

Explain the role of communication in crisis management

Some of the most critical instances of business communication occur during crises, which can include industrial accidents, crimes or scandals involving company employees, on-site hostage situations, terrorist attacks, information theft, product tampering incidents, and financial calamities. During a crisis, customers, employees, local communities, and others will demand information. In addition, rumors can spread unpredictably and uncontrollably (see "Business Communication 2.0: Controlling Rumors in a Social Media Environment"). You can also expect the news media to descend quickly, asking questions of anyone they can find.

Although you can't predict these events, you can prepare for them. Analysis of corporate crises over the past several decades reveals that companies that respond quickly with the

FIGURE 9.6 Effective E-Mail Providing Bad News About Company Operations
In this message to employees at Sybervantage, Frank Leslie shares the unpleasant news that a hoped-for licensing agreement with Warner Brothers has been rejected. Rather than dwell on the bad news, he focuses on options for the future. The upbeat close diminishes the effect of the bad news without hiding or downplaying the news itself.

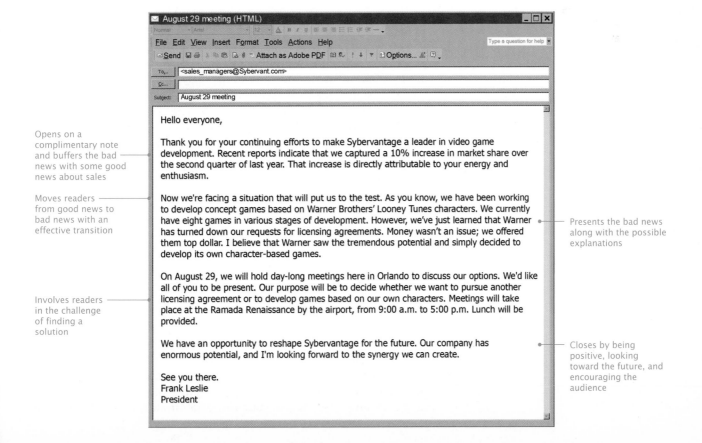

Business Communication 2.0

Controlling Rumors in a Social Media Environment

For all the benefits they bring to business, social media and other communication technologies have created a major new challenge: responding to online rumors and attacks on a company's reputation. Disappointed consumers can now communicate through blogs, social networking sites, social commerce sites, advocacy sites such as www.walmartwatch.com, general complaint websites such as www.planetfeedback.com, and company-specific sites such as www.verizonpathetic.com.

On the positive side, consumers who feel they have been treated unfairly can use the public exposure as leverage. Many companies appreciate the feedback from these sites, too, and even buy complaint summaries so they can improve products and services. However, false rumors and unfair criticisms can spread around the world in a matter of minutes. McDonald's, Coca-Cola, Pepsi, and Snapple are just a few of the brand names that have been harmed by false information.

Controlling rumors is difficult, but you can help contain them by taking five steps. First, monitor blogs and other online sources to catch and respond to negative messages. Second, decide whether each rumor or complaint justifies an official public response. If the rumor is not yet widespread, responding privately to a small number of people might be more effective than broadcasting a public response—which might just help spread the rumor to a wider audience. Also, some instances of misinformation might be so mild or vague that confronting them could cause more problems than it solves. In those cases,

your best course might be to ignore the rumor but communicate positive information that indirectly counters the rumor. Third, if you determine that a rumor requires a direct strategy, respond quickly with clear information. Some companies set up special websites, such as www.walmartfacts.com, to answer public criticisms. Fourth, respond to rumors wherever they appear, even if this means digging back through e-mail threads to respond personally to everyone who passed the message along. Fifth, enlist the help of government agencies such as the Centers for Disease Control and Prevention (www.cdc.gov) and debunking sites such as Snopes.com (www.snopes.com).

Whatever you do, don't bury your head in the sand and assume that a positive reputation doesn't need to be guarded and defended. Everybody has a voice now, and some of those voices don't care to play by the rules of ethical communication.

CAREER APPLICATIONS

1. A legitimate complaint about one of your products on PlanetFeedback.com also contains a statement that your company "doesn't care about its customers." How should you respond?
2. A few bloggers are circulating false information about your company, but the problem is not widespread—yet. Should you jump on the problem now and tell the world the rumor is false, even though most people haven't heard it yet? Explain your answer.

information people need tend to fare much better in the long run than those that go into hiding or release inconsistent or incorrect information.[15]

Anticipation and planning are key to successful communication in a crisis.

The key to successful communication efforts during a crisis is having a **crisis management plan.** In addition to defining operational procedures to deal with the crisis, this plan outlines communication tasks and responsibilities, which can include everything from media contacts to news release templates (see Table 9.3). The plan should clearly specify which people are authorized to speak for the company, contact information for all key executives, and a list of the media outlets and technologies that will be used to disseminate information. Many companies now go one step further by regularly testing crisis communications in realistic practice drills that last a full day or more.[16]

REAL-TIME UPDATES
Learn More

Take some of the sting out of delivering bad news

No one likes to deliver bad news, but these techniques can make it easier for you and the recipient. Go to **http://real-timeupdates.com/bct** and click on "Learn More." If you are using mybcommlab, you can access Real-Time Updates within each chapter or under Student Study Tools.

Sending Negative Employment Messages

Most managers must convey bad news about individual employees from time to time. Recipients have an emotional stake in your message, so taking the indirect approach is usually advised. In addition, use great care in choosing media for these messages. For instance, e-mail and other written forms let you control the message and avoid personal confrontation, but one-on-one conversations are more sensitive and facilitate questions and answers.

TABLE 9.3   How to Communicate in a Crisis

DO	DON'T
Prepare for trouble ahead of time by identifying potential problems, appointing and training a response team, and preparing and testing a crisis management plan.	Don't blame anyone for anything.
	Don't speculate in public.
Get top management involved as soon as the crisis hits.	Don't refuse to answer questions.
Set up a news center for company representatives and the media that is equipped with phones, computers, and other electronic tools for preparing news releases and online updates. At the news center, take the following steps:	Don't release information that will violate anyone's right to privacy.
	Don't use the crisis to pitch products or services.
• Issue frequent news updates and have trained personnel available to respond to questions around the clock.	Don't play favorites with media representatives.
• Provide complete information packets to the media as soon as possible.	
• Prevent conflicting statements and provide continuity by appointing a single person trained in advance to speak for the company.	
• Tell receptionists and other employees to direct all media calls to the designated spokesperson in the news center.	
• When new information is available, provide updates via blog postings, microblog updates, text messaging, and other appropriate tools.	
Tell the whole story—openly, completely, and honestly. If you are at fault, apologize.	
Demonstrate the company's concern through your statements and your actions.	

Refusing Requests for Employee References and Recommendation Letters

When sending refusals to prospective employers who have requested information about past employees, your message can be brief and direct:

> Our human resources department has authorized me to confirm that Yolanda Johnson worked for Tandy, Inc., for two years, from June 2005 to July 2007. Best of luck as you interview applicants.

Implies that company policy prohibits the release of any more information but does provide what information is available

Ends on a positive note

This message doesn't need to say, "We cannot comply with your request." It simply gives the reader all the information that is allowable.

Refusing an applicant's direct request for a recommendation letter is another matter. Any refusal to cooperate may seem to be a personal slight and a threat to the applicant's future. Diplomacy and preparation help readers accept your refusal:

> Thank you for letting me know about your job opportunity with Coca-Cola. Your internship there and the MBA you've worked so hard to earn should place you in an excellent position to land the marketing job.
>
> Although we do not send out formal recommendations here at PepsiCo, I can certainly send Coca-Cola a confirmation of your employment dates. And if you haven't considered this already, be sure to ask several of your professors to write evaluations of your marketing skills. Best of luck to you in your career.

Uses the indirect approach since the other party is probably expecting a positive response

Announces that the writer cannot comply with the request, without explicitly blaming it on "policy"

Offers to fulfill as much of the request as possible and offers an alternative

Ends on a positive note

This message tactfully avoids hurting the reader's feelings because it makes positive comments about the reader's recent activities, implies the refusal, suggests an alternative, and uses a polite close.

Poorly written rejection letters tarnish your company's reputation and can even invite legal troubles.

Rejecting Job Applicants

Tactfully telling job applicants that you won't be offering them employment is a common communication challenge. Poorly written rejection letters can have negative consequences, ranging from the loss of qualified candidates for future openings to the loss of potential customers (not only the rejected applicants but also their friends and family members).[17] Badly phrased rejection letters can even invite legal troubles. When delivering bad news to job applicants, follow three guidelines:[18]

- **Choose your approach carefully.** Experts disagree on whether the direct or indirect approach is best for rejection letters. On the one hand, job applicants know they won't get every position they apply for, so negative news during a job search is not generally a shock. On the other hand, people put their hopes and dreams on the line when they apply for work, so job applicants have a deep emotional investment in the process—which is one of the factors to consider in using the indirect approach. If you opt for the direct approach, be tactful in the opening. Tell your reader that the position has been filled rather than saying, "Your application has been rejected." If you opt for the indirect approach, be careful not to mislead the reader or delay the bad news for more than a sentence or two. A simple "Thank you for considering ABC as the place to start your career" is a quick, courteous buffer that shows your company is flattered to be considered. Don't mislead the reader in your buffer by praising his or her qualifications in a way that could suggest good news is soon to follow.
- **Clearly state why the applicant was not selected.** Make your rejection less personal by stating that you hired someone with more experience or whose qualifications match the position requirements more closely.
- **Close by suggesting alternatives.** If time permits, you might suggest other positions for which the applicant is qualified or professional organizations that could help the applicant find employment.

Compare the ineffective and effective versions of the message in Figure 9.7 to see how one writer followed these guidelines.

In the past, many professionals considered it basic business etiquette to respond to every job application, even if only to acknowledge that it had been received. However, some companies are now so swamped with e-mailed résumés and online applications that they no longer have time to respond to them all. However, a failure to respond to job applicants has traditionally been viewed as a fairly serious breach of business etiquette. Responding is not only good for your company's image but also initiates conversations that might lead to successful hiring when you have the right opportunities for the right people.[19] At the very least, companies can set up automated response systems that let applicants know that materials have been received and when jobs have been filled.

Giving Negative Performance Reviews

An important goal of any performance evaluation is to give the employee a plan of action for improving his or her performance.

The main purpose of a **performance review** is to improve employee performance by (1) emphasizing and clarifying job requirements, (2) giving employees feedback on their efforts toward fulfilling those requirements, and (3) guiding continued efforts by developing a plan of action, which includes rewards and opportunities. Performance reviews help companies set organizational standards and communicate organizational values.[20] Documentation of performance problems can also protect a company from being sued for unlawful termination.[21]

Criticizing others is difficult for most people, but discussing shortcomings is a necessary first step to improvement for both an employee and an organization. When you need to give a negative performance review, follow these guidelines:[22]

- **Confront the problem right away.** Avoiding mention of performance problems usually only makes them worse—and it robs the employee of the opportunity to improve. Moreover, if you don't document problems when they occur, you may make it more difficult to terminate employment later on if the situation comes to that.[23]

FIGURE 9.7 Ineffective and Effective E-Mails Rejecting a Job Applicant
This e-mail response was drafted by Marvin Fichter to communicate bad news to Carol DeCicco following her interview with Bradley Jackson. After reviewing the first draft, Fichter made several changes to improve the communication. The revised e-mail helps DeCicco understand that (1) she would have been hired if she'd had more tax experience and (2) she shouldn't be discouraged.

Ineffective

Dear Ms. DeCicco:

We were so impressed with your résumé and credentials. Your academic record and previous accounting experience are just what we were hoping to see. We just didn't expect to see such sterling qualifications in so many candidates. As you can imagine, with 30 applicants for this position, the selection process was quite difficult.

After much consideration, we were able to narrow down the choices to three, one of which was you. However, I'm sorry to say that you were not chosen to fill the tax accountant position.

If you wouldn't mind, we would like to keep your information on file for six months, on the off chance that another position might open up before you find another position.

Thank you for thinking of us.

Sincerely,
Marvin R. Fichter
Human Resources Director

Opens with an excessively positive tone that misleads the reader into thinking the answer will be positive

Includes an inappropriate apology; the company did nothing wrong so therefore has no need to apologize; also fails to explain why the candidate was not chosen

Closes with a weak, insincere request

Effective

Dear Ms. DeCicco:

Thank you for considering Bradley Jackson as the place to launch your career in accounting.

In light of the reporting complexities now imposed on the accounting profession by Sarbanes-Oxley and other recent legislation, the executive team has decided it would be wise to bolster our skill base with someone who has extensive industry experience. We have therefore filled the position with a more experienced candidate.

Your résumé and credentials show you to be a deserving candidate for entry-level positions. Your academic record and previous work experience certainly indicate your willingness to work hard. Those of us who had the opportunity to talk with you believe that your ability to communicate will certainly help you achieve an excellent position in a recognized accounting firm.

In the meantime, we would like to keep your information on file for six months, in case a position requiring less experience opens up in the near future.

I wish you the best of luck as you begin your new career.

Sincerely,
Marvin R. Fichter
Human Resources Director

Further sets the stage for the negative news by thoughtfully explaining the context in which the decision was made

Moderates the bad news with honest, specific encouragement

Buffers the upcoming bad news with a sincere thanks for being considered

Presents the bad news as a logical consequence of the decision-making process

Closes in a respectful, positive manner

- **Plan what to say.** Be clear about your concerns and include examples of the employee's specific actions. Think about any possible biases you may have and get feedback from others. Collect and verify all relevant facts (both strengths and weaknesses).
- **Deliver the message in private.** Whether in writing or in person, be sure to address the performance problem privately. Don't send performance reviews by e-mail or fax. If you're reviewing an employee's performance face to face, conduct that review in a

Address performance problems in private.

✓ **CHECKLIST:** **Writing Negative Employment Messages**

A. Refusing requests for employee references and recommendation letters
- Don't feel obligated to write a recommendation letter if you don't feel comfortable doing so.
- Take a diplomatic approach to minimize hurt feelings.
- Compliment the reader's accomplishments.
- Suggest alternatives, if available.

B. Rejecting job applicants
- If possible, respond to all applications, even if you use only a form message to acknowledge receipt.
- If you use the direct approach, take care to avoid being blunt or cold.
- If you use the indirect approach, don't mislead the reader in your buffer or delay the bad news for more than a sentence or two.
- Clearly state why the applicant was rejected.
- Suggest alternatives if possible.

C. Giving negative performance reviews
- Maintain an objective and unbiased tone.
- Use nonjudgmental language.
- Focus on problem resolution.
- Make sure negative feedback is documented and shared with the employee.
- Don't avoid confrontations by withholding negative feedback.
- Ask the employee for a commitment to improve.

D. Terminating employment
- State your reasons accurately and make sure they are objectively verifiable.
- Avoid statements that might expose your company to a wrongful termination lawsuit.
- Consult company lawyers to clarify all terms of the separation.
- End the relationship on terms as positive as possible.

meeting arranged expressly for that purpose and consider holding that meeting in a conference room or some other neutral area.

- **Focus on the problem.** Without attacking the employee, discuss the problems caused by his or her performance and explain how it doesn't meet expectations established for the position. In other words, "evaluate the work, not the worker."[24] Identify the consequences of continuing poor performance and show that you're committed to helping solve the problem.

- **Ask for a commitment from the employee.** Help the employee understand that planning for and making improvements are the employee's responsibility. However, finalize decisions jointly so that you can be sure any action to be taken is achievable. Set a schedule for improvement and for following up with evaluations of that improvement.

If an employee's performance has been disappointing, clearly and tactfully state how the employee can better meet the responsibilities of the job. If the performance review is to be effective, be sure to suggest ways that the employee can improve.[25] Remember that the ultimate goal is not to criticize but to help the employee succeed.

Terminating Employment

The decision to terminate employees is rarely easy or simple, but doing it effectively is an important managerial responsibility. When writing a termination message, you have three goals: (1) to present the reasons for this difficult action, (2) to avoid statements that might expose the company to a wrongful termination lawsuit, and (3) to leave the relationship between the terminated employee and the firm as favorable as possible. For both legal and personal reasons, present specific justification for asking the employee to leave and make sure that personnel policies have been applied consistently to avoid the appearance of unfair treatment.[26] Your company's lawyers will be able to tell you whether the employee's performance is legal grounds for termination.

Document Makeover

Improve This Memo

To practice correcting drafts of actual documents, visit the "Document Makeovers" section in either mybcommlab or the Companion Website for this text.

If mybcommlab is being used in your class, see your User Guide for specific instructions on how to access the content for this chapter. If you are accessing this feature through the Companion Website, click on "Document Makeovers" and then click Chapter 9. You will find a memo that contains problems and errors related to what you've learned in this chapter about handling negative messages. Use the Final Draft decision tool to create an improved version of this memo. Check the message for the use of buffers, apologies, explanations, subordination, embedding, positive action, conditional phrases, and upbeat perspectives.

Make sure that all your reasons are accurate and verifiable. Avoid words that are open to interpretation, such as *untidy* and *difficult.* You can help protect personal feelings as you end the relationship by telling the truth about the termination and by helping as much as you can to make the employee's transition as smooth as possible.[27] To review the tasks involved in this type of message, see "Checklist: Writing Negative Employment Messages." For the latest information on writing negative messages, visit http://real-timeupdates.com/bct and click on Chapter 9.

Carefully word a termination message to avoid creating undue ill will and grounds for legal action.

Communication Challenges at KPMG

Thanks to your good head for numbers and effective communication skills, you didn't take long to move up to a management position with KPMG. You're now an audit manager in the firm's Louisville, Kentucky, office. (An audit is the process of reviewing a firm's accounting records for accuracy and legal compliance.) Your responsibilities range from managing audits for KPMG's clients to helping members of your group develop their skills to coordinating with other managers in cross-functional team efforts. Not surprisingly, communication challenges are frequent and diverse.[28]

Individual Challenge: Another manager in the Louisville office stopped by this morning with a request to borrow two of your best auditors for a three-week emergency. Under normal conditions, you wouldn't hesitate to help, but your team has its own scheduling challenges to deal with. Plus, this isn't the first time this manager has run into trouble, and you are confident that poor project management is the

reason. In one or two sentences, diplomatically state your refusal to help while suggesting that your colleague's management skills need to be improved.

Team Challenge: You've found it easy to say yes to recommendation letter requests from former employees who were top performers, and you've learned to say no to those people who didn't perform so well. The requests you struggle with are from employees in the middle—people who didn't really excel but didn't really cause any trouble either. You've just received a request from a computer systems specialist who falls smack in the middle of the middle. Unfortunately, he's applying for a job at a firm that you know places high demands on its employees and generally hires the best of the best. He's a great person, and you'd love to help; but in your heart you know that if by some chance he does get the job, he probably won't last. Plus, you don't want to get a reputation in the industry for recommending weak candidates. With your team, brainstorm a sensitive but effective buffer that will help you set the stage for the negative news.

SUMMARY OF LEARNING OBJECTIVES

1 **Apply the three-step writing process to negative messages.** Because the way you convey negative information can be far more damaging than the fact that you're conveying it, planning your negative messages is crucial. Make sure your purpose is specific, necessary, and appropriate for written media. Find out how your audience prefers to receive bad news. Collect all the facts necessary to support your negative decision and adapt your tone to the situation as well as to your audience. Negative messages may be organized according to the direct or the indirect approach, and your choice depends on audience preference as well as on the situation. In addition, carefully choose positive words to construct diplomatic sentences. Finally, revision, design, and proofreading are necessary to ensure that you are saying exactly what you want to say in the best possible way.

2 **Explain the differences between the direct and the indirect approaches to negative messages, including**

when it's appropriate to use each one. The direct approach to negative messages puts the bad news up front, follows with the reasons (and perhaps offers an alternative), and closes with a positive statement. On the other hand, the indirect approach begins with a buffer (a neutral or positive statement), explains the reasons, clearly states the negative news without unduly emphasizing it, and closes with a positive statement. Use the direct approach when you know your audience prefers receiving bad news up front or if the bad news will cause readers little pain or disappointment. Otherwise, use the indirect approach.

3 **Identify the risks of using the indirect approach, and explain how to avoid such problems.** When using the indirect approach, you need to be careful to avoid obscuring the bad news or misleading your audience into thinking you're actually delivering good news. The key to avoiding both problems is remembering that the purpose of the indirect approach is to cushion the blow,

not to avoid delivering it. When using a buffer, you must be sure it is neither deceptive nor insincere. To write an effective buffer, look for opportunities to express your appreciation for being considered, to assure your reader of your attention to the request, or to indicate your understanding of the reader's needs.

4 **Explain the importance of maintaining high standards of ethics and etiquette when delivering negative messages.**   Ethics and etiquette are important in every message, of course, but they take on particular significance with negative messages for three reasons. First, in many cases, the communicator needs to adhere to a variety of laws and regulations when delivering negative messages. Second, good ethical practice demands care and sensitivity in the content and delivery of negative messages, as these messages can have a profoundly negative effect on the people who receive them. Third, communicators need to manage their own emotions when crafting and distributing negative messages while at the same time considering the emotional needs of their audiences.

5 **Explain the role of communication in crisis management.**   Preparation is key for successful crisis management. Although you can't anticipate the nature and circumstance of every possible crisis, you can prepare by deciding such issues as who is in charge of communications, where the press and the public can get information,

and what will be said in likely emergency scenarios. Rumor control is another important aspect; with the advent of instant messaging, text messaging on mobile phones, television, and other rapid communication vehicles, incorrect information can spread worldwide in seconds. A good crisis communication plan includes such items as e-mail and phone lists for important media contacts, website templates for various emergency scenarios, and after-hours contact information for key personnel in the company.

6 **List three guidelines for delivering bad news to job applicants, and give a brief explanation of each one.**   When rejecting job applicants, follow three guidelines: (1) Consider your approach carefully. Some managers advocate the direct approach on the grounds that job applicants realize they won't get every position they apply for, so bad news isn't necessarily a shock. Others assert that applicants have a significant emotional investment in the process, so while bad news may not be shocking, it is deeply disappointing. (2) State clearly why the applicant was not selected. This explanation can be specific without being personal if you explain that you hired someone with more experience or with qualifications that more closely match position requirements. (3) Suggest alternatives. Perhaps your company has other openings or you would be willing to consider the applicant for future openings.

PEARSON
mybcommlab™

Log on to **www.mybcommlab.com** to access the following study and assessment aids associated with this chapter:

- Video applications
- Real-Time Updates
- Peer review activity
- Quick Learning Guides

- Pre/post test
- Personalized study plan
- Model documents
- Sample presentations

If you are not using mybcommlab, you can access the Real-Time Updates and Quick Learning Guides through **http://real-timeupdates.com/bct**. The Quick Learning Guide (located under "Learn More" on the website) hits all the high points of this chapter in just two pages. This guide, especially prepared by the authors, will help you study for exams or review important concepts whenever you need a quick refresher.

Test Your Knowledge

1. What are the five main goals in delivering bad news?
2. Why is it particularly important to adapt your medium and tone to your audience's needs and preferences when writing a negative message?
3. What are the advantages of using the direct approach to deliver negative news at the beginning of a message?
4. What is the sequence of elements in a negative message that is organized using the indirect approach?
5. What is a buffer, and what steps must you take to ensure that buffers you write are ethical?
6. When using the indirect approach to announce a negative decision, what is the purpose of presenting your reasons before explaining the decision?

7. What are three techniques for de-emphasizing negative news?
8. Why is it important to have one designated contact person during a crisis?
9. What are three guidelines for writing rejection letters to job applicants?
10. When giving a negative review to an employee, what five guidelines should you follow?

Apply Your Knowledge

1. Why is it important to end a negative message on a positive note?
2. If company policy changes, should you explain those changes to employees and customers at about the same time? Why or why not?

3. Why is whistleblowing a controversial activity?
4. When a company suffers a setback, should you soften the impact by letting out the bad news a little at a time? Why or why not?
5. **Ethical Choices** Is intentionally de-emphasizing bad news the same as distorting graphs and charts to de-emphasize unfavorable data? Why or why not?

Practice Your Knowledge

Messages for Analysis

Read the following messages and then (1) analyze the strengths and weaknesses of each sentence and (2) revise each message so that it follows this chapter's guidelines.

Message 9.A: Providing Negative News About Company Operations

Date: Wed, 28 May 2010 4:20:15 -0800
From: M. Juhasz, Travel & Meeting Services <mjuhasz@blackanddecker.com>

To: [mailing list]

Subject: Travel

Dear Traveling Executives:

We need you to start using some of the budget suggestions we are going to issue as a separate memorandum. These include using videoconference equipment and web conferencing instead of traveling to meetings, staying in cheaper hotels, arranging flights for cheaper times, and flying from less-convenient but also less-expensive suburban airports.

The company needs to cut travel expenses by fifty percent, just as we've cut costs in all departments of Black & Decker. This means you'll no longer be able to stay in fancy hotels and make last-minute, costly changes to your travel plans.

You'll also be expected to avoid hotel surcharges for phone calls and Internet access. If the hotel you want to stay in doesn't offer free wireless, go somewhere else. And never, NEVER return a rental car with an empty tank! That causes the rental agency to charge us a premium price for the gas they sell when they fill it up upon your return.

You'll be expected to make these changes in your travel habits immediately.

Sincerely,

M. Juhasz

Travel & Meeting Services

Message 9.B: Refusing Requests for Claims and Adjustments

I am responding to your letter of about six weeks ago asking for an adjustment on your wireless hub, model WM39Z. We test all our products before they leave the factory; therefore, it could not have been our fault that your hub didn't work.

If you or someone in your office dropped the unit, it might have caused the damage. Or the damage could have been caused by the shipper if he dropped it. If so, you should file a claim with the shipper. At any rate, it wasn't our fault. The parts are already covered by warranty. However, we will provide labor for the repairs for $50, which is less than our cost, since you are a valued customer.

We will have a booth at the upcoming trade show there and hope to see you or someone from your office. We have many new models of hubs, routers, and other computer gear that we're sure you'll want to see. I've enclosed our latest catalog. Hope to see you there.

Message 9.C: Rejecting Job Applicants

I regret to inform you that you were not selected for our summer intern program at Equifax. We had over a thousand résumés and cover letters to go through and simply could not get to them all. We have been asked to notify everyone that we have already selected students for the 25 positions based on those who applied early and were qualified.

We're sure you will be able to find a suitable position for summer work in your field and wish you the best of luck. We deeply regret any inconvenience associated with our reply.

Exercises

Active links for all websites in this chapter can be found online. If mybcommlab is being used in your class, see your User Guide for instructions on accessing the content for this chapter. Otherwise, visit **www.pearsonglobaleditions.com/bovee**, locate *Business Communication Today*, Tenth Edition, click the Companion Website link, select Chapter 9, and then click on "Featured Websites." Please note that links to sites that become inactive after publication of the book will be removed from the Featured Websites section.

9.1 **Selecting the Approach** Select which approach you would use (direct or indirect) for the following negative messages.
   a. An e-mail message to your boss, informing her that one of your key clients is taking its business to a different accounting firm
   b. An e-mail message to a customer, informing her that one of the books she ordered over the Internet is temporarily out of stock
   c. An instant message to a customer, explaining that the DVD recorder he ordered for his new computer is on back order and that, as a consequence, the shipping of the entire order will be delayed
   d. A blog post to all employees, notifying them that the company parking lot will be repaved during the first week of June and that the company will provide a shuttle service from a remote parking lot during that period
   e. A letter from a travel agent to a customer, stating that the airline will not refund her money for the flight she missed but that her tickets are valid for one year
   f. A form letter from a U.S. airline to a customer, explaining that the company cannot extend the

expiration date of the customer's frequent flyer miles even though the customer was living overseas for the past three years and unable to use the miles during that time

g. A letter from an insurance company to a policyholder, denying a claim for reimbursement for a special medical procedure that is not covered under the terms of the customer's policy

h. A letter from an electronics store, stating that the customer will not be reimbursed for a malfunctioning mobile phone that is still under warranty (because the terms of the warranty do not cover damages to phones that were accidentally dropped from a moving car)

i. An announcement to the repairs department, listing parts that are on back order and will be three weeks late

9.2 Teamwork Working alone, revise the following statements to de-emphasize the bad news. (*Hint*: Minimize the space devoted to the bad news, subordinate it, embed it, or use the passive voice.) Then team up with a classmate and read each other's revisions. Did you both use the same approach in every case? Which approach seems to be most effective for each of the revised statements?

a. The airline can't refund your money. The "Conditions" section on the back of your ticket states that there are no refunds for missed flights. Sometimes the airline makes exceptions, but only when life and death are involved. Of course, your ticket is still valid and can be used on a flight to the same destination.

b. I'm sorry to tell you, we can't supply the custom decorations you requested. We called every supplier, and none of them can do what you want on such short notice. You can, however, get a standard decorative package on the same theme in time. I found a supplier that stocks these. Of course, it won't have quite the flair you originally requested.

c. We can't refund your money for the malfunctioning MP3 player. You shouldn't have immersed the unit in water while swimming; the users' manual clearly states that the unit is not designed to be used in adverse environments.

9.3 Using Buffers As a customer service supervisor for a telephone company, you're in charge of responding to customers' requests for refunds. You've just received an e-mail from a customer who unwittingly ran up a $500 bill for long-distance calls after mistakenly configuring his laptop computer to dial an Internet access number that wasn't a local call. The customer says it wasn't his fault because he didn't realize he was dialing a long-distance number. However, you've dealt with this situation before; you know that the customer's Internet service provider warns its customers to choose a local access number because customers are responsible for all long-distance charges. Draft a short buffer (one or two sentences) for your e-mail reply, sympathizing with the customer's plight but preparing him for the bad news (that company policy specifically prohibits refunds in such cases).

9.4 Internet Public companies occasionally need to issue news releases to announce or explain downturns in sales, profits, demand, or other business factors. Search the web to locate a company that has issued a press release that recently reported lower earnings or other bad news and access the news release on that firm's website. Alternatively, find the type of press release you're seeking by reviewing press releases at www.prnewswire.com or www.businesswire .com. How does the headline relate to the main message of the release? Is the release organized according to the direct or the indirect approach? What does the company do to present the bad news in a favorable light—and does this effort seem sincere and ethical to you?

9.5 Ethical Choices The insurance company where you work is planning to raise all premiums for health-care coverage. Your boss has asked you to read a draft of her letter to customers announcing the new, higher rates. The first two paragraphs discuss some exciting medical advances and the expanded coverage offered by your company. Only in the final paragraph do customers learn that they will have to pay more for coverage starting next year. What are the ethical implications of this draft? What changes would you suggest?

Expand Your Knowledge

Exploring the Best of the Web

Protect Yourself When Sending Negative Employment Messages

www.toolkit.com

A visit to Business Owner's Toolkit can help you reduce your legal liability, whether you are laying off an employee, firing an employee, or contemplating a companywide reduction in your workforce. Find out the safest way to fire someone from a legal standpoint before it's too late. Learn why it's important to document disciplinary actions. Discover why some bad news should be given face-to-face and never with a letter or over the phone. Read the site's advice under "Firing and Termination" to find answers to these questions:

1. What should a manager communicate to an employee during a termination meeting?

2. Why is it important to document employee disciplinary actions?

3. What steps should you take before firing an employee for misconduct or poor work?

Sharpening Your Career Skills Online

Bovée and Thill's Business Communication Web Search, at http://businesscommunicationblog.com/websearch, is a unique research tool designed specifically for business communication research. Use the Web Search function to find a website, video, PDF document, podcast, or PowerPoint presentation that offers advice on writing messages that convey negative information. Write a brief e-mail message to your instructor, describing the item that you found and summarizing the career skills information you learned from it.

CASES

Applying the Three-Step Writing Process to Cases

Apply each step to the following cases, as assigned by your instructor.

NEGATIVE MESSAGES ON ROUTINE BUSINESS MATTERS

TELEPHONE SKILLS

1. When a recall isn't really a recall: Voice recording informing customers that an unsafe product won't be replaced. Vail Products of Toledo, Ohio, manufactured a line of beds for use in hospitals and other institutions where there is a need to protect patients who might otherwise fall out of bed and injure themselves (including patients with cognitive impairments or patterns of spasms or seizures). These "enclosed bed systems" use a netted canopy to keep patients in bed rather than the traditional method of using physical restraints such as straps or tranquilizing drugs. The intent is humane, but the design is flawed: At least 30 patients have become trapped in the various parts of the mattress and canopy structure, and 8 of them have suffocated.

Working with the U.S. Food and Drug Administration (FDA), Vail issued a recall on the beds, as manufacturers often do in the case of unsafe products. However, the recall is not really a recall. Vail will not be replacing or modifying the beds, nor will it accept returns. Instead, the company is urging institutions to move patients to other beds, if possible. Vail has also sent out revised manuals and warning labels to be placed on the beds. The company also announced that it is ceasing production of enclosed beds.

Your task: A flurry of phone calls from concerned patients, family members, and institutional staff is overwhelming the support staff. As a writer in Vail's corporate communications office, you've been asked to draft a short script to be recorded on the company's phone system. When people call the main number, they'll hear "Press 1 for information regarding the recall of Model 500, Model 1000, and Model 2000 enclosed beds." After they press 1, they'll hear the message you're about to write, explaining that although the action is classified as a recall, Vail will not be accepting returned beds, nor will it replace any of the affected beds. The message should also assure customers that Vail has already sent revised operating manuals and warning labels to every registered owner of the beds in question. The phone system has limited memory, and you've been directed to keep the message to 75 words or less.[29]

E-MAIL SKILLS   PORTFOLIO BUILDER

2. Message to the boss: Refusing a project on ethical grounds. A not-so-secret secret is getting more attention than you'd really like after an article in *BusinessWeek* gave the world an inside look at how much money you and other electronics retailers make from extended warranties (sometimes called service contracts). The article explained that typically half of the warranty price goes to the salesperson as a commission and that only 20 percent of the total amount customers pay for warranties eventually goes to product repair.

You also know why extended warranties are such a profitable business. Many electronics products follow a predictable pattern of failure: a high failure rate early in their lives, then a "midlife" period during which failures go way down, and concluding with an "old age" period when failure rates ramp back up again (engineers refer to the phenomenon as the *bathtub curve* because it looks like a bathtub from the side—high at both ends and low in the middle). The early failures are usually covered by manufacturers' warranties, and the extended warranties you sell are designed to cover that middle part of the life span. In other words, many extended warranties cover the period of time during which consumers are *least* likely to need them and offer no coverage when consumers need them *most*. (Consumers can actually benefit from extended warranties in a few product categories, including laptop computers and plasma televisions. Of course, the more sense the warranty makes for the consumer, the less financial sense it makes for your company.)[30]

Your task: Worried that consumers will stop buying so many extended warranties, your boss has directed you to put together a sales training program that will help cashiers sell the extended warranties even more aggressively. The more you ponder this challenge, though, the more you're convinced that your company should change its strategy so it doesn't rely on profits from these warranties so much. In addition to offering questionable value to the consumer, the warranties risk creating a consumer backlash that could lead to lower sales of all your products. You would prefer to voice your concerns to your boss in person, but both of you are traveling on hectic schedules for the next week. You'll have to write an e-mail instead. Draft a brief message, explaining why you think the sales training specifically and the warranties in general are both bad ideas.

3. Not this time: Letter denying credit card annual fee waiver to United Overseas Bank customer. As a customer service officer in the credit card center at United Overseas Bank (UOB) in Singapore, your responsibilities include handling customers' credit card applications. When processing the applications, you may have to issue welcome gifts or credit card annual fee waivers to individual customers.

Yesterday, you received a letter from Mr. Michael Yew, who is a long-time privilege banking customer of UOB. Mr. Yew has accounts in privilege banking sections such as the UOB Global Currency Premium Account, Structured Deposits, and UOB Global Treasury. He also has a complimentary UOB Visa Signature Card with perpetual waiver of the annual fees. Last month, Mr. Yew applied for a new UOB Preferred Platinum Card for himself and two supplementary UOB Preferred Platinum Cards for his wife and his daughter. The fee for the principal card is $123 per year. It is free for the first supplementary card, while the second supplementary card is $61 per year. All three new cards and the first credit statement with the $184 annual fee charges for the principal card and the second supplementary card have already been sent to Mr. Yew.

Mr. Yew writes to the credit card center to request an annual fee waiver for both his principal card and the second supplementary card. In the letter, he mentions his privilege banking status and his accounts. He suggests giving up his complimentary UOB Visa Signature Card which has perpetual waiver of the annual fees in exchange of a perpetual annual fee wavier for his new principal UOB Preferred Platinum Card and the second supplementary card.

You decide to turn down Mr. Yew's request, as the complimentary UOB Visa Signature Card is issued to all privilege banking customers in conjunction with their accounts. Besides, the bank has a policy stating that each customer can only enjoy one supplementary card waiver, so Mr. Yew has to pay for the second supplementary card in any case. You must politely deny his request.

Your task: Write a letter to Mr. Michael Yew, Block 21, Fairview Park, Scott Road, Singapore. Explain your refusal of his request. Keep in mind that you don't want to lose this customer.[31]

BLOGGING SKILLS

4. Inconvenience for Mass Transit Rail Passengers: Alerting passengers about longer time needed. As the major rail system, Mass Transit Rail (MTR) not only runs through Hong Kong, but also connects Hong Kong with Shenzhen, on the border of China. Parallel-import traders have taken advantage of this convenience to smuggle parallel goods into China at Sheung Shui station. To save ticket fees, these traders often stay on the platform to meet their collaborators. MTR Corporation has decided to set up temporary barriers on Sheung Shui platform to separate boarding from alighting passengers. Although they obstruct the parallel-import traders, the barriers cause much inconvenience to normal passengers, as more time is needed to alight or board the train.[32]

Your task: Write a blog posting for the MTR Club (http://www.mtr.com.hk/eng/club/index.html) alerting passengers of the new policy and the possibility of using longer alighting and boarding times at the MTR Sheung Shui station. Tell them that the policy is only a temporary one and ask them to check the company website for any policy updates. Ask the passengers to cooperate, as MTR Corporation will prosecute passengers who ignore warnings.

IM SKILLS

5. Quick answer: Instant message turning down employee request at Hewlett-Packard. If she'd asked you a week ago, Lewinda Johnson might have been granted her request to attend a conference on the use of blogging for business, which is being held in New York City next month. Instead, Johnson waited until you were stuck in this meeting, and she needs your response within the hour. She'll have to take no for an answer: With travel budgets under tight restrictions, you would need at least three days to send her request up the chain of command. Furthermore, Johnson hasn't given you sufficient justification for her attendance since she's already familiar with blogging.

Your task: Write a 60- to 75-word instant message to Lewinda Johnson, declining her request. Decide whether the direct or indirect approach is appropriate.[33]

BLOGGING SKILLS   PORTFOLIO BUILDER

6. Coffee offer overflow: Undoing a marketing mistake at Starbucks. Marketing specialists usually celebrate when target audiences forward their messages to friends and family—essentially acting as unpaid advertising and sales representatives. In fact, the practice of viral marketing (see page 222) is based on this hope. For one Starbucks regional office, however, viral marketing started to make the company just a bit sick. The office sent employees in the Southeast an e-mail coupon for a free iced drink and invited them to share the coupon with family and friends. To the surprise of virtually no one who understands the nature of online life, the e-mail coupon multiplied rapidly, to the point that Starbucks stores all around the United States were quickly overwhelmed with requests for free drinks. The company decided to immediately terminate the free offer, a month ahead of the expiration date on the coupon.[34]

Your task: Write a one-paragraph message that can be posted on the Starbucks website and at individual stores, apologizing for the mix-up and explaining that the offer is no longer valid.

7. Retail rejection: Turning down a request to carry a product. G.O.D. (Goods of Desire) in Hong Kong (www.god.com.hk) is well-known for its blend of chic and traditional Oriental lifestyle concepts. The meticulously chosen shop name "G.O.D." assembles the phonetic sound of the Cantonese words meaning "to live better." With careful selection of the products it sells, G.O.D. has positioned itself as a trendsetter among young professionals who look for a certain lifestyle flair. The concept has proved successful, as can be seen in the popularity of its products and in the awards it received over the years.

G.O.D. offers a wide range of products such as furniture, household products, lighting, gift items, and clothing. Most of the products are designed and manufactured by G.O.D. Occasionally there are special crossover projects when G.O.D. works with well-established local brands in Hong Kong to create seasonal products. They also carry other brands locally or imported from the United States, the United Kingdom, France, the Netherlands, and Denmark.

As the merchandiser of G.O.D., you have to frequently review the list of suppliers to ensure their product quality and design are up to G.O.D.'s standard. You recently received a letter from one of the local suppliers asking if G.O.D. would like to carry a new line of bed linens that would cost more than the mass-market home-decor store models but less than G.O.D.'s own models. After reading the product descriptions, you realize that these are not a good fit for G.O.D. While these bed linen items certainly have a market, the designs are far too safe and old-fashioned. Besides, the textile contains 10 percent synthetic fibers and 90 percent cotton versus the 100 percent cotton linens manufactured by G.O.D. Additionally, their thread count is 400 while G.O.D.'s own linen products are normally above 600 thread count.[35]

Your task: Reply to this letter, explaining that the bed linens appear to be decent, but they don't fit G.O.D.'s concept and image of traditional yet chic. Support your decision with the criteria described above. Choose the direct or indirect approach carefully, taking into considering your company's future cooperation with this company.

8. Enough is enough: Alerting a service provider that its services will no longer be needed. Your company, PolicyPlan Insurance Services, is a 120-employee insurance claims processor based in Milwaukee. PolicyPlan has engaged Midwest Sparkleen for interior and exterior cleaning for the past five years. Midwest Sparkleen did exemplary work for the first four years, but after a change of ownership last year, the level of service has plummeted. Offices are no longer cleaned thoroughly, you've had to call the company at least six times to remind them to take care of spills and other messes that they're supposed to address routinely, and they've left toxic cleaning chemicals in a public hallway on several occasions. You have spoken with the owner about your concerns twice in the past three months, but his assurances that service would improve have not resulted in any noticeable improvements. When the evening cleaning crew forgot to lock the lobby door last Thursday—leaving your entire facility vulnerable to theft from midnight until 8 A.M. Friday morning—you decided it was time for a change.

Your task: Write a letter to Jason Allred, owner of Midwest Sparkleen, 4000 South Howell Avenue, Milwaukee, WI, 53207, telling him that PolicyPlan will not be renewing its annual cleaning contract with Midwest Sparkleen when the current contract expires at the end of this month. Cite the examples identified above, and keep the tone of your letter professional.

E-MAIL SKILLS

9. That's why we offer free trials: Rejecting a refund request. Like many other software companies, the Swiss company Fookes Software (www.fookes.com) lets potential customers download free evaluation copies of its software before deciding to purchase. By using the free trial versions, people can verify that the software meets their needs and is compatible with their PCs. Because it allows potential buyers to try products for 30 days before purchasing, the company does not provide refunds except in the case of accidental duplicate orders. Here is the company's refund policy, as shown on its website:

All of Fookes Software's products can be evaluated, **free of charge**, through a trial mode or separate trial version that can be downloaded directly from our web site. Use the trial **before you purchase** to ensure that the full product will be compatible with your computer systems and satisfy your requirements. If you do not, you accept that the product may not meet your needs and that this will not justify a refund or chargeback. If you experience an issue with our software, then please contact our customer support service for help in solving the problem.

All sales are final and refunds are provided only for accidental duplicate orders. Refunds will only be made to the credit card or PayPal account through which the original purchase was made. An administration fee may apply in such cases to cover processing costs and third-party commissions.

Ordering a software license signifies your acceptance of this Refund Policy.

In addition, the ordering page on the website asks potential buyers to read the refund policy before ordering and provides a link to the policy page.

This morning you received an e-mail message from a customer who purchased a copy of Album Express, a software package that helps people organize photos in attractive online albums and slide shows. After purchasing the program, the customer discovered that his computer has only 16 MB of memory, which is not enough to run the software effectively. He is now requesting a refund of the purchase price of $24.95. The website clearly states that Album Express requires at least 32 MB of memory, but the customer's e-mail doesn't mention whether he read this.[36]

Your task: Write an e-mail message, denying the customer's request for a refund.

E-MAIL SKILLS

10. Mobile phone violations: E-mail message to associates at Wilkes Artis Law Firm. "Company policy states that personnel are not to conduct business using mobile phones while driving," David Finch reminds you. He's a partner at the law firm Wilkes Artis in Washington, D.C., where you work as his administrative assistant.

You nod, waiting for him to explain. He already issued a memo about this rule last year, after a 15-year-old girl was hit and killed by an attorney from another firm. Driving back from a client meeting, the attorney was distracted while talking on her mobile phone. The girl's family sued the firm and won $30 million, but that's not the point. The point is that mobile phones can cause people to be hurt, even killed.

Finch explains, "Yesterday one of our associates called his secretary while driving his car. We can't allow this. According to the U.S. National Highway Transportation Safety Administration, 20 to 30 percent of all driving accidents are related to mobile phone usage. From now on, any violation of our mobile phone policy will result in suspension without pay, unless the call is a genuine health or traffic emergency."[37]

Your task: Finch asks you to write an e-mail message to all employees, announcing the new penalty for violating company policy.

NEGATIVE ORGANIZATIONAL NEWS

BLOGGING SKILLS

11. We're going to catch some flak for this: Alerting employees to the removal of a popular product. XtremityPlus is known for its outlandish extreme-sports products, and the Looney Launch is no exception. Fulfilling the dream of every childhood daredevil, the Looney Launch is an aluminum and fiberglass contraption that quickly unfolds to create the ultimate bicycle jump. The product has been selling as fast as you can make it, even though it comes plastered with warning labels proclaiming that its use is inherently dangerous.

As XtremityPlus's CEO, you were nervous about introducing this product, and your fears were just confirmed: You've been notified of the first lawsuit by a parent whose child broke several bones after crash-landing off a Looney Launch.

Your task: Write a post for your internal blog, explaining that the Looney Launch is being removed from the market immediately. Tell your employees to expect some negative reactions from enthusiastic customers and retailers but explain that (a) the company can't afford the risk of additional lawsuits; and (b) even for XtremityPlus, the Looney Launch pushes the envelope a bit too far. The product is simply too dangerous to sell in good conscience.

E-MAIL SKILLS

12. Looney Launch coming back to Earth: Informing retailers about the demise of a popular product. Now it's time to follow up the internal employee message about the Looney Launch (see Case 11) with a message to the retailers that carry the product.

Your task: Write an e-mail message to retailers, explaining that the Looney Launch is being removed from the market and explaining why you've reached this decision. Apologize for the temporary disruption this will cause to their businesses but emphasize that it's the right decision from both legal and social perspectives. Thank them for their continuing efforts to sell XtremityPlus products and assure them that your company will continue to offer exciting and innovative products for extreme-sports enthusiasts.

BLOGGING SKILLS   PORTFOLIO BUILDER

13. Communicating in a crisis: Informing the local community about a serious accident. An accident occurred last night at your company, Skyrail-ITM, the operator of the Ngong Ping Cable Car. The cable car ride, which runs from Tung Chung to Ngong Ping on Lantau Island, has been promoted as one of the "must-see" destinations in Hong Kong. Last night, an empty two-ton cable car fell off the ropeway and plunged more than 160 feet before it crashed into the hillside.

Your task: It's now Tuesday, the day after the accident. Write a brief post for the company's blog, covering the following points:

- A cabin fell off the ropeway and crashed onto a slope near the waterfront in Tung Chung.
- The accident happened at approximately 8 p.m. after operating hours on Monday, June 11, 2007.
- There were no passengers or staff in the cabin that fell.
- The police and firemen arrived at the scene immediately after the accident. They searched for anyone who may have been trapped, but no one was injured.
- During the time when the accident occurred, the company was conducting a brake test, which was part of the annual examination of the ropeway.
- The cause of the accident is not yet known.
- The company will conduct an investigation with the Engineering and Mechanical Services Department to find out the cause of the accident. All possible causes such as the weather or mechanical faults will be examined.
- The company will inform the public of the investigation results.
- The cable car service will be suspended indefinitely until the cable car system is examined thoroughly to guarantee passenger safety.

Conclude by thanking the police and firemen for their assistance and direct readers to Ngong Ping 360's official website for more information.[38]

E-MAIL SKILLS

14. The economy claims another one: Blog post announcing the closing of a Shaw Industries yarn plant. As the U.S. economy continued to sag in 2009 after receiving multiple blows from the housing and financial sectors, plant closures were a common tragedy across many industries. Shaw Industries, the world's largest manufacturer of carpeting, was among those suppliers to the housing industry that suffered as fewer houses were built or remodeled.

Your task: Write a brief message for Shaw's corporate blog, covering the following points:

- With more than $5 billion in annual sales, Shaw Industries is the world's number one carpet manufacturer.
- Shaw's Milledgeville, Georgia, plant makes yarn used in the manufacture of carpeting.

- The continuing struggles in the new-housing market and the inability of many current homeowners to afford remodeling projects have lowered demand for carpet. With less demand for carpet, the Milledgeville plant can no longer operate at a profit.
- Shaw is forced to close the Milledgeville plant and lay off all 150 employees at the plant.
- The plant will close in three to four weeks from the current date.
- As openings become available in other Shaw facilities, the company hopes to be able to place some of the workers in those jobs.
- Georgia Labor Commissioner Michael Thurmond promised to help the affected employees. "The layoff at Shaw Industries in Milledgeville will create a difficult situation for the workers and their families, and I want them to know they're not alone in dealing with this problem. Our staff will work closely with the laid-off workers, company officials, and local elected officials in determining how to best assist the affected employees."
- Assistance to be provided by the State of Georgia includes career counseling, unemployment benefits, and job retraining.[39]

E-MAIL SKILLS

15. Pulling the plug won't pull the plug: Alerting ATV owners to a serious safety problem. People who live for an adrenaline rush can find a way to go fast from Canada's Bombardier Recreational Products. Bombardier is one of the world's top makers of snowmobiles, personal watercraft, engines for motorboats, and all-terrain vehicles (ATVs)—all designed for fast fun.

Because it sends customers hurtling across snow, water, or land at high speeds, Bombardier takes safety quite seriously. However, problems do arise from time to time, requiring a rapid response with clear communication to the company's customer base. Bombardier recently became aware of a potentially hazardous situation with the "race-ready" version of its Can-Am DS 90 X ATVs. This model is equipped with a safety device called a tether engine shutoff switch, in which a cord is connected to a special switch that turns off the engine in the event of an emergency. On the affected units, pulling the cord might not shut off the motor, which is particularly dangerous if the rider falls off—the ATV will continue on its own until the engine speed returns to idle.

Your task: Write an e-mail message that will be sent to registered owners of 2008 and 2009 DS 90 X ATVs that include the potentially faulty switch. Analyze the situation carefully as you choose the direct or indirect approach for your message. Explain that the tether engine shutoff switch may not deactivate the engine when it is pulled in an emergency situation. To prevent riders from relying on a safety feature that might not work properly, Bombardier, in cooperation with transportation safety authorities in the United States and Canada, is voluntarily recalling these models to have the tether switch removed. Emphasize the serious nature of the situation by explaining that if the rider is ejected and the engine shutoff switch does not work properly, the ATV will run away on its own, potentially resulting in significant injuries or deaths. Owners should stop riding their vehicles immediately and make an appointment with an authorized dealer to have the switch removed. The service will be performed at no charge, and customers will receive a $50 credit voucher for future purchases of Bombardier accessories. Include the following contact information: www.can-am.brp.com and 1-888-638-5397.[40]

E-MAIL SKILLS PORTFOLIO BUILDER

16. Sorry, but we don't have a choice: E-mail about monitoring employee blogs. You can certainly sympathize with employees when they complain about having their e-mail and instant messages monitored, but you're implementing a company policy that all employees agree to abide by when they join the company. Your firm, Webcor Builders of San Mateo, California, is one of the estimated 60 percent of U.S. companies with such monitoring systems in place. More and more companies use these systems (which typically operate by scanning messages for keywords that suggest confidential, illegal, or otherwise inappropriate content) in an attempt to avoid instances of sexual harassment and other problems.

As the chief information officer, the manager in charge of computer systems in the company, you're often the target when employees complain about being monitored. Consequently, you know you're really going to hear it when employees learn that the monitoring program will be expanded to personal blogs as well.

Your task: Write an e-mail message to be distributed to the entire workforce, explaining that the automated monitoring program is about to be expanded to include employees' personal blogs. Explain that, while you sympathize with employee concerns regarding privacy and freedom of speech, it is the management team's responsibility to protect the company's intellectual property and the value of the company name. Therefore, employees' personal blogs will be added to the monitoring system to ensure that employees don't intentionally or accidentally expose company secrets or criticize management in a way that could harm the company.[41]

BLOGGING SKILLS PORTFOLIO BUILDER

17. Removing the obstacles on the on-ramp: Blog posting to Ernst & Young employees. Like many other companies these days, the accounting firm Ernst & Young is fighting a brain drain, as experienced executives and professionals leave midcareer to pursue charitable interests, devote more time to family matters, or pursue a variety of other dreams or obligations. The problem is particularly acute among women, because on average they step off the career track more often than men do. As general manager of the largest division in the company, you've been tapped to draft a set of guidelines to make it easier for employees who've taken some time off to move back into the company.

However, as soon as word gets out about what you're planning, several of your top performers, people who've never left the company for personal time off—or "taken the off-ramp," in current buzzword speak—march into your office to complain. They fear that encouraging the "off-rampers" to return isn't fair to the employees who've remained loyal to the firm, as they put it. One goes as far as to say that anyone who leaves the company doesn't deserve to be asked back. Two others claim that the additional experience and skills they've gained as they continued to work should guarantee them higher pay and more responsibilities than employees who took time off for themselves.

Your task: As unhappy as these several employees are, the program needs to be implemented if Ernst & Young hopes to bring "off-rampers" back into the company—thereby making sure they don't go to work for competitors instead. However, you also can't afford to antagonize the existing workforce; if the people who've already complained are any indication, you have a sizable morale problem on your hands. You decide that your first step is to clearly explain why the program is necessary, including how it will benefit everyone in the company by making Ernst & Young more competitive. Write a short posting for the company's internal blog, explaining that, despite the objections some employees have raised, the firm is going ahead with the program as planned. Balance this news (which some employees will obviously view as negative) with positive reassurances that all current employees will be treated fairly in terms of both compensation and promotion opportunities. Close with a call for continued communication on this issue, inviting people to meet with you in person or to post their thoughts on the blog.[42]

PORTFOLIO BUILDER

18. Listen to the music, partner: Delivering an ultimatum to a business associate. You're a marketing manager for Stanton, one of the premier suppliers of DJ equipment (turntables, amplifiers, speakers, mixers, and related accessories). Your company's latest creation, the FinalScratch system, has been flying off retailers' shelves. Both professional and amateur DJs love the way that FinalScratch gives them the feel of working with vinyl records by letting them control digital music files from any analog turntable or CD player while giving them access to the endless possibilities of digital music technology. (For more information about the product, go to www.stantondj.com.) Sales are strong everywhere except in Music99 stores, a retail chain in the Mid-Atlantic region. You suspect the cause: The owners of this chain refused to let their salespeople attend the free product training you offered when FinalScratch was introduced, claiming their people were smart enough to train themselves.

To explore the situation, you head out from Stanton headquarters in Hollywood, Florida, on an undercover shopping mission. After visiting a few Music99 locations, you're appalled by what you see. The salespeople in these stores clearly don't understand the FinalScratch concept, so they either give potential customers bad information about it or steer them to products from your competitors. No wonder sales are so bad at this chain.

Your task: You're tempted to pull your products out of this chain immediately, but you know how difficult and expensive it is to recruit new retailers in this market. However, this situation can't go on; you're losing thousands of dollars of potential business every week. Write a letter to Jackson Fletcher, the CEO of Music99 (14014 Preston Pike, Dover, DE 19901), expressing your disappointment in what you observed and explaining that the Music99 sales staff will need to agree to attend product training or else your company's management team will consider terminating the business relationship. You've met Mr. Fletcher in person once and talked to him on the phone several times, and you know him well enough to know that he will not be pleased by this ultimatum. Music99 does a good job selling other Stanton products—and he'll probably be furious to learn that you were "spying" on his sales staff.[43]

19. Refinancing rules: Letter explaining changes at PeopleFirst. When you began as a customer service representative at People-First.com, you worked with only five employees to pioneer a web-based auto loan brokerage. Customers loved it.

From your website, they filled out a single application and faxed in any necessary verification documents. Then PeopleFirst matched them with the best loan for which they qualified, chosen from a variety of lenders. You mailed them a no-obligation "Blank Check" to spend at any auto dealership up to the amount for which they qualified. The loan didn't begin until they spent the check. Later, if rates dropped, they could come back to PeopleFirst for refinancing.

All that changed when huge Capital One Financial Corporation bought out PeopleFirst The company changed your name to Capital One Auto Finance and converted all loans to Capital One loans. Under its new policies, Capital One will not refinance its own loans. However, your existing customers aren't charged a pre-payment penalty if they want to pay off their loans early by finding (on their own) another lender for refinancing. You might lose some business this way, but Capital One would lose a lot more if it refinanced all its loans every time rates dropped.

Your task: Explain the new policy in a letter to Faviola and Mary Franzone (7200 Poplar Ave., Memphis, TN 38197), who have inquired about refinancing their auto loan at today's lower rates.[44]

PODCASTING SKILLS

20. Say good-bye to the concierge: Podcast announcing the end of a popular employee benefit. An employee concierge seemed like a great idea when you added it as an employee benefit last year. The concierge handles a wide variety of personal chores for employees, everything from dropping off dry cleaning to ordering event tickets to sending flowers. Employees love the service, and you know that the time they save can be devoted to work or family activities. Unfortunately, profits are way down, and concierge usage is up—up so far that you'll need to add a second concierge to keep up with the demand. As painful as it will be for everyone, you decide that the company needs to stop offering the service.

Your task: Script a brief podcast, announcing the decision and explaining why it was necessary. Make up any details you need. If your instructor asks you to do so, record your podcast and submit the file.

WEB WRITING SKILLS

21. A rash of rashes: Alerting clothing customers to potential skin irritation. Sewn-in clothing tags carry essential information about size and garment care, but no matter where they are located inside a garment, they seem to have a knack for poking and scratching. Pestered consumers consequently welcomed the switch by many clothing makers to *tagless labels*, in which information is printed directly on the fabric, and no physical tag is sewn into the garment. Carter's, one of the leading manufacturers and retailers of children's clothing, is one of those companies. Unfortunately, a small number of parents have contacted Carter's to complain that their children have developed rashes where their skin came in contact with a tagless label.

Your task: Write an announcement for Carter's website, explaining that the company has heard some reports of babies whose skin

appeared to be irritated by the tagless labels. Cover the following points: (1) the situation applies only to clothes from the fall 2007 product line, in which the tagless label has a solid white printed background on which the label text is printed (as opposed to newer and older garments, in which the label text is printed directly on the fabric, without the solid background); (2) of the 100 million garments sold in the fall 2007 line, the company has received only 400 complaints of rashes; (3) based on a thorough analysis by the company, its suppliers, and several independent doctors and other specialists, Carter's has found that the labels contain no known skin irritants or abrasive chemicals, and the problem seems to affect only a very small number of children with sensitive skin; (4) because the problem is so limited in scope and the skin rashes are not serious, after discussions with the U.S. Consumer Products Safety Commission, the company has opted not to recall the clothes but is instead advising parents of affected children to switch to other garments; and (5) as is always the case with Carter's clothes, consumers can return unsatisfactory products for a full refund. You will be able to show two comparative photos on the website to help consumers identify the garments in question, one showing clothes from the fall 2007 line, with the solid-background labels, and one showing a newer line of clothes that have a different label style.[45]

NEGATIVE EMPLOYMENT MESSAGES

TELEPHONE SKILLS

22. Reacting to a lost contract: Phone call rescinding a job offer. As the human resources manager at Alion Science and Technology, a military research firm in McLean, Virginia, you were thrilled when one of the top computer visualization specialists in the United States accepted your job offer. Claus Gunnstein's skills would have made a major contribution to Alion's work in designing flight simulators and other systems. Unfortunately, the day after he accepted the offer, Alion received news that a major Pentagon contract had been canceled. In addition to letting several dozen current employees know that the company will be forced to lay them off, you need to tell Gunnstein that Alion has no choice but to rescind the job offer.

Your task: Outline the points you'll need to make in a telephone call to Gunnstein. Pay special attention to your opening and closing statements. (You'll review your plans for the phone call with Alion's legal staff to make sure everything you say follows employment law guidelines; for now, just focus on the way you'll present the negative news to Gunnstein. Feel free to make up any details you need.)[46]

23. Juggling diversity and performance: Memo giving a negative performance review at AT&T. As billing adjustments department manager at AT&T, you've been trained to handle a culturally diverse workforce. One of your best recent hires is 22-year-old Jorge Gutierrez. In record time, he was entering and testing complex price changes, mastering the challenges of your monumental computerized billing software. He was a real find—except for one problem: His close family ties often distract him from work duties.

His parents immigrated from Central America when Jorge and his sisters were young children, and you understand and deeply respect the importance that family plays in the lives of many Hispanic Americans. However, every morning, Gutierrez's mother calls to be sure he got to work safely. Then his father calls. And three times this month, his younger sister has called him away from work with three separate emergencies. Friends and extended family members seem to call at all hours of the day.

Gutierrez says he's asked friends and family members not to call his office number. Now they dial his mobile phone instead. He's reluctant to shut off his mobile phone during work hours in case someone in his family needs him.

At this point, you have given Gutierrez several oral warnings. You really can't afford to lose him, so you're hoping that a written negative review will give him greater incentive to persuade friends and relatives to respect his work commitments. You'll deliver the letter in a one-on-one meeting and help him find ways to resolve the issue within a mutually agreed-upon time frame.

Your task: Write the letter, using suggestions in this chapter to help put the bad news in a constructive light. Avoid culturally biased remarks or innuendo.

E-MAIL SKILLS

24. Career moves: E-mail refusing to write a recommendation. Tom Weiss worked in the office at Opal Pools and Patios for four months under your supervision (you're office manager). On the basis of what he told you he could do, you started him off as a file clerk. However, his organizational skills proved inadequate for the job, so you transferred him to logging in accounts receivable, where he performed almost adequately. Then he assured you that his "real strength" was customer relations, so you moved him to the complaint department. After he spent three weeks making angry customers even angrier, you were convinced that no place in your office was appropriate for his talents. Five weeks ago, you encouraged him to resign before being formally fired.

Today's e-mail brings a request from Weiss, asking you to write a letter recommending him for a sales position with a florist shop. You can't assess Weiss's sales abilities, but you do know him to be an incompetent file clerk, a careless bookkeeper, and an insensitive customer service representative. Someone else is more likely to deserve the sales job, so you decide that you have done enough favors for Tom Weiss for one lifetime and plan to refuse his request.

Your task: Write an e-mail reply to Weiss (tomweiss@mailnet.com), indicating that you have chosen not to write a letter of recommendation for him.

25. Bad news for 80: Form letter to unsuccessful job candidates. The dean's selection committee screened 85 applications for the position of dean of arts and sciences at your campus. After two rounds of eliminations, the top 5 candidates were invited to "airport interviews," in which the committee managed to meet with each candidate for an hour. Then the top 3 candidates were invited to the campus to meet with students, faculty, and administrators.

The committee recommended to the university president that the job be given to Constance Pappas, who has a doctorate in American studies and has been chairperson of the history department at Minneapolis Metropolitan College for the past three years. The president agreed, and Dr. Pappas accepted the offer.

One final task remains before the work of the dean's selection committee is finished: Letters must be sent to the 84 unsuccessful candidates. The 4 who reached the "airport interview" stage will receive personal letters from the chairperson of the committee. Your job, as secretary of the committee, is to draft the form letter that will be sent to the other 80 applicants.

Your task: Draft a letter of 100 to 200 words. All copies will be individually addressed to the recipients but will carry identical messages.

PORTFOLIO BUILDER

26. What we have here is a failure to communicate: Writing a negative performance review. Elaine Bridgewater, the former professional golfer you hired to oversee your golf equipment company's relationship with retailers, knows the business inside and out. As a former touring pro, she has unmatched credibility. She also has seemingly boundless energy, solid technical knowledge, and an engaging personal style. Unfortunately, she hasn't been quite as attentive as she needs to be when it comes to communicating with retailers. You've been getting complaints about voice-mail messages gone unanswered for days, confusing e-mails that require two or three rounds of clarification, and reports that are haphazardly thrown together. As valuable as Bridgewater's other skills are, she's going to cost the company sales if this goes on much longer. The retail channel is vital to your company's survival, and she's the employee most involved in this channel.

Your task: Draft a brief (one page maximum) informal performance appraisal and improvement plan for Bridgewater. Be sure to compliment her on the areas in which she excels but don't shy away from highlighting the areas in which she needs to improve, too: punctual response to customer messages; clear writing; and careful revision, production, and proofreading. Use what you've learned in this course so far to supply any additional advice about the importance of these skills.

Writing Persuasive Messages

Learning Objectives

After studying this chapter, you will be able to

1 Apply the three-step writing process to persuasive messages

2 Identify seven ways to establish credibility in persuasive messages

3 Describe the AIDA model for persuasive messages

4 Distinguish between emotional and logical appeals and discuss how to balance them

5 Describe seven essential steps in developing marketing and sales messages

6 Identify steps you can take to avoid ethical lapses in marketing and sales messages

Communication Close-up at CafeMom

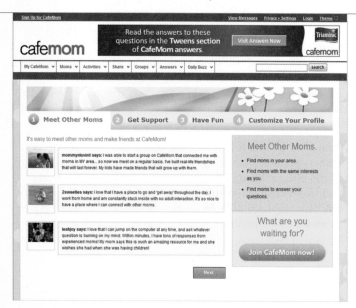

CafeMom appeals to new members with a variety of attractive images and brief, upbeat statements that emphasize the benefits of joining.

www.cafemom.com

Few roles in life require more information and insight than parenting. From prenatal care to early childhood development to education to socialization issues, parents are in continuous learning mode as their children grow. Parents also need to learn about themselves as they grow in their roles, from balancing work and home life to nurturing their own relationships. At the same time, parenting can be one of the most isolating experiences for people, often making it difficult for them to acquire the information and support they need to succeed as parents.

Two lifelong friends, actor and activist Andrew Shue and entrepreneur Michael Sanchez, pondered this age-old challenge and saw the web as a solution. The pair co-founded CafeMom, an online community and information resource that helps mothers find answers, insights, and each other.

Information resources and social networks abound on the web, and like any other web start-up, CafeMom faced the challenge of standing apart from the crowd and growing its membership large enough to create a viable business. One of the keys to its success is clear, audience-focused messages that make a compelling case for joining CafeMom. Using straightforward statements such as "CafeMom is an online community where thousands of moms come together every day to connect with each other" and "Whatever you're going through, chances are another mom has been there and can help," the company communicates the features of its various online services and the benefits of joining.

The persuasive communication effort certainly seems to have been successful: CafeMom is now the largest social networking community for mothers and continues to expand as more mothers join in search of helpful insights and friendly support from their peers.[1]

USING THE THREE-STEP WRITING PROCESS FOR PERSUASIVE MESSAGES

1 LEARNING OBJECTIVE

Apply the three-step writing process to persuasive messages

Professionals such as Michael Sanchez, CEO of CafeMom (profiled in the chapter-opening Communication Close-up), realize that successful businesses rely on persuasive messages in both internal and external communication. Whether you're trying to convince your boss to open a new office in Europe or encourage potential customers to try your products, you need to call on your abilities of **persuasion**—the attempt to change an audience's attitudes, beliefs, or actions.[2] Successful professionals understand that persuasion is not about trickery or getting people to make choices that aren't in their best interests; rather, persuasion lets your audience members know they have a choice and helps them choose to agree with you.[3] As with every other type of business message, the three-step writing process improves persuasive messages.

Step 1: Planning a Persuasive Message

Every day, untold numbers of good ideas go unheeded and good products go unsold simply because the messages meant to promote them aren't compelling enough. Even if audiences agree that your idea or product is attractive, they usually have other options to consider as well, so you will need to convince them that your choice is the best of all the attractive alternatives. Creating successful persuasive messages in these challenging situations starts with an insightful analysis of the situation.

Analyzing the Situation

A clear purpose is important in every message, of course, but clarity is doubly important in persuasive messages because you are asking the audience to do something—to take action, make decisions, and so on. Let's say you want to persuade members of top management to support a particular research project. But what does "support" mean? Do you want them to pat you on the back and wish you well? Or do you want them to give you a staff of five researchers and a $1 million annual budget? If you don't know what you want or can't express it clearly, you'll never be able to convince an audience to do anything.

In addition to having a clear purpose, the best persuasive messages are closely connected to audience members' desires and interests.[4] Consider their needs and motivations (the reasons they might respond favorably to your message), as well as their concerns and objections (the reasons they might *not* respond favorably). With these two insights as guides, you can work to find common ground with your audience while emphasizing positive points and minimizing negative ones.

To understand and categorize audience needs, you can refer to specific information such as **demographics** (the age, gender, occupation, income, education, and other quantifiable characteristics of the people you're trying to persuade) and **psychographics** (personality, attitudes, lifestyle, and other psychological characteristics). Be sure to consider cultural expectations so that you don't undermine your persuasive message by using an inappropriate appeal or by organizing your message in a way that seems unfamiliar or uncomfortable to your audience.

If you aim to change someone's attitudes, beliefs, or actions through a persuasive message, it is vital to understand his or her **motivation**—the combination of forces that drive people to satisfy their needs. Table 10.1 lists some of the needs that psychologists have identified or suggested as being important in

Persuasion is the attempt to change someone's attitudes, beliefs, or actions.

Failing to clarify your purpose is a common mistake with persuasive messages.

Demographics include characteristics such as age, gender, occupation, income, and education.

Psychographics include characteristics such as personality, attitudes, and lifestyle.

 REAL-TIME UPDATES
Learn More

Persuasion skills for every business professional

Persuasion is an essential business skill, no matter what career path you follow. Study these great tips for understanding, practicing, and applying persuasive skills. Go to **http://real-timeupdates.com/bct** and click on "Learn More." If you are using mybcommlab, you can access Real-Time Updates within each chapter or under Student Study Tools.

TABLE 10.1 Human Needs That Influence Motivation

NEED	IMPLICATIONS FOR COMMUNICATION
Basic physiological requirements: The needs for food, water, sleep, oxygen, and other essentials.	Everyone has these needs, but the degree of attention an individual gives to them often depends on whether the needs are being met; for instance, an advertisement for sleeping pills will have greater appeal to someone suffering from insomnia than to someone who has no problem sleeping.
Safety and security: The needs for protection from bodily harm, to know that loved ones are safe, and for financial security, protection of personal identity, career security, and other assurances.	These needs influence both consumer and business decisions in a wide variety of ways; for instance, advertisements for life insurance often encourage parents to think about the financial security of their children and other loved ones.
Affiliation and belonging: The needs for companionship, acceptance, love, popularity, etc.	The need to feel loved, accepted, or popular drives a great deal of human behavior, from the desire to be attractive to potential mates to wearing the clothing style that a particular social group is likely to approve.
Power and control: The need to feel in control of situations or to exert authority over others	You can see many examples appealing to this need in advertisements: *Take control of your life, your finances, your future, your career,* and so on. Many people who lack power want to know how to get it, and people who have power often want others to know they have it.
Achievement: The need to feel a sense of accomplishment—or to be admired by others for accomplishments	This need can involve both *knowing* (when people experience a feeling of accomplishment) and *showing* (when people are able to show others that they've achieved success); advertising for luxury consumer products frequently appeals to this need.
Adventure and distraction: The need for excitement or relief from daily routine	People vary widely in their need for adventure; some crave excitement—even danger—while others value calmness and predictability. Some needs for adventure and distraction are met *virtually,* such as through horror movies, thriller novels, etc.
Knowledge, exploration, and understanding: The need to keep learning	For some people, learning is usually a means to an end, a way to fulfill some other need; for others, acquiring new knowledge is the goal.
Aesthetic appreciation: The desire to experience beauty, order, symmetry, etc.	Although this need may seem "noncommercial" at first glance, advertisers appeal to it frequently, from the pleasing shape of a package to the quality of the gemstones in a piece of jewelry.
Self-actualization: The need to "be all that one can be," to reach one's full potential as a human being	Psychologists Kurt Goldstein and Abraham Maslow popularized self-actualization as the desire to make the most of one's potential, and Maslow identified it as one of the higher-level needs in his classic hierarchy; even if people met most or all of their other needs, they would still feel the need to self-actualize. An often-quoted example of appealing to this need is the U.S. Army's one-time advertising slogan "Be all that you can be."
Helping others: The need to believe that one is making a difference in the lives of other people	This need is the central motivation in fundraising messages and other appeals to charity.

Effective persuasive messages are closely aligned with audience motivations, those forces that drive people to satisfy their needs.

influencing human motivation. Obviously, the more closely a persuasive message aligns with a recipient's existing motivation, the more effective the message is likely to be. For example, if you try to persuade consumers to purchase a product on the basis of its fashion appeal, that message will connect with consumers who are motivated by a desire to be in style but probably won't connect with consumers driven by practical function or financial concerns.

Motivation is a complex psychological subject, and researchers have proposed a variety of theories to help explain why humans are driven to behave as they do. For instance, some theories suggest a process in which people take action to fulfill perceived needs and then evaluate the outcomes of those actions to determine whether the effort was worthwhile:

1. **Need.** The individual senses a need of some sort, from the basic need for food to a need for recognition or self-respect. We are all born with certain needs but can acquire other needs as we grow up, such as a need for achievement or a need to affiliate with compatible friends and colleagues.[5]

2. **Action.** To fulfill a need, the individual takes actions or adopts behaviors that he or she believes will result in the need being satisfied. The *quality* of the action is a matter of choosing which action to take, deciding how much effort to put into the action, and deciding how long to sustain that effort.[6]

3. **Outcome.** The individual observes the outcome of the action (sometimes called the *reward*) and determines whether the effort was worthwhile. Actions that result in positive outcomes are likely to be repeated; those that result in negative outcomes are less likely to be repeated.

Although this is a simplified view of motivation and not all theorists endorse this model, it helps emphasize the importance of understanding your audience's needs and why they would be driven to satisfy those needs. If you don't understand what motivates your audience, you won't be able persuade them to take the actions you'd like them to take.

Gathering Information

Once your situation analysis is complete, you need to gather the information necessary to create a compelling persuasive message. Chapter 11 offers advice on using the latest research techniques to find the information you need.

Selecting the Right Medium

Persuasive messages can be found in virtually every communication medium, from instant messages and podcasts to radio advertisements and skywriting. In fact, advertising agencies employ media specialists whose only jobs are to analyze the media options available and select the most cost-effective combination for each client and each advertising campaign.

In some situations, various members of your audience might prefer different media for the same message. Some consumers like to do all their car shopping in person, whereas others do most of their car-shopping research online. Some people don't mind promotional e-mails for products they're interested in; others resent every piece of commercial e-mail they receive. If you can't be sure you can reach most or all of your audience through a single medium, you need to use two or more, such as following up an e-mail campaign with printed letters.

You may need to use multiple media to reach your entire audience.

Social media (see Chapter 7) provide some exciting options for persuasive messages, particularly marketing and sales messages. However, as "Writing Persuasive Messages for Social Media" on page 331 explains, messages in these media require a unique approach.

Another important area of development is combining personal attention with technological reach and efficiency. For example, a customer support agent can carry on multiple instant messaging conversations at once, responding to one customer while other customers are typing messages. Even perceptions of human interaction created by animated *avatars* such as IKEA's "Anna" (www.ikea.com) can create a more sociable experience for shoppers, which can make websites more effective as a persuasive medium.[7]

Organizing Your Information

Successful persuasion requires close attention to all four aspects of organizing your information: defining your main idea, limiting your scope, choosing the direct or indirect approach, and grouping your points in a meaningful way. The most effective main ideas for persuasive messages have one thing in common: They are about the receiver, not the sender. For instance, if you're trying to convince others to join you in a business venture, explain how it will help them, not how it will help you.

To limit your scope effectively, include only the information needed to help your audience take the next step toward the ultimate decision or ultimate action you want. In simple scenarios such as persuading teammates to attend a special meeting, you might put everything you have to say into a single, short message. But if you want your company to invest several million dollars in your latest product idea, the scope of your first message might be limited to securing 10 minutes at the next executive committee meeting so that you can introduce your idea and get permission to explore it.

Limit your scope to include only the information needed to help your audience take the next step toward making a favorable decision.

Most persuasive messages use the indirect approach because it gives the writer the opportunity to explain his or her reasons and build interest before asking for a decision or action. However, consider using the direct approach whenever you know your audience is ready to hear your proposal. Similarly, if there's a good chance your audience members will

Use the direct approach if your audience is ready to hear your proposal.

Business Communication 2.0

Building an Audience Through Search Engine Optimization

Have you ever wondered why certain websites and blogs appear at the top of the list when you use an online search engine? Or why a site you might expect to find doesn't show up at all? Such questions are at the heart of one of the most important activities in online communication: *search engine optimization* (SEO). (SEO applies to the *natural* or *organic* search results, not the sponsored, paid results you see above, beside, or below the main search results listing.)

SEO involves three major parties: web users, website owners, and search engine developers such as Google, Yahoo!, and Microsoft. Most web users rely heavily on search engines to find relevant websites for shopping, research, and other online tasks. Website owners often rely on search engines to steer potential customers and other valuable visitors their way. To bring these two parties together while building lots of web traffic and advertising opportunities for themselves, search engine developers constantly fine-tune their engines to produce relevant, helpful search results.

And that's where things get interesting. Using sophisticated—and secret—algorithms, search engines rank search results by relevance to the user's input terms, starting with the most relevant results at the top of the list. Web users typically choose sites that show up in the first few pages of search results, so site owners naturally want to be ranked as high as possible.

Given the secrecy and the high stakes, the online search business has become something of a cat-and-mouse game in which website owners try to figure out what they can do improve their rankings, while search engine developers work to improve the quality of results—partly by blocking website owners' attempts to "game" the system. For instance, in the early days of online search, some website owners would embed dozens of popular search terms in their websites, even if those terms had nothing to do with their site content. Search engine developers responded with ways to detect such tactics and penalize sites that use them by either lowering the sites' rankings in the search results or leaving them out entirely.

SEO has become a complex topic as search engines and the web itself have continued to evolve and as motivated website owners have looked for ways to boost their rankings. For instance, Google now evaluates more than 100 factors to determine search rankings. Without becoming an expert in SEO, however, you can work toward improving rankings for your website by focusing on four important areas: (1) offer fresh, high-quality, audience-oriented content; (2) use relevant keywords judiciously, particularly in important areas such as the page title that displays at the top of the browser screen; and (3) encourage links to your site from other high-quality sites with relevant content. In addition, make sure search engines can find your valuable content, particularly if you have a lot of Web 2.0 and multimedia technologies on your site. For example, search engines tend to find blogs and wikis easily, but techniques for finding content in podcasts, online videos, and Flash animation are still developing. You can learn more from Google's Webmaster Guidelines, **www.google.com/support/ webmasters**.

CAREER APPLICATIONS

1. Locate a website for any company that sells products to consumers and write a new title for the site's homepage (the title that appears at the top of a web browser). Make the title short enough to read quickly while still summarizing what the company offers. Be sure to use one or more keywords that online shoppers would likely use when searching for the types of products the company sells.
2. Identify three high-quality websites that would be good sites to link to the site you chose in Question 1. For instance, if you chose a website that sells automotive parts and supplies, one of the three linking sites could be a popular blog that deals with automotive repair. Or if the site you chose sells golf equipment, you might find a sports website that covers the professional golf tours or one that provides information about golf courses around the world.

agree with your message, don't force them to wade through pages of reasoning before seeing your main idea (see Figure 10.1).

The choice of direct or indirect approach is influenced by your authority, expertise, or power within the organization.

Your choice between the direct and indirect approaches is also influenced by the extent of your authority, expertise, or power in an organization. Generally, the more of these qualities you have in a given situation, the more likely that the direct approach will work for you because audience members are more apt to accept whatever you have to say. Conversely, if you're writing on a subject outside your recognized expertise, or if you're trying to persuade higher-level managers, the indirect approach is usually better because it allows you to build credibility as you present your reasoning.

Step 2: Writing a Persuasive Message

Persuasive messages are often unexpected or even unwelcome, so the "you" attitude is crucial.

Persuasive messages are often uninvited and occasionally even unwelcome, so adopting the "you" attitude is particularly critical when you write them. Most people won't even pay attention to your message, much less respond to it, if it isn't about them. You can encourage a more welcome reception by (1) using positive and polite language, (2) understanding and

FIGURE 10.1 Proposal Using the Direct Approach

Bette McGiboney, an administrative assistant to the athletic director of Auburn University, presented a solution to the problem of high phone bills during the month of August. She already has a close relationship with her boss, who is likely to welcome the money-saving idea, so the direct approach is a fast, efficient way to communicate her proposal.

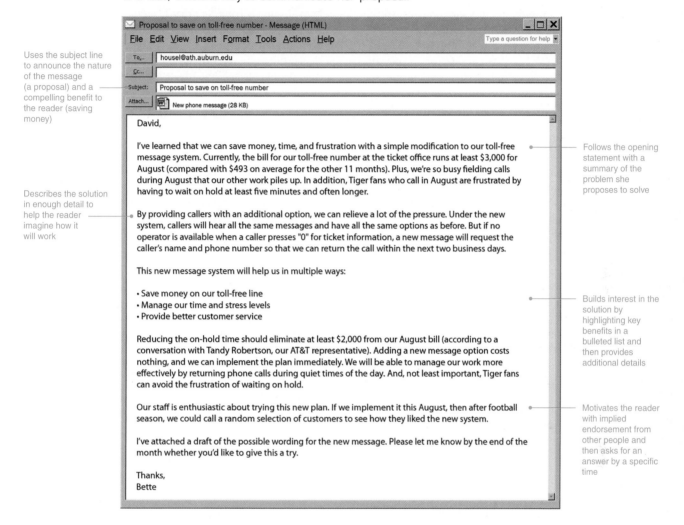

Uses the subject line to announce the nature of the message (a proposal) and a compelling benefit to the reader (saving money)

Describes the solution in enough detail to help the reader imagine how it will work

Follows the opening statement with a summary of the problem she proposes to solve

Builds interest in the solution by highlighting key benefits in a bulleted list and then provides additional details

Motivates the reader with implied endorsement from other people and then asks for an answer by a specific time

respecting cultural differences, (3) being sensitive to organizational cultures, and (4) taking steps to establish your credibility.

Positive language usually happens naturally with persuasive messages because you're promoting an idea or a product that you believe has benefits for your audience. However, polite language isn't as automatic as you might think. Don't insult the readers by implying that they are incapable of making smart decisions without your wise advice.

Demonstrating an understanding of and respect for cultural differences is crucial to persuasion. For example, an aggressive, hard-sell technique is likely to antagonize a French audience. In Germany, where people tend to focus on technical matters, make sure you provide solid supporting evidence for all messages. In Sweden, audiences tend to focus on theoretical questions and strategic implications, whereas U.S. audiences are usually concerned with more practical matters.[8]

The culture within an organization also affects persuasive efforts. For instance, some organizations handle disagreement and conflict in an indirect, behind-the-scenes way, whereas others accept and even encourage open discussion and the sharing of viewpoints. When you accept and follow these traditions, you show your audience members that you understand them and respect their values.

Finally, when trying to persuade a skeptical or hostile audience, you must convince people that you are credible before they will pay much attention to your message. According to

Make sure your persuasive messages consider the culture of your audience.

Ethics Detective

Solving the Case of the Incredible Credibility

As the director of human resources in your company, you're desperate for some help. You want to keep the costs of employee benefits under control while making sure you provide employees with a fair benefits package. However, you don't have time to research all the options for health insurance, wellness programs, retirement plans, family counseling, educational benefits, and everything else, so you decide to hire a consultant. You receive the following message from a consultant interested in working with you:

> I am considered the country's foremost authority on employee health insurance programs. My clients offer universally positive feedback on the programs I've designed for them. They also love how much time I save them—hundreds and hundreds of hours.

I am absolutely confident that I can thoroughly analyze your needs and create a portfolio that realizes every degree of savings possible. I invite you to experience the same level of service that has generated such comments as "Best advice ever!" and "Saved us an unbelievable amount of money."

You'd love to get results like that, but the message almost sounds too good to be true. Is it?

ANALYSIS

The consultant's message contains at least a dozen instances in which this writer's credibility might be questioned. Identify as many as you can and explain how you would bolster reader confidence by providing additional or different information.

---

2 LEARNING OBJECTIVE

Identify seven ways to establish credibility in persuasive messages

recent research, most managers overestimate their own credibility.[9] Chapter 5 lists characteristics essential to building and maintaining your credibility, including honesty, objectivity, awareness of audience needs, knowledge and expertise, endorsements, performance, and communication style. In addition to those elements, you can improve your credibility in persuasive messages with these techniques:

- **Using simple language.** In most persuasive situations, your audience will be cautious, watching for fantastic claims, insupportable descriptions, and emotional manipulation.
- **Supporting your message with facts.** Provide objective evidence for the claims and promises you make.
- **Identifying your sources.** Telling your audience where you got your information improves your credibility, especially if your audience already respects those sources.
- **Establishing common ground.** Beliefs, attitudes, and background experiences that you have in common with members of your audience will help them identify with you.
- **Being objective.** Your ability to understand and acknowledge all sides of an issue helps you present fair and logical arguments in your persuasive message.
- **Displaying your good intentions.** Your willingness to keep your audience's best interests in mind helps you create persuasive messages that are both effective and ethical.
- **Avoiding the "hard sell."** You've no doubt experienced a "hard sell," an aggressive approach that uses strong, emotional language and high-pressure tactics to convince people to make a firm decision in a hurry. Audiences tend to instinctively resist this approach because communicators who take this approach can come across as being more concerned with meeting their own goals than with satisfying the needs of their audiences. In contrast, a "soft sell" is more like a comfortable conversation in which the sender uses calm, rational persuasion to help the recipient make a smart choice.

Audiences resist the high-pressure tactics of the "hard sell" and tend to distrust communicators who take this approach.

Step 3: Completing a Persuasive Message

The pros know from experience that details can make or break a persuasive message, so they're careful not to skimp on this part of the writing process. For instance, advertisers may have a dozen or more people review a message before it's released to the public.

When you evaluate your content, try to judge your argument objectively and try not to overestimate your credibility. If possible, ask an experienced colleague who knows your audience well to review your draft. Make sure your design elements complement, rather than detract from, your persuasive argument. In addition, meticulous proofreading will help you identify any mechanical or spelling errors that would weaken your persuasive potential. Finally, make sure your distribution methods fit your audience's expectations and preferences.

With the three-step model in mind, you're ready to begin composing persuasive messages, starting with *persuasive business messages* (those that try to convince audiences to approve new projects, enter into business partnerships, and so on), followed by *marketing and sales messages* (those that try to convince audiences to consider and then purchase products and services).

DEVELOPING PERSUASIVE BUSINESS MESSAGES

Persuasive business messages comprise a broad and diverse category, with audiences that range from a single person in your own department to government agencies, investors, business partners, community leaders, and other external groups. Your success as a businessperson is closely tied to your ability to convince others to accept new ideas, change old habits, or act on your recommendations. As you move into positions of greater responsibility in your career, your persuasive messages could start to influence multimillion-dollar investments and the careers of hundreds or thousands of employees. Obviously, you need to match the increase in your persuasive skills with the care and thoroughly of your analysis and planning so that the ideas you convince others to adopt are sound.

No matter where your career leads, your success will depend on your ability to craft effective persuasive messages.

Strategies for Persuasive Business Messages

Even if you have the power to compel others to do what you want them to do, persuading them is more effective than forcing them. People who are forced into accepting a decision or plan are less motivated to support it and more likely to react negatively than if they're persuaded.[10] Within the context of the three-step process, effective persuasion involves four essential strategies: framing your arguments, balancing emotional and logical appeals, reinforcing your position, and anticipating objections. (Note that all these concepts in this section apply as well to marketing and sales messages, covered later in the chapter.)

Structuring Persuasive Business Messages

As noted earlier, most persuasive messages use the indirect approach. Experts in persuasive communication have developed a number of indirect models for such messages. One of the best known is the **AIDA model**, which organizes messages into four phases:

- **Attention.** Your first objective is to engage your readers or listeners in a way that encourages them to want to hear about your main idea. Write a brief and compelling sentence, without making extravagant claims or irrelevant points. Look for some common ground on which to build your case (see Figure 10.2). And while you want to be positive and confident, make sure you don't start out with a *hard sell*—a pushy, aggressive opening. Doing so often puts audiences on guard and on the defensive.
- **Interest.** Explain the relevance of your message to your audience. Continuing the theme you started with, paint a more detailed picture of the problem you propose to solve with the solution you're offering (whether it's a new idea, a new process, a new product, or whatever).
- **Desire.** Help audience members embrace your idea by explaining how the change will benefit them, either personally or professionally. Reduce resistance by identifying and answering in advance any questions the audience might have. If your idea is complex, you might need to explain how you would implement it. Back up your claims in order to increase audience willingness to take the action you suggest in the next section.
- **Action.** Suggest the action you want readers to take and phrase it in a way that emphasizes the benefits to them or to the organization they represent. Make the action as easy as possible to take, including offering to assist, if appropriate. Be sure to provide all the information the audience needs to take the action, including deadlines and contact details.

The AIDA model is tailor-made for using the indirect approach, allowing you to save your main idea for the action phase. However, you can also use it for the direct approach, in which case you use your main idea as an attention-getter, build interest with your argument,

3 LEARNING OBJECTIVE

Describe the AIDA model for persuasive messages

Using the AIDA model is an effective way to organize most persuasive messages:
- *Attention*
- *Interest*
- *Desire*
- *Action*

The AIDA model and similar plans are ideal for the indirect approach.

FIGURE 10.2 Persuasive Message Using the AIDA Model

Randy Thumwolt uses the AIDA model in a message about a program that would reduce Host Marriott's annual plastics costs and address consumer complaints about the company's recycling record. Note how Thumwolt "sells the problem" before attempting to sell the solution. Few people are interested in hearing about solutions to problems they don't know about or don't believe exist.

1 Plan → **2 Write** → **3 Complete**

Analyze the Situation
Verify that the purpose is to solve an ongoing problem, so the audience will be receptive.

Gather Information
Determine audience needs and obtain the necessary information on recycling problem areas.

Select the Right Medium
Verify that an e-mail message is appropriate for this communication.

Organize the Information
Limit the scope to the main idea, which is to propose a recycling solution; use the indirect approach to lay out the extent of the problem.

Adapt to Your Audience
Adjust the level of formality based on the degree of familiarity with the audience; maintain a positive relationship by using the "you" attitude, politeness, positive emphasis, and bias-free language.

Compose the Message
Use a conversational but professional style and keep the message brief, clear, and as helpful as possible.

Revise the Message
Evaluate content and review readability to make sure the information is clear and complete without being overwhelming.

Produce the Message
Emphasize a clean, professional appearance.

Proofread the Message
Review for errors in layout, spelling, and mechanics.

Distribute the Message
Verify that the right file is attached and then deliver the message.

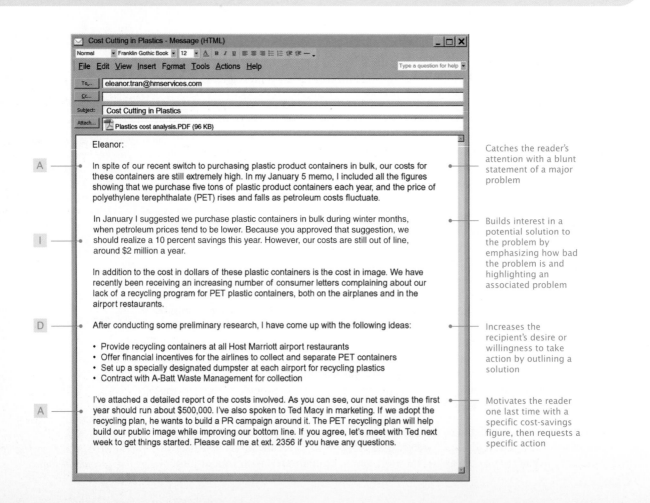

create desire with your evidence, and re-emphasize your main idea in the action phase with the specific action you want your audience to take.

When your AIDA message uses the indirect approach and is delivered by memo or e-mail, keep in mind that your subject line usually catches your reader's eye first. Your challenge is to make it interesting and relevant enough to capture reader attention without revealing your main idea. If you put your request in the subject line, you might just get a quick no before you've had a chance to present your arguments:

INSTEAD OF THIS	WRITE THIS
Request for development budget to add automated IM response system	Reducing the cost of customer support inquiries

With either the direct or indirect approach, AIDA and similar models do have limitations. First, AIDA is a unidirectional method that essentially talks *at* audiences, not *with* them. Second, AIDA is built around a single event, such as asking an audience for a decision, rather than on building a mutually beneficial, long-term relationship.[11] AIDA is still a valuable tool for the right purposes, but as you'll read later in the chapter, a conversational approach is more compatible with today's social media.

The AIDA model has limitations, and it needs to be modified for use with social media.

Balancing Emotional and Logical Appeals

Imagine you're sitting at a control panel with one knob labeled "logic" and another labeled "emotion." As you prepare your persuasive message, you carefully adjust each knob, tuning the message for maximum impact. Too little emotion, and your audience might not care enough to respond. Too much emotion, and your audience might think you are ignoring tough business questions or even being irrational.

Generally speaking, persuasive business messages rely more heavily on logical appeals than on emotional appeals because the main idea is usually to save money, increase quality, or improve some other practical, measurable aspect of business. To find the optimum balance, consider four factors: (1) the actions you hope to motivate, (2) your readers' expectations, (3) the degree of resistance you need to overcome, and (4) how far you feel empowered to go in order to sell your point of view.[12]

4 LEARNING OBJECTIVE

Distinguish between emotional and logical appeals and discuss how to balance them

Emotional Appeals   As its name implies, an **emotional appeal** calls on audience feelings and sympathies rather than facts, figures, and rational arguments. For instance, you can make use of the emotion surrounding certain words. The word *freedom* evokes strong feelings, as do words such as *success, prestige, compassion, security,* and *comfort.* Such words can help put your audience members in a positive frame of mind and help them accept your message. However, emotional appeals in business messages usually aren't effective by themselves because the audience wants proof that you can solve a business problem. Even if your audience members reach a conclusion based primarily on emotions, they'll look to you to provide logical support as well.

Emotional appeals attempt to connect with the reader's feelings or sympathies.

Logical appeals are based on the reader's notions of reason; these appeals can use analogy, induction, or deduction.

Logical Appeals   A **logical appeal** calls on reasoning and evidence. The basic approach with a logical appeal is to make a claim based on a rational argument, supported by solid evidence. When appealing to your audience's logic, you might use three types of reasoning:

- **Analogy.** With analogy, you reason from specific evidence to specific evidence. For instance, to convince management to buy a more robust firewall to protect your company's computer network, you might use the analogy of "circling the wagons," as when covered wagons crossing the continent gathered in a circle every night to form a safe space within.

REAL-TIME UPDATES
Learn More

Choose the most effective emotional appeal

Understand the different types of emotional appeals and select the most effective appeal for any marketing or sales message. Go to **http://real-timeupdates.com/bct** and click on "Learn More." If you are using mybcommlab, you can access Real-Time Updates within each chapter or under Student Study Tools.

REAL-TIME UPDATES
Learn More

Make sure your logic can stand on solid ground

Get sound advice on using logical appeals correctly and effectively. Go to **http://real-timeupdates.com/bct** and click on "Learn More." If you are using mybcommlab, you can access Real-Time Updates within each chapter or under Student Study Tools.

- **Induction.** With inductive reasoning, you work from specific evidence to a general conclusion. To convince your team to change to a new manufacturing process, for example, you could point out that every company that has adopted it has increased profits, so it must be a smart idea.
- **Deduction.** With deductive reasoning, you work from a generalization to a specific conclusion. To persuade your boss to hire additional customer support staff, you might point to industry surveys that show how crucial customer satisfaction is to corporate profits.

Every method of reasoning is vulnerable to misuse, both intentional and unintentional, so verify your rational arguments carefully. For example, in the case of the manufacturing process, are there any other factors that affect the integrity of your reasoning? What if that process works well only for small companies with few products, and your firm is a multinational behemoth with 10,000 products? To avoid faulty logic, follow these guidelines:[13]

Logical flaws include hasty generalizations, circular reasoning, attacks on opponents, oversimplifications, false assumptions of cause and effect, faulty analogies, and illogical support.

- **Avoid hasty generalizations.** Make sure you have plenty of evidence before drawing conclusions.
- **Avoid circular reasoning.** *Circular reasoning* is a logical fallacy in which you try to support your claim by restating it in different words. The statement "We know temporary workers cannot handle this task because temps are unqualified for it" doesn't prove anything because the claim and the supporting evidence are essentially identical. It doesn't prove *why* the temps are unqualified.
- **Avoid attacking an opponent.** If your persuasive appeal involves countering a competitive appeal made by someone else, make sure you attack the argument your opponent is making, not his or her character or qualifications.
- **Avoid oversimplifying a complex issue.** Make sure you present all the factors and don't reduce a wide range of choices to a simple "either/or" scenario if that isn't the case.
- **Avoid mistaken assumptions of cause and effect.** If you can't isolate the impact of a specific factor, you can't assume it's the cause of whatever effect you're discussing. The weather improves in spring, and people start playing baseball in spring. Does good weather cause baseball? No. There is a *correlation* between the two—meaning the data associated with them tend to rise and fall at the same time, but there is no *causation*—no proof that one causes the other. The complexity of many business situations makes cause and effect a particular challenge. You lowered prices, and sales went up. Were lower prices the cause of the increased sales? Perhaps, but the increase in sales might have been caused by a better advertising campaign, a competitor's delivery problems, or some other factor.
- **Avoid faulty analogies.** Be sure that the two objects or situations being compared are similar enough for the analogy to hold. For instance, the analogy between circling the wagons and using a network firewall isn't entirely valid because circling the wagons is a temporary move, and computer networks need permanent protection.
- **Avoid illogical support.** Make sure the connection between your claim and your support is truly logical and not based on a leap of faith, a missing premise, or irrelevant evidence.

Reinforcing Your Position

Choose your words carefully and use abstractions to enhance emotional content.

After you've worked out the basic elements of your argument, step back and look for ways to bolster the strength of your position. Can you find more powerful words to convey your message? For example, if your company is in serious financial trouble, talking about *fighting for survival* is a more powerful emotional appeal than talking about *ensuring continued operations*. Using vivid abstractions such as this along with basic facts and figures can bring your argument to life. As with any other powerful tool, though, vivid language and abstractions must be used carefully and honestly. If the company's survival isn't on the line, don't state or imply that it is.

In addition to individual word choices, consider using *metaphors* and other figures of speech. If you want to describe a quality-control system as being designed to catch every possible product flaw, you might call it a *spider web* to imply that it catches everything that comes its way. Similarly, anecdotes and stories can help your audience grasp the meaning and importance of your arguments. Instead of just listing the number of times the old laptop computers in your department have failed, you could describe how you lost a sale when your computer broke down during a critical sales presentation.

Beyond specific words and phrases, look for other factors that can reinforce your position. When you're asking for something, your audience members will find it easier to grant your request if they stand to benefit from it as well. The timing of your message can also help. Virtually all organizations operate in cycles of some sort—incoming payments from major customers, outgoing tax payments, seasonal demand for products, and so on. Study these patterns to see whether they might work for or against you. For example, the best time to ask for additional staff might be right after a cyclical period of intense activity that generated complaints about poor customer service, while the experience is still fresh in everyone's mind. If you wait too long before asking, the emotional aspect of the experience will have faded, and your request might look like just another cost increase.

Highlight the direct and indirect benefits of complying with your request.

Anticipating Objections

Even the most compelling ideas and proposals can be expected to encounter some initial resistance. The best way to deal with audience resistance is to anticipate as many objections as you can and address them in your message before your audience can even bring them up. For instance, if you know that your proposal to switch to lower-cost materials will raise concerns about product quality, address this issue head-on in your message. If you wait until people raise the concern after reading your message, they may gravitate toward a firm before you have a chance to address their concerns. By bringing up such potential problems right away, you also demonstrate a broad appreciation of the issue and imply confidence in your message.[14] This anticipation is particularly important in written messages, when you don't have the opportunity to detect and respond to objections on the spot.

Even powerful persuasive messages can encounter resistance from the audience.

To uncover potential audience objections, try to poke holes in your own theories and ideas before your audience does. Then find solutions to the problems you've uncovered. If possible, ask your audience members for their thoughts on the subject before you put together your argument; people are more likely to support solutions they help create.

Keep two things in mind when anticipating objections. First, you don't always have to explicitly discuss a potential objection. You could simply mention that the lower-cost materials have been tested and approved by the quality-control department. Second, if you expect a hostile audience, one biased against your plan from the beginning, present all sides of the story. As you cover each option, explain the pros and cons. You'll gain additional credibility if you present these options before presenting your recommendation or decision.[15]

Present both sides of an issue when you expect to encounter strong resistance.

To review the steps involved in developing persuasive messages, refer to "Checklist: Developing Persuasive Messages."

Common Examples of Persuasive Business Messages

Throughout your career, you'll have numerous opportunities to write persuasive messages within your organization, such as reports suggesting more efficient operating procedures or memos requesting money for new equipment. Similarly, you may produce a variety of persuasive messages for people outside the organization, such as websites shaping public opinions or letters requesting adjustments that go beyond a supplier's contractual obligations. In addition, many of the routine requests you studied in Chapter 8 can become persuasive messages if you want a nonroutine result or believe that you haven't received fair treatment. Most of these messages can be divided into persuasive requests for action, persuasive presentations of ideas, and persuasive claims and requests for adjustment.

✓ CHECKLIST: Developing Persuasive Messages

A. Get your reader's attention.
- Open with an audience benefit, a stimulating question, a problem, or an unexpected statement.
- Establish common ground by mentioning a point on which you and your audience agree.
- Show that you understand the audience's concerns.

B. Build your reader's interest.
- Expand and support your opening claim or promise.
- Emphasize the relevance of your message to your audience.

C. Increase your reader's desire.
- Make audience members want to change by explaining how the change will benefit them.
- Back up your claims with relevant evidence.

D. Motivate your reader to take action.
- Suggest the action you want readers to take.
- Stress the positive results of the action.
- Make the desired action clear and easy.

E. Balance emotional and logical appeals.
- Use emotional appeals to help the audience accept your message.
- Use logical appeals when presenting facts and evidence for complex ideas or recommendations.
- Avoid faulty logic.

F. Reinforce your position.
- Provide additional evidence of the benefits of your proposal and your own credibility in offering it.
- Use abstractions, metaphors, and other figures of speech to bring facts and figures to life.

G. Anticipate objections.
- Anticipate and answer potential objections.
- Present the pros and cons of all options if you anticipate a hostile reaction.

Persuasive Requests for Action

When making a persuasive request for action, explain why the request is reasonable.

The bulk of your persuasive business messages will involve requests for action. In some cases, your request will be anticipated or will require minimal effort on the recipient's part, so the direct approach is fine. In others, you'll need to introduce your intention indirectly. Open with an attention-getting device and show readers that you know something about their concerns. Use the interest and desire sections of your message to demonstrate that you have good reasons for making such a request and to cover what you know about the situation: the facts and figures, the benefits of helping, and any history or experience that will enhance your appeal. Your goals are (1) to gain credibility and (2) to make your readers believe that helping you will indeed help solve a significant problem. When you've demonstrated that your message is relevant to your readers, you can close with a request for some specific action or decision.

Sometimes the objective of persuasive messages is simply to encourage people to consider a new idea.

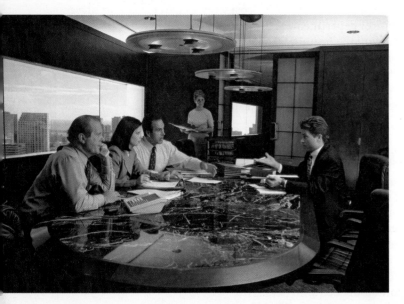

The ability to persuade others to accept and support your ideas is an essential career skill.

Persuasive Presentations of Ideas

Most internal persuasive messages focus on getting the audience to make a specific decision or take some specific action. However, you will encounter situations in which you simply want to change attitudes or beliefs about a particular topic, without asking the audience to decide or do anything—at least not yet. In complicated, multistep persuasive efforts, the goal of your first message might be nothing more than convincing your audience members to re-examine their opinions or assumption or to admit the possibility of new ways of thinking.

For instance, the World Wide Web Consortium (a global association that defines many of the guidelines and technologies behind the World Wide Web) has launched a campaign called the Web Accessibility Initiative. Although the consortium's ultimate goal is making websites more accessible to people who have disabilities or age-related limitations, a key interim goal is simply making website developers more aware of the need. As part of this effort, the consortium has developed a presentation that highlights the nature of the problems that many web visitors face.[16]

Persuasive Claims and Requests for Adjustments

Most claims and requests for adjustment are routine messages and use the direct approach discussed in Chapter 8. However, both consumers and business professionals sometimes encounter situations in which they believe they haven't received a fair deal by following normal procedures. These situations require a more persuasive message.

If a routine claim or request is unsuccessful, you may need to craft a more persuasive message to explain why you deserve a more satisfactory response.

The key ingredients of a good persuasive claim are a complete and specific review of the facts and a confident, positive tone. Assume that the other person is not trying to cheat you and that you have the right to be satisfied with the transaction. Begin persuasive claims by stating the basic problem or reviewing what has been done about the problem so far. Include a statement that you and your audience can agree with or that clarifies what you want to convince your audience about. Be as specific as possible about what you want to happen. Next, give your reader a good reason for granting your claim. Show how your audience is responsible for the problem and appeal to your reader's sense of fair play, goodwill, or moral responsibility. Explain how you feel about the problem but don't get carried away, don't complain too much, and don't make threats. People generally respond more favorably to requests that are calm and reasonable.

DEVELOPING MARKETING AND SALES MESSAGES

Marketing and sales messages use the same techniques as other persuasive messages, with the added emphasis of encouraging someone to participate in a commercial transaction. Although the terms *marketing message* and *sales message* are often used interchangeably, they represent separate but related efforts: Marketing messages usher potential buyers through the purchasing process without asking them to immediately make a decision. Marketing messages focus on such tasks as introducing new brands to the public, providing competitive comparison information, encouraging customers to visit websites for more information, reminding buyers that a particular product or service is available, and building relationships for the purpose of future sales activities (see Figure 10.3). In contrast, a sales message makes a specific request for people to purchase a particular product or service.

Marketing and sales messages use many of the same techniques as persuasive business messages.

Most marketing and sales messages, particularly in larger companies, are created and delivered by professionals with specific training in marketing, advertising, sales, or public relations. However, as a manager, you may be called on to review the work of these specialists or even to write such messages in smaller companies, and having a good understanding of how these messages work will help you be a more effective manager. The essential steps to address include assessing customer needs; analyzing your competition; determining key selling points and benefits; anticipating purchase objections; applying the AIDA model or a similar organizational plan; adapting your writing to social media, if appropriate; and maintaining high standards of ethics, legal compliance, and etiquette.

5 LEARNING OBJECTIVE

Describe seven essential steps in developing marketing and sales messages

Assessing Audience Needs

Successful marketing and sales messages start with an understanding of audience needs. For some products and services, this assessment is a fairly simple matter. For instance, customers compare only a few basic attributes when purchasing paper, including its weight, brightness, color, and finish. In contrast, they might consider dozens of features when shopping for real estate, cars, professional services, and other complex purchases. In addition, customer needs often extend beyond the basic product or service. For example, clothes do far more than simply keep you warm. What you wear can also make a statement about who you are, which social groups you want to be associated with (or not), and how you view your relationships with the people around you.

Purchasing decisions often involve more than just the basic product or service.

Begin by assessing audience needs, interests, and emotional concerns—just as you would for any other business message. Try to form a mental image of the typical buyer for the product you want to sell. Ask yourself what your audience members might want to know

FIGURE 10.3 Marketing Messages

The blog written by Jim Cosgrove of Newcastle Square Realty in Damariscotta, Maine, illustrates the key difference between marketing and sales messages. Cosgrove uses the blog to build a sense of community, educate potential buyers about the local housing market, and share opinions about the real estate business. None of these postings try to make an immediate sale, but they position Cosgrove and his company as knowledgeable guides who can help consumers when they are ready to buy houses in the area.

about this product. How can your product help them? Are they driven by price, or is quality more important to them?

Analyzing Your Competition

Most marketing and sales messages have to compete for the audience's attention.

Marketing and sales messages nearly always compete with messages from other companies trying to reach the same audience. When Nike plans a marketing campaign to introduce a new show model to current customers, the company knows that its audience has also been exposed to messages from New Balance, Reebok, and numerous other shoe companies. In crowded markets, writers sometimes have to search for words and phrases that other companies aren't already using. They might also want to avoid themes, writing styles, or creative approaches that are too similar to those of competitors' messages.

Determining Key Selling Points and Benefits

Selling points focus on the product; benefits focus on the user.

With some insight into audience needs and existing messages from the competition, you're ready to decide which benefits and features of your product or service to highlight. For all but the simplest products and services, you want to prioritize the items you plan to discuss. You also want to distinguish between the features of the product or service and the benefits

TABLE 10.2 Features Versus Benefits

PRODUCT OR SERVICE FEATURE	CUSTOMER BENEFIT
Carrier's Hybrid Heat dual-fuel system combines our Infinity 19 fuel pump with our Infinity 96 furnace.	Carrier's Hybrid Heat dual-fuel system provides the optimum balance of comfort and energy efficiency.
Our marketing communication audit accurately measures the impact of your advertising and public relations efforts.	Find out whether your message is reaching the target audience and whether you're spending your marketing budget in the best possible manner.
The spools in our fly-fishing reels are machined from solid blocks of aircraft-grade aluminum.	Go fishing with confidence: These lightweight reels will stand up to the toughest conditions.

that those features offer the customers. As Table 10.2 shows, **selling points** are the most attractive features of a product or service, whereas **benefits** are the particular advantages that readers will realize from those features. Put another way, selling points focus on the product or service, whereas benefits focus on the user.

For example, CafeMom doesn't stress the online networking feature of its services; rather, it stresses the opportunity to connect with other moms who have similar concerns and interests—which is the benefit enabled by the networking feature. A common approach to communicating features and benefits is to show them in a list or a table, identifying each feature and describing the benefits it offers (see Figure 10.4).

Anticipating Purchase Objections

As with persuasive business messages, marketing and sales messages often encounter objections; once again, the best way to handle them is to identify them up front and try to address as many as you can. Objections can include perceptions of high price, low quality, incompatibility, or unacceptable risk. Consumers might worry that a car won't be safe enough for

Anticipating objections is crucial to effective marketing and sales messages.

FIGURE 10.4 **Explaining the Benefits of Product Features**
This interactive webpage explains the user benefits made possible by key features of the BlackBerry Pearl smartphone. Website visitors simply click the "hotspot" associated with each feature to display an explanation of the benefits that feature provides.

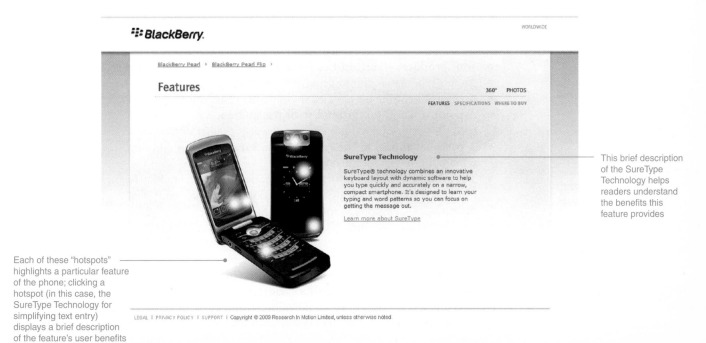

This brief description of the SureType Technology helps readers understand the benefits this feature provides

Each of these "hotspots" highlights a particular feature of the phone; clicking a hotspot (in this case, the SureType Technology for simplifying text entry) displays a brief description of the feature's user benefits a family, that a jacket will make them look unattractive, or that a hair salon will botch a haircut. Business buyers might worry about disrupting operations or failing to realize the financial returns on a purchase.

Price can be a particularly tricky issue in any message. Whether you highlight or downplay the price of your product, prepare your readers for it. Words such as *luxurious* and *economical* provide clues about how your price compares with that of competitors. Such words help your readers accept your price when you finally state it.

If price is a major selling point, give it a position of prominence, such as in the headline or as the last item in a paragraph. If price is not a major selling point, you can handle it in several ways: You can leave the price out altogether or de-emphasize it by putting the figure in the middle of a paragraph that comes well after you've presented the benefits and selling points. Here's an example:

Only 100 prints of this exclusive, limited-edition lithograph will be created. On June 15, they will be made available to the general public, but you can reserve one now for only $350, the special advance reservation price. Simply rush the enclosed reservation card back today so that your order is in before the June 15 publication date.

Whenever price is likely to cause an objection, look for ways to increase the perceived value of the purchase and decrease the perceived cost. For example, to help blunt the impact of the price of a home gym, you might say that it costs less than a year's worth of health club dues—plus, customers save on transportation costs by exercising at home. Of course, any attempts to minimize perceptions of price or other potential negatives must be ethical.

Applying AIDA or a Similar Model

Most marketing and sales messages are prepared according to the AIDA model or some variation of it. (But compare this approach with how *conversation marketing* messages are prepared in "Writing Persuasive Messages for Social Media" on page 331.) A typical AIDA-organized message begins with an attention-getting introduction, generates interest by describing some of the product's or service's unique features, increases desire by highlighting the benefits that are most appealing to the audience, and closes by suggesting the action the sender would like the audience members to take.

Getting Attention

You can use a variety of attention-getting devices in marketing and sales messages.

You can use a wide range of techniques to attract your audience's attention:

- **Your product's strongest feature or benefit.** "A little video for everyone" (promoting Apple's iPod nano with improved video-playing capabilities).[17]
- **A piece of genuine news.** "HealthGrades Reveals America's Best Hospitals."[18]
- **A point of common ground with the audience.** "An SUV adventurous enough to accommodate your spontaneity and the gear that comes with it."[19]
- **A personal appeal to the reader's emotions or values.** "Elastin Renewal: Our latest weapon in the fight against wrinkles."[20]
- **The promise of insider information.** "France may seem familiar, but nearly everything—from paying taxes to having a baby—is done quite differently. Get the practical answers to nearly 300 questions about making a life in France."[21]
- **The promise of savings.** "Through its initiative Save Energy Now, DOE's Industrial Technologies Program (ITP) helps industrial plants operate more efficiently and profitably by identifying ways to reduce energy use in key industrial process systems."[22]
- **A sample or demonstration of the product.** "In this real-time, online test drive, you'll be exploring the 2007 Microsoft Office release through your Web browser within minutes—with no product installation or download required!"[23]
- **A solution to a problem.** "This backpack's designed to endure all a kid's dropping and dragging."[24]

Of course, words aren't the only attention-getting device at your disposal. Strong, evocative images are common attention-getters. With online messages, you have even more options, including audio, animation, and video.

Even more so than in persuasive business messages, it's important to carefully balance emotion and logic in marketing and sales messages. Figure 10.5 suggests the range of logical and emotional appeals that marketing messages can achieve, based on the product and the target audience.

FIGURE 10.5 Emotional and Logical Appeals in Marketing and Sales Messages
Both these websites promote materials used in homes, but their respective messages use different blends of logical and emotional appeals. Premier Building Systems relies primarily on logical appeals in its messages to architectures and home builders. In contrast, in its messages to homeowners, Gladiator GarageWorks balances logical and emotional appeals in describing its garage organizers.

To help convince home builders to use its innovative panel system instead of traditional frame construction, Premier Building Systems focuses on logical factors such as cost, efficiency, and quality

Gladiator Garage Works uses a combination of logical and emotional appeals by promising to make your garage "a place to work, entertain, and show off to your friends and neighbors."

Website photograph used with permission of Whirlpool Corporation

Building Interest

To build interest, expand on and support the promises in your attention-getting opening.

Use the interest section of your message to build on the intrigue you created with your opening. This section should also offer support for any claims or promises you made in the opening. For instance, after opening with the headline "A little video for everyone," the Apple iPod nano webpage continues with the following:[25]

Explains the headline message of "a little video"

After establishing the key selling point (video), continues with other product features and benefits

> It's the small iPod with one very big idea: Video. Now the world's most popular music player lets you enjoy TV shows, movies, video podcasts, and more. The larger, brighter display means amazing picture quality. In six eye-catching colors, iPod nano is stunning all around. And with 4GB and 8GB models starting at just $149, little speaks volumes.

At this point in the message, Apple has offered enough information to help people understand how they might use the product, and it has spoken to a couple potential objections as well (the quality of the video experience on such a small display and the price). Anyone interested in a digital music player with video capability is probably intrigued enough to keep reading.

Increasing Desire

Add details and audience benefits to increase desire for the product or service.

To build desire for a product, a service, or an idea, continue to expand on and explain how accepting it will benefit the recipient. Think carefully about the sequence of support points and use plenty of subheadings, hyperlinks, and other devices to help people quickly find the information they need. For example, after reading this much about the iPod, some users might want to know more about the iTunes media store, whereas others will want technical specifications. The iPod product page continues with detailed discussions of various product features and benefits, and it offers numerous links to pages with other kinds of support information. The ability to provide flexible access to information is just one of the reasons the web is such a powerful medium for marketing and sales (see Figure 10.6).

FIGURE 10.6   **Flexible Communication on the Web**

Want to try on a thousand pairs of eyeglasses without leaving home? You can, thanks to interactive websites such as FramesDirect, which lets you upload a photo of yourself and then see how you look in a variety of eyeglass styles. Flexible media technologies make it easy to adapt promotional messages to the interests of individual audience members.

Throughout the body of your message, remember to keep the focus on the audience, not on your company or your product. When you talk about product features, remember to stress the benefits and talk in terms that make sense to users. For instance, after stating that the maximum memory capacity of the iPod nano is 8 GB, Apple "translates" that technical specification into various media storage capacities that have practical meaning to users, such as 2,000 songs, 7,000 photos, or 8 hours of video.[26]

As you work to build reader interest, be careful not to get so enthusiastic that you lose credibility. If Apple said that the video viewing experience on the iPod nano was as "satisfying as watching a full-size TV," most people would scoff at the notion of comparing a 2-inch display with a full-size television.

Avoid being so enthusiastic that you lose credibility.

To increase desire, as well as boost your credibility, provide support for your claims. Creative writers find many ways to provide support, including testimonials from satisfied users, articles written by industry experts, competitive comparisons, product samples and free demonstrations, independent test results, and movies or computer animations that show a product in action. You can also highlight guarantees that demonstrate your faith in your product and your willingness to back it up.

Motivating Action

After you have raised interest and built up the reader's desire for your product or service, you're ready to ask your audience to take action. Whether you want people to pick up the phone to place an order or visit your website to download a free demo version of your software, try to persuade them to do it right away with an effective *call to action*. You might offer a discount for the first 1,000 people to order, put a deadline on the offer, or simply remind them that the sooner they order, the sooner they'll be able to enjoy the product's benefits (see Figure 10.7). Even potential buyers who want the product can get distracted or forget to respond, so encouraging immediate action is important. Make the response action as simple and as risk-free as possible. If the process is confusing or time-consuming, you'll lose potential customers.

After you've generated sufficient interest and desire, you're ready to persuade readers to take the preferred action.

Take care to maintain the respectful, professional tone you've been using up to this point. Don't resort to gimmicks and desperate-sounding pleas for the customer's business. Make sure your final impression is compelling and positive. For instance, in a printed sales letter, the postscript (P.S.) below your signature is often one of the first or last parts people read. Use this valuable space to emphasize the key benefit you have to offer and to emphasize the advantages of ordering soon.

Writing Persuasive Messages for Social Media

The AIDA model and similar approaches have been successful with marketing and sales messages for decades, but communicating with customers in the social media landscape requires a different approach. As earlier chapters emphasize, potential buyers in a social media environment are no longer willing to be passive recipients in a structured, one-way information delivery process or to rely solely on promotional messages from marketers. This notion of interactive participation is the driving force behind **conversation marketing**, in which companies initiate and facilitate conversations in a networked community of customers, journalists, bloggers, and other interested parties. The term **social commerce** encompasses any aspect of buying and selling products and services or supporting customers through the use of social media.

Social commerce involves the use of social media in buying, selling, and customer support.

Given this shift from unidirectional speeches to multidirectional conversations, marketing and sales professionals must adapt their approach to planning, writing, and completing persuasive messages. Follow these guidelines:[27]

Promoting products and services through social media requires a more conversational approach.

- **Facilitate community building.** Make sure customers and other audiences can connect with your company and each other. Accomplishing this goal can be as simple as activating the commenting feature on a blog, or it may involve having a more elaborate *social commerce system.*
- **Initiate and respond to conversations within the community.** Through content on your website, blog postings, RSS newsfeeds, newsletters, and other tools, make sure

FIGURE 10.7 **The Call to Action in a Persuasive Message**
Notice how many calls to action are built into the homepage of the American Council on Exercise's website. ACE is a not-for-profit organization committed to encouraging physical fitness through safe and effective exercise. In pursuit of that goal, it offers certification and training for people who want to become personal trainers, and it helps consumers find certified trainers.

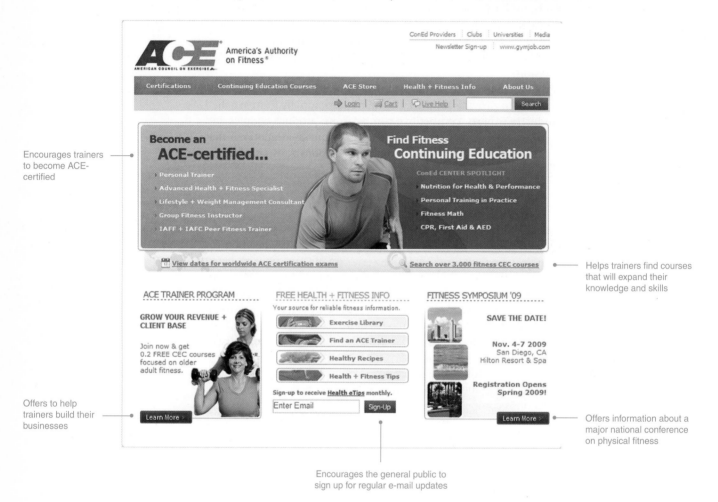

Encourages trainers to become ACE-certified

Offers to help trainers build their businesses

Helps trainers find courses that will expand their knowledge and skills

Offers information about a major national conference on physical fitness

Encourages the general public to sign up for regular e-mail updates

you provide the information customers need in order to evaluate your products and services (see Figure 10.8). Use an objective, conversational style; people in social networks want useful information, not "advertising speak."

- **Identify and support your champions.** In marketing, *champions* are enthusiastic fans of your company and its products. Champions are so enthusiastic that they help spread your message (through their blogs, for instance), defend you against detractors, and help other customers use your products.
- **Don't rely on the news media to distribute your message.** In traditional public relations efforts, marketers have to persuade the news media to distribute their messages to consumers and other audiences by producing news stories. These media are still important, but you can also speak directly to these audiences through blogs and other electronic tools.
- **Use the AIDA model at the right time and in the right places.** The AIDA approach is still valid for specific communication tasks, such as conventional advertising and the product promotion pages on your website.

For the latest information on using social media for persuasive communication, visit http://real-timeupdates.com/bct and click on Chapter 10.

FIGURE 10.8   Conversation Marketing

Talk about putting your money where your mouth is. To promote his book *Conversation Marketing*, Ian Lurie, the marketing strategist who helped popularize the concept of conversation marketing, gave everyone free access to the entire book online (a printed copy is also available for sale). By letting his blog subscribers, journalists, and potential clients of his consulting business read the book for free, Lurie stimulated multiple online conversations—some of which he discusses in brief updates inserted into the online text.

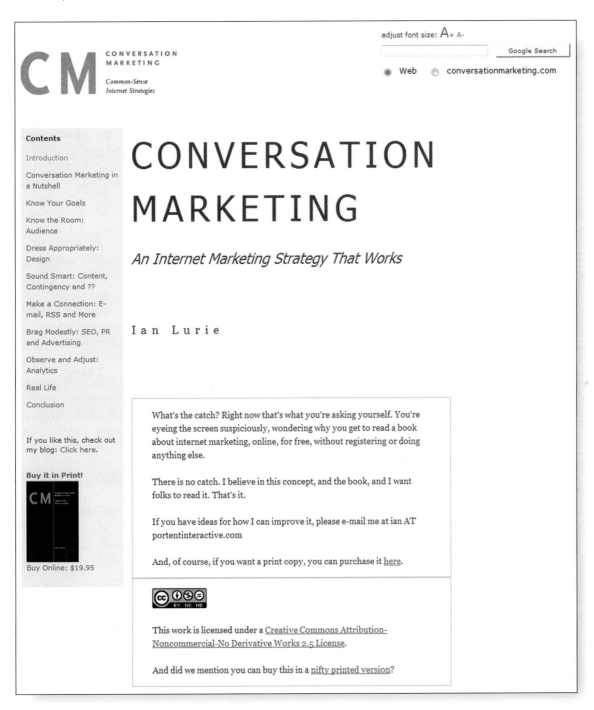

6 **LEARNING OBJECTIVE**

Identify steps you can take to avoid ethical lapses in marketing and sales messages

Marketing and sales messages are covered by a wide range of laws and regulations.

Maintaining High Standards of Ethics, Legal Compliance, and Etiquette

The word *persuasion* has negative connotations for some people, especially in a marketing or sales context. They associate persuasion with dishonest and unethical practices that lead unsuspecting audiences into accepting unworthy ideas or buying unneeded products. However, effective businesspeople view persuasion as a positive force, aligning their own interests with what is best for their audiences. They influence audience members by providing information and aiding understanding, which allows audiences the freedom to choose.[28] To maintain the highest standards of business ethics, always demonstrate the "you" attitude by showing honest concern for your audience's needs and interests.

A good example of ethical complexities in persuasive messages is **stealth marketing**, in which customers don't know they're being marketed to. One common stealth-marketing technique is sending people into public places to use particular products in a conspicuous manner and then discuss them with strangers—as though they were just regular people on the street, when in fact they are employed by a marketing firm. Another is paying consumers or rewarding them with insider information and other benefits to promote products to their friends without telling the friends it's a form of advertising. Critics complain that such techniques are deceptive because they don't give their targets the opportunity to raise their instinctive defenses against the persuasive powers of marketing messages.[29]

As marketing and selling grow increasingly complex, so do the legal ramifications of marketing and sales messages. In the United States, the Federal Trade Commission (FTC) has the authority to impose penalties (ranging from cease-and-desist orders to multimillion-dollar fines) against advertisers who violate national standards for truthful advertising. Other U.S. government agencies have authority over advertising in specific industries, such as transportation and financial services. Individual states have additional laws that apply. The legal aspects of promotional communication can be quite complex, from state to state and from country to country, and most companies require marketing and sales people to get clearance from company lawyers before sending messages. In any event, pay close attention to the following legal aspects of marketing and sales communication:[30]

- **Marketing and sales messages must be truthful and nondeceptive.** The FTC considers messages to be deceptive if they include statements that are likely to mislead reasonable customers and the statements are an important part of the purchasing decision. Failing to include important information is also considered deceptive. The FTC also looks at *implied claims*—claims you don't explicitly make but that can be inferred from what you do or don't say.

- **You must back up your claims with evidence.** According to the FTC, offering a money-back guarantee or providing letters from satisfied customers is not enough; you must still be able to support your claims with objective evidence such as a survey or scientific study. If you claim that your food product lowers cholesterol, you must have scientific evidence to support that claim.

- **Marketing and sales messages are considered binding contracts in many states.** If you imply or make an offer and then can't fulfill your end of the bargain, you can be sued for breach of contract.

- **In most cases, you can't use a person's name, photograph, or other identity without permission.** Doing so is considered an invasion of privacy. You can use images of people considered to be public figures as long as you don't unfairly imply that they endorse your message.

Before you launch a marketing or sales campaign, make sure you're up to date on the latest regulations affecting spam (or *unsolicited bulk e-mail*, as it's formally known), customer privacy, and data security. New laws are likely to appear in all three areas in the next few years.

Document Makeover

Improve This E-Mail Message

To practice correcting drafts of actual documents, visit the "Document Makeovers" section in either mybcommlab or the Companion Website for this text.

If mybcommlab is being used in your class, see your User Guide for specific instructions on how to access the content for this chapter. If you are accessing this feature through the Companion Website, click on "Document Makeovers" and then click Chapter 10. You will find an e-mail message that contains problems and errors related to what you've learned in this chapter about writing persuasive messages. Use the Final Draft decision tool to create an improved version of this persuasive e-mail request for action. Check the message for its effectiveness at gaining attention, building interest, stimulating desire, motivating action, focusing on the primary goal, and dealing with resistance.

Meeting your ethical and legal obligations will go a long way toward maintaining good communication etiquette as well. However, you may still face etiquette decisions within ethical and legal boundaries. For instance, you can produce a marketing campaign that complies with all applicable laws and yet is offensive or insulting to your audience. Taking an audience-centered approach, involving respect for your readers and their values, should help you avoid any such etiquette missteps.

Maintaining high ethical standards is a key aspect of good communication etiquette.

Technology also gives communicators new ways to demonstrate sensitivity to user needs. One example is automated RSS newsfeeds from blogs that alert customers to information in which they've expressed an interest. *Opt-in* e-mail newsletters are another technology that shows the "you" attitude at work. Unlike the unwelcome spam messages that litter e-mail in-boxes these days, opt-in messages are sent only to people who have specifically requested information.

Communication technologies such as opt-in e-mail and blog syndication can help you be sensitive to audience needs.

Communication Challenges at CafeMom

You're the vice president of member services at CafeMom, reporting to CEO Michael Sanchez. In addition to developing new online services, a key part of your job responsibility is crafting messages that describe the new services and persuade members to try them. Use what you've learned in this chapter and in your own experiences as a consumer (and as a parent, if applicable) to address these challenges.

Individual Challenge: You asked one of your staffers to write a benefit statement to communicate the advantages of the Groups section of the CafeMom website, which lets members find and join any of the thousands of existing groups or create new groups focused on just about any topic imaginable. She e-mails the following sentence: "We've worked hard to define and create a powerful online group capability; you can search far and wide on the Web, but you won't find anything as great as what we've created." Write an e-mail message in response, explaining why it's important to make marketing messages about the *customer*, not about the *company*. Include a revised version that illustrates this vital aspect of the "you" attitude. You can learn more about the Groups feature at the CafeMom website, **www.cafemom .com/groups**.

Team Challenge: A common challenge in marketing communication is distilling a long list of features to a single compelling message that can serve as the product's "headline." With your team, review this list of features and benefits:

- The experiences of thousands of moms are now aggregated in a single place online.
- Connect with moms like you; search for moms by personal and family challenges, interests, age of kids, or location.
- Get and give support; find support and swap advice with other moms on a wide range of topics that matter most to you.
- Post questions online and get input from mothers who've been there before.
- Joining CafeMom is absolutely free.
- Setting up your own personal profile is fast and easy.
- Join groups who share your likes and concerns.
- Write as much or as little as you want to share in your personal profile.
- You have complete control over the privacy of your information.

Brainstorm three one-sentence possibilities that could serve as the headline for a webpage promoting CafeMom and then choose the most compelling of the three options. Don't assume that every feature or benefit in the list needs to be incorporated in your high-level message.

SUMMARY OF LEARNING OBJECTIVES

1 **Apply the three-step writing process to persuasive messages.** The three-step process can easily be adapted to persuasive messages. These messages require careful planning because such messages are often unexpected and are at times unwelcome. To plan successfully, carefully clarify your purpose to make sure you focus on a single goal; clearly express your purpose to audience members so they are aware of what you would like them to feel, think, or do; and recognize that some audience decisions won't be made in a single step, and you'll need a series of persuasive messages to reach your ultimate objective. The information you need to gather involves a

combination of emotional and logical elements, which you then blend together based on your knowledge of audience wants and needs. Most persuasive messages use the indirect approach to establish awareness and interest before asking the audience to take action, although the direct approach is often better for routine persuasive messages or when you're in a position of authority relative to the audience. The "you" attitude is critical in persuasive messages, and successful writers take care to adapt their appeals to the specific wants and needs of their audiences. They also work hard to establish credibility with their readers. The steps involved in completing persuasive messages are essentially the same as for other message types, although even small errors can damage credibility, so persuasive communicators need to be doubly careful with presentation and proofreading.

2 **Identify seven ways to establish credibility in persuasive messages.**   The common ways to establish credibility include using simple language, supporting your message with factual evidence, naming your sources when you use information from others, demonstrating expertise (your own or others'), establishing common ground with the audience, being objective, and displaying good intentions.

3 **Describe the AIDA model for persuasive messages.** When using the AIDA model, you open your message by getting attention with a reader benefit, a problem, a stimulating question, a piece of news, or an unexpected statement. You build interest with facts, details, and additional reader benefits. You increase desire by providing more evidence and reader benefits and by anticipating and answering possible objections. You conclude by motivating a specific action, emphasizing the positive results of that action, and making it easy for the reader to respond.

4 **Distinguish between emotional and logical appeals, and discuss how to balance them.**   Emotional appeals call on feelings, using arguments that are based on audience needs or sympathies. Logical appeals call on reason using analogy, induction, or deduction. Most persuasive messages use a combination of emotion and logic; it's essential to use the right combination for each situation. To find the optimum balance, consider the actions you hope to motivate, your readers' expectations, the degree of resistance you need to overcome, and how far you feel empowered to go to sell your point of view. Persuasive business messages and marketing and sales messages directed at business buyers emphasize logic over emotion because business audiences want to know how a proposed idea, product, or service will improve financial results or produce some other practical business outcome. In contrast, marketing and sales messages directed at individual consumers often use a higher degree of emotion in the overall appeal.

5 **Describe seven essential steps in developing marketing and sales messages.**   To develop marketing and sales messages, follow these seven steps: (1) assess customer needs; (2) analyze your competition to make sure your messages don't overlap existing messages from competitors; (3) determine key selling points and customer-oriented benefits; (4) anticipate purchase objections and address as many as possible in your initial message; (5) apply the AIDA model or a similar organizational plan to ensure a successful sequence of persuasive points; (6) adapt your writing to social media, if appropriate; and (7) maintain high standards of ethics, legal compliance, and etiquette.

6 **Identify steps you can take to avoid ethical lapses in marketing and sales messages.**   Effective and ethical persuasive communicators focus on aligning their interests with the interests of their audiences. They help audiences understand how their proposals will provide benefits to the audience, using language that is persuasive without being manipulative. They choose words that are less likely to be misinterpreted and take care not to distort the truth. Throughout, they maintain a "you" attitude with honest concern for the audience's needs and interests.

PEARSON
mybcommlab

Log on to **www.mybcommlab.com** to access the following study and assessment aids associated with this chapter:

- Video applications
- Real-Time Updates
- Peer review activity
- Quick Learning Guides

- Pre/post test
- Personalized study plan
- Model documents
- Sample presentations

If you are not using mybcommlab, you can access the Real-Time Updates and Quick Learning Guides through http://real-timeupdates.com/bct. The Quick Learning Guide (located under "Learn More" on the website) hits all the high points of this chapter in just two pages. This guide, especially prepared by the authors, will help you study for exams or review important concepts whenever you need a quick refresher.

Test Your Knowledge

1. What are some questions to ask when gauging the audience's needs during the planning of a persuasive message?
2. What role do demographics and psychographics play in audience analysis during the planning of a persuasive message?
3. What are four of the ways you can build credibility with an audience when planning a persuasive message?
4. What is the AIDA model, and what are its limitations?
5. How do emotional appeals differ from logical appeals?
6. What three types of reasoning can you use in logical appeals?
7. What is conversation marketing?
8. What is likely to happen if you don't anticipate audience objections when crafting your messages?
9. How do benefits differ from features?
10. How does ethical behavior contribute to positive etiquette in persuasive messages?

Apply Your Knowledge

1. Why is it important to present both sides of an argument when writing a persuasive message to a potentially hostile audience?
2. How are persuasive messages different from routine messages?
3. Why do the AIDA model and similar approaches need to be modified when writing persuasive messages in social media?
4. What is likely to happen if your persuasive message starts immediately with a call to action? Why?
5. **Ethical Choices** Are emotional appeals ethical? Why or why not?

Practice Your Knowledge

Messages for Analysis

For Message 10.A and Message 10.B, read the following documents and then (1) analyze the strengths and weaknesses of each sentence and (2) revise each document so that it follows this chapter's guidelines.

Message 10.A: Writing Persuasive Claims and Requests for Adjustment

Dear Management of "Peranakan Classics":

I'm writing to express my total dismay at the horrendous service we received at your restaurant last Friday. We were truly excited about having our guests from London try Straits Chinese food for the first time but the excitement quickly transformed into dismay as a result of the lamentable service we got. Although at first I thought I would let it go and just never patronize your restaurant again, I figured I would be doing you a favor by writing to you because if you carry on like this, I'm afraid you won't stay open for long!

First, the waiter showed us to a table with three chairs for a party of four people and never came back with the fourth chair. We had to drag one over from the next table ourselves! Next we tried to make eye contact with him for a full 10 minutes to come and take our order but he kept avoiding us and the place wasn't even that crowded. And when the food finally came, my vegetarian friend who

had painstakingly explained that she didn't want meat or seafood in her "Peranakan Nasi Goreng" got her fried rice with prawns in it!

To top it all, we were charged an additional 10% of our bill, over and above the normal 7% for the Goods and Services Tax (GST), for service. Are you kidding me?

Message 10.B: Writing Sales Letters

Are you working parents? Do you have young, school-age children who need nutritious meals but you feel guilty about not being able to give them that every day? Despair no more as we will take care of it for you. At "Dial-a-Meal" our team of professionally trained cooks can whip up all of the following: Chinese, Western, Muslim-Halal, Indian Non-Vegetarian, and Vegetarian meals!

All you have to do is check the right boxes in the form we provide showing your choices for each day of the week. Your meals will be delivered to your home. Since we have just launched our business this month we are offering all meals at special promotional prices. Stop feeling guilty about being working parents and having little time to cook for your children. Call us today at 65879421 and sign up for a month of wholesome, home-cooked meals!.

Message 10.C: Making a Podcast More Persuasive

To access this message, visit http://real-timeupdates.com/bct, click on "Student Assignments," and select Chapter 10, page 337, Message 10.C. Download and listen to this podcast. Identify at least three ways in which the podcast could be more persuasive and draft a brief e-mail message that you could send to the podcaster with your suggestions for improvement.

Exercises

Active links for all websites in this chapter can be found online. If mybcommlab is being used in your class, see your User Guide for instructions on accessing the content for this chapter. Otherwise, visit www.pearsonglobaleditions.com/bovee, locate *Business Communication Today*, Tenth Edition, click the Companion Website link, select Chapter 10, and then click on "Featured Websites." Please note that links to sites that become inactive after publication of the book will be removed from the Featured Websites section.

10.1 **Teamwork** With another student, analyze the persuasive e-mail message to Eleanor Tran at Host Marriott (Figure 10.2) by answering the following questions:
   a. What techniques are used to capture the reader's attention?
   b. Does the writer use the direct or indirect organizational approach? Why?
   c. Is the subject line effective? Why or why not?
   d. Does the writer use an emotional or a logical appeal? Why?
   e. What reader benefits are included?
   f. How does the writer establish credibility?
   g. What tools does the writer use to reinforce his position?

10.2 **Composing Subject Lines** Compose effective subject lines for the following persuasive messages:
   a. A recommendation sent by e-mail to your branch manager to install wireless networking throughout the facility. Your primary reason is that management has encouraged more teamwork, but teams often

congregate in meeting rooms, the cafeteria, and other places that lack network access—without which they can't do much of the work they are expected to do.

b. A letter to area residents, soliciting customers for your new business, "Meals à la Car," a carryout dining service that delivers from most of the local restaurants. All local restaurant menus are on the Internet. Mom and Dad can dine on egg rolls and chow mein while the kids munch on pepperoni pizza.

c. An e-mail message to the company president, asking that employees be allowed to carry over their unused vacation days to the following year. Apparently, many employees canceled their fourth-quarter vacation plans to work on the installation of a new company computer system. Under their current contract, vacation days not used by December 31 can't be carried over to the following year.

10.3 Ethical Choices Your boss has asked you to post a message on the company's internal blog, urging everyone in your department to donate money to the company's favorite charity, an organization that operates a summer camp for physically challenged children. You wind up writing a lengthy posting, packed with facts and heartwarming anecdotes about the camp and the children's experiences. When you must work that hard to persuade your audience to take an action such as donating money to a charity, aren't you being manipulative and unethical? Explain.

10.4 Focusing on Benefits Determine whether the following sentences focus on features or benefits; rewrite as necessary to focus all the sentences on benefits.
   a. All-Cook skillets are coated with a durable, patented nonstick surface.
   b. You can call anyone and talk as long as you like on Saturdays and Sundays with our new FamilyTalk wireless plan.
   c. With 8-millisecond response time, the Samsung LN-S4095D 40-inch LCD TV delivers fast video action that is smooth and crisp.[31]

10.5 Internet Download the U.S. Federal Trade Commission document "Social Networking Sites: Safety Tips for Tweens and Teens" from www.ftc.gov/bcp/edu/pubs/consumer/tech/tec14.pdf. Keeping in mind the target audience, analyze the effectiveness of this publication. Do you think it does a good job of persuading young people to surf the Internet safely? Write a brief summary of your analysis, along with any recommendations you might have for conveying the message more persuasively.

10.6 Analyzing a Sales Package: Learning from the Direct-Mail Pros The daily mail often brings a selection of sales messages. Find a direct-mail package from your mailbox that includes a sales letter. Then answer the following questions to help analyze and learn from the approach used by the communication professionals who prepare these glossy sales messages. Your instructor might also ask you to share the package and your observations in a class discussion.
   a. Who is the intended audience?

b. What are some of the demographic and psychographic characteristics of the intended audience?

c. What is the purpose of the direct-mail package? Has it been designed to solicit a phone-call response, make a mail-order sale, obtain a charitable contribution, or do something else?

d. What technique was used to encourage you to open the envelope?

e. Did the letter writer follow the AIDA model or something similar? If not, explain the letter's organization.

f. What emotional appeals and logical arguments does the letter use?

g. What selling points and consumer benefits does the letter offer?

h. Did the letter and the rest of the package provide convincing support for the claims made in the letter? If not, what is lacking?

Expand Your Knowledge

Exploring the Best of the Web

Influence an Official and Promote Your Cause

http://thomas.loc.gov

At the Thomas site compiled by the Library of Congress, you'll discover voluminous information about U.S. government legislation, congressional members, and committee reports. You can also access committee homepages and numerous links to government agencies, current issues, and historical documents. You'll find all kinds of regulatory information, including laws and relevant issues that might affect you in the business world. Visit the site and stay informed. Maybe you'll want to convince a government official to support a business-related issue that affects you. Explore the data at the Thomas site and find an issue you can use to practice your skills at writing a persuasive message.

1. What key ideas would you include in an e-mail message to persuade your congressional representative to support an issue that is important to you?

2. In a letter to a senator or member of Congress, what information would you include to convince the reader to vote for an issue related to small business?

3. When sending a message to someone who receives hundreds of written appeals daily, what attention-getting techniques can you use? How can you get support for a cause that concerns you as a businessperson?

Sharpening Your Career Skills Online

Bovée and Thill's Business Communication Web Search, at http://businesscommunicationblog.com/websearch, is a unique research tool designed specifically for business communication research. Use the Web Search function to find a website, video, PDF document, podcast, or PowerPoint presentation that offers advice on writing persuasive messages (either persuasive business messages or marketing and sales messages). Write a brief e-mail message to your instructor, describing the item that you found and summarizing the career skills information you learned from it.

CASES

Applying the Three-Step Writing Process to Cases

Apply each step to the following cases, as assigned by your instructor.

PERSUASIVE BUSINESS MESSAGES

BLOGGING SKILLS   PORTFOLIO BUILDER

1. That's the point: E-mail encouraging your boss to blog. You've been trying for months to convince your boss, Will Florence, to start blogging. You've told him that top executives in many industries now use blogging as a way to connect with customers and other stakeholders without going through the filters and barriers of formal corporate communications. He was just about convinced—until he read the blog by Bob Lutz, the co-chair and design chief of General Motors.

"Look at this!" he calls from his office. "Bob Lutz is one of the most respected executives in the world, and all these people are criticizing him on his own blog. Sure, a lot of the responses are positive, but quite a few are openly hostile, disagreeing with GM strategy, criticizing the products, criticizing the subjects he chooses for his blog—you name it. If blogging is all about opening yourself up to criticism from every bystander with a keyboard, no way am I going to start a blog."

Your task: Write an e-mail message to Florence, persuading him that the freewheeling nature of blog communication is its key advantage, not a disadvantage at all. While they may not always agree with what he has to say, automotive enthusiasts and car buyers respect Lutz for communicating in his own words—and for giving them the opportunity to respond. For background information, read some of the postings from Lutz and other GM executives at http://fastlane.gmblogs.com.[32]

E-MAIL SKILLS

2. Give a little to get a lot: Suggesting more green comfort zones at the Benjamin Sheares University. As it stands now the only places where students can go to discuss projects or just enjoy some quiet reflection or reading time is the Central Library. The problem is that sometimes students like being out in natural settings to brainstorm or think. You have observed that there are actually many such areas all over the campus, and all the university has to do is to place wooden benches and some large umbrellas for shade. Alternatively, the benches could be placed under trees in wooded areas where the latter would provide natural shade from the sun. You are convinced that these would be hugely popular with students because, unlike the library, there would be no restrictions on talking, snacking, or even listening to music if students so desired.

The only problem is that recently the university announced that there would be serious budget cuts on all expenditures other than those on e-learning technology. However, you feel strongly that if the university backed your proposal you could approach some Singaporean philanthropists to sponsor these benches and umbrellas and get the job done without any cost to them.

Your task: Write a persuasive message to the university administration convincing them of the need for the Green Comfort Zones and of how, with their support, you could approach local philanthropists

for money. You can suggest that the sponsors be acknowledged for their contributions in all student magazines and newsletters as well as in the quarterly alumni magazine. You will post your persuasive message on the Student Suggestions website of the university.

E-MAIL SKILLS   PORTFOLIO BUILDER

3. Network disconnect: Building a business case for using social media at work. As someone who came of age in the "post e-mail" world of blogs, wikis, social networks, and other Web 2.0 technologies, you were rather disappointed to find your new employer solidly stuck in the age of e-mail. You use e-mail, of course, but it is only one of the tools in your communication toolbox. From your college years, you have hands-on experience with a wide range of social media tools, having used them to collaborate on school projects, to become involved in your local community, to learn more about various industries and professions, and to research potential employers during your job search. (In fact, without social media, you might've never heard about your current employer in the first place.) Moreover, your use of social media on the job has already paid several important dividends, including finding potential sales contacts at several large companies, connecting with peers in other companies to share ideas for working more efficiently, and learning about some upcoming legislative matters that could profoundly hamper your company's current way of doing business.

You hoped that by setting an example through your own use of social media at work, your new colleagues and company management would quickly adopt these tools as well. However, just the opposite has happened. Waiting in your e-mail in-box this morning was a message from the CEO, announcing that the company is now cutting off access to social networking websites and banning the use of any social media at work. The message says that using company time and company computers for socializing is highly inappropriate and might be considered grounds for dismissal in the future if the problem gets out of hand.

Your task: You are stunned by the message. You fight the urge to fire off a hotly worded reply to straighten out the CEO's misperceptions. Instead, you wisely decide to send a message to your immediate superior first, explaining why you believe the new policy should be reversed. Using your boss's favorite medium (e-mail, of course!), write a persuasive message, explaining why Facebook, Twitter, and other social networking technologies are valid—and valuable—business tools. Bolster your argument with examples from other companies and advice from communication experts. (To access a list of links to get your research started, visit http://real-timeupdates.com/bct, click on "Student Assignments," and select Chapter 10, page 339, Case 3.)

E-MAIL SKILLS

4. Life's little hassles: E-mail requesting satisfaction. It's hard to go through life without becoming annoyed at the way some things work. You have undoubtedly been dissatisfied with a product you've bought, a service you've received, or an action of some elected official or government agency.

Your task: Write a three- to five-paragraph persuasive e-mail message request, expressing your dissatisfaction in a particular case. Specify the action you want the reader to take.

5. Nap time: Memo requesting space for power nappers at Phidias & Associates. It's been one of those days. You were dragging by 10 A.M., ready to slump over into your computer monitor at the Phidias & Associates architectural firm in San Francisco. How are you supposed to be creatively inspired when you can barely get your eyes to focus and your head feels as if it's full of cotton? No, you weren't out partying last night; you've just been working long, late hours on a rush job for one of the firm's biggest clients. If only you could stretch out for a little catnap, you'd be good as new in 15 minutes.

Groggily, you recall an item you tore out of the *Wall Street Journal* a year ago—a paragraph or two in the "Work Week" column, all about companies adding "nap rooms" to help employees recharge during the day. You know that on weekends, a quick nap helps you get a lot more done during the day; and didn't they teach you in school that Thomas Edison kept a cot in his office and got his best ideas when he was napping? And the article quotes an expert, William A. Anthony, author of *The Art of Napping* and professor of rehabilitation counseling at Boston University. He says most people aren't sleep deprived, they're "nap ready."

There are plenty of other precedents and pioneers out there in the business world. At *Macworld* magazine, the human resources director, Shelly Ginenthal, says their two-person nap room was installed all the way back in 1986 and usually has a waiting line. At Yarde Metals in Bristol, Connecticut, President Bruce Yarde says, "A quick little nap can rejuvenate you." He's fighting employee stress with a 25-person nap room. You do some quick research for more evidence and turn up a report from the prestigious National Institutes of Health, indicating that power napping not only helps prevent burnout but also enhances information processing and learning.

Your task: After you've had a good night's sleep, write a memo to Jonas T. Phidias, persuading the senior partner that the distinguished offices of Phidias & Associates could benefit from the addition of a corporate nap room and an organizational embrace of power napping as a way to be more competitive. On a separate page, include a short note to your instructor, justifying your organizational approach (direct or indirect) and your selection of delivery medium (e-mail or interoffice mail).[33]

IM SKILLS

6. Helping children: Instant message holiday fund drive at IBM. At IBM, you're one of the coordinators for the annual Employee Charitable Contributions Campaign. Since 1978, the company has helped employees contribute to more than 2,000 health and human service agencies. These groups may offer child care; treat substance abuse; provide health services; or fight illiteracy, homelessness, and hunger. Some offer disaster relief or care for the elderly. All deserve support. They're carefully screened by IBM, one of the largest corporate contributors of cash, equipment, and people to nonprofit organizations and educational institutions around the world. As your literature states, the program "has engaged our employees more fully in the important mission of corporate citizenship."

During the winter holidays, you target agencies that cater to the needs of displaced families, women, and children. It's not difficult to raise enthusiasm. The prospect of helping children enjoy the holidays—children who otherwise might have nothing—usually awakens the spirit of your most distracted workers. But some of them wait until the last minute and then forget.

They have until December 16 to come forth with cash contributions. To make it in time for holiday deliveries, they can also bring in toys, food, and blankets through Tuesday, December 20. They shouldn't have any trouble finding the collection bins; they're everywhere, marked with bright red banners. But some will want to call you with questions or (you hope) to make credit card contributions: 800-658-3899, ext. 3342.

Your task: It's December 14. Write a 75- to 100-word instant message, encouraging last-minute holiday gifts.[34]

E-MAIL SKILLS

7. Tangled web: E-mail to PurelySoftware regarding an online order duplication. Last week you ordered new design software for your boss, Martin Soderburgh, at ArtAlive, the small art consulting business where you work. As he requested, you used his Visa card to order Adobe InDesign and Adobe Photoshop from an Internet vendor, PurelySoftware.com.

When you didn't receive the usual e-mail order confirmation, you called the company's toll-free number. The operator said the company's website was having problems, and he took a second order over the phone: $649 for Adobe InDesign, $564 for Adobe Photoshop, including tax and shipping. Four days later, ArtAlive received two shipments of the software, and your boss's credit card was charged $1,213 twice, for a total of $2,426.

Your task: Strictly speaking, you did authorize both orders. But you understood during the phone call that the first order was canceled, although you have no written proof. Send a persuasive e-mail to customerservice@purelysoftware.com, requesting (1) an immediate credit to your boss's Visa account and (2) a postage-paid return label for the duplicate order.[35]

E-MAIL SKILLS

8. Helping out: Message to Alhaque Food Chain (AFC) branch managers. Alhaque Food Chain (AFC) has become a famous name in Lahore, Pakistan, for its affordable, fast, and quality food. The top management of the company has practiced its strong commitment toward social responsibility and community service over the last five years. It has donated 7.5 percent of its after-tax profits toward providing the basic needs of food, clothing, and shelters for the downtrodden sectors of society. The company encourages its retail outlet staff to be compassionate toward the poor and to participate in voluntary community service in their free time as much as possible.

As the manager of an AFC outlet, in downtown Lahore, you have been successfully running the "Free Meal Coupon Service" program for the last four years, earning a good name for the company as well as for yourself. In view of the current economic downturn, AFC wants to expand its social and community activities, according to its corporate motto of "Sharing the Whole Meal with the Whole People."

You have been asked by the CEO to write a persuasive e-mail message to solicit more ideas from managers of the other retail outlets in the city so that the company's corporate motto is followed with extra vigor and zeal by all the retail outlets.

Your task: Write a persuasive e-mail message addressed to all managers of AFC outlets explaining the importance of the company's corporate motto and its implementation through their dedicated efforts. Also invite proposals for charitable projects in which their chain outlets can participate, within their budgetary limits, in the service of community.

E-MAIL SKILLS

9. No more driving: Telecommuting to Bachman, Trinity, and Smith. Sitting in your Dallas office at the accounting firm Bachman, Trinity, and Smith, clacking away on your computer, it seems as though you could be doing this work from your home. You haven't spoken to any co-workers in more than two hours. As long as you complete your work on time, does your location matter?

As an entry-level accountant, you've participated in on-location audits at major companies for nearly a year now. If your bosses trust you to work while staying at a hotel, why not let you work from home, where you already have an office with a computer, phone, and fax machine? You'd love to regain those two hours you lose commuting to and from work every day.

Your task: To gather support for this idea, visit the International Telework Coalition website, at www.telcoa.org. Find statistics and other support and write a memo persuading your boss, senior partner Marjorie Bachman, to grant you a six-month trial as a telecommuter.[36]

10. Always urgent: Memo pleading case for hosting a Red Cross blood drive. This morning as you drove to your job as food services manager at the Pechanga Casino Entertainment Center in Temecula, California, you were concerned to hear on the radio that the local Red Cross chapter put out a call for blood because national supplies have fallen dangerously low. During highly publicized disasters, people are emotional and eager to help out by donating blood. But in calmer times, only 5 percent of eligible donors think of giving blood. You're one of those few.

Not many people realize that donated blood lasts for only 72 hours. Consequently, the mainstay of emergency blood supplies must be replenished in an ongoing effort. No one is more skilled, dedicated, or efficient in handling blood than the American Red Cross, which is responsible for half the supply of blood and blood products in the United States.

Donated blood helps victims of accidents and disease, as well as surgery patients. Just yesterday you were reading about a girl named Melissa, who was diagnosed with multiple congenital heart defects and underwent her first open-heart surgery at one week of age. Now five years old, she's used well over 50 units of donated blood, and she wouldn't be alive without them. In a thank-you letter, her mother lauded the many strangers who had "given a piece of themselves" to save her precious daughter—and countless others. You also learned that a donor's pint of blood can benefit up to four other people.

Today, you're going to do more than just roll up your own sleeve. You know the local Red Cross chapter takes its Blood Mobile to corporations, restaurants, salons—anyplace willing to host public blood drives. What if you could convince the board of directors to support a blood drive at the casino? The slot machines

and gaming tables are usually full, hundreds of employees are on hand, and people who've never visited before might come down to donate blood. The positive publicity certainly couldn't hurt Pechanga's community image. With materials from the Red Cross, you're confident you can organize Pechanga's hosting effort and handle the promotion. (Last year, you headed the casino's successful Toys for Tots drive.)

To give blood, one must be healthy, be at least 17 years old (with no upper age limit), and weigh at least 110 pounds. Donors can give every 56 days. You'll be urging Pechanga donors to eat well, drink water, and be rested before the Blood Mobile arrives.

The local Red Cross chapter's mission statement says, in part, that the Red Cross is "a humanitarian organization led by volunteers and guided by the Fundamental Principles of the International Red Cross and Red Crescent Movement" that will "prevent and alleviate human suffering wherever it may be found." All assistance is given free of charge, made possible by "contributions of people's time, money, and skills"—and in the case of you and your co-workers, a piece of yourselves.

Your task: Write a memo persuading the Pechanga board of directors to host a public Red Cross blood drive. You can learn more about what's involved in hosting a blood drive at www.givelife.org (click on "Sponsor a Drive"). Ask the board to provide bottled water, orange juice, and snacks for donors. You'll organize food service workers to handle the distribution, but you'll need the board's approval to let your team volunteer during work hours. Use a combination of logical and emotional appeals.[37]

E-MAIL SKILLS   PORTFOLIO BUILDER

11. Message to a potential investor. You are a final-year student of the Environmental Science and Engineering department of the National University of Singapore, and as your final year project you have designed a fuzzy logic, water-saving, self-cleaning dishwasher that can be programmed to clean even delicate crystal ware. Although you have received accolades from your professors at the university, you would like to make it available to the general public, but as a student you lack the funds to promote and market the product.

As a Malaysian student in Singapore, you are more familiar with philanthropists in Malaysia who lend a helping hand to budding entrepreneurs with great ideas. One such person that you read about recently is Datuk Amar Leonard Linggi Tun Jugah, who works tirelessly to preserve Iban culture in Sarawak, East Malaysia. As an Iban yourself, you feel you would be able to communicate your excitement and eagerness to him quite easily.

Your task: Write an e-mail message to Datuk Amar, introducing yourself and your invention. Request a meeting, at which you would present your invention and business plan to him in greater detail. Explain clearly that you've done your research and found that working people as well as housewives in both Singapore and Malaysia would view this invention as a boon to their cleaning regimen, especially since it can be programmed to clean delicate crystal ware that previously had to be hand washed to prevent breakage. Draft a four-paragraph message following the AIDA model, ending with a request for a meeting with him when you go home for the semester break in two weeks. You can make up any other relevant information.

BLOGGING SKILLS   PORTFOLIO BUILDER

12. Web accessibility advocacy: It's not "World Wide" if it doesn't include everybody. Like most other companies today, your firm makes extensive use of the web for internal and external communication. However, after reading about the Web Accessibility Initiative (WAI), you've become concerned that your company's various websites haven't been designed to accommodate people with disabilities or age-related limitations. Fortunately, as one of the company's top managers, you have a perfect forum for letting everyone in the company know how important accessible web design is: Your internal blog is read by the vast majority of employees and managers throughout the company.

Your task: Visit the WAI website, at www.w3.org/WAI, and read the two articles "Introduction to Web Accessibility" (look in the "Introducing Accessibility" section) and "Developing a Web Accessibility Business Case for Your Organization" (in the "Managing Accessibility" section). Using the information you learn in these articles, write a post for your blog that emphasizes how important it is for your company's websites to be made more accessible. You don't have direct authority over the company's web developers, so it would be inappropriate for you to request them to take any specific action. Your goal is simply to raise awareness and encourage everyone to consider the needs of the company's online audiences. Don't worry about the technical aspects of web accessibility; focus instead on the benefits of improving accessibility.[38]

E-MAIL SKILLS

13. No wonder nobody ever calls me: E-mail to InstantCall, requesting adjustment. You thought it was strange that no one called you on your new mobile phone, even though you had given your family members, friends, and boss your new number. Two weeks after getting the new phone and agreeing to a $49 monthly fee, you called the service provider, InstantCall, just to see if everything was working. Sure enough, the technician discovered that your incoming calls were being routed to an inactive number. You're glad she found the problem, but then it took the company nearly two more weeks to fix it. When you called to complain about paying for service you didn't receive, the customer service agent suggests you send an e-mail to Judy Hinkley at the company's regional business office to request an adjustment.

Your task: Decide how much of an adjustment you think you deserve under the circumstances and then send an e-mail message to Hinkley, at judyh@instantcall.net, to request the adjustment to your account. Write a summary of events in chronological order, supplying exact dates for maximum effectiveness. Make up any information you need, such as problems that the malfunctioning service caused at home or at work.

14. Giro tales: Letter requesting clarification on loan repayment scheme. As someone who runs a small business, you run into minor cash flow problems every now and then, and you like to take advantage of the low-interest loan repayment schemes that local banks offer when they occur. You recently took one such loan for $6,795 with a local bank, which you can pay off over two years. You also signed up for the monthly repayments of your loan to be made through Giro deductions from an account you have

with the same bank. You prefer this electronic direct payment deduction system to monthly cash or check repayments because you don't want to forget to pay. Furthermore, you have been a customer of this bank for 14 years and pride yourself on your good reputation with them. Nevertheless the bank officer who attended to you did warn you that it would take about two months for the Giro deductions to begin because of the administrative work involved, so you did make two check payments for the first two months. But after two months you decided not to send a check anymore as you figured the Giro deductions should have kicked in. However, two weeks after the due date for the third month's payment, you received a call from the bank informing you that your payment was late. You repeated what you had been told by the bank officer at the time of application, and you were reassured that they would check and get back to you. They never got back to you. Instead, a week later, you got a pink notice from the bank with a terse message informing you that your payment was late, for which you would be charged a late fee, and that you should make your payment in the next three days.

Your task: You are annoyed that the bank has been giving you the wrong information and has handled a simple matter like Giro deductions so inefficiently. You are also upset by the accusing tone of the bank's note to you, which made you feel like you had no intentions of making the loan repayments. You decide that you're going to write a letter to clarify the whole matter. You also decide that since you've been a loyal customer for 14 years and have never faulted on any payments, you are going to demand that the late fee be waived, as you feel it is not your fault. You will write a letter to The Bank Manager, ST Bank, Tampines Branch, Singapore 456789.

MARKETING AND SALES MESSAGES

PORTFOLIO BUILDER

15. Foreign Direct Investment (FDI) opportunities in Pakistan. Pak-Saudi annual bilateral trade between Pakistan and Saudi Arabia was above $4 billion in 2008. Foreign Direct Investment (FDI) in Pakistan from Saudi Arabia was $278 million in 2006, which has decreased to $46 million in 2008. However, the Saudi Investment Authority (SAGIA) has been successful in attracting Pakistani investors to the Kingdom of Saudi Arabia. As a result, there are now more than 350 Pakistani investors who have established their businesses in various fields of construction and services. Pak-Saudi Joint Business Council (JBC) is going to hold its annual meeting in Riyadh (KSA) shortly, which leading Saudi/Pakistani investors are expected to attend.

Your task: Imagine yourself as CEO of the company that has been entrusted with promoting the FDI infusion into the Pakistani economy from the Saudi government as well as private companies in various sectors including infrastructure and industrial projects. Write a letter to be addressed to all the delegates of JBC giving data about Pakistan regarding its large market size of about 180 million people, tax holidays, potential of cheap and skilled labor, and chances of long-term prospects of business growth. Substantial web-based information about Pakistan and investment opportunities can also be found on http://www.pakistan.gov.pk/.

E-MAIL SKILLS

16. Slimming down: Shortening the Curves company history. Curves is a fitness center franchise that caters to women who may not feel at home in traditional gyms. With its customer-focused and research-based approach, Curves has become a significant force in the fitness industry and one of the most successful franchise operations in history.

Your task: Both potential customers and potential franchise owners can learn about the history of Curves at www.curves.com/about-curves/history.php. Using this 450-word article as a starting point, write a shorter version (no more than 150 words) that the company could use for automated e-mail and IM responses.

17. Give me liberty: Letter persuading customers to remain loyal to Colbar Art. For many people in the United States, the Statue of Liberty is something of a tourist cliché, so much a part of New York City's tourist hype that it's taken for granted. But for many immigrants, the first sight of Liberty as they enter the city brings tears along with hopes for a new life. Ovidiu Colea knows the feeling. He immigrated to the United States in the early 1980s, after a difficult past that included five long years in a Romanian hard-labor camp for trying to flee a Communist regime.

Colea worked two years as a cab driver to save enough money to start Colbar Art, a company that produces up to 80,000 hand-crafted replicas of the Liberty statue each year. He now helps other immigrants get a start in their new country by hiring them to design and produce Liberty models. Colea pays a royalty to the Liberty–Ellis Island Foundation for using Liberty's image. In fact, during the first year of operation, that royalty amounted to $250,000.

Painstaking labor is required to produce the acrylic and bonded marble statues with a hand-painted patina, and most of that work is done by the very immigrants lady Liberty welcomes to New York. Colea insists on keeping production in the United States. Although labor costs are lower outside the United States, he refuses to produce the statues in countries "where there is no liberty or no Statue of Liberty." By keeping jobs in the United States, he's doing his share to keep the American Dream alive.

But the meticulous labor also costs precious production time. With recent high demand for the replicas, the company has fallen behind on orders. To increase production to 120,000 statues per year, the company is leasing more space and training new employees. Meanwhile, the production deficits may continue for several months.

Your task: You work for Colbar Art as assistant manager, and Colea has asked you to write a persuasive form letter to all your customers, explaining the current delays and requesting patience. Be sure to explain the steps the company is taking to solve these delays and describe the quality and creativity that go into the replicas. You can quote Bradford Hill (owner of the Liberty Island gift shop), who says Colbar Art's models represent 65 percent of his sales. Make a convincing argument for your customers to remain loyal to Colbar Art.[39]

PORTFOLIO BUILDER

18. Taste it; you just might like it: Convincing consumers to sample agro-based protein products. Like so many new synthetic food products available these days in the supermarkets, substitute meat items made from soybean and other agro-based proteins have been available on food shelves along with other items made from fish, chicken, mutton, and beef. Consumers in Japan and China have accepted the substitute meat items based on their government certification (U.S. FDA equivalent) as healthier food substitutes for animal meats. The analysis provided in the table below shows the necessary nutritional data of the substitute meats on a comparative basis.

	PROTEIN (G)	CHOLESTEROL (MG)	SATURATED FATS (G)	CALORIES	RELATIVE PRICE $/KG
Fish	22.9	47	0.104	105	2.5
Chicken	31.0	85	1.0	165	1.5
Beef	25.9	88	8.5	305	2.0
Substitute Meat	30.7	58	2.7	188	1.0

Your task: Develop a flyer to be displayed in food stores that sell substitute meat items. The page size should be 8½ inches tall by 3¾ inches wide, so format your page accordingly. Allow room for a photograph of substitute meat items and do not try to fit too much text on the page.

TEXT MESSAGING SKILLS   E-MAIL SKILLS

19. Instant promotion: Text message/e-mail combo from Hilton Hotels to frequent guests. Quite a few members of the Hilton Hotels HHonors frequent-traveler program have signed up to receive special offers via text messaging. As a creative marketing writer, however, you've felt constrained by the 160-character limit of the text messaging system (and that includes spaces). Fortunately, an equally creative programmer has just figured out how to marry the company's text messaging system with its e-mail system. Now you can send text messages that announce an offer and invite recipients to request additional information, which will then be delivered automatically via e-mail.

Here is the offer you're working on today: For $575 per person per day (double room), valid through January 15, 2010, travelers can stay in the Hilton Pyramids Golf Resort in Cairo, Egypt, for seven nights/eight days, including breakfast, service charge, and tax. They'll be met at the airport, given transportation to the resort, plus two rounds of golf per person at Dreamland Golf course and two rounds of golf per person at Soleimaneia Pyramids Golf & Country Club course.

You also want to convey that the Dreamland course wraps like a serpent around the Hilton resort. Its lush greens and lakes, designed by Karl Litten, contrast sharply with the golden desert, culminating in a stunning view of the great Pyramids of Giza, one of the seven wonders of the ancient world. The Soleimaneia course features the "biggest floodlit driving course in Egypt." The travel package provides free transportation to this nearby course.

Rates are subject to availability, and other restrictions may apply.[40]

Your task: Write a text message, announcing this offer, staying within the 160-character limit. Any recipient who wants to learn more can simply reply "yes" to the message, and your system will then send an e-mail message to his or her e-mail account. Write a brief e-mail message that contains the full promotional message. Include the URL www.hilton.com/pyramid_golf, which readers can click on to make a reservation.

20. Selling your idea: Sales message promoting a product of your own invention. You never intended to become an inventor, but you saw a way to make something work more easily, so you set to work. You developed a prototype, found a way to mass-produce the product, and set up a small manufacturing studio in your home. You know that other people are going to benefit from your invention. Now all you need is to reach that market.

Your task: Imagine a useful product that you might have invented—perhaps something related to a hobby or sporting activity. List the benefits and features of your imaginary product. Then write a sales message for it, using what you've learned in this chapter and making up details as you need them.

PODCASTING SKILLS

21. Listen up: Podcast promoting a podcast station. Podcasting, the technique of recording individual sound files that people download from the Internet to listen to on their computers or music players, is quickly redefining the concept of radio. A growing crowd of musicians, essayists, journalists, and others with compelling content use podcasting to reach audiences they can't get to through traditional broadcast radio. The good news is that anyone with a microphone and a computer can record podcasts. That's also the bad news, at least from your perspective as a new podcaster: With so many podcasters now on the Internet, potential listeners have thousands and thousands of audio files to select from.

Your new podcast, School2Biz, offers advice to business students making the transition from college to career. You provide information on everything from preparing résumés to interviewing to finding one's place in the business world and building a successful career. As you expand your audience, you'd eventually like to turn School2Biz into a profitable operation (perhaps by selling advertising time during your podcasts). For now, you're simply offering free advice.

Your task: You've chosen The Podcast Bunker (www.podcast bunker.com) as the first website on which to promote School2Biz. The site lets podcasters promote their feeds with brief text listings, such as this description of Pet Talk Radio: "A weekly lifestyle show for people with more than a passing interest in pets. Hosted by Brian Pickering & Kaye Browne with Australia's favourite vet Dr Harry Cooper & animal trainer Steve Austin."

Option A: Write a 50-word description of your new podcast, making up any information you need to describe School2Biz. Be sure to mention who you are and why the information you

present is worth listening to. Option B: If your instructor tells you to do so, script and record a brief podcast (no more than three minutes long) that describes and promotes School2Biz.[41]

WEB WRITING SKILLS   PORTFOLIO BUILDER

22. Don't forget print: Using the web to promote Time Inc.'s magazine advertising. After getting a shaky start as the technology matured and advertisers tried to figure out this new medium, online advertising has finally become a significant force in consumer and business marketing. Companies in a wide variety of industries are shifting some of the advertising budgets from traditional media such as television and magazines to the increasing selection of advertising possibilities online—and more than a few companies now advertise almost exclusively online. That's fine for companies that sell advertising time and space for websites and blogs, but your job involves selling advertising in print magazines that are worried about losing market share to online publishers.

Online advertising has two major advantages that you can't really compete with: interactivity and the ability to precisely target individual audience members. On the other hand, you have several advantages going for you, including the ability to produce high-color photography, the physical presence of print (such as when a magazine sits on a table in a doctor's waiting room), portability, guaranteed circulation numbers, and close reader relationships that go back years or decades in many cases.

Your task: You work as an advertising sales specialist for the Time Inc. division of Time Warner, which publishes more than 150 magazines around the world. Write a brief persuasive message about the benefits of magazine advertising; the statement will be posted on the individual websites of Time Inc.'s numerous magazines, so you can't narrow in on any single publication. Also, Time Inc. coordinates its print publications with an extensive online presence (including thousands of paid online advertisements), so you can't bash online advertising, either.[42]

E-MAIL SKILLS   PORTFOLIO BUILDER

23. Insure.com: E-mail promoting a better way to buy insurance. The great thing about Insure.com is that no one is obligated to buy a thing, which makes your job in the company's marketing department easier. Free of charge, consumers can log on to your website, ask for dozens of insurance quotes, and then go off and buy elsewhere. They can look at instant price-comparison quotes from more than 200 insurers, covering every kind of insurance from term life and medical to private passenger auto insurance. All rates are guaranteed up-to-the-day accurate against a $500 reward. And so far the online service has received positive press from *Nation's Business, Kiplinger's Personal Finance, Good Housekeeping, The Los Angeles Times, Money, U.S. News & World Report,* and *Forbes.*

Insure.com generates revenues primarily from the receipt of commissions and fees paid by insurers based on the volume of business produced. Customers can purchase insurance from the company of their choice via the Insure.com website, or they can call a toll-free number to speak to one of the company's representatives. The reps are paid salaries versus commissions and do not directly benefit by promoting one insurance company's product over another.

And all this is free. Too bad more people don't know about your services.

Your task: It's your job to lure more insurance customers to Insure.com. You've decided to use direct e-mail marketing (using a list of consumers who have inquired about rates in the past but never committed to purchase anything). Write an e-mail sales message promoting the benefits of Insure.com's services. Be sure your message is suited to e-mail format, with an appropriate subject heading.[43]

PORTFOLIO BUILDER

24. Outsourcing: Letter from Kelly Services, offering solutions. Kelly Services is a global Fortune 500 company that offers staffing solutions that include temporary services, staff leasing, outsourcing, and vendor on-site and full-time placement. Kelly provides employees who have a wide range of skills across many disciplines, including office services, accounting, engineering, information technology, law, science, marketing, light industrial, education, health care, and home care.

Companies use Kelly Services to strategically balance workload and workforce during peaks and valleys of demand, to handle special projects, and to evaluate employees prior to making full-time hiring decisions. The dramatic changes in business have spurred the rapid growth of the contingent employment industry.

In turn, many individuals are choosing the flexibility of personal career management, increasing options of where, when, and how to work. Therefore, more and more workers are becoming receptive to being contract, temporary, or consulting employees.

The flexibility of a temporary services firm offers advantages to both the company and the employee. Both have the opportunity to evaluate one another prior to making a long-term commitment. Kelly Services earns a fee when its employees are hired permanently, but employers find that it's a small price to pay for such valuable preview time, which saves everyone the cost and pain of a bad hiring decision.

With 2,500 offices in 26 countries, Kelly provides its customers nearly 700,000 employees annually. The company provides staffing solutions to more than 90 percent of the Fortune 500 companies. Kelly has received many supplier awards for providing outstanding and cost-efficient staffing services, including Chrysler's Gold Award, Ford Motor Company's Q1 Preferred Quality Award, Intel Corporation's Supplier Continuous Quality Improvement (SCQI) Award, and DuPont Legal's Challenge Award.

As companies increasingly face new competitive pressures to provide better service and quality at lower prices, many are turning to outsourcing suppliers to deliver complete operational management of specific functions or support departments, allowing the company the necessary time to focus on its core competencies. One solution is to choose a single supplier such as the Kelly Management Services (KMS) division to deliver "full-service" outsourcing.

KMS combines management experience, people process improvements, technology enhancements, and industry expertise to optimize customer operations and reduce cost. KMS understands the unique challenges companies face in today's increasingly fast-paced business world and can provide customers with services across multiple functional offerings, including call center operations, warehousing, distribution and light assembly, back-office and administrative functions, and mail and reprographic services.

Your task: Write a sales letter to companies similar to Chrysler, Ford, Intel, and DuPont, explaining what Kelly has to offer. For current information, visit the Kelly website, at www.kellyservices.com.[44]

BLOGGING SKILLS

25. True green: Explaining why Hangers Cleaners is different. Other than possibly wrinkling their noses at that faint smell that wafts out of the plastic bags when they bring clothes home from the dry cleaner, many consumers probably don't pay much attention to the process that goes on behind the scenes at their neighborhood cleaner. However, traditional dry cleaning is a chemically intense process—so much so that these facilities require special environmental permits and monitoring by government agencies.

At Kansas City's Hangers Cleaners, the process is different—much different. The company's innovative machines use safe liquid carbon dioxide (CO_2) and specially developed detergents to clean clothes. The process requires no heat (making it easier on clothes) and has no need for the toxic, combustible perchloroethylene used in conventional dry cleaning (making it safer for employees and the environment). Customers can tell the difference, too. As one put it, "Since I started using Hangers, my clothes are softer, cleaner and they don't have that chemical smell."

Your task: Because many consumers aren't familiar with traditional dry cleaning, they don't immediately grasp why Hangers's method is better for clothes, employees, and the environment. Write a post for the company blog, explaining why Hangers is different. Limit yourself to 400 words. You can learn more about the company and its unique process at www.hangerskc.com.[45]

Part 4

Supporting Messages with Quality Information

■ **CHAPTER 11**   Finding, Evaluating, and Processing Information

■ **CHAPTER 12**   Designing Visual Communication

Follow a simple process for finding and analyzing information, and your readers will learn to trust your messages because they'll know you support your conclusions and recommendations with reliable information. The second major way to support your messages is with clear and compelling visuals. In fact, the visual presentation of information is one of the most exciting developments in business communication today. Even if you have no background in design, by following a few basic principles you can create powerful images to bolster your written messages.

Finding, Evaluating, and Processing Information

Learning Objectives

After studying this chapter, you will be able to

1 Describe an effective process for conducting business research

2 Define *primary research* and *secondary research* and explain when you use each method

3 Name ten criteria for evaluating the credibility of an information source

4 Provide five guidelines for conducting an effective online search

5 Outline the steps required to create and administer surveys and interviews

6 Describe the major tasks involved in processing and applying your research results

Communication Close-up at Tesco

British retail giant Tesco relies on extensive audience research to plan and craft its consumer messages.

www.tesco.com

Most consumers enjoy the benefits of stiff price competition among their local grocery stores, but the competition is anything but enjoyable for grocery retailers. In the United States, the average grocery store's after-tax profit margin hovers around 1 percent. With so little room for error, grocers need to stay on top of consumer behavior to make sure they offer the right mix of products at the right prices.

Tesco, the leading grocery retailer in the United Kingdom, is not only surviving but thriving in this tough industry. Under the leadership of Richard Brasher, the company's top marketing executive in the United Kingdom, Tesco devotes considerable effort to acquiring and processing information about its customers, information that is used in a variety of documents to drive both strategic and tactical decisions.

For example, when demographic research indicated a growing number of immigrants from Poland, the store reached out to Polish-speaking consumers to learn more about their wants and needs. After a successful experiment on a small scale, Tesco expanded its Polish foods selection to as many as 100 other stores. In another instance, the marketing team couldn't figure out why flowers and wine had become such hot sellers during a particular week at the beginning of summer that didn't coincide with any regular holidays. Analysis of sales data revealed that families were buying these items as gifts for their children's teachers at the end of the school year, so the company responded by making sure both items were stocked in plentiful supply during that week.

Tesco is now busy applying its information-driven approach to the competitive U.S. market. After studying the market for two decades, the company made its move in 2007 and now has more than 50 Fresh & Easy Neighborhood Markets in California, Nevada, and Arizona. True to form, Tesco is emphasizing research and information every step of the way in

every facet of the business. When the company approached the Phoenix-based dessert manufacturer Berto's Gelato and Sorbet about carrying its premium gelato in Fresh & Easy stores, Berto's CEO Ed DeBartolo was amazed at the amount of information the company demanded. Tesco even sent auditors and food scientists to the Berto's facility to conduct their own research. DeBartolo so admires Tesco's emphasis on information that he has applied the giant retailer's methods to all the products his company makes. And, he says, "I want to be a Tesco supplier for life."[1]

SUPPORTING YOUR MESSAGES WITH SOLID RESEARCH

Whether you're planning a simple blog posting or an entire business plan, you can follow the lead of Tesco (profiled in the chapter-opening Communication Close-up) and make sure your reporting, analysis, and recommendations are supported with solid research. Figure 11.1 outlines a five-step research process that will help you gather and use information efficiently; you'll learn more about these steps in the following sections.

1 **LEARNING OBJECTIVE**

Describe an effective process for conducting business research

PLANNING YOUR RESEARCH

You've learned to resist the temptation to dive into a new writing project without thoughtful planning; now you can apply that same level of discipline to research. With so much information online these days, it's tempting just to punch some keywords into a search engine and then dig through the results, looking for something, anything, that seems promising. However, such a lack of planning can limit both your effectiveness and your efficiency, and you can't afford either mistake in today's competitive business environment.

Jumping online and researching without a plan can be ineffective for several reasons: Your favorite search engine might not index the websites that have the information you need, the engine might use different terms to identify the information you're looking for, the information might not be online, or the information might not even exist. Poor planning also limits your efficiency, and because you'll rarely have enough time to research as thoroughly as you'd like, you can't afford to waste any time. If you don't frame the research challenge carefully before you start looking, chances are you'll discover something along the way that forces you to rethink the questions you're trying to answer or the approach you're taking. (Such discoveries can happen even when you are careful, but planning minimizes the chances.) Worse yet, you might move into the writing phase with inadequate information and waste additional time trying to construct a compelling message with insufficient support.

Researching without a plan wastes time and usually produces unsatisfactory results.

FIGURE 11.1 The Research Process
By following a methodical research process, you can save time and money while uncovering better information.

1 Plan	2 Locate data and information	3 Process data and information	4 Apply your findings	5 Manage information
• Maintain research ethics and etiquette • Familiarize yourself with the subject; develop problem statement • Identify information gaps • Prioritize research needs	• Evaluate sources • Collect secondary information at the library, online, or elsewhere • Document your sources • Collect primary information through surveys and interviews	• Quote, paraphrase, or summarize textual information • Analyze numerical information	• Summarize findings • Draw conclusions • Make recommendations	• Make research results available to others via your company's knowledge management system

The good news is that you can minimize or avoid all these problems with a few well-considered planning steps: Familiarize yourself with the subject so that you can frame insightful questions, identify the most critical gaps in your information, and then prioritize your research needs. However, before launching any research project, be sure to take a moment or two to consider the ethics and etiquette of your approach.

Maintaining Ethics and Etiquette in Your Research

Your research tactics can affect both the people from whom you gather information and the people who use your results. To avoid ethical lapses, keep the following points in mind:

- **Don't force a specific outcome by skewing your research.** Approach your research with an open mind and a willingness to accept whatever you find, even if it's not what you expect or want to see.
- **Respect the privacy of your research participants.** Privacy is a contentious issue today. Businesses believe they have a right to protect their confidential information from competitors, and consumers believe they have a right to protect their personal information from businesses.
- **Document sources and give appropriate credit.** Whether you are using published documents, personal interviews, or company records, citing your sources not only is fair to the people who created and provided the information but also helps your audience members confirm your information or explore it in more detail, if they so choose.

- **Respect the intellectual property and digital rights of your sources.** *Intellectual property* refers to the ownership of unique ideas that have commercial value in the marketplace.[2] For example, your research might turn up a great new way to sell services online, but that doesn't mean you're free to implement that process. It might be protected by one of the many patents that have been granted in recent years for business process models.
- **Don't extract more from your sources than they actually provide.** In other words, don't succumb to the temptation to put words in a source's mouth. For instance, if an industry expert says that a sales increase is possible, don't quote him or her as saying that a sales increase is probable.
- **Don't misrepresent who you are or what you intend to do with the research results.** One classic example of ethical lapses in this is area is known as *sugging*, short for *selling under the guise of research*. Another is *pretexting*, which is essentially lying about who you are (for example, claiming you are a journalist or a bill collector) in order to gain access to information that you couldn't get otherwise. Note that for some types of information, such as financial records, pretexting is illegal.[3]

Research etiquette deserves careful attention, too. For example, respect the time of anyone who agrees to be interviewed or to be a research participant and maintain courtesy throughout the interview or research process. For more information on research ethics and etiquette, review the *Code of Standards and Ethics for Survey Research* published by the Council of America Survey Research Organizations, at www.casro.org/codeofstandards.cfm.

Familiarizing Yourself with the Subject

Give yourself some unstructured time at the beginning of the project to explore the general subject area, perhaps by reading industry publications, visiting competitors' websites, and interviewing experts within your organization. Scan the tables of contents and indexes of books on the subject. Some of newest online search tools can be quite helpful in this regard; see "Taking Advantage of Innovative Research Technologies" on page 359.

When you have a basic grasp of the subject area, develop a **problem statement** that defines the problem or purpose of your research—the decision you need to make or the conclusion you need to reach at the end of the process. You may find it easier to phrase the problem as a question, such as "How can we improve customer satisfaction?" or "Does Nintendo's new system pose a competitive threat to us?"

Identifying Information Gaps

Your problem statement frames the purpose of your research, but it often doesn't tell you what specific information you need to find. You next task is to dig deeper to discover the specific *information gaps* that need to be filled through research. You or someone in your company may already have some of the information you need, and you don't want to waste time or money gathering information you already have in hand.

For instance, the question "How can we improve customer satisfaction?" is too vague because many separate factors contribute to customer satisfaction. To get useful information, you would break this topic down into specific issues, such as product reliability and customer service skills. Digging further, you may discover that you don't need to research product reliability because the company already tracks data on product repairs. However, if no one has ever measured the employees' customer service skills, you would identify that as a definite information gap. This example is oversimplified, but you can see how information gap analysis helps you focus on the most important issues to address in your research.

Focus your research by identifying the most important gaps in your information.

Prioritizing Research Needs

Prioritizing your research needs is important because you won't have the time or money to answer every question you might have. Moreover, if you'll be using interviewers or surveys, you'll need to limit the number of questions you ask so that you don't consume more time than people are willing to give. One simple way to prioritize is to divide your questions into "need to know" and "nice to know" and then toss out all the "nice to know" questions. If you started with a technique such as information gap analysis, you will get a clear idea of the information you truly need to collect.

You usually won't have enough time or money to answer every question that comes to mind, so setting priorities is a must.

LOCATING DATA AND INFORMATION

With a clear plan and careful prioritization, you're ready to conduct research—and the first step is to see whether anyone else has already done some or all of the research you need. Research done previously for another purpose is considered **secondary research**. The sources for such information include print and online periodicals, online databases, books, and other research reports. (Some companies specialize in reports on particular industries, companies, technologies, market regions, and other subjects.) Don't let the name *secondary* fool you, though. You want to start with secondary research because it can save you considerable time and money, although you may have to pay to see someone else's results. In contrast, **primary research** is new research done specifically for the current project. Primary sources include surveys, interviews, observations, and experiments.

2 **LEARNING OBJECTIVE**

Define *primary research* and *secondary research* and explain when you use each method

Evaluating Sources

No matter where you're searching, it is your responsibility to separate quality information from unreliable junk, so you don't taint your results or damage your reputation. Web 2.0 tools have complicated this challenge by making many new sources of information available. On the positive side, independent sources communicating through blogs, wikis, user-generated content sites, and podcasting channels can provide valuable and unique insights, often from experts whose voices might never be heard otherwise. On the negative side, these nontraditional information sources often lack the editorial boards and fact checkers commonly used in traditional publishing. You cannot assume that the information you find in blogs and other sources is accurate, objective, and current. Answer the following questions about each piece of material:

Evaluate your sources carefully to avoid embarrassing and potentially damaging mistakes.

- **Does the source have a reputation for honesty and reliability?** Naturally, you'll feel more comfortable using information from an established source that has a reputation for accuracy (see Figure 11.2). But don't let your guard down completely; even the finest reporters and editors can make mistakes. For sources that are new or relatively unknown, your safest bet is to corroborate anything you learn with information from several other sources.

3 **LEARNING OBJECTIVE**

Name ten criteria for evaluating the credibility of an information source

FIGURE 11.2   Getting Information from Reliable Sources
The U.S. Census Bureau is a trusted source of many types of facts and figures about the people and businesses in the United States.

- **Is the source potentially biased?** The individual or organization providing the information might have a particular bias or point of view regarding the information and its context. Such bias is neither inherently bad nor unethical, but you need to be aware of it so that you can interpret the information you find.
- **What is the purpose of the material?** Was the material designed to inform others of new research, advance a position, or stimulate discussion? Was it designed to promote or sell a product? Be sure to distinguish among advertising, advocating, and informing.
- **Is the author credible?** Find out whether the person or the publisher is well known in the field. Is the author an amateur? Merely someone with an opinion?
- **Where did the source get its information?** Many sources of secondary information get their material from other secondary sources, removing you even further from the original data.

Let your readers know if you were unable to verify critical pieces of information obtained in your research.

- **Can you verify the material independently?** Verification can uncover biases or mistakes—which is particularly important when the information goes beyond simple facts to include projections, interpretations, and estimates. If you can't verify critical information, let your audience know that.
- **Is the material current?** Make sure you are using the most current information available by checking the original publication date.
- **Is the material complete?** Have you accessed the entire document or only a selection from it? If it's a selection, which parts were excluded? Do you need more detail?
- **Are all claims supported with evidence?** Are opinions presented as facts? Does the writer make broad claims, such as "most people believe . . ." without citing any surveys to prove his or her point?
- **Do the source's claims stand up to logical scrutiny?** Finally, step back and ask whether the information makes sense. If that little voice in your head says that something sounds suspicious, listen!

You probably won't have time to conduct a thorough background check on all your sources, so focus your efforts on the most important or most suspicious pieces of information.

Conducting Secondary Research

Even if you intend to eventually conduct primary research, start with a review of any available secondary research. Inside the company, you might be able to find a variety of documents prepared for other projects that offer helpful information. Be sure to ask whether your company has a *knowledge management system*. (See "Managing Information" on page 370 for more on this topic.) Outside the company, you can choose from a wide range of print and online resources, some of which are included in Table 11.1. (Of course, the list in Table 11.1 represents a tiny fraction of the secondary resources available.)[4] For instance, if you want to know more about a specific company, one of the first things you'll need to find out is whether the company is public (sells shares of stock to the general public) or private. Public corporations, which are required to submit extensive financial reports to government agencies, generally have more information available than private companies. If your company doesn't have an in-house research librarian, consider beginning your search for secondary information at the nearest public or university library.

Start your research by conducting secondary research first.

Finding Information at the Library

Public, corporate, and university libraries offer an enormous array of business books, electronic databases, newspapers, periodicals, directories, almanacs, and government publications. Some of these printed sources provide information that is not available online, and some of the online sources provide information that is available by subscription. Don't assume that you can find everything you need through your own online research. Libraries are also where you'll find one of your most important resources: librarians. Reference librarians are trained in research techniques and can often help you find obscure information you can't find on your own. They can also direct you to many sources of business information. Also, many library websites now have a business portal, with links to helpful resources and advice on finding information.

Libraries offer information and resources you can't find anywhere else—including specialized research librarians.

TABLE 11.1 Important Resources for Business Research

COMPANY, INDUSTRY, AND PRODUCT RESOURCES (URLS ARE PROVIDED FOR ONLINE RESOURCES)

AnnualReports.com (www.annualreports.com). Free access to annual reports from thousands of public companies.

Brands and Their Companies/Companies and Their Brands. Contains data on more than 430,000 consumer products and 100,000 manufacturers, importers, marketers, and distributors. Also available as an online database; ask at your library.

CNN/Money (http://money.cnn.com). News, analysis, and financial resources covering companies, industries, and world markets.

D&B Directories. A variety of directories, including *America's Corporate Families* (ownership connections among companies), *Business Rankings* (25,000 leading companies), *Directory of Service Companies* (more than 50,000 companies in the service sector), and *Industrial Guide* (more than 120,000 manufacturing companies).

Hoover's Handbook of American Business. Profiles of 750 influential public and private corporations.

Hoover's Online (www.hoovers.com). Database of 12 million companies worldwide, including in-depth coverage of 35,000 leading companies around the world. Basic information available free; in-depth information requires a subscription.

Manufacturing and Distribution USA. Data on thousands of companies in the manufacturing, wholesaling, and retailing sectors.

NAICS Codes (www.census.gov/eos/www/naics). North American Industry Classification System.

Reference USA. Concise information on millions of U.S. companies; subscription database.

SEC filing (www.sec.gov/edgar.shtml). SEC filings, including 10Ks, 10Qs, annual reports, and prospectuses for U.S. public firms.

Standard & Poor's Industry Surveys. Concise investment profiles for a broad range of industries. Coverage is extensive, with a focus on current situation and outlook. Includes some summary data on major companies in each industry. Also available in a subscription database, as part of the NetAdvantage product line.

(continued)

TABLE 11.1 Important Resources for Business Research *(continued)*

Standard & Poor's Register of Corporations, Directors, and Executives. Index of major U.S. and international corporations. Lists officers, products, sales volume, and number of employees. Also available in a subscription database, as part of the NetAdvantage product line.

Thomas's Register of American Manufacturers (www.thomasnet.com). Information on thousands of U.S. manufacturers, indexed by company name and product.

RESEARCH DIRECTORIES AND INDEXES

Books in Print. Database indexes nearly 20 million book, audio book, and video titles from around the world. Available in print and professional online versions.

Directories in Print. Information on more than 15,000 business and industrial directories.

Encyclopedia of Associations. Index of thousands of associations, listed by broad subject category, specific subject, association, and location. Available as an online database as well.

Reader's Guide to Periodical Literature. Classic index of general-interest magazines, categorized by subject and author; also available in electronic format, including a version with the full text of thousands of articles.

TRADEMARKS AND PATENTS

Official Gazette of the United States Patent and Trademark Office (www.uspto.gov). Weekly publication (one for trademarks and one for patents) providing official record of newly assigned trademarks and patents, product descriptions, and product names.

United States Patent and Trademark Office (www.uspto.gov). Trademark and patent information records.

STATISTICS AND OTHER BUSINESS DATA

Bureau of Economic Analysis (www.bea.gov). Large collection of economic and government data.

Europa—The European Union Online (http://europa.eu/index_en.htm). A portal that provides up-to-date coverage of current affairs, legislation, policies, and EU statistics.

FedStats (www.fedstats.gov). Access to a full range of statistics and information from more than 70 U.S. government agencies.

Industry Norms and Key Business Ratios (Dun & Bradstreet). Industry, financial, and performance ratios.

Information Please Almanac. Compilation of broad-range statistical data, with strong focus on labor force.

Annual Statement Studies. Industry, financial, and performance ratios published by the Risk Management Association.

Statistical Abstract of the United States (www.census.gov). Annual compendium of U.S. economic, social, political, and industrials statistics.

STAT-USA (www.stat-usa.gov). Large collection of economic and government data.

The World Almanac and Book of Facts. Facts on economic, social, educational, and political events for major countries.

U.S. Bureau of Labor Statistics (www.bls.gov). Extensive national and regional information on labor and business, including employment, industry growth, productivity, the Consumer Price Index (CPI), and the overall U.S. economy.

U.S. Census Bureau (www.census.gov). Demographic data and analysis on consumers and businesses based on census results.

COMMERCIAL DATABASES (REQUIRE SUBSCRIPTIONS; CHECK WITH YOUR SCHOOL LIBRARY)

ABI/INFORM Trade & Industry. Access to more than 750 periodicals and newsletters that focus on specific trades or industries.

Business Source Premier (Ebsco). Access to a variety of databases on a wide range of disciplines from leading information providers.

Dialog. Hundreds of databases that include areas such as business and finance, news and media, medicine, pharmaceuticals, reference, social sciences, government and regulation, science and technology, and more.

HighBeam Research. Thousands of full-text newspaper, magazine, and newswire sources, plus maps and photographs.

Gale Business & Company Resource Center. A comprehensive research tool designed for undergraduate and graduate students, job searchers, and investors; offers a wide variety of information on companies and industries.

LexisNexis. Several thousand databases covering legal, corporate, government, and academic subjects.

ProQuest. Thousands of periodicals and newspapers; archives continue to expand through its program to digitize more than 5 billion pages of microfilm.

SRDS Media Solutions. A comprehensive database of magazine information and advertising rates, cataloging more than 100,000 U.S. and international media properties.

Whether you're trying to locate information in printed materials or in databases, each type of resource serves a special function:

- **Newspapers and periodicals.** Libraries offer access to a wide variety of popular magazines, general business magazines, *trade journals* (which provide information about specific professions and industries), and *academic journals* (which provide research-oriented articles from researchers and educators). Check the library's website or ask a librarian to see which periodicals are available in print or electronic formats.
- **Business books.** Although less timely than newspapers and periodicals, business books provide in-depth coverage of a variety of business topics. Many libraries now offer online access to their card catalogs so you can see if they have specific titles in their collections.
- **Directories.** Thousands of directories are published in print and electronic formats in many countries and many include membership information for all kinds of professions, industries, and special-interest groups.
- **Almanacs and statistical resources.** Almanacs are handy guides to factual and statistical information about countries, politics, the labor force, and so on. One of the most extensive, the *Statistical Abstract of the United States*, published annually by the U.S. Department of Commerce, contains statistics about occupations, government, population, health, business, crime, and the environment (also available online at www.census.gov).
- **Government publications.** Information on laws, court decisions, tax questions, regulatory issues, and other governmental concerns is often available in collections of government documents. A librarian can direct you to the information you want.
- **Electronic databases.** Databases offer vast collections of searchable information, often in specific areas, such as business, law, science, technology, and education. Some libraries offer remote online access to some or all databases; for others, you need to visit in person. The following section offers more information on using databases.

Local, state/province, and national government agencies publish a huge array of information that is helpful to business researchers.

Finding Information Online

Experienced researchers know that the Internet can be a tremendous source of business information, much of it free, and all of it available more-or-less instantly. They also know that the Internet can waste hours and hours of precious time and deliver inaccurate or biased information, exaggerated claims, and unsubstantiated rumors. If possible, try to learn something about an unfamiliar topic from a trusted source (such as an industry journal or an experienced colleague) before you start searching online. You'll be better able to detect skewed or erroneous information, and you can be more selective about which websites and documents to use.

Much of the information online has not been subjected to the same quality controls common in traditional offline publishing.

Two good places to start on the web are the Internet Public Library (www.ipl.org) and the Librarians' Internet Index (http://lii.org), two *web directories* that carefully select reliable websites to feature in subject-area collections. In their business sections, you can find such information as company profiles, trade data, business news, corporate tax and legal advice, small-business information, prepared forms and documents, biographies of executives, financial reports, job postings, online publications, and so on.

Start with a reliable web directory to learn more about a topic area.

If you're looking for information on a specific company, your best source may be the company's website. A company website generally includes detailed information about the firm's products, services, history, mission, strategy, financial performance, and employment needs. Many sites provide links to related company information, such as SEC filings, news releases, and more. Reputable companies are careful about the information they put online, but beware of the possibility of biases and mistakes.

You can gather a lot of information on companies from their websites, but remember that such information is designed to present the company in a positive light.

Understanding Search Engines, Web Directories, and Databases Many web users are in the habit of just punching a few words into one of the major search engines and pursuing whatever pops up. However, successful online searches require a lot more, in both the tools you use and how you use them. This section compares the three major categories of online research tools: search engines, web directories, and databases. Table 11.2 lists some of the most popular search engines, directories, metacrawlers, and specialized search tools available today. (*Note:* Some of these sites offer free toolbars for your web browser; unless

To be a successful online researcher, you need to expand your toolkit beyond the popular search engines.

TABLE 11.2   The Broad Spectrum of Online Search Tools

GENERAL-PURPOSE SEARCH ENGINES			
AOL Search	http://search.aol.com	Google	www.google.com
AlltheWeb	www.alltheweb.com	Viewzi	www.viewzi.com
AltaVista	www.altavista.com	Windows Live Search	www.live.com
Ask.com	www.ask.com	Yahoo! Search	http://search.yahoo.com

METACRAWLERS, CLUSTERING ENGINES, AND HYBRID SITES			
Clusty	http://clusty.com	Search.com	www.search.com
Dogpile	www.dogpile.com	SurfWax	www.surfwax.com
ixquick	www.ixquick.com	WebBrain	www.webbrain.com
jux2	www.jux2.com	WebCrawler	www.webcrawler.com
KartOO	www.kartoo.com	Yahoo!	www.yahoo.com
Mamma	www.mamma.com	ZapMeta	www.zapmeta.com
MetaCrawler	www.metacrawler.com		

WEB DIRECTORIES AND ONLINE LIBRARIES			
About	www.about.com	Library of Congress	www.loc.gov/rr/business
Answers.com	www.answers.com	Library Spot	www.libraryspot.com
Beaucoup!	www.beaucoup.com	Open Directory Project	www.dmoz.com
CEOExpress	http://ceoexpress.com	Questia (requires subscription)	www.questia.com
Digital Librarian	www.digital-librarian.com/business.html	USA.gov (U.S. government portal)	www.usa.gov
Google Directory	www.google.com/dirhp	Virtual Learning Resources Center	www.virtuallrc.com
INFOMINE	http://infomine.ucr.edu		
Internet Public Library	www.ipl.org		
Librarians' Internet Index	http://lii.org		

NEWS SEARCH ENGINES AND SOCIAL TAGGING SITES			
10 × 10	http://tenbyten.org	NewsNow	www.newsnow.co.uk
AlltheWeb News	http://www.alltheweb.com/?cat=news	Newseum	www.newseum.org
		Topix	www.topix.net
AltaVista News	http://news.altavista.com	WorldNews	www.wn.com
Delicious	http://delicious.com	Yahoo! News	http://news.yahoo.com
Digg	www.digg.com		
Google News	http://news.google.com		

BLOG, VIDEO, AND PODCAST SEARCH ENGINES AND DIRECTORIES			
American Rhetoric (speeches)	www.americanrhetoric.com	Podcast Bunker	www.podcastbunker.com
blinkx	www.blinkx.com	Podcast Pickle	www.podcastpickle.com
Bloglines	www.bloglines.com	Podcast Network	www.thepodcastnetwork.com
BlogPulse	www.blogpulse.com	podscope	www.podscope.com
Google Blog Search	http://blogsearch.google.com	Technorati	www.technorati.com
Google Video	http://video.google.com	Yahoo! Video search	http://video.search.yahoo.com
Podcast Alley	www.podcastalley.com	YouTube	www.youtube.com

PERIODICAL AND BOOK SEARCH ENGINES			
FindArticles.com	www.findarticles.com	Google Book Search	http://books.google.com
Google Scholar search	http://scholar.google.com		

you trust the website, don't download these toolbars. Some can install malicious software on your computer.)

Search engines identify individual webpages that contain specific words or phrases you've asked for. Search engines have the advantage of scanning millions or billions of individual webpages, and the best engines use powerful ranking algorithms to present the pages that are probably the most relevant to your search request. In addition, search engines such as Google Book Search now allow you to search through scanned copies of printed books (see Figure 11.3).

For all their ease and power, search engines have three main disadvantages you should be aware of: (1) No human editors are involved in evaluating the quality of the content you find on these pages; (2) various engines use different search techniques, so one engine might miss a site or page that another one finds; and (3) search engines can't reach all the content on many websites.

Today's search engines are powerful tools, but they still have important limitations.

The realm of out-of-reach pages is sometimes called the *hidden Internet* or the *deep web* because conventional search techniques can't access them. Webpages can be hidden from search engines for a variety of reasons, including password protection, links that some search engines can't follow (such as the links created with Adobe Flash animation software), pages that webmasters block from search engines, and *dynamic pages* that exist only when a visitor submits a query or request on a website. The hidden Internet is estimated to be at least several times larger than the visible Internet, and much of the material you might want to find for some reports could be unreachable through standard search engines.[5]

Specialized search engines can help reach information in the hidden Internet.

FIGURE 11.3   Google Book Search
The ability to search through printed texts electronically is a significant advantage for researchers in all subject areas. Google Book Search currently offers restricted previews but will soon offer full-access options.

Web directories benefit from having human editors evaluate and select websites.

Metacrawlers can save you time by employing multiple search engines at once.

Online databases give you access to some of the most important resources that search engines usually can't reach: millions of newspaper, magazine, and journal articles.

Make sure you know how each search engine, directory, database, or metacrawler works; they work in different ways, and you can get unpredictable results if you don't know how each one operates.

Fortunately, new search tools continue to reach more and more of this content; see the Real-Time Updates Learn More link to the left.

Web directories help address the first shortcoming of search engines, which is the lack of human editors to review and select the webpages on display. Directories such as those offered by the Internet Public Library, the Librarians' Internet Index, Yahoo!, and the Open Directory Project (at **http:// dmoz.org**) use human editors to categorize and evaluate websites and other media. For instance, the Open Directory Project lists nearly 250,000 business-related websites by category, from individual companies to industry associations, all of which have been evaluated and selected by a team of volunteer editors.[6] Specialized directories also let you browse collections of blogs, podcasts, and online video.

Metacrawlers or *metasearch engines* (such as Bovée and Thill's Web Search, at **http://businesscommunicationblog.com/websearch**) address the second shortcoming of search engines by formatting your search request for the specific requirements of multiple search engines and then telling you how many hits each engine was able to find for you.

Online databases address the third shortcoming of search engines by offering access to the newspapers, magazines, and journals that you're likely to need for many research projects. You can access such sources as *Fortune* and the *Wall Street Journal* either through the individual publishers' own sites or through a commercial database that offers access to multiple sources. Individual publisher sites sometimes require a subscription to that publication for anything beyond the current issue, and commercial databases require subscriptions to access all content. Some commercial databases, such as HighBeam Research (**www.highbeam.com**), offer individual pricing, whereas others, such as LexisNexis (**www.lexisnexis.com/corporate**) and ProQuest (**www.proquest.com**), are intended for use by companies, libraries, and other institutions. In addition to databases that primarily feature content from newspapers and periodicals, specialized databases such as Hoover's (**www.hoovers.com**) and OneSource's CorpTech (**www.corptech.com**) offer detailed information on thousands of individual companies. You can obtain company news releases from the free databases maintained by *PR Newswire* (**www .prnewswire.com**) and Business Wire (**www. businesswire.com**). News releases are good places to look for announcements of new products, management changes, earnings, dividends, mergers, acquisitions, and other company information. Ask your librarian for advice on accessing all these resources.

Using Search Tools Effectively   Search engines, metacrawlers, and databases offer a variety of ways to find information. Unfortunately, no two of them work in exactly the same way, and you have to learn how to use each one most effectively. The most basic form of searching is a *keyword search*, in which the engine or database attempts to find items that include all the words you enter. A *Boolean search* expands on this capability by using search operators that let you define a query with greater precision. Common operators include AND (the search must include both words before and after the AND), OR (the search can include either or both words), and NOT (the search ignores items with whatever word comes after NOT). For example:

- *corporate AND profits* finds webpages or database entries that contain both *corporate* and *profits*.
- *corporate OR profits* finds items that contain either *corporate* or *profits* but not necessarily both.
- *corporate NOT profits* finds items that contain *corporate* but excludes all those that contain the word *profits*.

Boolean searches can also include operators that let you find a particular word in close proximity to other words or use *wildcards* to find similar spellings (such as *profit*, *profits*, and *profitability*).

As a simpler alternative to Boolean searches, some search engines and databases offer *natural language searches*, which let you ask questions in normal, everyday English. (Natural language is what humans speak, as opposed to the languages computers speak.) For example, "Which video game companies are the most profitable?" is a natural language query. Be aware that some search tools let you select keyword, Boolean, or natural language searches, so make sure you know which method you're using.

Several search tools, including AlltheWeb, Google, and Microsoft's Live Search, have implemented *forms-based searches* that help you create powerful queries without needing to learn any special techniques.[7] As the name implies, you simply fill out an online form that typically lets you specify parameters such as date ranges, words to include or exclude, language, Internet domain name, and even file and media types. To access these forms, click on "advanced search" or a similar option.

To make the best use of any search engine or database, keep the following points in mind:

- **Read the instructions.** Unfortunately, there is no universal set of instructions that apply to every search tool. You can usually find a Help page that explains both basic and advanced functions, with advice on how to use a particular tool most effectively.
- **Pay attention to the details.** Details can make all the difference in a search. For instance, some search engines treat *AND* (uppercase) as a Boolean search operator and look only for pages or entries that contain both words. In contrast, *and* (lowercase) and similar basic words (called *stopwords*) are excluded from many searches because they are so common, they'll show up in every webpage or database entry. Similarly, some engines and databases interpret the question mark as a wildcard to let you search for variations of a given word, but Google searches for word variations automatically, so you don't need to use a wildcard.[8] Again, you need to know how to operate each search engine or database, and don't assume they all work in the same way.
- **Review the search and display options carefully.** Some sites and databases provide few options to control your queries, but others, such as Google's Advanced Search, let you make a variety of choices to include or exclude specific types of files and pages from specific sites. Also, when searching databases, pay close attention to whether you are searching in the title, author, subject, or document field. Each will return different results. Some databases default to searching only in the title field, meaning that you'll miss a lot of items unless you know the exact words used in the title. When the results are displayed, verify the presentation order; results might be sorted by date or by relevance.
- **Try variations of terms.** If you can't find what you're looking for, try abbreviations (*CEO, CPA*), synonyms (*man, male*), related terms (*child, adolescent, youth*), different spellings (*dialog, dialogue*), singular and plural forms (*woman, women*), nouns and adjectives (*manager, management, managerial*), and open and compound forms (*online, on line, on-line*). As mentioned earlier, Google searches for word variations automatically.
- **Adjust the scope of your search, if needed.** If a search yields little or no information, broaden your search by specifying fewer terms. Conversely, if you're inundated with too many hits, use more terms to narrow your search. For example, *Apple* yields many more hits than *Apple iPod*, which yields many more than *Apple iPod nano*.

Taking Advantage of Innovative Research Technologies As you conduct research throughout your career, keep an eye out for the latest technologies that can help you conduct your research more effectively and more efficiently. Four innovative tools now available are desktop and enterprise search engines, research and content managers, social bookmarking sites, and newsfeeds:

- **Desktop and enterprise search engines.** Unlike conventional search engines, which look for content on the web, **desktop search engines** look for content on a particular computer (see Figure 11.4). These tools are designed to identify and organize the many information and message fragments that most people have stored in various forms on

REAL-TIME UPDATES
Learn More

A practical guide to selecting the best online search tools

Different research projects require different search tools, and this article provides great advice for selecting search tools based on the requirements of each project. Go to **http://real-timeupdates.com/bct** and click on "Learn More." If you are using mybcommlab, you can access Real-Time Updates within each chapter or under Student Study Tools.

4 **LEARNING OBJECTIVE**

Provide five guidelines for conducting an effective online search

Take advantage of the latest research technologies, including desktop and enterprise search engines, research and content managers, social bookmarking sites, and newsfeeds.

FIGURE 11.4 Desktop Search Engines

Desktop search engines are part of the new generation of software tools that can help businesspeople find vital information on personal computers. In this example using Copernic Desktop Search (www.copernic.com), a user searching for *agreements* found 127 documents in a variety of formats.

their computers—e-mail messages, IM, PowerPoint presentations, audio and video clips, word-processing files, and so on. **Enterprise search engines** perform a similar task but across an entire network of computers.

- **Research and content managers.** A variety of tools known as *research managers* or *content managers* can be particularly helpful when your research involves numerous websites. These tools offer such features as letting you save and organize stored website links, providing permanent access to webpages you've visited even if the pages later change or disappear, and even automatically generating parts of reports such as tables of contents and bibliographies. Some of these tools, such as Zotero (www.zotero.org), are free to use.[9]

- **Social bookmarking sites.** The social bookmarking sites introduced in Chapter 7 can also assist with research. By highlighting websites, news articles, and other online items that other people find useful, bookmarking sites such as Digg (www.digg.com) and Delicious (http://delicious.com) can alert you to helpful resources and offer some indication of what online audiences are interested in at a particular moment in time. When using bookmarking or user-generated content sites for research, however, be aware of two potential problems. First, the lack of uniformity in tagging can lead you to miss sites of interest (although this problem may be resolved as sites evolve). Second, you can't assume that rankings truly represent any particular segment of the population. They aren't based on a statistically valid sample of the population, and they are vulnerable to manipulation by individuals and organizations trying to inflate popularity scores.[10]

To track a subject over time, sign up for newsfeeds from periodicals, blogs, and other sources that cover the subject.

- **Newsfeeds.** Newsfeeds, discussed in Chapter 7, are an ideal way to stay up to date on subjects that are likely to change or develop over time. For example, to stay on top of competitive moves in your industry, you can subscribe to newsfeeds from stock analysts who cover the industry, product user blogs, and blogs published by your competitors.

For more on the latest developments in online research tools, visit http://real-timeupdates .com/bct and click on Chapter 11.

Documenting Your Sources

Documenting the secondary sources you use in your writing serves three important functions: It properly and ethically credits the person who created the original material; it shows your audience that you have sufficient support for your message; and, as mentioned earlier, it helps your readers explore your topic in more detail, if desired. Your results might be used by people long after you conducted the research, and these people won't always have the opportunity to query you in person for more information.

Be sure to take advantage of source documentation tools whenever you can to help ensure that you accurately track all your sources in your word-processing program rather than attempt to track source notes by hand. Word-processing programs such as Microsoft Word automatically track and number endnotes for you, and you can use the "table of authorities" feature to create a bibliography of all the sources you've used. Also, tools such as Microsoft OneNote and Google Notebook can help you collect and organize your notes.[11] And research management tools such as Zotero make it easier to track sources found online.

You may document your sources through footnotes, endnotes, or some similar system (see Appendix B, "Documentation of Report Sources"). Whatever method you choose, documentation is necessary for books, articles, tables, charts, diagrams, song lyrics, scripted dialogue, letters, speeches, and anything else you take from someone else, including ideas and information that you've re-expressed through paraphrasing or summarizing.

However, you do not have to cite a source for general knowledge or for specialized knowledge that's generally known among your readers. For example, almost everyone knows that Nike is a large sporting goods company and that computers are pervasive in business today. You can say so on your own authority, even if you've read an article in which the author says the same thing.

Chapter 1 notes that copyright law covers the expression of creative ideas, and copyrights can cover a wide range of materials, including reports and other documents, web content, movies, musical compositions, lectures, computer programs, and even choreographed dance routines. Copyright protection is initiated the moment the expression is put into fixed form. Copyright law does not protect such elements as titles, names, short phrases, slogans, familiar symbols, or lists of ingredients or contents. It also doesn't protect ideas, procedures, methods, systems, processes, concepts, principles, discoveries, or devices, although it does cover their description, explanation, or illustration.[12] (Note that many of the entities that aren't covered under copyright law are covered under other legal protections, such as patents for devices and processes and trademarks for slogans.)

Merely crediting the source is not always enough. According to the *fair use doctrine*, you can use other people's work only as long as you don't unfairly prevent them from benefiting as a result. For example, if you reproduce someone else's copyrighted questionnaire in a report you're writing, even if you identify the source thoroughly, you may be preventing the author from selling a copy of that questionnaire to your readers.

In general, avoid relying to a great extent on someone else's work. However, when you can't avoid it, contact the copyright holder (usually the author or publisher) for permission to reprint. You'll often be asked to pay a fee.

For more information on copyrights, visit www.copyright.gov or www.creative commons.org.

Conducting Primary Research

If secondary research can't provide the information and insights you need, your next choice is to gather the information yourself with primary research. The two most common primary research methods are surveys and interviews, the focus of this section. Other primary techniques include *observations* and *experiments*, such as Tesco's test-marketing study with Polish foods (see page 348).

Proper documentation of the sources you use is an ethical responsibility—and an important resource for your readers.

Copyright protections may prevent you from using some materials without obtaining permission from the copyright holder.

5 LEARNING OBJECTIVE

Outline the steps required to create and administer surveys and interviews

Surveys and interviews are the most common primary research techniques.

Conducting Surveys

Surveys can provide invaluable insights on a wide variety of business topics, but they are useful only when they're reliable and valid. A survey is *reliable* if it produces identical results when repeated. A survey is *valid* if it measures what it's intended to measure. To generate results that are both reliable and valid, you need to choose research participants carefully and develop an effective set of questions. (A good survey handbook can guide you through the process of selecting participants. For surveys on high-risk topics, you're usually better off hiring a research specialist who knows how to avoid errors during planning, execution, and analysis.)

For a survey to produce valid results, it must be based on a representative sample of the population of interest.

When selecting the people who'll participate in your survey, the most critical task is getting a representative sample of the population in question. For instance, if you want to know how U.K. consumers feel about a particular product or company, don't just randomly survey people in the local mall and assume that their answers represent the opinions of everyone in the country. Different types of consumers shop at different times of the day and on different days of the week, some consumers don't shop at malls regularly, and many who do won't stop to talk with researchers.

To develop an effective survey questionnaire, start with the information gaps you identified earlier and then break these points into specific questions, choosing an appropriate type of question for each point. (Figure 11.5 shows various types of survey questions.) The following guidelines will help you produce results that are both valid and reliable:[13]

Provide clear instructions in questionnaires to prevent mistaken answers.

- **Provide clear instructions.** Respondents need to know exactly how to fill out your questionnaire.
- **Keep the questionnaire short and easy to answer.** Ask only questions that are relevant to your research. The longer the survey, the greater the chance that people will get frustrated and quit before finishing.
- **Whenever possible, formulate questions to provide answers that are easy to analyze.** Numbers and facts are easier to summarize than opinions, for instance. Of course, if you really want opinions, ask questions to elicit them.
- **Avoid leading questions.** Questions that lead to a particular answer will bias your survey. If you ask, "Do you prefer that we stay open in the evenings for customer convenience?" you'll no doubt get a "yes." Instead, ask, "What time of day do you normally do your shopping?"
- **Avoid ambiguous questions.** If you ask "Do you shop online often?" some people might interpret *often* to mean "every day," whereas others might think it means "once a week" or "once a month."
- **Ask only one question at a time.** A compound question such as "Do you read books and magazines?" doesn't allow for the respondent who reads one but not the other.
- **Make the survey adaptive.** With an online survey, you can program the software to branch automatically based on audience inputs. Not only does this sort of real-time adaptation deliver better answers, but it reduces frustration for survey respondents as well.[14]

Be sure to test your survey before using it.

Before you conduct your survey, test it on a sample group first to identify questions that might be confusing or that might generate answers you don't expect (see "Communication Miscues: The Art of the Question").

Online surveys are quick and inexpensive, but they require the same care in planning and analysis as offline surveys.

The Internet is now a preferred survey mechanism for many researchers, and dozens of companies offer online survey services (see Figure 11.6).[15] Compared to traditional mail and in-person techniques, online surveys are usually faster to create, easier to administer, faster to analyze, and less expensive overall. The interactive capabilities of the web can enhance all kinds of surveys, from simple opinion polls to complex purchase simulations. Many groupware systems now have polling features that make it easy to ask your fellow team members to vote on specific issues. However, don't let the speed and convenience of online surveys lower the requirements for careful planning; online surveys require the same care as any other type of survey, including being on guard against sampling bias.[16]

FIGURE 11.5   Types of Survey Questions
For each question you have in your survey, choose the type of question that will elicit
the most useful answers.

QUESTION TYPE   EXAMPLE

Open-ended   How would you describe the flavor of this ice cream?

Either-or   Do you think this ice cream is too rich?
_____ Yes
_____ No

Multiple choice   Which description best fits the taste of this ice cream?
(Choose only one.)
a. Delicious
b. Too fruity
c. Too sweet
d. Too intense
e. Bland
f. Stale

Scale   Please mark an X on the scale to indicate how you perceive the texture
of this ice cream.

Too light   Light   Creamy   Too creamy

Checklist   Which of the following ice cream brands do you recognize?
(Check all that apply.)
_____ Ben & Jerry's
_____ Breyers
_____ Carvel
_____ Dreyer's
_____ Häagen-Dazs

Ranking   Rank these flavors in order of your preference, from 1 (most preferred)
to 5 (least preferred):
_____ Vanilla
_____ Cherry
_____ Strawberry
_____ Chocolate
_____ Coconut

Short-answer   In the past 2 weeks, how many times did you buy ice cream
in a grocery store? _____

In the past 2 weeks, how many times did you buy ice cream
in an ice cream shop? _____

Conducting Interviews

Getting in-depth information straight from an expert can be a great method for collecting primary information. Interviews can take a variety of formats, from e-mail exchanges to group discussions. For example, Tesco invites thousands of customers to visit its stores every year for meetings known as Customer Question Time, when it asks customers how the company can serve them better.[17]

Be aware that the answers you receive in an interview are influenced by the types of questions you ask, by the way you ask them, and by each subject's cultural and language background. Potentially significant factors include the person's race, gender, age, educational level, and social status.[18]

Interviews are easy to conduct but require careful planning to produce useful results.

Communication Miscues

The Art of the Question

Poorly worded questions can produce unintended and unforeseen results. For example, assume that you receive regular surveys from the human resources department in your company, dealing with such issues as productivity, employee satisfaction, and employee benefits. This month's survey contains the following questions:

1. How would you rate the food in the company cafeteria? (Choose one.)

   Fantastic
   Nutritious
   Delicious
   Filling
   A good value for the money

2. What is your opinion of the improved insurance sign-up process we instituted last month?

3. If the dental benefits plan were modified relative to the current plan, wherein employees are expected to pay a $20 copayment at the time of each visit, with benefits subject to the normal companywide 80 percent co-insurance standard, provided the co-insurance ratio did not drop, would you continue to participate in the plan if copayment were increased to $50 but counterbalanced by a reduction in your monthly payroll deduction amount? _____ yes _____ no

4. Division supervisors continue to report problems with employees reporting for work late. Do the employees in your department tend to report for work

   Always on time
   Mostly on time
   Usually on time
   Occasionally late
   Frequently late

5. How many times did you personally report for work late last year?

6. Do you ever feel poorly trained or insufficiently motivated in your job? _____ yes _____ no

CAREER APPLICATIONS

1. Which of these questions might result in unusable information? Why?

2. How would you help the human resources manager rewrite the questions to improve the quality of information they generate?

FIGURE 11.6 Online Survey Tools
Online survey systems such as this one, offered by Object Planet, make it easy to create, administer, and analyze surveys.

<table>
<tr><td>✓ CHECKLIST:</td><td>Conducting Effective Information Interviews</td></tr>
</table>

- Learn about the person you will be interviewing.
- Formulate your main idea to ensure effective focus.
- Choose the length, style, and organization of the interview.
- Select question types to elicit the specific information you want.
- Design each question carefully to collect useful answers.
- Limit the number of questions you ask.
- Consider recording the interview if the subject permits.
- Review your notes as soon as the interview ends.

Ask **open-ended questions** (such as "Why do you believe that South America represents a better opportunity than Europe for this product line?") to solicit opinions, insights, and information. Ask **closed questions** to elicit a specific answer, such as yes or no. However, don't use too many closed questions in an interview, or the experience will feel more like a simple survey and won't take full advantage of the interactive interview setting.

Choose question types that will generate the specific types of information you need.

Think carefully about the sequence of your questions and the subject's potential answers so you can arrange questions in an order that helps uncover layers of information. Also consider providing the other person with a list of questions at least a day or two before the interview, especially if you'd like to quote your subject in writing or if your questions might require your subject to conduct research or think extensively about the answers. If you want to record the interview, ask the person ahead of time and respect his or her wishes.

As soon as possible after the interview, take a few moments to write down your thoughts, go over your notes, and organize your material. Look for important themes, helpful facts or statistics, and direct quotes. If you made a tape recording, *transcribe* it (take down word for word what the person said) or take notes from the tape just as you would while listening to someone in person.

Face-to-face interviews give you the opportunity to gauge reactions to your questions and observe the nonverbal signals that accompany the answers, but interviews don't necessarily have to take place in person. E-mail interviews are becoming more common, partly because they give subjects a chance to think through their responses thoroughly rather than rush to fit the time constraints of a face-to-face interview.[19] Also, e-mail interviews might be the only way you will be able to access some experts.

Face-to-face interviews give you the opportunity to gauge nonverbal responses.

In addition to individual interviews, business researchers can also use a form of group interview known as the **focus group**. In this format, a moderator guides a group through a series of discussion questions while the rest of the research team members observe through a one-way mirror. The key advantage of focus groups is the opportunity to learn from group dynamics as the various participants bounce ideas and questions off each other. Allowing a group to discuss topics and problems in this manner can uncover much richer information than can a series of individual interviews.[20]

As a reminder of the tasks involved in interviews, see "Checklist: Conducting Effective Information Interviews."

PROCESSING DATA AND INFORMATION

After you've collected all the necessary secondary and primary information, the next step is to transform it into the specific content you need. For simple projects, you may be able to insert your material directly into your report, presentation, or other application. However, when you have gathered a significant amount of information or raw data, you need to process the material before you can use it. This step can involve quoting, paraphrasing, or summarizing textual material; analyzing numeric data; drawing conclusions; and making recommendations.

6 LEARNING OBJECTIVE

Describe the major tasks involved in processing and applying your research results

Quoting, Paraphrasing, and Summarizing

You can use information from secondary sources in three ways. *Quoting* a source means you reproduce it exactly as you found it, and you either set it off with quotation marks (for shorter passages) or extract it in an indented paragraph (for longer passages). Use direct

After you collect your research, the next step is to convert it into usable information.

Quoting a source means reproducing the content exactly and indicating who created the information originally.

quotations when the original language will enhance your argument or when rewording the passage would lessen its impact. If the person you're quoting might not be well known to the audience, provide some context to help readers grasp the significance of the information and the credibility of the source. For example, you might introduce a quotation by saying, "After managing seven new product launches over the past decade, Annette Johnson had this to say about the use of independent distributors: . . ." Finally, take care not to include too many quotations, as doing so can create a choppy patchwork of varying styles and give the impression that all you've done is piece together the ideas of other people.

Paraphrasing is expressing someone else's ideas in your own words.

You can often maximize the impact of secondary material in your own writing by *paraphrasing* it—restating it in your own words and with your own sentence structures.[21] Paraphrasing helps you maintain consistent tone, present information using vocabulary more familiar to your audience, and avoid the choppy feel of too many quotations. Of course, you still need to credit the originator of the information but not with quotation marks or indented paragraphs.

To paraphrase effectively, follow these tips:[22]

- Reread the original passage until you fully understand its meaning.
- Record your paraphrase on a note card or in an electronic format.
- Use business language and jargon that your audience is familiar with.
- Check your version with the original source to verify that you have not altered the meaning.
- Use quotation marks to identify any unique terms or phrases you have borrowed exactly from the source.
- Record the source (including the page number) so that you can give proper credit if you use this material in your report.

Summarizing is similar to paraphrasing but distills the content into fewer words.

Summarizing is similar to paraphrasing but presents the gist of the material in fewer words than the original. An effective summary identifies the main ideas and major support points from your source material but leaves out minor details, examples, and other information that is less critical to your audience. Like quotations and paraphrases, summaries also require complete documentation of sources.

Of course, all three approaches require careful attention to ethics. When quoting directly, take care not to distort the original intent of the material by quoting selectively or out of context. If an interview subject said, "This market could grow dramatically next year if we invest heavily in new products," including just the phrase "this market could grow dramatically next year" in a report would be unethical.

When paraphrasing and summarizing, take care not to distort the original intent as you express the ideas in your own words and sentences. Remember that the goal is to help your audience relate to material that supports your message. Double-check your writing to make sure you didn't subconsciously skew the other writer's message to fit your own needs (see "Ethics Detective: Solving the Case of the Imaginary Good News").

Analyzing Your Data

Research often produces numeric data—everything from sales figures to population statistics to survey answers. By themselves, these numbers might not provide the insights you or your audience require. Are sales going up or going down? Are the age groups that represent your target markets growing or shrinking? What percentage of employees surveyed are so dissatisfied that they're ready to look for new jobs? These are the insights managers need in order to make good business decisions.

Gaining Insights

Mean, median, and mode provide insight into sets of data.

Even without advanced statistical techniques, you can use simple arithmetic to extract powerful insights from sets of research data. Three common and useful measures are shown in Table 11.3. The **mean** (which is what most people refer to when they use the term *average*) is the sum of all the items in the group divided by the number of items in that group. The **median** is the "middle of the road," or the midpoint of a series (with an equal number of

Ethics Detective

Solving the Case of the Imaginary Good News

To deal with a growing problem of employee turnover, your company recently hired a research firm to survey employees to find out why more employees are leaving than in past years. You and a colleague were assigned to work with the consultants and present their findings to upper management. Neither one of you welcomed the assignment because you suspect you'll have to present information that is critical of the management team.

As you feared, the researchers deliver a mixture of news that is mostly negative:

- Seventy-eight percent of employees believe management cares more about profits than people.
- Fifty-five percent aren't sure what's expected of them anymore.
- Forty percent believe wages at the company have not kept up with the industry average.
- Thirty-eight percent think management has done a good job of responding to competitive advances.
- Fifty-two percent expect to finish their careers at the company.

- Eighty percent believe the economy is too slow to support a productive job search.

While you're poring over the report, trying to figure out how you'll present the information tomorrow, an instant message from the CEO pops up on your partner's computer, asking for a quick summary of the results. She types the following and then asks you to review it before she sends it:

> As you'd expect in a no-holds-barred investigation like this, the researchers did uncover some areas for improvements. The good news: Only 20 percent of the workforce is even considering other options, and we could reasonably expect that only a fraction of that group will leave anytime soon.

ANALYSIS

You read your partner's summary twice, but something doesn't feel quite right. Does it present an accurate summary of the research? Why or why not? What's likely to happen when you present the complete research results to the CEO after first sending this IM?

---

items above and below). The **mode** is the number that occurs more often than any other in a sample. It's the best answer to a question such as "What is the usual amount?" Each of these three measures can give you different insights into a set of data.

Next, look at the data to spot **trends**—any repeatable patterns taking place over time, including growth, decline, and cyclical trends that vary between growth and decline. By examining data over a period of time, you can detect patterns and relationships that help you answer important questions.

Trends identify patterns that tend to repeat over time.

Statistical measures and trends identify *what* is happening. To help you understand *why* those things are happening, look at **causation** (the cause-and-effect linkage between two factors, where one of them causes the other to happen) and **correlation** (the simultaneous change in two variables that you're measuring, such as customer satisfaction dropping when product reliability drops). Bear in mind that causation can be easy to assume but difficult to prove. The

Causation shows cause-and-effect relationships; correlation indicates simultaneous changes in two variables that may not necessarily be causally related.

TABLE 11.3 Three Types of Data Measures: Mean, Median, and Mode

Wilson	$3,000	
Green	5,000	
Carrick	6,000	
Cho	7,000	——— Mean
Keeble	7,500	——— Median
Lopes	8,500	
O'Toole	8,500	Mode
Mannix	8,500	
Caruso	9,000	
Total	$63,000	

drop in customer satisfaction might have been caused by a new accounting system that fouled up customer invoices. To prove causation, you need to be able to isolate the suspected cause as the only potential source of the change in the measured effect. However, eliminating all but one possible cause isn't always feasible, so you often have to apply careful judgment to correlations. Researchers frequently explore the relationships between subsets of data using a technique called **cross-tabulation**. For instance, if you're trying to figure out why total sales rose or fell, you might look separately at sales data by age, gender, location, and product type.

Guarding Against Mistakes and Misinterpretations

Watch out for errors that might have crept in during collection and processing of data.

Numbers are easy to manipulate with spreadsheets and other computer tools, so be sure to guard against computational errors and misinterpretation of results. Double-check all calculations and document the operation of any spreadsheets you plan to share with colleagues. Common spreadsheet mistakes to watch for include errors in math formulas, references to unintended cells in the spreadsheet (resulting in the inclusion of data you don't want or the exclusion of data you do want), and failures to verify the specific operation of the spreadsheet's built-in math functions.

In addition to watching for computer errors, step back and look at your entire set of data before proceeding with any analysis. Do the numbers make sense, based on what you know about the subject? Are any data points suspicious? If the production numbers you've been measuring have never varied more than 10 percent month to month and then suddenly jumped 50 percent last month, is that new number real or an erroneous measurement?

Even when your data points are accurate and your analysis is technically correct, it's still possible to misinterpret or misrepresent the results. Many analysis errors require statistical expertise to identify and fix, but even without advanced skills, you can take these precautions:

- **Avoid faulty comparisons.** Make sure you compare "apples to apples" and not "apples to oranges," as the saying goes.
- **Don't push research results beyond their limits.** The temptation to extract insights and assurances that aren't really there can be quite strong, particularly in situations of great uncertainty. For instance, if you're about to recommend that your company invest millions of dollars in developing a new product, based on your consumer research, you're likely to "see" every possible justification in the data. If possible, have a trusted colleague review your data to see if he or she extracts the same conclusions.
- **Steer clear of misleading presentations.** As you'll see in Chapter 12, even valid data can be presented in invalid ways, and it's your responsibility to make sure the visual presentation of your data is accurate.

APPLYING YOUR FINDINGS

After all your planning, research, and processing, you're finally ready to apply your findings. This step can involve summarizing your results, drawing conclusions based on your results, and making recommendations.

Summarizing Your Research

A summary is an unbiased presentation of information regarding a particular topic, without attempts to draw conclusions or make recommendations.

If your boss has asked you to summarize the competitive strengths and weaknesses of another company or the recent trends in a particular market, it's crucial that you provide an unbiased summary that is free of your own opinions, conclusions, or recommendations. Summarizing is not always a simple task, and your boss will be judging your ability to separate significant issues from less-significant details. Identify the main idea and the key support points; separate them from details, examples, and other supporting evidence (see Table 11.4). Focus your efforts on your audience, highlighting the information that is most important to the person who assigned the project or to those who will be reading the report.

However, focusing on the audience doesn't mean you're supposed to convey only the information your audience wants to hear. A good summary might contain nothing but bad news, if that's what your research uncovered. Even if the summary isn't pleasant, effective managers always appreciate and respect honest, complete, and perceptive information from their employees.

TABLE 11.4 Summarizing Effectively

ORIGINAL MATERIAL (116 WORDS)	45-WORD SUMMARY	22-WORD SUMMARY
Our facilities costs spiraled out of control last year. The 23 percent jump was far ahead of every other cost category in the company and many times higher than the 4 percent average rise for commercial real estate in the Portland metropolitan area. The rise can be attributed to many factors, but **the major factors include repairs** (mostly electrical and structural problems at the downtown office), **energy** (most of our offices are heated by electricity, the price of which has been increasing much faster than for oil or gas), **and last but not least, the loss of two sublease tenants** whose rent payments made a substantial dent in our cost profile for the past five years.	**Our facilities costs jumped 23 percent last year,** far ahead of every other cost category in the company and many times higher than the 4 percent local average. The major factors contributing to the increase are repairs, energy, and the loss of two sublease tenants.	**Our facilities costs jumped 23 percent last year,** primarily because of rising repair and energy costs and the loss of sublease income.
Main idea		
Major support points		
Details		

Drawing Conclusions

A **conclusion** is a logical interpretation of the facts and other information in a report. Reaching good conclusions based on the evidence at hand is one of the most important skills you can develop in your business career. For a conclusion to be sound, it must meet two criteria. First, it must be based strictly on the information included in your report. You can't ignore anything—even if it doesn't support your conclusion. Moreover, you shouldn't introduce any new information in your conclusion. (If something is that important, it belongs in the body of your report.) Second, the conclusion must be logical, meaning it must follow accepted patterns of inductive or deductive reasoning. Conclusions that are based on unproven premises, appeal to emotion, make hasty generalizations, or contain any other logical fallacies are not valid.

A conclusion is a logical interpretation of research results.

Remember that your personal values or the organization's values may also influence your conclusions; just be sure that you're aware of how these biases affect your judgment. If a bias affects your conclusion, you should explain it to your audience. Also, don't expect all team members to examine the evidence and arrive at the same conclusion. One of the reasons for bringing additional people into a decision is to gain their unique perspectives and experiences.

Even though conclusions need to be logical, they may not automatically or obviously flow from the evidence. Many business decisions require assumptions, judgment calls, and creative thinking—in fact, the ability to see patterns and possibilities that others can't see is one of the hallmarks of innovative business leaders.

Making Recommendations

Whereas a conclusion interprets information, a **recommendation** suggests what to do about the information. The following example illustrates the difference between a conclusion and a recommendation:

A recommendation is a suggested course of action.

CONCLUSION	RECOMMENDATION
On the basis of its track record and current price, I conclude that this company is an attractive buy.	I recommend that we write a letter to the board of directors, offering to buy the company at a 10 percent premium over the current market value of its stock.

Knowledge management systems help organizations share research results and other valuable information and insights.

To be credible, recommendations must be based on logical analysis and sound conclusions. They must also be practical and acceptable to your readers, the people who have to make your recommendations work. Finally, when making a recommendation, be certain that you have adequately described the steps that come next. Don't leave your readers wondering what they need to do in order to act on your recommendation.

Document Makeover

Improve This List of Interview Questions

To practice correcting drafts of actual documents, visit the "Document Makeovers" section in either mybcommlab or the Companion Website for this text.

If mybcommlab is being used in your class, see your User Guide for specific instructions on how to access the content for this chapter. If you are accessing this feature through the Companion Website, click on "Document Makeovers" and then click Chapter 11. You will find a list of interview questions that contain problems and errors related to what you've learned in this chapter about finding, evaluating, and processing information. Use the Final Draft decision tool to create an improved version of these questions. Check questions for sequencing; appropriateness; perceptiveness; and respect for ethical, confidential, political, or sensitive issues.

MANAGING INFORMATION

Conducting your research well does more than provide strong support for your own writing projects. Your individual research projects are also an important contribution to your organization's collective knowledge base. To organize information and make it readily available to everyone in the company, many firms use some form of **knowledge management (KM)**, a set of technologies, policies, and procedures that let colleagues capture and share information throughout an organization. In recent years, social media tools have been enhancing the flexibility and capability of KM systems, making it easier for more people to contribute to and benefit from shared knowledge.[23]

Communication Challenges at Tesco

As a market development manager working for Richard Brasher, Tesco's top marketing executive in the United Kingdom, you are responsible for a variety of research, planning, and customer communication projects. Using what you've learned in this chapter about effective research methods, craft solutions to these two challenges.

Individual Challenge: Tesco has created several online stores (see **www.tesco.com**) and would like to expand the number of consumers who order goods and services online. What information would you need in order to devise a plan to attract more online shoppers?

Team Challenge: Shoppers often make numerous purchase decisions in the store rather than arrive with a preset list of specific brands to purchase. Brasher would like more information on why consumers choose one brand over another while standing in front of an array of products on the shelf. Is it the brand name? Something about the packaging? The price? Other factors? With your team, brainstorm ways to collect this information from at least 500 shoppers. Be sure to consider the practical considerations of data collection as well as privacy concerns. Summarize your plan in a short report for your instructor.

SUMMARY OF LEARNING OBJECTIVES

1 **Describe an effective process for conducting business research.** Begin the research process with careful planning to make sure you focus on the most important questions and identify the best place to find answers. Then locate the data and information, using primary and secondary research as needed. Process the results of your research, analyzing both textual and numeric information to extract averages, trends, and other insights. Apply your findings by summarizing information for someone else's benefit, drawing conclusions based on what you've learned, or developing recommendations.

Finally, manage information effectively so that you and others can retrieve it later and reuse it in other projects.

2 **Define *primary research* and *secondary research*, and explain when you use each method.** Primary research is research that is being conducted for the first time, whereas secondary research involves information that was originally gathered for another research project or another effort. Secondary research is generally used first, both to save time in case someone else has already gathered the

information needed and to offer additional insights into your research questions.

3 **Name ten criteria for evaluating the credibility of an information source.**   Information should come from a credible source that has a reputation for being honest and reliable; the source should also be unbiased. The purpose of the material should be known, and the author should be credible. The information should include references to sources (if obtained elsewhere), and it should be independently verifiable. The material should be current, complete, and supported with evidence. Finally, the information should seem logical.

4 **Provide five guidelines for conducting an effective online search.**   First and foremost, you need to read and understand the instructions for using each online research tool because they vary widely and may not search for or display results in the manner you expect. Second, pay attention to the details because even minor aspects of searching can influence results dramatically. Third, review search and display options carefully to optimize results. Fourth, try variations on your search terms if you can't find what you're looking for. Fifth, try narrower or broader searches to adjust the scope of what you're looking for.

5 **Outline the steps required to create and administer surveys and interviews.**   Conducting a survey involves selecting a representative set of respondents from the population you are studying, developing a questionnaire using carefully written and sequenced questions, and administering the actual survey to collect information. Conducting an interview starts with learning about the person(s) you plan to interview and then formulating your main idea to make sure your interview will stay focused. Choose the length, style, and organization of the interview and then select question types to elicit the sort of information you want, with each question designed to collect useful answers. Limit your questions to the most important queries. Record the interview, if the person allows, and review your notes as soon as the interview ends.

6 **Describe the major tasks involved in processing and applying your research results.**   In most cases, you need to process your research results in some fashion before applying them in reports and presentations. The three basic ways to process verbal information are *quoting* (using someone else's word directly, with appropriate attribution), *paraphrasing* (restating someone else's words in your own language), and *summarizing* (creating a shorter version of an original piece of writing). Processing numeric data can involve a variety of statistical analysis techniques. Three basic computations are the *mean* (what people mean when they say "average"), the *median* (the midpoint in a series, indicating an equal number of lesser and greater values), and the *mode* (the most frequently occurring value in a series). Processing results can also involve looking for trends and distinguishing causal relationships from correlations and mere coincidences. Research results can be applied in several ways, depending on the purpose of the report or presentation. A *summary* is a shortened version of one or more documents, research results, or other information; it filters out details and presents only the most important ideas. A *conclusion* is your analysis of what the findings mean (an interpretation of the facts). A *recommendation* is your opinion (based on reason and logic) about the course of action that should be taken.

PEARSON mybcommlab™

Log on to www.mybcommlab.com to access the following study and assessment aids associated with this chapter:

- Video applications
- Real-Time Updates
- Peer review activity
- Quick Learning Guides

- Pre/post test
- Personalized study plan
- Model documents
- Sample presentations

If you are not using mybcommlab, you can access the Real-Time Updates and Quick Learning Guides through http://real-timeupdates.com/bct. The Quick Learning Guide (located under "Learn More" on the website) hits all the high points of this chapter in just two pages. This guide, especially prepared by the authors, will help you study for exams or review important concepts whenever you need a quick refresher.

Test Your Knowledge

1. What are the five steps in the research process?
2. How does primary information differ from secondary information?
3. How can newsfeeds help you with research?
4. How does a search engine differ from a directory?

5. What is the purpose of information gap analysis?
6. What is the *hidden Internet*, or *deep web*?
7. What is paraphrasing, and what is its purpose?
8. What is the difference between the mean, median, and mode?
9. What are the characteristics of a sound conclusion?
10. How does a conclusion differ from a recommendation?

Apply Your Knowledge

1. Why is it important to plan your research effort?

2. Why must you be careful when citing information from online sources?

3. One of your employees submitted a report, comparing the market opportunities for two product ideas your company might develop. The report concludes that because the first idea yielded 340,000 hits in a Google search whereas the second idea yielded only 128,000 Google hits, the first idea clearly has more sales potential. Is this a valid conclusion? Why or why not?

4. While analyzing last year's sales data, you notice that sales were 10 to 15 percent higher than average during August, September, and November. The marketing department invested heavily in a search engine advertising campaign from August through December. Can you conclude that the advertising campaign caused the increase in sales? Why or why not?

5. **Ethical Choices** Companies occasionally make mistakes that expose confidential information, such as when employees lose laptop computers containing sensitive data files or webmasters forget to protect confidential webpages from search engine indexes. If you conducted a Google search that turned up competitive information on webpages that were clearly intended to be private, what would you do? Explain your answer.

Practice Your Knowledge

Message for Analysis

The following set of interview questions was prepared for a manager of Whirlpool Corporation. The goal of the interview was to learn some basic information about Whirlpool's meeting practices. Read the questions and then (1) critique them, as a whole, indicating what you like or dislike about this series of questions, and (2) select five questions and revise them to make them more effective.

1. What is your position in the company?

2. To whom do you report?

3. Do you attend or run many meetings?

4. Do your meetings start on time? Run late?

5. Do you distribute or receive a meeting agenda several days in advance of the meeting?

6. Do you like your job?

7. Do you travel a lot for your job?

8. Has your company cut back on travel expenditures? If so, how and why?

9. Does your company use videoconferencing or online meetings as an alternative to travel?

10. Does your company own its own videoconferencing equipment?

11. Are virtual meetings more or less effective than face-to-face meetings?

12. How long have you worked for Whirlpool?

13. Is Sears your largest retail customer?

14. How often does your management team meet with the managers of Sears?

15. Does your company produce only household appliances?

16. How do you keep your meetings on track?

17. Does someone prepare written minutes of meetings? Are the minutes distributed to meeting members?

Exercises

Active links for all websites in this chapter can be found online. If mybcommlab is being used in your class, see your User Guide for instructions on accessing the content for this chapter. Otherwise, visit www.pearsonglobaleditions.com/bovee, locate *Business Communication Today*, Tenth Edition, click the Companion Website link, select Chapter 11, and then click on "Featured Websites." Please note that links to sites that become inactive after publication of the book will be removed from the Featured Websites section.

11.1 **Understanding Your Topic: Subquestions** You and your business partners are considering buying several franchises in the fast-food business. You are all experienced managers or entrepreneurs, but none of you has experience in franchising. Visit www.amazon.com and search for books on this subject. Explore some of the books that you find by reading reviews and using the "search inside" feature.

    a. Use the information you find to develop a list of subquestions to help you narrow your focus.

    b. Write down the names of three books you might purchase to further aid your research.

    c. Summarize how a search like this can assist you with your research efforts and identify any risks of using this technique.

11.2 **Finding Secondary Information** Using online or printed sources, find the following information. Be sure to properly cite your sources, using the formats discussed in Appendix B.

    a. Contact information for the American Management Association

    b. Median weekly earnings of men and women by occupation

    c. Current market share for Perrier water

    d. Performance ratios for office supply retailers

    e. Annual stock performance for Hewlett-Packard

    f. Number of franchise outlets in the United States

    g. Composition of the U.S. workforce by profession

11.3 **Finding Secondary Information** Businesspeople have to know where to look for secondary information when they conduct research. Identify five periodicals or online resources (websites, blogs, and so on) in each the following professions:

    a. Marketing and advertising

    b. Insurance

    c. Telecommunications

    d. Accounting

11.4 **Finding Information: Industry Information** Locate the NAICS codes for the following industries:

    a. Hotels and motels

    b. Breakfast cereals

c. Bottled water
d. Automatic vending machines

11.5 Finding Information: Company Information Select any public company and find the following information:
a. Names of the company's current officers
b. List of the company's products or services (summarized by product lines or divisions, if the company offers many products and services)
c. Current issues in the company's industry
d. Outlook for the company's industry as a whole

11.6 Finding Information: Secondary Information You'd like to know if it's a good idea to buy banner advertisements on other websites to drive more traffic to your company's website. You're worried about the expense and difficulty of running an experiment to test banner effectiveness, so you decide to look for some secondary data. Identify three secondary sources that might offer helpful data on this question.

11.7 Finding Information: Search Techniques Analyze any recent school or work assignment that required you to conduct research. How did you approach your investigation? Did you rely mostly on sources of primary information or mostly on sources of secondary information? Now that you have studied this chapter, can you identify two ways to improve the research techniques you used during that assignment? Briefly explain.

11.8 Finding Information: Primary Information Deciding how to collect primary data is an important part of the research process. Which one or more of the five methods of data collection (examining documents, making observations, surveying people, conducting experiments, and performing interviews) would you use if you were researching these questions?
a. Has the litter problem on campus been reduced since the cafeteria began offering fewer take-out choices this year than in past years?
b. Has the school attracted more transfer students since it waived the formal application process and allowed students at other colleges simply to send their transcripts and a one-page letter of application?
c. Have the number of traffic accidents at the school's main entrance been reduced since a traffic light was installed?
d. Has student satisfaction with the campus bookstore improved now that students can order their books over the Internet and pick them up at several campus locations?

11.9 Finding Information: Surveys You work for a movie studio that is producing a young director's first motion picture, the story of a group of unknown musicians finding work and making a reputation in a competitive industry. Unfortunately, some of your friends leave the first complete screening, saying that the 182-minute movie is simply too long. Others said they couldn't imagine any sequences to cut out. Your boss wants to test the movie on a regular audience and ask viewers to complete a questionnaire that will help the director decide whether edits are needed and, if so, where. Design a questionnaire that you can use to solicit valid answers for a report to the director about how to handle the audience members' reactions to the movie.

11.10 Finding Information: Interviews Plan an informational interview with a professional working in your chosen field of study. Plan the structure of the interview and create a set of interview questions. Conduct the interview. Using the information you gathered, write a memo to another student, describing the tasks, advantages, and disadvantages of jobs in this field of study. (Assume that your reader is a person who also plans to pursue a career in this field of study.)

11.11 Finding Information: Interviews You're conducting an information interview with a manager in another division of your company. Partway through the interview, the manager shows clear signs of impatience. How should you respond? What might you do differently to prevent this from happening in the future? Explain your answers.

11.12 Teamwork: Evaluating Sources Break into small groups and surf the Internet to find websites that provide business information such as company or industry news, trends, analysis, facts, or performance data. Using the criteria discussed under "Evaluating Sources" on page 351, evaluate the credibility of the information presented at these websites.

11.13 Processing Information: Reading and Taking Notes Select an article from a business journal such as *BusinessWeek*, *Fortune*, or *Forbes*. Read the article and highlight the article's key points. Summarize the article in fewer than 100 words, paraphrasing the key points.

11.14 Processing Information: Documenting Sources Select five business articles from sources such as journals, books, newspapers, or websites. Develop a resource list, using Appendix B as a guideline.

11.15 Analyzing Data: Calculating the Mean Your boss has asked you to analyze and report on your division's sales for the first nine months of this year. Using the following data from company invoices, calculate the mean for each quarter and all averages for the year to date. Then identify and discuss the quarterly sales trends.

January	$24,600	June	26,800
February	25,900	July	$29,900
March	23,000	August	30,500
April	$21,200	September	26,600
May	24,600		

Expand Your Knowledge

Exploring the Best of the Web

Visit the Library That Never Closes

www.ipl.org

Start your business research by visiting the Internet Public Library, at www.ipl.org. Visit the reference center and explore the many online references available. These cover topics such as business, economics, law, government, science, technology, computers, education, and more. You can even submit questions for the IPL staff. Click on the "Business" subject collection and then click on "Business Directories" to perform these tasks:

1. Click on "Ready Reference" (left side of the page) and follow some of the reference links. How might these links help you when performing business research?
2. Click on "Business" under "Subject Collections" and locate the "Consumer Issues & Services" subheading. Find three sites that help consumers make better-informed decisions.

3. Click on "Business," find "Business Directories," and use one of the sites listed to select five companies. Find contact information (address, phone, website, officers' names, and so on) for each company. What kinds of contact information did you find at the company websites?

Sharpening Your Career Skills Online

Bovée and Thill's Business Communication Web Search, at http://businesscommunicationblog.com/websearch, is a unique research tool designed specifically for business communication research. Use the Web Search function to find a website, video, PDF document, podcast, or PowerPoint presentation that offers advice on using online search tools in business research. Write a brief e-mail message to your instructor, describing the item that you found and summarizing the career skills information you learned from it.

Designing Visual Communication

Learning Objectives

After studying this chapter, you will be able to

1 Discuss six principles of graphic design that help ensure effective visuals

2 Explain how to avoid ethical lapses when using visuals

3 Explain how to choose which points in your message to illustrate

4 Describe the most common options for presenting data in a visual format

5 Describe the most common options for presenting information, concepts, and ideas

6 List three criteria to review in order to verify the quality of your visuals

Communication Close-up at Xplane

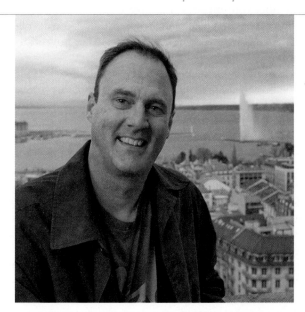

Founder Dave Gray helped establish XPLANE as one of the world's most innovative information design consultancies.

www.xplane.com

As its name suggests, Xplane is in the business of simplicity. According to CEO Aric Wood, "There's a reason the best business plans are sketched on napkins. Simple drawings are easier to understand than a 120-page document." Emphasizing *visual thinking*, Xplane distills complex business situations down to their simplest elements to make sure clients can understand the essential elements of a problem or opportunity, devise appropriate solutions, and communicate those results to diverse audiences.

Using eclectic teams of artists, writers, and business experts, Xplane applies visual thinking to some of the most difficult problems businesses face, including streamlining mergers and acquisitions, launching new ventures, educating investors, ensuring collaboration with external business partners, and training employees on complicated business processes. After a solution has been reached, Xplane's information designers create highly visual media pieces to help audiences grasp both the big picture and essentials details. (You can see an example of Xplane's work in Figure 4.5 on page 132.)

375

Xplane uses its techniques on its own problems and challenges, too. When the Portland, Oregon–based firm expanded into Europe through a new office in Spain, it used visual thinking to analyze the challenge of adopting Xplane's methods to European business practices.

The company's website emphasizes that "communication isn't a message sent. It's a message received." Clients are clearly receiving the message: Xplane's ever-expanding portfolio now includes projects for such A-list organizations as Apple, *BusinessWeek*, Lexus, Nokia, *Rolling Stone*, and the U.S. Marine Corps.[1]

UNDERSTANDING VISUAL COMMUNICATION

Project teams from Xplane (profiled in the chapter-opening Communication Close-up) look for new ways to connect and explore business ideas through creative visuals, often helping clients see important concepts and relationships that aren't obvious using text alone. Although the primary focus of this course is written messages, visual communication has become an important skill for today's business professionals and managers. This chapter helps you appreciate the power of images and the visual evolution of business communication. It then explains how to identify which points in your messages to illustrate, how to select the best visual for each of those points, and how to create effective visuals in any medium, from memos to reports to webpages to electronic presentations.

The Power of Images

Well-designed visual elements can enhance the communication power of textual messages and, in some instances, even replace textual messages. Visuals can often convey some message points (such as spatial relationships, correlations, procedures, and emotions) more effectively and more efficiently than words. Generally speaking, in a given amount of time, well-designed images can convey much more information than text.[2] In the numbers-oriented world of work, people rely heavily on trend lines, distribution curves, and visual presentations of numeric quantities. Visuals attract and hold people's attention, helping your audience understand and remember your message. Busy readers often jump to visuals to try to get the gist of a message, and attractive visuals can draw readers more deeply into your reports and presentations. Using pictures is also an effective way to communicate with the diverse audiences that are common in today's business environment.

Like words, visuals often carry connotative or symbolic meanings.

In addition to their direct information value, visuals often convey connotative meaning as well. As you read in Chapter 5, many words and phrases carry connotative meanings, which are all the mental images, emotions, and other impressions that the word or phrase evokes in audience members. A significant part of the power—and risk—of visual elements derives from their connotative meanings. Even something as simple as a watermark symbol embedded in letterhead stationery can boost reader confidence in the message that is printed on the paper.[3] Many colors, shapes, and other design elements have **visual symbolism**, and their symbolic, connotative meaning can evolve over time and mean different things in different cultures (see Figure 12.1). Being aware of these symbolic meanings and using them to your advantage are important aspects of being an effective business communicator.

Because they have so much power to communicate, visuals must be carefully planned, competently created, and seamlessly integrated with text. An awkward sentence or grammatical error deep within a report might not be noticed by the majority of readers, but a poorly chosen or clumsily implemented visual will be noticed by most—and can confuse or alienate audiences and damage your credibility. You don't need to be a professional designer to use visuals effectively, but you do need to be aware of some basic design principles if you want to avoid making high-visibility mistakes. This chapter gives you enough background to begin creating your own business visuals, and with some practice, you'll be able to craft effective visuals for nearly any communication project you might encounter.

The Visual Evolution in Business Communication

Thanks to advances in technology and changing audience expectations, business communication is becoming more visual.

Several technological and social factors are contributing to the increasing use—and importance—of visuals in business communication. The process of creating and working with visual elements used to be the domain of experts with complex and expensive tools. However, digital technology has changed this situation dramatically. Digital cameras that

FIGURE 12.1 Visual Symbolism

A red cross (with equal-length arms) on a white background is the well-known symbol of the Red Cross relief organization. It is also used to indicate the medical branches of many nations' military services. The red cross symbol is based on the flag of Switzerland (where the first Red Cross organization was formed), which over the course of hundreds of years developed from battle flags that originally used the Christian cross symbol. Although the Red Cross emblem is not based directly on the Christian symbol, the organization uses a red crescent in countries where Islam is the dominant religion and is known as the Red Crescent. To avoid any association with religious symbols, the International Federation of Red Cross and Red Crescent Societies (the global umbrella organization for all national Red Cross and Red Crescent organizations) recently adopted the Red Crystal as its new symbol.

can produce high-quality images and video are inexpensive and easy enough for anyone to use, and the software needed to create diagrams, process photos, edit video, and prepare other visual elements continues to get both easier and more powerful all the time. Plus, the global reach of the Internet makes it easy to send images almost instantly; and more Internet users have high-speed connections that can handle the larger computer files that visuals tend to require. Design and production tasks that used to take days can now be completed in hours or even minutes. As technologies such as wireless networking advance, business communicators will continue to reach wider audiences in less time, using equipment that costs less and requires fewer skills.[4]

While technology has been putting visual design and production into the hands of everyday business communicators in recent years, audience skills and expectations have been evolving as well. Two changes in particular could affect your communication efforts in the coming years. First, U.S. government research indicates that only half of the adult population in the United States now has the literacy skills considered necessary for success in today's workplace.[5] In other words, depending on the nature of your work, you could find yourself communicating with audiences whose skills could prevent them from successfully reading your documents. Visuals could play a vital role in communicating your messages to audiences with lower reading skills. Second, as technology has multiplied the ways in which communicators can create visuals and as people grow up and live in a more visual, media-saturated environment, audiences may well expect messages to be more visual.

REAL-TIME UPDATES
Learn More

See why visual design is a lot more than just "eye candy"

The visual design of a website is more than mere decoration—it is an essential, functional part of the website and a key factor in the communication process. Go to **http://real-timeupdates.com/bct** and click on "Learn More." If you are using mybcommlab, you can access Real-Time Updates within each chapter or under Student Study Tools.

As a result of these changes in both the tools and the communication environment, **visual literacy**, the ability to create effective images and to correctly interpret such images, has become a key business skill.[6] Whether you are using visuals to reach an audience with limited reading skills or to magnify the impact of your written messages, knowing how to help your audience see what you see will enable you to become a more effective communicator.

Visual literacy is the ability to both create and interpret visuals.

Visual Design Principles

Just as creating effective sentences and paragraphs requires working knowledge of the principles of good writing, creating effective visuals requires some knowledge of the principles of good design. Even though few businesspeople have the opportunity to formally study the "language" of line, mass, space, size, color, pattern, and texture, anyone can learn enough of the basic concepts to craft effective basic visuals.

1 LEARNING OBJECTIVE

Discuss six principles of graphic design that help ensure effective visuals

When you encounter visuals that you find appealing or unappealing, or effective or ineffective, stop and ask yourself what caused your response. Did a particular design grab you and practically force you to pay attention, or did you pass right by with hardly a notice? Did one chart reveal its information quickly and easily, while another made you spend time decoding its confusing message? Did one photo appeal to you at an emotional level and therefore draw you into a document, whereas another was offputting and caused you to lose interest in the document? By thinking about your own reactions to visual designs, you can become a more effective designer yourself.

Nearly every aspect of visual design is governed by conventions that set audience expectations.

As you consider your reactions to various designs and create designs of your own, you'll begin to see how six fundamental principles help distinguish ineffective and effective designs (see Figure 12.2):

Creating effective visuals requires basic knowledge of the principles of good design.

- **Consistency.** Audiences view a series of visuals as a whole and assume that design elements will be consistent from one page to the next. Think of consistency as *visual parallelism*, in the same way that textual parallelism helps audiences understand and compare a series of ideas.[7] You can achieve visual parallelism in a variety of ways, including through consistent use of color, shape, size, texture, position, scale, or typeface.

- **Contrast.** To emphasize differences, depict items in contrasting colors, shapes, or sizes. For example, to highlight the difference between two quantities in a pie chart, don't use two shades of blue; instead, use blue for one and yellow or some other dramatically contrasting color for the other.

- **Balance.** Balance can be either *formal*, in which the elements in the images are arranged symmetrically around a central point or axis, or *informal*, in which elements are not distributed evenly, but stronger and weaker elements are arranged in a way that achieves an overall effect of balance. A common approach to informal balance is weighing one visually dominant element against several smaller or weaker elements.[8] Generally speaking, formal balance is more calming and serious, whereas informal balance tends to feel more dynamic and engaging.

  - **Emphasis.** Audiences usually assume that the dominant element in a design is the most important, so make sure that the visually dominant element really does represent the most important information. You can do so through color, position, size, or placement, for example. Conversely, be sure to visually downplay less important items. For instance, avoid using strong colors for minor support points, and de-emphasize background features such as the grid lines on a chart.

  - **Convention.** Visual communication is guided by a variety of generally accepted rules or conventions, just as written communication is guided by an array of spelling, grammar, punctuation, and usage conventions. These conventions dictate virtually every aspect of design.[9] Moreover, many conventions are so ingrained that people don't even realize they are following these rules. For example, if English is your native language, you assume that ideas progress across the page from left to right because that's the direction in which English text is written. However, if you are a native Arabic or Hebrew speaker, you might automatically assume that flow on a page or screen is from right to left because that is the direction in which those languages are written. Similarly, Japanese audiences are used to reading publications from back to front, right to left. Flouting conventions often causes breakdowns in communication, but in some cases, it can be done to great effect.[10] For instance, flipping an organization chart upside down to put the customers at the top, with frontline employees directly beneath them and on down to the chief executive at the bottom, can be an effective way to emphasize that customers come first and that the managers are responsible for supporting employees in their efforts to satisfy customers.

  - **Simplicity.** As a general rule, simple is better when it comes to visuals for business communication. Remember that you're conveying information, not decorating an apartment or creating artwork. Limit the number of colors and design elements you use, and take care to avoid *chartjunk*, a term coined by visual communication

Creating effective visuals and correctly interpreting visuals that other people create are important business skills.

FIGURE 12.2   Ineffective and Effective Design
The slide in Figure 12.2a violates numerous principles of effective design, as you can see in the annotations. Figure 12.2b will never win any awards for exciting or innovative design, but it does its job efficiently and effectively.

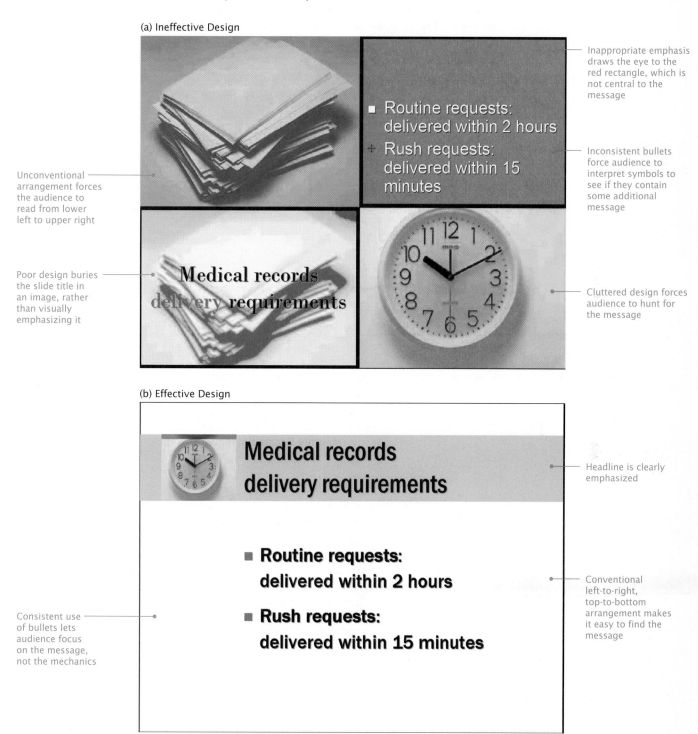

(a) Ineffective Design

Inappropriate emphasis draws the eye to the red rectangle, which is not central to the message

Inconsistent bullets force audience to interpret symbols to see if they contain some additional message

Unconventional arrangement forces the audience to read from lower left to upper right

Poor design buries the slide title in an image, rather than visually emphasizing it

- Routine requests: delivered within 2 hours
- Rush requests: delivered within 15 minutes

Medical records delivery requirements

Cluttered design forces audience to hunt for the message

(b) Effective Design

Medical records delivery requirements

Headline is clearly emphasized

- **Routine requests:** delivered within 2 hours
- **Rush requests:** delivered within 15 minutes

Conventional left-to-right, top-to-bottom arrangement makes it easy to find the message

Consistent use of bullets lets audience focus on the message, not the mechanics

specialist Edward R. Tufte for decorative elements that clutter documents and potentially confuse readers without adding any relevant information.[11] Computers make it far too easy to add chartjunk, from clip art illustrations to three-dimensional bar charts that display only two dimensions of data (see Figure 12.3). (For a great example of how multiple dimensions can add useful information to a graph, see Figure 12.14 on page 393.)

FIGURE 12.3   The Power of Simplicity

These two graphs contain the same information, but Figure 12.3a is much easier to interpret. None of the additional elements in Figure 12.3b, including the extra colors, background design, and three-dimensional structure, add any information value—and they make the graph harder to interpret. Adding a false third dimension to two-dimensional information such as these sales figures is a common mistake.

(a)

(b)

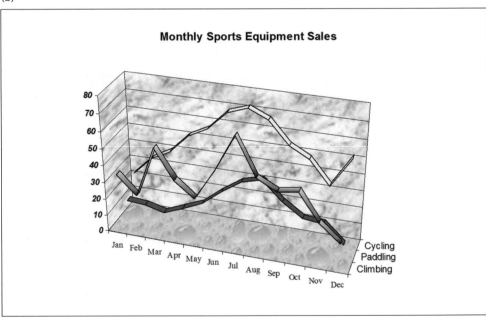

The Ethics of Visual Communication

Remember that the power to communicate with visuals comes with the responsibility to communicate ethically.

Power always comes with responsibility—and the potential power of visuals places an ethical burden on every business communicator. Ethical problems, both intentional and unintentional, can range from photos that play on racial or gender stereotypes to images that imply cause-and-effect relationships that may not exist to graphs that distort data (see Figure 12.4).

FIGURE 12.4 Influencing Perception Through Visual Design

Figure 12.4a shows impurities measured over the course of a 12-month period; the vertical scale is set from 0 to 120, sufficient to cover the range of variations in the data. However, what if you wanted to make the variations from month to month look more severe? Less severe? Figure 12.4b, with the scale "zoomed in" to a narrow range of 60 to 110, makes the variations look much more dramatic. The result could be a stronger emotional impact on the reader, creating the impression that these impurities are out of control. In contrast, Figure 12.4c expands the scale from 0 to 200, which minimizes the appearance of the variations in the data. This graph is visually "calmer," potentially creating the opposite impression from Figure 12.4b—that there's really nothing to worry about. The data shown in all three graphs are identical, but the graphs send three different messages to the reader. Are any of the graphs unethical? That depends on the communicator's intent and whether it inhibits the audience's ability to make informed decisions.

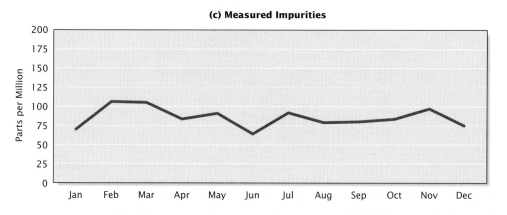

2 LEARNING
OBJECTIVE

Explain how to avoid
ethical lapses when
using visuals

*Visuals can't always speak for
themselves; make sure your
audience has enough context to
interpret your visuals correctly.*

Altering the scale of data charts is just one of many ways that visuals can be designed to emphasize or de-emphasize certain aspects of information. For example, to increase the perceived size of a product, an advertiser might show a close-up of it being held by someone with smaller-than-average hands. Conversely, a large hand would make the product seem smaller.

You can work to avoid ethical lapses in your visuals by following these guidelines:[12]

- **Consider all possible interpretations—and misinterpretations.** Try to view your visuals from your audience members' perspective; will their biases, beliefs, or backgrounds lead them to different conclusions than you've intended? For instance, assume that you want to show how easy your product is to use, and the photograph you've chosen just happens to show a woman operating the product. Will anyone conclude that what you really mean to say is that your product is so simple that "even a woman can use it"?
- **Provide context.** Even when they are completely accurate, all visuals can show only a partial view of reality. Part of your responsibility as a communicator is to provide not only accurate visuals but enough background information to help audiences interpret the visual information correctly.
- **Don't hide or minimize negative information that runs counter to your argument.** Obscuring information prevents your audiences from making fully informed decisions regarding your content.
- **Don't exaggerate information that supports your argument.** Similarly, you have a responsibility not to oversell information in support of your argument. You should also resist the temptation to alter or enhance photographs and other images in order to support your arguments.
- **Don't oversimplify complex situations.** By their very nature, visuals tend to present simplified views of reality. This is usually a benefit and one of the key reasons for using visuals. However, take care not to mislead an audience by hiding complications that are important to the audience's understanding of the situation.
- **Don't imply cause-and-effect relationships without providing proof that they exist.** For example, if you create a line chart that shows how increasing sales seem to track increasing advertising expenditures, you can claim a correlation but not necessarily a causal relationship between the two. You can claim a causal relationship (meaning that the increase in advertising spending caused the increase in sales) only if you can isolate advertising spending as the *only* factor that can account for the increase in sales.
- **Avoid emotional manipulation or other forms of coercion.** For instance, a photograph of an unhappy child being treated as a social outcast because he or she doesn't own the trendiest new toys could be considered an unethical way to persuade parents to buy those products for their children.
- **Be careful with the way you aggregate data.** Preparing charts, graphs, and tables that present data often involves decisions about *aggregating*, or grouping, data. The decisions you make about aggregating data can have a profound effect on the message your audience receives (see "Ethics Detective: Solving the Case of the Hidden Numbers"). For example, if you aggregate daily production levels to show only a single data point for each week, you might be obscuring important variations that happen from day to day.

*The ways in which you aggregate
data for display can affect the
messages and meanings that your
audience extracts from your
visuals.*

3 LEARNING
OBJECTIVE

Explain how to
choose which points
in your message to
illustrate

IDENTIFYING POINTS TO ILLUSTRATE

To help identify which parts of your message can benefit from visuals, step back and consider the flow of your message from the audience's point of view. Which parts of the message are likely to seem complex, open to misinterpretation, or even just a little bit dull? Are there any connections between ideas that might not be obvious if they are addressed only in text? Is there a lot of numeric data or other discrete factual content that would be difficult to read if presented in paragraph form? Is there a chance that the main idea won't "jump off the page" if it's covered only in text?

Ethics Detective

Solving the Case of the Hidden Numbers

You've been assigned to present the results of an industrywide study of the effects of insecticide. Your audience consists of the department heads in your company, whose experience and educational backgrounds vary widely, from chemical engineering to insurance to law. You're convinced you need to keep your report as simple and as jargon free as possible.

You're not a scientific expert in insecticides, but your supervisor has introduced you to a scientist who works for a trade association that represents chemical producers, including your firm. The scientist is familiar with the study you'll be reporting on, and she has experience in communicating technical subjects to diverse audiences. You jumped at the chance to have such a knowledgeable person review your presentation for technical accuracy, but you're uncomfortable with some of her feedback. In particular, you question her advice to replace the following line chart, which shows the number of insecticide poisonings and deaths by age.

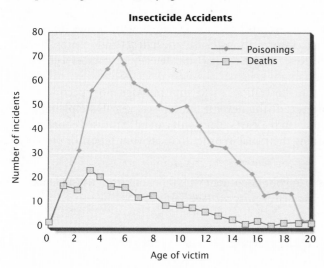

The scientist suggests that this chart is too busy and too difficult for nonspecialists to read. As an alternative, she provides a bar chart that selects four specific ages from the entire range. She says this chart communicates the same basic idea as the line chart but is much easier to read.

ANALYSIS

You agree with the scientist that the line chart is visually busy and takes more effort to process, but something bothers you about the bar chart. Does it present the insecticide situation accurately and honestly? Why or why not?

If you answer yes to any of these questions, you probably need one or more visuals. When you're deciding which points to present visually, think of the five Cs:

- **Clear.** The human mind is extremely adept at processing visual information, whether it's something as simple as the shape of a stop sign or as complicated as the floor plan for a new factory. If you're having difficultly conveying an idea in words, consider whether a visual element will do the job instead.
- **Complete.** Visuals, particularly tables, often serve to provide the supporting details for a main idea or recommendation. A table or another visual can provide these details without getting in the way of your main message.
- **Concise.** You've probably heard the phrase "A picture is worth a thousand words." If a particular section of your message seems to require extensive description or explanation, see whether there's a way to convey this information visually. With a

Effective visuals are clear, complete, concise, connected, and compelling.

TABLE 12.1 When to Use Visuals

PURPOSE	APPLICATION
To clarify	Support text descriptions of "graphic" topics: quantitative or numeric information, explanations of trends, descriptions.
To simplify	Divide complicated descriptions into components that can be depicted with conceptual models, flowcharts, organization charts, or diagrams.
To emphasize	Call attention to particularly important points by illustrating them with line, bar, and pie charts.
To summarize	Review major points in the narrative by providing a chart or table that sums up the data.
To reinforce	Present information in visual form to supplement descriptions in text.
To attract	Make material seem more interesting by decorating the cover or title page and by breaking up the text with visual aids.
To impress	Build confidence by using visual forms to convey authenticity and precision.
To unify	Depict the relationships among various elements of a whole.

picture working in conjunction with text, you may be able to reduce your word count considerably.

- **Connected.** A key purpose of many business messages is showing connections of some sort—similarities or differences, correlations, cause-and-effect relationships, and so on. Whenever you want readers to see such a connection, determine whether a chart, a diagram, or another illustration might help.

- **Compelling.** Will one or more illustrations make your message more persuasive, more interesting, more likely to get read? You never want to insert visuals simply for decorative purposes, of course, but even if a particular point can be expressed equally well via text or visuals, consider adding the visual in order to make your report or presentation more compelling.

As you identify which points in your document would benefit from a visual, make sure that each visual you decide on has a clear purpose (see Table 12.1).

SELECTING THE RIGHT TYPE OF VISUAL

After you have identified which points would benefit most from visual presentation, your next decision is choosing which type of visual to use for each message point. As you can see in Figure 12.5, you have many choices for business graphics. For certain types of information, the decision is usually obvious. For example, to present a large set of numeric values or detailed textual information, a table is the obvious choice in most cases. However, if you're presenting data broken down geographically, a color-coded map might be more effective, to show overall patterns rather than individual data points. Also, certain visuals are used more commonly for certain applications, as you'll see in the following sections.

Presenting Data

Business professionals have a tremendous number of choices for presenting data, from general-purpose line, bar, and pie charts to specialized charts for product portfolios, financial analysis, and other professional functions. The visuals most commonly used to present data include tables; line and surface charts; bar charts, pictograms, and Gantt charts; scatter and bubble diagrams; and pie charts. (Note that most people use the terms *chart* and *graph* interchangeably.)

4 LEARNING OBJECTIVE

Describe the most common options for presenting data in a visual format

You have many types of visuals to choose from, and each is best suited to particular communication tasks.

REAL-TIME UPDATES
Learn More

Quickly peruse dozens of data and information display techniques

This "periodic table of visualization methods" shows dozens of ways to display data, information, concepts, strategies, and more. Go to **http://real-timeupdates.com/bct** and click on "Learn More." If you are using mybcommlab, you can access Real-Time Updates within each chapter or under Student Study Tools.

FIGURE 12.5 Selecting the Best Visual

For each point you want to illustrate, make sure you choose the most effective type of visual.

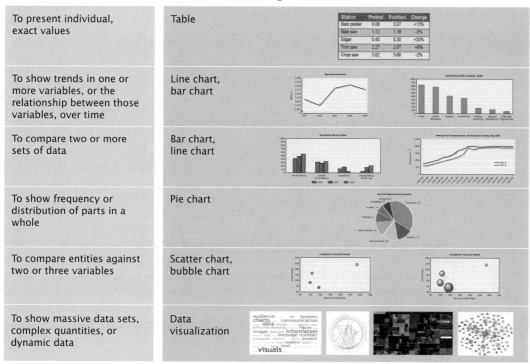

Communication Challenge	Effective Visual Choice

Presenting Data

Communication Challenge	Effective Visual Choice	
To present individual, exact values	Table	
To show trends in one or more variables, or the relationship between those variables, over time	Line chart, bar chart	
To compare two or more sets of data	Bar chart, line chart	
To show frequency or distribution of parts in a whole	Pie chart	
To compare entities against two or three variables	Scatter chart, bubble chart	
To show massive data sets, complex quantities, or dynamic data	Data visualization	

Presenting Information, Concepts, and Ideas

Communication Challenge	Effective Visual Choice	
To show geographic relationships or comparisons	Map	
To illustrate processes or procedures	Flowchart, diagram	
To show conceptual or spatial relationships (simplified)	Drawing	
To show spatial relationships (realistic)	Photograph	
To show processes, transformations, and other activities	Animation, video	

FIGURE 12.6 Parts of a Table

Here are the standard parts of a table. No matter which design you choose, make sure the layout is clear and that individual rows and columns are easy to follow.

	Multicolumn Heading			
Subheading	**Subheading**	**Subheading**	**Subheading**	**Single-Column Heading**
Row heading	x x x	x x x	x x x	x x x
Row heading	x x x	x x x	x x x	x x x
Subheading	x x x	x x x	x x x	x x x
Subheading	x x x	x x x	x x x	x x x
Total	x x x	x x x	x x x	x x x

Source: (In the same format as a text footnote; see Appendix B)

*Footnote (For an explanation of elements in the table, a superscript number or small letter may be used instead of an asterisk or other symbol.)

Tables

Printed tables can display extensive amounts of data, but tables for online display and electronic presentations need to be simpler.

When you need to present detailed, specific information, choose a **table**, a systematic arrangement of data in columns and rows. Tables are ideal when your audience needs information that would be either difficult or tedious to handle in the main text.

Most tables contain the standard parts illustrated in Figure 12.6. Every table includes vertical columns and horizontal rows, with useful headings along the top and side. For printed documents, you can adjust font size and column and row spacing to fit a considerable amount of information on the page and still maintain readability. For online documents, you'll need to reduce the number of columns and rows to make sure your tables are easily readable online. Tables for electronic presentations usually need to be the simplest of all because you can't expect audiences to read detailed information from the screen.

Although complex information may require formal tables that are set apart from the text, you can present some data more simply within the text. You make the table, in essence, a part of the paragraph, typed in tabular format. Such text tables are usually introduced with a sentence that leads directly into the tabulated information. Here's an example:[13]

Here is how the five leading full-service restaurant chains compare in terms of number of locations and annual revenue:

	OSI RESTAURANT PARTNERS	APPLEBEE'S	CARLSON	BRINKER	DARDEN
Major Chain(s)	Outback Steakhouse, Carrabba's	Applebee's	Friday's, Pick Up Stix	Chili's, On the Border, Romano's	Red Lobster, Olive Garden
Locations	1,400	1,970	1,000	1,800	1,700
Revenue ($ Million)	$4,150	$1,338	$2,400 (est. from 2004)	$4,235	$6,627

Source: Hoover's Online [accessed 3 December 2008] www.hoovers.com.

When you prepare tables, follow these guidelines to make your tables easy to read:

- Use common, understandable units and clearly identify the units you're using, whether it's dollars, percentages, price per ton, or some other units.
- Express all items in a column in the same unit and round off for simplicity whenever doing so won't eliminate essential details.

- Label column headings clearly and use a subheading if necessary.
- Separate columns or rows with lines or extra space to make the table easy to follow; in complex tables, consider highlighting every other row or column in a pale, contrasting color.
- Provide totals or averages of columns or rows when relevant.
- Document the source of the data, using the same format as a text footnote (see Appendix B).

Tables can contain numerals, words, symbols, or other facts and figures. Word tables are particularly appropriate for presenting survey findings or for comparing various items against a specific standard.

Line and Surface Charts

A **line chart** illustrates trends over time or plots the relationship of two or more variables. In line charts showing trends, the vertical, or *y*, axis shows the amount, and the horizontal, or *x*, axis shows the time or other quantity against which the amount is being measured. Both axes often start at zero in the lower-left corner, but you can exercise a fair amount of flexibility with both axes in order to present your data as clearly as possible. For instance, to show both positive and negative values (such as profit and loss), you can have the *y* axis span from a negative value up to a positive value, with zero somewhere in between. Of course, you should always avoid distorting the data in ways that could mislead your audience, as noted in the section "The Ethics of Visual Communication," on page 380.

Line charts are commonly used to show trends over time or the relationship between two or more variables.

If you need to compare two or more sets of data, you can plot them on the same chart for instant visual comparison (see Figure 12.7). Two or three lines on a single chart are usually easy to read, but beyond that, things can get confusing, particularly if the lines cross.

By their very nature, line charts often raise the question "What happens next?" For instance, if you present sales data for the past 12 months, your audience may well ask what you think will happen in the next 12 months. Predicting the future is always a risky endeavor, but you can use your spreadsheet's forecasting tools to extend a line into the future, using a statistical technique known as *regression analysis*. Check your spreadsheet's Help function for more information on using its *linear regression, trend line,* or *forecasting* functions. However, when using these tools, be aware that all they can do is extract patterns from past data and extend those patterns into the future. They don't have any awareness of the "real-life" factors that shaped that past data—and they may or may not produce that same pattern in the future.

Your spreadsheet offers ways to predict future values based on past values shown in a line chart.

A **surface chart**, also called an **area chart**, is a form of line chart with a cumulative effect; all the lines add up to the top line, which represents the total (see Figure 12.8). This presentation helps you illustrate changes in the composition of something over time. One

FIGURE 12.7 Line Chart
This line chart compares the temperatures measured inside two cement kilns from 8:00 A.M. to 5:00 P.M.

FIGURE 12.8 Surface Chart

Surface, or area, charts can show a combination of trends over time and the individual contributions of the components of a whole.

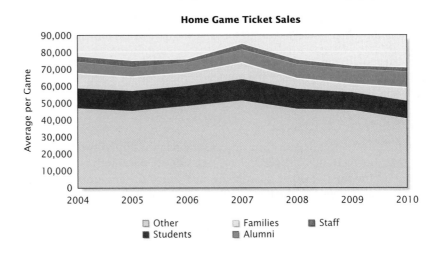

common use is to show how sales of individual products contribute to the company's overall revenue.[14] When preparing a surface chart, put the most important segment on the bottom and build up from there.

Bar Charts, Pictograms, and Gantt Charts

You can create bar charts in a wide variety of formats; choose the form that best illustrates the data and relationships in your message.

A **bar chart** portrays numbers by the height or length of its rectangular bars, making a series of numbers easy to read or understand. Bar charts are particularly valuable when you want to

- Compare the sizes of several items at one time
- Show changes in one item over time
- Indicate the composition of several items over time
- Show the relative sizes of components of a whole

As the charts in Figure 12.9 show, bar charts can appear in various forms. *Grouped* bar charts compare more than one set of data, using a different color or pattern for each set. *Deviation* bar charts identify positive and negative values, or winners and losers. *Segmented* bar charts, also known as *stacked* bar charts, show how individual components contribute to a total number, using a different color or pattern for each component. *Combination* bar and line charts compare quantities that require different intervals. *Paired* bar charts show the correlations between two items.

Figure 12.9 also suggests how creative you can be with bar charts. You might align the bars either vertically or horizontally, or you might use bar charts to show both positive and negative quantities. No matter what you do, however, be sure to space the bars evenly and place them in a logical order, such as chronological or alphabetical.

You can also convert the bars of a bar chart into lines of symbols, so that the number or length of the symbols indicates the relative value of each item. A chart that portrays data as symbols instead of words or numbers is known as a **pictogram** (see Figure 12.10). The chief value of pictograms is their novelty and ability to convey a more literal, visual message, but they can be more difficult to read if not designed with care and can present a less professional tone than a straightforward bar chart.

Closely related to the bar chart is the **time line chart**, which shows how much time is needed to complete each task in a given project. When you want to track progress toward completing a project, you can use a type of time line chart known as a **Gantt chart** (see Figure 12.11).

FIGURE 12.9 The Versatile Bar Chart

Here are six of the dozens of variations possible with bar charts: *singular* (12.9a), *grouped* (12.9b), *deviation* (12.9c), *segmented* (12.9d), *combination* (12.9e), and *paired* (12.9f).

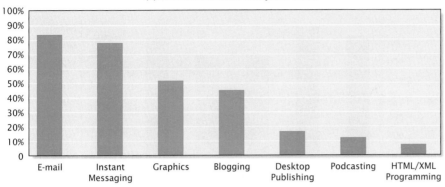

(a) CommuniCo Staff Computer Skills

(b) Worldwide Market Share

(c) CommuniCo Stock Price

(d) CommuniCo Preferred Communication Media

(continued)

FIGURE 12.9 The Versatile Bar Chart *(continued)*

FIGURE 12.10 Pictogram

Pictograms use symbols to represent quantities. In this example, Mozilla, the organization that develops the Firefox web browser, uses a calendar-style pictogram to make a competitive point. The stark difference shown with the two calendars has much greater visual impact than simply listing two numbers.

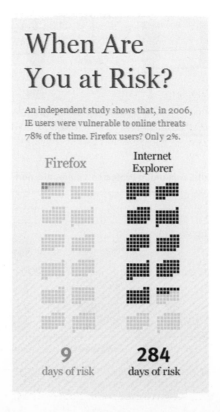

FIGURE 12.11   Gantt Chart

This Gantt chart shows the activities involved in designing the prototype and conducting the marketing research for a new product. The maroon bars indicate completed tasks, the blue bars indicate activities not yet completed, and the black diamond is a milestone—in this case the prototype's due date.

ID	Project Time line	Start Date	End Date	Duration	Percentage Complete	2010			
						June	July	August	September
1	**Design Phase**	**6/20/10**	**8/31/10**	**73d**	**90.00 %**				
2	Design Project	6/20/10	7/31/10	42d	100.00				
3	Prototype Design	8/3/10	8/21/10	19d	100.00				
4	Test Prototype	8/24/10	8/28/10	5d	0.00				
5	Prototype Complete	8/31/10	8/31/10	0d	0.00				
6	**Marketing Research Phase**	**8/3/10**	**9/25/10**	**54d**	**25.00**				
7	Preliminary Research	8/3/10	8/7/10	5d	100.00				
8	Conduct Focus Groups	8/10/10	8/11/10	2d	100.00				
9	Interviews	8/12/10	8/14/10	3d	100.00				
10	Analyze Research Results	8/17/10	8/28/10	12d	0.00				
11	Create Marketing Plan	8/31/10	9/25/10	26d	0.00				

Scatter and Bubble Diagrams

If you need to compare several entities (companies, markets, employees, and so on) on two variables, such as revenue and profit margin, use a **scatter diagram**, also known as an **XY diagram**. This diagram is similar to a line chart in the sense that one variable is plotted along the *x* (horizontal) axis and another along the *y* (vertical) axis. However, in a scatter diagram, individual points are plotted, not continuous lines. The **bubble diagram** expands to three variables, with the size of the bubble representing the third variable (see Figure 12.12).

Scatter diagrams compare entities against two variables; bubble diagrams compare them against three.

FIGURE 12.12   Bubble Diagram

A bubble diagram shows three variables: distance along the *x* and *y* axes, plus the diameter of each bubble. In this case, the rate of sales growth is plotted on the *x* axis, profit margin is plotted on the *y* axis, and the size of the bubbles represents annual sales. For instance, MooreComp has the greatest sales but the lowest profit margin, although it is growing faster than two of its three competitors.

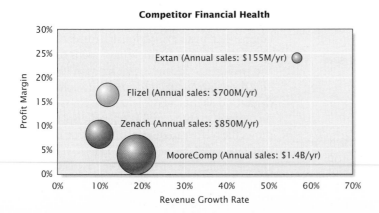

FIGURE 12.13 Pie Chart

When creating pie charts, use different colors or patterns to distinguish the various pieces. Label all the segments and indicate the value of each in either percentages or units of measure so that your readers will be able to judge the values of the wedges.

Year-End Head Count by Function

Executives, 8
Accounting, 14
Facilities, 14
Shipping, 17
Admin support, 25
Marketing/sales, 27
Engineers, 28
Assemblers, 67

Pie Charts

Readers expect pie charts to show the distribution of parts within a whole.

Like segmented bar charts and area charts, a **pie chart** shows how the parts of a whole are distributed (see Figure 12.13). However, pie charts have the advantage of familiarity; readers expect parts of a whole to be displayed via a pie chart. Each segment represents a slice of a complete circle, or *pie*. You can also combine pie charts with tables to expand the usefulness of such visuals.

To prevent pie charts from getting too cluttered, minimize the number of slices. If necessary, lump the smallest pieces together in an "other" category. Ideally, the largest or most important slice of the pie, the segment you want to emphasize, is placed at the 12 o'clock position; the rest are arranged clockwise either in order of size or in some other logical progression.

Use different colors (or patterns, if you'll be printing or reproducing charts in black and white) to distinguish the various pieces. If you want to draw attention to the segment that is of the greatest interest to your readers, use a brighter color for that segment, draw an arrow to the segment, or *explode* it by pulling the segment away from the rest of the pie. Remember, the segments must add up to 100 percent if percentages are used or to the total number if numbers are used.

Data Visualization

Data visualization displays can help readers make sense of massive data sets.

Conventional charts and graphs are limited in two ways: They can represent only numeric data, and most types show only a limited number of data points before the display becomes too cluttered to interpret. A diverse class of display capabilities known as **data visualization** overcome both of these drawbacks (see Figure 12.14). First, some types of data visualization displays can show hundreds, thousands, or even millions of data points, using a variety of graphical presentations. For instance, regional sales data can be displayed in three-dimensional "topography" maps to quickly show strong and weak areas. Second, other kinds of visualization tools combine data with textual information to communicate complex or dynamic data much faster than can conventional presentations. A common example of this type of display is a *tag cloud*, which shows the relative frequency of terms, or *tags* (user-applied content labels), in an article, a blog, a website, survey data, or another collection of text.[15] Data visualization in an exciting, dynamic field, and you can expect to see many innovations in the coming years.

FIGURE 12.14 Data Visualization

The range of data visualization displays is virtually endless; here are a few of the many different ways to display complex sets of data.

(a) Website Linkage Map Showing the Most Active Links to and from Apple's Homepage (**www.apple.com**)

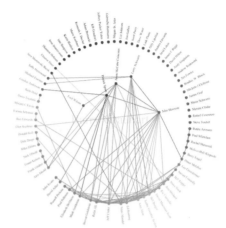

(b) Facebook "Friend Wheel" Showing How the Connections of One Facebook User Are Connected with One Another

audience avoid bar business charts color communication create data design detailed diagram easy effective elements example figure help images important information instance line maps message number photographs photos pie points present product professional re read readers report sales shows size sure tables text textual used usually value video visuals ways

(c) A Tag Cloud Showing the Relative Frequency of the 50 Most-Used Words in This Chapter (Other Than Common Words Such as *and, or,* and *the)*

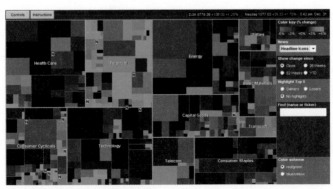

(d) A Real-Time "HeatMap" Showing Price Increases (Green) and Decreases (Red) for Stocks in Various Industry Sectors.

Presenting Information, Concepts, and Ideas

In addition to facts and figures, you'll need to present other types of information, from spatial relationships to abstract ideas. As Dave Gray and his colleagues at Xplane demonstrate, using words isn't always the best way to communicate information, concepts, or ideas, so these professionals often look for visual solutions to complement or even replace textual information. The most common types of visuals for these applications include flowcharts and organization charts; maps; drawings, diagrams, and photographs; and animation and video.

Flowcharts and Organization Charts

5 LEARNING OBJECTIVE

Describe the most common options for presenting information, concepts, and ideas

If you need to show physical or conceptual relationships rather than numeric ones, you might want to use a flowchart or an organization chart. A **flowchart** (see Figure 12.15) illustrates a sequence of events from start to finish; it is indispensable when illustrating processes, procedures, and sequential relationships. For general business purposes, you don't need to be too concerned about the specific shapes, although do keep them consistent. However, be aware that there is a formal flowchart "language" in which each shape has a specific meaning (diamonds are decision points, rectangles are process steps, and so on). If you're communicating with computer programmers and others who are accustomed to formal flowcharting, make sure you use the correct symbols to avoid confusion. Graphics programs that have flowchart symbols usually label their functions, making it easy to use the right ones.

FIGURE 12.15 Flowchart
Flowcharts show sequences of events and are most valuable when the process or procedure has a number of decision points and variable paths.

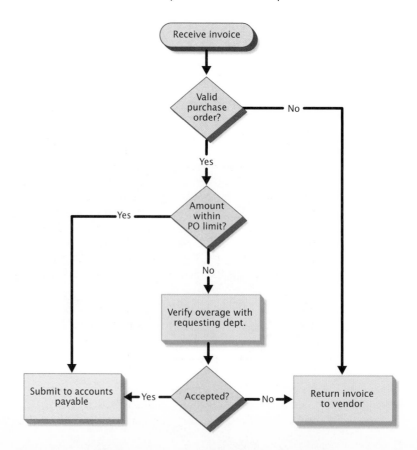

As the name implies, an **organization chart** illustrates the positions, units, or functions of an organization and the way they interrelate (refer to Figure 1.2 on page 40 for an example). These charts aren't limited to organizational structures, of course; as you saw in Chapter 4, they can also be used to outline messages.

Use organization charts to depict the interrelationships among the parts of a whole.

Maps

Maps can be used in a variety of ways to show location, distance, points of interest (such as competitive retail outlets), and geographic distribution of data, such as sales by region or population by state or province. In addition to presenting facts and figures, maps are useful for showing market territories, distribution routes, and facilities locations. Maps are sometimes used in conjunction with aerial photographs to provide a richer view (see Figure 12.16).

Use maps for such tasks as representing statistics by geographic area or showing spatial relationships.

Simple maps are available via clip art libraries for your word processor and presentation software, but more powerful uses (such as automatically generating color-coded maps based on data inputs) usually require the specialized capabilities of *geographic information systems*. You may also want to explore online resources such as Google Earth (http://earth.google.com) and Live Search (http://maps.live.com), which offer a variety of mapping and aerial photography features.

Drawings, Diagrams, and Photographs

The opportunities to use drawings, diagrams, and photographs are virtually endless (see Figure 12.17). Simple drawings can show the network of suppliers in an industry, the flow of funds through a company, or the process for completing the payroll each week. More complex diagrams can convey technical topics such as the operation of a machine or repair procedures.

Use drawings and diagrams to show how something works or how it is made or used; drawings are sometimes better than photographs because they let you focus on the most important details.

Word processors and presentation software provide basic drawing capabilities, but for more precise and professional illustrations, you'll need a specialized package such as Microsoft Visio, Adobe Illustrator, or Google SketchUp. Moving a level beyond those programs, *computer-aided design* (CAD) systems such as Autodesk's AutoCAD can produce extremely detailed architectural and engineering drawings.

Photographs offer both functional and decorative value, and with low-cost digital photography now widely available, virtually all writers can add photographs to print documents, presentations, and webpages. In addition, photo libraries such as Getty Images (www.gettyimages.com) and photo/image search engines such as AltaVista (www.altavista.com/image) and Google Image Search (http://images.google.com) make it easy to find digital photographs. Some of these photos are available for free, but the professional collections, such as Getty Images, require either a one-time payment for unlimited use (often called *royalty free*) or an annual payment or other limited-use purchase (often called *rights managed*). You can also find photos and other images through Creative Commons (http://creativecommons.org), with various levels of licensing terms.

Use photographs for visual appeal and to show exact appearances.

To use photographs successfully, consider these five guidelines:

- **Consider whether a diagram would be more effective than a photograph.** Photographs are often unmatched in their ability to communicate spatial relationships, sizes, shapes, and other physical parameters, but sometimes they communicate *too much* information. For example, to show how to adjust a specific part of a complicated machine, a photo can be confusing because it shows all the parts within the camera's view. A simplified diagram is often more effective because it allows you to emphasize the specific parts that are relevant to the problem at hand.
- **Learn how to use basic image-processing tools.** For instance, you can drop photographs directly into your word-processing or presentation file and then use that program to change the size of the file to fit the available space, but this isn't always the best approach. Rather than simply resizing, you might be better off *cropping*, or electronically cutting away part of the photo.
- **Match the file to the application.** Digital photos vary widely in *resolution*, which is the amount of detail in the image. Resolution can be expressed in one of two ways. Digital cameras are usually specified in *pixels*, the total number of *picture elements* in the file.

Match the resolution of your photo files to the application: Use higher resolution for print and lower resolution for electronic display.

FIGURE 12.16 Maps and Geographic Information Displays
Maps offer many opportunities for displaying data and information. The map in Figure 12.16a shows population projections for each state in the United States. When combined with databases in *geographic information systems (GIS)*, maps become extremely powerful visual reporting tools. The map in Figure 12.16b is a simple example of a GIS; more sophisticated systems can show overlays of population profiles, optimized transportation routes, and other information.

(a) Map Showing Statistical Data

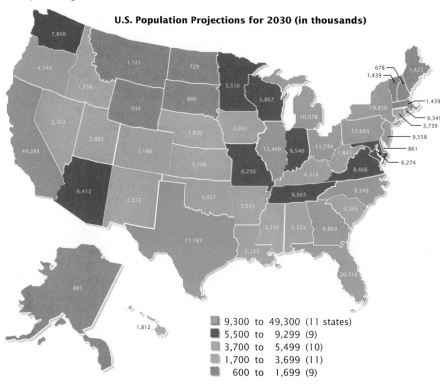

U.S. Population Projections for 2030 (in thousands)

■	9,300 to 49,300	(11 states)
■	5,500 to 9,299	(9)
■	3,700 to 5,499	(10)
■	1,700 to 3,699	(11)
■	600 to 1,699	(9)

(b) Simple Geographic Information System

FIGURE 12.17 Diagram
Clearly drawn diagrams can help audiences grasp technical information quickly.

For example, a 5-megapixel camera produces a photo with 5 million pixels in the image. Printers and scanners are usually specified in *dots per inch*, or *dpi*, which is the number of discrete points per linear inch. A 600 dpi office printer, therefore, creates 360,000 (600 × 600) discrete dots per square inch. Up to the limits of the printer, greater resolution is usually better for printed documents, but it isn't always helpful for online use. High-resolution image files are significantly larger than low-resolution image files, so they consume more storage space and take longer to transmit or download. In addition, many computer monitors and other electronic displays can't display all the fine detail in high-resolution images anyway (at least without zooming in and panning back and forth to see the entire image). If you plan to use photos on a website or an online report, use the "save for web" feature in your image-processing software to reduce the resolution and therefore the file size.

- **Make sure the photographs have communication value.** Except for covers, title slides, and other special uses, it's usually best to avoid including photographs simply for decorative value.

- **Be aware of copyrights and model permissions.** Just as with textual information you find online, you can't simply insert online photographs into your documents. Unless they are specifically offered for free, you have to assume that someone owns the photos and is entitled to payment or at least a photo credit. In addition, professional photographers are careful to have any person who poses in photos sign a model release form, which gives the photographer permission to use the person's image.

Technology makes it easy to use photographs in reports and presentations, but it also presents an important ethical concern. Software tools such as Photoshop allow you to easily make dramatic changes to photos without leaving a clue that they've been altered. Altering photos in small ways has been possible for a long time (more than a few students have

Altering or enhancing photographs can create ethical problems.

To show investors what a new building would look like in its environment, an artist combined a photograph of a scale model of the building with a photograph of the actual street scene. Because the target audience clearly understands that the proposed building doesn't exist, this sort of image manipulation is not unethical.

had blemishes airbrushed out of their yearbook photos), but computers make drastic changes easy and undetectable. You can remove people from photographs, put Person A's head on Person B's body, and make products look more attractive than they really are. Most people would agree that it's acceptable to make certain cosmetic improvements, such as brightening an underexposed photo to make it easier to view. But to avoid ethical lapses, don't make any alterations that mislead the viewer or substantially change the message conveyed by the photo.[16]

Animation and Video

Computer animation and video are among the most specialized forms of business visuals; when they are appropriate and done well, they offer unparalleled visual impact. At a simple level, you can animate shapes and text within electronic presentations (see Chapter 17). At a more sophisticated level, software such as Adobe Flash enables the creation of multimedia files that include computer animation, digital video, and other elements.

The combination of low-cost digital video cameras and video-sharing websites such as YouTube has spurred a revolution in business video applications in recent years. Product demonstrations, company overviews, promotional presentations, and training seminars are among the most popular applications of business video. With a little creativity, you can use video in everything from recruiting to contests that get customers or employees involved in the promotional process. For example, before moving into his career in the insurance industry, Hamline University graduate Eric Binfet used his creative and technical skills to write and produce the winning video in a Dairy Queen employee contest. The video did such a great job of showcasing some important new branding elements that the store owner pitched it to corporate as a potential commercial.[17]

PRODUCING AND INTEGRATING VISUALS

Now that you understand the communication power of visuals and have chosen the best visuals to illustrate key points in your report, website, or presentation, it's time to get creative. This section offers advice on creating visuals, integrating them with your text, and verifying the quality of your visual elements.

Creating Visuals

Computer software offers a variety of graphical tools but doesn't automatically give you the design sensibility that is needed for effective visuals.

Learning how to use your computer tools will help you save enormous amounts of time and produce better results.

Technology has put powerful graphics tools in the hands of virtually every business computer user, so you no longer have to rely on professional designers as much as businesspeople had to only a few years ago. Unfortunately, computers can't provide the specialized training and hands-on experience of a professional designer. Computers make it easy to create visuals, but they also make it easy to create ineffective, distracting, and even downright ugly visuals. However, by following the basic design principles discussed on pages 377 to 380, you can create all the basic visuals you need—visuals that are both attractive and effective.

Whether you're using the charting functions offered in a spreadsheet or the design features of a specialized graphics program, take a few minutes to familiarize yourself with the software's quirks and capabilities. For important visuals, try to have a professional designer set up a *template* for the various types of visuals you and your colleagues need to create. In addition to helping ensure an effective design, using templates saves you the time of making numerous design decisions every time you create a chart or graphic.

However, be careful with the templates included with some commercial software programs. Some are "overdesigned" and inappropriate for serious business uses, and some clutter the image with busy borders and backgrounds that can distract an audience from your real message.

No matter which tools you're using, take care to match the style and quality of your visuals with the subject matter and the situation at hand. The style of your visuals communicates a subtle message about your relationship with the audience. A simple sketch might be fine for a working meeting but inappropriate for a formal presentation or report. On the other hand, elaborate, full-color visuals may be viewed as extravagant for an informal report but may be entirely appropriate for a message to top management or influential outsiders.

The use of color in visuals improves learning, retention, and recall, as well as audience motivation and participation.

Integrating Visuals with Text

For maximum effectiveness and minimum disruption for the reader, visual elements need to be carefully integrated with the text of your message. In some instances, visual elements are somewhat independent from the text, as in the *sidebars* that occasionally accompany magazine articles. Such images are related to the content of the main story, but they aren't referred to by a specific title or figure number. This sort of treatment is often used in promotional materials such as brochures and advertisements.

A visual's level of sophistication should match the communication situation.

For reports and most other business documents, however, visuals are tightly integrated with the text so that readers can move back and forth between text and visuals with as little disruption as possible. Successful integration involves four decisions: maintaining a balance between visuals and text, referring to visuals in the text, placing the visuals in a document, and writing titles and other descriptions.

Maintaining a Balance Between Illustrations and Words

Strong visuals enhance the descriptive and persuasive power of your writing, but putting too many visuals into a report can distract your readers. If you're constantly referring to tables, drawings, and other visual elements, the effort to switch back and forth from words to visuals can make it difficult for readers to maintain focus on the thread of your message. The space occupied by visuals can also disrupt the flow of text on the page or screen.

Maintain a balance between text and visuals and place your visuals so that they help emphasize your key points.

Make sure your visuals match the needs, expectations, and interpretation skills of your audience.

The pacing of visuals throughout the text is also an important consideration. If most of your visuals are bunched in one section of the report, readers might spend more time there and less time in the text-heavy sections. Although it isn't always possible to have perfect distribution throughout a report, try to have a fairly even flow of text and visuals from page to page or screen to screen.

As always, take into account your readers' specific needs. If you're addressing an audience with multiple language backgrounds or widely varying reading skills, you can shift the balance toward more visual elements to help get around any language barriers. The professional experience, education, and training of your audience should influence your approach as well. For instance, detailed statistical plots and mathematical formulas are everyday reading material for quality-control engineers but not for most salespeople or top executives.

REAL-TIME UPDATES
Learn More

Jumpstart your visual creativity

The notion that visual creativity is a skill that only artists have—or should care about—is simply not true. Every professional can develop visual thinking and design skills that will improve problem solving and communication. Go to **http://real-timeupdates.com/bct** and click on "Learn More." If you are using mybcommlab, you can access Real-Time Updates within each chapter or under Student Study Tools.

Referencing Visuals

Unless a visual element clearly stands on its own, it should be clearly referred to by number in the text of your report. Some report writers refer to all visuals as "exhibits" and number them consecutively throughout the report; many others number tables and figures separately (everything that isn't a table is regarded as a figure). In a long report with numbered sections, illustrations may have a double number (separated by a period or a hyphen) representing the section number and the individual illustration number within that section. Whatever scheme you use, make sure it's clear and easy to follow.

Help your readers understand the significance of visuals by referring to them before readers encounter them in the document or on the screen. The following examples show how you can make this connection in the text:

> Figure 1 summarizes the financial history of the motorcycle division over the past five years, with sales broken into four categories.
>
> Total sales were steady over this period, but the mix of sales by category changed dramatically (see Figure 2).
>
> The underlying reason for the remarkable growth in our sales of youth golf apparel is suggested by Table 4, which shows the growing interest in junior golf around the world.

When describing the data shown in your visuals, be sure to emphasize the main point you are trying to make. Don't make the mistake of simply repeating the data to be shown. Paragraphs that do are guaranteed to put the reader to sleep:

> Among women who replied to the survey, 17.4 percent earn less than $5 per hour; 26.4 percent earn $5 to $7; 25.7 percent, $8 to $12; 18.0 percent, $13 to $24; 9.6 percent, $25 to $49; and 2.9 percent, $50 and over.

The visual will (or at least should) provide all these details; there is no need to repeat them in the text. Instead, use round numbers that sum up the message:

> As Table 4.2 shows, more than two-thirds of the women who replied earn less than $12 per hour.

Placing Visuals

Try to position your visuals so that your audience won't have to flip back and forth (in printed documents) or scroll (on-screen) between the visuals and the text. Ideally, it's best to place each visual within, beside, or immediately after the paragraph it illustrates so that readers can consult the explanation and the visual at the same time. This scheme works well both in print and online. If at all possible, avoid bunching visuals at the end of a section or the end of a document; doing so asks a lot of the reader. (Bunching is unavoidable in some cases, such as when multiple visuals accompany a single section of text—as in this chapter, for instance.) Word-processing, desktop-publishing, and web-design programs let you place graphical elements virtually anywhere you wish, so take advantage of this flexibility.

Writing Titles, Captions, and Legends

Titles, captions, and legends help connect your visual and textual messages and ensure a seamless reading experience. A **title** identifies the content and purpose of the visual, along with whatever label and number you're using to refer to the visual. A **descriptive title** simply identifies the topic of the illustration, whereas an **informative title** calls attention to the conclusion that ought to be drawn from the data. Here's an example of the difference:

DESCRIPTIVE TITLE	INFORMATIVE TITLE
Relationship Between Petroleum Demand and Refinery Capacity in the United States	Refinery Capacity Declines as Petroleum Demand Continues to Grow

An informative title saves readers the work of interpreting the visual to extract the main idea from it. Regardless of whether your titles and legends are informative or descriptive, phrase them consistently throughout a document.

A **caption** usually offers additional discussion of the visual's content and can be up to several sentences long, if appropriate. Captions can also alert readers that additional discussion is available in the accompanying text. A **legend** helps readers "decode" the visual by explaining what various colors, symbols, or other design choices mean (several of the figures in this chapter use legends, for example). Legends aren't necessary for simple graphs, such as a line chart or bar chart with only one series of data, but they are invaluable with more complex graphics.

Verifying the Quality of Your Visuals

Visuals have a particularly strong impact on your readers and on their perceptions of you and your work, so verifying the quality of your visuals is an essential step. Ask yourself three questions about every visual element:

- **Is the visual accurate?** Be sure to check for mistakes such as typographical errors, inconsistent color treatment, confusing or undocumented symbols, and misaligned elements. Also verify that information in visuals and text matches. For data presentations, particularly if you're producing charts with a spreadsheet, verify any formulas used to generate the numbers and make sure you've selected the right numbers for each chart. When you're in a hurry, it's easy to select the wrong column of numbers in a spreadsheet or the wrong set of numbers in a column. For flowcharts, organization charts, diagrams, photos, and other visuals, compare the visuals you created with the visuals you had planned to create. Does each visual deliver your message accurately? Have you inserted the right photos, maps, or other files?

- **Is the visual properly documented?** As with the textual elements in your reports and presentations, visuals based on other people's research, information, and ideas require full citation. (Even if the graphical design is entirely yours, any underlying information taken from other sources needs to be documented.) Also, try to anticipate any questions or concerns your audience may have and address them with additional information, as needed. For instance, if you're presenting the results of survey research, many readers will want to know who participated in the survey, how many people responded, and when the questions were asked. You could answer these questions with a note in the caption along the lines of "652 accountants, surveyed the week of January 17." Similarly, if you found a visual in a secondary source, list that source on or near the graphic to help readers assess the information. Alternatively, you can list sources in an appendix.

- **Is the visual honest?** As a final precaution, step back and verify that your visuals communicate truthful messages. Make sure they don't hide information the audience needs, imply conclusions that your information doesn't support, or play on audience emotions in manipulative or coercive ways.

For a review of the important points to remember when creating visuals, see "Checklist: Creating Effective Visuals." For more information on visual communication, including design principles, ethical matters, and the latest tools for creating and displaying visuals, visit **http://real-timeupdates .com/bct** and click on Chapter 12.

REAL-TIME UPDATES
Learn More

Understand why some visuals work and some don't

Learn from the insightful analysis of more than a dozen commonly used displays for data and information, along with redesigned visuals that address the identified problems. Go to **http:// real-timeupdates.com/bct** and click on "Learn More." If you are using mybcommlab, you can access Real-Time Updates within each chapter or under Student Study Tools.

6 LEARNING OBJECTIVE

List three criteria to review in order to verify the quality of your visuals

Review each visual to make sure it doesn't intentionally or unintentionally distort the meaning of the underlying information.

Document Makeover

Improve This Report Summary and Visuals

To practice correcting drafts of actual documents, visit the "Document Makeovers" section in either mybcommlab or the Companion Website for this text.

If mybcommlab is being used in your class, see your User Guide for specific instructions on how to access the content for this chapter. If you are accessing this feature through the Companion Website, click on "Document Makeovers" and then click Chapter 12. You will find a competitive analysis report summary that contains problems and errors related to what you've learned in this chapter about communicating information through visuals. Use the Final Draft decision tool to create an improved version of this summary. Check the message for appropriate formatting of visuals and proper use of text with visuals.

✓ **CHECKLIST:** **Creating Effective Visuals**

- Emphasize visual consistency to connect parts of a whole and minimize audience confusion.
- Avoid arbitrary changes of color, texture, typeface, position, or scale.
- Highlight contrasting points through color, position, and other design choices.
- Decide whether you want to achieve formal or informal balance.
- Emphasize dominant elements and de-emphasize less-important pieces in a design.
- Understand and follow (at least most of the time) the visual conventions your audience expects.
- Strive for simplicity and clarity; don't clutter your visuals with meaningless decoration.
- Follow the guidelines for avoiding ethical lapses.

- Carefully consider your message, the nature of your information, and your audience to choose which points to illustrate.
- Select the proper types of graphics for the information at hand and for the objective of the message.
- Be sure the visual contributes to overall understanding of the subject.
- Understand how to use your software tools to maximize effectiveness and efficiency.
- Integrate visuals and text by maintaining a balance between illustrations and words, clearly referring to visuals within the text, and placing visuals carefully.
- Use titles, captions, and legends to help readers understand the meaning and importance of your visuals.
- Verify the quality of your visuals by checking for accuracy, proper documentation, and honesty.

Communication Challenges at Xplane

Your passion for tackling complex problems led you to a position in Xplane's Portland, Oregon, home office after graduation. Using the principles of visual communication you learned in this chapter, tackle the following challenges. For inspiration, refer to Figure 4.5 on page 132 or visit Xplane's website, at www.xplane.com/work/solutions, to see other examples.

Individual Challenge: Using a flowchart as the foundation, create a visual guide to planning a fun weekend. In addition to labeling the individual shapes (see Figure 12.15 on page 394), feel free to add as many additional notes and other graphic elements as you need—but make sure your guide is clear and easy to use. If possible, create the piece

electronically or scan it and create a PDF file that you can submit to your instructor.

Team Challenge: As part of a team of three or four students, create a visual guide to getting into college that could help high schoolers plan and manage their way through this complicated process. Start by listing all the steps required to research colleges, take necessary tests, apply for financial aid, and so on. Then choose a visual *metaphor* that you can use to organize your information—a ladder, a road map, a treasure map, whatever works for you. Use this image as the foundation of your visual guide and then add labels and blocks of text to complete your work. If possible, create the piece electronically or scan it and create a PDF file that you can submit to your instructor.

SUMMARY OF LEARNING OBJECTIVES

1 **Discuss six principles of graphic design that help ensure effective visuals.** When preparing visuals, (1) use elements of design consistently so you don't confuse your audience; (2) use color and other elements to show contrast effectively; (3) strive for a visual balance, either formal or informal, that creates a feel that is appropriate for your overall message; (4) use design choices to draw attention to key elements and to visually

downplay less important items; (5) understand and follow design conventions that your audience expects (even if the expectation is subconscious), although you can consider unconventional design choices if they promise to convey your message more effectively; and (6) strive for simplicity in all your visuals, making design decisions that enhance the reception and understanding of information rather than obscure or confuse it.

2 **Explain how to avoid ethical lapses when using visuals.** Communicators are responsible for avoiding both intentional and unintentional ethical lapses when using visual elements. They can work to avoid these lapses by (1) considering all possible interpretations—and misinterpretations—of their messages and avoiding design choices that could lead to unwanted interpretations; (2) providing sufficient context, whether visual or verbal, for audiences to understand the meaning and significance of visuals; (3) not hiding or minimizing negative information that runs counter to their arguments; (4) not exaggerating information that supports their arguments; (5) not oversimplifying complex situations by hiding complications that are relevant to the audience's understanding; (6) not implying cause-and-effect relationships without providing proof that they exist; (7) avoiding emotional manipulation or other forms of coercion; and (8) being careful with the way they aggregate data.

3 **Explain how to choose which points in your message to illustrate.** To decide which points to illustrate, first step back and consider the overall flow of your message from the audience's point of view. Identify elements of the message that might be complex, vulnerable to misinterpretation, or even dull. Look for connections between ideas that should be highlighted or extensive collections of data and other discrete factual content that might be difficult to read in textual format.

4 **Describe the most common options for presenting data in a visual format.** The visuals most commonly used to present data include tables, line and surface charts, bar charts, pictograms, Gantt charts, scatter and bubble diagrams and pie charts. You will probably use line, bar, and pie charts most often in your business communication efforts. Moving beyond basic display formats, designers continue to invent new data visualization tools to present large or complex sets of data.

5 **Describe the most common options for presenting information, concepts, and ideas.** Among the most commonly used visual formats in business communication are flowcharts (which depict a sequence of events in a process), organization charts (which show the relationships among people or elements in an organization), various types of maps (including data-driven map displays made possible by geographic information systems), drawings (which are often used instead of photographs because they can focus attention on specific parts of an object), diagrams (used to convey designs, interrelated ideas, and other complex entities), photographs (used when realism or emotional impact is important), computer animation (which can range from simple motions in presentation software such as Microsoft PowerPoint to richly complex short "films"), and video (used for everything from résumé supplements to product demonstrations).

6 **List three criteria to review in order to verify the quality of your visuals.** Make sure every visual you use is accurate (there are no mistakes or missing information), properly documented (the creator of any underlying data used in the visual has been given complete credit), and honest (the visual honestly reveals the real meaning of the underlying data or information).

mybcommlab

Log on to **www.mybcommlab.com** to access the following study and assessment aids associated with this chapter:

- Video applications
- Real-Time Updates
- Peer review activity
- Quick Learning Guides

- Pre/post test
- Personalized study plan
- Model documents
- Sample presentations

If you are not using mybcommlab, you can access the Real-Time Updates and Quick Learning Guides through **http://real-timeupdates.com/bct**. The Quick Learning Guide (located under "Learn More" on the website) hits all the high points of this chapter in just two pages. This guide, especially prepared by the authors, will help you study for exams or review important concepts whenever you need a quick refresher.

Test Your Knowledge

1. What type of visual would you use to compare one part with a whole?
2. What type of visual would you use to present detailed, exact values?
3. Why is simplicity important in business visuals?
4. What type of visual would you use to illustrate trends over time?
5. Why might you use a simplified line drawing instead of a full-color digital photograph in a particular application?

6. For what purposes are Gantt charts used?

7. How does a flowchart differ from an organization chart?

8. When would you use a bubble diagram instead of a scatter diagram?

9. What is the purpose of adding titles, captions, and legends to visuals in reports?

10 How do you check a visual for quality?

Apply Your Knowledge

1. What similarities do you see between visuals and nonverbal communication? Explain your answer.

2. You're writing a report for the director of human resources on implementing team-based management throughout your company. You want to emphasize that since the new approaches were implemented six months ago, absenteeism and turnover have been sharply reduced in all but two departments. How do you visually present your data in the most favorable light while maintaining honest communication? Explain.

3. In addition to telling readers why an illustration is important, why else should you refer to it in the text of your document?

4. When you read a graph, how can you be sure that the visual impression you are receiving is an accurate reflection of reality? Explain.

5. **Ethical Choices** After studying the designs of corporate websites, Penn State University professor S. Shyam Sundar discovered quite an interesting phenomenon: The more interactive and engaging a website is, the more likely visitors are to "buy into whatever is being advocated" on the site. In other words, if two websites have identical content, the site with greater interactivity and more "bells and whistles" would be more persuasive.[18] Is it ethical to increase the persuasive power of a website simply by making it more interactive? Why or why not?

Practice Your Knowledge

Messages for Analysis

Message 12.A: Analyzing Pie Charts

Examine the pie charts in Figure 12.18 and point out any problems or errors you notice.

Message 12.B: Analyzing a Line Chart

Examine the line chart in Figure 12.19 and point out any problems or errors you notice.

Exercises

Active links for all websites in this chapter can be found online. If mybcommlab is being used in your class, see your User Guide for instructions on accessing the content for this chapter. Otherwise, visit **www.pearsonglobaleditions.com/bovee**, locate *Business Communication Today*, Tenth Edition, click the Companion Website link, select Chapter 12, and then click on "Featured Websites." Please note that links to sites that become inactive after publication of the book will be removed from the Featured Websites section.

12.1 **Improving Visual Design** Find a communication example that you believe could be improved by applying the visual design principles you learned in this chapter. It can be from any medium—a webpage, a magazine ad, a promotional e-mail message, an illustration from a report—anything that you can either copy or scan into a word-processing file. Import the image into your word processing program, annotate it with notes that identify visual weaknesses, and describe ways to fix those weaknesses. (In Microsoft Word, for example, you can use the "Callouts" feature to place notes wherever you'd like on the page.) In a paragraph of accompanying text, explain why you believe the message isn't as effective as it could be and how your suggestions would make it more effective.

FIGURE 12.18 Pie Charts for Analysis

What Types of Life Insurance Policies Are in Effect?

2008

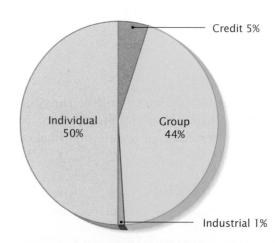

2009

FIGURE 12.19   Line Chart for Analysis

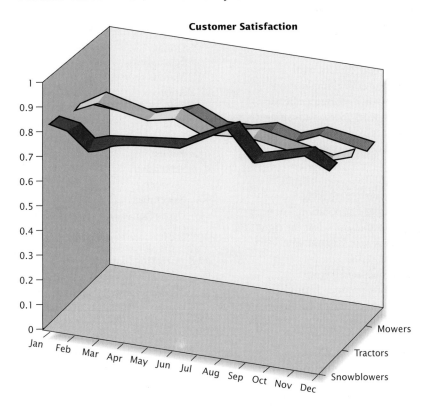

12.2   Preparing Bar and Pie Charts As a market researcher for a nationwide chain of car dealerships, you're examining car and truck ownership and lease patterns among single drivers in various age groups. By discovering which age groups have the highest percentages of owners, you will be better able to target advertising that promotes the leasing option. Using the information that follows, prepare a bar chart comparing the number of owners with the number of people who lease in each age category. Be sure to label your chart and include combined totals for owners and lessees ("total drivers"). Then prepare a pie chart showing the proportion of owners and lessees in the one age group that you think holds the most promise for leasing a new vehicle. Write a sentence that prepares your company's management for the information shown in the pie chart.

AGE GROUP	NUMBER OF OWNERS (IN THOUSANDS)	NUMBER OF LESSEES (IN THOUSANDS)
18–24	1,830	795
25–29	1,812	1,483
30–34	1,683	1,413
35–44	1,303	1,932
45–54	1,211	1,894
55–64	1,784	1,435
65–74	3,200	1,142
75+	3,431	854

12.3   Preparing Line Charts The pet food manufacturer you work for is interested in the results of a recent poll of U.S. pet-owning households. Look at the cat ownership statistics that follow and decide on the most appropriate scale for a chart; then create a line chart of the trends in cat ownership. What conclusions do you draw from the trend you've charted? Draft a paragraph or two discussing the results of this poll and the potential consequences for the pet food business. Support your conclusions by referring readers to your chart.

In 1995, 22 million U.S. households owned cats. In 2000, 24 million households owned cats. In 2005, 28 million households owned a cat. In 2010, 32 million households owned cats.

12.4   Creating Photographs As directed by your instructor, team up with other students, making sure that at least one of you has a digital camera or camera phone capable of downloading images to your word-processing software. Find a busy location on campus or in the surrounding neighborhood, someplace with lots of signs, storefronts, pedestrians, and traffic. Scout out two different photo opportunities, one that maximizes the visual impression of crowding and clutter, and one that minimizes this impression. For the first, assume that you are someone who advocates reducing the crowding and clutter, so you want to show how bad it is. For the second, assume that you are a real estate agent or someone else who is motivated to show people that even though the location offers lots of shopping, entertainment, and other attractions, it's actually a rather calm and quiet neighborhood. Insert the two images in a word-processing document and write a caption for each that emphasizes the two opposite messages just described. Finally, write a brief paragraph, discussing the ethical implications of what you've just done. Have you distorted reality or just presented it in ways that work to your advantage? Have you prevented audiences from gaining the information they would need to make informed decisions?

12.5 Selecting the Right Visual You're preparing the annual report for FretCo Guitar Corporation. For each of the following types of information, select the right chart or visual to illustrate the text. Explain your choices.
   a. Data on annual sales for the past 20 years
   b. Comparison of FretCo sales, product by product (electric guitars, bass guitars, amplifiers, acoustic guitars), for this year and last year
   c. Explanation of how a FretCo acoustic guitar is manufactured
   d. Explanation of how the FretCo Guitar Corporation markets its guitars
   e. Data on sales of FretCo products in each of 12 countries
   f. Comparison of FretCo sales figures with sales figures for three competing guitar makers over the past 10 years

12.6 Preparing Bar Charts Team up with a classmate to design charts based on a comparison of the total tax burden of the U.S. taxpayer with that of people in other nations. One teammate should sketch a horizontal or vertical bar chart, and the other should sketch a pictogram from the estimates that follow. Then exchange charts and analyze how well each conveys the situation of the U.S. taxpayer. Would the bar chart look best with vertical or horizontal bars? Why? What scale is best? How does the symbol used in the pictogram enhance or obscure the meaning or impact of the data? What suggestions can each student make for improving the other's visual aid?

> Estimates show that Swedish taxpayers spend 51 percent of their incomes on taxes, British taxpayers spend 48 percent, French taxpayers spend 37 percent, Japanese taxpayers spend 28 percent, and U.S. taxpayers spend 27 percent.

12.7 Selecting the Right Chart Here are last year's sales figures for the appliance and electronics megastore where you work. Construct charts based on these figures that will help you explain to the store's general manager seasonal variations in each department.

STORE SALES IN 2010 (IN $ THOUSANDS)

MONTH	HOME ELECTRONICS	COMPUTERS	APPLIANCES
January	$68	$39	$36
February	72	34	34
March	75	41	30
April	54	41	28
May	56	42	44
June	49	33	48
July	54	31	43
August	66	58	39
September	62	58	36
October	66	44	33
November	83	48	29
December	91	62	24

12.8 Creating Maps You work for C & S Holdings, a company that operates coin-activated, self-service car washes. Research shows that the farther customers live from a car wash, the less likely they are to visit. You know that 50 percent of customers at each of your car washes live within a 4-mile radius of the location, 65 percent live within 6 miles, 80 percent live within 8 miles, and 90 percent live within 10 miles. C & S's owner wants to open two new car washes in your city and has asked you to prepare a report, recommending locations. Using a map of your city, choose two possible locations for car washes and create a visual depicting the customer base surrounding each location.

12.9 Creating Organization Charts Create an organization chart for your college or university. Start with the school's website to learn the various offices and departments. Figure 1.2 on page 40 can serve as a model for how to structure your chart.

12.10 Creating Line Charts Re-create the line chart in Figure 12.7 on page 387 as a bar chart and as a pie chart. Which of these three formats does the best job of conveying the information? Are any of the formats definitely inappropriate for this information? Explain your answers.

12.11 Selecting the Right Chart With a team of two or three students, brainstorm and then sketch at least three types of charts you can use to compare the gross domestic product (GDP) of ten countries in southeast Asia. You can use any of the graphic ideas presented in the chapter, as well as any ideas or examples you find from other sources.

12.12 Internet Visit the website of the Census and Statistics Department of the Hong Kong Special Administrative Region (http://www.censtatd.gov.hk/home/index.jsp) and follow the link to Hong Kong Statistics. Compare the visual presentations of data in a table, a chart, and a map. Evaluate the effectiveness of the different visuals. Can the information be presented in a different visual?

12.13 Ethical Choices Using a spreadsheet, create a bar chart or line chart, using data you find online or in a business publication. Alter the horizontal and vertical scales in several ways to produce different displays of the original data. How do the alterations distort the information? How might a reader detect whether a chart's scale has been altered?

Expand Your Knowledge

Exploring the Best of the Web

Brush Up on Your Computer-Graphics Skills

http://graphicssoft.about.com

Need some help using graphics software? Get started at the About.com graphics software website. Take the tutorials and learn how to manage fonts, images, and a variety of other graphics-related tasks. View the illustrated demonstrations. Read the instructional articles. Learn how to use the most common file formats for graphics. Expand your knowledge of the basic principles of graphic design. And master some advanced color tips and theory. Don't leave without following the links to recommended books and magazines. Before you leave, answer these questions:

1. What are the most common file formats for online visuals?
2. What does color depth mean in computer visuals?
3. What is dithering, and how can it affect your visuals?

Sharpening Your Career Skills Online

Bovée and Thill's Business Communication Web Search, at http://businesscommunicationblog.com/websearch, is a unique research tool designed specifically for business communication research. Use the Web Search function to find a website, video, PDF document, podcast, or PowerPoint presentation that offers advice on creating effective visuals for documents and presentations. Write a brief e-mail message to your instructor, describing the item that you found and summarizing the career skills information you learned from it.

Planning, Writing, and Completing Reports and Proposals

Printed and online reports (including entire websites) are the major leagues of business communication. Here is where you analyze complex problems, educate audiences, address opportunities in the marketplace, win contracts, and even launch entire companies through compelling business plans. Adapt what you've learned so far to the particular challenges of long-format messages, including some special touches that can make formal reports stand out from the crowd.

Planning Reports and Proposals

Learning Objectives

After studying this chapter, you will be able to

1 Adapt the three-step writing process to reports and proposals

2 Explain the value of a work plan in the development of long reports

3 List the key elements of a business plan

4 Identify three steps you can take to ensure effective organization of online reports and other website content

5 Discuss three major ways to organize analytical reports

6 Explain how to choose an organizational strategy when writing a proposal

Communication Close-up at Kenwood U.S.A.

Kenwood relies heavily on reports to communicate market needs from managers and analysts in the United States to product designers in Japan.

www.kenwoodusa.com

If you've shopped for consumer electronics recently, and some specific feature jumped out at you, it probably wasn't an accident. Electronics companies constantly research consumer preferences to identify the features and capabilities that appeal to buyers looking for the latest in state-of-the art entertainment. As Keith Lehmann, senior vice president at Kenwood U.S.A., explains, "In rapidly changing markets such as consumer electronics, research gives us a road map for the products we need to build for the future, and communication with our customers helps us confirm the results of our research."

Recently, Lehmann's research team analyzed the mobile satellite radio market in the United States and determined that although fewer than 2 million drivers had satellite radio at the time, consumers were definitely enthusiastic about the new technology. The potential for market growth was tremendous, but despite the enthusiasm of Kenwood's marketing group, the product planning team was more cautious. Balancing risk and reward, they had detailed questions and needed more information about competitive offerings, projected prices, and other key issues before they could commit resources to a new product category.

Throughout its 50-plus years of worldwide operations, Kenwood has fostered close relationships with its base of dealers.

This strategy has allowed the company to learn valuable information about specific customer wants and needs. Lehmann's team decided to conduct a comprehensive dealer survey that sought answers to the key questions from the product planners.

The survey ultimately validated Lehmann's convictions that satellite radio was indeed poised for rapid growth. His team was able to convince the product planners that the technology should be prominently featured in Kenwood's new mobile audio components, which enabled the company to capture the leading edge of a significant market trend. As Lehmann said later, "Solid market research and strong communications with both our dealers and customers provide the tools we need to seize emerging product trends in advance of our competitors."[1]

CREATING EFFECTIVE REPORTS AND PROPOSALS

Like other business professionals, Kenwood's Keith Lehmann (profiled in the chapter-opening Communication Close-up) spends a lot of his time preparing reports and proposals. **Reports** are written accounts that objectively communicate information about some aspect of a business. **Informational reports** offer data, facts, feedback, and other types of information, without analysis or recommendations. **Analytical reports** offer both information and analysis, and they can also include recommendations. **Proposals** are a special category of reports that combine information delivery and persuasive communication.

The nature of these reports can vary widely, depending on the circumstances. Some of the reports you write will be voluntary, launched at your own initiative and following whatever structure you find most effective. Other reports will be in response to a manager's or customer's request, and you may or may not receive guidance regarding the organization and content. You'll also write reports that follow strict, specific guidelines for content and layout. You may write some reports only once in your career; others you may write or update annually, monthly, weekly, or even daily.

The purpose and content of business reports varies widely; in some cases you'll follow strict guidelines, but in others the organization and format will be up to you.

Your audience will sometimes be internal, which gives you more freedom to discuss sensitive information with less regard for potential misinterpretation. At other times, your audience might include customers, investors, community members, or news media, any of which can create additional demands as you present company information to such external groups.

Many of your reports will be written for internal audiences, but you're also likely to write reports for a wide range of outside readers.

Finally, your reports will vary widely in length and complexity. You may write one-page, memo-format reports that are simple and straightforward. Or you may write reports that cover complicated subjects, that run into hundreds or even thousands of pages, and that involve multiple writers and an array of technological tools.

No matter what the circumstances, these longer messages require all the skills and knowledge that you've gained throughout this course and will continue to gain on the job. View every business report as an opportunity to demonstrate your understanding of business challenges and your ability to contribute to your organization's success.

APPLYING THE THREE-STEP WRITING PROCESS TO REPORTS AND PROPOSALS

1 LEARNING OBJECTIVE

Adapt the three-step writing process to reports and proposals

By adapting the three-step writing process (see Figure 13.1), you can reduce the time required to write effective reports and still produce documents that make lasting and positive impressions on your audiences. The concepts are the same as those you explored in Chapters 4 through 6 and applied to shorter messages in Chapters 7 through 10. However, the emphasis on various tasks can vary considerably. For instance, planning can take days or weeks for a complex report or proposal.

Part 5 offers in-depth coverage of the three-step writing process for reports and proposals. This chapter discusses planning, Chapter 14 discusses writing, and Chapter 15 covers completing reports and proposals. Because much of the writing process has already been covered in Chapters 4 through 6, Chapters 13 through 15 focus on aspects that require special attention for longer messages.

Analyzing the Situation

The complexity of most reports and the magnitude of the work involved heighten the need to analyze the situation carefully. With an e-mail or another short message, you can change direction halfway through the first draft and perhaps lose only a few minutes of work. In

Given the length and complexity of many reports, it's crucial to define your purpose clearly so you don't waste time with unnecessary rework.

FIGURE 13.1   Three-Step Writing Process for Reports and Proposals
The three-step writing process is especially valuable with reports and proposals.
By guiding your work at each step, the process helps you make the most of the
time and energy you invest.

1   Plan   →

Analyze the Situation
Clarify the problem or
opportunity at hand, define
your purpose, develop an
audience profile, and develop
a work plan.

Gather Information
Determine audience needs
and obtain the information
necessary to satisfy those
needs; conduct a research
project, if necessary.

Select the Right Medium
Choose the best medium for
delivering your message;
consider delivery through
multiple media.

Organize the Information
Define your main idea, limit
your scope, select the direct
or indirect approach, and
outline your content using an
appropriate structure for an
informational report, an
analytical report, or a proposal.

2   Write   →

Adapt to Your Audience
Be sensitive to audience needs
with a "you" attitude, politeness,
positive emphasis, and bias-
free language. Build a strong
relationship with your audience
by establishing your credibility
and projecting your company's
image. Control your style with
a tone and voice appropriate
to the situation.

Compose the Message
Choose strong words that will
help you create effective
sentences and coherent
paragraphs throughout the
introduction, body, and close
of your report or proposal.

3   Complete

Revise the Message
Evaluate content and review
readability, then edit and rewrite
for conciseness and clarity.

Produce the Message
Use effective design elements
and suitable layout for a clean,
professional appearance;
seamlessly combine text and
graphical elements.

Proofread the Message
Review for errors in layout,
spelling, and mechanics.

Distribute the Message
Deliver your report using the
chosen medium; make sure all
documents and all relevant files
are distributed successfully.

contrast, if you change direction halfway through a major report, you could lose days, weeks, or even months. To minimize that chance, pay special attention to your statement of purpose. In addition, for anything beyond the simplest reports, take the time to prepare a work plan before you start writing.

Defining Your Purpose

In some cases, you'll be told the purpose of the report; in others, it's up to you to identify the purpose.

Informational reports often address a predetermined need and must meet specific audience expectations. For example, you may be asked to write reports that verify your company's compliance with government regulations, that summarize sales, or that monitor a process—all of which have audiences who expect certain information in a certain format. With other informational reports, you will need to uncover audience needs before you can define the optimum purpose.

Analytical reports and proposals are almost always written in response to a perceived problem or a perceived opportunity. A clear statement of this problem or opportunity helps frame the communication challenge by identifying *what* you're going to write about, but it's insufficient to guide your writing efforts. To plan effectively, address the problem or opportunity with a clear **statement of purpose** that defines *why* you are preparing the report (see Table 13.1).

The most useful way to phrase your purpose statement is to begin with an infinitive phrase (*to* plus a verb). Using an infinitive phrase encourages you to take control and decide where you're going before you begin. When you choose an infinitive phrase (such as *to*

TABLE 13.1 Problem Statements Versus Purpose Statements

PROBLEM STATEMENT	STATEMENT OF PURPOSE
Our company's market share is steadily declining.	To explore new ways of promoting and selling our products and to recommend the approaches most likely to stabilize our market share.
Our current computer network lacks sufficient bandwidth and cannot be upgraded to meet our future needs.	To analyze various networking options and to recommend the system that will best meet our company's current and future needs.
We need $2 million to launch our new product.	To convince investors that our new business would be a sound investment so that we can obtain desired financing.
Our current operations are too decentralized and expensive.	To justify the closing of the Newark plant and the transfer of East Coast operations to a single Midwest location in order to save the company money

inform, to confirm, to analyze, to persuade, or *to recommend*), you pin down your general goal in preparing the report. Consider these examples for informational reports:

> To update clients on the progress of the research project (progress report)
>
> To develop goals and objectives for the coming year (strategic plan)
>
> To identify customers and explain how the company will serve them (marketing plan)
>
> To submit monthly sales statistics to management (operating report)
>
> To summarize what occurred at the annual sales conference (personal activity report)
>
> To explain building access procedures (policy implementation report)
>
> To submit required information to the Securities and Exchange Commission (compliance report)

Your statement of purpose for an analytical report often needs to be more comprehensive than a statement for an informational report. Linda Moreno, the cost accounting manager for Electrovision, a high-tech company based in Los Gatos, California, was recently asked to find ways of reducing employee travel and entertainment costs. (Her complete report appears in Chapter 15.) Because Moreno was supposed to suggest specific ways to solve a problem, she phrased her statement of purpose accordingly:

> . . . to analyze the T&E [travel and entertainment] budget, evaluate the impact of recent changes in airfares and hotel costs, and suggest ways to tighten management's control over T&E expenses.

If Moreno had been assigned an informational report instead, she might have stated her purpose differently:

> To summarize Electrovision's spending on travel and entertainment

You can see from these two examples how much influence the purpose statement has on the scope of your report. If Moreno's manager had expected her to suggest ways to reduce costs but Moreno had collected only cost data, her report would have failed to meet expectations. Because she was assigned an analytical report rather than an informational report, Moreno had to go beyond merely collecting data; she had to draw conclusions and make recommendations.

Proposals must also be guided by a clear statement of purpose to help you focus on crafting a persuasive message. Here are several examples:

> To secure funding in next year's capital budget for a new conveyor system in the warehouse (funding proposal)
>
> To get management approval to reorganize the North American salesforce (general project proposal)
>
> To secure $2 million in venture capital funding to complete design and production of the new line of titanium mountain bikes (investment proposal as part of a business plan)
>
> To convince CommuniCo to purchase a trial subscription to our latest database offering (sales proposal)

Remember, the more specific your purpose statement, the more useful it will be as a guide to planning your report. Furthermore, always double-check your statement of purpose with the person who authorized the report. After seeing the purpose written down in black and white, the authorizer may decide that the report needs to go in a different direction. Once your statement of purpose is confirmed, you're ready to prepare your work plan.

2 LEARNING OBJECTIVE

Explain the value of a work plan in the development of long reports

A detailed work plan saves time and often helps produce a more effective report.

Preparing Your Work Plan

You're already accustomed to some schedule pressure with school reports. This is good practice for your business career, in which you'll be expected to produce quality reports quickly and efficiently. Carefully thinking out a work plan is the best way to make sure you produce good work on schedule. By identifying all the tasks that must be performed, you ensure that nothing is overlooked.

If you are preparing a work plan for yourself, it can be relatively informal: a simple list of the steps you plan to take and an estimate of their sequence and timing. However, for more complicated projects, particularly those that involve multiple team members, you'll want to prepare a formal, detailed work plan that can guide the performance of many tasks over a span of time. For consultants and others whose work output is a formal report, the work plan can also become the basis for a contract if the proposal is accepted. A formal work plan might include the following elements (especially the first two):

- **Statement of the problem or opportunity.** The problem statement clarifies the challenge you face, helps you (and anyone working with you) stay focused on the core issues, and helps everyone avoid the distractions that are likely to arise along the way.
- **Statement of the purpose and scope of your investigation.** The purpose statement describes what you plan to accomplish and therefore also defines the boundaries of your work. Delineating which subjects you will cover and which you won't is especially important for complex investigations.
- **Discussion of tasks to be accomplished.** For simple reports, the list of tasks to be accomplished will be short and probably obvious. However, longer reports and complex investigations require an exhaustive list so that you can reserve time with customers, with executives, or for outside services, such as market researchers or print shops.
- **Description of any additional products or activities that will result from your investigation.** In many cases, the only outcome of your efforts will be the report itself. In other cases, you'll need to produce something or perform some task in addition to completing the report. Make such expectations clear at the outset.
- **Review of project assignments, schedules, and resource requirements.** Indicate who will be responsible for what, when tasks will be completed, and how much the investigation will cost. If more than one person will be involved, you may also want to include a brief section on coordinating report writing and production, such as whether you'll use a wiki to develop the report content. If constraints on time, money, personnel, or data are likely to affect the quality of the report, identify these limitations up front.
- **Plans for following up after delivering the report.** Follow-up can be as simple as making sure people received the information they need or as complex as conducting

additional research to evaluate the results of proposals included in your report. Even informal follow-up can help you improve your future reports and communicate that you care about your work's effectiveness and its impact on the organization.

- **Working outline.** Some work plans include a tentative outline of the report, as does the plan in Figure 13.2.

Gathering Information

You may have to draw on a variety of techniques to gather the information required to meet audience needs. For instance, the market researchers at Kenwood U.S.A. (see page 410) gather information in numerous ways, from conducting surveys and one-on-one interviews

Some reports require formal research projects in order to gather all the necessary information.

FIGURE 13.2 Work Plan for a Report
A formal work plan such as this is a vital tool for planning and managing complex writing projects. The preliminary outline here helps guide the research; the report writers may modify the outline when they begin writing the report.

Clearly and succinctly defines the problem

Explains how the researchers will find the data and information they need

Clearly lists responsibilities and due dates

Identifies exactly what will be covered by the research and in the final report

Offers a preliminary outline with sufficient detail to guide the research and set reader expectations

STATEMENT OF THE PROBLEM
The rapid growth of our company over the past five years has reduced the sense of community among our staff. People no longer feel like part of an intimate organization that values teamwork.

PURPOSE AND SCOPE OF WORK
The purpose of this study is to determine whether social networking technology such as Facebook and Socialtext would help rebuild a sense of community within the workforce and whether encouraging the use of such tools in the workplace will have any negative consequences. The study will attempt to assess the impact of social networks in other companies in terms of community-building, morale, project communication, and overall productivity.

SOURCES AND METHODS OF DATA COLLECTION
Data collection will start with secondary research, including a review of recently published articles and studies on the use of social networking in business and a review of product information published by technology vendors. Primary research will focus on an employee and management survey to uncover attitudes about social networking tools. We will also collect anecdotal evidence from bloggers and others with experience using networks in the workplace.

PRELIMINARY OUTLINE
The preliminary outline for this study is as follows:
    I. What experiences have other companies had with social networks in the workplace?
        A. Do social networks have a demonstrable business benefit?
        B. How do employees benefit from using these tools?
        C. Has network security and information confidentiality been an issue?
    II. Is social networking an appropriate solution for our community-building needs?
        A. Is social networking better than other tools and methods for community building?
        B. Are employees already using social networking tools on the job?
        C. Will a company-endorsed system distract employees from essential duties?
        D. Will a company system add to managerial workloads in any way?
    III. If we move ahead, should we use a "business-class" network such as Socialtext or a consumer tool such as Facebook?
        A. How do the initial and ongoing costs compare?
        B. Do the additional capabilities of a business-class network justify the higher costs?
    IV. How should we implement a social network?
        A. Should we let it grow "organically," with employees choosing their own tools and groups?
        B. Should we make a variety of tools available and let employees improvise on their own
        C. Should we designate one system as the official company social network and make it a permanent, supported element of the information technology infrastructure?
    VI. How can we evaluate the success of a new social network?
        A. What are the criteria of success or failure?
        B. What is the best way to measure these criteria?

TASK ASSIGNMENTS AND SCHEDULE
Each phase of this study will be completed by the following dates:

Secondary research: Hank Waters	September 15, 2010
Employee and management survey: Julienne Cho	September 22, 2010
Analysis and synthesis of research: Hank Waters/Julienne Cho	October 6, 2010
Comparison of business and consumer solutions: Julienne Cho	October 13, 2010
Comparison of implementation strategies: Hank Waters	October 13, 2010
Final report: Hank Waters	October 20, 2010

to getting anecdotal feedback from consumers and retailers, combing through industry publications, and checking competitors' marketing materials.[2]

The sheer volume of information in most reports and proposals requires careful planning—and may even require a separate research project just to get the data and information you need. As Chapter 11 emphasizes, you should prioritize your information needs before you start and focus on the most important questions. Whenever possible, try to reuse or adapt existing information to save time.

Selecting the Right Medium

In some situations, you may be required to use a specific medium for your reports.

In addition to the general media selection criteria discussed in Chapter 4, consider several points for reports and proposals. Start with what you know about audience expectations. In some situations, audiences have specific media requirements, and you might not have a choice. For instance, executives in many corporations now expect to review reports via their in-house intranets, sometimes in conjunction with an *executive dashboard*, a customized online presentation of key operating variables such as revenue, profits, quality, customer satisfaction, and project progress.

Expect to deliver many or most of your reports in electronic format.

In other situations, your audience might be more flexible but still have preferences. If an audience of several managers is likely to make comments on your report, would the managers rather write on a paper copy or use the revision features in a word-processing file? Will you or someone else be revising or updating the report? Given the multiple benefits of electronic reports (including low distribution costs, searchability, and easy archiving), expect to deliver many or even most of your reports in electronic format in the future.

Consider delivering your report via multiple media, too. For instance, even the best-written reports can often benefit from in-person communication. To ensure effective communication, Kenwood employees in the United States and Japan discuss their reports frequently, via both teleconferences and meetings in both countries. Again, the decision comes down to a balance of what's best for both you and your audience.

Whatever you decide, bear in mind that your choice of medium also sends a message. A proposal that requests a venture capital investment of $5 million would look unimpressive as just a plain word-processing document. Conversely, a routine operating report dressed up in expensive multimedia will look like a waste of valuable company resources.

Organizing Your Information

Most business reports use the direct approach.

The length and complexity of most reports and proposals require extra emphasis on clear, reader-oriented organization. Your readers might have the patience to struggle through a short disorganized e-mail message but not through a poorly organized 200-page report. As Chapter 4 discusses, when an audience is likely to be receptive or at least open-minded, use the direct approach: Lead with a summary of your key findings, conclusions, recommendations, or proposal, whichever is relevant. This "up-front" arrangement is by far the most popular and convenient for business reports. It saves time and makes the rest of the report easier to follow. For those who have questions or want more information, later parts of the report provide complete findings and supporting details. The direct approach also produces a more forceful report. You sound sure of yourself when you state your conclusions confidently at the outset.

Use the indirect approach when you need to build support for your main idea or you want to avoid coming across as arrogant.

At times, however, confidence may be misconstrued as arrogance. If you're a junior member of a status-conscious organization, or if your audience is skeptical or hostile, consider the indirect approach: Introduce your complete findings and discuss all supporting details before presenting your conclusions and recommendations. The indirect approach gives you a chance to prove your points and gradually overcome your audience's reservations. By deferring the conclusions and recommendations to the end of your report, you imply that you've weighed the evidence objectively. You also imply that you're subordinating your judgment to that of the audience, whose members are capable of drawing their own conclusions when they have access to all the facts.

Although the indirect approach has advantages, some readers will always be in a hurry to get to the answer and will immediately flip to the recommendations anyway, thus defeating your purpose. Therefore, consider length before choosing the direct or indirect approach. In general, the longer the message, the less effective an indirect approach is likely to be.

FIGURE 13.3 Direct Approach Versus Indirect Approach in an Introduction
In the direct version of this introduction, the writer quickly presents the report's recommendation, followed by the conclusions that led to that recommendation. In the indirect version, the same topics are introduced in the same order, but no conclusions are drawn about them (the conclusions and the ultimate recommendation appear later, in the body of the report).

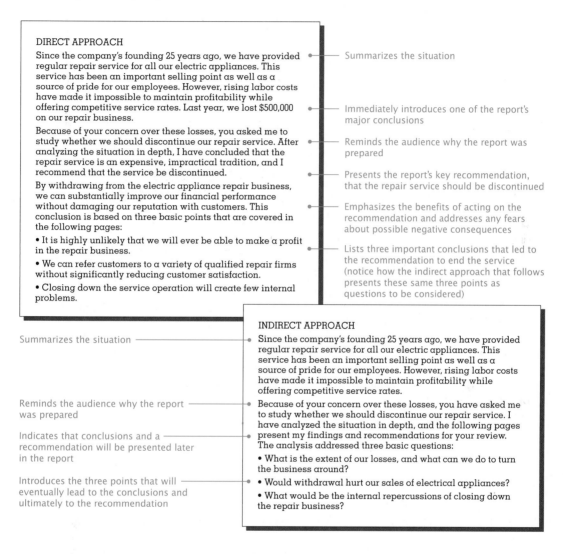

Because both direct and indirect approaches have merit, businesspeople often combine them. They reveal their conclusions and recommendations as they go along rather than put them either first or last. Figure 13.3 presents the introductions from two reports that follow the same general outline. In the direct version, a series of statements summarizes the conclusion reached in relation to each main topic on the outline. In the indirect version, the same topics are introduced in the same order but without drawing any conclusions about them. Instead, the conclusions appear within the body of the report.

Long reports sometimes combine direct and indirect approaches, building support for interim conclusions or recommendations along the way.

Regardless of the format, length, or order of your report, you must decide how your ideas will be subdivided and developed. Take care to choose the most logical argument structure—one that suits your topic and goals and that makes sense to your audience.

Regardless of how you structure your argument, keep the following points in mind when organizing a report or proposal:

- **Understand and meet audience expectations.** Certain audiences expect or even require a specific organization, and your report might be rejected if it doesn't meet those requirements. Other audiences give you room for some flexibility, as long as your

Audience expectations are one of the most important considerations when deciding on the organization of a report.

TABLE 13.2 Types of Outline Headings

DESCRIPTIVE (TOPICAL) OUTLINE	INFORMATIVE (TALKING) OUTLINE	
	QUESTION FORM	SUMMARY FORM

I. Industry Characteristics
  A. Annual sales
  B. Profitability
  C. Growth rate
    1. Sales
    2. Profit
	I. What is the nature of the industry?
	  A. What are the annual sales?
	  B. Is the industry profitable?
	  C. What is the pattern of growth?
	    1. Sales growth?
	    2. Profit growth?
		I. Flour milling is a mature industry.
		  A. Market is large.
		  B. Profit margins are narrow.
		  C. Growth is modest.
		    1. Sales growth averages less than 3 percent a year.
		    2. Profits are flat.

report contains the right categories of information. Whenever possible, study an example of a successful report before writing a similar one.

- **Select a format that's appropriate to the task.** For reports of five pages or less, a memo or letter (or an electronic equivalent) is often sufficient. For longer reports, you'll want to include many of the elements of a formal report, which you'll read about in Chapter 15.
- **Keep it as short as possible.** Your readers will appreciate your brevity, and you'll stand a better chance of getting your message across.
- **"Talk" your way through your outline.** When you outline your content, use informative ("talking") headings rather than simple descriptive ("topical") headings (see Table 13.2). With question or summary form, informative headings force you to really think through the content rather than simply identify the general topic area. Using informative headings also facilitates collaborative writing by reducing ambiguity about what each person needs to write.

For a quick review of adapting the three-step process to long reports, refer to "Checklist: Adapting the Three-Step Process to Reports and Proposals." The following sections provide specific advice on how to plan informational reports, analytical reports, and proposals.

PLANNING INFORMATIONAL REPORTS

Informational reports are used to monitor and control operations, to implement policies and procedures, to demonstrate compliance, and to document progress.

Informational reports provide the information that employees, managers, and others need in order to make decisions and take action. Although dozens of particular formats exist, they can be grouped into four general categories:

- **Reports to monitor and control operations.** Just as doctors rely on medical reports to see how well the various systems in a patient's body are functioning, business managers

✓ CHECKLIST: Adapting the Three-Step Process to Reports and Proposals

A. Analyze the situation.
- Clearly define your purpose before you start writing.
- If you need to accomplish several goals in the report, identify them all in advance.
- Prepare a work plan to guide your efforts.

B. Gather information.
- Determine whether you need to launch a separate research project to collect the necessary information.
- Reuse or adapt existing material whenever possible.

C. Select the right medium.
- Base your decision on audience expectations (or requirements, as the case may be).

- Consider the need for commenting, revising, distributing, and storing.
- Remember that the medium you choose also sends a message.

D. Organize your information.
- Use the direct approach if your audience is receptive.
- Use the indirect approach if your audience is skeptical.
- Use the indirect approach when you don't want to risk coming across as arrogant.
- Combine approaches if doing so will help build support for your primary message.

rely on a wide range of reports to see how well the various systems in their companies are functioning. *Plans* establish expectations and guidelines to direct future action (see "Creating Successful Business Plans" below). *Operating reports* provide feedback on a wide variety of an organization's functions, including sales, inventories, expenses, shipments, and other aspects of company operations. *Personal activity reports* provide information regarding an individual's experiences during sales calls, industry conferences, market research trips, and other activities.

- **Reports to implement policies and procedures.** Reports are the most common vehicle for conveying guidelines, approved procedures, and other organizational decisions. *Policy reports* outline procedures that employees are expected to follow. *Position papers* are a special type of policy report that outlines an individual executive's (or the entire organization's) official position on issues that affect a company's success.

- **Reports to demonstrate compliance.** Even the smallest businesses are required to show that they are in compliance with government regulations of one sort or another. Some compliance reports, such as quarterly and annual tax reports, affect all businesses. Others concern particular industries, companies using hazardous materials, specific professional functions, or other special factors. Compliance reports are usually created in specific formats that must be followed precisely.

- **Reports to document progress.** Progress reports range from simple updates to comprehensive reports that include such elements as measured progress toward goals, comparisons of budgeted versus actual expenses, and lists of ongoing concerns and risks.

Progress reports range from simple, informal updates to comprehensive status reports.

Figure 13.4 shows the major subcategories within each of the major report categories, along with examples of the most common types. Specific titles may vary, depending on the company you're with, but chances are you'll be called on to read nearly every one of these report types—and to write many of them, too.

Organizational Strategies for Informational Reports

Let the nature of whatever you're describing dictate your structure. Informational reports use a **topical organization**, arranging material according to one of the following topics:

A topical organization is built around the content itself, using such arrangements as comparison, importance, sequence, chronology, spatial orientation, geography, or category.

- **Comparison.** If you need to show similarities and differences (or advantages and disadvantages) between two or more entities, organize your report in a way that helps your readers see those similarities and differences clearly.
- **Importance.** If you're reviewing five product lines, you might organize your study according to the sales for each product line, beginning with the line that produces the most revenue and proceeding to the one that produces the least.
- **Sequence.** If you're studying a process, discuss it step by step, in sequence.
- **Chronology.** When investigating a chain of events, organize the study according to what happened in January, what happened in February, and so on.
- **Spatial orientation.** If you're explaining how a physical object works or how a physical space looks, describe it from left to right (or right to left, in some cultures), top to bottom, or outside to inside—in whatever order makes the most sense; just be consistent.
- **Geography.** If location is important, organize your study according to geography, such as by country or by state or province.
- **Category.** If you're asked to review several distinct aspects of a subject, look at one category at a time, such as sales, profit, cost, or investment.

Whichever pattern you choose, use it consistently so that readers can easily follow your discussion from start to finish. Of course, certain reports (such as compliance or monitor-and-control reports) must follow a prescribed flow.

Creating Successful Business Plans

The most important report you may ever get a chance to write is the business plan for a new venture. A comprehensive business plan forces you to think about personnel, marketing, facilities, suppliers, distribution, and a host of other issues vital to your success. If you are starting out on a small scale and using your own money, your business plan may be

3 LEARNING OBJECTIVE

List the key elements of a business plan

FIGURE 13.4 Common Types of Business Reports and Proposals
You will have the opportunity to read and write many types of reports in your career;
here are some of the most common.

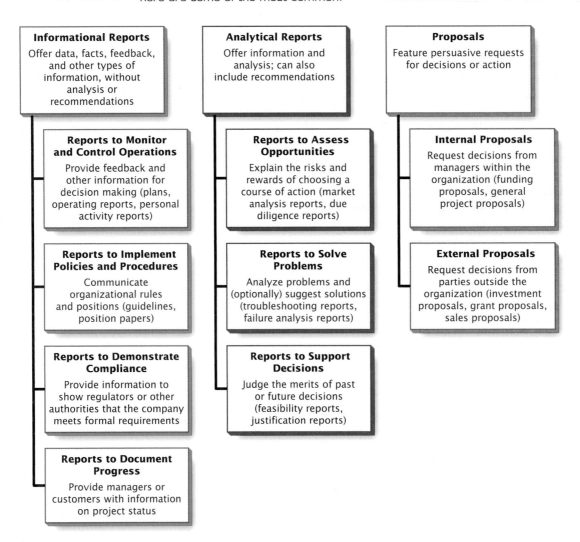

relatively informal. But at a minimum, you should describe the basic concept of the business and outline its specific goals, objectives, and resource requirements. A more formal plan, which is absolutely a necessity when you want to persuade other people to invest in or join your organization, should cover these points:[3]

Formal business plans, particularly those used to solicit outside investment, must meet a specific set of reader expectations.

- **Summary.** In one or two pages, summarize your business concept, particularly the *business model*, which defines how the company will generate revenue and produce a profit. Describe your product or service and its market potential. Highlight some things about your company and its leaders that will distinguish your firm from the competition. Summarize your financial projections and the amount of money investors can expect to make on their investment. Indicate how much money you will need from investors or lenders and where it will be spent.
- **Mission and objectives.** Explain the purpose of your business and what you hope to accomplish—and make sure this is a mission you can pursue with passion, through thick and thin, with every ounce of commitment and energy you can muster.
- **Company and industry.** Give full background information on the origins and structure of your venture and the characteristics of the industry in which you plan to compete.
- **Products or services.** Concisely describe your products or services, focusing on their unique attributes and their appeal to customers.

- **Market and competition.** Provide data that will persuade investors that you understand your target market and can achieve your sales goals. Be sure to identify the strengths and weaknesses of your competitors.
- **Management.** Summarize the background and qualifications of the key management personnel in your company. Include résumés in an appendix.
- **Marketing strategy.** Provide projections of sales volume and market share; outline a strategy for identifying and reaching potential customers, setting prices, providing customer support, and physically delivering your products or services. Whenever possible, include evidence of customer acceptance, such as advance product orders.
- **Design and development plans.** If your product requires design or development, describe the nature and extent of what needs to be done, including costs and possible problems. For new or unusual products, you may want to explain how the product will be manufactured.
- **Operations plan.** Provide information on facilities, equipment, and personnel requirements.
- **Overall schedule.** Forecast important milestones in the company's growth and development, including when you need to be fully staffed and when your products will be ready for the market.
- **Critical risks and problems.** Identify all negative factors and discuss them honestly.
- **Financial projections and requirements.** Include a detailed budget of start-up and operating costs, as well as projections for income, expenses, and cash flow for the first few years of business. Identify the company's financing needs and potential sources, if appropriate.
- **Exit strategy.** Explain how investors will be able to profit from their investment, such as through a public stock offering, sale of the company, or a buyback of the investors' interest.

Creating a complete business plan requires a considerable amount of work. However, by thinking your way through all these issues, you'll enjoy a smoother launch and a greater chance of success in your new adventure.

Organizing Website Content

Many websites, particularly company websites, function as informational reports, offering sections with information about the company, its history, its products and services, its executive team, and other key subjects. While most of what you've already learned about informational reports applies to website writing, the online experience requires some special considerations and practices.

As you begin to plan a website, start by recognizing the unique nature of online communication:

- **Web readers are demanding.** If your site can't meet readers' needs quickly, most people will move to another site that can. Most visitors won't bother to dig for information. They scan navigation buttons, headings, images, and hyperlinks, looking for possibilities. If nothing looks promising, they're gone.[4]
- **Reading online can be difficult.** For most people, reading on a computer monitor is more difficult than reading from the printed page. In fact, studies show that reading speeds are about 25 percent slower on a monitor than on paper.[5] Reading from computer screens can also be tiring on the eyes, even to the point of causing headaches, double vision, blurred vision, and other physical problems.[6]
- **The web is a nonlinear, multidimensional medium.** As a web writer, you can't expect your readers to follow a predefined path. Readers of printed reports can skim and skip through the material, of course, but the general scheme of reading proceeds in a linear fashion from the beginning, through the middle, to the end. In contrast, the navigational flexibility of the web makes it easy for readers to jump around in any direction, as they follow interesting links or search for specific content.

---

4 **LEARNING OBJECTIVE**

Identify three steps you can take to ensure effective organization of online reports and other website content

Although many websites and website sections function as information reports, the unique nature of online communication requires special consideration.

As you move on to define your purpose, bear in mind that most websites have to perform more than one communication function. Consequently, a single website could have a half-dozen purposes or more. Each of these individual purposes needs to be carefully defined and then integrated into an overall statement of purpose for the entire website. Then, as you develop the site, you'll need to clearly identify the specific purpose of each section of the site so that readers always know where to find the information they need.[7]

A typical company website has multiple purposes and multiple audiences that need to be addressed during the planning process.

Just as you probably will have a number of purposes for a single website, you're likely to have a number of audiences as well. The global reach of the web further complicates the audience analysis issue because you may get visitors from all parts of the world. After you've identified your multiple audiences, you need to analyze each group's unique information needs and then find a logical way to organize all that material. Professional website designers often use the term **information architecture** to describe the structure and navigational flow of all the parts of a website. In a sense, the information architecture is a three-dimensional outline of the site, showing (1) the vertical hierarchy of pages from the homepage down to the lower level; (2) the horizontal division of pages across the various sections of the site; and (3) the links that tie all these pages together, both internally (between various pages on the site) and externally (between your site and other websites).

As you develop the site architecture, you can begin to simulate how various audiences will use the site and refine the plan to meet everyone's needs (see Figure 13.5). For instance, can potential customers find new product information quickly? And can existing customers get support or warranty information quickly, without wading through pages of promotion for new products? You can also get a sense of how you'll need to assist visitors who enter the

FIGURE 13.5 Information Architecture
A carefully designed website considers the diverse needs of the target audience.

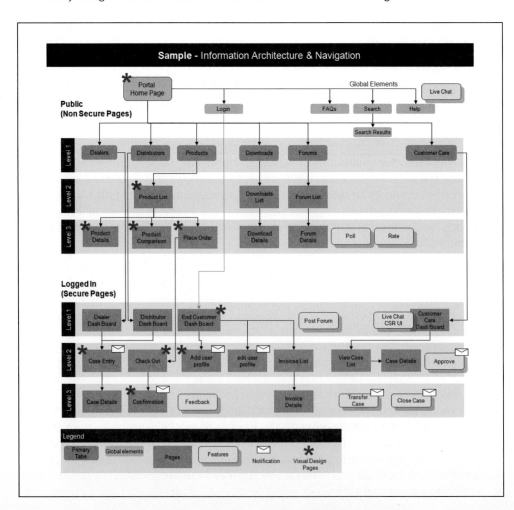

site at points other than the homepage, as often happens with search engine links. Accommodating these multiple entry points is one of the most difficult tasks in site design.[8]

To organize your site effectively, keep the following advice in mind:

- **Plan your navigation first.** Don't make the mistake of writing a traditional report and then adding some links to make it a website. To ensure that readers will be able to navigate your material effectively and efficiently, plan your site structure and navigation before you write.[9]
- **Let your readers be in control.** Help your readers get oriented by starting with a homepage that clearly points the way to various sections of the site; then offer plenty of descriptive labels, subheads, and other devices that let readers create their own paths through the site.
- **Break your information into chunks.** Help online readers scan and absorb information by breaking it into self-contained, easily readable chunks that are linked together logically. By doing so, you can provide comprehensive coverage that is easy to consume online.

Map out the various paths that different types of users are likely to take through your website and then develop content to fit this structure.

Effective Informational Reports: An Example

Effective informational reports are clearly and logically organized, with audience-centered content and generous use of previews and summaries. They are complete, without being unnecessarily long or detailed. One of the tasks your audience expects you to accomplish is to sort out the details and separate major points from minor points. In other words, readers expect you to take the time and effort needed to make the best use of their time. In addition, effective reports are honest and objective but not unduly harsh whenever negative information must be conveyed. Compare the differences between the report versions shown in Figures 13.6 and 13.7.

PLANNING ANALYTICAL REPORTS

The purpose of analytical reports is to analyze, to understand, to explain—to think through a problem or an opportunity and figure out how it affects the company and how the company should respond. In many cases, you'll also be expected to make a recommendation based on your analysis. As you saw in Figure 13.4, analytical reports fall into three basic categories:

- **Reports to assess opportunities.** Every business opportunity carries some degree of risk and also requires a variety of decisions and actions in order to capitalize on the opportunity. For instance, *market analysis reports* are used to judge the likelihood of success for new products or sales initiatives by identifying potential opportunities as well as competitive threats and other risks. *Due diligence reports* examine the financial aspects of a proposed decision, such as acquiring another company.
- **Reports to solve problems.** Managers often assign *troubleshooting reports* when they need to understand why something isn't working properly and what can be done to fix the situation. A variation, the *failure analysis report*, studies events that happened in the past, with the hope of learning how to avoid similar failures in the future.
- **Reports to support decisions.** *Feasibility reports* are called for when managers need to explore the ramifications of a decision they're about to make (such as replacing an advertising agency or switching materials used in a manufacturing process). *Justification reports* justify a decision that has already been made.

Analytical reports are used to assess opportunities, to solve problems, and to support decisions.

Writing analytical reports presents a greater challenge than writing informational reports, for three reasons. First, you're doing more than simply delivering information; you're also thinking through a problem or an opportunity and presenting your conclusions. The best writing in the world can't compensate for flawed analysis. Second, when your analysis is complete, you need to present your thinking in a credible manner. Third, analytical reports often convince other people to make significant financial and personnel decisions, so your reports carry the added responsibility of the consequences of these decisions.

FIGURE 13.6 Ineffective Informational Report
While this report looks professional at first glance, it contains a number of weaknesses in tone, content, and formatting. Compare with Figure 13.7.

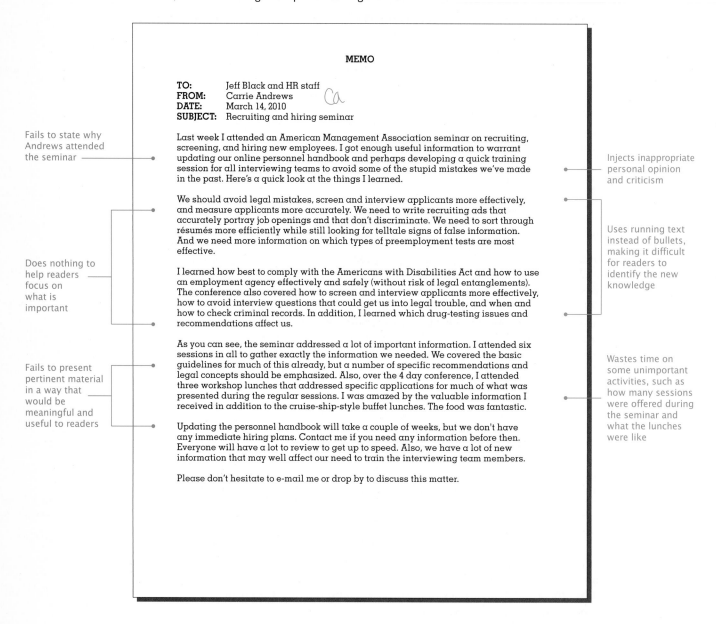

Fails to state why Andrews attended the seminar

Does nothing to help readers focus on what is important

Fails to present pertinent material in a way that would be meaningful and useful to readers

Injects inappropriate personal opinion and criticism

Uses running text instead of bullets, making it difficult for readers to identify the new knowledge

Wastes time on some unimportant activities, such as how many sessions were offered during the seminar and what the lunches were like

In some situations, the problem or opportunity you address in an analytical report may be defined by the person who authorizes the report. In other cases, you will have to define it yourself. Be careful not to confuse a simple topic (quarterly profits) with a problem (the decline in profits over the past six quarters). Moreover, if you're the only person who thinks a particular issue is a problem, your readers won't be interested in your solution unless your report first convinces them that a problem exists. Sometimes you need to "sell the problem" before you can sell the solution.

To help define the problem that your analytical report will address, answer these questions:

- What needs to be determined?
- Why is this issue important?
- Who is involved in the situation?
- Where is the trouble located?

Clarify the problem in an analytical report by determining what you need to analyze, why the issue is important, who is involved, where the trouble is located, and how and when the trouble started.

FIGURE 13.7 Effective Informational Report
This version of the report shown in Figure 13.6 is much easier to read and presents pertinent information in a clear, concise way.

States Andrews's reason for attending the seminar

Uses lists to help readers focus on key points

Concludes with information that the recipients need, along with an estimate of when it will be available

Captures reader interest with descriptive subject line

Respects readers' time by not including irrelevant information

- How did the situation originate?
- When did it start?

Not all these questions apply in every situation, but asking them helps you define the problem being addressed and limit the scope of your discussion.

Another effective way to tackle a complex problem is to divide it into a series of logical, connected questions, a process sometimes called **problem factoring**. You probably subconsciously approach most problems this way. When your car won't start, what do you do? You use the available evidence to organize your investigation, to start a search for cause-and-effect relationships. For example, if the engine doesn't turn over at all, you might suspect a dead battery. If the engine does turn over but won't fire, you can conclude that the battery

Use problem factoring to divide a complex problem into more manageable pieces.

TABLE 13.3 Common Ways to Structure Analytical Reports

ELEMENT	FOCUS ON CONCLUSIONS OR RECOMMENDATIONS	FOCUS ON LOGICAL ARGUMENT	
		USE 2 + 2 = 4 APPROACH	USE YARDSTICK APPROACH
Reader mindset	Are likely to accept	Hostile or skeptical	Hostile or skeptical
Approach	Direct	Indirect	Indirect
Writer credibility	High	Low	Low
Advantages	Readers quickly grasp conclusions or recommendations	Works well when you need to show readers how you built toward an answer by following clear logical steps	Works well when you have a list of criteria (standards) that must be considered in a decision; alternatives are all measured against the same criteria
Drawbacks	Structure can make topic seem too simple	Can make report longer	Readers must agree on criteria; can be lengthy because of the need to address each criterion for every alternative

is okay, but perhaps you're out of gas. When you speculate on the cause of a problem, you're forming a **hypothesis**, a potential explanation that needs to be tested. By subdividing a problem and forming hypotheses based on available evidence, you can tackle even the most complex situations. With a clear picture of the problem or opportunity in mind, you're ready to consider the best structure for your report.

Organizational Strategies for Analytical Reports

To create powerful analytical reports, consider your audience's likely reaction before choosing the most effective organizational strategy. When you expect your audience to agree with you, use the direct approach to focus attention on conclusions and recommendations. When you expect your audience to disagree with you or to be hostile, use the indirect approach to focus attention on the rationale behind your conclusions and recommendations.

Before you choose an approach, determine whether your audience is receptive or skeptical.

The three most common structural approaches for analytical reports are focusing on conclusions (direct), focusing on recommendations (direct), and focusing on logical arguments (indirect). See Table 13.3.

5 LEARNING OBJECTIVE

Discuss three major ways to organize analytical reports

Focusing on Conclusions

If you have already established credibility in the eyes of your target readers, and they're likely to accept your conclusions—whatever they may be—you can structure your report around those conclusions, using the direct approach (see Figure 13.8). However, the direct approach does have some risks. If your readers have reservations about you or your material, strong statements at the beginning may put them on the defensive. Also, focusing on conclusions may make everything you say seem too simple. Your readers could criticize your report as being superficial: "Why didn't you consider this angle?" or "Where did you get this number?"

Focusing on conclusions is often the best approach when you're addressing a receptive audience.

You can use a similar structure whether you're asked to analyze a problem or an opportunity. Readers who are interested mainly in your conclusions can grasp them quickly, and readers who want to know more about your analysis can look at the data you provide.

Focusing on Recommendations

In some situations, you'll be asked to provide advice on solving a problem or approaching an opportunity rather than simply analyze it. You can present your recommendations using a series of five steps:

When readers want to know what you think they should do, organize your report to focus on recommendations.

1. Establish or verify the need for action in the introduction by briefly describing the problem or opportunity.
2. Introduce the benefit that can be achieved, without providing any details.

FIGURE 13.8   Preliminary Outline of a Research Report Focusing on Conclusions
Cynthia Zolonka works on the human resources staff of a bank in Houston, Texas. Her company decided to have an outside firm handle its employee training, and a year after the outsourcing arrangement was established, Zolonka was asked to evaluate the results. Her analysis shows that the outsourcing experiment was a success, and she opens with that conclusion and supports it with clear evidence. Readers who accept the conclusion can stop reading, and those who desire more information can continue.

Opens with the conclusion that the program is a success

Supports the conclusion with evidence from two key areas

Completes the story by highlighting areas that still need improvement

MEASURING QUALITY IMPROVEMENTS

   I.   Introduction

   II.   Conclusion: Outsourcing employee training has reduced costs and improved quality

   III.   Cost reductions

      A. Exceeded 15 percent cost-reduction goal with 22 percent savings in first year

      B. Achieved actual reduction of 22 percent

      C. Reassigned three staffers who used to work on training full-time

      D. Reduced management time needed to oversee training

      E. Sold the computers that used to be reserved for training

   IV.   Quality improvements

      A. Employees say they are more confident in 7 out of 10 key skill areas

      B. Measurable mistakes have dropped by 12 percent

   V.   Areas needing improvement

      A. Three skill areas still need improvement

      B. Two trainers received approval ratings below 80 percent

      C. Outside trainers aren't always aware of internal company issues

      D. We have lost some flexibility for scheduling courses

   VI.   Summary

3. List the steps (recommendations) required to achieve the benefit, using action verbs for emphasis.
4. Explain each step more fully, giving details on procedures, costs, and benefits.
5. Summarize your recommendations.

If your recommendation carries any risks, be sure to clearly address them. Doing so not only makes your report more ethical but also offers you some protection in the event that your recommendation is implemented but doesn't work out as you had hoped. In short, make sure your readers know both the potential disadvantages and the potential benefits.

Whenever a recommendation carries some element of risk, you owe it to your audience to make this clear.

Focusing on Logical Arguments

When readers are likely to be skeptical or hostile to the conclusion or recommendation you plan to make, use the indirect approach. If you guide audience members along a logical path toward the answer, they are more likely to accept it when they encounter it. The two most common logical approaches are known as the *2 + 2 = 4 approach* and the *yardstick approach*.

Two common logical arguments are the 2 + 2 = 4 approach (adding everything up) and the yardstick approach (comparing solutions against criteria).

The 2 + 2 = 4 Approach   The **2 + 2 = 4 approach** is so named because it convinces readers of your point of view by demonstrating that everything adds up. The main points in your outline are the main reasons behind your conclusions and recommendations. You support each reason with the evidence you collected during your analysis.

Start by considering using the 2 + 2 = 4 approach; it's familiar and easy to develop.

Because of its natural feel and versatility, the 2 + 2 = 4 approach is generally the most persuasive and efficient way to develop an analytical report for skeptical readers. When organizing your own reports, try this structure first. You'll find that many business situations lend themselves nicely to this pattern of logical argumentation.

The yardstick approach compares a solution or several solutions to a set of predetermined standards.

The Yardstick Approach   The **yardstick approach** is useful when you need to use a number of criteria to evaluate one or more possible solutions. These criteria become the "yardstick" by which you measure the various alternatives. With this approach, you begin by discussing the problem or opportunity and then list the criteria that will guide the decision. The body of the report then evaluates the alternatives against those criteria. The main points of the outline are either the criteria themselves or the alternatives (see Figure 13.9).

The yardstick approach is particularly useful for proposals when the audience has provided a list of criteria the solution must meet. Say that your company has been asked to bid on a contract to design and install a factory-floor distribution system for a large corporation. The client has listed the requirements (criteria) for the system, and you've developed a

FIGURE 13.9   Outline of an Analytical Report Using the Yardstick Approach
This outline was prepared by J. C. Hartley, a market analyst for a large Sacramento company that makes irrigation equipment for farms and ranches. "We've been so successful in the agricultural market that we're starting to run out of customers to sell to," says Hartley. "To keep the company growing, we needed to find another market. Two obvious choices to consider were commercial buildings and residences," so she structured her report to compare these two opportunities.

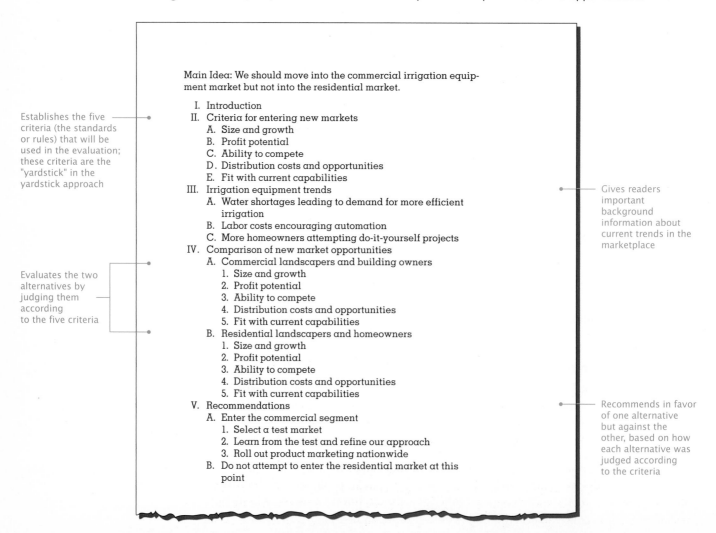

Main Idea: We should move into the commercial irrigation equipment market but not into the residential market.

I. Introduction
II. Criteria for entering new markets
   A. Size and growth
   B. Profit potential
   C. Ability to compete
   D. Distribution costs and opportunities
   E. Fit with current capabilities
III. Irrigation equipment trends
   A. Water shortages leading to demand for more efficient irrigation
   B. Labor costs encouraging automation
   C. More homeowners attempting do-it-yourself projects
IV. Comparison of new market opportunities
   A. Commercial landscapers and building owners
     1. Size and growth
     2. Profit potential
     3. Ability to compete
     4. Distribution costs and opportunities
     5. Fit with current capabilities
   B. Residential landscapers and homeowners
     1. Size and growth
     2. Profit potential
     3. Ability to compete
     4. Distribution costs and opportunities
     5. Fit with current capabilities
V. Recommendations
   A. Enter the commercial segment
     1. Select a test market
     2. Learn from the test and refine our approach
     3. Roll out product marketing nationwide
   B. Do not attempt to enter the residential market at this point

Establishes the five criteria (the standards or rules) that will be used in the evaluation; these criteria are the "yardstick" in the yardstick approach

Evaluates the two alternatives by judging them according to the five criteria

Gives readers important background information about current trends in the marketplace

Recommends in favor of one alternative but against the other, based on how each alternative was judged according to the criteria preliminary design to meet them. In the body of your proposal, you could use the client's list of requirements as the main headings and under each one explain how your preliminary design meets the requirement.

The yardstick approach has two potential drawbacks. First, your audience members need to agree with the criteria you're using in your analysis. If they don't, they won't agree with the results of the evaluation. If you have any doubt about their agreement, build consensus before you start your report, if possible, or take extra care to explain why the criteria you're using are the best ones in this particular case. Second, the yardstick approach can get tedious when you have many options to consider or many criteria to compare them against. One way to minimize the repetition is to compare the options in tables and then highlight the most unusual or important aspects of each alternative in the text so that you get the best of both worlds. This approach allows you to compare all the alternatives against the same yardstick while calling attention to the most significant differences among them.

Effective Analytical Reports: An Example

As national sales manager of a New Hampshire sporting goods company, Binh Phan was concerned about his company's ability to sell to its largest customers. His boss, the vice president of marketing, shared these concerns and asked Phan to analyze the situation and recommend a solution. As Phan says, "We sell to retail chains across the country. Large nationwide chains of superstores have been revolutionizing the industry, but we haven't had as much success with these big customers as we've had with smaller companies that operate strictly on a local or regional basis. With more and more of the industry in the hands of the large chains, we knew we had to fix the situation."

Phan's troubleshooting report appears in Figure 13.10. The main idea is that the company should establish separate sales teams for these major accounts rather than continue to service them through the company's four regional divisions. However, Phan knew his plan would be controversial because it requires a big change in the company's organization and in the way sales reps are paid. His thinking had to be clear and easy to follow, so he used the $2 + 2 = 4$ approach to focus on his reasons.

PLANNING PROPOSALS

Proposals are written for both internal and external audiences. Internal proposals request decisions from managers within the organization, such as proposals to buy new equipment or launch new research projects. Examples of external proposals include *investment proposals*, which request funding from external investors; *grant proposals*, which request funds from government agencies and other sponsoring organizations; and *sales proposals*, which suggest individualized solutions for potential customers and request purchase decisions.

The most significant factor in planning any proposal is whether the intended recipient has asked you to submit a proposal. *Solicited proposals* are generally prepared at the request of external parties that require a product or a service, but they may also be requested by such internal sources as management or the board of directors. When organizations require complex products, services, or systems, they often prepare a formal invitation to bid on the contract, called a **request for proposals (RFP)**, which includes instructions that specify exactly the type of work to be performed or products to be delivered, along with budgets, deadlines, and other requirements.

Buyers often solicit proposals by publishing a request for proposals (RFP).

To attract a large pool of qualified bidders, organizations send RFPs to firms with good performance records in the field, print them in trade publications, and post them on the web. U.S. government RFPs, for instance, can be found through Commerce Business Daily, at **www.cbd-net.com**.

To write a proposal in response to an RFP, you begin by reviewing the requirements. Next, you define the scope of the deliverables, determine the methods and procedures to be used, and estimate time requirements, personnel requirements, and costs. Then you put it all in writing—exactly as specified in the RFP, following the precise format it requires and responding meticulously to every point it raises.[10] RFPs can seem surprisingly picky, even

FIGURE 13.10 **Analytical Report Using the 2 + 2 = 4 Approach**
To make his logical argument both clear and compelling, Binh Phan used the 2 + 2 = 4 approach.

Clarifies who requested the report, when it was requested, and who wrote it

Explains how the information used in the analysis was collected

Describes the first problem and explains how it occurred, without blaming anyone personally

Highlights the serious nature of the problem

Organizational problems are the first "2" in Phan's 2 + 2 = 4 approach

MEMO

TO: Robert Mendoza, Vice President of Marketing
FROM: Binh Phan, National Sales Manager   BP
DATE: September 12, 2010
SUBJECT: Major accounts sales problems

As you requested on August 20, this report outlines the results of my investigation into the recent slowdown in sales to major accounts and the accompanying rise in sales- and service-related complaints from some of our largest customers.

Over the last four quarters, major account sales dropped 12%, whereas overall sales were up 7%. During the same time, we've all noticed an increase in both formal and informal complaints from larger customers, regarding how confusing and complicated it has become to do business with us.

My investigation started with in-depth discussions with the four regional sales managers, first as a group and then individually. The tension I felt in the initial meeting eventually bubbled to the surface during my meetings with each manager. Staff members in each region are convinced that other regions are booking orders they don't deserve, with one region doing all the legwork only to see another region get the sale, the commission, and the quota credit.

I followed up these formal discussions by talking informally and exchanging e-mail with several sales representatives from each region. Virtually everyone who is involved with our major national accounts has a story to share. No one is happy with the situation, and I sense that some reps are walking away from major customers because the process is so frustrating.

The decline in sales to our major national customers and the increase in their complaints stem from two problems: (1) sales force organization and (2) commission policy.

ORGANIZATIONAL PROBLEMS

When we divided the national sales force into four geographical regions last year, the idea was to focus our sales efforts and clarify responsibilities for each prospective and current customer. The regional managers have gotten to know their market territories very well, and sales have increased beyond even our most optimistic projections.

However, while solving one problem, we have created another. In the past 12 to 18 months, several regional customers have grown to national status, and a few retailers have taken on (or expressed interest in) our products. As a result, a significant portion of both current sales and future opportunities lies with these large national accounts.

I uncovered more than a dozen cases in which sales representatives from two or more regions found themselves competing with each other by pursuing the same customers from different locations. Moreover, the complaints from our major accounts about overlapping or nonexistent account coverage are a direct result of the regional organization. In some cases, customers aren't sure which of our representatives they're supposed to call with problems and orders. In other cases, no one has been in contact with them for several months.

(continued)

to the point of specifying the paper size for the proposal and the number of copies to send, but you must follow every detail.

Unsolicited proposals are created by organizations attempting to obtain business or funding without a specific invitation from a potential client. Such proposals may also be initiated by employees or managers who want to convince company insiders to adopt a program, a policy, or an idea. In other words, with an unsolicited proposal, the writer makes the first move. Even so, an unsolicited proposal should not come as a surprise to the recipient but, rather, should be the summation of a conversation that has been ongoing with the recipient.[11] Not only does this approach help ensure acceptance, but it gives you an opportunity to explore the recipient's needs and craft your proposal around them.

Unsolicited proposals also differ from solicited proposals in another important respect: Your audience may not be aware of the problem you are addressing, so your proposal must first convince readers that a problem or an opportunity exists before convincing them that you can address it. Thus, unsolicited proposals generally spend considerable time explaining why readers should take action and convincing them of the benefits of doing so.

Unsolicited proposals require additional persuasive elements because the audience isn't expecting a proposal and might not even be conscious of the problem you propose to solve.

FIGURE 13.10 (*Continued*)

2

For example, having retail outlets across the lower tier of the country, AmeriSport received pitches from reps out of our West, South, and East regions. Because our regional offices have a lot of negotiating freedom, the three were offering different prices. But all AmeriSport buying decisions were made at the Tampa headquarters, so all we did was confuse the customer. The irony of the current organization is that we're often giving our weakest selling and support efforts to the largest customers in the country.

Brings the first problem to life by complementing the general description with a specific example

COMMISSION PROBLEMS

Commission problems are the second "2" in Phan's 2 + 2 = 4 approach

The regional organization problems are compounded by the way we assign commissions and quota credit. Salespeople in one region can invest a lot of time in pursuing a sale, only to have the customer place the order in another region. So some sales rep in the second region ends up with the commission on a sale that was partly or even entirely earned by someone in the first region. Therefore, sales reps sometimes don't pursue leads in their regions, thinking that a rep in another region will get the commission.

Simplifies the reader's task by maintaining a parallel structure for the discussion of the second problem: a general description followed by a specific example

For example, Athletic Express, with outlets in 35 states spread across all four regions, finally got so frustrated with us that the company president called our headquarters. Athletic Express has been trying to place a large order for tennis and golf accessories, but none of our local reps seem interested in paying attention. I spoke with the rep responsible for Nashville, where the company is headquartered, and asked her why she wasn't working the account more actively. Her explanation was that last time she got involved with Athletic Express, the order was actually placed from their L.A. regional office, and she didn't get any commission after more than two weeks of selling time.

RECOMMENDATIONS

Phan concludes the 2 + 2 = 4 approach: organizational problems + commission problems = the need for a new sales structure

Our sales organization should reflect the nature of our customer base. To accomplish that goal, we need a group of reps who are free to pursue accounts across regional borders— and who are compensated fairly for their work. The most sensible answer is to establish a national account group. Any customers whose operations place them in more than one region would automatically be assigned to the national group.

Explains how the new organizational structure will solve both problems

In addition to solving the problem of competing sales efforts, the new structure will also largely eliminate the commission-splitting problem because regional reps will no longer invest time in prospects assigned to the national accounts team. However, we will need to find a fair way to compensate regional reps who are losing long-term customers to the national team. Some of these reps have invested years in developing customer relationships that will continue to yield sales well into the future, and everyone I talked to agrees that reps in these cases should receive some sort of compensation. Such a "transition commission" would also motivate the regional reps to help ensure a smooth transition from one sales group to the other. The exact nature of this compensation would need to be worked out with the various sales managers.

Acknowledges that the recommended solution does create a temporary compensation problem, but expresses confidence that a solution to that can be worked out

3

SUMMARY

The regional sales organization is effective at the regional and local levels but not at the national level. We should establish a national accounts group to handle sales that cross regional boundaries. Then we'll have one set of reps who are focused on the local and regional levels and another set who are pursuing national accounts.

Neatly summarizes both the problem and the recommended solution

To compensate regional reps who lose accounts to the national team, we will need to devise some sort of payment to reward them for the years of work invested in such accounts. This can be discussed with the sales managers once the new structure is in place.

Ethics Detective

Solving the Case of the Overblown Proposals

As the manager in charge of your company's New Ventures Group, you've read your share of proposals—hundreds, maybe thousands, of them. You've developed a sixth sense about these documents, an ability to separate cautious optimism from self-doubt and distinguish justified enthusiasm from insupportable hype.

Your company invests in promising smaller firms that could grow into beneficial business partners or even future acquisitions. In a typical scenario, a small company invents a new product but needs additional funding to manufacture and market it, so the owners approach you with funding proposals. Because you make the first major decision in this investment process, your choices and recommendations to the board of directors are crucial.

Moreover, the risks are considerable: If one of your recommendations doesn't pan out, the company could lose all the money it invested (often millions), and that's only the start. Failures consume your team's precious time and energy and can even put the company at risk for shareholder lawsuits and other serious headaches. In other words, mistakes in your line of work are costly.

The proposal in front of you today is intriguing. A small company in Oklahoma has designed a product called the Wireless Shopping List, and you think the idea might appeal to upscale homeowners. Small touchscreens are placed around the house, wherever occupants are likely to think of things they need to buy on the next shopping trip: on the refrigerator door, in the media room, in the nursery, in the garage, in the gardening shed. The system collects all these inputs, and on command it prints out a shopping list or downloads it to a PDA. It's a clever idea, but one paragraph in the proposal bothers you:

> Everybody in our test market audience was absolutely stunned when we demonstrated the simulated system. They couldn't believe something like this was even possible. It was so handy and so convenient—everyone said it would change their lives forever. We haven't even specified the price yet, but every single person in the room wanted to place an order, on the spot.

ANALYSIS

This proposal potentially oversells the idea in at least three different ways. Identify them and explain how they could lead you to decline the investment opportunity.

Every proposal competes for something, whether it's money, time, attention, or something else.

With virtually any proposal, whether solicited or unsolicited, whether for internal audiences or external, keep in mind that you are always competing for something—money, time, management attention, and so on. Even if yours is the only proposal on the table, you are still competing with all the other choices your audience members could make with their time, money, and attention.

Proposals can be significant writing projects, particularly when you are responding to a complex RFP. Fortunately, a variety of software products are available to lighten the load considerably. Basic features include the ability to automatically personalize the proposal, ensure proper structure, and organize storage of all your boilerplates (identical sections of text used in every proposal, such as a description of your company). At a more advanced level, products such as Sant's RFPMaster can scan RFPs to identify questions and requirements and fill in potential answers from a centralized knowledge base that contains input from all the relevant experts in your company.[12]

6 LEARNING OBJECTIVE

Explain how to choose an organizational strategy when writing a proposal

Using the indirect approach, following AIDA or a similar model, is often the best way to build your case in an unsolicited proposal.

Organizational Strategies for Proposals

Your choice of structure for proposals depends on whether your audience members expect the proposal and, if they do, whether you expect them to be receptive to your specific recommendation. In general, your audience is likely to be more receptive with solicited proposals because the problem and the solution have already been identified. Submit your proposal for the solution specified in the RFP and structure the proposal using the direct approach to focus on your recommendation. As soon as possible within the constraints of the RFP requirements, identify why your solution is unique and deserves close consideration.[13]

Depending on the circumstances and your relationship with the recipient, the indirect approach is often better for unsolicited proposals. When writing unsolicited proposals, you must first convince the audience that a problem exists and establish your credibility if you are unknown to the reader. At the same time, you need to give the reader a compelling reason to keep reading a document that he or she didn't request. Follow the AIDA model or a similar approach to grab the reader's attention quickly. For an external proposal, for instance, you might use in your introduction an attention-getter such as "In working with other companies in your industry, our productivity specialists were able to lower their operating costs by as much as 15 percent." And then to convince the reader that you can back up that claim, present your solution in a logical fashion, with solid evidence, leading up to a request for a decision.

Effective Proposals: An Example

A good proposal explains why a project or course of action is needed, what it will involve, how much it will cost, and how the recipient will benefit. You can see all these elements in Shandel Cohen's internal proposal for an automatic mail response system (see Figure 13.11, on pages 434–435).

Cohen manages the customer-response section of the marketing department at a personal computer manufacturer located in the Midwest. Her section sends out product information requested by customers and the field salesforce. Cohen has observed that the demand for information increases when a new product is released and that it diminishes as a product matures. This fluctuating demand causes drastic changes in her section's workload.

"Either we have more work than we can possibly handle," says Cohen, "or we don't have enough to keep us busy. But I don't want to get into a hiring-and-firing cycle." Cohen is also concerned about the amount of printed material that's discarded when products are upgraded or replaced. Her report describes the problem, her proposed solutions, the benefits to the company, and the projected costs, giving her audience all the information needed to make a decision.

For the latest information on planning reports and proposals, visit **www.real-timeupdates.com/bct** and click on Chapter 13.

Document Makeover

Improve This Report

To practice correcting drafts of actual documents, visit the "Document Makeovers" section in either mybcommlab or the Companion Website for this text.

If mybcommlab is being used in your class, see your User Guide for specific instructions on how to access the content for this chapter. If you are accessing this feature through the Companion Website, click on "Document Makeovers" and then select Chapter 13. You will find an informational report that contains problems and errors related to what you've learned in this chapter about planning business reports and proposals. Use the Final Draft decision tool to create an improved version of this report. Check the message for parallel construction, appropriate headings, suitable content, positive and bias-free language, and use of the "you" attitude.

Communication Challenges at Kenwood U.S.A.

You've joined Keith Lehmann's team at Kenwood as a consumer electronics business and marketing analyst. Kenwood's product portfolio in mobile electronics now includes not only satellite radio but also conventional CD players, video players, and navigation systems. Use your knowledge of business communication and report writing to address these challenges.

Individual Challenge: One of the latest mobile electronics innovations is onboard, high-speed Internet access for recreational vehicles (RVs) and a variety of trucks and other specialized vehicles. MotoSAT (**www.motosat.com**) is one of the leaders in this segment. Its products provide automated satellite Internet access with wireless networking throughout the vehicle. You plan to ask the product design team in Japan to explore the feasibility of creating a similar system for Kenwood, but you want to make sure the designers have a clear picture of the U.S. market (specifically, the RV market). Draft a one- or two-page informational report that describes typical vacation scenarios involving families who might be interested in purchasing a mobile Internet system from Kenwood. Be sure to give the designers a clear and vivid picture of what family road trips are like in the United States, from the types of vehicles used to the wide variety of vacation destinations. You want the designers to accurately visualize what such a vacation would be like, even if they've never spent much time in the United States.

Team Challenge: You would like the design team to have a solid assessment of strengths and potential weaknesses of the DataStorm G74 system offered by MotoSAT. With your team, review the material on the MotoSAT website and look for product reviews elsewhere online. Draft a short analytical report that summarizes what you've learned about the DataStorm G74, what its strengths and weaknesses appear to be, and what sort of product Kenwood might want to develop to compete with MotoSAT. Feel free to use your imagination to create any information you might need to describe the future Kenwood product.[14]

FIGURE 13.11   Internal Proposal

Shandel Cohen's internal proposal seeks management's approval to install an automatic mail response system. Because the company manufactures computers, she knows that her boss won't object to a computer-based solution. Also, because profits are always a concern, her report emphasizes the financial benefits of her proposal.

MEMO

TO: Jamie Engle
FROM: Shandel Cohen   *SC*
DATE: July 8, 2010
SUBJECT: Saving $145k/year with an automated e-mail response system

THE PROBLEM:
Expensive and Slow Response to Customer Information Requests

Our new product line has been very well received, and orders have surpassed our projections. This very success, however, has created a shortage of printed brochures, as well as considerable overtime for people in the customer response center. As we introduce upgrades and new options, our printed materials quickly become outdated. If we continue to rely on printed materials for customer information, we have two choices: Distribute existing materials (even though they are incomplete or inaccurate) or discard existing materials and print new ones.

THE SOLUTION:
Automated E-Mail Response System

With minor additions and modifications to our current e-mail system, we can set up an automated system to respond to customer requests for information. This system can save us time and money and can keep our distributed information current.

Automated e-mail response systems have been tested and proven effective. Many companies already use this method to respond to customer information requests, so we won't have to worry about relying on untested technology. Using the system is easy, too: Customers simply send a blank e-mail message to a specific address, and the system responds by sending an electronic copy of the requested brochure.

Benefit #1: Always-Current Information

Rather than discard and print new materials, we would only need to keep the electronic files up to date on the server. We could be able to provide customers and our field sales organization with up-to-date, correct information as soon as the upgrades or options are available.

Benefit #2: Instantaneous Delivery

Almost immediately after requesting information, customers would have that information in hand. Electronic delivery would be especially advantageous for our international customers. Regular mail to remote locations sometimes takes weeks to arrive, by which time the information may already be out of date. Both customers and field salespeople will appreciate the automatic mail-response system.

Benefit #3: Minimized Waste

With our current method of printing every marketing piece in large quantities, we discard thousands of pages of obsolete catalogs, data sheets, and other materials every year. By maintaining and distributing the information electronically, we would eliminate this waste. We would also free up a considerable amount of expensive floor space and shelving that is required for storing printed materials.

Catches the reader's attention with a compelling promise in subject line

Explains the proposed solution in enough detail to make it convincing, without burdening the reader with excessive detail

Describes the current situation and explains why it should be fixed

Builds reader interest in the proposed solution by listing a number of compelling benefits

(continued)

FIGURE 13.11 (*Continued*)

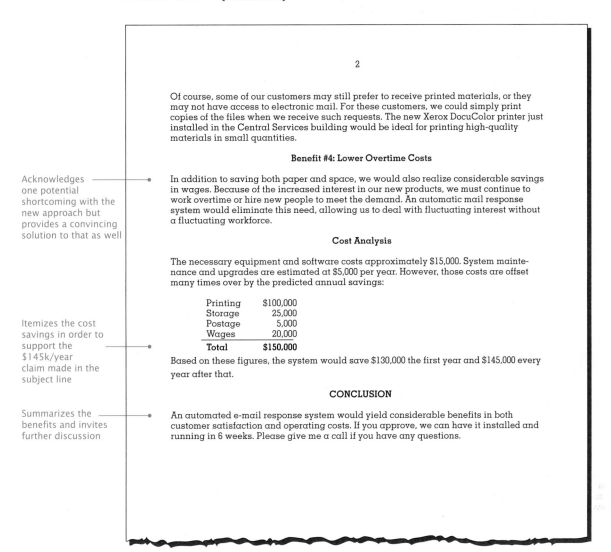

2

Of course, some of our customers may still prefer to receive printed materials, or they may not have access to electronic mail. For these customers, we could simply print copies of the files when we receive such requests. The new Xerox DocuColor printer just installed in the Central Services building would be ideal for printing high-quality materials in small quantities.

Benefit #4: Lower Overtime Costs

Acknowledges one potential shortcoming with the new approach but provides a convincing solution to that as well

In addition to saving both paper and space, we would also realize considerable savings in wages. Because of the increased interest in our new products, we must continue to work overtime or hire new people to meet the demand. An automatic mail response system would eliminate this need, allowing us to deal with fluctuating interest without a fluctuating workforce.

Cost Analysis

The necessary equipment and software costs approximately $15,000. System maintenance and upgrades are estimated at $5,000 per year. However, those costs are offset many times over by the predicted annual savings:

Itemizes the cost savings in order to support the $145k/year claim made in the subject line

Printing	$100,000
Storage	25,000
Postage	5,000
Wages	20,000
Total	**$150,000**

Based on these figures, the system would save $130,000 the first year and $145,000 every year after that.

CONCLUSION

Summarizes the benefits and invites further discussion

An automated e-mail response system would yield considerable benefits in both customer satisfaction and operating costs. If you approve, we can have it installed and running in 6 weeks. Please give me a call if you have any questions.

SUMMARY OF LEARNING OBJECTIVES

1 Adapt the three-step writing process to reports and proposals. The comprehensive nature of the three-step process is ideal for the work involved in most reports and proposals. Use all the advice you learned in Chapters 4 through 6, with added emphasis on a few specific points for longer documents: (1) Identify your purpose clearly to avoid rework, (2) prepare a work plan to guide the research and writing tasks, (3) determine whether a separate research project might be needed to gather the necessary information, (4) choose the appropriate medium (or media, in some cases) for your audience, and (5) organize your information by selecting the best approach for an informational or analytical report.

2 Explain the value of a work plan in the development of long reports. A formal work plan makes the writing process more efficient and more effective by guiding you through every step of the planning and writing process. A work plan usually includes (1) a problem statement defining what you're going to investigate; (2) a statement of purpose defining why you are preparing the report; (3) the tasks to be accomplished and the sequence in which they should be performed; (4) a description of any product that will result from your study; (5) a review of responsibilities, assignments, schedules, and resource requirements; (6) plans for following up after delivering the report; and (7) a working outline.

3 List the key elements of a business plan. Formal business plans—those that are shown to outside audiences such as investors and bankers—typically contain the following elements: a summary of the business concept, the company's mission and objectives, background on the company and the industry in which it competes, descriptions of its products and services, an analysis of target markets and key competitors, a discussion of the management team, a summary of the marketing strategy, design and development plans, an operations plan, a schedule with major milestones, an analysis of critical risks and problems, financial projections and requirements, and a description of the proposed exit strategy.

4 **Identify three steps you can take to ensure effective organization of online reports and other website content.** To help ensure effective organization of both online reports and websites in general, start by planning the structure and navigation paths before writing the content. Next, make sure you let readers be in control. Give them plenty of navigational flexibility so they can create their own paths according to the information they find interesting and useful. Don't force them to follow a rigid page-by-page scheme. Finally, break your information into chunks that can be scanned and absorbed quickly.

5 **Discuss three major ways to organize analytical reports.** The three most common ways to organize analytical reports are by focusing on conclusions, focusing on recommendations, and focusing on logical arguments.

6 **Explain how to choose an organizational strategy when writing a proposal.** The single most important factor to consider when organizing a proposal is whether the proposal is solicited or unsolicited. For a solicited proposal, the direct approach is nearly always better because the audience expects and wants to read your proposed solution. For an unsolicited proposal, the indirect approach is usually better because the reader isn't expecting the proposal and may not agree with you that a problem or an opportunity even exists.

PEARSON mybcommlab™

Log on to www.mybcommlab.com to access the following study and assessment aids associated with this chapter:

- Video applications
- Real-Time Updates
- Peer review activity
- Quick Learning Guides

- Pre/post test
- Personalized study plan
- Model documents
- Sample presentations

If you are not using mybcommlab, you can access the Real-Time Updates and Quick Learning Guides through http://real-timeupdates.com/bct. The Quick Learning Guide hits all the high points of this chapter in just two pages. This guide, especially prepared by the authors, will help you study for exams or review important concepts whenever you need a quick refresher.

Test Your Knowledge

1. How can your written reports influence your professional success?
2. What is the major difference between informational and analytical reports?
3. What does a statement of purpose convey?
4. What should you include in the work plan for a complex report or proposal?
5. What elements should be included in a formal business plan?
6. How are reports for monitoring and controlling operations used?
7. What are the seven major ways to organize an informational report?
8. How does a feasibility report differ from a justification report?
9. What is problem factoring?
10. What is an RFP, and how does it relate to proposal writing?

Apply Your Knowledge

1. In what ways are unsolicited proposals more challenging to write than solicited proposals?
2. Why is it important to identify all the paths that users are likely to take at a website before creating content for a new website?
3. If you want to make a specific recommendation in your report, should you include information that might support a different recommendation? Explain your answer.
4. If your report includes only factual information, is it necessarily objective? Please explain.
5. **Ethical Choices** If you were writing a troubleshooting report to help management decide how to reduce quality problems at a manufacturing plant, what ethical issues might you face? How might these ethical issues conflict with your need to report all the relevant facts and to offer evidence for your conclusions? Explain briefly.

Practice Your Knowledge

Message for Analysis

The Securities and Exchange Commission (SEC) requires all public companies to file a comprehensive annual report (form 10-K) electronically. Many companies post links to these reports on their websites, along with links to other company reports. Visit the website of Dell, at **www.dell.com**, and find the company's most recent annual reports (look in Investor Relations and then Financials): 10-K and Fiscal Year in Review. Compare the style and format of the two reports. For which audience(s) is the Year in Review targeted? Who besides the SEC might be interested in the Annual Report 10-K? Which report do you find easier to read? More interesting? More detailed?

Exercises

Active links for all websites in this chapter can be found online. If mybcommlab is being used in your class, see your User Guide for instructions on accessing the content for this chapter. Otherwise, visit **www.pearsonglobaleditions.com/bovee**, locate *Business Communication Today*, Tenth Edition, click the Companion Website link, select Chapter 13, and then click on "Featured Websites." Please note that links to sites that become inactive after publication of the book will be removed from the Featured Websites section.

13.1 Understanding Business Reports and Proposals: How Companies Use Reports Interview several people working in a career you might like to enter and ask them about the reports they receive and prepare. How do these reports tie in to the decision-making process? Who reads the reports they prepare? Do they write or read electronic online reports? Summarize your findings in writing, give them to your instructor, and be prepared to discuss them with the class.

13.2 Understanding Business Reports and Proposals: Report Classification Using the information presented in this chapter, identify the report type represented by each of the following examples. In addition, write a brief paragraph about each, explaining who the audience is likely to be, what type of data would be used, and whether conclusions and recommendations would be appropriate.
a. A statistical study of the pattern of violent crime in a large city during the past five years
b. A report prepared by a seed company, demonstrating the benefits of its seed corn for farmers
c. A report prepared by an independent testing agency, evaluating various types of nonprescription cold remedies
d. A trip report submitted at the end of a week by a traveling salesperson
e. A report indicating how 45 acres of undeveloped land could be converted into an industrial park
f. An annual report to be sent to the shareholders of a large corporation
g. A report from a U.S. National Park wildlife officer to Washington, D.C., headquarters showing the status of the California condor (an endangered species)

h. A report outlining the risks of closing a chain of retail stores and moving the entire business online

13.3 Internet Follow the step-by-step hints and examples for writing a funding proposal at **www.learnerassociates .com/proposal**. Review the writing hints and the entire sample proposal online. What details did the author decide to include in appendixes? Why was this material placed in the appendixes and not the main body of the report? According to the author's tips, when is the best time to prepare a project overview?

13.4 Informational Reports: Policy Report You're the vice president of operations for a Florida fast-food chain. In the aftermath of a major hurricane, you're drafting a report on the emergency procedures to be followed by personnel in each restaurant when storm warnings are in effect. Answer who, what, when, where, why, and how and then prepare a one-page outline of your report. Make up any details you need.

13.5 Unsolicited Proposal You're getting ready to launch a new lawn-care business that offers mowing, fertilizing, weeding, and other services. The lawn surrounding a nearby shopping center looks as if it could use better care, so you target that business for your first unsolicited proposal. To help prepare this proposal, write your answers to these questions:
a. What questions will you need to answer before you can write a proposal to solve the reader's problem? Be as specific as possible.
b. What customer benefits will you include in your proposal?
c. Will you use a letter or memo format for your proposal? Explain your answer.

13.6 Teamwork: Unsolicited Proposal Break into small groups and identify an operational problem occurring at your campus, involving one of the following: registration, university housing, food services, parking, or library services. Develop a workable solution to that problem. Finally, develop a list of pertinent facts that your team will need to gather to convince the reader that the problem exists and that your solution will work.

13.7 Analyzing the Situation: Statement of Purpose Sales at The Style Shop, a clothing store for men, have declined for the third month in a row. Your boss is not sure whether this decline is because the economy is weak or if it's because of another unknown reason. She has asked you to investigate the situation and to submit a report to her, highlighting some possible reasons for the decline. Develop a statement of purpose for your report.

13.8 Preparing the Work Plan South by Southwest (SXSW) is a family of conferences and festivals in Austin, Texas, that showcase some of the world's most creative talents in music, interactive media, and film. In addition to being a major entertainment venue for a week every March, SXSW is also an increasingly important *trade show*, an opportunity for companies to present products and services to potential customers and business partners. You work for a company that makes music training equipment such as an electronic keyboard with an integrated computer screen that guides learners through every step of learning to play a keyboard. Your manager has asked you to look into whether the company should rent an exhibition booth at SXSW next year. Prepare a work plan for an analytical report that will assess the promotional opportunities at SXSW and make a recommendation on exhibiting. Include the statement of purpose, a problem statement for any research you will conduct, a description of what will result from your investigation, the sources and methods of data collection, and a preliminary outline. Visit the SXSW website, at http://sxsw.com, for more information.[15]

13.9 Organizing Reports: Choosing the Direct or Indirect Approach For each of the following scenarios, determine whether the direct or indirect approach would be advisable and explain why.
a. The monthly financial report prepared by the accounting department for upper management
b. An accountant fresh out of college who wants to propose a new way to present those monthly financial results to upper management
c. An unsolicited proposal to provide payroll processing services
d. An analytical report, requested by the CEO, explaining why the company has been losing money in the eastern sales region for the past two years
e. An unsolicited proposal to the board of directors, outlining why it makes strategic sense for your company to expand into international markets; the board rejected a similar—but poorly presented—idea last year

13.10 Organizing Reports: Choosing the Direct or Indirect Approach Look through recent issues (print or online) of *BusinessWeek*, *Fortune*, or other business publications for an article that describes how an executive's conclusions about his or her company's current situation or future opportunities led to changes in policy, plans, or products. Construct an outline of the material, first using a direct approach and then using an indirect approach. Which approach do you think the executive would use when reporting these conclusions to stockholders? When reporting to other senior managers? Explain your answers.

13.11 Organizing Reports: Deciding on Format Go to the library or visit the website www.annualreportservice.com and review the annual reports recently released by two corporations in the same industry. Analyze each report and be prepared to discuss the following questions in class:
a. What organizational differences, if any, do you see in the way each corporation discusses its annual performance? Are the data presented clearly, so that shareholders can draw conclusions about how well the company performed?

b. What goals, challenges, and plans do top managers emphasize in their discussion of results?
c. How do the format and organization of each report enhance or detract from the information being presented?

13.12 Organizing Reports: Structuring Informational Reports Assume that your college president has received many student complaints about campus parking problems. You are appointed the chair of a student committee organized to investigate the problems and recommend solutions. The president gives you a file labeled "Parking: Complaints from Students," and you jot down the essence of the complaints as you inspect the contents. Your notes look like this:

- Inadequate student spaces at critical hours
- Poor night lighting near the computer center
- Inadequate attempts to keep resident neighbors from occupying spaces
- Dim marking lines
- Motorcycles taking up full spaces
- Discourteous security officers
- Spaces (often empty) reserved for college officials
- Relatively high parking fees
- Full fees charged to night students even though they use the lots only during low-demand periods
- Vandalism to cars and a sense of personal danger
- Inadequate total space
- Resident harassment of students parking on the street in front of neighboring houses

Prepare an outline for an informational report to be submitted to committee members. Use a topical organization that categorizes this information.

13.13 Organizing Reports: Structuring Analytical Reports Three years ago, your company (a carpet manufacturer) modernized its Georgia plant in anticipation of increasing demand for carpets. Because of the depressed housing market, the increase in demand for new carpets has been slow to materialize. As a result, the company has excess capacity at both its Georgia and California plants. On the basis of your research, you have recommended that the company close the California plant. The company president, J. P. Lawrence, has asked you to prepare a justification report to support your recommendation. Here are the facts you gathered by interviewing the respective plant managers:

Operational Statistics
- Georgia plant: This plant has newer equipment, has higher productivity, employs 100 nonunion production workers, and ships $12 million in carpets a year. Hourly base wage is $16.
- California plant: California plant employs 80 union production workers and ships $8 million in carpets a year. Hourly base wage is $20.

Financial Implications
- Savings by closing California plant: (1) Increase productivity by 17 percent; (2) reduce labor costs by 20 percent (total labor savings would be $1 million per

year; see assumptions); (3) annual local tax savings of $120,000 (Georgia has a more favorable tax climate).

- Sale of Pomona, California, land: Purchased in 1952 for $200,000. Current market value $2.5 million. Net profit (after capital gains tax) over $1 million.
- Sale of plant and equipment: Fully depreciated. Any proceeds a windfall.
- Costs of closing California plant: One-time deductible charge of $250,000 (relocation costs of $100,000 and severance payments totaling $150,000).

Assumptions
- Transfer five workers from California to Georgia.
- Hire 45 new workers in Georgia.
- Lay off 75 workers in California.
- Georgia plant would require a total of 150 workers to produce the combined volume of both plants.

a. Which approach (focus on conclusions, recommendations, or logical arguments) will you use to structure your report to the president? Why?

b. Suppose this report were to be circulated to plant managers and supervisors instead. What changes, if any, might you make in your approach?

c. List some conclusions that you might draw from the preceding information to use in your report.

d. Using the structure you selected for your report to the president, draft a final report outline with first- and second-level informative headings.

Expand Your Knowledge

Exploring the Best of the Web

Better Ideas for Better Business Plans

www.bizplanit.com/free.html
What's involved in a business plan? BizPlanIt.Com offers tips and advice, consulting services, a free e-mail newsletter, and a sample virtual business plan. You'll find suggestions on what details and

how much information to include in each section of a business plan. You can explore the site's numerous links to business plan books and software, online magazines, educational programs, government resources, women and minority resources, and even answers to your business plan questions. Review the articles on the site and answer the following questions:

1. Why is the executive summary such an important section of a business plan? What kind of information is contained in an executive summary?

2. What is the product/services section? What information should it contain? List some of the common errors to avoid when planning this part.

3. What type of business planning should you describe in the exit strategy section? Why?

Sharpening Your Career Skills Online

Bovée and Thill's Business Communication Web Search, at http://businesscommunicationblog.com/websearch, is a unique research tool designed specifically for business communication research. Use the Web Search function to find a website, video, PDF document, or PowerPoint presentation that offers advice on writing effective business proposals. Write a brief e-mail message to your instructor, describing the item that you found and summarizing the career skills information you learned from it.

Writing Reports and Proposals

Learning Objectives

After studying this chapter, you will be able to

1 Explain how to adapt to your audiences when writing reports and proposals

2 Name five characteristics of effective report content

3 List the topics commonly covered in the introduction, body, and close of formal reports

4 List six strategies to strengthen a proposal argument

5 Identify five characteristics of effective writing in online reports

6 Briefly describe three report elements that can help readers find their way in long documents

Communication Close-up at Tellabs

The annual reports written by Tellabs's George Stenitzer go beyond regulatory compliance to helping investors understand the business and its financial performance.

www.tellabs.com

Few reports get as much scrutiny as corporate annual reports, and the feedback from many readers of these reports is not particularly positive.

These compliance reports are required of every company listed on U.S. stock exchanges, and investors pore over them, looking for clues about a company's financial health and prospects. However, investor surveys suggest that many readers don't believe they are getting the information they need in order to make intelligent decisions about investing in a company's stock. Some companies have even been sued in recent years over their annual reports, with investors accusing them of withholding or obscuring vital information.

In this environment of uncertainty and outright mistrust, writers who communicate clearly and openly tend to stand out from the crowd. One such writer is George Stenitzer, vice president of corporate communication for Tellabs, a major producer of equipment for Internet service providers based in Naperville, Illinois. According to one widely respected consultant who assesses the quality of annual reports, Stenitzer's work practically demands to be read, thanks to its brevity, forthright style, full disclosure of important financial information, numerous features that enhance readability, and attractive design.

While annual report writers must comply with a complex array of legal compliance requirements, Stenitzer's view is that accuracy and compliance—while vital—are not enough. He recognizes that many companies still lean in the direction of minimal disclosure, saying just enough to satisfy government regulations, but Stenitzer's goal is to help investors truly understand the nature of Tellabs's business and its financial performance. As he puts it, "The test for investor communications is shifting from technical accuracy and legal compliance to clear communication and investor understanding."

The proof of his approach seems to be borne out in investor surveys. In an environment in which many investors are extremely skeptical of, or even confused by, what they read in annual reports, one of Tellabs's recent annual reports was rated "good" or "very good" by an overwhelming 83 percent of readers.[1]

WRITING REPORTS AND PROPOSALS

George Stenitzer (profiled in the chapter-opening Communication Close-up) and all other successful report writers will tell you how important the writing stage is in the development of effective reports and proposals. This chapter builds on the writing techniques and ideas you learned in Chapter 5, with issues that are particularly important when preparing longer messages. As with shorter messages, take a few moments before you start writing to make sure you're ready to adapt your approach to your audience.

ADAPTING TO YOUR AUDIENCE

Like all other messages, reports and proposals are most effective when they are adapted to the needs and interests of their intended audiences. To ensure your own success with reports, be sensitive to audience needs, build strong relationships with your audience, and control your style and tone.

> **1 LEARNING OBJECTIVE**
>
> Explain how to adapt to your audiences when writing reports and proposals

Being Sensitive to Your Audience's Needs

Chapter 5 discusses four aspects of audience sensitivity, and all four apply to reports and proposals: adopting the "you" attitude, maintaining a strong sense of etiquette, emphasizing the positive, and using bias-free language. Reports and proposals that are highly technical, complex, or lengthy can put heavy demands on readers, so the "you" attitude takes on special importance with these messages.

In addition, various audience members can have widely different information needs. For instance, if you're reporting on the results of a customer satisfaction survey, the service manager might want every detail, whereas the president might want only a top-level summary. With previews, summaries, appendixes, and other elements, you can meet the needs of a diverse audience—provided that you plan for these elements in advance.

Long and complex reports demand a lot from readers, making the "you" attitude especially important.

Building Strong Relationships with Your Audience

Building relationships with your readers starts with planning how to adapt your style and your language to meet their needs and expectations. Bear in mind that some reports—particularly any reports that can be transmitted online—can take on lives of their own, reaching a wider audience than you ever imagined and being read years after you write them. Consequently, choose your content and language with care. Also, because many companies have specific guidelines for communicating with public audiences, make sure you're aware of these preferences before you start writing.

As discussed in Chapter 5, establishing your credibility is vital to successful communication. To gain your audience's trust, research all sides of your topic and document your findings with credible sources. Also, be aware that setting audience expectations too high can lead to problems with your credibility if you can't deliver everything people expect you to, so take particular care with the introductory sections of important reports.

Your reports may continue to be read for months or years after you write them—and they may reach audiences you never envisioned.

Controlling Your Style and Tone

If you know your readers reasonably well and your report is likely to meet with their approval, you can adopt a fairly informal tone—provided that doing so is acceptable in the situation and in your company's culture. To make your tone less formal, refer to readers as *you*, and refer to yourself as *I* (or *we*, if there are multiple report authors).

Adjust the level of formality to match the situation and your audience's expectations.

FIGURE 14.1 Choosing the Right Tone for Business Reports
Yahoo! is known for a playful, informal tone in its advertising and in most communication with customers, but the company's tone is more formal when communicating with the public on more serious matters.

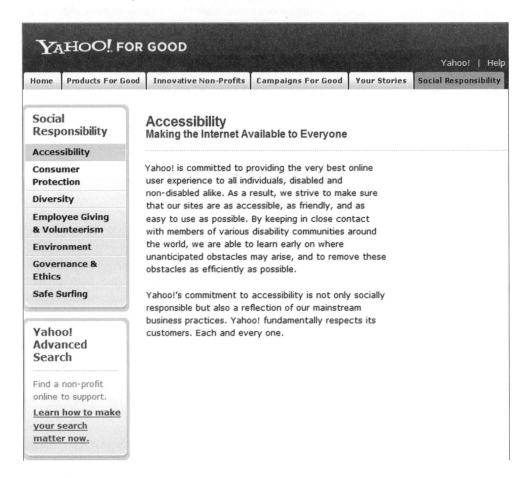

A more formal tone is usually appropriate for longer reports, especially those that deal with controversial or complex information. You'll also want to use a more formal tone when your report will be sent to other parts of the organization or to outsiders, such as customers, suppliers, or members of the community (see Figure 14.1).

If the situation calls for a more formal tone, use the impersonal journalism style, eliminating all references to *you* and *I* (including *we*, *us*, and *our*). When you use an impersonal style, you impose a controlled distance between you and your readers. Your tone is not only objective but also businesslike and unemotional. Be careful to avoid jokes and minimize the use of similes, metaphors, and overly colorful language.

However, when crafting a more formal tone, take care not to go overboard, or you'll end up sounding stiff or dull. In addition, don't inadvertently slip into the passive voice. You can avoid this potential weakness by making the report content itself the actor in a sentence. For example, to convert "I think we should buy TramCo" to a more formal tone, you could write "The financial analysis clearly shows that buying TramCo is the best alternative."

COMPOSING REPORTS AND PROPOSALS

Before you start writing, review your outline one more time and verify the wording of your headings and subheadings.

With a clear picture of how you need to adapt to your audience, you're ready to begin composing your first draft. Before you put those first words down on paper, though, review your outline one last time. Verify that the organization you've chosen makes sense, given everything you've learned about your topic so far. Also, review the wording of the headings and subheadings to make sure they establish the right tone. For a hard-hitting, direct tone, use informative phrasing ("Quality Problems Result in Nearly 500 Customer Defections Every Year"). For an objective, indirect tone, use descriptive phrasing ("Effects of Product Quality on Customer Retention").

Like other written business communications, reports and proposals have three main sections: an introduction (or *opening*), a body, and a close. The content and length of each section vary with the type and purpose of the document, the document's organizational structure, the length and depth of the material, the document's degree of formality, and your relationship with your audience.

An effective *introduction* accomplishes at least four things:

- Puts the report or proposal in a broader context by tying it to a problem or an assignment
- Introduces the subject or purpose of the report or proposal and indicates why the subject is important
- Previews the main ideas and the order in which they'll be covered
- Establishes the tone of the document and the writer's relationship with the audience

The introduction needs to provide context for the reader, introduce the subject, preview main ideas, and establish the tone of the document.

In the *body*, the middle section in your report or proposal, you present, analyze, and interpret the information gathered during your investigation. If appropriate, the body also contains the detailed proof necessary to support your conclusions and recommendations (see Figure 14.2).

The body of a report presents, analyzes, and interprets the information you gathered during your investigation.

The *close*, the final section of your report or proposal, has three important functions:

- Emphasizes the main points of the message and briefly reiterates the logic behind any conclusions or recommendations you've made
- Summarizes the benefits to the reader if the document suggests a change or some other course of action
- Brings all the action items together in one place and gives details about who should do what, when, where, and how

The close of your report should emphasize the main message, summarize audience benefits, gather together all the action items (if any), and indicate responsibilities for each one.

Research shows that the final section of a report or proposal leaves a strong lasting impression. The close gives you one last chance to make sure that your report says what you intended.[2] In fact, readers who are in a hurry might skip the body of the report and read only the summary, so make sure it carries a strong, clear message.

The close might be the only part of your report some readers have time for, so make sure it conveys the full weight of your message.

Drafting Report Content

Your credibility and prospects for the future are on the line with every business report you write, so make sure your content is

Effective report content is accurate, complete, balanced, clear, logical, and properly documented.

- **Accurate.** Information presented in a report must be factually correct. When writing reports, be sure to double-check your facts and references in addition to checking for typos. If an audience ever gets the inkling that your information is shaky, they'll start to view all your work with a skeptical eye.
- **Complete.** To help audiences make informed decisions, include all the information necessary for readers to understand the situation, problem, or proposal. Support all key assertions, using an appropriate combination of illustrations, explanations, and facts.[3] Tell your readers what they need to know—no more, no less—and present the information in a way that is geared to their needs. In a recent Tellabs annual report, for example, George Stenitzer and his team provided a concise and easily understandable overview of the company's complex and technical product line. Rather than burying the audience under technical details, the product overview clearly identifies how the company's products deliver the benefits that Internet users want and how the products offer business advantages to Tellabs's customers. The subject matter is presented in a way that any investor interested in the company's stock can comprehend.[4]
- **Balanced.** It's important to present all sides of the issue fairly and equitably and to include all the essential information, even if some of it doesn't support your line of reasoning. Omitting relevant information or facts can bias your report.

FIGURE 14.2 Effective Problem-Solving Report Focusing on Recommendations
In this report, recommending that her firm expand its website to full e-commerce capability, Alycia Jenn uses the body of the report to provide enough information to support her argument, without burdening her high-level readership with a lot of tactical details.

MEMO

TO: Board of Directors, Executive Committee members
FROM: Alycia Jenn, Business Development Manager
DATE: July 7, 2010
SUBJECT: Website expansion

Reminds readers of the origin and purpose of the report

In response to your request, my staff and I investigated the potential for expanding our website from its current "brochureware" status (in which we promote our company and its products but don't provide any way to place orders online) to full e-commerce capability (including placing orders and checking on order delivery status). After analyzing the behavior of our customers and major competitors and studying the overall development of electronic retailing, we have three recommendations:

1. We should expand our online presence from "brochureware" to e-commerce capability within the next 6 months.

2. We should engage a firm that specializes in online retailing to design and develop the new e-commerce capabilities.

3. We must take care to integrate online retailing with our store-based and mail-order operations.

Clarifies the recommendation by listing the necessary actions in clear, direct language

1. WE SHOULD EXPAND THE WEBSITE TO FULL E-COMMERCE CAPABILITY

Presents logical reasons for recommending that the firm expand its website to include e-commerce

First, does e-commerce capability make sense today for a small company that sells luxury housewares? Even though books and many other products are now commonly sold online, in most cases, this enterprise involves simple, low-cost products that don't require a lot of hands-on inspection before purchasing. As we've observed in our stores, shoppers like to interact with our products before purchasing them. However, a small but growing number of websites do sell specialty products, using such tactics as "virtual product tours" (in which shoppers can interactively view a product in three dimensions, rather than simply looking at a static photograph) and generous return policies (to reduce the perceived risk of buying products online).

Second, do we need to establish a presence now in order to remain competitive in the future? The answer is an overwhelming "yes." The initial steps taken by our competitors are already placing us at a disadvantage among those shoppers who are already comfortable buying online, and every trend indicates our minor competitive weakness today will turn into a major weakness in the next few years:

• Several of our top competitors are beginning to implement full e-commerce, including virtual product tours. Our research suggests that these companies aren't yet generating significant financial returns from these online investments, but their online sales are growing.

• Younger consumers who grew up with the World Wide Web will soon be reaching their peak earning years (ages 35–54). This demographic segment expects e-commerce in nearly every product category, and we'll lose them to the competition if we don't offer it.

Supports the reasoning with evidence

• The web is erasing geographical shopping limits, presenting both a threat and an opportunity. Even though our customers can now shop websites anywhere in the world (so that we have thousands of competitors instead of a dozen), we can now target customers anywhere in the world.

(continued)

• **Clear and logical.** Save your readers time by making sure your sentences are uncluttered, contain well-chosen words, and proceed logically. To help your readers move from one point to the next, make your transitions clear and logical. For a successful report, identify the ideas that belong together and organize them in a way that's easy to understand.[5]

• **Documented properly.** If you use primary and secondary sources for your report or proposal, be sure to properly document and give credit to your sources, as Chapter 11 explains.

Keeping these points in mind will help you draft an effective introduction, body, and close for your report (see Figure 14.3).

FIGURE 14.2 *(Continued)*

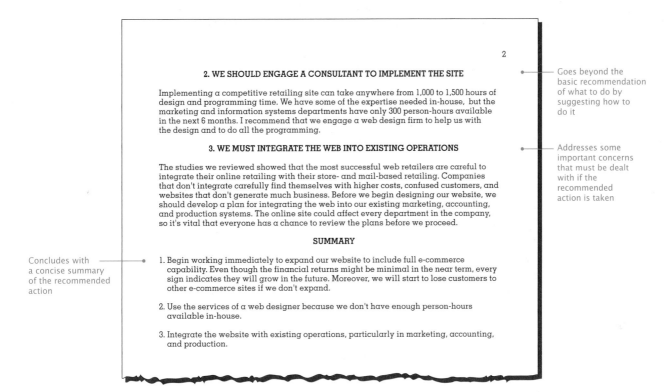

2. WE SHOULD ENGAGE A CONSULTANT TO IMPLEMENT THE SITE

Implementing a competitive retailing site can take anywhere from 1,000 to 1,500 hours of design and programming time. We have some of the expertise needed in-house, but the marketing and information systems departments have only 300 person-hours available in the next 6 months. I recommend that we engage a web design firm to help us with the design and to do all the programming.

3. WE MUST INTEGRATE THE WEB INTO EXISTING OPERATIONS

The studies we reviewed showed that the most successful web retailers are careful to integrate their online retailing with their store- and mail-based retailing. Companies that don't integrate carefully find themselves with higher costs, confused customers, and websites that don't generate much business. Before we begin designing our website, we should develop a plan for integrating the web into our existing marketing, accounting, and production systems. The online site could affect every department in the company, so it's vital that everyone has a chance to review the plans before we proceed.

SUMMARY

1. Begin working immediately to expand our website to include full e-commerce capability. Even though the financial returns might be minimal in the near term, every sign indicates they will grow in the future. Moreover, we will start to lose customers to other e-commerce sites if we don't expand.

2. Use the services of a web designer because we don't have enough person-hours available in-house.

3. Integrate the website with existing operations, particularly in marketing, accounting, and production.

Goes beyond the basic recommendation of what to do by suggesting how to do it

Addresses some important concerns that must be dealt with if the recommended action is taken

Concludes with a concise summary of the recommended action

Report Introduction

The specific elements you should include in a report's introduction depend on the nature and length of the report, the circumstances in which you're writing the report, and your relationship with the audience. An introduction could contain all of the following topics, although you'll want to pick and choose the best ones to include with each report you write:

- **Authorization.** When, how, and by whom the report was authorized; who wrote it; and when it was submitted. This material is especially important when no *letter of transmittal* is included.
- **Problem/opportunity/purpose.** The reason for the report's existence and what is to be accomplished as a result of your having written the report.
- **Scope.** What is and what isn't going to be covered in the report. The scope indicates the report's size and complexity; it also helps with the critical job of setting the audience's expectations.
- **Background.** The historical conditions or factors that led up to the report. This section enables readers to understand how the problem, situation, or opportunity developed and what has been done about it so far.
- **Sources and methods.** The primary and secondary sources of information used. As appropriate, this section explains how samples were selected, how questionnaires (which should be included in an appendix with any cover letters) were constructed, what follow-up was done, and so on. This section builds reader confidence in the work and in the sources and methods used.
- **Definitions.** A list of terms that might be unfamiliar to your audience, along with brief definitions. This section is unnecessary if readers are familiar with the terms you've used in your report—and they all agree on what the terms mean, which isn't always the case. Terms may also be defined where they appear in the body, in explanatory notes, or in a glossary.
- **Limitations.** Factors beyond your control that affect report quality, such as budget limitations, schedule constraints, or limited access to information or people. However, don't apologize for or try to explain away avoidable errors (such as having put off the report until the last minute).

3 LEARNING OBJECTIVE

List the topics commonly covered in the introduction, body, and close of formal reports

Carefully select the elements to include in your introduction; don't include anything your audience doesn't need.

FIGURE 14.3 **Effective Progress Report (Excerpt)**

Note how Carlyce Johnson offers her client a complete but concise update of her company's landscaping services. In addition to providing routine information, she also informs the client of progress on two problem areas, one that her firm has been able to resolve and one that they've just discovered. Johnson does the right thing by telling the client about the problems as early as possible, giving the client time to react and plan.

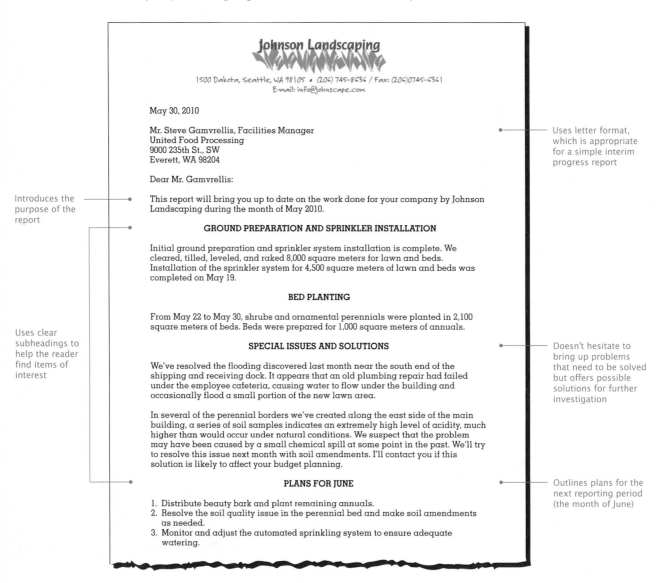

Uses letter format, which is appropriate for a simple interim progress report

Introduces the purpose of the report

Uses clear subheadings to help the reader find items of interest

Doesn't hesitate to bring up problems that need to be solved but offers possible solutions for further investigation

Outlines plans for the next reporting period (the month of June)

The letter content:

Johnson Landscaping

1500 Dakota, Seattle, WA 98105 • (206) 745-8636 / Fax: (206)0745-6361
E-mail: info@johnscape.com

May 30, 2010

Mr. Steve Gamvrellis, Facilities Manager
United Food Processing
9000 235th St., SW
Everett, WA 98204

Dear Mr. Gamvrellis:

This report will bring you up to date on the work done for your company by Johnson Landscaping during the month of May 2010.

GROUND PREPARATION AND SPRINKLER INSTALLATION

Initial ground preparation and sprinkler system installation is complete. We cleared, tilled, leveled, and raked 8,000 square meters for lawn and beds. Installation of the sprinkler system for 4,500 square meters of lawn and beds was completed on May 19.

BED PLANTING

From May 22 to May 30, shrubs and ornamental perennials were planted in 2,100 square meters of beds. Beds were prepared for 1,000 square meters of annuals.

SPECIAL ISSUES AND SOLUTIONS

We've resolved the flooding discovered last month near the south end of the shipping and receiving dock. It appears that an old plumbing repair had failed under the employee cafeteria, causing water to flow under the building and occasionally flood a small portion of the new lawn area.

In several of the perennial borders we've created along the east side of the main building, a series of soil samples indicates an extremely high level of acidity, much higher than would occur under natural conditions. We suspect that the problem may have been caused by a small chemical spill at some point in the past. We'll try to resolve this issue next month with soil amendments. I'll contact you if this solution is likely to affect your budget planning.

PLANS FOR JUNE

1. Distribute beauty bark and plant remaining annuals.
2. Resolve the soil quality issue in the perennial bed and make soil amendments as needed.
3. Monitor and adjust the automated sprinkling system to ensure adequate watering.

- **Report organization.** The organization of the report, along with a rationale for following this plan, if appropriate. This section is a road map that helps readers understand what's coming at each turn of the report and why.

In a relatively brief report, these topics may be discussed in only a paragraph or two. Here's an example of a brief indirect opening, taken from the introduction of a memo on why a new line of luggage has failed to sell well. The writer's ultimate goal is to recommend a shift in marketing strategy:

> Sales performance of the Venturer line can be improved. In the two years since its introduction, this product line has achieved a sales volume lower than we expected, resulting in a drain on the company's overall earnings. The purpose of this report is to review the luggage-buying habits of consumers in all markets where the Venturer line is sold, so that we can determine where to put our marketing emphasis.

This paragraph quickly introduces the subject (disappointing sales), tells why the problem is important (drain on earnings), and indicates the main points to be addressed in the body of the report (review of markets where the Venturer line is sold), without revealing what the conclusions and recommendations will be.

In a much longer formal report, the discussion of these topics may span several pages and constitute a significant section of the report.

Report Body

The body of a report can require some tough decisions about which elements to include and how much detail to offer. You should provide only enough detail in the body to support your conclusions and recommendations; you can put additional information in appendixes. The following topics are commonly covered in a report body:

The report body should contain only enough information to convey your message convincingly; don't overload the body with excessive details.

- Explanations of a problem or an opportunity
- Facts, statistical evidence, and trends
- Results of studies or investigations
- Discussion and analyses of potential courses of action
- Advantages, disadvantages, costs, and benefits of a particular course of action
- Procedures or steps in a process
- Methods and approaches
- Criteria for evaluating alternatives and options
- Conclusions and recommendations (in direct reports)
- Supporting reasons for conclusions or recommendations

For analytical reports using the direct approach, you can state your conclusions or recommendations in the introduction and use the body to provide your evidence and support (as illustrated in Figures 14.2 and 14.3). If you're using the indirect approach, you can use the body to discuss your logic and reserve your conclusions or recommendations until the close.

Report Close

The content and length of a report's close depend primarily on your choice of direct or indirect approach. If you're using the direct approach, you can end with a summary of key points, listed in the order in which they appear in the report body. If you're using the indirect approach, you can use the close to present your conclusions or recommendations if you didn't end the body with them. However, don't introduce new facts in your close; audience members should have all the information they need by the time they reach this point.

The nature of your close depends on the type of report (informational, analytical, or proposal) and the approach (direct or indirect).

If your report is intended to prompt others to action, use the close to spell out exactly what should happen next. If you'll be taking all the actions yourself, make sure your readers understand this fact so that they know what to expect from you (see Figure 14.4).

In a short report, the close may be only a paragraph or two. In a long report, however, the close might have separate sections for conclusions, recommendations, and actions. Separate sections help your reader locate this material and focus on each element. Such an arrangement also gives you a final opportunity to emphasize important content.

For long reports, you may need to divide your close into separate sections for conclusions, recommendations, and actions.

If you have multiple conclusions, recommendations, or actions, you may want to number and list them. An appropriate lead-in to such a list might be "The findings of this study lead to the following conclusions." A statement that could be used for a list of recommendations might be "Based on the conclusions of this study, we make the following recommendations." A statement that could be used for actions might be "In order to accomplish our goals on time, we must complete the following actions before the end of the year."

Drafting Proposal Content

If you're writing an unsolicited proposal, you have some latitude in the scope and organization of content. However, the scope and organization of a solicited proposal are usually governed by the request for proposals (RFP). Most RFPs spell

REAL-TIME UPDATES
Learn More

Need clarification about plagiarism?

Get helpful tips for avoiding plagiarism when researching and writing reports. Go to **http://real-timeupdates.com/bct** and click on "Learn More." If you are using mybcommlab, you can access Real-Time Updates within each chapter or under Student Study Tools.

FIGURE 14.4 Clarifying Expectations in a Report's Close
Roger Watson's personal activity report for July is a good example of efficiently conveying key information points, including a clear plan of action in the close. Note the use of hyperlinks to maps, photos, and a related report, all of which are stored on the same secure intranet site.

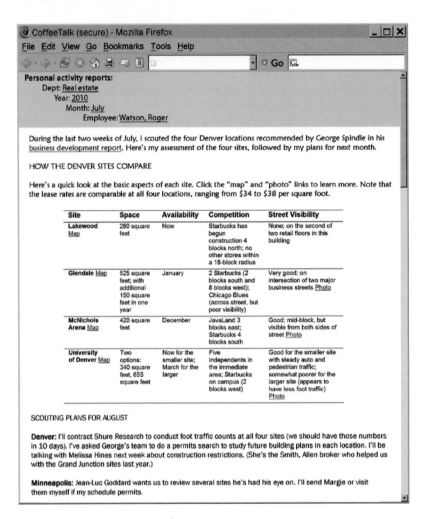

out precisely what you should cover and in what order. This uniformity lets the recipient evaluate competing proposals in a systematic way.

The AIDA model you learned in Chapter 10 works well for proposals, although you may need to adapt it if you're responding to an RFP.

The general purpose of any proposal is to persuade readers to do something, such as purchase goods or services, fund a project, or implement a program. Thus, your writing approach for a proposal is similar to that used for persuasive sales messages (see Chapter 10). Your proposal must sell your audience on your ideas, product, service, methods, and company. As with any other persuasive message, you can use the AIDA model to gain attention, build interest, create desire, and motivate action (of course, you may need to adapt if you're responding to an RFP or working within some other constraints). Here are some additional strategies to strengthen your persuasive argument:[6]

4 **LEARNING OBJECTIVE**

List six strategies to strengthen a proposal argument

Business proposals need to provide more than just attractive ideas; readers look for evidence of practical, achievable solutions.

- **Demonstrate your knowledge.** Everything you write should show the reader that you have the knowledge and experience to solve the problem or address the opportunity outlined in your proposal.
- **Provide concrete information and examples.** Avoid vague, unsupported generalizations such as "We are losing money on this program." Instead, provide quantifiable details such as the amount of money being lost, how, why, and so on. Explain how much money your proposed solution will save. Spell out your plan and give details on how the job will be done.

- **Research the competition.** Find out what alternatives your audience might choose over your proposal so that you can emphasize why your solution is the optimum choice. In some cases, potential customers face a "buy or build" decision, in which they must choose between buying a solution from an external party and building it themselves. In these cases, you are effectively competing against your target customers.
- **Prove that your proposal is workable.** Your proposal must be appropriate and feasible for your audience. It should be consistent with your audience's capabilities. For instance, your proposal would be pointless if it recommended a plan of action that requires three times the number of available employees or twice the available budget.
- **Adopt the "you" attitude.** Relate your product, service, or personnel to the reader's exact needs, either as stated in the RFP for a solicited proposal or as discovered through your own investigation for an unsolicited proposal.
- **Package your proposal attractively.** Make sure your proposal is letter perfect, inviting, and readable. Readers will prejudge the quality of your products or services by the proposal you submit. Errors, omissions, and inconsistencies will work against you—and may even cost you important career and business opportunities.

Proposals in various industries often have their own special challenges as well. For instance, management consultants have to convince every potential client that they have the skills and knowledge to solve the client's problem—without giving away the answer for free in the proposal. In other industries, such as transportation services, bidders may be asked to compute hundreds or thousands of individual pricing scenarios. Hands-on experience goes a long way when you're deciding what to include and exclude in a report; whenever possible, get advice from a senior colleague who's been through it before.

Proposal Introduction

The introduction presents and summarizes the problem you want to solve or the opportunity you want to pursue, along with your proposed solution. The introduction orients readers to the remainder of the report. If your proposal is solicited, its introduction should refer to the RFP so that readers know which RFP you're responding to. If your proposal is unsolicited, your introduction should mention any factors that led you to submit your proposal, such as prior conversations with members of the recipient organization's staff. The following topics are commonly covered in a proposal introduction:

- **Background or statement of the problem or opportunity.** Briefly reviews the reader's situation and establishes a need for action. Readers may not perceive a problem or an opportunity the same way you do. In unsolicited proposals, you need to convince them that a problem or an opportunity exists before you can convince them to accept your solution. In a way that is meaningful to your reader, discuss the current situation and explain how things could be better. Emphasize how your goals align with your audience's goals.

In an unsolicited proposal, your introduction may need to convince readers that a problem or an opportunity exists.

- **Solution.** Briefly describes the change you propose and highlights your key selling points and their benefits, showing how your proposal will help readers meet their business objectives. In long proposals, the heading for this section might be "Preliminary Analysis," "Overview of Approach," or some other wording that identifies this section as a preview of your solution.
- **Scope.** States the boundaries of the proposal, defining what you will and will not do. This section is sometimes called "Delimitations."
- **Organization.** Orients the reader to the remainder of the proposal and calls attention to the major divisions of information.

In short proposals, your discussion of these topics will be brief—perhaps only a sentence or two for each one. For long, formal proposals, each of these topics may warrant separate subheadings and several paragraphs of discussion.

Proposal Body

The proposal's body gives complete details on the proposed solution and specifies what the anticipated results will be. Because a proposal is by definition a persuasive message, your audience expects you to promote your offering in a confident, professional manner. Even

Readers understand that a proposal is a persuasive message, so they're willing to accommodate a promotional style—as long as it is professional and focused on their needs.

when you're expressing an idea that you believe in passionately, be sure to maintain an objective tone so that you don't risk overselling your message.

In addition to providing facts and evidence to support your conclusions, an effective body covers this information:

The work plan indicates exactly how you will accomplish the solution presented in the proposal.

- **Proposed solution.** Describes what you have to offer: your concept, product, or service. This section may also be titled "Technical Proposal," "Research Design," "Issues for Analysis," or "Work Statement." Focus on the strengths of your offer that are relevant to your readers' needs, and point out any advantages that you have over your competitors.
- **Work plan.** Describes how you'll accomplish what must be done, unless you'll be providing a standard, off-the-shelf item. (Note that *work plan* in this context describes the work you'll perform if your proposal is accepted, not the work plan you may have written to help guide the writing of the proposal itself.) Explain the steps you'll take, their timing, the methods or resources you'll use, and the person(s) responsible. Specifically include when the work will begin, how it will be divided into stages, when you will finish, and whether any follow-up is involved. If appropriate, include a time line or Gantt chart highlighting any critical dates. For solicited proposals, make sure your dates match those specified in the RFP. Keep in mind that if your proposal is accepted, the work plan is contractually binding, so don't promise to deliver more than you can realistically achieve within the stated time period.
- **Statement of qualifications.** Describes your organization's experience, personnel, and facilities—all in relation to reader needs. The qualifications section can be an important selling point, and it deserves to be handled carefully. You can supplement your qualifications by including a list of client references but get permission ahead of time to use these references.
- **Costs.** Covers pricing, reimbursable expenses, discounts, and cost factors. Coverage can vary widely, from a single price amount to detailed breakdowns by part number, service category, and so on. If you're responding to an RFP, follow its instructions. In other cases, your firm probably has a policy for discussing costs, including how much detail to provide.

In an informal proposal, discussion of some or all of these elements may be grouped together and presented in a letter format, as in the proposal shown in Figure 14.5. In a formal proposal, the discussion of these elements will be quite long and thorough. The format may resemble the format of long reports with multiple parts, as Chapter 15 discusses.

Proposal Close

The close is your last chance to convince the reader of the merits of your proposal, so make especially sure it's clear, compelling, and audience oriented.

The final section of a proposal generally summarizes the key points, emphasizes the benefits that readers will realize from your solution, summarizes the merits of your approach, restates why you and your firm are the ones to perform the service or provide the products in question, and asks for a decision from the client. The close is your last opportunity to persuade readers to accept your proposal. In both formal and informal proposals, make this section relatively brief, assertive (but not brash or abrupt), and confident.

5 **LEARNING OBJECTIVE**

Identify five characteristics of effective writing in online reports

Drafting Online Content

In addition to the other advice in this chapter about report writing, paying attention to five key aspects of web writing will help make your web content more effective. First, take special care to build trust with your intended audiences because careful readers can be skeptical of online content. Make sure your content is accurate, current, complete, and authoritative. Indicate the date material was originally posted and again when it is updated, so that readers can judge your content's currency.

Localizing web content involves both translating the content and adapting it to local cultural norms and practices.

Second, adapt your content for a global audience. This can be a complicated and expensive effort. Translating content is expensive, and *localizing* it so that it reflects not only the native language of your readers but their cultural norms, weights, measures, time, money, and so on is even more expensive. Some companies compromise by localizing the homepage and key secondary pages while keeping the deeper, more detailed content in its original language.

FIGURE 14.5 Solicited Proposal in Letter Format

This informal solicited proposal provides the information the customer needs to make a purchase. Note that by signing the proposal and returning it, the customer will enter into a legal contract to pay for the services described.

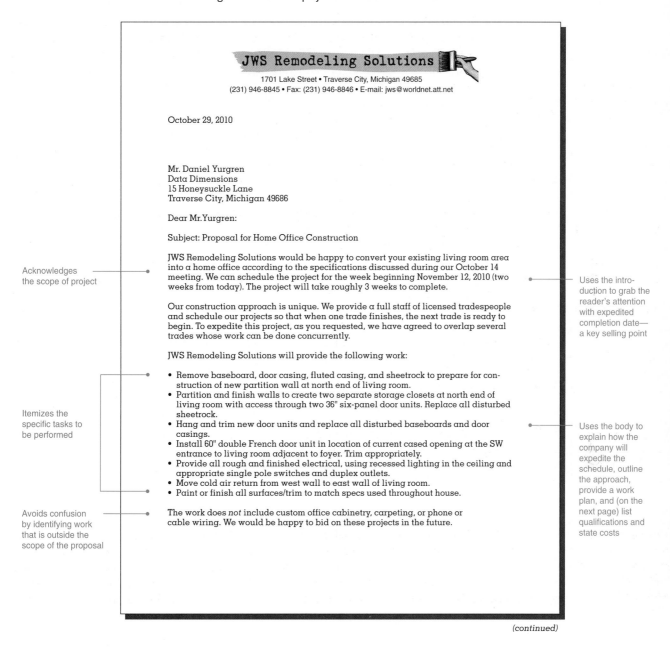

Acknowledges the scope of project

Itemizes the specific tasks to be performed

Avoids confusion by identifying work that is outside the scope of the proposal

Uses the introduction to grab the reader's attention with expedited completion date—a key selling point

Uses the body to explain how the company will expedite the schedule, outline the approach, provide a work plan, and (on the next page) list qualifications and state costs

(continued)

Third, present your information in a concise, skimmable format. Studies show that web readers typically read only a fraction of the words on a page—about 20 percent on the average—and the percentage goes down the longer the webpage gets.[7] Effective websites use a variety of means to help readers skim pages quickly, including lists, careful use of color and boldface, informative headings (clever headings with lots of wordplay are usually more annoying than effective), and helpful summaries that give readers a choice of learning more if they want to.

Fourth, write effective links because they help with both site navigation and content skimming. Above all, clearly identify where a link will take readers; don't force them to click through and try to figure out where they're going. If necessary, include a brief summary, explaining what readers will experience if they click on the link—particularly if the link does anything that might be unexpected, such as launch a video. Also, try to avoid using

Effective links in online reports let readers know exactly what to expect before they click on them.

FIGURE 14.5 *(Continued)*

Mr. Daniel Yurgren   Page 2   October 29, 2010

JWS Remodeling Solutions has been in business in the Michigan area for over 17 years.
We have a strong reputation for being a quality builder. We take great pride in our work
and we treat all projects with the same high-level attention, regardless of their size or
scope. Our tradespeople are all licensed, insured professionals with years of experience
in their respective crafts. Enclosed is a copy of our company brochure discussing our
qualifications in greater detail, along with a current client list. Please contact any of the
names on this list for references.

The total cost for this project is $6,800, broken down as follows:

Materials and supplies	$3,800
Labor	2,700
Disposal fees	300
Total	$6,800

An initial payment of $3,800 is due upon acceptance of this proposal. The remaining
$3,000 is due upon completion of the work.

If you would like to have JWS Remodeling Solutions complete this work, please sign one
copy of this letter and return it to us with your deposit in the enclosed envelope. We
currently anticipate no construction delays, since the materials needed for your job are
in stock and our staff of qualified workers is available during the period mentioned. If
you have any questions regarding the terms of this proposal, please call me.

Sincerely,

Jordan W. Spurrier
President

Enclosures (3)

Accepted by:

_____   _____
Daniel Yurgren   Date

Increases desire by highlighting qualifications

Helps reader accept the cost total by breaking it down into specific categories

Makes letter a binding contract, if signed

directional words such as *back, forward, next, above, below, bottom,* or *top.* Such words are
meaningful in a linear document but not necessarily in a hypertext document, where visitors can enter your site at many places and from many directions. Instead, use absolute
directions such as *Return to Tables, Next Learning Step,* or *Beginning of Tutorial.*[8]

Fifth, if you expect people to find your content through search engines, you need to pay
attention to **search engine optimization (SEO)**. In simple terms, SEO is fine-tuning your
content to make it more "findable" by the visitors you want to attract. Using sophisticated—
and secret—algorithms, search engines attempt to rank search results by relevance to the
user's input terms, putting the most relevant results at the top of the list. Web surfers tend to
select sites from the first few pages of search results, so getting high ranks from search engines
is crucial for websites that rely on search traffic. SEO has become a complex and controversial topic as search engines and the web itself have continued to evolve and as motivated website owners have kept looking for ways to boost their rankings. For instance, Google now

*If you rely on search engines for a
significant portion of your website
traffic, you need to optimize your
site to increase the chances that
search engines will give your site
high ranks in relevant searches.*

Business Communication 2.0

Identifying the Patterns That Help or Hinder Wiki Collaboration

Not too surprisingly, one of the most interesting websites on wiki collaboration is itself a wiki: Wikipatterns (www .wikipatterns.com). On this site, wiki practitioners share insights into patterns of behavior that either promote or inhibit the development and effective use of wikis.

On the positive side, the site identifies numerous "people patterns" (individual and group behaviors) and "adoption patterns" (techniques and strategies) that promote successful collaboration. For example, the adoption pattern "Critical Mass" describes the need to have a substantial amount of compelling content to encourage enough people in the group to use the wiki.

On the negative side, the site identifies what it calls "anti-patterns," which are behaviors, techniques, and strategies that inhibit wiki use and growth. A good example of a people anti-pattern is the "WikiTroll," someone who tends to leave inflammatory, unhelpful comments that do nothing but stir up controversy. One of the more interesting adoption anti-patterns is "Too much structure," which is imposing a rigid information architecture before the information has a chance to grow naturally.

As wikis continue to take over more and more of the communication tasks in many organizations, understanding the forces that support or impede wiki use will become an increasingly important element of business communication.

CAREER APPLICATIONS

1. Visit Wikipatterns and select one of the people patterns or adoption patterns. Next, briefly review what you learned about teamwork in Chapter 2. Does the positive wiki pattern you identified seem to correlate with the principles of successful teamwork? Why or why not?

2. As you peruse the various patterns and anti-patterns on the site, you'll notice that the wiki contributors don't always agree on the definition or importance of specific patterns. What does this tell you about the state of wiki use in business today?

---

evaluates more than 100 factors to determine search rankings. Without becoming an expert in SEO, however, you can work toward improving rankings for your website by focusing on three important areas: (1) Offer fresh, high-quality, audience-oriented content; (2) use relevant keywords judiciously, particularly in important areas such as the page title that displays at the top of the browser screen; and (3) encourage links to your site from other high-quality sites with relevant content.[9]

Collaborating on Wikis

As Chapter 2 points out, using wikis is a great way for teams and other groups to collaborate on writing projects, from brief articles to long reports and reference works. The benefits of wikis are compelling, but they do require a unique approach to writing.

Understanding the Wiki Philosophy

To be a valuable wiki contributor, keep these points in mind:[10]

- Writers need to let go of traditional expectations of authorship, including individual recognition and control. The value of a wiki stems from the collective insight of all its contributors.
- Team members sometimes need to be encouraged to edit and improve each other's work.
- Writers should use page templates and other formatting options to make sure the content fits the same style as the rest of the wiki.
- Many wikis provide both editing and commenting capabilities, and participants should use the appropriate tool for each. In other words, don't insert comments or questions into the main content; use the "talk page" or other commenting feature if you want to discuss the content.
- New users should take advantage of the *sandbox*, if available; this is a "safe," nonpublished section of the wiki where team members can practice editing and writing.

Wikis usually have guidelines to help new contributors integrate their work into the group's ongoing effort. Be sure to read and understand these guidelines; don't be afraid to ask for help.

REAL-TIME UPDATES
Learn More

A simple definition of search engine optimization

Internet marketing specialist Lee Odden provides a simple definition of *search engine optimization*. Go to **http://real-timeupdates.com/bct** and click on "Learn More." If you are using mybcommlab, you can access Real-Time Updates within each chapter or under Student Study Tools.

Becoming an effective wiki collaborator requires a shift in your mindset from the approach you use for individual writing.

Adapting the Three-Step Process for Successful Wiki Writing

If you are creating a new wiki, think through your long-term purpose carefully, just as you would with a new blog or podcast channel. Will the wiki be a one-time event (creating a report, for example) or an ongoing effort (such as maintaining Help files for a software program)? Who will be allowed to add or modify content? Will you or someone else serve as editor, reviewing all additions and changes? What rules and guidelines will you establish to guide the growth of the wiki? What security measures might be required? For instance, the PlayStation development team at Sony uses a wiki to keep top managers up to date on new products, and because this information is highly confidential, access to the wiki is tightly controlled.[11]

Whenever you add content to a wiki, make sure it fits in smoothly with the organization of the existing content.

If you are adding a page or an article to an existing wiki, figure out how this new material fits in with the existing organization. Find out whether any similar material already exists; if so, it might be better to expand an existing article or add a subpage rather than create a new item. Also, learn the wiki's preferred style for handling incomplete articles. For example, on the wiki that contains the user documentation for the popular WordPress blogging software, contributors are discouraged from adding new pages until the content is "fairly complete and accurate." Writers are instead encouraged to insert incomplete pages (usually called "stubs" in wiki parlance) and rough drafts under their personal pages until they are ready to be added to the main wiki content.[12]

If you are revising or updating an existing wiki article, use the checklist on page 190 in Chapter 6 to evaluate the content before you make changes. If you don't agree with published content and plan to revise it, you can use the wiki's discussion facility to share your concerns with other contributors. A well-run wiki encourages discussions and even robust disagreements, as long as everyone remains civil and respectful. If two or more contributors get into an "edit war," an editor may need to step in to resolve the conflict.[13]

Helping Readers Find Their Way

Help your audiences navigate through your reports by providing clear directions to key pieces of content.

Today's readers often lack the time or the inclination to plow through long reports page by page or screen by screen. They typically want to browse quickly, find a section of interest, dive in for details, browse for another section, and so on. If you want readers to understand and accept your message, help them navigate your document by using headings and links, smooth transitions, and previews and reviews.

Headings and Links

6 LEARNING OBJECTIVE

Briefly describe three report elements that can help readers find their way in long documents

As you learned in Chapter 6, headings are brief titles that cue readers about the content of sections that follow. They improve a document's readability and are especially useful for identifying the framework of a report. They also visually indicate shifts from one idea to the next, and when you use a combination of headings and subheadings, you help readers see the relationship between subordinate and main ideas. In addition, busy readers can quickly understand the gist of a document simply by scanning the headings. In online reports, headings serve all these functions, plus they can be used to provide links to other sections and other websites.

Many companies specify a format for headings, either through style guides or document templates. If yours does, use that recommended format. Otherwise, create a simple arrangement that clearly distinguishes levels and is applied consistently throughout your document. Figure 14.6 shows an example of a simple scheme that's easy for readers to follow. Whatever scheme you use, keep it clean and professional and make sure readers can easily distinguish different levels of headings and subheadings.

Transitions

Transitions connect ideas by helping readers move from one thought to the next.

Successful report writers use transitions (see Chapter 5) to help readers move from one section of a report to the next and from key point to key point within sections. Transitions can be words, sentences, or complete paragraphs. Here's an example:

> . . . As you can see, our profits have decreased by 12 percent over the past eight months.

FIGURE 14.6   Simple Heading Format for Reports
This simple arrangement will work well for most reports. However, your company may have a standard style guide or template for report headings, and if it does, you should use it.

TITLE

The title is centered at the top of the page in all capital letters, usually bold-faced (or underlined if typewritten), often in a large font (type size), and often using a sans serif typeface. When the title runs to more than one line, the lines are usually double-spaced and arranged as an inverted pyramid (the longer line on the top).

FIRST-LEVEL HEADING

A first-level heading indicates what the following section is about, perhaps by describing the subdivisions. All first-level headings are grammatically parallel, with the possible exception of such headings as "Introduction," "Conclusions," and "Recommendations." Some text appears between every two headings, regardless of their levels. Still boldfaced and sans serif, the font may be smaller than that used in the title but still larger than the typeface used in the text and still in all capital letters.

Second-Level Heading

Like first-level headings, second-level headings indicate what the following material is about. All second-level headings within a section are grammatically parallel. Still boldfaced and sans serif, the font may either remain the same or shrink to the size used in the text, and the style is now initial capitals followed with lowercase. Never use only one second-level heading under a first-level heading. (The same is true for every other level of heading.)

Third-Level Heading

A third-level heading is worded to reflect the content of the material that follows. All third-level headings beneath a second-level heading should be grammatically parallel.

Fourth-Level Heading. Like all the other levels of heading, fourth-level headings reflect the subject that will be developed. All fourth-level headings within a subsection are parallel.

Fifth-level headings are generally the lowest level of heading used. However, you can indicate further breakdowns in your ideas by using a list:

1. *The first item in a list.* You may indent the entire item in block format to set it off visually. Numbers are optional.
2. *The second item in a list.* All lists have at least two items. An introductory phrase or sentence may be italicized for emphasis, as shown here.

To counteract this decline in profits, we can explore alternatives. First, we can raise our selling prices. Second, we can work to reduce our manufacturing costs. Third, we can introduce new products that will support higher profit margins. However, each of these alternatives has both advantages and disadvantages.

The phrase *As you can see* alerts readers to the fact that they are reading a summary of the information just presented. The phrase *this decline in profits* refers to the previous paragraph, to let readers know that the text will be saying something else about that topic. The words *first, second,* and *third* help readers stay on track as the three alternatives are introduced, and the word *however* alerts readers to the fact that evaluating the three alternatives requires some additional discussion. Effective transitions such as these can help readers summarize and remember what they've learned so far while giving them a mental framework to process new information.

Previews and Reviews

Previews help readers prepare for upcoming information, and reviews help them verify and clarify what they've just read.

Preview sections introduce important topics by helping readers get ready for new information; they are particularly helpful when the information is complex, unexpected, or unfamiliar. Think of a preview as an opportunity for readers to arrange their mental file folders before you start giving them information to put in those folders.

Review sections come after a body of material and summarize the information just covered. They help readers absorb details while keeping track of the big picture. Long reports and those dealing with complex subjects can often benefit from multiple review sections, one at the end of every major subject block, as well as a more comprehensive review at the very end of a document.

Previews and reviews can be written in sentence format, in bulleted lists, or using a combination of the two. Both are effective, but bullets can increase your document's readability by adding white space to the document design. Consider the following preview, which is written using both formats:

SENTENCE FORMAT	BULLETED LIST
The next section discusses the advantages of online advertising. Among them are currency, global reach, affordability, and interactivity.	As the next section shows, online advertising has four advantages: • Currency • Global reach • Affordability • Interactivity

For more on writing effective bullets and lists, see "Using Lists and Bullets to Clarify and Emphasize" on page 185 in Chapter 6. To review the tasks discussed in this section, see "Checklist: Composing Business Reports and Proposals."

✓ **CHECKLIST:**   **Composing Business Reports and Proposals**

A. Review and fine-tune your outline.
- Match your parallel headings to the tone of your report.
- Understand how the introduction, body, and close work together to convey your message.

B. Draft report content.
- Use the introduction to establish the purpose, scope, and organization of your report.
- Use the body to present and interpret the information you gathered.
- Use the close to summarize major points, discuss conclusions, or make recommendations.

C. Draft proposal content.
- Use the introduction to discuss the background or problem, your solution, the scope, and organization.
- Use the body to persuasively explain the benefits of your proposed approach.
- Use the close to emphasize reader benefits and summarize the merits of your approach.

D. Draft online content.
- Establish your credibility with information that is accurate, current, complete, and authoritative.
- Adapt your content to local audiences as much as possible.

- Compose compelling, web-friendly content in the inverted pyramid style.
- Present concise, scannable content.
- Create user-friendly links that clearly identify where the reader will be taken upon clicking.

E. Collaborate on wikis.
- Adopt the wiki philosophy, starting with letting go of traditional expectations of authorship and control.
- Encourage everyone to contribute.
- Use wiki capabilities wisely.
- Carefully think through the purpose of new wikis before creating them.
- Before adding content to an existing wiki, make sure it will fit the organization of the existing content.
- Evaluate wiki articles carefully before editing them.

F. Help readers find their way.
- Provide headings to improve readability and clarify the framework of your ideas.
- Create transitions that tie together ideas and show how one thought relates to another.
- Preview important topics to help readers get ready for new information.
- Review information to help readers absorb details and keep the big picture in mind.

USING TECHNOLOGY TO CRAFT REPORTS AND PROPOSALS

Creating lengthy reports and proposals can be a huge task, so take advantage of technological tools to help throughout the process. You've read about some of these tools in earlier chapters; here are some of the most important ones for developing reports and proposals:

- **Templates.** Beyond simply formatting documents, report templates can identify the specific sections required for each type of report and even automatically insert headings for each section.
- **Linked and embedded documents.** In many reports and proposals, you'll include graphics, spreadsheets, databases, and other elements produced in other software programs. For instance, in Microsoft Office, you can choose to either *link* to another file (which ensures that changes in that file are reflected in your file) or *embed* another file (which doesn't include this automatic updating feature). Just make sure you know how your tools work.
- **Electronic forms.** For recurring forms such as sales reports and compliance reports, consider creating files that combine boilerplate text for material that doesn't change from report to report.
- **Electronic documents.** Portable document format (PDF) files are widely used in business today, and a variety of tools are available to convert reports and proposals to PDF files that are easy and safe to share electronically.
- **Multimedia documents.** When the written word isn't enough, combine your report with video clips, animation, presentation software slides, and other elements. As you'll see in Chapter 17, tools such as Microsoft Producer let you merge a variety of file types to create compelling multimedia presentations that supplement or replace traditional reports.
- **Proposal-writing software.** Chapter 13 mentions proposal-writing software; such semi-automated systems can save enormous amounts of time and energy for companies that prepare numerous proposals every year.

For the latest information on writing business reports and proposals, visit **www.real-timeupdates.com/bct** and click on Chapter 14.

Look for ways to utilize technology to reduce the mechanical work involved in writing long reports.

Document Makeover

Improve This Policy Report

To practice correcting drafts of actual documents, visit the "Document Makeovers" section in either mybcommlab or the Companion Website for this text.

If mybcommlab is being used in your class, see your User Guide for specific instructions on how to access the content for this chapter. If you are accessing this feature through the Companion Website, click on "Document Makeovers" and then select Chapter 14. You will find a policy report that contains problems and errors related to what you've learned in this chapter about writing business reports and proposals. Use the Final Draft decision tool to create an improved version of this report. Check the message for an effective opening; consistent levels of formality or informality; and the use of headings, lists, transitions, and previews and reviews to help orient readers.

Communication Challenges at Tellabs

You wanted to start your career in corporate communications with an opportunity to learn from one of the best, so you're excited to be on George Stenitzer's team at Tellabs. Using the skills you've been practicing in your course, respond to these challenges.

Individual Challenge: Like many other companies associated with the Internet, Tellabs's business declined when the dot-com boom of the late 1990s began to fizzle out by early 2001. The following excerpt from a recent Tellabs annual report describes the effect this had on the company's operations. (The *carriers* and *service providers* referred to are the

companies that buy Tellabs's products; *material charges* are expenses that are significant enough to affect the company's stock price.) As you review these two paragraphs (don't worry about all the technical and financial details), you can see that the first discusses the period from 2001 to 2003, when the company's financial results suffered. The second discusses the upturn that began in 2003 and continued through 2005. Write a transition sentence for the beginning of the second paragraph, signaling to readers that the story is about to change from the negative news of 2001–2003 to the more positive results that began in 2003.

The markets for our products have undergone dynamic change over the last few years. Beginning in 2001, carrier overcapacity, a softening economy and other factors caused our customers to reduce their capital spending significantly. The impact on Tellabs was a dramatic decline in revenue for each of the years 2001 through 2003. In addition, we had manufacturing overcapacity, excess inventories and a cost structure that could not be supported by our smaller revenue base. We responded by closing manufacturing facilities, reducing global head count, consolidating office space, exiting certain product lines and instituting cost controls across the organization. We also reviewed our product portfolio and cut back or stopped development efforts on some products. In addition, at the end of 2003, we moved to outsource the majority of our remaining manufacturing operations to third-party electronics manufacturing services providers to take advantage of their greater purchasing power and other efficiencies. These actions caused us to record material charges in 2001 through 2005 for excess and obsolete inventory and excess purchase commitments, severance costs, facilities shutdown costs, including accelerated depreciation on certain manufacturing and office buildings and equipment due to shortened useful lives, and various contractual obligations. We also recorded charges for other impaired and surplus assets.

Market stability began in 2003 and continued in 2004 and 2005 as service providers invested in their networks at levels at or above 2003. This stability enabled us to post year-over-year revenue growth in 2004 for the first time since fiscal 2000. Growing demand for wireless services, including third-generation (3G) services, drove capital investments by both wireless and wireline service providers and helped drive sales of our transport and managed access products.

Team Challenge: Stenitzer's audience-oriented approach to writing extends to the web, through such key elements as carefully worded hyperlinks that let website visitors know exactly what to expect before they click. He wants to make sure that the links on the Investor Relations page (**www.tellabs.com/investors**) are as good as they can possibly be. With your team, establish criteria that you believe make effective links and then review the investor pages on four other corporate websites (choose any four companies in any industries that interest you). Create a table that compares the four sites with Tellabs, using the criteria you established. Write a one-paragraph summary of the information in the table, along with a list of any improvements that you think could be made to the Tellabs investor section.

SUMMARY OF LEARNING OBJECTIVES

1 **Explain how to adapt to your audiences when writing reports and proposals.** Adapt to your audience by demonstrating sensitivity to their needs (adopting the "you" attitude, maintaining a strong sense of etiquette, emphasizing the positive, and using bias-free language), building a strong relationship with your audience (making sure your writing reflects the desired image of your organization and building your credibility), and controlling your style and tone to achieve the appropriate degree of formality, given the nature of the material and your relationship with the audience.

2 **Name five characteristics of effective report content.** Effective report content is accurate if it is factually correct and error free. It is complete if it includes all necessary information and supports all key assertions. It is balanced if it presents all sides of an argument. It is clear and logical if it is well written and organized logically. It is properly documented if credit is given to all primary and secondary sources of information used.

3 **List the topics commonly covered in the introduction, body, and close of formal reports.** The introduction highlights who authorized the report, the purpose and scope of a report, necessary background material, the sources or methods used to gather information, important definitions, any limitations, and the order in which the various topics are covered. The body can discuss such details as problems, opportunities, facts, evidence, trends, results of studies or investigations, analysis of potential courses of action and their advantages and disadvantages, process procedures and steps, methods and approaches, evaluation criteria for options, conclusions, recommendations, and supporting reasons. The close summarizes key points, restates conclusions and recommendations, if appropriate, and lists action items.

4 **List six strategies to strengthen a proposal argument.** To strengthen your argument, you should demonstrate your knowledge, provide concrete examples, research the competition, prove that your proposal is workable, adopt a "you" attitude, and make your proposal attractive and error free.

5 **Identify five characteristics of effective writing in online reports.** First, effective web content builds trust with often-skeptical online audiences by being accurate, current, complete, and authoritative. Second, as much as

possible, the content is adapted to global audiences, including localizing for specific languages and cultural norms. Third, good web content is easy to scan quickly because online readers often take a quick look at a webpage to see if anything promises to meet their information needs. Fourth, effective online reports make good use of links to enable both the scanning of content and navigation of the website. Fifth, good web content is "findable" by search engines through the use of search engine optimization.

6 **Briefly describe three report elements that can help readers find their way in long documents.**   Effective reports help readers navigate the document by using three elements: (1) headings (and links for online reports), which set off important ideas and provide the reader with clues as to the report's framework and shifts in discussion; (2) transitions, which tie together ideas and keep readers moving along; and (3) previews and reviews, which prepare readers for new information and summarize previously discussed information.

PEARSON mybcommlab™

Log on to **www.mybcommlab.com** to access the following study and assessment aids associated with this chapter:

- Video applications
- Real-Time Updates
- Peer review activity
- Quick Learning Guides

- Pre/post test
- Personalized study plan
- Model documents
- Sample presentations

If you are not using mybcommlab, you can access the Real-Time Updates and Quick Learning Guides through **http://real-timeupdates.com/bct**. The Quick Learning Guide hits all the high points of this chapter in just two pages. This guide, especially prepared by the authors, will help you study for exams or review important concepts whenever you need a quick refresher.

Test Your Knowledge

1. Why is the "you" attitude especially important with long, complex reports?
2. What writing choices can you make to adjust the formality of your reports?
3. Why is it helpful to review your outline one last time before you begin writing a report?
4. What is the function of a report introduction?
5. What information might you include in the close of a report?
6. How do the introductions of solicited and unsolicited proposals differ?
7. Why is the work plan a key component of a proposal?
8. How does giving dates for online content help your readers?
9. How does the inverted pyramid style help online readers?
10. What elements can you use to help readers follow the structure and flow of information in a long report?

Apply Your Knowledge

1. Should a report always explain the writer's method of gathering evidence or solving a problem? Why or why not?
2. What are the risks of not explaining the purpose of a proposal within the introduction?
3. Why do experts recommend that online content be shorter than printed content, wherever possible?
4. Why do you need to approach wiki writing with a different attitude than the one you take with conventional writing?
5. **Ethical Choices** If a company receives a solicited proposal from a management consulting firm, is it ethical for the company to adopt the recommendations discussed in the proposal even though the company does not hire the submitting firm? Why or why not?

Practice Your Knowledge

Messages for Analysis

Message 14.A: Revising Web Content with a "You" Attitude

To access this wiki exercise, visit **http://real-timeupdates.com/bct**, click on "Student Assignments," and select Chapter 14, page 459, Message 14.A. Follow the instructions for evaluating the existing content and revising it to make it more reader oriented.

Message 14.B: Improving the Effectiveness of a Wiki Article

To access this wiki exercise, go to **http://real-timeupdates.com/bct**, click on "Student Assignments," and select Chapter 14, Page 459, Message 14.B. Follow the instructions for evaluating the existing content and revising it to make it clear and concise.

Message 14.C: Improving a Solicited Proposal

Read the solicited proposal in Figure 14.7. (1) Analyze the strengths and weaknesses of this document and (2) revise the document so that it follows this chapter's guidelines.

Exercises

Active links for all websites in this chapter can be found online. If mybcommlab is being used in your class, see your User Guide for instructions on accessing the content for this chapter. Otherwise, visit **www.pearsonglobaleditions.com/bovee**, locate *Business Communication Today*, Tenth Edition, click the Companion Website link, select Chapter 14, and then click on "Featured Websites." Please note that links to sites that become inactive after publication of the book will be removed from the Featured Websites section.

FIGURE 14.7   Solicited Proposal

Morning Star Travel Service Ltd.
Room 201, Bank Centre,
35 Nathan Road, Kowloon, Hong Kong.

April 15, 2009

PROJECT: Incentive Travel Scheme 89UX2 Contract No. 9194

Dear Mr. Wong:

Morning Star Travel Service Ltd. proposes to be the sole organizer for the Incentive Travel Scheme 89UX2 for 90 staff of your company. The itinerary and the price are shown in the following table:

Incentive Travel Scheme Details

Destination	Length of Stay	Tour Group Size	Price/head*	Total
Beijing	4 days 3 nights	30	HK$3,200.00	HK$96,000.00
Tokyo	5 days 4 nights	30	HK$7,000.00	HK$210,000.00
Seoul	5 days 4 nights	30	HK$4,000.00	HK$120,000.00

*Price/head refers to the total price covering the whole length of stay for each tour member. It includes all taxes but excludes high-season surcharge.

The following items clarify and qualify the scope of our services:
1. Morning Star Travel Service Ltd. will send one tour guide and one escort for each tour group.
2. Accommodation will be four-star hotels or equivalent. All meals are included.
3. One air-conditioned coach will be provided to each tour group.
4. Every member joining the above-mentioned tour groups is responsible for obtaining the entry visa for the respective countries.
5. Travel Service shall not be liable for the travel insurance of individual travelers.
6. The itinerary may be altered in case of adverse weather conditions.
7. The minimum and maximum number per tour group is 20 and 35. Morning Star Travel Service Ltd. shall be paid strictly based on the actual number of travelers in each group.
8. Morning Star Travel Service Ltd. may withdraw this bid if we do not receive a written confirmation from your company within 10 days of your receipt of this proposal.
9. Morning Star Travel Service Ltd. shall not provide a refund for travelers who withdraw from the tour group 5 working days before the tour commencement.
10. A deposit of $129 is required of each traveler.

If you have any questions, feel free to contact me at the phone number listed below.

Sincerely,

William Fung
Marketing Manager
Morning Star Travel Service Ltd.
Office: (852) 2771 2208
Fax: (852) 2771 8800
E-mail: William_Fung@morningstar.com.hk

Adapted from: Morning Star Travel Service Ltd. website (http:www.morning-star.com.hk) Accessed on 15 April 2009.

14.1   **Adapting Reports to the Audience**   Review the reports shown in Figures 14.1 to 14.4. Give specific examples of how each of these reports establishes a good relationship with the audience. Consider such things as using the "you" attitude, emphasizing the positive, establishing credibility, being polite, using bias-free language, and projecting a good company image.

14.2   **Composing Reports: Report Content**   You are writing an analytical report on the U.S. sales of your newest product. Of the following topics, identify where in the report each element should be included—the introduction, body, or close. Briefly explain your decisions.
   a.   Regional breakdowns of sales across the country
   b.   Date the product was released in the marketplace
   c.   Sales figures from competitors selling similar products worldwide
   d.   Predictions of how the struggling U.S. economy will affect sales over the next six months
   e.   The method used for obtaining the preceding predictions
   f.   The impact of similar products being sold in the United States by Japanese competitors
   g.   Your recommendation about whether the company should sell this product internationally
   h.   Actions that must be completed by year end if the company decides to sell this product internationally

14.3   **Composing Reports**   Find an article in a business newspaper or journal (in print or online) that recommends a solution to a problem. Identify the problem, the recommended solution(s), and the supporting evidence provided by the author to justify his or her recommendation(s). Did the author cite any formal or informal studies as evidence? What facts or statistics did the author include? Did the author cite any criteria for evaluating possible options? If so, what were they?

14.4 Composing Web Content: Effective Links Write an effectively worded link for each of the following content sections on a website (make up any information you need):

  a. A page that summarizes the company's most recent quarterly financial results
  b. A page that lists the phone numbers and e-mail addresses for key contacts within the company
  c. A page containing a news release announcing that the company is being investigated by the Securities and Exchange Commission (SEC) for possible accounting irregularities
  d. A page that announces the launch of a major new product

14.5 Composing Reports: Navigational Clues Review a long business article in a journal or newspaper. Highlight examples of how the article uses headings, transitions, and previews and reviews to help the readers find their way.

14.6 Ethical Choices Your boss has asked you to prepare a feasibility report to determine whether the company should advertise its custom-crafted cabinetry in the weekly neighborhood newspaper. Based on your primary research, you think they should. As you draft the introduction to your report, however, you discover that the survey administered to the neighborhood newspaper subscribers was flawed. Several of the questions were poorly written and misleading. You used the survey results, among other findings, to justify your recommendation. The report is due in three days. What actions might you want to take, if any, before you complete your report?

14.7 Composing Business Reports Your boss, Len Chow (vice president of corporate planning), has asked you to research opportunities in the cosmetics industry and to prepare a report that presents your findings and your recommendation for where you think the company should focus its marketing efforts. Here's a copy of your note cards (data were created for this exercise):

Subject: Demand   ref: 1.1
Industrywide sales have grown consistently for several decades, fueled by both a growing population and increased per capita consumption

Subject: Competition   ref: 1.2
700 companies currently in cosmetics industry

Subject: Niches   ref: 1.3
Focusing on special niches avoids head-on competition with industry leaders

Subject: Competition   ref: 1.4
Industry dominated by market leaders: Revlon, Procter & Gamble, Avon, Gillette

Subject: Demand   ref: 1.5
Industry no longer recession-proof: Past year, sales sluggish; consumer spending is down; most affected were mid- to high-priced brands; consumers traded down to less expensive lines

Subject: Competition   ref: 1.6
Smaller companies (Neutrogena, Mary Kay, Soft Soap, and Noxell) survive by: specializing in niches, differentiating product line, focusing on market segment

Subject: Demand   ref: 1.7
Consumption of cosmetics relatively flat for past five years

Subject: Competition   ref: 1.8
Prices are constant while promotion budgets are increasing

Subject: Niches   ref: 1.9
Men: 50 percent of adult population; account for one-fifth of cosmetic sales; market leaders have attempted this market but failed

Subject: Demand   ref: 1.10
Cosmetic industry is near maturity, but some segments may vary. Total market currently produces annual retail sales of $14.5 billion: Cosmetics/lotions/fragrances—$5.635 billion; Personal hygiene products—$4.375 billion; Hair-care products—$3.435 billion; shaving products—$1.055 billion

Subject: Niches   ref: 1.11
Ethnic groups: Some firms specialize in products for African Americans; few firms oriented toward Hispanic, Asian, or Native Americans, which tend to be concentrated geographically

Subject: Demand   ref: 1.12
Average annual expenditure per person for cosmetics is $158

Subject: Competition   ref: 1.13
Competition is intensifying, and dominant companies are putting pressure on smaller ones

Subject: Demand   ref: 1.14
First quarter of current year, demand is beginning to revive; trend expected to continue well into next year

Subject: Niches   ref: 1.15
Senior citizens: large growing segment of population; account for 6% of cosmetic sales; specialized needs for hair and skin not being met; interested in appearance

Subject: Demand   ref: 1.16
Demographic trends: (1) Gradual maturing of baby boomer generation will fuel growth by consuming greater quantities of skincare products, hair replenishment and coloring products, and anti-aging products; (2) population is increasing in the South and Southwest, where some brands have strong distribution

List the main idea of your message (your recommendation), the major points (your conclusions), and supporting evidence. Then construct a final report outline with first- and second-level informative headings focusing on your conclusions. Because Chow requested this report, you can feel free to use the direct approach. Finish by writing a draft of your memo report to Chow.

Expand Your Knowledge

Exploring the Best of the Web

Research Before You Report

www.corporateinformation.com

Research your competition at Corporate Information and find out what you need to know before you write your next report or proposal. This website has links to thousands of company profiles, data on many industries in dozens of countries, and current economic information for more than 100 countries. You'll also find research reports analyzing sales, dividends, earnings, and profit ratios on thousands of companies, current foreign exchange rates, and definitions of commonly used global company extensions, such as GmbH SA de CV, and more. Scan the site and answer these questions:

1. Select an industry of your choice from one of the listed countries and follow the links to reports, analyses, and data on that industry. What specific types of information did you find on the industry? How might you use this information when writing a report or proposal?
2. Review one of the sample company research reports that are available for free. What types of specific information are available in these reports? How might you use this information when writing a report or proposal?
3. What do the company extensions GmbH, KK, LLC, OHG, SA, and SNC mean?

Sharpening Your Career Skills Online

Bovée and Thill's Business Communication Web Search, at http://businesscommunicationblog.com/websearch, is a unique research tool designed specifically for business communication research. Use the Web Search function to find a website, video, PDF document, or PowerPoint presentation that offers advice on writing website content. Write a brief e-mail message to your instructor, describing the item that you found and summarizing the career skills information you learned from it.

CASES

Applying the Three-Step Writing Process to Cases

Apply each step to the following cases, as assigned by your instructor.

INFORMAL INFORMATIONAL REPORTS

1. My progress to date: Interim progress report on your academic career. As you know, the procedural requirements involved in getting a degree or certificate can be nearly as challenging as any course you could take.

Your task: Prepare an interim progress report that details the steps you've taken toward completing your graduation or certification requirements. After examining the requirements listed in your college catalog, indicate a realistic schedule for completing those that remain. In addition to course requirements, include steps such as completing the residency requirement, filing necessary papers, and paying necessary fees. Use a memo format for your report and address it to anyone who is helping or encouraging you through school.

2. Passing on the message: Create an activity report of a meeting by interviewing one of the participants. Seminars, symposia, and conferences are an integral part of academia. Last month one of your professors participated in an International Conference on Education.

Your task: Prepare a report in the memo format, to be circulated among your fellow students, by interviewing the professor who participated in the conference and who can provide you with the copy of the program and proceedings of the conference.

3. Check that price tag: Informational report on trends in college costs. Are tuition costs going up, going down, or remaining the same? Your college's administration has asked you to compare your college's tuition costs with those of a nearby college and determine which has risen more quickly. Research the trend by checking your college's annual tuition costs for each of the most recent four years. Then research the four-year tuition trends for a neighboring college. For both colleges, calculate the percentage change in tuition costs from year to year and between the first and fourth years.

Your task: Prepare an informal report (using the letter format), presenting your findings and conclusions to the president of your college. Include graphics to explain and support your conclusions.

SOCIAL NETWORKING SKILLS   BLOGGING SKILLS

4. With experience comes wisdom: Sharing your wisdom with future college students. If you're like many other college students, your first year was more than you expected: more difficult, more fun, more frustrating, more expensive, more exhausting, more rewarding—more of everything, positive and negative. Oh, the things you know now that you didn't know then!

Your task: With several other students, identify five or six things you wish you would've realized or understood better before you started your first year of college. These can relate to your school life (such as "I didn't realize how much work I would have for my classes" or "I should've asked for help as soon as I got stuck") and your personal and social life ("I wish I would've been more open to meeting people"). Use these items as the foundation of a brief informational report that you could post on a blog that is read by high school students and their families. Your goal with this report is to help the next generation of students make a successful and rewarding transition to college.

INFORMAL ANALYTICAL REPORTS

5. Learning opportunity: Analyzing a significant mistake or failure in your life. Mistakes can be wonderful learning opportunities if we're honest with ourselves and receptive to learning from the mistake.

Your task: Identify a mistake you've made—something significant enough to have cost you a lot of money, wasted a lot of time, harmed your health, damaged a relationship, created serious problems at work, prevented you from pursuing what could've been a rewarding opportunity, or otherwise had serious consequences. Now figure out why you made that mistake. Did you let emotions get in the way of clear thinking? Did you make a serious financial blunder because you didn't take the time to understand the consequences of a decision? Were you too cautious? Not cautious enough? Perhaps several factors led to a poor decision.

Write a brief analytical report to your instructor that describes the situation and outlines your analysis of why the failure occurred and how you can avoid making a similar mistake in the future. If you can't think of a significant mistake or failure that you're comfortable sharing with your instructor, write about a mistake that a friend or family member made (without revealing the person's identify or potentially causing him or her any embarrassment).

6. Staying the course: Unsolicited proposal using the 2 + 2 = 4 approach. Think of a course you would love to see added to the core curriculum at your school. Conversely, if you would like to see a course offered as an elective rather than being required, write your e-mail report accordingly.

Your task: Write a short e-mail proposal, using the 2 + 2 = 4 approach. Prepare your proposal to be submitted to the academic dean by e-mail. Be sure to include reasons supporting your idea.

7. Planning my program: Problem-solving report using the yardstick method. Assume that you will have time for only one course next term.

Your task: List the pros and cons of four or five courses that interest you and use the yardstick method to settle on the course that is best for you to take at this time. Write your report in memo format, addressing it to your academic adviser.

8. Restaurant review: Troubleshooting report on a restaurant's food and operations. Visit any restaurant, possibly your school cafeteria. The workers and fellow customers will assume that you are an ordinary customer, but you are really a spy for the owner.

Your task: After your visit, write a short letter to the owner, explaining (1) what you did and what you observed, (2) any violations of policy that you observed, and (3) your recommendations for improvement. The first part of your report (what you did and what you observed) will be the longest. Include a description of the premises, inside and out. Tell how long it took for each step in ordering and receiving your meal. Describe the service and food thoroughly. You are interested in both the good and bad aspects of the establishment's décor, service, and food. For the second section (violations of policy), use some common sense. If all the servers but one have their hair covered, you may assume that policy requires hair to be covered; a dirty window or restroom obviously violates policy. The last section (recommendations for improvement) involves professional judgment. What management actions would improve the restaurant?

9. On the books: Troubleshooting report on improving the campus bookstore. Imagine that you are a consultant, hired to improve the profits of your campus bookstore.

Your task: Visit the bookstore and look critically at its operations. Then draft a letter to the bookstore manager, offering recommendations that would make the store more profitable, perhaps suggesting products it should carry, hours that it should remain open, or added services that it should make available to students. Be sure to support your recommendations.

10. Day and night: Problem-solving report on stocking a 24-hour convenience store. When a store is open all day, every day, when's the best time to restock the shelves? That's the challenge at Store 24, a retail chain that never closes. Imagine you're the assistant manager of a Store 24 branch that just opened near your campus. You want to set up a restocking schedule that won't conflict with prime shopping hours. Think about the number of customers you're likely to serve in the morning, afternoon, evening, and overnight hours. Consider, too, how many employees you might have during these four periods.

Your task: Write a problem-solving report in letter form to the store manager (Isabel Chu) and the regional manager (Eric Angstrom), who must agree on a solution to this problem. Discuss the pros and cons of each of the four periods and include your recommendation for restocking the shelves.

PROPOSALS

11. "Would you carry it?" Unsolicited sales proposal, recommending a product to a retail outlet. Select a product you are familiar with and imagine that you are the manufacturer, trying to get a local retail outlet to carry it. Use the Internet and other resources to gather information about the product.

Your task: Write an unsolicited sales proposal in letter format to the owner (or manager) of the store, proposing that the item be stocked. Use the information you gathered to describe some of the product's features and benefits to the store. Then make up some reasonable figures, highlighting what the item costs, what it can be sold for, and what services your company provides (return of unsold items, free replacement of unsatisfactory items, necessary repairs, and so on).

PORTFOLIO BUILDER

12. Where is everybody? Proposal to sell GPS fleet-tracking system.
As a sales manager for Air-Trak, one of your responsibilities is writing sales proposals for potential buyers of your company's Air-Trak tracking system. The system uses the global positioning system (GPS) to track the location of vehicles and other assets. For example, the dispatcher for a trucking company can simply click a map display on a computer screen to find out where all the company's trucks are at that instant. Air-Trak lists the following as benefits of the system:

- Making sure vehicles follow prescribed routes with minimal loitering time
- "Geofencing," in which dispatchers are alerted if vehicles leave assigned routes or designated service areas
- Route optimization, in which fleet managers can analyze routes and destinations to find the most time- and fuel-efficient path for each vehicle

- Comparisons between scheduled and actual travel
- Enhanced security, protecting both drivers and cargo

Your task: Write a brief proposal to Doneta Zachs, fleet manager for Midwest Express, 338 S.W. 6th, Des Moines, Iowa, 50321. Introduce your company, explain the benefits of the Air-Trak system, and propose a trial deployment in which you would equip five Midwest Express trucks. For the purposes of this assignment, you don't need to worry about the technical details of the system; focus on promoting the benefits and asking for a decision regarding the test project. (You can learn more about the Air-Trak system at www.air-trak.com.)[14]

Completing Reports and Proposals

Learning Objectives

After studying this chapter, you will be able to

1 Summarize the four tasks involved in completing business reports and proposals

2 Identify the major components of a formal report

3 Identify the circumstances in which you should include letters of authorization and letters of acceptance in your reports

4 Explain the difference between a synopsis and an executive summary

5 Identify the major components of a formal proposal

6 Identify the major components to include in a request for proposals (RFP)

Communication Close-up at the Bill & Melinda Gates Foundation

In his role as CEO of the Bill & Melinda Gates Foundation, Jeff Raikes (left) relies on numerous reports and proposals to guide the foundation's long-term strategy, monitor results, and build partnerships.

www.gatesfoundation.org

Microsoft co-founder Bill Gates is accustomed to creating change on a global scale, and he now applies that same energy and strategic thinking to charitable causes. Backed by billions of dollars in endowments, the Bill & Melinda Gates Foundation acts as a catalyst, bringing resources together in a way that "increases the momentum, scale, and sustainability of change." The strategy is applied to such important social challenges as containing the AIDS epidemic, eradicating malaria, improving high schools, and making sure people everywhere have access to the digital revolution made possible by the Internet.

Meeting challenges of such staggering complexity and coordinating the resources of organizations all over the world is no small task, and communication plays a vital role in this effort. In particular, reports and proposals link the various groups involved in the foundation's activities and inform the public about ongoing challenges and progress. As just one measure of the foundation's enormous scope, it receives several thousand formal grant requests each month.

The foundation is staffed with people who have demonstrated effective leadership and communication skills. Jeff Raikes, a former Microsoft executive who took over as chief executive officer in 2008, is deeply involved in reports and proposals—as a writer and as a reader. Raikes examines

465

proposals from various angles, listening to his colleagues' perspectives and asking probing questions: Does this proposal align with our core values and goals? Is this really the best approach? What's going to make the biggest difference? How do we define *success* in this effort? Could this proposal be a catalyst that attracts other organizations to participate? Raikes and other staffers have learned to read between the lines, too. As his predecessor Patty Stonesifer put it, "It's amazing what people won't tell you when you have billions of dollars to give away."

Raikes and his colleagues recognize that they are tackling problems of almost unimaginable complexity, but with systematic thinking, unstoppable optimism, unmatched financial resources, and effective communication skills, they remain committed to improving life for people the world over.[1]

---

1 **LEARNING OBJECTIVE**

Summarize the four tasks involved in completing business reports and proposals

PUTTING THE FINAL TOUCHES ON REPORTS AND PROPOSALS

Experienced business communicators such as Jeff Raikes (profiled in the chapter-opening Communication Close-up) recognize that the process of writing a report or proposal doesn't end with a first draft. This chapter addresses all four tasks involved in completing longer messages: revising, producing, proofreading, and distributing. Although the tasks covered in this chapter are similar in concept to those you studied for short messages in Chapter 6, the completion stage for reports and proposals can require a lot more work. And as you've probably already experienced while doing school reports, computers, copiers, and other resources have an uncanny knack for going haywire when you're frantic to finish and have no time to spare. When you're completing an important report on the job, try to leave yourself double or even triple the amount of time you think you'll need so that last-minute glitches don't compromise the quality of all your hard work.

Formal reports have a higher degree of polish and production quality, and they often contain elements not found in informal reports.

Most of the discussion in this chapter applies to *formal* reports and proposals, documents that require an extra measure of polish and professionalism. Few reports and proposals require every component described in this chapter, but be sure to carefully select the elements you want to include in each of your documents.

REVISING REPORTS AND PROPOSALS

The revision process is essentially the same for reports as for any other business message, although it may take considerably more time, depending on the length of your document. Evaluate your organization, style, and tone, making sure that you've said what you want to say and that you've said it in the most logical order and in a way that responds to your audience's needs. Then work to improve the report's readability by varying sentence length, keeping paragraphs short, using lists and bullets, and adding headings and subheadings. Keep revising the content until it is clear, concise, and compelling.

Revising for clarity and conciseness is especially important for online reports because reading online can be difficult.

Tight, efficient writing that is easy to skim is always a plus, but it's especially important for impatient online audiences.[2] Review online report content carefully; strip out all information that doesn't meet audience needs and condense everything else as much as possible. Audiences will gladly return to sites that deliver quality information quickly—and they'll avoid sites that don't.

PRODUCING REPORTS AND PROPOSALS

When you are satisfied with the quality of your text, you're ready to produce your report by incorporating the design elements discussed in Chapter 6. At this point, you should also start to add charts, graphs, and other visuals.

In today's leanly staffed companies, you should be prepared to produce formal reports with little or no assistance from design specialists or other professionals.

In some organizations, you'll be able to rely on the help of specialists in design and production, particularly when you are working on important, high-visibility reports or proposals. You may also have clerical help available to assist with the mechanical assembly and distribution. However, for most reports in many of today's leanly staffed companies, you should count on doing most or all of the production work yourself.

The good news is that computer tools are now generally easy enough for the average businessperson to use productively. The bad news is that continual improvements in computer tools increase your audience's expectations. People are influenced by packaging, and a handsomely bound report with full-color graphics will impress your audience more than a plain report, even though the two documents may contain the same information. In other words, you may find yourself spending extra time on production in order to keep your audience's attention.

Components of a Formal Report

The parts you include in a report depend on the type of report you are writing, its length, your audience's expectations and requirements, and your organization's preferences. The components listed in Figure 15.1 fall into three categories: prefatory parts, text of the report, and supplementary parts. For an illustration of how the various parts fit together, see Linda Moreno's Electrovision report in "Report Writer's Notebook: Analyzing a Formal Report."

A component of a formal report may start on a new page, but not always. Inserting page breaks consumes more paper and adds to the bulk of your report. On the other hand, starting a section on a new page helps your readers navigate the report and recognize transitions between major sections or features.

Prefatory Parts

Prefatory parts are front-end materials that provide key preliminary information so that readers can decide whether and how to read the report.[3] Note that many of these parts—such as the table of contents, list of illustrations, and executive summary—are easier to

(Text continued on page 483)

> **REAL-TIME UPDATES**
> **Learn More**
>
> **Get practical advice on developing research reports**
>
> The Online Writing Lab offers advice on developing all the sections of a typical research report. Go to **http://real-timeupdates.com/bct** and click on "Learn More." If you are using mybcommlab, you can access Real-Time Updates within each chapter or under Student Study Tools.

2 LEARNING OBJECTIVE

Identify the major components of a formal report

Formal reports can contain a variety of prefatory parts, from a cover page to a synopsis or executive summary.

FIGURE 15.1   Parts of a Formal Report
Depending on the level of formality you need to achieve, you can select from these elements to complete a formal report.

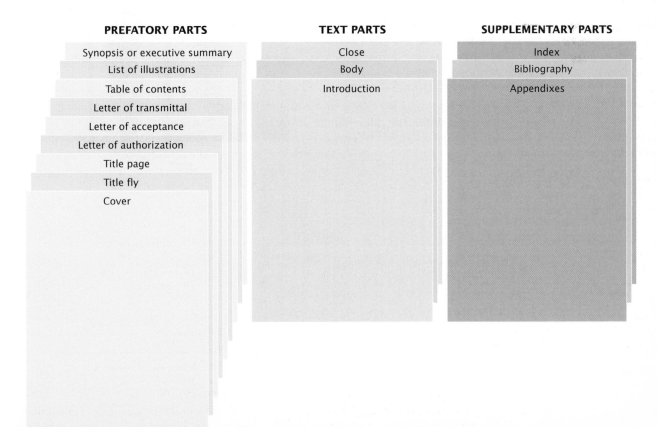

PREFATORY PARTS	TEXT PARTS	SUPPLEMENTARY PARTS
Synopsis or executive summary	Close	Index
List of illustrations	Body	Bibliography
Table of contents	Introduction	Appendixes
Letter of transmittal		
Letter of acceptance		
Letter of authorization		
Title page		
Title fly		
Cover		

Report Writer's Notebook: Analyzing a Formal Report

Analyzing a Formal Report

The report presented in the following pages was prepared by Linda Moreno, manager of the cost accounting department at Electrovision, a high-tech company based in Los Gatos, California. Electrovision's main product is optical character recognition equipment, which is used by the U.S. Postal Service for sorting mail. Moreno's job is to help analyze the company's costs. She has this to say about the background of the report:

> For the past three or four years, Electrovision has been on a roll. Our A-12 optical character reader was a real breakthrough, and the post office grabbed up as many as we could make. Our sales and profits kept climbing, and morale was fantastic. Everybody seemed to think that the good times would last forever. Unfortunately, everybody was wrong. When the Postal Service announced that it was postponing all new equipment purchases because of cuts in its budget, we woke up to the fact that we are essentially a one-product company with one customer. At that point, management started scrambling around looking for ways to cut costs until we could diversify our business a bit.
>
> The vice president of operations, Dennis McWilliams, asked me to help identify cost-cutting opportunities in travel and entertainment. On the basis of his personal observations, he felt that Electrovision was overly generous in its travel policies and that we might be able to save a significant amount by controlling these costs more carefully. My investigation confirmed his suspicion.
>
> I was reasonably confident that my report would be well received. I've worked with Dennis for several years and know what he likes: plenty of facts, clearly stated conclusions, and specific recommendations for what should be done next. I also knew that my report would be passed on to other Electrovision executives, so I wanted to create a good impression. I wanted the report to be accurate and thorough, visually appealing, readable, and appropriate in tone.

When writing the analytical report that follows, Moreno based the organization on conclusions and recommendations presented in direct order. The first two sections of the report correspond to Moreno's two main conclusions: that Electrovision's travel and entertainment costs are too high and that cuts are essential. The third section presents recommendations for achieving better control over travel and entertainment expenses. As you review the report, analyze both the mechanical aspects and the way Moreno presents her ideas. Be prepared to discuss the way the various components convey and reinforce the main message.

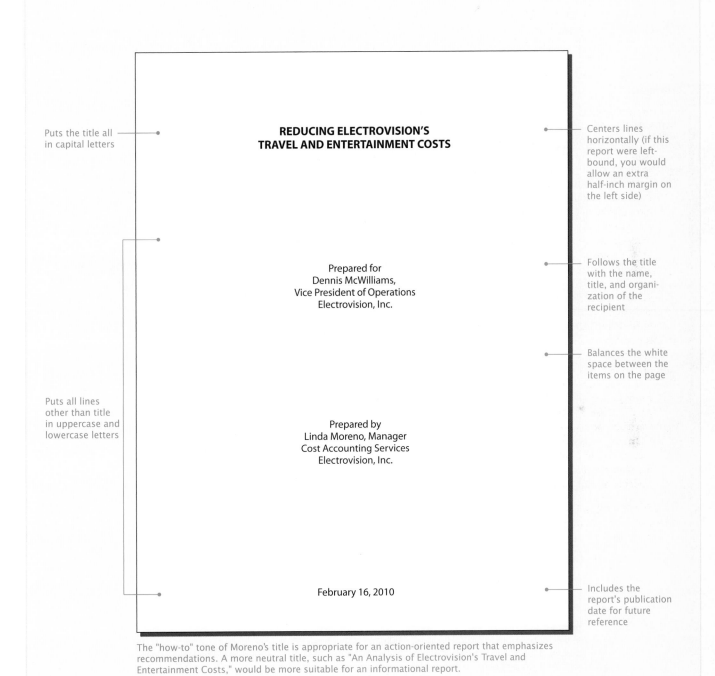

Puts the title all in capital letters

Puts all lines other than title in uppercase and lowercase letters

**REDUCING ELECTROVISION'S
TRAVEL AND ENTERTAINMENT COSTS**

Prepared for
Dennis McWilliams,
Vice President of Operations
Electrovision, Inc.

Prepared by
Linda Moreno, Manager
Cost Accounting Services
Electrovision, Inc.

February 16, 2010

Centers lines horizontally (if this report were left-bound, you would allow an extra half-inch margin on the left side)

Follows the title with the name, title, and organization of the recipient

Balances the white space between the items on the page

Includes the report's publication date for future reference

The "how-to" tone of Moreno's title is appropriate for an action-oriented report that emphasizes recommendations. A more neutral title, such as "An Analysis of Electrovision's Travel and Entertainment Costs," would be more suitable for an informational report.

Uses memo format for transmitting this internal report; otherwise, letter format would be used for transmitting external reports

Uses a conversational style

Acknowledges help that has been received

Presents the main conclusion right away (because Moreno expects a positive response)

Closes with thanks and an offer to discuss results (when appropriate, you could also include an offer to help with future projects)

MEMORANDUM

TO: Dennis McWilliams, Vice President of Operations
FROM: Linda Moreno, Manager of Cost Accounting Services   *LM*
DATE: February 16, 2010
SUBJECT: Reducing Electrovision's Travel and Entertainment Costs

Here is the report you requested January 28 on Electrovision's travel and entertainment costs.

Your suspicions were right. We are spending far too much on business travel. Our unwritten policy has been "anything goes," leaving us with no real control over T&E expenses. Although this hands-off approach may have been understandable when Electrovision's profits were high, we can no longer afford the luxury of going first class.

The solutions to the problem seem rather clear. We need to have someone with centralized responsibility for travel and entertainment costs, a clear statement of policy, an effective control system, and a business-oriented travel service that can optimize our travel arrangements. We should also investigate alternatives to travel, such as videoconferencing. Perhaps more important, we need to change our attitude. Instead of viewing travel funds as a bottomless supply of money, all traveling employees need to act as if they were paying the bills themselves.

Getting people to economize is not going to be easy. In the course of researching this issue, I've found that our employees are deeply attached to their generous travel privileges. I think some would almost prefer a cut in pay to a loss in travel status. We'll need a lot of top management involvement to sell people on the need for moderation. One thing is clear: People will be very bitter if we create a two-class system in which top executives get special privileges while the rest of the employees make the sacrifices.

I'm grateful to Mary Lehman and Connie McIllvain for their help in rounding up and sorting through five years' worth of expense reports. Their efforts were truly Herculean.

Thanks for giving me the opportunity to work on this assignment. It's been a real education. If you have any questions about the report, please give me a call.

In this report, Moreno decided to write a brief memo of transmittal and include a separate executive summary. Short reports (fewer than 10 pages) often combine the synopsis or executive summary with the memo or letter of transmittal.

Doesn't include any elements that appear before the "Contents" page

Words the headings exactly as they appear in the text

Numbers figures consecutively throughout the report

Numbers the contents page with lowercase Roman numerals centered at the bottom margin

Includes only the page numbers where sections begin

CONTENTS

LIST OF ILLUSTRATIONS

iii

Moreno included only first- and second-level headings in her table of contents, even though the report contains third-level headings. She prefers a shorter table of contents that focuses attention on the main divisions of thought. She used informative titles, which are appropriate for a report to a receptive audience.

Begins by stating
the purpose of
the report

Presents the points
in the executive
summary in the
same order as they
appear in the
report, using
subheadings
that summarize the
content of the
main sections of
the report

Continues
numbering the
executive
summary pages
with lowercase
Roman numerals

EXECUTIVE SUMMARY

This report analyzes Electrovision's travel and entertainment (T&E) costs and
presents recommendations for reducing those costs.

Travel and Entertainment Costs Are Too High

Travel and entertainment is a large and growing expense category for
Electrovision. The company spends over $16 million per year on business travel,
and these costs have been increasing by 12 percent annually. Company employees
make roughly 3,390 trips each year at an average cost per trip of $4,720. Airfares
are the biggest expense, followed by hotels, meals, and rental cars.

The nature of Electrovision's business does require extensive travel, but the
company's costs are excessive: Our employees spend more than twice the national
average on travel and entertainment. Although the location of the company's
facilities may partly explain this discrepancy, the main reason for our high costs
is a management style that gives employees little incentive to economize.

Cuts Are Essential

Electrovision management now recognizes the need to gain more control over this
element of costs. The company is currently entering a period of declining profits,
prompting management to look for every opportunity to reduce spending. At the
same time, rising airfares and hotel rates are making T&E expenses more significant.

Electrovision Can Save $6 Million per Year

Fortunately, Electrovision has a number of excellent opportunities for reducing
T&E costs. Savings of up to $6 million per year should be achievable, judging by
the experience of other companies. A sensible travel-management program can
save companies as much as 35 percent a year (Gilligan 39–40), and we should be
able to save even more, since we purchase many more business-class tickets than
the average. Four steps will help us cut costs:

1. Hire a director of travel and entertainment to assume overall responsibility for
   T&E spending, policies, and technologies, including the hiring and
   management of a national travel agency.
2. Educate employees on the need for cost containment, both in avoiding
   unnecessary travel and reducing costs when travel is necessary.
3. Negotiate preferential rates with travel providers.
4. Implement technological alternatives to travel, such as virtual meetings.

As necessary as these changes are, they will likely hurt morale, at least in the
short term. Management will need to make a determined effort to explain the
rationale for reduced spending. By exercising moderation in their own travel
arrangements, Electrovision executives can set a good example and help other
employees accept the changes. On the plus side, using travel alternatives such as
web conferencing will reduce the travel burden on many employees and help
them balance their business and personal lives.

iv

Targets a receptive
audience with a
hard-hitting tone in
the executive
summary (a more
neutral approach
would be better for
hostile or skeptical
readers)

Executive summary
uses the same font
and paragraph
treatment as the
text of the report

Moreno decided to include an executive summary because her report is aimed at a mixed
audience, some of whom are interested in the details of her report and others who just want the
"big picture." The executive summary is aimed at the second group, giving them enough information to make a decision without burdening them with the task of reading the entire report.

Her writing style matches the serious nature of the content without sounding distant or stiff.
Moreno chose the formal approach because several members of her audience are considerably
higher up in the organization, and she did not want to sound too familiar. In addition, her
company prefers the impersonal style for formal reports.

Centers the title of the report on the first page of the text, 2 inches from the top of the page

REDUCING ELECTROVISION'S TRAVEL AND ENTERTAINMENT COSTS

INTRODUCTION

Electrovision has always encouraged a significant amount of business travel. To compensate employees for the stress and inconvenience of frequent trips, management has authorized generous travel and entertainment (T&E) allowances. This philosophy has been good for morale, but last year Electrovision spent $16 million on travel and entertainment—$7 million more than it spent on research and development.

Opens by establishing the need for action

This year's T&E costs will affect profits even more, due to increases in airline fares and hotel rates. Also, the company anticipates that profits will be relatively weak for a variety of other reasons. Therefore, Dennis McWilliams, Vice President of Operations, has asked the accounting department to explore ways to reduce the T&E budget.

The purpose of this report is to analyze T&E expenses, evaluate the effect of recent hotel and airfare increases, and suggest ways to tighten control over T&E costs. The report outlines several steps that could reduce Electrovision's expenses, but the precise financial impact of these measures is difficult to project. The estimates presented here provide a "best guess" view of what Electrovision can expect to save.

In preparing this report, the accounting department analyzed internal expense reports for the past five years to determine how much Electrovision spends on travel and entertainment. These figures were then compared with average statistics compiled by Dow Jones (publisher of the *Wall Street Journal*) and presented as the Dow Jones Travel Index. We also analyzed trends and suggestions published in a variety of business journal articles to see how other companies are coping with the high cost of business travel.

Mentions sources and methods to increase credibility and to give readers a complete picture of the study's background

THE HIGH COST OF TRAVEL AND ENTERTAINMENT

Although many companies view travel and entertainment as an incidental cost of doing business, the dollars add up. At Electrovision the bill for airfares, hotels, rental cars, meals, and entertainment totaled $16 million last year. Our T&E budget has increased by 12 percent per year for the past five years. Compared to the average U.S. business traveler, Electrovision's expenditures are high, largely because of management's generous policy on travel benefits.

Uses the arabic numeral 1 for the first page, centering the number about 1 inch from the bottom of the page

1

In her brief introduction, Moreno counts on topic sentences and transitions to indicate that she is discussing the purpose, scope, and limitations of the study.

2

Uses arabic numerals to number the second and succeeding pages of the text in the upper right-hand corner where the top and right-hand margins meet

$16 Million per Year Spent on Travel and Entertainment

Electrovision's annual budget for travel and entertainment is only 8 percent of sales. Because this is a relatively small expense category compared with such things as salaries and commissions, it is tempting to dismiss T&E costs as insignificant. However, T&E is Electrovision's third-largest controllable expense, directly behind salaries and information systems.

Last year Electrovision personnel made about 3,390 trips at an average cost per trip of $4,720. The typical trip involved a round-trip flight of 3,000 kilometers, meals, and hotel accommodations for two or three days, and a rental car. Roughly 80 percent of trips were made by 20 percent of the staff—top management and sales personnel traveled most, averaging 18 trips per year.

Figure 1 illustrates how the T&E budget is spent. The largest categories are airfares and lodging, which together account for $7 out of $10 that employees spend on travel and entertainment. This spending breakdown has been relatively steady for the past five years and is consistent with the distribution of expenses experienced by other companies.

Places the visual as close as possible to the point it illustrates

Figure 1
Airfares and Lodging Account for Over
Two-Thirds of Electrovision's T&E Budget

Although the composition of the T&E budget has been consistent, its size has not. As mentioned earlier, these expenditures have increased by about 12 percent per year for the past five years, roughly twice the rate of the company's sales growth (see Figure 2). This rate of growth makes T&E Electrovision's fastest-growing expense item.

Gives each visual a title that clearly indicates what it's about; titles are consistently placed to the left of each visual

Figure 2
T&E Expenses Continue to Increase as a
Percentage of Sales

Moreno opens the first main section of the body with a topic sentence that introduces an important fact about the subject of the section. Then she orients the reader to the three major points developed in the section.

3

Electrovision's Travel Expenses Exceed National Averages

Much of our travel budget is justified. Two major factors contribute to Electrovision's high T&E budget:

- With our headquarters on the West Coast and our major customer on the East Coast, we naturally spend a lot of money on cross-country flights.

- A great deal of travel takes place between our headquarters here on the West Coast and the manufacturing operations in Detroit, Boston, and Dallas. Corporate managers and division personnel make frequent trips to coordinate these disparate operations.

However, even though a good portion of Electrovision's travel budget is justifiable, the company spends considerably more on T&E than the average business traveler (see Figure 3).

Figure 3
Electrovision Employees Spend Over Twice as Much as the Average Business Traveler

Source: *Wall Street Journal* and company records

Dollars Spent per Day

The Dow Jones Travel Index calculates the average cost per day of business travel in the United States, based on average airfare, hotel rates, and rental car rates. The average fluctuates weekly as travel companies change their rates, but it has been running at about $1,000 per day for the last year or so. In contrast, Electrovision's average daily expense over the past year has been $2,250—a hefty 125 percent higher than average. This figure is based on the average trip cost of $4,720 listed earlier and an average trip length of 2.1 days.

Spending Has Been Encouraged

Although a variety of factors may contribute to this differential, Electrovision's relatively high T&E costs are at least partially attributable to the company's philosophy and management style. Since many employees do not enjoy business travel, management has tried to make the trips more pleasant by authorizing business-class airfare, luxury hotel accommodations, and full-size rental cars. The sales staff is encouraged to entertain clients at top restaurants and to invite them to cultural and sporting events.

Numbers the visuals consecutively and refers to them in the text by their numbers

Introduces visuals before they appear and indicates what readers should notice about the data

The chart in Figure 3 is simple but effective; Moreno includes just enough data to make her point. Notice how she is as careful about the appearance of her report as she is about the quality of its content.

4

The cost of these privileges is easy to overlook, given the weakness of Electrovision's system for keeping track of T&E expenses:

- The monthly financial records do not contain a separate category for travel and entertainment; the information is buried under Cost of Goods Sold and under Selling, General, and Administrative Expenses.

- Each department head is given authority to approve any expense report, regardless of how large it may be.

- Receipts are not required for expenditures of less than $100.

- Individuals are allowed to make their own travel arrangements.

- No one is charged with the responsibility for controlling the company's total spending on travel and entertainment.

GROWING IMPACT ON THE BOTTOM LINE

During the past three years, the company's healthy profits have resulted in relatively little pressure to push for tighter controls over all aspects of the business. However, as we all know, the situation is changing. We're projecting flat to declining profits for the next two years, a situation that has prompted all of us to search for ways to cut costs. At the same time, rising airfares and hotel rates have increased the impact of T&E expenses on the company's financial results.

Lower Profits Underscore the Need for Change

The next two years promise to be difficult for Electrovision. After several years of steady increases in spending, the Postal Service is tightening procurement policies for automated mail-handling equipment. Funding for the A-12 optical character reader has been canceled. As a consequence, the marketing department expects sales to drop by 15 percent. Although Electrovision is negotiating several other promising R&D contracts, the marketing department does not foresee any major procurements for the next two to three years.

At the same time, Electrovision is facing cost increases on several fronts. As we have known for several months, the new production facility now under construction in Salt Lake City, Utah, is behind schedule and over budget. Labor contracts in Boston and Dallas will expire within the next six months, and plant managers there anticipate that significant salary and benefits concessions may be necessary to avoid strikes.

Moreover, marketing and advertising costs are expected to increase as we attempt to strengthen these activities to better cope with competitive pressures. Given the expected decline in revenues and increase in costs, the Executive Committee's prediction that profits will fall by 12 percent in the coming fiscal year does not seem overly pessimistic.

Moreno designed her report to include plenty of white space so even those pages that lack visuals are still attractive and easy to read.

5

Airfares and Hotel Rates Are Rising

Business travelers have grown accustomed to frequent fare wars and discounting in the travel industry in recent years. Excess capacity and aggressive price competition, particularly in the airline business, made travel a relative bargain.

However, that situation has changed as weaker competitors have been forced out and the remaining players have grown stronger and smarter. Airlines and hotels are better at managing inventory and keeping occupancy rates high, which translates into higher costs for Electrovision. Last year saw some of the steepest rate hikes in years. Business airfares (tickets most likely to be purchased by business travelers) jumped more than 40 percent in many markets. The trend is expected to continue, with rates increasing another 5 to 10 percent overall (Phillips 331; "Travel Costs Under Pressure" 30; Dahl B6).

Given the fact that air and hotel costs account for almost 70 percent of our T&E budget, the trend toward higher prices in these two categories will have serious consequences, unless management takes action to control these costs.

METHODS FOR REDUCING T&E COSTS

By implementing a number of reforms, management can expect to reduce Electrovision's T&E budget by as much as 40 percent. This estimate is based on the general assessment made by American Express (Gilligan 39) and on the fact that we have an opportunity to significantly reduce air travel costs by eliminating business-class travel. However, these measures are likely to be unpopular with employees. To gain acceptance for such changes, management will need to sell employees on the need for moderation in T&E allowances.

Four Ways to Trim Expenses

By researching what other companies are doing to curb T&E expenses, the accounting department has identified four prominent opportunities that should enable Electrovision to save about $6 million annually in travel-related costs.

Institute Tighter Spending Controls

A single individual should be appointed director of travel and entertainment to spearhead the effort to gain control of the T&E budget. More than a third of all U.S. companies now employ travel managers ("Businesses Use Savvy Managers" 4). The director should be familiar with the travel industry and should be well versed in both accounting and information technology. The director should also report to the vice president of operations. The director's first priorities should be to establish a written T&E policy and a cost-control system.

Electrovision currently has no written policy on travel and entertainment, a step that is widely recommended by air travel experts (Smith D4). Creating a policy

6

would clarify management's position and serve as a vehicle for communicating the need for moderation. At a minimum, the policy should include the following:

- All travel and entertainment should be strictly related to business and should be approved in advance.

- Except under special circumstances to be approved on a case-by-case basis, employees should travel by coach and stay in mid-range business hotels.

- The T&E policy should apply equally to employees at all levels.

To implement the new policy, Electrovision will need to create a system for controlling T&E expenses. Each department should prepare an annual T&E budget as part of its operating plan. These budgets should be presented in detail so that management can evaluate how T&E dollars will be spent and can recommend appropriate cuts. To help management monitor performance relative to these budgets, the director of travel should prepare monthly financial statements showing actual T&E expenditures by department.

The director of travel should also be responsible for retaining a business-oriented travel service that will schedule all employee business trips and look for the best travel deals, particularly in airfares. In addition to centralizing Electrovision's reservation and ticketing activities, the agency will negotiate reduced group rates with hotels and rental car firms. The agency selected should have offices nationwide so that all Electrovision facilities can channel their reservations through the same company. This is particularly important in light of the dizzying array of often wildly different airfares available between some cities. It's not uncommon to find dozens of fares along commonly traveled routes (Rowe 30). In addition, the director can help coordinate travel across the company to secure group discounts whenever possible (Barker 31; Miller B6).

Reduce Unnecessary Travel and Entertainment

One of the easiest ways to reduce expenses is to reduce the amount of traveling and entertaining that occurs. An analysis of last year's expenditures suggests that as much as 30 percent of Electrovision's travel and entertainment is discretionary. The professional staff spent $2.8 million attending seminars and conferences last year. Although these gatherings are undoubtedly beneficial, the company could save money by sending fewer epresentatives to each function and perhaps by eliminating some of the less valuable seminars.

Similarly, Electrovision could economize on trips between headquarters and divisions by reducing the frequency of such visits and by sending fewer people on each trip. Although there is often no substitute for face-to-face meetings, management could try to resolve more internal issues through telephone, electronic, and written communication.

Electrovision can also reduce spending by urging employees to economize. Instead of flying business class, employees can fly coach class or take advantage

---

Breaks up text with bulleted lists, which not only call attention to important points but also add visual interest

Specifies the steps required to implement recommendations

Moreno takes care not to overstep the boundaries of her analysis. For instance, she doesn't analyze the value of the seminars that employees attend every year, so she avoids any absolute statements about reducing travel to seminars.

7

of discount fares. Rather than ordering a $50 bottle of wine, employees can select a less expensive bottle or dispense with alcohol entirely. People can book rooms at moderately priced hotels and drive smaller rental cars.

Obtain Lowest Rates from Travel Providers

Apart from urging employees to economize, Electrovision can also save money by searching for the lowest available airfares, hotel rates, and rental car fees. Currently, few employees have the time or knowledge to seek out travel bargains. When they need to travel, they make the most convenient and comfortable arrangements. A professional travel service will be able to obtain lower rates from travel providers.

Judging by the experience of other companies, Electrovision may be able to trim as much as 30 to 40 percent from the travel budget simply by looking for bargains in airfares and negotiating group rates with hotels and rental car companies. Electrovision should be able to achieve these economies by analyzing its travel patterns, identifying frequently visited locations, and selecting a few hotels that are willing to reduce rates in exchange for guaranteed business. At the same time, the company should be able to save up to 40 percent on rental car charges by negotiating a corporate rate.

The possibilities for economizing are promising; however, making the best travel arrangements often requires trade-offs such as the following:

- The best fares might not always be the lowest. Indirect flights are usually cheaper, but they take longer and may end up costing more in lost work time.

- The cheapest tickets often require booking 14 or even 30 days in advance, which is often impossible for us.

- Discount tickets are usually nonrefundable, which is a serious drawback when a trip needs to be canceled at the last minute.

Replace Travel with Technological Alternatives

Less-expensive travel options promise significant savings, but the biggest cost reductions over the long term might come from replacing travel with virtual meeting technology. Both analysts and corporate users say that the early kinks that hampered online meetings have largely been worked out, and the latest systems are fast, easy to learn, and easy to use (Solheim 26). For example, Webex (a leading provider of webconferencing services) offers everything from simple, impromptu team meetings to major online events with up to 3,000 participants ("Online Meeting Solutions").

One of the first responsibilities of the new travel director should be an evaluation of these technologies and a recommendation for integrating them throughout Electrovision's operations.

Points out possible difficulties to show that all angles have been considered and to build confidence in her judgment

Note how Moreno makes the transition from section to section. The first sentence under the second heading on this page refers to the subject of the previous paragraph and signals a shift in thought.

8

The Impact of Reforms

By implementing tighter controls, reducing unnecessary expenses, negotiating more favorable rates, and exploring alternatives to travel, Electrovision should be able to reduce its T&E budget significantly. As Table 1 illustrates, the combined savings should be in the neighborhood of $6 million, although the precise figures are somewhat difficult to project.

Table 1
Electrovision Can Trim Travel and Entertainment Costs
by an Estimated $6 Million per Year

SOURCE OF SAVINGS	ESTIMATED SAVINGS
Switching from business-class to coach airfare	$2,300,000
Negotiating preferred hotel rates	940,000
Negotiating preferred rental car rates	460,000
Systematically searching for lower airfares	375,000
Reducing interdivisional travel	675,000
Reducing seminar and conference attendance	1,250,000
TOTAL POTENTIAL SAVINGS	**$6,000,000**

To achieve the economies outlined in the table, Electrovision will incur expenses for hiring a director of travel and for implementing a T&E cost-control system. These costs are projected at $115,000: $105,000 per year in salary and benefits for the new employee and a one-time expense of $10,000 for the cost-control system. The cost of retaining a full-service travel agency is negligible, even with the service fees that many are now passing along from airlines and other service providers.

The measures required to achieve these savings are likely to be unpopular with employees. Electrovision personnel are accustomed to generous T&E allowances, and they are likely to resent having these privileges curtailed. To alleviate their disappointment

- Management should make a determined effort to explain why the changes are necessary.
- The director of corporate communication should be asked to develop a multifaceted campaign that will communicate the importance of curtailing T&E costs.
- Management should set a positive example by adhering strictly to the new policies.
- The limitations should apply equally to employees at all levels in the organization.

Note how Moreno calls attention in the first paragraph to items in the following table, without repeating the information in the table.

9

Uses a descriptive heading for the last section of the text (in informational reports, this section is often called "Summary"; in analytical reports, it is called "Conclusions" or "Conclusions and Recommendations")

Summarizes conclusions in the first two paragraphs—a good approach because Moreno organized her report around conclusions and recommendations, so readers have already been introduced to them

CONCLUSIONS AND RECOMMENDATIONS

Electrovision is currently spending $16 million per year on travel and entertainment. Although much of this spending is justified, the company's costs are high relative to competitors' costs, mainly because Electrovision has been generous with its travel benefits.

Electrovision's liberal approach to travel and entertainment was understandable during years of high profitability; however, the company is facing the prospect of declining profits for the next several years. Management is therefore motivated to cut costs in all areas of the business. Reducing T&E spending is particularly important because the bottom-line impact of these costs will increase as airline fares increase.

Electrovision should be able to reduce T&E costs by as much as 40 percent by taking four important steps:

Emphasizes the recommendations by presenting them in list format

1. *Institute tighter spending controls.* Management should hire a director of travel and entertainment who will assume overall responsibility for T&E activities. Within the next six months, this director should develop a written travel policy, institute a T&E budget and a cost-control system, and retain a professional, business-oriented travel agency that will optimize arrangements with travel providers.

2. *Reduce unnecessary travel and entertainment.* Electrovision should encourage employees to economize on T&E spending. Management can accomplish this by authorizing fewer trips and by urging employees to be more conservative in their spending.

3. *Obtain lowest rates from travel providers.* Electrovision should also focus on obtaining the best rates on airline tickets, hotel rooms, and rental cars. By channeling all arrangements through a professional travel agency, the company can optimize its choices and gain clout in negotiating preferred rates.

4. *Replace travel with technological alternatives.* With the number of computers already installed in our facilities, it seems likely that we could take advantage of desktop videoconferencing and other distance-meeting tools. Technological alternatives won't be quite as feasible with customer sites, since these systems require compatible equipment at both ends of a connection, but such systems are certainly a possibility for communication with Electrovision's own sites.

Because these measures may be unpopular with employees, management should make a concerted effort to explain the importance of reducing travel costs. The director of corporate communication should be given responsibility for developing a plan to communicate the need for employee cooperation.

Moreno doesn't introduce any new facts in this section. In a longer report she might have divided this section into subsections, labeled "Conclusions" and "Recommendations," to distinguish between the two.

10

WORKS CITED

Barker, Julie. "How to Rein in Group Travel Costs." *Successful Meetings* Feb. 2008: 31.

"Businesses Use Savvy Managers to Keep Travel Costs Down." *Christian Science Monitor* 17 July 2008: 4.

Dahl, Jonathan. "2000: The Year Travel Costs Took Off." *Wall Street Journal* 29 Dec. 2007: B6.

Gilligan, Edward P. "Trimming Your T&E Is Easier Than You Think." *Managing Office Technology* Nov. 2008: 39–40.

"Meet With Anyone, Anywhere, Anytime, "*Webex.com*. 2009. WebEx, 2 February 2009, <http://www.webex.com/solutions/online-meeting-suc.html>.

Miller, Lisa. "Attention, Airline Ticket Shoppers." *Wall Street Journal* 7 July 2007: B6.

Phillips, Edward H. "Airlines Post Record Traffic." *Aviation Week & Space Technology* 8 Jan. 2007: 331.

Rowe, Irene Vlitos. "Global Solution for Cutting Travel Costs." *European* 12 Oct. 2008: 30.

Smith, Carol. "Rising, Erratic Airfares Make Company Policy Vital." *Los Angeles Times* 2 Nov. 2007: D4.

Solheim, Shelley. "Web Conferencing Made Easy." *eWeek* 22 Aug. 2008: 26.

"Travel Costs Under Pressure." *Purchasing* 15 Feb. 2007: 30.

Lists references alphabetically by the author's last name, and when the author is unknown, by the title of the reference (see Appendix B for additional details on preparing reference lists)

Moreno's list of references follows the style recommended in The MLA Style Manual. The box below shows how these sources would be cited following APA style.

10

REFERENCES

Barker, J. (2008, February). How to rein in group travel costs. *Successful Meetings*, 31.

Businesses use savvy managers to keep travel costs down. (2008, July 17). *Christian Science Monitor*, 4.

Dahl, J. (2007, December 29). 2000: The year travel costs took off. *Wall Street Journal*, B6.

Gilligan, E. (2008, November). Trimming your T&E is easier than you think. *Managing Office Technology*, 39–40.

Miller, L. (2007, July 7). Attention, airline ticket shoppers. *Wall Street Journal*, B6.

Phillips, E. (2007, January 8). Airlines post record traffic. *Aviation Week & Space Technology*, 331.

Rowe, I. (2008, October 12). Global solution for cutting travel costs. *European*, 30.

Smith, C. (2007, November 2). Rising, erratic airfares make company policy vital. *Los Angeles Times*, D4.

Solheim, S. (2008, August 22). Web conferencing made easy. *eWeek*, 26.

Travel costs under pressure. (2007, February 15). *Purchasing*, 30.

Webex.com. (2009). *Meet With Anyone, Anywhere, Anytime*. Retrieved 2 February 2009, from http://www.webex.com/solutions/online-meeting-suc.html.

prepare after the text has been completed because they are based on the main text of the report. When your text is complete, you can also use your word-processing software to automatically compile the table of contents and the list of illustrations.

Cover   Many companies have standard covers for reports, made of heavy paper and imprinted with the company's name and logo. If your company doesn't have such covers, you can usually find something suitable in a good stationery or office supply store. Look for cover stock that is attractive, convenient, and appropriate to the subject matter.

Covers are typically labeled with the report title, the writer's name (optional), and the submission date (also optional). Think carefully about the title. You want it be concise while still communicating the essence of the subject matter.

Title Fly and Title Page   The **title fly** is a single sheet of paper with only the title of the report on it. It adds a touch of formality, but it isn't really necessary, and it consumes additional paper. The **title page** includes four blocks of information: (1) the title of the report; (2) the name, title, and address of the person, group, or organization that authorized the report (if anyone); (3) the name, title, and address of the person, group, or organization that prepared the report; and (4) the date on which the report was submitted. On some title pages, the second block of information is preceded by the words *Prepared for* or *Submitted to*, and the third block of information is preceded by *Prepared by* or *Submitted by*. In some cases, the title page serves as the cover of the report, especially if the report is relatively short and is intended solely for internal use.

Letter of Authorization and Letter of Acceptance   If you received written authorization to prepare a report, you might want to include that **letter of authorization** (or *memo of authorization*) in your report. If you wrote a **letter of acceptance** (or *memo of acceptance*) in response to that communication, accepting the assignment and clarifying any conditions or limitations, you might also include that letter here, in the report's prefatory parts. In general, letters of authorization and acceptance are included in only the most formal reports. However, consider including one or both if a significant amount of time has passed since you started the project or if you do not have a close working relationship with the audience. These pieces help make sure everyone is clear about the report's intent and the approach you took to create it.

3 **LEARNING OBJECTIVE**

Identify the circumstances in which you should include letters of authorization and letters of acceptance in your reports

A letter of authorization is a document that instructs you to produce a report; a letter of acceptance is your written agreement to produce the report.

Letter of Transmittal   The **letter of transmittal** (or *memo of transmittal*), a specialized form of a cover letter that is usually positioned right before the table of contents, introduces your report to the audience. This piece says what you would say if you were handing the report directly to the person who authorized it, so the style is often less formal than the rest of the report.

If your readers are likely to be skeptical of or even hostile to something in your report, the letter of transmittal is a good place to acknowledge their concerns and explain how the report addresses the issues they care about. Also, if you need to convey sensitive information to selected audience members, you can opt to include the letter in just those copies.

Depending on the nature of your report, your letter of transmittal can follow either the direct approach for routine or positive messages described in Chapter 8 or the indirect approach for negative messages described in Chapter 9. Open by introducing the report and summarizing its purpose, with a statement such as "Here is the report you asked me to prepare on . . ." The rest of the introduction includes information about the scope of the report, the methods used to complete the study, limitations, and any special messages you need to convey. If the report does not have a synopsis, the letter of transmittal may summarize the major findings, conclusions, and recommendations.

In the body of the letter, you may also highlight important points or sections of the report, make comments on side issues, give suggestions for follow-up studies, and offer any details that will help readers understand and use the report. You may also want to acknowledge help given by others. The conclusion of the transmittal letter often includes a note of thanks for having been given the report assignment, an expression of willingness to discuss the report, and an offer to assist with future projects.

A letter or memo of transmittal introduces your report to your audience.

If you don't include a synopsis, you can summarize the report's content in your letter of transmittal.

Table of Contents   The table of contents (often titled simply "Contents") indicates in outline form the coverage, sequence, and relative importance of the information in the report. The headings used in the text of the report are the basis for the table of contents. Depending on the length and complexity of the report, you may need to decide how many levels of headings to show in the contents; it's a trade-off between simplicity and completeness. Contents that show only first-level heads are easy to scan but could frustrate people looking for specific subsections in the report. Conversely, contents that show every level of heading—down to fourth or fifth level in detailed reports—identify all the sections but can intimidate readers and blur the focus by detracting from your most important message points. Where the detailed table of contents could have dozens or even hundreds of entries, consider including two tables: a high-level table that shows only major headings, followed by a detailed table that includes everything (as this and many other textbooks do). No matter how many levels you include, make sure readers can easily distinguish between them.

Also, take extra care to verify that your table of contents is accurate, consistent, and complete. Even minor errors could damage your credibility if readers turn to a given page and don't find what they expect to see there, or if they find headings that seem similar to those in the table of contents but aren't worded quite the same. To ensure accuracy, construct the table of contents after your report is complete, thoroughly edited, and proofed. This way, the headings and subheadings aren't likely to change or move from page to page. And if at all possible, use the automatic features in your word-processing software to generate the table of contents. Doing so helps improve accuracy by eliminating typing mistakes, and it keeps your table current in the event that you have to repaginate or revise headings late in the process.

List of Illustrations   If you have more than a handful of illustrations in your report, or if you want to call attention to your illustrations, include a list of illustrations after the table of contents. For simplicity's sake, some reports refer to all visuals as *illustrations* or *exhibits*. In other reports, as in Moreno's Electrovision report, tables are labeled separately from other types of visuals, which are called *figures*. Regardless of the system you use, be sure to include titles and page numbers.

If you have enough space on a single page, include the list of illustrations directly beneath the table of contents. Otherwise, put this list on the page after the contents page. When tables and figures are numbered separately, they should also be listed separately.

Synopsis or Executive Summary   A **synopsis** is a brief overview (one page or less) of a report's most important points, designed to give readers a quick preview of the contents (see Figure 15.2). It's often included in long informational reports dealing with technical, professional, or academic subjects and can also be called an **abstract**. Because it's a concise representation of an entire report, it may be distributed separately to a wide audience; interested readers can then request a copy of the entire report. A synopsis or an abstract is not a lengthy element, but take your time with it. In a sense, it's an advertisement for the entire report, so you want it to represent the report accurately.

The phrasing of a synopsis can be either informative or descriptive. An informative synopsis presents the main points of the report in the order in which they appear in the text. A descriptive synopsis, on the other hand, simply tells what the report is about, using only moderately greater detail than the table of contents; the actual findings of the report are omitted. Here are examples of statements from each type:

INFORMATIVE SYNOPSIS	DESCRIPTIVE SYNOPSIS
Sales of super-premium ice cream make up 11 percent of the total ice cream market.	This report contains information about super-premium ice cream and its share of the market.

The way you handle a synopsis reflects the approach you use in the text. If you're using the indirect approach in your report, you're better off with a descriptive synopsis because an informative synopsis "gives away the ending" of your report. No matter which type of synopsis you use, be sure to present an accurate picture of the report's contents.[4]

To save time and reduce errors, use the table of contents generator in your word-processing software.

4 **LEARNING OBJECTIVE**

Explain the difference between a synopsis and an executive summary

A synopsis is a brief preview of the most important points in your report.

However, if your report will be distributed to outsiders, include additional information on where you obtained the data. Most college students are familiar with citation methods suggested by the Modern Language Association (MLA) or the American Psychological Association (APA). *The Chicago Manual of Style* is a reference often used by typesetters and publishers. All these sources encourage the use of in-text citations (inserting the author's last name and a year of publication or a page number directly in the text).

Index   An **index** is an alphabetical list of names and subjects mentioned in a report, along with the pages on which they occur (see the indexes in this book for examples). If you think your readers will need to access specific points of information in a lengthy report, consider including an index that lists all key topics, product names, markets, or important persons—whatever is relevant to your subject matter. As with your table of contents, accuracy in an index is critical. The good news is that you can also use your word-processing software to compile the index. Just be sure to update the index (and any other automatically generated elements, such as the table of contents) right before you produce and distribute your report.

If your report is lengthy, an index can help readers locate specific topics quickly.

Components of a Formal Proposal

The goal of a proposal is to make your offering and the organization you represent stand out from the competition. Consequently, proposals addressed to external audiences, including potential customers and investors, are nearly always formal. For smaller projects and situations in which you already have a working relationship with the audience, a proposal can be less formal and skip some of the components described in this section.

Formal proposals contain many of the same components as other formal reports (see Figure 15.3). The difference lies mostly in the text, although a few of the prefatory

5 LEARNING OBJECTIVE

Identify the major components of a formal proposal

Formal proposals must have a high degree of polish and professionalism.

FIGURE 15.3   Parts of a Formal Proposal
As with formal reports, you can select from a variety of components to complete a formal proposal.

PREFATORY PARTS	TEXT PARTS	SUPPLEMENTARY PARTS
Synopsis or executive summary	Close	Appendixes
List of illustrations	Body	
Table of contents	Introduction	
Letter of transmittal		
Request for proposals		
Title page		
Title fly		
Cover		

parts are also different. With the exception of an occasional appendix, most proposals have few supplementary parts. As always, if you're responding to an RFP, follow its specifications to the letter, being sure to include everything it asks for and nothing it doesn't ask for.

Prefatory Parts

The cover, title fly, title page, table of contents, and list of illustrations are handled the same in a formal proposal as in other formal reports. However, you'll want to handle other prefatory parts a bit differently, such as the copy of the RFP, the synopsis or executive summary, and the letter of transmittal.

An RFP may require you to include a copy of the RFP in your prefatory section; be sure to follow instructions carefully.

Copy of the RFP   RFPs usually have specific instructions for referring to the RFP itself in your proposal because the organizations that issue RFPs need a methodical way to track all their active RFPs and the incoming responses. Some organizations require that you include a copy of the entire RFP in your proposal; others simply want you to refer to the RFP by name or number or perhaps include just the introductory section of the RFP. Just make sure you follow the instructions in every detail. If the RFP offers no specific instructions, use your best judgment, based on the length of the RFP and whether you received a printed copy or accessed it online.

Synopsis or Executive Summary   Although you may include a synopsis or an executive summary for your reader's convenience when your proposal is quite long, these components are often less useful in a formal proposal than they are in a formal report. If your proposal is unsolicited, your transmittal letter will already have caught the reader's interest, making a synopsis or an executive summary redundant. It may also be less important if your proposal is solicited because the reader is already committed to studying your proposal to find out how you intend to satisfy the terms of a contract. The introduction of a solicited proposal would provide an adequate preview of the contents.

Letter of Transmittal   The way you handle the letter of transmittal depends on whether the proposal is solicited or unsolicited. If the proposal is solicited, approach the letter of transmittal as a positive message, highlighting those aspects of your proposal that may give you a competitive advantage. If the proposal is unsolicited, approach the letter as a persuasive message that must convince the reader that you have something worthwhile to offer, something that justifies the time required to read the entire proposal.

Text of the Proposal

Just as with reports, the text of a proposal is composed of three main parts: the introduction, body, and close. As Chapter 14 notes, the content and depth of each part depend on whether the proposal is solicited or unsolicited, formal or informal. Here's a brief review:[6]

- **Introduction.** This section presents and summarizes the problem you intend to solve and your solution to that problem, including any benefits the reader will receive from your solution.
- **Body.** This section explains the complete details of the solution: how the job will be done, how it will be broken into tasks, what method will be used to do it (including the required equipment, material, and personnel), when the work will begin and end, how much the entire job will cost (including a detailed breakdown, if required or requested), and why you are qualified.
- **Close.** This section emphasizes the benefits that readers will realize from your solution, and it urges readers to act.

Figure 15.4 provides an example of an informal proposal.

FIGURE 15.4 Informal Solicited Proposal
This proposal was submitted by Dixon O'Donnell, vice president of O'Donnell & Associates, a geotechnical engineering firm that conducts a variety of environmental testing services. As you review this document, pay close attention to the specific items addressed in the proposal's introduction, body, and close.

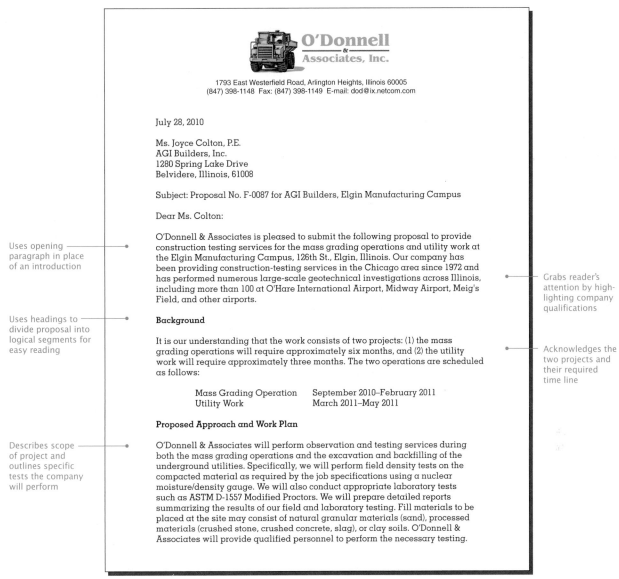

Uses opening paragraph in place of an introduction

Uses headings to divide proposal into logical segments for easy reading

Describes scope of project and outlines specific tests the company will perform

Grabs reader's attention by highlighting company qualifications

Acknowledges the two projects and their required time line

(continued)

PROOFREADING REPORTS AND PROPOSALS

After you have assembled all the components of your report or proposal, revised the entire document's content for clarity and conciseness, and designed the document to ensure readability and a positive impression on your readers, you have essentially produced your document in its final form. Now you need to review it thoroughly one last time, looking for inconsistencies, errors, and missing components. Proofing can catch minor flaws that might diminish your credibility—and major flaws that might damage your career.

Proofreading the textual part of your report is essentially the same as proofreading any other business message—you check for typos, spelling errors, and mistakes in punctuation. However, reports often have elements that may not be included in other messages, so don't forget to proof your visuals thoroughly and make sure they are positioned correctly. If you need specific tips on proofreading documents, look back at Chapter 6 for some reminders on what to look for when proofreading text and how to proofread like a pro.

FIGURE 15.4 (*Continued*)

Explains who will be responsible for the various tasks

O'Donnell & Associates, Inc.   Page 2   July 28, 2010

Kevin Patel will be the lead field technician responsible for the project. A copy of Mr. Patel's résumé is included with this proposal for your review. Kevin will coordinate field activities with your job site superintendent and make sure that appropriate personnel are assigned to the job site. Overall project management will be the responsibility of Joseph Proesel. Project engineering services will be performed under the direction of Dixon O'Donnell, P.E. All field personnel assigned to the site will be familiar with and abide by the Project Site Health and Safety Plan prepared by Carlson Environmental, Inc., dated April 2010.

Encloses résumé rather than listing qualifications in the document

Qualifications

O'Donnell & Associates has been providing quality professional services since 1972 in the areas of

Grabs attention by mentioning compelling qualifications

- Geotechnical engineering
- Materials testing and inspection
- Pavement evaluation
- Environmental services
- Engineering and technical support (CADD) services

The company provides Phase I and Phase II environmental site assessments, preparation of LUST site closure reports, installation of groundwater monitoring wells, and testing of soil/groundwater samples for environmental contaminants. Geotechnical services include all phases of soil mechanics and foundation engineering, including foundation and lateral load analysis, slope stability analysis, site preparation recommendations, see page analysis, pavement design, and settlement analysis.

O'Donnell & Associates materials testing laboratory is certified by AASHTO Accreditation Program for the testing of Soils, Aggregate, Hot Mix Asphalt and Portland Cement Concrete. A copy of our laboratory certification is included with this proposal. In addition to in-house training, field and laboratory technicians participate in a variety of certification programs, including those sponsored by the American Concrete Institute (ACI) and Illinois Department of Transportation (IDOT).

Gains credibility by describing certifications (approvals by recognized industry associations or government agencies)

Costs

On the basis of our understanding of the scope of the work, we estimate the total cost of the two projects to be $100,260.00, as follows:

(*continued*)

Ask for proofreading assistance from someone who hasn't been involved in the development of your proposal; he or she might see errors that you've been overlooking.

Whenever possible, arrange for someone with "fresh eyes" to proofread the report, somebody who hasn't been involved with the text so far. At this point in the process, you are so familiar with the content that your mind will fill in missing words, fix misspelled words, and subconsciously compensate for other flaws, without your even being aware of it. Someone else might see mistakes that you've passed over a dozen times without noticing. An ideal approach is to have two people review it, one who is an expert in the subject matter and one who isn't. The first person can ensure its technical accuracy, and the second can ensure that a wide range of readers will understand it.[7]

DISTRIBUTING REPORTS AND PROPOSALS

All the distribution issues explored in Chapter 6 apply to reports and proposals, but pay particular attention to the length and complexity of your documents. For physical distribution, consider spending the few extra dollars for a professional courier or package delivery service, if that will help your document stand apart from the crowd. The online tracking

FIGURE 15.4   (*Continued*)

O'Donnell & Associates, Inc.   Page 3   July 28, 2010

Cost Estimates

Cost Estimate: Mass Grading	Units	Rate ($)	Total Cost ($)
Field Inspection			
Labor	1,320 hours	$38.50	$ 50,820.00
Nuclear Moisture Density Meter	132 days	35.00	4,620.00
Vehicle Expense	132 days	45.00	5,940.00
Laboratory Testing			
Proctor Density Tests (ASTM D-1557)	4 tests	130.00	520.00
Engineering/Project Management			
Principal Engineer	16 hours	110.00	1,760.00
Project Manager	20 hours	80.00	1,600.00
Administrative Assistant	12 hours	50.00	600.00
Subtotal			**$ 65,860.00**

Cost Estimate: Utility Work	Units	Rate ($)	Total Cost ($)
Field Inspection			
Labor	660 hours	$ 38.50	$ 25,410.00
Nuclear Moisture Density Meter	66 days	5.00	2,310.00
Vehicle Expense	66 days	45.00	2,970.00
Laboratory Testing			
Proctor Density Tests (ASTM D-1557)	2 tests	130.00	260.00
Engineering/Project Management			
Principal Engineer	10 hours	110.00	1,100.00
Project Manager	20 hours	80.00	1,600.00
Administrative Assistant	15 hours	50.00	750.00
Subtotal			**$ 34,400.00**

| **Total Project Costs** | | | **$100,260.00** |

This estimate assumes full-time inspection services. However, our services may also be performed on an as-requested basis, and actual charges will reflect time associated with the project. We have attached our standard fee schedule for your review. Overtime rates are for hours in excess of 8.0 hours per day, before 7:00 a.m., after 5:00 p.m., and on holidays and weekends.

Itemizes costs by project and gives supporting details

Provides alternative option in case full-time service costs exceed client's budget

(*continued*)

offered by FedEx, UPS, and other services can verify that your document arrived safely. On the other hand, if you've prepared the document for a single person or small group, delivering it in person can be a nice touch. In addition to answering any immediate questions about it, you can promote the results in person—reminding the recipient of the benefits contained in your report or proposal.

For electronic distribution, unless your audience specifically requests a word-processor file, provide documents as PDF files. Many people are reluctant to open word-processor files these days, particularly from outsiders, given the vulnerability of such files to macro viruses and other contaminations. Moreover, using PDF files lets you control how your document is displayed on your audience's computer, ensuring that your readers see your document as you intended. In addition, making documents available as downloadable PDF files is almost universally expected these days, if only for the sake of convenience.

Using portable document format (PDF) is a safe and common way to distribute reports electronically.

If your company or client expects you to distribute your reports via a web-based content management system, intranet, or extranet, be sure to upload the correct file(s) to the correct online location. Verify the onscreen display of your report after you've posted it, too; make sure graphics, charts, links, and other elements are in place and operational.

FIGURE 15.4 (*Continued*)

O'Donnell & Associates, Inc.   Page 4   July 28, 2010

Authorization

With a staff of over 30 personnel, including registered professional engineers, resident engineers, geologists, construction inspectors, laboratory technicians, and drillers, we are convinced that O'Donnell & Associates is capable of providing the services required for a project of this magnitude.

If you would like our firm to provide the services as outlined in this proposal, please sign this letter and return it to us along with a certified check in the amount of $10,000 (our retainer) by August 13, 2010. Please call me if you have any questions regarding the terms of this proposal or our approach.

Sincerely,

Dixon O'Donnell

Dixon O'Donnell
Vice President

Enclosures

Accepted for AGI BUILDERS, INC.

By_____   Date _____

Uses brief close to emphasize qualifications and ask for client decision

Provides deadline and makes response easy

Makes letter a binding contract, if signed

When you've completed your formal report or proposal and sent it off to your audience, your next task is to wait for a response. If you don't hear from your readers within a week or two, you might want to ask politely whether the report arrived. (Some RFPs specify a response time frame. In such a case, *don't* pester the recipient ahead of schedule, or you'll hurt your chances.) In hope of stimulating a response, you might ask a question about the report, such as "How do you think accounting will react to the proposed budget increase?" You might also offer to answer any questions or provide additional information. To review the ideas presented in this chapter, see "Checklist: Producing Formal Reports and Proposals," and for the latest information on completing business reports and proposals, visit http://real-timeupdates.com/bct and click on Chapter 15.

✓ **CHECKLIST: Producing Formal Reports and Proposals**

A. Prefatory parts.
- Use your company's standard report covers, if available.
- Include a concise, descriptive title on the cover.
- Include a title fly only if you want an extra-formal touch.
- On the title page, list (1) report title; (2) name, title, and address of the group or person who authorized the report; (3) name, title, and address of the group or person who prepared the report; and (4) date of submission.
- Include a copy of the letter of authorization, if appropriate.
- Include a copy of the RFP (or its introduction only, if the document is long), if appropriate.
- Include a letter of transmittal that introduces the report.
- Provide a table of contents in outline form, with headings worded exactly as they appear in the body of the report.
- Include a list of illustrations if the report contains a large number of them.
- Include a synopsis (brief summary of the report) or an executive summary (a condensed, "mini" version of the report) for longer reports.

B. Text of the report.
- Draft an introduction that prepares the reader for the content that follows.
- Provide information that supports your conclusions, recommendations, or proposals in the body of the report.
- Don't overload the body with unnecessary detail.
- Close with a summary of your main idea.

C. Supplementary parts.
- Use appendixes to provide supplementary information or supporting evidence.
- List in a bibliography any secondary sources you used.
- Provide an index if your report contains a large number of terms or ideas and is likely to be consulted over time.

WRITING REQUESTS FOR PROPOSALS

At some point in your career, you might be the one receiving proposals, and learning how to request effective proposals will simplify the process considerably. Various organizations handle RFPs in different ways. For example, the Bill & Melinda Gates Foundation's education program does not accept unsolicited proposals, so grant proposals must be written in response to published RFPs. The Gates health program also emphasizes RFPs but does invite inquiries regarding projects that align with its funding priorities, even if a specific RFP has not been issued for a particular project area. In these cases, organizations are asked to submit a letter of inquiry (LOI) via an online form. If an LOI is accepted, the organization is then invited to submit a grant proposal.[8]

When writing an RFP, remember that it is more than just a request; it's an informational report that provides potential bidders with the information they need to craft effective proposals. Writing an RFP demands careful consideration because it starts a process that leads to a proposal, a contract, and eventually the delivery of a product or the performance of a service. In other words, mistakes at the RFP stage can ripple throughout the process and create costly headaches for everyone involved.

An RFP's specific content will vary widely from industry to industry, but all RFPs should include some combination of the following elements:[9]

- **Company background.** Give potential bidders some background information on your organization, your business priorities, and other information they might need in order to respond in an informed manner.
- **Project description.** Put your requirements in context; are you seeking bids for routine supplies or services, or do you need a major computer system?
- **Requirements.** The requirements section should spell out everything you expect from potential vendors; don't leave anything to unstated assumptions. Will potential vendors provide key equipment, or will you? Will you expect vendors to work under confidentiality restrictions, such as a nondisclosure agreement? Who will pay if costs run higher than expected? Will you require ongoing service or support? Providing this information can be a lot of work, but again, overlooking anything at this point is likely to create considerable problems once the project gets rolling.

When writing an RFP, be sure to give potential respondents all the information they need to craft a meaningful response to your request.

6 LEARNING OBJECTIVE

Identify the major components to include in a request for proposals (RFP)

- **Decision criteria.** Let bidders know how you'll be making the decision. Is quality more important than cost? Will you consider only certain types of vendors or only those that use certain processes or technologies? Will you entertain bids from companies that have never worked in your particular industry? The answers to such questions not only help bidders determine whether they're right for your project but also help them craft proposals that meet your needs.
- **Proposal requirements.** Explain exactly what you expect to see in the proposal itself—which sections, what media, how many copies, and so on.
- **Submission and contact information.** A well-written RFP answers most potential questions, and it also tells people when, where, and how to respond. In addition, effective RFPs always give bidders the name of a contact within the organization who can answer detailed questions.

Document Makeover

Improve This Executive Summary

To practice correcting drafts of actual documents, visit the "Document Makeovers" section in either mybcommlab or the Companion Website for this text.

If mybcommlab is being used in your class, see your User Guide for specific instructions on how to access the content for this chapter. If you are accessing this feature through the Companion Website, click on "Document Makeovers" and then select Chapter 15. You will find an excerpt from an executive summary that contains problems and errors related to what you've learned in this chapter about completing formal reports and proposals. Use the Final Draft decision tool to create an improved version of this document. Check the executive summary for an appropriate degree of formality, parallel structures, and the skillful inclusion or exclusion of detail.

A smart approach to managing RFPs can minimize the work involved for everyone and maximize the effectiveness of the RFP. First, identify your decision criteria and then brainstorm the information you need to measure against those criteria. Don't ask bidders to submit information about every aspect of their operations if such details aren't relevant to your decision. Making such unreasonable demands is unfair to bidders, will unnecessarily complicate your review process, and will discourage some potentially attractive bidders from responding.

Second, to get quality responses that match your unique business needs, give bidders plenty of time to respond. Successful companies are usually busy responding to other RFPs and working on other projects, and you can't expect them to drop everything to focus solely on your RFP.

Third, if your company generates numerous RFPs, tracking proposals can become a full-time job. Consider establishing an online system for tracking responses automatically.[10]

Communication Challenges at the Bill & Melinda Gates Foundation

Jeff Raikes and his colleagues at the Bill & Melinda Gates Foundation not only read numerous reports and proposals every year, they also write and produce many reports, for both internal and external audiences. In fact, communication is one of the foundation's most important functions, as it seeks to improve the health and education of children worldwide. In addition, the foundation is known as one of the most efficiently managed charities in the world, so cost-effectiveness is a vital concern in every phase of the communication process. Raikes recently hired you as an assistant director of communication, and your responsibilities include developing new ways for the foundation to produce effective reports as efficiently as possible.

Individual Challenge: Review several of the reports and other publications posted online (as PDF files) at **www.gatesfoundation.org**. Compare the design and layout of these documents. Do you see evidence of standardized design across documents? Write a brief e-mail to Raikes, explaining the financial advantages of using a single design scheme for all external foundation documents.

Team Challenge: As a champion of new technologies, Raikes has a strong interest in applying information technology to the challenge of global communication. As part of a small team, research the opportunities for electronic delivery of health information to remote villages in India. Prepare a one-page report summarizing your findings.

SUMMARY OF LEARNING OBJECTIVES

1 Summarize the four tasks involved in completing business reports and proposals. To complete a business report or proposal, you first need to revise, produce, and proofread the document just as you would any other business message. Revising reports and proposals involves evaluating content, style, organization, and tone; reviewing for readability; and editing for clarity and conciseness. After you've verified a report's quality, the fourth step is distributing the report and all supporting materials to the intended audience.

2 Identify the major components of a formal report. Report components can be divided into prefatory parts, text parts, and supplementary parts. *Prefatory parts*, which present and package your report, can include a synopsis or executive summary, a list of illustrations, the table of contents, a letter of transmittal, a letter of acceptance, a letter of authorization, a title page, a title fly, and a cover. *Text parts* include the standard message elements of introduction, body, and close. *Supplementary parts* can include an index, a bibliography, and one or more appendixes.

3 Identify the circumstances in which you should include letters of authorization and letters of acceptance in your reports. If you received a letter of authorization to begin work on a report and you wrote a letter of acceptance when you took on the assignment, it's a good idea to include both items in your report if there's a chance that your audience might not expect the material you're about to deliver. Either or both of these documents can help clarify what you did and why you did it.

4 Explain the difference between a synopsis and an executive summary. A synopsis is a brief overview of an entire report and may either highlight the main points as they appear in the text or simply tell the reader what the report is about. It is designed to entice the audience to read the report, but it is not intended to replace the report. In contrast, an executive summary is more comprehensive than a synopsis; it is essentially a "mini" version of the report. It may contain headings, visual aids, and enough information to help busy executives make quick decisions. Although an executive summary is not designed to replace the report, in some cases it may be the only thing that a busy executive reads carefully.

5 Identify the major components of a formal proposal. Like a formal report, a formal proposal consists of prefatory parts, text parts, and supplementary parts. *Prefatory parts* that package and present the proposal include a synopsis or an executive summary, a list of illustrations, a table of contents, a letter of transmittal, a copy of or reference to the RFP (for solicited proposals), a title page, a title fly, and a cover. *Text parts* include the standard introduction, body, and close. Proposals typically don't have a significant number of *supplementary parts*, other than possibly an appendix or two that provide supporting information.

6 Identify the major components to include in a request for proposals (RFP). The content of RFPs varies widely from industry to industry and project to project, but most include background on the company, a description of the project, solution requirements, the criteria that will be used to make selection decisions, expectations for submitted proposals, and any relevant submission and contact information.

PEARSON mybcommlab™

Log on to www.mybcommlab.com to access the following study and assessment aids associated with this chapter:

- Video applications
- Real-Time Updates
- Peer review activity
- Quick Learning Guides
- Pre/post test
- Personalized study plan
- Model documents
- Sample presentations

If you are not using mybcommlab, you can access the Real-Time Updates and Quick Learning Guides through http://real-timeupdates.com/bct. The Quick Learning Guide hits all the high points of this chapter in just two pages. This guide, especially prepared by the authors, will help you study for exams or review important concepts whenever you need a quick refresher.

Test Your Knowledge

1. What are the tasks involved in revising a report or proposal?
2. When should you start a report section on a new page?
3. What information is included on the title page of a report?
4. What is the difference between a letter of authorization and a letter of acceptance?
5. What is a letter of transmittal, and where is it positioned within a report?
6. When are executive summaries useful?
7. What are three supplementary parts often included in formal reports?
8. What types of material does an appendix contain?
9. Why do some writers cite references in the report text?
10. What is the equivalent of a letter of authorization for a proposal?

Apply Your Knowledge

1. Is an executive summary a persuasive message? Explain your answer.
2. Under what circumstances would you include more than one table of contents in a report?
3. If you were submitting a solicited proposal to build a small shopping center, would you include as references the names and addresses of other clients for whom you recently built similar facilities? Where in the proposal would you include these references? Why?
4. If you included a bibliography in your report, would you also need to include in-text citations? Please explain.
5. **Ethical Choices** How would you report on a confidential survey in which employees rated their managers' capabilities? Both employees and managers expect to see the results. Would you give the same report to employees and managers? What components would you include or exclude for each audience? Explain your choices.

Practice Your Knowledge

Message for Analysis

Visit the website of the U.S. Citizenship and Immigration Services (a division of the U.S. Department of Homeland Security), at http://uscis.gov. Click on "About USCIS," followed by "Reports and Studies," and find the report titled "The Triennial Comprehensive Report on Immigration." Download this PDF file and read the executive summary. Using the information in this chapter, analyze the executive summary and offer specific suggestions for revising it.

Exercises

Active links for all websites in this chapter can be found online. If mybcommlab is being used in your class, see your User Guide for instructions on accessing the content for this chapter. Otherwise, visit www.pearsonglobaleditions.com/bovee, locate *Business Communication Today*, Tenth Edition, click the Companion Website link, select Chapter 15, and then click on "Featured Websites." Please note that links to sites that become inactive after publication of the book will be removed from the Featured Websites section.

15.1 **Revising for Clarity and Conciseness** The following sentence appears in your first draft of a report that analyzes perceived shortcomings in your company's employee health benefits:

> Among the many criticisms and concerns expressed by the workforce, at least among the 376 who responded to our online survey (out of 655 active employees), the issues of elder care, health insurance during retirement, and the increased amount that employees are being forced to pay every month as the company's contribution to health insurance coverage has declined over the past two years were identified as the most important.

Revise this 69-word sentence to make it shorter, more direct, and more powerful.

15.2 **Teamwork** You and a classmate are helping Linda Moreno prepare her report on Electrovision's travel and entertainment costs (see "Report Writer's Notebook"). This time, however, the report is to be informational rather than analytical, so it will not include recommendations. Review the existing report and determine what changes would be needed to make it an informational report. Be as specific as possible. For example, if your team decides the report needs a new title, what title would you use? Now draft a transmittal memo for Moreno to use in conveying this informational report to Dennis McWilliams, Electrovision's vice president of operations.

15.3 **Producing Reports: Letter of Transmittal** You are president of the Friends of the Library, a nonprofit group that raises funds and provides volunteers to support your local library. Every February, you send a report of the previous year's activities and accomplishments to the County Arts Council, which provides an annual grant of $1,000 toward your group's summer reading festival. Now it's February 6, and you've completed your formal report. Here are the highlights:

- Back-to-school book sale raised $2,000.
- Holiday craft fair raised $1,100.
- Promotion and prizes for summer reading festival cost $1,450.
- Materials for children's program featuring local author cost $125.
- New reference databases for library's career center cost $850.
- Bookmarks promoting library's website cost $200.

Write a letter of transmittal to Erica Maki, the council's director. Because she is expecting this report, you can use the direct approach. Be sure to express gratitude for the council's ongoing financial support.

15.4 **Internet** Government reports vary in purpose and structure. Read through the Department of Education's report "Helping Your Child Become a Reader," available at www.ed.gov. What is the purpose of this document? Does the title communicate this purpose? What type of report is this, and what is the report's structure? Which prefatory and supplementary parts are included? Now analyze the visuals. What types of visuals are included in this report? Are they all necessary? Are the titles and legends sufficiently informative? How does this report take advantage of the online medium to enhance readability?

15.5 **Ethical Choices: Team Challenge** You submitted what you thought was a masterful report to your boss over three weeks ago. The report analyzes current department productivity and recommends several steps that you think will improve employee output without increasing individual workloads. Brilliant, you thought. But you haven't heard a word from your boss. Did you overstep your boundaries by making recommendations that might imply that she has not been doing a good job? Did you overwhelm her with your ideas? You'd like some feedback. In your last e-mail to her, you asked if she had read your report. So far you've received no reply. Then yesterday, you overheard the company vice president talk about some productivity changes in your department. The changes were ones that you recommended in your report. Now you're worried that your boss submitted your report to senior management and will take full credit for your terrific ideas. What, if anything, should you do? Should you confront your boss about this? Should you ask to meet with the company vice president? Discuss this situation with your teammates and develop a solution to this sticky situation. Present your solution to the class, explaining the rationale behind your decision.

Expand Your Knowledge

Exploring the Best of the Web

Preview Before You Produce

www.dogpile.com

A good way to get ideas for the best style, organization, and format of a report is by looking at copies of professional business reports. To find samples of various types of reports, you can use a metasearch engine such as Dogpile. Choose a metasearch engine (refer to Table 11.2 on page 356). Try several search terms, such as *status report, progress report, sales report, business plan,* or *marketing plan,* until you uncover an interesting-looking report. Review the report and then answer the following questions:

1. What is the purpose of the report you read? Who is its target audience? Explain why the structure and style of the report make it easy or difficult to follow the main idea.
2. What type of report did you read? Briefly describe the main message. Is the information well organized? If you answer yes, explain how you can use the report as a guide for a report you might write. If you answer no, explain why the report is not helpful.
3. Drawing on what you know about the qualities of a good business report, review a report and describe the features that contribute to its readability.

Sharpening Your Career Skills Online

Bovée and Thill's Business Communication Web Search, at http://businesscommunicationblog.com/websearch, is a unique research tool designed specifically for business communication research. Use the Web Search function to find a website, video, PDF document, or PowerPoint presentation that offers advice on producing formal reports and proposals. Write a brief e-mail message to your instructor, describing the item that you found and summarizing the career skills information you learned from it.

CASES

Applying the Three-Step Writing Process to Cases

Apply each step to the following cases, as assigned by your instructor.

SHORT FORMAL REPORTS REQUIRING NO ADDITIONAL RESEARCH

PORTFOLIO BUILDER

1. Giving it the online try: Report analyzing the advantages and disadvantages of corporate online learning. As the newest member of the corporate training division of Paper Products, Inc., you have been asked to investigate and analyze the merits of creating online courses for the company's employees. The president of your company thinks e-learning might be a good employee benefit as well as a terrific way for employees to learn new skills that they can use on the job. You've already done your research, and here's a copy of your notes:

Online courses open up new horizons for working adults, who often find it difficult to juggle conventional classes with jobs and families.
Adults over 25 now represent nearly half of higher-ed students; most are employed and want more education to advance their careers.
Some experts believe that online learning will never be as good as face-to-face instruction.
Online learning requires no commute and is appealing for employees who travel regularly.
Enrollment in courses offered online by postsecondary institutions is expected to increase from 4 million students in 2009 to 7 million students in 2014.
E-learning is a cost-effective way to get better-educated employees.
More than one-third of the $50 billion spent on employee training every year is spent on e-learning.
At IBM, some 200,000 employees received education or training online last year, and 75 percent of the company's Basic Blue course for new managers is online. E-learning cut IBM's training bill by $350 million last year—mostly because online courses don't require travel.
There are no national statistics, but a recent report from the *Chronicle of Higher Education* found that institutions are seeing dropout rates that range from 20 to 50 percent for online learners. The research does not adequately explain why the dropout rates for e-learners are higher.
A recent study of corporate online learners reported that employees want the following things from their online courses: college credit or a certificate; active correspondence with an online facilitator who has frequent virtual office hours; access to 24-hour, seven-day-a-week technical support; and the ability to start a course anytime.

Corporate e-learners said that their top reason for dropping a course was lack of time. Many had trouble completing courses from their desktops because of frequent distractions caused by co-workers. Some said they could only access courses through the company's intranet, so they couldn't finish their assignments from home.
Besides lack of time, corporate e-learners cited the following as e-learning disadvantages: lack of management oversight, lack of motivation, problems with technology, lack of student support, individual learning preferences, poorly designed courses, substandard/inexperienced instructors.
A recent study by GE Capital found that finishing a corporate online course was dependent on whether managers gave reinforcement on attendance, how important employees were made to feel, and whether employee progress in the course was tracked.
Sun Microsystems found that interactivity can be a critical success factor for online courses. Company studies showed that only 25 percent of employees finish classes that are strictly self-paced. But 75 percent finish when given similar assignments and access to tutors through e-mail, phone, or online discussion groups.
Company managers must supervise e-learning just as they would any other important initiative.
For online learning to work, companies must develop a culture that takes online learning just as seriously as classroom training.
For many e-learners, studying at home is optimal. Whenever possible, companies should offer courses through the Internet or provide intranet access at home. Having employees studying on their own time will more than cover any added costs.
Corporate e-learning has flared into a $2.3 billion market, making it one of the fastest-growing segments of the education industry.
Rather than fly trainers to 7,000 dealerships, General Motors University now uses interactive satellite broadcasts to teach salespeople the best way to highlight features of the new Buick.
Fast and cheap, e-training can shave companies' training costs while it saves employees' travel time.
Pharmaceutical companies such as Merck are conducting live, interactive classes over the web, allowing sales reps to learn about the latest product information at home rather than fly to a conference center.
McDonald's trainers can log into Hamburger University to learn such skills as how to assemble a made-to-order burger or properly place a drink on a tray.

One obstacle to the spread of online corporate training is the mismatch between what employees really need—customized courses that are tailored to a firm's products and its unique corporate culture—and what employers can afford.

Eighty percent of companies prefer developing their own online training courses in-house. But creating even one customized e-course can take months, involve armies of experts, and cost anywhere from $25,000 to $50,000. Thus, most companies either stick with classroom training or buy generic courses on such topics as how to give performance appraisals, understanding basic business ethics, and so on. Employers can choose from a wide selection of noncustomized electronic courses.

For online learning to be effective, content must be broken into short "chunks" with lots of pop quizzes, online discussion groups, and other interactive features that let students demonstrate what they've learned. For instance, Circuit City's tutorial on digital camcorders consists of three 20-minute segments. Each contains audio demonstrations of how to handle customer product queries, tests on terminology, and "try-its" that propel trainees back onto the floor to practice what they've learned.

Dell expects 90 percent of its learning solutions to be totally or partially technology enabled.

The Home Depot has used e-training to cut a full day from the time required to train new cashiers.

Online training has freed up an average of 17 days every year for Black & Decker's sales representatives.

Your task: Write a short (three to five pages) memo report to the director of human resources, Kerry Simmons, presenting the advantages and disadvantages of e-learning and making a recommendation about whether Paper Products, Inc., should invest time and money in training its employees this way. Be sure to organize your information so that it is clear, concise, and logically presented. Simmons likes to read the "bottom line" first, so be direct: Present your recommendation up-front and support your recommendation with your findings.[11]

PORTFOLIO BUILDER

2. Grumbling in the ranks: When departments can't agree on the value of work. You've been in your new job as human resources director for only a week, and already you have a major personnel crisis on your hands. Some employees in the marketing department got their hands on a confidential salary report, only to learn that, on average, marketing employees earn less than engineering employees. In addition, several top performers in the engineering group make significantly more money than anybody in marketing. The report was passed around the company instantly by e-mail, and now everyone is discussing the situation. You'll deal with the data security issue later; for now, you need to address the dissatisfaction in the marketing group.

Table 1 lists the salary and employment data you were able to pull from the employee database. You also had the opportunity to interview the engineering and marketing directors to get their opinions on the pay situation; their answers are listed in Table 2.

Your task: The CEO has asked for a short report, summarizing the data and information you have on engineering and marketing salaries. Feel free to offer your own interpretation of the situation as well (make up any information you need), but keep in mind that as a new manager with almost no experience in the company, your opinion might not have a lot of influence.

PORTFOLIO BUILDER

3. Building a new magazine: Finding opportunity in the remodeling craze. Spurred on in part by the success of numerous television shows and even entire cable networks devoted to remodeling, homeowners are redecorating and rebuilding like never before. Many people are content with superficial changes, such as new paint or new accessories, but some are

TABLE 1 Selected Employment Data for Engineers and Marketing Staff

EMPLOYMENT STATISTIC	ENGINEERING DEPARTMENT	MARKETING DEPARTMENT
Average number of years of work experience	18.2	16.3
Average number of years of experience in current profession	17.8	8.6
Average number of years with company	12.4	7.9
Average number of years of college education	6.9	4.8
Average number of years between promotions	6.7	4.3
Salary range	$58–165k	$45–85k
Median salary	$77k	$62k

TABLE 2   Summary Statements from Department Director Interviews

QUESTION	ENGINEERING DIRECTOR	MARKETING DIRECTOR
1. Should engineering and marketing professionals receive roughly similar pay?	In general, yes, but we need to make allowances for the special nature of the engineering profession. In some cases, it's entirely appropriate for an engineer to earn more than a marketing person.	Yes.
2. Why or why not?	Several reasons: (1) Top engineers are extremely hard to find, and we need to offer competitive salaries; (2) the structure of the engineering department doesn't provide as many promotional opportunities, so we can't use promotions as a motivator the way marketing can; (3) many of our engineers have advanced degrees, and nearly all pursue continuous education to stay on top of the technology.	Without marketing, the products the engineers create wouldn't reach customers, and the company wouldn't have any revenue. The two teams make equal contributions to the company's success.
3. If we decide to balance pay between the two departments, how should we do it?	If we do anything to cap or reduce engineering salaries, we'll lose key people to the competition.	If we can't increase payroll immediately to raise marketing salaries, the only fair thing to do is freeze raises in engineering and gradually raise marketing salaries over the next few years.

more ambitious. These homeowners want to move walls, add rooms, redesign kitchens, convert garages to home theaters—the big stuff.

With many consumer trends, publishers try to create magazines that appeal to carefully identified groups of potential readers and the advertisers who'd like to reach them. The do-it-yourself (DIY) market is already served by numerous magazines, but you see an opportunity in those homeowners who tackle the heavy-duty projects. Tables 3 through 5 summarize the results of some preliminary research you asked your company's research staff to conduct.

TABLE 3   Rooms Most Frequently Remodeled by DIYers

ROOM	PERCENTAGE OF HOMEOWNERS SURVEYED WHO HAVE TACKLED OR PLAN TO TACKLE AT LEAST A PARTIAL REMODEL
Kitchen	60
Bathroom	48
Home office/study	44
Bedroom	38
Media room/home theater	31
Den/recreation room	28
Living room	27
Dining room	12
Sun room/solarium	8

TABLE 4   Average Amount Spent on Remodeling Projects

ESTIMATED AMOUNT	PERCENTAGE OF SURVEYED HOMEOWNERS
Under $5k	5
$5–10k	21
$10–20k	39
$20–50k	22
More than $50k	13

Your task: You think the data show a real opportunity for a "big projects" DIY magazine, although you'll need more extensive research to confirm the size of the market and refine the editorial direction of the magazine. Prepare a brief analytical report that presents the data you have, identifies the opportunity or opportunities you've found (suggest your own ideas based on the tables), and requests funding from the editorial board to pursue further research.

SHORT FORMAL REPORTS REQUIRING ADDITIONAL RESEARCH

PORTFOLIO BUILDER

4. Reconciling the experts: Resolving the advice on writing business plans. Like any other endeavor that combines hardnosed factual analysis and creative freethinking, the task of writing business plans generates a range of opinions.

TABLE 5 Tasks Performed by Homeowner on a Typical Remodeling Project

TASK	PERCENTAGE OF SURVEYED HOMEOWNERS WHO PERFORM OR PLAN TO PERFORM MOST OR ALL OF THIS TASK THEMSELVES
Conceptual design	90
Technical design/ architecture	34
Demolition	98
Foundation work	62
Framing	88
Plumbing	91
Electrical	55
Heating/cooling	22
Finish carpentry	85
Tile work	90
Painting	100
Interior design	52

Your task: Find at least six sources of advice on writing successful business plans (focus on start-up businesses that are likely to seek outside investors). Use at least two books, two magazine or journal articles, and two websites or blogs. Analyze the advice you find and identify points where most or all the experts agree and points where they don't agree. Wherever you find points of significant disagreement, identify which opinion you find most convincing and explain why. Summarize your findings in a brief formal report.

TEAM SKILLS   PORTFOLIO BUILDER

5. Averse to verse? Report suggesting ways to increase sales of poetry. Anyone looking at the fragmented 21st-century landscape of media and entertainment options might be surprised to learn that poetry was once a dominant medium for not only creative literary expression but philosophical, political, and even scientific discourse. Alas, such is no longer the case.

Your task: With a team of fellow students, your challenge is to identify opportunities to increase sales of poetry—any kind of poetry, in any medium. The following suggestions may help you get started:

- Research recent bestsellers in the poetry field and try to identify why they have been popular.
- Interview literature professors, professional poets, librarians, publishers, and bookstore personnel.
- Conduct surveys and interviews to find out why consumers don't buy more poetry.
- Review professional journals that cover the field of poetry, including *Publishers Weekly* and *Poets & Writers*, from both business and creative standpoints.

Summarize your findings in a brief formal report; assume that your target readers are executives in the publishing industry.

PORTFOLIO BUILDER

6. A ready-made business: Finding the right franchise opportunity. After 15 years in the corporate world, you're ready to strike out on your own. Rather than building a business from the ground up, however, you think that buying a franchise is a better idea. Unfortunately, some of the most lucrative franchise opportunities, such as the major fast-food chains, require significant start-up costs—some more than a half-million dollars. Fortunately, you've met several potential investors who seem willing to help you get started in exchange for a share of ownership. Between your own savings and money from these investors, you estimate that you can raise from $350,000 to $600,000, depending on how much ownership share you want to concede to the investors.

You've worked in several functional areas already, including sales and manufacturing, so you have a fairly well-rounded business résumé. You're open to just about any type of business, too, as long as it provides the opportunity to grow; you don't want to be so tied down to the first operation that you can't turn it over to a hired manager and expand into another market.

Your task: To convene a formal meeting with the investor group, you need to first draft a report that outlines the types of franchise opportunities you'd like to pursue. Write a brief report, identifying five franchises that you would like to explore further. (Choose five based on your own personal interests and the criteria already identified.) For each possibility, identify the nature of the business, the financial requirements, the level of support the company provides, and a brief statement of why you could run such a business successfully (make up any details you need). Be sure to carefully review the information you find about each franchise company to make sure you can qualify for it. For instance, McDonald's doesn't allow investment partnerships to buy franchises, so you won't be able to start up a McDonald's outlet until you have enough money to do it on your own.

For a quick introduction to franchising, see How Stuff Works (www.howstuffworks.com/franchising). You can learn more about the business of franchising at Franchising.com (www.franchising.com) and search for specific franchise opportunities at Francorp Connect (www.francorpconnect.com). In addition, many companies that sell franchises, such as Subway, offer additional information on their websites.

LONG FORMAL REPORTS REQUIRING NO ADDITIONAL RESEARCH

PORTFOLIO BUILDER

7. You can get anything online these days: Shopping for automobiles on the Internet. As a researcher for your local consumer protection agency, you're frequently called on to investigate consumer topics and write reports for the agency's website. Thousands of consumers have arranged the purchase of cars online, and millions more do at least some of their research online before heading to a dealership. Some want to save time and money, some want to be armed with as much information as possible before talking to a dealer, while others want to completely avoid the often-uncomfortable experience of negotiating prices with car salespeople. In response, a variety of online services have emerged to meet these consumer needs. Some let you compare information on various car models, some connect you to local dealers to complete the transaction, and some complete nearly all of the transaction details for you, including negotiating the price. Some search the inventory of thousands of dealers, whereas others search only a single dealership or a network of affiliated dealers. In other words, a slew of new tools are available for car buyers, but it's not always easy to figure out where to go and what to expect. That's where your report will help.

By visiting a variety of car-related websites and reading magazine and newspaper articles on the car-buying process, you've compiled a variety of notes related to the subject:

- **Process overview.** The process is relatively straightforward and fairly similar to other online shopping experiences, with two key differences. In general, a consumer identifies the make and model of car he or she wants, and then the online car-buying service searches the inventories of car dealers nationwide and presents the available choices. The consumer chooses a particular car from that list, and the service handles the communication and purchase details with the dealer. When the paperwork is finished, the consumer then visits the dealership and picks up the car. The two biggest differences with online auto buying are that (1) you can't actually complete the purchase over the Internet (in most cases, you must visit a local dealer to pick up the car and sign the papers, although in some cities, a dealer or a local car-buying service will deliver it to your home), and (2) in many places, it's illegal to purchase a new car from anyone other than a franchise dealer (i.e., you can't buy directly from the manufacturer, the way you can buy a Dell computer directly from Dell, for instance).
- **Information you can find online (not all information is available at all sites).** The information you can find online includes makes, models, colors, options, option packages (often, specific options are available only as part of a package; you need to know these constraints before you select your options), photos, specifications (everything from engine size to interior space), fuel efficiency estimates, performance data, safety information, predicted resale value, reviews, comparable models, insurance costs, consumer ratings, repair and reliability histories, available buyer incentives and rebates, true ownership costs (including fuel, maintenance, repairs, etc.), warranty information, loan and lease payments, and maintenance requirements.
- **Advantages of shopping online.** Advantages of shopping online include shopping from the comfort and convenience of home, none of the dreaded negotiating at the dealership (in many cases), the ability to search far and wide for a specific car (even nationwide, on many sites), rapid access to considerable amounts of data and information, and reviews from both professional automotive journalists and other consumers. In general, online auto shopping reduces a key advantage that auto dealers used to have: control of most of the information in the purchase transaction. Now consumers can find out how reliable each model is, how quickly it will depreciate, how often it is likely to need repairs, what other

drivers think of it, how much the dealer paid the manufacturer for it, and so on.
- **Changing nature of the business.** The relationship between dealers and third-party websites (such as CarsDirect.com and Vehix.com) continues to evolve. At first, the relationship was antagonistic, as some third-party sites and dealers frequently competed for the same customers, and each side made bold proclamations about driving the other out of business. However, the relationship is more collaborative in many cases now, with dealers realizing that some third-party sites already have wide brand awareness and nationwide audiences. As the percentage of new car sales that originate via the Internet continues to increase, dealers are more receptive to working with third-party sites.
- **Comparing information from multiple sources.** Consumers shouldn't rely solely on the information from a single website. Each site has its own way of organizing information, and many have their own ways of evaluating car models and connecting buyers with sellers.
- **Understanding what each site is doing.** For instance, some search thousands of dealers, regardless of ownership connections. Others, such as AutoNation, search only affiliated dealers. A search for a specific model might yield only a half-dozen cars on one site but dozens of cars on another site. Find out who owns the site and what their business objectives are, if you can; this will help you assess the information you receive.
- **Leading websites.** Consumers can check out a wide variety of websites, some of which are full-service operations, offering everything from research to negotiation; others provide more specific and limited services. For instance, CarsDirect (www.carsdirect.com) provides a full range of services, whereas Carfax (www.carfax.com) specializes in uncovering the repair histories of individual used cars. Table 6 lists some of the leading car-related websites.

Your task: Write an informational report, based on your research notes. The purpose of the report is to introduce consumers to the basic concepts of integrating the Internet into their car-buying activities and to educate them about important issues.[12]

PORTFOLIO BUILDER

8. Moving the workforce: Understanding commute patterns. Your company is the largest private employer in your metropolitan area, and the 43,500 employees in your workforce have a tremendous impact on local traffic. A group of city and county transportation officials recently approached your CEO with a request to explore ways to reduce this impact. The CEO has assigned you the task of analyzing the workforce's transportation habits and attitudes as a first step toward identifying potential solutions. He's willing to consider anything from subsidized bus passes to company-owned shuttle buses to telecommuting, but the decision requires a thorough understanding of employee transportation needs. Tables 7 through 11 summarize data you collected in an employee survey.

Your task: Present the results of your survey in an informational report, using the data provided in Tables 7 through 11.

TABLE 6 Leading Automotive Websites

SITE	URL
AutoAdvice	www.autoadvice.com
Autobytel	www.autobytel.com
Autos.com	www.autos.com
AutoVantage	www.autovantage.com
Autoweb	www.autoweb.com
CarBargains	www.carbargains.com
Carfax	www.carfax.com
CarPrices.com	www.carprices.com
Cars.com	www.cars.com
CarsDirect	www.carsdirect.com
CarSmart	www.carsmart.com
Consumer Reports	www.consumerreports.org
eBay Motors	www.motors.ebay.com
Edmunds	www.edmunds.com
iMotors	www.imotors.com
IntelliChoice	www.intellichoice.com
InvoiceDealers	www.invoicedealers.com
JDPower	www.jdpower.com
Kelly Blue Book	www.kbb.com
MSN Autos	http://autos.msn.com
PickupTrucks.com	www.pickuptrucks.com
The Car Connection	www.thecarconnection.com
Vehix.com	www.vehix.com
Yahoo! Autos	http//autos.yahoo.com

TABLE 7 Employee Carpool Habits

FREQUENCY OF USE: CARPOOLING	PORTION OF WORKFORCE
Every day, every week	10,138 (23%)
Certain days, every week	4,361 (10%)
Randomly	983 (2%)
Never	28,018 (64%)

TABLE 8 Use of Public Transportation

FREQUENCY OF USE: PUBLIC TRANSPORTATION	PORTION OF WORKFORCE
Every day, every week	23,556 (54%)
Certain days, every week	2,029 (5%)
Randomly	5,862 (13%)
Never	12,053 (28%)

TABLE 9 Effect of Potential Improvements to Public Transportation

WHICH OF THE FOLLOWING WOULD ENCOURAGE YOU TO USE PUBLIC TRANSPORTATION MORE FREQUENTLY (CHECK ALL THAT APPLY)	PORTION OF RESPONDENTS
Increased perceptions of safety	4,932 (28%)
Improved cleanliness	852 (5%)
Reduced commute times	7,285 (41%)
Greater convenience: fewer transfers	3,278 (18%)
Greater convenience: more stops	1,155 (6%)
Lower (or subsidized) fares	5,634 (31%)
Nothing could encourage me to take public transportation	8,294 (46%)

Note: This question was asked of respondents who use public transportation randomly or never, a subgroup that represents 17,915 employees, or 41 percent of the workforce.

TABLE 10 Distance Traveled to/from Work

DISTANCE YOU TRAVEL TO WORK (ONE WAY)	PORTION OF WORKFORCE
Less than 1 kilometer	531 (1%)
1–3 kilometers	6,874 (16%)
4–10 kilometers	22,951 (53%)
11–20 kilometers	10,605 (24%)
More than 20 kilometers	2,539 (6%)

TABLE 11 Is Telecommuting an Option?

DOES THE NATURE OF YOUR WORK MAKE TELECOMMUTING A REALISTIC OPTION?	PORTION OF WORKFORCE
Yes, every day	3,460 (8%)
Yes, several days a week	8,521 (20%)
Yes, random days	12,918 (30%)
No	18,601 (43%)

LONG FORMAL REPORTS REQUIRING ADDITIONAL RESEARCH

PORTFOLIO BUILDER

9. Face-off: Informational report comparing two companies in the same industry. The partners in your accounting firm have agreed to invest some of the company's profits in the stock market. A previous team effort identified two leading companies in each of five different industries:

- Boeing; Airbus (aerospace)
- Hewlett-Packard; Dell (computers and software)

- Applebee's; OSI Restaurant Partners (casual dining)
- Barnes & Noble; Amazon.com (retailing)
- UPS; FedEx (delivery and logistics)

The partners have already done an in-depth financial analysis of all 10 firms, and they have asked you to look for more qualitative information, such as

- Fundamental philosophical differences in management styles, launch and handling of products and services, marketing of products and services, and approach to e-commerce that sets one rival company apart from the other
- Future challenges that each competitor faces
- Important decisions made by the two competitors and how those decisions affected their company
- Fundamental differences in each company's vision of its industry's future (for instance, do they both agree on what consumers want, what products to deliver, and so on?)
- Specific competitive advantages of each rival
- Past challenges each competitor has faced and how each met those challenges
- Strategic moves made by one rival that might affect the other
- Company success stories
- Brief company background information
- Brief comparative statistics, such as annual sales, market share, number of employees, number of stores, types of equipment, number of customers, sources of revenue, and so on

Your task: Select two competitors from the preceding list (or another list provided by your instructor) and write a long formal informational report comparing how the two companies are addressing the topics outlined by the partners. Of course, not every topic will apply to each company, and some will be more important than others—depending on the companies you select. The partners will invest in only one of the two companies in your report. (*Note:* Because these topics require considerable research, your instructor may choose to make this a team project.)

10. Is there any justice? Report critiquing legislation. Plenty of people complain about their legislators, but few are specific about their complaints. Here's your chance.

Your task: Write a long formal report about a law that you believe should not have been enacted or that should be enacted. Be objective. Write the report using specific facts to support your beliefs. Reach conclusions and offer a recommendation at the end of the report. As a final step, send a copy of the report to an appropriate official or legislator.

11. Travel opportunities: Report comparing two destinations. You are planning to take a two-week trip abroad sometime within the next year. Because there are a couple destinations that appeal to you, you are going to have to do some research before you can make a decision.

Your task: Prepare a lengthy comparative study of two countries that you would like to visit. Begin by making a list of important questions you will need to answer. Do you want a relaxing vacation or an educational experience? What types of services will you require? What will your transportation needs be? Where will you have the least difficulty with the language? Using resources in your library, the Internet, and perhaps travel agencies, analyze the suitability of these two destinations with respect to your own

travel criteria. At the end of the report, recommend the better country to visit this year.

PORTFOLIO BUILDER

12. Secondary sources: Report based on library and online research. As a college student and an active consumer, you may have considered one or more of the following questions at some point in the past few years:

   a. What criteria distinguish the top-rated MBA programs in your country? How well do these criteria correspond to the needs and expectations of business? Are the criteria fair for students, employers, and business schools?
   b. Which of three companies you might like to work for has the strongest corporate ethics policies?
   c. What will the music industry look like in the future? What's next after online stores such as Apple iTunes and digital players such as the iPod?
   d. Which industries and job categories are forecast to experience the greatest growth—and therefore the greatest demands for workers—in the next 10 years?
   e. What has been the impact of Starbucks's aggressive growth on small, independent coffee shops? On midsized chains or franchises? In the United States or in another country?
   f. How large is the "industry" of major college sports? How much do the major football or cricket programs contribute—directly or indirectly—to other parts of a typical university?
   g. How much have minor league sports—baseball, hockey, arena U.S.-style football—grown in small- and medium-market cities? What is the local economic impact when these municipalities build stadiums and arenas?

Your task: Answer one of these questions, using secondary research sources for information. Be sure to document your sources in the correct form. Make conclusions and offer recommendations where appropriate.

PORTFOLIO BUILDER

13. Doing business abroad: Report summarizing the social and business customs of a foreign country. Your company would like to sell its products overseas. Before they begin negotiating on the international horizon, however, the management team members must have a clear understanding of the social and business customs of the countries where they intend to do business.

Your task: Choose a non-English-speaking country and write a long formal report, summarizing the country's social and business customs. Review Chapter 3 and use Table 3.1 as a guide for the types of information you should include in your report.

FORMAL PROPOSALS

PORTFOLIO BUILDER

14. Polishing the presenters: Offering your services as a presentation trainer. Presentations can make or break both careers and businesses. A good presentation can bring in millions of dollars in new sales or fresh investment capital. A bad presentation might cause a number of troubles, from turning away potential customers to upsetting fellow employees to derailing key projects. To help business professionals plan, create, and deliver more effective presentations, you offer a three-day workshop that covers the essentials of good presentations:

- Understanding your audience's needs and expectations
- Formulating your presentation objectives
- Choosing an organizational approach
- Writing openings that catch your audience members' attention
- Creating effective graphics and slides
- Practicing and delivering your presentation
- Leaving a positive impression on your audience
- Avoiding common mistakes with Microsoft PowerPoint
- Making presentations online using webcasting tools
- Handling questions and arguments from the audience
- Overcoming the top 10 worries of public speaking (including How can I overcome stage fright? and I'm not the performing type; can I still give an effective presentation?)

Here is some additional information about the workshop:

- **Workshop benefits:** Students will learn how to prepare better presentations in less time and deliver them more effectively.
- **Who should attend:** Top executives, project managers, employment recruiters, sales professionals, and anyone else who gives important presentations to internal or external audiences.
- **Your qualifications:** 18 years of business experience, including 14 years in sales and 12 years in public speaking. Experience speaking to audiences as large as 5,000 people. More than a dozen speech-related articles published in professional journals. Have conducted successful workshops for nearly 100 companies.
- **Workshop details:** Three-day workshop (9 A.M. to 3:30 P.M.) that combines lectures, practice presentations, and both individual and group feedback. Minimum number of students: 6. Maximum number of students per workshop: 12.
- **Pricing:** The cost is $3,500, plus $100 per student. 10 percent discount for additional workshops.
- **Other information:** Each attendee will have the opportunity to give three practice presentations that will last from three to five minutes. Everyone is encouraged to bring PowerPoint files containing slides from actual business presentations. Each attendee will also receive a workbook and a digital video recording of his or her final class presentation. You'll also be available for phone or e-mail coaching for six months after the workshop.

Your task: Identify a company in your local area that might be a good candidate for your services. Learn more about the company by visiting its website so you can personalize your proposal. Using the information listed earlier in this exercise, prepare a sales proposal that explains the benefits of your training and what students can expect during the workshop.

PORTFOLIO BUILDER

15. Healthy alternatives: Proposal to sell snacks and beverages at local schools. For years, a controversy has been brewing over the amount of junk food and soft drinks being sold through vending machines in local schools. Schools benefit from revenue-sharing arrangements, but many parents and health experts are concerned about the negative effects of these snacks and beverages. You and your brother have almost a decade of experience running espresso

and juice stands in malls and on street corners, and you'd love to find some way to expand your business into schools. After a quick brainstorming session, the two of you craft a plan that makes good business sense while meeting the financial concerns of school administrators and the nutritional concerns of parents and dietitians. Here are the notes from your brainstorming session:

- Set up portable juice bars on school campuses, offering healthy fruit and vegetable drinks along with simple healthy snacks.
- Offer schools 30 percent of profits in exchange for free space and long-term contracts.
- Provide job training opportunities for students (during athletic events, etc.).
- Provide detailed dietary analysis of all products sold.
- Establish a nutritional advisory board composed of parents, students, and at least one certified health professional.
- Assure schools and parents that all products are safe (e.g., no stimulant drinks, no dietary supplements, and so on).
- Support local farmers and specialty food preparers by buying locally and giving these vendors the opportunity to test-market new products at your stands.

Your task: Based on the ideas listed, draft a formal proposal to the local school board, outlining your plan to offer healthier alternatives to soft drinks and prepackaged snack foods. Invent any details you need to complete your proposal.

PORTFOLIO BUILDER

16. Career connections: Helping employees get the advice they need to move ahead. Seems like everybody in the firm is frustrated. On the one hand, top executives complain about the number of lower-level employees who want promotions but just don't seem to "get it" when it comes to dealing with customers and the public, recognizing when to speak out and when to be quiet, knowing how to push new ideas through the appropriate channels, and performing other essential but difficult-to-teach tasks. On the other hand, ambitious employees who'd like to learn more feel that they have nowhere to turn for career advice from people who've been there. In between, a variety of managers and midlevel executives are overwhelmed by the growing number of mentoring requests they're getting, sometimes from employees they don't even know.

You've been assigned the challenge of proposing a formal mentoring program—and a considerable challenge it is:

- The number of employees who want mentoring relationships far exceeds the number of managers and executives willing and able to be mentors. How will you select people for the program?
- The people most in demand for mentoring also tend to be some of the busiest people in the organization.
- After several years of belt tightening and staff reductions, the entire company feels overworked; few people can imagine adding another recurring task to their seemingly endless to-do lists.
- What's in it for the mentors? Why would they be motivated to help lower-level employees?
- How will you measure success or failure of the mentoring effort?

Your task: Identify potential solutions to the issues (make up any information you need) and draft a proposal to the executive committee for a formal, companywide mentoring program that would match selected employees with successful managers and executives.

Part 6

Designing and Delivering Oral and Online Presentations

Presentations give you the opportunity to put all your communication skills on display, from audience analysis and research to the design of presentation materials to public speaking. Learn how to plan effective presentations, overcome the anxieties that every speaker feels, and respond to questions from the audience. Complement your talk with compelling visual materials and learn how to create presentation slides that engage and excite your audience. Finally, discover some tips and techniques for succeeding with online presentations, an increasingly common mode of communication in today's environment.

16

Developing Oral and Online Presentations

Learning Objectives

After studying this chapter, you will be able to

1 Explain the importance of oral and online presentations in your career success and explain how to adapt the three-step writing process to oral presentations

2 Identify the two primary reasons that limiting your scope is especially important for oral presentations

3 Discuss the three functions of an effective introduction

4 Identify six ways to get your audience's attention and six ways to hold it

5 Describe the techniques you can use to feel more confident in front of an audience

6 List six steps you can take to handle questions during a presentation

Communication Close-up at Fitch

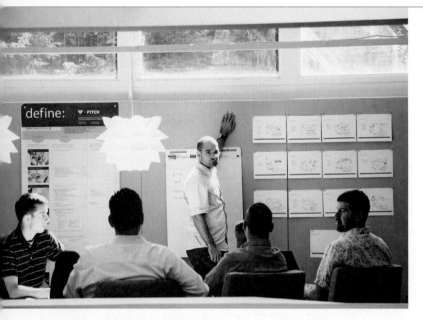

Presenters at Fitch often take chances in their presentations by going against audience expectations. The strategy works if it stimulates new thinking and ultimately meets audience needs.

www.fitch.com

Figure out what the audience expects to get from a presentation—and then *don't* give it to them? A risky strategy, indeed, but it's working for Fitch, a global design consultancy with offices in North America, Europe, Asia, and the Middle East. Fitch designs everything from restaurants and retail stores to consumer products and packaging to corporate events and websites.

For most professional services firms, a sales presentation follows a predictable pattern: Speak about the company's capabilities, introduce a small army of talented people to impress the potential client, present examples of work done for other clients, and then ask the potential client for a decision. Most presenters prefer this approach because they get to speak from a position of confidence (based on all the great work they've done for other clients), and their level of risk is low (they don't have to present any new ideas until they get a contract).

Even though potential clients expect a traditional "pitch" with all this information, Fitch doesn't offer it. Instead, the company's designers study the client's business, develop a strong point of view regarding the challenge at hand, and work on a design concept—all before making a presentation. When it comes time for the pitch, Fitch essentially says, "Here's the design we think is right for you. Love it or leave it." According to Eric Ashworth, a Fitch marketing executive, the goal is to inspire an "Aha!" moment that makes the client excited—and maybe just a little nervous.

Does this brash approach work? Ashworth says this style of presentation is 30 percent more effective in generating sales than the traditional approach and has led to contracts with such clients as 3M, LEGO, Nissan, Nokia, and the BBC. Recent high-profile engagements include Microsoft's Xbox launch event in Spain, the Harrods store in London's Heathrow Airport, and the luxury Atlantis resort in Dubai. However, Ashworth does offer a caution: The approach can work wonders—or it can "get you pushed out of the room."[1]

BUILDING YOUR CAREER WITH ORAL AND ONLINE PRESENTATIONS

1 LEARNING OBJECTIVE

No matter how expected or unexpected your next presentation might be, Fitch's Eric Ashworth (profiled in the chapter-opening Communication Close-up) can verify that presentations offer you important opportunities to put all your communication skills on display—not only in research, planning, writing, and visual design but in interpersonal and nonverbal communication, too. Presentations can also give you a chance to demonstrate your abilities to think on your feet, grasp complex issues, and handle challenging situations—all attributes that executives look for when searching for talented employees to promote within an organization. Perhaps best of all, oral presentations let your personality shine through in ways that even the best-written reports can't provide.

Explain the importance of oral and online presentations in your career success and explain how to adapt the three-step writing process to oral presentations

If the thought of giving a speech or presentation makes you nervous, try to keep three points in mind. First, everybody gets nervous when speaking in front of a group. Even after years of experience, professional speakers and entertainers get nervous. Second, being nervous is actually a good thing; it means you care about the topic, your audience, and your career success. With practice, you can convert those nervous feelings into positive energy. Third, you don't have to be a victim of your own emotions when it comes to oral presentations. You can take control of the situation by using the planning and development techniques that you'll learn in this chapter—starting with how to adapt the three-step writing process to the unique challenges of oral and online presentations.

Feeling nervous is perfectly normal when you're faced with an oral presentation; the good news is there are positive steps you can take to reduce your anxiety.

You will rarely write out a presentation word for word, but nearly every task in the three-step writing process applies to oral presentations, with some modifications (see Figure 16.1). In addition, a few extra steps will help you prepare both your material and yourself for the actual presentation. As with written reports, people often judge the quality of the content by the quality of the presentation, so your delivery style and the packaging of any visual support materials can be as important as your message. For important presentations, make sure you give yourself plenty of time to plan, create, and practice your presentation. Creating a top-notch presentation and being ready to deliver it smoothly and confidently can take far longer than many beginners imagine.[2] This chapter walks you through the three-step development process, and Chapter 17 offers advice on creating visual materials to enhance your presentation.

While you don't usually write your oral presentations word for word, the three-step writing process is easily adaptable to oral presentations.

PLANNING YOUR PRESENTATION

Planning presentations is much like planning any other business message: You (1) analyze the situation, (2) gather information, (3) select the right medium, and (4) organize the information. Gathering information for oral presentations is essentially the same as it is for written communication projects (see Chapter 11). The other three planning tasks have some special applications when it comes to oral and online presentations; they are covered in the following sections.

REAL-TIME UPDATES
Learn More

Practical advice for making presentations that stick

Presentation expert Andy Bounds describes his simple RAP method for great presentations: start with the desired **r**esults in mind, understand **a**udience motivations, and only then can you **p**repare effectively. Go to http://real-timeupdates.com/bct and click on "Learn More." If you are using mybcommlab, you can access Real-Time Updates within each chapter or under Student Study Tools.

FIGURE 16.1   The Three-Step Process for Developing Oral and Online Presentations
Although you rarely "write" a presentation or speech in the sense of composing every word ahead of time, the tasks in the three-step writing process adapt quite well to the challenge of planning, creating, and delivering both oral and online presentations.

1 Plan → **2 Write** → **3 Complete**

Analyze the Situation
Define your purpose and develop a profile of your audience, including their likely emotional states and language preferences.

Gather Information
Determine audience needs and obtain the information necessary to satisfy those needs.

Select the Right Medium
Choose the best medium or combination of media for delivering your presentation, including handouts and other support materials.

Organize the Information
Define your main idea, limit your scope and verify timing, select the direct or indirect approach, and outline your content.

Adapt to Your Audience
Adapt your content, presentation style, and room setup to the audience and the specific situation. Be sensitive to audience needs and expectations with a "you" attitude, politeness, positive emphasis, and bias-free language. Plan to establish your credibility as required.

Compose Your Presentation
Outline an attention-getting introduction, body, and close. Prepare supporting visuals and speaking notes.

Revise the Message
Evaluate your content and speaking notes.

Master Your Delivery
Choose your delivery mode and practice your presentation.

Prepare to Speak
Verify facilities and equipment, including online connections and software setups. Hire an interpreter if necessary.

Overcome Anxiety
Take steps to feel more confident and appear more confident on stage.

Analyzing the Situation

The purpose of most business presentations is to inform or persuade; you may also give presentations designed primarily to collaborate with others.

As with written communications, analyzing the situation for an oral presentation involves defining your purpose and developing an audience profile. The purpose of most of your presentations will be to inform or to persuade, although you may occasionally need to make a collaborative presentation, such as when you're leading a problem-solving or brainstorming session. Given the time limitations of most presentations and the "live" nature of the event, make sure your purpose is crystal clear. For instance, with Fitch's unusual presentation strategy, the company skips something audience members expect to hear (descriptions of work done in the past) in order to focus on something audience members really want to hear (how Fitch can help them in the future).

Knowing your audience's state of mind will help you adjust both your message and your delivery.

When you develop your audience profile, try to anticipate the likely emotional state of your audience members. Here are tips for dealing with a variety of audience mindsets:

- **Supportive.** Whenever you're fortunate enough to be speaking to people who welcome both you and your message, reward their goodwill with a presentation that is clear, concise, and upbeat. Speak in a relaxed, confident manner and provide just enough information to confirm their belief in you and your message.
- **Interested but neutral.** Plan to build your credibility as you present your main idea and key support points. Address possible objections as you move along to show that you've considered all sides of the issue. Be confident in what you have to say but remain open to questions and challenges.
- **Uninterested.** In some respects, an uninterested audience can be even more challenging than an apprehensive or hostile audience. If people don't care, it doesn't matter how

COMMUNICATING ACROSS CULTURES

Five Tips for Making Presentations Around the World

When speaking to an international audience, keep in mind that audience members' language fluency might vary widely. So take special care to ensure clear communication:

1. **Speak slowly and distinctly.** The most common complaint of international audiences is that English speakers talk too fast. Articulate each word carefully, emphasize consonants for clarity, and pause frequently.
2. **Repeat key words and phrases.** When audiences are not very familiar with your language, they need to hear important information more than once. Also, they may not be familiar with synonyms, so word key points in the same way throughout your presentation.
3. **Aim for clarity.** Keep your message simple. Eliminate complex sentence structure, abbreviations, and acronyms. Replace two-word verbs with one-word alternatives (such as *review* instead of *look over*). Such verbs are confusing because the definition of each separate word differs from the meaning of the two words combined. Similarly, avoid cultural idioms, such as *once in a blue moon*, which may be unfamiliar to an international audience.
4. **Communicate with body language.** Emphasize and clarify verbal information with gestures and facial expressions. For

instance, smile to emphasize positive points and use gestures to illustrate the meaning of words such as *up*, *down*, or *under*.
5. **Support your spoken message with visuals.** Simple, clear visuals, from flip charts to electronic slides, can help you describe your key points. If possible, prepare captions in both English and your audience's native language.

CAREER APPLICATIONS

1. One of the most important changes speakers need to make when addressing audiences in other cultures is to avoid colloquial figures of speech. Replace such phrases (for example, "hit one out of the park," "go for broke," "get your ducks in a row") with wording that is more likely to be understood by nonnative English speakers or audiences in other countries.
2. Make a list of 10 two-word verbs. How does the meaning of each separate word differ from the definition of the combined words? Replace each two-word verb with a single, specific word that will be clearer to an international audience.

---

good your presentation is. Think creatively to find a way to connect your message with some aspect of their personal or professional lives (see "Arousing Audience Interest" on page 518).

- **Apprehensive.** If listeners are worried about your message, treat their emotions with respect. Don't try to diffuse the situation with humor or trivialize their concerns. If your message will calm their fears, use the direct approach to share the good news immediately. If your message will confirm their fears, consider using the indirect approach to build up rational support for the negative message.
- **Hostile.** No one looks forward to addressing an angry audience, but you do have one major factor working in your favor: People definitely care about your message. As with an apprehensive audience, treat their emotions with respect and avoid humor. Prepare thoroughly so you can provide complete information in a calm, rational manner. Consider using the indirect approach to build support for your message while addressing points of concern along the way. Remain calm and don't engage in emotional exchanges with the audience.

You also need to determine whether your audience is comfortable listening to the language you speak. Listening to an unfamiliar language is much more difficult than reading that language, so an audience that might be able to read a written report might not be able to understand an oral presentation covering the same material (see "Communicating Across Cultures: Five Tips for Making Presentations Around the World").

Also consider the specific circumstances in which you'll be making your presentation. Will you speak to five people in a conference room, where you can control everything from light to sound to temperature? Or will you be demonstrating a product on the floor of a trade show, where you might have from 1 to 100 listeners and little control over the environment? Will everyone be in the same room, or will some or all of your audience participate from remote locations via the Internet? What equipment will you have at your disposal?

Try to learn as much as you can about the setting and circumstances of your presentation, from the size of the audience to potential interruptions.

For in-person presentations, pay close attention to seating arrangements. The four basic formats have distinct advantages and disadvantages:

- **Classroom or theater seating**, in which all chairs or desks face forward, helps keep attention focused on the speaker and is usually the best method for accommodating large audiences. However, this arrangement inhibits interaction among audience members, so it is not desirable for brainstorming or other collaborative activities.
- **Conference table seating**, in which people sit along both sides of a long table and the speaker stands at one end, is a common arrangement for smaller meetings. It promotes interaction among attendees, but it tends to isolate the speaker at one end of the room.
- **Horseshoe, or "U"-shaped, seating**, in which tables are arranged in the shape of a "U," improves on conference table seating by allowing the speaker to walk between the tables to interact with individual audience members.
- **Café seating**, in which people sit in groups at individual tables, is best for breakout sessions and other small-group activities. However, this arrangement is less than ideal for anything more than short presentations because it places some in the audience with their backs to the speaker, making it awkward for both them and the presenter.

If you can't control the seating arrangement, at least be aware of what it is so you can adjust your plans if needed.

All these variables can influence not only the style of your presentation but the content. For instance, in a public environment full of distractions and uncertainties, you're probably better off keeping your content simple and short because chances are you won't be able to keep everyone's attention for the duration of your presentation.

Table 16.1 offers a summary of the key steps in analyzing an audience for oral presentations. For even more insight into audience evaluation (including emotional and cultural issues), consult a good public-speaking textbook.

Selecting the Right Medium

The task of selecting the right medium might seem obvious—after all, you are speaking, so it's an oral medium. However, technology offers an array of choices these days, ranging from live, in-person presentations to podcasts to online video to webcasts that people view on

TABLE 16.1 Analyzing an Audience for Oral Presentations

TASK	ACTIONS
To determine audience size and composition	• Estimate how many people will attend and whether they will all attend in person, online, or a mix of both. • Find out if the audience members share professional interests or other affiliations that can help you establish common ground with them. • Analyze demographic and psychographic variables to see any significant differences or similarities should influence the content and style of your presentation.
To predict the audience's probable reaction	• Analyze why audience members are attending the presentation. • Predict the mood that people will be in when you speak to them: supportive, interested but neutral, uninterested, apprehensive, or hostile. • Find out what kind of backup information will impress and influence the audience: technical data, historical information, financial data, demonstrations, samples, and so on. • Consider whether the audience has any biases that might work against you. • Anticipate possible objections or questions.
To gauge the audience's level of understanding	• Analyze whether everybody has the same background and experience. • Determine what the audience already knows about the subject. • Decide what background information the audience will need to better understand the subject. • Consider whether the audience is familiar with your vocabulary. • Analyze what the audience expects from you. • Think about the mix of general concepts and specific details you will need to present.

your website whenever doing so fits their individual schedules. Explore these options early on so that you can take full advantage of the ones at your disposal. For example, to reach an international audience, you might want to conduct a live presentation with a question-and-answer session for the on-site audience and post a video archive of this meeting on your website for audience members in other time zones.

Organizing Your Presentation

Organizing a presentation involves the same tasks as organizing a written message: Define your main idea, limit your scope, select the direct or indirect approach, and outline your content. As you work through these tasks, keep in mind that oral media have certain restraints. When reading written reports, audiences can skip back and forth, backing up if they miss a point or become confused and jumping ahead if they aren't interested in a particular part or are already familiar with the content. However, audiences for oral presentations are more or less trapped in your time frame and sequence. Aside from interrupting you, they have no choice but to listen to your content in the exact order in which you present it. (Of course, if you've made your presentation available as a webcast, video, or podcast, listeners do have the option of moving back and forth at their own pace.)

Defining Your Main Idea

If you've ever heard a speaker struggle to get his or her point across ("What I really mean to say is . . ."), you know how frustrating such an experience can be for an audience. To avoid that struggle, identify the most important message you want audience members to take away with them. Then compose a one-sentence summary that links this idea to your audience's frame of reference, much as an advertising slogan points out how a product can benefit consumers. Here are some examples:

If you can't express your main idea in a single sentence, you probably haven't defined it clearly enough.

> Convince management that reorganizing the technical support department will improve customer service and reduce employee turnover.
>
> Convince the board of directors that we should build a new plant in Texas to eliminate manufacturing bottlenecks and improve production quality.
>
> Address employee concerns regarding a new health-care plan by showing how the plan will reduce costs and improve the quality of their care.

Each of these statements puts a particular slant on the subject, one that directly relates to the audience's interests. Make sure your purpose is based on a clear understanding of audience needs so that you can deliver information your audience truly cares about.[3] For example, a group of new employees will be much more responsive to your discussion of plant safety procedures if you focus on how the procedures can save lives and prevent injuries rather than on how they will save the company money or conform to government regulations.

Limiting Your Scope

Limiting your scope is important with any message, but it's particularly vital with presentations, for two reasons. First, for many presentations, you must work within strict time limits. For example, at DEMO and TechCrunch, two influential conferences in which entrepreneurs present their business plans to potential investors, presentations are limited to six and eight minutes, respectively.[4] To accomplish in six or eight minutes the complex task of introducing your company and convincing people to invest in it, you must distill your message down to its essential points. No matter what the time constraints, if you overestimate the amount of material you can cover within your allotted time, you're left with only unpleasant alternatives: rushing through your presentation, skipping some of the information you've so carefully prepared, or trying to steal a few minutes from the next presenter. At the other extreme, if you don't have enough material prepared to fill your time slot, you might be left standing in front of the audience trying to ad lib information you haven't prepared.

2 LEARNING OBJECTIVE

Identify the two primary reasons that limiting your scope is especially important for oral presentations

Limiting you scope is important for two reasons: to ensure that your presentation fits the allotted time and to make sure you respect your audience members' time and attention.

Second, you can count on having audience attention for only a finite amount of time, and you'll lose the audience if you try to cover too much material. For example, studies show that audience attention levels and retention rates drop sharply after 20 minutes.[5]

The only sure way to measure the length of your presentation is to complete a practice run.

After you've decided on the right amount of information to cover, make sure your material matches the time you've been allotted. The only sure way to do so is to do a practice run and time how long it takes. Alternatively, you can try several techniques for estimating time requirements. First, if you're in one of those rare situations in which you're reciting your material verbatim or reading from a prepared script (more on that later in the chapter), you can divide your word count by 125 (if you speak slower than average) or 150 (if you're faster than average) to get a rough idea of how many minutes you'll need. Second, you can measure how long it takes to talk through a small portion of your presentation and then extrapolate how long the entire presentation will take. This method isn't terribly accurate, but it can help identify major timing problems. Third, after you get some experience giving presentations with either overhead transparencies or electronic slides, you'll get a feel for the time you typically need to cover a single slide. As a general guideline, figure on 3 or even 4 minutes per slide if you are using conventional structured slides (see "Choosing Structured or Free-Form Slides" on page 535 in Chapter 17 for more information).[6] For instance, if you have 20 minutes, plan on roughly five to seven slides. If you're whipping through slides faster than that, chances are you might be simply reading bullet points from your slides or not engaging the audience with enough discussion about each slide.

Of course, be sure to factor in time for introductions, coffee breaks, demonstrations, question-and-answer sessions, and anything else that takes away from your speaking time.

Choosing Your Approach

Organize a short presentation the same way you would a brief written message; organize a longer presentations as you would a report.

If you have 10 minutes or less to deliver your message, organize your presentation much as you would a brief written message: Use the direct approach if the subject involves routine information or good news; use the indirect approach if the subject involves negative news or persuasion. Plan to spend a minute or two during your introduction to arouse interest and to give a preview of what's to come. For the body of the presentation, be prepared to explain the who, what, when, where, why, and how of your subject. In the final few moments, review the points you've made, and close with a statement that will help your audience remember the subject of your speech (see Figure 16.2).

Longer presentations are organized like reports. If the purpose is to inform, use the direct approach and a structure imposed naturally by the subject: importance, sequence, chronology, spatial orientation, geography, or category (as discussed in Chapter 13). If your purpose is to analyze, persuade, or collaborate, organize your material around conclusions and recommendations or around a logical argument. Use the direct approach if the audience is receptive and the indirect approach if you expect resistance.

As you develop your presentation, keep in mind that oral reports have one important advantage over written reports: You can adjust your outline on the fly if you need to. Identify the critical points in your presentation and ask yourself some "what if" questions to address possible audience reactions. For instance, if you're worried that the audience might not agree with the financial assumptions you've made, you might prepare a detailed analysis that you can include in your presentation in case you sense that a negative reaction is building or if someone openly questions you about it. As you'll see in Chapter 17, presentation software such as Microsoft PowerPoint makes it easy to adjust your presentation as you move along, allowing you to skip over any parts you decide not to use or to insert backup material at the last minute.

Simplicity is critical in the organization of oral and online presentations.

Regardless of the length of your presentation, remember that simplicity of organization is especially valuable in oral communication. If listeners lose the thread of your presentation, they'll have a hard time catching up and following your message in the remainder of your speech. Explain at the beginning how you've organized your material and try to limit the number of main points to three or four.

Finally, remind yourself that just like other good business messages, an effective presentation has a clear introduction, body, and close. In fact, one noted presentation expert even advises a three-act storytelling structure (the approach used in many novels, movies, and TV shows). Act I introduces the "story" you're about to tell and grabs the audience's attention.

FIGURE 16.2 Effective Outline for a 10-Minute Progress Report
Here is an outline of a short presentation that updates management on the status of a key project; the presenter has some bad news to deliver, so she opted for the indirect approach to lay out the reasons for the delay before sharing the news of the schedule slip.

Progress Report: August 2010

Purpose: To update the Executive Committee on our product development schedule.

I. Review goals and progress.
   A. Mechanical design:
      1. Goal: 100%
      2. Actual: 80%
      3. Reason for delay: Unanticipated problems with case durability
   B. Software development:
      1. Goal: 50%
      2. Actual: 60%
   C. Material sourcing:
      1. Goal: 100%
      2. Actual: 45% (and materials identified are at 140% of anticipated costs)
      3. Reason for delay: Purchasing is understaffed and hasn't been able to research sources adequately.
II. Discuss schedule options.
   A. Option 1: Reschedule product launch date.
   B. Option 2: Launch on schedule with more expensive materials.
III. Suggest goals for next month.
IV. Q&A

Act II explores the complications, evidence, support points, and other information needed to understand the story and its conclusion. Act III resolves all the complications and presents a solution that addresses the problem introduced in Act I and that is strongly supported by all the evidence introduced in Act II.[7]

Preparing Your Outline

A presentation outline (see Figure 16.3) performs the same function as an outline for a written document: It helps you organize the message in a way that maximizes its impact on your audience. However, a presentation outline can also serve as the foundation of your speaking notes, so as you write your outline, start thinking about the words you'll want to use when you deliver your presentation. To ensure effective organization, prepare your outline in several stages:[8]

- **State your purpose and main idea.** As you develop your outline, check frequently to be sure that the points, organization, connections, and title relate to your purpose and main idea.
- **Organize your major points and subpoints.** Express each major point as a single, complete sentence to help you keep track of the one specific idea you want to convey in that point. Then look at the order of points to make sure their arrangement is logical and effective.
- **Identify your introduction, body, and close.** Start with the body, numbering each major point and subpoint according to its level in your outline. Then lay out the points for your introduction and close.

In addition to planning your speech, a presentation outline helps you plan your speaking notes as well.

FIGURE 16.3 **Effective Outline for a 30-Minute Presentation**
This outline clearly identifies the purpose and the distinct points to be made in the introduction, body, and close. Notice how the speaker wrote her major transitions in full sentence form to be sure she can clearly phrase these critical passages when it's time to speak.

Includes the statement of purpose

Highlights the purpose in the introduction

Explains the investigation process

Uses a logical and simple organization

Explains why the problem exists

OUR TRAVEL AND ENTERTAINMENT COSTS ARE OUT OF CONTROL

Purpose: To explain why Electrovision's travel and entertainment (T&E) costs are so high and to propose a series of changes to bring them under control.

INTRODUCTION

I. Our T&E costs are way above average, and they pose a threat to the company's financial health; fortunately, we can fix the problem in four straightforward steps that could save as much as $6 million a year.

II. How we approached the investigation
   A. We analyzed internal expense reports.
   B. We compared our cost data with nationwide averages.
   C. We analyzed published information on trends and cost-control suggestions.

(Transition: This presentation reviews Electrovision's spending patterns, analyzes the impact on company profits, and recommends four steps for reducing the budget.)

BODY

I. Analysis of spending patterns
   A. The amount we've been spending on T&E:
      1. Airfares, hotels, rental cars, restaurants, and entertainment totaled $16 million last year.
      2. T&E budget increased by 12 percent per year for the past five years.
   B. Where the money goes:
      1. We took 3,390 trips last year at an average cost per trip of $4,725.
      2. Airfares and lodging represent 70 percent of T&E expenses.
   C. How our spending compares with national averages:
      1. Facilities and customers spread from coast to coast force us to spend a lot on travel.
      2. However, we spend 125 percent more than the national average for every day of travel. (Source: Dow Jones)
   D. Why do we spend so much?
      1. First-class travel has been viewed as compensation for the demands of extensive travel.
      2. The sales staff is encouraged to entertain clients.
      3. T&E costs are hard for managers to view and study.
      4. No one has central responsibility for controlling costs.

(Transition: We need to control spending for two reasons: (1) profits are projected to be flat or declining over the next two years, and (2) hotel rates and airfares continue to rise sharply.)

- **Show your connections.** Write out in sentence form the transitions you plan to use to move from one part to the next.
- **Show your sources.** Prepare your bibliography and be prepared to mention key sources during your talk.
- **Choose a title.** Not all presentations have a title, but a title can be useful if your presentation will be publicized ahead of time or introduced by someone else. The title sets audience members' expectations, so make it compelling and audience centered.

The outline in Figure 16.3 is for a 30-minute analytical presentation that uses the direct approach, organized around conclusions. This outline is based on Chapter 15's Electrovision report, written by Linda Moreno.

FIGURE 16.3 *(Continued)*

II. Impact on profits

    A. T&E costs continue to rise, as do other company costs.
    B. Revenue is projected to decline in coming years.
    C. Bottom line: We're headed for trouble.

Explains why T&E costs are a problem

(Transition: By implementing a number of reforms, management can expect to reduce Electrovision's T&E budget by as much as 40 percent. We can cut expenses in four ways.)

III. Solution

    A. We should institute tighter spending controls:
        1. Hire a travel manager to control costs and negotiate group discounts.
        2. Develop a formal, written policy to contain costs.
        3. Give departmental managers the data they need to make smarter decisions.
    B. We can reduce unnecessary travel and entertainment costs:
        1. Cut down on discretionary trips (seminars, etc.).
        2. Reduce the number of intracompany trips and employees sent on each trip.
        3. Encourage employees to economize.
    C. We can find lower travel rates:
        1. Negotiate corporate discounts.
        2. Plan trips more carefully to take advantage of lower fares.
    D. We can replace some travel with technological alternatives:
        1. Conference calls
        2. Videoconferences
        3. Other possibilities
    E. Potential impact of all these changes: As much as $6 million in reduced costs (Source: American Express)

Maintains the logical organization throughout

Provides the four-step solution mentioned in the introduction, then makes a recommendation for implementing the steps

(Transition: This presentation reviews Electrovision's spending patterns, analyzes the impact on company profits, and recommends four steps for reducing the budget.)

CLOSE

I. We spend more on T&E than we should
II. Four fairly obvious steps will yield significant cost savings

    A. Establish tighter controls
    B. Rein in unnecessary T&E costs
    C. Find lower travel rates
    D. Reduce travel by using technological alternatives

Restates the four recommended steps

Many speakers like to prepare both a detailed *planning outline* and a simpler *speaking outline* that provides all the cues and reminders they need to present their material.[9] Here are some guidelines for preparing an effective speaking outline:[10]

You may find it helpful to create a simpler speaking outline from your planning outline.

- **Follow the planning outline.** Start with the planning outline and strip away anything you don't want to actually say to your audience (including statements of general purpose and specific purpose, the main idea, and a detailed bibliography).
- **Condense points and transitions to keywords.** Choose words that will prompt you to remember what each point is about so that you can speak fluently. Be sure to write out statistics, quotations, and other specifics so that you don't stumble over them. You may also want to write complete sentences for transitions that connect main points or for critical points in your introduction or your close.
- **Add delivery cues.** During rehearsals, note the places in your outline where you plan to pause for emphasis, speak more slowly, use a visual, and so on.
- **Arrange your notes.** Make sure your note cards are legible and numbered so that you can keep them in order before and during your presentation.

WRITING YOUR PRESENTATION

Although you may never actually write out a presentation word for word, you need to engage in the writing process—developing your ideas, structuring support points, phrasing your transitions, and so on. Depending on the situation and your personal style, you might follow these initial words closely during your presentation, or you might express your thoughts in fresh, spontaneous language. Before you get to the actual writing phase, consider how you should adapt your style to your audience.

Adapting to Your Audience

Adapting to your audience addresses a number of issues, from speaking style to technology choices.

Audience expectations, subject matter, purpose, budget, and time constraints all influence the style of your presentation. If you're speaking to a small group, particularly people you already know, you can use a casual style that encourages audience participation. A small conference room, with your audience seated around a table, may be appropriate. Use simple visuals and invite your audience to interject comments. Deliver your remarks in a conversational tone, using notes to jog your memory, if necessary.

If you're addressing a large audience and the event is an important one, you'll want to establish a more formal atmosphere. A formal style is well suited to announcements about mergers or acquisitions, new products, financial results, and other business milestones. During formal presentations, speakers often stand on a podium or stage, behind a lectern that can hold their notes, a microphone, and controls for the presentation equipment.

Composing Your Presentation

Just like written documents, presentations consist of three distinct elements: the introduction, the body, and the close.

Introduction

3 **LEARNING OBJECTIVE**

Discuss the three functions of an effective introduction

A good introduction arouses the audience's interest in your topic, establishes your credibility, and prepares the audience for what will follow. That's a lot to pack into the first few minutes of your presentation, so give yourself plenty of time to prepare the words and visuals you'll use to get your presentation off to a great start.

Arousing Audience Interest Some subjects are naturally more interesting to some audiences than others. If you will be discussing a matter of profound significance that will personally affect the members of your audience, chances are they'll listen, regardless of how you begin. All you really have to do is announce your topic, and you'll have their attention. Other subjects call for more imagination. Here are six ways to arouse audience interest:[11]

4 **LEARNING OBJECTIVE**

Identify six ways to get your audience's attention and six ways to hold it

- **Unite the audience around a common goal.** Invite listeners to help solve a problem, capitalize on an opportunity, or otherwise engage in the topic of your presentation.
- **Tell a story.** Well-told stories are naturally interesting and can be compelling. Of course, make sure your story illustrates an important and relevant point.
- **Pass around an example.** Psychologists say that you can get people to remember your points by appealing to their senses. A great way to do so is to pass around an example. If your company is in the textile business, let the audience handle some of your fabrics. If you sell chocolates, give everybody a taste.
- **Ask a question.** Asking questions will get the audience actively involved in your presentation and, at the same time, will give you information about them and their needs.
- **Share a startling statistic.** An intriguing, unexpected, or shocking detail can often grab the attention of your listeners.
- **Use humor.** Opening with an amusing observation about yourself, the subject matter of the presentation, or the circumstances surrounding the presentation can be an effective way to lighten the "pre-presentation jitters" for you and the audience or to make an emotional connection with your listeners. However, humor must be used with great care. Make sure any comments are relevant, appropriate, and not offensive to anyone in the audience. In general, avoid humor when you and the audience don't share the same native language or culture; it's too easy for humor to fall flat or backfire.

Regardless of which technique you choose, make sure you can give audience members a reason to care and to believe that the time they're about to spend listening to you will be worth their while.[12]

Building Your Credibility   In addition to grabbing the audience's attention, your introduction needs to establish your credibility. If you're a well-known expert in the subject matter or have earned your audience's trust in other situations, you're already ahead of the game. However, if you have no working relationship with your audience or if you're speaking in an area outside your known expertise, you need to establish credibility and do so quickly; people tend to decide within a few minutes whether you're worth listening to.[13] For instance, in its presentations to potential clients, Fitch (see page 508) seeks to build credibility by showing how well its designers understand the client's business needs.

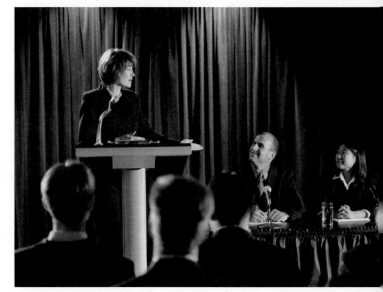

If you will be introduced by a master of ceremonies or another speaker, that person may be able to briefly itemize your qualifications as a way to build your credibility with the audience.

Techniques for building credibility vary, depending on whether you will be introducing yourself or having someone else introduce you. If a master of ceremonies, a conference chair, or another person will introduce you, he or she can present your credentials so that you won't appear boastful. However, make sure that the person introducing you doesn't exaggerate your qualifications; your credibility will probably go down rather than up if this happens.

If you will be introducing yourself, keep your comments simple. At the same time, don't be afraid to mention your accomplishments. Your listeners will be curious about your qualifications, so tell them briefly who you are and why you're the right person to be giving this presentation. Here's an example:

> I'm Karen Whitney, a market research analyst with Information Resources Corporation. For the past five years, I've specialized in studying high-technology markets. Your director of engineering, John LaBarre, has asked me to talk to you about recent trends in computer-aided design so that you'll have a better idea of how to direct your research efforts.

This speaker establishes credibility by tying her credentials to the purpose of her presentation, without boasting. By mentioning her company's name, her specialization and position, and the name of the audience's boss, she lets her listeners know immediately that she is qualified to tell them something they need to know. She connects her background to their concerns.

Previewing Your Message   In addition to arousing audience interest and building your credibility, a good introduction gives your audience members a preview of what's ahead, helping them understand the structure and content of your message. A reader can learn these things by looking at the table of contents and scanning the headings, but in a presentation, you need to provide that framework with a preview.

Use the preview to help your audience understand the importance, structure, and content of your message.

Your preview should summarize the main idea of your presentation, identify major supporting points, and indicate the order in which you'll develop those points. Tell your listeners in so many words, "This is the subject, and these are the points I will cover." Once you've established the framework, you can be confident that the audience will understand how the individual facts and figures are related to your main idea as you move into the body of your presentation.

Body

The bulk of your speech or presentation is devoted to a discussion of the three or four main points in your outline. Whether you're using the direct or indirect approach, make sure the organization of your presentation is clear and your presentation holds the audience's attention.

Connecting Your Ideas   In written documents, you can show how ideas are related on the page or screen by using a variety of design clues, such as headings, paragraph indentations, and lists. However, with oral communication—particularly when you aren't using visuals for support—you have to rely primarily on words to link various parts and ideas.

Use transitions to repeat key ideas and help the audience follow along, particularly in longer presentations.

For links between sentences and paragraphs, use transitional words and phrases: *therefore, because, in addition, in contrast, moreover, for example, consequently, nevertheless,* or *finally.* To link major sections of a presentation, use complete sentences or paragraphs, such as "Now that we've reviewed the problem, let's take a look at some solutions." Every time you shift topics, be sure to stress the connection between ideas. Summarize what's been said and then preview what's to come. You might also want to call attention to the transitions by using gestures, changing your tone of voice, or introducing a visual, as Chapter 17 points out.

Holding Your Audience's Attention   After you've successfully captured your audience's attention in your introduction, you need to work to keep it throughout the body of your presentation. In addition to the general challenge of keeping readers interested, you have to compensate for another inescapable fact of oral presentations: Your audience can think and read faster than you can speak. And with online presentations, where people in remote locations are sitting alone at their computers, they may be tempted by numerous distractions. Here are a few helpful tips for keeping the audience tuned into your message:

The most important way to hold audience members' attention is to show how your message relates to their individual needs and concerns.

- **Relate your subject to your audience's needs.** People are naturally most interested in things that affect them personally.
- **Anticipate your audience's questions.** Try to anticipate as many questions as you can and address these questions in the body of your presentation. You'll also want to prepare and reserve additional material to use during the question-and-answer period, in case the audience asks for greater detail.
- **Use clear, vivid language.** If your presentation will involve abstract ideas, show how those abstractions connect with everyday life. Use familiar words, short sentences, and concrete examples. Be sure to use some variety as well; repeating the same words and phrases puts people to sleep.
- **Explain the relationship between your subject and familiar ideas.** Show how your subject is related to ideas that audience members already understand and give people a way to categorize and remember your points.[14]
- **Ask for opinions or pause occasionally for questions or comments.** Audience feedback helps you determine whether your listeners understand a key point before you launch into another section. Asking questions or providing comments also gives your audience members a chance to switch for a time from listening to participating, which helps them engage with your message and develop a sense of shared ownership.
- **Illustrate your ideas with visuals.** As Chapter 17 discusses, you might want to develop visuals for your presentation and coordinate them with your delivery. Visuals enliven your message, help you connect with audience members, and help people remember your message more effectively.

When attempting to hold an audience's attention, public speakers sometimes face distractions in the background. A focused speaker can overcome such physical interruptions and get his or her message across.

Close

The close of a speech or presentation is critical for two reasons. First, audience members' attention tends to peak at this point because they anticipate moving on to the next activity in their busy day. Second, audience members will leave with your final words ringing in their ears. Before closing your presentation, tell listeners that you're about to finish so that they'll make one final effort to listen intently. Don't be afraid to sound obvious. Consider saying something such as "In conclusion" or "To sum it all up." You want people to know that this is the final segment of your presentation.

Restating Your Main Points   After you've decided how to announce your close, repeat your main idea. Emphasize what you want your audience members to do or to think and stress the key motivating factor that will encourage them to respond that way. Finally, reinforce your theme by succinctly restating your main supporting points. A few sentences are generally enough to refresh people's memories. For example, to close a presentation on your company's executive compensation program, you could repeat your specific recommendations and then conclude with a memorable statement to motivate your audience to take action:

Plan your close carefully so that your audience leaves with your main idea fresh in their minds.

> We can all be proud of the way our company has grown. However, if we want to continue that growth, we need to adjust our executive compensation program to reflect competitive practices. If we don't, our best people will look for opportunities elsewhere. In summary, our survey has shown that we need to do four things to improve executive compensation:
>
> - Increase the overall level of compensation
> - Install a cash bonus program
> - Offer a variety of stock-based incentives
> - Improve our health insurance and pension benefits
>
> By making these improvements, we can help our company cross the threshold of growth to face our industry's largest competitors.

Such repetition of key ideas greatly improves the chance that your audience will hear your message in the way you intended.

Describing Next Steps   Some presentations require the audience to reach a decision or agree to take specific action, in which case the close offers an opportunity to verify these steps. If audience members agree on an issue covered in the presentation, review the consensus in a sentence or two. If they don't agree, make the lack of consensus clear by saying something like "We seem to have some fundamental disagreement on this question." Then be ready to suggest a method of resolving the differences. If you're not sure in advance how your audience will respond, prepare alternative closes so that you don't have to scramble for an ending if things don't work as you had planned.

If you need to have the audience make a decision or agree to take action, make sure the responsibilities for doing so are clear.

If you expect any action to occur as a result of your speech, be sure to identify who is responsible for doing what and by when. One effective technique is to list the action items, with an estimated completion date and the name of the person or team responsible. You can present this list in a visual and ask each person on the list to agree to accomplish his or her assigned task by the target date. This public commitment to action helps ensure that things will get done.

Plan your final statement carefully so you can end on a strong, positive note.

Ending on a Strong Note   Your final remarks need to make a memorable impression, and you can achieve this goal by thinking ahead about what you'll say and how you'll say it. If you don't have a strong finish planned, you run the risk of just fizzling out and dissipating the energy you've worked to build up.

Let your purpose and your main idea drive the content and emotional tone of your final statement. For example, if you're making a persuasive presentation, use the final statement to sum up the benefits of responding—and make sure you finish on a positive, confident note. Conversely, if your presentation is meant to deliver a negative message, such as a warning that if efficiency isn't improved soon, profits will suffer, make your warning clear and your tone serious. By all means, express as much confidence and hope as the situation

REAL-TIME UPDATES
Learn More

Get a quick reminder of the elements of a successful presentation

The Memphis Public Library offers succinct reminders of the planning and design choices that lead to successful presentations. Go to **http://real-timeupdates.com/bct** and click on "Learn More." If you are using mybcommlab, you can access Real-Time Updates within each chapter or under Student Study Tools.

warrants, but if you try to inject false optimism or phony cheer, you will undermine your vital message and leave people wondering if things are really as bad as you say they are. If the tone of your presentation is more neutral, such as when delivering a routine status update, end on a confident note that tells the audience you're on top of the situation, and everything is under control.

COMPLETING YOUR PRESENTATION

With an outline and speaking notes in hand, you're ready to complete the development of your presentation. As with written communication, this third step starts with the all-important task of revising your message to ensure appropriate content. Edit for clarity and conciseness, as you would any business message. And for presentations, you'll need to go beyond these now-familiar tasks and pay special attention to four additional aspects: mastering the art of delivery, preparing to speak, overcoming anxiety, and handling questions responsively.

Mastering the Art of Delivery

After you've written your presentation and created any necessary visuals, you're ready to work on your delivery. You have a variety of delivery methods to choose from, some of which are easier to handle than others:

- **Memorizing.** Memorizing an entire presentation is generally not advisable, especially if it's a long one. In the best of circumstances, you'll probably sound stilted; in the worst, you might forget your lines. Besides, you'll often need to address audience questions during your speech, so you need to be flexible enough to adjust your speech as you go. However, memorizing a quotation, an opening paragraph, and some strong finishing remarks can bolster your confidence and strengthen your delivery.
- **Reading.** If you're delivering a technical or complex presentation, you may want to read it. For instance, policy statements are sometimes read in full because the wording can be critical. However, unless you're required or expected to read your presentation verbatim, reading is usually not your best option. If you read from a prepared script, chances are you won't speak as naturally as you would otherwise, and the result will be a monotonous, uninspiring presentation.[15] After all, if all you're doing is reading, why not just write a report and let your audience members read it themselves? If you do plan to read your speech for some reason, practice enough so that you can still make periodic eye contact with your audience and make sure the printout of your speech is easy to read.

Speaking from carefully prepared notes is the easiest and most effective delivery mode for most presenters.

- **Speaking from notes.** Speaking with the help of an outline or note cards is usually the easiest and most effective delivery mode. The outline or notes guide you through the flow of the speech while giving you the freedom to speak naturally and spontaneously, to maintain eye contact with your listeners, and to respond and improvise as circumstances warrant. If you print note cards, use heavy note cards instead of regular paper. They're quieter and easier to flip through as you talk.
- **Impromptu speaking.** From time to time, you may have to give an *impromptu*, or unrehearsed, speech, without the benefit of any planning or practice. Take 5 or 10 seconds to identify the one key idea you want to share with the audience. The silence might feel uncomfortable, but there's no harm in "looking thoughtful" while you decide what to say. If it helps to avoid the feeling of just sitting or standing there, you can engage in some innocent activity while you gather your thoughts, such as calmly rearranging some papers in front of you or tidying the contents of your briefcase. If you absolutely cannot say something intelligent and effective on the subject at hand, it's usually better to explain that you can't and ask for an opportunity to prepare some remarks for a later time or date.

Regardless of which delivery mode you use, be sure that you're thoroughly familiar with your subject. Knowing what you're speaking about is the best way to build your self-confidence. If you stumble, get interrupted, or suffer equipment failures, your expertise will help you get back on track.

Practice is key to the success of a presenter, no matter how much experience you have. Apple co-founder and CEO Steve Jobs, who is widely admired for his new-product presentations and has decades of experience speaking in front of massive crowds, still spends hours practicing his delivery.[16] If you rehearse in front of a mirror, try to visualize the room filled with listeners. If possible, record your speech to check the sound of your voice, as well as your timing, phrasing, and emphasis. And if you have the equipment to do so, rehearse on video to see yourself as your audience will.

Schedule plenty of practice time when you're developing a high-profile presentation.

Preparing to Speak

In addition to knowing your material thoroughly and practicing your delivery, make sure that your location is ready, you have everything you'll need, and you're prepared to address audiences from other cultures, if that applies.

Whenever you can, scout the location for your presentation in advance. Check the seating arrangement to make sure it's appropriate for both your needs and the audience's. Verify the availability and operation of all the equipment and supplies you're counting on, from a laptop and LCD projector to simple but vital necessities such as flip charts and marking pens. Many corporate conference rooms now have permanent projection systems that require you to e-mail your presentation file ahead of time or bring it on a disk or flash drive. Make sure that you know what to expect in advance.

If possible, visit the speaking venue ahead of time to familiarize yourself with the facilities and the equipment.

If you're addressing audience members who speak a different native language, consider using an interpreter. Working with an interpreter does constrain your presentation somewhat. For instance, you must speak slowly enough for the interpreter to keep up with you. Send your interpreter a copy of your speaking notes and your visuals as far in advance of your presentation as possible. If your audience is likely to include persons with hearing impairments, be sure to team up with a sign-language interpreter as well.

When you deliver an oral presentation to people from other cultures, you may need to adapt the content of your presentation. It is also important to take into account any cultural preferences for appearance, mannerisms, and other customs. Your interpreter or host will be able to suggest appropriate changes for a specific audience or particular occasion.

Overcoming Anxiety

Even polished speakers with years of experience feel some anxiety about getting up in front of an audience. The difference is that they know how to use this *stage fright* to their advantage. Think of nervousness as a positive indication that you care about your audience, your topic, and the occasion. Let feeling of anticipation give you the extra energy you need to make your presentation sparkle. Here are some ways to harness your nervous energy to become a more confident speaker:[17]

5 LEARNING OBJECTIVE

Describe the techniques you can use to feel more confident in front of an audience

Preparation is the best antidote for anxiety.

- **Prepare more material than necessary.** Extra knowledge will reduce your anxiety.
- **Practice, practice, practice.** The more familiar you are with your material, the less panic you'll feel.
- **Think positively.** See yourself as polished and professional, and your audience will, too.
- **Visualize your success.** Visualize yourself in front of the audience, feeling confident, prepared, and able to handle any situation that might arise.[18]
- **Take a few deep breaths.** Before you begin to speak, remember that your audience wants you to succeed, too.
- **Be ready.** Memorize your first sentence so you can open on a confident note.
- **Be comfortable.** Dress appropriately for the situation but as comfortably as possible. Drink plenty of water before your scheduled presentation time to ensure that your voice is well hydrated (bring a bottle of water with you, too).
- **Don't panic.** If you sense that you're starting to race, pause and arrange your notes or perform some other small task while taking several deep breaths. Then start again at your normal pace. If you feel that you're losing your audience members, try to pull them back by asking for comments or questions.

Communication Miscues

Recovering from Disasters

You've researched your topic, analyzed your audience, prepared a compelling message, crafted eye-catching visuals, and practiced until you're running like a smooth machine. You're ready to go.

Then you wake up with a sore throat and half a voice. You grab a few lozenges, hope for the best, and drive to the conference facility in plenty of time to set up your equipment. Oops, somebody forgot to tell you that your presentation has been moved up by an hour, and your audience is already in the room waiting for you. You scramble to turn on your laptop and get it connected to the projector, only to discover that you forgot to pack the power cord for your laptop, and your battery is low. But that won't be a problem: Your laptop is dead anyway. Feeling smart, you pull out a CD-ROM with a backup copy of your PowerPoint slides and ask to use one of the several laptops you see scattered around the room. Nice idea, but they're equipped only with USB flash drives, so your CD is useless. The audience is getting restless; a few people get up to leave. You keep hoping you'll wake up from this bad dream so that your great day can really start. Sorry. This *is* your day.

Ask any business speaker with a few years of experience, and you'll hear all these horror stories and a few more. People who've driven to the wrong conference center, hit themselves in the head with a microphone, tripped over wires, started with a sure-fire joke that generated nothing but cold stares, or been rendered speechless by tough questions. Hoping you'll be spared isn't an effective response. You must be prepared for when—not if—something goes wrong.

If you assume that something *will* go wrong at some point, you can make peace with the possibility and focus on backup planning. Experts suggest that you make a list of every major problem you might encounter and imagine how you'll respond when these calamities strike you on the day of a big presentation. As much as possible, create a backup plan, such as calling ahead to reserve a second projector in the event that yours gets lost in transit. You won't be able to put backup resources in place for every possible glitch, but by at least thinking through the possibilities, you can decide how you'll respond. When disaster does strike, you'll look like a polished pro instead of a befuddled novice.

CAREER APPLICATIONS

1. If you spy trouble ahead in your presentation, such as noticing that your laptop battery is about to go dead or that you somehow have an old copy of the presentation file, should you tell your audience what's wrong? Or should you try to "wing it"? Explain your answer.
2. What steps can you take to make absolutely sure that you have a usable backup copy of your electronic presentation slides outside your office? Why is this important?

- **Concentrate on your message and your audience, not on yourself.** When you're busy thinking about your subject and observing your audience's response, you tend to forget your fears.
- **Maintain eye contact with friendly audience members.** Be sure to maintain eye contact with your audience, shifting your gaze around the room periodically to connect with individual audience members.[19]
- **Keep going.** Things usually get better as you move along, with each successful minute giving you more confidence.

No one enjoys mistakes, equipment failures, and other troubles, but they are survivable. To learn how several experienced presenters have overcome some serious glitches, see "Communication Miscues: Recovering from Disasters."

Confident delivery starts as soon as you become the focus of attention, before you even begin to speak, so don't rush. As you approach the front of the room, walk with confidence, breathe deeply, and stand up straight. Face your audience, adjust the microphone and other equipment, as needed, count to three slowly, and then scan the audience. When you find a friendly face, make eye contact and smile. Look away, count to three again, and then begin your presentation.[20] If you are nervous, this slow, controlled beginning will help you establish rapport and appear more confident. Make sure your nonverbal signals send a message of confidence.

Nonverbal signals tell the audience how you're feeling, so pay attention to the signals you send.

Your posture is important in projecting more confidence. Stand tall, with your weight on both feet and your shoulders back. Avoid gripping the lectern or other physical structure. Use your hands to emphasize your remarks with appropriate gestures. Meanwhile, vary your facial expressions to make the message more dynamic.

Finally, think about the sound of your voice. Studies indicate that people who speak with lower pitches at a slightly faster-than-average rate are perceived as being more credible.[21] Try to sound poised and confident, varying your pitch and speaking rate to add emphasis. For instance, slow down slightly when you're making an important point.[22] Speak clearly and crisply, articulating all the syllables, and sound enthusiastic about what you're saying. Use silence instead of meaningless filler words such as *um, you know, okay,* and *like.* Silence adds dramatic punch and gives the audience time to think about your message.

Handling Questions Responsively

The question-and-answer period is often one of the most important parts of an oral presentation, so don't leave it to chance. Anticipate questions you are likely to get and think through the answers you want to give. Questions give you a chance to obtain important information, to emphasize your main idea and supporting points, and to build enthusiasm for your point of view. The following sections offer specific advice that will help you shine during a question-and-answer session.

Don't leave the question-and-answer period to chance: Anticipate likely questions and think through your answers.

Focusing on the Questioner

When someone poses a question, focus your attention on that individual. Pay attention to the questioner's body language and facial expression to help determine what he or she really means. Nod your head to acknowledge the question; then repeat it aloud to confirm your understanding and to ensure that the entire audience has heard it. If the question is vague or confusing, ask for clarification; then give a simple, direct answer. If you're asked to choose between two alternatives, don't feel you must do so. Offer your own choice instead, if it makes more sense.[23]

For online presentations, you may not be able to use body language to help assess a questioner's real intent. Listen carefully to his or her voice if you have an audio connection. If you're not sure you've picked up the unspoken part of the question (such as sarcasm or a challenge to your authority), ask the questioner to clarify exactly what he or she would like to know.

6 LEARNING OBJECTIVE

List six steps you can take to handle questions during a presentation

Responding Appropriately

This might sound like obvious advice, but be sure to answer the question you're asked. Don't sidestep it, ignore it, laugh it off, or take off on a tangent and forget to address the original question. If you don't know the answer, don't pretend that you do. Instead, say something like "I don't have those figures. I'll get them for you as quickly as possible." In some cases, you won't have time to answer every question that is asked; if possible, arrange another means to give people the information they need. If giving an adequate answer would take too long, simply say, "I'm sorry, we don't have time to get into that issue right now, but if you'll see me after the presentation, I'll be happy to discuss it with you."

Maintaining control during the question-and-answer session can be challenging, particularly if any audience members outrank you in the corporate hierarchy.

Maintaining Control

Unlike in the delivery phase of your presentation, you have less control during the question-and-answer session. However, you can help maintain control during this crucial period by establishing some ground rules up front (although you won't have the authority to do so in some instances). Before you begin, announce a time limit or a question limit per person. Give as many audience members as possible a chance to participate by calling on people from different parts of the room. If the same person keeps angling for attention, restate the question limit or say something like "Several other people have questions; I'll get back to you if time permits." Engaging as many people as possible is particularly important during online presentations because it's easy to feel excluded as a remote member of the audience.

The question-and-answer session is often the most valuable part of a presentation, so prepare for it by researching answers to likely questions.

If someone tries to take over the presentation by arguing with you or making speeches of his or her own instead of asking questions, remember that it's up to you to stay in control. If appropriate, you might ask audience members to identify themselves before they ask questions. People are more likely to behave themselves when everyone knows their names.[24] If you can't resolve a disagreement, you can state that you and the questioner have differing opinions and, before calling on someone else, offer to get back to the questioner after you've done more research.

Surviving the Hot Seat

If you ever face hostile questions, don't duck; respond honestly and directly while keeping your cool.

Whether it's an overdue project or quarterly financial results that didn't meet investor expectations, chances are you'll have to answer some tough questions during a presentation. In such a situation, look the person in the eye, answer the question as well as you can, and keep your emotions under control. Whatever the case, avoid getting into a heated argument. Even if you win, you'll leave the audience feeling uncomfortable about both the situation and your ability to handle conflict. Recognize that questioners who challenge your ideas, logic, or facts may just be trying to push you into overreacting. Defuse hostility by paraphrasing the question and asking the questioner to confirm that you've understood it correctly. Divide complicated questions into parts that you can answer simply. State your response accurately and factually; then move on to the next question. Avoid postures or gestures that might seem antagonistic. Maintain a businesslike tone of voice and a pleasant expression.[25] And never resort to insults; they will most likely backfire and make the audience more sympathetic to the questioner.

Encouraging Questions

A situation in which listeners are quiet can be just as uncomfortable as having a noisy, hostile audience. If there's a chance that your audience members will be too timid or too angry to ask questions, consider arranging a few questions ahead of time with a cooperative member of the audience. If a friend or the meeting organizer gets the ball rolling, others in the audience will probably join in. You might ask a question yourself: "Would you like to know more about . . . ?" If someone in the audience responds, act as if the question came from that person in the first place. When all else fails, say something like, "I know from experience that most questions are asked after the question-and-answer period. So I'll be around afterward to talk."[26]

Concluding Your Presentation

No matter how the presentation has gone, conclude in a strong, confident manner.

When the time allotted for your presentation is up, signal a halt to the question-and-answer session. Prepare the audience for the end by saying something along the lines of, "Our time is almost up. Let's have one more question." After you've made your reply, summarize the

CHECKLIST: Developing Oral and Online Presentations

A. Plan your presentation.
- Analyze the situation by defining your purpose and developing an audience profile.
- Select the right medium.
- Organize your presentation by defining the main idea, limiting the scope, choosing your approach, and preparing your outline.

B. Write your presentation.
- Adapt to your audience by tailoring your style and language.
- Compose your presentation by preparing an introduction, a body, and a close.
- Use your introduction to arouse audience interest, build your credibility, and preview your message.

- Use the body to connect your ideas and hold your audience's attention.
- Use the close to restate your main points and describe the next steps.

C. Complete your presentation.
- Master the art of delivery by choosing a delivery method, knowing your material, and practicing your delivery.
- Check the location and equipment, including online setups, if needed, in advance.
- Determine whether you should use an interpreter.
- Overcome anxiety by preparing thoroughly.
- Handle questions responsively.

main idea of the presentation and thank people for their attention. Conclude the way you opened, by looking around the room and making eye contact. Then gather your notes and leave the stage, maintaining the same confident demeanor you've had from the beginning.

For a reminder of the steps to take in developing an oral presentation, refer to "Checklist: Developing Oral and Online Presentations." For the latest advice on planning presentations, visit http://real-timeupdates.com/bct and click on Chapter 16.

Document Makeover

Improve This Presentation

To practice correcting drafts of actual documents, visit the "Document Makeovers" section in either mybcommlab or the Companion Website for this text.

If mybcommlab is being used in your class, see your User Guide for specific instructions on how to access the content for this chapter. If you are accessing this feature through the Companion Website, click on "Document Makeovers" and then click Chapter 16. You will find a presentation draft that contains problems and errors related to what you've learned in this chapter about preparing effective oral presentations. Use the Final Draft decision tool to create an improved version of this presentation. Check the message for effective choices in scope, style, opening, use of transitions, and closing.

Communication Challenges at Fitch

 Pacific Theaters, a Southern California movie-theater operator, is launching a new chain called ArcLight Cinemas (www.arclightcinemas.com). The company wants to present ArcLight as a more enjoyable, upscale movie-going experience, something clearly differentiated from the run-of-the-mill theaters across the United States. Yesterday, Fitch's Eric Ashworth met with Pacific Theaters's management to discuss the need to create a compelling image for ArcLight. Today, he selected you and three others to form the account team and asked that your group start developing ideas. From his meeting notes, it's clear that the client envisions a typical presentation about logos, marketing slogans, and color schemes—the usual stuff in a traditional agency pitch. Not the Fitch way, for sure.

Individual Challenge: Two weeks have passed and, true to the Fitch mentality, you and your teammates have developed a strong vision for ArcLight. Your concept centers on the notion of recapturing the old-time glamour and excitement of going to the movies—back when going to the movies was a special event. Now it's time to outline your sales presentation, from introduction to body to close. How will you grab and hold the audience's attention? How can you make audience members excited and inspire the big "Aha!" that Fitch aims for? Prepare a one-page outline.

Team Challenge: In a small group, brainstorm ways to describe the glamour of old-time Hollywood to younger audiences who may have grown up on teen comedies and horror movies. Assume that you're going to speak to a group of young managers at Pacific Theaters and outline a short presentation that would help them get a sense of what Hollywood was like in the days of Clark Gable, Vivien Leigh, Rita Hayworth, and Cary Grant. Provide your instructor with an outline and a brief description of the visuals you might use.

SUMMARY OF LEARNING OBJECTIVES

1 **Explain the importance of oral and online presentations in your career success, and explain how to adapt the three-step writing process to oral presentations.** Oral and online presentations give you the opportunity to use all of your communication skills, from research to writing to speaking. Presentations also demonstrate your ability to think quickly, to adapt to challenging situations, and to handle touchy questions and complex issues. They also let your personality shine through in ways that aren't always possible in written media. Although you rarely want to write out a presentation

word for word, the three-step writing process is easy to adapt to oral presentations. The steps you take in planning oral presentations are generally the same as with any other business message: analyze the situation, gather information, select the right medium, and organize the information. Next, whereas you don't actually write your presentation in most cases, plan your word and phrase choices so you can speak in a way that delivers planned messages in a spontaneous way. This step also includes creating whatever visual support materials you plan to use. And, of course, adapting to your audience is every bit as important with oral messages as with written messages. Completing the third step in the three-step process is where oral and online presentations differ the most from written messages. You still want to revise carefully and proofread all handouts and visual materials to ensure clarity and accuracy. You also need to practice and perfect your delivery, prepare to speak by verifying facilities and equipment, take steps to manage anxiety, and plan your approach to handling questions. For online presentations, make sure your audience can access your presentation materials, including audio and video feeds.

2 **Identify the two primary reasons that limiting your scope is especially important for oral presentations.** Limiting the scope of presentations is crucial because (1) you generally have a fixed amount of time in which to speak, so you need to fit your material to the time allotted; and (2) audience members have limited attention spans, and you must respect their time.

3 **Discuss the three functions of an effective introduction.** An effective introduction arouses audience interest in your topic, builds your credibility, and gives your audience a preview of your message. If your topic doesn't naturally interest the audience, you need to work extra hard in your introduction (and throughout the presentation) to relate the material to the audience in as personal a manner as possible. Speaker credibility is a crucial aspect of any presentation because audiences are most likely to pay attention to messages coming from someone they perceive to be an expert in the subject area. If you can't demonstrate credibility in your subject area, you can "borrow" credibility from recognized experts by incorporating their insights and opinions into your presentation (giving proper credit, of course). Previewing your message in the introduction helps the audience members recognize the importance of your material and gives them a chance to prepare for it by understanding how you plan to present it.

4 **Identify six ways to grab your audience's attention and six ways to hold it.** To grab your audience's attention during your introduction, you can unite the audience around a common goal, tell a story, pass around a sample, ask a question, state a startling statistic, or use humor (although humor must be approached with great care and avoided if there is any chance that it will not go over well with your audience). To hold your audience's attention after you've captured it with a compelling introduction, continue to relate your subject to your audience's needs, anticipate audience questions and prepare effective responses, use clear and vivid language, relate your subject to ideas the audience is already familiar and comfortable with, ask for questions or comments, and illustrate your ideas with visuals.

5 **Describe the techniques you can use to feel more confident in front of an audience.** To overcome anxiety and feel more confident as a speaker, prepare more material than necessary so that the extra knowledge will reduce your nervousness. Rehearse your oral presentation to become as familiar as possible with your topic. Think positively and see yourself as a polished professional. Right before speaking, visualize your success and tell yourself you're ready. Take a few deep breaths and remember that your audience actually wants you to succeed. Be ready by memorizing your first sentence. Be comfortable by sipping some water. If you feel you're losing your audience members, don't panic; instead, pull them back by asking for their opinions or questions and involving them in the action. Keep going no matter what, because you'll likely get better as you go.

6 **List six steps you can take to handle questions during a presentation.** To handle questions effectively, start by focusing on the questioner, paying attention to nonverbal signals. Second, respond appropriately, even if that means explaining that you don't have an answer but will arrange to get one. Third, as much as circumstances allow, maintain control of the question-and-answer session. Fourth, when faced with difficult or hostile questions, maintain a calm demeanor and avoid getting into arguments. Fifth, if you need to, encourage questions from the audience. Sixth, when the question-and-answer time is about to expire, let the audience know that time is almost up so that you can conclude gracefully.

PEARSON
mybcommlab™

Log on to www.mybcommlab.com to access the following study and assessment aids associated with this chapter:

- Video applications
- Real-Time Updates
- Peer review activity
- Quick Learning Guides

- Pre/post test
- Personalized study plan
- Model documents
- Sample presentations

If you are not using mybcommlab, you can access the Real-Time Updates and Quick Learning Guides through http://real-timeupdates.com/bct. The Quick Learning Guide hits all the high points of this chapter in just two pages. This guide, especially prepared by the authors, will help you study for exams or review important concepts whenever you need a quick refresher.

Test Your Knowledge

1. What skills do oral and online presentations give you the opportunity to practice and demonstrate?
2. What are the two most common purposes for giving oral presentations?
3. Why do you have to limit your scope when planning a presentation?
4. Why is simplicity of organization important in oral communication?
5. How can outlines help you with the writing and delivery of an oral presentation?
6. What three goals should you accomplish during the introduction of an oral presentation?
7. How can you get and keep the audience's attention?
8. How does the delivery method of impromptu speaking differ from the delivery method of speaking from notes?
9. As a speaker, what nonverbal signals can you send to appear more confident?
10. What can speakers do to maintain control during the question-and-answer period of a presentation?

Apply Your Knowledge

1. Would you rather (a) deliver an oral presentation to an external audience, (b) be interviewed for a news story that involves a serious accident at your company, or (c) make a presentation to a departmental meeting? Why? How do the communication skills differ among those situations? Explain.
2. How might the audience's attitude affect the amount of audience interaction during or after a presentation? Explain your answer.
3. If you were giving an oral presentation on the performance of a company product, what three attention-getters might you use to enliven your speech?
4. From the speaker's perspective, what are the advantages and disadvantages of responding to questions from the audience throughout an oral presentation rather than just afterward? From the listener's perspective, which approach would you prefer? Why?
5. **Ethical Choices** Is it ethical to use design elements and special effects to persuade an audience? Why or why not?

Practice Your Knowledge

Messages for Analysis

Message 16.A: Analyzing the Structure of a Presentation

Find the transcript of a business-oriented speech or presentation by searching online for "speech transcription" or "presentation transcription." You can also browse **www.americanrhetoric.com**, which has thousands of transcriptions from speeches on a variety of subjects. Examine both the introduction and the close and analyze how these two sections work together to emphasize the main idea. Does the speaker want the audience to take any specific actions? To change any particular beliefs or feelings?

Next, identify the transitional sentences or phrases that clarify the speech's structure for the listener, especially those that help the speaker shift between supporting points. Using these transitions as clues, list the main message and supporting points; then indicate how each transitional phrase links the current supporting point to the succeeding one. Finally, prepare a brief (two- to three-minute) oral presentation summarizing your analysis for your class.

Message 16.B: Did the Introduction Get Your Attention?

To access this message, visit **http://real-timeupdates.com/bct**, click on "Student Assignments," and select Chapter 16, page 529, Message 16.B. Download and listen to this podcast, which is the introduction of a presentation to college seniors. Identify at least two techniques the speaker uses to try to grab your attention.

Exercises

Active links for all websites in this chapter can be found online. If mybcommlab is being used in your class, see your User Guide for instructions on accessing the content for this chapter. Otherwise, visit **www.pearsonglobaleditions.com/bovee**, locate *Business Communication Today*, Tenth Edition, click the Companion Website link, select Chapter 16, and then click on "Featured Websites." Please note that links to sites that become inactive after publication of the book will be removed from the Featured Websites section.

16.1 **Internet** For many years, Toastmasters has been dedicated to helping its members give speeches. Instruction, good speakers as models, and practice sessions aim to teach members to convey information in lively and informative ways. Visit the Toastmasters website, at **www.toastmasters.org**, and gather the information required to outline a three-minute presentation to your class, explaining how Toastmasters could help you and your classmates write and deliver effective speeches.

16.2 **Mastering Delivery: Analysis** Attend a presentation at your school or in your town or watch a speech on television. Categorize the speech as one that motivates or entertains, one that informs or analyzes, or one that persuades or urges collaboration. Then compare the speaker's delivery with this chapter's "Checklist: Developing Oral and Online Presentations." Write a two-page report, analyzing the speaker's performance and suggesting improvements.

16.3 **Mastering Delivery: Nonverbal Signals** Observe and analyze the delivery of a speaker in a school, work, or other setting. What type of delivery did the speaker use (reciting a memorized speech, reading a printed speech, speaking from an outline or notes, or delivering an impromptu speech)? Was this delivery appropriate for the occasion? What nonverbal signals did the speaker use to emphasize key points? Were these signals effective? Which nonverbal signals would you suggest to further enhance the delivery of this oral presentation—and why?

16.4 **Ethical Choices** Think again about the oral presentation you observed and analyzed in exercise 16.3. How could the speaker have used nonverbal signals to unethically manipulate the audience's attitudes or actions?

16.5 **Teamwork** You've been asked to give an informative 10-minute presentation on vacation opportunities in your home town. Draft your introduction, which should last no more than two minutes. Then pair off with a classmate and analyze each other's introductions. How well do these two introductions arouse the audience's interest, build credibility, and preview the presentation? Suggest how these introductions might be improved.

16.6 **Delivering Oral Presentations: Possible Topics** Browse through the following topics to see which ones interest you:
  a. What I expect to learn in this course
  b. Past public speaking experiences: the good, the bad, and the ugly
  c. I would be good at teaching _____.
  d. I am afraid of _____.
  e. It's easy for me to _____.
  f. I get angry when _____.
  g. I am happiest when I _____.
  h. People would be surprised if they knew that I _____.
  i. My favorite older person
  j. My favorite charity
  k. My favorite place
  l. My favorite sport
  m. My favorite store
  n. My favorite television show
  o. The town you live in suffers from a great deal of juvenile vandalism. Explain to a group of community members why juvenile recreational facilities should be built instead of a juvenile detention complex.

  p. You are speaking to the Humane Society. Support or oppose the use of animals for medical research purposes.
  q. You are talking to civic leaders of your community. Try to convince them to build an art gallery.
  r. You are speaking to a first-grade class at an elementary school. Explain why they should brush their teeth after meals.
  s. You are speaking to a group of traveling salespeople. Convince them that they should wear their seatbelts while driving.
  t. You are speaking to a group of elderly people. Convince them to adopt an exercise program.
  u. Energy issues (supply, conservation, alternative sources, national security, global warming, pollution, etc.)
  v. Financial issues (banking, investing, family finances, etc.)
  w. Government (domestic policy, foreign policy, social security taxes, welfare, etc.)
  x. Interesting new technologies (virtual reality, geographic information systems, nanotechnology, bioengineering, etc.)
  y. Politics (political parties, elections, legislative bodies and legislation, the presidency, etc.)
  z. Sports (amateur and professional, baseball, football, golf, hang gliding, hockey, rock climbing, tennis, etc.)

Choose a topic and prepare a brief presentation (5–10 minutes) to be given to your class.

16.7 **Completing Oral Presentations: Self-Assessment** How good are you at planning, writing, and delivering oral presentations? In the following table, rate yourself on each of the elements of the oral presentation process. Then examine your ratings to identify where you are strongest and where you can improve, using the tips in this chapter.

ELEMENTS OF THE PRESENTATION PROCESS	ALWAYS	FREQUENTLY	OCCASIONALLY	NEVER
1. I start by defining my purpose.	_____	_____	_____	_____
2. I analyze my audience before writing an oral presentation.	_____	_____	_____	_____
3. I match my presentation length to the allotted time.	_____	_____	_____	_____
4. I begin my oral presentations with an attention-getting introduction.	_____	_____	_____	_____
5. I look for ways to build credibility as a speaker.	_____	_____	_____	_____
6. I cover only a few main points in the body of my presentation.	_____	_____	_____	_____
7. I use transitions to help listeners follow my ideas.	_____	_____	_____	_____
8. I review main points and describe next steps in the close.	_____	_____	_____	_____
9. I practice my presentation beforehand.	_____	_____	_____	_____
10. I prepare in advance for questions and objections.	_____	_____	_____	_____
11. I conclude oral presentations by summarizing my main idea.	_____	_____	_____	_____

Expand Your Knowledge

Exploring the Best of the Web

Learn from the Presentation Pros

www.presentations.com

The online home of *Presentations* magazine offers a wealth of articles that give practical advice on creating and delivering business presentations. Under the "Presentations" tab, browse the Creation, Delivery, Venue, Technology, and Products sections to find resources that will help you complete the following tasks.

1. Find several articles that discuss the unique challenges of making presentations at trade shows. Identify three to five tips that will help you succeed in these environments.
2. Find a recent article that discusses tips, techniques, or traps of using PowerPoint for business presentations. Summarize the article's advice in a brief message that could be posted on your company's internal blog.
3. Find one or more articles that discuss techniques for improving vocal delivery. Identify three points that speakers can use to make more effective use of their voice during presentations.

Sharpening Your Career Skills Online

Bovée and Thill's Business Communication Web Search, at http://businesscommunicationblog.com/websearch, is a unique research tool designed specifically for business communication research. Use the Web Search function to find a website, video, PDF document, podcast, or PowerPoint presentation that offers advice on public speaking or oral presentations in business. Write a brief e-mail message to your instructor, describing the item that you found and summarizing the career skills information you learned from it.

Enhancing Presentations with Slides and Other Visuals

Learning Objectives

After studying this chapter, you will be able to

1 Explain how visuals enhance oral presentations and list several popular types of visuals

2 Explain the difference between structured and free-form slides

3 Explain the importance of design consistency in electronic slides and other visuals

4 Describe the effective use of transitions and builds in electronic presentations

5 Identify three types of noncontent slides you can use to support a presentation

6 Highlight nine major issues to consider when you're preparing to give a presentation online

Communication Close-up at Hewlett-Packard

Dan Talbott (far right) led a team whose presentation skills helped land a multibillion-dollar contract for Hewlett-Packard.

www.hp.com

Presentations make everyone nervous, but imagine how nervous you might be if you were making a presentation with millions or billions of dollars on the line. That's business as usual for Dan Talbott of HP Managed Services, a unit of Hewlett-Packard that manages computer operations for other companies.

A great example of a high-stakes situation was HP's pursuit of a huge contract with Procter & Gamble (P&G), the consumer-products giant that markets more than 300 brands, including Charmin, Crest, and Tide. P&G was looking to lower its costs by hiring an outside organization to take over its global information system—a network of more than 80,000 computers. HP was facing two tough competitors for the contract, Electronic Data Systems and IBM, and had to be considered a distant third-place contender because it had never landed a contract the size of the P&G deal. And as if that weren't enough, P&G had published a 10,000-page request for proposals (RFP) and limited the response time to just 56 days—9 to 12 months is typical on projects of this magnitude.

As a seasoned industry veteran but a rookie at HP, Talbott was eager to show that he could bring his new employer this mammoth piece of business. He moved his team into an HP office near P&G's Cincinnati headquarters, tapped the brainpower of 80 colleagues from around the world, and began developing the series of presentations that were specified in the RFP. Talbott told the group, "Our job is to ensure that every conversation is a win." However, HP's initial presentation was shaky, so he asked the presenters to print their PowerPoint slides—more than 200 in all—and post them on the walls of a conference room. He conducted a slide-by-slide critique, questioning every slide that lacked a clear message. The team revised and kept revising until the presentation was audience centered and crystal clear from beginning to end.

That rigorous review produced a string of successful presentations that ultimately helped Talbott and his team win a 10-year contract worth $3 billion—a stunning success that announced HP's arrival as a serious contender in computer services. As HP continues to rack up successes in the services business, it looks to be not only a significant force in the market but one of the relatively few large technology companies positioned to ride out the global economic storm.[1]

PLANNING YOUR PRESENTATION VISUALS

You may never be on stage with $3 billion at stake (see the chapter-opening Communication Close-up), but you can take Dan Talbott's rigorous approach to presentation quality and make every one of your presentations a success. By following the three-step development process in Chapter 16, you'll have a well-crafted, audience-focused message. The techniques in this chapter will help you enhance the delivery of that message with creative and effective visuals.

Visuals can improve the quality and impact of an oral presentation by creating interest, illustrating points that are difficult to explain with words alone, adding variety, and increasing the audience's ability to absorb and remember information. Behavioral research has shown that visuals can improve learning by up to 400 percent because humans can process visuals 60,000 times faster than text.[2]

For all the communication power of visuals, however, don't make the mistake of thinking that your visuals *are* a presentation. Particularly when using presentation software such as Microsoft PowerPoint, Apple Keynote, or Google Presentations, communicators sometimes fall into the trap of letting the slides take center stage. Remember that you and your message are the presentation, not your visuals; your visuals are there to help support and clarify what you have to say.[3]

1 LEARNING OBJECTIVE

Explain how visuals enhance oral presentations and list several popular types of visuals

Remember that the purpose of visuals is to support your presentation, not replace it.

Selecting the Type of Visuals to Use

You can select from a variety of visuals to enhance oral presentations, each with unique advantages and disadvantages:

In most businesses, electronic presentations are now the presentation technology of choice, although they're certainly not the only option.

- **Electronic slides.** Electronic presentations created with Microsoft PowerPoint or similar programs are the visuals of choice in most business situations today. An **electronic presentation**, or *slide show*, consists of a series of individual **electronic slides**. To display an electronic presentation, you simply connect your computer to a portable projector or a built-in unit that's part of a multimedia system in a conference room. Electronic presentations have numerous advantages: They are easy to edit and update; you can add to them sound, photos, video, and animation; they can be incorporated into online meetings and webcasts; and you can record self-running presentations for trade shows, websites, and other uses. The primary disadvantages are the equipment requirements, the potential complexity involved in creating multimedia presentations, and the risk that your hardware or software won't cooperate when it's show time.

- **Overhead transparencies.** Overhead transparencies are the very definition of old school, but they do have advantages. You can create overheads using software such as Microsoft PowerPoint, other graphics programs, your word-processing software, a typewriter, or even a pen. Moreover, simple transparencies don't require the latest computer or projection equipment. You can write on them during a presentation, and they never malfunction. On the downside, they're limited to static displays, they're impossible to edit once you've printed them, and you or a partner are forced to stand next to the projector throughout your entire presentation.

- **Chalkboards and whiteboards.** Chalkboards and whiteboards are effective tools for recording points made during small-group sessions. With electronic whiteboards, you can print and e-mail copies of whatever is written, too.

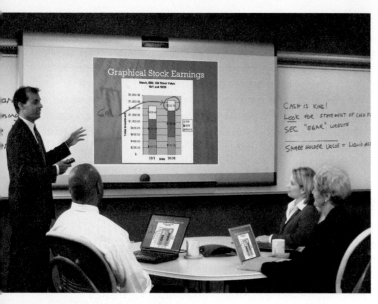

Electronic whiteboards let you capture notes and feedback during presentations and then print or e-mail them to audience members.

- **Flip charts.** Flip charts are another dependable low-tech tool for meetings and presentations. They are great for recording comments and questions during a presentation or for creating a "group memory" during brainstorming sessions, keeping track of all the ideas the team generates.
- **Other visuals.** Be creative when choosing visuals to support your presentation. A video of a focus group talking about your company can have a lot more impact than a series of slides that summarize what the group said. In technical or scientific presentations, a sample of a product or type of material lets your audience experience your subject directly. Designers and architects use mock-ups and models to help people envision what a final creation will look like. You might also want to incorporate other software in your presentation, such as a spreadsheet to show financial data or a computer-aided design program to show a new product's design. If you're demonstrating the use of a particular software program, for instance, you can create a **screencast**, which records everything you do on-screen—moving the mouse, opening windows, making menu selections, and so on. Most screencasting software also lets you add on-screen annotations and record an audio track to explain what is happening on-screen.

This chapter focuses on electronic presentations, the mainstay of business presentations today, although most of these design tips apply to overhead transparencies as well.

Verifying Your Design Plans

Think through your presentation outline carefully before designing your visuals.

After you have chosen the medium or media for your visuals, think through your presentation plan carefully before you start creating anything. Discerning audience members—the sort of people who can influence the direction of your career—are not easily fooled by visual razzle-dazzle. If your analysis is shaky or your conclusions are suspect, an over-the-top visual production won't help your presentation succeed.

Review the plan for each visual and ask yourself how it will help your audience understand and appreciate your message. This simple test alone can eliminate the twin scourges of the modern conference room: PowerPoint presentations that are (1) festooned with flying objects, dancing text, swirling transitions, meaningless sound effects, and other electronic distractions; or (2) nothing but one dry list of bullet points after another. Think through what you'll say while displaying each visual, making sure your words and visuals will work in harmony.

Next, make sure your presentation style is appropriate for the subject matter, the audience, and the setting (see Figure 17.1). Take the time to double-check any cultural assumptions that might be inappropriate. Are you highlighting with a color that has negative emotional connotations in your audience's culture? Would your materials be too playful for a serious audience? Too serious for an audience that values creativity?

Accuracy and simplicity are keys to effective visuals.

When it comes time to make design choices, from selecting fonts to deciding whether to include a photo, remember the advice from Chapter 16 and let simplicity be your guide. Doing so has several advantages. First, it takes less time to create simple materials, and time is the most precious commodity in today's business environment. Second, simple visuals reduce the chances of distraction and misinterpretation. Third, the more "bells and whistles" you have in your presentation, the more likely something will go wrong.

Finally, use your time wisely. Presentation software in particular can eat up hours and hours of time you probably don't have. Based on your audience and situation, decide up-front how much sophistication is good enough and then stop when you get there. Use the time you'll save to rehearse your presentation and get a good night's sleep before the big day.

FIGURE 17.1   Presentation Style
Presentation software makes it easy to create an endless variety of visual styles.
Compare the staid, "quiet" style on the left with the more dynamic style on the right.

CREATING EFFECTIVE SLIDES

Microsoft's PowerPoint software holds a curious distinction in the business world: Virtually everyone seems to use it—and virtually everyone seems to hate it. This is a bit of an exaggeration, to be sure, but enough people have grown weary of mind-numbing slide presentations for "death by PowerPoint" to become a common complaint.

The problem is not with PowerPoint itself (or with any other presentation program)—it is just a tool, and like all other tools, it can be used well or used poorly. When it is used poorly, the result can be messy slides that are difficult to read and sleep-inducing presentations that are difficult to follow. As you read this section and create your next presentation, always keep the audience's experience in mind: What will it be like to view this slide while listening to a speaker? The guidelines in this chapter will help you create slides that enhance the presentation experience for both you and your audience.

Creating effective slides requires both rational and creative instincts. As you create each slide, start by verifying the message it needs to convey, write the text that will be displayed on the slide and then add graphics and other visual elements. If you start with special effects or multimedia, these aspects are likely to become the focus of your slides rather than the message. Get your message and text in place first and then think about graphics. This approach can rescue you from schedule nightmares, too; if you run out of time, at least you'll have the message in place, even if you didn't have time to dress it up with as many graphic elements as you had planned.

Develop the message and text for each slide first and then move on to graphics and special effects.

Choosing Structured or Free-Form Slides

Perhaps the most important design choice you face when creating slides is whether to use conventional *structured slides* or the looser, *free-form slides* that many presentation specialists now advocate. Compare the two rows of slides in Figure 17.2. The structured slides in the top row follow the same basic format throughout the presentation; in fact, they're based directly on the templates built into PowerPoint. The free-form slides in the bottom row don't follow a rigid structure—and most definitely not a PowerPoint template. However, this doesn't mean free-form designs are just random from one slide to the next. Effectively designed slides should still be unified by design elements such as color and font selections, for example, as Figures 17.2c and 17.2d are. Also, note how Figure 17.2d combines visual and textual messages to convey the point about listening without criticizing. This complementary approach of pictures and words is a highlight of free-form design.

Because the amount of content varies so dramatically between the two design approaches, the number of slides in a presentation also varies dramatically. For instance, someone using structured slides might have 5 or 6 slides for a 20-minute presentation and

2 LEARNING OBJECTIVE

Explain the difference between structured and free-form slides

Structured slides are usually based on templates that give all the slides in a presentation the same general look; free-form slides typically don't follow any set design plan.

FIGURE 17.2 Structured Versus Free-Form Slide Design

Compare the rigid, predictable design of the two slides in the top row with the free-form designs in the bottom row. Although the two free-form slides don't follow the same design structure, they are visually linked by color and font choices. (Note that Figure 17.2d is a humorous way of conveying the first bullet point in Figure 17.2b.)

Figure 17.2a

Figure 17.2b

Figure 17.2c

Figure 17.2d

Free-form slides often have far less content per slide than structured designs, which requires many more slides to cover a presentation of equal length.

spend 3 or 4 minutes on each one. In contrast, someone using free-form slides for the same presentation might have 60 or 80 slides or more and spend only 15 or 20 seconds on each one. In the extreme, a 20-minute free-form presentation could have *hundreds* of slides, with individual slides often displayed for less than a second.[4] Both design strategies have advantages and disadvantages, and one or the other can be a better choice for specific situations.

Structured Slides

Structured slides are usually the best choice for project updates and other routine information presentations, particularly if the slides are intended to be used only once.

Structured slides have the advantage of being fast and easy to create; you simply choose an overall design scheme for the presentation, select a template for a new slide, and start typing your information. Of course, making things easier on the presenter won't necessarily make them easy for the audience, but if you're in a schedule crunch, going the structured route might save the day because at least you'll have *something* ready to show. Also, because more information can usually be packed on each slide, structured slides can be more effective at conveying complex ideas or sets of interrelated data to the right audiences. For example, if you are talking to a group of executives who must decide where to make budget cuts across the company's eight divisions, at some point in the presentation, they will want to see summary data for all eight divisions on a single slide for easy comparison. Such a slide would be overcrowded by the usual definition, but this might be the only practical way to get a "big picture" view of the situation. Finally, structured slides can be more effective as stand-alone documents that people can read on their own, without a presenter. It can certainly be argued that PowerPoint was never intended to produce such stand-alone documents, but the fact is that slide sets are frequently "read" without the benefit of a speaker or any supplemental documents, and having the additional information on the slides makes them more comprehensible. Given the speed and ease of creating them, structured slides can be a more practical choice for routine presentations such as project status updates.

The primary disadvantage of structured design is the mind-numbing effect of text-heavy slides that all look alike. Slide after slide of dense, highly structured bullet points with no visual relief can indeed put an audience to sleep, particularly if the presenter puts too many bullet points on a slide, writes the bullet points as complete sentences, or simply reads the bullet points to the audience. Multimedia expert Richard Mayer of the University of California, Santa Barbara, explains that this is a common problem—presenters focusing on delivering information without considering how the audience can convert that information to usable meaning.[5]

Free-Form Slides

The goal of free-form slide design is to overcome the drawbacks of text-heavy structured design by fulfilling three criteria that Mayer and other researchers have identified as important for successful presentations: (1) providing complementary information through both textual and visual means; (2) limiting the amount of information delivered at any one time to prevent cognitive overload; and (3) helping viewers process information by identifying priorities and connections, such as by highlighting the most important data points in a graph.[6] (Of course, well-designed structured slides can also meet these criteria, but the constraints of prebuilt templates make doing so more of a challenge.) With appropriate imagery, free-form designs can also create a more dynamic and engaging experience for the audience. Given their ability to excite and engage, free-form designs are particularly good for motivational, educational, and persuasive presentations—particularly when the slides will be used multiple times and therefore compensate for the extra time and effort required to create them.

In addition to benefits, free-form slides have several potential disadvantages. First, effectively designing slides with both visual and textual elements is more creatively demanding and more time-consuming than simply typing text into preformatted templates. Second, because less textual information tends to be displayed on-screen, the speaker is responsible for conveying more of the content of the presentation—which can be a problem for novice speakers or speakers who are not entirely comfortable with the material. (Of course, a thoroughly prepared presenter shouldn't need this much information, but circumstances sometimes prevent adequate preparation.) Third, if not handled carefully, dividing information into such small chunks can make it difficult to present complex subjects in a cohesive, integrated manner.

Writing Readable Content

No matter which style of slides you choose for a particular presentation, the text of your slides needs to be readable from all vantage points in the room. The three keys to readability are (1) using appropriate fonts in the right size (see "Fonts and Type Styles" on page 541), (2) limiting the amount of text on each slide, and (3) using words and phrases that help your viewers process the information you are conveying.

Structured slide designs, particularly screen after screen of identical-looking bullet points, can be boring and overwhelming.

Well-designed free-form slides help viewers understand, process, and remember the speaker's message.

The key disadvantages of free-form slide designs are the time and effort often required to create them.

No matter which design strategy you use, limit the amount of information on each slide to avoid overloading your viewers.

One of the most common mistakes beginners make—and one of the chief criticisms leveled at structured slide designs in general—is stuffing slides with too much text. Doing so creates several problems: It overloads the audience with too much information too fast; it takes attention away from the speaker by forcing people to read more; and it requires the presenter to use smaller type, which in turn makes the slides even harder to read. Keep in mind that slide text is not supposed to display your entire speaking script or highlight every point you intend to make.[7] Following the "30-point rule" explained under "Fonts and Type Styles" is an easy way to prevent all three problems.

Use your slides as guides to the content, not as the content themselves.

To choose effective words and phrases, think of the text on your slides as a guide to the content, not the content itself. In a sense, slide text serves as the headings and subheadings for your presentation. Accordingly, choose words and short phrases that help your audience follow the flow of ideas, without forcing them to read in depth. You primarily want your audience to *listen*, not to *read*. Use your slides to highlight key points, summarize and preview your message, signal major shifts in thought, illustrate concepts, or help create interest in your spoken message.

Reducing word count and making careful wording choices help you focus each slide on a single, clear message. When HP's first presentation to Procter & Gamble (see page 532) was not as successful as he had hoped, Dan Talbott reviewed and edited every single one of more than 200 slides to make sure each carried a clear, audience-focused message.[8]

When writing content for text slides, keep your message short and simple (see Figure 17.3):

- Limit each slide to one thought, concept, or idea (without dividing things so far that the audience has trouble seeing the big picture).
- Limit text content to four or five lines with four or five words per line. For selected slides, it might make sense to exceed these limits, but do so infrequently.
- Don't show a large number of text-heavy slides in a row; give the audience some visual relief.
- Write short bulleted phrases rather than long sentences.
- Use sentences only when you need to share a quotation or some other text item verbatim.[9]
- Phrase list items in parallel grammatical form to facilitate quick reading.
- Use the active voice.
- Include short, informative titles.

Modifying Graphics for Slides

Just as text needs to be simplified for projection, so do many charts, graphs, tables, and other visual elements. Detailed visuals that might look fine on the printed page can be too dense and complicated for presentations. Don't make the audience study your charts and graphs in order to get the message. You can create effective presentation visuals by following these guidelines:

Many graphics that work quite well in printed form need to be simplified for use in presentations because they are too dense and too complicated to be easily viewed on-screen.

- **Reduce the detail.** Eliminate anything that is not absolutely essential to the message. If necessary, break information into more than one graphic illustration. If a deeper level of detail is helpful or necessary, hand out printed visuals that people can review during or after the presentation.
- **Simplify.** For example, if a bar chart is segmented by week, don't write "Week of 12/01," "Week of 12/08," and so on. Use the "Week of" label once and then just include the dates. Similarly, you might be able to remove the vertical scale from the left side of the chart and just show individual values above each bar.[10]
- **Shorten numbers.** If doing so doesn't hide essential details, you can round off numbers such as $12,500.72 to $12 or $12.5 and then label the axis to indicate thousands.
- **Limit the amount of data shown.** Line graphs look busy when they have more than two or three lines, bar charts look crowded with more than five or six bars, and tables are difficult to read if they have too many rows or columns.

FIGURE 17.3   Writing Readable Content

Effective text slides are clear, simple guides that help the audience understand and remember the speaker's message. Notice the progression toward simplicity in these slides: Figure 17.3a is a paragraph that would distract the audience for an extended period of time. Figure 17.3b simplifies the message somewhat, but these bullet points are too long, and the slide is too crowded. Figure 17.3c offers concise, readable bullets, although too many slides in a row in this structured design would become tedious. Figure 17.4d distills the message down to a single compelling thought, without even a headline. It is easy to read, but the speaker will need to fill in the missing parts of the message.

Figure 17.3a

Figure 17.3b

Figure 17.3c

Figure 17.3d

- **Highlight key points.** Use arrows, boldface type, and color to direct your audience's eyes to the main point of a visual. Summarize the intent of the graphic in one clear title, such as "Earnings have increased by 15%."
- **Adjust the size and design.** Modify the size of a graphic to accommodate the size of a slide. Leave plenty of white space so that audience members can view and interpret content from a distance. Use colors that stand out from the slide's background and choose a font that's clear and easy to read.

Selecting Design Elements

Poorly designed slides detract from good content. However, by paying attention to a few design basics, you can transform a dull presentation into one that is not only dynamic but also readable. Chapter 12 highlights six principles of effective design: consistency, contrast,

To design effective slides, you need to consider six principles of effective design: consistency, contrast, balance, emphasis, convention, and simplicity.

TABLE 17.1 Color and Emotion

COLOR	SELECTED EMOTIONAL ASSOCIATIONS (CAN VARY BY CULTURE)	BEST USES
Blue	Peaceful, soothing, tranquil, cool, trusting	Background for presentation slides (usually dark blue); safe and conservative
White	Neutral, innocent, pure, wise	Font color of choice for most presentation slides that have a dark background
Yellow	Warm, bright, cheerful, enthusiastic	Text bullets and subheadings on a dark background
Red	Passionate, dangerous, active, painful	To promote action or stimulate the audience; seldom used as a background. ("In the red" specifically refers to financial losses.)
Green	Assertive, prosperous, envious, relaxed	Highlight and accent color. (Green symbolizes money in the United States but not in other countries.)

balance, emphasis, convention, and simplicity. Pay close attention to these principles as you select the color, background design, artwork, fonts, and type styles for your slides.

Color

Color is much more than mere decoration: It provides emphasis, isolation, and contrast; it increases readability and retention; and it can stimulate desired emotional responses.

Color is a critical design element, far more than mere decoration. It grabs the viewer's attention, emphasizes important ideas, creates contrast, and isolates slide elements. It can also play a key role in the overall acceptance of your message. Research shows that color visuals can account for 60 percent of an audience's acceptance or rejection of an idea. Color can increase willingness to read by up to 80 percent, and it can enhance learning and improve retention by more than 75 percent.[11]

Your color choices can also stimulate various emotions, as Table 17.1 suggests. For instance, if you want to excite your audience, add some warm colors, such as red and orange, to your slides. If you want to achieve a more relaxed and receptive environment, blue is a better choice.[12] Remember, color may have a different meaning in certain cultures, so if you are creating slides for international audiences, research these cultural differences.

When selecting color, limit your choices to a few compatible ones and keep in mind that some colors work better together than others. Contrasting colors, for example, increase readability, so when selecting color for backgrounds, titles, and text, avoid choosing colors that are close in hue, such as brown on green or blue on purple.[13] If you'll be presenting in a dark room, use dark colors such as blue for the background, a midrange of brightness for illustrations, and light colors for text. If you are presenting in well-lit rooms, reverse the colors: Use light colors for the background and dark colors for text. If you have some reason to change colors between slides, don't switch back and forth from very dark to very bright; the effect is jarring to the audience's eyes.[14]

Background Designs and Artwork

Every visual has two layers or levels of graphic design: the background and foreground. The *background* is the equivalent of paper in a printed report and normally stays the same from slide to slide. The *foreground* contains the unique text and graphic elements that make up each individual slide.

The background should stay in the background, not compete with the foreground.

Generally speaking, the less your background does, the better. Cluttered or flashy backgrounds tend to distract from your message. Look through the design templates next time you use PowerPoint; you'll find a selection of designs with backgrounds that range from the subtle and visually "quiet" to some that are quite colorful and too playful for business use. The background needs to stay in the background; it shouldn't compete with the foreground elements. When in doubt, go for subtle and simple.

You may also want to add your company logo, the date, the presentation title, and a running slide number to help both you and the audience follow along. Just be sure to keep all

FIGURE 17.4   Distractions from Decorative Artwork

Clip art and other pieces of purely decorative artwork must be used with great care to avoid distracting your audience by giving them extra visual elements to decode— particularly if the artwork is inconsistent from piece to piece or slide to slide. The clip art in this slide doesn't add any information value, and it creates a cartoony, unprofessional look.

these elements small and unobtrusive. Also, be sure to check whether your company has a standard design; many companies now have custom-designed PowerPoint templates that ensure consistency for all their presentations.

In the foreground, artwork can be either functional or decorative. *Functional artwork* includes photos, technical drawings, charts, and other visual elements containing information that's part of your message. In contrast, *decorative artwork* is there simply to enhance the look of your slides. Decorative artwork is the least important element of any slide, but it tends to cause the most trouble for anyone inexperienced in designing slides. Clip art is probably the biggest troublemaker in decorative art. You can find thousands of pieces of clip art, but few of them have any information value. Use them judiciously, or they'll give your slides a cartoony feel (see Figure 17.4).

Artwork can be either decorative or functional; use decorative artwork sparingly.

Fonts and Type Styles

When selecting fonts and type styles for slides, follow these guidelines:

- Avoid script or decorative fonts.
- Limit the number of fonts to one or two per slide (if two fonts are used, use one for headings and the other for slide text).
- When using thinner fonts, use boldface type so that letters won't look washed out.
- Avoid italicized type; it is usually difficult to read when projected.
- Avoid all-capitalized words and phrases.
- Allow extra white space between lines of text.
- Be consistent with fonts, type styles, colors, and sizes.

Many of the fonts available on your computer are difficult to read when projected, so they aren't good choices for presentation slides.

When selecting type sizes, consider the room(s) in which you'll be presenting. The farther the audience is from the screen, the larger your type needs to be in order to be readable

FIGURE 17.5 **Selecting Fonts for Projection**
Times New Roman is a standard font for many print documents; however, as Figure 17.5a illustrates, the serif design makes it difficult to read on-screen—as does the italicized type. As Figure 17.5b shows, sans serif fonts such as Calibri are a better choice for slides; they are cleaner and easier to read from a distance.

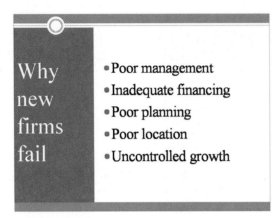

Figure 17.5a Times New Roman (serif) font

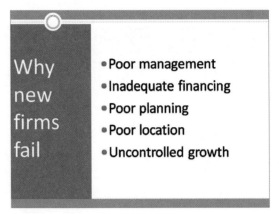

Figure 17.5b Calibri (sans serif) font

from everywhere in the room. Venture capitalist and investor Guy Kawasaki, who has sat through hundreds and hundreds of PowerPoint presentations, suggests using no type smaller than 30 points. Doing so not only ensures readable slides but forces you to distill every idea down to its essential core, simply because you won't have room to be wordy.[15] After you have selected your fonts and type styles, test them for readability by viewing sample slides from your audience's viewing location (see Figure 17.5).

Achieving Design Consistency

3 **LEARNING OBJECTIVE**

Explain the importance of design consistency in electronic slides and other visuals

Design inconsistencies confuse and annoy audiences; don't change colors and other design elements randomly throughout your presentation.

With some practice (as both a presenter and an audience member), you'll get a feel for how much consistency is too much— when a design goes from being cohesive to being bland and uninteresting.

Audiences start to assign meaning to visual elements beginning with your first slide. For instance, if the first slide presents the most important information in bright yellow, 36-point Arial, your audience will expect the same font treatment for the most important information on the second and third slides as well; so when choosing fonts and point size, be consistent. Also be consistent in your layout. Make sure that items that repeat on every slide, such as the date and the company logo, are in the same location on every slide. Otherwise, you'll distract your readers as they try to figure out the arrangement of each new slide.

Fortunately, software designed specifically for presentations makes consistency easy to achieve (at least for structured slide designs). You simply adjust the slide master using the colors, fonts, and other design elements you've chosen; these choices will then automatically show up on every slide in the presentation (see Figure 17.6). In addition, you can maintain consistency by choosing a predefined layout from those available in your software—which helps ensure that bulleted lists, charts, graphics, and other elements show up in predictable places on each slide. Something as simple as switching from a single column of bullet points to two columns can cause problems for readers, as they try to figure out the meaning of the new arrangement. The less work readers have to do to interpret your slide designs, the more attention they can pay to your message.

Now, after all this advice about simplicity and consistency, a word of caution: Too much of a good thing can make your slides dull and lifeless. Particularly in a long presentation, one identical-looking slide after another can lull your audience to sleep. Even if you are using templates and a structured design, look for opportunities to provide some visual variety within the framework of your overall design, such as making use of animation and special effects.

FIGURE 17.6 Presentation Slide Master

The slide master feature in PowerPoint and other presentation programs makes it easy to create consistent slides. Simply adjust the master as you need, and all the slides of that type in your presentation will change accordingly. Note that many slide design templates contain more levels of bullet points than you would ever want to use for normal presentation purposes.

Click to edit Master title style	Why new firms fail

Click to edit Master text styles
  Second level
   Third level
    Fourth level
     Fifth level
	Poor management
	  Weak strategies
	   Unclear priorities
	   Unstable plans
	  Uninspired leadership
	Inadequate financing
	  Weak marketing and sales efforts
	  Inability to survive until breakeven

Figure 17.6a Slide master for bullet slides   Figure 17.6b Example of how content is displayed

Adding Animation and Special Effects

Today's presentation software offers a wide array of options for livening up your slides, including sound, animation, video clips, transition effects from one slide to the next, and hyperlinks to websites and other resources. As with every other visual element, the key is to make sure that any effects you use support your message. Always consider the impact that all these effects will have on your audience and use only those special effects that support your message.[16]

Animation and special effects can be grouped into four categories: functional animation, transitions and builds, hyperlinks, and multimedia. These capabilities are briefly discussed in the following sections, but to learn more about them, consult the Help menu in your software or visit http://real-timeupdates.com/bct and click on Chapter 17.

Although you can animate just about everything in an electronic presentation, resist the temptation to do so—make sure each animation has a purpose.

Functional Animation

PowerPoint and other presentation packages offer a mind-boggling set of tools for moving and changing things on-screen. You can have a block of text cartwheel in from outer space, change colors, change font and font size, spin around in circles, blink on and off, wave back and forth, crawl around the screen following a predefined path, and then disappear one letter at a time, like some sort of erasing typewriter. You *can* do all this, but *should* you?

Just as static graphic elements can be either functional or decorative, so too can animated elements. For instance, having each bullet point fly in from the left side of the screen doesn't add any functional value to your communication effort. In contrast, a highlight arrow or color bar that moves around the screen to emphasize specific points in a technical diagram can be an effective use of animation and a welcome alternative to a laser pointer. You can control every aspect of the animation, so it's easy to coordinate the movement with the points you're making in your presentation. Using controlled animation is also a great way to demonstrate sequences and procedures. For a training session on machinery repair, for example, you can show a schematic diagram of the machinery and walk your

 REAL-TIME UPDATES
Learn More

Five words of wisdom for successful slide design

Satyajeet Singh advises presenters to focus on five attributes: big, simple, clear, consistent, and progressive. (View this presentation in slide show mode for full impact.) Go to **http://real-timeupdates.com/bct** and click on "Learn More." If you are using mybcommlab, you can access Real-Time Updates within each chapter or under Student Study Tools.

Business Communication 2.0

Presentations Get Social

When you're looking for creative inspiration, collaboration, or feedback, don't limit yourself to the people in your office. With a presentation sharing website such as SlideShare (www .slideshare.net), you can learn from and collaborate with the entire world. Sometimes described as "YouTube for Power-Point," SlideShare offers free storage and controlled access for presentation slides; it now hosts thousands of presentations, with more added every day.

If you'd like to find presentations on just about any topic imaginable, you can search for slides by keyword, browse by category, select popular topics from a tag cloud, or sort by popularity. For inspiration and design ideas, simply browse until something catches your eye. You can view any publicly available presentation in the viewer window right on the SlideShare website or download presentations to your computer (if the person who uploaded the presentation you select allows it to be downloaded).

If you want to share your slides, you can upload presentations as a guest or create a profile much as you can on a social networking site. With your profile established, you can continue to add new presentations to your *slidespace* and expand your online community by adding new contacts. As with Flickr and some other content-sharing sites, SlideShare lets you set various levels of access permission, from your eyes only to selected contacts to the entire world. This controlled sharing aspect is a great way to share slides with conference attendees, business partners, and team members. You can also embed your presentations in your blog so all your blog visitors can see them, or embed them on an intranet so that only your co-workers can see them.

In the spirit of community, SlideShare offers tools to alert your followers on the Twitter microblogging service and your contacts on LinkedIn and other social networking sites. With SlideShare, your friends, fans, and customers can see your inspiring content as soon as you publish it.

CAREER APPLICATIONS

1. Visit SlideShare and find two presentations on the same business topic, such as public relations, financial matters, leadership, or even giving presentations. View and compare the two presentations in terms of content. Which presentation is clearer? More credible? More convincing? What specific steps did this presenter take to ensure clarity and confidence?

2. Now compare those two presentations in terms of their visual design. Do their designs help or hinder the communication effort? If you see any weaknesses, what improvements would you suggest?

---

4 LEARNING OBJECTIVE

Describe the effective use of transitions and builds in electronic presentations

audience through each step of the troubleshooting process, highlighting each step on-screen as you address it verbally. Again, use animation in support of your message, not simply for animation's sake.

Transitions and Builds

In addition to animating specific elements on your slides, you can choose from PowerPoint's options for adding motion *between* slides. These **transitions** control how one slide replaces another on-screen. Subtle transitions can ease your viewers' gaze from one slide to the next—such as having the current slide gently fade out before the next one fades in. However, most of the transitions currently available (such as checkerboards, pinwheels, and spinning "newsflashes") are like miniature animated shows themselves and are therefore too distracting. You can even add sound effects, from drumrolls to explosions. These exaggerated transition effects not only disrupt the flow of your presentation, they can make the whole thing seem amateurish. If you use a transition effect, use the same one throughout the presentation (so that audiences don't wonder if there is some significance to a new transition at some point during the presentation) and choose the effect carefully. Aim for a smooth, subtle, artful effect that is easy on the eye. And unless a sound effect is somehow integral to the message, there is no reason to add audio to a transition.

Builds are similar to transitions but much more useful. These effects control the release of text, graphics, and other elements on individual slides. For instance, with builds you

REAL-TIME UPDATES
Learn More

How not to use PowerPoint

Comedian Don McMillan presents a humorous and insightful viewpoint on how not to use PowerPoint. Go to **http://real-timeupdates .com/bct** and click on "Learn More." If you are using mybcommlab, you can access Real-Time Updates within each chapter or under Student Study Tools.

can make your bullet points appear one at a time rather than having all of them appear on a slide at once, which makes it difficult to focus on a single point. This controlled release of information helps draw audience members' attention to the point being discussed and keeps them from reading ahead.

Using carefully designed builds can be a great way to present information in easy-to-process pieces.

As with transitions, stick with the subtle, basic options for builds. The point of a build, after all, is to release information in a controlled fashion, not to distract or entertain the audience. Another useful option is to change the color of bullet points as you discuss each one. For instance, if your primary text color is a strong blue, you might have the text in each bullet point change to a light gray after you've finished talking about it. This approach adds some subtle activity to the screen and keeps the audience's attention focused on the current bullet point.

After you've assigned builds to your slides, you can control the build activity with a mouse or a remote control device. Experiment with the options in your software to find the most effective build scheme. In addition to building up text, you can build up graphical elements. For instance, to discuss monthly sales of three products over the past year, you can have a line graph of the first product appear by itself while you discuss it, and then you can click the mouse to display the second product's sales line, then the third.

Hyperlinks and Action Buttons

Hyperlinks and action buttons can be quite handy when you need flexibility in your presentations or want to share different kinds of files with the audience. A **hyperlink** instructs your computer to jump to another slide in your presentation, to a website, or to another program entirely. Hyperlinks can be simple underlined text (like most of the links you see on a website), or they can be assigned to **action buttons**, which are a variety of preprogrammed hyperlink icons available in PowerPoint.

You can increase the flexibility of your presentation slides with hyperlinks that let you jump to different slides, websites, or other software screens with the click of a mouse.

Using hyperlinks is also a great way to customize your presentations. For instance, if you work in sales and call on a variety of customers, you can't be sure what sort of situation you'll encounter at each customer's site. You might be prepared to give an in-depth technical presentation to a group of engineers, only to have the company president walk in and request a five-minute overview. Or you might prepare a set of detailed technical slides but not show them unless the audience asks detailed questions. Another common situation is finding out at the last minute that you have only a fraction of the time you thought you had to make your presentation. With some foresight and planning, you won't need to rush through your entire presentation or scramble on the spot to find the most important slides. Instead, you can simply click an action button labeled "Five-minute overview" and jump right to the two or three most important slides in your presentation. With hyperlinks, you can even switch from the indirect approach to the direct approach or vice versa, based on the response you're getting from your audience. By building in links that accommodate these various scenarios, you can adjust your presentation at a moment's notice—and look polished and professional while you do it (see Figure 17.7).

Multimedia Elements

Using audio and video clips can be a great way to complement your textual message. You can incorporate various media elements with PowerPoint by using tools such as the Microsoft Producer add-in. In addition, dozens of software programs are now available to assist with video editing, from basic tools sometimes included with digital cameras or camcorders to professional packages such as Adobe Premiere Pro.

Video clips can add memorable, engaging content to your presentations—as long as they are relevant, interesting, and brief.

COMPLETING SLIDES AND SUPPORT MATERIALS

Just as you would review any message for content, style, tone, readability, clarity, and conciseness, you should apply the same quality control to your slides and other visuals. As you look over your presentation for the final time, make sure that all visuals are

Review each slide carefully to make sure it is clear and readable.

- **Readable.** Can text be read from the back of the room? Does the text stand out from the background?
- **Consistent.** Are colors and design elements used consistently?

FIGURE 17.7 **Adapting a Presentation on the Fly**
With hyperlinks that jump to various slides throughout a presentation, you can easily adapt your presentation in response to audience needs. In this simple presentation, for example, the speaker can jump to detailed discussions about engineering, marketing, or finance with one click of the mouse.

- **Simple.** Is each slide and the entire presentation as simple as possible? Can you eliminate any slides?
- **Audience centered.** Are the message and the design focused on the audience?
- **Clear.** Is the main point of a slide obvious? Easy to understand? Can the audience grasp the main point in five to eight seconds?
- **Concise and grammatical.** Is text written in concise phrases? Are the phrases parallel?
- **Focused.** Does each slide cover only one thought, concept, or idea? Does the slide grab the viewer's attention in the right place and support the key points of the message? Are arrows, symbols, or other techniques used to draw the audience's attention to the key sections of a chart or diagram?
- **Fully operational.** Have you verified every slide in your presentation? Do all the animations and other special effects work as you intended?

Remember, you want the audience to listen to you, not study the slides, so make sure your slides are not distracting in any way.

Use the slide sorter view to verify and modify the organization of your slides.

Electronic presentation software can help you during the editing and revision process. As Figure 17.8 shows, using the *slide sorter* makes it easy to add and delete slides, reposition them, and check for design consistency. You can also use this view to preview animation and transition effects and experiment with design elements. For instance, if you want to experiment with a different background design or different font, select a new design element and preview it in your slides. If you choose to keep the new design, execute the "apply all" command to update all existing slides and to change the slide master, which will apply the design changes to any new slides you create. Note that you can also use the slide sorter view as a *storyboard* to plan your presentation.[17]

With your slides working properly and in clear, logical order, you're just a few steps away from being ready. Now is a good time to think about a backup plan. What will you do if your laptop won't turn on or the projector dies? Can you get by without your slides? For important presentations, consider having backup equipment on standby, loaded with your presentation, and ready to go. At the very least, have enough printed handouts ready to give the audience so that, as a last resort, you can give your presentation "on paper."

FIGURE 17.8 Slide Sorter View

Examining thumbnails of slides on one screen is the best way to check the overall design of your final product. The slide sorter also makes it easy to review the order and organization of your presentation; you can even use this screen to storyboard your presentation before creating slides.

Creating Navigation and Support Slides

At this point, you've created the slides that will deliver the content of your presentation. You can enhance your presentation with a few additional slides that add "finish" to your presentation and provide additional information to benefit your audience:

- **Title slide(s).** Make a good first impression on your audience with one or two title slides, the equivalent of a report's cover and title page (see Figures 17.9a and 17.9b) A title slide should contain the title of your presentation (and subtitle, if appropriate), your name, your department affiliation (for internal audiences), and your company affiliation (for external audiences). You may also include the presentation date and an appropriate graphic element. Depending on the amount of information you need to convey at this point, two title slides might be appropriate: one focusing on the topic of the presentation and a second slide with your affiliation and other information. This second slide can also be used to introduce the speaker and list his or her credentials.

- **Agenda and program details.** You can optionally use slides to communicate both the agenda for your presentation and any additional information that your audience might need. Because presentations pull your audience members away from their daily routines and work responsibilities, people can have questions about anything from break times or lunch plans to opportunities to plug into a network to check their e-mail (see Figures 17.9c and 17.9d). By answering these questions at the beginning of your presentation, you'll minimize disruptions later and help the audience stay focused on your message.

- **Navigation slides.** To tell your audience where you're going and where you've been, you can use a series of **navigation slides** based on your outline or agenda. This technique is most useful in longer presentations with several major sections. As you complete each section, repeat the slide but indicate which material has been covered and which section you are about to begin (see Figure 17.10). This sort of slide is sometimes referred to as a *moving blueprint.* You can then use the original slide again in the close of your presentation to review the points you've covered. As an alternative to the repeating agenda slide, you can insert a simple *bumper slide* at each major section break, announcing the title of the section you're about to begin.[18]

5 LEARNING OBJECTIVE

Identify three types of noncontent slides you can use to support a presentation

Navigational slides help your audience keep track of what you've covered already and what you plan to cover next.

FIGURE 17.9 Navigation and Support Slides

You can use a variety of navigation and support slides to introduce yourself and your presentation, to let the audience know what your presentation covers, and to provide essential details.

Figure 17.9a Title slide

Figure 17.9b Title slide 2

Figure 17.9c Agenda

Figure 17.9d Program details

FIGURE 17.10 Navigation Slides

Here are two of the ways you can use a *blueprint slide* as a navigational aid to help your audience stay on track with the presentation. Figure 17.10a visually "mutes" and checks off the sections of the presentation that have already been covered. In contrast, Figure 17.10b uses a sliding highlight box to indicate the next section to be covered.

Figure 17.10a "Muting" topics already covered

Figure 17.10b Highlighting the next topic

Creating Effective Handouts

Providing handouts is a great way to offer your audience additional material without overloading your slides with information. Possibilities for good handout materials include the following:[19]

- **Complex charts and diagrams.** Charts and tables that are too unwieldy for the screen or that demand thorough analysis make good handouts. A common approach is to create a stripped-down version of a chart or graphic for the presentation slide and include a more detailed version in your handouts.
- **Articles and technical papers.** Magazine articles that supplement the information in your presentation make good handout materials, as do technical papers that provide in-depth coverage of the material you've highlighted in your presentation.
- **Case studies.** Summaries of case studies along with references and contact information make good supplemental reading material.
- **Websites.** Lists of websites related to your topic are useful; provide each site's URL and a one- or two-sentence summary of its content.
- **Copies of presentation slides.** In many cases, audiences like to have print versions of the slides used by a speaker, containing the speaker's comments about each slide and blank lines for note taking. PowerPoint gives you several options for printing handouts, from a single slide per page to as many as nine per page.

Use handout materials to support the points made in your presentation and to offer the audience additional information on your topic.

Other good handout materials include brochures, pictures, outlines, a copy of the presentation agenda, and other program details. Make sure the information is all useful and relevant.

Timing the distribution of handouts depends on the content of your handouts, the nature of your presentation, and your personal preference. Some speakers prefer to distribute handout copies of their slides before the presentation begins so that the audience can take notes. Doing so can be risky, however, if you've organized your talk with the indirect approach, because the audience can read ahead and reach the conclusion and recommendations before you're able to build up to them yourself. Other speakers simply advise the audience of the types of information they are including in handouts but delay distributing anything until they have finished speaking.

The more you practice a presentation, the more confidence you'll have in yourself and your material.

Practicing Your Delivery

Many things can go wrong in a major presentation, including equipment glitches, confusing slides, and the unpleasant discovery that you're out of time but only halfway through your material. That's why experienced speakers always practice important presentations. If you can arrange an audience of several helpful colleagues, by all means do so. They can tell you if your slides are understandable and whether your delivery is effective. A day or two before you're ready to step on stage for an important talk, make sure you can give a positive response to each of the following questions:

- **Can you present your material naturally, without reading your slides word for word?** Reading your slides is one of the worst mistakes a presenter can make. Practice until you can speak naturally from notes or an outline.
- **Is the equipment working—and do you know how to work it?** Verify that your computer will work with the projector and that you're comfortable operating any equipment that will be needed.
- **Is your timing on track?** Now is the time to trim if you need to, not when you're live on stage.

Learning to focus on audience members and interact with them while using electronic slides or other visuals takes practice.

- **Can you easily pronounce all the words you plan to use?** Everyone stumbles over certain words, and your tongue is most likely to get tied up when you're under pressure and your mouth is dry.
- **Have you decided how you're going to introduce your slides?** Some presenters prefer to introduce each slide before displaying it. Doing so allows you to set the stage before your audience starts reading the slide and jumping to their own conclusions.
- **Have you anticipated likely questions and objections?** Put yourself in the audience's shoes and try to imagine what issues the various audience members might have about your content. Then think through your answers ahead of time. Don't assume that you can handle whatever comes up.[20]
- **Does your message come through clearly?** Step back and look at everything you plan to present. Are you presenting the right material in the right quantity to get your message across? Don't make the common mistake of worrying so much about the supporting evidence that your message gets lost in the all details.[21]

You'll know you've practiced enough when you can present the material at a comfortable pace and in a conversational tone, without the need to read your slides or constantly refer to your notes.

With experience, you'll get a feel for how much practice is enough in any given situation. Your credibility is dramatically enhanced when you move seamlessly through your presentation, matching effective words with each slide. Practicing helps keep you on track, helps you maintain a conversational tone with your audience, and boosts your confidence and composure.

For a quick review of the key steps in creating effective visuals, see "Checklist: Enhancing Presentations with Visuals." For the latest information on presentation design, visit http://real-timeupdates.com/bct and click on Chapter 17.

✓ **CHECKLIST:** **Enhancing Presentations with Visuals**

A. Plan your presentation visuals.
- Make sure you and your message, not your visuals, remain the focus of your presentation.
- Select your visuals carefully to support your message; use a combination of visuals if needed.
- Review your plan for each visual to make sure it truly supports your message.
- Follow effective design principles, with an emphasis on accuracy and simplicity.
- Use your time wisely so that you have plenty of time to practice your presentation.

B. Create effective slides.
- Choose structured or free-form slides, based on the content and situation.
- Write content that will be readable from everywhere in the room.
- Write short, active, parallel phrases that support, not replace, your spoken message.
- Avoid complete sentences unless you need to quote verbatim.
- Limit the amount of text so that your audience can focus on listening, not reading.
- Simplify print graphics for use on slides but don't oversimplify.
- Use color to emphasize important ideas, create contrast, and isolate visual elements.
- Limit color to a few compatible choices and use them consistently.
- Make sure your slide background doesn't compete with the foreground.

- Use decorative artwork sparingly; focus on functional artwork that supports your message.
- Choose fonts that are easy to read on-screen; limit the number of fonts and use them consistently.
- Use slide masters to maintain consistency throughout your presentation.
- Use functional animation when it can support your message.
- Make sure slide transitions are subtle.
- Use builds carefully to control the release of information.
- Use hyperlinks and action buttons to add flexibility to your presentation.
- Incorporate multimedia elements that can help engage your audience and deliver your message.

C. Complete slides and support materials.
- Review every slide carefully to ensure accuracy, consistency, and clarity.
- Make sure that all slides are fully operational.
- Use the slide sorter to verify and adjust the sequence of slides, if needed.
- Have a backup plan in case your electronic presentation plan fails.
- Create navigation and support slides.
- Create handouts to back up your presentation message.
- Practice your delivery to ensure a smooth presentation.

GIVING PRESENTATIONS ONLINE

You should expect to give some presentations online during your career. Depending on the system, you'll communicate through combination of audio, video, and electronic slides. Your audience will view your presentation either on individual computer screens or via a projector in a conference room. Capabilities vary from one system to another, so it's a good idea to make sure you're familiar with the system you'll be using well in advance of your presentation.

Online presentations give you a way to reach more people in less time, but they require special preparation and skills.

The benefits of online presentations (sometimes called *webinars*, for *web seminars*) are considerable, including the opportunity to communicate with a geographically dispersed audience at a fraction of the cost of travel and the ability for a project team or an entire organization to meet at a moment's notice. Online presentations can also be less disruptive for the members of your audience, giving them the options of viewing your presentation from their desk and listening to only those parts that apply to them.

However, the challenges for an online presenter can also be considerable, thanks to that layer of technology between you and your audience. Many of those "human moments" that guide and encourage you through an in-person presentation won't travel across the digital divide, particularly if you don't have a live video link. However, online systems continue to improve, and presenters who master this new mode of communication will definitely have an advantage in tomorrow's business environment.

Once you master the technology, you can spend less time thinking about it and more time thinking about the most important elements of the presentation: your message and your audience.

To ensure successful online presentations, keep the following advice in mind:

- **Consider all your alternatives.** Microsoft PowerPoint is far and away the dominant presentation software in business, but a growing number of alternatives are now available—including some designed specifically for online presentations.[22]
- **Consider sending preview study materials ahead of time.** If your presentation covers complicated or unfamiliar material, consider sending "prestudy" materials ahead of time so audience members can familiarize themselves with any important background information. In addition to preview materials, also consider sending technical "how-to" information to help inexperienced users connect to the system.[23] Also, by using a free service such as SlideShare (see page 544), you can distribute your presentation slides to either public or private audiences, and you can record audio narrative to make your presentations function on their own.[24]
- **Keep your content—and your presentation of it—as simple as possible.** Break complicated slides down into multiple slides, if necessary, and keep the direction of your discussion clear so that no one gets lost. Moreover, make sure any streaming video presentations are short; viewers don't like to sit through recorded speeches online.[25]
- **Ask for feedback frequently.** Depending on the video connection, you probably won't have much visual feedback that alerts you when audience members are confused (such as perplexed looks or blank stares), and many online viewers will be reluctant to call attention to themselves by interrupting you to ask for clarification. To make sure you're not losing people, ask for feedback as you go.
- **Consider the viewing experience from the audience's side.** Will participants be able to see what you think they can see? For instance, webcast video is typically displayed in a small window on-screen, which can make it difficult to see tiny details.
- **Make sure your audience can receive the sort of content you intend to use.** For instance, some corporate firewalls (electronic "safety gates") don't allow streaming media, so your webcast video might not survive the trip.[26]
- **Allow plenty of time for everyone to get connected and familiar with the screens they're viewing.** Also, if people need to download any software to participate, be sure to tell them ahead of time so they don't waste precious meeting time trying to configure their computers.

6 **LEARNING OBJECTIVE**

Highlight nine major issues to consider when you're preparing to give a presentation online

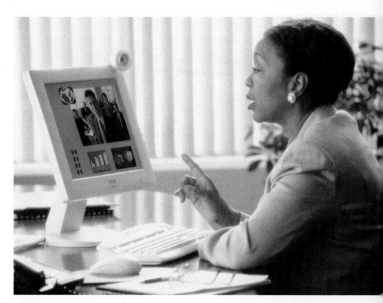

Online presentations let you reach a wider audience, but the lack of direct contact forces you to take a more active role in engaging your audience.

Document Makeover

Improve These Slides

To practice correcting drafts of actual documents, visit the "Document Makeovers" section in either mybcommlab or the Companion Website for this text.

If mybcommlab is being used in your class, see your User Guide for specific instructions on how to access the content for this chapter. If you are accessing this feature through the Companion Website, click on "Document Makeovers" and then click Chapter 17. You will find a series of slides containing problems and errors related to what you've learned in this chapter about enhancing oral presentations with electronic slides. Use the Final Draft decision tool to create an improved version of these slides. Check the slides for wordiness, clarity, consistency, complexity, necessity, readability, active versus passive voice, appropriateness of ideas, spelling, and grammar.

- **Consider assigning a moderator to host the event and handle the software.** For anything beyond basic presentations to internal audiences, trying to play the triple role of host, technical expert, and presenter can be overwhelming. By assigning a colleague to handle all the logistics, you can focus on delivering your message.
- **Engage the audience frequently.** Without the social pressure of being in the same room with the presenter and other audience members, failing to pay attention or even virtually "leaving" by shutting off the presentation are much easier to during online presentations.[27] To help avoid this situation, plan to engage the audience at regular intervals. For instance, many meeting systems let you conduct online polls, in which audience members are asked to vote on issues or respond to questions.[28]

Last but not least, don't get lost in the technology. With virtual whiteboards, real-time polling, collaborative editing, and other powerful features, electronic communication systems provide lots of gadgets that can distract both you and your audience. Use these tools whenever they'll help but remember that the most important aspect of any presentation is getting the audience to receive, understand, and embrace your message. For the latest information on creating and delivering online presentations, visit http://real-timeupdates.com/bct and click on Chapter 17.

Communication Challenges at Hewlett-Packard

HP continues to pursue major contracts with other global companies, and you've recently joined the company as a sales representative. Dan Talbott's group is pursuing a big project with Walt Disney Imagineering, the organization that unites the artistic, engineering, production, and installation teams responsible for creating Disney theme parks. As with the Procter & Gamble deal, Talbott has assembled a team—including you—in an HP sales office near Disney's headquarters in Burbank, California.

Individual Challenge: In his first meeting with the team, Talbott mentioned two significant links between the companies.

First, in 1939, when HP was just starting out (as a maker of electronic instrumentation), Disney was one of its first customers, buying equipment that was used in the production of the movie *Fantasia*. Second, both companies value innovation, imagination, and creativity. To help prepare your part of the presentation—and get ready for Dan's rigorous review—create a list of the images and electronic presentation capabilities that can help convey HP's passion for innovation.

Team Challenge: As part of a small group, discuss the risks and rewards of using visual effects, sound effects, and animation in an electronic presentation when you'll be facing a visually sophisticated audience such as Walt Disney Imagineering. List the major pros and cons in an e-mail message to your instructor.

SUMMARY OF LEARNING OBJECTIVES

1 **Explain how visuals enhance oral presentations, and list several popular types of visuals.** Visuals create interest, illustrate and clarify important points, add variety, and help the listener absorb the information you're presenting. In most businesses today, electronic presentations are the most common tool, but you might also use overhead transparencies, chalkboards and whiteboards (including electronic whiteboards), flip charts, product samples, models, video, and various software programs.

2 **Explain the difference between structured and free-form slides.** Structured slides follow the same design plan for most or all the slides in a presentation. They are often created by using the templates provided with PowerPoint and other electronic presentation programs. Structured slides tend to convey most of their information through bullet points. In contrast, free-form slides do not follow any set design scheme from slide to slide, although they can and should use color, font selection, and other design choices to create a unified feel across a presentation. Free-form slides often have just a single thought or statement on each slide, requiring many more slides to cover the same amount of material as the typical structured design.

3 **Explain the importance of design consistency in electronic slides and other visuals.** Consistency is important because your audience looks for patterns in the way you use color, font size, and other design elements. If the first slide shows major points in blue text and minor points in green text, your audience will expect that pattern to continue throughout the presentation. If you change color assignments from slide to slide, you'll lose viewers' attention as they try to figure out what's important on each slide. Anything that distracts audience members diminishes the concentration they can direct toward your presentation.

4 **Describe the effective use of transitions and builds in electronic presentations.** Transitions between slides can ease the viewer from one slide to the next, provided that they are chosen artfully, with an emphasis on visual calm and subtlety. In contrast, hyperactive visuals with excessive motion and noise distract audience members and can disrupt the train of thought you're trying hard to keep them on as you move through your presentation. Whereas transitions are effects that occur between slides, builds are transitions within a single slide and affect the way that the various text and graphic elements are presented. A common build effect is displaying a bulleted list one item at a time rather than all at once. Used judiciously, builds can be a good way to layer information as you work toward a conclusion.

5 **Identify three types of noncontent slides you can use to support a presentation.** In addition to the slides that convey your content, you can create one or more *title slides* to introduce your presentation (and yourself, if necessary), *agenda and program detail slides* that tell viewers what to expect during the presentation and provide information to help them plan their time, and *navigation slides* that help you and your audience keep track of where you are in the presentation.

6 **Highlight nine major issues to consider when you're preparing to give a presentation online.** Review these points to help plan a successful online presentation: (1) Consider all your options; PowerPoint is far and away the most common presentation software in business, but other options are available, including some designed specifically for online presentations. (2) Consider sending preview materials ahead of time so your audience members can familiarize themselves with the issues you plan to discuss. (3) Keep your content and presentation as simple as possible. (4) Plan to ask for feedback frequently because you might not get all the nonverbal signals that normally alert you to confusion or disagreement. (5) Consider the viewing experience from the audience's side to make sure your intended content is easy to view. (6) Make sure your audience can receive the sort of content you intend to use, such as video clips. (7) Allow plenty of time for everyone to get connected and familiar with the screen they're viewing. (8) Consider assigning a moderator to manage the logistics of the online session so you can focus on the message and the audience. (9) Find creative ways to engage the audience at regular intervals, such as by using online polling.

PEARSON
mybcommlab™

Log on to **www.mybcommlab.com** to access the following study and assessment aids associated with this chapter:

- Video applications
- Real-Time Updates
- Peer review activity
- Quick Learning Guides

- Pre/post test
- Personalized study plan
- Model documents
- Sample presentations

If you are not using mybcommlab, you can access the Real-Time Updates and Quick Learning Guides through **http://real-timeupdates.com/bct**. The Quick Learning Guide hits all the high points of this chapter in just two pages. This guide, especially prepared by the authors, will help you study for exams or review important concepts whenever you need a quick refresher.

Test Your Knowledge

1. How do structured and free-form slide designs differ from one another?
2. What is the recommended number of fonts to use per slide?
3. How can hyperlinks be used in electronic slides?
4. How does slide sorter view facilitate the editing process for an electronic presentation?
5. How is a moving blueprint slide used in a presentation?
6. When should you distribute handouts? Why?
7. What is the difference between decorative and functional artwork and animation?
8. What is the advantage of practicing an oral presentation with visuals in front of a live audience?
9. How do slide transitions differ from builds?
10. Why should you ask for feedback and otherwise engage the audience frequently during online presentations?

Apply Your Knowledge

1. How does the "30-point rule" for fonts help ensure readable and memorable slide content?
2. How might you modify a graph appearing in a printed document to make it appropriate for a slide?
3. Would you choose a structured or free-form design plan for a presentation to an audience of possible investors in your company? Why?
4. How can you use slide masters to enhance the effectiveness of your slides?
5. **Ethical Choices** Is it ethical to use design elements and special effects to persuade an audience? Why or why not?

Practice Your Knowledge

Messages for Analysis

Message 17.A: Improving a Slide

Examine the slide in Figure 17.11 and point out any problems you notice. How would you correct these problems?

Message 17.B: Modifying for Presentation

Examine the graph in Figure 17.12 and explain how to modify it for an electronic presentation, using the guidelines discussed in this chapter.

Message 17.C: Analyzing the Animation

To access this PowerPoint presentation, visit http://real-time updates.com/bct, click on "Student Assignments," and select Chapter 17, page 554, Message 17.C. Download and watch the presentation in slide show mode (after you select Slide Show from the View menu, simply click your mouse to advance through the slides). After you've watched the presentation, identify at least three ways in which various animations, builds, and transitions either enhanced or impeded your understanding of the subject matter.

Exercises

Active links for all websites in this chapter can be found online. If mybcommlab is being used in your class, see your User Guide for instructions on accessing the content for this chapter. Otherwise, visit www.pearsonglobaleditions.com/bovee, locate *Business Communication Today*, Tenth Edition, click the Companion Website link, select Chapter 17, and then click on "Featured Websites." Please note that links to sites that become inactive after publication of the book will be removed from the Featured Websites section.

FIGURE 17.11 Piece of Cake Bakery Customer Survey

FIGURE 17.12
CommuniCo Employee
Training Costs

17.1 **Creating Effective Slides: Content** Look through recent issues (print or online) of *BusinessWeek*, *Fortune*, or other business publications for articles that discuss issues a specific company or industry is facing. Based on the articles and the guidelines discussed in this chapter, create three to five slides summarizing these issues. If you don't have access to computer presentation software or a word processor, you can draw the slides on plain paper.

17.2 **Creating Effective Slides: Content and Design** You've been asked to give an informative 10-minute talk to a group of convention attendees on great things to see and do while visiting your hometown. Write the content for three or four slides (including a title slide). Then think about the design elements for your slides. Describe design choices you would make, particularly in terms of colors, fonts, drawings, and photography. If your instructor directs, create the slides that you've described.

17.3 **Completing Electronic Presentations: Slide Sorter View** PowerPoint comes with a number of content templates for presentations. Use the software's AutoContent Wizard to create a short presentation by selecting a presentation type and supplying information for the slide templates (feel free to make up material). Then, using the slide sorter view, critique the content, layout, and design elements of your presentation. Edit and revise the slides to improve their overall effectiveness.

17.4 **Creating Effective Slides: Structured Versus Free-Form Design** Find a business-related slide presentation on SlideShare (www.slideshare.net) and analyze the design. Do you consider it structured or free form? Does the design help the audience understand and remember the message? Why or why not? What improvements would you suggest to the design?

17.5 **Internet** Creating hyperlinks to live websites can perk up an electronic presentation, but it requires being prepared for the unexpected. What are some of the obstacles you might encounter when creating live Internet links for use during a presentation? How can you prepare in advance to overcome such obstacles?

Expand Your Knowledge

Exploring the Best of the Web
Presentation Design with Zen-like Simplicity

www.presentationzen.com

Garr Reynolds is a widely read and widely admired expert on presentation design, and his blog, Presentation Zen, offers numerous tips, techniques, and insights that can help presenters. In addition to his own great advice, Reynolds provides links to a variety of effective presentations on numerous topics. Click through the archives to find these three posts and answer the associated questions:

1. **October 6, 2008: "Financial crisis simplified" (a whiteboard presentation).** Watch this video and explain why a whiteboard is a more effective medium for conveying Paddy Hirsch's message than a series of electronic slides would have been. (Imagine that you are in the room with Hirsch and can therefore see the entire whiteboard all the time, rather than relying on the camera operator to pan back and forth. Even with the visual restrictions of panning, however, the benefit of using the whiteboard in this case is obvious.)
2. **June 8, 2006: "You are creative (who the %$#@! says you're not?)."** How might you apply Brenda Ueland's advice on finding and nurturing your creative instincts?
3. **December 10, 2008: "Benjamin Zander at Pop!Tech 2008: How Fascinating!"** How does Zander use visuals in his presentation? (Think about visual aids in the broadest possible perspective here.) Would this presentation be as effective using only PowerPoint? Why or why not?

Sharpening Your Career Skills Online

Bovée and Thill's Business Communication Web Search, at http://businesscommunicationblog.com/websearch, is a unique research tool designed specifically for business communication research. Use the Web Search function to find a website, video, PDF document, podcast, or PowerPoint presentation that offers advice on creating slides and other presentation visuals. Write a brief e-mail message to your instructor, describing the item that you found and summarizing the career skills information you learned from it.

CASES

Applying the Three-Step Writing Process to Cases

Apply each step to the following cases, as assigned by your instructor.

PORTFOLIO BUILDER

1. Is anybody out there? Explaining Loopt's social mapping service. How many times have you been out shopping or clubbing and wondered if any of your friends were in the neighborhood? A new *social mapping* service from Loopt can provide the answer. It lets you put yourself on a map that your friends can see on their mobile phones, and you can see their locations as well. You can even get automatic alerts whenever friends are near.

Your task: Create a brief presentation, explaining the Loopt concept to someone who is comfortable using text messaging and other mobile phone features. Be sure to explain how to find out whether a particular phone model supports Loopt and include a slide that discusses safety issues. You can learn more about it at www.loopt.com.[29]

PORTFOLIO BUILDER

2. I'll find my space somewhere else, thanks: Promoting alternatives to MySpace. With a user base well on its way toward 200 million people, MySpace is the king of social networking sites. However, it doesn't appeal to everyone. Some people want to be able to customize their online presence more than MySpace allows, while others want more control over who sees what aspects of their online profiles.

Your task: Choose one of the lesser-known alternatives to MySpace, such as the customizable social networking site Ning (www.ning.com), the blogging site Vox (www.vox.com), the content sharing site eSnips (www.esnips.com), or any other site that offers some degree of social networking. Compare its features and functions to those of MySpace and prepare a brief presentation that highlights the similarities and differences of the two sites. In your presentation, identify the sort of people most likely to prefer the site you've chosen over MySpace.[30]

3. Face to face: Updating management on your monthly progress. Imagine that you've just completed the impressive-looking online progress report shown in Figure 14.4 (page 448), when your boss decides he'd like to hear a presentation from you instead.

Your task: Adapt the information in Figure 14.4 to a brief electronic slide show. Your boss might want to see maps of the four locations listed, so have slides with maps ready. (Because you don't have the specific addresses, just capture an online map for each general area; Lakewood and Glendale are both suburbs of Denver, and Pepsi Center is a sports arena in Denver.)

PORTFOLIO BUILDER

4. Hot topics: Identifying key elements in an important business issue. In your job as a business development researcher for a major corporation, you're asked to gather and process information on a wide variety of subjects. Management has gained confidence in your research and analysis skills and would now like you to begin making regular presentations at management retreats and other functions. Topics are likely to include the following:

- Offshoring of U.S. jobs
- Foreign ownership of U.S. firms
- Employment issues involving immigrants
- Tax breaks offered by local and state/provincial governments to attract new businesses
- Economic impact of environmental regulations
- Government bailouts of troubled industries

Your task: Choose one of the topics from the list and conduct enough research to familiarize yourself with the topic. Identify at least three important issues that anyone involved with this topic should know about. Prepare a 10-minute presentation that introduces the topic, comments on its importance to the U.S. economy, and discusses the issues you've identified. Assume that your audience is a cross-section of business managers who don't have any particular experience in the topic you've chosen.

PORTFOLIO BUILDER

5. Check out my skill set: Describing five skills you've learned or developed in this class. Depending on the sequence your instructor chose for this course, you've probably covered at least a dozen chapters at this point and learned or improved many valuable skills. Think through your progress and identify five business communication skills that you've either learned for the first time or developed during this course.

Your task: Create a six-slide presentation (using PowerPoint or another software or online solution, as directed by your instructor), with a title slide and five slides that describe each of the five skills you've identified. Be sure to explain how each skill could help you in your career. Use any visual style that you feel is appropriate for the assignment.

6. Verizon on the horizon: Promoting the benefits of joining this communications giant. In its competitive battles with AT&T, Sprint, T-Mobile, and other carriers, Verizon competes to attract and keep not just customers but top employees. Engineers and technicians obviously play a vital role in a technology company such as Verizon, but the firm also needs specialists in everything from accounting to public relations to real estate.

Your task: Prepare a brief presentation that Verizon recruiters could use at job fairs and other venues to entice both new graduates and experienced professionals to consider joining the company. Choose a structured or free-form design and then create an appropriate number of slides for a presentation that is at least 10 minutes but no longer than 15 (not including a question-and-answer period). Assume that the audience members have heard of Verizon but don't have any in-depth knowledge about the company. You can learn more about the company and the benefits of working there by visiting www22.verizon.com/jobs.

Part 7

Writing Employment Messages and Interviewing for Jobs

The same techniques you use to succeed in your career can also help you launch and manage that career. Understand the employer's perspective on the hiring process so that you can adapt your approach and find the best job in the shortest possible time. Learn the best ways to craft a résumé and the other elements in your job search portfolio. Understand the interviewing process to make sure you're prepared for every stage and every type of interview.

18

Building Careers and Writing Résumés

Learning Objectives

After studying this chapter, you will be able to

1 Describe the approach most employers take to finding potential new employees

2 Explain the importance of networking in your career search

3 Discuss how to choose the appropriate résumé organization and list the advantages and disadvantages of the three common options

4 List the major sections of a traditional résumé

5 Identify six different formats in which you can produce a résumé

6 Describe what you should do to adapt your résumé to a scannable format

Communication Close-up at Hersha Hospitality Management

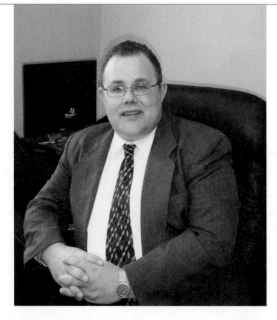

An applicant tracking system has helped Jeffrey Wade and his team at Hersha Hospitality Management efficiently recruit the customer service–driven employees on which Hersha relies.

www.hershahotels.com

For applicants, the job search process might be long and grueling, but at least it has a definite beginning, middle, and end. But for managers in charge of recruiting, such as Hersha Hospitality Management's vice president of human resources, Jeffrey Wade, the process never ends. Hersha provides operational management services to a growing number of hotels in the eastern United States, and as the company grows, its need to add top-quality employees continues.

Expansion is not the only force that puts demands on Wade and his team. "Recruiting in the hospitality industry is always a challenge because many of the positions are lower-wage jobs, and front-office positions are often filled by college students who want to move on with their careers," he explains. In other words, even as the company expands and needs to bring in more new employees, many existing employees are looking to move up and out. The result is relentless pressure to select new people to join the Hersha family. Moreover, Wade isn't interested in hiring just anybody; the company has extremely high customer service standards for everyone from entry-level hotel workers to top management.

Many managers in Wade's position, particularly in small to midsize companies, *outsource* the recruiting function, paying an outside company to find and filter candidates. However, Wade believes that recruiting is too essential to Hersha's success to be left in the hands of an outsider.

His answer to the challenge of endless hiring is to use an *applicant tracking system*, a computer-based solution that integrates the entire recruiting and employee records management effort—from job seekers' submission of online résumés and applications through interviewing, hiring, orientation, promotions, and eventual leaving of the company. Although it is highly computerized, the process is far from impersonal. In fact, by managing all the details, the system frees up Wade and his staff to spend time with applicants, assessing their personalities and potential fit with Hersha's service-oriented culture.[1]

SECURING EMPLOYMENT IN TODAY'S JOB MARKET

Hersha's approach to managing the employee application process (profiled in the chapter-opening Communication Close-up) highlights the ever-evolving nature of the job market. To keep up with the demand for good employees—and the flood of résumés coming in from all over the Internet—many companies now use some form of automation to find the best candidates and shepherd them through the selection process.

Understanding how employers approach the hiring process is just one of many insights and skills you need in order to conduct a successful job search. After you've armed yourself with knowledge of today's workplace and your potential role in it, it's time to launch an efficient, productive process to find the ideal position. (Before you read this chapter, make sure you've read the Prologue, "Building a Career with Your Communication Skills," which starts on page 25.) Figure 18.1 shows the six most important tasks in the job search process. This chapter and the Prologue discuss the first two, and Chapter 19 explores the final four.

Understanding Employers' Approach to the Employment Process

You can save considerable time and effort in your job search by understanding how employers approach the recruiting process. Look at Figure 18.2, and you'll notice that the easiest way for you to find out about new opportunities—through the employer's outside advertising—is the employer's *least-preferred* way of finding new employees. Some top employers find as

1 | **LEARNING OBJECTIVE**

Describe the approach most employers take to finding potential new employees

It's important to understand that the easiest way for you to find jobs (that is, through companies' help-wanted advertising) is the least-preferred channel for many companies to find new employees.

FIGURE 18.1   The Employment Search
Finding the ideal job opportunity is a six-step process that you might repeat a number of times during your career.

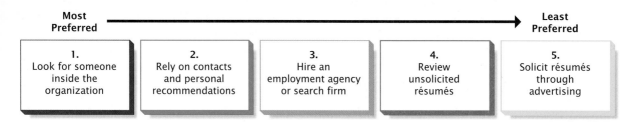

FIGURE 18.2 How Organizations Prefer to Find New Employees
Employers often prefer to look at their existing workforce to find candidates for new jobs and promotions. If no suitable candidates can be found, they begin to look outside the firm, starting with people company insiders already know.

many as 40 percent of new hires through employee referrals.[2] In fact, according to some estimates, up to 80 percent of all job openings are never advertised, a phenomenon known as the *hidden job market*.[3] In other words, employers have looked in quite a few other places before they come looking for you. To find the best opportunities, it's up to you to take action to get yourself noticed.

Beyond personal referrals, employers use a variety of methods to identify potential employees. According to one recent survey of large employers, companies' own websites are the number-one source of external hires.[4] Many employers also send representatives to college campuses and job fairs to interview students. Employers also recruit candidates through employment agencies, state-run employment services, temporary staffing services, the employment bureaus operated by some trade associations, and *headhunters* (recruiters who specialize in finding experienced executives and professionals for specific job openings). A growing number of employers now use social networking sites such as Facebook and LinkedIn to develop relationships with potential employees.[5] Employers advertise job openings in a variety of news media, through search-engine advertising, and on *job boards* such as Monster and CareerBuilder.

Major job boards such as Monster and CareerBuilder have grown so popular that some employers feel deluged with résumés from these sources, and some job seekers fear it's becoming impossible to stand out from the crowd when hundreds or thousands of people are applying for the same jobs. As a result, many specialized websites are now springing up to focus on narrow parts of the job market or offer technology that promises to do a better job of matching employers and job searchers. For example, Jobfox (**www.jobfox.com**) uses in-depth questionnaires to match employers and employees,[6] while Jobster (**www.jobster.com**) uses the latest social networking technologies to create a vast referral network that its corporate clients use to find potential employees.[7]

To keep tabs on all the applicants in various stages of the recruiting process, companies such as Hersha now use computerized **applicant tracking systems** to capture and store the hundreds or thousands of résumés they receive each year. These systems use a variety of filtering techniques to help recruiters find good prospects for current openings, so having the right terminology on your résumé is essential (see the information on keyword summaries on page 577).[8]

REAL-TIME UPDATES
Learn More

Innovative job searches using social networking

Entrepreneur Willy Franzen describes a fascinating experiment he conducted in which job seekers used advertising on Facebook to target specific employers. Go to **http://real-time updates.com/bct** and click on "Learn More." If you are using mybcommlab, you can access Real-Time Updates within each chapter or under Student Study Tools.

Organizing Your Approach to the Employment Process

The employment process can be time-consuming, so organize your efforts carefully to be efficient and maximize your chances. Begin by finding out where the job opportunities are, which industries are strong, which parts of the country are growing, and which specific job categories offer the best prospects for the future. From there you can investigate individual organizations, doing your best to learn as much about them as possible.

Staying Abreast of Business and Financial News

Thanks to the Internet, staying on top of business news is easy today. In fact, your biggest challenge will be selecting new material from the many available sources. To help you get started, here is a selection of websites of periodicals that offer business news (in some cases, you need to be a subscriber to access all the material, including archives):

- *Wall Street Journal*: http://online.wsj.com/public/us
- *New York Times*: www.nyt.com
- *USA Today*: www.usatoday.com
- *BusinessWeek*: www.businessweek.com
- *Business 2.0*: www.business2.com
- *Fast Company*: www.fastcompany.com
- *Fortune*: www.fortune.com
- *Forbes*: www.forbes.com

With so many print and electronic resources available today, it's easy to stay in touch with what's happening in the business world.

In addition, thousands of bloggers and podcasters offer news and commentary on the business world. To identify some that you might find helpful, start with directories such as Technorati (www.technorati.com/blogs/tag/business) for blogs or Podcast Alley (www.podcastalley.com; select the "Business" genre) for podcasts. For all these online resources, use a newsfeed aggregator to select the type of stories you're interested in and have them delivered to your screen automatically.

Of course, with all the business information available today, it's easy to get lost in the details. Try not to get too caught up in the daily particulars of business. Start by examining "big picture" topics—trends, issues, industrywide challenges, and careers—before delving into specific companies that look attractive.

Researching Specific Companies

Chapter 11 discusses how to find information on individual industries and companies, and it provides a list of helpful research resources. Review those sources, as well as professional journals and websites in the fields that interest you. When you've identified a promising industry and career field, consult directories of employers at your college library, at your career center, or on the web and compile a list of specific organizations that appeal to you.

In addition to using the web to find detailed information about prospective employers, you can use it to look for and respond to job openings. Most companies, even small firms, offer at least basic information about themselves on their websites. Look for the "About Us" or "Company" part of the site to find a company profile, executive biographies, press releases, financial information, and information on employment opportunities. You'll often find information about an organization's mission, products, annual reports, and employee benefits. Plus, you can often download annual reports, brochures, and other materials. Any company's website is going to present the firm in the most positive light possible, of course, so look for outside sources as well, including the business sections of local newspapers and trade publications that cover the company's industries and markets.

Go beyond every company's own communication materials; find out what others in their industries and communities think about them.

Don't limit your research to easily available sources, however. Companies are likely to be impressed by creative research, such as interviewing their customers to learn more about how the firm does business. "Detailed research, including talking to our customers, is so rare it will almost guarantee you get hired," explains the recruiting manager at Alcon Laboratories.[9]

Table 18.1 lists some of the many websites where you can learn more about companies and find job openings. Start with The Riley Guide, www.rileyguide.com, which offers links to hundreds of specialized websites that post openings in specific industries and professions. Your college's career center placement office probably maintains an up-to-date list as well.

 REAL-TIME UPDATES
Learn More

Use these checklists to organize your job search

A job search can be a long, exhausting process, but getting organized with these handy checklists will help you make the best use of your time. Go to **http://real-timeupdates.com/bct** and click on "Learn More." If you are using mybcommlab, you can access Real-Time Updates within each chapter or under Student Study Tools.

TABLE 18.1   Netting a Job on the Web

WEBSITE	URL	HIGHLIGHTS
Riley Guide	www.rileyguide.com	Vast collection of links to both general and specialized job sites for every career imaginable; don't miss this one—it'll save you hours and hours of searching
CollegeRecruiter.com	www.collegerecruiter.com	Focused on opportunities for graduates with less than three years of work experience
Monster	www.monster.com	One of the most popular job sites, with hundreds of thousands of openings, many from hard-to-find small companies; extensive collection of advice on the job search process
MonsterTrak	www.monstertrak.com	Focused on job searches for new college grads; your school's career center site probably links here
Yahoo! Hotjobs	http://hotjobs.yahoo.com	Another leading job board; like Monster and CareerBuilder, offers extensive advice for job seekers
CareerBuilder	www.careerbuilder.com	One of the largest job boards; affiliated with more than 150 newspapers around the United States
Jobster	www.jobster.com	Relatively new site that uses social networking to link employers with job seekers
USAJOBS	www.usajobs.opm.gov	The official job search site for the U.S. government, featuring everything from jobs for economists to astronauts to border patrol agents
IMDiversity	www.imdiversity.com	Good resource on diversity in the workplace, with job postings from companies that have made a special commitment to promoting diversity in their workforces
Dice.com	www.dice.com	One of the best sites for high-technology jobs
Net-Temps	www.nettemps.com	Popular site for contractors and freelancers looking for short-term assignments
WetFeet	www.wetfeet.com	Posts listings from companies looking for interns in a wide variety of professions
Simply Hired Indeed	www.simplyhired.com www.indeed.com	Specialized search engines that look for job postings on hundreds of websites worldwide; they find many postings that aren't listed on job board sites such as Monster.

*Note: This list represents only a small fraction of the hundreds of job-posting sites and other resources available online; be sure to check with your college's career center for the latest information.

2 LEARNING OBJECTIVE

Explain the importance of networking in your career search

Start networking now; your classmates could turn out to be some of your most important business contacts.

Networking

Networking is the process of making informal connections with mutually beneficial business contacts. Networking takes place wherever and whenever people talk: at industry functions, at social gatherings, at sports events and recreational activities, at alumni reunions, and so on. Social networking technologies, particularly business-oriented websites such as www.linkedin.com, www.ryze.com, and www.spoke.com, have become powerful networking resources. Read news sites, blogs, and other online sources. Participate in student business organizations, especially those with ties to professional organizations. Visit *trade shows* to learn about various industries and rub shoulders with people who work in those industries.[10] Don't overlook volunteering; you not only meet people but also demonstrate your ability to solve problems, plan projects, and so on. You can do some good while creating a network for yourself.

Remember that networking is about people helping each other, not just about other people helping you. Pay close attention to networking etiquette: Try to learn something about the people you want to connect with, don't overwhelm others with too many messages or requests, be succinct in all your communication efforts, don't give out other people's names and contact information without their permission to do so, never e-mail your résumé to complete strangers, and remember to say thank you every time someone helps you.[11]

To become a valued network member, you need to be able to help others in some way. You may not have any influential contacts yet, but because you're actively researching a number of industries and trends in your own job search, you probably have valuable information you can share. Or you might simply be able to connect one person with another who can help. The more you network, the more valuable you become in your network—and the more valuable your network becomes to you.

Remember that you need to contribute to the networking process, too.

Seeking Career Counseling

Your college's career center probably offers a wide variety of services, including individual counseling, job fairs, on-campus interviews, and job listings. Counselors can give you advice on résumé-writing software and provide workshops in job search techniques, résumé preparation, job readiness training, interview techniques, self-marketing, and more.[12] You can also find career planning advice online. Many of the websites listed in Table 18.1 offer articles and online tests to help you choose a career path, identify essential skills, and prepare to enter the job market.

Don't overlook the many resources available through your college's placement office.

PREPARING RÉSUMÉS

The job search process involves many forms of communication, but the centerpiece of this effort is a well-written résumé. Some job seekers are intimidated by the prospect of writing a résumé, but it is really just another specialized business message. Follow the three-step writing process, and it'll be easier than you think (see Figure 18.3).

Planning Your Résumé

Your résumé must be more than a simple list of the jobs you've held. It needs to tell the "story of you"—who you are, what you've accomplished, and, most importantly, what you can contribute to an organization that hires you. As with other business messages, planning a résumé means analyzing your purpose and your audience, gathering information, choosing the best medium, and organizing your content. Be prepared to craft several versions; by making simple changes in wording or organization, you can match your presentation more closely to the specific opportunities offered by particular employers.

Analyzing Your Purpose and Audience

A **résumé** is a structured, written summary of a person's education, employment background, and job qualifications. Before you begin writing a résumé, make sure you understand its true function: It is a persuasive business message intended to stimulate an employer's interest in meeting you and learning more about you (see Table 18.2). A successful résumé inspires a prospective employer to invite you to interview with the company. In other words, your purpose in writing your résumé is to create interest—*not* to tell readers every little detail.[13]

When you view your résumé as a persuasive business message, it's easier to decide what should and shouldn't be in it.

Because you've already completed a good deal of research on specific companies, you should know quite a bit about the organizations you'll be applying to. But take some time now to learn what you can about the individuals who may be reading your résumé. For example, if you learned of an opportunity through your networking efforts, chances are you'll have both a contact name and some personalized advice to help fine-tune your writing. Search online using the person's name; you might find him or her mentioned in a news release, magazine article, or blog. Any bit of information can help you craft a more effective message. Even if you can't identify a specific hiring manager, try to put yourself in his or her shoes so that you can tailor your résumé to satisfy your audience's needs. Why would that person be interested in learning more about you?

By the way, if employers ask to see your "CV," they're referring to your *curriculum vitae,* the term used instead of *résumé* in some professions and in many countries outside the

FIGURE 18.3 Three-Step Writing Process for Résumés
Following the three-step writing process will help you create a successful résumé in a short time. Remember to pay particular attention to the "you" attitude and presentation quality; your résumé will probably get tossed aside if it doesn't speak to audience needs or if it contains mistakes.

1 Plan →

Analyze the Situation
Recognize that the purpose of your résumé is to get an interview, not to get a job.

Gather Information
Research target industries and companies so that you know what they're looking for in new hires; learn about various jobs and what to expect; learn about the hiring manager, if possible.

Select the Right Medium
Start with a traditional paper résumé and develop scannable, electronic plain-text, HTML, or PDF versions, as needed. Consider using PowerPoint and video for your e-portfolio.

Organize the Information
Choose an organizational model that highlights your strengths and downplays your shortcomings; use the chronological approach unless you have a strong reason not to.

2 Write →

Adapt to Your Audience
Plan your wording carefully so that you can catch a recruiter's eye within seconds; translate your education and experience into attributes that target employers find valuable.

Compose the Message
Write clearly and succinctly, using active, powerful language that is appropriate to the industries and companies you're targeting; use a professional tone in all communications, even when using e-mail.

3 Complete

Revise the Message
Evaluate content and review readability and then edit and rewrite for conciseness and clarity.

Produce the Message
Use effective design elements and suitable layout for a clean, professional appearance; seamlessly combine text and graphical elements.

Proofread the Message
Review for errors in layout, spelling, and mechanics; mistakes can cost you interview opportunities.

Distribute the Message
Deliver your résumé following the specific instructions of each employer or job board website.

TABLE 18.2 Fallacies and Facts About Résumés

FALLACY	FACT
The purpose of a résumé is to list all your skills and abilities.	The purpose of a résumé is to kindle employer interest and generate an interview.
A good résumé will get you the job you want.	All a résumé can do is get you in the door.
Your résumé will always be read carefully and thoroughly.	In most cases, your résumé needs to make a positive impression within 30 or 45 seconds; only then will someone read it in detail. Moreover, it may be screened by a computer looking for keywords first—and if it doesn't contain the right keywords, a human being may never see it.
The more good information you present about yourself in your résumé, the better, so stuff your résumé with every positive detail you can think of.	Recruiters don't need that much information about you at the initial screening stage, and they probably won't read it.
If you want a really good résumé, have it prepared by a résumé service.	You have the skills needed to prepare an effective résumé, so prepare it yourself—unless the position is especially high level or specialized. Even then, you should check carefully before using a service.

United States. Résumés and CVs are essentially the same, although CVs can be more detailed. If you need to adapt a U.S.-style résumé to CV format, or vice versa, see Monster.com, which offers helpful guidelines on the subject.

Gathering Pertinent Information

If you haven't been building an employment portfolio thus far, you may need to do some research on yourself at this point. Gather all the pertinent personal history you can think of, including all the specific dates, duties, and accomplishments from any previous jobs you've held. Collect every piece of relevant educational experience that adds to your qualifications—formal degrees, skills certificates, academic awards, or scholarships. Also, gather any relevant information about personal endeavors: dates of your membership in associations, offices you have held in any club or professional organization, any presentations you have given to community groups. You probably won't use every piece of information you come up with, but you'll want to have it at your fingertips before you begin composing your résumé.

Selecting the Best Medium

You should expect to produce your résumé in several media; "Producing Your Résumé" on page 575 explores the various options. No matter how many different media you eventually use, however, it's always a good idea to prepare a traditional paper résumé and keep copies on hand. You never know when someone might ask for it, and not all employers want to bother with electronic media when all they want to know is your basic profile. In addition, starting with a paper résumé is a great way to organize your background information and identify your unique strengths.

Organizing Your Résumé Around Your Strengths

Organize your résumé to highlight several qualities employers seek: that you (1) think in terms of results, (2) know how to get things done, (3) are well rounded, (4) show signs of career progress and professional development, (5) have personal standards of excellence, (6) are flexible and willing to try new things, and (7) communicate effectively.

In each category, emphasize the information that does the best job of aligning your career objectives with the needs of your target employers—and that does so without distorting or misrepresenting the facts.[14] While you're pondering your strengths, you also need to consider any perceived weaknesses you may have. Do you have something in your history that might trigger an employer's red flag? Here are some common problems and quick suggestions for overcoming them:[15]

- **Frequent job changes.** If you've had a number of short-term jobs of a similar nature, such as independent contracting and temporary assignments, try to group them under a single heading. Also, if past job positions were eliminated as a result of layoffs or mergers, find a subtle way to convey that information (if not in your résumé, then in your cover letter). Reasonable employers understand that many otherwise stable employees have been forced to job hop in recent years.
- **Gaps in work history.** Mention relevant experience and education you gained during employment gaps, such as volunteer or community work. If gaps are due to personal circumstances such as injuries, illness, or caring for a relative, you can use a cover letter to offer honest but general explanations about your absences ("I had serious health concerns and had to take time off to fully recover").
- **Inexperience.** Mention related volunteer work. List relevant course work and internships. If appropriate, offer hiring incentives such as "willing to work nights and weekends."
- **Overqualification.** Tone down your résumé, focusing exclusively on the experience and skills that relate to the position.
- **Long-term employment with one company.** Itemize each position held at the firm to show career progress with increasing responsibilities.
- **Job termination for cause.** Be honest with interviewers. Show that you're a hardworking employee and counter their concerns with proof, such as recommendations and examples of completed projects.

---

3 LEARNING OBJECTIVE

Discuss how to choose the appropriate résumé organization and list the advantages and disadvantages of the three common options

The key to organizing a résumé is aligning your personal strengths with both the general and specific qualities that your target employers are looking for.

Frequent job changes and gaps in your work history are two of the most common issues that employers may perceive as weaknesses, so plan to address these if they pertain to you.

- **Criminal record.** You don't necessarily need to disclose on your résumé a criminal record or time spent incarcerated, but you may be asked about it on a job application form. Laws regarding what employers may ask (and whether they can conduct a criminal background check) vary by country and profession, but if you are asked and the question applies to you, you must answer truthfully, or you risk being terminated later if the employer finds out. Use the interview process to explain any mitigating circumstances and to emphasize your rehabilitation and commitment to being a law-abiding, trustworthy employee.[16]

To focus attention on your strongest points, adopt the appropriate organizational approach for your résumé, based on your background and your goals.

The Chronological Résumé   In a **chronological résumé**, the work experience section dominates and is placed in the most prominent slot, immediately after your name and address and optional objective. Develop this section by listing your jobs sequentially in reverse order, beginning with the most recent position. Under each listing, describe your responsibilities and accomplishments, giving the most space to the most recent and most relevant positions. If you're just graduating from college and have limited professional experience, you can vary this chronological approach by putting your educational qualifications before your experience, thereby focusing attention on your academic credentials.

The chronological résumé is the most common résumé approach, but it might not be right for you at a particular stage in your career.

The chronological approach is the most common way to organize a résumé, and many employers prefer it. This approach has three key advantages: (1) Employers are familiar with it and can easily find information, (2) it highlights growth and career progression, and (3) it highlights employment continuity and stability.[17] As vice president with Korn/Ferry International, Robert Nesbit speaks for many hiring managers and recruiters when he says, "Unless you have a really compelling reason, don't use any but the standard chronological format. Your résumé should not read like a treasure map, full of minute clues to the whereabouts of your jobs and experience. I want to be able to grasp quickly where a candidate has worked, how long, and in what capacities."[18]

The chronological approach is especially appropriate if you have a strong employment history and are aiming for a job that builds on your current career path (see Figures 18.4 and 18.5).

The functional résumé is often used by people with little employment history or with gaps in their work history, but some employers suspect that people who use this approach are trying to hide weaknesses in their backgrounds.

The Functional Résumé   A **functional résumé**, sometimes called a *skills résumé*, emphasizes your skills and capabilities while identifying employers and academic experience in subordinate sections. This pattern stresses individual areas of competence, so it's useful for people who are just entering the job market, who want to redirect their careers, or who have little continuous career-related experience. The functional approach also has three advantages: (1) Without having to read through job descriptions, employers can see what you can do for them; (2) you can emphasize earlier job experience; and (3) you can de-emphasize any lengthy unemployment or lack of career progress. However, you should be aware that because a functional résumé can obscure your work history, many employment professionals are suspicious of it—and some assume that candidates who use it are trying to hide something. In fact, Monster lists the functional résumé as one of employers' "Top 10 Pet Peeves."[19] If you don't have a strong, uninterrupted history of relevant work, the combination résumé might be a better choice.

If you don't have a lot of work history, consider a combination résumé to highlight your skills while still providing a chronological history of your employment.

The Combination Résumé   A **combination résumé** includes the best features of the chronological and functional approaches (see Figure 18.6). Nevertheless, it is not commonly used, and it has two major disadvantages: (1) It tends to be longer than a chronological résumé, and (2) it can be repetitive if you have to list your accomplishments and skills in both the functional section and the chronological job descriptions.[20]

As you look at a number of sample résumés, you'll probably notice variations on the three basic formats presented here. Study these other options in light of effective communication principles; if you find one that seems like a good fit for your unique situation, by all means use it.

FIGURE 18.4   Ineffective Chronological Résumé
This chronological résumé exhibits a wide range of problems. The language is self-centered and unprofessional, and the organization forces the reader to dig out essential details—and today's recruiters don't have the time or the patience for that. Compare this with the improved version in Figure 18.5.

Fails to provide an introductory statement of any kind, forcing the reader to piece together what this applicant is all about

Uses bulleted lists ineffectively: items are poorly organized, lack parallelism, use "I" too often, use too many words, and fail to highlight most important skills

Uses too many words to describe education and lacks parallelism

Organizes information chronologically but hides that fact with awkward format

Fails to highlight skills and attributes that will be valuable to a future employer

Fails to use headings, making it difficult to find key information

---

Roberto Cortez

5687 Crosswoods Drive, Falls Church, Virginia 22046
Home: (703) 987-0086   Office: (703) 549-6624
Email: rcortez@silvernet.com

I have been staff accountant/financial analyst at Inter-American Imports in Alexandria, Virginia, from March 2002 to present.

- I have negotiated with major suppliers.

- I speak both Spanish and German fluently, and I was recently encouraged to implement an electronic funds transfer for vendor disbursements.

- In my current position, I am responsible for preparing accounting reports.

- I have audited financial transactions.

- I have also been involved in the design of a computerized model to adjust accounts for fluctuations in currency exchange rates.

- I am skilled in the use of Excel, Access, Microsoft Dynamics, and SAP business One.

- I am deeply knowledgeable regarding Sarbox reporting.

Was staff accountant with Monsanto Agricultural Chemicals in Mexico City, Mexico (October 2001 to March 2005).

- While with Monsanto in Mexico City, I was responsible for budgeting and billing.

- I am responsible for credit-processing functions.

- I was also responsible for auditing the travel and entertainment expenses for the sales department.

- I launched an online computer system to automate all accounting functions.

- Also during this time, I was able to travel extensively in Latin America.

I have my Master of Business Administration with emphasis on international business, which I earned while attending George Mason University in Fairfax, Virginia, from 1991 to 2001.

Bachelor of Business Administration, Accounting (1996–1999), earned while attending University of Texas in Austin, Texas.

Writing Your Résumé

Your résumé is one of the most important documents you will ever write. Even so, you needn't work yourself into a panic; all the advice you need for writing effective résumés is presented in this chapter. Follow the three-step process and help ensure success by remembering four key points. First, treat your résumé with the respect it deserves. Until employers have a chance to learn more about you, you *are* your résumé, and a single mistake or oversight can cost you interview opportunities. Second, give yourself plenty of time. Don't put off preparing your résumé until the last second and then try to write it in one sitting. Third, learn from good models. You can find thousands of sample résumés online at college websites and job sites such as Monster. Fourth, don't get frustrated by the conflicting advice you read about résumés. Résumés are more art than science, and there is more than one way to be successful with them. Consider the alternatives and choose the approach that makes the most sense to you, given everything you know about successful business communication.

Early in the evaluation process, your résumé might be the only information employers have about you, so make sure that information is clear and compelling.

FIGURE 18.5 Effective Chronological Résumé

This version does a much better job of presenting the candidate's ability to contribute to a new employer. Notice in particular how easy it is to scan through this résumé to find sections of interest.

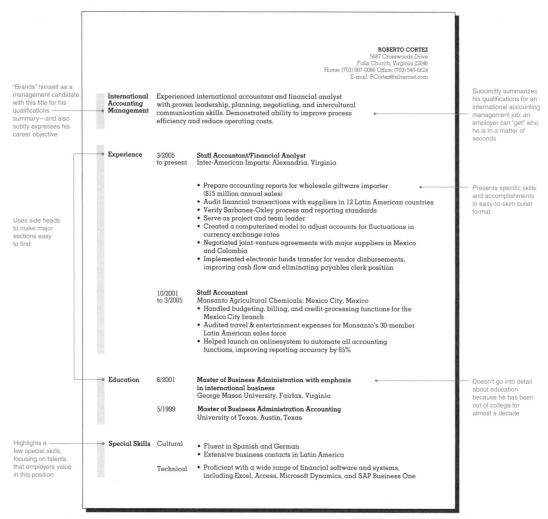

"Brands" himself as a management candidate with this title for his qualifications summary—and also subtly expresses his career objective

Uses side heads to make major sections easy to find

Highlights a few special skills, focusing on talents that employers value in this position

ROBERTO CORTEZ
5687 Crosswoods Drive
Falls Church, Virginia 22046
Home: (703) 987-0086 Office: (703) 549-6624
E-mail: RCortez@silvernet.com

International Accounting Management

Experienced international accountant and financial analyst with proven leadership, planning, negotiating, and intercultural communication skills. Demonstrated ability to improve process efficiency and reduce operating costs.

Experience

3/2005 to present

Staff Accountant/Financial Analyst
Inter-American Imports: Alexandria, Virginia

- Prepare accounting reports for wholesale giftware importer ($15 million annual sales)
- Audit financial transactions with suppliers in 12 Latin American countries
- Verify Sarbanes-Oxley process and reporting standards
- Serve as project and team leader
- Created a computerized model to adjust accounts for fluctuations in currency exchange rates
- Negotiated joint-venture agreements with major suppliers in Mexico and Colombia
- Implemented electronic funds transfer for vendor disbursements, improving cash flow and eliminating payables clerk position

10/2001 to 3/2005

Staff Accountant
Monsanto Agricultural Chemicals: Mexico City, Mexico
- Handled budgeting, billing, and credit-processing functions for the Mexico City branch
- Audited travel & entertainment expenses for Monsanto's 30-member Latin American sales force
- Helped launch an onlinesystem to automate all accounting functions, improving reporting accuracy by 65%

Education

6/2001

Master of Business Administration with emphasis in international business
George Mason University, Fairfax, Virginia

5/1999

Master of Business Administration Accounting
University of Texas, Austin, Texas

Special Skills

Cultural
- Fluent in Spanish and German
- Extensive business contacts in Latin America

Technical
- Proficient with a wide range of financial software and systems, including Excel, Access, Microsoft Dynamics, and SAP Business One

Succinctly summarizes his qualifications for an international accounting management job; an employer can "get" who he is in a matter of seconds

Presents specific skills and accomplishments in easy-to-skim bullet format

Doesn't go into detail about education because he has been out of college for almost a decade

---

1 Plan →

Analyze the Situation
Decide on the best way to combine finance and international experience.

Gather Information
Research target positions to identify key employer needs.

Select the Right Medium
Start with a traditional paper résumé and develop scannable or plain-text versions as needed.

Organize the Information
Open with a qualifications summary that also signals the career objective; choose the chronological format since it fits this strong employment history perfectly.

2 Write →

Adapt to Your Audience
Translate specific experience into general qualifications that all multinational companies will find valuable.

Compose the Message
Write clearly and succinctly, using active, powerful language that is appropriate to the accounting management profession.

3 Complete

Revise the Message
Evaluate content and review readability, clarity, and accuracy.

Produce the Message
Use effective design elements and suitable layout for a clean, professional appearance.

Proofread the Message
Review for errors in layout, spelling, and mechanics.

Distribute the Message
Deliver the résumé and other employment messages following the specific instructions of each employer or job board website.

FIGURE 18.6 Combination Résumé

With her limited work experience in her field of interest, Erica Vorkamp opted for a combination résumé to highlight her skills. Her employment history is complete and easy to find, but it isn't featured to the same degree as the other elements. Note that even though this is a webpage, she mimicked a conventional résumé design to make her information easy to find. Having an HTML version as part of her e-portfolio also lets her provide instant links to other information, such as samples of her work and testimonials from people who have worked with her in the past.

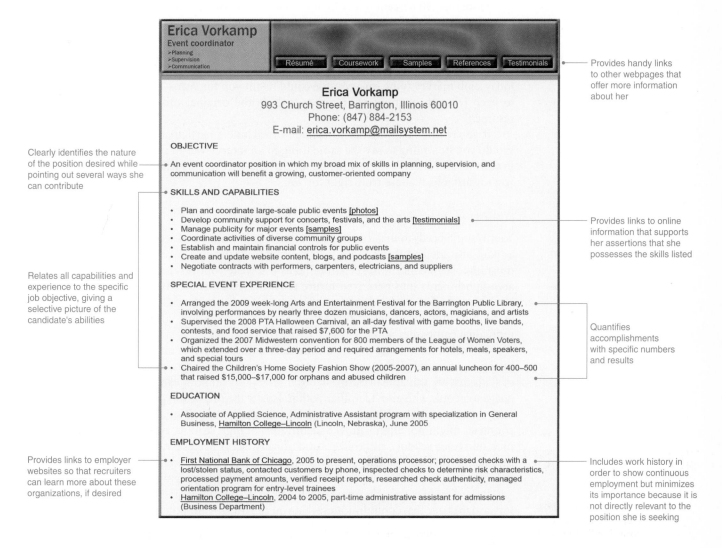

Provides handy links to other webpages that offer more information about her

Clearly identifies the nature of the position desired while pointing out several ways she can contribute

Relates all capabilities and experience to the specific job objective, giving a selective picture of the candidate's abilities

Provides links to online information that supports her assertions that she possesses the skills listed

Quantifies accomplishments with specific numbers and results

Provides links to employer websites so that recruiters can learn more about these organizations, if desired

Includes work history in order to show continuous employment but minimizes its importance because it is not directly relevant to the position she is seeking

If you feel uncomfortable writing about yourself, you're not alone. Many people, even accomplished writers, find it difficult to write their own résumés. If you get stuck, find a classmate or friend who is also writing a résumé and swap projects for a while. By working on each other's résumés, you might be able to speed up the process for both of you.

Keeping Your Résumé Honest

Somehow, the idea that "everybody lies on their résumés" has crept into popular consciousness, and dishonesty in the job search process has reached epidemic proportions. Estimates vary, but one comprehensive study uncovered lies about work history in more than 40 percent of the résumés tested.[21] And it's not just the simple fudging of facts here and there. Dishonest applicants are getting bolder all the time—going so far as to buy fake diplomas online, pay a computer hacker to insert their names into prestigious universities' graduation records, and sign up for services that offer phony employment verification.[22]

Applicants with integrity know they don't need to stoop to lying to compete in the job market. If you are tempted to stretch the truth, bear in mind that professional recruiters

Applicants with integrity know they don't need to lie on their résumés to catch the attention of potential employers.

have seen every trick in the book, and employers who are fed up with the dishonesty are getting more aggressive at uncovering the truth. Nearly all employers do some form of background checking, from contacting references to verifying employment to checking for criminal records. In addition to using their own resources, U.S. companies now spend more than $2 billion each year on outside services that specialize in verifying résumés and application information.[23] Employers are also beginning to craft certain interview questions specifically to uncover dishonest résumé entries.[24]

More than 90 percent of companies that find lies on résumés refuse to hire the offending applicants, even if that means withdrawing formal job offers.[25] And even if you do sneak past these filters and get hired, you'll probably be exposed on the job when you can't live up to your own résumé. Résumé fabrications have been known to catch up to people many years into their careers, with embarrassing consequences. Given the networked nature of today's job market, lying on a résumé could haunt you for years—and you could be forced to keep lying throughout your career to hide the original misrepresentations on your résumé.[26]

If you're not sure whether to include or exclude a particular point, ask yourself this: Would you be willing to say the same thing to an interviewer in person? If not, don't say it in your résumé. Keep your résumé honest so that it represents who you really are and leads you toward jobs that are truly right for you.

Adapting Your Résumé to Your Audience

One of the biggest challenges in writing a résumé is to make your unique qualities quickly apparent to readers; they won't search through details if you don't look like an appealing candidate.

Your résumé needs to make a positive impression in a matter of seconds, so be sure to adopt a "you" attitude and think about your résumé from the employer's perspective. The single most important concept to keep in mind as you write your résumé is to translate your past accomplishments into perceived future potential. In other words, employers are certainly interested in what you've done for other organizations in the past, but they're more interested in what you can do for them in the future. If necessary, customize your résumé for individual companies, too.

You may also need to translate your skills and experiences into the terminology of the hiring organization. For instance, military experience can help a person develop a number of skills that are valuable in business, but military terminology can sound like a foreign language to people who aren't familiar with it. Isolate the important general concepts and present them in common business language. Similarly, educational achievements in other countries might not align with U.S. definitions of high schools, community colleges, technical and trade schools, and colleges and universities. If necessary, include a brief statement explaining how your degree or certificate relates to U.S. expectations—or how your U.S. degree relates to expectations in other countries, if you're applying for work abroad.

Although your résumé is a highly factual document, it should still tell the "story of you," giving readers a clear picture of the sort of employee you are.

Regardless of your background, it's up to you to combine your experiences into a straightforward message that communicates what you can do for your potential employer.[27] Think in terms of an image or a theme you'd like to project. Are you academically gifted? A strong leader? A well-rounded person? A creative genius? A technical wizard? By knowing yourself and your audience, you'll be able to focus on the strengths that potential employers want.

Composing Your Résumé

Draft your résumé using short, crisp phrases built around strong verbs and nouns.

Write your résumé using a simple and direct style. Use short, crisp phrases instead of whole sentences and focus on what your reader needs to know. Avoid using the word *I*, which can sound both self-involved and repetitive by the time you outline all your skills and accomplishments. Instead, start your phrases with strong action verbs such as these:[28]

accomplished	assumed	coordinated	explored	initiated
achieved	budgeted	created	forecasted	installed
administered	chaired	demonstrated	generated	introduced
approved	changed	developed	identified	investigated
arranged	compiled	directed	implemented	joined
assisted	completed	established	improved	launched

maintained	participated	recommended	set up	supervised
managed	performed	reduced	simplified	systematized
motivated	planned	reorganized	sparked	targeted
operated	presented	resolved	streamlined	trained
organized	proposed	saved	strengthened	transformed
oversaw	raised	served	succeeded	upgraded

For instance, you might say, "Created a campus organization for students interested in entrepreneurship" or "Managed a fast-food restaurant and four employees." Whenever you can, quantify the results so that your claims don't come across as empty puffery. Don't just say you're a team player or detail oriented—show you are by offering concrete proof.[29] Here are some examples of phrasing accomplishments using active statements that show results:

AVOID WEAK STATEMENTS	USE ACTIVE STATEMENTS THAT SHOW RESULTS
Responsible for developing a new filing system	Developed a new filing system that reduced paperwork by 50 percent
I was in charge of customer complaints and all ordering problems	Handled all customer complaints and resolved all product order discrepancies
I won a trip to Europe for opening the most new customer accounts in my department	Generated the highest number of new customer accounts in my department
Member of special campus task force to resolve student problems with existing cafeteria assignments	Assisted in implementing new campus dining program that balances student wishes with cafeteria capacity

Providing specific supporting evidence is vital but make sure you don't go overboard with small details.[30]

Name and Contact Information Your name and contact information constitute the heading of your résumé; include the following:

- Name
- Physical address (both permanent and temporary, if you're likely to move during the job search process; however, if you're posting a résumé in an unsecured location online, leave off your physical address for security purposes)
- E-mail address
- Phone number(s)
- The URL of your personal webpage or e-portfolio (if you have one)

Be sure that everything in your résumé heading is well organized and clearly laid out on the page.

If the only e-mail address you have is through your current employer, get a free personal e-mail address from one of the many services that offer them. It's not fair to your current employer to use company resources for a job search; moreover, it sends a bad signal to potential employers. Also, if your personal e-mail address is anything like precious .princess@something.com or PsychoDawg@something.com, get a new e-mail address for your business correspondence.

Introductory Statement Of all the parts of a résumé, the brief introductory statement that follows your name and contact information probably generates the most disagreement. You can put one of three things here:[31]

- **Career objective.** A career objective identifies either a specific job you want to land or a general career track you would like to pursue. Some experts advise against including a career objective because it can categorize you so narrowly that you miss out on interesting opportunities, and it is essentially about fulfilling your desires, not about meeting the employer's needs. In the past, most résumés included a career objective, but in

4 LEARNING OBJECTIVE

List the major sections of a traditional résumé

Be sure to provide complete and accurate contact information; mistakes in this section of the résumé are surprisingly common.

If you don't already have one, get a professional-sounding e-mail address for business correspondence (such as firstname.lastname@ something.com), *if you don't already have one.*

If you choose to open with a career objective, make sure it is phrased in terms of meeting an employer's *needs, not* your *needs.*

recent years more job seekers are using a qualifications summary or a career summary. However, if you have little or no work experience in your target profession, a career objective might be your best option. If you do opt for an objective, word it in a way that relates your qualifications to employer needs (see Figure 18.6 on page 569). Avoid such self-absorbed (but all too common) statements as "A fulfilling position that provides ample opportunity for career growth and personal satisfaction."

A qualifications summary gives a quick overview of the value you can offer an employer.

- **Qualifications summary.** A qualifications summary offers a brief view of your key qualifications. The goal is to let a reader know within a few seconds what you can deliver. You can title this section generically as "Qualifications Summary" or "Summary of Qualifications," or if you have one dominant qualification, you can use that as the title (see the career summary in Figure 18.5 on page 568 for an example). Consider using a qualifications summary if you have one or more important qualifications but don't yet have a long career history. Also, if haven't been working long but your college education has given you a dominant professional "theme," such as multimedia design or taxation, you can craft a qualifications summary that highlights your educational preparedness.
- **Career summary.** A career summary offers a brief recap of your career, with the goal of presenting increasing levels of responsibility and performance. A career summary can be particularly useful for executives who have demonstrated the ability to manage increasingly larger and more complicated business operations—a key consideration when companies look to hire upper-level managers.

Your education is likely to be one of your strongest selling points, so think carefully about how to present it.

Education   If you're still in school, education is probably your strongest selling point. Present your educational background in depth, choosing facts that support your "theme." Give this section a heading such as "Education," "Technical Training," or "Academic Preparation," as appropriate. Then, starting with the most recent, list the name and location of each school you have attended, the month and year of your graduation (say "anticipated graduation in _____" if you haven't graduated yet), your major and minor fields of study, significant skills and abilities you've developed in your course work, and the degrees or certificates you've earned. If you're still working toward a degree, include in parentheses the expected date of completion. Showcase your qualifications by listing courses that have directly equipped you for the job you are seeking and indicate any scholarships, awards, or academic honors you've received.

The education section should also include relevant training sponsored by business or government organizations. Mention high school or military training only if the associated achievements are pertinent to your career goals.

Whether you list your grade point average depends on the job you want and the quality of your grades. If you don't show your GPA on your résumé—and there's no rule saying you have to—be prepared to answer questions about it during the interview process because many employers will assume that your GPA is not spectacular if you didn't show it on your résumé. If you choose to show a grade point average, be sure to mention the scale, especially if it isn't a four-point scale. If your grades are better within your major than in other courses, you can also list your GPA as "Major GPA" and include only those courses within your major.

When you describe past job responsibilities, be sure to relate them to the needs of potential employers; identify the skills and knowledge from these previous jobs that you can apply to a future job.

Work Experience, Skills, and Accomplishments   Like the education section, the work experience section should focus on your overall theme. Align your past with the employer's future. Call attention to the skills you've developed on the job and to your ability to handle increasing responsibility.

List your jobs in reverse chronological order (starting with the most recent). Include military service and any internships and part-time or temporary jobs related to your career objective. Include the name and location of the employer, and if readers are unlikely to recognize the organization, briefly describe what it does. When you want to keep the name of your current employer confidential, you can identify the firm by industry only ("a large video game developer"). If an organization's name or location has changed since you worked there, state the current name and location and include the old information preceded by "formerly . . ." Before or after each job listing, state your job title and list the years you worked in the job; use the phrase "to present" to denote current employment. Indicate whether a job was part time.

Devote the most space to the jobs that are related to your target position. If you were personally responsible for something significant, be sure to mention it ("Devised a new collection system that accelerated payment of overdue receivables"). Facts about your skills and accomplishments are the most important information you can give a prospective employer, so quantify them whenever possible:

Whenever you can, quantify your accomplishments in numeric terms: sales increases, customer satisfaction scores, measured productivity, and so on.

> Created an online ad campaign that increased sales by 9 percent
> Raised $2,500 in 15 days for cancer research

One helpful exercise is to write a 30-second "commercial" for each major skill you want to highlight. The commercial should offer proof that you really do possess the skill. For your résumé, distill the commercials down to brief phrases; you can use the more detailed proof statements in cover letters and as answers to interview questions.[32]

If you've held a number of part-time, temporary, or entry-level jobs that don't relate to your career objective, you have to use your best judgment when it comes to including or excluding them. On the one hand, employers will be impressed by the fact that you can land and keep jobs while you're progressing toward your career goals. On the other hand, too many minor and irrelevant work details can clutter your résumé, particularly if you've been in the professional workforce for a few years. Generally speaking, if you don't have a long employment history, use these jobs to show your ability and willingness to work.

You can also include information describing other aspects of your background that pertain to your career objective, such as fluency in multiple languages. If samples of your work might increase your chances of getting a job, insert a line at the end of your résumé, offering to supply them on request or indicating that they're available in your e-portfolio.

Activities and Achievements Include activities and achievements outside of a work context only if they make you a more attractive job candidate. For example, membership in the Toastmasters public-speaking organization shows an interest in becoming a better communicator, which is something every smart employer values. Similarly, artistic awards could weigh in your favor if you are applying for work at a web design company or an advertising agency. However, unless you are applying to a running-shoe company such as Nike or New Balance, the fact that you are a long-distance runner is irrelevant. Also consider mentioning publications and other accomplishments that required relevant business skills.

Don't overlook personal accomplishments that indicate special skills or qualities, but make sure they are relevant to the jobs you're seeking.

Because many employers are involved in their local communities, they tend to look positively on applicants who are active and concerned members of their communities as well. Consider including community service activities that suggest leadership, teamwork, communication skills, technical aptitude, or other valuable attributes.

You should generally avoid indicating membership or significant activity in religious or political organizations (unless, of course, you're applying to such an organization) because doing so might raise concerns for people with differing beliefs or affiliations. However, if you want to highlight skills you developed while involved with such a group, you can refer to it generically as a "not-for-profit organization."

Finally, if you have little or no job experience and not much to discuss outside your education, indicating involvement in athletics or other organized student activities lets employers know that you don't spend all your free time hanging around your apartment, playing video games. However, this information becomes increasingly irrelevant the longer you have been out of school.

Personal Data In nearly all instances, your résumé should not include any personal data beyond the information described in the previous sections. When applying to U.S. companies, never include any of the following: physical characteristics, age, gender, marital status, sexual orientation, religious or political affiliations, race, national origin, salary history,

Do not include any personal data unless there is a specific reason to do so (there rarely is).

Communication Miscues

Don't. Just Don't.

Even though employment recruiters might think they've seen it all by now, innovative job applicants will keep finding new ways to get their résumés tossed into the recycling bin. Here are a few examples for your amusement—and warning, if you're inclined to share a little too much information:

- The passing of a beloved pet is never easy, but should grief over a departed cat keep someone out of the workforce for three months? That's how one job applicant explained a three-month gap in his employment history.
- One applicant's résumé arrived in an envelope that had a picture of a car on it, along with an explanation saying this would be a gift for the hiring manager.
- A person's family medical history is obviously important to him or her, but it's not something to put on a résumé, as one job seeker did, for reasons unknown.
- In a valiant effort to cram as many mistakes as possible onto a single page, one creative candidate included a full body photo of herself—in thigh-high boots, no less—and used oversized, fluorescent pink paper. This résumé probably did look pretty as it fluttered off a recruiter's desk into the trash can.

- Expressing strong interest in a job is good, but not if that interest in expressed like this: "to keep my parole officer from putting me back in jail."
- One applicant's mother was proud of her, to be sure, but including a letter from her with a résumé made the applicant look like, well, a child.

These cringe-inducing blunders are worth more than a quick chuckle: They're a great reminder of why it is crucial to understand the purpose of a résumé and the effect a résumé has on hiring managers.

CAREER APPLICATIONS

1. Is it a good idea to "show some personality" in your résumé? Explain your answer.
2. How should you handle the employment section of your résumé if you really did take three months off work to grieve the loss of a pet?

---

reasons for leaving jobs, names of previous supervisors, names of references, Social Security number, or student ID number. Also, never include a photo on or with your résumé—some employers won't even look at résumés with photos for fear of being accused of discrimination based on personal characteristics.[33]

Note that standards can vary in other countries. For example, you might be expected to include your citizenship, nationality, or marital status.[34] However, verify such requirements before including any personal data.

Prepare a list of references, using the same design and layout as your résumé.

The availability of references is usually assumed, so you don't need to put "References available upon request" at the end of your résumé. However, be sure to have a list of several references ready when you begin applying for jobs; you will probably be asked for it at some point in the selection process. Prepare your reference sheet with your name and contact information at the top. For a finished look, use the same design and layout you use for your résumé. Then list three or four people who have agreed to serve as references. (Don't list anyone who hasn't agreed to be listed.) Include each person's name, job title, organization, address, telephone number, and e-mail address (if the reference prefers to be contacted by e-mail).

Completing Your Résumé

As with any other business message, completing your résumé involves revising it for quality, producing it in an appropriate form, and proofreading it for any errors before distributing it to your target employers.

The ideal length of your résumé depends on the depth of your experience and the level of the positions for which you are applying. As a general guideline, if you have fewer than 10 years of professional experience, try to keep your résumé to one page. If you have more experience and are applying for a higher-level position, you may need to prepare a somewhat longer résumé.[35] For highly technical positions, longer résumés are often the norm as well because the qualifications for such jobs can require more description.

Revising Your Résumé

Ask professional recruiters to list the most common mistakes they see on résumés, and you'll hear the same things over and over again. Keep your résumé out of the recycling bin by avoiding these flaws:

- **Too long.** The résumé is not concise, relevant, and to the point.
- **Too short or sketchy.** The résumé does not give enough information for a proper evaluation of the applicant.
- **Difficult to read.** The résumé lacks enough white space and devices such as indentations and boldfacing to make the reader's job easier.
- **Wordy.** Descriptions are verbose, using numerous words to describe simple concepts.
- **Amateurish.** The résumé includes the wrong information or presents it awkwardly, which indicates that the applicant has little understanding of the business world or of a particular industry.
- **Poorly produced.** The print is faint and difficult to read or the paper is cheap and inappropriate.
- **Full of spelling and grammar errors.** The document contains spelling and grammar mistakes which indicate that the candidate lacks communication skills and attention to quality.
- **Boastful.** The overconfident tone makes the reader wonder whether the applicant's self-evaluation is realistic.
- **Too generic.** The applicant failed to show how his or her qualifications match the needs of the specific job opening.
- **Gimmicky.** The words, structure, decoration, or material used in the résumé depart so far from the usual as to make the résumé ineffective.

Avoid common errors that will get your résumé excluded from consideration.

Producing Your Résumé

Good design is a must, and it's not difficult to achieve. As you can see in Figures 18.5 and 18.6, good designs are simple, are clearly organized, have plenty of white space, and use straightforward typefaces such as Times Roman or Arial. (Keep in mind that many of the fonts on your computer are not appropriate for a résumé.) Make your subheadings easy to find and easy to read, placing them either above each section or in the left margin. Use lists to itemize important points. Color is not necessary by any means, but if you add color, make it subtle and sophisticated, such as using a thin horizontal line under your name and address. The most common way to get into trouble with résumé design is going overboard (see Figure 18.7). An amateurish design could end your chances of getting an interview. As one experienced recruiter put it recently, "At our office, these résumés are rejected without even being read."[36] Of course, if you are applying for a graphic design position or some other opportunity in which visual creativity is expected, you can certainly use your résumé as a way to demonstrate your design skills.[37]

Effective résumé designs are simple, clean, and professional—not gaudy, clever, or cute.

Depending on the companies you apply to, you might want to produce your résumé in as many as six forms (all are explained in the following sections):

- Printed traditional résumé
- Printed scannable résumé
- Electronic plain-text file
- Microsoft Word file
- HTML format
- PDF file

5 LEARNING OBJECTIVE

Identify six different formats in which you can produce a résumé

Some applicants also create PowerPoint presentations or videos to supplement a conventional résumé. Two key advantages of a PowerPoint supplement are flexibility and multimedia capabilities. For instance, you can present a menu of choices on the opening screen and allow viewers to click through to such items as a brief biography or photos that document important accomplishments (such as screen shots of websites you designed).

Start with a traditional printed résumé but realize that you may need to create several other versions during your job search.

A video résumé can be a compelling supplement as well, but videos are not without controversy. Some employment law experts advise employers not to view videos, at least not until

Using a PowerPoint presentation or a video can be a great way to supplement your résumé, but not all employers will view them.

FIGURE 18.7   Ineffective Résumé Design

This résumé tries too hard to be creative and eye-catching, resulting in a document that is difficult to read—and that probably won't get read. Recruiters have seen every conceivable design gimmick, so don't try to stand out from the crowd with unusual design. Instead, provide compelling, employer-focused information that is easy to find.

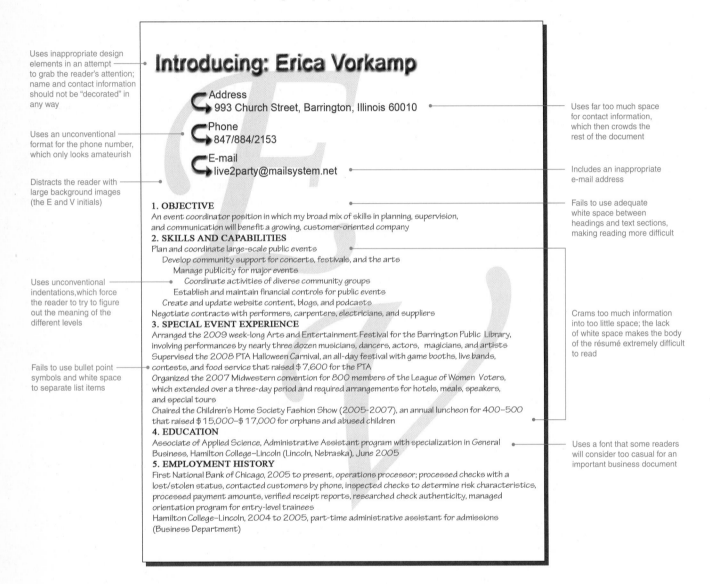

after candidates have been evaluated solely on their credentials. The reason for this caution is the same as with photographs: Seeing visual cues of the age, ethnicity, and gender of candidates early in the selection process exposes employers to complaints of discriminatory hiring practices. In addition, videos are more cumbersome to evaluate than paper or electronic résumés.[38]

Strive for a clean, classy look in your printed résumé, using professional-grade paper and a clean, high-quality printer.

Printing a Traditional Résumé   The traditional paper résumé still has a place in this world of electronic job searches, if only to have a few copies ready whenever one of your networking contacts asks for one. Avoid basic, low-cost white bond paper intended for general office use and gimmicky papers with borders and backgrounds. Choose a heavier, higher-quality paper designed specifically for résumés and other important documents. White or slightly off-white is the best color choice. This paper is more expensive than general office paper, but you don't need much, and it's a worthwhile investment.

When you're ready to print your résumé, use a well-maintained, quality printer. Don't tolerate any streaks, stray lines, or poor print quality. You wouldn't walk into an interview looking messy, so make sure your résumé doesn't look that way, either.

Printing a Scannable Résumé   To cope with the flood of unsolicited paper résumés in recent years, many companies now optically scan incoming résumés into applicant tracking systems that hiring managers can search for attractive candidates. Whether they use simpler keyword matching or sophisticated linguistic analysis, these systems display lists of possible candidates, each with a percentage score indicating how closely the résumé reflects a given position's requirements.[39] Nearly all large companies now use these systems, as do many midsized companies and even some small firms.[40]

The use of scanning has important implications for your résumé. First, computers are interested only in matching information to search parameters, not in artistic attempts at résumé design. In fact, complex designs can cause errors in the scanning process. Second, *optical character recognition* (*OCR*) software doesn't technically "read" anything; it merely looks for shapes that match stored profiles of characters. If OCR software can't make sense of your fancy fonts or creative page layout, it will enter gibberish into the database (for instance, your name might go in as "W<$..3r·?00!#" instead of "Walter Jones"). Third, even the most sophisticated databases cannot conduct a search with the nuance and intuition of an experienced human recruiter.

For job searchers, this situation creates two requirements for a successful scannable résumé: (1) Use a plain font and simplified design and (2) compile a **keyword summary** that lists all the terms that could help match your résumé to the right openings. Other than the keyword summary, a scannable résumé contains the same information as your traditional résumé but is formatted to be OCR friendly (see Figure 18.8):[41]

- Use a clean sans serif font such as Verdana or Arial and size it between 10 and 14 points.
- Make sure characters do not touch one another, including the slash (/).
- Don't use side-by-side columns.
- Don't use ampersands (&), percent signs (%), accented characters (such as é and ö), or bullet symbols (use a hyphen, not a lowercase *o*, in place of a bullet symbol).
- Put each phone number and e-mail address on its own line.
- Print on plain white paper.

Your scannable résumé will probably be longer than your traditional résumé because you can't compress text into multiple columns and because you need plenty of white space between headings and sections. If your scannable résumé runs more than one page, make sure your name appears on each subsequent page (in case the pages become separated). Before sending a scannable résumé, check the company's website or call the human resources department to see whether it has any specific requirements other than those discussed here.

When adding a keyword summary (see Figure 18.8) to your résumé, keep your audience in mind. Employers generally search for nouns (because verbs tend to be generic rather than specific to a particular position or skill), so make your keywords nouns as well. Use abbreviations sparingly and only when they are well known and unambiguous, such as *MBA*. List 20 to 30 words and phrases that define your skills, experience, education, and professional affiliations as they relate to your target position. Place this list right after your name and address. Note that you can also use your keywords as tags on your blog, social networking profile, or other elements of your online presence.[42]

One good way to identify which keywords to include in your summary is to find all the skills listed in ads for the types of jobs you're interested in. Another advantage of staying up to date with industry news and networking widely is that you'll develop a good ear for current terminology.

If you're tempted to toss in impressive keywords that don't really apply to you, don't. Increasingly sophisticated résumé analysis systems can now detect whether your keywords truly relate to the job descriptions and other information on your résumé. If a system suspects that you've padded your keyword list, it could move you to the bottom of the ranking or delete your résumé.[43]

6 LEARNING OBJECTIVE

Describe what you should do to adapt your résumé to a scannable format

Think carefully about the keywords you include in your scannable résumé; they need to appeal to recruiters and reflect your qualities accurately.

REAL-TIME UPDATES
Learn More

Practical advice on preparing a scannable résumé

Take advantage of these great tips on successfully transforming your résumé for optical scanning. Go to **http://real-timeupdates.com/bct** and click on "Learn More." If you are using mybcommlab, you can access Real-Time Updates within each chapter or under Student Study Tools.

FIGURE 18.8 Scannable Résumé

This version of the chronological résumé from Figure 18.5 shows the changes necessary to ensure successful scanning. Notice that the résumé doesn't have any special characters, formatting, or design elements that are likely to confuse the scanning software.

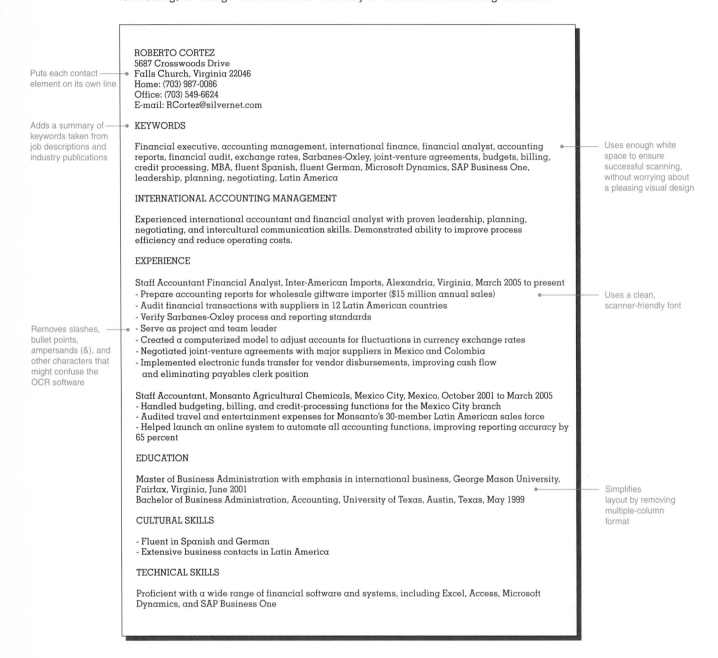

Puts each contact element on its own line

Adds a summary of keywords taken from job descriptions and industry publications

Removes slashes, bullet points, ampersands (&), and other characters that might confuse the OCR software

Uses enough white space to ensure successful scanning, without worrying about a pleasing visual design

Uses a clean, scanner-friendly font

Simplifies layout by removing multiple-column format

ROBERTO CORTEZ
5687 Crosswoods Drive
Falls Church, Virginia 22046
Home: (703) 987-0086
Office: (703) 549-6624
E-mail: RCortez@silvernet.com

KEYWORDS

Financial executive, accounting management, international finance, financial analyst, accounting reports, financial audit, exchange rates, Sarbanes-Oxley, joint-venture agreements, budgets, billing, credit processing, MBA, fluent Spanish, fluent German, Microsoft Dynamics, SAP Business One, leadership, planning, negotiating, Latin America

INTERNATIONAL ACCOUNTING MANAGEMENT

Experienced international accountant and financial analyst with proven leadership, planning, negotiating, and intercultural communication skills. Demonstrated ability to improve process efficiency and reduce operating costs.

EXPERIENCE

Staff Accountant Financial Analyst, Inter-American Imports, Alexandria, Virginia, March 2005 to present
- Prepare accounting reports for wholesale giftware importer ($15 million annual sales)
- Audit financial transactions with suppliers in 12 Latin American countries
- Verify Sarbanes-Oxley process and reporting standards
- Serve as project and team leader
- Created a computerized model to adjust accounts for fluctuations in currency exchange rates
- Negotiated joint-venture agreements with major suppliers in Mexico and Colombia
- Implemented electronic funds transfer for vendor disbursements, improving cash flow
  and eliminating payables clerk position

Staff Accountant, Monsanto Agricultural Chemicals, Mexico City, Mexico, October 2001 to March 2005
- Handled budgeting, billing, and credit-processing functions for the Mexico City branch
- Audited travel and entertainment expenses for Monsanto's 30-member Latin American sales force
- Helped launch an online system to automate all accounting functions, improving reporting accuracy by 65 percent

EDUCATION

Master of Business Administration with emphasis in international business, George Mason University, Fairfax, Virginia, June 2001
Bachelor of Business Administration, Accounting, University of Texas, Austin, Texas, May 1999

CULTURAL SKILLS

- Fluent in Spanish and German
- Extensive business contacts in Latin America

TECHNICAL SKILLS

Proficient with a wide range of financial software and systems, including Excel, Access, Microsoft Dynamics, and SAP Business One

---

A plain-text version of your résumé is simply a computer file without any of the formatting that you typically apply using a word-processing program.

Creating a Plain-Text File of Your Résumé Many employers now prefer to enter résumé information directly into their tracking systems through the use of **plain-text versions** (sometimes referred to as *ASCII text versions*). This approach has the same goal as a scannable résumé, but it's faster, easier, and less prone to errors than the scanning process. If you have the option of mailing a scannable résumé or submitting plain text online, go with plain text. Note that a plain-text version should include a keyword summary (see the previous section).

In addition, when employers or networking contacts ask you to e-mail your résumé, they'll often want to receive it in plain-text format in the body of your e-mail message. Thanks to the prevalence of computer viruses these days, many employers will refuse to open an e-mail attachment. Plain text is also helpful when you're completing online application forms; simply copy and paste from your plain-text file into the appropriate fields.

Plain text is just what it sounds like: no font selections, no bullet symbols, no colors, no lines or boxes, and so on. A plain-text version is easy to create with word-processing software. Start with the file you used to create your traditional printed résumé, use the "Save As" choice to save it as "plain text" or whichever similarly labeled option your software has, and then verify the result.

The verification step is crucial because you need to be sure about what happens to your layout. Open the text file to view the layout but don't use your word-processing software; instead, open the file with a basic text editor (such as Microsoft's Notepad) so that the text doesn't get reformatted in any way. If necessary, adjust the page manually, moving text and inserting spaces as needed. For simplicity's sake, left justify all your headings rather than try to center them manually. You can put headings in all caps to separate them from blocks of text.

Make sure you verify the plain-text file that you create with a word-processing program and adjust it as needed.

Creating a Word File of Your Résumé   In some cases, an employer or a job-posting website will let you upload a Microsoft Word file directly. (Although there are certainly other word-processing programs on the market, Microsoft Word is the de facto standard in business these days.) Read the instructions on each site carefully. For instance, you can upload a Word résumé to Monster, but the site asks you to follow some specific formatting instructions to make sure your file doesn't become garbled.[44]

Before you submit a Word file to anyone, make sure your computer system is virus free. Infecting a potential employer's PC is not a way to make a good first impression.

Creating an HTML Version of Your Résumé   You can probably find several uses for an HTML (webpage) version of your résumé, including sending it as a fully formatted e-mail message and including it in your e-portfolio. A key advantage of an HTML version is that you can provide links to supporting details and other materials from within your résumé. Even if you don't have HTML experience, you can save your résumé as a webpage from within Word. This method won't necessarily create the most spectacularly beautiful webpage, but it should at least be functional.

You have many options for posting your résumé online. Remember that you could be displaying your personal information for all the world to see, so think carefully about privacy and security.

As you design your HTML résumé, think of important keywords to use as hyperlinks—words that will grab an employer's attention and make the recruiter want to click on that hyperlink to learn more about you. You can link to papers you've written, recommendations you've received, and sound or video clips that directly support your résumé. However, be sure to have permission to publish or link to material created for a previous employer.

Creating a PDF Version of Your Résumé   Creating a PDF version of your résumé is a simple procedure, but you need the right software. Adobe Acrobat (not the free Adobe Reader) is the best-known program, but many others are available, including some free versions. You can also use Adobe's online service at **http://createpdf.adobe.com** to create PDFs without buying software.

Proofreading Your Résumé

Employers view your résumé as a concrete example of your attention to quality and detail. Your résumé doesn't need to be good or pretty good—it needs to be *perfect*. In a recent survey, an overwhelming majority of executives said that just one or two errors in the job application package are enough to doom a candidate's chances.[45] Job seekers have committed every conceivable error, from forgetting to put their own names on their résumés to misspelling "Education."[46] Your résumé is one of the most important documents you'll ever write, so don't cut corners when it comes to proofreading. Check all headings and lists for clarity and parallelism and be sure that your grammar, spelling, and punctuation are correct. Ask at least three other people to read it, too. As the creator of the material, you could stare at a mistake for weeks and not see it.

Your résumé can't be "pretty good" or "almost perfect"—it needs to be perfect, so proofread it thoroughly and ask several other people to verify it, too.

You also need to make sure your résumé works in every format you create, so double- and triple-check your scannable, plain-text, and HTML versions closely. Many personal computer users now have low-cost scanners with OCR software, so you can even test the scannability of your résumé. These OCR tools aren't as accurate as commercial systems, but you'll get a rough idea of what your résumé will look like on the other end of the scanning process. Test your plain-text version by copying it into an e-mail message and sending it to yourself and several friends on different e-mail systems.

Distributing Your Résumé

How you distribute your résumé depends on the number of employers you target and their preferences for receiving résumés. Employers usually list their preferences on their websites, so verify this information to make sure your résumé ends up in the right format and in the right channel. Beyond that, here are some general distribution tips:

- **Mailing your traditional and scannable résumés.** Take some care with the packaging. Spend a few extra cents to mail these documents in a flat 9×12 envelope, or better yet, use a Priority Mail flat-rate envelope, which gives you a sturdy cardboard mailer and faster delivery for just a few more dollars. Consider sending both standard and scannable versions to each employer. In your cover letter, explain that for the employer's convenience, you're sending both formats. However, if an employer provides the means to submit a résumé electronically, go with that option, as it increases the chances that your information will get into the applicant tracking system quickly and correctly.

- **Faxing your traditional and scannable résumés.** If you know that an employer prefers résumés via fax, be sure to send a standard fax cover sheet, along with your cover letter, followed by your résumé. Set the fax machine to "fine" mode to help ensure a high-quality printout on the receiving end. Note that a faxed résumé is probably the least desired format for many employers, so choose this route only if the employer requests faxes.

- **E-mailing your résumé.** Unless someone specifically asks for a Word document as an e-mail attachment, chances are a Word file won't get opened (because of virus concerns). Instead, insert plain text into the body of the e-mail message, attach a PDF file, or include a hyperlink in the e-mail that links to a résumé on your website or in your e-portfolio. If you have a reference number or a job ad number, include it in your e-mail subject line.

- **Posting your résumé online.** The range of options for posting résumés online seems to grow every year, particularly with the emergence of social networks and specialized job search websites. Consider all the following in your job search: (1) create an e-portfolio (see the Prologue for an example); (2) create a personal website, which can include your e-portfolio; (3) create a profile on one or more social networking sites; (4) post your résumé on "general-purpose" job websites, such as Monster and CareerBuilder; (5) post your résumé on specialized websites, such as Jobster and Jobfox (note that some specialized sites focus on higher-level positions, so they might not be available to you early in your career); (6) post your résumé with a staffing service, such as Volt (**http://jobs .volt.com**); and (7) keep an eye out for any new channels that emerge in the coming years. In every case, pay close attention to the instructions. For instance, some sites let you upload a Word file, whereas others want you to copy and paste individual sections of résumé into an online application form.

CHECKLIST: Writing an Effective Résumé

A. Plan your résumé.
- Analyze your purpose and audience carefully to make sure your message meets employers' needs.
- Gather pertinent information about your target companies.
- Select the best medium by researching the preferences of each employer.
- Organize your résumé around your strengths, choosing the chronological, functional, or combination structure. (Be careful about using the functional structure.)

B. Write your résumé.
- Keep your résumé honest.
- Adapt your résumé to your audience to highlight the qualifications each employer is looking for.

- Use powerful language to convey your name and contact information, career objective or summary of qualifications, education, work experience, skills, work or school accomplishments, and personal activities and achievements.

C. Complete your résumé.
- Revise your résumé until it is clear, concise, and compelling.
- Produce your résumé in all the formats you might need: traditional printed résumé, scannable, plain-text file, Microsoft Word file, HTML format, or PDF.
- Proofread your résumé to make sure it is absolutely perfect.
- Distribute your résumé using the means that each employer prefers.

Before you upload your résumé to any site, learn about its confidentiality protection. Some sites allow you to specify levels of confidentiality, such as letting employers search your qualifications without seeing your personal contact information or preventing your current employer from seeing your résumé. In any case, carefully limit the amount of personal information you provide online. Never put your Social Security number, student ID number, or driver's license number online, and don't post your résumé to any website that doesn't give you the option of restricting the display of your contact information. (Only employers that are registered clients of the service should be able to see your contact information.)[47]

For a quick summary of the steps to take when planning, writing, and completing your résumé, refer to "Checklist: Writing an Effective Résumé." For the latest information on résumé writing and distribution, visit **http://real-timeupdates .com/bct** and click on Chapter 18.

Document Makeover

Improve This Résumé

To practice correcting drafts of actual documents, visit the "Document Makeovers" section in either mybcommlab or the Companion Website for this text.

If mybcommlab is being used in your class, see your User Guide for specific instructions on how to access the content for this chapter. If you are accessing this feature through the Companion Website, click on "Document Makeovers" and then click Chapter 18. You will find a résumé that contains problems and errors related to what you've learned in this chapter about writing effective résumés and application letters. Use the Final Draft decision tool to create an improved version of this document. Check the résumé for spelling and grammatical errors, effective use of verbs and pronouns, inclusion of unnecessary information, and omission of important facts.

Communication Challenges at Hersha Hospitality Management

You recently joined Jeffrey Wade's recruiting team at Hersha, and your responsibilities include analyzing résumés and applications to help the company identify the most promising candidates to be interviewed. Study the two scenarios that follow and apply what you learned in this chapter about recruiting and résumés.

Individual Challenge: One of today's tasks is selecting candidates to be interviewed for a management trainee position. This position involves significant interaction with other departments, so communication skills are vital. The applicant tracking system has turned up two candidates with almost identical qualifications. You have time to interview only one of them, however. Based on the way the two candidates described their education, which one would you invite in for an interview—and why?

a. Morehouse College, Atlanta, GA, 2003–2007. Received BA degree with a major in Business Administration and a minor in Finance. Graduated with a 3.65 grade-point average. Played varsity U.S.-style football and basketball. Worked 15 hours per week in the library. Coordinated the local student chapter of the American Management Association. Member of Alpha Phi Alpha social fraternity.

b. I attended Wayne State University in Detroit, Michigan, for two years and then transferred to the University of Michigan at Ann Arbor, where I completed my studies. My major was economics, but I also took many business management courses, including employee motivation, small business administration, history of business start-ups, and organizational behavior. I selected courses based on the professors' reputation for excellence, and I received mostly As and Bs. Unlike many other college students, I viewed the acquisition of knowledge—rather than career preparation—as my primary goal. I believe I have received a well-rounded education that has prepared me to approach management situations as problem-solving exercises.

Team Challenge: To find candidates for an accounting associate position (a job typically filled by college graduates rather than more experienced professionals), you searched the application tracking system and found the following rather unconventional résumé. With one or two other students, study the résumé in light of what you know about both the recruiting process at Hersha and effective résumés. Then decide whether you should (1) invite this candidate for an interview; (2) reject the application without further analysis; (3) review the candidate's web-based e-portfolio, then make a decision about inviting him in for an interview; or (4) compare the candidate's qualifications relative to those of other applicants and invite him in for an interview only if you cannot find several qualified applicants. Explain your choice.

Darius Jaidee
809 N. Perkins Rd, Stillwater, OK 74075
Phone: (405) 369-0098
E-mail: dariusj@okstate.edu

Career Objective: To build a successful career in financial management

Summary of Qualifications: As a student at the University of Oklahoma, Stillwater, completed a wide variety of assignments that demonstrate skills related to accounting and management. For example:

Planning skills: As president of the university's foreign affairs forum, organized six lectures and workshops featuring 36 speakers from 16 foreign countries within a nine-month period. Identified and recruited the speakers, handled their travel arrangements, and scheduled the facilities.

Communication skills: Wrote more than 25 essays and term papers on various academic topics, including at least 10 dealing with business and finance. As a senior, wrote a 20-page analysis of financial trends in the petroleum industry, interviewing five high-ranking executives in accounting and finance positions at ConocoPhillip's refinery in Ponca City, Oklahoma, and company headquarters in Houston, Texas.

Accounting and computer skills: Competent in all areas of Microsoft Office, including Excel spreadsheets and Access databases. Assisted with bookkeeping activities in parents' small business, including the conversion from paper-based to computer-based accounting (Peachtree software). Have taken courses in accounting, financial planning, database design, web design, and computer networking.

For more information, including employment history, please access my e-portfolio at **http://dariusjaidee.tripod.com**.

SUMMARY OF LEARNING OBJECTIVES

1 Describe the approach most employers take to finding potential new employees. Employers look for new employees using as many as five different approaches, and most have definite preferences from among these five. The preferred source is the employer's current workforce (most employers try to promote and hire from within before looking anywhere else), followed by the hiring manager's own personal contacts and personal recommendations from other trusted professionals. If these sources don't yield the right candidates or enough of them, employers will consider hiring an employment agency or a search firm (sometimes called a "headhunter") and begin to review unsolicited résumés (often with the computerized assistance of a résumé database or applicant tracking system). Finally, employers will solicit applications from the general public, through their own websites, job boards such as Monster, and a variety of advertising efforts.

2 Explain the importance of networking in your career search. Networking is vital in today's job market because many job opportunities are never advertised to the public, or at least not until an employer has exhausted other opportunities. As an active networker, you might hear about opportunities that you would never know about otherwise. In addition, networking often allows you to learn information about employers and hiring managers that isn't available to the general public. Finally, your network contacts can often endorse your qualifications to a potential employer, giving you an advantage over other applicants.

3 Discuss how to choose the appropriate résumé organization, and list the advantages and disadvantages of the three common options. Each organizational approach emphasizes different strengths. If you have a lot of

employment experience, you would choose the chronological approach because it focuses on your work history. The advantages of the chronological résumé are that (1) it helps employers easily locate necessary information, (2) it highlights your professional growth and career progress, and (3) it emphasizes continuity and stability in your employment background. The functional approach focuses on particular skills and competencies you've developed. The advantages of the functional résumé are that (1) it helps employers easily see what you can do for them, (2) it allows you to emphasize earlier job experience, and (3) it lets you downplay any lengthy periods of unemployment or a lack of career progress. However, many employers are suspicious of the functional résumé for this very reason. The combination approach uses the best features of the other two, but it has two disadvantages: (1) It tends to be longer, and (2) it can be repetitious if you must list accomplishments and skills in the functional section as well as in the individual job descriptions.

4 List the major sections of a traditional résumé. Your résumé must include three sections: (1) your contact information (including name, address, telephone number, and e-mail address), (2) your education background (with related skills and accomplishments), and (3) your work experience (with related skills and accomplishments). Options include listing your career objective, a qualifications summary, or a career summary; describing related activities and achievements; and perhaps providing relevant personal data.

5 Identify six different formats in which you can produce a résumé. The six formats are traditional printed résumé, scannable, electronic plain text, Word file, HTML, and PDF.

6 **Describe what you should do to adapt your résumé to a scannable format.** A scannable résumé requires two significant changes to the traditional printed format: removing all formatting (including multiple columns of bullet points) and adding a list of keywords. You can remove all the formatting manually, but it's easier to just save a plain-text version of your traditional résumé file and then verify its appearance, using a simple text editor such as Notepad. You may need to move a few items around and insert or remove blank lines and spaces to make sure all the items line up appropriately. Then add a list of keywords (nouns) that define your skills, experience, and education. Make sure the résumé also includes important jargon that is characteristic of the language in your field.

PEARSON mybcommlab

Log on to www.mybcommlab.com to access the following study and assessment aids associated with this chapter:

- Video applications
- Real-Time Updates
- Peer review activity
- Quick Learning Guides
- Pre/post test
- Personalized study plan
- Model documents
- Sample presentations

If you are not using mybcommlab, you can access the Real-Time Updates and Quick Learning Guides through http://real-timeupdates.com/bct. The Quick Learning Guide hits all the high points of this chapter in just two pages. This guide, especially prepared by the authors, will help you study for exams or review important concepts whenever you need a quick refresher.

Test Your Knowledge

1. What is the most-preferred source of new employee leads for most employers?
2. Why is it important to have an organized approach to finding a new job?
3. Why is it important to contribute to any networks you belong to, in addition to looking for assistance for your own career?
4. What is a résumé, and why is it important to adopt a "you" attitude when preparing one?
5. How does a chronological résumé differ from a functional résumé, and when is each appropriate?
6. Why are some employers suspicious of the functional résumé?
7. Explain the difference between a qualifications summary and a career summary.
8. What are some of the most common problems with résumés?
9. Why is it important to provide a keyword summary in a scannable or electronic résumé?
10. Should you include personal data on a résumé? Explain your answer.

companies are using this approach to deal with the flood of résumés they receive. Do you think that scanning is a good idea? Explain.

3. Can you use a qualifications summary if you don't yet have extensive professional experience in your desired career? Why or why not?
4. Some people don't have a clear career path when they enter the job market. If you're in this situation, how would your uncertainty affect the way your write your résumé?
5. **Ethical Choices** Between your sophomore and junior years, you quit school for a year to earn the money to finish college. You worked as a loan-processing assistant in a finance company, checking references on loan applications, typing, and filing. Your manager made a lot of the fact that he had never attended college. He seemed to resent you for pursuing your education, but he never criticized your work, so you thought you were doing okay. After you'd been working there for six months, he fired you, saying that you'd failed to be thorough enough in your credit checks. You were actually glad to leave, and you found another job right away at a bank, doing similar duties. Now that you've graduated from college, you're writing your résumé. Will you include the finance company job in your work history? Explain.

Apply Your Knowledge

1. How should you present a past job that is unrelated to your current career plans?
2. One of the disadvantages of computerized résumé scanning is that some qualified applicants will be missed because the technology isn't perfect. However, more and more

Practice Your Knowledge

Message for Analysis

Read the following résumé information and then (1) analyze the strengths or weaknesses of the information and (2) revise the résumé so that it follows the guidelines presented in this chapter.

Message 18.A: Writing a Résumé

Sylvia Manchester
765 Belle Fleur Blvd.
New Orleans, LA 70113
(504) 312-9504
smanchester@rcnmail.com

PERSONAL: Single, excellent health, 5'8", 116 lbs.; hobbies include cooking, dancing, and reading.

JOB OBJECTIVE: To obtain a responsible position in marketing or sales with a good company.

EDUCATION: BA degree in biology, University of Louisiana, 1998. Graduated with a 3.0 average. Member of the varsity cheerleading squad. President of Panhellenic League. Homecoming queen.

WORK EXPERIENCE

Fisher Scientific Instruments, 2004 to now, field sales representative. Responsible for calling on customers and explaining the features of Fisher's line of laboratory instruments. Also responsible for writing sales letters, attending trade shows, and preparing weekly sales reports.

Fisher Scientific Instruments, 2001–2003, customer service representative. Was responsible for handling incoming phone calls from customers who had questions about delivery, quality, or operation of Fisher's line of laboratory instruments. Also handled miscellaneous correspondence with customers.

Medical Electronics, Inc., 1998–2001, administrative assistant to the vice president of marketing. In addition to handling typical secretarial chores for the vice president of marketing, I was in charge of compiling the monthly sales reports, using figures provided by members of the field sales force. I also was given responsibility for doing various market research activities.

New Orleans Convention and Visitors Bureau, 1995–1998, summers, tour guide. During the summers of my college years, I led tours of New Orleans for tourists visiting the city. My duties included greeting conventioneers and their spouses at hotels, explaining the history and features of the city during an all-day sightseeing tour, and answering questions about New Orleans and its attractions. During my fourth summer with the bureau, I was asked to help train the new tour guides. I prepared a handbook that provided interesting facts about the various tourist attractions, as well as answers to the most commonly asked tourist questions. The Bureau was so impressed with the handbook they had it printed up so that it could be given as a gift to visitors.

University of Louisiana, 1995–1998, part-time clerk in admissions office. While I was a student in college, I worked 15 hours a week in the admissions office. My duties included filing, processing applications, and handling correspondence with high school students and administrators.

Exercises

Active links for all websites in this chapter can be found online. If mybcommlab is being used in your class, see your User Guide for instructions on accessing the content for this chapter. Otherwise, visit www.pearsonglobaleditions.com/bovee, locate *Business Communication Today*, Tenth Edition, click the Companion Website link, select Chapter 18, and then click on "Featured Websites." Please note that links to sites that become inactive after publication of the book will be removed from the Featured Websites section.

18.1 **Internet** Based on the preferences you identified in your career self-assessment (see page 28) and the academic,

professional, and personal qualities you have to offer, perform an online search for a career that matches your interests (starting with the websites listed in Table 18.1). Draft a brief report for your instructor, indicating how the career you select and the job openings you find match your strengths and preferences.

18.2 **Teamwork** Working with another student, change the following statements to make them more effective for a résumé by using action verbs.

   a. Have some experience with database design.

   b. Assigned to a project to analyze the cost accounting methods for a large manufacturer.

   c. I was part of a team that developed a new inventory control system.

   d. Am responsible for preparing the quarterly department budget.

   e. Was a manager of a department with seven employees working for me.

   f. Was responsible for developing a spreadsheet to analyze monthly sales by department.

   g. Put in place a new program for ordering supplies.

18.3 **Résumé Preparation: Work Accomplishments** Using your team's answers to exercise 18.2, make the statements stronger by quantifying them. (Make up any numbers you need.)

18.4 **Ethical Choices** Assume that you achieved all the tasks shown in exercise 18.2 not as an individual employee but as part of a work team. In your résumé, must you mention other team members? Explain your answer.

18.5 **Résumé Preparation: Electronic Plain-Text Version** Using your revised version of Message for Analysis 18.A, prepare a fully formatted print résumé. What formatting changes would Sylvia Manchester need to make if she were uploading her résumé to a website as a plain-text file? Develop a keyword summary and make all the changes needed to complete this plain-text résumé.

18.6 **Résumé Preparation: HTML Version** Using your revised version of the résumé in Message for Analysis 18.A, prepare a webpage version. Your instructor may direct you to a particular HTML editing tool, or you can use the "Save as Web Page" function in Microsoft Word. Word also lets you insert hyperlinks, so somewhere in the Work Experience section, create a hyperlink that takes the reader to a secondary page in order to show a work sample. For this new page, you can either use one of your own assignments from this course or simply create a blank page titled "Work Sample for Sylvia Manchester." On this page, create a hyperlink that takes the reader back to the main résumé page.

   Be sure to test your finished files using a web browser. Adjust your formatting as necessary to ensure a clean, professional design. When your files are complete, submit as your instructor indicates.

18.7 **It's Show Time: Creating a Vidcast to Supplement Your Application** Imagine that you are applying for work in a field that involves speaking in front of an audience, such as sales, consulting, management, or training. Using material you created for any of the exercises or cases in Chapter 14, plan a two- to three-minute video demonstration of your speaking and presentation skills. Using a digital camcorder, a digital camera with video capability, or a webcam, record yourself speaking to an imaginary audience. If possible, use PowerPoint slides or other visuals. As your instructor directs, either submit this movie clip or use it to create a video podcast. For a good tutorial on creating vidcasts on Apple computers running Mac OS X, visit **www.apple.com/quicktime/tutorials/videopodcasts.html**; for Windows computers, visit **www.apple.com/quicktime/tutorials/videopodcasts_win.html**.

Expand Your Knowledge

Exploring the Best of the Web

Post a Résumé Online

www.careerbuilder.com

At CareerBuilder, you'll find sample résumés, tips on preparing different types of résumés (including scannable ones), links to additional articles, and expert advice on creating résumés that bring positive results. After you've polished your résumé-writing skills, you can search for jobs online, using the site's numerous links to national and international industry-specific websites. You can access the information at CareerBuilder to develop your résumé and then post it with prospective employers—all free of charge. Use the site's advice to complete these tasks:

1. Before writing a new résumé, make a list of action verbs that describe your skills and experience.
2. Describe the advantages and disadvantages of chronological and functional résumé formats. Do you think a combination résumé would be an appropriate format for your new résumé? Explain why or why not.
3. List some of the tips you learned for preparing a résumé for online posting.

Sharpening Your Career Skills Online

Bovée and Thill's Business Communication Web Search, at http://businesscommunicationblog.com/websearch, is a unique research tool designed specifically for business communication research. Use the Web Search function to find a website, video, PDF document, podcast, or PowerPoint presentation that offers advice on creating an effective résumé. Write a brief e-mail message to your instructor, describing the item that you found and summarizing the career skills information you learned from it.

CASES

Applying the Three-Step Writing Process to Cases

Apply each step to the following cases, as assigned by your instructor.

1. The right job, right now: Imagining your ideal résumé. Think about yourself. What are some things that come easily to you? What do you enjoy doing? In what part of the country would you like to live? Do you like to work indoors? Outdoors? A combination of the two? How much do you like to travel? Would you like to spend considerable time on the road? Do you like to work closely with others or more independently? What conditions make a job unpleasant? Do you delegate responsibility easily, or do you like to do things yourself? Are you better with words or numbers? Better at speaking or writing? Do you like to work under fixed deadlines? How important is job security to you? Do you want your supervisor to state clearly what is expected of you, or do you like the freedom to make many of your own decisions?

Your task: After answering these questions, gather information about possible jobs that suit your current qualifications by consulting reference materials (from your college library or placement center) and by searching online. Next, choose a location, a company, and a job that interests you. Write a résumé that matches your qualifications and the job description; use whatever format your instructor specifies.

E-MAIL SKILLS

2. The dream job in the future: What will it take to get there? Chances are you won't be able to land your dream job right out of college, but that doesn't mean you shouldn't start planning right now to make that dream come true.

Your task: Using online job search tools, find a job that sounds just about perfect for you, even if you're not yet qualified for it. It might even be something that would take 10 or 20 years to reach. Don't settle for something that's not quite right—find a job that is so "you" and so exciting that you would jump out of bed every morning, eager to go to work (such jobs really do exist!). Start with the job description you found online and then supplement it with additional research so that you get a good picture of what this job and career path are all about. Compile a list of all the qualifications you would need in order to have a reasonable chance of landing such a job. Now compare this list with your current résumé. Write a brief e-mail to your instructor that identifies all the areas in which you would need to improve your skills, work experience, education, and other qualifications in order to land your dream job.

PRESENTATION SKILLS   PORTFOLIO BUILDER

3. The multimedia me: Job interview via web cam. Live job interviewing over an Internet web cam is a growing trend. Instead of flying job applicants for face-to-face interviews, companies turn to interviewing with web cams to save both cost and time.

Your task: With a student partner, test run a live web cam interview for a job you pick. Take turns being the interviewer and the interviewee. Dress professionally. The ideal location for setting up the equipment is a quiet and neutral location. Check the lighting and sound quality. When answering questions, practice smiling naturally and using hand gestures. As there may be a delay in signal emission, time yourself carefully during the conversation. Tape record your interviews and evaluate your performance in terms of the quality of your answers, your physical appearance, and nonverbal signals. List 10 areas for improvement.

Applying and Interviewing for Employment

Learning Objectives
After studying this chapter, you will be able to

1 Define the purpose of application letters and explain how to apply the AIDA model to them

2 Describe the typical sequence of job interviews

3 Describe briefly what employers look for during an employment interview and preemployment testing

4 List six tasks you need to complete to prepare for a successful job interview

5 Explain the three stages of a successful employment interview

6 Identify the most common employment messages that follow an interview and explain when you would use each one

Communication Close-up at Google

Arnnon Geshuri heads Google's recruiting effort as the company looks to hire thousands of the most innovative online business and technical specialists in the world.

www.google.com

As you prepare for your job interviews, knowing just the basic facts and figures about a company isn't always enough to impress top recruiters. For instance, most web surfers know Google as the leading online search engine, but the company is also helping to revolutionize advertising, publishing, geographic information systems, shopping—if it involves digital information, chances are that Google has looked into opportunities to build a business out of it.

As Google continues its rapid growth, recruiting manager Arnnon Geshuri and his staff dedicate considerable time, energy, and resources to employee recruiting. However, finding the right people is so important to the company that contributing to the recruiting effort is considered the responsibility of virtually every manager and employee. In fact, John Sullivan of San Francisco State University, who has studied the company's recruiting efforts closely, says that recruiting permeates the company so thoroughly that Google has created what he terms the world's first "recruiting culture." Acting on the belief that hiring choices are the most important decisions a company can make, Google has been known to wait several years to find the right people to fill some posts—even though it receives more than a million résumés a year.

Moreover, as befits a company focused on innovation, Google pursues people who don't fit the traditional corporate mold. Most are either risk takers with adventurous outside interests or experienced superstars from top research labs or respected technology firms. Googlers, as employees are informally known, hail from every corner of the business world—and beyond. As the company puts it, "Googlers have been Olympic athletes and Jeopardy champions; professional chefs and independent filmmakers."

You may never apply to Google, but gaining similar insights about the companies you are interested in will give you a competitive edge. Google provides quite a bit of information on its website about work life at the company, but you can't always hop on a company website to find these insights. Doing some extra digging through magazines, reading employment-related blogs, networking with others in your chosen field, and taking other opportunities to learn will help you prepare for every stage of the employment search process.[1]

WRITING APPLICATION LETTERS AND OTHER EMPLOYMENT MESSAGES

Whether you plan to apply to Google (profiled in the chapter-opening Communication Close-up) or any other company, your résumé will usually be the centerpiece of your job search package. However, it needs support from several other employment messages, including application letters, job-inquiry letters, application forms, and follow-up notes.

Application Letters

Whenever you submit your résumé, accompany it with an **application letter** to let readers know what you're sending, why you're sending it, and how they can benefit from reading it. (Application letters are sometimes called *cover letters*, and they can be either printed or e-mailed.) The process of planning, writing, and completing an application letter involves the same three steps you've used throughout this course. Start by researching the organization and then focus on your audience so that you can show you've done your homework. During your research, try to find out the name, title, and department of the person you're writing to. If you can't find a specific name, use something like "Dear Hiring Manager."[2] If you're applying for work in another country, be sure to research the hiring practices that are prevalent in that culture and adjust your letter format as needed.

Remember that your reader's in-box is probably overflowing with résumés and application letters, and respect his or her time. Avoid gimmicks and don't repeat information that already appears in your résumé. Keep your letter straightforward, fact based, short, upbeat, and professional. Here are some quick tips to help you write effective application letters:[3]

1 LEARNING OBJECTIVE

Define the purpose of application letters and explain how to apply the AIDA model to them

Use the three-step process to create attention-getting application letters.

Impress your reader with knowledge and professionalism— not gimmicks.

- Be as clear as possible about the kind of opportunity you seek.
- Show that you understand the company and the position.
- Never volunteer salary information unless an employer asks for it.
- Keep it short—and keep e-mail application letters especially short; in just two or three paragraphs, convey how your strengths and character would fit the position.
- Show some personality; doing so will help balance the choppy, shorthand style of your résumé.
- Meticulously check your spelling, mechanics, and grammar; errors will send your message directly to the recycling bin. And be aware that potential employers will treat your e-mail messages every bit as seriously as formal, printed letters.[4]

If you're sending a **solicited application letter** in response to an announced job opening, you'll usually know what qualifications the organization is seeking (see Figure 19.1). In contrast, if you're sending an **unsolicited application letter** to an organization that has not announced an opening, you'll need to do some research to identify the requirements the position is likely to have (see Figure 19.2).

Solicited and unsolicited application letters present your qualifications similarly. The main difference is in the opening paragraph. In a solicited letter, you need no special attention-getter because you have been invited to apply. In an unsolicited letter, you need to start by capturing the reader's attention and interest.

FIGURE 19.1 **Effective Solicited Application Message**

In this response to an online job posting, Dalton Smith highlights his qualifications while mirroring the requirements specified in the posting. Following the AIDA model, he grabs attention immediately by letting the reader know that he is familiar with the company and the global transportation business.

Position			Supply Chain Pricing Analyst Apply		
Position code	T23-6678	Location	Tacoma, WA	Status	Full-time

Sea-Air Global Transport has an immediate opening for a supply chain pricing analyst in our Tacoma, WA, headquarters. This challenging position requires excellent communication skills in a variety of media, a polished customer service presence both in person and over the phone, and proven aptitude in statistical analysis and business mathematics.

The minimum educational requirement for this position is a bachelors degree or equivalent, preferably in business, statistical methods, or applied mathematics. Experience in customer service is highly desirable, and experience in transportation or logistics is a major plus.

Click here to learn more about Sea-Air or click here to explore the attractive compensation and benefits packages we offer all employees.

Smith's application letter mirrors the language of the job posting

27225 Eucalyptus Avenue
Long Beach, CA 90806
March 12, 2010

Sea-Air Global Transport
5467 Port of Tacoma Rd., Suite 230
Tacoma, WA 98421

Dear Hiring Manager:

Sea-Air Global Transport consistently appeared as a top transportation firm in the research I did for my senior project in global supply chain management, so imagine my delight when I discovered the opening for an export pricing analyst in your Tacoma headquarters (Position Code: T23-6678). With a major in business and a minor in statistical methods, my education has been ideal preparation for the challenges of this position.

In fact, my senior project demonstrates most of the skills listed in your job description, including written communication skills, analytical abilities, and math aptitude. I enjoyed the opportunity to put my math skills to the test as part of the statistical comparison of various freight modes.

As you can see from my résumé, I also have more than three years of part-time experience working with customers in both retail and commercial settings. This experience taught me the importance of customer service, and I want to start my professional career with a company that truly values the customer. In reviewing your website and reading several articles on Lloyd's List and other trade websites, I am impressed by Sea-Air's constant attention to customer service in this highly competitive industry.

My verbal communication skills would be best demonstrated in an interview, of course. I would be happy to meet with a representative of your company at the earliest convenience. I can be reached at dalton.k.smith@gmail.com or by phone at (562) 555-3737.

Sincerely,

Dalton Smith

Immediately grabs attention by indicating knowledge of the company and its industry

Emphasizes his customer service orientation and also shows he has done his homework by researching the company

Doesn't include a handwritten signature because the letter was uploaded to a website along with his résumé

Identifies the specific job to which he is applying

Echoes qualifications stated in the job posting

Politely asks for an interview in a way that emphasizes yet another job-related skill

Getting Attention

Like your résumé, your application letter is a form of advertising, so organize it as you would a marketing or sales message: Use the AIDA model, focus on your audience, and emphasize reader benefits (as discussed in Chapter 10). Make sure your style projects confidence without being arrogant.

The opening paragraph of your application letter has two important tasks to accomplish: (1) clearly stating your reason for writing and (2) giving the recipient a reason to keep reading. Why would a recruiter want to keep reading your letter instead of the hundred others piling up on his or her desk? Because you show some immediate potential for meeting the company's

The opening paragraph of your application letter needs to clearly convey the reason you're writing and give the recipient a compelling reason to keep reading.

FIGURE 19.2 Effective Unsolicited Application Letter
Glenda Johns's experience as a clerk and an assistant manager gives her a good idea of the qualities that Walmart is likely to be looking for in future managers. She uses these insights to craft the opening of her letter.

457 Mountain View Rd.
Clear Lake, IA 50428
June 16, 2010

Ms. Patricia Downings, Store Manager
Walmart
840 South Oak
Iowa Falls, IA 50126

Dear Ms. Downing:

Gains attention in the first paragraph by speaking directly to the reader's needs

You want retail clerks and managers who are accurate, enthusiastic, and experienced. You want someone who cares about customer service, who understands merchandising, and who can work with others to get the job done. When you're ready to hire a manager trainee or a clerk who is willing to work toward promotion, please consider me for the job.

Points out personal qualities that aren't specifically stated in her résumé

Working as a clerk and then as an assistant manager in a large department store has taught me how to anticipate customer problems and deliver the type of service that keeps customers coming back. Moreover, my recent BA degree in retailing, which encompassed such courses as retailing, marketing, management, and business information systems, will provide your store with a well-rounded associate. (Please refer to my enclosed résumé for more information.) You'll find that I'm interested in every facet of retailing, eager to take on responsibility, and willing to continue learning throughout my career.

Builds the reader's interest by demonstrating knowledge of the company's policy regarding promotion

I understand that Walmart prefers to promote its managers from within the company, and I would be pleased to start out with an entry-level position until I gain the necessary experience. Do you have any associate positions opening up soon? Could we discuss my qualifications? I will phone you early next Wednesday to arrange a meeting at your convenience.

Focuses on the reader and displays the "you" attitude, even though the last paragraph uses the word "I"

Sincerely,

Glenda Johns

Glenda Johns

Enclosure

needs. You've researched the company and the position, and you know something about the industry and its current challenges. Consider this opening:

> With the recent slowdown in corporate purchasing, I can certainly appreciate the challenge of new fleet sales in this business environment. With my high energy level and 16 months of new-car sales experience, I believe I can produce the results you listed as vital in your September 23 advertisement in the *Baltimore Sun*.

This applicant does a smooth job of mirroring the company's stated needs while highlighting his personal qualifications, along with evidence that he understands the broader market.

Table 19.1 highlights some ways you can spark interest and grab attention in your opening paragraph. All these openings demonstrate the "you" attitude, and many indicate how the applicant can serve the employer.

TABLE 19.1 Tips for Getting Attention in Application Letters

TIP	EXAMPLE
UNSOLICITED APPLICATION LETTERS	
• Show how your strongest skills will benefit the organization.	If you need a regional sales specialist who consistently meets sales targets while fostering strong customer relationships, please consider my qualifications.
• Describe your understanding of the job's requirements and show how well your qualifications fit them.	Your annual report stated that improving manufacturing efficiency is one of the company's top priorities for next year. Through my postgraduate research in systems engineering and consulting work for several companies in the industry, I've developed reliable methods for quickly identifying ways to cut production time while reducing resource use.
• Mention the name of a person known to and highly regarded by the reader.	When Janice McHugh of your franchise sales division spoke to our business communication class last week, she said you often need promising new marketing graduates at this time of year.
• Refer to publicized company activities, achievements, changes, or new procedures.	Today's issue of the *Detroit News* reports that you may need the expertise of computer programmers versed in robotics when your Lansing tire plant automates this spring.
• Use a question to demonstrate your understanding of the organization's needs.	Can your fast-growing market research division use an interviewer with two years of field survey experience, a B.A. in public relations, and a real desire to succeed? If so, please consider me for the position.
• Use a catchphrase opening if the job requires ingenuity and imagination.	*Haut monde*—whether referring to French, Italian, or Arab clients, it still means "high society." As an interior designer for your Beverly Hills showroom, not only could I serve and sell to your distinguished clientele, but I could do it in all these languages. I speak, read, and write them fluently.
SOLICITED APPLICATION LETTERS	
• Identify where you discovered the job opening; describe what you have to offer.	Your ad in the April issue of *Travel & Leisure* for a cruise-line social director caught my eye. My eight years of experience as a social director in the travel industry would allow me to serve your new Caribbean cruise division well.

Building Interest and Increasing Desire

Use the middle section of your letter to expand on your opening, presenting a more complete picture of your strengths.

The middle section of your application letter presents your strongest selling points in terms of their potential benefit to the organization, thereby building interest in you and creating a desire to interview you. As with the opening, the more specific you can be in the middle section, the better. And back up your assertions with some convincing evidence of your ability to perform:

> **Poor:** I completed three college courses in business communication, earning an A in each course, and have worked for the past year at Imperial Construction.
>
> **Improved:** Using the skills gained from three semesters of college training in business communication, I developed a collection system for Imperial Construction that reduced annual bad-debt losses by 25 percent. Emphasizing a win–win scenario for the company and its clients with incentives for on-time payment, the system was also credited with improving customer satisfaction.

When writing a solicited letter, be sure to discuss each requirement specified in the advertisement. If you are deficient in any of these requirements, stress other solid selling points to help strengthen your overall presentation.

Don't restrict your message to just core job duties. Also highlight personal characteristics that apply to the targeted position, such as your diligence or your ability to work hard, learn quickly, handle responsibility, or get along with people:

> While attending college full-time, I trained 3 hours a day with the varsity track team. In addition, I worked part-time during the school year and up to 60 hours a week each summer in order to be totally self-supporting while in college. I can offer your organization the same level of effort and perseverance.

Another matter you might bring up in this section is your salary requirements—but *only* if the organization has asked you to state them. If you don't know the salary that's appropriate for the position and someone with your qualifications, you can find salary ranges for hundreds of jobs at the Bureau of Labor Statistics website (**www.bls.gov**) or a number of commercial sites, including Monster.com. If you do state a target salary, tie it to the benefits you would bring to the organization:

Don't bring up salary in your application letter unless the recipient has previously asked you to include your salary requirements.

> For the past two years, I have been helping a company similar to yours organize its database marketing efforts. I would therefore like to receive a salary in the same range (the mid-60s) for helping your company set up a more efficient customer database.

Toward the end of this section, refer the reader to your résumé by citing a specific fact or general point covered there:

> As you can see in the enclosed résumé, I've been working part-time with a local publisher since my sophomore year. During that time, I've used client interactions as an opportunity to build strong customer service skills.

Motivating Action

The final paragraph of your application letter has two important functions: to ask the reader for a specific action and to facilitate a reply. Don't demand an interview, however; try to sound natural and appreciative. Offer to come to the employer's office at a convenient time or, if the firm is some distance away, to meet with its nearest representative or arrange a telephone interview. Make the request easy to fulfill by stating your phone number and the best time to reach you—or, if you want to be in control, by mentioning that you will follow up with a phone call in a few days. Refer again to your strongest selling point and, if desired, your date of availability:

In the final paragraph of your application letter, respectfully ask for specific action and make it easy for the reader to respond.

> After you have reviewed my qualifications, could we discuss the possibility of putting my marketing skills to work for your company? Because I will be on spring break the week of March 8, I would like to arrange a time to talk then. I will call in late February to schedule a convenient time when we could discuss employment opportunities at your company.

After you have edited and proofread your application letter, give it a final quality check by referring to "Checklist: Writing Application Letters." Then send it along with your résumé promptly, especially if you are responding to an advertisement or online job posting.

Application Follow-ups

If your application letter and résumé fail to bring a response within a month or so, follow up with a second letter to keep your file active. This follow-up letter also gives you a chance to update your original application with any recent job-related information:

> Since applying to you on May 3 for a position in your management training program, I have completed three courses in business and management at South River Community College and received straight A's.
>
> Please keep my application in your active file; I would welcome another opportunity to apply for the program.

✓ **CHECKLIST:** **Writing Application Letters**

- Open the letter by capturing the reader's attention in a businesslike way.
- Use specific language to clearly state your interests and objectives.
- Build interest and desire in your potential contribution by presenting your key qualifications for the job.
- Link your education, experience, and personal qualities to the job requirements.

- Outline salary requirements only if the organization has requested that you provide them.
- Request an interview at a time and place that is convenient for the reader.
- Make it easy to comply with your request by providing your complete contact information and good times to reach you.
- Adapt your style for cultural variations, if required.

Even if you've received a letter acknowledging your application and saying that it will be kept on file, don't hesitate to send a follow-up letter three months later to show that you are still interested:

> Three months have elapsed since I applied to you for an underwriting position, but I want to let you know that I am still very interested in joining your company.
>
> I recently completed a four-week temporary work assignment at a large local insurance agency. I learned several new verification techniques and gained experience in using the online computer system. This experience could increase my value to your underwriting department.
>
> Please keep my application in your active file and let me know when a position opens for a capable underwriter.

Think creatively about a follow-up message; show that you've continued to add to your skills or that you've learned more about the company or the industry.

You can write this sort of follow-up message even if you have no new accomplishments to share. Do some quick research on the company and its industry to find something that you can feature in your message ("I've been reading about the new technical challenges facing your industry..."). Your initiative and knowledge will impress recruiters. Without a follow-up communication from you, the human resources office is likely to assume that you've already found a job and are no longer interested in the organization. Moreover, a company's requirements change. A follow-up letter can demonstrate that you're sincerely interested in working for the organization, persistent in pursuing your goals, and committed to upgrading your skills. And it might just get you an interview.

UNDERSTANDING THE INTERVIEWING PROCESS

All recruiters, including Google's Arnnon Geshuri, have lists of qualities and accomplishments they are looking for in job candidates. An **employment interview** is a formal meeting during which you and a prospective employer ask questions and exchange information. These meetings have a dual purpose: (1) The organization's main objective is to find the best person available for the job by determining whether you and the organization are a good match, and (2) your main objective is to find the job best suited to your goals and capabilities. While recruiters are trying to decide whether you are right for them, you must decide whether a company is right for you.

Large organizations that hire hundreds of new employees every year typically take a more systematic approach to the recruiting and interviewing process than small local businesses that hire only a few new people each year. In many cases, the easiest way to connect with a big company is through your campus career center,

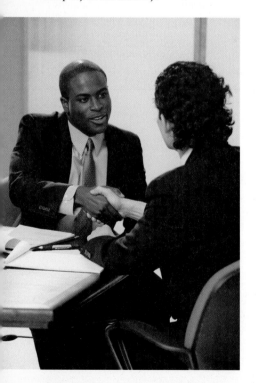

Asking questions of your own is as important as answering the interviewer's questions. Not only do you get vital information, you show initiative and curiosity.

while the most efficient way to reach a smaller business is often by contacting the company directly.

Regardless of what approach you take, interviewing takes time, so begin the process well in advance of the date you want to start work. During downturns in the economy, early planning is especially crucial. In these periods, employers become more selective, and many corporations reduce their campus visits and campus hiring programs, so more of the job-search burden falls on you. Whatever shape the economy is in, try to secure as many interviews as you can, both to improve your chances of receiving a job offer and to give yourself more options when you do get offers.

REAL-TIME UPDATES
Learn More

Looking for an international adventure?

Finding a job in another country is a long and complex process, but these tips can help you reach your goal as quickly as possible. Go to **http://real-timeupdates.com/bct** and click on "Learn More." If you are using mybcommlab, you can access Real-Time Updates within each chapter or under Student Study Tools.

The Typical Sequence of Interviews

Most employers interview an applicant multiple times before deciding to make a job offer. At the most selective companies, you might have a dozen or more individual interviews across several stages.[5] Depending on the company and the position, the process may stretch out over many weeks, or it may be completed in a matter of days.[6]

The interviewing process starts with a *screening stage*, in which an employer filters out applicants who are unqualified or otherwise not a good fit for the position. Screening can take place on campus, at company offices, or via telephone or computer. Time is limited in screening interviews, so keep your answers short while providing a few key points that differentiate you from other candidates. If your screening interview will take place by phone, try to schedule it for a time when you can be focused and free from interruptions.[7] Also, don't make the mistake of treating the phone call as a casual conversation; you are being interviewed just as seriously as you would be if you were meeting in person.

Your best approach to an interview at the screening stage is to follow the interviewer's lead. Keep your responses short and to the point. Time is limited, so talking too much can be a big mistake. However, to give the interviewer a way to differentiate you from other candidates and to demonstrate your strengths and qualifications, try to emphasize the "theme" you used in developing your résumé.

The next stage of interviews helps the organization narrow the field a little further. Your best approach during this *selection stage* of interviews is to show interest in the job, relate your skills and experience to the organization's needs, listen attentively, ask insightful questions that show you've done your research, and display enthusiasm. Typically, if you're invited to visit a company, you will talk with several people in succession, such as a member of the human resources department, one or two potential colleagues, and one or more managers, including your potential supervisor. At Google, for example, recruits talk with at least four interviewers, both managers and potential colleagues.[8]

If the interviewers agree that you're a good candidate, you may receive a job offer, either on the spot or a few days later by phone, mail, or e-mail. In other cases, you may be invited back for a final evaluation, often by a higher-ranking executive. The objective of this *final stage* is often to sell you on the advantages of joining the organization.

Common Types of Interviews

Employers can use a number of interviewing methods, so you need to recognize the various types and be prepared for each one. These methods can be distinguished by the way they are structured, the number of people involved, and the purpose of the interview.

Structured Versus Unstructured Interviews

In a **structured interview**, the interviewer (or a computer) asks a series of prepared questions in a set order. Structured interviews help employers identify candidates who don't meet basic job criteria, and they allow the interview team to compare answers from multiple candidates.[9]

2 **LEARNING OBJECTIVE**

Describe the typical sequence of job interviews

Most organizations interview an applicant several times before extending a job offer.

During the screening stage, try to differentiate yourself from other candidates.

During the selection stage, you may interview with several people, perhaps at the same time.

During the final stage, the interviewer may try to sell you on working for the firm.

A structured interview follows a set sequence of questions, allowing the interview team to compare answers from all candidates.

In an open-ended interview, the interviewer adapts the line of questioning based on your responses and questions.

In contrast, in an **open-ended interview**, the interviewer adapts his or her line of questioning based on the answers you give and any questions you ask. Even though it may feel like a conversation, remember that it's still an interview, so keep your answers focused and professional.

Panel and Group Interviews

In a panel interview, you meet with several interviewers at once; in a group interview, several candidates meet with one or more interviewers at once.

Many of your interviews will be conventional one-on-one interviews, with just you and a single interviewer. However, in a **panel interview**, you will meet with several interviewers at once (some companies have up to 50 employees on the panel, but that is unusual).[10] Try to make a connection with each person on the panel and remember that each one has a different perspective, so tailor your responses accordingly.[11] For example, an upper-level manager is likely to be interested in your overall business sense and strategic perspective, whereas a potential colleague might be more interested in your technical skills and ability to work as part of a team.

Some organizations perform **group interviews**, in which one or more interviewers meet with several candidates simultaneously. A key purpose of the group interview is to observe how the candidates interact.[12]

Behavioral, Situational, Working, and Stress Interviews

Behavioral interviews, in which you are asked to describe how you handled situations from your past, are commonly used.

Perhaps the most common type of interview these days is the **behavioral interview**, in which you are asked to relate specific incidents and experiences from your past.[13] Whereas traditional, generic interview questions can often be answered with "canned" responses, behavioral questions require candidates to use their own experiences and attributes to craft answers. Employers use these questions to assess such areas as your job-related technical skills and your ability to work under pressure, coordinate with others, and resolve conflict.[14]

Interviewers also look to see if the ways you handled challenges in the past reflect the organization's core values. To prepare for a behavioral interview, start by researching these values, which you can usually find discussed in the "About Us" section of the company's website. For example, one firm might emphasize innovation and technical excellence, while another might emphasize teamwork and commitment to customers. Next, review your work history and experience on school projects to recall several instances in which you demonstrated an important job-related skill or attribute that can be expressed in terms of those values. By discussing your experiences and accomplishments in the context of the company's values, you demonstrate that you understand what is important to the company and that you can be counted on to uphold those values.

In situational interviews, you're asked to explain how you would handle various hypothetical situations.

A **situational interview** is similar to a behavioral interview except that the questions focus on how you would handle various hypothetical situations on the job. The situations will likely relate to the job you're applying for, so the more you know about the position, the better prepared you'll be.

In a working interview, you perform real or simulated work-related tasks.

A **working interview** is the most realistic of all: You actually perform a job-related activity during the interview. You may be asked to lead a brainstorming session (sometimes with other job candidates), solve a business problem, engage in role playing, or even make a presentation.[15]

Stress interviews help recruiters see how you handle yourself under pressure.

The most unnerving type of interview is the **stress interview**, during which you might be asked questions designed to unsettle you or even subject you to long periods of silence, criticism, interruptions, and or hostile reactions by the interviewer. The theory behind this approach is that you'll reveal how well you handle stressful situations, although some experts find the technique of dubious value.[16] If you find yourself in a stress interview, recognize what is happening and collect your thoughts for a few seconds before you respond.

Interview Media

Expect to use a variety of media when you interview, from in-person conversations to virtual meetings.

In addition to encountering a variety of interview formats, expect to be interviewed through a variety of media. Employers trying to cut travel costs and the demands on staff time now interview candidates via telephone, e-mail, instant messaging, virtual online systems, and videoconferencing, in addition to traditional face-to-face meetings. These alternative media options are used most frequently in the screening stage but can be used into the selection stage as well.

To succeed at a telephone interview, make sure you treat it as seriously as an in-person interview. Be ready with a copy of all the materials you have sent the employer, including your résumé and any correspondence. In addition, prepare some note cards with key message points you'd like to make and your supporting evidence (such as an impressive success story from your current job). If possible, arrange to speak on a landline so you don't have to worry about mobile phone reception problems. And remember that you won't be able to use a pleasant smile, a firm handshake, and other nonverbal signals to create a good impression. A positive, alert tone of voice is therefore vital.[17]

Treat a telephone interview as seriously as you would an in-person interview.

E-mail and IM are sometimes used in the screening stage. While you have even less opportunity to send and receive nonverbal signals with these formats, you do have the major advantage of being able to review and edit each response before you send it. Maintain a professional style in your responses and be sure to ask questions that demonstrate your knowledge of the company and the position.[18]

When interviewing via e-mail or IM, be sure to take a moment to review your responses before sending them.

Many employers use video technology for both live and recorded interviews. Live video interviews can involve a videoconferencing facility or simply a webcam attached to your personal computer. (Some companies will arrange to send you a webcam if you don't have one.) With recorded video interviews, an online system asks a set of questions and records each respondent's answers. Recruiters then watch the videos as part of the screening process. Some systems also include online questionnaires in which you type your answers.[19] Prepare for a video interview as you would for an in-person interview and take the extra steps needed to become familiar with the equipment and the process. If you're interviewing from home, arrange the space so that the webcam doesn't pick anything distracting or embarrassing in the background. During any video interview, remember to sit up straight and focus on the camera.

In a video interview, speak to the camera as though you are addressing the interviewer in person.

Virtual online interviews can range from simple structured interviews to sophisticated job simulations that are similar to working interviews. People applying for teller positions at Sun-Trust, a regional bank based in Atlanta, interact with video-game-like characters while performing job-related tasks. These job simulations not only identify good candidates but also reduce the risk of employment discrimination lawsuits because they closely mimic actual job skills.[20] The latest development in simulators uses prerecorded video of real people asking questions and records the candidate's answers on video as well.[21] And as one might expect from an innovator in search technology, Google is testing an extensive online interview system that measures attitudes, behaviors, personality, and personal history in an attempt to find candidates who match the profiles of successful Google employees.[22] Virtual worlds such as Second Life are also likely to see increased use in the interviewing process in years to come (see Figure 19.3).[23]

Computer-based virtual interviews range from simple structured interviews to realistic job simulations to meetings in virtual worlds.

What Employers Look for in an Interview

Interviews give employers the chance to go beyond the basic data of your résumé to get to know you and to answer two essential questions. The first is whether you can handle the responsibilities of the position. You'll probably be asked to describe your education, previous job experiences, and skill set. You may also be asked how you would apply those skills to hypothetical situations on the job. By learning as much as you can about the company, the industry, and the specific job, you have a great opportunity to stand apart from the competition.

The second essential question is whether you will be a good fit with the organization and the target position. This line of inquiry includes both a general aspect and a specific aspect. The general aspect concerns your overall personality and approach to work. All good employers want people who are confident, dedicated, positive, curious, courteous, ethical, and willing to commit to something larger than their own individual goals. You could have superstar qualifications, but if an employer suspects that you might be a negative presence in the workplace, you probably won't get a job offer.

The specific aspect involves the fit with a particular company and position. Just like people, companies have different "personalities." Some are more intense; others are more laid back. Some emphasize teamwork; others expect employees to forge their own way and even to compete with one another. Expectations also vary from job to job within a company and from industry to industry. An outgoing personality is essential for sales but less so for

3 LEARNING OBJECTIVE

Describe briefly what employers look for during an employment interview and preemployment testing

Suitability for a specific job is judged on the basis of
- *Academic preparation*
- *Work experience*
- *Job-related personality traits*

Compatibility with an organization and a position is judged on the basis of personal background, attitudes, and style.

FIGURE 19.3 **Finding Real Jobs in a Virtual World**
Virtual job fairs, such as the Working Worlds event hosted by Luxembourg's GAX Technologies, allow candidates and recruiters to interact without the time and expense of travel.

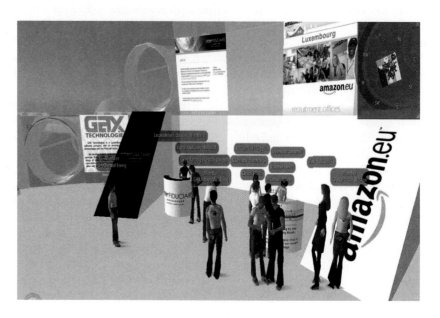

research, for instance. Numerous candidates might have the technical qualifications for a particular job, but not all will have the right mix of personal attributes.

Expect some questions about personal interests, world events, and other topics that help recruiters judge your personality and curiosity.

Some interviewers believe that personal background indicates how well a candidate will fit in, so they might ask about your interests, hobbies, awareness of world events, and so forth. You can expand your potential along these lines by reading widely, making an effort to meet new people, and participating in discussion groups, seminars, and workshops. For instance, Google values diverse interests and experiences, and rampant curiosity about virtually any subject is welcome.

Beyond your organizational fit, interviewers are likely to consider your personal style as well. You're likely to impress an employer by being open, enthusiastic, and interested. Some interviewers also look for courtesy, sincerity, willingness to learn, and a style that is positive and self-confident. All these qualities help a new employee adapt to a new workplace and new responsibilities.

Preemployment Testing and Background Checks

Preemployment tests attempt to provide objective, quantitative information about a candidate's skills, attitudes, and habits.

In an effort to improve the predictability of the selection process and reduce the reliance on the brief interaction that an interview allows, many employers now conduct a variety of preemployment tests.[24] Testing is a complex topic that varies widely by industry and position, and it also involves a wide range of legal and ethical issues, including discrimination and privacy issues. For instance, any testing that can be construed as a preemployment medical examination is prohibited by the Americans with Disabilities Act.[25] Here is an overview of the most common types of tests:

- **Integrity tests.** You might not think that a test could identify job candidates who are likely to steal from their employers or commit other ethical or legal infractions, but employers have had some success in using integrity tests.[26]
- **Personality tests.** Some employers use personality tests to profile overall intellectual ability, attitudes toward work, interests, managerial potential, dependability, commitment, honesty, and motivation.[27] The use of personality tests in hiring is controversial, however; recent research suggests that current tests are not reliable predictors of job success.[28]
- **Job skills tests.** The most common type of preemployment tests are those designed to assess the competency or specific abilities needed to perform a job.[29] Some large

employers, including Google and Capital One, have created custom evaluation systems that test applicants and continue to track employees after they're hired.[30] Google uses testing in creative ways not only to measure skills of potential hires but also to build interest in the company as a fun place to work. Thousands of computer programmers compete in the annual Google Code Jam, vying for valuable prizes and the chance to visit Google to explore job opportunities.[31]

- **Substance tests.** Testing for substance use or abuse is one of the most controversial issues in business today. Some employers believe such testing is absolutely necessary to maintain workplace safety and protect companies from lawsuits, whereas others view it as an invasion of employee privacy and a sign of disrespect. In recent years, as many as 80 percent of U.S. employers have conducted drug testing, but that percentage appears to be declining.[32]
- **Background checks.** In addition to testing, most companies conduct some sort of *background check* on job candidates.[33] Such investigations can include reviewing your credit record, checking to see whether you have a criminal history, and verifying your education. To help prevent a background check from tripping you up, make sure your college transcript and credit record are correct and up to date.[34] And if you have anything posted on MySpace, Facebook, or anywhere else that might be potentially embarrassing, take it down now. Recruiters routinely search for information about candidates online.[35] Employers can also find "unscripted references" from online social networks—that is, people who know you in some capacity but whom you haven't listed as references.[36]

If you're concerned about any preemployment test, ask the employer for more information or ask your college placement office for advice. You can also get more information from the Equal Employment Opportunity Commission, at **www.eeoc.gov**.

PREPARING FOR A JOB INTERVIEW

The more prepared you are, the less nervous you'll be about the interviewing process. To prepare for a successful interview, learn about the organization (including any relevant cultural issues that may be involved), think ahead about questions, bolster your confidence, polish your interview style, plan to look good, and be ready when you arrive.

Learning About the Organization

A potential employer expects serious candidates to demonstrate an understanding of the company's operations, its markets, and its strategic and tactical challenges.[37] You've already done some initial research to identify companies of interest, but when you're invited to interview, it's time to dig a little deeper (see Table 19.2). Making this effort demonstrates your interest in the company, and it identifies you as a business professional who knows the importance of investigation and analysis.

Thinking Ahead About Questions

Planning ahead for the interviewer's questions will help you handle them more confidently and successfully. As you consider answers to questions you might encounter, think in terms of how you can relate your qualifications to the organization's needs. In addition, you will want to prepare insightful questions of your own.

Planning for the Employer's Questions

In addition to questions about specific jobs and organizational needs, you can expect to be asked a variety of questions about your skills, achievements, goals, attitudes toward work and school, relationships with others, and occasionally your hobbies and interests. You'll also need to anticipate and give a little extra thought to a few particularly tough questions, such as these:

- **What is the hardest decision you've ever had to make?** Be prepared with a good example, explaining why the decision was difficult and how you finally made it.
- **What are your greatest weaknesses?** This question seems to be a stock favorite of some interviewers, although it probably rarely yields useful information. One recommended

4 LEARNING OBJECTIVE

List six tasks you need to complete to prepare for a successful job interview

Interviewers expect serious candidates to know some basic information about the company and its industry.

As you plan your responses to potential interview questions, be prepared to relate your qualifications to the organization's needs.

TABLE 19.2 Investigating an Organization and a Job Opportunity

WHERE TO LOOK AND WHAT YOU CAN LEARN

- *Company website:* Overall information about the company, including key executives, products and services, locations and divisions, employee benefits, and job descriptions
- *Competitors' websites:* Similar information from competitors, including the strengths those companies claim to have
- *Industry-related websites:* Objective analysis and criticism of the company, its products, its reputation, and its management
- *Marketing materials (brochures, catalogs, etc.):* The company's marketing strategy and customer communication style
- *Company publications (both print and electronic):* Key events, stories about employees, and new products
- *Blogs:* Analysis and criticism (not always fair or unbiased) of the company, its products and services, its reputation, and its management
- *Social networks:* Names and job titles of potential contacts in a company
- *Periodicals (newspapers and trade journals, both print and online):* In-depth stories about the company and its strategies, products, successes, and failures; you may find profiles of top executives
- *Career center at your college:* A wide array of information about companies that hire graduates
- *Current and former employees:* Insights into the work environment

POINTS TO LEARN ABOUT THE ORGANIZATION

- Full name
- Location (headquarters and divisions, branches, subsidiaries, or other units)
- Ownership (public or private; whether it is owned by another company)
- Age and brief history
- Products and services
- Industry position (whether the company is a leader or a minor player; whether it is an innovator or more of a follower)
- Key financial points (such as stock price and trend, if a public company)
- Growth prospects (whether the company is investing in its future through research and development; whether it is in a thriving industry)

POINTS TO LEARN ABOUT THE POSITION

- Title
- Functions and responsibilities
- Qualifications and expectations
- Possible career paths
- Salary range
- Travel expectations and opportunities
- Relocation expectations and opportunities

way to answer this question is to mention a relatively minor shortcoming and explain how you're working to improve in that area.

- **What didn't you like about previous jobs you've held?** Answer this one carefully: The interviewer is trying to predict whether you'll be an unhappy or difficult employee.[38] Describe something that you didn't like in a way that puts you in a positive light, such as having limited opportunities to apply your skills or education. Avoid making negative comments about former employers or colleagues.
- **Where do you want to be five years from now?** This questions tests (1) whether you're merely using this job as a stopover until something better comes along and (2) whether you've given thought to your long-term goals. Whatever you plan to say, your answer should reflect your desire to contribute to the employer's long-term goals. Whether this question yields useful information is a matter of debate but be prepared to answer it.[39]
- **Tell me something about yourself.** Ask if the interviewer would like to know about your specific skills or attributes. If this point is clarified, respond accordingly. If it isn't, explain how your skills can contribute to the job and the organization. This is a great chance to sell yourself.

COMMUNICATING ACROSS CULTURES

Successfully Interviewing Across Borders

Interviewing for a job in another country can be one of the most exciting steps in your career. To succeed, you need to pay especially close attention to the important elements of the interviewing process, including personal appearance, an awareness of what interviewers are really trying to learn about you, and what you should learn about the organization you're hoping to join.

Some countries and cultures place a much higher importance on dress and personal grooming than many employees in the United States are accustomed to; moreover, expectations of personal appearance can vary dramatically from country to country. Ask people who've been to the country before and observe local businesspeople when you arrive. Many people interpret inappropriate dress as more than a simple fashion mistake; they view it as an inability or unwillingness to understand another culture.

Whether or not these things should matter isn't the question; they do matter, and successful job candidates learn how to respond to different expectations. For instance, business image consultant Ashley Rothschild points out that you could get away with wearing a boldly colored suit in Italy but probably not in Japan. Business professionals do tend to dress formally in Italy, but as a worldwide fashion leader, the country has a broad definition of what is appropriate business attire.

Smart U.S. recruiters always analyze both nonverbal signals and verbal messages to judge whether an applicant truly has the qualities necessary for a job. In international employment situations, you'll probably be under even closer scrutiny. Recruiters abroad will want to know if you really have what it takes to succeed in unfamiliar social settings, how your family will handle the transition, and whether you can adapt your personal work style and habits enough to blend in with the hiring organization.

Remember to ask plenty of questions and do your research, both before and after the interview. Some employees view overseas postings as grand adventures, only to collide headfirst with the reality of what it's like to live and work in a completely different culture. For instance, if you've grown accustomed to the independent work style you enjoy in your current job or in school, could you handle a more structured work environment with a hierarchical chain of command? Make sure to get a sense of the culture both within the company and within its social community before you commit to a job in another country.

CAREER APPLICATIONS

1. Explain how you could find out what is appropriate dress for a job interview in South Africa.
2. Would it be appropriate to ask an interviewer to describe the culture in his or her country? Explain your answer.

Continue your preparation by jotting down a brief answer to each question in Table 19.3. You can also find typical interview questions at websites such as InterviewUp (www.interviewup.com), where candidates share actual questions they have faced in recent interviews.[40]

Planning Questions of Your Own

Remember that an interview is a two-way street: The questions you ask are just as important as the answers you provide. By asking insightful questions, you can demonstrate your understanding of the organization, you can steer the discussion into areas that allow you to present your qualifications to best advantage, and you can verify for yourself whether this is a good opportunity. Plus, interviewers expect you to ask questions; if you don't have any questions, the interviewer is likely to wonder if you're really interested in the job or whether you've done any research into the company. Plan to ask questions that will help you collect the following sorts of information:

- **Are these my kind of people?** Observe the interviewers, and if you can, arrange to talk with other employees.
- **Can I do this work?** Compare your qualifications with the requirements described by the interviewer.
- **Will I enjoy the work?** Will the work give you real feelings of accomplishment and satisfaction?

REAL-TIME UPDATES
Learn More

Study the classics to ace your next interview

No, not Homer and Ovid—classic interview questions. Prepare answers to these old standbys so you can respond with clarity and confidence. Go to **http://real-timeupdates.com/bct** and click on "Learn More." If you are using mybcommlab, you can access Real-Time Updates within each chapter or under Student Study Tools.

Practice answering typical interview questions so that you can respond with confidence and complete answers.

Plan questions that will help you decide whether the work and the organization are compatible with your goals and values.

TABLE 19.3 Twenty-Five Common Interview Questions

QUESTIONS ABOUT COLLEGE

1. What courses in college did you like most? Least? Why?
2. Do you think your extracurricular activities in college were worth the time you spent on them? Why or why not?
3. When did you choose your college major? Did you ever change your major? If so, why?
4. Do you feel you did the best scholastic work you are capable of?
5. How has your college education prepared you for this position?

QUESTIONS ABOUT EMPLOYERS AND JOBS

6. What jobs have you held? Why did you leave?
7. What percentage of your college expenses did you earn? How?
8. Why did you choose your particular field of work?
9. What are the disadvantages of your chosen field?
10. Have you served in the military? What rank did you achieve? What jobs did you perform?
11. What do you think about how this industry operates today?
12. Why do you think you would like this particular type of job?

QUESTIONS ABOUT PERSONAL ATTITUDES AND PREFERENCES

13. Do you prefer to work in any specific geographic location? If so, why?
14. How much money do you hope to be earning in 5 years? In 10 years?
15. What do you think determines a person's progress in a good organization?
16. What personal characteristics do you feel are necessary for success in your chosen field?
17. Tell me a story.
18. Do you like to travel?
19. Why should I hire you?

QUESTIONS ABOUT WORK HABITS

20. Do you prefer working with others or by yourself?
21. What type of boss do you prefer?
22. Have you ever had any difficulty getting along with colleagues or supervisors? With instructors? With other students?
23. What would you do if you were given an unrealistic deadline for a task or project?
24. How do you feel about overtime work?
25. What have you done that shows initiative and willingness to work?

- **Is the job what I want?** Will it make use of your best capabilities? Does it offer a career path to the long-term goals you've set?
- **Does the job pay what I'm worth?** By comparing jobs and salaries before you're interviewed, you'll know what's reasonable for someone with your skills in your industry.
- **What kind of person would I be working for?** If the interviewer is your prospective boss, watch how others interact with that person, tactfully query other employees, or pose a careful question or two during the interview. If your prospective boss is someone else, discretely ask about that person's name, job title, and responsibilities as a way to learn more.
- **What sort of future can I expect with this organization?** Is this organization in healthy financial shape? Will it grow enough to offer you opportunities to advance?

Think ahead about ways to relate your skills and accomplishments through brief, memorable stories.

For a list of good questions that you might use as a starting point, see Table 19.4.

As you prepare answers, look for ways to frame your responses as brief stories (30 to 90 seconds) rather than simple declarative statements.[41] Instead of just saying you are good at finding ways to reduce costs, tell a story of a time you did just that. Cohesive stories tend to stick in the listener's mind more effectively than disconnected facts and statements.

Bolstering Your Confidence

The best way to build your confidence is to prepare thoroughly and address shortcomings as best you can—in other words, to take action.

Interviewing is stressful for everyone, so some nervousness is natural. However, you can take steps to feel more confident. Start by reminding yourself that you have value to offer the employer, and the employer already thinks highly enough of you to invite you to an interview.

TABLE 19.4 Ten Questions to Ask an Interviewer

QUESTION	REASON FOR ASKING
1. What are the job's major responsibilities?	A vague answer could mean that the responsibilities have not been clearly defined, which is almost guaranteed to cause frustration if you take the job.
2. What qualities do you want in the person who fills this position?	This will help you go beyond the job description to understand what the company really wants.
3. How do you measure success for someone in this position?	A vague or incomplete answer could mean that the expectations you will face are unrealistic or ill defined.
4. What is the first problem that needs the attention of the person you hire?	Not only will this help you prepare, but it can signal whether you're about to jump into a problematic situation.
5. Would relocation be required now or in the future?	If you're not willing to move often or at all, you need to know those expectations now.
6. Why is this job now vacant?	If the previous employee got promoted, that's a good sign. If the person quit, that might not be such a good sign.
7. What makes your organization different from others in the industry?	The answer will help you assess whether the company has a clear strategy to succeed in its industry and whether top managers communicate it to lower-level employees.
8. How would you define your organization's managerial philosophy?	You want to know whether the managerial philosophy is consistent with your own working values.
9. What is a typical workday like for you?	The interviewer's response can give you clues about daily life at the company.
10. What systems and policies are in place to help employees stay up to date in their professions and continue to expand their skills?	If the company doesn't have a strong commitment to employee development, chances are it isn't going to stay competitive very long.

If some aspect of your appearance or background makes you uneasy, correct it if possible or offset it by emphasizing positive traits such as warmth, wit, intelligence, or charm. Instead of dwelling on your weaknesses, focus on your strengths. Instead of worrying about how you will perform in the interview, focus on how you can help the organization succeed. As with public speaking, the more prepared you are, the more confident you'll be.

Polishing Your Interview Style

Competence and confidence are the foundation of your interviewing style, and you can enhance them by giving the interviewer an impression of poise, good manners, and good judgment. You can develop an adept style by staging mock interviews with a friend or using an interview simulator. Record these mock interviews so you can evaluate yourself. Your career center may have computer-based systems for practicing interviews as well (see Figure 19.4).

After each practice session, look for opportunities to improve. Have your mock interview partner critique your performance, or critique yourself if you're able to record your practice interviews, using the list of warning signs shown in Table 19.5. Pay close attention to the length of your planned answers as well. Interviewers want you to give complete answers, but they don't want you to take up valuable time or test their patience by chatting about minor or irrelevant details.[42]

Staging mock interviews with a friend is a good way to hone your style.

Evaluate your nonverbal behavior as well. In the United States and most other Western cultures, you are more likely to have a successful interview if you maintain eye contact, smile frequently, sit in an attentive position, and use frequent hand gestures. These nonverbal signals convince the interviewer that you're alert, assertive, dependable, confident, responsible, and energetic.[43]

Nonverbal behavior has a significant effect on the interviewer's opinion of you.

FIGURE 19.4 Interview Simulators
Experts recommend practicing your interview skills as much as possible. You can use a friend or classmate as a practice partner, or you might be able to use one of the interview simulators now available, such as this system from Perfect Interview. Ask at your career center for more information.

The way you speak is almost as important as what you say.

The sound of your voice can also have a major impact on your success in a job interview.[44] Recording your voice can help you overcome voice problems. If you tend to speak too rapidly, practice speaking more slowly. If your voice sounds too loud or too soft, practice adjusting it. Work on eliminating speech mannerisms such as *you know*, *like*, and *um*, which make you sound hesitant or inarticulate.

Dress conservatively and be well groomed for every interview; you will be judged on how well you can sense what is appropriate in the work environment.

Presenting a Professional Image

Clothing and grooming are important elements of preparation because they reveal something about a candidate's personality, professionalism, and ability to sense the unspoken "rules" of a situation. Your research into various industries and professions should give

TABLE 19.5 Warning Signs: 25 Attributes That Interviewers Don't Like to See

1. Poor personal appearance
2. Overbearing, overaggressive, or conceited demeanor; a "superiority complex"; a know-it-all attitude
3. Inability to express ideas clearly; poor voice, diction, or grammar
4. Lack of knowledge or experience
5. Poor preparation for the interview
6. Lack of interest in the job
7. Lack of planning for career; lack of purpose or goals
8. Lack of enthusiasm; passive and indifferent demeanor
9. Lack of confidence and poise; appearance of being nervous and ill at ease
10. Insufficient evidence of achievement
11. Failure to participate in extracurricular activities
12. Overemphasis on money; interest only in the best dollar offer
13. Poor scholastic record; just got by
14. Unwillingness to start at the bottom; expecting too much too soon
15. Tendency to make excuses
16. Evasive answers; hedging on unfavorable factors in record
17. Lack of tact
18. Lack of maturity
19. Lack of courtesy; being ill mannered
20. Condemnation of past employers
21. Lack of social skills
22. Marked dislike for schoolwork
23. Lack of vitality
24. Failure to look interviewer in the eye
25. Limp, weak handshake

you insight into expectations for business attire. If you're not sure what to wear, refer to Table 2.4 on page 88 for tips on selecting appropriate business attire or ask someone who works in the same industry. And don't be afraid to call the company for advice.

You don't need to spend a fortune on interview clothes, but your clothes must be clean, pressed, and appropriate. The following conservative look will serve you well in just about any interview situation:[45]

REAL-TIME UPDATES
Learn More

Do you know the difference between business casual and business formal?

Go shopping with a business style expert to select the appropriate wear for any interview. Go to http://real-timeupdates.com/bct and click on "Learn More." If you are using mybcommlab, you can access Real-Time Updates within each chapter or under Student Study Tools.

- Neat, "adult" hairstyle
- Conservative business suit (for women, that means no exposed midriffs, no short skirts, and no plunging necklines), in a dark solid color or a subtle pattern such as pinstripes
- White shirt for men; coordinated blouse for women
- Conservative tie (classic stripes or subtle patterns) for men
- Limited jewelry (men should wear very little jewelry)
- No visible piercings other than one or two earrings (for women only)
- No visible tattoos
- Stylish but professional-looking shoes (no high heels or casual shoes)
- Clean hands and nicely trimmed fingernails
- Little or no perfume or cologne (some people are allergic, and many people are put off by strong smells)
- Subtle makeup (for women)
- Exemplary personal hygiene

If you want to be taken seriously, dress and act seriously.

Remember, an interview is not the place to express your individuality or to let your inner rebel run wild. Send a clear signal that you understand the business world and know how to adapt to it. You won't be taken seriously otherwise.

Being Ready When You Arrive

When you go to your interview, take a small notebook, a pen, a list of the questions you want to ask, several copies of your résumé (protected in a folder), an outline of what you have learned about the organization, and any past correspondence about the position. You may also want to take a small calendar, a transcript of your college grades, a list of references, and a portfolio containing samples of your work, performance reviews, and certificates of achievement.[46]

Be sure you know when and where the interview will be held. The worst way to start an interview is to be late, and arriving in a stressed-out state isn't much better. Check the route you will take but don't rely on time estimates from a bus or subway service or from an online mapping service. If you're not familiar with the route, the safest choice is to travel to the location a few days before the interview, if possible, to verify it for yourself. Leave yourself plenty of time for unforeseen problems.

When you arrive, remind yourself that you are fully prepared and confident and then try to relax. You may have to wait, so bring along something business oriented to read. If company literature is available in the lobby, read it while you wait. At every step, show respect for everyone you encounter. If the opportunity presents itself, ask a few questions about the organization or express enthusiasm for the job. Refrain from smoking before the interview (nonsmokers can smell smoke on the clothing of interviewees) and avoid chewing gum or otherwise eating or drinking in the waiting room. Anything you do or say while you wait may well get back to the interviewer, so make sure your best qualities show from the moment you enter the premises. To review the steps for planning a successful interview, see "Checklist: Planning for a Successful Job Interview."

Make a positive first impression with careful grooming and attire. You don't need to spend a fortune on new clothes, but you do need to look clean, prepared, and professional.

Be ready to go the minute you arrive at the interviewing site; don't fumble around for your résumé or your list of questions.

✓ **CHECKLIST:**   **Planning for a Successful Job Interview**

- Learn about the organization, including its operations, markets, and challenges.
- Plan for the employer's questions, including questions about tough decisions you've made, your perceived shortcomings, what you didn't like about previous jobs, and your career plans.
- Plan questions of your own to find out whether this is really the job and the organization for you and to show that you've done your research.
- Bolster your confidence by removing as many sources of apprehension as you can.

- Polish your interview style by staging mock interviews.
- Present a professional appearance with appropriate dress and grooming.
- Be ready when you arrive and bring along a pen, paper, a list of questions, copies of your résumé, an outline of your research on the company, and any correspondence you've had regarding the position.
- Double-check the location and time of the interview and map out the route beforehand.
- Relax and be flexible; the schedule and interview arrangements may change when you arrive.

5 LEARNING OBJECTIVE

Explain the three stages of a successful employment interview

The first minute of an interview is crucial, so be ready and stay on your toes.

You could face substantial questions as soon as interview starts, so make sure you are prepared and ready to go.

Tailor your answers to emphasize your strengths.

INTERVIEWING FOR SUCCESS

At this point, you have a good sense of the overall process and know how to prepare for your interviews. The next step is to get familiar with the three stages of every interview: the warm-up, the question-and-answer session, and the close.

The Warm-up

Of the three stages, the warm-up is the most important, even though it may account for only a small fraction of the time you spend in the interview. Studies suggest that many interviewers, particularly those who are poorly trained in interviewing techniques, make up their minds within the first 20 seconds of contact with a candidate.[47] Don't let your guard down if the interviewer wants to engage in what feels like small talk; these exchanges are every bit as important as structured questions.

Body language is crucial at this point. Stand up or sit up straight, maintain regular but natural eye contact, and don't fidget. When the interviewer extends a hand, respond with a firm but not overpowering handshake. Repeat the interviewer's name when you're introduced ("It's a pleasure to meet you, Ms. Litton"). Wait until you're asked to be seated or the interviewer has taken a seat. Let the interviewer start the discussion and be ready to answer one or two substantial questions right away. Common openers include[48]

- Why do you want to work here?
- What do you know about us?
- Tell me a little about yourself.

The Question-and-Answer Stage

Questions and answers will consume the greatest part of the interview. The interviewer will ask you about your qualifications and discuss many of the points mentioned in your résumé. You'll also be asking questions of your own.

Dealing with Questions

Let the interviewer lead the conversation and never answer a question before he or she has finished asking it. Not only is doing so rude, but the last few words of the question might alter how you respond. As much as possible, avoid one-word, yes-or-no answers. Use the opportunity to expand on a positive response or explain a negative response. If you're asked a difficult question, pause before responding. Think through the implications of the question; for instance, the recruiter may know that you can't answer a question and only want to know how you'll handle the situation.

Whenever you're asked if you have any questions, or whenever doing so naturally fits the flow of the conversation, ask a question from the list you've prepared. Probe for what the company is looking for in its new employees so that you can show how you meet the firm's

Communication Miscues

Make Sure You Don't Talk Yourself Out of a Job

Even well-qualified applicants sometimes talk themselves right out of an opportunity by making avoidable blunders during a job interview. Take care to avoid these all-too-common mistakes:

- **Being defensive.** An interview isn't an interrogation, and the interviewer isn't out to get you. Treat interviews as business conversations, an exchange of information in which both sides have something of value to share. You'll give (and get) better information that way.
- **Failing to ask questions.** Interviewers expect you to ask questions, both during the interview and at its conclusion, when they ask if you have any questions. If you have nothing to ask, you come across as someone who isn't really interested in the job or the company. Prepare a list of questions before every interview.
- **Failing to answer questions—or trying to bluff your way through difficult questions.** If you can't answer a question, don't try to talk your way around it or fake your way through it. Remember that sometimes interviewers ask strange questions just to see how you'll respond. What kind of fish would you like to be? How would you go about nailing jelly to the ceiling? Why are manhole covers round? Some of these questions are designed to test your grace under pressure, whereas others are used to get you to think through a logical answer. (Manhole covers are round because a circle is the only shape that can't fall through an open hole of slightly smaller size, by the way.) Don't act like the question is stupid or refuse to answer it. As Lynne Sarikas, director of the MBA Career Center at Northeastern

University, explains, these questions offer an opportunity to "demonstrate quick thinking, poise, creativity, and even a sense of humor."[49]

- **Freezing up.** The human brain seems to have the capacity to just freeze up in stressful situations. An interviewer might have asked you a simple question, or perhaps you are halfway through an intelligent answer, and poof!—all your thoughts disappear and you can't organize words in any logical order. Try to quickly replay the last few seconds of the conversation in your mind to see if you can recapture the conversational thread. If that fails, you're probably better off explaining to the interviewer that your mind has gone blank and asking him or her to repeat the question. Doing so is embarrassing but not as embarrassing as chattering on and on with no idea of what you're saying, hoping you'll stumble back onto the topic.
- **Failing to understand your potential to contribute to the organization.** Interviewers care less about your history than about how you can help their organization in the future. Be sure to understand ahead of time how your skills can help the company meet its challenges.

CAREER APPLICATIONS

1. What should you do if you suddenly realize that something you said earlier in the interview is incorrect or incomplete? Explain your answer.
2. How would you answer the following question: "How do you respond to colleagues who make you angry?" Explain your answer.

---

needs. Also try to zero in on any reservations the interviewer might have about you so that you can dispel them.

Listening to the Interviewer

Paying attention when an interviewer speaks can be as important as giving good answers or asking good questions. Review the tips on listening offered in Chapter 2. The interviewer's facial expressions, eye movements, gestures, and posture may tell you the real meaning of what is being said. Be especially aware of how your comments are received. Does the interviewer nod in agreement or smile to show approval? If so, you're making progress. If not, you might want to introduce another topic or modify your approach.

Paying attention to both verbal and nonverbal messages can help you turn the question-and-answer stage to your advantage.

Handling Discriminatory Questions

In many countries, employers cannot legally discriminate against a job candidate on the basis of race, color, gender, age (at least if you're 40 or older), marital status, religion, national origin, or disability. Accordingly, governments have regulations in place to prevent interviewers from asking questions in ways that would allow them to discriminate according to any of these factors. Individual states/provinces and cities have enacted a variety of laws concerning interview questions, so you may have additional protections beyond the national standards.[50] Table 19.6 compares specific questions that may and may not be asked during an employment interview in the United States.

Well-trained interviewers are aware of questions they shouldn't ask.

TABLE 19.6 Interview Questions That U.S. Employers Are and Are Not Allowed to Ask

INTERVIEWERS MAY ASK THIS...	BUT NOT THIS
What is your name?	What was your maiden name?
Are you over 18?	When were you born?
Did you graduate from high school?	When did you graduate from high school?
[No questions about race are allowed.]	What is your race?
Can you perform [specific tasks]?	Do you have physical or mental disabilities? Do you have a drug or alcohol problem? Are you taking any prescription drugs?
Would you be able to meet the job's requirement to frequently work weekends?	Would working on weekends conflict with your religion?
Do you have the legal right to work in the United States?	What country are you a citizen of?
Have you ever been convicted of a felony?	Have you ever been arrested?
This job requires that you speak Spanish. Do you?	What language did you speak in your home when you were growing up?

Think about how you might respond if you are asked a potentially unlawful question.

If your interviewer asks unlawful personal questions, how you respond depends on how badly you want the job, how you feel about revealing the information asked for, what you think the interviewer will do with the information, and whether you want to work for a company whose employees ask such questions. Remember that you always have the option of simply refusing to answer or of telling the interviewer that you think a particular question is unethical—although either of these responses is likely to leave an unfavorable impression.[51] If you do want the job, you might (1) ask how the question is related to your qualifications, (2) explain that the information is personal, (3) respond to what you think is the interviewer's real concern, or (4) answer both the question and the concern.

If you do answer an unethical or unlawful question, you run the risk that your answer may hurt your chances, so think carefully before answering.[52] In any event, don't forget the two-way nature of the interview process: The organization is learning about you, and you're learning about the organization. Would you want to work for an organization that condones illegal or discriminatory questions or that doesn't train its employees to avoid them?

If you believe an interviewer's questions are unreasonable, unrelated to the job, or an attempt to discriminate, you can complain to the nearest field office of the Equal Employment Opportunity Commission (find offices online at **www.eeoc.gov**) or to the agency in your area that regulates fair employment practices.

The Close

Like the warm-up, the end of the interview is more important than its brief duration would indicate. These last few minutes are your last opportunity to emphasize your value to the organization and to correct any misconceptions the interviewer might have. Be aware that many interviews will ask if you have any more questions at this point, so save one or two from your list.

Concluding Gracefully

Conclude an interview with courtesy and enthusiasm.

You can usually tell when the interviewer is trying to conclude the session. He or she may ask whether you have any more questions, check the time, sum up the discussion, or simply tell you that the allotted time for the interview is up. When you get the signal, be sure to thank the interviewer for the opportunity and express your interest in the organization. If you can do so comfortably, try to pin down what will happen next, but don't press for an immediate decision.

If this is your second or third visit to the organization, the interview may end with an offer of employment. If you have other offers or need time to think about this offer, it's perfectly acceptable to thank the interviewer for the offer and ask for some time to consider it. If no job offer is made, the interview team may not have reached a decision yet, but you may tactfully ask when you can expect to know the decision.

Discussing Salary

If you receive an offer during an interview, you'll naturally want to discuss salary. However, let the interviewer raise the subject. If you are asked your salary requirements during the interview or on a job application, you can say that your salary requirements are open or negotiable or that you would expect a competitive compensation package.[53] If you have added qualifications, point them out: "With my 18 months of experience in the field, I would expect to start in the middle of the normal salary range." You can find industry salary ranges at the Bureau of Labor Statistics website (www.bls.gov) and at several of the popular job websites.

If you don't like the offer, you can ask if there is any room for negotiation. How far you can negotiate depends on several factors, including market demand for your particular skills, the overall strength of the job market, the company's compensation policies, the company's financial health, and whether you currently have other job offers. Remember that you're negotiating a business deal, not asking for personal favors, so focus on the unique value you can bring to the job. The more information you have, the stronger your position will be.

Salary will probably be the most important component of your compensation and benefits package, but it's not the only factor by any means. And even if salary isn't negotiable, you may find flexibility in a signing bonus, profit sharing, pension and other retirement benefits, health coverage, vacation time, stock options, and other valuable elements in the overall compensation and benefits package.[54]

To review the important tips for successful interviews, see "Checklist: Making a Positive Impression in Job Interviews."

Interview Notes

If yours is a typical job search, you'll have many interviews before you accept an offer. For that reason, keeping a notebook or simple database of interview notes can help you refresh your

REAL-TIME UPDATES
Learn More

Evaluating a job offer

Explore the many steps needed to determine whether a job offer is right for you, your family, and your future. Go to **http://real-timeupdates .com/bct** and click on "Learn More." If you are using mybcommlab, you can access Real-Time Updates within each chapter or under Student Study Tools.

Research salary ranges in your job, industry, and geographic region before you try to negotiate salary.

Negotiating benefits may be one way to get more value from an employment package.

REAL-TIME UPDATES
Learn More

Follow these negotiating tips to get the best job offer

Make sure you get the best compensation package when you get a job offer. Go to **http://real-time updates.com/bct** and click on "Learn More." If you are using mybcommlab, you can access Real-Time Updates within each chapter or under Student Study Tools.

✓ **CHECKLIST:** **Making a Positive Impression in Job Interviews**

A. Be ready for the warm-up stage.
- Stay on your toes; even initial small talk is part of the interviewing process.
- Greet the interviewer by name, with a smile and direct eye contact.
- Offer a firm (not crushing) handshake if the interviewer extends a hand.
- Take a seat only after the interviewer invites you to sit or has taken his or her own seat.
- Listen for clues about what the interviewer is trying to get you to reveal about you and your qualifications.

B. Understand the question-and-answer stage.
- Let the interviewer lead the conversation.
- Never answer a question before the interviewer finishes asking it.
- Listen carefully to the interviewer and watch for nonverbal signals.
- Don't limit yourself to simple yes-or-no answers; expand on the answer to show your knowledge of the company (but don't ramble on).

- If you encounter a potentially discriminatory question, decide how you want to respond before you say anything.
- When you have the opportunity, ask questions from the list you've prepared; remember that interviewers expect you to ask questions.

C. Close on a strong note.
- Watch and listen for signs that the interview is about to end.
- Quickly evaluate how well you've done and correct any misperceptions the interviewer might have.
- If you receive an offer and aren't ready to decide, it's entirely appropriate to ask for time to think about it.
- Don't bring up salary but be prepared to discuss it if the interviewer raises the subject.
- End with a warm smile and a handshake and thank the interviewer for meeting with you.

Keep a written record of your job interviews and keep your notes organized so that you can compare companies and opportunities.

memory of each conversation. As soon as you leave the interview facility, jot down the names and titles of the people you met. Briefly summarize the interviewer's answers to your questions. Then quickly evaluate your performance during the interview, listing what you handled well and what you didn't. Going over these notes can help you improve your performance in the future.[55] In addition to improving your performance during interviews, interview notes help you keep track of any follow-up messages you'll need to send.

For the latest information on interviewing strategies, visit **http://real-timeupdates .com/bct** and click on Chapter 19.

6 LEARNING OBJECTIVE

Identify the most common employment messages that follow an interview and explain when you would use each one

Six types of follow-up messages:
- *Thank-you message*
- *Message of inquiry*
- *Request for a time extension*
- *Letter of acceptance*
- *Letter declining a job offer*
- *Letter of resignation*

FOLLOWING UP AFTER THE INTERVIEW

Staying in contact with a prospective employer after an interview shows that you really want the job and are determined to get it. Doing so also gives you another chance to demonstrate your communication skills and sense of business etiquette. You have several opportunities to communicate after an interview, starting with a thank-you message.

Thank-You Message

Write a thank-you message within two days of the interview, even if you feel you have little chance of being offered the job. Not only is this good etiquette, but it can be an essential step in promoting yourself to the employer. The thank-you message gives you the opportunity to reinforce the reasons that you are a good choice for the position, and it lets you respond to any negatives that might have arisen in the interview.[56] Acknowledge the interviewer's time and courtesy, convey your continued interest, reinforce the reasons that you are a good fit for the position, and then ask politely for a decision (see Figure 19.5).

FIGURE 19.5 Thank-You Message
In three brief paragraphs, Michael Espinosa acknowledges the interviewer's time and consideration, expresses his continued interest in the position, explains a crucial discussion point that he has reconsidered, and asks for a decision.

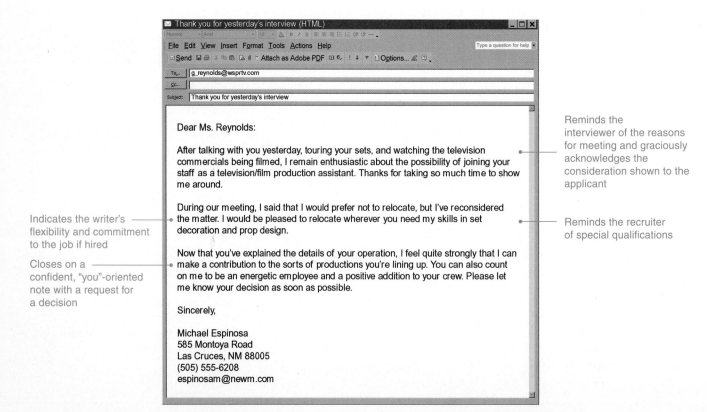

Reminds the interviewer of the reasons for meeting and graciously acknowledges the consideration shown to the applicant

Reminds the recruiter of special qualifications

Indicates the writer's flexibility and commitment to the job if hired

Closes on a confident, "you"-oriented note with a request for a decision

Depending on the company and the relationship you've established with the interviewer, the thank-you message can be handled via letter or e-mail. Keep your thank-you message brief, and organize it like a routine message. Demonstrate the "you" attitude and sound positive without sounding over-confident.

Message of Inquiry

If you're not advised of the interviewer's decision by the promised date or within two weeks, you might make an inquiry. A message of inquiry is particularly appropriate if you've received a job offer from a second firm and don't want to accept it before you have an answer from the first. The following message illustrates the general plan for a direct request; the writer assumes that a simple oversight or routine delay, and not outright rejection, is the reason for the delay:

> Document Makeover
>
> **Improve This Letter**
>
> To practice correcting drafts of actual documents, visit the "Document Makeovers" section in either mybcommlab or the Companion Website for this text.
>
> If mybcommlab is being used in your class, see your User Guide for specific instructions on how to access the content for this chapter. If you are accessing this feature through the Companion Website, click on "Document Makeovers" and then click Chapter 19. You will find a letter that contains problems and errors related to what you've learned in this chapter about applying and interviewing for employment. Use the Final Draft decision tool to create an improved version of this request for a time extension. Check the letter for all the elements necessary to reassure the potential employer, ask for the extension, explain the reasons for the request, offer to compromise, and facilitate a quick reply.

When we talked on April 7 about the fashion coordinator position in your Park Avenue showroom, you indicated that a decision would be made by May 1. I am still enthusiastic about the position and eager to know what conclusion you've reached. — Identifies the position and introduces the main idea

To complicate matters, another firm has now offered me a position and has asked that I reply within the next two weeks. — Places the reason for the request second

Because your company seems to offer a greater challenge, I would appreciate knowing about your decision by Thursday, May 12. If you need more information before then, please let me know. — Makes a courteous request for specific action last, while clearly stating a preference for this organization

Request for a Time Extension

If you receive a job offer while other interviews are still pending, you can ask the employer for a time extension. Open with a strong statement of your continued interest in the job, ask for more time to consider the offer, provide specific reasons for the request, and assure the reader that you will respond by a specific date (see Figure 19.6).

Letter of Acceptance

When you receive a job offer that you want to accept, reply within five days. Begin by accepting the position and expressing thanks. Identify the job that you're accepting. In the next paragraph, cover any necessary details. Conclude by saying that you look forward to reporting for work. As always, a positive message such as this should convey your enthusiasm and eagerness to cooperate:

Use the model for positive messages when you write a letter of acceptance.

I'm delighted to accept the graphic design position in your advertising department at the salary of $2,975 a month. — Confirms the specific terms of the offer with a good-news statement at the beginning

Enclosed are the health insurance forms you asked me to complete and sign. I've already given notice to my current employer and will be able to start work on Monday, January 18. — Covers miscellaneous details in the middle

The prospect of joining your firm is exciting. Thank you for giving me this opportunity for what I'm sure will be a challenging future. — Closes with another reference to the good news and a look toward the future

Be aware that a job offer and a written acceptance of that offer can constitute a legally binding contract—for you and the employer. Before you write an acceptance letter, be sure you want the job.

FIGURE 19.6 Request for a Time Extension

If you need to request more time to make a decision about a job offer, be sure to explain why you need the extension and reaffirm that you are still interested in the job.

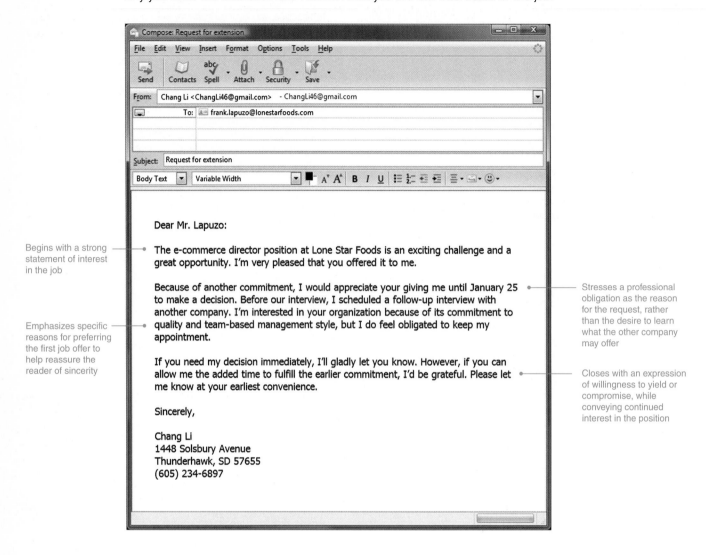

Begins with a strong statement of interest in the job

Emphasizes specific reasons for preferring the first job offer to help reassure the reader of sincerity

Stresses a professional obligation as the reason for the request, rather than the desire to learn what the other company may offer

Closes with an expression of willingness to yield or compromise, while conveying continued interest in the position

Dear Mr. Lapuzo:

The e-commerce director position at Lone Star Foods is an exciting challenge and a great opportunity. I'm very pleased that you offered it to me.

Because of another commitment, I would appreciate your giving me until January 25 to make a decision. Before our interview, I scheduled a follow-up interview with another company. I'm interested in your organization because of its commitment to quality and team-based management style, but I do feel obligated to keep my appointment.

If you need my decision immediately, I'll gladly let you know. However, if you can allow me the added time to fulfill the earlier commitment, I'd be grateful. Please let me know at your earliest convenience.

Sincerely,

Chang Li
1448 Solsbury Avenue
Thunderhawk, SD 57655
(605) 234-6897

Letter Declining a Job Offer

A letter declining a job offer should follow the model for negative messages.

After all your interviews, you may find that you need to write a letter declining a job offer. Use the techniques for negative messages (see Chapter 9): Open warmly, state the reasons for refusing the offer, decline the offer explicitly, and close on a pleasant note, expressing gratitude. By taking the time to write a sincere, tactful letter, you leave the door open for future contact:

Uses a buffer in the opening paragraph

Precedes the bad news with tactfully phrased reasons for the applicant's unfavorable decision and leaves the door open

Lets the reader down gently with a sincere and cordial ending

Thank you for your hospitality during my interview at your Durham facility last month. I'm flattered that you would offer me the computer analyst position that we talked about.

I was fortunate to receive two job offers during my search. Because my desire to work abroad can more readily be satisfied by another company, I have accepted that job offer.

I deeply appreciate the time you spent talking with me. Thank you again for your consideration and kindness.

Letter of Resignation

If you get a job offer and are currently employed, you can maintain good relations with your current employer by writing a letter of resignation to your immediate supervisor. Follow the approach for negative messages and make the letter sound as positive as possible, regardless of how you feel. Don't take this letter as an opportunity to vent any frustrations you may have. Say something favorable about the organization, the people you work with, or what you've learned on the job. Then state your intention to leave and give the date of your last day on the job. Be sure you give your current employer at least two weeks' notice:

Letters of resignation should always be written in a gracious and professional style that avoids criticism of your employer or your colleagues.

My sincere thanks to you and to all the other Emblem Corporation employees for helping me learn so much about serving the public these past two years. You have given me untold help and encouragement.

You may recall that when you first interviewed me, my goal was to become a customer relations supervisor. Because that opportunity has been offered to me by another organization, I am submitting my resignation. I will miss my friends and colleagues at Emblem, but I want to take advantage of this opportunity.

I would like to terminate my work here two weeks from today but can arrange to work an additional week if you want me to train a replacement.

Best wishes to all of you.

Uses an appreciative opening to serve as a buffer

States reasons before the bad news itself, using tactful phrasing to help keep the relationship friendly, should the writer later want letters of recommendation

Discusses necessary details in an extra paragraph

Tempers any disappointment with a cordial close

To verify the content and style of your follow-up messages, consult the tips in "Checklist: Writing Follow-up Messages."

✔ **CHECKLIST:** **Writing Follow-up Messages**

A. Thank-you messages.
- Write a brief thank-you letter within two days of the interview.
- Acknowledge the interviewer's time and courtesy.
- Restate the specific job you're applying for.
- Express your enthusiasm about the organization and the job.
- Add any new facts that may help your chances.
- Politely ask for a decision.

B. Messages of inquiry.
- If you haven't heard from the interviewer by the promised date, write a brief message of inquiry.
- Use the direct approach: main idea, necessary details, specific request.

C. Requests for a time extension.
- Request an extension if you have pending interviews and need time to decide about an offer.
- Open on a friendly note.
- Explain why you need more time and express continued interest in the company.
- In the close, promise a quick decision if your request is denied and ask for a confirmation if your request is granted.

D. Letters of acceptance.
- Send this message within five days of receiving the offer.
- State clearly that you accept the offer, identify the job you're accepting, and confirm vital details such as salary and start date.
- Make sure you want the job; an acceptance letter can be treated as a legally binding contract.

E. Letters declining a job offer.
- Use the model for negative messages.
- Open on a warm and appreciative note and then explain why you are refusing the offer.
- End on a sincere, positive note.

F. Letters of resignation.
- Send a letter of resignation to your current employer as soon as possible.
- Begin with an appreciative buffer.
- In the middle section, state your reasons for leaving and actually state that you are resigning.
- Close cordially.

Communication Challenges at Google

After a few years of experience in the human resources department of a publishing company, you recently joined Google's recruiting team under Arnnon Geshuri. Today, Geshuri asked you to help with the recruiting and hiring of the project coordinators. These people will provide administrative help to the various engineering teams in the company and also serve as liaisons to other departments.

Individual Challenge: Geshuri is looking for experienced administrative support people who remain calm when things get chaotic and are flexible enough to interact successfully not only with engineers but also with accountants, marketing managers, salespeople, facilities staff, and others. With those requirements in mind, create a list of three or four questions to use during the screening interviews for project coordinators.

Team Challenge: Seven candidates survived the screening process and now you're planning the onsite interviews. In a small group, discuss the types of people to include on the interview team (consult a management textbook if you're unfamiliar with positions in a typical corporation): Who should serve as host and handle the warm-up stage? Who should be involved in the question-and-answer stage? Who should handle the close? In all cases, explain why.

SUMMARY OF LEARNING OBJECTIVES

1 **Define the purpose of application letters, and explain how to apply the AIDA model to them.** In addition to explaining why you're sending a résumé, the purpose of an application letter is to convince readers to look at your résumé. This makes application letters a type of persuasive message and therefore ideal for the AIDA organizational approach. Get attention in the opening paragraph by showing how your work skills could benefit the organization, by explaining how your qualifications fit the job, or by demonstrating an understanding of the organization's needs. Build interest and desire by showing how you can meet the job requirements and, near the end of this section, be sure to refer your reader to your résumé. Finally, motivate action by making your request easy to fulfill and by including all necessary contact information.

2 **Describe the typical sequence of job interviews.** The typical sequence of interviews involves three stages. During the first stage, the *screening stage*, an employer administers fairly structured interviews to eliminate unqualified applicants. During the second stage, the *selection stage*, the pool of applicants is narrowed considerably. The employer administers a series of structured and unstructured interviews to find the best candidates for the job. Candidates who advance to the third stage, the *final stage*, of the sequence have a good chance of receiving a job offer. During this stage, candidates meet with executives who have the authority to offer the job and set compensation. The underlying objective of this final stage is to select the final candidate(s) and convince the candidate(s) to accept a job offer.

3 **Describe briefly what employers look for during an employment interview and preemployment testing.** Employers look for two things during an employment interview. First, they look for evidence that an applicant is qualified for the position. Even though interviewers have already reviewed your résumé, they want to see how well your skills match their requirements and perhaps get a sense of your ability to be flexible and apply diverse skills in more than one area. Sometimes, interviewers use preemployment tests to help gather the evidence they need to make a decision. Second, employers try to assess whether an applicant will be compatible with the other people in the organization. Whether interviewers focus on personal background or personal style, they are interested in finding someone who will easily adapt to a new workplace and new responsibilities.

4 **List six tasks you need to complete to prepare for a successful job interview.** To prepare for a successful job interview, begin by (1) refining the research you did when planning your résumé. Knowing as much as you can about the company and its needs helps you highlight the aspects of your background and qualifications that will appeal to the organization. (2) Next, think ahead about questions—both those you'll need to answer and those you'll want to ask. (3) Bolster your confidence by focusing on your strengths to overcome any apprehension. (4) Polish your style by staging mock interviews and paying close attention to nonverbal behaviors, including voice problems. (5) Plan to look your best with businesslike clothing and good grooming. (6) Finally, arrive on time and ready to begin.

5 **Explain the three stages of a successful employment interview.** All employment interviews have three stages. The warm-up stage is the most important because first impressions greatly influence an interviewer's decision. The question-and-answer stage is the longest, during which you will answer and ask questions. Listening carefully and watching the interviewer's nonverbal clues help you determine how the interview is going. The close is also important because you need to evaluate your performance to determine whether the interviewer has any misconceptions that you must correct.

6 **Identify the most common employment messages that follow an interview and explain when you would use each one.** The two most common types of follow-up messages are usually in letter form but can also be effective by phone or e-mail. You send the *thank-you* message within two days after your interview to show appreciation, express your continued interest in the job, and politely ask for a decision. You send an *inquiry* if you haven't received the interviewer's decision by the date promised or within two weeks of the interview—especially if you've received a job offer from another firm. The remaining four employment messages are best sent in letter form, to document any official action. You request a *time extension* if you receive a job offer while other interviews are pending and you want more time to complete those interviews before making a decision. You send a *letter of acceptance* within five days of receiving a job offer that you want to take. You send a *letter declining a job offer* when you want to refuse an offer tactfully and leave the door open for future contact. You send a *letter of resignation* when you receive a job offer that you want to accept while you are currently employed.

PEARSON mybcommlab

Log on to www.mybcommlab.com to access the following study and assessment aids associated with this chapter:

- Video applications
- Real-Time Updates
- Peer review activity
- Quick Learning Guides
- Pre/post test
- Personalized study plan
- Model documents
- Sample presentations

If you are not using mybcommlab, you can access the Real-Time Updates and Quick Learning Guides through http://real-timeupdates.com/bct. The Quick Learning Guide hits all the high points of this chapter in just two pages. This guide, especially prepared by the authors, will help you study for exams or review important concepts whenever you need a quick refresher.

Test Your Knowledge

1. How can you apply the AIDA model to an application letter?
2. Why do many employers now use situational or behavioral interviews?
3. What is the purpose of a working interview?
4. Why do employers conduct preemployment testing?
5. Why are the questions you ask during an interview as important as the answers you give to the interviewer's questions?
6. What are the three stages of every interview, and which is the most important?
7. How should you respond if an interviewer at a company where you want to work asks you a question that seems too personal or unethical?
8. What should you say in a thank-you message after an interview?
9. What is the purpose of sending a letter of inquiry after an interview?
10. What is the legal significance of a letter of acceptance?

Apply Your Knowledge

1. How can you distinguish yourself from other candidates in a screening interview and still keep your responses short and to the point? Explain.
2. How can you prepare for a situational or behavioral interview if you have no experience with the job for which you are interviewing?
3. If you want a new job because you can't work with your current supervisor, how can you explain this situation to a prospective employer? Give an example.
4. If you lack one important qualification for a job but have made it past the initial screening stage, how should you

prepare to handle this issue during the next round of interviews? Explain your answer.

5. **Ethical Choices** Why is it important to distinguish unethical or illegal interview questions from acceptable questions? Explain.

Practice Your Knowledge

Messages for Analysis

Read the following documents and then (1) analyze the strengths or weaknesses of each document and (2) revise each document so that it follows this chapter's guidelines.

Message 19.A: Writing an Application Letter

I'm writing to let you know about my availability for the brand manager job you advertised. As you can see from my enclosed résumé, my background is perfect for the position. Even though I don't have any real job experience, my grades have been outstanding, considering that I went to a top-ranked business school.

I did many things during my undergraduate years to prepare me for this job:

- Earned a 3.4 out of a 4.0, with a 3.8 in my business courses
- Elected representative to the student governing association
- Selected to receive the Lamar Franklin Award
- Worked to earn a portion of my tuition

I am sending my résumé to all the top firms, but I like yours better than any of the rest. Your reputation is tops in the industry, and I want to be associated with a business that can pridefully say it's the best.

If you wish for me to come in for an interview, I can come on a Friday afternoon or anytime on weekends when I don't have classes. Again, thanks for considering me for your brand manager position.

Message 19.B: Writing Application Follow-up Messages

Did you receive my résumé? I sent it to you at least two months ago and haven't heard anything. I know you keep résumés on file, but I just want to be sure that you keep me in mind. I heard you are hiring health-care managers and certainly would like to be considered for one of those positions.

Since I last wrote you, I've worked in a variety of positions that have helped prepare me for management. To wit, I've become lunch manager at the restaurant where I work, which involved a raise in pay. I now manage a waitstaff of 12 girls and take the lunch receipts to the bank every day.

Of course, I'd much rather be working at a real job, and that's why I'm writing again. Is there anything else you would like to know about me or my background? I would really like to know more about your company. Is there any literature you could send me? If so, I would really appreciate it.

I think one reason I haven't been hired yet is that I don't want to leave Atlanta. So I hope when you think of me, it's for a position that wouldn't require moving. Thanks again for considering my application.

Message 19.C: Thank-You Message

Thank you for the really marvelous opportunity to meet you and your colleagues at Starret Engine Company. I really enjoyed touring your facilities and talking with all the people there. You have quite a crew! Some of the other companies I have visited have been so rigid and uptight that I can't imagine how I would fit in. It's a relief to run into a group of people who seem to enjoy their work as much as all of you do.

I know that you must be looking at many other candidates for this job, and I know that some of them will probably be more experienced than I am. But I do want to emphasize that my two-year hitch in the Navy involved a good deal of engineering work. I don't think I mentioned all my shipboard responsibilities during the interview.

Please give me a call within the next week to let me know your decision. You can usually find me at my dormitory in the evening after dinner (phone: 877-9080).

Message 19.D: Letter of Inquiry

I have recently received a very attractive job offer from the Warrington Company. But before I let them know one way or another, I would like to consider any offer that your firm may extend. I was quite impressed with your company during my recent interview, and I am still very interested in a career there.

I don't mean to pressure you, but Warrington has asked for my decision within 10 days. Could you let me know by Tuesday whether you plan to offer me a position? That would give me enough time to compare the two offers.

Message 19.E: Letter Declining a Job Offer

I'm writing to say that I must decline your job offer. Another company has made me a more generous offer, and I have decided to accept. However, if things don't work out for me there, I will let you know. I sincerely appreciate your interest in me.

Exercises

Active links for all websites in this chapter can be found online. If mybcommlab is being used in your class, see your User Guide for instructions on accessing the content for this chapter. Otherwise, visit **www.pearsonglobaleditions.com/bovee**, locate *Business Communication Today*, Tenth Edition, click the Companion Website link, select Chapter 19, and then click on "Featured Websites." Please note that links to sites that become inactive after publication of the book will be removed from the Featured Websites section.

19.1 **Internet** Select a large company (one that you can easily find information on) where you might like to work. Use Internet sources to gather some preliminary research on the company; don't limit your search to the company's own website.

1. What did you learn about this organization that would help you during an interview there?
2. What Internet sources did you use to obtain this information?
3. Armed with this information, what aspects of your background do you think might appeal to this company's recruiters?
4. Based on what you've learned about this company's culture, what aspects of your personality should you try to highlight during an interview?

19.2 Teamwork Divide the class into two groups. Half the class will be recruiters for a large chain of national department stores, looking to fill manager trainee positions (there are 16 openings). The other half of the class will be candidates for the job. The company is specifically looking for candidates who demonstrate these three qualities: initiative, dependability, and willingness to assume responsibility.

1. Have each recruiter select and interview an applicant for 10 minutes.
2. Have all the recruiters discuss how they assessed the applicant in each of the three desired qualities. What questions did they ask or what did they use as an indicator to determine whether the candidate possessed the quality?
3. Have all the applicants discuss what they said to convince the recruiters that they possessed each of these qualities.

19.3 Interviews: Understanding Qualifications Write a short e-mail to your instructor, discussing what you believe are your greatest strengths and weaknesses from an employment perspective. Next, explain how these strengths and weaknesses would be viewed by interviewers evaluating your qualifications.

19.4 Interviews: Being Prepared Prepare written answers to 10 of the questions listed in Table 19.3.

19.5 Ethical Choices You have decided to accept a new position with a competitor of your company. Write a letter of resignation to your supervisor, announcing your decision.

1. Will you notify your employer that you are joining a competing firm? Explain.
2. Will you use the direct or the indirect approach? Explain.
3. Will you send your letter by e-mail, send it by regular mail, or place it on your supervisor's desk?

Expand Your Knowledge

Exploring the Best of the Web

Prepare and Practice Before That First Interview

www.job-interview.net

How can you practice for a job interview? What are some questions you might be asked? How should you respond? What questions are you not obligated to answer? Job-interview.net provides mock interviews based on actual job openings. It provides job descriptions, questions and answers for specific careers and jobs, and links to company guides and annual reports. You'll find a step-by-step plan that outlines key job requirements, lists practice interview questions, and helps you put together practice interviews. The site offers tips on the keywords to look for in a job description, which will help you narrow your search and anticipate the questions you might be asked on your first or next job interview. Explore the site and then answer these questions:

1. What are some problem questions you might be asked during a job interview? How would you handle these questions?
2. Choose a job title from the list and read more about it. What did you learn that could help during an actual interview for the job you selected?
3. Developing an "interview game plan" ahead of time helps you make a strong, positive impression during an interview. What are some of the things you can practice to help make everything you do during an interview seem to come naturally?

Sharpening Your Career Skills Online

Bovée and Thill's Business Communication Web Search, at http://businesscommunicationblog.com/websearch, is a unique research tool designed specifically for business communication research. Use the Web Search function to find a website, video, PDF document, or PowerPoint presentation that offers advice on interviewing. Write a brief e-mail message to your instructor, describing the item that you found and summarizing the career skills information you learned from it.

CASES

Applying the Three-Step Writing Process to Cases

Apply each step to the following cases, as assigned by your instructor.

PREPARING OTHER TYPES OF EMPLOYMENT MESSAGES

1. Online application: Electronic application letter introducing a résumé. While researching a digital camera purchase, you stumble on the webzine *Megapixel* (www.megapixel.net), which offers product reviews on a wide array of camera models. The quality of the reviews and the stunning examples of photography on the site inspire you to a new part-time business idea: You'd like to write a regular column for *Megapixel*. The webzine does a great job addressing the information needs of experienced camera users, but you see an opportunity to write for "newbies," people who are new to digital photography and need a more basic level of information.

Your task: Write an e-mail message that will serve as your application letter and address your message to Denys Bouton, who edits the English edition of *Megapixel*. (It is also published in French.) Try to limit your message to one screen (generally 20–25 lines). You'll need a creative "hook" and a reassuring approach that identifies you as the right person to launch this new feature in the webzine. (Make up any details about your background that you may need to complete the letter.)

2. All over the map: Application letter to Google Earth. You've applied yourself with vigor and resolve for four years, and you're just about to graduate with your business degree. While cruising the web to relax one night, you stumble on something called Google Earth. You're hooked instantly by the ability to zoom all around the globe and look at detailed satellite photos of places you've been to or dreamed of visiting. You can even type in the address of your apartment and get an aerial view of your neighborhood. You're amazed at the three-dimensional renderings of major U.S. cities. Plus, the photographs and maps are linked to Google's other search technologies, allowing you to locate everything from ATMs to coffees shops in your neighborhood.

You've loved maps since you were a kid, and discovering Google Earth is making you wish you'd majored in geography. Knowing how important it is to follow your heart, you decide to apply to Google anyway, even though you don't have a strong background in geographic information systems. You do have a ton of passion for maps and a good head for business.

Your task: Visit http://earth.google.com and explore the system's capabilities. (You can download a free copy of the software.) In particular, look at the business and government applications of the technology, such as customized aerial photos and maps for real estate sales, land use and environmental impact analysis, and emergency planning for homeland security agencies. Be sure to visit the Community pages as well, where you can learn more about the many interesting applications of this technology. Draft an application e-mail to Google (address it to jobs@google.com), asking to be considered for the Google Earth team. Think about how you could help the company develop the commercial potential of this product line and make sure your enthusiasm shines through in the message.

INTERVIEWING WITH POTENTIAL EMPLOYERS

3. Digging for insights: Compiling a list of questions to ask in an interview. Research is a critical element of the job search process. With information in hand, you increase the chance of finding the right opportunity (and avoiding bad choices), and you impress interviewers in multiple ways by demonstrating initiative, curiosity, research and analysis skills, an appreciation for the complex challenges of running a business, and willingness to work to achieve results.

Your task: With a small team of classmates, use online job listings to identify an intriguing job opening that at one least member of the team would seriously consider pursuing as graduation approaches. (You'll find it helpful if the career is related to at least one team member's college major or on-the-job experience so that the team can benefit from some knowledge of the profession in question.) Next, research the company, its competitors, its markets, and this specific position to identify five questions that would (1) help the team member decide if this is a good opportunity and (2) show an interviewer that you've really done your homework. Go beyond the basic and obvious questions to identify current, specific, and complex issues that only deep research can uncover. For example, is the company facing significant technical, financial, legal, or regulatory challenges that threaten its ability to grow or perhaps even survive in the long term? Or is the market evolving in a way that positions this particular company for dramatic growth? In a brief report, list your five questions, identify how you uncovered the issue, and explain why each is significant.

4. Interviewers and interviewees: Classroom exercise in interviewing. Interviewing is clearly an interactive process that involves at least two people. The best way to practice for interviews is to work with others.

Your task: You and all other members of your class are to write letters of application for an entry-level or management-trainee position that requires a pleasant personality and intelligence but a minimum of specialized education or experience. Sign your letter with a fictitious name that conceals your identity. Next, polish (or create) a résumé that accurately identifies you and your educational and professional accomplishments.

Now, three members of the class who volunteer as interviewers divide up all the anonymously written application letters. Then each interviewer selects a candidate who seems the most pleasant and convincing in his or her letter. At this time, the selected candidates identify themselves and give the interviewers their résumés.

Each interviewer then interviews his or her chosen candidate in front of the class, seeking to understand how the items on the résumé qualify the candidate for the job. At the end of the interviews, the class may decide who gets the job and discuss why this candidate was successful. Afterward, retrieve your letter, sign it with your name, and submit it to the instructor for credit.

5. Internet interview: Exercise in interviewing. Locate the website of a company in an industry in which you might like to work and then identify an interesting position within the company. Study the company, using any of the online business resources discussed in Chapter 11, and prepare for an interview with that company.

Your task: Working with a classmate, take turns interviewing each other for your chosen positions. Interviewers should take notes during the interview. When the interview is complete, critique each other's performance. (Interviewers should critique how well candidates prepared for the interview and answered the questions; interviewees should critique the quality of the questions asked.) Write a follow-up letter, thanking your interviewer, and submit the letter to your instructor.

FOLLOWING UP AFTER AN INTERVIEW

6. Letter asking for delay of an employment decision. After graduating with a degree in Telecommunication Engineering, you applied to the University Communication Department (UCD) for the post of Telecommunication Engineer. You gave the interview and submitted necessary documents to the UCD. However, the process at the UCD was not only slow but involved many bureaucratic delays. Although during the interview you were assured that you were selected for the job, due to the unnecessary delays you got frustrated. In the meantime, someone from a multinational telecommunications organization approached you and offered you a job abroad. You went abroad for the interview, were selected, and immediately started the internship. During the initial days of the internship you realized that you may not be able to adjust to the company culture, even though your immediate boss called you and gave you encouragement. You discussed the matter with your father back home, who asked you to write a letter to UCD. In the letter, you should request that the UCD keep your job offer open for about a month, so that you can decide whether you will join the UCD or not.

Your task: Write a letter to the University Communication Department Director, Mr. Muhammad Inam Ulhaque, requesting a few weeks' delay in your job offer.

7. Job hunt: Set of employment-related letters to a single company. Where would you like to work? Choose one of your favorite products, find out what company either manufactures it or sells it in the United States (if it's manufactured in another country). Assume that a month ago you sent your résumé and application letter. Not long afterward, you were invited to come for an interview, which seemed to go very well.

Your task: Use your imagination to write the following: (1) a thank-you letter for the interview, (2) a note of inquiry, (3) a request for more time to decide, (4) a letter of acceptance, and (5) a letter declining the job offer.

8. Breaking up is hard to do: Resignation letter to a valued mentor. Leaving a job is rarely stress free, but it's particularly difficult when you are parting ways with a mentor who played an important role in advancing your career. A half-dozen years into your career, you have benefited greatly from the advice, encouragement, and professional connections offered by your mentor, who also happens to be your current boss. She seemed to believe in your potential from the very beginning and went out of her way on numerous occasions to help you. You returned the favor by becoming a stellar employee who has made important contributions to the success of the department your boss leads.

Unfortunately, you find yourself at a career impasse. You believe you are ready to move into a management position, but your company is not growing enough to create many opportunities. Worse yet, you joined the firm during a period of rapid expansion, so there are many eager and qualified internal candidates at your career level interested in the few managerial jobs that do become available. You fear it may be years before you get the chance to move up in the company. Through your online networking activities, you found an opportunity with a firm in another industry and have decided to pursue it.

Your task: You have a close relationship with your boss, so you will announce your intention to leave the company in a private, one-on-one conversation. However, you also recognize the need to write a formal letter of resignation, which you will hand to your boss during this meeting. This letter is addressed to your boss, but as formal business correspondence that will become part of your personnel file, it should not be a "personal" letter. Making up whatever details you need, write a brief letter of resignation.

Appendix A
Format and Layout of Business Documents

The format and layout of business documents vary from country to country; they even vary within regions of the United States. In addition, many organizations develop their own variations of standard styles, adapting documents to the types of messages they send and the kinds of audiences they communicate with. The formats described here are more common than others.

FIRST IMPRESSIONS

Your documents tell readers a lot about you and about your company's professionalism. So all your documents must look neat, present a professional image, and be easy to read. Your audience's first impression of a document comes from the quality of its paper, the way it is customized, and its general appearance.

Paper

To give a quality impression, businesspeople consider carefully the paper they use. Several aspects of paper contribute to the overall impression:

- **Weight.** Paper quality is judged by the weight of four reams (each a 500-sheet package) of letter-size paper. The weight most commonly used by U.S. business organizations is 20-pound paper, but 16- and 24-pound versions are also used.
- **Cotton content.** Paper quality is also judged by the percentage of cotton in the paper. Cotton doesn't yellow over time the way wood pulp does, plus it's both strong and soft. For letters and outside reports, use paper with a 25 percent cotton content. For memos and other internal documents, you can use a lighter-weight paper with lower cotton content. Airmail-weight paper may save money for international correspondence, but make sure it isn't too flimsy.[1]
- **Size.** In the United States, the standard paper size for business documents is 8½ by 11 inches. Standard legal documents are 8½ by 14 inches. Executives sometimes have heavier 7-by-10-inch paper on hand (with matching envelopes) for personal messages such as congratulations.[2] They may also have a box of note cards imprinted with their initials and a box of plain folded notes for condolences or for acknowledging formal invitations.
- **Color.** White is the standard color for business purposes, although neutral colors such as gray and ivory are sometimes used. Memos can be produced on pastel-colored paper to distinguish them from external correspondence. In addition, memos are sometimes produced on various colors of paper for routing to separate departments. Light-colored papers are appropriate, but bright or dark colors make reading difficult and may appear too frivolous.

Customization

For letters to outsiders, U.S. businesses commonly use letterhead stationery, which may be either professionally printed or designed in-house using word processing templates and graphics. The letterhead includes the company's name and address, usually at the top of the page but sometimes along the left side or even at the bottom. Other information may be included in the letterhead as well: the company's telephone number, fax number, cable address, website address, product lines, date of establishment, officers and directors, slogan, and symbol (logo). Well-designed letterhead gives readers[3]

- Pertinent reference data
- A favorable image of the company
- A good idea of what the company does

For as much as it's meant to accomplish, the letterhead should be as simple as possible. Too much information makes the page look cluttered, occupies space needed for the message, and might become outdated before all the stationery can be used. If you correspond frequently with people abroad, your letterhead must be intelligible to foreigners. It must include the name of your country in addition to your cable, telex, e-mail, or fax information.

In the United States, businesses always use letterhead for the first page of a letter. Successive pages are usually plain sheets of paper that match the letterhead in color and quality. Some companies use a specially printed second-page letterhead that bears only the company's name. Other countries have other conventions.

Many companies also design and print standardized forms for memos and frequently written reports that always require the same sort of information (such as sales reports and expense reports). These forms may be printed in sets for use with carbon paper or in carbonless-copy sets that produce multiple copies automatically. More and more organizations use computers to generate their standardized forms, which can save them both money and time.[4]

Appearance

Nearly all business documents are produced using an inkjet or laser printer; make sure to use a clean, high-quality printer. Certain documents, however, should be handwritten (such as a short informal memo or a note of condolence). Be sure to handwrite, print, or type the envelope to match the document. However, even a letter on the best-quality paper with the best-designed letterhead may look unprofessional if it's poorly produced. So pay close attention to all the factors affecting appearance, including the following:

- **Margins.** Companies in the United States make sure that documents (especially external ones) are centered on the page, with margins of at least 1 inch all around. Using word processing software, you can achieve this balance simply by defining the format parameters.
- **Line length.** Lines are rarely justified, because the resulting text looks too much like a form letter and can be hard to read (even with proportional spacing). Varying line length makes the document look more personal and interesting.
- **Line spacing.** You can adjust the number of blank lines between elements (such as between the date and the inside address) to ensure that a short document fills the page vertically or that a longer document extends at least two lines of the body onto the last page.
- **Character spacing.** Use proper spacing between characters and after punctuation. For example, U.S. conventions include leaving one space after commas, semicolons, colons, and sentence-ending periods. Each letter in a person's initials is followed by a period and a single space. However, abbreviations such as U.S.A. or MBA may or may not have periods, but they never have internal spaces.
- **Special symbols.** Take advantage of the many special symbols available with your computer's selection of fonts. (In Microsoft Word, click on the Insert menu, then select Symbol.) Table A.1 shows some of the more common symbols used in business documents. In addition, see if your company has a style guide for documents, which may include other symbols you are expected to use.
- **Corrections.** Messy corrections are unacceptable in business documents. If you notice an error after printing

a document with your word processor, correct the mistake and reprint. (With informal memos to members of your own team or department, the occasional small correction in pen or pencil is acceptable, but never in formal documents.)

LETTERS

All business letters have certain elements in common. Several of these elements appear in every letter; others appear only when desirable or appropriate. In addition, these letter parts are usually arranged in one of three basic formats.

Standard Letter Parts

The letter in Figure A.1 shows the placement of standard letter parts. The writer of this business letter had no letterhead available but correctly included a heading. All business letters typically include these seven elements.

Heading

Most companies have preprinted *letterhead* sheets that show the company name, address, telephone number, website URL, and a general e-mail address. Executive letterhead also bears the name of an individual within the organization. Computers allow you to design your own letterhead (either one to use for all correspondence or a new one for each piece of correspondence). If letterhead stationery is not available, the heading includes a return address (but no name) and starts 13 lines from the top of the page, which leaves a 2-inch top margin.

Date

If you're using letterhead, place the date at least one blank line beneath the lowest part of the letterhead. Without letterhead, place the date immediately below the return address. The standard method of writing the date in the United States uses the full name of the month (no abbreviations), followed by the day (in numerals, without *st*, *nd*, *rd*, or *th*), a comma, and then the year: July 14, 2010 (7/14/2010). Some organizations follow other conventions (see Table A.2). To maintain the utmost clarity in international correspondence, always spell out the name of the month in dates.[5]

When communicating internationally, you may also experience some confusion over time. Some companies in the United States refer to morning (A.M.) and afternoon (P.M.), dividing a 24-hour day into 12-hour blocks so that they refer to four o'clock in the morning (4:00 A.M.) or four o'clock in the afternoon (4:00 P.M.). The U.S. military and European companies refer to one 24-hour period so that 0400 hours (4:00 A.M.) is always in the morning and 1600 hours (4:00 P.M.) is always in the afternoon.[6] Make sure your references to time are as clear as possible, and be sure you clearly understand your audience's time references.

TABLE A.1   Special Symbols on a Computer

	COMPUTER SYMBOL
Case fractions	½
Copyright	©
Registered trademark	®
Cents	¢
British pound	£
Paragraph	¶
Bullets	●, ♦, ■, □, ✓, ☑, ⊗
Em dash	—
En dash	–

FIGURE A.1 Standard Letter Parts

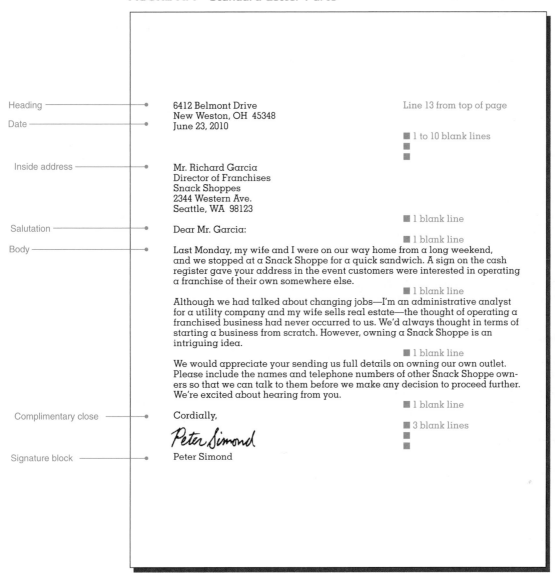

Heading — 6412 Belmont Drive
New Weston, OH 45348
Date — June 23, 2010

Line 13 from top of page

■ 1 to 10 blank lines
■
■

Inside address — Mr. Richard Garcia
Director of Franchises
Snack Shoppes
2344 Western Ave.
Seattle, WA 98123

■ 1 blank line

Salutation — Dear Mr. Garcia:

■ 1 blank line

Body — Last Monday, my wife and I were on our way home from a long weekend, and we stopped at a Snack Shoppe for a quick sandwich. A sign on the cash register gave your address in the event customers were interested in operating a franchise of their own somewhere else.

■ 1 blank line

Although we had talked about changing jobs—I'm an administrative analyst for a utility company and my wife sells real estate—the thought of operating a franchised business had never occurred to us. We'd always thought in terms of starting a business from scratch. However, owning a Snack Shoppe is an intriguing idea.

■ 1 blank line

We would appreciate your sending us full details on owning our own outlet. Please include the names and telephone numbers of other Snack Shoppe owners so that we can talk to them before we make any decision to proceed further. We're excited about hearing from you.

■ 1 blank line

Complimentary close — Cordially,

■ 3 blank lines
■
■

Peter Simond

Signature block — Peter Simond

Inside Address

The inside address identifies the recipient of the letter. For U.S. correspondence, begin the inside address at least one line below the date. Precede the addressee's name with a courtesy title, such as *Dr.*, *Mr.*, or *Ms.* The accepted courtesy title for women in business is *Ms.*, although a woman known to prefer the title *Miss* or *Mrs.* is always accommodated.

If you don't know whether a person is a man or a woman (and you have no way of finding out), omit the courtesy title. For example, *Terry Smith* could be either a man or a woman. The first line of the inside address would be just *Terry Smith*, and the salutation would be *Dear Terry Smith*. The same is true if you know only a person's initials, as in *S. J. Adams.*

TABLE A.2 Common Date Forms

CONVENTION	DESCRIPTION	DATE—MIXED	DATE—ALL NUMERALS
U.S. standard	Month (spelled out) day, year	July 14, 2010	7/14/10
U.S. government and some U.S. industries	Day (in numerals) month (spelled out) year	14 July 2010	14/7/10
European	Replace U.S. solidus (diagonal line) with periods	14 July 2010	14.7.2010
International standard	Year month day	2010 July 14	2010,7,14

TABLE A.3 Forms of Address

PERSON	IN ADDRESS	IN SALUTATION
Personal Titles		
Man	Mr. [first & last name]	Dear Mr. [last name]:
Woman*	Ms. [first & last name]	Dear Ms. [last name]:
Two men (or more)	Mr. [first & last name] and Mr. [first & last name]	Dear Mr. [last name] and Mr. [last name] *or* Messrs. [last name] and [last name]:
Two women (or more)	Ms. [first & last name] and Ms. [first & last name]	Dear Ms. [last name] and Ms. [last name] *or* Mses. [last name] and [last name]:
One woman and one man	Ms. [first & last name] and Mr. [first & last name]	Dear Ms. [last name] and Mr. [last name]:
Couple (married)	Mr. [husband's first name] and Mrs. [wife's first name] [couple's last name]	Dear Mr. and Mrs. [last name]:
Couple (married with different last names)	Mr. [first & last name of husband] Ms. [first & last name of wife]	Dear Mr. [husband's last name] and Ms. [wife's last name]:
Couple (married professionals with same title and same last name)	[title in plural form] [husband's first name] and [wife's first name] [couple's last name]	Dear [title in plural form] [last name]:
Couple (married professionals with different titles and same last name)	[title] [first & last name of husband] and [title] [first & last name of wife]	Dear [title] and [title] [last name]:
Professional Titles		
President of a college or university	[title] [first & last name], President	Dear [title] [last name]:
Dean of a school of college	Dean [first & last name] *or* Dr., Mr., or Ms. [first & last name], Dean of [title]	Dear Dean [last name]: *or* Dear Dr., Mr., or Ms. [last name]:
Professor	Professor *or* Dr. [first & last name]	Dear Professor *or* Dr. [last name]:
Physician	[first & last name], M.D.	Dear Dr. [last name]:
Lawyer	Mr. *or* Ms. [first & last name] Attorney at Law	Dear Mr. *or* Ms. [last name]:
Military personnel	[full rank, first & last name, abbreviation of service designation] (add *Retired* if applicable)	Dear [rank][last name]:
Company or corporation	[name of organization]	Ladies and Gentlemen: *or* Gentlemen and Ladies:
Governmental Titles		
President of the United States	The president	Dear Mr. *or* Madam President:
Senator of the United States	Honorable [first & last name]	Dear Senator [last name]:
Cabinet member	Honorable [first & last name]	Dear Mr. *or* Madam Secretary:
Postmaster General		Dear Mr. *or* Madam Postmaster General:
Attorney General		Dear Mr. *or* Madam Attorney General:
Mayor	Honorable [first & last name], Mayor of [name of city]	Dear Mayor [last name]:
Judge	The Honorable [first & last name]	Dear Judge [last name]:

*Use *Mrs.* or *Miss* only if the recipient has specifically requested that you use one of these titles; otherwise *always* use *Ms.* in business correspondence. Also, never refer to a married woman by her husband's name (e.g., Mrs. Robert Washington) unless she specifically requests that you do so.

Spell out and capitalize titles that precede a person's name, such as *Professor* or *General* (see Table A.3 for the proper forms of address). The person's organizational title, such as *Director*, may be included on this first line (if it is short) or on the line below; the name of a department may follow. In addresses and signature lines, don't forget to capitalize any professional title that follows a person's name:

Mr. Ray Johnson, Dean

Ms. Patricia T. Higgins

Assistant Vice President

However, professional titles not appearing in an address or signature line are capitalized only when they directly precede the name:

President Kenneth Johanson will deliver the speech.

Maria Morales, president of ABC Enterprises, will deliver the speech.

The Honorable Helen Masters, senator from Arizona, will deliver the speech.

If the name of a specific person is unavailable, you may address the letter to the department or to a specific position within the department. Also, be sure to spell out company names in full, unless the company itself uses abbreviations in its official name.

Other address information includes the treatment of buildings, house numbers, and compass directions (see Table A.4). The following example shows all the information that may be included in the inside address and its proper order for U.S. correspondence:

Ms. Linda Coolidge, Vice President
Corporate Planning Department
Midwest Airlines
Kowalski Building, Suite 21-A
7279 Bristol Ave.
Toledo, OH 43617

Canadian addresses are similar, except that the name of the province is usually spelled out:

Dr. H. C. Armstrong
Research and Development
Commonwealth Mining Consortium
The Chelton Building, Suite 301
585 Second St. SW
Calgary, Alberta T2P 2P5

The order and layout of address information vary from country to country. So when addressing correspondence for other countries, carefully follow the format and information that appear in the company's letterhead. However, when you're sending mail from the United States, be sure that the name of the destination country appears on the last line of the address in capital letters. Use the English version of the country name so that your mail is routed from the United States to the right country. Then, to be sure your mail is routed correctly within the destination country, use the foreign spelling of the city name (using the characters and diacritical marks that would be commonly used in the region). For example, the following address uses *Köln* instead of *Cologne*:

H. R. Veith, Director	Addresses
Eisfieren Glaswerk	Company name
Blaubachstrasse 13	Street address
Postfach 10 80 07	Post office road
D-5000 Köln I	District, city
GERMANY	Country

For additional examples of international addresses, see Table A.5.

Be sure to use organizational titles correctly when addressing international correspondence. Job designations vary around the world. In England, for example, a managing director is often what a U.S. company would call its chief executive officer or president, and a British deputy is the equivalent of a vice president. In France, responsibilities are assigned to individuals without regard to title or organizational structure, and in China the title *project manager* has meaning, but the title *sales manager* may not.

To make matters worse, businesspeople in some countries sign correspondence without their names typed below. In Germany, for example, the belief is that employees represent the company, so it's inappropriate to emphasize personal names.[7] Use the examples in Table A.5 as guidelines when addressing correspondence to countries outside the United States.

Salutation

In the salutation of your letter, follow the style of the first line of the inside address. If the first line is a person's name, the salutation is *Dear Mr.* or *Ms. Name*. The formality of the salutation depends on your relationship with the addressee. If in conversation you would say "Mary," your letter's salutation should be *Dear Mary*, followed by a colon. Otherwise, include the courtesy title and last name, followed by a colon. Presuming to write *Dear Lewis* instead of *Dear Professor Chang* demonstrates a disrespectful familiarity that the recipient will probably resent.

If the first line of the inside address is a position title such as *Director of Personnel*, then use *Dear Director*. If the addressee is unknown, use a polite description, such as *Dear Alumnus, Dear SPCA Supporter*, or *Dear Voter*. If the first line is plural (a department or company), then use *Ladies and*

TABLE A.4 Inside Address Information

DESCRIPTION	EXAMPLE
Capitalize building names.	Empire State Building
Capitalize locations within buildings (apartments, suites, rooms).	Suite 1073
Use numerals for all house or building numbers, except the number *one*.	One Trinity Lane; 637 Adams Ave., Apt. 7
Spell out compass directions that fall within a street address	1074 West Connover St.
Abbreviate compass directions that follow the street address	783 Main St., N.E., Apt. 27

TABLE A.5 International Addresses and Salutations

COUNTRY	POSTAL ADDRESS	ADDRESS ELEMENTS	SALUTATIONS
Argentina	Sr. Juan Pérez Editorial Internacional S.A. Av. Sarmiento 1337, 8° P. C. C1035AAB BUENOS AIRES–CF ARGENTINA	S.A. = Sociedad Anónima (corporation) Av. Sarmiento (name of street) 1337 (building number) 8° – 8th. P = Piso (floor) C (room or suite) C1035AAB (postcode + city) CF = Capital Federal (federal capital)	Sr. – Señor (Mr.) Sra. – Señora (Mrs.) Srta. – Señorita (Miss) Don't use given names except with people you know well.
Australia	Mr. Roger Lewis International Publishing Pty. Ltd. 166 Kent Street, Level 9 GPO Box 3542 SYDNEY NSW 2001 AUSTRALIA	Pty. Ltd. – Proprietory Limited (corp.) 166 (building number) Kent Street (name of street) Level (floor) GPO Box (P.O. box) City + state (abbrev.) + postcode	Mr. and Mrs. used on first contact. Ms. not common (avoid use). Business is informal—use given name freely.
Austria	Herrn Dipl.-Ing.J.Gerdenitsch International Verlag Ges.m.b.H. Glockengasse 159 1010 WIEN AUSTRIA	Herrn – To Mr. (separate line) Dipl.-Ing. (engineering degree) Ges.m.b.H. (a corporation) Glockengasse (street name) 159 (building number) 1010 (postcode + city) WIEN (Vienna)	Herr (Mr.) Frau (Mrs.) Fräulein (Miss) obsolete in business, so do not use. Given names are almost never used in business.
Brazil	Ilmo. Sr. Gilberto Rabello Ribeiro Editores Internacionais S.A. Rua da Ajuda, 228–6° Andar Caixa Postal 2574 20040–000 RIO DE JANEIRO–RJ BRAZIL	Ilmo. = Ilustrissimo (honorific) Ilma. = Ilustrissima (hon. female) S.A. – Sociedade Anônima (corporation) Rua = street, da Ajuda (street name) 228 (building number) 6° = 6th. Andar (floor) Caixa Postal (P.O. box) 20040–000 (postcode + city)–RJ (state abbrev.)	Sr. = Senhor (Mr.) Sra. = Senhora (Mrs.) Srta. = Senhorita (Miss) Family name at end, e.g., Senhor Ribeiro (Rabello is mother's family name) Given names readily used in business.
China	Xia Zhiyi International Publishing Ltd. 14 Jianguolu Chaoyangqu BEIJING 100025 CHINA	Ltd. (limited liability corporation) 14 (building number) Jianguolu (street name), lu (street) Chaoyangqu (district name) (city + postcode)	Family name (single syllable) first. Given name (2 syllables) second, sometimes reversed. Use Mr. or Ms. at all times (Mr. Xia).
France	Monsieur LEFÈVRE Alain Éditions Internationales S.A. Siège Social Immeuble Le Bonaparte 64–68, av. Galliéni B.P. 154 75942 PARIS CEDEX 19 FRANCE	S.A. = Société Anonyme (corporation) Siège Social (head office) Immeuble (building + name) 64–68 (building occupies 64, 66, 68) av. = avenue (no initial capital) B.P. = Boîte Postale (P.O. box) 75942 (postcode + city) CEDEX (postcode for P.O. box)	Monsieur (Mr.) Madame (Mrs.) Mademoiselle (Miss) Best not to abbreviate. Family name is sometimes in all caps with given name following.
Germany	Herrn Gerhardt Schneider International Verlag GmbH Schillerstraße 159 44147 DORTMUND GERMANY	Herrn = To Mr. (on a separate line) GmbH (inc.—incorporated) –straße (street—'ß' often written 'ss') 159 (building number) 44147 (postcode – city)	Herr (Mr.) Frau (Mrs.) Fräulein (Miss) obsolete in business. Business is formal: (1) do not use given names unless invited, and (2) use academic titles precisely.

COUNTRY	POSTAL ADDRESS	ADDRESS ELEMENTS	SALUTATIONS
India	Sr. Shyam Lal Gupta International Publishing (Pvt.) Ltd. 1820 Rehaja Centre 214, Darussalam Road Andheri East BOMBAY–400049 INDIA	(Pvt.) (privately owned) Ltd. (limited liability corporation) 1820 (possibly office #20 on 18th floor) Rehaja Centre (building name) 214 (building number) Andheri East (suburb name) (city + hyphen + postcode)	Shri (Mr.), Shrimati (Mrs.) but English is common business language, so use Mr., Mrs., Miss. Given names are used only by family and close friends.
Italy	Egr. Sig. Giacomo Mariotti Edizioni Internazionali S.p.A. Via Terenzio, 21 20138 MILANO ITALY	Egr. = Egregio (honorific) Sig. = Signor (not nec. a separate line) S.p.A. = Società per Azioni (corp.) Via (street) 21 (building number) 20138 (postcode + city)	Sig. = Signore (Mr.) Sig.ra = Signora (Mrs.) Sig.a (Ms.) Women in business are addressed as Signora. Use given name only when invited.
Japan	Mr. Taro Tanaka Kokusai Shuppan K.K. 10–23, 5-chome, Minamiazabu Minato-ku TOKYO 106 JAPAN	K.K. = Kabushiki Kaisha (corporation) 10 (lot number) 23 (building number) 5-chome (area #5) Minamiazabu (neighborhood name) Minato-ku (city district) (city + postcode)	Given names not used in business. Use family name + job title. Or use family name + "-san" (Tanaka-san) or more respectfully, add "-sama" or "-dono."
Korea	Mr. Kim Chang-ik International Publishers Ltd. Room 206, Korea Building 33–4 Nonhyon-dong Kangnam-ku SEOUL 135–010 KOREA	English company names common Ltd. (a corporation) 206 (office number inside the building) 33–4 (area 4 of subdivision 33) -dong (city neighborhood name) -ku (subdivision of city) (city + postcode)	Family name is normally first but sometimes placed after given name. A two-part name is the given name. Use Mr. or Mrs. in letters, but use job title in speech.
Mexico	Sr. Francisco Pérez Martínez Editores Internacionales S.A. Independencia No. 322 Col. Juárez 06050 MEXICO D.F.	S.A. – Sociedad Anónima (corporation) Independencia (street name) No. = Número (number) 322 (building number) Col. = Colonia (city district) Juárez (locality name) 06050 (postcode + city) D.F. = Distrito Federal (federal capital)	Sr. – Señor (Mr.) Sra. = Señora (Mrs.) Srta. = Señorita (Miss) Family name in middle: e.g., Sr. Pérez (Martínez is mother's family). Given names are used in business.
South Africa	Mr. Mandla Ntuli International Publishing (Pty.) Ltd. Private Bag X2581 JOHANNESBURG 2000 SOUTH AFRICA	Pty. = Proprietory (privately owned) Ltd. (a corporation) Private Bag (P.O. Box) (city + postcode) or (postcode + city)	Mnr = Meneer (Mr.) Mev. = Mevrou (Mrs.) Mejuffrou (Miss) is not used in business. Business is becoming less formal, so the use of given names is possible.
United Kingdom	Mr. N. J. Lancaster International Publishing Ltd. Kingsbury House 12 Kingsbury Road EDGEWARE Middlesex HA8 9XG ENGLAND	N. J. (initials of given names) Ltd. (limited liability corporation) Kingsbury House (building name) 12 (building number) Kingsbury Road (name of street/road) EDGEWARE (city—all caps) Middlesex (county—not all caps) HA8 9XG	Mr. and Ms. used mostly. Mrs. and Miss sometimes used in North and by older women. Given names—called Christian names—are used in business after some time. Wait to be invited.

Gentlemen (look again at Table A.3). When you do not know whether you're writing to an individual or a group (for example, when writing a reference or a letter of recommendation), use *To whom it may concern*.

In the United States some letter writers use a "salutopening" on the salutation line. A salutopening omits *Dear* but includes the first few words of the opening paragraph along with the recipient's name. After this line, the sentence continues a double space below as part of the body of the letter, as in these examples:

> Thank you, Mr. Brown,
> for your prompt payment of your bill.   Salutopening Body

> Congratulations, Ms. Lake!
> Your promotion is well deserved.   Salutopening Body

Whether your salutation is informal or formal, be especially careful that names are spelled right. A misspelled name is glaring evidence of carelessness, and it belies the personal interest you're trying to express.

Body

The body of the letter is your message. Almost all letters are single-spaced, with one blank line before and after the salutation or salutopening, between paragraphs, and before the complimentary close. The body may include indented lists, entire paragraphs indented for emphasis, and even subheadings. If it does, all similar elements should be treated in the same way. Your department or company may select a format to use for all letters.

Complimentary Close

The complimentary close begins on the second line below the body of the letter. Alternatives for wording are available, but currently the trend seems to be toward using one-word closes, such as *Sincerely* and *Cordially*. In any case, the complimentary close reflects the relationship between you and the person you're writing to. Avoid cute closes, such as *Yours for bigger profits*. If your audience doesn't know you well, your sense of humor may be misunderstood.

Signature Block

Leave three blank lines for a written signature below the complimentary close, and then include the sender's name (unless it appears in the letterhead). The person's title may appear on the same line as the name or on the line below:

> Cordially,
>
> Raymond Dunnigan
> Director of Personnel

Your letterhead indicates that you're representing your company. However, if your letter is on plain paper or runs to a second page, you may want to emphasize that you're speaking legally for the company. The accepted way of doing that is to

place the company's name in capital letters a double space below the complimentary close and then include the sender's name and title four lines below that:

> Sincerely,
> WENTWORTH INDUSTRIES
>
> (Ms.) Helen B. Taylor
> President

If your name could be taken for either a man's or a woman's, a courtesy title indicating gender should be included, with or without parentheses. Also, women who prefer a particular courtesy title should include it:

> Mrs. Nancy Winters
> (Ms.) Juana Flores
> Ms. Pat Li
> (Mr.) Jamie Saunders

Additional Letter Parts

Letters vary greatly in subject matter and thus in the identifying information they need and the format they adopt. The letter in Figure A.2 shows how these additional parts should be arranged. The following elements may be used in any combination, depending on the requirements of the particular letter:

- **Addressee notation.** Letters that have a restricted readership or that must be handled in a special way should include such addressee notations as *Personal, Confidential,* or *Please Forward*. This sort of notation appears a double space above the inside address, in all-capital letters.
- **Attention line.** Although not commonly used today, an attention line can be used if you know only the last name of the person you're writing to. It can also direct a letter to a position title or department. Place the attention line on the first line of the inside address and put the company name on the second.[8] Match the address on the envelope with the style of the inside address. An attention line may take any of the following forms or variants of them:

  Attention Dr. McHenry
  Attention Director of Marketing
  Attention Marketing Department

- **Subject line.** The subject line tells recipients at a glance what the letter is about (and indicates where to file the letter for future reference). It usually appears below the salutation, either against the left margin, indented (as a paragraph in the body), or centered. It can be placed above the salutation or at the very top of the page, and it can be underscored. Some businesses omit the word *Subject*, and some organizations replace it with *Re:* or *In re:* (meaning "concerning" or "in the matter of"). The

FIGURE A.2 Additional Letter Parts

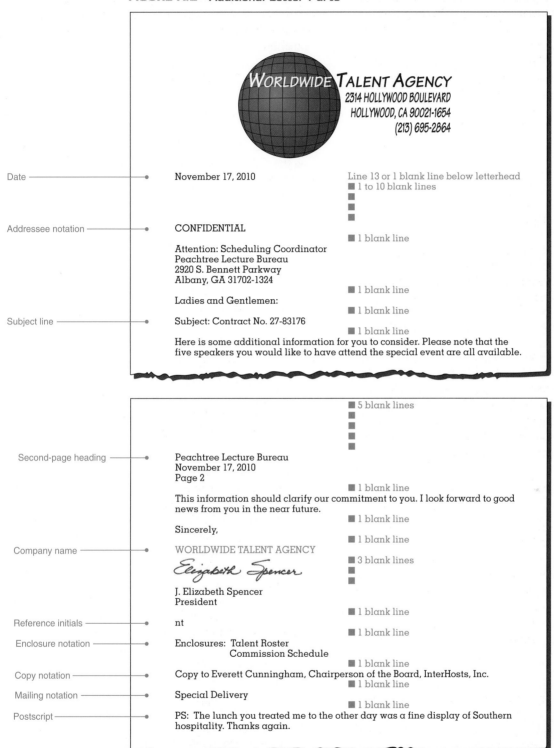

Date ——————— •   November 17, 2010   Line 13 or 1 blank line below letterhead
                                         ■ 1 to 10 blank lines

Addressee notation ——— •   CONFIDENTIAL

Attention: Scheduling Coordinator
Peachtree Lecture Bureau
2920 S. Bennett Parkway
Albany, GA 31702-1324

Ladies and Gentlemen:

Subject line ——————— •   Subject: Contract No. 27-83176

Here is some additional information for you to consider. Please note that the five speakers you would like to have attend the special event are all available.

Second-page heading ——— •   Peachtree Lecture Bureau
November 17, 2010
Page 2

This information should clarify our commitment to you. I look forward to good news from you in the near future.

Sincerely,

Company name ——————— •   WORLDWIDE TALENT AGENCY

Elizabeth Spencer

J. Elizabeth Spencer
President

Reference initials ——————— •   nt

Enclosure notation ——————— •   Enclosures: Talent Roster
                  Commission Schedule

Copy notation ——————— •   Copy to Everett Cunningham, Chairperson of the Board, InterHosts, Inc.

Mailing notation ——————— •   Special Delivery

Postscript ——————— •   PS: The lunch you treated me to the other day was a fine display of Southern hospitality. Thanks again.

subject line may take a variety of forms, including the following:

Subject: RainMaster Sprinklers

About your February 2, 2010, order

FALL 2010 SALES MEETING

Reference Order No. 27920

● **Second-page heading.** Use a second-page heading whenever an additional page is required. Some companies have second-page letterhead (with the company name and address on one line and in a smaller typeface). The heading bears the name (person or organization) from the first line of the inside address, the page number, the date, and perhaps a reference number. Leave two blank lines before the body. Make sure that at least two lines of a continued paragraph appear on the first and second pages. Never allow the closing lines to appear alone on a continued page. Precede the complimentary close or signature lines with at least two lines of the body. Also, don't hyphenate the last word on a page. All the following are acceptable forms for second-page headings:

Ms. Melissa Baker

May 10, 2010

Page 2

Ms. Melissa Baker, May 10, 2010, Page 2

Ms. Melissa Baker -2- May 10, 2010

- **Company name.** If you include the company's name in the signature block, put it all in capital letters a double space below the complimentary close. You usually include the company's name in the signature block only when the writer is serving as the company's official spokesperson or when letterhead has not been used.
- **Reference initials.** When businesspeople keyboard their own letters, reference initials are unnecessary, so they are becoming rare. When one person dictates a letter and another person produces it, reference initials show who helped prepare it. Place initials at the left margin, a double space below the signature block. When the signature block includes the writer's name, use only the preparer's initials. If the signature block includes only the department, use both sets of initials, usually in one of the following forms: *RSR/sm, RSR:sm,* or *RSR:SM* (writer/ preparer). When the writer and the signer are different people, at least the file copy should bear both their initials as well as the typist's: *JFS/RSR/sm* (signer/writer/ preparer).
- **Enclosure notation.** Enclosure notations appear at the bottom of a letter, one or two lines below the reference initials. Some common forms include the following:

Enclosure

Enclosures (2)

Enclosures: Résumé

  Photograph

  Attachment

- **Copy notation.** Copy notations may follow reference initials or enclosure notations. They indicate who's receiving a *courtesy copy* (*cc*). Some companies indicate copies made on a photocopier (*pc*), or they simply use *copy* (*c*). Recipients are listed in order of rank or (rank being equal) in alphabetical order. Among the forms used are the following:

cc: David Wentworth, Vice President

pc: Dr. Martha Littlefield

Copy to Hans Vogel

748 Chesterton Road

Snohomish, WA 98290

c: Joseph Martinez with brochure and technical sheet

When sending copies to readers without other recipients knowing, place *bc, bcc,* or *bpc* ("blind copy," "blind courtesy copy," or "blind photocopy") along with the name and any other information only on the copy, not on the original.

- **Mailing notation.** You may place a mailing notation (such as *Special Delivery* or *Registered Mail*) at the bottom of the letter, after reference initials or enclosure notations (whichever is last) and before copy notations. Or you may place it at the top of the letter, either above the inside address on the left side or just below the date on the right side. For greater visibility, mailing notations may appear in capital letters.
- **Postscript.** A postscript is an afterthought to the letter, a message that requires emphasis, or a personal note. It is usually the last thing on any letter and may be preceded by *P.S., PS,, PS:,* or nothing at all. A second afterthought would be designated *P.P.S.* (post postscript). Since postscripts usually indicate poor planning, generally avoid them. However, they're common in sales letters as a punch line to remind readers of a benefit for taking advantage of the offer.

Letter Formats

A letter format is the way of arranging all the basic letter parts. Sometimes a company adopts a certain format as its policy; sometimes the individual letter writer or preparer is allowed to choose the most appropriate format. In the United States, three major letter formats are commonly used:

- **Block format.** Each letter part begins at the left margin. The main advantage is quick and efficient preparation (see Figure A.3).
- **Modified block format.** Same as block format, except that the date, complimentary close, and signature block start near the center of the page (see Figure A.4). The modified block format does permit indentions as an option. This format mixes preparation speed with traditional placement of some letter parts. It also looks more balanced on the page than the block format does.
- **Simplified format.** Instead of using a salutation, this format often weaves the reader's name into the first line or two of the body and often includes a subject line in capital letters (see Figure A.5). With no complimentary close, your signature appears after the body, followed by your printed (or typewritten) name (usually in all capital letters). This format is convenient when you don't know the reader's name; however, some people object to it as mechanical and impersonal (a drawback you can overcome with a warm writing style). Because certain letter parts are eliminated, some line spacing is changed.

These three formats differ in the way paragraphs are indented, in the way letter parts are placed, and in some punctuation. However, the elements are always separated by at least one blank line, and the printed (or typewritten) name is always separated from the line above by at least three blank

FIGURE A.3 Block Letter Format

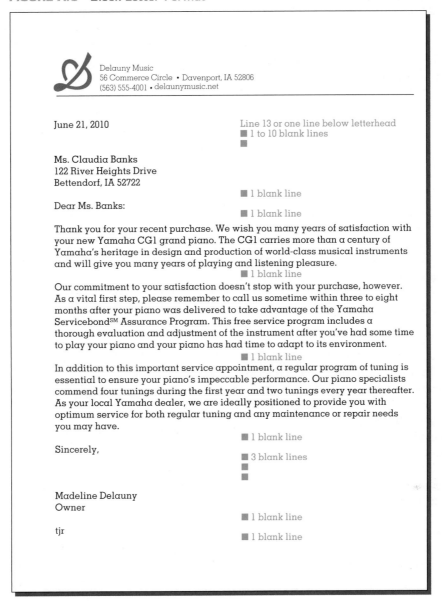

Delauny Music
56 Commerce Circle • Davenport, IA 52806
(563) 555-4001 • delaunymusic.net

June 21, 2010   Line 13 or one line below letterhead
                                       ■ 1 to 10 blank lines
                                       ■

Ms. Claudia Banks
122 River Heights Drive
Bettendorf, IA 52722
                                       ■ 1 blank line
Dear Ms. Banks:
                                       ■ 1 blank line
Thank you for your recent purchase. We wish you many years of satisfaction with
your new Yamaha CG1 grand piano. The CG1 carries more than a century of
Yamaha's heritage in design and production of world-class musical instruments
and will give you many years of playing and listening pleasure.
                                       ■ 1 blank line
Our commitment to your satisfaction doesn't stop with your purchase, however.
As a vital first step, please remember to call us sometime within three to eight
months after your piano was delivered to take advantage of the Yamaha
Servicebond^SM Assurance Program. This free service program includes a
thorough evaluation and adjustment of the instrument after you've had some time
to play your piano and your piano has had time to adapt to its environment.
                                       ■ 1 blank line
In addition to this important service appointment, a regular program of tuning is
essential to ensure your piano's impeccable performance. Our piano specialists
commend four tunings during the first year and two tunings every year thereafter.
As your local Yamaha dealer, we are ideally positioned to provide you with
optimum service for both regular tuning and any maintenance or repair needs
you may have.
                                       ■ 1 blank line
Sincerely,
                                       ■ 3 blank lines
                                       ■
                                       ■
Madeline Delauny
Owner
                                       ■ 1 blank line
tjr
                                       ■ 1 blank line

lines to allow space for a signature. If paragraphs are indented, the indention is normally five spaces. The most common formats for intercultural business letters are the block style and the modified block style.

In addition to these three letter formats, letters may also be classified according to their style of punctuation. *Standard*, or *mixed, punctuation* uses a colon after the salutation (a comma if the letter is social or personal) and a comma after the complimentary close. *Open punctuation* uses no colon or comma after the salutation or the complimentary close. Although the most popular style in business communication is mixed punctuation, either style of punctuation may be used with block or modified block letter formats. Because the simplified letter format has no salutation or complimentary close, the style of punctuation is irrelevant.

ENVELOPES

For a first impression, the quality of the envelope is just as important as the quality of the stationery. Letterhead and envelopes should be of the same paper stock, have the same color ink, and be imprinted with the same address and logo. Most envelopes used by U.S. businesses are No. 10 envelopes (9½ inches long), which are sized for an 8½-by-11-inch piece of paper folded in thirds. Some occasions call for a smaller, No. 6¾, envelope or for envelopes proportioned to fit special stationery. Figure A.6 shows the two most common sizes.

Addressing the Envelope

No matter what size the envelope, the address is always single-spaced with all lines aligned on the left. The address on the envelope is in the same style as the inside address and

FIGURE A.4 Modified Block Letter Format

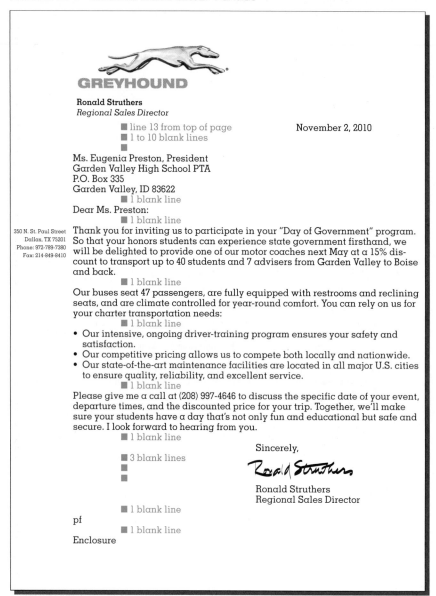

presents the same information. The order to follow is from the smallest division to the largest:

1. Name and title of recipient
2. Name of department or subgroup
3. Name of organization
4. Name of building
5. Street address and suite number, or post office box number
6. City, state, or province, and zip code or postal code
7. Name of country (if the letter is being sent abroad)

Because the U.S. Postal Service uses optical scanners to sort mail, envelopes for quantity mailings, in particular, should be addressed in the prescribed format. Everything is in capital letters, no punctuation is included, and all mailing instructions of interest to the post office are placed above the address area (see Figure A.6). Canada Post requires a similar

format, except that only the city is all in capitals, and the postal code is placed on the line below the name of the city. The post office scanners read addresses from the bottom up, so if a letter is to be sent to a post office box rather than to a street address, the street address should appear on the line above the box number. Figure A.6 also shows the proper spacing for addresses and return addresses.

The U.S. Postal Service and the Canada Post Corporation have published lists of two-letter mailing abbreviations for states, provinces, and territories (see Table A.6). Postal authorities prefer no punctuation with these abbreviations, but some executives prefer to have state and province names spelled out in full and set off from city names by a comma. The issue is unresolved, although the comma is most often included. Quantity mailings follow post office requirements. For other letters, a reasonable compromise is to use traditional punctuation,

FIGURE A.5 Simplified Letter Format

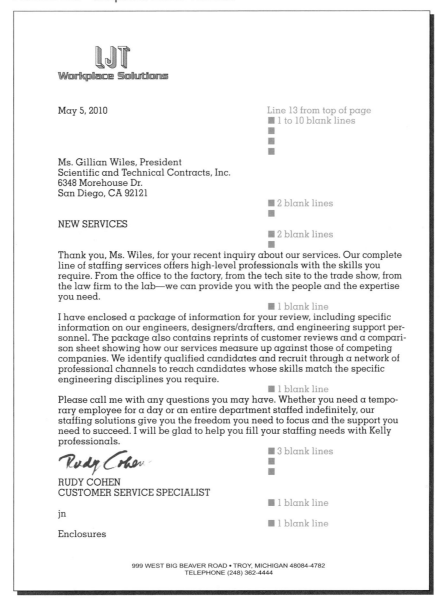

uppercase and lowercase letters for names and street addresses, but two-letter state or province abbreviations, as shown here:

Mr. Kevin Kennedy

2107 E. Packer Dr.

Amarillo, TX 79108

For all out-of-office correspondence, use zip and postal codes that have been assigned to speed mail delivery. The U.S. Postal Service has divided the United States and its territories into 10 zones (0 to 9); this digit comes first in the zip code. The second and third digits represent smaller geographical areas within a state, and the last two digits identify a "local delivery area." Canadian postal codes are alphanumeric, with a three-character "area code" and a three-character "local code" separated by a single space (K2P 5A5). Zip and postal codes should be separated from state and province names by one space. Canadian postal codes may be treated the same or may be put in the bottom line of the address all by itself.

The U.S. Postal Service has added zip 4 codes, which add a hyphen and four more numbers to the standard zip codes. The first two of the new numbers may identify an area as small as a single large building, and the last two digits may identify one floor in a large building or even a specific department of an organization. The zip 4 codes are especially useful for business correspondence. The Canada Post Corporation achieves the same result with special postal codes assigned to buildings and organizations that receive a large volume of mail.

FIGURE A.6 Prescribed Envelope Format

Small envelope, No. 6³/₄, is 6¹/₂ by 3⁵/₈ inches.

TABLE A.6 Two-Letter Mailing Abbreviations for the United States and Canada

STATE/ TERRITORY/ PROVINCE	ABBREVIATION	STATE/ TERRITORY/ PROVINCE	ABBREVIATION	STATE/ TERRITORY/ PROVINCE	ABBREVIATION
United States		Massachusetts	MA	Texas	TX
Alabama	AL	Michigan	MI	Utah	UT
Alaska	AK	Minnesota	MN	Vermont	VT
American Samoa	AS	Mississippi	MS	Virginia	VA
Arizona	AZ	Missouri	MO	Virgin Islands	VI
Arkansas	AR	Montana	MT	Washington	WA
California	CA	Nebraska	NE	West Virginia	WV
Canal Zone	CZ	Nevada	NV	Wisconsin	WI
Colorado	CO	New Hampshire	NH	Wyoming	WY
Connecticut	CT	New Jersey	NJ	**Canada**	
Delaware	DE	New Mexico	NM	Alberta	AB
District of Columbia	DC	New York	NY	British Columbia	BC
Florida	FL	North Carolina	NC	Labrador	NL
Georgia	GA	North Dakota	ND	Manitoba	MB
Guam	GU	Northern Mariana	MP	New Brunswick	NB
Hawaii	HI	Ohio	OH	Newfoundland	NL
Idaho	ID	Oklahoma	OK	Northwest Territories	NT
Illinois	IL	Oregon	OR	Nova Scotia	NS
Indiana	IN	Pennsylvania	PA	Nunavur	NU
Iowa	IA	Puerto Rico	PR	Ontario	ON
Kansas	KS	Rhode Island	RI	Prince Edward Island	PE
Kentucky	KY	South Carolina	SC	Quebec	PQ
Louisiana	LA	South Dakota	SD	Saskatchewan	SK
Maine	ME	Tennessee	TN	Yukon Territory	YT
Maryland	MD	Trust Territories	TT		

Folding to Fit

The way a letter is folded also contributes to the recipient's overall impression of your organization's professionalism. When sending a standard-size piece of paper in a No. 10 envelope, fold it in thirds, with the bottom folded up first and the top folded down over it (see Figure A.7); the open end should be at the top of the envelope and facing out. Fit smaller stationery neatly into the appropriate envelope simply by folding it in half or in thirds. When sending a standard-size letterhead in a No. 6¾ envelope, fold it in half from top to bottom and then in thirds from side to side.

International Mail

Postal service differs from country to country, so it's always a good idea to investigate the quality and availability of various services before sending messages and packages internationally. Also, compare the services offered by delivery companies such as UPS and FedEx to find the best rates and options for each destination and type of shipment. No matter which service you choose, be aware that international mail requires more planning than domestic mail. For example, for anything beyond simple letters, you generally need to prepare *customs forms* and possibly other documents, depending on the country of destination and the type of shipment. You are responsible for following the laws of the United States and any countries to which you send mail and packages.

The U.S. Postal Service currently offers four classes of international delivery, listed here from the fastest (and most expensive) to the slowest (and least expensive):

- **Global Express Guaranteed** is the fastest option. This service, offered in conjunction with FedEx, provides delivery in one to three business days to more than 190 countries and territories.
- **Express Mail International** guarantees delivery in three to five business days to a limited number of countries, including Australia, China, Hong Kong, Japan, and South Korea.
- **Priority Mail International** offers delivery guarantees of 6 to 10 business days to more than 190 countries and territories.
- **First Class Mail International** is an economical way to send correspondence and packages weighing up to four pounds to virtually any destination worldwide.

To prepare your mail for international delivery, follow the instructions provided at www.usps.com/international. There you'll find complete information on the international services available through the U.S. Postal Service, along with advice on addressing and packaging mail, completing customs forms, and calculating postage rates and fees. The *International Mail Manual*, also available on this website, offers the latest information and regulations for both outbound and inbound international mail. For instance, you can click on individual country names to see current information about restricted or prohibited items and materials, required customs forms, and rates for various classes of service.[9] Various countries have specific and often extensive lists of items that may not be sent by mail at all or that must be sent using particular postal service options.

MEMOS

Many organizations have memo forms preprinted, with labeled spaces for the recipient's name (or sometimes a checklist of all departments in an organization or all persons

FIGURE A.7 Folding Standard-Size Letterhead

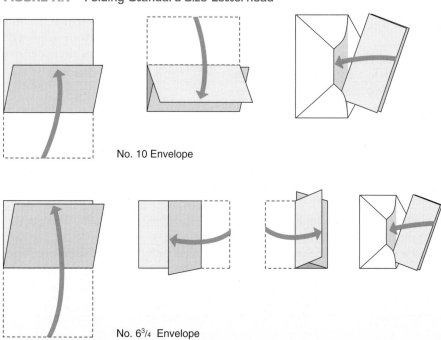

No. 10 Envelope

No. 6³/₄ Envelope

FIGURE A.8 Preprinted Memo Form

MEMO

TO: _____

DEPT: _____   FROM: _____

DATE: _____   TELEPHONE: _____

SUBJECT: _____   *For your* ☐ APPROVAL ☐ INFORMATION ☐ COMMENT

in a department), the sender's name, the date, and the subject (see Figure A.8). If such forms don't exist, you can use a memo template (which comes with word processing software and provides margin settings, headings, and special formats), or you can use plain paper.

On your document, include a title such as MEMO or INTEROFFICE CORRESPONDENCE (all in capitals) centered at the top of the page or aligned with the left margin. Also at the top, include the words *To, From, Date,* and *Subject*—followed by the appropriate information—with a blank line between as shown here:

MEMO

TO:

FROM:

DATE:

SUBJECT:

Sometimes the heading is organized like this:

MEMO

TO: DATE:

FROM: SUBJECT:

You can arrange these four pieces of information in almost any order. The date sometimes appears without the heading *Date.* The subject may be presented with the letters *Re:* (in place of *SUBJECT:*) or may even be presented without any heading (but in capital letters so that it stands out clearly). You may want to include a file or reference number, introduced by the word *File.*

The following guidelines will help you effectively format specific memo elements:

- **Addressees.** When sending a memo to a long list of people, include the notation *See distribution list* or *See below* in the *To* position at the top; then list the names at the end of the memo. Arrange this list alphabetically, except when high-ranking officials deserve more prominent placement. You can also address memos to groups of people—*All Sales Representatives, Production Group, New Product Team.*

- **Courtesy titles.** You need not use courtesy titles anywhere in a memo; first initials and last names, first names, or even initials alone are often sufficient. However, use a courtesy title if you would use one in a face-to-face encounter with the person.

- **Subject line.** The subject line of a memo helps busy colleagues quickly find out what your memo is about. Although the subject "line" may overflow onto a second line, it's most helpful when it's short (but still informative).

- **Body.** Start the body of the memo on the second or third line below the heading. Like the body of a letter, it's usually single-spaced with blank lines between paragraphs. Indenting paragraphs is optional. Handle lists, important passages, and subheadings as you do in letters. If the memo is very short, you may double-space it.

- **Second page.** If the memo carries over to a second page, head the second page just as you head the second page of a letter.

- **Writer's initials.** Unlike a letter, a memo doesn't require a complimentary close or a signature, because your name is already prominent at the top. However, you may initial the memo—either beside the name appearing at the top of the memo or at the bottom of the memo—or you may even sign your name at the bottom, particularly if the memo deals with money or confidential matters.

- **Other elements.** Treat elements such as reference initials, enclosure notations, and copy notations just as you would in a letter.

Memos may be delivered by hand, by the post office (when the recipient works at a different location), or through interoffice mail. Interoffice mail may require the use of special reusable envelopes that have spaces for the recipient's name and department or room number; the name of the previous recipient is simply crossed out. If a regular envelope is used, the words *Interoffice Mail* appear where the stamp normally goes, so that it won't accidentally be stamped and mailed with the rest of the office correspondence.

Informal, routine, or brief reports for distribution within a company are often presented in memo form. Don't include report parts such as a table of contents and appendixes, but write the body of the memo report just as carefully as you'd write a formal report.

E-MAIL

Because e-mail messages can act both as memos (carrying information within your company) and as letters (carrying information outside your company and around the world), their format depends on your audience and purpose. You may choose to have your e-mail resemble a formal letter or a detailed report, or you may decide to keep things as simple as an interoffice memo. A modified memo format is appropriate for most e-mail messages.[10] All e-mail programs include two major elements: the header and the body (see Figure A.9).

Header

The e-mail header depends on the particular program you use. Some programs even allow you to choose between a shorter and a longer version. However, most headers contain similar information:

- **To:** Contains the audience's e-mail address (see Figure A.10). Most e-mail programs also allow you to send mail to an entire group of people all at once. First, you create a distribution list. Then you type the name of the list in the *To:* line instead of typing the addresses of every person in the group.[11] The most common e-mail addresses are addresses such as

nmaa.betsy@c.si.edu (Smithsonian Institute's National Museum of American Art)

webwsj@dowjones.com (*Wall Street Journal*)

relpubli@mairie-toulouse.mipnet.fr (Municipal Services, Toulouse, Fraance)

- **From:** Contains your e-mail address.
- **Date:** Contains the day of the week, date (day, month, year), time, and time zone.

FIGURE A.9 A Typical E-Mail Message

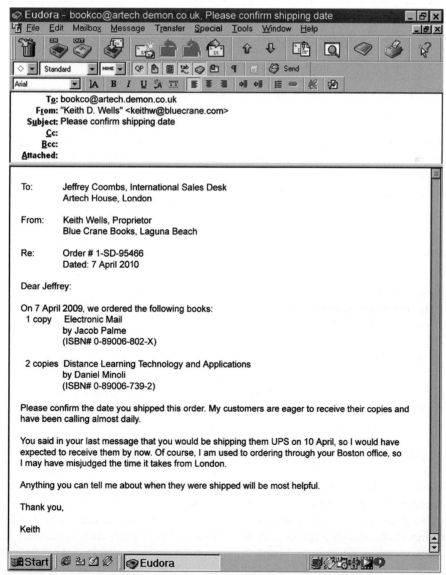

FIGURE A.10 Anatomy of an E-Mail Address

Everything on the left side of the @ symbol is the user name.

Everything on the right side describes the computer where that user has an account.

Charles.Rathcome@elementalsgroup.com

TLD	Type of User
.com	business and commercial
.edu	educational institutions
.gov	nonmilitary government and related groups
.mil	military-related groups
.net	network providers
.org	organizations and nonprofit groups
.biz	business
.pro	professions
.coop	cooperative
.info	information
.museum	museums
.aero	air transport
.name	name

The machine name usually ends with a country code (such as fr for France, dk for Denmark, hk for Hong Kong). But within the United States, the country code is replaced with a top-level domain (TLD) that indicates the type of organization operating that particular website.

- **Subject:** Describes the content of the message and presents an opportunity for you to build interest in your message.
- **Cc:** Allows you to send copies of a message to more than one person at a time. It also allows everyone on the list to see who else received the same message.
- **Bcc:** Lets you send copies to people without the other recipients knowing—a practice considered unethical by some.[12]
- **Attachments:** Contains the name(s) of the file(s) you attach to your e-mail message. The file can be a word processing document, a digital image, an audio or video message, a spreadsheet, or a software program.[13]

Most e-mail programs now allow you the choice of hiding or revealing other lines that contain more detailed information, including

- **Message-Id:** The exact location of this e-mail message on the sender's system
- **X-mailer:** The version of the e-mail program being used
- **Content type:** A description of the text and character set that is contained in the message
- **Received:** Information about each of the systems your e-mail passed through en route to your mailbox[14]

Body

The rest of the space below the header is for the body of your message. In the *To:* and *From:* lines, some headers actually print out the names of the sender and receiver (in addition to their e-mail addresses). Other headers do not. If your mail program includes only the e-mail addresses, you

might consider including your own memo-type header in the body of your message, as in Figure A.9. The writer even included a second, more specific subject line in his memo-type header. Some recipients may applaud the clarity of such second headers; however, others will criticize the space it takes. Your decision depends on how formal you want to be.

Do include a greeting in your e-mail. As pointed out in Chapter 7, greetings personalize your message. Leave one line space above and below your greeting to set it off from the rest of your message. You may end your greeting with a colon (formal), a comma (conversational), or even two hyphens (informal)—depending on the level of formality you want.

Your message begins one blank line space below your greeting. Just as in memos and letters, skip one line space between paragraphs and include headings, numbered lists, bulleted lists, and embedded lists when appropriate.

One blank line space below your message, include a simple closing, often just one word. A blank line space below that, include your signature. Whether you type your name or use a signature file, including your signature personalizes your message.

REPORTS

Enhance your report's effectiveness by paying careful attention to its appearance and layout. Follow whatever guidelines your organization prefers, always being neat and consistent throughout. If it's up to you to decide formatting questions, the following conventions may help you decide how to handle margins, headings, and page numbers.

FIGURE A.11   Margins for Formal Reports

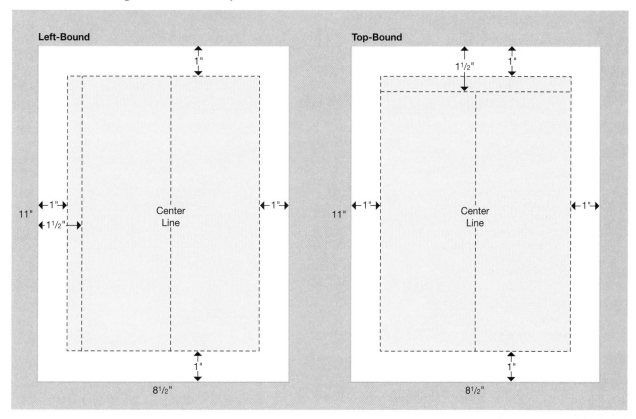

Margins

All margins on a report page are at least 1 inch wide. For double-spaced pages, use 1-inch margins; for single-spaced pages, set margins between 1¼ and 1½ inches. The top, left, and right margins are usually the same, but the bottom margins can be 1½ times deeper. Some special pages also have deeper top margins. Set top margins as deep as 2 inches for pages that contain major titles: prefatory parts (such as the table of contents or the executive summary), supplementary parts (such as the reference notes or bibliography), and textual parts (such as the first page of the text or the first page of each chapter).

If you're going to bind your report at the left or at the top, add half an inch to the margin on the bound edge (see Figure A.11): The space taken by the binding on left-bound reports makes the center point of the text a quarter inch to the right of the center of the paper. Be sure to center headings between the margins, not between the edges of the paper. The "center" paragraph format setting in your word processor does this automatically.

Headings

Headings of various levels provide visual clues to a report's organization. Figure 14.6, on page 455, illustrates one good system for showing these levels, but many variations exist. No matter which system you use, be sure to be consistent.

Page Numbers

Remember that every page in the report is counted; however, not all pages show numbers. The first page of the report, normally the title page, is unnumbered. All other pages in the prefatory section are numbered with a lowercase roman numeral, beginning with *ii* and continuing with *iii, iv, v,* and so on. The unadorned (no dashes, no period) page number is centered at the bottom margin.

Number the first page of the text of the report with the unadorned arabic numeral 1, centered at the bottom margin (double- or triple-spaced below the text). In left-bound reports, number the following pages (including the supplementary parts) consecutively with unadorned arabic numerals (2, 3, and so on), placed at the top right-hand margin (double- or triple-spaced above the text). For top-bound reports and for special pages having 2-inch top margins, center the page numbers at the bottom margin.

Appendix B
Documentation of Report Sources

By providing information about your sources, you improve your own credibility as well as the credibility of the facts and opinions you present. Documentation gives readers the means for checking your findings and pursuing the subject further. Also, documenting your report is the accepted way to give credit to the people whose work you have drawn from.

What style should you use to document your report? Experts recommend various forms, depending on your field or discipline. Moreover, your employer or client may use a form different from those the experts suggest. Don't let this discrepancy confuse you. If your employer specifies a form, use it; the standardized form is easier for colleagues to understand. However, if the choice of form is left to you, adopt one of the styles described here. Whatever style you choose, be consistent within any given report, using the same order, punctuation, and format from one reference citation or bibliography entry to the next.

A wide variety of style manuals provide detailed information on documentation. These publications explain the three most commonly used styles:

- American Psychological Association, *Publication Manual of the American Psychological Association*, 5th ed. (Washington, D.C.: American Psychological Association, 2001). Details the author–date system, which is preferred in the social sciences and often in the natural sciences as well.
- *The Chicago Manual of Style*, 15th ed. (Chicago: University of Chicago Press, 2003). Often referred to only as "*Chicago*" and widely used in the publishing industry; provides detailed treatment of source documentation and many other aspects of document preparation.
- Joseph Gibaldi, *MLA Style Manual and Guide to Scholarly Publishing*, 3rd ed. (New York: Modern Language Association, 2008). Serves as the basis for the note and bibliography style used in much academic writing and is recommended in many college textbooks on writing term papers; provides a lot of examples in the humanities.

For more information on these three guides, visit http://real-timeupdates.com/bct and click on Appendix B. Although many schemes have been proposed for organizing the information in source notes, all of them break the information into parts: (1) information about the author (name), (2) information about the work (title, edition, volume number), (3) information about the publication (place, publisher), (4) information about the date, and (5) information on relevant page ranges.

In the following sections, we summarize the major conventions for documenting sources in three styles: *The Chicago Manual of Style* (Chicago), the *Publication Manual of the American Psychological Association* (APA), and the *MLA Style Manual* (MLA).

CHICAGO HUMANITIES STYLE

The Chicago Manual of Style recommends two types of documentation systems. The *documentary-note*, or *humanities*, style gives bibliographic citations in notes—either footnotes (when printed at the bottom of a page) or endnotes (when printed at the end of the report). The humanities system is often used in literature, history, and the arts. The other system strongly recommended by *Chicago* is the *author-date* system, which cites the author's last name and the date of publication in the text, usually in parentheses, reserving full documentation for the reference list (or bibliography). For the purpose of comparing styles, we will concentrate on the humanities system, which is described in detail in *Chicago*.

In-Text Citation—*Chicago* Humanities Style

To document report sources in text, the humanities system relies on superscripts—arabic numerals placed just above the line of type at the end of the reference:

> Toward the end of his speech, Myers sounded a note of caution, saying that even though the economy is expected to grow, it could easily slow a bit.[10]

The superscript lets the reader know how to look for source information in either a footnote or an endnote (see Figure B-1). Some readers prefer footnotes so that they can simply glance at the bottom of the page for information. Others prefer endnotes so that they can read the text without a clutter of notes on the page. Also, endnotes relieve the writer from worrying about how long each note will be and how much space it will take away from the page. Both footnotes and endnotes are handled automatically by today's word processing software.

For the reader's convenience, you can use footnotes for **content notes** (which may supplement your main text with asides about a particular issue or event, provide a cross-reference to another section of your report, or direct the reader to a related source). Then you can use endnotes for **source notes** (which document direct quotations, paraphrased passages, and visual aids). Consider which type of note is most common in your report, and then choose whether to present these notes all as endnotes or all as footnotes. Regardless of the method you choose for referencing textual information in your report, notes for visual aids (both content notes and source notes) are placed on the same page as the visual.

FIGURE B-1   Sample Endnotes—*Chicago* Humanities Style

NOTES

Journal article with volume and issue numbers

1. Jonathan Clifton, "Beyond Taxonomies of Influence," *Journal of Business Communication* 46, no. 1 (2009): 57–79.

Brochure

2. BestTemp Staffing Services, *An Employer's Guide to Staffing Services,* 2d ed. (Denver: BestTemp Information Center, 2008), 31.

Newspaper article, no author

3. "Might Be Harder Than It Looks," *Los Angeles Times,* 30 January 2009, sec. A, p. 22.

Annual report

4. The Walt Disney Company, *2007 Annual Report* (Burbank, Calif.: The Walt Disney Company, 2008), 48.

Magazine article

5. Kerry A. Dolan, "A Whole New Crop" *Forbes*, 2 June 2008, 72–75.

Television broadcast

6. Daniel Han, "Trade Wars Heating Up Around the Globe," *CNN Headline News* (Atlanta: CNN, 5 March 2002).

Internet, World Wide Web

7. "Intel—Company Capsule," Hoover's Online [cited 19 June 2008], 3 screens; available from www.hoovers.com/intel/-ID_13787-/free-co-factsheet.xhtml.

Book, component parts

8. Sonja Kuntz, "Moving Beyond Benefits," in *Our Changing Workforce,* ed. Randolf Jacobson (New York: Citadel Press, 2001), 213–27.

Unpublished dissertation or thesis

9. George H. Morales, "The Economic Pressures on Industrialized Nations in a Global Economy" (Ph.D. diss., University of San Diego, 2001), 32–47.

Paper presented at a meeting

10. Charles Myers, "HMOs in Today's Environment" (paper presented at the Conference on Medical Insurance Solutions, Chicago, Ill., August 2001), 16–17.

Online magazine article

11. Leo Babauta, "17 Tips to Be Productive with Instant Messaging," in *Web Worker Daily* [online] (San Francisco, 2007 [updated 14 November 2007; cited 14 February 2008]); available from http://webworkerdaily.com.

CD-ROM encyclopedia article, one author

12. Robert Parkings, "George Eastman," *The Concise Columbia Encyclopedia* (New York: Columbia University Press, 1998) [CD-ROM].

Interview

13. Georgia Stainer, general manager, Day Cable and Communications, interview by author, Topeka, Kan., 2 March 2000.

Newspaper article, one author

14. Evelyn Standish, "Global Market Crushes OPEC's Delicate Balance of Interests," *Wall Street Journal,* 19 January 2002, sec. A, p. 1.

Book, two authors

15. Miriam Toller and Jay Fielding, *Global Business for Smaller Companies* (Rocklin, Calif.: Prima Publishing, 2001), 102–3.

Government publication

16. U.S. Department of Defense, *Stretching Research Dollars: Survival Advice for Universities and Government Labs* (Washington, D.C.: GPO, 2002), 126.

Bibliography—*Chicago* Humanities Style

The humanities system may or may not be accompanied by a bibliography (because the notes give all the necessary bibliographic information). However, endnotes are arranged in order of appearance in the text, so an alphabetical bibliography can be valuable to your readers. The bibliography may be titled *Bibliography, Reference List, Sources, Works Cited* (if you include only those sources you actually cited in your report), or *Works Consulted* (if you include uncited sources as well). This list of sources may also serve as a reading list for those who want to pursue the subject of your report further, so you may want to annotate each entry—that is, comment on the subject matter and viewpoint of the source, as well as on its usefulness to readers. Annotations may be written in either complete or incomplete sentences. (See the annotated list of style manuals early in this appendix.) A bibliography may also be more manageable if you subdivide it into categories (a classified bibliography), either by type of reference (such as books, articles, and unpublished material) or by subject matter (such as government regulation, market forces, and so on). Following are the major conventions for developing a bibliography according to *Chicago* style (see Figure B-2):

- Exclude any page numbers that may be cited in source notes, except for journals, periodicals, and newspapers.
- Alphabetize entries by the last name of the lead author (listing last name first). The names of second and succeeding authors are listed in normal order. Entries without an

FIGURE B-2 Sample Bibliography—*Chicago* Humanities Style

BIBLIOGRAPHY

Journal article with volume and issue numbers

Clifton, Jonathan. "Beyond Taxonomies of Influence." *Journal of Business Communication* 46, no. 1 (2009): 57–79.

Online magazine article

Babauta, Leo. "17 Tips to Be Productive with Instant Messaging," In *Web Worker Daily* [online], San Francisco, 2007 [updated 14 November 2007, cited 14 February 2008]. Available from http://webworkerdaily.com.

Brochure

BestTemp Staffing Services. *An Employer's Guide to Staffing Services.* 2d ed. Denver: BestTemp Information Center, 2008.

Newspaper article, no author

"Might Be Harder Than It Looks." *Los Angeles Times,* 30 January 2009, sec. A, p. 22.

Magazine article

Dolan, Kerry A. "A Whole New Crop," *Forbes*, 2 June 2008, 72–75.

Television broadcast

Han, Daniel. "Trade Wars Heating Up Around the Globe." *CNN Headline News.* Atlanta: CNN, 5 March 2002.

Internet, World Wide Web

"Intel—Company Capsule." *Hoover's Online* [cited 19 June 2008]. 3 screens; Available from www.hoovers.com/intel/-ID_13787-/free-co-factsheet.xhtml.

Book, component parts

Kuntz, Sonja. "Moving Beyond Benefits." In *Our Changing Workforce*, edited by Randolf Jacobson. New York: Citadel Press, 2001.

Unpublished dissertation or thesis

Morales, George H. "The Economic Pressures on Industrialized Nations in a Global Economy." Ph.D. diss., University of San Diego, 2001.

Paper presented at a meeting

Myers, Charles. "HMOs in Today's Environment." Paper presented at the Conference on Medical Insurance Solutions, Chicago, Ill., August 2001.

CD-ROM encyclopedia article, one author

Parkings, Robert. "George Eastman." *The Concise Columbia Encyclopedia.* New York: Columbia University Press, 1998. [CD-ROM].

Interview

Stainer, Georgia, general manager, Day Cable and Communications. Interview by author. Topeka, Kan., 2 March 2000.

Newspaper article, one author

Standish, Evelyn. "Global Market Crushes OPEC's Delicate Balance of Interests." *Wall Street Journal,* 19 January 2002, sec. A, p. 1.

Book, two authors

Toller, Miriam, and Jay Fielding. *Global Business for Smaller Companies.* Rocklin, Calif.: Prima Publishing, 2001.

Government publication

U.S. Department of Defense. *Stretching Research Dollars: Survival Advice for Universities and Government Labs.* Washington, D.C.: GPO, 2002.

Annual report

The Walt Disney Company, *2007 Annual Report,* Burbank, Calif.: The Walt Disney Company, 2008.

author name are alphabetized by the first important word in the title.

- Format entries as hanging indents (indent second and succeeding lines three to five spaces).
- Arrange entries in the following general order: (1) author name, (2) title information, (3) publication information, (4) date, (5) periodical page range.
- Use quotation marks around the titles of articles from magazines, newspapers, and journals. Capitalize the first and last words, as well as all other important words (except prepositions, articles, and coordinating conjunctions).
- Use italics to set off the names of books, newspapers, journals, and other complete publications. Capitalize

the first and last words, as well as all other important words.

- For journal articles, include the volume number and the issue number (if necessary). Include the year of publication inside parentheses and follow with a colon and the page range of the article: *Journal of Business Communication* 46, no. 1 (2009): 57–79. (In this source, the volume is 46, the number is 1, and the page range is 57–79.)
- Use brackets to identify all electronic references: [Online database] or [CD-ROM].
- Explain how electronic references can be reached: Available from www.spaceless.com/WWWVL.
- Give the citation date for online references: Cited 23 August 2010.

APA STYLE

The American Psychological Association (APA) recommends the author–date system of documentation, which is popular in the physical, natural, and social sciences. When using this system, you simply insert the author's last name and the year of publication within parentheses following the text discussion of the material cited. Include a page number if you use a direct quote. This approach briefly identifies the source so that readers can locate complete information in the alphabetical reference list at the end of the report. The author–date system is both brief and clear, saving readers time and effort.

In-Text Citation—APA Style

To document report sources in text using APA style, insert the author's surname and the date of publication at the end of a statement. Enclose this information in parentheses. If the author's name is referred to in the text itself, then the name can be omitted from parenthetical material.

> Some experts recommend both translation and back-translation when dealing with any non-English-speaking culture (Clifton, 2009).
>
> Toller and Fielding (2001) make a strong case for small companies succeeding in global business.

Personal communications and interviews conducted by the author would not be listed in the reference list at all. Such citations would appear in the text only.

> Increasing the role of cable companies is high on the list of Georgia Stainer, general manager at Day Cable and Communications (personal communication, March 2, 2009).

List of References—APA Style

For APA style, list only those works actually cited in the text (so you would not include works for background or for further reading). Report writers must choose their references judiciously. Following are the major conventions for developing a reference list according to APA style (see Figure B-3):

- Format entries as hanging indents.
- List all author names in reversed order (last name first), and use only initials for the first and middle names.
- Arrange entries in the following general order: (1) author name, (2) date, (3) title information, (4) publication information, (5) periodical page range.
- Follow the author name with the date of publication in parentheses.
- List titles of articles from magazines, newspapers, and journals without underlines or quotation marks. Capitalize only the first word of the title, any proper nouns, and the first word to follow an internal colon.
- Italicize titles of books, capitalizing only the first word, any proper nouns, and the first word to follow a colon.

- Italicize names of magazines, newspapers, journals, and other complete publications. Capitalize all the important words.
- For journal articles, include the volume number (in italics) and, if necessary, the issue number (in parentheses). Finally, include the page range of the article: *Journal of Business Communication, 46*(1), 57–79. (In this example, the volume is 46, the number is 1, and the page range is 57–79.)
- Include personal communications (such as letters, memos, e-mail, and conversations) only in text, not in reference lists.
- Electronic references include author, date of publication, title of article, name of publication (if one), volume, date of retrieval (month, day, year), and the source.
- For electronic references, indicate the actual year of publication and the exact date of retrieval.
- For electronic references, specify the URL; leave periods off the ends of URLs.

MLA STYLE

The style recommended by the Modern Language Association of America is used widely in the humanities, especially in the study of language and literature. Like APA style, MLA style uses brief parenthetical citations in the text. However, instead of including author name and year, MLA citations include author name and page reference.

In-Text Citation—MLA Style

To document report sources in text using MLA style, insert the author's last name and a page reference inside parentheses following the cited material: (Matthews 63). If the author's name is mentioned in the text reference, the name can be omitted from the parenthetical citation: (63). The citation indicates that the reference came from page 63 of a work by Matthews. With the author's name, readers can find complete publication information in the alphabetically arranged list of works cited that comes at the end of the report.

> Some experts recommend both translation and back-translation when dealing with any non-English-speaking culture (Clifton 57).
>
> Toller and Fielding make a strong case for small companies succeeding in global business (102–03).

List of Works Cited—MLA Style

The *MLA Style Manual* recommends preparing the list of works cited first so that you will know what information to give in the parenthetical citation (for example, whether to add a short title if you're citing more than one work by the same author, or whether to give an initial or first name if you're citing two authors who have the same last name). The list of works cited appears at the end of your report, contains all the works that you cite in your text, and lists them in alphabetical order. Following are the major conventions

FIGURE B-3 Sample References—APA Style

REFERENCES

Journal article with volume and issue numbers

Clifton, J. (2009). Beyond Taxonomies of Influence. *Journal of Business Communication 46* (1), 57.

Online magazine article

Babauta, L. (2007, November 14), 17 tips to be productive with instant messaging. *Web Worker Daily*. Retrieved February 14, 2008, from http://webworkerdaily.com.

Brochure

BestTemp Staffing Services. (2008). *An employer's guide to staffing services* (2d ed.) [Brochure]. Denver: BestTemp Information Center.

Newspaper article, no author

Might be harder than it looks. (2009, January 30). *Los Angeles Times,* p. A22.

Magazine article

Dolan, K. A. (2008, June 2). A whole new crop. *Forbes*, 72–75.

Television broadcast

Han, D. (2002, March 5). Trade wars heating up around the globe. *CNN Headline News*. [Television broadcast]. Atlanta, GA: CNN.

Internet, World Wide Web

Hoover's Online. (2003). *Intel—Company Capsule*. Retrieved June 19, 2008, from http://www.hoovers.com/intel/-ID_13787-/free-co-factsheet.xhtml.

Book, component parts

Kuntz, S. (2001). Moving beyond benefits. In Randolph Jacobson (Ed.), *Our changing workforce* (pp. 213–227). New York: Citadel Press.

Unpublished dissertation or thesis

Morales, G. H. (2001). *The economic pressures on industrialized nations in a global economy*. Unpublished doctoral dissertation, University of San Diego.

Paper presented at a meeting

Myers, C. (2001, August). *HMOs in today's environment*. Paper presented at the Conference on Medical Insurance Solutions, Chicago, IL.

CD-ROM encyclopedia article, one author

Parkings, R. (1998). George Eastman. On *The concise Columbia encyclopedia*. [CD-ROM]. New York: Columbia University Press.

Interview

Cited in text only, not in the list of references.

Newspaper article, one author

Standish, E. (2002, January 19). Global market crushes OPEC's delicate balance of interests. *Wall Street Journal*, p. A1.

Book, two authors

Toller, M., & Fielding, J. (2001). *Global business for smaller companies*. Rocklin, CA: Prima Publishing.

Government publication

U.S. Department of Defense. (2002). *Stretching research dollars: Survival advice for universities and government labs*. Washington, DC: U.S. Government Printing Office.

Annual report

The Walt Disney Company. (2008). *2007 Annual Report*. Burbank, Calif.: The Walt Disney Company.

for developing a reference list according to MLA style (see Figure B-4):

- Format entries as hanging indents.
- Arrange entries in the following general order: (1) author name, (2) title information, (3) publication information, (4) date, (5) periodical page range.
- List the lead author's name in reverse order (last name first), using either full first names or initials. List second and succeeding author names in normal order.
- Use quotation marks around the titles of articles from magazines, newspapers, and journals. Capitalize all important words.

- Italicize the names of books, newspapers, journals, and other complete publications, capitalizing all main words in the title.
- For journal articles, include the volume number and the issue number (if necessary). Include the year of publication inside parentheses and follow with a colon and the page range of the article: *Journal of Business Communication* 46, 1 (2009): 57. (In this source, the volume is 46, the number is 1, and the page is 57.)
- Electronic sources are less fixed than print sources, and they may not be readily accessible to readers. So citations for electronic sources must provide more information.

FIGURE B-4 Sample Works Cited—MLA Style

WORKS CITED

Journal article with volume and issue numbers	Clifton, Jonathan. "Beyond Taxonomies of Influence." *Journal of Business Communication* 46, 1 (2009): 57–79.
Online magazine article	Babauta, Leo. "17 Tips to Be Productive with Instant Messaging," *Web Worker Daily* 14 Nov. 2007. 14 Feb. 2008. <http://webworkerdaily.com>.
Brochure	BestTemp Staffing Services. *An Employer's Guide to Staffing Services*. 2d ed. Denver: BestTemp Information Center, 2008.
Newspaper article, no author	"Might Be Harder Than It Looks." *Los Angeles Times,* 30 Jan. 2009: A22.
Magazine article	Dolan, Kerry A. "A Whole New Crop" *Forbes*, 2 June 2008: 72–75.
Television broadcast	Han, Daniel. "Trade Wars Heating Up Around the Globe." *CNN Headline News*. CNN, Atlanta. 5 Mar. 2002.
Internet, World Wide Web	"Intel—Company Capsule." *Hoover's Online*. 2008. Hoover's Company Information. 19 June 2008 <http://www.hoovers.com/intel/-ID_13787/free-co-factsheet.xhtml.
Book, component parts	Kuntz, Sonja. "Moving Beyond Benefits." *Our Changing Workforce*. Ed. Randolf Jacobson. New York: Citadel Press, 2001. 213–27.
Unpublished dissertation or thesis	Morales, George H. "The Economic Pressures on Industrialized Nations in a Global Economy." Diss. U of San Diego, 2001.
Paper presented at a meeting	Myers, Charles. "HMOs in Today's Environment." Conference on Medical Insurance Solutions. Chicago. 13 Aug. 2001.
CD-ROM encyclopedia article, one author	Parkings, Robert. "George Eastman." *The Concise Columbia Encyclopedia*. CD-ROM. New York: Columbia UP, 1998.
Interview	Stainer, Georgia, general manager, Day Cable and Communications. Telephone interview. 2 Mar. 2000.
Newspaper article, one author	Standish, Evelyn. "Global Market Crushes OPEC's Delicate Balance of Interests." *Wall Street Journal,* 19 Jan. 2002: A1.
Book, two authors	Toller, Miriam, and Jay Fielding. *Global Business for Smaller Companies*. Rocklin, CA: Prima Publishing, 2001.
Government publication	United States. Department of Defense. *Stretching Research Dollars: Survival Advice for Universities and Government Labs*. Washington: GPO, 2002.
Annual report	The Walt Disney Company, *2007 Annual Report*. Calif.: The Walt Disney Company, 2008.

Always try to be as comprehensive as possible, citing whatever information is available (however, see the note below about extremely long URLs).

- The date for electronic sources should contain both the date assigned in the source and the date accessed by the researcher.
- The URL for electronic sources must be as accurate and complete as possible, from access-mode identifier (such as http or ftp) to all relevant directory and file names. If the URL is extremely long, use the URL of the website's home page or the URL of the site's search page if you used the site's search function to find the article. Be sure to enclose this path inside angle brackets: http://www.hoovers.com/capsules/13787.html.

Appendix C
Correction Symbols

Instructors often use these short, easy-to-remember correction symbols and abbreviations when evaluating students' writing. You can use them too, to understand your instructor's suggestions and to revise and proofread your own letters, memos, and reports. Refer to the Handbook of Grammar, Mechanics, and Usage (pages H-1–H-26) for further information.

CONTENT AND STYLE

Acc	Accuracy. Check to be sure information is correct.
ACE	Avoid copying examples.
ACP	Avoid copying problems.
Adp	Adapt. Tailor message to reader.
App	Follow proper organization approach. (Refer to Chapter 4.)
Assign	Assignment. Review instructions for assignment.
AV	Active verb. Substitute active for passive.
Awk	Awkward phrasing. Rewrite.
BC	Be consistent.
BMS	Be more sincere.
Chop	Choppy sentences. Use longer sentences and more transitional phrases.
Con	Condense. Use fewer words.
CT	Conversational tone. Avoid using overly formal language.
Depers	Depersonalize. Avoid attributing credit or blame to any individual or group.
Dev	Develop. Provide greater detail.
Dir	Direct. Use direct approach; get to the point.
Emph	Emphasize. Develop this point more fully.
EW	Explanation weak. Check logic; provide more proof.
Fl	Flattery. Avoid compliments that are insincere.
FS	Figure of speech. Find a more accurate expression.
GNF	Good news first. Use direct order.
GRF	Give reasons first. Use indirect order.
GW	Goodwill. Put more emphasis on expressions of goodwill.
H/E	Honesty/ethics. Revise statement to reflect good business practices.
Imp	Imply. Avoid being direct.
Inc	Incomplete. Develop further.
Jar	Jargon. Use less specialized language.

Log	Logic. Check development of argument.
Neg	Negative. Use more positive approach or expression.
Obv	Obvious. Do not state point in such detail.
OC	Overconfident. Adopt humbler language.
OM	Omission.
Org	Organization. Strengthen outline.
OS	Off the subject. Close with point on main subject.
Par	Parallel. Use same structure.
Pom	Pompous. Rephrase in down-to-earth terms.
PV	Point of view. Make statement from reader's perspective rather than your own.
RB	Reader benefit. Explain what reader stands to gain.
Red	Redundant. Reduce number of times this point is made.
Ref	Reference. Cite source of information.
Rep	Repetitive. Provide different expression.
RS	Resale. Reassure reader that he or she has made a good choice.
SA	Service attitude. Put more emphasis on helping reader.
Sin	Sincerity. Avoid sounding glib or uncaring.
SL	Stereotyped language. Focus on individual's characteristics instead of on false generalizations.
Spec	Specific. Provide more specific statement.
SPM	Sales promotion material. Tell reader about related goods or services.
Stet	Let stand in original form.
Sub	Subordinate. Make this point less important.
SX	Sexist. Avoid language that contributes to gender stereotypes.
Tone	Tone needs improvement.
Trans	Transition. Show connection between points.
UAE	Use action ending. Close by stating what reader should do next.
UAS	Use appropriate salutation.
UAV	Use active voice.
Unc	Unclear. Rewrite to clarify meaning.
UPV	Use passive voice.
USS	Use shorter sentences.
V	Variety. Use different expression or sentence pattern.
W	Wordy. Eliminate unnecessary words.
WC	Word choice. Find a more appropriate word.
YA	"You" attitude. Rewrite to emphasize reader's needs.

GRAMMAR, MECHANICS, AND USAGE

Ab	Abbreviation. Avoid abbreviations in most cases; use correct abbreviation.
Adj	Adjective. Use adjective instead.
Adv	Adverb. Use adverb instead.
Agr	Agreement. Make subject and verb or noun and pronoun agree.
Ap	Appearance. Improve appearance.
Apos	Apostrophe. Check use of apostrophe.
Art	Article. Use correct article.
BC	Be consistent.
Cap	Capitalize.
Case	Use cases correctly.
CoAdj	Coordinate adjective. Insert comma between coordinate adjectives; delete comma between adjective and compound noun.
CS	Comma splice. Use period or semicolon to separate clauses.
DM	Dangling modifier. Rewrite so that modifier clearly relates to subject of sentence.
Exp	Expletive. Avoid expletive beginnings, such as it is, there are, there is, this is, and these are.
F	Format. Improve layout of document.
Frag	Fragment. Rewrite as complete sentence.
Gram	Grammar. Correct grammatical error.
HCA	Hyphenate compound adjective.
lc	Lowercase. Do not use capital letter.
M	Margins. Improve frame around document.
MM	Misplaced modifier. Place modifier close to word it modifies.
NRC	Nonrestrictive clause (or phrase). Separate from rest of sentence with commas.
P	Punctuation. Use correct punctuation.
Par	Parallel. Use same structure.
PH	Place higher. Move document up on page.
PL	Place lower. Move document down on page.
Prep	Preposition. Use correct preposition.
RC	Restrictive clause (or phrase). Remove commas that separate clause from rest of sentence.
RO	Run-on sentence. Separate two sentences with comma and coordinating conjunction or with semicolon.
SC	Series comma. Add comma before *and*.
SI	Split infinitive. Do not separate *to* from rest of verb.
Sp	Spelling error. Consult dictionary.
S-V	Subject–verb pair. Do not separate with comma.
Syl	Syllabification. Divide word between syllables.
WD	Word division. Check dictionary for proper end-of-line hyphenation.
WW	Wrong word. Replace with another word.

PROOFREADING MARKS

Symbol	Meaning	Symbol Used in Context	Corrected Copy
═══	Align horizontally	meaningful result	meaningful result
‖	Align vertically	1. Power cable 2. Keyboard	1. Power cable 2. Keyboard
bf	Boldface	Recommendations bf	**Recommendations**
≡	Capitalize	Pepsico, Inc.	PepsiCo, Inc.
⊐⊏	Center	Awards Banquet	Awards Banquet
◠	Close up space	self- confidence	self-confidence
ℓ	Delete	harrassment and abuse	harassment
ds	Double-space	text in first line text in second line ds	text in first line text in second line
∧	Insert	" and white tirquoise shirts	turquoise and white shirts
∨	Insert apostrophe	our teams goals	our team's goals
∧	Insert comma	a, b and c	a, b, and c
⹀	Insert hyphen	third quarter sales	third-quarter sales
⊙	Insert period	Harrigan et al	Harrigan et al.
∜	Insert quotation marks	This team isn't cooperating.	This "team" isn't cooperating.
#	Insert space	real estate testcase	real estate test case
ital	Italics	Quarterly Report ital	*Quarterly Report*
/	Lowercase	TULSA, South of here	Tulsa, south of here
⌴	Move down	Sincerely,	Sincerely,
⊏	Move left	Attention: Security	Attention: Security
⊐	Move right	February 2, 2010	February 2, 2010
⌐	Move up	THIRD-QUARTER SALES	THIRD-QUARTER SALES
STET	Restore	staff talked openly and frankly STET	staff talked openly
∽	Run lines together	Manager, Distribution	Manager, Distribution
ss	Single space	text in first line text in second line ss	text in first line text in second line
⬭	Spell out	COD	cash on delivery
sp	Spell out	sp Assn. of Biochem. Engrs.	Association of Biochemical Engineers
⌐┘	Start new line	Marla Fenton, Manager, Distribution	Marla Fenton, Manager, Distribution
¶	Start new paragraph	¶The solution is easy to determine but difficult to implement in a competitive environment like the one we now face.	The solution is easy to determine but difficult to implement in a competitive environment like the one we now face.
∼	Transpose	airy, light, casual tone	light, airy, casual tone

Video Guide

Your instructor may elect to show you one or more of the videos described on the following pages. These programs supplement course concepts with real-life examples of business-people meeting important communication challenges. This video guide includes several review and analysis questions as well as exercises for each video. Be sure to review the appropriate page ahead of time so that you'll know what to look for when you watch the video. (To access backup copies of the online articles mentioned in the follow-up assignments and research projects, visit and click on "Student Assignments.")

EFFECTIVE COMMUNICATION

Learning Objectives

After viewing this video, you will be able to

1. Recognize the importance of communication in the business environment
2. Recognize the elements that distinguish effective from ineffective communication
3. Understand why brevity is an important part of effective communication

Background Information

Effective communication delivers a number of business benefits, including stronger decision making and faster problem solving, earlier warning of potential problems, increased productivity and steadier workflow, stronger business relationships, clearer and more persuasive marketing messages, enhanced professional images for both employers and companies, lower employee turnover and higher employee satisfaction, better financial results, and higher return for investors. To be considered effective, communication efforts need to provide practical information, give facts rather than vague impressions, present information concisely, clarify expectations and responsibilities, and offer persuasive arguments and recommendations.

The Video

This video portrays a new employee at an advertising agency as he learns the importance of effective communication—and learns how to improve his communication efforts. As he goes through a typical day accompanied by a "message mentor," he observes the results of both effective and ineffective communication.

Discussion Questions

1. Why might new hires fresh out of college face challenges in learning how to communicate in the workplace?
2. How should you handle situations in which you are asked to provide solid information but the only information available to you is imprecise and potentially unreliable?
3. How can effective communication improve employee morale?
4. How can you judge how much information to provide your audience in any given situation?
5. Can communication efforts be both effective and unethical? For example, what about a marketing campaign that uses compelling information to persuade people to buy an inferior product when a better product is available from the competition?

Follow-up Assignment

Most companies make an effort to define external communication strategies, but many don't have a formal strategy for internal communication—which is every bit as essential to their success. Read the article, "Internal Communication Strategies—The Neglected Strategic Element," at **http://workhelp.org/content/view/171/46/** and then answer the following questions:

1. What are the advantages of effective internal communication?
2. How does communication help align the efforts of everyone in the organization toward common goals?
3. Why is it important to have a companywide strategy for internal communication?

For Further Research

The *HR Magazine* article "Great Communicators, Great Communication" emphasizes the role communication plays in creating great workplaces. Visit **www.shrm.org**, use the search function to find the article, and then summarize the steps companies have taken to be included among the magazine's list of the 50 best small and medium companies to work for in the United States.

ETHICAL COMMUNICATION

Learning Objectives

After viewing this video, you will be able to

1. Describe a process for deciding what is ethical or unethical
2. Explain the importance of meeting your personal and professional responsibilities in an ethical manner
3. Discuss the possible consequences of ethical and unethical choices and talk about the impact of these choices on direct and related audiences

Background Information

Communication is ethical when it includes all relevant information, when it's true in every sense, and when it isn't deceptive in any way. In contrast, communication is unethical when it includes false information, fails to include important information, or otherwise misleads an audience. To avoid unethical choices in your communication efforts, you must consider not only legal issues but also the needs of your audience and the expectations of society and your employer. In turn, companies that demonstrate high standards of ethics maintain credibility with employees, customers, and other stakeholders.

The Video

This video identifies two important tools in a communicator's toolbox: honesty and objectivity. These tools help businesspeople resolve ethical dilemmas and avoid ethical lapses, both within the company and during interactions with outside audiences. Poor ethical choices can damage a company's credibility and put employees, customers, and the surrounding community at risk. Unfortunately, some ethical choices are neither clear nor simple, and you may face situations in which the needs of one group or individual must be weighed against the needs of another.

Discussion Questions

1. Would you ever consider compromising your ethics for self-gain? If so, under what circumstance? If not, why?
2. The video mentions the role of misrepresentations in the collapse of Enron. If you were the head of communications at Enron and had some knowledge of the true nature of the company's financial condition, what would you have done?
3. Identify risks involved when you choose to act in an unethical manner.
4. How can you be an effective business communicator without credibility?
5. Is it ethical to call in sick to work, even though you are not ill? What happens to your credibility if someone finds out you were not sick?

Follow-up Assignment

Many businesses, from small companies to large corporations, formulate codes of ethics that outline ethical standards for employees. Download IBM's Business Conduct Guidelines from www.ibm.com/investor/pdf/BCG2009.pdf and answer the following questions:

1. What does IBM want employees to do if they are aware of unethical situations within the organization?
2. How does IBM view misleading statements or innuendos about competitors?
3. What advice does IBM give employees on the subject of receiving gifts from people outside the company?

For Further Research

Advertising communications, particularly advertising aimed at children, can present a variety of ethical concerns. Visit the American Psychological Association's website, at www.apa.org, and search for the article "Advertising to children: Is it ethical?" After reading this article, do you believe it is unethical for psychologists to advise companies on how to target children more effectively through advertising? Why or why not?

BUSINESS ETIQUETTE

Learning Objectives

After viewing this video, you will be able to

1. Recognize the negative impact that poor etiquette can have in the workplace
2. Identify the five goals that every bad-news message should seek to achieve
3. Identify situations in which the indirect approach is likely to be more effective than the direct approach

Background Information

Etiquette strikes some people as a fine idea for tea parties but something that has little relevance in the contemporary workplace. However, the stresses and strains of today's business environment make etiquette more important than ever. Poor etiquette harms relationships, hinders communication, lowers morale and productivity, and limits career potential. Successful professionals know that taking the time and effort to treat others with respect—through their words and their actions—pays off for everyone in the long run.

The Video

This video shows a young employee learning firsthand the value of business etiquette. A business associate whom he has offended through clumsy communication turns the tables and helps him understand the negative effect that poor etiquette has on people in the workplace. She then helps him grasp the steps needed to present himself respectably and to communicate in ways that get his point across without unnecessarily stirring up negative emotions.

Discussion Questions

1. Is paying attention to standards of etiquette likely to save time or cost time in the workplace? Why?
2. If you need to deliver bad news to a person with whom you will probably never interact again, how can you justify taking extra time and effort to communicate carefully and respectfully? Are you wasting your company's money by spending time on such efforts?
3. How does a well-written buffer in an indirect negative message help the receiver accept the bad news?
4. Can a buffer also make the task of delivering negative messages less stressful? Why or why not?

5. Is the indirect approach to negative messages deceptive? Shouldn't communication always be straightforward and direct? Be prepared to explain your answer.

Follow-up Assignment

Visit www.executiveplanet.com and click on any country that interests you. Explore the Public Behaviour section(s) for that country and identify three tips that would help anyone from the United States who is preparing to do business there.

For Further Research

Take the brief business etiquette quiz at http://www.gradview .com/articles/careers/etiquette.html. Were you able to figure out answers to these situations? Do you agree with the responses that the website identifies as being correct?

LEARNING TO LISTEN: SECOND CITY COMMUNICATIONS
CREATIVITY: SECOND CITY COMMUNICATIONS

Learning Objectives

After viewing this video, you will be able to

1. Understand the functions of interpersonal communication in the workplace
2. Identify the ways to overcome barriers to effective communication
3. Discuss the importance of active listening both socially and professionally

Background Information

Chicago's Second City Improv is more than the world's best-known comedy theater. Second City now brings its famous brand of humor to corporate giants such as Coca-Cola, Motorola, and Microsoft. With over 40 years of experience in corporate services, Second City's teachers help business professionals develop communication skills through lessons in improvisational theater. Business communications training is Second City's fastest-growing practice, fueled by the demands of more than 200 Fortune 500 companies. Workshops are tailored to clients' needs in such areas as listening and giving presentations, collaborative leadership and team skills, interviewing, breaking down barriers to successful communication, and using humor to convey important messages. The next time you watch improvisational sketch comedy, ask yourself how a lesson in the art of "improv" might give your career a boost.

The Video

In these two video segments, you'll see Second City's training techniques in action. The first segment addresses the need to listen actively, and the second explores techniques for

encouraging innovation. The second clip is less focused on communication, but you can see how the techniques for stimulating innovation work equally well for fostering meaningful, two-way conversation that encourages people to open up rather than shut down.

Discussion Questions

1. How do the exercises featured in this video address the contrasting needs of the trial lawyer, the divorce lawyer, and the media buyer?
2. Would ABC's talkative guest Kay Jarman, the 47-year-old award-winning salesperson, be a good candidate for Second City's training workshop?
3. What other workshops might Tom Yorton want to offer companies in response to the current economic and political climate?
4. How might the "Yes and" rule of improvisation be used to train customer service representatives at an L.L. Bean or a Dell call center? Without physical cues, such as facial expression and body language, is the "Yes and" rule still effective?
5. As president and managing director of Second City Communications, Tom Yorton says the following: "You have to be willing to fail to be able to get the results you want . . . to connect with an audience." Do you agree that this statement is as true in business as it is in comedy? Support your chosen position.

Follow-up Assignment

Enjoy Second City Communications's website, at www .secondcity. com. If you are a loyal fan, you might want to check out the book titles offered and read more about the group's history. Now explore Second City's Corporate Services: Scan the client roster, read the testimonials, and select a case study that you find compelling. If you are currently employed, which workshop would be most beneficial to you and to your work team? Explain your choice. If you are not currently employed, how might you and your fellow business students benefit from a Second City workshop? Which workshop would you most like to participate in? Explain how you think it might help you in terms of your social life, your career planning, and your interviewing skills.

For Further Research

The importance of active listening is at the core of *consultative selling*, an approach that emphasizes posing questions to the potential buyer in order to identify needs and expectations—rather than rattling off a prepared sales speech. PublicSpeaking Skills.com (www.publicspeakingskills.com) is one of many companies that offer training in consultative selling. Review the description of the company's Consultative Selling and Negotiating Skills course. Do the principles espoused match the concept of the "you" attitude and the elements of ethical communication that you've learned so far?

COMMUNICATING IN THE GLOBAL WORKPLACE

Learning Objectives

After viewing this video, you will be able to

1. Discuss the challenges of communicating in the global workplace
2. Identify barriers to effective communication across borders
3. Explain the critical role of time in global communication efforts

Background Information

Many businesses are crossing national boundaries to engage in international business. However, operating in a global environment presents a variety of challenges related to culture and communication. Understanding and respecting these challenges can mean the difference between success and failure, so executives must make sure that employees are educated on cultural issues before attempting to do business in other countries.

The Video

This video identifies the challenges to effective communication in the global marketplace, including the barriers posed by language, culture, time, and technology. You will see that a significant amount of research needs to be conducted before a company can engage in successful global business ventures. For instance, if communicators are unaware of differences in gestures, expressions, and dialect, they can inadvertently offend or confuse their audiences. In addition, time zone differences require organizations to plan carefully in advance so that they can develop, translate, and deliver information in a timely manner.

Discussion Questions

1. Language can be a barrier to effective communication. What steps can a company take to minimize language barriers across borders?
2. What characteristics of a country's culture need to be researched to ensure business success across borders?
3. How does a company ensure that a message is properly translated into the local language and dialect of the people it conducts business with?
4. What challenges does a company face when trying to hold a conference call or video meeting with affiliates and employees around the world?
5. The video mentions that some companies have trusted contacts in a country they wish to do business with, while other companies rely on a significant amount of research to learn more about culture and other local characteristics. What method do you feel is most effective for gathering useful, accurate, and up-to-date information regarding cultural issues?

Follow-up Assignment

The Coca-Cola Company has local operations in more than 200 countries throughout the world. Visit www.coca-cola.com and click on "Change Country" at the top of the page to learn more about the company's business activities in a variety of countries. What steps does Coke take to communicate through its website with customers around the world? Does the company strive to develop products that meet local tastes and needs? If so, how and why?

For Further Research

Choose a country other than the United States and research your selection, using both online and library resources to identify important cultural characteristics specific to that country. For example, you might want to gather information about gestures and other nonverbal communication that would be considered offensive, about work habits, or about laws related to conducting business in that country. The characteristics you identify should be useful and accurate.

Based on what you've learned about this country and your personal beliefs, values, and life experiences, is there any risk that you might have a prejudiced or ethnocentric viewpoint regarding people from this country? Why or why not?

IMPACT OF CULTURE ON BUSINESS: SPOTLIGHT ON LATIN AMERICA

Learning Objectives

After viewing this video, you will be able to

1. List key aspects of Latin American cultures and indicate the influences on their development
2. Identify factors that might lead to cultural change in Latin America
3. Explain some of the major cultural contrasts within Latin America and their impact on international business operations

Background Information

To a large degree, culture defines the way all human beings interpret and respond to life's changing circumstances. When you interact with people from your own culture, your shared experiences and expectations usually enhance the communication process by providing a common language and frame of reference. However, when you communicate across cultural boundaries, a lack of awareness of your audience's culture—and the subconscious ways that your own culture shapes your perceptions—can result in partial or even total failure of the communication process. Moreover, culture is rarely static, so impressions you may have gathered at one point in your life may need to be revisited and revised over time.

The Video

This video takes a broad look at Latin America's various countries and cultures and explores the business implications of cultural similarities and differences. You'll learn how cultural groups that may appear identical on the surface can in fact have subtle but profound differences. Although communication is just one of many topics discussed in the video, you will get a sense of just how important—and challenging—communication can be when conducting business across cultural boundaries.

Discussion Questions

1. Explain what the video means when it says that your own culture can "sneak up on you."
2. How is business influencing the economic gulf between urban and rural populations in Latin America?
3. How have imperial conquests and slavery affected the populations and cultures of Latin America?
4. How do many outsiders view the issue of business and government corruption in Latin America?
5. Is business etiquette in most of Latin America considered relatively formal or relatively informal?

Follow-up Assignment

The World Bank plays an important role in today's fast-changing, closely meshed global economy. Visit the bank's website, at www.worldbank.org, and explore the programs and initiatives under way in the Latin American region. How is the bank using this website to foster better communication between Latin America and the rest of the world?

For Further Research

In today's global marketplace, knowing as much as possible about your international customers' business practices and customs could give you a strategic advantage. To help you successfully conduct business around the globe, visit www.buyusainfo.net and select any country from the drop-down menu. How can resources such as this website help U.S. businesses communicate more successfully with customers, employees, and other groups in Latin America?

EFFECTIVE ORAL PRESENTATIONS

Learning Objectives

After viewing this video, you will be able to

1. Reiterate the importance of knowing your audience before creating and delivering oral presentations
2. Discuss the role of teamwork in preparing and delivering complex presentations
3. Explain the importance of anticipating objections likely to be raised during a presentation

Background Information

Oral presentations are a vital communication medium in most companies. In particular, important decisions often involve one or more presentations, either in person or online, in which people advocating a specific choice present their case to the people responsible for making the decision. Such presentations usually combine informational and analytical reporting, along with the persuasive aspects of a proposal. Beyond the mere delivery of information, however, presentations also involve an element of performance. Audiences search for both verbal and nonverbal clues to help them assess presenters' knowledge, confidence, and credibility.

The Video

This video follows three colleagues as they create and deliver a presentation that seeks to convince the audience to approve the purchase of a particular software system that will be used to manage the company's sales force. The presenters explain the importance of understanding the expectations of their audience, from the types of visuals they prefer to the objections they are likely to raise. The team also explains how they took advantage of each member's individual strengths to create a more effective presentation.

Discussion Questions

1. How did the presenters demonstrate their knowledge of the audience?
2. Why did one presenter use a $100 bill as a prop?
3. What are the risks of using props such as the $100 bill?
4. How did the presenters prepare for objections raised by the audience?
5. How would the team need to modify its presentation for an online webcast instead of an in-person oral presentation?

Follow-up Assignment

Podcasts (audio only) and vidcasts (podcasts with video) are quickly catching on as a medium for business presentations. Visit www.technorati.com and click on the Business channel. Select any three podcasts. Listen to them, taking careful notes so that you can compare the three selections in terms of grabbing your attention, keeping your attention, and effectively communicating the podcast's information. Which of the three podcasts is the most effective? Why?

For Further Research

Musicians, actors, jugglers—virtually everyone who performs in public experiences *performance anxiety*, or *stage fright*, as it is commonly known. This anxiety is simply the natural outcome of caring about how well you do. After all, if you didn't care, you wouldn't feel anxious. Seasoned performers not only recognize that anxiety is natural but they also have learned how to use this emotion to their advantage by giving them extra energy. Visit www.petethomas.co.uk/performance-nerves.html and www.jugglingdb.com (search for "stage fright" and then click on the "Collective wisdom on stage fright") and read how these accomplished performers handle the anxiety of performing in public. How can you adapt their techniques to business presentations?

INTERVIEWING SKILLS

Learning Objectives

After viewing this video, you will be able to

1. Explain how the AIDA approach helps create effective application letters
2. Identify mistakes that can cause an otherwise qualified candidate to lose out on a job opportunity
3. Explain why planning for tough questions is such an important part of your interviewing strategy

Background Information

Most companies would admit that an employment interview is an imperfect test of a candidate's skills and personality fit with the organization. In response, some are beginning to add testing, job simulations, and other evaluation tools to the selection process. However, the classic face-to-face interview remains the dominant decision-making tool in the hiring process, so developing your interviewing skills will be vital to your success at every stage in your career.

The Video

This video follows the progress of two candidates applying and interviewing for a technical writing position. One candidate has more experience in this area, but his approach to the interview process ends up costing him the job opportunity. In contrast, a candidate with less experience takes a confident and creative approach that nets her the job.

Discussion Questions

1. Why are multiple StayCom managers involved in this interviewing process? Couldn't one manager handle it?
2. Why does one of the managers compare an application letter to a news story?
3. What steps did Cheryl Yung take to overcome a potential shortcoming in her qualifications?
4. What mistakes did candidate Buddy McCoy make in his interview?
5. Why would the interviewers care about the interpersonal skills of someone who will be writing for a living?

Follow-up Assignment

Nonverbal cues are important in every communication scenario, but they are perhaps never more important than in job interviews. Not only are interviewers looking for any clues they can find that will guide their decisions but they tend to make up their minds quickly—perhaps even before the candidate has said anything at all. Use the Web Search feature at http://businesscommunicationblog.com/ websearch to find advice on nonverbal communication in interviews. Distill this information down to a half dozen or so key points that you can write on a note card to study before you step into your next job interview.

For Further Research

You look great in your new interview outfit, your hair is perfect but not too perfect, your smile radiates positive energy, and you're ready to dazzle the interviewer. Then, oops—you discover that your first interview will be held over the telephone, so none of your visual cues will help you at this stage. Don't fret; read the telephone interviewing advice at www.collegegrad.com/jobsearch/phone-Interviewing-Success/, and you'll be ready to dazzle the interviewer long distance.

Handbook of Grammar, Mechanics, and Usage

The rules of grammar, mechanics, and usage provide the guidance every professional needs in order to communicate successfully with colleagues, customers, and other audiences. Understanding and following these rules helps you in two important ways. First, the rules determine how meaning is encoded and decoded in the communication process. If you don't encode your messages using the same rules your readers or listeners use to decode them, chances are your audiences will not extract your intended meaning from your messages. Without a firm grasp of the basics of grammar, mechanics, and usage, you risk being misunderstood, damaging your company's image, losing money for your company, and possibly even losing your job. In other words, if you want to get your point across, you need to follow the rules of grammar, mechanics, and usage. Second, apart from transferring meaning successfully, following the rules tells your audience that you respect the conventions and expectations of the business community.

You can think of *grammar* as the agreed-upon structure of a language, the way that individual words are formed and the manner in which those words are then combined to form meaningful sentences. *Mechanics* are style and formatting issues such as capitalization, spelling, and the use of numbers and symbols. *Usage* involves the accepted and expected way in which specific words are used by a particular community of people—in this case, the community of businesspeople who use English. This handbook can help you improve your knowledge and awareness in all three areas. It is divided into the following sections:

- **Diagnostic Test of English Skills.** Testing your current knowledge of grammar, mechanics, and usage helps you find out where your strengths and weaknesses lie. This test offers 50 items taken from the topics included in this handbook.
- **Assessment of English Skills.** After completing the diagnostic test, use the assessment form to highlight the areas you most need to review.
- **Essentials of Grammar, Mechanics, and Usage.** This section helps you quickly review the basics. You can study the things you've probably already learned but may have forgotten about grammar, punctuation, mechanics (including capitalization, abbreviation, number style, and word division), and vocabulary (including frequently confused words, frequently misused words, frequently misspelled words, and transitional words and phrases). Practice sessions throughout this section help you test yourself and reinforce what you learn. Use this essential review not only to study and improve your English skills but also as a reference for any questions you may have during this course.

DIAGNOSTIC TEST OF ENGLISH SKILLS

Use this test to determine whether you need more practice with grammar, punctuation, mechanics, or vocabulary. When you've answered all the questions, ask your instructor for an answer sheet so that you can score the test. On the Assessment of English Skills form (page H-3), record the number of questions you answered incorrectly in each section.

The following choices apply to items 1–5. Write in each blank the letter of the choice that best describes the part of speech that is underlined.

A. noun
B. pronoun
C. verb
D. adjective
E. adverb
F. preposition
G. conjunction
H. article

_____ 1. The new branch location will be decided <u>by</u> next week.
_____ 2. We must hire only <u>qualified</u>, ambitious graduates.
_____ 3. After their <u>presentation,</u> I was still undecided.
_____ 4. See <u>me</u> after the meeting.
_____ 5. Margaret, pressed for time, turned in <u>unusually</u> sloppy work.

In the blanks for items 6–15, write the letter of the word or phrase that best completes each sentence.

_____ 6. (A. Russ's, B. Russ') laptop was stolen last week.
_____ 7. Speaking only for (A. me, B. myself), I think the new policy is discriminatory.
_____ 8. Of the five candidates we interviewed yesterday, (A. who, B. whom) do you believe is the best choice?
_____ 9. India has increased (A. it's, B. its) imports of corn and rice.
_____ 10. Anyone who wants to be (A. their, B. his or her) own boss should think about owning a franchise.
_____ 11. If the IT department can't (A. lie, B. lay) the fiber-optic cable by March 1, the plant will not open on schedule.
_____ 12. Starbucks (A. is, B. are) opening five new stores in San Diego in the next year.
_____ 13. The number of women-owned small businesses (A. has, B. have) increased sharply in the past two decades.
_____ 14. Greg and Bernyce worked (A. good, B. well) together.
_____ 15. They distributed the supplies (A. among, B. between) the six staff members.

The following choices apply to items 16–20. Write in each blank the letter of the choice that best describes the sentence structure problem with each item.

A. sentence fragment
B. comma splice
C. misplaced modifier
D. fused sentence
E. lack of parallelism
F. unclear antecedent

_____ 16. The number of employees who took the buyout offer was much higher than expected, now the entire company is understaffed.

_____ 17. The leader in Internet-only banking.

_____ 18. Diamond doesn't actually sell financial products rather it acts as an intermediary.

_____ 19. Helen's proposal is for not only the present but also for the future.

_____ 20. When purchasing luxury products, quality is more important than price for consumers.

For items 21–30, circle the letter of the preferred choice in each of the following groups of sentences.

21. A. What do you think of the ad slogan "Have it your way?"
    B. What do you think of the ad slogan "Have it your way"?

22. A. Send copies to Jackie Cross, Uniline, Brad Nardi, Peale & Associates, and Tom Griesbaum, MatchMakers.
    B. Send copies to Jackie Cross, Uniline; Brad Nardi, Peale & Associates; and Tom Griesbaum, MatchMakers.

23. A. They've recorded 22 complaints since yesterday, all of them from long-time employees.
    B. They've recorded 22 complaints since yesterday; all of them from long-time employees.

24. A. We are looking for two qualities in applicants: experience with computers and an interest in people.
    B. We are looking for two qualities in applicants; experience with computers and an interest in people.

25. A. At the Center for the Blind the clients we serve have lost vision, due to a wide variety of causes.
    B. At the Center for the Blind, the clients we serve have lost vision due to a wide variety of causes.

26. A. Replace your standard light bulbs with new, compact fluorescent bulbs.
    B. Replace your standard light bulbs with new, compact, fluorescent bulbs.
    C. Replace your standard light bulbs with new compact fluorescent bulbs.

27. A. Blue Cross of California may have changed its name to Anthem Blue Cross but the company still has the same commitment to California.
    B. Blue Cross of California may have changed its name to Anthem Blue Cross, but the company still has the same commitment to California.

28. A. Only eight banks in this country—maybe nine can handle transactions of this magnitude.
    B. Only eight banks in this country—maybe nine—can handle transactions of this magnitude.

29. A. Instead of focusing on high-growth companies, we targeted mature businesses with only one or two people handling the decision making.
    B. Instead of focusing on high growth companies, we targeted mature businesses with only one or two people handling the decision-making.

30. A. According to board president Damian Cabaza "having a crisis communication plan is a high priority."
    B. According to board president Damian Cabaza, "Having a crisis communication plan is a high priority."

For items 31–40, select the best choice from among those provided.

31. A. At her previous employer, Mary-Anne worked in Marketing Communications and Human Resources.
    B. At her previous employer, Mary-Anne worked in marketing communications and human resources.

32. A. By fall, we'll have a dozen locations between the Mississippi and Missouri rivers.
    B. By Fall, we'll have a dozen locations between the Mississippi and Missouri Rivers.

33. A. The Board applauded President Donlan upon her reelection for a fifth term.
    B. The board applauded president Donlan upon her reelection for a fifth term.
    C. The board applauded President Donlan upon her reelection for a fifth term.

34. A. If you want to travel to France, you need to be au courant with the business practices.
    B. If you want to travel to France, you need to be "au courant" with the business practices.

35. A. As the company's CEO, Thomas Spurgeon handles all dealings with the FDA.
    B. As the company's C.E.O., Thomas Spurgeon handles all dealings with the F.D.A.

36. A. The maximum speed limit in most states is 65 mph.
    B. The maximum speed limit in most states is 65 m.p.h.

37. A. Sales of graphic novels increased nine percent between 2008 and 2009.
    B. Sales of graphic novels increased 9 percent between 2008 and 2009.

38. A. Our store is open daily from nine a.m. to seven P. M.
    B. Our store is open daily from 9:00 A.M. to 7:00 P.M.

39. A. The organizing meeting is scheduled for July 27, and the event will be held in January 2010.
    B. The organizing meeting is scheduled for July 27th, and the event will be held in January, 2010.

40. A. We need six desks, eight file cabinets, and 12 trashcans.
    B. We need 6 desks, 8 file cabinets, and 12 trashcans.

For items 41–50, write in each blank the letter of the word that best completes each sentence.

_____ **41.** Will having a degree (A. affect, B. effect) my chances for promotion?

_____ **42.** Try not to (A. loose, B. lose) this key; we will charge you a fee to replace it.

_____ **43.** I don't want to discuss my (A. personal, B. personnel) problems in front of anyone.

_____ **44.** Let us help you choose the right tie to (A. complement, B. compliment) your look.

_____ **45.** The repairman's whistling (A. aggravated, B. irritated) all of us in accounting.

_____ **46.** The bank agreed to (A. loan, B. lend) the Smiths $20,000 for their start-up.

_____ **47.** The credit card company is (A. liable, B. likely) to increase your interest rate if you miss a payment.

_____ **48.** The airline tries to (A. accommodate, B. accomodate) disabled passengers.

_____ **49.** Every company needs a policy regarding sexual (A. harrassment, B. harassment).

_____ **50.** Use your best (A. judgment, B. judgement) in selecting a service provider.

ASSESSMENT OF ENGLISH SKILLS

In the space provided, record the number of questions you answered incorrectly.

QUESTIONS	SKILLS AREA	NUMBER OF INCORRECT ANSWERS
1–5	Parts of speech	_____
6–15	Usage	_____
16–20	Sentence structure	_____
21–30	Punctuation	_____
31–40	Mechanics	_____
41–50	Vocabulary	_____

If you had more than two incorrect answers in any of the skills areas, focus on those areas in the appropriate sections of this handbook.

ESSENTIALS OF GRAMMAR, MECHANICS, AND USAGE

The following sentence looks innocent, but is it really?

We sell tuxedos as well as rent.

You sell tuxedos, but it's highly unlikely that you sell rent—which is what this sentence says. Whatever you're selling, some people will ignore your message because of a blunder like this. The following sentence has a similar problem:

Vice President Eldon Neale told his chief engineer that he would no longer be with Avix, Inc., as of June 30.

Is Eldon or the engineer leaving? No matter which side the facts are on, the sentence can be read the other way. Now look at this sentence:

The year before we budgeted more for advertising sales were up.

Confused? Perhaps this is what the writer meant:

The year before, we budgeted more for advertising. Sales were up.

Or maybe the writer meant this:

The year before we budgeted more for advertising, sales were up.

These examples show that even short, simple sentences can be misunderstood because of errors on the part of the writer. As you've learned in numerous courses over your schooling, an English sentence consists of the parts of speech being combined with punctuation, mechanics, and vocabulary to convey meaning. Making a point of brushing up on your grammar, punctuation, mechanics, and vocabulary skills will help ensure that you create clear, effective business messages.

1.0 GRAMMAR

Grammar is the study of how words come together to form sentences. Categorized by meaning, form, and function, English words fall into various parts of speech: nouns, pronouns, verbs, adjectives, adverbs, prepositions, conjunctions, articles, and interjections. You will communicate more clearly if you understand how each of these parts of speech operates in a sentence.

1.1 Nouns

A **noun** names a person, a place, a thing, or an idea. Anything you can see or detect with one of your senses has a noun to name it. Some things you can't see or sense are also nouns—ions, for example, or space. So are things that exist as ideas, such as accuracy and height. (You can see that something is accurate or that a building is tall, but you can't see the idea of accuracy or the idea of height.) These names for ideas are known as **abstract nouns**. The simplest nouns are the names of things you can see or touch: *car, building, cloud, brick;* these are termed **concrete nouns**. A few nouns, such as *algorithm, software,* and *code,* are difficult to categorize as either abstract or concrete but can reasonably be considered concrete even though they don't have a physical presence.

1.1.1 Proper Nouns and Common Nouns

So far, all the examples of nouns have been **common nouns**, referring to general classes of things. The word *building* refers to a whole class of structures. Common nouns such as *building* are not capitalized.

If you want to talk about one particular building, however, you might refer to the Glazier Building. The name is capitalized, indicating that *Glazier Building* is a **proper noun**.

Here are three sets of common and proper nouns for comparison:

Common	Proper
city	Kansas City
company	Blaisden Company
store	Books Galore

1.1.2 Nouns as Subject and Object

Nouns may be used in sentences as subjects or objects. That is, the person, place, thing, or idea that is being or doing (subject) is represented by a noun. So is the person, place, idea, or thing that is being acted on (object). In the following sentence, the nouns are underlined:

The web designer created the homepage.

The web designer (subject) is acting in a way that affects the home page (object). The following sentence is more complicated:

The installer delivered the carpet to the customer.

Installer is the subject. *Carpet* is the object of the main part of the sentence (acted on by the installer), and *customer* is the object of the phrase *to the customer*. Nevertheless, both *carpet* and *customer* are objects.

1.1.3 Plural Nouns

Nouns can be either singular or plural. The usual way to make a plural noun is to add *s* or *es* to the singular form of the word:

Singular	Plural
file	files
tax	taxes
cargo	cargoes

Many nouns have other ways of forming the plural. Some plurals involve a change in a vowel (*mouse/mice, goose/ geese, woman/women*), the addition of *en* or *ren* (*ox/oxen, child/children*), the change from *y* to *ies* (*city/cities, specialty/ specialties*), or the change from *f* to *v* (*knife/knives, half/halves;* some exceptions: *fifes, roofs*). Some words of Latin origin offer a choice of plurals (*phenomena/phenomenons, indexes/ indices, appendixes/appendices*). It's always a good idea to consult a dictionary if you are unsure of the correct or preferred plural spelling of a word.

The plurals of compound nouns are usually formed by adding *s* or *es* to the main word of the compound (*fathers-in-law, editors-in-chief, attorneys-at-law*).

Some nouns are the same whether singular or plural (*sleep, deer, moose*). Some nouns are plural in form but singular in use (*ethics, measles*). Some nouns are used in the plural only (*scissors, trousers*).

Letters, numbers, and words used as words are sometimes made plural by adding an apostrophe and an *s* (*A's, Ph.D.'s, I's*). However, if no confusion would be created by leaving off the apostrophe, it is common practice to just add the *s* (*1990s, RFPs, DVDs*).

1.1.4 Possessive Nouns

A noun becomes possessive when it's used to show the ownership of something. Then you add *'s* to the word:

the man's car   the woman's apartment

However, ownership does not need to be legal:

the secretary's desk   the company's assets

Also, ownership may be nothing more than an automatic association:

a day's work   the job's prestige

An exception to the rule about adding *'s* to make a noun possessive occurs when the word is singular and already has two "s" sounds at the end. In cases like the following, an apostrophe is all that's needed:

crisis' dimensions   Mr. Moses' application

When the noun has only one "s" sound at the end, however, retain the *'s*:

Chris's book   Carolyn Nuss's office

With compound (hyphenated) nouns, add *'s* to the last word:

Compound Noun	Possessive Noun
mother-in-law	mother-in-law's
mayor-elect	mayor-elect's

To form the possessive of plural nouns, just begin by following the same rule as with singular nouns: add *'s*. However, if the plural noun already ends in an *s* (as most do), drop the one you've added, leaving only the apostrophe:

the clients' complaints   employees' benefits

To denote joint possession by two or more proper nouns, add the *'s* to the last name only (*Moody, Nation, and Smith's* ad agency). To denote individual possession by two or more persons, add an *'s* to each proper noun (*Moody's, Nation's, and Smith's* ad agencies).

1.1.5 Collective Nouns

Collective nouns encompass a group of people or objects: *crowd, jury, committee, team, audience, family, couple, herd, class.* They are often treated as singular nouns. (For more on collective nouns, see Section 1.3.4, Subject–Verb Agreement.)

1.2 Pronouns

A **pronoun** is a word that stands for a noun; it saves repeating the noun:

> Employees have some choice of weeks for vacation, but *they* must notify the HR office of *their* preference by March 1.

The pronouns *they* and *their* stand in for the noun *employees.* The noun that a pronoun stands for is called the **antecedent** of the pronoun; *employees* is the antecedent of *they* and *their.*

When the antecedent is plural, the pronoun that stands in for it has to be plural; *they* and *their* are plural pronouns because *employees* is plural. Likewise, when the antecedent is singular, the pronoun has to be singular:

> We thought the contract had expired, but we soon learned that *it* had not.

1.2.1 Multiple Antecedents

Sometimes a pronoun has a double (or even a triple) antecedent:

> Kathryn Boettcher and Luis Gutierrez went beyond *their* sales quotas for January.

If taken alone, *Kathryn Boettcher* is a singular antecedent. So is *Luis Gutierrez.* However, when together they are the plural antecedent of a pronoun, so the pronoun has to be plural. Thus the pronoun is *their* instead of *her* or *his.*

1.2.2 Unclear Antecedents

In some sentences the pronoun's antecedent is unclear:

> Sandy Wright sent Jane Brougham *her* production figures for the previous year. *She* thought they were too low.

To which person does the pronoun *her* refer? Someone who knew Sandy and Jane and knew their business relationship might be able to figure out the antecedent for *her.* Even with such an advantage, however, a reader might receive the wrong meaning. Also, it would be nearly impossible for any reader to know which name is the antecedent of *she.*

The best way to clarify an ambiguous pronoun is usually to rewrite the sentence, repeating nouns when needed for clarity:

> Sandy Wright sent her production figures for the previous year to Jane Brougham. Jane thought they were too low.

The noun needs to be repeated only when the antecedent is unclear.

1.2.3 Pronoun Classes

Personal pronouns consist of *I, you, we/us, he/him, she/her, it,* and *they/them.*

Compound personal pronouns are created by adding *self* or *selves* to simple personal pronouns: *myself, ourselves, yourself, yourselves, himself, herself, itself, themselves.* Compound personal pronouns are used either *intensively*, to emphasize the identity of the noun or pronoun (I *myself* have seen the demonstration), or *reflexively*, to indicate that the subject is the receiver of his or her own action (I promised *myself* I'd finish by noon). Compound personal pronouns are used incorrectly if they appear in a sentence without their antecedent:

> Walter, Virginia, and *I* (not *myself*) are the top salespeople.

> You need to tell *her* (not *herself*) about the mixup.

Relative pronouns refer to nouns (or groups of words used as nouns) in the main clause and are used to introduce clauses:

> Purina is the brand *that* most dog owners purchase.

The relative pronouns are *which, who, whom, whose,* and *what.* Other words used as relative pronouns include *that, whoever, whomever, whatever,* and *whichever.*

Interrogative pronouns are those used for asking questions: *who, whom, whose, which,* and *what.*

Demonstrative pronouns point out particular persons, places, or things:

> *That* is my desk.   *This* can't be correct.

The demonstrative pronouns are *this, these, that,* and *those.*

Indefinite pronouns refer to persons or things not specifically identified. They include *anyone, someone, everyone, everybody, somebody, either, neither, one, none, all, both, each, another, any, many,* and similar words.

1.2.4 Case of Pronouns

The case of a pronoun tells whether it's acting or acted upon:

> *She* sells an average of five packages each week.

In this sentence, *she* is doing the selling. Because *she* is acting, *she* is said to be in the **nominative case**. Now consider what happens when the pronoun is acted upon:

> After six months, Ms. Browning promoted *her.*

In this sentence, the pronoun *her* is acted upon and is thus said to be in the **objective case**.

Contrast the nominative and objective pronouns in this list:

Nominative	Objective
I	me
we	us
he	him
she	her
they	them
who	whom
whoever	whomever

Objective pronouns may be used as either the object of a verb (such as *promoted*) or the object of a preposition (such as *with*):

> Rob worked with *them* until the order was filled.

In this example, *them* is the object of the preposition *with* because Rob acted upon—worked with—them. Here's a sentence with three pronouns, the first one nominative, the second the object of a verb, and the third the object of a preposition:

> *He* paid *us* as soon as the check came from *them*.

He is nominative; *us* is objective because it's the object of the verb *paid*; *them* is objective because it's the object of the preposition *from*.

Every writer sometimes wonders whether to use *who* or *whom*:

> (*Who, Whom*) will you hire?

Because this sentence is a question, it's difficult to see that *whom* is the object of the verb *hire*. You can figure out which pronoun to use if you rearrange the question and temporarily try *she* and *her* in place of *who* and *whom*: "Will you hire *she?*" or "Will you hire *her?*" *Her* and *whom* are both objective, so the correct choice is "Whom will you hire?" Here's a different example:

> (*Who, Whom*) logged so much travel time?

Turning the question into a statement, you get:

> He logged so much travel time.

Therefore, the correct statement is:

> Who logged so much travel time?

1.2.5 Possessive Pronouns

Possessive pronouns work like possessive nouns—they show ownership or automatic association:

her job	their preferences
his account	its equipment

However, possessive pronouns are different from possessive nouns in the way they are written. Possessive pronouns never have an apostrophe:

Possessive Noun	**Possessive Pronoun**
the woman's estate	her estate
Roger Franklin's plans	his plans
the shareholders' feelings	their feelings
the vacuum cleaner's attachments	its attachments

The word *its* is the possessive of *it*. Like all other possessive pronouns, *its* has no apostrophe. Some people confuse *its* with *it's*, the contraction of *it is*. (Contractions are discussed in Section 2.9, Apostrophes.)

1.2.6 Pronoun–Antecedent Agreement

Like nouns, pronouns can be singular or plural. Pronouns must agree in number with their antecedents—a singular antecedent requires a singular pronoun:

> The president of the board tendered *his* resignation.

Multiple antecedents require a plural pronoun:

> The members of the board tendered *their* resignations.

A pronoun referring to singular antecedents connected by *or* or *nor* should be singular:

> Neither Sean nor Terry made *his* quota.

But a pronoun referring to a plural and a singular antecedent connected by *or* or *nor* should be plural:

> Neither Sean nor the twins made *their* quotas.

Formal English prefers the nominative case after the linking verb *to be*:

> It is *I*.   That is *he*.

However, for general usage it's perfectly acceptable to use the more natural "It's me" and "That's him."

1.3 Verbs

A **verb** describes an action or acts as a link between a subject and words that define or describe that subject:

> They all *quit* in disgust.
> Working conditions *were* substandard.

The English language is full of **action verbs**. Here are a few you'll often run across in the business world:

verify	perform	fulfill
hire	succeed	send
leave	improve	receive
accept	develop	pay

You could undoubtedly list many more.

The most common linking verbs are all the forms of *to be*: I *am, was,* or *will be*; you *are, were,* or *will be*. Other words that can serve as linking verbs include *seem, become, appear, prove, look, remain, feel, taste, smell, sound, resemble, turn,* and *grow*:

> It *seemed* a good plan at the time.
> She *sounds* impressive at a meeting.
> The time *grows* near for us to make a decision.

These verbs link what comes before them in the sentence with what comes after; no action is involved. (See Section 1.7.5 for a fuller discussion of linking verbs.)

An **auxiliary verb** is one that helps another verb and is used for showing tense, voice, and so on. A verb with its helpers is called a **verb phrase**. Verbs used as auxiliaries include *do, did, have, may, can, must, shall, might, could, would,* and *should*.

1.3.1 Verb Tenses

English has three simple verb tenses: present, past, and future.

Present:	Our branches in Hawaii *stock* other items.
Past:	We *stocked* Purquil pens for a short time.
Future:	Rotex Tire Stores *will stock* your line of tires when you begin a program of effective national advertising.

With most verbs (the regular ones), the past tense ends in *ed*, and the future tense always has *will* or *shall* in front of it. But the present tense is more complex, depending on the subject:

	First Person	Second Person	Third Person
Singular	I stock	you stock	he/she/it stocks
Plural	we stock	you stock	they stock

The basic form, *stock*, takes an additional *s* when *he, she,* or *it* precedes it. (See Section 1.3.4 for more on subject–verb agreement.)

In addition to the three simple tenses, the three **perfect tenses** are created by adding forms of the auxiliary verb *have*. The present perfect tense uses the past participle (regularly the past tense) of the main verb, *stocked*, and adds the present-tense *have* or *has* to the front of it:

(I, we, you, they) *have stocked.*

(He, she, it) *has stocked.*

The past perfect tense uses the past participle of the main verb, *stocked*, and adds the past-tense *had* to the front of it:

(I, you, he, she, it, we, they) *had stocked.*

The future perfect tense also uses the past participle of the main verb, *stocked*, but adds the future-tense *will have*:

(I, you, he, she, it, we, they) *will have stocked.*

Verbs should be kept in the same tense when the actions occur at the same time:

When the payroll checks *came in*, everyone *showed up* for work.

We *have found* that everyone *has pitched* in to help.

When the actions occur at different times, you may change tense accordingly:

The shipment *came* last Wednesday, so if another one *comes* in today, please return it.

The new employee *had been* ill at ease, but now she *has become* a full-fledged member of the team.

1.3.2 Irregular Verbs

Many verbs don't follow some of the standard patterns for verb tenses. The most irregular of these verbs is *to be*:

Tense	Singular	Plural
Present:	I *am*	we *are*
	you *are*	you *are*
	he, she, it *is*	they *are*
Past:	I *was*	we *were*
	you *were*	you *were*
	he, she, it *was*	they *were*

The future tense of *to be* is formed in the same way that the future tense of a regular verb is formed.

The perfect tenses of *to be* are also formed as they would be for a regular verb, except that the past participle is a special form, *been*, instead of just the past tense:

Present perfect:	you have been
Past perfect:	you had been
Future perfect:	you will have been

Here's a sampling of other irregular verbs:

Present	Past	Past Participle
begin	began	begun
shrink	shrank	shrunk
know	knew	known
rise	rose	risen
become	became	become
go	went	gone
do	did	done

Dictionaries list the various forms of other irregular verbs.

1.3.3 Transitive and Intransitive Verbs

Many people are confused by three particular sets of verbs:

lie/lay   sit/set   rise/raise

Using these verbs correctly is much easier when you learn the difference between transitive and intransitive verbs.

Transitive verbs require a receiver; they "transfer" their action to an object. Intransitive verbs do not have a receiver for their action. Some intransitive verbs are complete in themselves and need no help from other words (prices *dropped*; we *won*). Other intransitive words must be "completed" by a noun or adjective called a **complement**. Complements occur with linking verbs.

Here are some sample uses of transitive and intransitive verbs:

Intransitive	Transitive
We should include in our new offices a place to *lie* down for a nap.	The workers will be here on Monday to *lay* new carpeting.
Even the way an interviewee *sits* is important.	That crate is full of stemware, so *set* it down carefully.
Salaries at Compu-Link, Inc., *rise* swiftly.	They *raise* their level of production every year.

The workers *lay* carpeting, you *set down* the crate, they *raise* production; each action is transferred to something. In the intransitive sentences, a person *lies down*, an interviewee *sits*, and salaries *rise* without affecting anything else. Intransitive sentences are complete with only a subject and a verb; transitive sentences are not complete unless they also include an object; or something to transfer the action to.

Tenses are a confusing element of the lie/lay problem:

Present	Past	Past Participle
I *lie*	I *lay*	I *have lain*
I *lay* (something down)	I *laid* (something down)	I *have laid* (something down)

The past tense of *lie* and the present tense of *lay* look and sound alike, even though they're different verbs.

1.3.4 Subject–Verb Agreement

Whether regular or irregular, every verb must agree with its subject, both in person (first, second, or third) and in number (single or plural).

	First Person	Second Person	Third Person
Singular	I *am*	you *are*	he/she/it *is*
	I *write*	you *write*	he/she/it *writes*
Plural	we *are*	you *are*	they *are*
	we *write*	you *write*	they *write*

In a simple sentence, making a verb agree with its subject is a straightforward task:

Hector Ruiz *is* a strong competitor. (third-person singular)

We *write* to you every month. (first-person plural)

Confusion sometimes arises when sentences are a bit more complicated. For example, be sure to avoid agreement problems when words come between the subject and verb. In the following examples, the verb appears in italics, and its subject is underlined:

The <u>analysis</u> of existing documents *takes* a full week.

Even though *documents* is a plural, the verb is in the singular form. That's because the subject of the sentence is *analysis*, a singular noun. The phrase *of existing documents* can be disregarded. Here is another example:

The <u>answers</u> for this exercise *are* in the study guide.

Take away the phrase *for this exercise* and you are left with the plural subject *answers*. Therefore, the verb takes the plural form.

Verb agreement is also complicated when the subject is a collective noun or pronoun or when the subject may be considered either singular or plural. In such cases, you often have to analyze the surrounding sentence to determine which verb form to use:

The <u>staff</u> *is* quartered in the warehouse.

The <u>staff</u> *are* at their desks in the warehouse.

The <u>computers</u> and the <u>staff</u> *are* in the warehouse.

Neither the staff nor the <u>computers</u> *are* in the warehouse.

<u>Every</u> computer *is* in the warehouse.

Many a <u>computer</u> *is* in the warehouse.

Did you notice that words such as *every* use the singular verb form? In addition, when an *either/or* or a *neither/nor* phrase combines singular and plural nouns, the verb takes the form that matches the noun closest to it.

In the business world, some subjects require extra attention. Company names, for example, are considered singular and therefore take a singular verb in most cases—even if they contain plural words:

Stater Brothers *offers* convenient grocery shopping.

In addition, quantities are sometimes considered singular and sometimes plural. If a quantity refers to a total amount, it takes a singular verb; if a quantity refers to individual, countable units, it takes a plural verb:

Three hours *is* a long time.

The eight dollars we collected for the fund *are* tacked on the bulletin board.

Fractions may also be singular or plural, depending on the noun that accompanies them:

One-third of the warehouse *is* devoted to this product line.

One-third of the products *are* defective.

To decide whether to use a singular or plural verb with subjects such as *number* and *variety*, follow this simple rule: If the subject is preceded by *a*, use a plural verb:

A number of products *are* being displayed at the trade show.

If the subject is preceded by *the*, use a singular verb:

The variety of products on display *is* mind-boggling.

For a related discussion, see Section 1.7.1, Longer Sentences.

1.3.5 Voice of Verbs

Verbs have two voices, active and passive. When the subject comes first, the verb is in **active voice;** when the object comes first, the verb is in **passive voice:**

Active:	The buyer *paid* a large amount.
Passive:	A large amount *was paid* by the buyer.

The passive voice uses a form of the verb *to be,* which adds words to a sentence. In the example, the passive-voice sentence uses eight words, whereas the active-voice sentence uses only six to say the same thing. The words *was* and *by* are unnecessary to convey the meaning of the sentence. In fact, extra words usually clog meaning. So be sure to opt for the active voice when you have a choice.

At times, however, you have no choice:

Several items *have been taken,* but so far we don't know who took them.

The passive voice becomes necessary when you don't know (or don't want to say) who performed the action; the active voice is bolder and more direct.

1.3.6 Mood of Verbs

Verbs can express one of three moods: indicative, imperative, or subjunctive. The **indicative mood** is used to make a statement or to ask a question:

The secretary mailed a letter to each supplier.

Did the secretary mail a letter to each supplier?

Use the **imperative mood** when you wish to command or request:

Please mail a letter to each supplier.

With the imperative mood, the subject is the understood *you.*

The **subjunctive mood** is used to express doubt or a wish or a condition contrary to fact:

If I *were* you, I wouldn't send that e-mail.

The subjunctive is also used to express a suggestion or a request:

I asked that Rosario *be* [not *is*] present at the meeting.

1.3.7 Verbals

Verbals are verbs that are modified to function as other parts of speech. They include infinitives, gerunds, and participles.

Infinitives are formed by placing a *to* in front of the verb (*to go, to purchase, to work*). They function as nouns. Although many of us were taught that it is "incorrect" to split an infinitive—that is, to place an adverb between the *to* and the verb—that rule is not a hard and fast one. In some cases, the adverb is best placed in the middle of the infinitive to avoid awkward constructions or ambiguous meaning:

Production of steel is expected to *moderately exceed* domestic use.

Gerunds are verbals formed by adding *ing* to a verb (*going, having, working*). Like infinitives, they function as nouns. Gerunds and gerund phrases take a singular verb:

Borrowing from banks *is* preferable to getting venture capital.

Participles are verb forms used as adjectives. The present participle ends in *ing* and generally describes action going on at the same time as other action:

Checking the schedule, the contractor was pleased with progress on the project.

The past participle is usually the same form as the past tense and generally indicates completed action:

When *completed,* the project will occupy six city blocks.

The **perfect participle** is formed by adding *having* to the past participle:

Having completed the project, the contractor submitted his last invoice.

1.4 Adjectives

An **adjective** modifies (tells something about) a noun or pronoun. Each of the following phrases says more about the noun or pronoun than the noun or pronoun would say alone:

an *efficient* staff	a *heavy* price
brisk trade	*light* web traffic

Adjectives modify nouns more often than they modify pronouns. When adjectives do modify pronouns, however, the sentence usually has a linking verb:

They were *attentive.*	It looked *appropriate.*
He seems *interested.*	You are *skillful.*

1.4.1 Types of Adjectives

Adjectives serve a variety of purposes. **Descriptive adjectives** express some quality belonging to the modified item (*tall, successful, green*). **Limiting or definitive adjectives,** on the other hand, point out the modified item or limit its meaning without expressing a quality. Types include:

- Numeral adjectives (one, fifty, second)
- Articles (a, an, the)
- Pronominal adjectives: pronouns used as adjectives (his desk, each employee)
- Demonstrative adjectives: this, these, that, those (these tires, that invoice)

Proper adjectives are derived from proper nouns:

Chinese customs	*Orwellian* overtones

Predicate adjectives complete the meaning of the predicate and are introduced by linking verbs:

The location is *perfect.*	Prices are *high.*

1.4.2 Comparative Degree

Most adjectives can take three forms: simple, comparative, and superlative. The simple form modifies a single noun or pronoun. Use the comparative form when comparing two items. When comparing three or more items, use the superlative form:

Simple	Comparative	Superlative
hard	harder	hardest
safe	safer	safest
dry	drier	driest

The comparative form adds *er* to the simple form, and the superlative form adds *est*. (The *y* at the end of a word changes to *i* before the *er* or *est* is added.)

A small number of adjectives are irregular, including these:

Simple	Comparative	Superlative
good	better	best
bad	worse	worst
little	less	least

When the simple form of an adjective has two or more syllables, you usually add *more* to form the comparative and *most* to form the superlative:

Simple	Comparative	Superlative
useful	more useful	most useful
exhausting	more exhausting	most exhausting
expensive	more expensive	most expensive

The most common exceptions are two-syllable adjectives that end in *y*:

Simple	Comparative	Superlative
happy	happier	happiest
costly	costlier	costliest

If you choose this option, change the *y* to *i* and tack *er* or *est* onto the end.

Some adjectives cannot be used to make comparisons because they themselves indicate the extreme. For example, if something is perfect, nothing can be more perfect. If something is unique or ultimate, nothing can be more unique or more ultimate.

1.4.3 Hyphenated Adjectives

Many adjectives used in the business world are actually combinations of words: *up-to-date* report, *last-minute* effort, *fifth-floor* suite, *well-built* engine. As you can see, they are hyphenated when they come before the noun they modify. However, when such word combinations come after the noun they modify, they are not hyphenated. In the following example, the adjectives appear in italics and the nouns they modify are underlined:

The <u>report</u> is *up to date* because of our team's *last-minute* <u>efforts</u>.

Hyphens are not used when part of the combination is a word ending in *ly* (because that word is usually not an adjective). Hyphens are also omitted from word combinations that

are used so frequently that readers are used to seeing the words together:

We live in a *rapidly shrinking* world.

Our *highly motivated* employees will be well paid.

Please consider renewing your *credit card* account.

Send those figures to our *data processing* department.

Our new intern is a *high school* student.

1.5 Adverbs

An **adverb** modifies a verb, an adjective, or another adverb:

Modifying a verb:	Our marketing department works *efficiently*.
Modifying an adjective:	She was not dependable, although she was *highly* intelligent.
Modifying another adverb:	When signing new clients, he moved *extremely* cautiously.

An adverb can be a single word (*clearly*), a phrase (*very clearly*), or a clause (*because it was clear*).

1.5.1 Types of Adverbs

Simple adverbs are simple modifiers:

The door opened *automatically*.

The order arrived *yesterday*.

Top companies were *there*.

Interrogative adverbs ask a question:

Where have you been?

Conjunctive adverbs connect clauses:

We can't start *until* Maria gets here.

Jorge tried to explain *how* the new software works.

Words frequently used as conjunctive adverbs include *where, wherever, when, whenever, while, as, how, why, before, after, until,* and *since*.

Negative adverbs include *not, never, seldom, rarely, scarcely, hardly,* and similar words. Negative adverbs are powerful words and therefore do not need any help in conveying a negative thought. Avoid using double negatives like these:

I don't want no mistakes.
(Correct: "I don't want any mistakes," or "I want no mistakes.")

They couldn't hardly read the report.
(Correct: "They could hardly read the report," or "They couldn't read the report.")

They scarcely noticed neither one.
(Correct: "They scarcely noticed either one," or "They noticed neither one.")

1.5.2 Adverb–Adjective Confusion

Many adverbs are adjectives turned into adverbs by adding *ly*: *highly, extremely, officially, closely, really*. In addition, many words can be adjectives or adverbs, depending on their usage in a particular sentence:

The *early* bird gets the worm. [adjective]	We arrived *early*. [adverb]
It was a *hard* decision. [adjective]	He hit the wall *hard*. [adverb]

Because of this situation, some adverbs are difficult to distinguish from adjectives. For example, in the following sentences, is the underlined word an adverb or an adjective?

They worked <u>well</u>.

The baby is <u>well</u>.

In the first sentence, *well* is an adverb modifying the verb *worked*. In the second sentence, *well* is an adjective modifying the noun *baby*. To choose correctly between adverbs and adjectives, remember that linking verbs are used to connect an adjective to describe a noun. In contrast, you would use an adverb to describe an action verb:

Adjective	Adverb
He is *good* worker. (What kind of worker is he?)	He works *well*. (How does he work?)
It is a *real* computer. (What kind of computer is it?)	It *really* is a computer. (To what extent is it a computer?)
The traffic is *slow*. (What quality does the traffic have?)	The traffic moves *slowly*. (How does the traffic move?)
This food tastes *bad* without salt. (What quality does the food have?)	This food *badly* needs salt. (How much is it needed?)

1.5.3 Comparative Degree

Like adjectives, adverbs can be used to compare items. Generally, the basic adverb is combined with *more* or *most*, just as long adjectives are. However, some adverbs have one-word comparative forms:

One Item	Two Items	Three Items
quickly	more quickly	most quickly
sincerely	less sincerely	least sincerely
fast	faster	fastest
well	better	best

1.6 Other Parts of Speech

Nouns, pronouns, verbs, adjectives, and adverbs carry most of the meaning in a sentence. Four other parts of speech link them together in sentences: prepositions, conjunctions, articles, and interjections.

1.6.1 Prepositions

A preposition is a word or group of words that describes a relationship between other words in a sentence. A simple preposition is made up of one word: *of, in, by, above, below*. A *compound preposition* is made up of two prepositions: *out of, from among, except for, because of*.

A **prepositional phrase** is a group of words introduced by a preposition that functions as an adjective (an adjectival phrase) or as an adverb (adverbial phrase) by telling more about a pronoun, noun, or verb:

The shipment will be here *by next Friday*.

Put the mail *in the out-bin*.

Prepositional phrases should be placed as close as possible to the element they are modifying:

Shopping *on the Internet* can be confusing for the uninitiated. (*not* Shopping can be confusing for the uninitiated *on the Internet*.)

Some prepositions are closely linked with a verb. When using phrases such as *look up* and *wipe out*, keep them intact and do not insert anything between the verb and the preposition.

You may have been told that it is unacceptable to put a preposition at the end of a sentence. However, that is not a hard-and-fast rule, and trying to follow it can sometimes be a challenge. You can end a sentence with a preposition as along as the sentence sounds natural and as long as rewording the sentence would create awkward wording:

I couldn't tell what they were interested in.

What did she attribute it to?

What are you looking for?

Avoid using unnecessary prepositions. In the following examples, the prepositions in parentheses should be omitted:

All (of) the staff members were present.

I almost fell off (of) my chair with surprise.

Where was Mr. Steuben going (to)?

They couldn't help (from) wondering.

The opposite problem is failing to include a preposition when you should. Consider these two sentences:

Sales were over $100,000 for Linda and Bill.

Sales were over $100,000 for Linda and for Bill.

The first sentence indicates that Linda and Bill had combined sales over $100,000; the second, that Linda and Bill each had sales over $100,000, for a combined total in excess of $200,000. The preposition *for* is critical here.

When the same preposition can be used for two or more words in a sentence without affecting the meaning, only the last preposition is required:

We are familiar (with) and satisfied with your company's products.

But when different prepositions are normally used with the words, all the prepositions must be included:

> We are familiar with and interested in your company's products.

Some prepositions have come to be used in a particular way with certain other parts of speech. Here is a partial list of some prepositions that have come to be used with certain words:

according to	independent of
agree to (a proposal)	inferior to
agree with (a person)	plan to
buy from	prefer to
capable of	prior to
comply with	reason with
conform to	responsible for
differ from (things)	similar to
differ with (person)	talk to (without interaction)
different from	talk with (with interaction)
get from (receive)	wait for (person or thing)
get off (dismount)	wait on (like a waiter)

If you are unsure of the correct idiomatic expression, check a dictionary.

Some verb–preposition idioms vary depending on the situation: You agree *to* a proposal but *with* a person, *on* a price, or *in* principle. You argue *about* something, *with* a person, and *for* or *against* a proposition. You compare one item *to* another to show their similarities; you compare one item *with* another to show differences.

Here are some other examples of preposition usage that have given writers trouble:

among/between: *Among* is used to refer to three or more (Circulate the memo *among* the staff); *between* is used to refer to two (Put the copy machine *between* Judy and Dan)

as if/like: *As if* is used before a clause (It seems *as if* we should be doing something); *like* is used before a noun or pronoun (He seems *like* a nice guy).

have/of: *Have* is a verb used in verb phrases (They should *have* checked first); *of* is a preposition and is never used in such cases.

in/into: *In* is used to refer to a static position (The file is *in* the cabinet); *into* is used to refer to movement toward a position (Put the file *into* the cabinet).

1.6.2 Conjunctions

Conjunctions connect the parts of a sentence: words, phrases, and clauses. A coordinating conjunction connects two words, phrases, or clauses of equal rank. The simple coordinating conjunctions include *and, but, or, nor, for, yet,* and *so.* Correlative conjunctions are coordinating conjunctions used in pairs: *both/and, either/or, neither/nor, not only/but also.* Constructions

with correlative conjunctions should be parallel, with the same part of speech following each element of the conjunction:

> The purchase was *not only* expensive *but also* unnecessary.
>
> The purchase *not only* was expensive *but also* was unnecessary.

Conjunctive adverbs are adverbs used to connect or show relationships between clauses. They include *however, nevertheless, consequently, moreover,* and *as a result.*

A **subordinate conjunction** connects two clauses of unequal rank; it joins a dependent (subordinate) clause to the independent clause on which it depends (for more on dependent and independent clauses, see Section 1.7.1). Subordinate conjunctions include *as, if, because, although, while, before, since, that, until, unless, when, where,* and *whether.*

1.6.3 Articles and Interjections

Only three articles exist in English: *the, a,* and *an.* These words are used, like adjectives, to specify which item you are talking about. *The* is called the *definite article* because it indicates a specific noun; *a* and *an* are called the *indefinite articles* because they are less specific about what they are referring to.

If a word begins with a vowel (soft) sound, use *an;* otherwise, use *a.* It's *a* history, not *an* history, *a* hypothesis, not *an* hypothesis. Use *an* with an "h" word only if it is a soft "h," as in *honor* and *hour.* Use *an* with words that are pronounced with a soft vowel sound even if they are spelled beginning with a consonant (usually in the case of abbreviations): *an SEC application, an MP3 file.* Use *a* with words that begin with vowels if they are pronounced with a hard sound: *a university, a Usenet account.*

Repeat an article if adjectives modify different nouns: *The red house and the white house are mine.* Do not repeat an article if all adjectives modify the same noun: *The red and white house is mine.*

Interjections are words that express no solid information, only emotion:

Wow!	Well, well!
Oh, no!	Good!

Such purely emotional language has its place in private life and advertising copy, but it only weakens the effect of most business writing.

1.7 Sentences

Sentences are constructed with the major building blocks, the parts of speech. Take, for example, this simple two-word sentence:

> Money talks.

It consists of a noun (*money*) and a verb (*talks*). When used in this way, the noun works as the first requirement for a sentence, the **subject**, and the verb works as the second requirement, the **predicate**. Without a subject (who or what does something) and a predicate (the doing of it), you have merely a collection of words, not a sentence.

1.7.1 Longer Sentences

More complicated sentences have more complicated subjects and predicates, but they still have a simple subject and a predicate verb. In the following examples, the subject is underlined once, the predicate verb twice:

> Marex and Contron enjoy higher earnings each quarter.

Marex [and] *Contron* do something; *enjoy* is what they do.

> My interview, coming minutes after my freeway accident, did not impress or move anyone.

Interview is what did something. What did it do? It *did* [not] *impress* [or] *move*.

> In terms of usable space, a steel warehouse, with its extremely long span of roof unsupported by pillars, makes more sense.

Warehouse is what *makes*.

These three sentences demonstrate several things. First, in all three sentences, the simple subject and predicate verb are the "bare bones" of the sentence, the parts that carry the core idea of the sentence. When trying to find the subject and predicate verb, disregard all prepositional phrases, modifiers, conjunctions, and articles.

Second, in the third sentence, the verb is singular (*makes*) because the subject is singular (*warehouse*). Even though the plural noun *pillars* is closer to the verb, *warehouse* is the subject. So *warehouse* determines whether the verb is singular or plural. Subject and predicate must agree.

Third, the subject in the first sentence is compound (*Marex* [and] *Contron*). A compound subject, when connected by *and*, requires a plural verb (*enjoy*). Also, the second sentence shows how compound predicates can occur (*did* [not] *impress* [or] *move*).

Fourth, the second sentence incorporates a group of words—*coming minutes after my freeway accident*—containing a form of a verb (*coming*) and a noun (*accident*). Yet, this group of words is not a complete sentence for two reasons:

- Not all nouns are subjects: *Accident* is not the subject of *coming*.
- Not all verbs are predicates: A verb that ends in *ing* can never be the predicate of a sentence (unless preceded by a form of *to be*, as in *was coming*).

Because they don't contain a subject and a predicate, the words *coming minutes after my freeway accident* (called a **phrase**) can't be written as a sentence. That is, the phrase cannot stand alone; it cannot begin with a capital letter and end with a period. So a phrase must always be just one part of a sentence.

Sometimes a sentence incorporates two or more groups of words that do contain a subject and a predicate; these word groups are called **clauses**:

> My interview, because it came minutes after my freeway accident, did not impress or move anyone.

The **independent clause** is the portion of the sentence that could stand alone without revision:

> My interview did not impress or move anyone.

The other part of the sentence could stand alone only by removing *because*.

> (because) It came minutes after my freeway accident.

This part of the sentence is known as a **dependent clause**; although it has a subject and a predicate (just as an independent clause does), it's linked to the main part of the sentence by a word (*because*) showing its dependence.

In summary, the two types of clauses—dependent and independent—both have a subject and a predicate. Dependent clauses, however, do not bear the main meaning of the sentence and are therefore linked to an independent clause. Nor can phrases stand alone, because they lack both a subject and a predicate. Only independent clauses can be written as sentences without revision.

1.7.2 Types of Sentences

Sentences come in four main types, depending on the extent to which they contain clauses. A simple sentence has one subject and one predicate; in short, it has one main independent clause:

> Boeing is the world's largest aerospace company.

A **compound sentence** consists of two independent clauses connected by a coordinating conjunction (*and, or, but*, etc.) or a semicolon:

> Airbus outsold Boeing for several years, but Boeing has recently regained the lead.

A **complex sentence** consists of an independent clause and one or more dependent clauses:

> Boeing is betting [independent clause] that airlines will begin using moderately smaller planes to fly passengers between smaller cities [dependent clause introduced by *that*].

A **compound-complex sentence** has two main clauses, at least one of which contains a subordinate (dependent clause):

> Boeing is betting [independent clause] that airlines will begin using moderately smaller planes to fly passengers between smaller cities [dependent clause], and it anticipates that new airports will be developed to meet passenger needs [independent clause].

1.7.3 Sentence Fragments

An incomplete sentence (a phrase or a dependent clause) that is written as though it were a complete sentence is called a **fragment.** Consider the following sentence fragments:

> Marilyn Sanders, having had pilferage problems in her store for the past year. Refuses to accept the results of our investigation.

This serious error can easily be corrected by putting the two fragments together:

> Marilyn Sanders, having had pilferage problems in her store for the past year, refuses to accept the results of our investigation.

The actual details of a situation will determine the best way for you to remedy a fragment problem.

The ban on fragments has one exception. Some advertising copy contains sentence fragments, written knowingly to convey a certain rhythm. However, advertising is the only area of business in which fragments are acceptable.

1.7.4 Fused Sentences and Comma Splices

Just as there can be too little in a group of words to make it a sentence, there can also be too much:

> All our mail is run through a postage meter every afternoon someone picks it up.

This example contains two sentences, not one, but the two have been blended so that it's hard to tell where one ends and the next begins. Is the mail run through a meter every afternoon? If so, the sentences should read:

> All our mail is run through a postage meter every afternoon. Someone picks it up.

Perhaps the mail is run through a meter at some other time (morning, for example) and is picked up every afternoon;

> All our mail is run through a postage meter. Every afternoon someone picks it up.

The order of words is the same in all three cases; sentence division makes all the difference. Either of the last two cases is grammatically correct. The choice depends on the facts of the situation.

Sometimes these so-called **fused sentences** have a more obvious point of separation:

> Several large orders arrived within a few days of one another, too many came in for us to process by the end of the month.

Here, the comma has been put between two independent clauses in an attempt to link them. When a lowly comma separates two complete sentences, the result is called a **comma splice**. A comma splice can be remedied in one of three ways:

- Replace the comma with a period and capitalize the next word: ". . . one another. Too many ". . ."
- Replace the comma with a semicolon and do not capitalize the next word: " . . . one another; too many . . ." This remedy works only when the two sentences have closely related meanings.
- Change one of the sentences so that it becomes a phrase or a dependent clause. This remedy often produces the best writing, but it takes more work.

The third alternative can be carried out in several ways. One is to begin the sentence with a subordinating conjunction:

> Whenever several large orders arrived within a few days of one another, too many came in for us to process by the end of the month.

Another way is to remove part of the subject or the predicate verb from one of the independent clauses, thereby creating a phrase:

> Several large orders arrived within a few days of one another, too many for us to process by the end of the month.

Finally, you can change one of the predicate verbs to its *ing* form:

> Several large orders arrived within a few days of one another, too many coming in for us to process by the end of the month.

In many cases, simply adding a coordinating conjunction can separate fused sentences or remedy a comma splice:

> You can fire them, or you can make better use of their abilities.
>
> Margaret drew up the designs, and Matt carried them out.
>
> We will have three strong months, but after that sales will taper off.

Be careful with coordinating conjunctions: Use them only to join simple sentences that express similar ideas.

Also, because they say relatively little about the relationship between the two clauses they join, avoid using coordinating conjunctions too often: *and* is merely an addition sign; *but* is just a turn signal; *or* only points to an alternative. Subordinating conjunctions such as *because* and *whenever* tell the reader a lot more.

1.7.5 Sentences with Linking Verbs

Linking verbs were discussed briefly in the section on verbs (Section 1.3). Here, you can see more fully the way they function in a sentence. The following is a model of any sentence with a linking verb:

> A *(verb)* B.

Although words such as *seems* and *feels* can also be linking verbs, let's assume that the verb is a form of *to be*:

> A *is* B.

In such a sentence, A and B are always nouns, pronouns, or adjectives. When one is a noun and the other is a pronoun, or when both are nouns, the sentence says that one is the same as the other:

> She is president.
>
> Rachel is president.
>
> She is forceful.

Recall from Section 1.3.3 that the noun or adjective that follows the linking verb is called a *complement*. When it is a noun or noun phrase, the complement is called a *predicate nominative*, when the complement is an adjective, it is referred to as a *predicate adjective*.

1.7.6 Misplaced Modifiers

The position of a modifier in a sentence is important. The movement of *only* changes the meaning in the following sentences:

> Only we are obliged to supply those items specified in your contract.

> We are obliged only to supply those items specified in your contract.

> We are obliged to supply only those items specified in your contract.

> We are obliged to supply those items specified only in your contract.

In any particular set of circumstances, only one of those sentences would be accurate. The others would very likely cause problems. To prevent misunderstanding, place such modifiers as close as possible to the noun or verb they modify.

For similar reasons, whole phrases that are modifiers must be placed near the right noun or verb. Mistakes in placement create ludicrous meanings:

> Antia Information Systems bought new computer chairs for the programmers with more comfortable seats.

The anatomy of programmers is not normally a concern of business writers. Obviously, the comfort of the chairs was the issue:

> Antia Information Systems bought programmers the new computer chairs with more comfortable seats.

> Here is another example:

> I asked him to file all the letters in the cabinet that had been answered.

In this ridiculous sentence, the cabinet has been answered, even though no cabinet in history is known to have asked a question. *That had been answered* is too far from *letters* and too close to *cabinet*. Here's an improvement:

> I asked him to file in the cabinet all the letters that had been answered.

The term **dangling modifier** is often used to refer to a clause or phrase that because of its position in the sentence seems to modify a word that it is not meant to modify. For instance:

> Lying motionless, co-workers rushed to Barry's aid.

Readers expect an introductory phrase to modify the subject of the main clause. But in this case it wasn't the *co-workers* who were lying motionless but rather *Barry* who was in this situation. Like this example, most instances of dangling modifiers occur at the beginning of sentences. The source of some danglers is a passive construction:

> To find the needed information, the whole book had to be read.

In such cases, switching to the active voice can usually remedy the problem:

> To find the needed information, you will need to read the whole book.

1.7.7 Parallelism

Two or more sentence elements that have the same relation to another element should be in the same form. Otherwise, the reader is forced to work harder to understand the meaning of the sentence. When a series consists of phrases or clauses, the same part of speech (preposition, gerund, etc.) should introduce them. Do not mix infinitives with participles or adjectives with nouns. Here are some examples of nonparallel elements:

> Andersen is hiring managers, programmers, and people who work in accounting. [nouns not parallel]

> Andersen earns income by auditing, consulting, and by bookkeeping. [prepositional phrases not parallel]

> Andersen's goals are to win new clients, keeping old clients happy, and finding new enterprises. [infinitive mixed with gerunds]

2.0 PUNCTUATION

On the highway, signs tell you when to slow down or stop, where to turn, and when to merge. In similar fashion, punctuation helps readers negotiate your prose. The proper use of punctuation keeps readers from losing track of your meaning.

2.1 Periods

Use a period (1) to end any sentence that is not a question, (2) with certain abbreviations, and (3) between dollars and cents in an amount of money.

2.2 Question Marks

Use a question mark after any direct question that requests an answer:

> Are you planning to enclose a check, or shall we bill you?

Don't use a question mark with commands phrased as questions for the sake of politeness:

> Will you send us a check today.

A question mark should precede quotation marks, parentheses, and brackets if it is part of the quoted or parenthetical material; otherwise, it should follow:

> This issue of *Inc.* has an article titled "What's Your Entrepreneurial IQ?"

> Have you read the article "Five Principles of Guerrilla Marketing"?

Do not use the question mark with indirect questions or with requests:

> Mr. Antonelli asked whether anyone had seen Nathalia lately.

Do not use a comma or a period with a question mark; the question mark takes the place of these punctuation marks.

2.3 Exclamation Points

Use exclamation points after highly emotional language. Because business writing almost never calls for emotional language, you will seldom use exclamation points.

2.4 Semicolons

Semicolons have three main uses. One is to separate two closely related independent clauses:

> The outline for the report is due within a week; the report itself is due at the end of the month.

A semicolon should also be used instead of a comma when the items in a series have commas within them:

> Our previous meetings were on November 11, 2004; February 20, 2005; and April 28, 2006.

Finally, a semicolon should be used to separate independent clauses when the second one begins with a conjunctive adverb such as *however, therefore,* or *nevertheless* or a phrase such as *for example* or *in that case:*

> Our supplier has been out of part D712 for 10 weeks; however, we have found another source that can ship the part right away.

> His test scores were quite low; on the other hand, he has a lot of relevant experience.

Section 4.4 provides more information on using transitional words and phrases.

> Semicolons should always be placed outside parentheses.

> Events Northwest has the contract for this year's convention (August 23–28); we haven't awarded the contract for next year yet.

2.5 Colons

Use a colon after the salutation in a business letter. You should also use a colon at the end of a sentence or phrase introducing a list or (sometimes) a quotation:

> Our study included the three most critical problems: insufficient capital, incompetent management, and inappropriate location.

A colon should not be used when the list, quotation, or idea is a direct object of the verb or preposition. This rule applies whether the list is set off or run in:

> We are able to supply
> staples
> wood screws
> nails
> toggle bolts

> This shipment includes 9 DVDs, 12 CDs, and 4 USB flash drives.

Another way you can use a colon is to separate the main clause and another sentence element when the second explains, illustrates, or amplifies the first:

> Management was unprepared for the union representatives' demands: this fact alone accounts for their arguing well into the night.

However, in contemporary usage, such clauses are frequently separated by a semicolon.

> Like semicolons, colons should always be placed outside parentheses.

> He has an expensive list of new demands (none of which is covered in the purchase agreement): new carpeting, network cabling, and a new security system.

2.6 Commas

Commas have many uses; the most common is to separate items in a series:

> He took the job, learned it well, worked hard, and succeeded.

> Put paper, pencils, and paper clips on the requisition list.

Company style may dictate omitting the final comma in a series. However, if you have a choice, use the final comma; it's often necessary to prevent misunderstanding.

A second place to use a comma is between independent clauses that are joined by a coordinating conjunction (*and, but,* or *or*).

> She spoke to the sales staff, and he spoke to the production staff.

> I was advised to proceed, and I did.

A third use for the comma is to separate a dependent clause at the beginning of a sentence from an independent clause:

> Because of our lead in the market, we may be able to risk introducing a new product.

However, a dependent clause at the end of a sentence is separated from the independent clause by a comma only when the dependent clause is unnecessary to the main meaning of the sentence:

> We may be able to introduce a new product, although it may involve some risk.

A fourth use for the comma is after an introductory phrase or word:

> Starting with this amount of capital, we can survive in the red for one year.

> Through more careful planning, we may be able to serve more people.

> Yes, you may proceed as originally planned.

However, with short introductory prepositional phrases and some one-syllable words (such as *hence* and *thus*), the comma is often omitted:

> Before January 1 we must complete the inventory.

> Thus we may not need to hire anyone.

> In July we will complete the move to Tulsa.

Fifth, paired commas are used to set off nonrestrictive clauses and phrases. A **restrictive clause** is one that cannot be omitted without altering the meaning of the main clause, whereas a **nonrestrictive clause** can be:

> The *Time Magazine* website, which is produced by Steve Conley, has won several design awards. [nonrestrictive: the material set off by commas could be omitted]

> The website that is produced by Steve Conley has won several design awards. [restrictive: no commas are used before and after *that is produced by Steve Conley* because this information is necessary to the meaning of the sentence—it specifies which website]

A sixth use for commas is to set off appositive words and phrases. (An **appositive** has the same meaning as the word it is in apposition to.) Like nonrestrictive clauses, appositives can be dropped without changing or obscuring the meaning of the sentence:

> Conley, a freelance designer, also produces the websites for several nonprofit corporations.

Seventh, commas are used between adjectives modifying the same noun (coordinate adjectives):

> She left Monday for a long, difficult recruiting trip.

To test the appropriateness of such a comma, try reversing the order of the adjectives: *a difficult, long recruiting trip.* If the order cannot be reversed, leave out the comma (a *good old friend* isn't the same as an *old good friend*). A comma should not be used when one of the adjectives is part of the noun. Compare these two phrases:

> a distinguished, well-known figure

> a distinguished public figure

The adjective–noun combination of *public* and *figure* has been used together so often that it has come to be considered a single thing: *public figure.* So no comma is required.

Eighth, commas are used both before and after the year in sentences that include month, day, and year:

> It will be sent by December 15, 2007, from our Cincinnati plant.

Some companies write dates in another form: 15 December 2007. No commas should be used in that case. Nor is a comma needed when only the month and year are present (December 2007).

Ninth, commas are used to set off a variety of parenthetical words and phrases within sentences, including state names, dates, abbreviations, transitional expressions, and contrasted elements:

> They were, in fact, prepared to submit a bid.

> Habermacher, Inc., went public in 1999.

> Our goal was increased profits, not increased market share.

> Service, then, is our main concern.

> The factory was completed in Chattanooga, Tennessee, just three weeks ago.

> Joanne Dubiik, M.D., has applied for a loan from First Savings.

> I started work here on March 1, 2003, and soon received my first promotion.

Tenth, a comma is used to separate a quotation from the rest of the sentence:

> Your warranty reads, "These conditions remain in effect for one year from date of purchase."

However, the comma is left out when the quotation as a whole is built into the structure of the sentence:

> He hurried off with an angry "Look where you're going."

Finally, a comma should be used whenever it's needed to avoid confusion or an unintended meaning. Compare the following:

> Ever since they have planned new ventures more carefully.

> Ever since, they have planned new ventures more carefully.

2.7 Dashes

Use dashes to surround a comment that is a sudden turn in thought:

> Membership in the IBSA—it's expensive but worth it—may be obtained by applying to our New York office.

A dash can also be used to emphasize a parenthetical word or phrase:

> Third-quarter profits—in excess of $2 million—are up sharply.

Finally, use dashes to set off a phrase that contains commas:

> All our offices—Milwaukee, New Orleans, and Phoenix—have sent representatives.

Don't confuse a dash with a hyphen. A dash separates and emphasizes words, phrases, and clauses more strongly than commas or parentheses can; a hyphen ties two words so tightly that they almost become one word.

When using a computer, use the em dash symbol. When typing a dash in e-mail, type two hyphens with no space before, between, or after.

A second type of dash, the en dash, can be produced with computer word processing and page-layout programs. This kind of dash is shorter than the regular dash and longer than a hyphen. It is reserved almost exclusively for indicating "to" or "through" with numbers such as dates and pages: *2001–2002, pages 30–44.*

2.8 Hyphens

Hyphens are mainly used in three ways. The first is to separate the parts of compound words beginning with such prefixes as *self-, ex-, quasi-,* and *all-*:

self-assured	quasi-official
ex-wife	all-important

However, do not use hyphens in words that have prefixes such as *pro, anti, non, re, pre, un, inter,* and *extra:*

prolabor	nonunion
antifascist	interdepartmental

Exceptions occur when (1) the prefix occurs before a proper noun or (2) the vowel at the end of the prefix is the same as the first letter of the root word:

pro-Republican	anti-American
anti-inflammatory	extra-atmospheric

When in doubt, consult your dictionary.

Hyphens are used in some types of spelled-out numbers. For instance, they are used to separate the parts of a spelled-out number from *twenty-one* to *ninety-nine* and for spelled-out fractions: *two-thirds, one-sixth* (although some style guides say not to hyphenate fractions used as nouns).

Certain compound nouns are formed by using hyphens: *secretary-treasurer, city-state.* Check your dictionary for compounds you're unsure about.

Hyphens are also used in some compound adjectives, which are adjectives made up of two or more words. Specifically, you should use hyphens in compound adjectives that come before the noun:

an interest-bearing account	well-informed executives

However, you need not hyphenate when the adjective follows a linking verb:

This account is interest bearing.

Their executives are well informed.

You can shorten sentences that list similar hyphenated words by dropping the common part from all but the last word:

Check the costs of first-, second-, and third-class postage.

Finally, hyphens may be used to divide words at the end of a typed line. Such hyphenation is best avoided, but when you have to divide words at the end of a line, do so correctly (see Section 3.5). Dictionaries show how words are divided into syllables.

2.9 Apostrophes

Use an apostrophe in the possessive form of noun (but not in a pronoun):

On his desk was a reply to Bette *Ainsley's* application for the *manager's* position.

Apostrophes are also used in place of the missing letter(s) of a contraction:

Whole Words	Contraction
we will	we'll
do not	don't
they are	they're

2.10 Quotation Marks

Use quotation marks to surround words that are repeated exactly as they were said or written:

The collection letter ended by saying, "This is your third and final notice."

Remember: (1) When the quoted material is a complete sentence, the first word is capitalized. (2) The final comma or period goes inside the closing quotation marks.

Quotation marks are also used to set off the title of a newspaper story, magazine article, or book chapter:

You should read "Legal Aspects of the Collection Letter" in *Today's Credit.*

Quotation marks may also be used to indicate special treatment for words or phrases, such as terms that you're using in an unusual or ironic way:

Our management "team" spends more time squabbling than working to solve company problems.

When you are defining a word, put the definition in quotation marks:

The abbreviation *etc.* means "and so forth."

When using quotation marks, take care to insert the closing marks as well as the opening ones.

Although periods and commas go inside any quotation marks, colons and semicolons generally go outside them. A question mark goes inside the quotation marks only if the quotation is a question:

All that day we wondered, "Is he with us?"

If the quotation is not a question but the entire sentence is, the question mark goes outside:

What did she mean by "You will hear from me"?

For quotes within quotes, use single quotation marks within double:

As David Pottruck, former co-CEO of Charles Schwab, told it, "I assembled about 100 managers at the base of the Golden Gate Bridge and gave them jackets emblazoned with the phrase 'Crossing the Chasm' and then led them across the bridge."

Otherwise, do not use single quotation marks for anything, including titles of works—that's British style.

2.11 Parentheses and Brackets

Use parentheses to surround comments that are entirely incidental or to supply additional information:

Our figures do not match yours, although (if my calculations are correct) they are closer than we thought.

These kinds of supplements do not require FDA (Food and Drug Administration) approval.

Parentheses are used in legal documents to surround figures in arabic numerals that follow the same amount in words:

Remittance will be One Thousand Two Hundred Dollars ($1,200).

Be careful to put punctuation marks (period, comma, and so on) outside the parentheses unless they are part of the statement in parentheses. And keep in mind that parentheses have both an opening and a closing mark; both should always be used, even when setting off listed items within text: *(1)*, not *1)*.

Brackets are used for notation, comment, explanation, or correction within quoted material:

> In the interview, multimillionaire Bob Buford said, "One of my major influences was Peter [Drucker], who encourages people and helps them believe in themselves."

Brackets are also used for parenthetical material that falls within parentheses:

> Drucker's magnum opus *(Management: Tasks, Responsibilities, Practices* [Harper & Row, 1979]) has influenced generations of entrepreneurs.

2.12 Ellipses

Use ellipsis points, or three evenly spaced periods, to indicate that material has been left out of a direct quotation. Use them only in direct quotations and only at the point where material was left out. In the following example, the first sentence is quoted in the second:

> The Dow Jones Industrial Average fell 276.39 points, or 2.6%, during the week to 10292.31.
>
> According to the *Wall Street Journal*, "The Dow Jones Industrial Average fell 276.39 points . . . to 10,292.31."

The number of dots in ellipses is not optional; always use three. Occasionally, the points of an ellipsis come at the end of a sentence, where they seem to grow a fourth dot. Don't be fooled: One of the dots is a period. Ellipsis points should always be preceded and followed by a space.

Avoid using ellipses to represent a pause in your writing; use a dash for that purpose:

> At first we had planned to leave for the conference on Wednesday—but then we changed our minds. [not *on Wednesday . . . but then*]

3.0 MECHANICS

The most obvious and least tolerable mistakes that a business writer makes are probably those related to grammar and punctuation. However, a number of small details, known as writing mechanics, demonstrate the writer's polish and reflect on the company's professionalism.

When it comes to mechanics, also called *style*, many of the "rules" are not hard and fast. Publications and organizations vary in their preferred styles for capitalization, abbreviations, numbers, italics, and so on. Here, we'll try to differentiate between practices that are generally accepted and those that can vary. When you are writing materials for a specific company or organization, find out the preferred style (such as *The Chicago Manual of Style* or Webster's *Style*

Manual). Otherwise, choose a respected style guide. The key to style is consistency: If you spell out the word *percent* in one part of a document, don't use the percent sign in a similar context elsewhere in the same document.

3.1 Capitalization

With capitalization, you can follow either an "up" style (when in doubt, capitalize: *Federal Government, Board of Directors*) or a "down" style (when in doubt, use lowercase: *federal government, board of directors*). The trend over the last few decades has been toward the down style. Your best bet is to get a good style manual and consult it when you have a capitalization question. Following are some rules that most style guides agree on.

Capital letters are used at the beginning of certain word groups:

- **Complete sentence:** Before hanging up, he said, "We'll meet here on Wednesday at noon."
- **Formal statement following a colon:** She has a favorite motto: Where there's a will, there's a way.
- **Phrase used as sentence:** Absolutely not!
- **Quoted sentence embedded in another sentence:** Scott said, "Nobody was here during lunch hour except me."
- **List of items set off from text:** Three preliminary steps are involved:

  Design review

  Budgeting

  Scheduling

Capitalize proper adjectives and proper nouns (the names of particular persons, places, and things):

> Darrell Greene lived in a Victorian mansion.
>
> We sent Ms. Larson an application form, informing her that not all applicants are interviewed.
>
> Let's consider opening a branch in the West, perhaps at the west end of Tucson, Arizona.
>
> As office buildings go, the Kinney Building is a pleasant setting for TDG Office Equipment.
>
> We are going to have to cancel our plans for hiring French and German sales reps.

Larson's name is capitalized because she is a particular applicant, whereas the general term *applicant* is left uncapitalized. Likewise, *West* is capitalized when it refers to a particular place but not when it means a direction. In the same way, *office* and *building* are not capitalized when they are general terms (common nouns), but they are capitalized when they are part of the title of a particular office or building (proper nouns). Some proper adjectives are lowercased when they are part of terms that have come into common use, such as *french fries* and *roman numerals*.

Titles within families or companies as well as professional titles may also be capitalized:

> I turned down Uncle David when he offered me a job. I wouldn't be comfortable working for one of my relatives.
>
> We've never had a president quite like President Sweeney.

People's titles are capitalized when they are used in addressing a person, especially in a formal context. They are not usually capitalized, however, when they are used merely to identify the person:

> Address the letter to Chairperson Anna Palmer.
>
> I wish to thank Chairperson Anna Palmer for her assistance.
>
> Anna Palmer, chairperson of the board, took the podium.

Also capitalize titles if they are used by themselves in addressing a person:

> Thank you, Doctor, for your donation.

Always capitalize the first word of the salutation and complimentary close of a letter:

> *Dear* Mr. Andrews: *Yours* very truly,

The names of organizations are capitalized, of course; so are the official names of their departments and divisions. However, do not use capitals when referring in general terms to a department or division, especially one in another organization:

> Route this memo to Personnel.
>
> Larry Tien was transferred to the Microchip Division.
>
> Will you be enrolled in the Psychology Department?
>
> Someone from the personnel department at EnerTech stopped by the booth.

Capitalization is unnecessary when using a word like *company, corporation,* or *university* alone:

> The corporation plans to issue 50,000 shares of common stock.

Likewise, the names of specific products are capitalized, although the names of general product types are not:

> Apple Inc. Xerox machine
>
> Tide laundry detergent

When it comes to government terminology, here are some guides to capitalization: (1) Lowercase *federal* unless it is part of an agency name; (2) capitalize names of courts, departments, bureaus, offices, and agencies but lowercase such references as *the bureau* and *the department* when the full name is not used; (3) lowercase the titles of government officers unless they precede a specific person's name: *the secretary of state, the senator, the ambassador, the governor, and the mayor* but *Mayor Gonzalez* (Note: style guides vary on whether to capitalize *president* when referring to the president of the United States without including the person's name); capitalize the names of laws and acts: *the Sherman Antitrust Act, the Civil Rights Act*; (5) capitalize the names of political parties but lowercase the word *party: Democratic party, Libertarian party.*

One problem that often arises in writing about places is the treatment of two or more proper nouns of the same type.

When the common word comes before the specific names, it is capitalized; when it comes after the specific names, it is not:

> Lakes Ontario and Huron
>
> Allegheny and Monongahela rivers

The names of languages, races, and ethnic groups are capitalized: Japanese, Caucasian, Hispanic. But racial terms that denote only skin color are not capitalized: black, white.

When referring to the titles of books, articles, magazines, newspapers, reports, movies, and so on, you should capitalize the first and last words and all nouns, pronouns, adjectives, verbs, and adverbs, and capitalize prepositions and conjunctions with five letters or more. Except for the first and last words, do not capitalize articles:

> *Economics During the Great War*
>
> "An Investigation into the Market for Long-Distance Services"
>
> "What Successes Are Made Of"

When *the* is part of the official name of a newspaper or magazine, it should be treated this way too:

> *The Wall Street Journal*

Style guides vary in their recommendations regarding capitalization of hyphenated words in titles. A general guide is to capitalize the second word in a temporary compound (a compound that is hyphenated for grammatical reasons and not spelling reasons), such as *Law-Abiding Citizen*, but to lowercase the word if the term is always hyphenated, such as *Son-in-law*).

References to specific pages, paragraphs, lines, and the like are not capitalized: *page 73, line 3*. However, in most other numbered or lettered references, the identifying term is capitalized:

> *Chapter 4* *Serial No. 382-2203* *Item B-11*

Finally, the names of academic degrees are capitalized when they follow a person's name but are not capitalized when used in a general sense:

> I received a bachelor of science degree.
>
> Thomas Whitelaw, Doctor of Philosophy, will attend.

Similarly, general courses of study are not capitalized, but the names of specific classes are:

> She studied accounting as an undergraduate.
>
> She is enrolled in Accounting 201.

3.2 Underscores and Italics

Usually a line typed underneath a word or phrase either provides emphasis or indicates the title of a book, magazine, or newspaper. If possible, use italics instead of an underscore. Italics (or underlining) should also be used for defining terms and for discussing words as words:

> In this report, *net sales* refers to after-tax sales dollars.
>
> The word *building* is a common noun and should not be capitalized.

Also use italics to set off foreign words, unless the words have become a common part of English:

> Top Shelf is considered the *sine qua non* of comic book publishers.
>
> Chris uses a laissez-faire [no italic] management style.

3.3 Abbreviations

Abbreviations are used heavily in tables, charts, lists, and forms. They're used sparingly in prose. Here are some abbreviation situations to watch for:

- In most cases do not use periods with acronyms (words formed from the initial letter or letters of parts of a term): *CEO, CD-ROM, DOS, YWCA, FDA;* but *Ph.D., M.A., M. D.*
- Use periods with abbreviations such as *Mr., Ms., Sr., Jr., a.m., p.m., B.C.,* and *A.D.*
- The trend is away from using periods with such units of measure as *mph, mm,* and *lb.*
- Use periods with such Latin abbreviations as *e.g., i.e., et al.,* and *etc.* However, style guides recommend that you avoid using these Latin forms and instead use their English equivalents (*for example, that is, and others,* and *and so on,* respectively). If you must use these abbreviations, such as in parenthetical expressions or footnotes, do not put them in italics.
- Some companies have abbreviations as part of their names (*&, Co., Inc., Ltd.*). When you refer to such firms by name, be sure to double-check the preferred spelling, including spacing: *AT&T; Barnes & Noble; Carson Pirie Scott & Company; PepsiCo; Kate Spade, Inc.; National Data Corporation; Siemens Corp.; Glaxo Wellcome PLC; US Airways; U.S. Business Reporter.*
- Most style guides recommend that you spell out *United States* as a noun and reserve *U.S.* as an adjective preceding the noun modified.

One way to handle an abbreviation that you want to use throughout a document is to spell it out the first time you use it, follow it with the abbreviation in parentheses, and then use the abbreviation in the remainder of the document.

3.4 Numbers

Numbers may be correctly handled many ways in business writing, so follow company style. In the absence of a set style, however, generally spell out all numbers from one to nine and use arabic numerals for the rest.

There are some exceptions to this general rule. For example, never begin a sentence with a numeral:

> Twenty of us produced 641 units per week in the first 12 weeks of the year.

Use numerals for the numbers one through nine if they're in the same list as larger numbers:

> Our weekly quota rose from 9 to 15 to 27.

Use numerals for percentages, time of day (except with o'clock), dates, and (in general) dollar amounts:

> Our division is responsible for 7 percent of total sales.
>
> The meeting is scheduled for 8:30 a.m. on August 2.
>
> Add $3 for postage and handling.

When using numerals for time, be consistent: It should be *between 10:00 a.m. and 4:30 p.m.,* not *between 10 a.m. and 4:30 p.m.* Expressions such as *4:00 o'clock* and *7 a.m. in the morning* are redundant.

Use a comma in numbers expressing thousands (1,257), unless your company specifies another style. When dealing with numbers in the millions and billions, combine words and figures: 7.3 million, 2 billion.

When writing dollar amounts, use a decimal point only if cents are included. In lists of two or more dollar amounts, use the decimal point either for all or for none:

> He sent two checks, one for $67.92 and one for $90.00.

When two numbers fall next to each other in a sentence, use figures for the number that is largest, most difficult to spell, or part of a physical measurement; use words for the other:

> I have learned to manage a classroom of 30 twelve-year-olds.
>
> She won a bonus for selling 24 thirty-volume sets.
>
> You'll need twenty 3-inch bolts.

In addresses, all street numbers except One are in numerals. So are suite and room numbers and zip codes. For street names that are numbered, practice varies so widely that you should use the form specified on an organization's letterhead or in a reliable directory. All the following examples are correct:

> One Fifth Avenue   297 Ninth Street
>
> 1839 44th Street   11026 West 78 Place

Telephone numbers are always expressed in numerals. Parentheses may separate the area code from the rest of the number, but a slash or a hyphen may be used instead, especially if the entire phone number is enclosed in parentheses:

> 382-8329   (602/382-8329)   602-382-8329

Percentages are always expressed in numerals. The word *percent* is used in most cases, but % may be used in tables, forms, and statistical writing.

Ages are usually expressed in words—except when a parenthetical reference to age follows someone's name:

> Mrs. Margaret Sanderson is seventy-two.
>
> Mrs. Margaret Sanderson, 72, swims daily.

Also, ages expressed in years and months are treated like physical measurements that combine two units of measure: *5 years 6 months.*

Physical measurements such as distance, weight, and volume are also often expressed in numerals: *9 kilometers, 5 feet 3 inches, 7 pounds 10 ounces.*

Decimal numbers are always written in numerals. In most cases, add a zero to the left of the decimal point if the number is less than one and does not already start with a zero:

1.38   .07   0.2

In a series of related decimal numbers with at least one number greater than one, make sure that all numbers smaller than one have a zero to the left of the decimal point: 1.20, 0.21, 0.09.

Simple fractions are written in words, but more complicated fractions are expressed in figures or, if easier to read, in figures and words:

two-thirds   9/32   2 hundredths

Most style guides recommend that you use a comma with numbers consisting of four digits: *2,345*, not *2345*.

When typing ordinal numbers, such as *3rd edition* or *21st century*, your word processing program may automatically make the letters *rd* (or *st*, *th*, or *nd*) into a superscript. Do yourself a favor and turn that formatting function off in your "Preferences," as superscripts should not be used in regular prose or even in bibliographies.

3.5 Word Division

In general, avoid dividing words at the end of lines. When you must do so, follow these rules:

- Don't divide one-syllable words (such as *since*, *walked*, and *thought*), abbreviations (*mgr.*), contractions (*isn't*), or numbers expressed in numerals (*117,500*).
- Divide words between syllables, as specified in a dictionary or word-division manual.
- Make sure that at least three letters of the divided words are moved to the second line: *sin-cerely* instead of *sincere-ly*.
- Do not end a page or more than three consecutive lines with hyphens.
- Leave syllables consisting of a single vowel at the end of the first line (*impedi-ment* instead of *imped-iment*), except when the single vowel is part of a suffix such as *-able*, *-ible*, *-ical*, or *-ity* (*re-spons-ible* instead of *re-sponsi-ble*).
- Divide between double letters (*tomor-row*), except when the root word ends in double letters (*call-ing* instead of *cal-ling*).
- Wherever possible, divide hyphenated words at the hyphen only: instead of *anti-inde-pendence*, use *anti-independence*.
- Whenever possible, do not break URLs or e-mail addresses. If you have to break a long URL or e-mail address, do not insert a hyphen at the end of the first line.

4.0 VOCABULARY

Using the right word in the right place is a crucial skill in business communication. However, many pitfalls await the unwary.

4.1 Frequently Confused Words

Because the following sets of words sound similar, be careful not to use one when you mean to use the other:

Word	Meaning
accede	to comply with
exceed	to go beyond
accept	to take
except	to exclude
access	admittance
excess	too much
advice	suggestion
advise	to suggest
affect	to influence
effect	the result
allot	to distribute
a lot	much or many
all ready	completely prepared
already	completed earlier
born	given birth to
borne	carried
capital	money; chief city
capitol	a government building
cite	to quote
sight	a view
site	a location
complement	complete amount; to go well with
compliment	expression of esteem; to flatter
corespondent	party in a divorce suit
correspondent	letter writer
council	a panel of people
counsel	advice; a lawyer
defer	to put off until later
differ	to be different
device	a mechanism
devise	to plan
die	to stop living; a tool
dye	to color
discreet	careful
discrete	separate
envelop	to surround
envelope	a covering for a letter
forth	forward
fourth	number four
holey	full of holes
holy	sacred
wholly	completely
human	of people
humane	kindly
incidence	frequency
incidents	events

Word	Meaning
instance	example
instants	moments
interstate	between states
intrastate	within a state
later	afterward
latter	the second of two
lead	a metal; to guide
led	guided
lean	to rest at an angle
lien	a claim
levee	embankment
levy	tax
loath	reluctant
loathe	to hate
loose	free; not tight
lose	to mislay
material	substance
materiel	equipment
miner	mineworker
minor	underage person
moral	virtuous; a lesson
morale	sense of well-being
ordinance	law
ordnance	weapons
overdo	to do in excess
overdue	past due
peace	lack of conflict
piece	a fragment
pedal	a foot lever
peddle	to sell
persecute	to torment
prosecute	to sue
personal	private
personnel	employees
precedence	priority
precedents	previous events
principal	sum of money; chief; main
principle	general rule
rap	to knock
wrap	to cover
residence	home
residents	inhabitants
right	correct
rite	ceremony
write	to form words on a surface
role	a part to play
roll	to tumble; a list

Word	Meaning
root	part of a plant
rout	to defeat
route	a traveler's way
shear	to cut
sheer	thin, steep
stationary	immovable
stationery	paper
than	as compared with
then	at that time
their	belonging to them
there	in that place
they're	they are
to	a preposition
too	excessively; also
two	the number
waive	to set aside
wave	a swell of water; a gesture
weather	atmospheric conditions
whether	if
who's	contraction of "who is" or "who has"
whose	possessive form of who

In the preceding list, only enough of each word's meaning is given to help you distinguish between the words in each group. For more complete definitions, consult a dictionary.

4.2 Frequently Misused Words

The following words tend to be misused for reasons other than their sound. Reference books (including the *Random House College Dictionary*, revised edition; Follett's *Modern American Usage*; and Fowler's *Modern English Usage*) can help you with similar questions of usage:

a lot: When the writer means "many," *a lot* is always two separate words, never one.

aggravate/irritate: *Aggravate* means "to make things worse." Sitting in the smoke-filled room *aggravated* his sinus condition. *Irritate* means "to annoy." Her constant questions *irritated* [not *aggravated*] me.

anticipate/expect: *Anticipate* means "to prepare for": Macy's *anticipated* increased demand for athletic shoes in spring by ordering in November. In formal usage, it is incorrect to use *anticipate* for *expect*: I *expected* (not *anticipated*) a better response to our presentation than we actually got.

compose/comprise: The whole comprises the parts:

The company's distribution division *comprises* four departments.

It would be incorrect usage to say

The company's distribution division *is comprised of* four departments.

In that construction, *is composed of* or *consists of* would be preferable. It might be helpful to think of *comprise* as meaning "encompasses" or "contains."

continual/continuous: *Continual* refers to ongoing actions that have breaks:

Her *continual* complaining will accomplish little in the long run.

Continuous refers to ongoing actions without interruptions or breaks:

A *continuous* stream of paper came out of the fax machine.

convince/persuade: One is *convinced* of a fact or that something is true; one is *persuaded* by someone else to do something. The use of *to* with *convince* is unidiomatic—you don't convince someone to do something, you persuade them to do it.

correspond with: Use this phrase when you are talking about exchanging letters. Use *correspond to* when you mean "similar to." Use either *correspond with* or *correspond to* when you mean "relate to."

dilemma/problem: Technically, a *dilemma* is a situation in which one must choose between two undesirable alternatives. It shouldn't be used when no choice is actually involved.

disinterested: This word means "fair, unbiased, having no favorites, impartial." If you mean "bored" or "not interested," use *uninterested.*

etc.: This abbreviated form of the Latin phrase *et cetera* means "and so on" or "and so forth," so it is never correct to write *and etc.* The current tendency among business writers is to use English rather than Latin.

example/sample: An *example* is a model to be followed or one item that represents a group. A *sample* is a preview of a product or another entity, intended to demonstrate the product's qualities. In statistics, a sample is selected to represent the characteristics of a larger population.

flaunt/flout: To *flaunt* is to be ostentatious or boastful; to *flout* is to mock or scoff at.

impact: Avoid using *impact* as a verb when *influence* or *affect* is meant.

imply/infer: Both refer to hints. Their great difference lies in who is acting. The writer *implies,* the reader *infers,* sees between the lines.

lay: This word is a transitive verb. Never use it for the intransitive *lie.* (See Section 1.3.3.)

lend/loan: *Lend* is a verb; *loan* is a noun. Usage such as "Can you *loan* me $5?" is therefore incorrect.

less/fewer: Use *less* for uncountable quantities (such as amounts of water, air, sugar, and oil). Use *fewer* for countable quantities (such as numbers of jars, saws, words, pages, and humans). The same distinction applies to *much* and *little* (uncountable) versus *many* and *few* (countable).

liable/likely: *Liable* means "responsible for": I will hold you *liable* if this deal doesn't go through. It is incorrect to use *liable* for "possible": Anything is *likely* (not *liable*) to happen.

literally: *Literally* means "actually" or "precisely"; it is often misused to mean "almost" or "virtually." It is usually best left out entirely or replaced with *figuratively.*

many/much: See *less/fewer.*

regardless: The *less* suffix is the negative part. No word needs two negative parts, so don't add *ir* (a negative prefix) to the beginning. There is no such word as *irregardless.*

try: Always follow with *to,* never *and.*

verbal: People in the business community who are careful with language frown on those who use *verbal* to mean "spoken" or "oral." Many others do say "verbal agreement." Strictly speaking, *verbal* means "of words" and therefore includes both spoken and written words. Follow company usage in this matter.

4.3 Frequently Misspelled Words

All of us, even the world's best spellers, sometimes have to check a dictionary for the spelling of some words. People who have never memorized the spelling of commonly used words must look up so many that they grow exasperated and give up on spelling words correctly.

Don't expect perfection and don't surrender. If you can memorize the spelling of just the words listed here, you'll need the dictionary far less often and you'll write with more confidence:

absence	changeable
absorption	clientele
accessible	collateral
accommodate	committee
accumulate	comparative
achieve	competitor
advantageous	concede
affiliated	congratulations
aggressive	connoisseur
alignment	consensus
aluminum	convenient
ambience	convertible
analyze	corroborate
apparent	criticism
appropriate	
argument	definitely
asphalt	description
assistant	desirable
asterisk	dilemma
auditor	disappear
	disappoint
bankruptcy	disbursement
believable	discrepancy
brilliant	dissatisfied
bulletin	dissipate
calendar	eligible
campaign	embarrassing
category	endorsement
ceiling	exaggerate

exceed
exhaust
existence
extraordinary

fallacy
familiar
flexible
fluctuation
forty

gesture
grievous

haphazard
harassment
holiday

illegible
immigrant
incidentally
indelible
independent
indispensable
insistent
intermediary
irresistible

jewelry
judgment
judicial

labeling
legitimate
leisure
license
litigation

maintenance
mathematics
mediocre
minimum

necessary
negligence
negotiable
newsstand
noticeable

occurrence
omission

parallel
pastime
peaceable
permanent
perseverance
persistent
personnel
persuade
possesses
precede
predictable
preferred
privilege
procedure
proceed
pronunciation
psychology
pursue

questionnaire

receive
recommend
repetition
rescind
rhythmical
ridiculous

salable
secretary
seize
separate
sincerely
succeed
suddenness
superintendent
supersede
surprise

tangible
tariff
technique
tenant
truly

unanimous
until

vacillate
vacuum
vicious

4.4 Transitional Words and Phrases

The following sentences don't communicate as well as they could because they lack a transitional word or phrase:

> Production delays are inevitable. Our current lag time in filling orders is one month.

A semicolon between the two sentences would signal a close relationship between their meanings, but it wouldn't even hint at what that relationship is. Here are the sentences again, now linked by means of a semicolon, with a space for a transitional word or phrase:

> Production delays are inevitable; _____, our current lag time in filling orders is one month.

Now read the sentence with *nevertheless* in the blank space. Then try *therefore, incidentally, in fact,* and *at any rate* in the blank. Each substitution changes the meaning of the sentence.

Here are some transitional words (conjunctive adverbs) that will help you write more clearly:

accordingly	furthermore	moreover
anyway	however	otherwise
besides	incidentally	still
consequently	likewise	therefore
finally	meanwhile	

The following transitional phrases are used in the same way:

as a result	in other words
at any rate	in the second place
for example	on the other hand
in fact	to the contrary

When one of these words or phrases joins two independent clauses, it should be preceded by a semicolon and followed by a comma:

> The consultant recommended a complete reorganization; moreover, she suggested that we drop several products.

References

PROLOGUE

1. "Advocacy Small Business Statistics and Research," U.S. Small Business Administration [accessed 3 July 2007] www.sba.gov; Malik Singleton, "Same Markets, New Marketplaces," *Black Enterprise*, September 2004, 34; Edmund L. Andrews, "Where Do the Jobs Come From?" *New York Times*, 21 September 2004, E1, E11; Maureen Jenkins, "Yours for the Taking," *Boeing Frontiers Online*, June 2004 [accessed 25 September 2005] www.boeing.com; "Firm Predicts Top 10 Workforce/Workplace Trends for 2004," *Enterprise*, 8–14 December 2003, 1–2; Scott Hudson, "Keeping Employees Happy," *Community Banker*, September 2003, 34+; Marvin J. Cetron and Owen Davies, "Trends Now Changing the World: Technology, the Workplace, Management, and Institutions," *Futurist* 35, no. 2 (March/April 2001): 27–42.
2. "Career Planning: Do It Directionally," Leadership Now blog, 27 June 2007 [accessed 7 July 2008] www.leadershipnow.com.
3. Vivian Yeo, "India Still Top Choice for Offshoring," *BusinessWeek* online, 27 June 2008 [accessed 7 July 2008] www.businessweek.com; Jim Puzzanghera, "Coalition of High-Tech Firms to Urge Officials to Help Keep U.S. Competitive," *San Jose Mercury News*, 8 January 2004 [accessed 14 February 2004] www.ebscohost.com.
4. Amanda Bennett, "GE Redesigns Rungs of Career Ladder," *Wall Street Journal*, 15 March 1993, B1, B3.
5. Robin White Goode, "International and Foreign Language Skills Have an Edge," *Black Enterprise*, May 1995, 53.
6. Nancy M. Somerick, "Managing a Communication Internship Program," *Bulletin of the Association for Business Communication* 56, no. 3 (1993): 10–20.
7. Fellowforce website [accessed 8 February 2009] www.fellowforce.com.
8. Joan Lloyd, "Changing Workplace Requires You to Alter Your Career Outlook," *Milwaukee Journal Sentinel*, 4 July 1999, 1; Camille DeBell, "Ninety Years in the World of Work in America," *Career Development Quarterly* 50, no.1 (September 2001): 77–88.
9. Jeffrey R. Young, "'E-Portfolios' Could Give Students a New Sense of Their Accomplishments," *The Chronicle of Higher Education*, 8 March 2002, A31.
10. Brian Carcione, e-portfolio [accessed 20 December 2006] http://portfolio.psu.edu.

CHAPTER 1

1. Six Apart website [accessed 26 July 2008] www.sixapart.com; David Kirkpatrick and Daniel Roth, "Why There's No Escaping the Blog," *Fortune*, 10 January 2005, 44–50; "People of the Year," *PC Magazine*, 12 December 2004 [accessed 21 June 2005] www.pcmag.com; Thomas Mucha, "A Motor City Marketing Lesson," *Business 2.0*, 10 March 2005 [accessed 13 March 2005] www.business2.com; Lee Gomes, "How the Next Big Thing in Technology Morphed into a Really Big Thing," *Wall Street Journal*, 4 October 2004, B1; David Kirkpatrick, "It's Hard to Manage if You Don't Blog," *Fortune*, 4 October 2004, 46.
2. Caroline Kealey, "Web 2.0: The Medium Is the Message, but What's the Result?" *CW Bulletin*, October 2007 [accessed 24 July 2008] www.iabc.com.
3. Julie Connelly, "Youthful Attitudes, Sobering Realities," *New York Times*, 28 October 2003, E1, E6; Nigel Andrews and Laura D'Andrea Tyson, "The Upwardly Global MBA," *Strategy + Business 36*: 60–69; Jim McKay, "Communication Skills Found Lacking,"

Pittsburgh Post-Gazette, 28 February 2005 [accessed 28 February 2005] www.delawareonline.com.
4. Richard L. Daft, *Management*, 6th ed. (Cincinnati: Thomson South-Western, 2003), 580.
5. "Majority of Global Companies Face an Engagement Gap," Internal Comms Hub website, 23 October 2007 [accessed 5 July 2008] www.internalcommshub.com; Gary L. Neilson, Karla L. Martin, and Elizabeth Powers, "The Secrets to Successful Strategy Execution," *Harvard Business Review*, June 2008, 61–70; Nicholas Carr, "Lessons in Corporate Blogging," *BusinessWeek*, 18 July 2006, 9; Susan Meisinger, "To Keep Employees, Talk—and Listen—to Them!" *HR Magazine*, August 2006, 10.
6. Charlotte Huff, "Why Business Can't Write—and What to Do About It," *Workforce Management*, October 2008 [accessed 14 October 2008] www.workforce.com.
7. Daft, *Management*, 147.
8. Gareth R. Jones and Jennifer M. George, *Contemporary Management*, 3rd ed. (New York: McGraw-Hill Irwin, 2003), 512, 517.
9. Philip C. Kolin, *Successful Writing at Work*, 6th ed. (Boston: Houghton Mifflin, 2001), 17–23.
10. Tim Laseter and Rob Cross, "The Craft of Connection," *Strategy + Business*, Autumn 2006, 26–32.
11. "CEOs to Communicators: 'Stick to Common Sense,'" Internal Comms Hub website, 23 October 2007 [accessed 11 July 2008] www.internalcommshub.com; "A Writing Competency Model for Business," BizCom 101.com, 14 December 2007 [accessed 11 July 2008] www.business-writing-courses.com; Sue Dewhurst and Liam FitzPatrick, "What Should Be the Competency of Your IC Team?" white paper, 2007 [accessed 11 July 2008] http://competentcommunicators.com.
12. Don Hellriegel, Susan E. Jackson, and John W. Slocum, Jr., *Management: A Competency-Based Approach* (Cincinnati: Thomson South-Western, 2002), 447.
13. Paul Martin Lester, *Visual Communication: Images with Messages* (Belmont, Calif.: Thomson South-Western, 2006), 6–8.
14. Michael R. Solomon, *Consumer Behavior: Buying, Having, and Being*, 6th ed. (Upper Saddle River, N.J.: Pearson Prentice Hall, 2004), 65.
15. Anne Field, "What You Say, What They Hear," *Harvard Management Communication Letter*, Winter 2005, 3–5.
16. Chuck Williams, *Management*, 2nd ed. (Cincinnati: Thomson South-Western, 2002), 690.
17. Charles G. Morris and Albert A. Maisto, *Psychology: An Introduction*, 12th ed. (Upper Saddle River, N.J.: Pearson Prentice Hall, 2005), 226–239; Saundra K. Ciccarelli and Glenn E. Meyer, *Psychology* (Upper Saddle River, N.J.: Prentice Hall, 2006), 210–229; Mark H. Ashcraft, *Cognition*, 4th ed. (Upper Saddle River, N.J.: Prentice Hall, 2006), 44–54.
18. Stephanie Armour, "Music Hath Charms for Some Workers—Others It Really Annoys," *USA Today*, 24 March 2006, B1–B2.
19. Hellriegel et al., *Management: A Competency-Based Approach*, 451.
20. Laura L. Myers and Mary L. Tucker, "Increasing Awareness of Emotional Intelligence in a Business Curriculum," *Business Communication Quarterly*, March 2005, 44–51.
21. John Owens, "Good Communication in Workplace Is Basic to Getting Any Job Done," *Knight Ridder/Tribune Business News*, 9 July 2003, 1.
22. Williams, *Management*, 706–707.

23. Tara Craig, "How to Avoid Information Overload," *Personnel Today*, 10 June 2008, 31; Jeff Davidson, "Fighting Information Overload," *Canadian Manager*, Spring 2005, 16+.

24. Information Overload Research Group website [accessed 19 July 2008] www.iorgforum.org.

25. "Are You Addicted to Your BlackBerry?" *Forbes*, 3 April 2008 [accessed 23 July 2008] www.forbes.com; "Employers, Beware: 'Techno Addicts' May Be More Liability Than Boon," Lockergnome.com, 18 August 2006 [accessed 23 August 2006] www .lockergnome.com.

26. Sushil K. Sharma and Jatinder N. D. Gupta, "Improving Workers' Productivity and Reducing Internet Abuse," *Journal of Computer Information Systems*, Winter 2003–2004, 74–78.

27. Jack Trout, "Beware of 'Infomania,'" *Forbes*, 11 August 2006 [accessed 5 October 2006] www.forbes.com.

28. Eric J. Sinrod, "Perspective: It's My Internet—I Can Do What I Want," News.com, 29 March 2006 [accessed 12 August 2006] www.news.com.

29. Eric J. Sinrod, "Time to Crack Down on Tech at Work?" News.com, 14 June 2006 [accessed 12 August 2006] www.news.com.

30. Steve Lohr, "As Travel Costs Rise, More Meetings Go Virtual," *New York Times*, 22 July 2008 [accessed 23 July 2008] www.nytimes .com.

31. A. Thomas Young, "Ethics in Business: Business of Ethics," *Vital Speeches*, 15 September 1992, 725–730.

32. Kolin, *Successful Writing at Work*, 24–30.

33. Nancy K. Kubasek, Bartley A. Brennan, and M. Neil Browne, *The Legal Environment of Business*, 3rd ed. (Upper Saddle River, N.J.: Prentice Hall, 2003), 172.

34. Rich Phillips and John Zarrella, "Live Bombs Haunt Orlando Neighborhood," CNN.com, 1 July 2008 [accessed 24 July 2008] www.cnn.com.

35. Daft, *Management*, 155.

36. "Less Than Half of Companies Encourage Discussion of Ethical Issues at the Workplace," press release, International Association of Business Communicators Research Foundation website, 23 May 2006 [accessed 12 August 2006] www.iabc.com.

37. Kent Hoover, "Most Employees See Ethical Misconduct at Work," *Washington Business Journal*, 10 December 2007 [accessed 24 July 2008] www.bizjournals.com.

38. Gap, Inc., "Code of Business Conduct," updated 4 January 2005 [accessed 24 July 2008] www.gapinc.com.

39. Based in part on Robert Kreitner, *Management*, 9th ed. (Boston: Houghton Mifflin, 2004), 163.

40. Henry R. Cheeseman, *Contemporary Business and E-Commerce Law*, 4th ed. (Upper Saddle River, N.J.: Prentice Hall, 2003), 841–843.

41. Cheeseman, *Contemporary Business and E-Commerce Law*, 201.

42. John Jude Moran, *Employment Law: New Challenges in the Business Environment*, 2nd ed. (Upper Saddle River, N.J.: Prentice Hall, 2002), 186–187; Kubasek et al., *The Legal Environment of Business*, 562.

43. Cheeseman, *Contemporary Business and E-Commerce Law*, 325.

44. Kubasek et al., *The Legal Environment of Business*, 306.

CHAPTER 2

1. Evelyn Nussenbaum, "Boosting Teamwork with Wikis," *Fortune Small Business*, 12 February 2008 [accessed 15 August 2008] http://money.cnn.com; Doug Cornelius, "Wikis at the Rosen Law Firm," KM Space blog, 28 February 2008 [accessed 15 August 2008] http://kmspace.blogspot.com; Rosen Law Firm website [accessed 15 August 2008] www.rosen.com.

2. Courtland L. Bovée and John V. Thill, *Business in Action*, 3rd ed. (Upper Saddle River, N.J.: Pearson Prentice Hall, 2005), 175.

3. "Five Case Studies on Successful Teams," *HR Focus*, April 2002, 18+.

4. Stephen R. Robbins, *Essentials of Organizational Behavior*, 6th ed. (Upper Saddle River, N.J.: Prentice Hall, 2000), 98.

5. Max Landsberg and Madeline Pfau, "Developing Diversity: Lessons from Top Teams," *Strategy + Business*, Winter 2005, 10–12.

6. "Groups Best at Complex Problems," *Industrial Engineer*, June 2006, 14.

7. Lynda McDermott, Bill Waite, and Nolan Brawley, "Executive Teamwork," *Executive Excellence*, May 1999, 15.

8. Nicola A. Nelson, "Leading Teams," *Defense AT&L*, July–August 2006, 26–29; Larry Cole and Michael Cole, "Why Is the Teamwork Buzz Word Not Working?" *Communication World*, February–March 1999, 29; Patricia Buhler, "Managing in the 90s: Creating Flexibility in Today's Workplace," *Supervision*, January 1997, 241; Allison W. Amason, Allen C. Hochwarter, Wayne A. Thompson, and Kenneth R. Harrison, "Conflict: An Important Dimension in Successful Management Teams," *Organizational Dynamics*, Autumn 1995, 201.

9. Richard L. Daft, *Management*, 6th ed. (Cincinnati: Thomson South-Western, 2003), 614.

10. Geoffrey Colvin, "Why Dream Teams Fail," *Fortune*, 12 June 2006, 87–92.

11. Vijay Govindarajan and Anil K. Gupta, "Building an Effective Global Business Team," *MIT Sloan Management Review*, Summer 2001, 631.

12. Louise Rehling, "Improving Teamwork Through Awareness of Conversational Styles," *Business Communication Quarterly*, December 2004, 475–482.

13. Jon Hanke, "Presenting as a Team," *Presentations*, January 1998, 74–82.

14. William P. Galle, Jr., Beverly H. Nelson, Donna W. Luse, and Maurice F. Villere, *Business Communication: A Technology-Based Approach* (Chicago: Irwin, 1996), 260.

15. Mary Beth Debs, "Recent Research on Collaborative Writing in Industry," *Technical Communication*, November 1991, 476–484.

16. "TWiki Success Stories," TWiki website [accessed 18 August 2006] www.twiki.org.

17. Mark Choate, "What Makes an Enterprise Wiki?" CMS Watch website, 28 April 2006 [accessed 18 August 2006] www.cmswatch.com.

18. Choate, "What Makes an Enterprise Wiki?"

19. Tony Kontzer, "Learning to Share," *InformationWeek*, 5 May 2003, 28; Jon Udell, "Uniting Under Groove," *InfoWorld*, 17 February 2003 [accessed 9 September 2003] www.elibrary.com; Alison Overholt, "Virtually There?" *Fast Company*, 14 February 2002, 108.

20. Colvin, "Why Dream Teams Fail," 87–92.

21. Tiziana Casciaro and Miguel Sousa Lobo, "Competent Jerks, Lovable Fools, and the Formation of Social Networks," *Harvard Business Review*, June 2005, 92–99.

22. Stephen P. Robbins and David A. DeCenzo, *Fundamentals of Management*, 4th ed. (Upper Saddle River, N.J.: Prentice Hall, 2004), 266–267; Jerald Greenberg and Robert A. Baron, *Behavior in Organizations*, 8th ed. (Upper Saddle River, N.J.: Prentice Hall, 2003), 279–280.

23. "Team Building: Managing the Norms of Informal Groups in the Workplace," Accel-Team website [accessed 16 August 2006] www.accel-team.com.

24. B. Aubrey Fisher, *Small Group Decision Making: Communication and the Group Process*, 2nd ed. (New York: McGraw-Hill, 1980), 145–149; Robbins and De Cenzo, *Fundamentals of Management*, 334–335; Daft, *Management*, 602–603.

25. Michael Laff, "Effective Team Building: More Than Just Fun at Work," *Training + Development*, August 2006, 24–35.

26. Claire Sookman, "Building Your Virtual Team," *Network World*, 21 June 2004, 91.

27. Jared Sandberg, "Brainstorming Works Best if People Scramble for Ideas on Their Own," *Wall Street Journal*, 13 June 2006, B1.

28. Mark K. Smith, "Bruce W. Tuckman—Forming, Storming, Norming, and Performing in Groups," Infed.org [accessed 5 July 2005] www.infed.org.

29. Robbins and DeCenzo, *Fundamentals of Management*, 258–259.

30. Daft, *Management*, 609–612.

31. Andy Boynton and Bill Fischer, *Virtuoso Teams: Lessons from Teams That Changed Their Worlds* (Harrow, UK: FT Prentice Hall, 2005), 10.
32. Thomas K. Capozzoli, "Conflict Resolution—A Key Ingredient in Successful Teams," *Supervision*, November 1999, 14–16.
33. Jesse S. Nirenberg, *Getting Through to People* (Paramus, N.J.: Prentice Hall, 1973), 134–142.
34. Nirenberg, *Getting Through to People,* 134–142.
35. Nirenberg, *Getting Through to People,* 134–142.
36. Christopher Carfi and Leif Chastaine, "Social Networking for Businesses & Organizations" (white paper), Cerado website [accessed 13 August 2008] www.cerado.com.
37. David Pescovitz, "Technology of the Year: Social Network Applications," *Business 2.0*, November 2003, 113–114.
38. "Better Meetings Benefit Everyone: How to Make Yours More Productive," *Working Communicator Bonus Report*, July 1998, 1.
39. Ken Blanchard, "Meetings Can Be Effective," *Supervisory Management*, October 1992, 5.
40. Cyrus Farivar, "How to Run an Effective Meeting," BNET website [accessed 12 August 2008] www.bnet.com.
41. "Better Meetings Benefit Everyone."
42. Steve Lohr, "As Travel Costs Rise, More Meetings Go Virtual," *New York Times*, 22 July 2008 [accessed 23 July 2008] www.nytimes.com.
43. IBM Jam program website [accessed 15 August 2006] www.collaborationjam.com; "Big Blue Brainstorm," *BusinessWeek,* 7 August 2006 [accessed 15 August 2006] www.businessweek.com; Roger O. Crockett, "The 21st Century Meeting," *BusinessWeek*, 26 February 2007, 72–79.
44. Augusta M. Simon, "Effective Listening: Barriers to Listening in a Diverse Business Environment," *Bulletin of the Association for Business Communication* 54, no. 3 (September 1991): 73–74.
45. Judi Brownell, *Listening*, 2nd ed. (Boston: Allyn & Bacon, 2002), 9, 10.
46. Anne Fisher, "The Trouble with MBAs," *Fortune International*, 30 April 2007, 33–34.
47. Robyn D. Clarke, "Do You Hear What I Hear?" *Black Enterprise*, May 1998, 129.
48. Dennis M. Kratz and Abby Robinson Kratz, *Effective Listening Skills* (New York: McGraw-Hill, 1995), 45–53; J. Michael Sproule, *Communication Today* (Glenview, Ill.: Scott Foresman, 1981), 69.
49. Brownell, *Listening*, 230–231.
50. Kratz and Kratz, *Effective Listening Skills*, 78–79; Sproule, *Communication Today*.
51. Bill Brooks, "The Power of Active Listening," *American Salesman*, June 2003, 12; "Active Listening," Study Guides and Strategies website [accessed 5 February 2005] www.studygs.net.
52. Bob Lamons, "Good Listeners Are Better Communicators," *Marketing News*, 11 September 1995, 13+; Phillip Morgan and H. Kent Baker, "Building a Professional Image: Improving Listening Behavior," *Supervisory Management*, November 1985, 35–36.
53. Clarke, "Do You Hear What I Hear?"; Dot Yandle, "Listening to Understand," *Pryor Report Management Newsletter Supplement* 15, no. 8 (August 1998): 13.
54. Brownell, *Listening*, 14; Kratz and Kratz, *Effective Listening Skills*, 8–9; Sherwyn P. Morreale and Courtland L. Bovée, *Excellence in Public Speaking* (Orlando, Fla.: Harcourt Brace, 1998), 72–76; Lyman K. Steil, Larry L. Barker, and Kittie W. Watson, *Effective Listening: Key to Your Success* (Reading, Mass.: Addison Wesley, 1983), 21–22.
55. Patrick J. Collins, *Say It with Power and Confidence* (Upper Saddle River, N.J.: Prentice Hall, 1997), 40–45.
56. Morreale and Bovée, *Excellence in Public Speaking*, 296.
57. Judee K. Burgoon, David B. Butler, and W. Gill Woodall, *Nonverbal Communication: The Unspoken Dialog* (New York: McGraw-Hill, 1996), 137.
58. Dale G. Leathers, *Successful Nonverbal Communication: Principles and Applications* (New York: Macmillan, 1986), 19.
59. Gerald H. Graham, Jeanne Unrue, and Paul Jennings, "The Impact of Nonverbal Communication in Organizations: A Survey of Perceptions," *Journal of Business Communication* 28, no. 1 (Winter 1991): 45–62.
60. Virginia P. Richmond and James C. McCroskey, *Nonverbal Behavior in Interpersonal Relations* (Boston: Allyn & Bacon, 2000), 153–157.
61. Richmond and McCroskey, *Nonverbal Behavior in Interpersonal Relations*, 2–3.
62. John Hollon, "No Tolerance for Jerks," *Workforce Management*, 12 February 2007, 34.
63. Marilyn Pincus, *Everyday Business Etiquette* (Hauppauge, N.Y.: Barron's Educational Series, 1996), 136.
64. Dan May Casperson, *Power Etiquette: What You Don't Know Can Kill Your Career* (New York: AMACOM, 1999), 23.
65. Maggie Jackson, "Turn Off That Cellphone. It's Meeting Time," *New York Times*, 2 March 2003, sec. 3, 12.
66. Casperson, *Power Etiquette*, 10–14; Ellyn Spragins, "Introducing Politeness," *Fortune Small Business*, November 2001, 30.
67. Tanya Mohn, "The Social Graces as a Business Tool," *New York Times*, 10 November 2002, sec. 3, 12.
68. Casperson, *Power Etiquette*, 44–46.
69. Casperson, *Power Etiquette*, 109–110.
70. Pete Babb, "The Ten Commandments of Blog and Wiki Etiquette," *InfoWorld*, 28 May 2007 [accessed 3 August 2008] www.infoworld.com; Judith Kallos, "Instant Messaging Etiquette," NetM@nners blog [accessed 3 August 2008] www.netmanners.com; Michael S. Hyatt, "E-Mail Etiquette 101," From Where I Sit blog, 1 July 2007 [accessed 3 August 2008] www.michaelhyatt.com.

CHAPTER 3

1. "IBM Innovation Embraces All Races, Cultures and Genders," Diversity Careers website [accessed 16 August 2008] www.diversitycareers.com; Regina Tosca and Rima Matsumoto, "Diversity and Inclusion: A Driving Force for Growth and Innovation at IBM," 2 February 2007, Hispanic Association on Corporate Responsibility website [accessed 12 February 2007] www.hacr.org; IBM website [accessed 16 August 2008] www.ibm.com; "Executive Corner: Letter from IBM's Vice President, Global Workforce Diversity," IBM website [accessed 12 February 2007] www.ibm.com; "IBM—Diversity as a Strategic Imperative," TWI website [accessed 6 July 2005] www.diversityatwork.com; Cliff Edwards, "The Rewards of Tolerance," *BusinessWeek*, 15 December 2003 [accessed 6 July 2005] www.businessweek.com; David A. Thomas, "IBM Finds Profit in Diversity," *HBS Working Knowledge*, 27 September 2004 [accessed 5 July 2005] http://hbswk.hbs.edu; "IBM Diversity Executive to Speak at the University of Virginia," *University of Virginia News*, 7 November 2003 [accessed 5 July 2005] www.virginia.edu.
2. Michael R. Carrell, Everett E. Mann, and Tracey Honeycutt Sigler, "Defining Workforce Diversity Programs and Practices in Organizations: A Longitudinal Study," *Labor Law Journal*, Spring 2006, 5–12.
3. "Top Trading Partners—Total Trade, Exports, Imports June 2008," U.S. Census Bureau website [accessed 16 August 2008] www.census.gov.
4. Nancy R. Lockwood, "Workplace Diversity: Leveraging the Power of Difference for Competitive Advantage," *HR Magazine*, June 2005, special section 1–10.
5. Podcast interview with Ron Glover, IBM website [accessed 17 August 2008] www.ibm.com.
6. "More Than 300 Counties Now 'Majority–Minority,'" press release, U.S. Census Bureau website, 9 August 2007 [accessed 16 August 2008] www.census.gov; Robert Kreitner, *Management*, 9th ed. (Boston: Houghton Mifflin, 2004), 84.
7. Linda Beamer and Iris Varner, *Intercultural Communication in the Workplace*, 2nd ed. (New York: McGraw-Hill Irwin, 2001), xiii.
8. Tracy Novinger, *Intercultural Communication, A Practical Guide* (Austin, Tex.: University of Texas Press, 2001), 15.

9. Larry A. Samovar and Richard E. Porter, "Basic Principles of Intercultural Communication," in *Intercultural Communication: A Reader*, 6th ed., edited by Larry A. Samovar and Richard E. Porter (Belmont, Calif.: Wadsworth, 1991), 12.

10. "Cross Cultural Etiquette Awareness," Kwintessential website [accessed 17 August 2008] www.kwintessential.co.uk.

11. Beamer and Varner, *Intercultural Communication in the Workplace*, 3.

12. "Languages of the USA," Ethnologue website [accessed 22 August 2006] www.ethnologue.com.

13. Philip R. Harris and Robert T. Moran, *Managing Cultural Differences*, 3rd ed. (Houston: Gulf, 1991), 394–397, 429–430.

14. Lillian H. Chaney and Jeanette S. Martin, *Intercultural Business Communication*, 2nd ed. (Upper Saddle River, N.J.: Prentice Hall, 2000), 6.

15. Beamer and Varner, *Intercultural Communication in the Workplace*, 4.

16. Chaney and Martin, *Intercultural Business Communication*, 2nd ed., 9.

17. Richard L. Daft, *Management*, 6th ed. (Cincinnati: Thomson South-Western, 2003), 455.

18. Lillian H. Chaney and Jeanette S. Martin, *Intercultural Business Communication*, 4th ed. (Upper Saddle River, N.J.: Pearson Prentice Hall, 2007), 53.

19. Project Implicit website [accessed 17 August 2008] http://implicit.harvard.edu/implicit.

20. Linda Beamer, "Teaching English Business Writing to Chinese-Speaking Business Students," *Bulletin of the Association for Business Communication* 57, no. 1 (1994): 12–18.

21. Edward T. Hall, "Context and Meaning," in *Intercultural Communication*, 6th ed., edited by Larry A. Samovar and Richard E. Porter (Belmont, Calif.: Wadsworth, 1991), 46–55.

22. Daft, *Management*, 459.

23. Charley H. Dodd, *Dynamics of Intercultural Communication*, 3rd ed. (Dubuque, Ia.: Brown, 1991), 69–70.

24. Daft, *Management*, 459.

25. Beamer and Varner, *Intercultural Communication in the Workplace*, 230–233.

26. James Wilfong and Toni Seger, *Taking Your Business Global* (Franklin Lakes, N.J.: Career Press, 1997), 277–278.

27. Guo-Ming Chen and William J. Starosta, *Foundations of Intercultural Communication* (Boston: Allyn & Bacon, 1998), 288–289.

28. Mark Landler and Michael Barbaro, "Wal-Mart Finds That Its Formula Doesn't Fit Every Culture," *New York Times*, 2 August 2006 [accessed 23 August 2006] www.nytimes.com.

29. Mary A. DeVries, *Internationally Yours* (New York: Houghton Mifflin, 1994), 194.

30. Robert O. Joy, "Cultural and Procedural Differences That Influence Business Strategies and Operations in the People's Republic of China," *SAM Advanced Management Journal*, Summer 1989, 29–33.

31. Chaney and Martin, *Intercultural Business Communication*, 2nd ed., 122–123.

32. Mansour Javidan, "Forward-Thinking Cultures," *Harvard Business Review*, July–August 2007, 20.

33. IBM website [accessed 17 August 2008] www.ibm.com; Wendy Harris, "Out of the Corporate Closet," *Black Enterprise*, May 2007, 64–66; David A. Thomas, "Diversity as Strategy," *Harvard Business Review*, September 2004, 98–108; Joe Mullich, "Hiring Without Limits," *Workforce Management*, June 2004, 53–58; Mike France and William G. Symonds, "Diversity Is About to Get More Elusive, Not Less," 7 July 2003, *BusinessWeek* [accessed 24 January 2005] www.businessweek.com.

34. Novinger, *Intercultural Communication: A Practical Guide*, 54.

35. Peter Coy, "Old. Smart. Productive." *BusinessWeek*, 27 June 2005 [accessed 24 August 2006] www.businessweek.com; Beamer and Varner, *Intercultural Communication in the Workplace*, 107–108.

36. Beamer and Varner, *Intercultural Communication in the Workplace*, 107–108.

37. Nancy Sutton Bell and Marvin Narz, "Meeting the Challenges of Age Diversity in the Workplace," *The CPA Journal*, February 2007 [accessed 17 August 2008] www.nysscpa.org.

38. Tonya Vinas, "A Place at the Table," *IndustryWeek*, 1 July 2003, 22.

39. Daft, *Management*, 445.

40. John Gray, *Mars and Venus in the Workplace* (New York: HarperCollins, 2002), 10, 25–27, 61–63.

41. Chaney and Martin, *Intercultural Business Communication*, 4th ed., 62.

42. Todd Henneman, "A New Approach to Faith at Work," *Workforce Management*, October 2004, 76–77.

43. Mark D. Downey, "Keeping the Faith," *HR Magazine*, January 2008, 85–88.

44. Vadim Liberman, "What Happens When an Employee's Freedom of Religion Crosses Paths with a Company's Interests?" *Conference Board Review*, September/October 2007, 42–48.

45. IBM Accessibility Center [accessed 24 August 2006] www-03.ibm.com/able; AssistiveTech.net [accessed 24 August 2006] www.assistivetech.net; Business Leadership Network website [accessed 24 August 2006] www.usbln.org; National Institute on Disability and Rehabilitation Research website [accessed 24 August 2006] www.ed.gov/about/offices/list/osers/nidrr; Rehabilitation Engineering & Assistive Technology Society of North America website [accessed 24 August 2006] www.resna.org.

46. Daphne A. Jameson, "Reconceptualizing Cultural Identity and its Role in Intercultural Business Communication," *Journal of Business Communication*, July 2007, 199–235.

47. Leslie Knudson, "Diversity on a Global Scale," *HR Management* [accessed 17 August 2008] www.hrmreport.com.

48. Craig S. Smith, "Beware of Green Hats in China and Other Cross-Cultural Faux Pas," *New York Times*, 30 April 2002, C11.

49. Sana Reynolds and Deborah Valentine, *Guide for Internationals: Culture, Communication, and ESL* (Upper Saddle River, N.J.: Pearson Prentice Hall, 2006), 3–11, 14–19, 25.

50. P. Christopher Earley and Elaine Mosakowsi, "Cultural Intelligence," *Harvard Business Review*, October 2004, 139–146.

51. Wendy A. Conklin, "An Inside Look at Two Diversity Intranet Sites: IBM and Merck," *The Diversity Factor*, Summer 2005.

52. Paul Johnson, "Must the Whole World Speak English?" *Forbes*, 29 November 2004, 39; Randolph E. Schmid, "Study Says English Language Is Losing Cultural Dominance," *Desert Sun*, 29 February 2004, A25.

53. Mary Beth Sheridan, "Learning the New Language of Labor," *Washington Post*, 20 August 2002, A1.

54. Phillip M. Perry, "Found in Translation," *Kitchen & Bath Business*, September 2006, 44–46.

55. Bob Nelson, "Motivating Workers Worldwide," *Global Workforce*, November 1998, 25–27.

56. Mona Casady and Lynn Wasson, "Written Communication Skills of International Business Persons," *Bulletin of the Association for Business Communication* 57, no. 4 (1994): 36–40.

57. Lynn Gaertner-Johnston, "Found in Translation," Business Writing blog, 25 November 2005 [accessed 18 August 2008] www.businesswritingblog.com.

58. "From Plain English to Global English," Quality Web Content website [accessed 24 August 2006] www.webpagecontent.com.

59. Myron W. Lustig and Jolene Koester, *Intercultural Competence*, 4th ed. (Boston: Allyn & Bacon, 2003), 196.

60. Wilfong and Seger, *Taking Your Business Global*, 232.

61. Mark Lasswell, "Lost in Translation," *Business 2.0*, August 2004, 68–70.

62. Sheridan Prasso, ed., "It's All Greek to These Sites," *BusinessWeek*, 22 July 2002, 18.

CHAPTER 4

1. Shel Israel, "Twitterville Notebook: HR Block's Paula Drum," Global Neighbourhoods blog, 22 December 2008 [accessed 25 January 2009] http://redcouch.typepad.com/weblog; "H&R Block's Paula Drum Talks up Value of Online 'Presence,'" The Deal website, video interview, 6 June 2008 [accessed 28 August 2008] www.thedeal.com; Shel Israel, "SAP Global Survey: H&R Block's Paula Drum," Global

Neighbourhoods blog, 4 April 2008 [accessed 28 August 2008] http://redcouch.typepad.com/weblog; "Tango in Plain English," video [accessed 27 August 2008] www.youtube.com; "H&R Block, Inc.," Hoovers [accessed 27 August 2008] www.hoovers.com; Linda Zimmer, "H&R Block Tangoes into Second Life," Business Communicators of Second Life blog, 17 March 2007 [accessed 27 August 2008] http://freshtakes.typepad.com/sl_communicators; H&R Block website [accessed 25 January 2009] www.hrblock.com; "H&R Block Launches First Virtual Tax Experience in Second Life," press release [accessed 27 August 2008] www.hrblock.com.

2. Laurey Berk and Phillip G. Clampitt, "Finding the Right Path in the Communication Maze," *IABC Communication World*, October 1991, 28–32.

3. Linda Duyle, "Get Out of Your Office," *HR Magazine*, July 2006, 99–101.

4. Frank Martin Hein, "Making the Best Use of Electronic Media," *Communication World*, November–December 2006, 20–23.

5. Caroline McCarthy, "The Future of Web Apps Will See the Death of E-Mail," Webware blog, 29 February 2008 [accessed 25 August 2008] http://news.cnet.com; Kris Maher, "The Jungle," *Wall Street Journal*, 5 October 2004, B10; Kevin Maney, "Surge in Text Messaging Makes Cell Operators :-)," *USA Today*, 28 July 2005, B1–B2.

6. David Kirkpatrick, "It's Hard to Manage if You Don't Blog," *Fortune*, 4 October 2004, 46; Lee Gomes, "How the Next Big Thing in Technology Morphed into a Really Big Thing," *Wall Street Journal*, 4 October 2004, B1; Jeff Meisner, "Cutting Through the Blah, Blah, Blah," *Puget Sound Business Journal*, 19–25 November 2004, 27–28; Lauren Gard, "The Business of Blogging," *BusinessWeek*, 13 December 2004, 117–119; Heather Green, "Online Video: The Sequel," *BusinessWeek*, 10 January 2005, 40; Michelle Conlin and Andrew Park, "Blogging with the Boss's Blessing," *BusinessWeek*, 28 June 2004, 100–102.

7. Berk and Clampitt, "Finding the Right Path in the Communication Maze."

8. Samantha R. Murray and Joseph Peyrefitte, "Knowledge Type and Communication Media Choice in the Knowledge Transfer Process," *Journal of Managerial Issues*, Spring 2007, 111–133.

9. Berk and Clampitt, "Finding the Right Path in the Communication Maze."

10. Raymond M. Olderman, *10 Minute Guide to Business Communication* (New York: Alpha Books, 1997), 19–20.

11. Mohan R. Limaye and David A. Victor, "Cross-Cultural Business Communication Research: State of the Art and Hypotheses for the 1990s," *Journal of Business Communication* 28, no. 3 (Summer 1991): 277–299.

12. Mind Mapping Software Weblog [accessed 1 February 2008] http://mindmapping.typepad.com; bubbl.us website [accessed 1 February 2008] http://bubbl.us.

13. Holly Weeks, "The Best Memo You'll Ever Write," *Harvard Management Communication Letter*, Spring 2005, 3–5.

CHAPTER 5

1. "An Interview with Joi Ito, CEO of Creative Commons," audio interview [accessed 6 September 2008] www.businessweek.com; Kenji Hall, "Online Sharing with Creative Commons," *BusinessWeek*, 15 August 2008 [accessed 6 September 2008] www.businessweek.com; Creative Commons website [accessed 6 September 2008] www.creativecommons.org; Ariana Eunjung Cha, "Creative Commons Is Rewriting Rules of Copyright," *Washington Post*, 15 March 2005 [accessed 3 August 2005] www.washingtonpost.com; Steven Levy, "Lawrence Lessig's Supreme Showdown," Wired, October 2002 [accessed 3 August 2005] www.wired.com; "Happy Birthday: We'll Sue," Snopes.com [accessed 3 August 2005] www.snopes.com.

2. Annette N. Shelby and N. Lamar Reinsch, Jr., "Positive Emphasis and You Attitude: An Empirical Study," *Journal of Business Communication* 32, no. 4 (1995): 303–322.

3. Sherryl Kleinman, "Why Sexist Language Matters," *Qualitative Sociology* 25, no. 2 (Summer 2002): 299–304.

4. Judy E. Pickens, "Terms of Equality: A Guide to Bias-Free Language," *Personnel Journal*, August 1985, 24.

5. Lisa Taylor, "Communicating About People with Disabilities: Does the Language We Use Make a Difference?" *Bulletin of the Association for Business Communication* 53, no. 3 (September 1990): 65–67.

6. Susan Benjamin, *Words at Work* (Reading, Mass.: Addison-Wesley, 1997), 136–137.

7. Stuart Crainer and Des Dearlove, "Making Yourself Understood," *Across the Board*, May/June 2004, 23–27.

8. Plain English Campaign website [accessed 3 October 2003] www.plainenglish.co.uk.

9. Plain Language website [accessed 3 September 2008] www.plainlanguage.gov.

10. Creative Commons website [accessed 2 September 2008] www.creativecommons.org.

11. Joseph Kimble, "Answering the Critics of Plain Language," The Plain Language Network website, 12 April 2003 [accessed 22 September 2006] www.plainlanguagenetwork.org.

12. Susan Jaderstrom and Joanne Miller, "Active Writing," *Office Pro*, November/December 2003, 29.

13. Gap website [accessed 20 September 2006] www.gap.com.

14. Mary Munter, *Guide to Managerial Communication*, 7th ed. (Upper Saddle River, N.J.: Pearson Prentice Hall, 2006), 41.

15. Portions of this section are adapted from Courtland L. Bovée, *Techniques of Writing Business Letters, Memos, and Reports* (Sherman Oaks, Calif.: Banner Books International, 1978), 13–90.

16. Catherine Quinn, "Lose the Office Jargon; It May Sunset Your Career," *The Age* (Australia), 1 September 2007 [accessed 5 February 2008] www.theage.com.au.

17. Robert Hartwell Fiske, *The Dimwit's Dictionary* (Oak Park, Ill.: Marion Street Press, 2002), 16–20.

18. Visuwords website [accessed 5 February 2008] www.visuwords.com.

19. Beverly Ballaro and Christina Bielaszka-DuVernay, "Building a Bridge over the River Boredom," *Harvard Management Communication Letter*, Winter 2005, 3–5.

20. David A. Fryxell, "Lost in Transition?" *Writers Digest*, January 2005, 24–26.

21. Food Allergy Initiative website [accessed 5 September 2008] www.foodallergyinitiative.org; Diana Keough, "Snacks That Can Kill; Schools Take Steps to Protect Kids Who Have Severe Allergies to Nuts," *Plain Dealer*, 15 July 2003, E1; "Dawdling over Food Labels," *New York Times*, 2 June 2003, A16; Sheila McNulty, "A Matter of Life and Death," *Financial Times*, 10 September 2003, 14.

22. Apple iTunes website [accessed 23 September 2006] www.apple.com/itunes.

CHAPTER 6

1. Mercedes-AMG website [accessed 7 September 2008] www.mercedes-amg.com; Razorfish website [accessed 25 September 2006] www.razorfish.com; "Mercedes-AMG Website Wins Webby Award," 12 June 2006, eMercedesBenz website [accessed 25 September 2006] www.emercedesbenz.com.

2. Adapted from "ParknShop Fined over Oilfish Scandal," *South China Morning Post*, 18 December 2007. Centre for Food Safety, The Hong Kong Special Administrative Region, "Guidelines on Identification and Labelling of Oilfish/Cod." www.cfs.gov.hk [accessed 14 April 2008).

3. William Zinsser, *On Writing Well*, 5th ed. (New York: Harper-Collins, 1994), 9.

4. Zinsser, *On Writing Well*, 7, 17.

5. Zinsser, *On Writing Well*, 126.

6. Deborah Gunn, "Looking Good on Paper," *Office Pro*, March 2004, 10–11.

7. Jennifer Saranow, "Memo to Web Sites: Grow Up!" *Wall Street Journal*, 15 November 2004, R14–R15.

8. Jacci Howard Bear, "Desktop Publishing Rules of Page Layout," About.com [accessed 22 August 2005] www.about.com.

9. Jacci Howard Bear, "Desktop Publishing Rules for How Many Fonts to Use," About.com [accessed 22 August 2005] www.about.com.

10. The writing samples in this exercise were adapted from material on the Mercedes-AMG website [accessed 2 October 2006 and 9 September 2008] www.mercedes-amg.com.

11. The writing sample in this exercise was adapted from material on the Marsh Risk Consulting website [accessed 2 October 2006] www.marshriskconsulting.com.

CHAPTER 7

1. Bill Owens, "Why Can't I Make Reservations Further in Advance?" Nuts About Southwest blog, 24 January 2007 [accessed 15 May 2007] www.blogsouthwest.com; Bill Owens, "I Blogged. You Flamed. We Changed." Nuts About Southwest blog, 18 April 2007 [accessed 10 May 2007] www.blogsouthwest.com; "Welcome to the 'New and Improved' Nuts About Southwest—A User's Guide," Nuts About Southwest blog [accessed 13 September 2008] www.blogsouthwest.com; "Southwest Airlines Is Nuts About Blogging," Southwest Airlines press release, 27 April 2007 [accessed 15 May 2007] www.prnewswire.com.

2. Specialized Bicycle Components website [accessed 14 September 2008] www.specialized.com; Specialized Riders Club website [accessed 14 September 2008] www.specializedriders.com; Steven Outing, "Enabling the Social Company," white paper, September 2007 [accessed 14 September 2008] www.enthusiastgroup.com.

3. Kate Maddox, "Warrillow Finds 39% of Small-Business Owners Use Text Messaging," BtoB, 1 August 2008 [accessed 15 September 2008] www.btobonline.com; Dave Carpenter, "Companies Discover Marketing Power of Text Messaging," *Seattle Times*, 25 September 2006 [accessed 25 September 2006] www.seattletimes.com.

4. Catherine Toole, "My 7 Deadly Sins of Writing for Social Media—Am I Right?" Econsultancy blog, 19 June 2007 [accessed 16 September 2008] www.econsultancy.com; Muhammad Saleem, "How to Write a Social Media Press Release," Copyblogger [accessed 16 September 2008] www.copyblogger.com; Melanie McBride, "5 Tips for (Better) Social Media Writing," Melanie McBride Online, 11 June 2008 [accessed 16 September 2008] http://melaniemcbride.net.

5. Hilary Potkewitz and Rachel Brown, "Spread of E-Mail Has Altered Communication Habits at Work," *Los Angeles Business Journal*, 18 April 2005 [accessed 30 April 2006] www.findarticles.com; Nancy Flynn, *Instant Messaging Rules* (New York: AMACOM, 2004), 47–54.

6. "Employee Communication Is Cause for Concern," Duane Morris LLP website, 23 August 2006 [accessed 4 October 2006] www.duanemorris.com.

7. Greg Burns, "For Some, Benefits of E-Mail Not Worth Risk," *San Diego Union-Tribune*, 16 August 2005, A1, A8; Pui-Wing Tam, Erin White, Nick Wingfield, and Kris Maher, "Snooping E-Mail by Software Is Now a Workplace Norm," *Wall Street Journal*, 9 March 2005, B1+.

8. Matt Cain, "Managing E-Mail Hygiene," ZD Net Tech Update, 5 February 2004 [accessed 19 March 2004] www.techupdate.zdnet.com.

9. Lizette Alvarez, "Got 2 Extra Hours for Your E-Mail?" *New York Times*, 10 November 2005 [accessed 10 November 2005] www.nytimes.com.

10. Jack Trout, "Beware of Infomania,'" *Forbes*, 11 August 2006 [accessed 5 October 2006] www.forbes.com.

11. Reid Goldsborough, "Creeping Informality Can Be Big Mistake in Business E-Mails," *New Orleans City Business*, 14 March 2005, 18; Jack E. Appleman, "Bad Writing Can Cost Insurers Time & Money," *National Underwriter*, 27 September 2004, 34; Adina Genn, "RE: This Is an Important Message, Really," *Long Island Business News*, 5–11 December 2003, 21A; Lynn Lofton, "Regardless of What You Thought, Grammar Rules *Do* Apply to E-Mail," *Mississippi Business Journal*, 23–29 May 2005, 1.

12. Mary Munter, Priscilla S. Rogers, and Jone Rymer, "Business E-Mail: Guidelines for Users," *Business Communication Quarterly*, March 2003, 26+; Renee B. Horowitz and Marian G. Barchilon, "Stylistic Guidelines for E-Mail," *IEEE Transactions on Professional Communication* 37, no. 4 (December 1994): 207–212.

13. "E-Mail Is So Five Minutes Ago," *BusinessWeek* online, 28 November 2005 [accessed 3 May 2006] www.businessweek.com.

14. Robert J. Holland, "Connected—More or Less," Richmond.com, 8 August 2006 [accessed 5 October 2006] www.richmond.com.

15. Douglas MacMillan, "The End of Instant Messaging (As We Know It), *BusinessWeek*, 16 November 2008 [accessed 16 December 2008] www.businessweek.com.

16. Vayusphere website [accessed 22 January 2006] www.vayusphere.com; Christa C. Ayer, "Presence Awareness: Instant Messaging's Killer App," *Mobile Business Advisor*, 1 July 2004 [accessed 22 January 2006] www.highbeam.com; Jefferson Graham, "Instant Messaging Programs Are No Longer Just for Messages," *USA Today*, 20 October 2003, 5D; Todd R. Weiss, "Microsoft Targets Corporate Instant Messaging Customers," *Computerworld*, 18 November 2002, 12; "Banks Adopt Instant Messaging to Create a Global Business Network," *Computer Weekly*, 25 April 2002, 40; Michael D. Osterman, "Instant Messaging in the Enterprise," *Business Communications Review*, January 2003, 59–62; John Pallato, "Instant Messaging Unites Work Groups and Inspires Collaboration," *Internet World*, December 2002, 14+.

17. Paul Mah, "Using Text Messaging in Business," Mobile Enterprise blog, 4 February 2008 [accessed 16 September 2008] http://blogs.techrepublic.com.com/wireless; Paul Kedrosky, "Why We Don't Get the (Text) Message," *Business 2.0*, 2 October 2006 [accessed 4 October 2006] www.business2.com; Carpenter, "Companies Discover Marketing Power of Text Messaging."

18. Mark Gibbs, "Racing to Instant Messaging," *NetworkWorld*, 17 February 2003, 74.

19. "E-Mail Is So Five Minutes Ago."

20. *SANS Top-20 2007 Security Risks*, SANS Institute [accessed 16 September 2008] www.sans.org; Tom Espiner, "Spim, Splog on the Rise," CNET News, 6 July 2006 [accessed 16 September 2008] http://news.cnet.com; Anita Hamilton, "You've Got Spim!" *Time*, 2 February 2004 [accessed 1 March 2004] www.time.com; Elizabeth Millard, "Instant Messaging Threats Still Rising," Newsfactor.com, 6 July 2005 [accessed 5 October 2006] www.newsfactor.com.

21. Clint Boulton, "IDC: IM Use Is Booming in Business," InstantMessagingPlanet.com, 5 October 2005 [accessed 22 January 2006] www.instantmessagingplanet.com; Jenny Goodbody, "Critical Success Factors for Global Virtual Teams," *Strategic Communication Management*, February/March 2005, 18–21; Ann Majchrzak, Arvind Malhotra, Jeffrey Stamps, and Jessica Lipnack, "Can Absence Make a Team Grow Stronger?" *Harvard Business Review*, May 2004, 131–137; Christine Y. Chen, "The IM Invasion," *Fortune*, 26 May 2003, 135–138; Yudhijit Bhattacharjee, "A Swarm of Little Notes," *Time*, September 2002, A3–A8; Mark Bruno, "Taming the Wild Frontiers of Instant Messaging," *Bank Technology News*, December 2002, 30–31; Richard Grigonis, "Enterprise-Strength Instant Messaging," Convergence.com, 10–15 [accessed March 2003] www.convergence.com.

22. Pallato, "Instant Messaging Unites Work Groups and Inspires Collaboration," 14+.

23. Dr. Laundry blog [accessed 15 September 2008] www.drlaundryblog.com.

24. GM FastLane blog [accessed 15 September 2008] http://fastlane.gmblogs.com.

25. Fredrik Wackå, "Six Types of Blogs—A Classification," CorporateBlogging.Info website, 10 August 2004 [accessed 5 October 2006] www.corporateblogging.info; Stephen Baker, "The Inside Story on Company Blogs," *BusinessWeek* 14 February 2006 [accessed 15 February 2006] www.businessweek.com; Jeremy Wright, *Blog Marketing* (New York: McGraw-Hill, 2006), 45–56; Paul Chaney, "Blogs: Beyond the Hype!" 26 May 2005 [accessed 4 May 2006] http://radiantmarketinggroup.com.

26. Evolve24 website [accessed 15 September 2008] www.evolve24.com.

27. Ann Smarty, "16 Examples of Huge Brands Using Twitter for Business," *Search Engine Journal*, 7 October 2008 [accessed 16 October

2008] www.searchenginejournal.com; Heather Green, "Creative Business Uses of Twitter," *BusinessWeek*, 30 April 2006 [accessed 15 September 2008] www.businessweek.com.

28. Adam C. Haver, personal communication, 25 November 2008.

29. Stephen Baker and Heather Green, "Blogs Will Change Your Business," *BusinessWeek*, 2 May 2005, 57–67.

30. Julie Moran Alterio, "Podcasts a Hit Inside and Outside IBM," *The Journal News* (White Plains, N.Y.), 9 January 2006 [accessed 5 May 2006] www.thejournalnews.com.

31. "Turn Your Feed into a Podcast," Lifehacker blog, 12 January 2006 [accessed 6 May 2006] www.lifehacker.com.

32. "Set Up Your Podcast for Success," FeedForAll website [accessed 4 October 2006] www.feedforall.com.

33. Shel Holtz, "Ten Guidelines for B2B Podcasts," WebProNews, 12 October 2005 [accessed 9 March 2006] www.webpronews.com.

34. Todd Cochrane, *Podcasting: The Do-It-Yourself Guide* (Indianapolis, Ind.: Wiley, 2005), 107–109.

35. Michael W. Geoghegan and Dan Klass, *Podcast Solutions: The Complete Guide to Podcasting* (Berkeley, Calif.: Friends of Ed, 2005), 57–86; Cochrane, *Podcasting: The Do-It-Yourself Guide*, 87–136.

36. "Syndication Format," Answers.com [accessed 5 October 2006] www.answers.com.

37. FeedBurner website [accessed 15 September 2008] www.feedburner.com.

38. Adapted from Comic-Con website [accessed 16 January 2007] www.comic-con.org; Tom Spurgeon, "Welcome to Nerd Vegas: A Guide to Visiting and Enjoying Comic-Con International in San Diego, 2006!" The Comics Reporter, 11 July 2006 [accessed 16 January 2007] www.comicsreporter.com; Rebecca Winters Keegan, "Boys Who Like Toys," *Time*, 19 April 2007 [accessed 15 May 2007] www.time.com.

39. Adapted from Tom Lowry, "ESPN.COM: Guys and Dollars," *BusinessWeek* online, 17 October 2005 [accessed 16 January 2007] www.businessweek.com.

40. Adapted from Lisa Marsh, "Why Fashion Loves Skinny," MSN Lifestyle [accessed 17 September 2008] http://lifestyle.msn.com.

41. Adapted from Crutchfield website [accessed 17 January 2007] www.crutchfield.com.

42. Adapted from *Logan* website [accessed 16 January 2007] www.loganmagazine.com.

43. Adapted from job description for Global Marketing Manager–Apparel, New Balance website [accessed 24 August 2005] www.newbalance.com.

44. Adapted from "Major New Study Shatters Stereotypes About Teens and Video Games," MacArthur Foundation, 16 September 2008 [accessed 18 September 2008] www.macfound.org.

45. Adapted from "Side Impact Protection Explained," Britax website [accessed 18 September 2008] www.britaxusa.com.

46. JetBlue Twitter website [accessed 18 September 2008] http://twitter.com/JetBlue; "JetBlue Lands on eBay," JetBlue website [accessed 18 September 2008] http://jetblue.com/ebay.

47. Adapted from Liz Moyer, "California Dreaming," *Forbes*, 8 May 2006 [accessed 8 May 2006] www.forbes.com; "Wachovia to Acquire Golden West Financial, Nation's Most Admired and 2nd Largest Savings Institution," 7 May 2006, Wachovia website [accessed 8 May 2006] www.wachovia.com.

CHAPTER 8

1. Get Satisfaction website [accessed 2 October 2008] http://getsatisfaction.com; Dan Fost, "On the Internet, Everyone Can Hear You Complain," *New York Times*, 25 February 2008 [accessed 2 October 2008] www.nytimes.com.

2. "Review Offer Letters Carefully to Avoid Binding Promises," *Fair Employment Practices Guidelines*, 15 May 2001, 5–6.

3. Fraser P. Seitel, *The Practice of Public Relations*, 9th ed. (Upper Saddle River, N.J.: Prentice Hall, 2004), 402–411; *Techniques for Communicators* (Chicago: Lawrence Ragan Communication, 1995), 34, 36.

4. David Meerman Scott, *The New Rules of Marketing and PR* (Hoboken, N.J.: Wiley, 2007), 62.

5. Mary Mitchell, "The Circle of Life—Condolence Letters," LiveandLearn.com [accessed 18 July 2005] www.liveandlearn.com; Donna Larcen, "Authors Share the Words of Condolence," *Los Angeles Times*, 20 December 1991, E11.

6. Adapted from an answer on Get Satisfaction website, 26 September [accessed 3 October 2008] http://getsatisfaction.com.

7. Adapted from Tom Abate, "Need to Preserve Cash Generates Wave of Layoffs in Biotech Industry," *San Francisco Chronicle*, 10 February 2003 [accessed 18 July 2005] www.sfgate.com.

8. Adapted from Lisa DiCarlo, "IBM Gets the Message—Instantly," Forbes.com, 7 July 2002 [accessed 22 July 2003] www.forbes.com; "IBM Introduces Breakthrough Messaging Technology for Customers and Business Partners," *M2 Presswire*, 19 February 2003 [accessed 24 July 2003] www.proquest.com; "IBM and America Online Team for Instant Messaging Pilot," *M2 Presswire*, 4 February 2003 [accessed 24 July 2003] www.proquest.com.

9. Adapted from CES website [accessed 18 July 2005] www.cesweb.org.

10. Adapted from Floorgraphics website [accessed 25 October 2006] www.floorgraphics.com; John Grossman, "It's an Ad, Ad, Ad, Ad World," *Inc.*, March 2000, 23–26; David Wellman, "'Floor' Toons," *Supermarket Business*, 15 November 1999, 47; "Floorshow," *Dallas Morning News*, 4 September 1998, 11D.

11. Adapted from Jamba Juice website [accessed 26 October 2006] http://www.jambajuice.com/#/ jobs_careers/; Brenda Paik Sunoo, "Blending a Successful Workforce," *Workforce*, March 2000, 44–48; Michael Adams, "Kirk Perron: Jamba Juice," *Restaurant Business*, 15 March 1999, 38; "Live in a Blender," *Restaurant Business*, 1 December 2000, 48–50; David Goll, "Jamba Juices Up 24-Hour Fitness Clubs," *East Bay Business Times*, 30 June 2000, 6.

12. Adapted from Burt Helm, "Wal-Mart, Please Don't Leave Me," *BusinessWeek*, 9 October 2006, 84–89.

13. Adapted from Jane Costello, "Check Your Insurance Before Renting an SUV," *Wall Street Journal*, 13 June 2001 [accessed 14 June 2001] http://online.wsj.com.

14. Adapted from Michael Mescon, Courtland Bovée, and John Thill, *Business Today*, 10th ed. (Upper Saddle River, N.J. Prentice Hall, 2002), 220.

15. "Entrepreneurs Across America," *Entrepreneur Magazine* [accessed 12 June 1997] www.entrepreneur. com.

16. Adapted from SitePoint website [accessed 12 May 2006] www.sitepoint.com; Dylan Tweney, "The Defogger: Slim Down That Homepage," *Business 2.0*, 13 July 2001 [accessed 1 August 2001] www.business2.com.

17. Adapted from Public Relations Society of America website [accessed 18 June 2005] www.prsa.org.

18. Adapted from Keith H. Hammonds, "Difference Is Power," *Fast Company*, 36, 258 [accessed 11 July 2000] www.fastcompany.com; Terri Morrison, Wayne A. Conaway, and George A. Borden, Ph.D., *Kiss, Bow, or Shake Hands* (Holbrook, Mass.: Adams Media Corporation, April 1995).

19. Adapted from Jeff Nachtigal, "It's Easy and Cheap Being Green," *Fortune*, 16 October 2006, 53; "Adobe Wins Platinum Certification Awarded by U.S. Green Building Council," press release, 3 July 2006 [accessed 15 October 2006] www.adobe.com.

CHAPTER 9

1. Larry Neumeister, "U.S. Tries to Resurrect KPMG Tax Shelter Case," *Washington Post*, 26 March 2008 [accessed 9 October 2008] www.washingtonpost.com; "Revised KPMG Tax-Shelter Settlement Gets Final Approval," *Public Accounting Report*, 15 June 2006, 6–7; "Inside the KPMG Mess," *BusinessWeek*, 1 September 2005 [accessed 1 September 2005] www.businessweek.com; KPMG Careers website [accessed 19 August 2005] www.kpmgcareers.com; "KPMG LLP Statement Regarding Department of Justice Matter,"

press release, 16 June 2005 [accessed 19 August 2005] www.us.kpmg.com; "KPMG May Avoid Indictment as U.S. Pushes Settlement, People Say," Bloomberg.com, 4 August 2005 [accessed 19 August 2005] www.bloomberg.com; "KPMG Offers Apology Over Illegal Tax Shelters," *Boston Globe,* 17 June 2005 [accessed 19 August 2005] www.boston.com; Jeff Bailey and Lynnley Browning, "KPMG May Dodge One Bullet, Only to Face Another," *New York Times,* 21 June 2005 [accessed 19 August 2005] www.nytimes.com.

2. Katie Grasso, "Deliver Bad News to Workers Face-to-Face, with Empathy," *Courier-Post* (Camden, N.J.), 8 February 2006 [accessed 14 May 2006] www.courierpostonline.com.

3. Letter from Sheila Zuckerman, Countrywide Office of the President, 6 September 2008.

4. Carol David and Margaret Ann Baker, "Rereading Bad News: Compliance-Gaining Features in Management Memos," *Journal of Business Communication,* October 1994 [accessed 1 December 2003] www.elibrary.com.

5. Ian McDonald, "Marsh Can Do $600 Million, but Apologize?" *Wall Street Journal,* 14 January 2005, C1, C3; Adrienne Carter and Amy Borrus, "What if Companies Fessed Up?" *BusinessWeek,* 24 January 2005, 59–60; Patrick J. Kiger, "The Art of the Apology," *Workforce Management,* October 2004, 57–62.

6. Golnar Motevalli, "Reputational Risk: Is It Time for Bankers to Risk an Apology?" *Insurance Journal,* 20 October 2008 [accessed 30 January 2009] www.insurancejournal.com; Del Jones, "Why 'Sorry' Isn't in Many CEOs' Vocabularies Anymore," *USA Today,* 21 October 2008 [accessed 29 October 2008] www.usatoday.com.

7. Ameeta Patel and Lamar Reinsch, "Companies Can Apologize: Corporate Apologies and Legal Liability," *Business Communication Quarterly,* March 2003 [accessed 1 December 2003] www.elibrary.com.

8. John Guiniven, "Sorry! An Apology as a Strategic PR Tool," *Public Relations Tactics,* December 2007, 6.

9. Iris I. Varner, "A Comparison of American and French Business Correspondence," *Journal of Business Communication* 24, no. 4 (Fall 1988): 55–65.

10. Susan Jenkins and John Hinds, "Business Letter Writing: English, French, and Japanese," *TESOL Quarterly* 21, no. 2 (June 1987): 327–349; Saburo Haneda and Hiosuke Shima, "Japanese Communication Behavior as Reflected in Letter Writing," *Journal of Business Communication* 19, no. 1 (1982): 19–32.

11. James Calvert Scott and Diana J. Green, "British Perspectives on Organizing Bad-News Letters: Organizational Patterns Used by Major U.K. Companies," *Bulletin of the Association for Business Communication* 55, no. 1 (March 1992): 17–19.

12. "Advice from the Pros on the Best Way to Deliver Bad News," Report on *Customer Relationship Management,* 1 February 2003 [accessed 1 December 2003] www.elibrary.com.

13. Ben Levisohn, "Getting More Workers to Whistle," *BusinessWeek,* 28 January 2008, 18.

14. "Less Than Half of Privately Held Businesses Support Whistleblowing," Grant Thornton website [accessed 13 October 2008] www.internationalbusinessreport.com.

15. Courtland L. Bovée, John V. Thill, George P. Dovel, and Marian Burk Wood, *Advertising Excellence* (New York: McGraw-Hill, 1995), 508–509; John Holusha, "Exxon's Public-Relations Problem," *New York Times,* 12 April 1989, D1.

16. "Throw Out the Old Handbook in Favor of Today's Crisis Drills," *PR News,* 27 January 2003, 1.

17. Thomas S. Brice and Marie Waung, "Applicant Rejection Letters: Are Businesses Sending the Wrong Message?" *Business Horizons,* March-April 1995, 59–62.

18. Gwendolyn N. Smith, Rebecca F. Nolan, and Yong Dai, "Job-Refusal Letters: Readers' Affective Responses to Direct and Indirect Organizational Plans," *Business Communication Quarterly* 59, no. 1 (1996): 67–73; Brice and Waung, "Applicant Rejection Letters."

19. John Zappe, "Building on Brand to Attract Top Employees," *Workforce Management,* 27 February 2006, 31.

20. Judi Brownell, "The Performance Appraisal Interviews: A Multipurpose Communication Assignment," *Bulletin of the Association for Business Communication* 57, no. 2 (1994): 11–21.

21. Gary Dessler, A *Framework for Human Resource Management,* 3rd ed. (Upper Saddle River, N.J.: Pearson Prentice Hall, 2004), 198.

22. Patricia A. McLagan, "Advice for Bad-News Bearers: How to Tell Employees They're Not Hacking It and Get Results," *IndustryWeek,* 15 February 1993, 42; Michael Lee Smith, "Give Feedback, Not Criticism," *Supervisory Management,* 1993, 4; "A Checklist for Conducting Problem Performer Appraisals," *Supervisory Management,* December 1993, 7–9.

23. Carrie Brodzinski, "Avoiding Wrongful Termination Suits," *National Underwriter Property & Casualty—Risk & Benefits Management,* 13 October 2003 [accessed 2 December 2003] www.elibrary.com.

24. "Writing Effective Employee Evaluations," *Healthcare Executive,* September/October 2008, 82.

25. Jane R. Goodson, Gail W. McGee, and Anson Seers, "Giving Appropriate Performance Feedback to Managers: An Empirical Test of Content and Outcomes," *Journal of Business Communication* 29, no. 4 (1992): 329–342.

26. "A Legal Termination," *Supervision,* September 2008, 22–25; Craig Cox, "On the Firing Line," Business Ethics, May–June 1992, 33–34.

27. Cox, "On the Firing Line."

28. See Note 1.

29. Adapted from "FDA Notifies Public That Vail Products, Inc., Issues Nationwide Recall of Enclosed Bed Systems," FDA press release, 30 June 2005 [accessed 18 August 2005] www.fda.gov.

30. Adapted from "Bathtub Curve," *Engineering Statistics Handbook,* National Institute of Standards and Technology website [accessed 16 April 2005] www.nist.gov; Robert Berner, "The Warranty Windfall," *BusinessWeek,* 20 December 2004, 84–86; Larry Armstrong, "When Service Contracts Make Sense," *BusinessWeek,* 20 December 2004, 86.

31. Adapted from United Overseas Bank website [accessed on April 15, 2009] http:www.uob.com.sg.

32. Adapted from "MTR Corp in move against parallel traders," *South China Morning Post,* 2 March 2009.

33. Adapted from Sean Doherty, "Dynamic Communications," *Network Computing,* 3 April 2003, 26 [accessed 24 July 2003] http://search.epnet.com; Todd Wasserman, "Post-Merger HP Invents New Image to Challenge Tech Foes IBM and Dell," Brandweek, 18 November 2002, 9 [accessed 24 July 2003] http://search.epnet.com; R. P. Srikanth, "IM Tools Are Latest Tech Toys for Corporate Users," *Express Computer,* 1 July 2002 [accessed 21 July 2003] www.expresscomputeronline.com.

34. "Viral Effect of Email Promotion," Alka Dwivedi blog [accessed 19 October 2006] www.alkadwivedi.net; Teresa Valdez Klein, "Starbucks Makes a Viral Marketing Misstep," Blog Business Summit website [accessed 19 October 2006] www.blogbusinesssummit.com.

35. Adapted from G.O.D. website [accessed April 15, 2009] http://www.god.com.hk.

36. Adapted from Fookes Software website [accessed 28 October 2008] www.fookes.com.

37. Adapted from Associated Press, "Employers Restricting Use of Cell Phones in Cars," CNN.com/Sci-Tech, 27 August 2001 [accessed 27 August 2001] www.cnn.com; Julie Vallese, "Study: All Cell Phones Distract Drivers," CNN.com/U.S., 16 August 2001 [accessed 7 September 2001] www.cnn.com.

38. Adapted from "Cable car closed after cabin plunges," *South China Morning Post,* 12 June 2007.

39. Adapted from Rodney Manley, "Milledgeville Plant to Close; 150 to Lose Jobs," Macon.com , 28 January 2009 [accessed 1 February 2009] www.macon.com; Jamie Jones, "Shaw Plant Closing in Milledgeville," *The Daily Citizen* (Dalton, Georgia), 29 January 2009 [accessed 1 February 2009] www.northwestgeorgia.com.

40. Adapted from "Recall Safety Notice," Bombardier Recreational Products website, 10 September 2008 [accessed 30 October 2008]

www.brp.com; Bombardier Recreational Products website [accessed 30 October 2008] www.brp.com.

41. Adapted from Pui-Wing Tam, Erin White, Nick Wingfield, and Kris Maher, "Snooping E-Mail by Software Is Now a Workplace Norm," *Wall Street Journal,* 9 March 2005, B1+.

42. Adapted from Sylvia Ann Hewlett and Carolyn Buck Luce, "Off-ramps and On-ramps," *Harvard Business Review,* March 2005, 43–54.

43. Adapted from Stanton website [accessed 18 August 2005] www.stantondj.com.

44. Adapted from Capital One Auto Finance (formerly People First.com) website [accessed 23 December 2003] www.capital oneautofinance.com.

45. Adapted from "Feds Warn Carter's Baby Clothes May Cause Rash," CNN.com, 25 October 2008 [accessed 30 October 2008] www.cnn.com; "A Message from Carter's on 'Tag-Less' Labels," Carter's website [accessed 30 October 2008] www.carters.com.

46. Adapted from Alion website [accessed 19 August 2005] www .alionscience.com.

CHAPTER 10

1. CafeMom website [accessed 10 November 2008] www.cafemom .com; "ClubMom Introduces the MomNetwork—The Web's First Social Network for Moms," press release, 8 May 2006 [accessed 22 October 2006] www.hcp.com; "Laura Fortner Named Senior Vice President, Business Development at ClubMom," press release, 20 September 2006 [accessed 22 October 2006] http://newyork .dbusinessnews.com.

2. Jay A. Conger, "The Necessary Art of Persuasion," *Harvard Business Review,* May–June 1998, 84–95; Jeanette W. Gilsdorf, "Write Me Your Best Case for...," *Bulletin of the Association for Business Communication* 54, no. 1 (March 1991): 7–12.

3. "Vital Skill for Today's Managers: Persuading, Not Ordering Others," *Soundview Executive Book Summaries,* September 1998, 1.

4. Mary Cross, "Aristotle and Business Writing: Why We Need to Teach Persuasion," *Bulletin of the Association for Business Communication* 54, no. 1 (March 1991): 3–6.

5. Stephen P. Robbins and David A. DeCenzo, *Fundamentals of Management,* 4th ed. (Upper Saddle River, N.J.: Prentice Hall, 2004), 284.

6. Edwin A. Locke and Gary P. Latham, "What Should We Do About Motivation Theory? Six Recommendations for the Twenty-First Century," *Academy of Management Review,* July 2004, 388+.

7. IKEA website [accessed 3 March 2008] www.ikea.com; Liz C. Wang, Julie Baker, Judy A. Wagner, and Kirk Wakefield, "Can a Retail Web Site Be Social?" *Journal of Marketing* 71, no. 3 (July 2007), 143–157.

8. Robert T. Moran, "Tips on Making Speeches to International Audiences," *International Management,* April 1980, 58–59.

9. Conger, "The Necessary Art of Persuasion."

10. Wesley Clark, "The Potency of Persuasion," *Fortune,* 12 November 2007, 48; W. H. Weiss, "Using Persuasion Successfully," *Supervision,* October 2006, 13–16.

11. Tom Chandler, "The Copywriter's Best Friend," *The Copywriter Underground blog,* 20 December 2006 [accessed 4 March 2008] http://copywriterunderground.com.

12. Raymond M. Olderman, *10-Minute Guide to Business Communication* (New York: Macmillan Spectrum/Alpha Books, 1997), 57–61.

13. John D. Ramage and John C. Bean, *Writing Arguments: A Rhetoric with Readings,* 3rd ed. (Boston: Allyn & Bacon, 1995), 430–442.

14. Philip Vassallo, "Persuading Powerfully: Tips for Writing Persuasive Documents," *Et Cetera,* Spring 2002, 65–71.

15. Dianna Booher, *Communicate with Confidence* (New York: McGraw-Hill, 1994), 102.

16. *Overview of the Web Accessibility Initiative,* W3C website [accessed 20 October 2006] www.w3.org.

17. iPod nano main product page, Apple website [accessed 4 March 2008] www.apple.com/ipodnano.

18. "HealthGrades Reveals America's Best Hospitals," 27 February 2008 [accessed 4 March 2008] www.ivanhoe.com.

19. Saturn VUE product page, Saturn website [accessed 8 December 2003] www.saturn.com.

20. Lancôme website [accessed 4 March 2008] www.lancome-usa .com.

21. *Living in France* product page, Insider Paris Guides website [accessed 4 March 2008] www.insiderparisguides.com.

22. U.S. Department of Energy, Energy Efficiency and Renewable Energy website [accessed 4 March 2008] www.eere.energy.gov.

23. Microsoft Office website [accessed 4 March 2008] http:// office.microsoft.com.

24. Fast Break Backpack product page, Lands' End website [accessed 8 December 2003] www.landsend.com.

25. iPod nano main product page, Apple website [accessed 4 March 2008] www.apple.com/ipodnano.

26. "Technical Specifications," iPod nano, Apple website [accessed 4 March 2008] www.apple.com/ipodnano.

27. Larry Weber, *Marketing to the Social Web* (Hoboken, N.J.: Wiley, 2007), 12–14; David Meerman Scott, *The New Rules of Marketing and PR* (Hoboken, N.J.: Wiley, 2007), 62; Paul Gillin, *The New Influencers* (Sanger, Calif.: Quill Driver Books, 2007), 34–35; Jeremy Wright, *Blog Marketing: The Revolutionary Way to Increase Sales, Build Your Brand, and Get Exceptional Results* (New York: McGraw-Hill, 2006), 263–365.

28. Gilsdorf, "Write Me Your Best Case for...."

29. "Undercover Marketing Uncovered," CBSnews.com, 25 July 2004 [accessed 11 April 2005] www.cbsnews.com; Stephanie Dunnewind, "Teen Recruits Create Word-of-Mouth 'Buzz' to Hook Peers on Products," *Seattle Times,* 20 November 2004 [accessed 11 April 2005] www.seattletimes.com.

30. *Frequently Asked Advertising Questions: A Guide for Small Business,* U.S. Federal Trade Commission website [accessed 9 December 2003] www.ftc.gov.

31. Adapted from Samsung website [accessed 22 October 2006] www.samsung.com.

32. Adapted from GM Fastlane Blog [accessed 6 November 2008] http://fastlane.gmblogs.com.

33. Adapted from "'Power Nap' Prevents Burnout; Morning Sleep Perfects a Skill," National Institutes of Health press release, 2 July 2002 [accessed 31 October 2006] www.nih.gov; Albert R. Karr, "Work Week: Wake Up and Read This," *Wall Street Journal,* 6 May 1997, A1.

34. Adapted from IBM website [accessed 15 January 2004] www .ibm.com; "DAS Faces an Assured Future with IBM," IBM website [accessed 16 January 2004] www.ibm.com; "Sametime," IBM website [accessed 16 January 2004] www.ibm.com.

35. Adapted from CNET Shopper.com [accessed 1 October 2001] http://shopper.cnet.com.

36. Adapted from Courtland L. Bovée and John V. Thill, *Business in Action,* 3rd ed. (Upper Saddle River, N.J.: Prentice Hall, 2005), 236–237; International Telework Coalition website [accessed 24 August 2005] www.telcoa.org; Jason Roberson, "Rush-Hour Rebellion," *Dallas Business Journal,* 22 June 2001, 31; Carole Hawkins, "Ready, Set, Go Home," *Black Enterprise,* August 2001, 118–124; Wayne Tompkins, "Telecommuting in Transition," *Courier-Journal* (Louisville, Ky.), 9 July 2001, 1C.

37. Adapted from Give Life website [accessed 23 August 2005] www.givelife.org; American Red Cross website [accessed 3 October 2001] www.redcross.org; American Red Cross San Diego Chapter website [accessed 3 October 2001] www.sdarc.org.

38. Adapted from Web Accessibility Initiative, World Wide Web Consortium website [accessed 7 November 2008] www.w3.org.

39. Adapted from Norimitsu Onishi, "Making Liberty His Business: Ex-Political Prisoner Turns Freedom's Icon into a Career," *New York Times,* 18 April 1996, B1; Colbar Art website [accessed 9 January 2004] www.colbarart.com.

40. Adapted from Sarah Plaskitt, "Case Study: Hilton Uses SMS with Success," *B&T Marketing & Media,* 27 June 2002 [accessed

22 July 2003] www.bandt.com.au; "Wireless Messaging Briefs," *Instant Messaging Planet*, 4 October 2002 [accessed 22 July 2003] www.instantmessagingplanet.com; Hilton Hotels Corporation, *Hoover's Company Capsules*, 1 July 2003 [accessed 24 July 2003] www.proquest.com; Matthew G. Nelson, "Hilton Takes Reservations Wireless," *InformationWeek*, 25 June 2001, 99 [accessed 24 July 2003] www.web22.epnet.com; Hilton Hotels website [accessed 15 January 2004] www.hilton.com.

41. Adapted from The Podcast Bunker website [accessed 25 August 2005] www.podcastbunker.com.

42. Adapted from Time Inc. website [accessed 25 August 2005] www.timewarner.com.

43. Adapted from Insure.com website [accessed 24 August 2005] www.insure.com.

44. Adapted from Kelly Services website [accessed 9 January 2004] www.kellyservices.com.

45. Adapted from Hangers Cleaners (Kansas City) website [accessed 7 November 2008] www.hangerskc.com; Charles Fishman, "The Greener Cleaners," Fast Company website [accessed 11 July 2000] http://fastcompany.com; Micell Technologies website [accessed 1 September 2000] www.micell.com; Cool Clean Technologies, Inc., website [accessed 9 January 2004] www.co2olclean.com.

CHAPTER 11

1. Fresh & Easy website [accessed 23 November 2008] www.freshandeasy.com; Tesco website [accessed 23 November 2008] www.tesco.com; "Competition and Profit," Food Marketing Institute website [accessed 5 November 2006] www.fmi.org; John E. Forsyth, Nicolo Galante, and Todd Guild, "Capitalizing on Customer Insights," *McKinsey Quarterly*, 2006 Issue 3, 42–53; "Company Spotlight: Tesco PLC," *MarketWatch: Global Round-Up*, July 2006, 76–81; James Quilter, "Tesco Hands Senior Role to Brand Planning Chief," *Marketing*, 2 August 2006, 4; Don Longo, "The British Are Coming," *Progressive Grocer*, 15 April 2006, 66–75.

2. LegalDefinitions.com [accessed 17 December 2003] www.legaldefinitions.com.

3. Tom Krazit, "FAQ: The HP 'Pretexting' Scandal," ZDNet.com, 6 September 2006 [accessed 26 October 2006] www.zdnet.com.

4. Information for this section was obtained from "Finding Industry Information" [accessed 3 November 1998] www.pitt.edu/~buslibry/industries.htm; Thomas P. Bergman, Stephen M. Garrison, and Gregory M. Scott, *The Business Student Writer's Manual and Guide to the Internet* (Upper Saddle River, N.J.: Prentice Hall, 1998), 67–80; Ernest L. Maier, Anthony J. Faria, Peter Kaatrude, and Elizabeth Wood, *The Business Library and How to Use It* (Detroit: Omnigraphics, 1996), 53–76; Sherwyn P. Morreale and Courtland L. Bovée, *Excellence in Public Speaking* (Fort Worth: Harcourt Brace College Publishers, 1998), 166–171.

5. Joe Barker, "Invisible or Deep Web: What It Is, Why It Exists, How to Find It, and Its Inherent Ambiguity," 1 August 2006, UC Berkeley-Teaching Library Internet Workshops [accessed 25 October 2006] www.lib.berkeley.edu.

6. Open Directory [accessed 24 November 2008] http://dmoz.com.

7. AlltheWeb.com advanced search page [accessed 24 November 2008] www.alltheweb.com; Google advanced search page [accessed 24 November 2008] www.google.com; Live Search website [accessed 24 November 2008] www.live.com.

8. Google Help Center [accessed 24 November 2008] www.google.com.

9. Zotero website [accessed 24 November 2008] www.zotero.org; RefWorks website [accessed 24 November 2008] www.refworks.com; Net Snippets website [accessed 3 November 2006] www.netsnippets.com.

10. Kevin J. Delaney, "Web Sites' Lists of 'Most Viewed' Too Easy to Game?" *Wall Street Journal*, 15 May 2007, B1–B2; Noam Cohen, "Spinning a Web of Lies at Digital Speed," *New York Times*, 13 October 2008, B3; Antone Gonsalves, "Digg Dogged by Allegations of Manipulation," *TechWeb*, 7 September 2006 [accessed 3 November 2006] www.techweb.com.

11. "Top 10 Benefits of OneNote 2007," Microsoft website [accessed 8 March 2008] www.microsoft.com; "Welcome to Google Notebook," Google website [accessed 8 March 2008] www.google.com.

12. "Copyright Office Basics," U.S. Copyright Office website [accessed 2 November 2006] www.copyright.gov.

13. "How to Design and Conduct a Study," *Credit Union Magazine*, October 1983, 36–46.

14. Product features page, SurveyMonkey.com [accessed 29 October 2006] www.surveymonkey.com.

15. American Marketing Association website [accessed 14 December 2003] www.marketingpower.com.

16. Karen J. Bannan, "Companies Save Time, Money with Online Surveys," *B to B*, 9 June 2003, 1+; Allen Hogg, "Online Research Overview," American Marketing Association website [accessed 15 December 2003] www.marketingpower.com.

17. Tesco website [accessed 5 November 2006] www.tesco.com.

18. Morreale and Bovée, *Excellence in Public Speaking*, 177.

19. Morreale and Bovée, *Excellence in Public Speaking*, 182.

20. A. B. Blankenship and George Edward Breen, *State of the Art Marketing Research* (Lincolnwood, Ill.: NTC Business Books, 1992), 225.

21. Lynn Quitman Troyka, *Simon & Schuster Handbook for Writers*, 6th ed. (Upper Saddle River, N.J.: Simon & Schuster, 2002), 481.

22. "How to Paraphrase Effectively: 6 Steps to Follow," Researchpaper.com [accessed 26 October 1998] www.researchpaper.com.

23. Venkatesh Rao, "Social Media vs. Knowledge Management: A Generational War," *Social Computing*, 17 November 2008 [accessed 23 November 2008] www.socialcomputingmagazine.com; Jeff Kelly, "KM vs. Social Media: Beware the Warmongers," 17 November 2008 [accessed 23 November 2008] www.socialcomputingmagazine.com.

CHAPTER 12

1. Xplane website [accessed 4 December 2008] www.xplane.com; "Small & Global," CNN, 23 June 2008 [accessed 4 December 2008] www.cnn.com; "Visionary Leaders," *Portland Monthly*, October 2007, 82–88.

2. Alexis Gerard and Bob Goldstein, *Going Visual* (Hoboken, N.J.: Wiley, 2005), 18.

3. Charles Kostelnick and Michael Hassett, *Shaping Information: The Rhetoric of Visual Conventions* (Carbondale, Ill.: Southern Illinois University Press, 2003), 177.

4. Gerard and Goldstein, *Going Visual*, 25–27.

5. "Fact Sheet Overview," *2003 National Assessment of Adult Literacy*, National Institute for Literacy [accessed 22 November 2006] www.nifl.gov.

6. Gerard and Goldstein, *Going Visual*, 103–106.

7. Edward R. Tufte, *Visual Explanations: Images and Quantities, Evidence and Narrative* (Cheshire, Conn.: Graphics Press, 1997), 82.

8. Joshua David McClurg-Genevese, "The Principles of Design," *Digital Web Magazine*, 13 June 2005 [accessed 23 November 2006] www.digital-web.com.

9. Kostelnick and Hassett, *Shaping Information: The Rhetoric of Visual Conventions*, 17.

10. Kostelnick and Hassett, *Shaping Information: The Rhetoric of Visual Conventions*, 216.

11. Edward R. Tufte, *The Visual Display of Quantitative Information* (Cheshire, Conn.: Graphic Press, 1983), 113.

12. Based in part on Tufte, *Visual Explanations: Images and Quantities, Evidence and Narrative*, 29–37, 53; Paul Martin Lester, *Visual Communication: Images with Messages*, 4th ed. (Belmont, Calif.: Thomson Wadsworth, 2006), 95–105, 194–196.

13. Data from Hoover's Online [accessed 3 December 2008] www.hoovers.com.

14. Robert L. Harris, *Information Graphics: A Comprehensive Illustrated Reference* (New York: Oxford University Press, 1999), 14.

15. "Data Visualization: Modern Approaches," *Smashing Magazine*, 2 August 2007 [accessed 15 March 2008] www.smashingmagazine.com; "7 Things You Should Know About Data Visualization,"

EDUCAUSE Learning Initiative website [accessed 15 March 2008] www.educause.edu; TagCrowd website [accessed 15 March 2008] www.tagcrowd.com.

16. Sheri Rosen, "What Is Truth?" *IABC Communication World*, March 1995, 40.

17. Eric Binfet, personal communication, 26 November 2008.

18. "Interactive Web Sites Draw Minds, Shape Public Perception," *ScienceDaily*, 27 May 2008 [accessed 3 December 2008] www.sciencedaily.com.

CHAPTER 13

1. Doug Walmisley, Kenwood USA, personal communication, 8 February 2007; Kenwood USA website [accessed 9 December 2008] www.kenwoodusa.com; MotoSAT website [accessed 9 December 2008] www.motosat.com; "Kenwood Announces Strategic Organization Changes," Kenwood Corporation press release, 2 October 2006 [accessed 7 November 2006] http://biz.yahoo.com; Amy Gilroy, "Vendors Retool Lines to Combat Sales Slump," *TWICE*, 13 October 2003, 28; Amy Gilroy, "Car Audio in Double-Digit Slump," *TWICE*, 7 July 2003, 8; Martin Fackler, "Japan Profiles: Haruo Kawahara, Kenwood Chief," Dow Jones Newswires, *Far Eastern Economic Review*, 24 September 2003 [accessed 9 December 2003] http://online.wsj.com; Corey Goldman, "Satellite Radio's Future Still Up in the Air," *Toronto Star*, 11 August 2003 [accessed 9 December 2003] www.elibrary.com; Denis Storey, "Kenwood Chief Touts Turnaround," Mobile Radio Technology website, 1 February 2003 [accessed 9 December 2003] www.iwce-mrt.com; Erin Strout, "Ask SMM," *Sales and Marketing Management*, October 2002, 59.

2. See Note 1.

3. Adapted from Michael Gerber, "The Business Plan That Always Works," *Her Business*, May/June 2004, 23–25; J. Tol Broome, Jr., "How to Write a Business Plan," *Nation's Business*, February 1993, 29–30; Albert Richards, "The Ernst & Young Business Plan Guide," *R & D Management*, April 1995, 253; David Lanchner, "How Chitchat Became a Valuable Business Plan," *Global Finance*, February 1995, 54–56; Marguerita Ashby-Berger, "My Business Plan—And What Really Happened," *Small Business Forum*, Winter 1994–1995, 24–35; Stanley R. Rich and David E. Gumpert, *Business Plans That Win $$$* (New York: Harper & Row, 1985).

4. Jakob Nielsen, "Reading on the Web" [accessed 11 November 2004] www.useit.com/alertbox/9710a.html.

5. Reid Goldsborough, "Words for the Wise," *Link-Up*, September–October 1999, 25–26.

6. Julie Rohovit, "Computer Eye Strain: The Dilbert Syndrome," Virtual Hospital website [accessed 9 November 2004] www.vh.org.

7. Nick Usborne, "Two Pillars of a Successful Site," *Excess Voice*, May 2004 [accessed 8 November 2004] www.excessvoice.com.

8. Shel Holtz, *Writing for the Wired World* (San Francisco: International Association of Business Communicators, 1999), 6–9.

9. Holtz, *Writing for the Wired World*, 28–29.

10. Iris Varner, *Contemporary Business Report Writing*, 2nd ed. (Chicago: Dryden Press, 1991), 170.

11. Curt Kampmeier, "How to Write a Proposal That's Accepted Every Time," *Consulting to Management*, September 2000, 62.

12. Dan MacDougall, "Orchestrating Your Proposal," *Canadian Consulting Engineer*, March–April 2003, 51–56; Sant Corporation website [accessed 7 December 2008] www.santcorp.com.

13. "Why What You Learned in School About Writing Was Wrong," CapturePlanning.com [accessed 9 December 2008] www.captureplanning.com.

14. See Note 1.

15. Adapted from Catherine Holahan and Spencer E. Ante, "SXSW: Where Tech Mingles with Music," *BusinessWeek*, 7 March 2008 [accessed 9 March 2008] www.businessweek.com; SXSW website [accessed 9 March 2008] http://sxsw.com.

CHAPTER 14

1. Adapted from Tellabs website [accessed 12 December 2008] www.tellabs.com; Sid Cato, "World's Best 2005 Reports," Sid Cato's Office Annual Report Website [accessed 11 November 2006] www.sidcato.com; George Stenitzer, "New Challenges for Annual Reports," Presentation to National Investor Relations Institute, November 2005 [accessed 11 November 2006] www.niri-chicago.org.

2. A. S. C. Ehrenberg, "Report Writing—Six Simple Rules for Better Business Documents," *Admap*, June 1992, 39–42.

3. Michael Netzley and Craig Snow, *Guide to Report Writing* (Upper Saddle River, N.J.: Prentice Hall, 2001), 15.

4. "Tellabs Solutions and Applications," Tellabs 2005 Annual Report [accessed 11 November 2006] www.tellabs.com.

5. David A. Hayes, "Helping Students Grasp the Knack of Writing Summaries," *Journal of Reading* (November 1989): 96–101.

6. Philip C. Kolin, *Successful Writing at Work*, 6th ed. (Boston: Houghton Mifflin, 2001), 552–555.

7. Jakob Nielsen, "How Little Do Users Read?" 6 May 2008, UseIt.com [accessed 11 December 2008] www.useit.com.

8. Shel Holtz, "Writing for the Wired World," *International Association of Business Communicators*, 1999, 6–9.

9. Christopher Null, "Search Engine Optimization for Your Web Site," *PC World*, 4 December 2008 [accessed 11 December 2008] www.pcworld.com; "Law Firm Marketing Now Dependent on Search Engine Optimization," *Law Office Management & Administration Report*, June 2006, 1, 10–12; *Pandia Search Engine Marketing 101*, Pandia Search Central website [accessed 25 March 2007] www.pandia.com; Mike Grehan, "Does Textbook SEO Really Work Anymore?" 17 April 2006, ClickZ.com [accessed 25 March 2007], www.clickz.com; Shari Thurow, "Web Positioning Metrics and SEO," 24 October 2005, ClickZ.com [accessed 25 March 2007] www.clickz.com.

10. "Codex: Guidelines," WordPress website [accessed 16 February 2008] http://wordpress.org; Michael Shanks, "Wiki Guidelines," Traumwerk website [accessed 18 August 2006] http://metamedia.stanford.edu/projects/traumwerk/home; Joe Moxley, MC Morgan, Matt Barton, and Donna Hanak, "For Teachers New to Wikis," Writing Wiki [accessed 18 August 2006] http://writingwiki.org; "Wiki Guidelines," Psi [accessed 18 August 2006] http://psi-im.org.

11. Rachael King, "No Rest for the Wiki," *BusinessWeek*, 12 March 2007 [accessed 14 February 2008] www.businessweek.com.

12. "Codex: Guidelines," WordPress website [accessed 14 February 2008] http://wordpress.org.

13. "Wikipedia: Edit War," Wikipedia.com [accessed 14 February 2008] http://en.wikipedia.org.

14. Adapted from Air-Trak website [accessed 9 March 2008] www.air-trak.com.

CHAPTER 15

1. "CEO's Letter: A Message from Patty Stonesifer," Bill & Melinda Gates Foundation 2007 Annual Report [accessed 13 December 2008] www.gatesfoundation.org; Bill & Melinda Gates Foundation website [accessed 13 December 2008] www.gatesfoundation.org; Richard Klausner and Pedro Alonso, "An Attack on All Fronts," *Nature*, 19 August 2004, 930–931; "Richard Klausner Spends to Save Lives," *Fast Company*, November 2002, 128; Kent Allen, "The Gatekeeper," *U.S. News & World Report*, 8 December 2003, 64–66.

2. John Morkes and Jakob Nielsen, "Concise, Scannable, and Objective: How to Write for the Web," UseIt.com [accessed 13 November 2006] www.useit.com.

3. Michael Netzley and Craig Snow, *Guide to Report Writing* (Upper Saddle River, N.J.: Prentice Hall, 2001), 57.

4. Oswald M. T. Ratteray, "Hit the Mark with Better Summaries," *Supervisory Management*, September 1989, 43–45.

5. Netzley and Snow, *Guide to Report Writing*, 43.

6. Alice Reid, "A Practical Guide for Writing Proposals" [accessed 31 May 2001] http://members.dca.net/areid/proposal.htm.

7. Toby B. Gooley, "Ocean Shipping: RFPs That Get Results," *Logistics Management*, July 2003, 47–52.

8. See Note 1.

9. Andrea Obana, "How to Write a Request for Proposals (RFP)," Fine Brand Media website [accessed 22 January 2004] www.finebrand.com; Gooley, "Ocean Shipping: RFPs That Get Results," 47–52.

10. Obana, "How to Write a Request for Proposals (RFP)"; Gooley, "Ocean Shipping: RFPs That Get Results," 47–52; "Writing a Good RFP," *Infrastructure Issues*, September 1998, Mead & Hunt website [accessed 23 January 2004] www.meadhunt.com.

11. Adapted from "Home Depot Says E-Learning Is Paying for Itself," *Workforce Management*, 25 February 2004 [accessed 28 February 2004] www.workforce.com; Robert Celaschi, "The Insider: Training," *Workforce Management*, August 2004, 67–69; Joe Mullich, "A Second Act for E-Learning," *Workforce Management*, February 2004, 51–55; Gail Johnson, "Brewing the Perfect Blend," *Training*, December 2003, 30+; Tammy Galvin, "2003 Industry Report," *Training*, October 2003, 21+; William C. Symonds, "Giving It the Old Online Try," *BusinessWeek*, 3 December 2001, 76–80; Karen Frankola, "Why Online Learners Drop Out," *Workforce*, October 2001, 52–60; Mary Lord, "They're Online and on the Job; Managers and Hamburger Flippers Are Being E-Trained at Work," *U.S. News & World Report*, 15 October 2001, 72–77.

12. Adapted from Ieva M. Augstumes, "Buyers Take the Driver's Seat," *Dallas Morning News*, 20 February 2004 [accessed 30 June 2004] www.highbeam.com; Jill Amadio, "A Click Away: Automotive Web Sites Are Revved Up and Ready to Help You Buy," *Entrepreneur*, 1 August 2003 [accessed 30 June 2004] www.highbeam.com; Dawn C. Chmielewski, "Car Sites Lend Feel-Good Info for Haggling," *San Jose Mercury News*, 1 August 2003 [accessed 30 June 2004] www.highbeam.com; Cromwell Schubarth, "Autoheroes Handle Hassle of Haggling," *Boston Herald*, 24 July 2003 [accessed 30 June 2004] www.highbeam.com; Rick Popely, "Internet Doesn't Change Basic Shopping Rules," *Chicago Tribune*, 28 February 2004 [accessed 30 June 2004] www.highbeam.com; Matt Nauman, "Walnut Creek, Calif., Firm Prospers as Online Car Buying Becomes More Popular," *San Jose Mercury News*, 21 June 2004 [accessed 30 June 2004] www.highbeam.com; Cliff Banks, "e-Dealer 100," Ward's Dealer Business, 1 April 2004 [accessed 30 June 2004] www.highbeam.com; Cars.com website [accessed 30 June 2004] www.cars.com; CarsDirect website [accessed 30 June 2004] www.carsdirect.com.

CHAPTER 16

1. Fitch website [accessed 20 December 2008] www.fitch.com; "Fitch Fact Sheet," Fitch website [accessed 26 November 2006] www.fitch.com; "Fitch: Worldwide—A Different View," Fitch website [accessed 15 December 2003] www.fitch.com; "About Fitch: Worldwide," Fitch website [accessed 10 October 2003] www.fitch.com; Fara Warner, "How Fitch Makes Its (Fast) Pitch," *Fast Company*, March 2002, 126.

2. Carmine Gallo, "How to Deliver a Presentation Under Pressure," *BusinessWeek*, 22 September 2008, 30.

3. Irwin Pollack, "Don't Just Give Presentations, Impact Your Audience," *Fort Worth Business Press*, 1 May 2006, 10.

4. Gallo, "How to Deliver a Presentation Under Pressure."

5. Carmine Gallo, "Loaded for Bore," *BusinessWeek* online, 5 August 2005 [accessed 19 September 2005] www.businessweek.com.

6. Sarah Lary and Karen Pruente, "Powerless Point: Common PowerPoint Mistakes to Avoid," *Public Relations Tactics*, February 2004, 28.

7. Cliff Atkinson, *Beyond Bullet Points: Using Microsoft PowerPoint to Create Presentations That Inform, Motivate, and Inspire* (Redmond, Wash.: Microsoft Press, 2005), 29, 55, 65.

8. Sherwyn P. Morreale and Courtland L. Bovée, *Excellence in Public Speaking* (Fort Worth: Harcourt Brace, 1998), 234–237.

9. Morreale and Bovée, *Excellence in Public Speaking*, 230.

10. Morreale and Bovée, *Excellence in Public Speaking*, 241–243.

11. Adapted from Eric J. Adams, "Management Focus: User-Friendly Presentation Software," *World Trade*, March 1995, 92.

12. Carmine Gallo, "Grab Your Audience Fast," *BusinessWeek*, 13 September 2006, 19.

13. Walter Kiechel III, "How to Give a Speech," *Fortune*, 8 June 1987, 180.

14. *Communication and Leadership Program* (Santa Ana, Calif.: Toastmasters International, 1980), 44, 45.

15. Steve Adubato, "Throw Away That Script, Use an Outline Instead," *NJBiz*, 23 October 2006, 17.

16. Peter Burrows and Ronald Grover, "Steve Jobs' Magic Kingdom," *BusinessWeek* online, 6 February 2006 [accessed 25 November 2006] www.businessweek.com.

17. Morreale and Bovée, *Excellence in Public Speaking*, 24–25.

18. Jennifer Rotondo and Mike Rotondo, Jr., *Presentation Skills for Managers* (New York: McGraw-Hill, 2002), 9.

19. Lillian H. Chaney and Catherine G. Green, "Presenter Behaviors: Actions Often Speak Louder Than Words," *American Salesman*, April 2006, 22–27.

20. Judy Linscott, "Getting On and Off the Podium," *Savvy*, October 1985, 44.

21. Iris R. Johnson, "Before You Approach the Podium," *MW*, January–February 1989, 7.

22. "Advice from a Voice Coach: Say It and Sell It," *Presentations*, 6 November 2006 [accessed 27 November 2006] www.presentations.com.

23. "Control the Question-and-Answer Session," *Soundview Executive Book Summaries* 20, no. 6, pt. 2 (June 1998): 4.

24. "Control the Question-and-Answer Session."

25. Robert L. Montgomery, "Listening on Your Feet," *The Toastmaster*, July 1987, 14–15.

26. Adapted from Ronald L. Applebaum and Karl W. E. Anatol, *Effective Oral Communication: For Business and the Professions* (Chicago: Science Research Associates, 1982), 240–244.

CHAPTER 17

1. James Rogers, "The Tech Investor's Guide to 2009," 26 December 2008, TheStreet.com [accessed 27 December 2008] www.thestreet.com; "Culture and Philosophy" and "Procter & Gamble Case Study," HP website [accessed 20 September 2005] www.hp.com; Paul McDougall, "Procter & Gamble's Deal with HP Grows," *InformationWeek*, 16 August 2004 [accessed 20 September 2005] www.outsourcingpipeline.com; Bill Breen, "The Big Score," *Fast Company*, September 2003, 64; "HP Finalizes $3 Billion Outsourcing Agreement to Manage Procter & Gamble's IT Infrastructure," press release, HP website, 6 May 2003 [accessed 10 October 2003] www.hp.com; "HP Selected by P&G for $3 Billion, 10-Year Services Contract," press release, HP website, 11 April 2003 [accessed 10 October 2003] www.hp.com.

2. "Polishing Your Presentation," 3M Meeting Network [accessed 8 June 2001] www.mmm.com/meetingnetwork/readingroom/meetingguide_pres.html.

3. Michael Hyatt, "Five Rules to Better PowerPoint Presentations," 21 June 2005, Working Smart blog [accessed 2 December 2006] www.michaelhyatt.com.

4. An example of such a presentation is Dick Hardt's keynote presentation at OSCON 2005; the presentation can be viewed at www.identity20.com/media/OSCON2005.

5. Cliff Atkinson, "The Cognitive Load of PowerPoint: Q&A with Richard E. Mayer," Sociablemedia.com [accessed 22 December 2008] www.sociablemedia.com.

6. Atkinson, "The Cognitive Load of PowerPoint: Q&A with Richard E. Mayer."

7. Claudyne Wilder and David Fine, *Point, Click & Wow* (San Francisco: Jossey-Bass Pfeiffer, 1996), 50.
8. See Note 1.
9. Jerry Weissman, *Presenting to Win: The Art of Telling Your Story* (Upper Saddle River, N.J.: Pearson Prentice Hall, 2006), 124.
10. Weissman, *Presenting to Win*, 144–147.
11. Margo Halverson, "Choosing the Right Colors for Your Next Presentation," 3M Meeting Network [accessed 8 June 2001] www.mmm.com/meetingnetwork/readingroom/meetingguide_right_color.html.
12. Carol Klinger and Joel G. Siegel, "Computer Multimedia Presentations," *CPA Journal*, June 1996, 46.
13. Jon Hanke, "Five Tips for Better Visuals," 3M Meeting Network [accessed 25 May 2007] http://www.3m.com/meetingnetwork/presentations/pmag_better_visuals.html.
14. Hanke, "Five Tips for Better Visuals."
15. Guy Kawasaki, "Rule of Thumb," *Entrepreneur*, May 2008, 44.
16. Sarah Lary and Karen Pruente, "Powerless Point: Common PowerPoint Mistakes to Avoid," *Public Relations Tactics*, February 2004, 28.
17. Cliff Atkinson, *Beyond Bullet Points: Using Microsoft PowerPoint to Create Presentations That Inform, Motivate, and Inspire* (Redmond, Wash.: Microsoft Press, 2005), 16.
18. Weissman, *Presenting to Win*, 162.
19. Ted Simons, "Handouts That Won't Get Trashed," *Presentations*, February 1999, 47-50.
20. Jennifer Rotondo and Mike Rotondo, Jr., *Presentation Skills for Managers* (New York: McGraw-Hill, 2002), 151.
21. Roly Grimshaw, "Communication by the Numbers," *Harvard Management Communication Letter*, Summer 2005, 3–4.
22. Sean P. Aune, "Forget PowerPoint: 13 Online Presentation Apps," Mashable, 16 February 2008 [accessed 24 December 2008] www.mashable.com.
23. Julia Chang, "Best Practices for Web Presentations," *Sales & Marketing Management*, November 2005, 52.
24. SlideShare website [accessed 24 December 2008] www.slideshare.net.
25. Jeff Yocom, "TechRepublic Survey Yields Advice on Streaming Video," TechRepublic website [accessed 16 February 2004] www.techrepublic.com.
26. "Webcasting Tips & Advice," Spider Eye Studios [accessed 13 February 2004] www.spidereye.com.
27. Allison Rossett, "What Stinks About Webinars?" *Chief Learning Officer*, August 2008, 46–49.
28. "Best Practices for Online Marketing Events with WebEx Event Center," WebEx Communications [accessed 3 December 2006] www.webex.com.
29. Adapted from Loopt website [accessed 27 December 2008] www.loopt.com; Boost Mobile website [accessed 9 December 2006] www.boostmobile.com.
30. Adapted from Vox website [accessed 27 December 2008] www.vox.com; eSnips website [accessed 27 December 2008] www.esnips.com; Robert D. Hof, "There's Not Enough 'Me' in MySpace," *BusinessWeek*, 4 December 2006, 40.

CHAPTER 18

1. Hersha Hospitality Management website [accessed 30 December 2008] www.hershahotels.com; Charles Handler, "What You Need to Know About What's Happening in the Pre-Employment Assessment Market," Ere.net, 20 July 2006 [accessed 12 December 2006] www.ere.net; Fay Hansen, "Growing into Applicant Tracking Systems, *Workforce Management*, 10 October 2006 [accessed 12 December 2006] www.workforce.com; Connie Winkler, "Job Try-outs Go Virtual," *HR Magazine*, September 2006, 131–134; "Hersha Hospitality Management Selects ERC's Selectech Workforce Management Recruiting Solution," 7 December 2006, ERC Dataplus website [accessed 12 December 2006] www.ercdataplus.com.

2. Anne Fisher, "How to Get Hired by a 'Best' Company," *Fortune*, 4 February 2008, 96.
3. Caroline A. Drakeley, "Viral Networking: Tactics in Today's Job Market," *Intercom*, September–October 2003, 4–7.
4. "CareerXroads 6th Annual Sources of Hire Study, 2006," CareerXroads website [accessed 30 March 2008] www.careerxroads.com.
5. Caroline Kealey, "Web 2.0: The Medium Is the Message, but What's the Result?" IABC website [accessed 29 December 2008] www.iabc.com; Alina Tugend, "Job Hunting Is, and Isn't, What It Used to Be," *New York Times*, 26 September 2008 [accessed 29 December 2008] www.nytimes.com.
6. Jobfox website [accessed 29 December 2008] www.jobfox.com; Olga Kharif, "The Job of Challenging Monster," *BusinessWeek* online, 6 September 2005 [accessed 25 September 2005] www.businessweek.com; "Job Sites: The 'Second Generation,'" *BusinessWeek* online, 7 September 2005 [accessed 25 September 2005] www.businessweek.com.
7. Jobster website [accessed 29 December 2008] www.jobster.com; Jeanette Borzo, "Taking on the Recruiting Monster," *FSB*, May 2007, 89–90.
8. Douglas MacMillan, "The Art of the Online Résumé," *BusinessWeek*, 7 May 2007, 86.
9. Fisher, "How to Get Hired by a 'Best' Company."
10. Anne Fisher, "Greener Pastures in a New Field," *Fortune*, 26 January 2004, 48.
11. Liz Ryan, "Etiquette for Online Outreach," Yahoo! Hotjobs website [accessed 26 March 2008] http://hotjobs.yahoo.com.
12. Career and Employment Services, Danville Area Community College website [accessed 23 March 2008] www.dacc.edu/career; Career Counseling, Sarah Lawrence College website [accessed 23 March 2008] www.slc.edu/occ/index.php; Cheryl L. Noll, "Collaborating with the Career Planning and Placement Center in the Job-Search Project," *Business Communication Quarterly* 58, no. 3 (1995): 53–55.
13. Rockport Institute, "How to Write a Masterpiece of a Résumé" [accessed 24 March 2008] www.rockportinstitute.com.
14. Pam Stanley-Weigand, "Organizing the Writing of Your Resume," *Bulletin of the Association for Business Communication* 54, no. 3 (September 1991): 11–12.
15. Susan Vaughn, "Answer the Hard Questions Before Asked," *Los Angeles Times*, 29 July 2001, W1–W2.
16. John Steven Niznik, "Landing a Job with a Criminal Record," About.com [accessed 12 December 2006] http://jobsearchtech.about.com.
17. Richard H. Beatty and Nicholas C. Burkholder, *The Executive Career Guide for MBAs* (New York: Wiley, 1996), 133.
18. Adapted from Burdette E. Bostwick, *How to Find the Job You've Always Wanted* (New York: Wiley, 1982), 69–70.
19. Norma Mushkat Gaffin, "Recruiters' Top 10 Resume Pet Peeves," Monster.com [accessed 19 February 2004] www.monster.com; Beatty and Burkholder, *The Executive Career Guide for MBAs*, 151.
20. Rockport Institute, "How to Write a Masterpiece of a Résumé."
21. "How to Ferret Out Instances of Résumé Padding and Fraud," *Compensation & Benefits for Law Offices*, June 2006, 1+.
22. "Resume Fraud Gets Slicker and Easier," CNN.com [accessed 11 March 2004] www.cnn.com.
23. Lisa Takeuchi Cullen, "Getting Wise to Lies," *Time*, 1 May 2006, 59; "Resume Fraud Gets Slicker and Easier"; Employment Research Services website [accessed 18 March 2004] www.erscheck.com.
24. "How to Ferret Out Instances of Résumé Padding and Fraud."
25. Jacqueline Durett, "Redoing Your Résumé? Leave Off the Lies," *Training*, December 2006, 9; "Employers Turn Their Fire on Untruthful CVs," *Supply Management*, 23 June 2005, 13.
26. Cynthia E. Conn," Integrating Writing Skills and Ethics Training in Business Communication Pedagogy: A Résumé Case Study Exemplar," *Business Communication Quarterly*, June 2008, 138–151;

Marilyn Moats Kennedy, "Don't Get Burned by Résumé Inflation," *Marketing News*, 15 April 2007, 37–38.

27. Sal Divita, "If You're Thinking Résumé, Think Creatively," *Marketing News*, 14 September 1992, 29.

28. Rockport Institute, "How to Write a Masterpiece of a Résumé."

29. Lora Morsch, "25 Words That Hurt Your Resume," CNN.com, 20 January 2006 [accessed 20 January 2006] www.cnn.com.

30. Liz Ryan, "The Reengineered Résumé," *BusinessWeek*, 3 December 2007, SC12.

31. Anthony Balderrama, "Resume Blunders That Will Keep You from Getting Hired," CNN.com, 19 March 2008 [accessed 26 March 2008] www.cnn.com; Michelle Dumas, "5 Resume Writing Myths," Distinctive Documents blog, 17 July 2007 [accessed 26 March 2008] http://blog.distinctiveweb.com; Kim Isaacs, "Resume Dilemma: Recent Graduate," Monster.com [accessed 26 March 2008] http://career-advice.monster.com.

32. Karl L. Smart, "Articulating Skills in the Job Search," *Business Communication Quarterly* 67, no. 2 (June 2004): 198–205.

33. "25 Things You Should Never Include on a Resume," HR World website 18 December 2007 [accessed 25 March 2008] www.hrworld.com.

34. "When to Include Personal Data," ResumeEdge.com [accessed 25 March 2008] www.resumeedge.com.

35. "Résumé Length: What It Should Be and Why It Matters to Recruiters," *HR Focus*, June 2007, 9.

36. Ed Tazzia, "Wanted: A Résumé That Really Works," *Brandweek*, 15 May 2006, 26.

37. Rachel Zupek, "Seven Exceptions to Job Search Rules," CNN.com, 3 September 2008 [accessed 29 December 2008] www.cnn.com.

38. John Sullivan, "Résumés: Paper, Please," *Workforce Management*, 22 October 2007, 50; "Video Résumés Offer Both Pros and Cons During Recruiting," *HR Focus*, July 2007, 8.

39. Ellen Joe Pollock, "Sir: Your Application for a Job Is Rejected; Sincerely, Hal 9000," *Wall Street Journal*, 30 July 1998, A1, A12.

40. "Scannable Resume Design," ResumeEdge.com [accessed 19 February 2004] www.resumeedge.com.

41. Kim Isaacs, "Tips for Creating a Scannable Resume," Monster.com [accessed 19 February 2004] www.monster.com.

42. Christian Anderson, "New Year's Resolutions—Jobster Style," Jobster blog, 21 December 2007 [accessed 28 March 2008] www.jobster.blogs.com.

43. Sarah E. Needleman, "Why Sneaky Tactics May Not Help Resume; Recruiters Use New Search Technologies to Ferret Out Bogus Keywords," *Wall Street Journal*, 6 March 2007, B8.

44. Kim Isaacs, "Enhance Your Resume for Monster Upload," Monster.com [accessed 19 February 2004] www.monster.com.

45. "10 Reasons Why You Are Not Getting Any Interviews," *Miami Times*, 7–13 November 2007, 6D.

46. "The Rogue's Gallery of 25 Awful Résumé Mistakes," CareerExplorer.net [accessed 19 February 2004] www.careerexplorer.net.

47. "Protect Yourself From Identity Theft When Hunting for a Job Online," *Office Pro*, May 2007, 6.

CHAPTER 19

1. Guy Logan, "Hiring Policy Makes Google Best Place to Work in the UK," *Personnel Today*, 3 June 2008, 3; John Sullivan, "A Case Study of Google Recruiting," 5 December 2005, *Electronic Recruiting Exchange* [accessed 16 December 2006] www.ere.net; "What's It Like to Work at Google?" Google website [accessed 26 September 2005] www.google.com; Fred Vogelstein, "Can Google Grow Up?" *Fortune*, 8 December 2003, 102; Quentin Hardy, "All Eyes on Google," *Forbes*, 26 May 2003, 100; Keith H. Hammonds, "Growth Search," *Fast Company*, April 2003, 74–81; Stanley Bing, "How Not to Success (*sic*) in Business," *Fortune*, 30 December 2002, 210; Pierre Mornell, "Zero Defect Hiring," *Inc.*, March 1998, 74.

2. "The Writer Approach," *Los Angeles Times*, 17 November 2002, W1.

3. Toni Logan, "The Perfect Cover Story," *Kinko's Impress* 2 (2000): 32, 34.

4. James Gonyea, "Money Talks: Salary History Versus Salary Requirements," Monster.com [accessed 19 October 2004] www.monster.com; Marguerite Higgins, "Tech-Savvy Job Hunters Not So Suave in Writing; E-Mail Résumés Appall Employers," *Washington Times*, 17 December 2002 [accessed 22 February 2004] www.highbeam.com; "Keep Goal in Mind When Crafting a Résumé," *Register-Guard* (Eugene, Ore.), 3 August 2003 [accessed 22 February 2004] www.highbeam.com; Anis F. McClin, "Effects of Spelling Errors on the Perception of Writers," *Journal of General Psychology*, January 2002 [accessed 22 February 2004] www.highbeam.com.

5. Anne Fisher, "How to Get Hired by a 'Best' Company," *Fortune*, 4 February 2008, 96.

6. Sarah E. Needleman, "Speed Interviewing Grows as Skills Shortage Looms; Strategy May Help Lock in Top Picks; Some Drawbacks," *Wall Street Journal*, 6 November 2007, B15.

7. Scott Beagrie, "How to Handle a Telephone Job Interview," *Personnel Today*, 26 June 2007, 29.

8. "Hiring Process," Google website [accessed 2 January 2009] www.google.com.

9. John Olmstead, "Predict Future Success with Structured Interviews," *Nursing Management*, March 2007, 52–53.

10. Fisher, "How to Get Hired by a 'Best' Company."

11. Erinn R. Johnson, "Pressure Sessions," *Black Enterprise*, October 2007, 72.

12. "What's a Group Interview," About.com Tech Careers [accessed 5 April 2008] http://jobsearchtech.about.com.

13. Fisher, "How to Get Hired by a 'Best' Company."

14. "FAQs About Behavioral Based Interviewing," University of Wisconsin–Eau Clair website [accessed 5 April 2008] www.uwec.edu; "Advice on Mastering the 'Behavioral' Interview," *Financial Executive*, November 2007, 11.

15. Chris Pentilla, "Testing the Waters," *Entrepreneur*, January 2004 [accessed 27 May 2006] www.entrepreneur.com; Terry McKenna, "Behavior-Based Interviewing," *National Petroleum News*, January 2004, 16; Nancy K. Austin, "Goodbye Gimmicks," *Incentive*, May 1996, 241.

16. William Poundstone, "Beware the Interview Inquisition," *Harvard Business Review*, May 2003, 18+.

17. Peter Vogt, "Mastering the Phone Interview," Monster.com [accessed 13 December 2006] www.monster.com; Nina Segal, "The Global Interview: Tips for Successful, Unconventional Interview Techniques," Monster.com [accessed 13 December 2006] www.monster.com.

18. Segal, "The Global Interview: Tips for Successful, Unconventional Interview Techniques."

19. HireVue website [accessed 4 April 2008] www.hirevue.com; in2View website [accessed 4 April 2008] www.in2view.biz; Victoria Reitz, "Interview Without Leaving Home," *Machine Design*, 1 April 2004, 66.

20. Connie Winkler, "Job Tryouts Go Virtual," *HR Magazine*, September 2006, 131–134.

21. Steven Isbitts, "Virtual Interview," *Tampa Tribune*, 20 March 2006 [accessed 13 December 2006] www.ebscohost.com.

22. Saul Hansell, "Google Answer to Filling Jobs Is an Algorithm," *New York Times*, 3 January 2007 [accessed 3 January 2007] www.nytimes.com.

23. Gina Ruiz, "Job Candidate Assessment Tests Go Virtual," *Workforce Management*, January 2008 [accessed 1 January 2009] www.workforce.com.

24. Dino di Mattia, "Testing Methods and Effectiveness of Tests," *Supervision*, August 2005, 4–5.

25. Steven Mitchell Sack, "The Working Woman's Legal Survival Guide: Testing," FindLaw [accessed 22 February 2004] www.findlaw.com; David W. Arnold and John W. Jones, "Who the Devil's Applying Now?" *Security Management*, March 2002, 85–88.

26. Arnold and Jones, "Who the Devil's Applying Now?"
27. Arnold and Jones, "Who the Devil's Applying Now?" 86.
28. Frederick P. Morgeson, Michael A. Campion, Robert L. Dipboye, John R. Hollenbeck, Kevin Murphy, and Neal Schmitt, "Are We Getting Fooled Again? Coming to Terms with Limitations in the Use of Personality Tests in Personnel Selection," *Personnel Psychology*, 60, Winter 2007, 1029–1049.
29. Adam Agard, "Preemployment Skills Testing: An Important Step in the Hiring Process," *Supervision*, June 2003, 7+.
30. Ashlea Ebeling, "Corporate Moneyball," *Forbes*, 23 April 2007, 102+.
31. Sullivan, "A Case Study of Google Recruiting."
32. "Drug Test Company Official Disputes Report Pre-Employment Tests Falling," *Drug Detection Report*, 23 March 2006, 43.
33. Matthew J. Heller, "Digging Deeper," *Workforce Management*, 3 March 2008, 35–39.
34. "Check Yourself Before Employer Does," *CA Magazine*, June/July 2005, 12.
35. Scott Medintz, "Talkin' 'Bout MySpace Generation," *Money*, February 2006, 27.
36. Michael Kaplan, "Job Interview Brainteasers," *Business 2.0*, September 2007, 35–37.
37. Nancy K. Austin, "Goodbye Gimmicks," *Incentive*, May 1996, 241.
38. Katherine Spencer Lee, "Tackling Tough Interview Questions," *Certification Magazine*, May 2005, 35.
39. Nick Corcodilos, "How to Answer a Misguided Interview Question," *Seattle Times*, 30 March 2008 [accessed 5 April 2008] www.seattletimes.com.
40. InterviewUp website [accessed 5 April 2008] www.interviewup.com.
41. Joe Turner, "An Interview Strategy: Telling Stories," Yahoo! HotJobs [accessed 5 April 2008] http://hotjobs.yahoo.com.
42. "A Word of Caution for Chatty Job Candidates," *Public Relations Tactics*, January 2008, 4.
43. Robert Gifford, Cheuk Fan Ng, and Margaret Wilkinson, "Nonverbal Cues in the Employment Interview: Links Between Applicant Qualities and Interviewer Judgments," *Journal of Applied Psychology* 70, no. 4 (1985): 729.
44. Dale G. Leathers, *Successful Nonverbal Communication* (New York: Macmillan, 1986), 225.
45. Randall S. Hansen, "When Job-Hunting: Dress for Success," QuintCareers.com [accessed 5 April 2008] www.quintcareers.com; Alison Doyle, "Dressing for Success," About.com [accessed 5 April 2008] http://jobsearch.about.com.
46. William S. Frank, "Job Interview: Pre-Flight Checklist," *The Career Advisor* [accessed 28 September 2005] http://careerplanning.about.com.
47. T. Shawn Taylor, "Most Managers Have No Idea How to Hire the Right Person for the Job," *Chicago Tribune*, 23 July 2002 [accessed 29 September 2005] www.ebsco.com.
48. "10 Minutes to Impress," *Journal of Accountancy*, July 2007, 13.
49. "Because You Asked: Interviews Get a Little Strange," ManageSmarter, 25 September 2008 [accessed 2 January 2009] www.managesmarter.com.
50. Sack, "The Working Woman's Legal Survival Guide."
51. Gerald L. Wilson, "Preparing Students for Responding to Illegal Selection Interview Questions," *Bulletin of the Association for Business Communication* 54, no. 2 (1991): 44–49.
52. Jeff Springston and Joann Keyton, "Interview Response Training," *Bulletin of the Association for Business Communication* 54, no. 3 (1991): 28–30; Gerald L. Wilson, "An Analysis of Instructional Strategies for Responding to Illegal Selection Interview Questions," *Bulletin of the Association for Business Communication* 54, no. 3 (1991): 31–35.
53. "Negotiating Salary: An Introduction," *InformationWeek* online [accessed 22 February 2004] www.infoweek.com.
54. "Negotiating Salary: An Introduction."
55. Harold H. Hellwig, "Job Interviewing: Process and Practice," *Bulletin of the Association for Business Communication* 55, no. 2 (1992): 8–14.
56. Joan S. Lublin, "Notes to Interviewers Should Go Beyond a Simple Thank You," *Wall Street Journal*, 5 February 2008, B1.

Acknowledgments

TEXT

39 (Business Communication 2.0: Putting Their Communication Skills to Work) Adapted from Matthew Nederlanden, personal communication, 1 November 2008; Liz Wise, personal communication, 27 October 2008; Meg Stivison, personal communication, 25 October 2008; Melissa Popp, personal communication, 3 November 2008; Philip Beech, personal communication, 28 October 2008; Aga Westfal, personal communication, 25 October 2008; Matthew Meyer, personal communication, 27 October 2008; Ted Rubin, personal communication, 27 October 2008; Chris Millichap, personal communication, 30 October 2008; Jerrold Thompson, personal communication, 22 November 2008. **62 (Business Communication 2.0: Who's Responsible Here?)** Adapted from Louise Story, "Can a Sandwich Be Slandered?" *New York Times*, 29 January 2008 [accessed 1 August 2008] www.nytimes.com; David Ardia, "Slandering Sandwiches and User Submitted Content," Citizen Media Law Project website, 29 January 2008 [accessed 1 August 2008] www.citmedialaw.org; "Doctor's Associates Inc. vs. QIP Holders LLC: Complaint for Injunctive Relief and Damages," Citizen Media Law Project website, 27 October 2006 [accessed 1 August 2008] www.citmedialaw.org; "MTV to Run User Generated Ads," *Marketing*, 15 November 2006, 3. **85 (Checklist: Overcoming Barriers to Effective Listening)** Robert A. Luke, Jr., "Improving Your Listening Ability," *Supervisory Management*, June 1992, 7; Madelyn Burley-Allen, "Listening for Excellence in Communication," *The Dynamics of Behavior Newsletter* 2, no. 2 (Summer 1992): 1; Bob Lamons, "Good Listeners Are Better Communicators," *Marketing News*, 11 September 1995, 13+. **86 (Communicating Across Cultures: Actions Speak Louder Than Words All Around the World)** Adapted from Lillian H. Chaney and Jeanete S. Martin, *Intercultural Business Communication*, 4th ed. (Upper Saddle River, N.J.: Pearson Prentice Hall, 2007), 126; David A. Victor, *International Business Communication* (New York: HarperCollins, 1992); David Wallace, "Mind Your Manners," *World Trade*, October 1992, 52, 54–55; Hannele Duvfa, "Innocents Abroad: The Politics of Cross-Cultural Communication," *Communication and Discourse Across Cultures and Languages*, 1991, 73–89; M. Katherine Glover, "Do's and Taboos: Cultural Aspects of International Business," *Business America*, 13 August 1990, 2–6; C. Barnum and N. Woniansky, "Taking Cues from Body Language," *Management Review*, June 1989, 59–60. **87 (Checklist: Improving Nonverbal Communication Skills)** Gerald H. Graham, Jeanne Unrue, and Paul Jennings, "The Impact of Nonverbal Communication in Organizations: A Survey of Perceptions," *Journal of Business Communication* 28, no. 1 (Winter 1991): 45–62; Dianna Booher, *Communicate with Confidence* (New York: McGraw-Hill, 1994), 363–370. **101 (Communicating Across Cultures: Test Your Intercultural Knowledge)** Adapted from David A. Ricks, "International Business Blunders: An Update," *Business & Economic Review*, January–March 1988, 25; Valerie Frazee, "Keeping Up on Chinese Culture," *Global Workforce*, October 1996, 16–17; Valerie Frazee, "Establishing Relations in Germany," *Global Workforce*, April 1997, 16–17; James Wilfong and Toni Seger, *Taking Your Business Global* (Franklin Lakes, N.J.: Career Press, 1997), 282. **111 (Business Communication 2.0: The Web 2.0 Way to Learn a New Language)** Adapted from Palabea website [accessed 5 December 2008] www.palabea.net; Free Language website [accessed 5 December 2008] http://freelanguage.org. **161 (Communicating Across Cultures: Communicating with a Global Audience on the Web)** Adapted from Laura Morelli, "Writing for a Global Audience on the Web," *Marketing News*, 17 August 1998, 16; Yuri and Anna Radzievsky, "Successful Global Web Sites Look Through Eyes of the Audience,"

Advertising Age's Business Marketing, January 1998, 17; Sari Kalin, "The Importance of Being Multiculturally Correct," *Computerworld*, 6 October 1997, G16–G17; B. G. Yovovich, "Making Sense of All the Web's Numbers," *Editor & Publisher*, November 1998, 30–31; David Wilford, "Are We All Speaking the Same Language?" *The Times*, (London), 20 April 2000, 4. **258 (Communication Miscues:** When Recommendation Letters Lead to Lawsuits) Adapted from Diane Cadrain, "HR Professionals Stymied by Vanishing Job References," *HR Magazine*, November 2004, 31–40; "Five (or More) Ways You Can Be Sued for Writing (or Not Writing) Recommendation Letters," *Fair Employment Practice Guidelines*, July 2006, 1, 3–4; Rochelle Kaplan, "Writing a Recommendation Letter," National Association of Colleges and Employers website [accessed 12 October 2006] www.naceweb.org; Maura Dolan and Stuart Silverstein, "Court Broadens Liability for Job References," *Los Angeles Times*, 28 January 1997, A1, A11; David A. Price, "Good References Pave Road to Court," *USA Today*, 13 February 1997, 11A; Frances A. McMorris, "Ex-Bosses Face Less Peril Giving Honest Job References," *Wall Street Journal*, 8 July 1996, B1, B8; Dawn Gunsch, "Gray Matters: Centralize Control of Giving References," *Personnel Journal*, September 1992, 114, 116–117; Betty Southard Murphy, Wayne E. Barlow, and D. Diane Hatch, "Manager's Newsfront: Job Reference Liability of Employees," *Personnel Journal*, September 1991, 22, 26; Ross H. Fishman, "When Silence Is Golden," *Nation's Business*, July 1991, 48–49. **283 (Photo Caption)** Ken Ward, Jr., "Bayer Admits 'We Fell Short' in Fire Response, redOrbit, 9 October 2008 [accessed 11 October 2008] www.redorbit.com; "Plant Manager Apologizes for Lack of Communication," *Charleston Daily Mail*, 11 October 2008 [accessed 11 October 2008] www.dailymail.com. **296 (Business Communication 2.0: Controlling Rumors in a Social Media Environment)** Augie Ray, "Combating Rumors in Social Media: Sarah Palin and Babygate," Experience: The Blog, 1 September 2008 [accessed 18 October 2008] www.experiencetheblog.com; Michelle Conlin, "Web Attack," *BusinessWeek* online, 16 April 2007 [accessed 27 February 2008] www.businessweek.com; Melissa Allison, "Corporations Seek to Clean Up Online Rumors," *Seattle Times*, 4 March 2007 [accessed 4 March 2007] www.seattletimes.com; Charles Wolrich, "Top Corporate Hate Web Sites," *Forbes*, 8 March 2005 [accessed 16 August 2005] www.forbes.com; PlanetFeedback.com [accessed 27 February 2008] www.planetfeedback.com; "Health Related Hoaxes and Rumors," Centers for Disease Control and Prevention website [accessed 16 August 2005] www.cdc.gov; Snopes.com [accessed 16 August 2005] www.snopes.com; "Pranksters, Activists and Rogues: Know Your Adversaries and Where They Surf," *PR News*, 26 June 2000 [accessed 3 December 2003] www.elibrary.com. **316 (Business Communication 2.0: Building an Audience Through Search Engine Optimization)** Adapted from P.J. Fusco, "How Web 2.0 Affects SEO Strategy," ClickZ, 23 May 2007 [accessed 6 November 2008] www.clickz.com; "Law Firm Marketing Now Dependent on Search Engine Optimization," *Law Office Management & Administration Report*, June 2006, 1, 10–12; *Pandia Search Engine Marketing 101*, Pandia website [accessed 25 March 2007] www.pandia.com; Mike Grehan, "Does Textbook SEO Really Work Anymore?" ClickZ, 17 April 2006 [accessed 25 March 2007], www.clickz.com; Shari Thurow, "Web Positioning Metrics and SEO," ClickZ, 24 October 2005 [accessed 25 March 2007], www.clickz.com. **383 (Ethics Detective: Solving the Case of the Hidden Numbers)** Adapted from A. S. C. Ehrenberg, "The Problem of Numeracy," *Admap*, February 1992, 37–40; Mary S. Auvil and Kenneth W. Auvil, *Introduction to Business Graphics: Concepts and Applications* (Cincinnati: South-Western, 1992), 40, 192–193;

Peter H. Selby, *Using Graphs and Tables: A Self-Teaching Guide* (New York: Wiley, 1979), 8–9. **453 (Business Communication 2.0: Identifying the Patterns That Help or Hinder Wiki Collaboration)** Adapted from Wikipatterns.com [accessed 12 December 2008] www.wikipatterns.com; Luis Suarez, "Wikipatterns—Getting the Most Out of Your Own Wiki Experience by Learning from Others," elsua: The Knowledge Management Blog [accessed 12 December 2008] http://it.toolbox.com/blogs/elsua. **511 (Communicating Across Cultures: Five Tips for Making Presentations Around the World)** Adapted from Patricia L. Kurtz, *The Global Speaker* (New York: AMACOM, 1995), 35–47, 56–68, 75–82, 87–100; David A. Victor, *International Business Communication* (New York: HarperCollins, 1992), 39–45; Lalita Khosla, "You Say Tomato," *Forbes*, 21 May 2001, 36; Stephen Dolainski, "Are Expats Getting Lost in the Translation?" *Workforce*, February 1997, 32–39. **524 (Communication Miscues: Recovering from Disasters)** Adapted from C. Peter Guiliano and Frank J. Currilo, "Going Blank in the Boardroom," *Public Relations Quarterly*, Winter 2003, 35+; Jennifer Rotondo and Mike Rotondo, Jr., *Presentation Skills for Managers* (New York: McGraw-Hill, 2002), 160–162; Mark Merritt, "No More Nightmares," *Presentations*, April 2001, 44+. **544 (Business Communication 2.0: Presentations Get Social)** Adapted from SlideShare website [accessed 28 December 2008] www.slideshare.net; "SlideShare Presentations," LinkedIn website [accessed 28 December 2008] www.linkedin.com; Jason Kincaid, "SlideShare Sends PowerPoint to the Cloud with New Plugin," TechCrunch, 15 December 2008 [accessed 28 December 2008] www.techcrunch.com. **574 (Communication Miscues: Don't. Just Don't.)** Adapted from Rosemary Haefner, "Biggest Resume Mistakes," CNN.com, 21 May 2007 [accessed 30 December 2008] www.cnn.com; Sue Campbell, "Eight Worst Resume Mistakes," 1st-Writer.com [accessed 30 December 2008] www.1st-writer.com; "150 Funniest Resume Mistakes, Bloopers, and Blunders Ever," The Best Article Every Day blog, 2 June 2008 [accessed 30 December 2008] www.bspcn.com; "Hiring Managers Share Top 12 Wackiest Resume Blunders in New CareerBuilder.com Survey," CareerBuilder.com, 25 April 2007 [accessed 30 December 2008] www.careerbuilder.com. **599 (Communicating Across Cultures: Successfully Interviewing Across Borders)** Adapted from Jean-Marc Hachey, "Interviewing for an International Job," excerpt from *The Canadian Guide to Working and Living Overseas*, 3rd ed. [accessed 23 February 2004] www.workingoverseas.com; Rebecca Falkoff, "Dress to Impress the World: International Business Fashion," Monster.com [accessed 23 February 2004] www.monster.com; Mary Ellen Slater, "Navigating the Details of Landing an Overseas Job," *Washington Post*, 11 November 2002, E4567. **605 (Communication Miscues: Make Sure You Don't Talk Yourself Out of a Job)** Adapted from Thomas Pack, "Good Answers to Job Interview Questions," *Information Today*, January 2004, 35+; John Lees, "Make Them Believe You Are the Best," *The Times* (London), 21 January 2004, 3; "Six Interview Mistakes," Monster.com [accessed 23 February 2004] www.monster.com.

FIGURES AND TABLES

72 (Figure 2.1) Used by permission of Wikia, Inc. **76 (Table 2.2: Business Uses of Social Networking Technology)** Adapted from Christopher Carfi and Leif Chastaine, "Social Networking for Businesses & Organizations" (white paper), Cerado website [accessed 13 August 2008] www.cerado.com; Anusorn Kansap, "Social Networking," PowerPoint presentation, Silpakorn University [accessed 14 August 2008] http://real-timeupdates.com; "Social Network Websites: Best Practices from Leading Services," white paper, 28 November 2007, faberNovel Consulting website [accessed 14 August 2008] www.fabernovel.com. **81 (Figure 2.6: Web-Based Meetings)** Courtesy of InstantPresenter. **82 (Figure 2.7: Virtual Meetings in a Virtual World)** Courtesy of Cranial Tap. **84 (Table 2.3: What Makes an Effective Listener?)** Madelyn Burley-Allen, *Listening: The Forgotten Skill* (New York: Wiley, 1995), 70–71, 119–120; Judi Brownell, *Listening: Attitudes, Principles, and Skills* (Boston: Allyn & Bacon, 2002); 3, 9, 83, 89, 125; Larry Barker and Kittie Watson, *Listen Up* (New York: St. Martin's, 2000), 8, 9, 64. **90 (Table 2.5: Quick Tips for Improving Your Phone Skills)** Alf Nucifora, "Voice Mail Demands Good Etiquette from Both Sides," *Puget Sound Business*

Journal, 5–11 September 2003, 24; Ruth Davidhizar and Ruth Shearer, "The Effective Voice Mail Message," *Hospital Material Management Quarterly*, 45–49; "How to Get the Most Out of Voice Mail," *The CPA Journal*, February 2000, 11; Jo Ind, "Hanging On the Telephone," *Birmingham Post*, 28 July 1999, PS10; Larry Barker and Kittie Watson, *Listen Up* (New York: St. Martin's Press, 2000), 64–65; Lin Walker, *Telephone Techniques* (New York: AMACOM, 1998), 46–47; Dorothy Neal, *Telephone Techniques*, 2nd ed. (New York: Glencoe McGraw-Hill, 1998), 31; Jeannie Davis, *Beyond "Hello"* (Aurora, Col.: Now Hear This, Inc., 2000), 2–3; "Ten Steps to Caller-Friendly Voice Mail," *Managing Office Technology*, January 1995, 25; Rhonda Finniss, "Voice Mail: Tips for a Positive Impression," *Administrative Assistant's Update*, August 2001, 5; Ruth Davidhizar and Ruth Shearer, "The Effective Voice Mail Message," *Hospital Material Management Quarterly*, 45–49; "How to Get the Most Out of Voice Mail," *The CPA Journal*, February 2000, 11. **98 (Figure 3.1: Languages of the World)** Copyright © 2005, SIL International, from the database of Ethnologue Languages of the World, 15th ed., www.ethnologue.com. **102 (Figure 3.2: How Cultural Context Affects Business)** Mary O'Hara-Devereaux and Robert Johansen, *Global Work: Bridging Distance, Culture, and Time* (San Francisco: Jossey-Bass, 1994), 55, 59. Used with permission of John Wiley & Sons, Inc. **104 (Figure 3.3: Future Orientation and National Competitiveness)** Mansour Javidan, "Forward-Thinking Cultures," *Harvard Business Review*, July–August 2007, 20. Copyright © 2007 by the Harvard Business School Publishing Corporation; All Rights Reserved. **105 (Figure 3.4: Avoiding Nonverbal Mishaps)** Adapted from Roger Axtell, *Gestures: The Do's and Taboos of Body Language Around the World* (New York: Wiley, 1991), 117–119. Used with permission of John Wiley & Sons, Inc. **123 (Figure 4.1: The Three-Step Writing Process)** Adapted from Kevin J. Harty and John Keenan, *Writing for Business and Industry: Process and Product* (New York: Macmillan Publishing Company, 1987), 3–4; Richard Hatch, *Business Writing* (Chicago: Science Research Associates, 1983), 88–89; Richard Hatch, *Business Communication Theory and Technique* (Chicago: Science Research Associates, 1983), 74–75; Center for Humanities, *Writing as a Process: A Step-by-Step Guide, Four Filmstrips and Cassettes* (Mount Kisko, NY: Center for Humanities, 1987); Michael L. Keene, *Effective Professional Writing* (New York: D.C. Heath, 1987), 28–34. **130 (Figure 4.4: An Audience-Focused Report)** Used by permission of Alderwood Water & Wastewater. **133 (Figure 4.6: Electronic Oral Media)** Used by permission of World Voyager Vacations. **181 (Figure 6.1: Improving a Customer Letter Through Careful Revision)** Letterhead provided by Yamaha Corporation of America; text written by the authors. **182 (Figure 6.2: Revised Customer Letter)** Letterhead provided by Yamaha Corporation of America; text written by the authors. **197 (Figure 6.6: Multimedia Tools)** Photo by Ryan Lackey. Adobe product screen shot(s) reprinted with permission from Adobe Systems Incorporated. **199 (Figure 6.7: A Typical Business Memo)** Used with permission of Carnival Corporation. **220 (Figure 7.3: Video Blogging)** Used with permission of Joe Foley. **222 (Table 7.2: Tips for Effective Business Blogging)** Robert Scoble and Shel Israel, *Naked Conversations* (Hoboken, N.J.: John Wiley & Sons, 2006), 78–81, 190–194; Paul McFedries, *The Complete Idiot's Guide to Creating a Web Page & Blog*, 6th ed. (New York: Alpha, 2004), 206–208, 272–276; Shel Holtz and Ted Demopoulos, *Blogging for Business* (Chicago: Kaplan, 2006), 54–59, 113–114; Denise Wakeman, "Top 10 Blog Writing Tips," Blogarooni.com [accessed 1 February 2006] www.blogarooni.com; Dennis A. Mahoney, "How to Write a Better Weblog," 22 February 2002, A List Apart [accessed 1 February 2006] www.alistapart.com. **229 (Figure 7.7: Viewing Blog Updates in Web Browsers)** Used with permission of David Meerman Scott. **244 (Figure 8.1: Routine Messages)** Google blog screenshot © Google Inc. and is used with permission. **254 (Figure 8.6: Personalized Reply to a Request for Information)** Courtesy Herman Miller. **259 (Figure 8.8: Effective Recommendation Letter)** Letterhead provided by Airbus Americas, Inc.; text written by the authors. **282 (Figure 9.2: Negative Message Using the Direct Approach)** Used with permission of Spherion Corporation. **314 (Table 10.1: Human Needs That Influence Motivation)** Adapted from Saundra K. Ciccarelli and Glenn E. Meyer, *Psychology* (Upper

Saddle River, N.J.: Prentice Hall, 2006), 336–346; Courtland L. Bovée, John V. Thill, and Michael H. Mescon, *Excellence in Business*, 3rd ed. (Upper Saddle River, N.J.: Prentice Hall, 2006), 327–333; Abraham H. Maslow, "A Theory of Human Motivation," *Psychological Review* 50 (1943): 370–396. **326 (Figure 10.3: Marketing Messages)** Used with permission of Maine Coast Properties. **327 (Table 10.2)** Adapted from "What Is the HYBRID HEAT Dual Fuel System by Carrier?" Carrier website [accessed 5 November 2008] www.residential.carrier.com. **327 (Figure 10.4: Explaining the Benefits of Product Features)** Blackberry®, RIM®, Research in Motion®, Sure Type®, SurePress™ and related trademarks, names and logos are the property of Research in Motion Limited and are registered and/or used in the U.S. and countries around the world. **329 (Figure 10.5b: Emotional and Logical Appeals in Marketing and Sales Messages)** Gladiator GarageWorks website photograph used with permission of Whirlpool Corporation. **332 (Figure 10.7: The Call to Action in a Persuasive Message)** Reprinted with permission from the American Council on Exercise. **353 (Table 11.1: Important Resources for Business Research)** Adapted from H.W. Wilson website [accessed 20 November 2008] www.hwwilson.com; Bowker website [accessed 20 November 2008] www.bowker.com; University of Washington Libraries online card catalog [accessed 20 November 2008] http://uwashington.worldcat.org; D&B website [accessed 20 November 2008] www.dnb.com; "Industry Information," Thomas J. Long Business and Economics Library website, University of California, Berkeley [accessed 6 November 2006] www.lib.berkeley.edu; Hoovers website [accessed 20 November 2008] www.hoovers.com; MarketResearch.com [accessed 6 November 2006] www.marketresearch.com; Risk Management Association website [accessed 6 November 2006] www.rmahq.org; "Subscribed Sites," Sno-Isle Regional Library System [accessed 18 December 2003] www.sno-isle.org; "Business Directories: A Research Guide," University of Delaware Library website [accessed 6 November 2006] www.lib.udel.edu; Thomas P. Bergman, Stephen M. Garrison, and Gregory M. Scott, *The Business Student Writer's Manual and Guide to the Internet* (Paramus, N.J.: Prentice Hall, 1998), 67–80; Ernest L. Maier, Anthony J. Faria, Peter Kaatrude, and Elizabeth Wood, *The Business Library and How to Use It* (Detroit: Omnigraphics, 1996), 53–76. **357 (Figure 11.3: Google Book Search)** © Google, Inc. **360 (Figure 11.4: Desktop Search Engines)** Used with permission of Copernic. **390 (Figure 12.10: Pictogram)** Copyright 2005-2009 Mozilla. All Rights Reserved. All rights in the names, trademarks, and logos of the Mozilla Foundation, including without limitation, Firefox®, as well as the Firefox logo are owned exclusively by the Mozilla Foundation. **393 (Figure 12.14: Data Visualization)** (a) Used with permission of TouchGraph. (b) Used with permission of Barry Graubart. (d) Copyright 2009 SmartMoney. All rights reserved. **422 (Figure 13.5: Information Architecture)** Used with permission of Danny Aldo, a Certified Usability Analyst. **485 (Figure 15.2: Report Synopsis)** Reprinted by permission of Sprint Nextel. **540 (Table 17.1: Color and Emotion)** Adapted from Claudyne Wilder and David Fine, *Point, Click & Wow* (San Francisco: Jossey-Bass Pfeiffer, 1996), 63, 527. **560 (Figure 18.2: How Organizations Prefer to Find New Employees)** Reprinted with permission from Richard Nelson Bolles, *What Color Is Your Parachute?* (Berkeley, Calif.: Ten Speed Press, 2009), www.tenspeed.com. **562 (Table 18.1: Netting a Job on the Web)** The Riley Guide [accessed 30 March 2008] www.rileyguide.com; SimplyHired website [accessed 30 March 2008] www.simplyhired.com; Indeed website [accessed 30 March 2008] www.indeed.com; CollegeRecruiter.com [accessed 30 March 2008] www.collegerecruiter.com; Jobster website [accessed 30 March 2008] www.jobster.com; WetFeet [accessed 30 March 2008] http://wetfeet.com. **596 (Figure 19.3: Finding Real Jobs in a Virtual World)** Used with permission of Working Worlds. **600 (Table 19.3: Twenty-Five Common Interview Questions)** Adapted from InterviewUp website [accessed 6 April 2008] www.interviewup.com; *The Northwestern Endicott Report* (Evanston, Ill.: Northwestern University Placement Center). **601 (Table 19.4: Ten Questions to Ask an Interviewer)** Adapted from Joe Conklin, "Turning the Tables: Six Questions to Ask Your Interviewer," *Quality Progress*, November 2007, 55; Andrea N. Browne, "Keeping the Momentum at the Interview; Ask Questions, Do Your Research, and Be a Team Player," *Washington Post*, 29 July 2007, K1; Marilyn Sherman, "Questions R Us: What to Ask at a Job Interview," *Career World*, January 2004, 20; H. Lee Rust, *Job Search: The Completion Manual for Jobseekers* (New York: American Management Association, 1979), 56. **602 (Table 19.5: Warning Signs: 25 Attributes That Interviewers Don't Like to See)** Adapted from InterviewUp website [accessed 6 April 2008] www.interviewup.com; *The Northwestern Endicott Report* (Evanston, Ill.: Northwestern University Placement Center). **606 (Table 19.6: Interview Questions That Employers Are and Are Not Allowed to Ask)** Deanna G. Kucler, "Interview Questions: Legal or Illegal?" *Workforce Management* [accessed 28 September 2005] www.workforce.com; "Illegal Interview Questions," *USA Today*, 29 January 2001 [accessed 28 September 2005] www.usatoday.com; "Dangerous Questions," *Nation's Business*, May 1999, 22.

PHOTOS

Cover Getty Images—Stockbyte. **35** Marco Cappalunga, Shutterstock. **36 and 63** Mena & Ben Trott, Co-founders of Six Apart, Ltd. **43** Walter Hodges, Getty Images Inc.—Stone Allstock. **47** Ellen Isaacs/age Fotostock, Art Life Images. **54, left top** Belkin International, Inc. **54, top right** Getty Images – Digital Vision. **54, left bottom** Lance Davies Photography, Polyvision, A Steelcase Company. **55, right top** Instant-Presenter. **55, right bottom** Ethan Hill Photography. **55, left bottom** Studio M, Stock Connection. **56, right bottom** Peter Christopher, Masterfile Corporation. **57, right top** Photolibrary.com. **57, left bottom** Marcio Jose Sanchez, AP Wide World Photo. **57, right bottom** Staples, Inc. **pages 68 and 91** Rosen Law Firm. **79** Peter Wynn Thompson/The New York Times, Redux Pictures. **89** Rob Lewine, CORBIS-NY. **96 and 116** IBM Corporation. **99** Mark Richards, PhotoEdit, Inc. **106** Steve Cole, Getty Images – Photodisc. **115** Diego Azubel/epa, CORBIS-NY. **121** Asia Images Group, Getty Images, Inc. Asia Images Group—Royalty Free. **122 and 145** H&R Block World Headquarters. **131** JUPITERIMAGES/ Comstock Images, Alamy Images Royalty Free. **150 and 173** Mizuka Ito, Creative Commons. **179 and 202** Daimler Chrysler AG. **209** Stockbyte, Getty Images, Inc.—Stockbyte Royalty Free. **210 and 230** Southwest Airlines Co. **211** Chris Strangemore. **221** Ric Feld, AP Wide World Photos. **227** Promethius Consulting, LLC. **242 and 265** Thor Muller. **255** David Deal. **278 and 301** Landov Media. **283** Tom Hindman, AP Wide World Photos. **324** ImageState, Alamy Images. **347** Image Source, Getty Images Inc.—Image Source Royalty Free. **348 and 370** Getty Images Editorial. **375 and 402** seangilligan.com/XPLANE. **378** Britt Erlanson, Getty Images Inc.—Image Bank. **379** Alan Gough, Alan Gough Photography. **399** Juan Fuertes, Shutterstock. David Gilder, Shutterstock. **410 and 433** Kenwood USA Corporation. **440 and 457** Robert Seale, Tellabs. **465 and 494** Paul Sakuma, AP Wide World Photos. **507** Nabil John Elderkin, Getty Images. **508 and 527** Fitch. **519** Comstock/SuperStock, Inc. **520** Jeff Greenberg, PhotoEdit, Inc. **525** Noel Hendrickson, Getty Images, Inc.—Image Bank. **532 and 552** Hewlett Packard. **534** Lance Davies Photography, Polyvision, A Steelcase Company. **549** Dennis MacDonald, PhotoEdit, Inc. **551** CORBIS-NY. **557** Matt Carr, Getty Images. **558 and 581** Hersha Hospitality Management. **586 and 612** Google, Inc. **592** AGE Fotostock America, Inc.—Royalty-free. **603** Jon Feingersh/Zefa.

Brand, Organization, Name, and Website Index

Subject Index